UNION STEAMSHIP COMPANY MARINA
SNUG COVE, BOWEN ISLAND

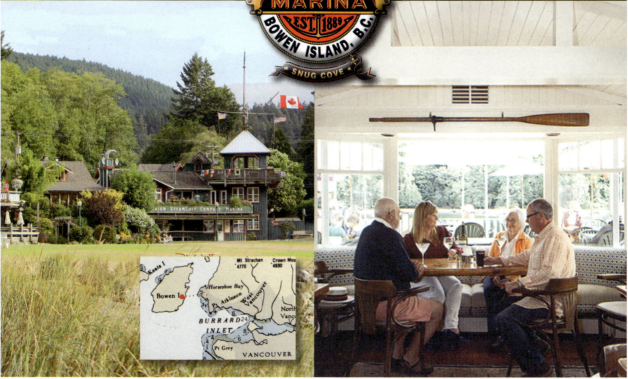

A first-class marina & resort just eight nautical miles from Vancouver.
Guest Moorage to 210', Doc Morgan's Restaurant, 8 Historical Cottage Rentals, Chandlery & Gift Shop.

604.947.0707 • VHF 66A
www.ussc.ca • marina@ussc.ca

INTRODUCTION   Page 5

2024 Northwest Boat Travel

TRUSTED SINCE 1978

General Information

Title:	Page:
Cap Sante Marina	Inside Front Cover
Pleasant Harbor Marina	Inside Back Cover
Montague Harbour Marina	Outside Back Cover
Union SteamShip Co. Marina	1
Chapter Locations	2 & 3
Table of Contents	5
What is Northwest Boat Travel?	6
Mariner's Library	8
U. S. Geographical Chapters (see contents below)	10
Important Notices, Customs Info, Boating Resources	108
Basic Boat Maneuvering	118
Basic Boat Anchoring	119
Canada Geographical Chapters (See contents below)	120
Crossing The Straits	284
VHF Marine Radio Information	286
Distance Tables	288
Index of Ports-of-Call, Anchorages, Facilities, Places to Go, Things to See and Do	293
Index of Advertisers	304

Puget Sound

Chapter:	Page:
1. South: Vashon Island to Shelton	10
2. West Central: Port Madison to Sinclair Inlet	28
3. East Central: Elliott Bay to Lake Washington	37
4. Hood Canal to Northern Olympic Peninsula	51
5. North: Possession Sound & Saratoga Passage	67

Gateway Area & San Juan Islands

6. Swinomish Channel to Point Roberts	76
7. Blakely to San Juan & Sucia Islands	90

Vancouver Island & Gulf Islands

8. Victoria, Saanich Peninsula & Inlet	120
9. Southeast: South Pender Island to Mayne Island	131
10. Central: Salt Spring Island to Maple Bay	137
11. North: Kulleet Bay to Departure Bay (Nanaimo)	150

City of Vancouver to Discovery Passage

12. Vancouver, Fraser River & Howe Sound	157
13. Sunshine Coast: Gibsons to Lund	173
14. Desolation Sound: Redonda & Cortes Islands	185
15. Northwest Georgia Strait: Nanoose to Oyster River	192
16. Discovery Passage: Campbell River to Stuart Island	198

North Vancouver Island & West Coast

Chapter:	Page:
17. Johnstone & Queen Charlotte Straits, & Adjacent Islands	208
18. West Coast of Vancouver Island	224

Northern B.C. & Southeast Alaska

19. Blunden Harbour to Dixon Entrance, Including Haida Gwaii	238
20. Ketchikan to Skagway, Glacier Bay, Sitka	259

PUBLICATION INFORMATION

Founders: Phil & Gwen Cole

Customer Service Representative: Debbie Brickman

Email: debbie@vernonpublications.com

Mailing Address: Post Office Box 970, Woodinville, WA 98072-0970

Phone: (425) 488-3211

Email: info@vernonpublications.com

Publisher: Trevor Vernon

Conditor: Robert Walters

Home Page: www.boattravel.com

ISBN: 978-1-7343975-4-3

© 2024 Vernon Publications, LLC   All rights reserved. Printed in Seattle, Washington

Cover: Echo Bay, Sucia Island (p. 106)
Photo © Keith Ross, Keith's Frame of Mind

Inset: Dent Island Lodge (p. 206)
Photo © Michael Poliza

Disclaimer & Warning: Use of this publication implies acceptance of the following: **1.** Charts and maps are included solely for artistic and general information purposes. Only government approved charts should be used for navigation. **2.** Hazards, navigation information, waypoints, chart numbers, tide & current tables, distance tables, and warnings are not an exhaustive and complete listing of such items, nor are they necessarily accurate for your travels, since weather, water, tides, currents, and wind conditions can vary widely from time-to-time and the precise location of your vessel cannot be accurately predicted for such purposes. Only proper instruments and government approved publications should be used for navigation. **3.** Although a good faith effort has been made to provide useful and helpful information, because of the ever present possibility of human or mechanical error by ourselves, our sources of information, or others, the publishers and editors cannot guarantee the accuracy or completeness of any information contained in this publication, nor assume liability for direct, indirect, or consequential damages resulting from errors or omissions.

© 2024 Vernon Publications, LLC

WHAT IS NORTHWEST BOAT TRAVEL AND HOW DO I USE IT?

Now in its 46th year, *Northwest Boat Travel* is a unique cruising guide written by Northwest Boaters for Northwest Boaters. It is a compilation of information collected over years of boating experience, with additions and updates made yearly in order to provide the information that boaters who cruise these waters need to know.

Enjoy the journey with Northwest Boat Travel – and if, as you travel, you can adapt your needs and desires to the surroundings, you will open yourself to a variety of experiences, ranging from gourmet restaurants and posh hotels to remote anchorages and wilderness campsites. Please remember that buildings, floats, owners, and establishments are subject to change and it is impossible to guarantee the actual availability or nature of the services or facilities described. We can only describe our experiences and those our readers have shared with us. We invite you to explore these wonderful waters of adventure as we have, and to partake of the good life along the way. We welcome your comments, information, and suggestions.

Shoal Bay Public Dock (p. 211) — Photo © Victor Davare

How To Use This Guide

The Chapter Locations Map: Located on pages 2 and 3, this map is a quick way to locate the information that interests you in the book. For instance, if you want to know about the West Coast of Vancouver Island, just find that location on the map and note the chapter number.

Chapter Organization and Content: Twenty geographically arranged chapters, from south to north, present descriptions and useful information about the waterways, bays, anchorages, facilities, and services along the Inside Passage from Olympia, Washington to Skagway, Alaska.

Symbols and Chart List: At the beginning of each chapter are two boxes marked "Symbols" and "Chart List." "Symbols" is a key for all of the icons used in the book. Such icons make it easier to spot what you are looking for at a glance. For instance, if you need to find a boat launch in a particular area, look on the page for the ⛵. The Chart List box contains a list of the NOAA and Canadian Hydrographic Services charts that cover the geographical areas within that chapter. Other nautical atlases are referenced here as well.

Waypoints and Maps: Each chapter contains maps that provide a general idea of the area. Each map is marked with numbers that correspond to numbers in the text. It is a quick, easy way to locate the place on the map that you are reading about in the chapter. For instance, the entry titled "Vashon Island (1)" tells you that Vashon Island is marked by a number 1 on the map. Latitude and longitude coordinates of many of the marinas are listed in the text, as well. As always, we try very hard to make sure these are helpful and accurate, but only proper instruments and government approved publications should be used for navigation.

Essential Supplies and Services: At each chapter's end is a classified listing of contact information for area businesses and services that boaters might need. Listings appear alphabetically under various headings. We've included boating essentials like fuel, marine supplies, marinas, repairs & services, as well as a few "nonessentials" like golf courses, parks and visitor information.

Important Notices: Located between Chapters 7 and 8 are pages containing information for U.S. and Canada regarding crossing the border, rules, regulations, contacts, procedures, and resources for a variety of subjects.

Tables, Indexes, and Articles: Included in the guide book are articles (*Crossing the Big Waters, Basic Anchoring*), Distance Tables, VHF Radio operation, Index of Sponsors, and an Index to places, facilities, and services.

The ★ (Steering Star) symbol, used throughout this guide, was inspired by the John Masefield poem, *Sea Fever*. The star guides readers to recommended destinations, facilities, and services.

Visit us at boattravel.com

Mariner's Library Recommended Publications

Patos Island Lighthouse (p. 105) Photo © Chris Teren / TerenPhotography.com

Editor's Note: Because of rapid changes along the Inside Passage, not ALL of these books are necessarily recommended to be used as guides to current facilities, places, dangers, and conditions. Some are classics of primary value for their pictures, articles, and charts. Some are reprints from earlier editions while others, especially charts, are revised and reprinted annually or every few years. And some are just entertaining reads!

Adventuring to Princess Louisa Inlet: By Betty Wright. Betty's story of her incredible trip in 1957 with her husband, Jim, traveling in their 16-foot outboard boat from Anacortes to Princess Louisa Inlet.

Afoot & Afloat Series: By Ted & Marge Mueller. These books for land and sea travelers describes the terrain and covers activities for beachcombers, divers, walkers, and hikers from South Puget Sound through the San Juan Islands.

Alaska Harbors Directory: Download a copy of this helpful guide by the Alaska Dept. of Transportation and Public Facilities at www.dot.alaska.gov/stwdmno/ports/assets/pdf/directory/directory.pdf Includes drawings and lists of available facilities.

Alaska's Southeast: (2004, 9th ed.) By Sarah Eppenbach. Information on history, geography, flora, fauna, and what to see while cruising.

Anchorages & Marine Parks: By Peter Vassilopoulos. A guide to sheltered anchorages, marine parks, and recommended areas for kayaking and scuba diving in the San Juan Islands, Gulf Islands, Desolation Sound, the West Coast of Vancouver Island, and the Inside Passage.

Bring Me A Minstrel - Shared Songs of the Salish Sea: By Robert B. Greene. An informative and humorous travel memoir revolving around an 11-day voyage from Sequim to Princess Louisa Inlet. To learn more visit www.robertbgreene.com.

British Columbia Tidal Waters Sport Fishing Guide/Fresh Water Salmon Supplement: Fisheries & Oceans Canada, Communications Branch, Ste 200-401 Burrard St, Vancouver, B.C. Canada V6C 3S4. Phone 604-666-0384. Download at www.pac.dfo-mpo.gc.ca.

Canadian Hydrographic Service, Official charts for British Columbia waters: Comprehensive chart collection. Chart #3313, spiral bound, large size with comprehensive coverage Victoria to Nanaimo and Gulf Islands.

Canadian Tide & Current Tables (Volumes 5-7): Daily Canadian Hydrographic Service. Daily tide and current tables. Full size, easy to read & updated annually. Vol. 5 covers Juan de Fuca Strait and the entire Strait of Georgia. Also includes tables for Seattle and Port Townsend and currents for Juan de Fuca Strait and Deception Pass. Vol. 6 covers West Coast of Vancouver Island and East Coast of Vancouver Island as far south as Campbell River. Vol. 7 covers coast of Northern British Columbia, including the Queen Charlotte Islands to Dixon Entrance. mpo.gc.ca.

Sailing Directions: by Canadian Hydrographic Service. The following five volumes cover from the Strait of Juan de Fuca north to Dixon Entrance-

- **Sailing Directions: British Columbia Coast (South Portion), Vol. 1, 2004 (P118)**
- **Sailing Directions, Inner Passage – Queen Charlotte Sound to Chatham Sound, 2002 (PAC 205E)**
- **Sailing Directions, Hecate Strait, Dixon Entrance, Portland Inlet and Adjacent Waters and Haida Gwaii, 2015 (PAC 206E)**
- **Sailing Directions, General Information, Pacific Coast, 2006 (PAC 200E)**
- **Sailing Directions, Juan de Fuca Strait and Strait of Georgia, 2012 (PAC 201E)**

Challenge the Wilderness: By George D. Tomlinson. The true account of Robert and Alice Woods Tomlinson's life as missionaries along British Columbia's north coast. Historical facts about William Duncan's mission at Metlakatla and Native culture in the 1860's.

Compact Chart Book for Washington Waters. Large scale NOAA charts covering all Washington coastal waters, San Juan Islands, Puget Sound, Lake Washington. West coast and Columbia River bar advisory charts. Multiple indexes. From Evergreen Pacific Publishing.

Cruising Atlas for Northwest Waters: Reproductions of government charts covering Olympia to Queen Sound on the inside of Vancouver Island. Aerial photos; detailed harbor charts; magnetic headings. From Evergreen Pacific Publishing.

Curve of Time: By M. Wylie Blanchett. Delightful accounts of a family's adventures when a widow and her five children cruise the British Columbia coast in the days when few pleasure craft plied these waters.

Day By Day To Alaska: By Dale R. Petersen. The author takes his dream cruise in the 21-ft Bayliner Trophy, Day by Day, from Puget Sound to Sitka, Alaska and return via the outside of Vancouver Island.

Exploring Series Cruising Guides: By Don Douglass & Reanne Hemingway-Douglass. Publications include Vancouver Island's West Coast, South Coast of British Columbia, North Coast of British Columbia, and San Juan and Gulf Islands, Southeast Alaska. Suggested itineraries, distance tables, background information, author's observations, detailed descriptions, diagrams and photos.

Glaciers, Bears and Totems-Sailing in Search of the Real Southeast Alaska: By Elsie Hulsizer. A wonderful adventure travel book gleaned from three summers of sailing, writing, and photographing the wild beauty of Southeast Alaska.

Gunkholing Series: *South Puget Sound, San Juan Islands, Gulf Islands, Desolation Sound and Princess Louisa Inlet:* By Jo Bailey, Al Cummings & Carl Nyberg. Four separate books. By kayak and sailboats, the writers explored nooks and crannies. Interesting narratives, historical information and native lore.

Hell on High Seas: By Rob Mundle. Remarkable stories of survival and daring on the world's oceans. Amazing feats of courage: some verging on madness, others eluding death through sheer bravery, determination and innovation - or even divine intervention?

How to Read a Nautical Chart: 2nd edition By Nigel Calder. A complete guide to understanding and using electronic and paper charts.

Local Knowledge The Skipper's Reference – Tacoma to Ketchikan: By Keven Monahan. Great book for the pilot house. Navigational tips, distance tables and other resources.

Visit us at boattravel.com

Mariner's Library Recommended Publications

Marine Atlas, The Original: By Bayless Enterprises. Two volumes containing detailed cruise charts covering the waters of British Columbia, Puget Sound, and Alaska. Pre-plotted magnetic courses, aerial photos, and marine parks list. Both volumes 14" x 11", plastic spiral (nonmagnetic) bound. Index and speed tables. Volume 1: Olympia to Malcolm Island, North end of Vancouver Island, B.C. 2018. Volume 2: Port Hardy to Skagway, Alaska. 2020. Email: tipsbay@outlook.com. Bayless Enterprises, Inc. 2728 211th St SE, Bothell WA 98021. (206) 291-4049.

Mariners Guide to Nautical Information: By Pricilla Travis. A truly useful reference work for new and not so new boaters. Over 2,000 modern nautical topics including navigation rules, cruising under sail & power, electronics, communication, safety, weather, commonly-used nautical language.

Navigation Rules & Regulations Handbook: By the Department of Homeland Security, US Coast Guard. Current Edition 5/2018.

Passage to Juneau-A Sea and It's Meaning: By Jonathan Raban. A wonderfully written travelogue of Raban's own trip by boat from Seattle to Juneau, presented alongside with an account of Captain George Vancouver's voyage in 1792-94 and his encounters along the coast.

Proven Cruising Routes, Seattle To Ketchikan, Vol. 1: By Kevin Monahan and Don Douglass. Actual routes-waypoint to waypoint, with a diagram of each waypoint-from Seattle to Ketchikan.

Sailing a Serious Ocean: Sailboats, Storms, Stories and Lessons Learned from 30 Years at Sea: By John Kretschmer. Author, teacher, and experienced sailor, John Kretschmer, shares the lessons he has learned over 30 years on the sea. You'll glean all sorts of helpful information on storm tactics, classic sailing books, rig design and more while enjoying true accounts of John's adventures and challenges at sea.

San Juan Islands Cruising Atlas: (By Evergreen Pacific Publishing. Detailed coverage of the San Juan Islands including the Canadian Gulf Islands and SE Vancouver Island. Harbor charts, aerial photos and more.

Sea Salt – Recipes from the West Coast Galley: by Alison Malone Eathorne, Hilary Malone, and Lorna Malone. These sailing authors bring readers on a voyage around Vancouver Island and draw inspiration from local seafood, wineries, and farmer's markets. 100+ recipes, colour photographs.

South Islander - Memoirs of a Cruising Dog: By Amanda Spottiswoode. A light-hearted memoir of the adventures and misadventures of over a decade of cruising between Vancouver Island and the mainland. 31 beautifully hand drawn illustrated maps and tips for some of the best dog walks on the coast. Perfect for anyone cruising with dogs or for boat-bound humans. To order, http://southislander.ca.

Taken By the Wind: The Northwest Coast: A Guide to Sailing the Coasts of British Columbia and Southeast Alaska: By Marilyn Johnson. A well-researched guide that helps you use the unique winds and tidal currents of each area to keep you under sail as much as possible along this beautiful wilderness coastline.

The One Minute Guide to the Nautical Rules of the Road: 2nd edition By Charles Wing. Quick access guide to international and U.S. navigational rules of the road. Rules are explained and illustrated, running light pattern guide included.

Tranquility: A Memoir of an American Sailor: By Billy Sparrow. A three week summer voyage in an old wooden sailboat begins an uexpected, epic adventure. A "sea story, a land story, a life story."

United States Coast Pilot: Published by the National Oceanographic Survey. Depths, characteristics, hazards, anchorages, and navigational information for coastal waters. Volume 7-California, Oregon, Hawaii, and Washington. Volume 8-Dixon Entrance and Alaska to Cape Spencer. Volume 9-Cape Spencer, Alaska to the Bering Sea.

Voyaging With Kids - A Guide to Family Life Afloat: By Behan Gifford, Sara Dawn Johnson, and Michael Robertson. Knowledge gleaned after voyaging thousands of miles with children. Practical and specialized information for parents who want to cruise as a family.

Walker Common Sense Log Book: By Milo & Terri Walker. Now on its 14th printing, this best selling log book includes tabbed sections for vessel information, inventory, maintenance, fuel and radio logs.

Gorge Harbour (p. 190) — Photo © Gorge Harbour Marina

Freshwater Bay, Alaska (p. 275) — Photo © Cynthia Meyer

Arabella's Landing Marina - photo © Arabella's Landing

Chapter 1:
South Puget Sound

Vashon Island to Hammersley Inlet. Des Moines, Tacoma, Gig Harbor, Olympia, Shelton; Carr, Case, & Budd Inlets.

Browns Point Lighthouse Park marks the entrance to Commencement Bay — Photo © Laurie Littlefield-Wells

Symbols
- [ ]: Numbers between [ ] are chart numbers.
- { }: Numbers & letters between { } are waypoints.
- ★ Recommended destinations, facilities, and services
- ⚓: Park, ⛵: Boat Launch, ▲: Campgrounds,
- ⚑: Hiking Trails, ⊼: Picnic Area, ⚲: Biking,
- ⚓: Scuba

Chart List
NOAA Charts:
  18445, 18448, 18453, 18456, 18457, 18474
Marine Atlas Vol 1 (2018): Pages 2-3
Evergreen Cruising Atlas: Pages 151, 155, 156, 158, 159, 169, 172, 173, 176

★ See "Important Notices" between Chapters 7 and 8 for specific information on boating related topics such as boating safety, weather, U.S. & Canadian marine radio use, Vessel Traffic Service, security zones, Canadian & U.S. Customs, etc. Due to changing regulations, call ahead to verify latest customs information.

Puget Sound
[18445]

★ **Puget Sound:** When glaciers dug deep troughs in the basin between the Cascade and Olympic Mountains, they left depths to 900 feet that filled with ocean water, creating a sound that extends nearly 90 miles. In 1792, Captain George Vancouver named this extensive waterway "Puget Sound" to honor Peter Puget, leader of the expedition to the southern portion of the sound. The sound stretches from Olympia northward to the Strait of Juan de Fuca and affords over 2,000 miles of shoreline.

Although much of Puget Sound is deep, the southernmost waters culminate in shoals and drying flats. Tidal differences vary greatly from north to south. At Port Townsend, on the north, the range is eight feet, while, on the south at Olympia, the change can be as much as 15 feet. Currents generally flow north or south with velocities of one-half knot to seven knots, depending on land constrictions. Current and tide tables are necessary publications to have on board. Storm winds usually blow from the south or southeast. In late spring and summer, the prevailing winds are from the west and northwest. Except during storms, overnight winds are usually calm and there are rising afternoon breezes. In summer, a change to a southerly wind may indicate the approach of a storm front. Fog is common along the Puget Sound. April and May are the most fog-free months, while October, November, January and February tend to have the most fog. Monitor weather conditions on VHF WX-1.

Leisure, educational, and sports activities of all kinds are available on and around Puget Sound. Each port-of-call is unique, with its own personality and attractions. Along with boating adventures from any size craft, other activities include picnicking on a beach, hiking on the many trails, and camping at sites in state and county parks.

The Sound is home to various species of fish and marine mammals such as the harbor seal, harbor porpoise, Dall's porpoise, and Orca whale. Gray and Minke whales and California and Steller sea lions are seasonal visitors. Fish and shellfish harvesting are a big part of the state's economy. These include oysters, clams, scallops, crabs, geoducks, and shrimp. Several beaches offer shellfish harvesting to the public. Before digging, call 1-800-562-5632 or visit www.doh.wa.gov (search "beach closures").

Vashon & Maury Islands
[18445, 18448, 18474]

★ **Vashon Island & Vashon Center (1):** Captain George Vancouver named this large island to honor James Vashon, a British Naval officer under whose command Vancouver once served. Steep cliffs and forested hillsides are prominent landmarks. The shoreline is indented with curving beaches and small coves such as Fern Cove and Paradise Cove (site of the Campfire's Camp Sealth), and a few sharper niches such as Lisabuela and Cove (where ruins mark the wharf where the Virginia V once made scheduled stops). Overnight anchorage is recommended only in settled weather. Quartermaster Harbor, a large natural anchorage, is located between Vashon and its neighbor, Maury Island.

In the days of the Mosquito Fleet, steamers plied the waters of Colvos, East, and Dalco Passages, which fringe the island, making regular stops at such ports of call as Olalla, Cove, and Lisabuela. Later, the Black Ball Line developed the ferry landing at the north end. Eventually the Washington State Ferry system took over operations, building a wharf on the north shore between Dolphin Point and Point Vashon. Today, a commuter, passenger-only ferry makes early morning and late afternoon runs on weekdays between downtown Seattle and the island. Car/passenger ferries connect with Fauntleroy in West Seattle, as well as Southworth on the Kitsap Peninsula. Another Ferry Terminal is found at Tahlequah, on the extreme south end of the island. Here a car/passenger ferry makes regular crossings to and from Tacoma's Point Defiance.

The largest community, Vashon, is situated along the main north-south road. There are restaurants, a bakery, hardware, grocery, and liquor stores, as well as specialty shops, a gas station, theater, and post office. Vashon's Farmers Market at the Village Green is open every Saturday from April through mid-December and dozens of Farm Stands offering fresh produce dot the island. Vashon is renowned for its large artist community. During the first two weeks of May and December local artists display works at various galleries and their private studios for the semi-annual *ArtsTour*. Each July, the community also hosts the popular *Strawberry Festival*, a two day event filled with family fun. For more information about events, lodging and dining options visit www.vashonchamber.com.

King County Metro bus Route #119 runs weekdays only to downtown Vashon from Dockton County Park and Burton, a short walk from Quartermaster Marina. You can flag down the bus whether or not you are at a bus stop. Route #118 runs daily from the north end ferry terminal to the Tahlequah ferry. Public boat moorage is available at King County Dockton Park on Maury Island and Quartermaster Marina located in inner Quartermaster Harbor in the small community of Burton. Quartermaster Yacht Club participates in a reciprocal moorage program.

Colvos Passage: This mile-wide passage is free of obstructions and extends about 11 miles along the western shore of Vashon Island. Lights mark the passage, follow a mid-channel course. The current in Colvos Passage sets north on both the ebb and flood tides. Northbound currents are stronger on the ebb tide and the weakest at maximum flood tide. The constant north bound current is a plus for vessels headed north, but for those traveling south (especially against a North wind) a decision must be made - take the much longer route east of Vashon or fight the current and weather in Colvos.

Olalla: This small community is located on the opposite shore of the passage. There is a launch

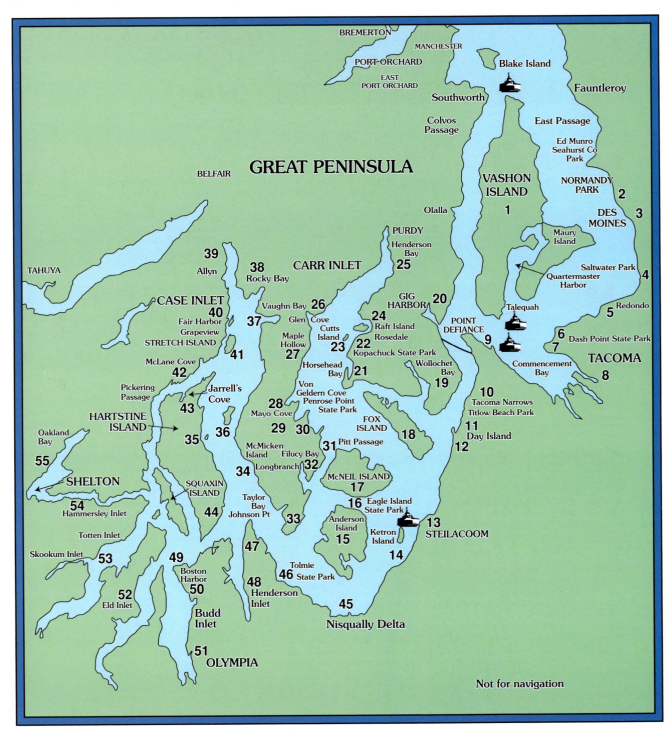

Sunset on the Des Moines Marina   Photo © Ernest Wead

ramp and a picnic area accessible by dinghy. The Olalla Bay Market (former landmark waterfront Al's Grocery Store) offers groceries, wine, craft beer, pizza, ice cream, pretzels and sandwiches. 253-858-6567. There is a dock in front of the store. No dock access at low tide. At high tide (around 12') there is approximately 8' depth at the dock. Watch depths carefully. The nearby bridge is the site of the annual *New Year's Day Polar Bear Club Plunge*. The *Olalla Americana Music Festival* in August is held at the Little League Ballfield.

★⚓ **Lisabuela Park:** Located on the island's west side, 4.5 miles north of the south end of the island, Lisabuela Park was once the site of a resort. Be aware of fast currents near shore. There is a hand-carried boat launch ramp, picnic table, portapotty, and WA Water Trails Association camping sites. There are two sites in the park for a max of 1-night and capacity for 2 tents per site (4 adults max), May-October. Campsites are by reservation only. Contact Vashon Adventures at info@vashonadventures.com or 206-259-3978. More info on camping https://www.vashonadventure.com/camping-at-point-robinson-lisabeula.

East Passage: [18474] See current tables for The Narrows, Washington. Be aware that East Passage is a main shipping channel, with Vessel Traffic Separation lanes. Tugs and freighters are common sights. While currents in East and Colvos Passages are not particularly strong, many boaters heading south will go down East Passage and return north by Colvos Passage. This is because the current in Colvos nearly always flows north.

★⚓ **Wingehaven Park:** The park on the northeast end of Vashon Island was once a large estate owned by the Winge family. Temporary anchorage with some protection from westerly winds is possible, but wakes from passing ships may be a nuisance. Vashon Adventures may be offering bike-in and boat-in camping in 2024. Please contact Vashon Adventures (info@vashonadventures.com) and/or the Vashon Park District for more information. 206-463-9602

Tramp Harbor: Formed by the easternmost part of Vashon Island and the north end of Maury Island this curving beach has shoals along much of its length, extending about 0.2 miles from shore. Point Heyer is a sandspit to the north. Temporary anchorage is possible, but is open to north winds and wakes of passing ships. There is no moorage float, a fishing pier, a picnic area, and a good beach for beachcombing. Off shore, buoys mark the boundaries of an artificial reef at the KVI Tower that is popular with divers.

Maury Island: [18474] This "island" is actually a five-mile long peninsula of Vashon Island, connected by a highway at a narrow neck of land. This is the site of the small community of Portage, whose name recalls its history as a place where Native Tribes used the area for a canoe portage.

★⚓ **Point Robinson Park/Point Robinson Lighthouse:** The beach gradient around Point Robinson is very shallow, and then drops off rapidly. Beachable boats can easily land here, but check the tide tables to avoid having a beached boat float away on the flood or end up on the high level mark on the ebb. The park runs along the water and on up the hillside. Open dawn to dusk, the park offers a place to picnic, beachcomb, fish, fly kites and enjoy other outdoor activities. No fires allowed, portable restrooms are available.

The light station celebrated its centennial in 2015 and the original lighthouse keepers quarters are now historic vacation rentals. Email Eric Wyatt, Recreation Manager, at lodgings@vashonparks.org for reservations or visit www.vashonparks.org/lodging for information.

Point Robinson Lighthouse, a working lighthouse with a fifth-order Fresnel lens offers public tours on Sundays, 12-4 p.m. during high season (mid-May to mid-Sept). South of the lighthouse, is the Ship's Store gift shop, open on weekends during the high season. To arrange a lighthouse tour or a visit to The Ship's Store outside of normal operating hours, contact Captain Joe Wubbold, U.S. Coast Guard (ret.) at captainjoe@centurytel.net. Captain Wubbold is president of The Keepers of Point Robinson volunteer group. Advance notice for requests is appreciated. Two WA Water Trails Association campsites, as well as additional picnic tables, trails and a rock sculpture are located on the bluff above the lighthouse. There are two camping sites in the park for a max of 1-night and capacity for 2 tents per site (4 adults max), May-October. Campsites are by reservation only. Contact Vashon Adventures at info@vashonadventures.com or 206-259-3978. More info on camping https://www.vashonadventure.com/camping-at-point-robinson-lisabeula.

★⚓ **Maury Island Marine Park:** This King County Park, on the east side of Maury Island, is on the site of an old gravel mine. Its open location leaves it exposed to the surf, and wave action has created a rather steep beach. The upper beach (above 0 feet) is composed mostly of loose gravel while the lower beach (below 0 feet) is flatter and sandy in some areas. Rare stands of Pacific Madrone trees are found at the park. A salt marsh is located at the end of the beach. Scuba diving and walking the beach and upland trails are possible activities. There is a porta potty, picnic shelter, no water, no fires allowed. May-Oct primitive campsites can be reserved, vashonadventures.com.

★ **Quartermaster Harbor:** Vashon and Maury Islands come together to form this five-mile long harbor. When entering between Neill Point and Piner Point, be aware of a two fathom shoal off Neill Point and a buoy-marked shoal off Manzanita, on Maury Island. Quartermaster Harbor is favored for its variety of anchoring sites and park lands. North and south winds can enter, but sites are available that offer protection from a particular wind. Anchorage is on a mud bottom in depths of 20-50 feet. The harbor shallows in the bay north of Burton Peninsula. Private homes, many with mooring buoys are located in this area. A marina and Quartermaster Yacht Club (with reciprocal moorage) are on the southwest side of the inner harbor. Use caution at low tide or in windy conditions. The small community of Burton with stores, post office, art gallery and several B & B's are nearby. Daily bus service connects Burton with Dockton County Park and other Vashon Island sites.

Several parks have waterfront access. A public tidelands beach, north of Neill Point and accessible only by small boat, has clams and geoducks. There is an undeveloped park at Lost Lake, north of the beach. Burton Acres Park and Jensen Point Park are on Burton Peninsula. The latter is day use park with restrooms, a swimming beach, hiking trails, picnic areas, and a launching ramp that is located at the park's northeast point. Anchor some distance off shore to avoid shallow water at low tide. This is a popular site for dinghies, canoes, kayaks, and inflatable craft. Kayak & SUP rentals, classes, and tours offered on-site, 206-259-3978, info@vashonadventures.com.

Quartermaster Marina: {47° 23.44' N, 122° 27.96' W} Permanent, seasonal, transient moorage, 30/50 amp power on 50' slips, water, shower, pump-out (call ahead), small trailerable boat lift (under 20'). 206-463-3624.

★⚓ **Dockton Park:** {47° 22' 20" N, 122° 27 14.5" W} The Dockton Marina renovation is complete and provides space for 30 boats on a first come/first served basis.. Dockton Park, on the harbor's east shore, is protected from all but strong north winds. Anchorage is also possible in 18-30 feet of water, on a mud bottom. Check depths with fathometer. Some boaters have reported problems with anchor dragging. Mooring buoys are private. On-land park amenities include a paved launch ramp, restrooms, parking, play area, and picnic shelter. Some 12 miles of trails for hiking and mountain biking are accessible from the trailhead

SOUTH PUGET SOUND Chapter 1 Page 13

across the street. From the park, you can also take a historical walking tour of the neighborhood - look for signs near the play area. King County Metro bus route #119 stops nearby and goes through Vashon's commercial district to the ferry terminal. To reserve the picnic shelter, contact King County Parks at 206-477-6150 or regional.scheduling@kingcounty.gov.

Tahlequah: This small community is the terminus of the ferry to Point Defiance. No marine facilities.

Dalco Passage: This passage separates the southern tip of Vashon Island from Point Defiance in Tacoma. The current in the middle of Dalco Passage almost always sets west or northwest.

East Passage Mainland
[18445, 18448, 18474]

Fauntleroy: This is the site of the ferry terminal with service to Vashon Island and Southworth (on the Kitsap Peninsula). Lincoln Park is to the north, however Seattle City Park regulations prohibit the beaching of boats.

★ **Seahurst Park (2):** No moorage, but small boats can be beached here. Offshore, buoys mark a sunken, largely decomposed barge where scuba diving is popular. Park facilities include picnic tables, BBQ's, restrooms, trails, playground and the Environmental Science Center (for family events and program information call, 206-248-4266).

★ **Des Moines (3):** Des Moines, coined "The Waterland City," is bordered on the west by six miles of shoreline along Puget Sound. If you love beaches, parks and trails, outdoor festivals and great dining; point yourself in the direction of the Des Moines waterfront and explore the full array of attractions and activities. Des Moines Beach Park Event Center (a national historic district) is adjacent to the Des Moines Marina with its 840-slips, guest docks, fishing pier, restaurants, boat repair facilities and opportunities for beachcombing, kayaking and paddleboarding, as well as diving tours. During the summer there are lots of fun events like the Farmers Market (10am-2pm, Sat. June-Sept), Fireworks Over Des Moines, the Waterland Festival and Parade, Wednesday evening concerts in Beach Park, free outdoor movies, the Poverty Bay Blues & Brews Festival and an Arts Gala. Downtown Marina District shopping is only a few blocks away and includes a variety of shops, services, lodging and dining establishments, public art and a historic museum. Saltwater State Park and Redondo Beach are to the south with reefs for scuba diving, camping and a public aquarium open on Saturdays. SeaTac International Airport and a Sound Transit Light Rail Station are only 10 minutes away by automobile and public transportation. Visit desmoineswa.gov, tothebeachwa.com or seattlesouthside.com and make Des Moines your next stop for an unforgettable Puget Sound experience.

★ **Des Moines Marina:** {47° 24.106' N, 122° 20.8' W} This well maintained, city-owned facility has moorage, 30/50 amp power, gas, diesel, water, propane, repairs, haul-out, showers, waste pump-out, and restrooms. Enter south of the fishing pier, between the fishing pier and the north end of the rip rap breakwater. Convenient to restaurants, groceries, and downtown Des Moines. Reservations accepted for groups of 5 or more boats. One month minimum notice for groups. See our advertisement on this page. Website: www.desmoinesmarina.com. Email: marinainfo@desmoineswa.gov. Address: 22307 Dock Avenue South, Des Moines, Washington 98198. Telephone: 206-824-5700.

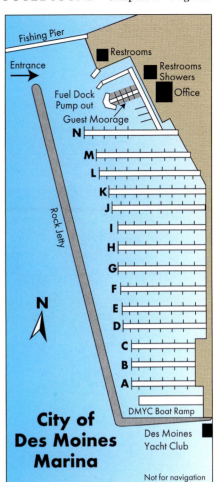

City of Des Moines Marina

Not for navigation

★ **City of Des Moines Marina:** To enjoy one of the finest views of the Olympic Mountains, come to this Marina located on the east side of Puget Sound, just a few miles south of Seattle and north of Tacoma (47-24' N lat. 22-20' long.). The Marina entrance is between the fishing pier and the north end of the breakwater. At night, look for the green entrance buoy, along with the three yellow navigation lights on the fishing pier and the single red marker light on the end of the breakwater. After clearing the breakwater, turn starboard and proceed to the fuel dock and guest moorage area. Approximately 1,200' of guest moorage space available on a first come first served basis. Water and 30/50 amp shore power are available. Check in at the fuel dock. No charge for moorage for vessels moored under 4 hours. There is  a waiting list for permanent moorage. Please visit the Marinas website for current waitlist time frames. Since its opening in 1970, this well maintained facility has served the community of Des Moines and provided boaters access to the city's business district, located a few blocks east. Nearby are banks, shops, groceries, restaurants, and lodging. Also located in the Marina is Anthony's Homeport, Classic Yacht Sales, Ranger Tugs, Quarterdeck Coffee, Beer & Wine Bar, and CSR Marine boatyard. Fuel dock with gas, diesel, propane, and lubricants are available. Showers, restrooms and a pump-out are available free of charge. Families and large gatherings enjoy the picnic and meeting facilities at adjacent Des Moines Beach Park. Visit the marina's website for more information. www.desmoinesmarina.com. Address: 22307 Dock Ave S, Des Moines, WA 98198. Telephone: 206-824-5700. Email: marinainfo@desmoineswa.gov.

The Tacoma Dome and Thea Foss Waterway looking to Commencement Bay Photo © City of Tacoma

CSR Marine: (Located at Des Moines Marina) Haul-outs to 50'/50,000 lbs. Full service boatyard. 206-878-4414.

Saltwater State Park (4): This park lies south of Des Moines in an attractive valley beside McSorley Creek, a salmon spawning bed. Facilities include campsites, picnic tables, two picnic shelters, seasonal food concession, fresh water, restroom, showers, two mooring buoys (day use only), hiking trails, a scuba rinse station, and an underwater artificial reef, which is a protected marine sanctuary. The upper trails have beautiful views of Maury and Vashon Islands. Open hours 8am-dusk. A seasonal "teach on the beach" program for children includes marine identification and beach walks. 253-661-4955.

Redondo (5): Site of Redondo Waterfront Park. Anchoring is possible. There is a seasonal mooring float and a two lane concrete launching ramp with 360' of side tie dock for launching personal water crafts. There are nearby shops, restaurants, a boardwalk, lighted fishing pier, fish cleaning station, restrooms, boat parking and boat washing. Artificial reefs, including a VW bug, make this a popular dive spot. Captain Vancouver originally named this site Poverty Bay because of a "poverty" of winds.

Dash Point State Park (6): Located in Federal Way, this park rims a warm, sandy beach. Fishing, swimming, and skim boarding are popular here. Because the water is shallow for some distance off the beach, it is necessary to anchor quite a distance out from shore. The anchorage is open to winds and wakes. There are miles of hiking and biking trails, as well as picnic tables/shelters, tent and RV campsites, cabins, trailer dump station, fresh water restroom and showers. Park Office: 253-661-4955.

Dash Point Park & Pier: A 300' fishing pier marks this site. There are picnic sites, a sandy beach for portable boats, a playground, and protected waters for swimming. Shallow water extends some distance offshore. Scuba diving is popular at a wreck off the park.

Browns Point Lighthouse Park (7): This park has 1,500 feet of waterfront. Anchorage, open to the north, is possible in the deeper water offshore. This historic beacon across from Tacoma marks the entrance to Commencement Bay. The beacon sits in an attractive three-acre property that the USCG leases to Metro Parks Tacoma. Points Northeast Historical Society maintains the historic, fully restored lightkeepers cottage as a history museum and vacation rental (available year-round, see VRBO and Airbnb web sites for more information). A boat house displays a replica Coast Guard surf boat and maritime artifacts. The original 19th century fog bell hangs in what was the pump house. Free tours on Sat., May-Sept. 1-4pm. Picnic area and restrooms available. A small shopping center with fine and casual dining nearby. www.pointsnortheast.org. 253-927-2536.

Tacoma & Commencement Bay

[18445, 18448, 18453, 18474]

Tacoma (8): [18453] Although Tacoma's renaissance is the talk of the town, this city has been on the cutting edge for years. It is the first city in Washington to offer light rail service, boasts the largest municipally owned telecommunications system in the U.S., and is among North America's largest container ports. With its location on Commencement Bay, one of the largest natural deep-water ports in the world, much of the commercial development by the Port of Tacoma is on the flatlands around the waterways. By boat, entry is from Puget Sound, via Commencement Bay to Hylebos and Thea Foss Waterways. A five knot speed limit is enforced. At the head of Commencement Bay there are several small marinas along Hylebos and Thea Foss Waterways. Marinas along the Thea Foss Waterway offer access to repair facilities, chandleries, museums, shops, art galleries, specialty boutiques, restaurants, and waterfront parks. A public dock in front of the Museum of Glass now lets boaters arrive in Tacoma's Museum District by water. From there, they can easily walk across the Chihuly Bridge of Glass to the Washington State History Museum, historic Union Station (filled with Chihuly glass art) and the Tacoma Art Museum. There are no moorage facilities in the Blair Waterway, but a trip in and out of this waterway permits seeing the rails at the mouth where Todd Shipyards built the "Baby Flattops" during World War II.

Many community celebrations are held on Tacoma's waterfront. Each April, Commencement Bay is the site of the *Daffodil Festival Marine Parade*. Another event centered around Commencement Bay and Ruston Way parks is an annual *Fourth of July Extravaganza* featuring an air show, arts and crafts booths, and fireworks. The last weekend of June, *Taste of Tacoma* features food and wine tasting, entertainment, and other fun activities at Point Defiance Park. Many sailing races and regattas are also held on Commencement Bay throughout the year. To highlight the holiday season, there is a marine Christmas parade along the Ruston Way shore and into Thea Foss Waterway.

Thea Foss Waterway comes alive each summer with *The Tacoma Maritime Fest*, headquartered at the Foss Waterway Seaport Museum. Traditional highlights of the festival are free Port of Tacoma boat tours, free admission to the Foss Waterway Seaport, plenty of children's activities, food vendors and a variety of boats, from vintage crafts to the most modern working vessels. For details visit, www.tacomawaterfront.org.

The Port of Tacoma: The Port of Tacoma is an economic engine for the South Puget Sound. Nearly $3 billion in labor income is generated from the more than 42,000 jobs derived from port activity. As a partner in The Northwest Seaport Alliance, the Port of Tacoma connects the U.S. to Asian markets and to Alaska. Container ships are common sights on Commencement Bay and are larger than ever before, nearly tripling in capacity over the past two decades. Grain ships waiting for corn and soybeans, as well as roll-on/roll-off vessels carrying new automotibles, are also regularly spotted on the Bay.

Puyallup River: The Puyallup River system is one of Puget Sound's largest. It supports a large fish run, and much of the river basin has historical and archaeological significance.

Marine View Drive & Hylebos Waterway

[18445, 18448]

Marine View Drive, Hylebos Waterway: [18453] Marinas along Hylebos Waterway offer moorage, launching, provisions, and repairs, along with views of downtown Tacoma, the Port of Tacoma, and Mount Rainier. Native tribes once called the area, Tahoma, meaning Mother of Waters. Marine View Drive, along the northeast shore of Commencement Bay, is an aptly named street which ascends the edge of a bluff.

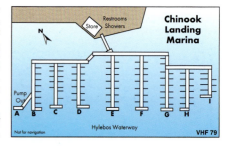

Visit us at boattravel.com

Chinook Landing Marina: {47° 16.90' N, 122° 24.20' W} Permanent and transient moorage, 30/50 amp power (125 volt), water, restrooms, laundry, showers, cable, free WiFi, pump-out, trash, recycling, convenience store, security. Open all year. 253-627-7676. VHF 79.

Modutech Marine Inc.: Full service boat yard. Covered moorage, 3 marine lifts, 100 ton railway, insurance repair, custom fiberglass, aluminum, steel and custom woodwork. 253-272-9319.

Tyee Marina: {47° 17' 33" N, 122° 25' 5" W} Permanent moorage (covered to 36', uncovered to 60'), 30/50 amp power, water, showers, public pump-out, wifi, storage units, security. 253-383-5321.

Marina at Browns Point: {47° 17' 43" N, 122° 25' 04" W} Permanent moorage, liveaboards. 30/50 amp power, water, showers, laundry, restrooms, wifi, secured parking. Public pump-out. 253-272-2827.

Hylebos Marina: {47° 16' 35.364" N, 122° 23' 21.444" W} Permanent moorage to 80', no liveaboards, 30/50amp power & 120/240 volt, boatyard services or DIY, 35 & 75-ton Travelifts, supplies, storage. 253-272-6623.

The East 21st Streed Bridge spans the Thea Foss Waterway   Photo © City of Tacoma

Thea Foss Waterway

[18453]

★ **Thea Foss Waterway:** [18453] In 1900, the Puyallup River was channeled into a straight course, forming two large waterways. One of these, City Waterway, was home to Tacoma Municipal Dock. Built in 1911, it was the State's first publically owned dock. In 1989, City Waterway was renamed "Thea Foss Waterway" to honor the pioneer tug boating family headed by Thea Foss.

No anchoring is permitted along the waterway, but free, short-term moorage is available in several places. An attractive new esplanade follows the shore, making it convenient to access many downtown Tacoma attractions including hotels, restaurants, the Broadway Theater District, Antique Row, and the Tacoma Farmer's Market (May to Oct.). Light rail service (currently free) carries passengers to and from the Theater District and the Dome District, with many attractions along the way, including the Museum District and the UW Tacoma campus.

On the very north end of the waterway is Thea's Park, a small park with no facilities that is owned and maintained by Metro Parks Tacoma. Nearby is a seasonal seaplane dock, as well as docks for visiting boaters that are managed by the Foss Waterway Seaport. The Foss Waterway Seaport is housed in the restored, historic Balfour Dock Building. This maritime heritage and marine education center offers exhibits showcasing Tacoma's working waterfront, as well as "The Boat Shop" where active boat builders are observed at work. The Seaport's popular signature event, the Tacoma Maritime Fest, is held in July. For information, visit www.fosswaterwayseaport.org or call 253-272-2750.

Just past the Seaport on the west side of the waterway is Foss Harbor Marina. Continuing along the shoreline about mid-way down is the 15th Street Public Dock. From here, many points of interest in downtown Tacoma, as well as several restaurants and a seafood market are easily reached on foot.

Further into the waterway on the west side, Dock Street Marina sits directly in front of the Museum of Glass, one of the District's numerous museums. The Museum of Glass connects to the Washington State History Museum by way of the famed Chihuly Bridge of Glass; adjacent is historic Union Station (free to the public), the Tacoma Art Museum and the Children's Museum of Tacoma.

Across on the eastern shore is the Foss Landing Marina and Delin Docks. The LeMay America's Car Museum, the Tacoma Dome and Freighthouse Station Marketplace (with international food court and a variety of interesting shops) are a short walk away in the Dome District. Across the street from Freighthouse Square a Tacoma Link Light Rail Station allows further citywide exploration. The service is free from one end of downtown to the other.

★ **Dock Street Marina:** {47° 14' 45" N, 122° 25' 59" W} Guest moorage for individuals or clubs, 36' to 60' slips, with pier ends to 127'. Gated concrete docks with ADA features. 30/50/100 amp power, water, slip-side pump-outs, restrooms, free showers, laundry, kayak/SUP rentals. Pet friendly and environmentally sensitive EnviroStars marina! 253-572-2524. Dockmaster 253-250-1906.

Delin Docks Marina: {47° 14' 53" N, 122° 25' 48" W} Permanent moorage, liveaboards, 30'-60' slips, 30/50 amp power, water, showers, laundry, garbage/oil disposal, slip-side pump-outs, parking. 253-572-2524.

Foss Harbor Marina: {47° 15' 27" N, 122° 26' 10.4" W} Transient & live-aboard moorage, fuel dock (discounts available), restrooms, showers, Wi-Fi, grocery store, slip-side pump-out service, watercraft rentals, secure gated access. 253-272-4404. VHF 71.

Foss Landing Marina: {47° 14' 39" N, 122° 25' 53"W} Permanent wet moorage, dry storage, 30/50 amp power, water, shower, cable TV, slip-side pump-outs, secure parking. 253-627-4344.

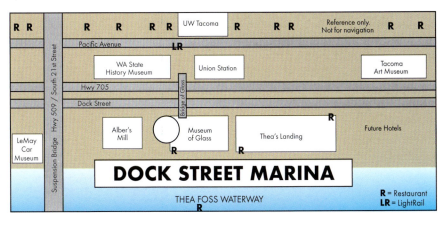

Page 16 Chapter 1 SOUTH PUGET SOUND

Dune Peninsula at Point Defiance Park   Photo © City of Tacoma

Foss Waterway Seaport: Located on the historic Thea Foss Waterway on the southwest side of Commencement Bay, the Foss Waterway Seaport celebrates Tacoma's rich maritime heritage - past, present and future. Located on the waterfront in a century-old wooden wheat warehouse known as the Balfour Dock building. Listed on the National Registry of Historic Places, the Seaport is one of two remaining wooden warehouses with others that stretched almost a mile long and were originally built to accommodate cargo "arriving by rail and departing by sail" during the early years of Tacoma's history. Activities at the Seaport include: Maritime Heritage Exhibits, Heritage Boat Shop, Land and Boat based Education Programs, Event Rental Space and Guest Boat Moorage Space. The Seaport offers 1,200 feet of side-tie moorage, 30 and 50 amp power, water, and easy access to local restaurants and participates in the Museum Pass Program. Please ask about the Seaport Family Membership/NARM Combo ($125 or higher) The North American Reciprocal Museum (NARM) Program offers member priced admission to over 896 museums and member discounts at museum stores. Address: 705 Dock St., Tacoma, WA 98402. Phone: 253-272-2750 ext. 100. Website: www. fosswaterwayseaport.org.

Johnny's Dock Marina: {47° 14' 45" N, 122° 25' 50" W} Monthly moorage for boats 20' to 60'. Slipside potable water, electrical hookups, gated secure parking, onside caretaker. 253-666-6840.

Tacoma Fuel Dock at Commencement Bay Marine Services: {47° 15' 20" N, 122° 25' 56" W} Ethanol free gas, diesel, oil, free pump-out, ice & snacks in summer. 253-383-0851. On-site vessel repair, parts, haul-out to 16 ton/40'. 253-572-2666.

★ **15th Street Public Dock:** Also known as the "Fish Peddler Dock" (named after the restaurant that fronts it), this dock is open all year. 220' of side-tie day moorage only, 2-hr moorage limit. No services, no ADA access. For information call 253-272-4352.

Old Town & Ruston Way
[18445, 18448]

★ **Ruston Way [18453]:** This shoreline is part of scenic Kla How Ya Drive and offers panoramic views of Commencement Bay, Vashon Island, the Port of Tacoma, the city skyline, and the Cascade and Olympic mountain ranges. Within the two mile stretch of waterfront are beaches for walking or beach combing, parks, picnic tables, a jogging and bicycle trail, a fishing pier, public parking, and restaurants (several have docks for boats to moor while dining).

★ **Jack Hyde Park on Commencement Bay:** A large sundial is a landmark in this park at the south end of Ruston Way. Picnic area available.

★ **Old Town Historic District:** The shopping district, one block from the Ruston Way waterfront, offers specialty foods, gifts, and artists' wares. In 1864, when Job Carr established claim to the land now known as Old Town it was the beginning of Tacoma. The first house, church, post office, school, hospital, and lumber mill were built here. Many old buildings still remain, including Tacoma's oldest existing building, St. Peter's Church built in 1873. By 1900, Slavonian immigrants settled in the Old Town, near Ruston Way. They introduced purse seining, a new and better method of fishing. This sparked a boom in commercial fishing, boat building and shipping along the shoreline.

★ **Old Town Dock:** The original dock was built in 1873. By 1880, visitors could rent a boat, board a steamer bound for other Puget Sound ports, or purchase wood, grains and farm produce from the stores and businesses operating on the dock. Today, a renovated dock offers two short term moorage slips (up to 40' and 60'). No power. Off the main dock are free board floats for kayaks and smaller boats (day time moorage only). An underwater artificial reef makes an excellent habitat and feeding ground for sea life. No fishing or diving off pier. A sandy beach with picnic tables and restrooms is nearby. West of the Old Town Dock, a large pier extends in front of the Silver Cloud Inn where boats tie up during the summer - first come, first served.

Dickman Mill Park: Site of the historic Dickman Lumber Mill that operated here from the 1890's until 1974. Restrooms and trails.

Hamilton Park: A small park with promenades, benches, picnic table, water, gardens and a fitness station.

★ **Puget Creek Natural Area/Puget Park:** Located on Alder Street just 600-feet across Ruston Way, this natural area is bisected by one of only three salmon-bearing streams within the city limits. Miles of trails wind through the gulch to Puget Park where there is a playground and picnic tables.

★ **Les Davis Fishing Pier:** This public fishing pier is a major attraction in the area. It is open 24 hours, with shelters, rod holders, and night lights. Restrooms are available during daylight hours only. During summer months, concessions are offered nearby. Stairs that access the water are a popular starting place for divers bound for the artificial reef located offshore.

★ **Marine Park:** Located next to the Les Davis Fishing Pier, this park has benches, lawn areas, restrooms, and is a popular embarkation point for scuba divers. Tacoma's original fireboat is berthed at the east end of Marine Park. Memorial sculptures recognize Tacoma's sister city, Kunsan City, Korea and the sister port of Kitakyushu, Japan. Several restaurants are nearby.

★ **Point Defiance Park (9):** Point Defiance Park is accessible by land and sea, and offers year-round seasonal activities and special events for visitors of every age. This is the site of the Tacoma Yacht Club, two marinas, an 8-lane public launch ramp, a public fishing pier, the Point Defiance-Vashon Island Ferry Terminal, a restaurant, and Point Defiance Park. The 760-acre park has panoramic vistas of the water, Vashon Island, the Olympics and majestic Mount Rainier. Eight themed botanical gardens including the formal rose, rhododendron, and Japanese gardens, along with miles of trails through old growth forest and a shoreline promenade offer peaceful moments in the park. Nearby are sandy beaches, tennis

Foss Harbor Marina

courts, playgrounds, and signature rental and picnic facilities. Scuba diving is possible off the shores of Owen Beach. Extensive hiking, running, walking and bicycling routes are accessible. Point Defiance Park, with its Zoo and Aquarium and historic 1855 Fort Nisqually Living History Museum, serves more than 3 million visitors annually and is rated as one of the best parks in the country. Events in this park include *Candlelight Tours* held in October at Fort Nisqually, and *Zoolights* at Point Defiance Zoo & Aquarium during the month of December. Parks & Recreation: 253-305-1022, www.metroparkstacoma.org. Zoo: 253-404-3800.

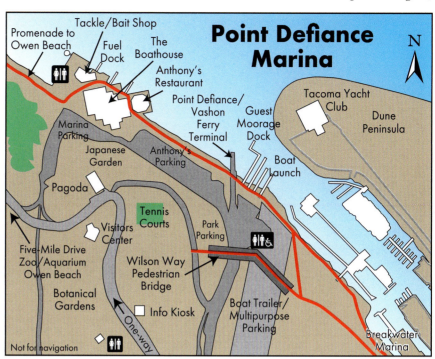

★ **Point Defiance Marina & Boathouse at Point Defiance Park:** {47° 18.29' N, 122° 31.41' W} is one of Tacoma's premier waterfront destinations on the shores of Commencement Bay. Point Defiance Marina is a 5 Star Certified Clean Marina. Boaters and visitors are invited to stop inside the Bait and Tackle Shop where they will be greeted by knowledgeable staff and experienced anglers. The Bait and Tackle Shop offers food & beverage, fuel, souvenirs, boating & fishing supplies, clothing and WSDFW license sales. No kayak, no boat - no problem!

Our friendly staff can help you rent a kayak or motor boat by the hour or for the day. We have plenty of rental boats with 9.9 horsepower motors which allow you to cruise or fish the Puget Sound with ease. Point Defiance Marina also offers a wide variety of classes and events throughout the year to enrich your marine experience. Located next to the Bait & Tackle Shop are two transient daytime floats and a fuel float with ethanol-free gas for purchase. Nearby is an 8-lane public boat launch offering 72 hour maximum transient moorage with available power and pump-out station all with convenient and easy access to ample boat trailer parking. Point Defiance Marina also offers year-round individual boat storage spaces for rent including access to boat lifts to the water. The 300-unit dry storage facility accommodates vessels up to 17'. The Marina is open 363 days a year from dawn to dusk. Plan for a full day or a long weekend and enjoy all the features and amenities Port Defiance Park has to offer including: Fort Nisqually Living History Museum, Point Defiance Zoo & Aquarium, old growth forest, botanical gardens, hiking trails, off-leash dog park, and signature rental facilities and historical picnic shelters. Anthony's Restaurant, next door to Point Defiance Marina, offers fine dining and breathtaking views of Puget Sound. Access to Point Defiance Marina by land is through Point Defiance Park and by water WDFW Area 11 Tacoma-Vashon east of Owen Beach. See our advertisement on this page. 5912 N. Waterfront Dr., Tacoma, WA 98407. www.pointdefiancemarina.com. Facebook "Point Defiance Marina." Telephone: 253-404-3960.

Breakwater Marina: {47° 18.30' N, 122° 30.69' W} Permanent moorage, limited guest moorage call ahead. 15/30 amp power, water, restrooms, showers, laundry, public pump-out (fee), yacht sales, full-service marine shop, grid, repairs. 253-752-6663.

Tacoma Yacht Club: Located off Ruston Way, next to Point Ruston on Yacht Club Rd. 290+ slips for members plus guest & reciprocal moorage. Clubhouse at {47° 18' 24.6816" N 122° 30' 44.6004" W}. 253-752-3555.

Salmon Beach: When rounding Point Defiance, heading south toward the Narrows, one passes the unique, secluded, turn-of-the-century Salmon Beach residential community (listed on the Washington Heritage Register). Homes built on stilts over the water are accessed only by water or steep trails from the top of the bluff.

Tacoma Narrows (10): [18445, 18448, 18474] See The Narrows, Washington current tables. When the water from the up-to-12 foot tidal changes in the South Sound flows through this passage, currents can run more than five knots. Currents generally flow northerly along the east side of the passage and southerly on the west side. Maximum flood and ebb currents occur about four hours after low and high tides in Seattle. The Tacoma Narrows Bridge, the fifth longest suspension bridge in the U.S., spans the Narrows and connects Tacoma to the Kitsap Peninsula. The waters of the Narrows lead to the South Sound, Longbranch Peninsula, Olympia, Horsehead Bay, Wollochet Bay, and more.

★ **Titlow Park (11):** Pilings from the old Olympic Peninsula Ferry Landing mark the location of this 75-acre park. Inhabited by octopus, crab, sea urchins, bullheads, perch and ratfish, the

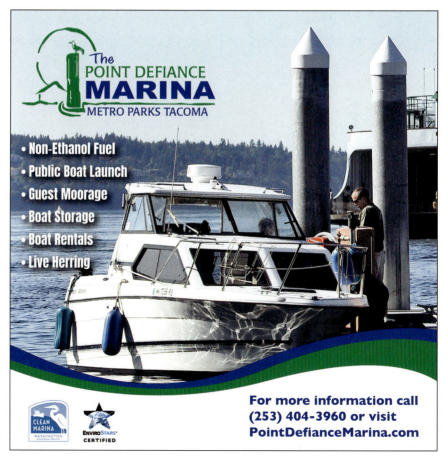

Chapter 1 SOUTH PUGET SOUND

Gig Harbor Marina Photo © Chance Busey

pilings draw scuba divers to the site. The historic Titlow Lodge, circa 1911 is found here as are picnic sites, athletic fields, sports courts, trails, a hand carried boat launch, a lagoon, a playground, and "sprayground" for water fun. Restaurants and a small grocery store are nearby.

Aaron's Marine Service: Boat, outboard, trailer service & repair. 253-564-1644

Narrows Marina: {47° 15' 22" N, 122° 36' 19" W} Overnight guest moorage (first come, first served), gas, diesel, pump-out, covered and uncovered moorage as well as dry boat storage. Narrows Marina Bait & Tackle store is stocked with snacks, beer, ice, live and frozen bait, fishing and crabbing gear. 253-564-3032.

Day Island (12): A 3-knot speed limit is enforced in the area. A dredged waterway, spanned by a bridge, separates this island (actually a peninsula) from the mainland. The best course favors the Day Island side. Entrance to the waterway is restricted until there is a +4 foot tide. Upon entry to basin, be aware of the tides and the draft of your vessel. There is a minimum low tide depth of one foot. A large drying shoal is in the entrance. Keep the shoal and the three green day markers to port. There are several permanent moorage facilities on Day Island. Some local residents anchor shallow draft boats in Day Island Lagoon, which is also the site of the Day Island Yacht Club (members or reciprocal guest moorage only). From here, you can walk to a restaurant, brewery, and a park with picnic area. Bait, ice, snacks, beverages, supplies, and fuel are available nearby at the Narrows Marina where there is also a marine mechanic and parts store on-site. It is also possible to anchor east of the north tip of Day Island.

Day Island Yacht Harbor: {47° 14' 34" N, -122° 33' 42" W} Privately owned boathouses, permanent moorage, haul-outs to 15,000 lbs. 253-565-4814.

★ **Steilacoom (13):** This is the terminus for the ferry between Anderson, Ketron, and McNeil Islands. There is short-term visitor moorage for boats up to 26' long at a small float tucked in near the ferry landing. Anchorage is found off Sunnyside Beach Park. This park has a small pebble beach, picnic facilities, playground, and restroom. Founded by Lafayette Balch, a sea captain, Steilacoom began as a bustling frontier seaport. It was the first incorporated town (1854) in Washington Territory. Several historic homes have been restored, and 32 buildings are on the National Registry of Historic Places. A self-guided walking or driving tour is possible. Don't miss the Historical Museum that includes the furnished 1857 Nathaniel Orr pioneer home site with wagon shop and historic orchard. (For hours call, 253-584-4133), or the Steilacoom Tribal Cultural Center featuring a changing gallery, tribal exhibits, and gift/snack shop (Open Sat., 10am-4pm, 253-584-6308). The latter is housed in the former Oberlin Congregational Church building, circa 1903. The Bair Drug & Hardware Store, a local landmark, has found new life as a restaurant. Built in 1895, the store housed a post office, and carried hardware, patent medicines, and sweet treats at its 1906 soda fountain. Steilacoom has a number of other eateries as well, including a coffee shop, a deli and pub, and for a deck with a view the Topside is a popular choice. Plan a summer visit and enjoy a farmers market or concert every Wednesday from late-June through August or a Salmon Bake on the last Sunday in July. For a fall visit, have fresh cider at the *Apple Squeeze* held the first Sunday in October.

Ketron Island (14): This is a private island with no public facilities.

★ **Anderson Island, Oro Bay, & Amsterdam Bay (15):** Anderson Island is the southernmost island in Puget Sound. It is a small, densely wooded island, encircled by 14 miles of beachfront property. Known for its serene pasture land and casual lifestyle, it is popular with bicyclists and boaters, though its shoreline is mostly private. A ferry connects Anderson Island to Steilacoom. A 5-knot speed limit is enforced in the area. Between the Ferry Landing and Sandy Point is the private Riviera Club Marina (20 slips, 3 mooring buoys, members only). There is anchorage in Oro and Amsterdam Bays. Oro Bay, on the southeast side has a shallow entrance, but offers good anchorage inside. This is the site of the private Oro Bay Marina and Yacht Club (reciprocal moorage only, first come first serve. Boats to 50 feet, 20 amp power). Amsterdam Bay, on the east side of the Island is very shallow especially at low tide. Favored anchorage is near the center of the bay. Good fishing is found year-round in the vicinity. The island is home to B & B's, several stores, a museum and private golf course. In September the annual Island Fair is held.

★ **Eagle Island Marine State Park (16):** This island in Balch Passage, between Anderson and McNeil Islands, is accessible only by boat. A buoy marks a nearby reef. One mooring buoy is provided, 3 day limit. Strong currents in Balch Passage can shift the buoys into shallow water at low tides. Seals are often spotted in the shoal near the buoys. The Island has some sandy beaches. No drinking water, garbage deposit, or restrooms. The island was named for Harry Eagle, a member of the Wilkes Expedition. Park Info, 360-426-9226.

McNeil Island (17): The oldest prison facility in the Northwest closed here in 2011. Home to a Territorial Jail (1875), Federal Penitentiary (1879-1980), and State Corrections Center (1981-2011). Now the only facility left is the Special Commitment Center where civilly committed sex offenders who have completed their prison sentences receive specialized mental health treatment. Boaters should maintain a distance of at least 100 yards off the island. Part of the island is a Wildlife Area that also includes Pitt and Gertrude Islands. The latter has the largest haul-out site for harbor seals in southern Puget Sound. The islands are home to many bald eagles and blue herons.

★ **Fox Island & Tanglewood Island (18):** This peaceful residential island is connected to the mainland by a bridge. (See Hale Passage below.) Strong currents in this vicinity can affect launching from Fox Island ramp. The ramp is in poor condition and usable at high tide. The Island has no public floats. Tanglewood Island, the private island next to Fox Island, was once the site of a boys camp. A landmark faux "lighthouse" was built here in 1947. Today, the "Light" of the lighthouse has been restored by island residents, however the landmark clubhouse building adjacent to the lighthouse was demolished several years ago. Because of aquaculture operations, anchor on the west side of Tanglewood Island and also farther in, behind the island. Echo Bay has good anchorage, but buoys in the bay are private. It is possible to land a dinghy in the southeast corner of this bay where there are no homes. One block up from the shore, on 6th Avenue, is a grocery store with gas and propane, deli, beer pub and occasional live music. All floats and shorelines are private with the exception of the Fox Island Sand Spit at Nearns Point that curves around to cradle an anchorage basin. Owned by PenMet Parks, the spit is open for day use. A public concrete fishing pier with picnic areas and beach access is found on the eastern tip of the island. Further up the shoreline, the Fox Island Yacht Club is located in Cedrona Bay (members and reciprocal moorage). An historical museum is located about mid-island. For Island information visit, www.FoxIslandWA.net.

Visit us at boattravel.com

Hale Passage: Separating Fox Island from the mainland, this four mile passage has maximum currents in excess of three knots. The ebb flows east and is stronger than the westerly flood current. Near the west end of the passage, a fixed highway bridge has a clearance of 31' at mean high water. A drying shoal, marked on its northeast side by a green buoy, is 350 yards southeast of the bridge and near the middle of the channel. Pass north of the buoy.

★ **Wollochet Bay (19):** [18448] Many private homes and private mooring buoys line this two-mile-long inlet located off Hale Passage. Anchorage is possible near the center farther into the bay where the bay narrows abruptly. Slow to no wake speed in the bay. Private buoys and the Tacoma Yacht Club Outstation occupy most of the shallow basin at the head. There are launching ramps to starboard at the mouth of the bay and on the west shore in the inner harbor. Wollochet Bay Estuary Park is located along the north end of the bay near the mouth of Artondale Creek.

Gig Harbor at dusk with Mount Rainier in the background — Photo © Jim Nelson

Gig Harbor
[18445, 18448, 18474]

★ **Gig Harbor (20):** A 5-MPH speed limit and/or no wake is enforced. When traversing the shallow and narrow, 50-yard-wide channel at low tide that rims the spit at the entrance, keep to mid-channel if possible. The shallowest part of the channel is just outside the bay and is approximately nine feet at a zero tide. Tidal currents can affect maneuvering near the spit. Within the harbor, shallow areas extend from shore and a drying flat is at the extreme head. Good anchorage on a mud bottom is found in the center in 40 feet of water. Anchorage is encouraged on the north side and center of the harbor, not on the south side. Visitor moorage is found at Arabella's Landing Marina, Pleasurecraft Marina and Gig Harbor Marina. Jerisich Dock, on the southern shore also has guest moorage, and some restaurants have moorage floats for customers. A launch ramp is located on the northeast shore at the end of Randall Drive. No fuel available in Gig Harbor. The harbor is popular and sometimes crowded with kayak and SUP enthusiasts. A voluntary safety program called "Go With The Flow" was introduced in 2019 (https://www.gigharborwa.gov/683/Go-With-The-Flow).

Located at the southern end of the Kitsap Peninsula, Gig Harbor is home to spectacular views of Mount Rainier, the Olympics and the Cascades. Coined "The Maritime City," the harbor was so sheltered that in 1851, Lt. Wilkes refused to enter until his gig was dispatched to explore the entry channel. The picturesque and photogenic waterfront is often featured in magazines. Croatian descendants have given this community a European heritage, with fishing and tourism as major industries. A variety of restaurants are found here (many serving fresh seafood). Local shops feature wearable art, quilts, antiques, photographs, original paintings, pottery, concrete sculptures and books. The Harbor History Museum on the downtown waterfront showcases the unique heritage of the Gig Harbor Peninsula. Free admission; for information: 253-858-6722. Near the museum, the historic Eddon Boatyard is home to the Gig Harbor Boat Shop where the tradition and craft of wooden boat building is preserved through programs and workshops. The Boat Shop's classic small craft livery service has rowboats and two electric boats available for public use. For open hours call 253-857-9344. Eddon Boatyard has a pier and float, although access is limited by shallow depth. The float's south face is available for 3-hr bow-tie small-craft moorage. The north face is used for Gig Harbor Boat Shop programming. Beach access at the site is tide dependent.

The Waterfront Farmers Market at Skansie Brothers Park downtown is held from June through August every Thursday, 1pm-6pm. During summer months Skansie Brothers Park also hosts free Tuesday night concerts. On the first weekend in June, 16,000 people come to celebrate the popular Maritime Gig Festival with free live entertainment, food, parade and more. Other annual events include the Film Festival and Cider Swig in September, and Girls Night Out in November. For 2024 information on the lighted boat parade, visit www.visitgigharborwa.com for updates.

For information on the vintage-styled trolley that runs between the historic downtown waterfront and the uptown shopping area visit www.piercetransit.org. By car, Gig Harbor is reached by State Highway 16 west from Interstate 5 in Tacoma. Gig Harbor, 30 minutes from Bremerton, is accessible via the Seattle-Bremerton ferry.

Need more Gig Harbor information? Stop by the Visitor Information Center at the Gig Harbor Chamber of Commerce on Judson St. or visitgigharborwa.com for a calendar of events, an online Visitors Guide, and other visitor information online.

Maritime Pier: {47° 19' 48.2" N, 122° 34' 41.3' W} Drive-aboard pier only for pedestrians and authorized commercial fishing vehicles. Public parking area and restrooms at the base of the pier. Lower 12-ft x 40-ft float is available for pick-up/drop-off access for the general public. 15 minute limit, no transient moorage. Pump-out station on north end of float, open year round. 253-851-6170.

★⚓ **Community Paddler's Dock at Ancich Waterfront Park:** {47° 20' 03.5" N, 122° 35' 08.9' W} This dock, is located on the water in front of the City's Ancich Waterfront Park. Moorage of any kind is prohibited at the dock but human-powered watercraft are allowed to launch into/out of the water. Restrooms are available at Ancich Waterfront Park. Park hours are from dawn to dusk. 253-851-6170.

★⚓ **Jerisich Dock at Skansie Brothers Park:** {47° 19' 55.6" N, 122° 34' 49.5' W} Look for the large American flag and long moorage float extending from the southern shore. Check depth and low tide prediction, especially on the east side of the float near the ramp. Guest moorage with water (seasonal) and 30 amp power on both sides of the pier (rafting and stern tie on east side only). Two buoys are available for boats under 32' in length. Rates are posted, use automatic payment kiosk. No reservations, first come-first served. Maximum moorage stay is three overnights, whether continuous or not, within any 10-day period. Pump-out on the end of the dock, open seasonally April 1 - Nov 1. Picnic areas, restrooms, showers, map & visitor information. 253-851-6170.

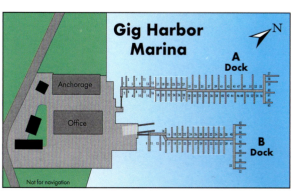

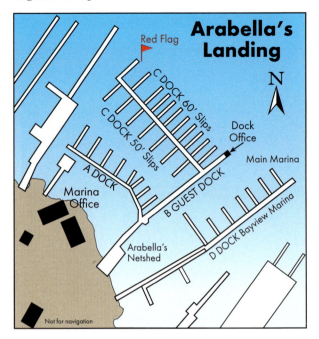

The Magic Bus under sail in Gig Harbor Photo © Chance Busey

★ **Arabella's Landing Marina:** {47° 20' 0.26" N, -122° 34' 59" W} Open year-round. For Guest moorage go to our easy-to-access online reservations system. Log into our website at www.arabellasland-ing.com then click on the "Overnight Moorage" tab. Click on "Book Reservation". Slips vary in length from 30 feet to 95 feet. For yachts longer than 95 feet, please call the office at 253-851-1793. Moorage fees are based on the length of the slip. 30-amp and 50-amp power, water, restrooms and showers are included in the moorage fee. Laundry facilities are available for a nominal fee. Stan and Judy Stearns developed this lovely marina, located in the heart of Historic downtown Gig Harbor. Arabella's well-trained staff offers docking assistance seasonally during office hours. Arabella's has impeccable concrete docks, well-groomed lawns, lush flower gardens, brick walkways, complete wheelchair access, and a clubhouse and lounge for group gatherings. See our advertisement on this page. E-Mail: info@arabellaslanding.com. Address: 3323 Harborview Drive, Gig Harbor, Washington 98332. Telephone: 253-851-1793. Fax: 253-851-3967.

Gig Harbor Marina & Boatyard: Full service boatyard with a 50-ton Travelift. Monthly and overnight moorage, free WiFi, 30 amp power, bathrooms with showers, food trolley and a rentable event space located between the boatyard and beautiful Skansie Brothers Park. 253-858-3535. VHF 69.

Harborview Marina: Privately owned covered slips to 46', sold as condos. 253-851-3948.

Lighthouse Marine Gig Harbor LLC: Marine repair. Specializing in outboards and stern drives. 253-858-8160.

Murphy's Landing: {47° 20' 6" N, 122° 35' 24" W} Permanent moorage. Slips for sale. 253-851-3093.

Peninsula Yacht Basin: {47° 20' 20" N, 122° 35' 28" W} Permanent moorage only. Homeport for Gig Harbor Yacht Club (members and reciprocal moorage, 253-851-1807.) 253-858-2250.

Pleasurecraft Marina: {47° 19.81' N, 122° 34.74' W} Permanent covered moorage. 253-858-2350. Houseboat rentals on-site. 253-549-6639.

Ship to Shore Marine: (At Arabella's Landing Marina). Marine supplies/hardware, charts, kayaks/SUPs, accessories. 253-858-6090.

Tides Tavern: {47° 19' 39" N, 122° 34' 40" W} World famous clam chowder, beer-battered fish-n-chips, pizzas, sandwiches, burgers, salads and fresh local seafood, wine, beer and spirits. Come by foot, boat, floatplane or car! Must be 21+. 253-858-3982.

West Shore Marina: {47° 20' 13" N, 122° 35' 24" W} Long term moorage only. 253-851-1793.

SOUTH PUGET SOUND   Chapter 1   Page 21

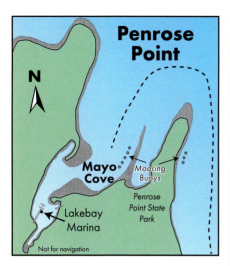

Arabella's Landing in bloom   Photo © Arabella's Landing

Carr Inlet
[18445, 18448, 18474]

★ **Horsehead Bay (21):** Good, but limited, anchorage is found on a sandy mud bottom in 15-25 feet of water. A sandspit, shaped like a horse head restricts the entrance and cuts off westerly seas. Private homes rim the bay, but there is a strip of public beach in the southeast part of the bay. A launching ramp is to port upon entry.

★⚓ **Kopachuck State Park (22):** Located .7 miles north of Horsehead Bay. Two mooring buoys are available. Anchorage is possible on a good mud bottom. No protection from winds. Facilities include picnic areas (some with beautiful sunset views), forest trails, and water. No overnight camping. About 1.5 miles from the park, groceries are available at a small store. There is a sunken artificial reef offshore for scuba divers. Avoid the area near the white buoy. 253-265-3606.

★⚓ **Cutts Island (Deadman Island) Marine State Park (23):** Located in Carr Inlet, this two-acre marine park offers 8 mooring buoys, a beach for picnicking and great views from the top of the clay cliffs. A spit between Cutts and Raft Islands is exposed at low tide. No drinking water, no fires, no camping. Beware of poison oak. Give resident seals a very wide berth. Scuba diving is popular in the Kopachuck-Cutts Island vicinity. 360-902-8844.

★ **Rosedale and Raft Island (24):** Good anchorage is possible in the lee of Raft Island. Raft Island is private, no services available. A bridge connects the south shore of Raft Island to the mainland. The height from the mud at mid-channel to the underside of the bridge structure is 36' 6". The channel goes dry at low tide. Depending on the tide and boat size, you may be able to pass under the bridge at high tide (at least 4-5ft). Recommended entry is around the north side of Raft Island. Island View Market, on the Gig Harbor side, has a dock for patrons (dock is open when Market is open), hand-carry gas, some groceries & a popular public house with a great selection of wine & beer. Call the store, 253-851-9882 if unsure of the tides.

★ **Henderson Bay (25):** Leading to the community of Purdy, this bay stretches to Burley Lagoon at the extreme head. The lagoon dries and is private oyster lease land. Purdy has no marine facilities, however anchorage is good. Open to the south. Purdy Sand Spit divides Burley Lagoon from Henderson Bay. This public waterfront area includes a boat launching ramp located at Wauna near the highway bridge. DNR beaches, found along the north shore of Henderson Bay, are marked with white posts.

Glen Cove (26): A spit protects the entrance to this very shallow bay. Do not attempt entry on a minus tide. A launching ramp is located to port near the entrance. There is limited, if any, anchorage.

★ **Maple Hollow (27):** Anchorage in the bay is possible. Avoid the Naval Acoustic Range marked by a red triangle with a flashing red light. Located below a steep, thickly forested hillside. A circular hiking trail leads from the beach to a park with picnic area.

★ **Von Geldern Cove (28):** Limited anchorage space lies near the entrance to this shallow cove. A shoal extends from the north shore and the area is also exposed to north winds. Watch depths, especially at low tide. A launching ramp is on the west shore. The quiet residential town of Home includes a store, service station, tiny restaurant, laundromat and post office.

★ **Mayo Cove (29):** Shoals lie off of both sides of Penrose Point, extending from the northeast side and on the west in Mayo Cove. When entering Mayo Cove, stay toward the center of Carr Inlet until Lakebay Marina comes into view. Turn to enter, staying in the center channel. A shoal, about a half-mile in length, extends from the beach about 300 yards west of Penrose Point. Mayo Cove is shallow, so be aware of tides, depths and the draft of your boat. Stay in center channel. The channel makes a bend to starboard. A marina and private homes lie near the head. Penrose Point State Park is located on the east shore.

Lakebay Marina Resort: {47° 15' 29" N, 122° 45' 29" W} The Recreational Boating Association (RBAW) partnered with State Agencies to purchase the marina in December 2021. The cooperative arrangement calls for DNR to oversee the aquatic lands and lease; State Parks to manage the uplands area; and RBAW to develop plans for renovation of the marina over the next several years. The goal is to operate it as a marine park for all to enjoy. The marina and land property is currently closed and inaccessible to the public while renovations are in progress.

★⚓ **Penrose Point Marine State Park (30):** Caution advised when approaching this area. To avoid unmarked shoals, keep Penrose Point well off to port. This lovely state park has over 2 miles of saltwater frontage on Mayo Cove and Carr Inlet. Mooring floats with an accessible pumpout in Mayo Cove. The floats dry on extreme low tides. The tidal range is 12 feet. Mooring buoys are in outer Mayo Cove and along the east shore toward Delano Bay. Anchorage is possible off Delano Beach on either end of the mooring buoys in about 5 fathoms. A park ranger is on duty. Showers, restrooms, RV & tent camp sites (no hookups), fresh water, dump station, picnic tables, hiking & biking trails. Open daily. 253-884-2514, 1-888-CAMPOUT for reservations.

Pitt Passage (31): [18445] See current table for The Narrows, Washington. This narrow, two-mile-long channel is on the west side of McNeil Island. The ebb current flows north through Pitt Passage at the maximum rate of two and one-half knots. When traversing the passage, avoid the buoy-marked Pitt Passage Rocks, located off the McNeil Island shore, south of Pitt Island. At Pitt Island itself, pass in the channel on the east side of the island. Least depth within the passage at zero tide is 11 feet. Another buoy-marked shoal is a hazard north of Pitt Island. White posts on the beach along the west side of the Pitt Passage mark a public beach.

Many groundings occur at Wyckoff Shoal, a drying shoal located farther north of Pitt Island. Watch the depths and use chart. Pass west of green buoy #3 and north of green buoy #1. Wyckoff Shoal is managed by DNR and is the site of commercial geoduck harvesting.

★ **Filucy Bay & Longbranch (32):** Filucy Bay is a lovely, sheltered bay with good anchorage in 25-35 feet of water on a mud bottom. A marina is located inside the bay. Anchorage, with protection from southeast winds, may be found in fairly shallow water inside the spit at McDermott Point and in the inlet that extends to the north. A launching ramp is south of McDermott Point. Near the marina is a wooded, nature walk and ballfield.

Longbranch Improvement Club Marina: {47° 12' 56" N, 122° 45' 28" W} Permanent, monthly and guest moorage (first-come, first-served), 30 amp power, water, restroom, garbage disposal, covered pavilion, ice. 253-202-2056. VHF 68.

2024 Northwest Boat Travel

View from the Fair Harbor Marina Photo © Fair Harbor Marina

Case Inlet
[18445, 18448]

Taylor Bay (33): There is limited anchorage near the entrance. Much of the shoreline is private, but Taylor Bay Park has 600 feet of shoreline access for non-motorized boats.

★⚓ **Joemma Beach State Park (34):** Located in Whitman Cove, this Cascadia Marine Trail Campsite has a large camp and 2 water trail sites. There is one boat ramp, 4 mooring buoys and 500-feet of dock space (docks available from mid-May to mid-October, offering 30-feet of moorage at low tide). Primitive tent sites, vault toilets, and picnic sites are available. The covered picnic shelter can be reserved, 253-884-1944. Fees charged. Open year round, 8am to dusk. Activities include walking the trails and beachcombing. The Park is named for Joe and Emma Smith who lived on the premises from 1917 to 1932. 253-884-1944, 360-902-8844.

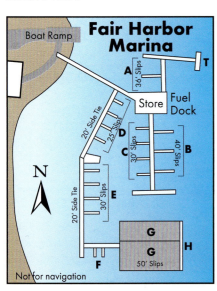

★⚓ **McMicken Island Marine State Park (35):** Mooring buoys are north and south of the island. Fees apply. There is good anchorage on a mud bottom. This 11 acre park is located off the east shore of Harstine Island. It is accessible only by boat. There is a large rock on the south covered at high tide. A drying shoal about 30 ft. wide lies between Harstine and McMicken Islands and connects them at low tide. An artificial reef, constructed of old tires, lies north of the island. Divers are likely to be in the vicinity. On Harstine Island, behind the reef, is a public beach marked by white posts. There are clams, oysters, rock crab, and mussels here. Vault toilets, and hiking trails are on park land. No fresh water or camping on land. Campfires and dogs are not allowed on the island. The extreme south tip of the island is privately owned. 360-426-9226, 360-902-8844.

★⚓ **Harstine Island State Park:** (aka as "Hartstene.") Located near the center of the east side of the island, this park has 1,600 feet of saltwater shoreline on Case Inlet. Anchor along the shoreline in two fathoms at low tide. By land, a parking lot is at the trail head and a one half mile trail leads down to the beach. Hiking, beachcombing, clamming, and fishing are popular. The public beach extends along the Inlet giving beach walkers access to McMicken Island State Park at low tide by way of a sand spit. There is no camping allowed on the island. The DNR manages all the tidelands. 360-426-9226, 360-902-8844.

Herron Island (36): A ferry connects this private island of 120 residents with the mainland. Only riders with valid guest passes are allowed to board.

★ **Vaughn Bay (37):** This good, protected anchorage should be entered only at mid-tide or higher. Watch your depths. Tidal changes cause strong currents in the pass and an incoming tide is preferable when entering. Enter mid-channel off the spit and follow the north shore for 200 yards. Then turn south, cross the bay staying parallel to the spit. There is anchorage in two to four fathoms on a mud bottom at the south end of the spit, but no public buoys. A public beach where one might find littleneck and butter clams and red rock crab is located on the outside of Vaughn Spit. On the north shore of Vaughn Bay is a launching ramp (unusable at low tide). If you walk about .6 miles from this ramp by road to the 3-way intersection and turn right on S. Vaughn Rd., it is a short walk to the Key Peninsula Historical Museum. The museum is an interesting place to visit and hosts many events throughout the year. Free admission, 1-4pm on Tuesdays and Saturdays. Also open by appointment- call Judy at 253-225-9759.

Rocky Bay (38): Rocky Point provides some protection in north and west winds, however it is exposed to southerlies. A very shallow channel leads into the lagoon back of the sandspit. Watch for rocks. Travel around the small sandy island before turning to go behind the sandspit.

★ **Allyn (39):** A 200-foot long pier with a mooring float extends from shore. Twelve transient moorage slips are available for up to 50-foot vessels. The bay is shallow at low tide and extreme caution is advised for deep draft boats. Approach along the east side of the bay until opposite the pier, then turn in toward the pier. Drying flats extend from the head of Case Inlet. This public Port of Allyn on North Bay is the site of a boat launch and the float -which was newly rebuilt in late 2019, as well as the Allyn Waterfront Park offering a playground, restrooms, and a rentable gazebo. There is no marine fuel facility. There is a bus stop near the dock, but visitors will find this a walkable town with three restaurants, two gourmet coffee outlets, a historic church, and gift shops, all in the downtown area. The unique George Kenny Chainsaw Carving School offers competitions, instruction, and a gallery of carvings for sale (360-275-9570). Weekend wine tasting is right next door. Additional conveniences include a grocery store, beauty shop, gas station, pizza shop, and a mechanic. About half of a mile from town is the Lakeland Village Golf Course, which features 27 holes of PGA-level golf.. The third weekend in July brings thousands to the annual *Allyn Days* featuring a Salmon Bake on Saturday, and *Geoduck Festival* and *Taylor Shellfish Oyster Roast* on Sunday. For more information visit www.portofallyn.com, www.allynwa.org or www.explorehoodcanal.com.

Allyn Waterfront Park Dock: {47° 22' 58.8" N, 122° 49' 30" W} Limited transient, seasonal moorage, 30/50 amp power, water, launch ramps, restrooms, shower for $5 (call ahead to arrange key check out), pump-out. Five feet of water at dock at low tide. Easy walk to restaurants and shops. 360-275-2430.

★ **Fair Harbor & Grapeview (40):** Enter from the south, in the channel between Stretch Island and Reach Island (also known locally as Treasure Island). The waterway under the bridge to Reach Island is dry on a minus tide. Deeper water is found near the marina. This harbor offers limited anchorage. Additional anchorage is found between the north tip of Reach Island and the mainland. Approach from the north. Across from the Island, farming once fueled the economy of the now residential community of Grapeview. From its name, one can easily surmise the identity of the areas number one crop. Many new, expensive waterfront homes are lining the shores as people discover the beauty and serenity of the area. Each year on the last Saturday in July the Grapeview Community Association and Fair Harbor Marina hosts the *Grapeview Water & Art Festival* at the marina. The festival features art, music, food, kids' activities and contests.

Fair Harbor Marina: {47° 20' 11" N, 122° 50' 2" W} Nestled in South Puget Sound's Case Inlet. Fuel, showerss, restrooms, laundry, car rental and paddelboard rental. 253-315-1629

SOUTH PUGET SOUND   Chapter 1   Page 23

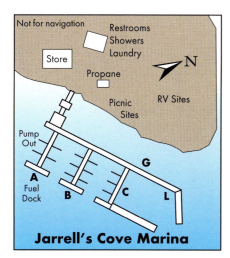

Jarrell Cove Marine State Park   *Photo © gdeakins*

★ **Stretch Island (41):** Stretch Island, east of Grapeview on Case Inlet, is connected to the mainland by a bridge. There is no clear channel on the west side of the island and the area dries on any low tide. The famous "Island Belle" grape used for winemaking is grown here and at one time, several wineries and juice companies flourished here. This Island is also home to Stretch Point Marine State Park.

★⚓ **Stretch Point Marine State Park:** This four acre park situated on both sides of Stretch Point on the northeast corner of Stretch Island is accessible only by boat. Five mooring buoys are east of the sandy point and west of the point in the bight. Stretch Point has no pay station, but boaters can pay mooring fees at Jarrell Cove State Park. Anchorage in the bight is open to northerly wind. Smaller boats can pull up onto a nice sandy, gravelly beach. There is no fresh water, but mussels, swimming beaches, and scuba diving spots are plentiful. 360-426-9226.

★ **McLane Cove (42):** This small indent off Pickering Passage has adequate depths for anchorage. A shoal is on the east side.

Pickering Passage: [18448] This nine-mile-long passage connects Case Inlet with Peale Passage and Totten Inlet (See current table for The Narrows, Washington). Pass mid-channel. The flood current sets to the south toward Hammersley Inlet. Velocities in the area of Hammersley Inlet can reach 2.5 knots. A fixed bridge at Graham Point, clearance 31' at mean high water, connects Harstine Island with the mainland. Latimer's Landing County Park, adjacent to the bridge near Graham Point, has a concrete ramp that can handle somewhat larger boats, a dock, and a pit toilet. About one mile west of Dougall Point on the north shore of Harstine, is a private marina with moorage open only to property owners.

★⚓ **Jarrell Cove Marine State Park (43):** This park is in the lovely inlet on the northern side of Harstine Island. Beware of the shallow waters at minus tides and near the head of the cove. Moorage floats include one located to port near the entrance, and another larger float that lies to port farther into the bay. There is a pump-out and there are 14 mooring buoys. The 67-acre park is accessible by land or by boat and offers visitors two kitchen shelters, picnic tables, restroom, shower, 21 tent campsites and one Cascadia Marine Trail site. Kitchen shelters can be reserved, 1-888-226-7688. Fresh water is available. User fees are charged year around. Anglers of all ages fish for perch and other marine creatures. Activities include canoeing, fishing, scuba diving, and hiking. 360-426-9226.

★ **Jarrell's Cove Marina:** {47° 17.00' N, 122° 53.40' W} Located on Harstine Island, opposite Jarrell's Cove State Park, this very clean marina has permanent and guest moorage, 30 ampere power, fresh water, Valvtect marine fuel (contains no ethanol), diesel (biodegradable), gas (no ethanol & good additives), ice, bait, fishing tackle, laundry, showers, waste pump-out and dump, picnic sites, and a nice beach. Three RV sites are equipped with electricity, water, and a dump station. The well stocked store has groceries, beer, wine, pop, and gifts. Moorage is available on a first come-first serve basis. Open every day in the summer (Memorial Day weekend through Labor Day) and by appointment in the winter. Address: 220 E. Wilson Road, Shelton, Washington 98584. Fax: 360-432-8494. Telephone: 360-426-8823.

★ **Squaxin Island (44):** Squaxin Island is Squaxin Island Tribal land.

★⚓ **Hope Island Marine State Park:** Peace and serenity can be found at this lovely 106 acre state park. A resident caretaker is on-site. Two mile hiking trail, vault toilets, picnic tables, eight tent sites, one Cascade Marine Trail site. No potable water, no fires, no pets allowed. There are five mooring buoys available. Anchorage is possible off the eastern shore. Watch depths. Fishing is good in this area. There are no campfires or dogs allowed on the island. Boaters and paddlers outside the Squaxin Tribe are not allowed to land on neighboring Squaxin Island. 360-463-1861.

Nisqually Delta, Budd Inlet, & Olympia

[18445, 18448, 18456]

Nisqually Delta (45): The largest undeveloped river delta in South Sound, the Nisqually Estuary has an outstanding accumulation of shore birds, marine mammals, and other wildlife. It is such an important and unique habitat that about 15,000 acres have been set aside as the Nisqually Reach Aquatic Reserve. The Reserve extends from the Nisqually River Delta across Nisqually Reach, including all state-owned aquatic lands in these areas, plus state-owned bedlands and beaches surrounding Anderson, Ketron and Eagle Islands to the shores of McNeil Island. A boat ramp at Luhr Beach, on Nisqually Head, provides access at high water. (See current tables for Dupont Wharf, Washington.) Nearby, the Nisqually Reach Nature Center has three tidal aquariums, study bird mounts, and varied activities for visitors. Open noon-4pm Wed., Sat., Sun. 360-459-0387. WDFW Vehicle Access Pass or Discover Pass is required to access Luhr Beach or the Nature Center (inquire at the Center about a temporary parking pass for center access). Across McAlister Creek, the 4,500 acre Billy Frank Jr. Nisqually National Wildlife Refuge has a Visitor Center and over four miles of trails for wildlife viewing. For fees, hours and information about boating at the Refuge, 360-753-9467.

★⚓ **Tolmie Marine State Park (46):** Five mooring buoys lie well out from shore because the beach extends some distance. Anchorage is possible. This day use park is located on the mainland about half way between Johnson Point and the Nisqually River delta and is accessible by land or sea. It has a picturesque saltwater lagoon and one of the South Sound's finest sandy beaches. A man-made reef 500 yards off shore provides scuba diving territory where octopus, perch, moon snails and sand dollars are common sights. Hiking is possible on over three miles of trails. There are picnic tables and two kitchen shelters with electricity. Call the Park to reserve at 360-456-6464.

Johnson Point (47): Zittel's Marina is located in Baird Cove. Further down the shoreline toward Tolmie Park, is a boat storage and repair facility.

Puget Marina: {47° 8' 56.256" N, 122° 47' 33.8778" W} Private boat launch, dry boat storage, new/used boat sales, boat and motor service/repair. 360-491-7388.

2024 Northwest Boat Travel

Olympia's Swantown Marina Photo © Port of Olympia

The other Port of Olympia facility, Port Plaza, with moorage and viewing tower, is on the main channel, past the marine shipping terminal. At the head of the inlet, next to the boat houses, is Percival Landing Park. This historically significant site was named in 1853 after Captain Samuel Percival.

The downtown heart of Olympia has many restored buildings which house gift shops, grocery stores, a Farmers Market, book shops, marine businesses, art galleries, antique, clothing and specialty shops, and a variety of popular restaurants and bars featuring live entertainment. The Washington Center For The Performing Arts also features live stage productions with local and regional actors. If you have kids in tow, the Hands On Children Museum is a great stop, designed to entertain and educate children of all ages.

Rimming the waterfront is a landscaped, mile-long, wooden promenade with benches and tables built over pilings. The main promenade heads north, past a carved Orca Whale and a tangle of docks, to a tower that offers gulls-eye, 360° view of the Olympics and the port. At the corner of Fourth and Water Streets, a life-sized sculptured couple leans against the boardwalk rail, locked in an endless kiss while the boats come and go.

Parks found within easy walking distance include Capitol Lake, Sylvester, and Port Plaza where you can enjoy the boating and sailing activities, picnic areas, and trails - all in the shadow of the Capitol Buildings. Music-In-The-Park concerts entertain visitors every Saturday at 1pm during July at Sylvester Park. Visit http://downtownolympia.org/Events/Music-In-the-Park for more information.

Nearby, the Old Capitol is all stone arches and turrets. Built in 1892 as the Thurston County Courthouse, this served as the capitol from 1905 to 1928.

Another noteworthy building, the Legislative Building, was completed in 1928 with a design reminiscent of the U.S. Capitol in Washington DC. Louis Comfort Tiffany Studios designed the building's floor lamps, sconces, and chandeliers. Tours offered weekdays 10am-3pm and weekends 11:30am-2:30pm. Next to the capitol stands the red brick, Georgian Style home of the governor. Executive Mansion Tours are conducted on occasional Wednesdays, by reservation only. Reservations for mansion tours must be made online at least 24 hours in advance. Call 360-902-8880 or go to https://des.wa.gov/services/facilities-and-leasing-managment/capitol-campus/tours for capitol campus tours information.

Special events featured during the year include the *Capitol City Marathon* in May, *Lakefair* in July, and *Harbor Days*, with the *Vintage Tugboat Race* on Labor Day weekend. Contact Experience Olympia & Beyond for information regarding area events, attractions, and transportation. 360-763-5656, www.ExperienceOlympia.com.

Zittel's Marina: {47° 9' 55.7496" N, 122° 48' 29.8332" W} Permanent & guest moorage, gas, diesel, 20/30 amp power, water, restrooms, showers, pump-out, boatyard (onsite service or DIY), haul-out to 48', boat sling, ramp, marina store, snack bar, boat rentals. 360-459-1950.

★ **Henderson Inlet (48):** Locally known as South Bay, Henderson Inlet extends over four miles to extensive drying flats. Keep to the center, avoid private buoys and submerged pilings on the west. There is good anchorage inside the entrance in 35 feet of water on a mud bottom. Open to north winds. This is a wildlife conservation area. It is possible to explore Woodard Bay by dinghy.

★ **Boston Harbor (49):** The entrance to this attractive half-moon shaped harbor is identified by a lighthouse on Dofflemyer Point, at the mouth of Budd Inlet. A marina and public launch ramp are located here. The cement ramp is rather steep and usable for most boats at +1.0 tide or higher. Around the turn of the century this site was frequented by smugglers. From here, boaters can access Nisqually Reach and other nearby attractions.

Boston Harbor Marina: {47° 8' 23.5104" N, 122° 54' 17.5998" W} Permanent and guest moorage, marine grade gas, diesel, 20 amp power, restrooms, private beach, wifi available. Groceries, beer/wine, snack shack, gifts, SUP/kayak rentals. 360-357-5670. VHF 16.

★ **Budd Inlet [18448, 18456]:** The entrance to Budd Inlet is a mile wide between Dofflemyer and Cooper Points and is deep enough for all recreational vessels. To reach downtown Olympia from the north, round Dofflemyer Point and head toward Olympia by continuing past Olympia Shoal, marked by lighted beacons on the shoal's east and west sides. From Olympia Shoal, pick up the 28' dredged and buoyed channel that leads into the harbor. A spoils bank from channel dredging, lies east of the channel. This bank is quite shoal, with parts of it drying, so stay in the channel. The channel branches at a piling intersection marker. Follow the eastern leg to Swantown Marina and Boatworks.

★ **Burfoot County Park (50):** This day-use park is a small niche south of Boston Harbor. It has trails, picnic areas, a playground, volleyball courts, and horseshoes. It is accessed by land or water. An artificial reef is marked by buoys.

★ **Squaxin Park (formerly Priest Point Park):** Located on East Bay Drive, this park has a good beach and extensive tide flats, picnic tables, shelters, playground, water, restrooms, and looped trail. Shelter reservations, 360-753-8380.

Walk-around: The Ellis Cove Trail, three mile loop trail with Interpretive Stations, describe different aspects of the ecology, forest, birds, plant life, wildlife, and history of the area. Beach access is possible in several places.

★ **Olympia (51)** (See Budd Inlet chart numbers and navigation information above): There is overnight moorage at Swantown Marina, Port Plaza, and Percival Landing Park. Swantown Marina, Fuel Dock and Boatyard, operated by the Port of Olympia, is located on the east side of the peninsula that juts out from the head of Budd Inlet.

★ **Port Plaza (Port of Olympia):** Located north of Percival Landing. Water, no power. Free four-hour moorage, then guest rate for over four hours. This Plaza frequently serves as a concert and event site for outdoor events. Bronze artwork reflects maritime and natural history. The colored and textured concrete and paved surfaces, unique planting areas and raised lawn invite visitors to enjoy a relaxing respite onshore. For more information, call Swantown Marina 360-528-8049.

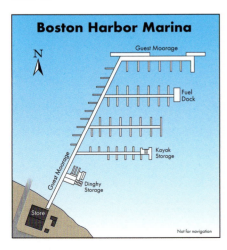

Visit us at boattravel.com

SOUTH PUGET SOUND   Chapter 1   Page 25

The Swantown Marina framed by the Olympic Mountains   Photo © Port of Olympia

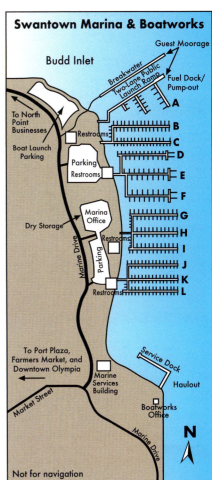

★ **Swantown Marina and Boatworks:** {47° 03.50' N, 122° 36.65 W} Owned and operated by Port of Olympia. Swantown offers 656 permanent moorage slips ranging from 20-92 ft in length, 70+ guest moorage slips for boats up to 100 ft in length and a state-of-the-art fueling station offering ValvTect Marine gas & diesel. Amenities include 24 hour security, 30 & 50 amp shore power, concrete two-lane launch ramp, pump-out station, restrooms, showers, laundry, 1.2 mile Billy Frank Jr. walking trail, free WiFi, repairs & 24-hour emergency haul-out. Swantown's 3.6 acre boatyard is fully fenced, lighted & secured and has the capacity to store up to 60 vessels. Swantown's 82 ton Marine Travelift is capable of hauling vessels from 17 ft - 80 ft in length and up to 21 ft wide. Swantown is a Certified Clean Marina & Boatworks is a Certified Clean Boatyard. Open year round. See our advertisement on this page. Begin your journey at www.Swantownmarina.com. Email: marina@portolympia.com. Marina address: 1022 Marine Drive N.E., Olympia, Washington 98501. Marina Telephone: 360-528-8049. Fax: 360-528-8094. Boatworks address: 650 Marine Drive NE, Olympia, Washington 98501. Boatworks Telephone: 360-528-8059. Fax: 360-528-8095. VHF 16 & 65A.

Martin Marina: {47° 2' 50.784" N, 122° 54' 12.3114" W} Permanent moorage, liveaboards, parking, laundry, power, restrooms, water. 360-357-5433.

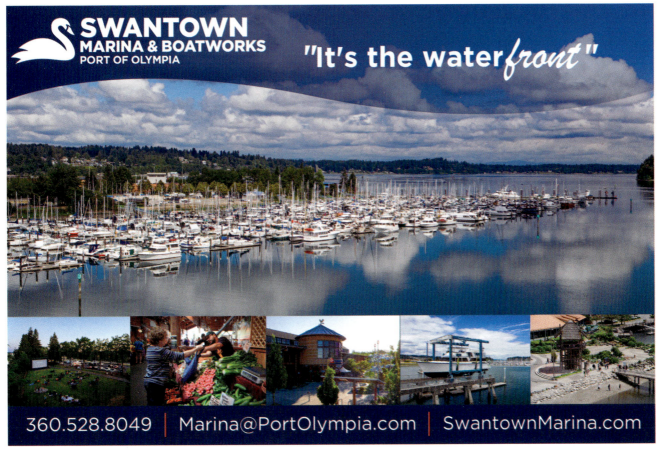

2024 Northwest Boat Travel

Eld Inlet
Photo © Mark M. Matthies

Percival Landing Marine Park: {47° 2" 49.1856" N, 122° 54' 16.9056" W} Guest moorage on docks D (no power or water) and E (power & water). No fee for daytime moorage. Overnight moorage requires registration and fees apply. Seven day maximum stay within any 30-day period. Showers (access codes provided at registration), restrooms (open dawn to dusk), waste pump-out, and light garbage disposal. Check in and pay at the Olympia Center Pay Station on Columbia St. and Olympia Ave. If the Center is closed, place moorage payments at the boater registration area on the east side of the boardwalk. For information, Olympia Parks & Rec 360-753-8380. Picnic areas, playfields, an observation tower, shoreline boardwalk, the Olympia Farmers Market, restaurants, and grocery store are in and around the park. The historic 1910 Sand Man tug moored here is open to the public on most weekends. No fee. The Harbor House is a rentable venue on-site.

West Bay Marina: {47° 3' 52.5348" N, 122° 54' 59.148" W} Permanent, guest and group/club moorage, liveaboards, 30 amp power, pump-out, garbage/oil deposit, laundry, showers, restrooms, restaurant (free moorage at guest dock while dining), kayak rentals. 360-943-2022.

★ **Eld Inlet (52):** This inlet extends five miles. Limited anchorage is possible, however caution advised because of shallow depths and a lack of protection from winds. A spit extends some distance off Cooper Point and there is shoaling, allow at least 400 yards as you round the point. Enter the inlet on an incoming tide and favor mid-channel. Homes are along the shore. The east shore is undeveloped and offers niches for anchoring. Frye Cove County Park, north of Flapjack Point, has two miles of trails for nature walks, a playground and picnic area. Anchorage is possible. There is an artificial reef for and scuba diving. A pay launch ramp is on the north shore of Young Bay, south of Flapjack Point. It is best to enter this cove on an incoming tide. Limited anchorage is possible. See Current Table for The Narrows, Washington.

★ **Totten Inlet (53):** [18448] The warm waters of Totten and Skookum Inlets have been oyster producing grounds since the mid-1800's. Rock walls and poles used to mark the beds can be hazards for boats. There are no public beaches in the inlet. Anchorage is possible away from obstructions. A 2-lane launch ramp with parking is located at Arcadia Point on the eastern entrance to Totten Inlet. Depths in Skookum Inlet allow for dinghy exploration only. Tidal range is 12 feet. See Current Table for The Narrows, Washington. The Squaxin Island Tribal Headquarters in Kamilche is located on the mainland between Totten and Skookum Inlets. The Tribe owns and operates the Salish Cliffs Golf Course, as well as Little Creek Casino Resort & Spa with gaming, dining, lodging, concerts and spa services. There is also an interesting Tribal Museum Library and Research Center, known as the Squaxin Island Museum with displays of cultural items, including rare artifacts from a 500 year-old village site. Call 360-432-3839 for open hours. The closest moorage is Shelton's Oakland Bay Marina. Mason County Transit Route 6 runs between Shelton and the casino, call 1-800-374-3747.

★ **Hammersley Inlet (54):** [18445, 18448, 18457] See Current Table for The Narrows, Washington. This eight mile, narrow, fish-hook shaped passage leads to Oakland Bay and the City of Shelton. Controlling depth in the inlet is eight feet. Flood tides flow toward the head at a maximum rate of two and one half knots and are strongest near Cape Horn. The shallowest portion of the inlet is near the entrance, where there are drying flats. When entering, stay close to the north shore. Silting makes it important to make a wide turn and stay close to the Hungerford Side. At present, no navigation buoys are in the inlet. Some aids are marked on shore. After Church Point, passage is easier. Vessels with tows have the right of way. Traverse near the end of the flood tide when the tide is high and currents are weakest.

★ **Shelton & Oakland Bay (55):** The Oakland Bay Marina and the Shelton Yacht Club are located in Oakland Bay, about 1/2 mile from the town of Shelton along State Hwy 3. A Visitor Information Center in downtown Shelton is housed in the historic Peninsula Railway Caboose #700 (staffed by volunteers, hours vary). The Caboose is steps away from quaint shops and restaurants along Railroad Avenue, with grocery stores and other amenities close by. WiFi is available at the marina and at downtown coffee shops and stores. The Mason County Historical Museum, the Post Office, and four city parks are also found in historic downtown. Just a short drive away are several county parks, including Shorecrest County Park with picnic sites and a small boat launch (low tide advisory launch/load). Much of Oakland Bay is devoted to log storage and oyster cultivation. Shellfish farming is the second largest employer in Mason County. *OysterFest*, held the first weekend in October, celebrates the industry. Shelton is also known as Christmas Town USA, a nickname from the 1950's when several million Christmas trees were shipped from Shelton each year. The *Forest Festival* in June is a nod to this local heritage. For more information about Shelton, contact 360-426-2021, 1-800-576-2021. www.explorehoodcanal.com.

Oakland Bay Marina: {47° 12' 45" N, 123° 4' 55" W} Now owned & operated by the Shelton Yacht Club, 360-426-9476. Permanent moorage, 226' of guest moorage, (self register). 30 amp power, water, pump-out, restrooms, free wifi, boat launch (tide dependant).

Shelton Yacht Club: {47° 12.835' , 123° 5.096' W} Located at the Oakland Bay Marina. Guest dock for reciprocal moorage (48hr max, call 360-426-9476). Boat lift for club members only.

Essential Supplies & Services

AIR TRANSPORTATION
NW Seaplanes ... 425-277-1590, 1-800-690-0086
San Juan Airlines............ 1-800-874-4434
Seattle Seaplanes 1-800-637-5553

BOOKS / CHARTS
Evergreen Pacific Publishing......425-493-1451
The Marine Atlas.................. 253-872-5707
Narrows Marina Bait & Tackle 253-564-3032
Point Defiance Marina & Boathouse 253-404-3960

BUS TRANSPORTATION
Greyhound 1-800-231-2222
Mason County Transit..........1-800-374-3747
Olympia Intercity Transit............. 360-786-1881
Pierce Co. Transit 253-581-8000
Vashon Metro Rider 206-553-3000

COAST GUARD
Emergencies 911, 206-217-6001, or VHF 16
Sector Puget Sound (office) 206-217-6200

Vessel Traffic 206-217-6152

FERRY TRANSPORTATION
Washington State 1-800-843-3779

FISHING/SHELLFISHING INFO
https://wdfw.wa.gov/fishing/shellfish
Fishing Regulations 360-902-2500
24-hour Red Tide Hotline 1-800-562-5632
Shellfish Rule Change Hotline........1-866-880-5431

Visit us at boattravel.com

Essential Supplies & Services — continued

FUELS

Boston Harbor Marina, Olympia: Gas. Diesel
.... 360-357-5670
Des Moines: Gas, Diesel ... 206-824-5700 VHF 16
Fair Harbor Marina, Grapevile: Gas. ... 360-426-4028
Foss Harbor Marina ....253-272-4404, VHF 71
Jarrell's Cove Marina: Hartstine Island. Gas,
 Diesel (no ethanol) 360-426-8823
Narrows Marina, Tacoma: Gas, Diesel .. 253-564-3032
Point Defiance Marina & Boathouse 253-404-3960
Swantown Marina, Olympia. 360-528-8049
Tacoma Fuel Dock, Tacoma: Gas, Diesel .. 253-383-0851
Zittel's Marina, Olympia: Gas, Diesel . 360-459-1950

GOLF COURSES

Capitol City: from Olympia 360-491-5111
Lakeland Village: from Allyn or Fair Harbor
.... 360-275-6100
North Shore: from Tacoma Marine Drive Moorages
.... 253-927-1375
Tumwater Valley: from Olympia 360-943-9500

HAUL-OUTS

Commencement Bay Marine, Tacoma .. 253-572-2666
CSR Marine, Des Moines ...... 206-878-4414 VHF 16
Gig Harbor Marina & Boatyard 253-858-3535
Hylebos Marina, Tacoma 253-272-6623
Modutech Marine Inc 253-272-9319
Narrows Marina, Tacoma: 253-564-3032
Swantown Boatworks, Olympia
 .... 360-528-8059 VHF 16 & 65A
Zittel's, Olympia 360-459-1950

HOSPITALS

Capitol Medical Ctr, Olympia 360-754-5858
Providence St Peters Olympia 360-491-9480
Mason General Hospital Shelton 360-426-1611
St. Anthony's, Gig Harbor 253-530-2000
Tacoma General Hospital 253-403-1000

MARINAS / MOORAGE FLOATS

Allyn Waterfront Park Dock Seasonal 360-275-2430
Arabella's Landing Marina, Gig Harbor
253-851-1793
Boston Harbor Marina,
 Olympia.................. 360-357-5670 VHF 16
Breakwater Marina, Point Defiance..... 253-752-6663
Chinook Landing, Tacoma ..... 253-627-7676 VHF 79
Des Moines Marina ...... 206-824-5700 VHF 16
Dock Street Marina 253-250-1906
Dockton County Park, Maury Island
Fair Harbor Marina, Grapeview........ 360-426-4028
Foss Harbor Marina ....253-272-4404, VHF 71
Foss Waterway Seaport ...... 253-272-2750 ext. 100
Gig Harbor Marina & Boatyard 253-858-3535
Jarrell's Cove, Hartstine Is. 360-426-8823
Jerisich Dock, Gig Harbor............ 253-851-6170
Johnny's Dock Marina............. 253-627-3186
Longbranch Marina........... 253-202-2056 VHF 68
Maritime Pier 253-851-6170
Narrows Marina, Tacoma: 253-564-3032
Oakland Bay Marina 360-426-6435
Penrose Point Park.................. 253-884-2514
Percival Landing, Olympia 360-753-8380
Point Defiance Marina & Boathouse 253-404-3960
Quartermaster Marina................ 206-463-3624
Swantown Marina, Olympia
 .... 360-528-8049 VHF 16 & 65A

West Bay Marina.................. 360-943-2022
Tyee Marina, Tacoma 253-383-5321
Zittel's Marina, Olympia 360-459-1950

MARINE SUPPLIES

Fair Harbor Marina, Grapeview........ 360-426-4028
Narrows Marina Bait & Tackle 253-564-3032
Point Defiance Marina & Boathouse 253-404-3960
Ship to Shore Marine, Gig Harbor....... 253-858-6090

MARITIME MUSEUMS

Foss Waterway Seaport ...... 253-272-2750 ext. 100

PARKS

Camping Reservations 1-888-226-7688
Department of Natural Resources..... 360-825-1631
King County Parks (shelter reservations) 206-477-6150
MetroParks Tacoma 253-305-1030
Vashon Park District............... 206-463-9602
Washington State 360-902-8844

PROPANE

Des Moines Marina 206-824-5700
Foss Harbor Marina 253-272-4404

RAMPS

Allyn, Arcadia Point, Boston Harbor, Burton County
 Park, Dockton County Park, Eld Inlet, Fox Island, Glen
 Cove, Graham Point, Pickering Passage, Henderson
 Bay-Horsehead Bay, Johnson Point, Longbranch,
 Luhr Beach, Nisqually Delta, Redondo Beach, Shelton,
 Steilacoom, Totten Inlet, Vaughn Bay, Von Geldern
 Cove, Wauna, Wollochet Bay, Young Point, Eld Inlet
Fair Harbor Marina, Grapeview 360-426-4028
Narrows Marina, Tacoma: 253-564-3032
Point Defiance Marina & Boathouse 253-404-3960
Swantown Boatworks, Olympia
 .... 360-528-8059 VHF 16 & 65A
Zittel's, Olympia 360-459-1950

REPAIRS & SERVICES

Aarons Marine Service 253-564-1644
Breakwater Marina, Point Defiance..... 253-752-6663
Commencement Bay Marine, Tacoma .. 253-572-2666
CSR Marine, Des Moines 206-878-4414
Gig Harbor Marina & Boatyard 253-858-3535
Hylebos Marina..................... 253-272-6623
Lighthouse Marine Gig Harbor LLC 253-858-8160
Modutech Marine Inc 253-272-9319
Puget Marina, Olympia 360-491-7388
Swantown Boatworks: Olympia 360-528-8059
Zittel's Marina, Olympia 360-459-1950

RESTAURANTS

Anthony's @ Point Defiance Marina
253-591-5325
Arabella's Landing Marina, Gig Harbor
253-851-1793
Boathouse 19, Tacoma 253-565-1919
Narrows Brewing Co............... 253-327-1400
Tides Tavern, Gig Harbor 253-858-3982

RV FACILITIES

Dash Point Park
Jarrell's Cove, Hartstine Island 360-426-8823
Kopachuck State Park, Penrose Point State Park

SCUBA SITES

Dash Point State Park   Saltwater State Park
Eld Inlet   Stretch Island State Park
Jarrell's Cove State Park   Titlow Beach
Kopachuck State Park   Tolmie State Park
Point Robinson County Park   Tramp Harbor, Vashon
Ruston Way, Tacoma   Island
Redondo Beach   Tacoma Marine Park

SEWAGE DISPOSAL SITES

Allyn: Pump....................... 360-275-2430
Arabella's Landing, Gig Harbor:
 Pump........................253-851-1793
Breakwater Marina, Point Defiance: Pump
.... 253-752-6663
Chinook Landing, Tacoma ..... 253-627-7676 VHF 79
Delin Docks Marina................ 253-572-2524
Des Moines Marina: Pump, Dump...206-824-5700
Dock Street Marina 253-250-1906
Foss Harbor Marina, Tacoma: Pump ... 253-272-4404
Jarrell's Cove Marina: Pump Dump..360-426-8823
Jarrell's Cove State Park: Pump-Out.... 360-426-9226
Marina at Browns Point 253-272-2827
Narrows Marina, Tacoma: Pump 253-564-3032
Oakland Bay Marina: Pump........... 360-426-6435
Penrose Point Mayo Cove: Pump, Dump . 253-884-2514
Percival Landing, Olympia: Pump,
 Dump........................ 360-753-8380
Point Defiance Marina & Boathouse
253-404-3960
Pumpout Guy: Mobile Pumpout 206-437-6764
Quartermaster Marina.............. 206-463-3624
Swantown Marina, Olympia: Pump. .360-528-8049
Tacoma Fuel Dock 253-383-0851
Tyee Marina 253-383-5321
West Bay Marina, Olympia Pump..... 360-943-2022
Zittel's Marina, Olympia, Pump........ 360-459-1950

TAXI

Gig Harbor .... 253-241-6701 or 360-621-8819
Olympia (D.C. Cab)................ 360-786-5226
Shelton 360-426-8294
Tacoma........................... 253-472-3303

TOWING

Tow Boat U.S.- Dispatch........... 1-800-367-8222
Tow Boat U.S.- Tacoma/Olympia 253-312-2927

TRAILER REPAIR (MOBILE)

Trailer Techs.................206-889-0286

VISITOR INFORMATION

Gig Harbor C of C 253-851-6865
Hood Canal & S. Puget Sound 1-800-576-2021
Experience Olympia & Beyond 360-704-7544,
 or........................... 1-877-704-7500
Mason County C of C (Shelton) 360-426-2021
Tacoma/Pierce County 253-284-3254,
 or........................... 1-800-272-2662

WEATHER

NOAA Recorded Message........... 360-357-6453
VHF WX-1, WX-3

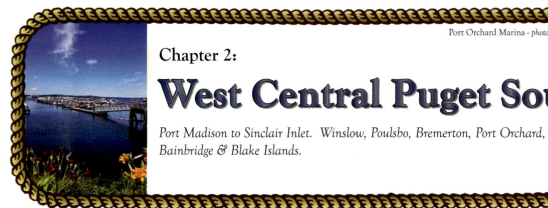

Chapter 2:
West Central Puget Sound

Port Madison to Sinclair Inlet. Winslow, Poulsbo, Bremerton, Port Orchard, Bainbridge & Blake Islands.

Port Orchard Marina - photo © Port of Bremerton

Symbols

[ ]: Numbers between [ ] are chart numbers.
{ }: Numbers & letters between { } are waypoints.
★ Recommended destinations, facilities, and services
⛱: Park, ⛵: Boat Launch, ▲: Campgrounds,
🥾: Hiking Trails, ⛱: Picnic Area, 🚴: Biking,
🤿: Scuba

★ See "Important Notices" between Chapters 7 and 8 for specific information on boating related topics such as boating safety, weather, U.S. & Canadian marine radio use, Vessel Traffic Service, security zones, Canadian & U.S. Customs, etc. Due to changing regulations, call ahead to verify latest customs information.

Bainbridge Island
[18441, 18445, 18448]

★ **Bainbridge Island:** Circumnavigating Bainbridge Island is a boater's delight. One can anchor in a bay where the atmosphere seems to hang heavy with memories of the past and, at the same time, one can view the setting sun on Seattle's modern skyscrapers and enjoy the twinkling night lights of the metropolis, just across Puget Sound. One could easily spend several days just exploring the many bays, parks, and the community of Winslow. For a shore excursion from moorage at Winslow, it is possible to rent a car or bicycle and ride along the relatively flat road which heads north toward Murden Cove. On the water, places of interest include Eagle Harbor, Fay Bainbridge Park, Point Monroe, Port Madison, Agate Passage, Manzanita Bay, Fort Ward State Park, and Blakely Harbor.

Bainbridge Islanders are extremely proud of their home and its colorful history of Native settlements, shipyards, sawmills, and agriculture. Traces of this heritage are found among miles of gently rolling hills, farms, vineyards, pristine seashore, and abundant streams where salmon return each year to spawn.

History records that over 150 years ago, timber and ship building industries thrived. Although the square riggers and down-easters that once loaded lumber at the Port Madison mill and plied the waters of Puget Sound en route to far corners of the world are gone, it is easy to imagine them sailing by. The Blakely Harbor docks, which provided moorage for ships, are also gone as is Hall Brother's Shipyard, once an Eagle Harbor landmark. Port Blakely, once a thriving, wide-open town, has only a few crumbling pilings as souvenirs of those days.

★ **Blakely Harbor (1):** This one mile indentation has a wide entrance that narrows to a lagoon at the head. Good anchorage may be found well into the harbor. Favor the center of the bay and southern shore. There are shoals and submerged pilings near shore. Private homes edge the low bank shore line. Port Blakely Mill, one of the world's largest sawmills was located here in the 1800's with mill buildings and employee houses fronting a boardwalk that rimmed the town and harbor. Paintings of the harbor show it filled to capacity with windjammers flying the flags of many nations. A park is being developed on the property and now includes restrooms, trails, interpretive displays, and a launch for hand carried boats.

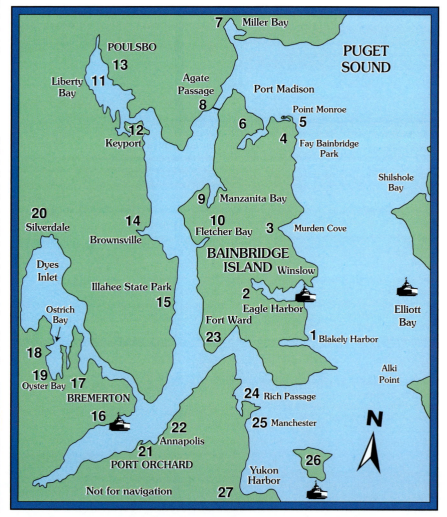

Chart List

NOAA Charts:
18441, 18445-46, 18448-49, 18452, 18474

Marine Atlas Vol 1 (2018): Page 4

Evergreen Cruising Guide: Pages 151, 154, 155, 161, 170, 171, 174

Visit us at boattravel.com

WEST CENTRAL PUGET SOUND Chapter 2 Page 29

★ **Eagle Harbor (2):** [18449] Terminus for the Winslow-Seattle ferry, Eagle Harbor has a great deal of vessel traffic. Located on the eastern shore of Bainbridge Island opposite Seattle's Elliott Bay, this two-mile-long harbor narrows, curves, and ends in a drying flat. When approaching, note the obstructions on the northern side of the entrance at Wing Point. This tree-lined point is approximately 30 feet in height. About 500 yards of rocks and foul ground extend in a southerly direction from this point. The number '2' buoy marks the end of the foul area. Round this buoy, keeping it to starboard. Turn west in the channel, keeping markers '3' and '5' to port. The harbor speed limit of 5 knots begins at the U.S. Coast Guard Buoy #5. Ferries traversing this narrow corridor have the right-of-way. Be aware of the no-anchor zone that extends from the south shore of the harbor entrance (outlined in red dashes on Chart 18449). Anchoring is permitted in the main harbor west of the Ferry repair facility and 200' south of the marinas on the north side. All anchor area is public access only. The maximum state allowed time at anchor is 30 days. Moorage is available at several marinas in the harbor and at Eagle Harbor Waterfront Park, no fuel facilities. Stores and services are found in Winslow on the north shore of Eagle Harbor. From south shore moorage they are accessed by dinghy, taxi or bus.

Eagle Harbor Marina: {47° 36' 58"N, 122° 30.49'W} On Eagle Harbor's south shore. No access to town. Permanent moorage, 30/50/100 amp power, WiFi, showers, restrooms, laundry, pump-out. 206-842-4003.

The Harbour Marina: {47° 37' 11" N, 122° 31.28'W} On Eagle Harbor's north shore. Permanent & transient moorage, 30 amp power, water, showers, restrooms, sauna, laundry, pump-out, pub. Free tie up for pub patrons if space is available first come/first served. Other visitors pay $5 hr./4 hr. min. Dockmaster: 206-550-5340.

Winslow Wharf Marina: {47° 37' 2"N, 122° 31.5'W} On Eagle Harbor's north shore. Limited transient moorage (advance reservations required), restrooms, showers, 30/50 amp power, laundry, pump-out, Wi-Fi available upon request. Reciprocal moorage for Eagle Harbor Yacht Club Request for reciprocity must be done in person at time of check-in. The Chandlery next door offers snacks, drinks and marine supplies for boaters in addition to general supplies. 206-842-4202.

★ **Winslow:** Winslow is the terminal city for the Bainbridge Island-Seattle ferry. A bridge links the island to Kitsap and Olympic Peninsulas. Within walking distance of moorage you can explore locally-owned specialty shops, retail stores, restaurants, wine tasting rooms featuring local wine, art galleries and museums along the main downtown street, Winslow Way. To get started, pick up a copy of the Walkabout Guide, available at many of these establishments as well as the ferry terminal information kiosk and the Chamber of Commerce Visitor Center (206-842-3700). Known for its thriving art community, the Island's unique artistic spirit and character is reflected throughout downtown Winslow. The new Bainbridge Island Museum of Art with free admission is located one block from ferry. Local artists display works on First Friday Gallery Walks and at a twice-yearly island-wide studio tour. B.I. Ride bus transportation with scheduled routes and destination-on-request service is available Mon.- Sat. year-round. Visit Bloedel Reserve public garden, the Bainbridge Island Historical Museum, the Japanese American Exclusion Memorial (a National Park Service National Historic Site), microbrewery & organic distillery (World's Best Vodka 2014). Monthly winery tour weekends offer the opportunity to visit the island's seven wineries. Bicycle and car rentals are available in Winslow. www.VisitBainbridgeIsland.org.

Walk-Around: The mile-long Waterfront Trail, rims the waterfront, passes the site of historic Hall Brothers Shipyard, and leads to Eagle Harbor Waterfront Park.

★⚓ **Eagle Harbor Waterfront Park Float:** {47° 37' 16.3" N, 122° 31.04.3W} Madronas overhanging the water and a long float mark the site of Eagle Harbor Waterfront Park. Watch the depths and the tide chart. A 900' linear moorage system and four public buoys lies southwest of the park. A dinghy dock is found on the northeast section of the recently expanded City Dock. A concrete launch ramp is nearby. The park is a wonderful gathering place and hosts annual concerts and festivals. It also features a play area, picnic sites, and tennis courts. A grocery store, chandlery, small boat rental, shops and restaurants are within walking distance.

Bainbridge Island City Dock: Transient moorage for boats to 70' (2 days max), no reservations, prepare to raft. 30/50 amp power, water, restrooms, showers, pump-out, launch ramp. 206-842-5211 (during business hours) or 911 Non Emergency (after business hours).

Murden Cove (3): This bowl-shaped bay can be used to drop a lunch hook, but is not a good overnight moorage. Much of the inner bay dries at low tide. Skiff Point, farther north, has a constantly shifting shoal area. Clearance of at least 250 yards is advisable. There is good crabbing in this area.

★⚓ **Fay Bainbridge Park (4):** A steep hillside is the backdrop for this park with sandy beaches. Tent/RV camp sites with water & power at RV sites (camp sites are reservable), 3 cabins, picnic tables & 2 reservable picnic shelters, water, portable toilet or restrooms & showers. A Cascadia Marine Trail tent site is south of the day-use area. 206-842-2302.

Point Monroe (5): This low, narrow sand spit curves like a hooked finger. The entrance dries at low spring tides. It is possible to anchor in the bay. Enter at high water and check the expected low tide with present depth readings. The bay is exposed to winds from the north. Private floats extend from shore into the bay. Tightly clustered homes rim the spit and shore. A lagoon-like bay is between the spit and shore. There is fishing off Point Monroe. Bottom fish such as perch and ling cod are prevalent.

★ **Port Madison (6):** [18446, 18478] Port Madison is actually the body of water that separates Bainbridge Island from the mainland shore to the north.

★ **Inner Port Madison & Hidden Cove:** To the south, the mile long indentation into Bainbridge Island is known as either Port Madison or Inner Port Madison. This lovely inlet is very popular, and is the site of summer homes, a yacht club, and the residential community of Port Madison. The entrance is fairly narrow with shallow water to starboard near Treasure Island and a cluster of rocks 100 yards off the entrance. A marked rock, covered six feet, is south-southwest of Treasure Island. Caution is advised regarding other sunken debris, created because ballast was dumped from early-day ships. A bight on the port side just inside the entrance has adequate depths, but limited room for anchorage. Because of boat traffic, the more popular anchorages are farther in, closer to the head of the bay, especially in an area known as Hidden Cove. Hidden Cove is home to the Port Madison Yacht Club (member and reciprocal moorage, depth at dock is approximately 8' at a 0 tide.) The community of Port Madison was named to honor President James Madison. A sawmill was in operation from 1853-1892, the first brass and iron foundry in the territory opened in 1859, and shipyards were on both sides of the harbor. Later, it became home to the first fish oil refinery north of San Francisco, and for 36 years it was the Kitsap County seat.

Indianola: [18473, 18446] This rural community is situated within the borders of the Port Madison Reservation. On the north shore of Port Madison, is a long wharf that serves as a fishing pier and viewing site. Although the wharf has been rebuilt, it marks the spot where steamers once docked. A small float provides short-term only shore access during the summer. Check depths when approaching. Anchorage is possible outside of the pier, however it is exposed. A country store & deli and post office are walkable from the pier.

Miller Bay (7): Much of this sheltered bay, including the entrance, is shallow and some of it dries on low tides. Depending on your boat's draft, you'll want at least a 5' tide or higher to enter the bay. Shallow anchorage is possible.

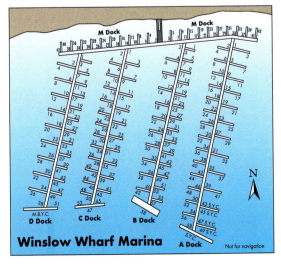

Poulsbo   Photo © Patricia Thomas

of historic torpedoes as well as displays about submarine history, the Ocean Environment, diving and salvage, a reproduction of the control room from the submarine USS Greenling and an exhibit of unmanned underwater vehicles. Outdoor exhibits include the deep submergence vehicles Mystic, Trieste II. Open daily 10am - 4pm, closed Tues. Call 360-396-4148.

★ **Keyport (12):** This community, known as "Torpedo Town USA," is next to the navy base. Permanently moored boats fill most moorage slips, however there is 250' of guest dock space for transient moorage. There are restaurants, a general store, a B & B, auto repair shop, post office and parks within walking distance. Central Park has picnic tables, gazebo and play area. Saltwater Park has tables and benches overlooking Dog Fish Bay and, like the Port, is a Kitsap Peninsula Water Trail site. Each September, *Keyport Fest* features local musicians, free activities for kids, and a classic car show.

Port of Keyport: Permanent and guest moorage (3 hours free, fee is $1.00 per foot, per night. Limit 3 nights per month), 30 amp power, water, new launch ramp. 206-910-7644.

Miller Bay Marine: Permanent & transient moorage (tide dependent, call ahead). Repairs, haul-outs, marine parts, boat/trailer sales, launch ramp (boats to 30', $5 fee). 360-598-4900.

Agate Passage (8): See current table for Admiralty Inlet. Agate Passage, a straight channel about one mile in length, connects Port Orchard and Port Madison. Depths average 20 feet. Currents run to six knots at springs, ebbing northeast and flooding southwest. The Agate Pass Bridge (75 foot clearance at mean high water) connects Bainbridge to the peninsula. Shoal areas, some marked with buoys, fringe both shores. Scuba divers spearfish here for cod, sole, and flounder. In 1841, Wilkes named Agate Pass, not for the rocks, but for Alfred Agate, the expedition's itinerant artist. Clearwater Casino Resort is located on the west shore.

Suquamish: Suquamish is the site of a community dock with a large float for temporary mooring. A launch ramp, best for small to medium sized boats is located slightly to the north. The House of Awakened Culture, Chief Seattle's gravesite, and the Museum and Cultural Center are all within walking distance of the float. Both the House of Awakened Culture and museum were built with a shed style roof reminiscent of the roof of Old Man House where Chief Seattle was born in 1786. The Museum Store sells Native American art and other items. For open hours, 360-394-7105. For a bite to eat, stop by Sully's Bistro for coffee and pastries. Both are located on the waterfront. Fresh fruit and vegetables, seafood and local handmade goods are available June through mid-October at the Farmers Market adjacent to the museum. Each year, on the third weekend in August enjoy *A Northwest Indian Festival* honoring Chief Seattle. Traditional food, dances, art, canoe races and more mark this special celebration.

★ **Old Man House Park & Chief Seattle Park:** Owned and operated by the Suquamish Tribe, this park is approximately one half mile south of Suquamish, on the west shore of Agate Passage. Temporary anchorage may be possible, depending on currents. Dinghy to the sandy beach where water, a fire ring, toilet, and picnic facilities are available. A cable sign marks the northern boundary of the park. Do not anchor in this vicinity. A gas station, mini-mart, and deli are located near the park.

★ **Manzanita Bay (9):** [18446] This bay is next to Arrow Point. There is good anchorage in 25-30 feet on a mud bottom at the center of the bay. Once a stop on the Mosquito Fleet, submerged pilings are near the shore.

Walk-around: It is possible to row to a public access area in the northeast corner of the bay. Look for the road end where concrete formations with steps are set between rock walls.

Fletcher Bay (10): This shallow bay is used extensively by local residents. Property is private, no public access. It is limited both in shelter and in swinging room. The entrance dries at half tide.

Liberty Bay
[18441, 18445]

★ **Liberty Bay (11):** Once known as Dog Fish Bay, this four mile indentation is the water access to the City of Poulsbo. The naval facility, Naval Undersea Warfare Center Division, Keyport, lies in the entrance channel to Liberty Bay. When navy underwater vehicle testing is in progress, there will be a naval vessel present with a red flashing light. The navy also conducts acoustic monitoring in the area, as indicated by an amber flashing light on their test barge at the facility's pier. The navy recommends that boaters stay as far east in the channel as possible, look for either of these indicators that testing is in progress, and monitor Marine Band channel 16 whenever in the area. The head of the bay is a drying flat. Anchorage is good near the head in the shelter of Port of Poulsbo yacht basin. The bay is open to southeast winds.

★ **Keyport Naval:** Slow to three knots in this vicinity. Moor at the Keyport Marina, located east of the Naval Facility, on Grandview Blvd. The U.S. Naval Undersea Museum is an official U.S. Navy museum. Exhibits include the nation's best collection

★ **Poulsbo (13):** Known as "Little Norway," this quaint town of Norwegian heritage is nestled along the waterfront of Liberty Bay. A south-facing, full-service marina also has a waterfront park at the top of the dock. The town is walkable and provides a wide variety of attractions. A thriving art community has spawned several first-class art galleries, as well as a monthly Art Walk. Two museums celebrate Poulsbo's heritage-one in City Hall and a Maritime Museum on Front Street. For foodies, there are a dozen excellent restaurants, serving different styles and flavors. For beer aficionados, there is a growing craft brewery industry. And, of course, the famous Sluys Poulsbo Bakery features lefse and other Scandinavian treats, as well as the giant Viking donut. Paint a bowl, create a mosaic, sample wines, have high tea—there is plenty to see and do.

Poulsbo was founded in the 1880s by Norwegian cod fishermen who found it reminiscent of their homeland. Today the town is still home to a large Norwegian population and has one of the State's largest Sons of Norway Lodges. During the Christmas season, Norwegian Christmas scenes adorn shop windows. The community's biggest festival, *Viking Fest*, is a three-day, weekend blowout marking Norway's Independence Day, *Sytennde Mai* (Seventeenth of May). *Fireworks on the Fjord* is celebrated on July 3rd; the annual *Lutefisk Dinner* is in October; *Jule Fest*, kicks off the holiday season as Vikings row ashore with the Lucia bride, a local girl, often with Norwegian heritage.

Six parks within the town blend with the green of surrounding hillsides—the perfect setting for families to picnic and play. An 800' long pedestrian boardwalk connects waterfront parks. Separating the downtown core from the guest marina, Waterfront Park has picnic facilities and the Kvelstad Pavilion—great for entertainment, weddings, and campfire pits. Visitors can rent electric boats, kayaks, SUP's, and other watercraft locally. By car, three ferry routes bring visitors to the Kitsap Peninsula from Greater Seattle: the Edmonds-Kingston ferry, the Seattle-Bainbridge ferry, and the Seattle-Bremerton ferry. Kitsap Transit provides bus service with connections to Bainbridge Island, Kingston, Bremerton, and Silverdale.

★ **Poulsbo Marina** {47° 44.017' N, 122° 38.854' W} Located in the heart of downtown Poulsbo within walking distance of many fine shops and restaurants. The facility features 130 guest moorage slips and is open 7 days a week, all year (except for Thanksgiving, Christmas and New Years Day) and offers winter moorage October 1st - April 30th. Water and 30 amp power available on all docks. Limited 50 amp power available. The fuel dock sells ethanol free gasoline and diesel fuel. On location are restrooms, showers and laundry. Self serve pump-out available 27/7. Free Wi-Fi, public boat launch, covered activity barge and picnic area. Group and individual reservations accepted. Please check website for details. See our advertisement on this page. Address: 18809 Front St., Poulsbo, WA 98370. Telephone: 360-779-3505. Website: www.portofpoulsbo.com. VHF 66A.

Liberty Bay Marina: {47° 43' 27 N, 122° 38'38"W} Permanent moorage. 360-779-7762.

Longship Marine: Provision up at Longship Marine. A new, used and consignment outlet for all your cruising, off-grid living, and boat maintenance needs. The eclectic store is easily accessible by boat, just a stone's throw from the guest moorage docks at the Port of Poulsbo. A boat store run by boaters with over 3,000 consigners bringing "new" treasures daily AND daily deliveries from Seattle for special orders. Check out the current loot at www.longshipmarine.com. Address: 18969 Anderson Pkwy NE, Poulsbo, WA 98370. Telephone: 360-779-2378

Bremerton Area
[18441, 18445, 18449]

★ **Brownsville (14)** [18446, 18449]: Burke Bay is the site of the Port of Brownsville Marina, fuel facilities (at the south end of A dock), launching ramps, and the Brownsville Yacht Club. The Bay is shallow with some drying areas. Stay inside the green buoys as you enter or depart the marina. Nearby, Overlook Park has a covered picnic area, picnic tables, fire pit, bbq's, and horse shoe and volleyball areas. Five Cascadia Marine Trail camp sites are located at the Port of Brownsville. There is also a full service Deli offering food, beer, wine and ice. The Daily Stop grocery store and Sweeney's Country Style Meats are within walking distance (less than 1/4 mile.) In September, the Port hosts *Brownsville Appreciation Day* to support local schools. It is a fun day with live music, a car show, arts & crafts, food, dinghy rides, and kids games.

Port of Brownsville: {47° 39' 7.9 N, 122° 36' 59.07 W} Permanent, and guest moorage, water, 120 volt 30 amp power, boat ramp with free parking, fuel dock, two free sanitary pump-outs and dump-sites, bathrooms and showers. 360-692-5498.

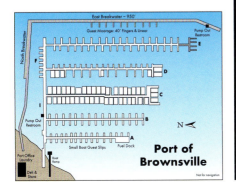

Illahee: Illahee is a Native word meaning "earth," "country" or "resting place." Located about 4 miles south of Brownsville Marina, Illahee has a community fishing pier with two floats. Watch depths when approaching the floats. Shoals are south of the pier. Moorage is available for up to 72 hours. At this time there are no provisions or gas nearby. For Port info: www.portofillahee.com.

★ **Illahee Marine State Park (15):** This 86-acre park contains a boat launch ramp, a pier, 356-feet of moorage dock {47° 35' 56.97" N, 122° 35' 31.92" W} and five moorage buoys. A rock is reported to be about 50 yards southeast of the pier. A floating breakwater gives some protection, however vessel wakes enter this bay. The park has a Veteran's war memorial honoring members from Bremerton who died in World War I. It is also home to one of the nation's largest Yew trees and Kitsap County's last stand of old growth timber. Water activities include fishing, water-skiing, swimming, scuba diving, oyster beds, clamming and crabbing. Horseshoes, volleyball, softball, geocaching and metal detecting are popular onshore pastimes. Facilities include restrooms, showers, campsites, and covered kitchen shelters. Park Info: 360-478-6460. Kitchen shelter reservations: 888-226-7688 or visit www.parks.wa.gov.

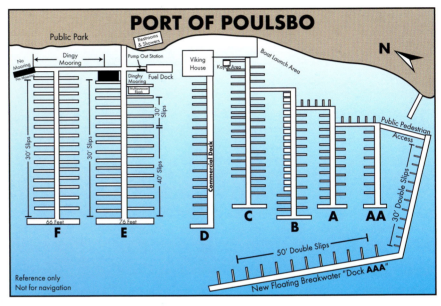

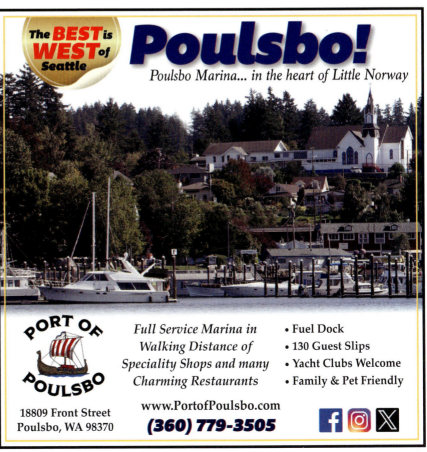

★ **Bremerton & Bremerton Waterfront Park (16) [18449]:** When cruising along the north shore of Sinclair Inlet, maintain a 1,500 foot distance from the shore, especially near the Puget Sound Naval Shipyard. Bremerton got its start in 1891 when founder, William Bremer, sold a 190 acre parcel to the US Navy for a shipyard. Today this yard includes several miles of waterfront, 688 acres of land, 268 buildings, six dry docks and seven piers. The mothball fleet is located at the west end of the shipyard.

Although the shipyard is not open to the public, visitors can tour the USS Turner Joy (DD-951). The destroyer is moored northeast of the ferry terminal on the Bremerton waterfront just north of the marina. Built in Seattle and commissioned in 1959, the Turner Joy's crew saw combat in the Gulf of Tonkin conflict at the onset of the Vietnam War, earning nine battle stars. Most spaces on the ship are accessible on the self-guided tour, including the engine room, bridge, and berths. The ship also features a Vietnam POW memorial. 360-792-2457.

Next to the shipyard on Pacific Avenue is the Puget Sound Naval Shipyard Memorial Plaza. The town's rich heritage as a naval base supporting aircraft carriers, cruisers, destroyers and submarines continues to be a source of pride and is reflected in the Puget Sound Navy Museum located a few blocks above the waterfront, at 251 1st Street. Visitors experience life as a sailor on the USS John C. Stennis, explore what it was like to serve on a Special Operations Submarine during the Cold War, and much more. The museum offers a gift shop, research library, and children's area. Free admission, summer hours 10 am - 4 pm Monday and Wednesday- Sunday. 360-479-7447.

The City of Bremerton's dramatic revitalization over the past several years is especially notable in the historic town near the waterfront. The downtown core adjacent to the marina now reflects a vibrant "walkable" neighborhood which connects the Bremerton boardwalk at the marina and the downtown. The Bremerton Harborside, with conference center, hotel, restaurant, shops and musical fountains is located here. The four-block Bremerton Waterfront Park offers spectacular views of Puget Sound as well as picnic sites, statues, and an observation platform. Look for the enormous propeller. At the south terminus of the waterfront, the Bremerton Transportation Center is the connection point for ferry travelers going to and from Seattle, and also for Kitsap Transit bus passengers.

Downtown Bremerton, up from the waterfront, offers restaurants and good browsing at art galleries featuring Northwest artists and at specialty stores. The Kitsap History Museum displays interesting vignettes of Bremerton's early days along with rotating exhibits. Located with the History Museum, the Aurora Valentinetti Puppet Museum has an amazing collection of puppets from all over the world, as well as tours, workshops, a gift shop, and hands-on activities. For hours and information call 360-479-6226. The Admiral Theatre, a handsome art-deco performing arts venue, offers a wide variety of programing, 360-373-6743. In front of the Admiral, at 5th and Pacific, look for the plaque commemorating Harry S. Truman's speech that elicited the famous shout "Give 'em hell, Harry!" The Pacific Planetarium is currently not doing public or private events. Visit www.pacificplanetarium for more information.

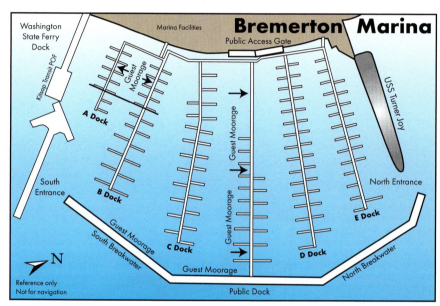

Come to Bremerton the third Saturday in May for the *Armed Forces Festival and Parade*, one of the country's largest Armed Forces celebrations with more than 100 parade units. The day begins with a pancake breakfast, followed by the parade and a Military Culinary Arts competition. On Memorial Day weekend, the *Kitsap Harbor Festival* has events in both Bremerton and Port Orchard. Enjoy live entertainment on the Bremerton boardwalk along with dozens of food and craft booths, car shows, and street markets. From May through mid-Oct a Farmers Market features fresh food and produce, kids' activities and demonstrations on Thursday at Evergreen Park 4-7pm. *The Blackberry Festival* on Labor Day weekend is a popular end-of-summer event with food and craft booths, kid's activities, outdoor movies, and live entertainment on the Bremerton Boardwalk. The marina fills up for these events, reservations are recommended.

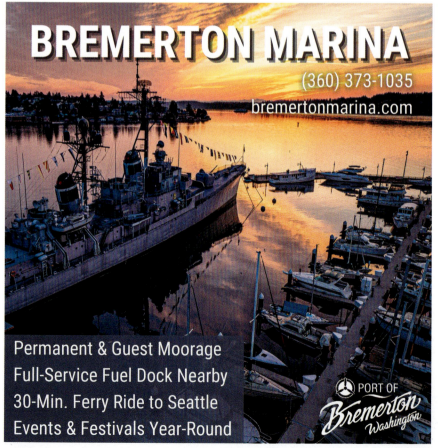

★ **Bremerton Marina:** {47° 33' 7.6 N, 122°37'39W} Certified Clean Marina. Let the Bremerton Marina's wonderful staff welcome you to the finest facility and service in the Puget Sound. Located between the Seattle ferry dock and the historic USS Turner Joy, the Bremerton Marina is the highlight of Bremerton's revitalization project and offers excellent docks and breakwater protection against ferry wakes. Guest moorage is available year-round with over 60 slips and 990' of inside side-tie moorage. Amenities include 30 and 50 amp power, water, restrooms, free showers, laundry, free WiFi and two pump-out stations. Other amenities include two tented activity areas with BBQs available seasonally. Kitsap Transit buses service the marina and most of Kitsap County. See our advertisement on this page. Website: www.bremertonmarina.com. Street Address: 120 Washington Beach, Bremerton. Telephone: 360-373-1035. VHF 66A.

Bridgeview Marina: {47° 34' 41" N, 122° 38' 37.5"W} Permanent moorage, water, restrooms, showers, laundry, and private pump-out. 360-876-2522.

Port Washington Narrows: [18449, 18452] See current table for Admiralty Inlet. This waterway, approximately three miles long, leads to Dyes Inlet. Currents, which run to approximately four knots, occasional rips, shallow areas, an unmarked, drying shoal on the north shore, and a large amount of boat traffic make caution necessary when navigating this channel. Because of these conditions, and the numerous piers and moorage floats, wakes must be minimized. The Manette Bridge and the Warren Bridge both traverse the channel; clearance is not a concern.

Boat Shed Restaurant: Dock conveniently located across from Bremerton Marina and ferry landing. Mid-size and dinghies encouraged on the dock although we can accommodate up to 70 feet. 360-377-2600.

★⚓ **Evergreen Rotary Park:** On the west side, between the two bridges, this park has an accessible launching ramp and dock, picnic tables, group shelters, sand volleyball, basketball courts, and the County's first accessible playground.

★⚓ **Lions Park:** This 15-acre park includes nearly 2,000 feet of shoreline on the north side of Port Washington Narrows. Launch ramp, picnic tables, group shelters, restrooms, walking trails, marine themed play area and ballfields.

★ **Phinney Bay (17):** [18449] Phinney Bay is located on the south side of Port Washington Narrows. On the west side of the bay at {47° 35' 14.44" N, 122° 39' 57.82" W} is the Bremerton Yacht Club (reciprocal moorage offered.) Sheltered anchorage can be found beyond the club, toward the head of the bay. Anchor in about 30 feet of water. A wreck is charted in the southern area of the bay. Shoals extend from shore. It has adequate water above it, even at a minus tide, however it can catch ground tackle. Mud Bay, back-to-back with Phinney Bay, dries on a low tide, however it can be explored by dinghy or shallow draft boats on higher tides.

★ **Ostrich Bay (18)** [18474] : This long indentation near Madrona Point has anchorage at the head of the bay. Caution advised of shoals off the point. US Coast Guard requests mariners and divers not to disturb the bottom sediment in the small back of the bay and near navy ammo loading pier due to unexploded ammunition. An undeveloped park with public tidelands, is on the west shore. A narrow passage, with a minimum depth of 10', leads farther inland to Oyster Bay.

★ **Oyster Bay (19):** High hills surround this beautiful, sheltered anchorage. Depths are 25-35'.

★ **Dyes Inlet (20):** The inlet is a wide, shallow bay that is exposed to most winds. Because of contamination, shellfish harvesting is often prohibited. Caution advised regarding a drying shoal, known as Clam Island, in the east half of the inlet.

Chico: The Chico launching ramp is on the west shore of Dyes Inlet, south of Silverdale. Ramp is closed from dusk to dawn. Beaches on both sides of the ramp are private.

Tracyton: On the east side of Dyes Inlet, is the community of Tracyton. A launching ramp has a porta-potty, an artistic bench facing the fantastic view and kayak rack onsite. From here, trailerable boats can access the many bays on the opposite shore and possibly drop a lunch hook and dinghy to shore. The Tracyton Public House and mini-mart/gas station are two blocks up from ramp.

Overview of the Bremerton Marina   Photo © Chad Stockton, CS Creative Productions

★⚓ **Anna Smith County Park:** Located near Barker Creek on the northeast side of Dyes Inlet, this interesting park is known for its Master Gardners demonstration garden and nature trail. Picnic tables, restrooms, outdoor amphitheater and 600' of public beach are also found here. Adjacent beach is private, no trespassing allowed. Look for the old concrete wall south of Barker Creek. Temporary anchorage is possible, however avoid the drying shoal.

★ **Silverdale:** [18449] At the head of Dyes Inlet lies the town of Silverdale. With a population of over 20,000 residents, this community offers many of the conveniences of the "big city" yet retains hometown appeal. As you approach, look for the gazebo that marks the location of Silverdale Waterfront Park. Moorage is west of the gazebo. Directly north of the dock is the park and main street for Old Town Silverdale featuring historic murals, bakery/cafe, fish & chips and brewery stop. Several other dining options, including a local favorite seafood/steak restaurant and specialty crepe's is located within walking distance. Within a one mile radius are many other shops, restaurants, Kitsap Mall and The Trails shopping malls, and a large multiplex movie theater. Boats, kayaks and SUP's are a common sight on Dyes Inlet. A leg of the Kitsap Peninsula Water Trail, the first nationally designated trail routed exclusively on salt water, is found here. Each June the Silverdale Waterfront is the site of the Silverdale Sprints Regatta featuring outrigger canoes. Another fun event, *The Whaling Days Community Festival,* held the last weekend in July in Old Town includes a street fair, 5K run, entertainment, parade, beer garden, Dyes Inlet Dash/Outrigger Canoe Races and fireworks all connected to the Silverdale Waterfront Park.

★⚓ **Silverdale Waterfront Park:** The park has a picnic area with a shelter, restrooms, fresh water, a new ADA accessible playground and beach access. Shopping within a mile. Kayak/SUP rentals are available May-Sept. Call 360-297-4659. The Clear Creek Trail system, stretching seven miles, connects to the park. The boat ramp is west of the park.

Port of Silverdale: {47° 38' 31" N, 122° 41' 46" W} Moorage (max 10 nights), 30 amp power (under maintenance), pier, restroom, showers, security, parking, boat launch. Seasonal fresh water, pump-out (Fri-Sun, 6am-9pm, May 1-Oct 1). Group/yacht clubs with advanced reservations ($75 fee). 360-698-4918.

Dyes Inlet & Mount Rainier   Photo © Ted Moore

Sinclair Inlet & Port Orchard

[18441, 18445]

★ **Port Orchard Strait:** This waterway extends along the coast of Kitsap Peninsula, separating the mainland from Bainbridge Island. It turns toward the southwest, extending a branch into Port Washington Narrows to the northwest, passing the City of Bremerton to starboard, the City of Port Orchard to port, and ending in Sinclair Inlet. The Sinclair Inlet Wildlife Viewing Area is at the head (access by car or beachable boat). Views of migratory waterfowl are possible. Nearby, on the southern shore is Elandan Gardens featuring a collection of about 300 bonsai, an exquisite garden (admission fee applies), a gift shop and gallery, 360-373-8260. Because of exposure to winds and highway noise, anchorage in this area is not recommended. Moorage is possible at the Port Orchard Marina. Close to the launch ramp at the Port Orchard Marina, is the Annapolis/Retsil fishing pier and float. Be aware of the shoal between Annapolis and the marina.

★ **City of Port Orchard:** Port Orchard and the popular Port Orchard Marina have long been a favored boating destination. For trailered boats, a public launching ramp directly off Bay Street hooks into the Port Orchard Marina and is equipped with a 1.5 acre parking lot, bathrooms with wheelchair access, park benches, picnic tables, and a trail. Anchorage can also be found at the head of Sinclair Inlet.

Many of the City's attractions are within easy distance of the Port Orchard Marina. Bay Street, with its historic buildings, is a photographer's delight. Browse through dozens of shops, pubs and restaurants; there's something for everyone, including many antiques and vintage collectibles and the Western WA Center for the Arts with live community theatre year round. If visiting from April to October, take in the Port Orchard Farmer's Market on the waterfront boardwalk each Saturday from 9am-2pm. Take a picnic lunch and enjoy the view from the Public Pier at the Marina. Local parks and playgrounds offer swimming, picnic sites, and tennis courts. In 20 minutes visitors can find themselves at three top notch popular golf courses.

On Memorial Day weekend, the *Kitsap Harbor Festival* has events in both Bremerton & Port Orchard. Special events include the *West Sound Marine Swap Meet* and the *Seagull Calling Festival and Wings Cook-Off*, and the *Seagull Splat 5K Run/Walk*. Free *Concerts by the Bay* are held downtown on Thursday evenings June through August. The summer festival *Fathoms O' Fun*, with a parade, arts & crafts and fireworks is the last weekend in June through July 4th. July is also the month for *The Chris Craft Rendezvous and Mustangs on the Bay*, as well as the *Arts and Antiques Fair*. The second Sunday in August brings *The Cruz* hot rod and custom car show and the third weekend is the *Pirate's Rendezvous Craft and Vendor Show and Tall Ships*.

On the hill above downtown you will find the Sidney Art Gallery and Museum and the Historic Log Cabin as well as dozens of beautiful craftsman and Victorian homes. Three restored homes offer B&B accommodations.

Port Orchard, Kitsap County's first incorporated city, was originally named Sidney. Port Orchard, became the County Seat in 1893 and with its beautiful Sidney Hotel, was the scene of fashion and entertainment for naval officers and their families. Along with a string of other Puget Sound ports, Port Orchard was served by steamers of the Mosquito Fleet.

The *Carlisle II*, affectionately called the "foot ferry", spearheads the last of Washington's original operating Mosquito Fleet that moved people and goods by water before roads were built. Riders can board the Carlisle II from a dock near the Port Orchard Marina and take a 12 minute ride to Bremerton. The ferry departs on the hour and half hour. 360-373-2877. Port Orchard can also be reached by air at the Bremerton airport, and by car via the Fauntleroy-Southworth ferry from Seattle, the Seattle-Bremerton ferry, and from Tacoma via Highway 16. Transit buses stop near the floats with service in the Port Orchard/South Kitsap area. For more information, www.skchamber.org.

★ **Port Orchard Marina:** {47° 32'69N, 122°38'37W} Certified Clean Marina. Located on the pristine waters of Puget Sound, the Port Orchard Marina delivers easy access to boating locations from Olympia, Tacoma, Seattle, and to the San Juan Islands and beyond! Guest moorage is available year-round with 50 slips along 1,300' of the marina's inside breakwater. Amenities include 30 amp and 125V power, water, restrooms, free showers, laundry, free WiFi, fuel dock, and pump-out stations. Other amenities include a waterfront park and gazebo with covered seating as well as an activity float with heaters and BBQs available. The marina is conveniently located close to all Port Orchard attractions and is serviced by

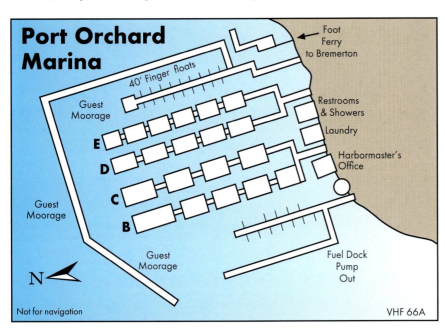

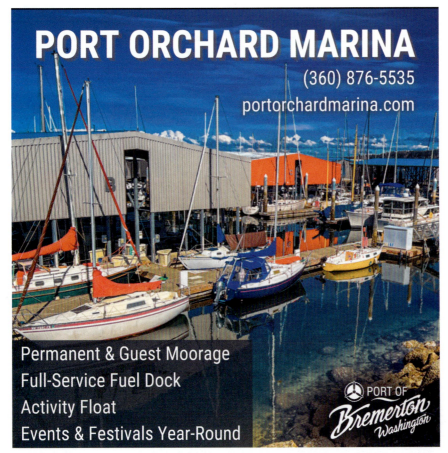

Visit us at boattravel.com

WEST CENTRAL PUGET SOUND   Chapter 2   Page 35

Kitsap Transit buses. See our advertisement on page 34. Website: www.portorchardmarina.org. Street Address: 707 Sidney Pkwy, Port Orchard. Telephone: 360-876-5535. VHF 66A.

Kitsap Marina: Permanent moorage under 50', stern-drive/outboard haulouts to 30', repairs on engine outboards, out-drives, trailer sales & service. 360-895-2193.

Port Orchard Railway Marina: {47° 32' 29.44" N, 122° 38' 42.79"W} Annual & monthly moorage to 70', 30 & 50 dual amp power, water, restrooms, showers, laundry, pump-out, WiFi. 360-876-2522.

Sinclair Inlet Marina: {47° 32' 26.3" N, 122° 38' 28.3"W} Permanent moorage, showers, restroom, laundry, private pump-out. 360-338-6596.

Yachtfish Marine N.W.: {47° 32' 14.5" N, 122° 38' 52.2"W} Permanent and transient moorage. 50 ton travelift, repairs, full service boatyard. 360-876-9016.

Annapolis (22): A public float and launching ramp are east of the old ferry pier at Retsil. The float grounds at low water, and is open to northerly winds. Commuter transit buses leave from the parking lot at the Annapolis Ferry in Retsil in the morning and afternoon. 1-800-501-RIDE.

Waterman Pier: Once a steamer stop, the 200-foot-long pier now serves as a public recreational and fishing pier. Limited beach area.

Rich Passage: This passage separates Kitsap Peninsula from Bainbridge Island. Frequent ferry traffic can be a hazard. Be aware of seasonal spring tides that can run up to 4 knots. See current table for Admiralty Inlet.

★ **Fort Ward Park (23):** This day use park on Bainbridge Island has a two lane boat ramp, vault toilets, walking trails, picnic tables, water (no charge) and Cascadia Marine Trail campsites. Because of strong currents and traffic in Rich Passage, anchoring and/or overnight stays are not advised.. Two gun batteries in the park recall the establishment of Fort Ward in 1903 to protect the Bremerton Naval Shipyard. During World War II, the site housed a Naval radio station and communications training center. A walk along the beach reveals unusual sandstone formations carved by wind and water erosion. Scuba diving is popular off Orchard Rocks. Fishing, crabbing, and sailboarding are also enjoyed in the area. 206-842-2302.

★ **Manchester State Park (24):** Extensive eddies and strong currents often make this bight between Middle Point and Point Glover inhospitable, but temporary anchorage is possible. The park, on Middle Point, six miles northeast of Port Orchard, is part of the Cascadia Marine Trail. Manchester has campsites, including a group camping site, restrooms, showers, picnic tables, and three reservable picnic shelters. There is an unguarded swimming beach, a volleyball court, horseshoe pits, and hiking trails. Fishing and scuba diving are also popular pursuits. A large brick structure, once used as a torpedo warehouse, is a reminder of the park's origin as a military fort. Park Info: 360-871-4065.

★ **Manchester (25):** In the late 1800's the residents of this small town chose the name of "Manchester," reflecting their vision of creating a busy seaport equal to the namesake port of Manchester, England. Today, the community of Manchester is largely residential and known for spectacular views of Seattle, Blake Island State Park and Mt. Rainier. Annual community events include a

Blake Island Marine State Park   Photo © VPLLC

Salmon Bake in June and the *Celebrate Manchester Day* in August. There are two docks and a small park. No fresh water or overnight moorage. The floating docks are in shallow water and not usable during extreme minus tides. A park with picnic area and launching ramp are adjacent. Purchase a $7 single launch, $10 overnight (includes launch and parking) or yearly pass. Restrooms, family restaurant, pub, post office and library are nearby. Port of Manchester: 360-871-0500.

★ **Blake Island Marine State Park (26):** {N47° 54' 25" W-122° 48'.25} This popular park hosts over 13,000 visiting vessels a year. It is located two miles south of Bainbridge Island and five miles west of Seattle. There are no natural harbors, but 24 moorage buoys are scattered offshore and there are beaches for landing dinghies. Boats 37' and longer are not allowed on buoys on south end of the island. Limits are posted on buoys. A breakwater on the island's northeast side protects the moorage floats, but not in all winds. Approach the floats through the shallow, dredged channel. Overnight moorage fees are collected year around. Thirty amp power is available, $6 per night. An artificial reef, for scuba divers, lies on the south side of the island. Strong currents in the area can be hazardous.

Camping sites, include 3 Cascadia Marine Trail sites, picnic areas, shelters, waste pump-out, porta potti dump, volleyball courts, hiking trails, restrooms, fresh water, and hot showers are provided. Swimming and clamming are possible on some of the beaches. This site was the ancestral camping ground of the Suquamish tribe, and it is believed that Chief Seattle was born here.

Named after George Blake who led a survey from 1837-1848, the island was purchased at the turn of the century by William Trimble. Renamed Trimble Island, it became one of the most beautiful private estates in the country, housing a magnificent library collection. In 1929, William's wife drowned when the family car plunged off an Elliott Bay pier. Mr. Trimble never returned to the island. Some remains of the Trimble home and gardens are still visible not far from the floats. This island became a state park in 1959. Park Info: 360-731-8330. To reserve picnic shelter or group campsite: 888-226-7688.

Southworth: This is the terminus for the Kitsap Peninsula-Vashon Island-Fauntleroy (West Seattle) ferry. Small downtown area includes a grocery store and post office.

Harper: The tiny town of Harper is located on the south shore of Yukon Harbor. The 400' Harpers Ferry Fishing Pier has restrooms and parking. A gravel launching ramp is accessible at higher tides. Small boats can be beached. Scuba divers often use the waters surrounding the pier where the wreck of the Barbara G is found.

★ **Yukon Harbor (27):** Anchorage is possible in this wide bight with protection from southwest winds. Tide flats extend from the head.

On anchor off Manchester State Park
Photo © Roger Hunsperger

2024 Northwest Boat Travel

Essential Supplies & Services

Chris Craft Rendezvous at the Port Orchard Marina Photo © Port of Bremerton

AIR TRANSPORTATION
NW Seaplanes . . . 425-277-1590, 1-800-690-0086
San Juan Airlines. 1-800-874-4434
Seattle Seaplanes 1-800-637-5553

BOOKS / BOOK STORES
Evergreen Pacific Publishing. 425-493-1451
The Marine Atlas. 253-872-5707

BUS TRANSPORTATION
Kitsap Transit . . . . . . 360-697-2877 or 1-800-501-7433

CNG CYLINDERS
The Chandelery, Bainbridge Island 206-842-7245

COAST GUARD
Emergencies . . . . 911, 206-217-6001, VHF 16
Sector Puget Sound (office) 206-217-6200
Vessel Traffic 206-217-6152

FERRY TRANSPORTATION
Bremerton-Port Orchard, Passenger only
. . . . 1-800-501-RIDE
Washington State 1-800-843-3779

FISHING/SHELLFISHING INFO
Fishing Regulations 360-902-2500
24-hr Red Tide Hotline. 800-562-5632
Shellfish Rule Change Hotline. 1-866-880-5431

FUELS
Port of Brownsville Marina . . 360-692-5498 VHF 16, 66
Port Orchard Marina: Gas, Diesel. . . 360-876-5535
Port of Poulsbo Marina: Gas, Diesel
. . . . 360-779-3505

GOLF COURSES
These courses are accessible from moorage and have rental clubs.
Gold Mountain: Port Orchard/Bremerton
. . . . 360-415-5432
Horseshoe Lake: Gig Harbor/Port Orchard
. . . . 253-857-3326
McCormick Woods: Port Orchard 360-895-0130
Meadowmeer: Winslow/Poulsbo 206-842-2218
Rolling Hills: Brownsville 360-479-1212
Trophy Lake Golf Course: Port Orchard. 360-874-8337
Village Greens: Port Orchard 360-871-1222

HAUL-OUTS
Kitsap Marina 360-895-2193
Port of Brownsville Marina . . 360-692-5498 VHF 16, 66
Yachtfish Marine. 360-876-9016

HOSPITALS/MEDICAL CLINICS
Bainbridge Island Urgen Care 206-341-0001
Bremerton. 360-744-3911
Harrison Medical Center (Silverdale) . . . 360-744-8800
Port Orchard Urgent Care 360-744-6275

MARINAS / MOORAGE FLOATS
Blake Island State Park
Bremerton Marina . . . . . . 360-373-1035 VHF 66A
Bridgeview Marina 360-876-2522
Eagle Harbor Marina (Permanent) 206-842-4003
Eagle Harbor Waterfront Park: Winslow. 206-780-3733
Illahee Marine State Park 360-478-6460
Keyport, Port of: Keyport 541-760-0176
Kitsap Marina (permanent) 360-895-2193
Port Orchard Marina. . . . . 360-876-5535 VHF 66A
Port Orchard Railway Marina, permanent 360-876-2522
Port of Brownsville Marina . . 360-692-5498 VHF 16, 66
Port of Poulsbo Marina. 360-779-3505
Port of Silverdale 360-698-4918
The Harbour Marina: Eagle Harbor. 206-550-5340
Winslow Wharf Marina 206-842-4202

MARINE SUPPLIES & PARTS
Longship Marine. 360-779-2378

PARKS
Department of Natural Resources. 360-902-1000
Washington State Park Info 360-902-8844
Camping Reservations 888-226-7688

PROPANE
Port of Brownsville Marina . . 360-692-5498 VHF 16, 66

RAMPS
Annapolis
Miller Bay Marine 360-598-4900
Port of Brownsville . . . . 360-692-5498 VHF 16, 66
Chico
Eagle Harbor Waterfront Park
Evergreen City Park: Bremerton
Fay Bainbridge Park
Fort Ward Park
Harper Park, Southworth
Illahee State Park 360-478-6460
Keyport Port of 541-760-0176
Lebo Street, Washington Narrows
Manchester
Miller Bay: Miller Bay Marine 360-598-4900
Port Orchard
Poulsbo Marina 360-779-3505
Retsil: Sinclair Inlet
Silverdale, Port of 360-698-4918
Suquamish
Tracyton

REPAIRS / SERVICE
Kitsap Marine Marina 360-895-2193
Miller Bay Marine 360-598-4900
Yachtfish Marine N.W.: Port Orchard . . . 360-876-9016

RESTAURANT / PUB
Boat Shed Restaurant. 360-377-2600
Harbour Public House, Eagle Harbor . . . 206-842-0969

SCUBA SITES
Agate Passage, Blake Island Marine State Park
Illahee Marine State Park, Yukon Harbor
Fort Ward State Park

SEWAGE DISPOSALS
Blake Island State Park: Pump, Dump . . 360-731-8330
Eagle Harbor Marina: Pump 206-842-4003
Eagle Harbor Waterfront Park: Winslow. Pump, Dump.
. . . . 206-786-7627
Port of Brownsville Marina . . 360-692-5498 VHF 16, 66
Port Orchard Marina: Pump, Dump . . 360-876-5535
Poulsbo Marina: Poulsbo. Pump . . . 360-779-3505
Port of Silverdale: Pump, Seasonal. 360-698-4918
Pumpout Guy: Mobile Pumpout 206-437-6764
The Harbour Marina: Eagle Harbor. 206-842-6502

TAXI
Bainbridge Island 360-244-4420
Bremerton. 360-782-1966
Port Orchard -Red Top 360-876-4949
Silverdale 360-473-6996

TOWING
TowBoat U.S. (Puget Sound Area) 206-300-0486

VISITOR INFORMATION
Bainbridge Island 206-842-3700
Bremerton. 360-479-3579
Kitsap Peninsula Visitors Bureau 360-683-1084
Port Orchard. 360-876-3505
Poulsbo. 360-779-4848
Silverdale 360-692-6800

WEATHER:
NOAA Recorded Message. 206-526-6087
VHF WX-1

Visit us at boattravel.com

Chapter 3:
East Central Puget Sound

Elliott Bay to Lake Washington. Seattle, Kirkland, Bellevue, Renton, Hiram M. Chittenden Locks, Lake Washington Ship Canal, Lake Union, Mercer Island.

Lake Union - photo © The Center for Wooden Boats

Symbols

[   ]: Numbers between [ ] are chart numbers.

{   }: Numbers & letters between { } are waypoints.

★ Recommended destinations, facilities, and services

⛺: Park, 🚤: Boat Launch, ▲: Campgrounds,

🚶: Hiking Trails, ⛱: Picnic Area, 🚲: Biking,

🤿: Scuba

★ See "Important Notices" between Chapters 7 and 8 for specific information on boating related topics such as boating safety, weather, U.S. & Canadian marine radio use, Vessel Traffic Service, security zones, Canadian & U.S. Customs, etc. Due to changing regulations, call ahead to verify latest customs information.

★ **The Lakes to Locks Water Trail:** This regional fresh water, day use trail is designed for small, non-motorized vessels and has over 100 public access sites located on Lake Sammamish, Lake Washington, and Lake Union. These sites are joined by sloughs, cuts, and waterways, culminating at the Hiram M. Chittenden Locks where the fresh water of the lakes meets the salt water of the Puget Sound. Contact Washington Water Trails Assn. 206-545-9161, www.wwta.org.

Seattle
[18441, 18445, 18450, 18474]

★ **Seattle:** When you sail into Seattle, you are reaching a destination city that is one of the most beautiful in the world. Resembling an hourglass fitted between Puget Sound and Lake Washington, it is the air and sea gateway to Alaska and Asia. Seattle is a cosmopolitan center, with great natural beauty, intriguing points-of-interest, and many attractions. Because of its location, there are hundreds of marine related businesses, industries, and services. The Port of Seattle alone operates 19 major terminals, including Bell Harbor Marina for pleasure boats, located on Elliott Bay; Shilshole Bay Marina, for pleasure boats; and Fishermen's Terminal, for commercial fishing vessels and pleasure boats. The shorelines of Portage Bay, Salmon Bay, and Lake Union are also home to a number of marine supply stores, moorage facilities, and boat yards.

Traversing the locks, from the salt water of Puget Sound to the lake waters inland, is a unique experience possible in only a few places in the world. Restaurants, stores, theaters, major hotels, night life, tours, professional sports facilities, and

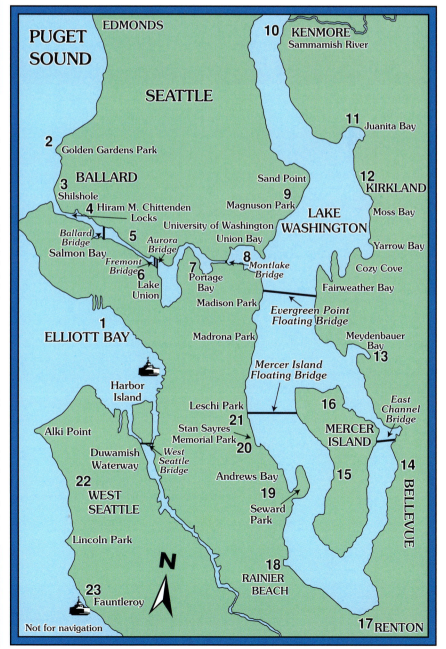

Chart List

NOAA Charts: 18441, 18445-450, 18474

Marine Atlas Vol 1 (2018): Pages 1, 4

Evergreen Cruising Atlas: 151, 154, 155, 162, 163, 164, 165, 166, 167, 168

The ever changing Seattle skyline from Elliott Bay Photo © Daniel

beautiful parks, all await exploration. Each May, the *Opening Day Parade* ushers in the yachting season. Since the 1950's, *Seafair*, with its parades, unlimited Hydroplane races, and community celebrations is a major attraction each summer.

Coined *The Emerald City*, Seattle, named after Chief Sealth of the Duwamish Tribe, has what many people consider to be an unusually romantic history. In 1851, Seattle's first white settlers arrived at Alki Point on the schooner *Exact*. Their primary source of revenue was selling logs for pilings for the San Francisco docks. They cleared land for homesteads and businesses along what is now Elliott Bay and a sawmill operated in the location of Pioneer Square. By 1889, the settlement, of 20,000, was a regular stop on shipping routes. In June 1889 a fire destroyed 50 downtown blocks. Undaunted, the re-building began immediately. On July 17, 1897, the steamship *Portland* arrived with $1 million in gold from the Yukon. The subsequent Alaska Gold Rush boosted the area's economy and focused attention on Seattle's strategic location. Many destined for the gold fields in Alaska changed their minds and stayed to help build the town. Immigrants came from around the world, especially from Scandinavian countries because the climate and surroundings were similar to their homelands. Other large migrations have come from Asia, as exemplified in the International District of today. A definite feather in Seattle's cap came with winning the right to host the 1909 Alaska Yukon Exhibition held on what is now the University of Washington campus. By 1910, the population had grown to 235,000. Another event designed to attract international attention took place in 1962 when Century 21 Exposition, *Seattle's World's Fair* attracted nearly 10 million visitors. The Space Needle and Pacific Science Center stand as a tribute to this event.

During World War II, Seattle's deep water port became a center for naval operations and ship building. Without a doubt, the Boeing Airplane Company has played a major role in Seattle's growth.

Today, Seattle is a leader in a number of industries including aerospace, software, and biotechnology. It is also considered to be a leading center for the arts, with renown ballet, opera, theatre and symphony companies, as well as hundreds of galleries and museums. In professional sports, it has Mariners baseball, Storm WNBA basketball, Seahawks football, Sounders FC soccer, Seawolves rugby and Kraken hockey.

Alki Point: This point is the site of a lighthouse that is part of an active USCG facility. No floats or mooring buoys and no anchoring is permitted off the shoreline. Power boats may not come ashore at the public beach area. Hand carried, non-motorized small boats can be beached in a designated area northeast of the open sandy public beach. Do not approach the fence. Free public lighthouse tours are conducted by Coast Guard Auxiliary volunteers most Sunday afternoons, 1-3:45pm, from Memorial Day weekend through Labor Day weekend. Note: there are dates when no tours are available. Extending around Duwamish Head, Alki beach reaches Don Armeni Park and Seacrest Park.

Elliott Bay
[18441, 18445, 18450]

Safety Zones in Elliott Bay: No unauthorized person or vessel may enter or remain in these safety zones. USCG Base at Pier 36 described as all waters east of a line from {47-35.450'N 122-20.585'W} to {47-35.409'N 122-20.585'W}. All waters extending 1,000 yards due south from the end of Pier 91 during the arrival/departure of large passenger cruise vessels at Pier 91. All waters within 100 yards surrounding cruise vessels moored at Pier 91.

★ **Elliott Bay (1):** Speed limit is seven knots within 200 yards of shore. More and more pleasure craft are cruising into this, Seattle's major harbor, and the center of maritime commerce. Moorage is available at several sites. Anchoring by pleasure craft is not permitted. Notable are the large freighters frequently at anchor and large cranes that faintly resemble huge insect-like creatures as they manipulate containers into the cargo ships. Cruise ship piers await passenger arrivals, fireboats practice streaming water out over the harbor, kayaks and canoes maneuver in and out among the piers and, amidst it all, a steady parade of Washington State ferries arrive and depart. The following description of Elliott Bay attractions begins on the West Seattle shore and circles around through the downtown core to the northern shore and Magnolia Bluff. See current tide table for Admiralty Inlet.

★ **Don Armeni Park:** On the west shore of Elliott Bay, Don Armeni Park is located just inside Duwamish Head. The park has a four lane launch ramp with side floats (launch fees apply.) During evening hours, limit your time on the boat ramp as lights shine directly into the homes across the street. Headlights are required for vehicles in operation so don't turn them off, just be as courteous as possible. If extra time is needed to prepare your boat, use the flat staging area near the street. This park also features picnic tables, restrooms, and spectacular views of downtown Seattle, especially at sunset when the setting sun reflects off the skyscrapers. (206) 684-7249.

★ **Seacrest Park:** Located immediately south of Don Armeni Park, this park has a concrete dock with gangway, finger-piers for kayaks and a 70-ft section of dock for the King County Water Taxi. Private vessels may moor for up to 2 hours on the portion of the dock that runs parallel to the Fishing Pier; but are not allowed on the southern "T" dock that the Water Taxi accesses. There is a boathouse with concessions, restrooms, restaurant, and picnic area. Alki Kayak Tours has skates, kayak, SUP, and bike rentals, 206-953-7669. Scuba diving is possible, no diving within 150' of the fishing pier.

★ **Harbor Island & Duwamish Waterway:** Watch the commercial operations of this port facility and enjoy a change of scenery by exploring the Duwamish River vicinity. A marina, with floating breakwater, is located at the southern tip of Harbor Island where the Duwamish River separates into the East and West Waterways before flowing around Harbor Island and into Elliott Bay. Port of Seattle operated parks are found along the Duwamish River. These parks include a variety of amenities such as picnic areas, waterfront shoreline, benches, fishing piers, look-outs, and some launch ramps for hand carried craft. Port parks and Shoreline Paths are also found at a number of terminals where visitors can enjoy up-close views of shipping operations, harbor tour boats, and an occasional canoe or kayak wending its way among the piers. www.portseattle.org/community/waterfront-parks.

Harbor Island Marina: {47° 34' 12.741" N, 122° 20' 47.9148" W} Monthly recreational and commercial moorage for vessels 26'-70', liveaboards (call for availability), water, 30/50 amp power, restrooms, showers, public pump-out, garbage deposit, security, parking. 206-787-3006.

Downtown Seattle Waterfront

The Olympic Sculpture Park is a short walk from the Bell Harbor Marina Photo © Richard Serra

★ **Downtown Seattle Waterfront:** Downtown is the epicenter of Seattle's culture and commerce. Its vibrant urban lifestyle continues to grow in popularity. Visitors enjoy the area's 1,145 restaurants, cafes and bars, 29 parks, 12 museums, 117 art galleries and 1,000 plus shops and retail stores–all mostly found within walking distance. For those that are not, Metro Buses run along 3rd Ave., parallel to the downtown Seattle waterfront connecting Belltown with Pike Place Market, the downtown retail area, Pioneer Square, the International District and beyond. Call 206-553-3000 for trip planning.

The International District, or Chinatown, is an interesting stop. This vibrant inner-city neighborhood is the cultural hub for Asian Americans in the area. It is a jumble of Korean, Vietnamese, Chinese and Japanese restaurants, unique specialty shops and grocery stores. The Wing Luke Asian Museum and the Nippon Kan Theatre are local notables. The *Lunar New Year Celebration* and *Dragon Fest* are popular community events.

The piers along the waterfront are numbered progressively from south to north. A great way to get a general lay-of-the land is to take a bus tour or a harbor cruise on a sight-seeing boat.

Beginning at Pier 36, this is the U.S. Coast Guard Base Seattle, home of the Coast Guard Museum. There is no cost to visit the museum and it is open Mon., Wed., and Fri. from 9am to 2pm. Be prepared to provide identification papers. Proof of US citizenship such as a passport may be rquested to enter. 206-217-6993. Proceeding north, and curving with the shoreline, is Pier 48, a former cargo terminal that currently serves as an equipment staging area for the Alaskan Way Viaduct Replacement Project. Once past the Washington State Ferry Terminal the landscape changes to tourism. From this location, it is possible to walk to Pioneer Square, considered by many to be the heart of Seattle. Visit restored buildings housing pubs, restaurants, antique stores, galleries, boutiques and other area shops. Parks provide benches and statues. The Pioneer Building, on the east border of Pioneer Square, is one of the oldest and most ornate.

Much of the vehicular traffic along the waterfront turns into the large Washington State Ferry Terminal on Coleman Dock, located at Piers 50 and 52. Ferries depart for Winslow, Bremerton, and (passenger only) to Vashon Island.

Continuing northwest, a fun stop is Pier 53 to see the fireboats. Then, for the next few blocks, there are restaurants and sightseeing tour opportunities to fill every wish. On Pier 57 take a ride on the 175' Seattle Great Wheel at the end of the dock or on a vintage carousel inside Miners Landing. Between Piers 57 and 59 a waterfront park provides picnic sites and a public fishing pier. Piers 59 and 60 house the highly respected Seattle Aquarium featuring award-winning exhibits of marine life, including a spectacular 20 x 40 foot viewing window. 206-386-4300. Across the street is the Pike Street Hillclimb, where you can walk to world famous Pike Place Market, the nation's oldest working Farmer's Market.

Back on the waterfront, stroll out Piers 62/63 for wonderful views of Elliott Bay and beyond. The Port of Seattle's Bell Harbor Marina is at Pier 66. The Bell Street Pier development includes restaurants, a gourmet grocery/deli, ATM machine, cruise ship terminal, and the Bell Harbor International Conference Center. Panoramic views, telescopes, historical information, and outdoor seating are found at the Public Plaza, located on the roof of the center. On the pier level there is an interactive children's fountain. Pedestrian bridges at the site and at Lenora Street, a few blocks to the south, allow convenient access. Moorage is within walking distance to the Pike Place Market, grocery store, hotels, restaurants, jogging paths, parks, and the Seattle Aquarium. If you are moored at Bell Harbor, a short bus or taxi ride could take you to the architecturally acclaimed Central Library, T-Mobile Park and Lumen Field, Benaroya Hall, medical facilities, churches, historic residential neighborhoods, or to the 74 acre Seattle Center. The Center features the 605 foot high Space Needle with observation platform and revolving restaurant at the top with panoramic views of the city, Puget Sound, and the Cascade and Olympic Mountain ranges. Also at Seattle Center is a children's museum and theater, the McCaw Hall, Museum of Pop Culture, the Pacific Science Center, Climate Pledge Arena, and the Chihuly Garden and Glass Museum. Center information: 206-684-7200. The Monorail, a legacy from the 1962 World's Fair, runs from Seattle Center into downtown Seattle where it is possible to take the bus, or even walk back down to the waterfront. For current schedule, 206-905-2620.

Continuing north along the waterfront, other retail outlets and cruise lines occupy space to Pier 70. As the beach curves northwest, it becomes a 1.25 mile stretch of waterfront known as Myrtle Edwards Park featuring benches, biking lanes, and walkways. Adjacent to the park is the unique

Page 40 Chapter 3 EAST CENTRAL PUGET SOUND

Bell Harbor Marina neighbors some of Seattle's most famous attractions Photo © Sean Pavone

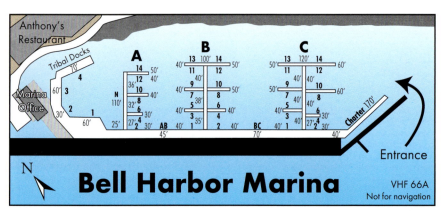

Olympic Sculpture Park. From here, the shoreline winds around, past the grain elevators to Pier 86 and Centennial Park. A tackle shop, restrooms, rose garden, Native American totem pole, exercise station, and a walking & biking path are accessible. An underwater reef on the north end is marked by orange buoys. This park-like waterfront ends at massive Piers 90 and 91. Smith Cove Park, a small park that offers big views and shore access, as well as picnic tables, benches and restrooms is tucked between Pier 91 and the Elliott Bay Marina complex. Lights mark the entrances on both sides of the Elliott Bay Marina breakwater.

★ **Bell Harbor Marina:** {47° 36' 38" N, 122° 20' 56" W} This Port of Seattle marina is Seattle's only downtown facility and open for guest moorage. Amenities include: moorage, power, water, showers, restrooms, garbage deposit and waste pump-out. Individuals and groups are welcome. Reservations advised. Bell Harbor Marina is walking distance to downtown Seattle and many of its iconic attractions–Seattle Space Needle, Seattle Great Wheel, Seattle Aquarium, Chihuly Glass and Garden Museum, Seattle Art Museum and Pike Place Market. Enjoy the Pacific Northwest's cuisine at Anthony's Restaurant located at the marina or discover farm to table freshness at the many eateries nearby. This year-around facility includes dock power at 30/110, 50/220 amps/voltage, and new 100-amp power with wide, concrete docks that are wheelchair accessible. Other amenities include: drinking and hose down water, locked gates, security cameras, and 24-hour staffing. Boaters are advised to radio the marina office on VHF Channel 66A prior to arrival. Reserve your slip at 206-787-3952. **Certified Clean Marina.** See our advertisement on this page. Website: www.portseattle.org. Email: bhm@portseattle.org. Address: Pier 66, 2203 Alaskan Way, Seattle, Washington 98121. Telephone: 206-787-3952. After-Hours: 206-465-0554. VHF 66A.

Visit us at boattravel.com

EAST CENTRAL PUGET SOUND Chapter 3 Page 41

★ **Elliott Bay Marina:** {47° 37.75 N, 122° 23.80 W} Permanent and guest moorage, vessels to 300'. Power (30amp, 125 volt & 50amp, 125/250 volt, 100amp single phase, 100amp 3 phase 480v), water, showers, laundry, gas, diesel, oil, pump-out, repairs, boat supplies, light groceries, beer, wine, bait/tackle, ice, restaurants, kayak/SUP rentals. See our advertisement on this page. Marina: 206-285-4817. VHF 78A. Fuel dock: "G" Dock, 206-282-8424. VHF 78A.

Shilshole Bay
[18441, 18446, 18447]

★ **Golden Gardens Park (2):** This popular park, known for swimming, sunbathing, sandy beaches, and sweeping views, stretches from Shilshole Bay to Meadow Point. There is a hand carried boat launch, hiking trails, picnic shelters, tables, concessions, fishing pier, off-leash dog area and play equipment. Park hours are 4am-11:30pm. Meadow Point has been noted for good fishing, (hook and line fin-fishing only).

★ **Shilshole Bay (3):** Located near the entrance to the locks, this curving shoreline is home to the Port of Seattle Shilshole Bay Marina. Speed limit within 200 yards of shore is seven knots. Stay in the marked channel because of shallow water and a drying flat off the bluff that is directly across from the marina breakwater. Condominiums, an assortment of restaurants and marine-related businesses and a statue of Leif Erikson that honors Seattle's Scandinavian immigrants overlook the moorage basin. The Eddie Vine boat ramp is located between the marina and Golden Gardens Park. Buses run along the waterfront into Ballard where riders can easily transfer to other city locales. See current table for Admiralty Inlet.

Elliott Bay Marina Photo © Linda Harms

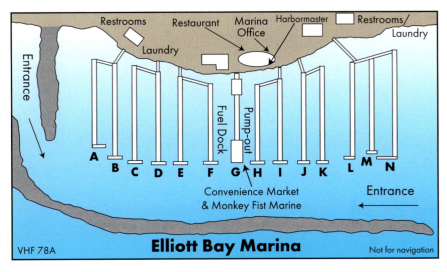

ELLIOTT BAY MARINA
2601 West Marina Place | Seattle, WA 98199 | 206.285.4817 | www.elliottbaymarina.net

Shilshole Bay Marina Photo © Don Wilson, Port of Seattle

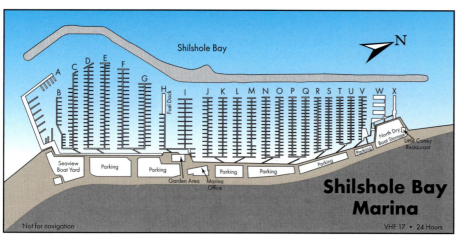

★ **Shilshole Bay Marina:** {47° 40' 39" N, 122° 24' 39" W} This Port of Seattle marina, with its convenient location on Central Puget Sound, has been called the *Gateway to Puget Sound Recreational Cruising*. Floating concrete piers are fully equipped with all the conveniences boaters require year-around. Power and water equipped guest moorage is found at several locations. The marina boasts a variety of slip sizes and wide berths. On-site laundry, showers, restrooms, recycling, and trash receptacles. Gas, diesel, oils, small grocery, beer, wine, ice, and porta potti dump are available at the fuel facility. Free sewage pump at A and H docks. Launch ramps and a 25-ton marine crane (located at CSR) accommodates haul outs. Individuals and groups welcome. Large garden area, bring your own bocce ball set and enjoy our bocce court right onsite on the plaza, BBQ's and plaza space available for guest activities. Pet friendly, please follow leash policy, etc .It's walking distance to Golden Gardens Park, Ray's Boathouse and Little Coney. **Certified Clean Marina.** See our advertisement on this page. Website: www.portseattle. org. E-mail: sbm@portseattle.org. Mailing address: 7001 Seaview Avenue NW, Suite 100, Seattle, Washington 98117. Telephone: 206-787-3006. After-Hours: 206-601-4089. Staff on duty 24 hours a day/seven days a week. VHF 17.

Shilshole Bay Fuel Dock: Gas, diesel #2 and kerosene, porta potti dump, marine batteries, groceries, snacks, ice, beer, wine, bait/tackle. 206-783-7555. VHF 17.

Hiram M. Chittenden Locks
[18441, 18447]

★ **Hiram M. Chittenden Locks (4):** [18447] Built in 1916, these locks are also known as the "Government" or "Ballard Locks." More than a million visitors a year watch the boats being raised or lowered. By allowing gravity to move water into and out of lock chambers, the two locks lift and lower vessels navigating between the sea level of Puget Sound and the higher elevation of the ship canal and Lakes Union and Washington, a difference of as much as 26 feet, depending on tide and lake level fluctuations. The locks are in operation 24 hours a day, unless closed for maintenance. Locking time is about 25 minutes for the large lock and ten minutes for the small lock.

Visit us at boattravel.com

Navigating the Locks

The locks handle a large volume of traffic and it may be necessary to wait for a turn, so it is wise to be flexible and plan to take more time. Being prepared with the proper equipment is also important. Boaters need two 50-foot lines with 12-inch eye splices for locking. Lines, one in the bow and one in the stern, should be arranged neatly in preparation. Because your final placement in the locks is unknown, fenders are vital equipment and should be placed on both sides of the boat prior to entry. The lock authority also recommends that the captain check the reverse gear at this time. Crewmembers should be stationed at both the bow and the stern of the boat, and children should be inside the cabin. Be careful to keep hands away from cleats and do not hang arms or legs over the sides of the boat.

Do not use sound signals to signal a lock tender. Tie up at the holding pier and wait for the green lights. Directions given over a public address system tell boaters to proceed at 2½ knots into the appropriate lock. If your boat is larger than 85' in length, wait for the entrance to the big lock. If your boat's draft is over 14', you will need to request that the salt water barrier be lowered.

Small lock: Most pleasure boat traffic is accommodated in the small lock which has usable space of 123 feet in length, 28 feet in width. Boaters are directed to the moss covered sides, the boater wraps their line around one of the mushroom-shaped buttons attached to the movable inner walls. These tie-up posts will raise or lower along with the water. This eliminates the work and danger of a fixed tie-up, like the ones used in the big lock. The attendant will instruct boats about rafting to other boats. During the locking process boaters should keep an eye on the lines just in case the floating wall hang-ups. In that case, slacken the lines as needed and notify a lock attendant. When the water levels are equal, boaters will be asked to tie-down their lines while awaiting their turn to leave the chamber. When the locks are opened, strong currents occur due to the flow of a large volume of water.

Large lock: Commercial traffic, large ships, and sometimes, pleasure boats are directed to use the large lock. It has usable space of 760 feet in length and 80 feet in width, and can accommodate up to 100 boats. The procedures differ in the large lock because there is no movable inner wall with tie-up posts on it. When entering from Puget Sound, the lock attendant will throw a line down to the boat. The boater uses a slip knot to tie the eye of his line to the lock attendant's line. The attendant then hauls up the line to his level and secures it to his cleat. On the boat, the crewman will wrap his end around the deck cleat and tend the line, bringing it in as the water rises in the lock. Keep the line taut around the cleat at all times, but do not tie down. When at lake level, the attendant will release the line from his cleat and hand it to you.

When heading out from the lake, you are at the higher water level, you will hand the line to the lock attendant when requested to do so. The attendant will wrap his end around his cleat, while you wrap your end around the deck cleat. Do not tie. The line must be tended and paid-out as the water level falls. Keep the line taut around the cleat at all times. Serious damage or injury can result from a line that snags on a cleat or other object, or a person during the descent.

When the water levels are equal, boaters will be asked to tie off their lines or the lines of another vessel rafting alongside while awaiting their turns to exit the lock chamber.

Need more help? The Seattle District Corps of Engineers offer a free "Locking Through" program (classes conducted January-September). Or stop by the locks and pick up a copy of *Guidelines for Boaters*. For more information visit, www.nws.usace.army.mil or call 206-764-3750.

Walk around: Visitors to the Locks park in a lot located at 3015 NW 54th. A walkway leads to the Locks and Visitors Center with exhibits and gift shop. Enjoy the beautiful Carl S. English Jr. Botanical Gardens or check out the fish ladder from an underwater viewing room. For information or tours: 206-783-7059.

★ **Lake Washington Ship Canal:** [18447] Construction of this eight mile long canal was completed on July 4, 1917. Minimum width is 100 feet, with depths dredged to 30 feet. The waterway extends from Puget Sound through Shilshole Bay, Salmon Bay, Lake Union, Portage Bay, Union Bay to Lake Washington. A speed limit of seven knots is enforced in the canal and on the lakes within 100 yards of any shoreline, pier, or shore installation. No anchoring is permitted along the canal.

Lake Washington Ship Canal Bridge Information: Several bridges affect passage of tall masted vessels. Minimum clearances are: Burlington Northern Bridge (west of the locks) 42' (check the Clearance Gauge since clearance may vary as much as two feet), Ballard Bridge 44', Fremont Bridge 30', University Bridge 42.5' and Montlake Bridge 46'.

On weekdays, except national holidays, the Ballard, Fremont, and University Bridges remain closed during peak rush hours (7am-9am and 4pm-6pm). Otherwise, from 7am to 11pm boaters should signal the bridge operator by horn, using one long blast (four to six seconds) followed by one short blast (one second) when the vessel is at least 100 yards from the bridge. The bridge operator will acknowledge the signal and open the bridge as soon as possible. If the bridge cannot be opened immediately, the bridge operator will respond with five or more short blasts (danger signal). If you hear the danger signal, stand off. The bridge operator will signal with one prolonged and one short blast once the bridge can be opened. From 11pm-7am, bridge openings are made by appointment. Call at least one hour ahead of time by phone, 206-386-4251 or by VHF 13 to the "Bridge Shop."

The Montlake Bridge has a seasonal schedule. From May 1 to Aug. 31, drawbridge openings for marine traffic are restricted on weekdays between 7am and 9am and between 3:30pm and 6:30pm. Between 12:30 to 3:30pm and from 6 to 6:30pm, openings are limited to the hour and half hour. There are no closures on weekends or national holidays. From Sept. 1 - April 30, weekday rush hour closures are extended from 7am- 10am and 3:30pm-7pm. To contact the Montlake Bridge to request an opening, signal by horn, call by phone at 206-720-3048, or radio VHF 13.

★ **Ballard (5):** Ballard was settled by Scandinavians, many of whom became loggers and fishermen. The Ballard neighborhood includes the downtown center along Market Street, the marine-oriented companies along the Salmon Bay waterfront, and the residential area on the hills above the shoreline that curves south and then westward to Shilshole Bay on Puget Sound. A downtown core offers unique shops, a wide array of fine restaurants, coffee shops, pubs, and a theater. The renown Nordic Heritage Museum, reopened in it's new home on Market Street in 2018.

★ **Ballard Pier - 24th Avenue Landing:** The Ballard Pier is being replaced by a new pedestrian pier and will be unavailable to boaters through the summer of 2024. Boaters will need to avoid temporary mooring dolphins and barging activities. There are docks on either side of the pier, but boats cannot moor on the sides next to the pier. This is part of the off-limit area.

★ **Salmon Bay (5):** This bay extends from the east end of the locks to the Ballard Bridge. Before the locks and the Lake Washington Ship Canal were built, this was a shallow, unnavigable harbor. Today, it is an active marine supply and industrial center. There are fuel docks, and permanent moorage facilities for pleasure and commercial boats along the shore. Fishermen's Terminal is on the southern shore. In the shadow of the Ballard Bridge, on the north shore, is the 14th Avenue Boat Ramp with two piers, two launch lanes, no fee to launch. Also on the north shore, located between the Ballard and Fremont Bridges, is Canal Boatyard, a full service boatyard with a wide variety of onsite services and a 55-ton Travelift. Call 206-784-8408 for details.

★ **Fishermen's Terminal Moorage:** {47° 39' 6" N, 122° 22' 47" W} Located just inside the Ballard Locks, this Port of Seattle facility is homeport to the North Pacific Fishing Fleet. Recreational boaters are also welcome to tie up at this landmark facility which offers both transient and monthly freshwater moorage. This year-around facility includes dock power at 30 and 50 amps, water, showers, laundry, three-day parking, 24-hour security, bilge and sewage pump-out, marine repairs, and groceries on-site. Fishermen's also offers three distinct on-site eateries to explore: Chinooks, The Highliner Public House and The Bay Cafe'. The site was dedicated in 1914 and is now home to the state's largest salmon and halibut fishing fleets, groundfish, longliners, and factory trawlers. Staff is on duty 24 hours/seven days a week. **Certified Clean Marina.** E-mail: ft@portseattle.org. Address: 3919 18th Avenue West, Seattle, Washington 98119. Telephone: 206-787-3395. Website: www.portseattle.org.

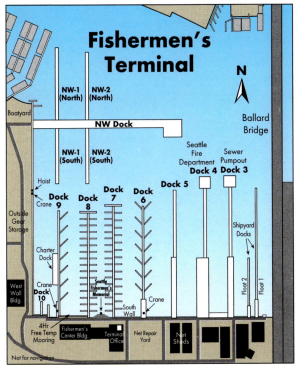

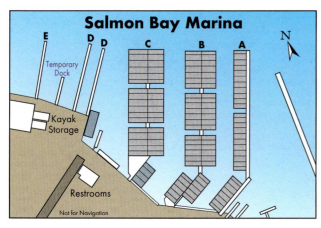

Salmon Bay Marina — Not for Navigation

★ **Salmon Bay Marina**: {47° 39' 37.6524" N, 122° 22' 44.9574" W} This Port of Seattle marina is located just inside the Ballard Locks, just west of the Ballard Bridge, and west of Fishermen's Terminal. It offers both covered and uncovered freshwater monthly moorage, plus other on-site amenities including: dock power at 30 and 50 amps, water, showers, restrooms, garbage deposit, nearby waste pumpout, locked gates, and 24-hour security. Enjoy fine dining, family restaurants, a pub and shops at nearby Fishermen's Terminal. Marina open year-around and staff available 24 hours/seven days a week. Email: salmonbay@portseattle.org. Physical address: 2100 W Commodore Way, Seattle, Washington 98199. Mailing address: 3919 18th Avenue West, Seattle, Washington 98119. Telephone: 206-787-3395. Website: www.portseattle.org. Ballard Mill Marina: {47° 39' 45" N, 122° 23' 6" W} Permanent moorage, liveaboards, 20/30 amp power, water, restrooms, laundry, showers. 206-789-4777.

Ballard Mill Marina: {47° 39' 45" N, 122° 23' 6" W} Permanent moorage, liveaboards, 20/30 amp power, water, restrooms, laundry, showers. 206-789-4777.

Covich-Williams (Ballard): Gas, diesel, oils, filters, water. Mon-Fri 8am-4:30pm, Sat. 8am-11:30am. 206-784-0171, 1-800-833-3132.

Ewing Street Moorings: Permanent moorage, very limited guest moorage, liveaboards, 20/30 amp power, restrooms, water. Used boats, parts, marine equipment for sale. 206-283-1075.

Waypoint Marine Group: {47° 40' 0.142" N, 122° 23' 41.899 W} Long/short term moorage (in and out of water), power up to 480 volts, water, repairs, parts, inflatables/boat/trailer sales. Located at Ballard Locks Jacobsen Terminal. 206-284-0200.

Lake Union
[18441, 18447]

★ **Lake Union (6)**: In 1854, Thomas Mercer a prominent Seattleite, named this lake in anticipation of the day when a canal would create a "union" between the lakes and the Puget Sound. Years later his vision would be realized and since that day Lake Union's waterfront has been continuously changing. Moorages, condos, floathouses, restaurants, marine supply stores, boat brokerages, charter agencies, boatyards, and marine repair businesses thrive. Transient moorage may be arranged at some marinas when slips of permanent tenants are vacant. Temporary moorage can be found at several waterfront restaurants. Speed limit is seven knots and no anchoring is permitted.

The Seattle Police Harbor Patrol Office, Gas Works Park, and a Seattle Parks and Recreation boat launch off Northlake Way at the foot of Sunnyside Street, are on the north shore. Gas Works Park is easy to locate by the large remnants of machinery from the days when the plant manufactured gas from coal. The park features a Play Barn, picnic sites, trails, restrooms, and one of the city's best kite flying hills. Offshore, four yellow buoys mark an area for boat testing on this north side of the lake. Caution advised.

On the east shore, restaurants, boatyards, a seaplane base and houseboats line the waterfront. The warehouses and docks of the old Wards Cove fish packing company, a familiar sight for nearly a century, is now a new waterfront community with high-end floating homes and a private marina. A buoy-marked shoal is near the southwest shore. On the southern shore is Lake Union Park, the Museum of History & Industry, and The Center for Wooden Boats.

The Center for Wooden Boats is a maze of docks loaded with classic wooden craft of all kinds. There is never a charge to walk the CWB docks. The Craftsman-style buildings house the Boatshop and the Boathouse Gallery. In the Boatshop you'll often see students building a boat from the keel up or volunteers restoring one of CWB's many boats. The Boathouse is home to a wonderful collection of old photographs from the Oregon Historical Society and a rotating exhibit. Hanging from the ceiling are old rowing shells, a Greenland kayak, and the driftwood skeleton of an old Eskimo kayak. There are over one hundred and fifty boats of historic significance, some of which you can rent for a row or sail. On Sundays, CWB offers public rides on a rotating selection of boats that include a classic steamer, a skin-on-frame canoe and an open fishing sailboat that is more than a century old. Get there early-seats fill up fast! (Please note this is a monthly program, it only happens one Sunday of every month, usually the 4th Sunday and occasionally on a Saturday). 206-382-2628.

★ **Fisheries Supply**: Fisheries Supply is the largest supplier of marine products in the Pacific Northwest. For over 90 years, this family-owned business has provided the best customer service and largest inventory of quality marine products to both professional and recreational boaters. Our customer service staff includes many avid boaters with a wealth of experience available to you to solve any of your boating-related needs. We ship anywhere in the world, including directly to your boat in the San Juan Islands via Kenmore Air, and you can place your order either with one of our customer service representatives or on our easy-to-use website. If you can't find the part you need on our website, give us a call and we will do our best to locate it for you. Fisheries Supply is located on the north end of Lake Union directly across from Gas Works Park in Seattle, Washington at 1900 N. Northlake Way, Seattle, WA 98103. Shop online at www.fisheriessupply.com or call us at (800) 426-6930. See our advertisement on page 45.

★ **Seattle Seaplanes**: Located on Lake Union, this company's motto is "We Fly Everywhere!" Scheduled and charter flights in Washington, to and from British Columbia, and Alaska. Fly-in passengers, parts, and supply service direct to your boat. See our advertisement on this page. Website: www.seattleseaplanes.com Address: 1325 Fairview Avenue East, Seattle, Washington 98102. Fax: 206-329-9617. Telephones: 206-329-9638, 1-800-637-5553.

Don't let a broken pump, clogged fuel filter or lost anchor ruin your vacation. Fisheries Supply has a full range of shipping options throughout the Pacific NW and Alaska, including custom solutions via Kenmore Air to almost anywhere in the San Juans, BC and the Inside Passage.

Largest Selection
of Marine Supplies in the Pacific Northwest

Same-Day Shipping
for Orders Placed by 2pm

Custom Shipping
to the San Juans, BC and Inside Passage*

*via Kenmore Air, certain restrictions apply

Kenmore Air / Michael Bertrand Photography

Where Boating Adventures Begin

Call us 800.426.6930   FisheriesSupply.com   1900 N. Northlake Way, Seattle

Chapter 3 EAST CENTRAL PUGET SOUND

Duck Dodge Sailing on Lake Union Photo © VPLLC

Dunato's Towing & Salvage: {47° 38' 59.6358" N, 122° 19' 52.6218" W} Emergency towing & salvage. 2309 N. Northlake Way, 206-730-7227.

Fairview Marinas: {47° 37' 49.2594" N, 122° 19' 46.7286" W} Permanent moorage, 30/50 amp power, water, shower, restroom, garbage deposit, recycling, parking, public pumpout. 1109 & 1151 Fairview Ave. N. 206-786-1753.

Gallery Marine: (N Lake Union) Inboard engine service (under 65'), electrical & generator repairs. 717 N.E. Northlake Way, 206-547-2477.

Marina Mart: (SW Lake Union) Annual moorage only, boats 15'-94'. No liveaboards. Covered/uncovered slips, power, restrooms, showers, private pump-out. 1264-1530 Westlake Ave N. 206-447-5575.

Morrison's North Star Marine: {47° 38' 42" N, 122° 20' 46" W} Gas, diesel, filters, oils, oil changes, water, pump-out, restrooms, convenience store items, snacks, wine/beer, marine supplies, ice. 2732 Westlake Ave N. 206-284-6600.

Nautical Landing Marina: (Western shore) {47 38' 33.4" N, 122 20' 37.4" W} Permanent and transient moorage (50' - 350'). 30/50/100 amp power, 240v and 100amp/480v. WiFi, security, parking. 206-464-4614.

Yachtfish Marine: (eastern shore) Full service boatyard, 60-ton Travelift (boats 19' to 75'). 1141 Fairview Ave N. 206-623-3233.

Portage Bay (7): This bay is almost entirely filled with yacht club facilities and houseboats. Montlake Cut, a concrete-sided man-made canal, connects Portage Bay with Union Bay. See directions for bridge openings included in this chapter in the entry for Lake Washington Ship Canal.

★ **Washington Sea Grant:** Washington Sea Grant (WSG) is all about water - and the people and businesses that live and work around the waters in Washington State. WSG partners with Washington State Parks Clean Vessel Act program to educate boaters about marine sewage pumpouts. For over 50 years, WSG has served Washington residents by funding marine research and working with communities to help them better understand and sustain use of ocean and coastal resources, from fishing and aquaculture farming practices to safe boating and tsunami preparedness. Based at the University of Washington, WSG is part of a national network of 34 Sea Grant colleges within the National Oceanic and Atmospheric Administration (NOAA). WSG also works with many other colleges and academic and research institutions throughout the Pacific Northwest to support communities and the health of our ocean and waters. See our advertisement on page 4. Website: www.wsg.washington.edu or contact Aaron Barnett at aaronb5@uw.edu. Telephone: 206-616-8929.

Boat Street Marina: {47° 39' 1" N, 122° 18' 50" W} Long term moorage, no liveaboards, power, water, garbage deposit, recycling, public pump-out. 206-634-2050.

Union Bay (8): This shallow bay, next to the University of Washington, has mooring buoys and a dock that is not attached to shore. This is a popular destination whenever the University of Washington has a sporting event at the stadium. Anchoring is permitted only during Husky football games. Boats visiting Husky Stadium must keep out of the area north and west of the green buoy. Anchorage is possible in other areas. Use a heavy anchor and adequate chain because the bottom is poor holding. Flag down a UW shuttle boat to make a free trip to shore. The shuttle back to your anchored boat is $10 per person. There will be limited shuttle service in late October & November. Please check with UW about shuttle arrangements before game day for later games. Only boats with permits are allowed to land on the Husky docks. For single game or season permit information email: uwharbor@uw.edu. Restrooms and telephone are on shore.

The Washington Park Arboretum, a botanical research center, is located on the southern shore. The park's Visitor Center is open Tuesday thru Sunday from 10am to 4pm and has interpretive displays, as well as a free guided tour on the first

Visit us at boattravel.com

Thursday of each month at 11:30 am. Call 206-543-8800 to verify dates/times. Rent a canoe, kayak or rowboat at the University Waterfront Activities Center at Husky Stadium and paddle across the ship canal to explore the Arboretum's secluded waterways. For information, call the Activities Center at 206-543-9433.

Lake Washington

[18441, 18447, 18448]

★ **Lake Washington:** Nearly 17 miles in length, Lake Washington stretches from the communities of Kenmore on the north to Renton on the south. Seattle borders the lake on the west, while Kirkland and Bellevue rim the eastern shore. Mercer Island, located in the southern portion of the lake, is connected by bridges to the mainland. Enforced seven knot speed restrictions exist within 100 yards of shore and under the bridges. City of Seattle policy does not allow anchoring along its shores, whether in Lake Washington or on Puget Sound. Andrews Bay is an exception, and a specific code of conduct is in force. See entry for Seward Park in this chapter. The Seattle Police Harbor Patrol supervises traffic and handles requests for aid. 206-684-4071. VHF 13 or emergency VHF 16.

Opposite Seattle, on the eastern shore of Lake Washington, the only anchorage is in Juanita Bay off of St. Edward State Park (short-term overnight moorage only).

Many parks with swimming beaches and fishing piers line the Lake Washington shore. Private docks, often jut out from beautifully landscaped properties. Swimming, sailing, cruising, water-skiing, and fishing are popular activities. Launching ramp sites include the Sammamish River, Magnuson Park at Sand Point, Moss Bay, Stan Sayres Park, Newport Shores, Atlantic City Park, Ferdinand Street at Seward Park (hand launch only), and east of the Boeing plant at Renton. Fishing piers are located at North Leschi Moorage, Madison Park, Mount Baker Park, Madrona Park, and Seward Park on Bailey Peninsula.

Swimming beaches, both public and private, dot the shore between houses. These are usually marked by buoys, anchored rafts, or floats. Seattle Park Beaches operate from the end of June through Labor Day, 12 pm-7 pm weekdays, 11 am-7 pm weather permitting. Beaches are located at Matthews Beach, Magnuson Park, Madison Park, Madrona Park, Mount Baker Park, Seward Park, and Pritchard Beach. Hydroplane activity reaches a peak in August during the *Seafair* celebration. The headquarters for the Hydroplane installation is in the Stan Sayres Memorial Park on the west shore, south of the Mercer Island Floating Bridge. The University of Washington crew team also races on the lake.

Lake Washington Bridges: The southernmost bridge is the Mercer Island Floating Bridge (Interstate 90) connecting Seattle with Mercer Island. Vertical clearance at either end is 29 feet. Clearance is 35' at East and West Center Span. There is a marked nautical mile check course on the bridge. Keep clear of anchor cables which are within 1,250 feet of both sides of the bridge. Underwater remains of piers of a former fixed bridge are southeast of the I-90 bridge. Stay in the main navigation channel. The new State Route 520 Bridge is the northernmost bridge. It extends from Foster Island to Fairweather Point on the east. Large, bright, reflective orange buoys are at both ends of the bridge near the navigation channels to indicate the location of shallow, submerged anchor cables that secure the floating bridge. The west navigation channel has a navigational height of 43 feet. In the East navigation channel, the final navigational height of the pontoon located at the west side of the east channel is 70 feet. The typical clearance by the fixed, east approach column along the east side of the channel is 65 feet, but may rise to approximately 67 feet with lower water levels. For updates about boating activities and navigation restrictions in the area, visit www.wsdot.wa.gov/construction-planning.

Kirkland's Carillon Point Marina   Photo © Merrill Images

★⚓ **Sand Point & Magnuson Park (9):** Sand Point, site of a former Naval Air Station from 1920-1970, is now NW District Headquarters for the National Oceanic and Atmospheric Administration. A small marina belongs to the Navy. Also located at Sand Point is Seattle's second largest park, Magnuson Park. Within its 350 acres there is something for everyone - sports courts and fields, sailing center, swimming beach, biking and walking trails, off-leash dog area, picnic sites, playground and wading pools. There are three long piers and four boat launch lanes at the SE end of the park. Use the NE 65th Street entrance. Hand-carried, non-motorized vessels can be launched in two areas, one just south of the public piers and one south of the swimming beach. 206-684-4946. ⚓🎣🚴

Kenmore (10): Located at the northern tip of Lake Washington, Kenmore is the gateway to the Sammamish River. Follow the lighted markers outlining the channel, passing the red CG Buoys #2 and #4. Watch your depths as shoaling and grounding has occurred. Be alert for seaplanes landing and taking off. A WDFW boat launch, just east of the Sammamish River Bridge, provides access to Lake Washington and features a double water entry/exit, restrooms, and parking. ⚓

★ **Kenmore Air:** Taking a seaplane flight is a quintessential Northwest experience, and Kenmore Air makes it easy to enjoy the unique thrill of flying off the water and soaring over one of the most beautiful regions in the world. With Kenmore Air fly between Seattle and the San Juans or Victoria, BC in about 45 minutes! No long ferry lines and no hoards of people at the border. Kenmore Air also offers scheduled service to over 45 spectacular seasonal destinations including the BC Gulf Islands, Sunshine Coast, Desolation Sound, Blind Channel and the Northern Inside Passage. It's fast, convenient and stress-free! For the ultimate in flexibility, consider chartering an aircraft as you determine exactly when and where the flight goes. Our fleet of 24 aircraft can accommodate 1-10 passengers, thereby giving us the opportunity to fly groups larger than the capacity of any single aircraft. See our ad on page 45. Information and reservations at KenmoreAir.com or 1-866-435-9524.

★⚓ **Tracy Owen Station** at Log Boom Park: This Kenmore park offers picnic tables, benches, restrooms, trails, fishing pier, and play area. From May through September there is a 62x10 float for day moorage only, no power. Anchorage is possible south of the park. Canoes, kayaks, SUPs, and bikes can be rented seasonally, or experience our EcoTour on the Sammamish River, call 425-417-8637. The northern end of the 18-mile Burke-Gilman Trail to Gas Works Park in Seattle starts here. 🎣🚴

Harbour Village Marina: {47° 45' 13" N, 122° 15' 32" W} Long term and off-season moorage, slips to 51', some sublets, 30/50amp power, water, laundry, shower, free pump-out. 425-485-7557.

North Lake Marina: {47° 45' 26.3592" N, 122° 15' 34.6248" W} Permanent moorage. Non-ethanol gas, lubes, oil filters, dry storage, haul-outs to 30,000 lbs, (max width 12.5') service/ repairs, parts, chandlery, ice. 425-482-9465.

★⚓ **Saint Edwards State Park:** This day-use park contains 326 acres and is primarily accessed by car. Site of a former seminary, there are trails to the beach where good fishing is found. Equestrian and hiking trails, picnic sites, playground, sports fields, horseshoe pits. When arriving by water, look for the park sign. Because of shoaling and uneven depths, anchoring may be difficult. Anchor out in deeper water. 425-823-2992. 🎣🚴

★ **Sammamish River (10):** It is possible for flat bottom, shallow draft boats to navigate the dredged waterway all the way to Redmond. Bothell's first white settler, Columbus Greenleaf, arrived in 1870 and built a cabin on the river. The river played an important role in commerce and for years was navigable by large barges headed to Bothell Landing, an important steamboat landing. In 1917, the level of the lake dropped nine feet with the opening of the Washington Ship Canal, marking the end of large scale transportation up the river.

★⚓ **Bothell Landing:** Located about two miles up the Sammamish River, this city park has a launch for canoes and small boats, an amphitheater that hosts a number of popular community events, a playground, restrooms, trails, picnic tables and BBQ's. The Hannan House, built in 1893 by

Chapter 3 EAST CENTRAL PUGET SOUND

Looking south from Bellevue on Lake Washington toward Mount Rainier Photo © George Cole

William Hannan for his bride, Mima, is the main museum building. The 1884 Beckstrom Log Cabin, as well as Bothell's first one-room 1885 Schoolhouse are also on the grounds. These historic buildings are free to visit on Sundays, 1-4pm, April-Oct. For museum information, bothellhistoricalmuseum.org. Visitors to Bothell Landing can wander into town or bike ride on trails along the river. For information regarding park events go to www.bothellwa.gov.

★ **Marymoor Park:** Located at the north end of Sammamish Lake, Marymoor Park is King County's most popular park with more than 3 million visitors each year. The park features a climbing rock, exercise circuit, sports fields, picnic areas, off-leash dog area, trails, and the state's only Velodrome (offering competitive racing as well as public drop-in use). During summer months a popular Concert Series features internationally known acts. www.marymoorconcerts.com. It is possible to launch hand-carried boats at the Sammamish Rowing Assn Boathouse and float down the eight-mile stretch, past Woodinville and Bothell to Lake Washington. Call 425-653-2583 for information. Park Office: 206-477-7275.

★ **Kirkland (12):** Kirkland's stunning setting on Lake Washington includes two miles of lakefront footage, the largest publicly owned waterfront on the Eastside. Moss Bay has marina facilities at Kirkland's Marina Park. This lovely park with its pavilion, picnic tables, free wifi, amphitheatre, restrooms, fishing area and sandy beach makes a lovely stop. Marina Park also hosts many popular community events like *Kirkland Uncorked*, a regional showcase of art, food and wine held each July, *Summmerfest Music & Arts Festival* in July and *Kirkland Oktoberfest* in September. June through September a Wednesday Farmers Market features local produce, flowers, products and arts & crafts from 3-7pm. Free concerts are held at the pavilion on Thursday nights during the summer. Within walking distance of Marina Park are boutiques, eateries, a library, and performance center that features dance, theatre and music, 425-893-9900. Following the shoreline several waterfront restaurants maintain private floats for guest moorage while dining. Carillon Point is the site of a marina, the Woodmark Hotel and Still Spa, restaurants, coffee bars, retail shops and services, as well as a central plaza that hosts outdoor movies in the summer. A public guest pier at the Carillon Point Marina is first come/first served, no overnight moorage, 2 hour maximum, boats over 32' must use outside of the pier. For activities and events in Kirkland, visit www.explorekirkland.com.

Carillon Point Marina: {47° 39' 24.3354" N, 122° 12' 23.364" W} Permanent moorage, guest moorage by reservation only, 30/50 amp power, water, showers, restrooms, pump-out. 425-822-1700.

Kirkland Homeport Marina: Next to City of Kirkland Marina. Permanent moorage, 100 amps/240 volts power in some slips, parking. 425-827-4849.

Kirkland Marina at Marina Park: {47° 40' 27.1194" N, 122° 12' 32.0394" W} 72 overnight slips, no reservations. Power in some slips on the south side of marina dock (pay on arrival for these slips). Pay stations onsite (credit/debit cards). Three hours free loading 8am-10pm; after 10pm pay on arrival. Max stay of 5 consecutive days year-round. Boat launch (boats 24' or less; credit/debit cards), free use Nov 1-March 31, Boat Launch Card optional (purchase at City Hall during working hours). 425-587-3300.

Yarrow Bay Marina: {47° 39' 14.382 N, 122° 12' 24.5226"} Permanent moorage, regular and premium gas, oil, repairs, parts/accessories, Marina Store with refreshments, supplies & sundries, boat rentals/sales, haul-out to 30', public pump-out. 425-822-6066.

★ **Cozy Cove:** Cozy Cove is nestled between the Cities of Hunts Point and Yarrow Point. As one would expect in these affluent communities, large waterfront mansions, private mooring buoys and docks line the shore.

★ **Fairweather Bay:** Give a wide berth to Hunts Point when crossing between Cozy Cove to Fairweather Bay.

★ **Meydenbauer Bay (13):** Meydenbauer Bay Marina and the smaller Bellevue Yacht Basin are now owned by the City of Bellevue and future plans are being made for the facilities. A private yacht club is also located in the area, as is Meydenbauer Beach Park, with its swimming beach, picnic area and playground. Private docks dot the southwest shore of the bay. Beaux Arts Village, south of Meydenbauer Bay, is the site of a private marina. Though hard to imagine, a fleet of whaling ships, belonging to the American-Pacific Whaling Company used to winter in Meydenbauer Bay as recently as the 1930's.

Bellevue Marina at Meydenbauer Bay: {47° 37' 9.408" N, 122° 12' 13.536" W} Permanent moorage, covered/uncovered. Visitor moorage between piers 2 & 3 from 8am-9pm, 4 hour limit, no overnight. Water, 30/50 amp power, oil disposal, restroom, security gate. 425-452-4883.

Bellevue (14): Bellevue, incorporated in 1953, is now the fifth largest city in the state. The city's marina is on Meydenbauer Bay, near downtown Bellevue. The large new park on Meydenbauer Bay also hosts a seasonal canoe, kayak and SUP rental program. Enatai Beach, a park south of the East Channel Bridge has a dock, swimming beaches, picnic area, restrooms, and seasonal canoe, kayak, and SUP rentals. Newcastle Beach is the largest city park on Lake Washington. Beautiful lake views, a swimming beach, picnic and playground areas, and nature trail are popular features. Call 425-452-6885 for park information. Between the two parks, the SE 40th Boat Launch, at 118th and SE 40th St., also provides access to Lake Washington. Parking available, fee charged. For boat launch info, Julie Byers at 425-452-4444. Fuel, permanent moorage, and a yacht club are found near the launch.

Newport Yacht Basin Association: {47° 34' 30.6984" N, 122° 11' 15.1368" W} Private condo marina, no guest moorage, limited reciprocal moorage. Buy, own, or rent slips. Marina office: 425-746-7225.

Seattle Boat Co.: (Next to 40th St. Boat Launch) Sales, service, SkyLaunch Marina, boat club, valet/dockside service, storage. Fuel Dock: gas, diesel, oil, lube, ice, snacks. 425-641-2090.

★ **Mercer Island (15):** This beautiful island, just two miles wide and about five miles long is home to about 25,000 residents. Luxurious homes front the shoreline, many with private docks extending into the lake. There are plans to close the boat dock at Luther Burbank Park during 2023 and 2024. A total renovation of the waterfront will make for a fantastic day use destination starting in 2025. A launch ramp is found at 3600 E. Mercer Way on Barnabie Point where the East Channel Bridge (vertical clearance 65') crosses East Channel.

★ **Luther Burbank Park (16):** This extensive waterfront park situated north of Barnabie Point stretches all the way to Calkins Point. Docks with finger piers can accommodate 30 boats (dock may be closed in 2024 for renovations). Day moorage only. A popular sailing program leaves from the docks. Expansive lawn areas are great for picnics and games. Trails for hiking and jogging can be found throughout the park. Other attractions include an Off Leash Dog area, playground, tennis courts, fishing pier, picnic sites, restrooms for day moorage only, a swimming beach, and an amphitheater that hosts the Wooden-O Theatre's Shakespearean plays in July and August. Shops in the town center are less than a mile from this park. 206-275-7609.

Renton (17): This city on Lake Washington's southern shore offers an abundance of natural beauty from spectacular views of the Olympics,

EAST CENTRAL PUGET SOUND Chapter 3 Page 49

the Cascades and Mount Rainier, to the Cedar River that runs through the heart of its downtown. At the mouth of that river, the Cedar River Trail Park has a non-motorized boat launch, picnic and play areas, a 4.5 mile trail, and the Renton Rowing Center offering kayak/SUP rentals and rowing programs, 425-902-4848.

★ **Northwest Seaplanes:** Serving boaters since 1988. Scheduled and Charter Flights from Seattle to British Columbia's Inside Passage and Vancouver Island: April Point, Barkley Sound, Blind Channel, Bliss Landing, Campbell River, Cortes Bay, Dent Island, Desolation Sound, Discovery Islands, Lagoon Cove, Mansons Landing, Nootka Sound, Port McNeill, Prideaux Haven, Sullivan Bay, Tahsis, Tofino, and 100's more of your favorite cruising destinations. We provide passenger, freight and professionally tailored services. Located just 15 minutes from the Seattle Airport and downtown Seattle. Free Shuttle Service to SeaTac Airport. See our advertisement on this page. Website: www.nwseaplanes.com. Address: 860 W Perimeter Road, Renton, Washington 98057. Telephone: 425-277-1590 for reservations and information.

★ **Trailer Techs: Mobile Trailer Repair.** Our professional certified staff have over 20 years of experience. We come to your location. Our work vans are fully stocked to complete most repairs in the same day. We service and repair wheel bearings, surge brakes, electric brakes, electric over hydraulic brakes, lights, suspension, axles and more. We also do full LED light upgrades. We work on all non air brake trailers, including boat, camper, utility and equipment trailers. Our service area includes Tacoma, Bellevue, Seattle, Maple Valley, Everett, the southern San Juan Islands, and everywhere in between. Pricing depends on location and travel times. Please call, text or email with any questions. See our advertisement on page 6. Website: www.trailertechs.net. Email: service@trailertechs.net. Telephone: 206-889-0286.

★ **Gene Coulon Memorial Park:** This beautiful waterfront park has some daytime moorage slips with no power and an eight lane boat launch ramp (open 24/7, for boats less than 30' and under 10,000 lbs, fee charged). On shore are swimming beaches, a bathhouse with hot showers, restroom, walking paths, tennis courts, horseshoe pits, sand volleyball courts, a playground, a viewing tower, picnic sites and restaurants. Of special interest are the bronze statues and the unusual floating patio-decks, connected by ramps with the main walkway. A number of community events are hosted here, starting with the annual *Polar Bear Dip*, followed by a summer concert series and outdoor films, a 4th of July celebration and finally, *Clam Lights* in December. Park information, rates, fee, and hours. 425-430-6600. www.rentonwa.gov/parks.

Rainier Beach/Atlantic City Boat Ramp (18): Speed limit three knots within 100 yards of shore. The only public facility located here is the Atlantic City launching ramp found in the cove south of Beer Sheva Park. This wide ramp has dock space accommodating up to six launches/retrievals at a time. Fee applies. Other facilities are private yacht clubs and marinas.

Parkshore Marina: {47° 31' 17.886" N, 122° 15' 45.0792" W} Private homeowners association moorage, buy/rent slips, owner liveaboards only, showers, laundry, public pump-out. 206-725-3330.

★ **Seward Park & Andrews Bay (19):** This park encompasses Andrews Bay and Bailey Peninsula. A Code of Conduct is enforced regarding speed (three knot limit), noise, pollution, and environmental damage. The anchorage area can accommodate approximately 80 vessels. It extends from the Seward Park shoreline out to buoys in place 150 yards off the western shore. There is a 300 yard buffer zone off the extreme head of the bay. The approved area is defined by two buoys marked with an "A" (indicating the northwest and southwest corners) and two shore markers (indicating NE and SE corners). Place the hook where you are assured of not swinging out of the designated area or into your neighbor. Anchoring is limited to 72 hours within any 7 day period. There is a launching ramp for hand carried boats. The only access to land is at the launch ramp on the western shore, however there is no float for dinghy-ties. In the park are picnic spots, tennis courts, swimming beach, an art studio, and environmental learning center. A nature trail skirts the peninsula. Bird watchers will enjoy this park, home to 100 species of birds.

Lakewood Moorage: {47° 33' 48.7" N, 122° 15' 59.3" W} Permanent moorage (accepting waitlist applications), 20/30 amp power, water, restrooms & laundry for tenants only. 206-722-0660.

★ **Stan Sayres Memorial Park (20):** This park is located a mile south of the I-90 bridge on a north facing point. The peninsula upon which it sits was created when water levels in Lake Washington lowered with the building of the Ship Canal in 1917. Named for hydroplane racer, Stan Sayres, this park has a launching ramp, walking trails, restrooms, and day moorage facilities for small boats. It is also the site of the Mount Baker Rowing and Sailing Center offering rowing and sailing programs, as well as kayak, windsurfing and SUP classes. 206-386-1913.

★ **Leschi (21):** Leschi is located between the Mount Baker and Madrona neighborhoods along the shores of Lake Washington. In the late 1800's an amusement park, serviced by a cable-car system running between Leschi and Pioneer Square, was located here. The park is long gone, but people still enjoy the tranquility and beauty of this neighborhood. The waterfront is the site of a fishing pier and two Seattle Park Department moorages that are separated by a commercial center that also has a marina, as well as offices, grocery and wine store, coffee shop, hair salon, and several restaurants.

Leschi Moorage: North {47° 36' 12.4" N, 122° 17' 2" W} South {47° 36' 4" N, 122° 17' 6" W} Dry & wet permanent moorage (accepting waitlist applications), 20/30 amp power, water. 206-722-0660.

Leschi Yacht Basin: {47° 36' 1" N, 122° 17' 13" W} Permanent moorage, power, water, restrooms, restaurant onsite. 206-722-0660.

West Seattle
[18445, 18448]

West Seattle's Western Shore (22): See current table for Admiralty Inlet. This is the site of the Alki Point Lighthouse, and several saltwater beaches including Alki Beach. No mooring facilities. Only hand carried, non-motorized small boats may be beached in a designated area northeast of the open public sandy beach. Me-Kwa-Mooks Natural Area is to the south, as are Lowman Beach Park and Lincoln Park.

★ **Lincoln Park:** This lovely 135-acre park, accessed by car, borders Puget Sound north of the Fauntleroy-Vashon Island ferry landing. Anchoring, and/or the beaching of power craft is not permitted. In the park are trails, athletic fields, horseshoe pits, tennis courts, picnic sites, a seasonal heated saltwater pool, and locales for scuba diving, beachcombing, and fishing.

Fauntleroy (23): Site of the Fauntleroy Vashon-Southworth ferry. No marine facilities.

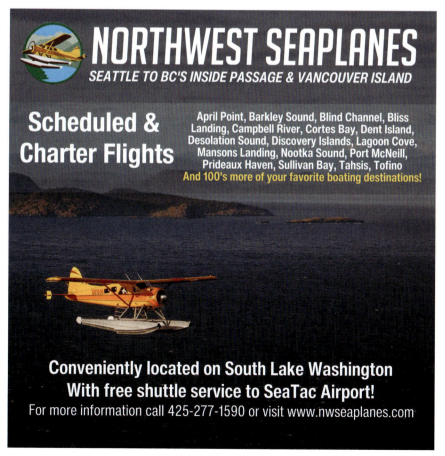

Essential Supplies & Services

AIR TRANSPORTATION
Kenmore Air 1-866-435-9524
NW Seaplanes . . . 425-277-1590, 1-800-690-0086
San Juan Airlines 1-800-874-4434
Seattle Seaplanes   206-329-9638, 1-800-637-5553

AMBULANCES: Medic 1 911

BOOKS / CHARTS
Captain's Nautical . . 206-283-7242, 1-800-448-2278
Evergreen Pacific Publishing 425-493-1451
Fisheries Supply 1-800-426-6930
The Marine Atlas 253-872-5707

BUS TRANSPORTATION
Greyhound 1-800-231-2222, 206-624-0618
Metro 206-553-3000
Sound Transit 1-888-889-6368

CNG CYLINDERS
Sure Marine (Call Ahead) 1-800-562-7797
Emergencies . . . . 911, 206-217-6001, VHF 16
Sector Puget Sound (office) 206-217-6200
Vessel Traffic 206-217-6152

FERRY TRANSPORTATION
Victoria Clipper (passenger only) 206-448-5000
. . . . 1-800-888-2535
Washington State 206-464-6400; 1-800-843-3779

FISHING/SHELLFISHING INFO
Fishing Regulations 360-902-2500
24-hour Red Tide Hotline 1-800-562-5632
Shellfish Rule Change Hotline 1-866-880-5431

FUELS
Ballard Oil: Ballard. Diesel 206-783-0241
Covich-Williams: Ballard. Gas, Diesel . . . 206-784-0171
Elliott Bay Fuel Dock: Gas, Diesel . . 206-282-8424
North Lake Marina: Gas 425-482-9465
Seattle Boat Co. Gas, Diesel 425-641-2090
Morrison's North Star: Lake Union. Gas, Diesel.
. . . . 206-284-6600
Shilshole Bay Fuel Dock: Ballard. Gas, Diesel
. . . . 206-783-7555, VHF 17
Yarrow Bay Marina: Kirkland. Gas, Diesel 425-822-6066

HAUL-OUTS
Canal Boatyard 206-784-8408
North Lake Marina 425-482-9465
Seaview West 206-783-6550
Shilshole Bay Marina: Ballard 206-787-3006
Yarrow Bay Marina: 425-822-6066
Yachtfish Marine 206-623-3233

HOSPITALS
Swedish Medical Center Ballard 206-782-2700
Bellevue Overlake Medical 425-688-5000
Evergreen Health, Kirkland 425-899-1000
Virginia Mason, Seattle 1-888-862-2737

LIQUOR STORE
Elliott Bay Marina 206-285-4817

MARINAS / MOORAGE FLOATS
Ballard Mill Marina, Permanent 206-789-4777
Bell Harbor: Pier 66 . . . 206-787-3952 VHF 66A
Bellevue Marina at Meydenbauer 425-452-4883
Carillon Point Marina: Kirkland 425-822-1700
Elliott Bay Marina . . . 206-285-4817 VHF 78A
Ewing Street Moorings: Seattle 206-283-1075
Fairview Marinas, Permanent 206-786-1753
Fisherman's Terminal: Seattle 206-787-3395 VHF 17
Harbor Island Marina 206-787-3006
Harbour Village Marina 425-485-7557
Kirkland Marina 425-587-3300
Kirkland Homeport Marina 425-827-4849
Lakewood Moorage: Andrews Bay, Permanent . . . .
. . . . 206-722-0660
Leschi Moorage, Permanent 206-722-0660
Luther Burbank Park: Mercer Island. (day only)
Marina Mart, Permanent 206-447-5575
Nautical Landing: 206-464-4614
Salmon Bay Marina . . . . . 206-787-3395 VHF 17
Shilshole Bay Marina: Ballard   206-787-3006 VHF 17
Waypoint Marine Group 206-284-0200
Yarrow Bay Marina, Permanent 425-822-6066

MARINE STORE
Fisheries Supply 1-800-426-6930

PARKS
King County Parks 206-477-4527
Seattle Parks 206-684-4075
Washington State Park Info 360-902-8844

POLICE
King County Marine Patrol 206-296-7559
Mercer Island Marine Patrol 206-275-7953
Seattle Harbor Patrol 206-684-4071
(in times of distress call 9-1-1 or VHF 16)

RAMPS
Atlantic City Boat Ramp SW shore Lake Washington
Barnabie Point: Mercer Island
Don Armeni Boat Ramp: Duwamish Head, Elliott Bay
14th Avenue NW Ramp: Ballard
Gene Coulon Park, Renton 425-430-6700
Eddie Vine Ramp, Ballard
Kirkland Marina Park: Moss Bay
Lake Union: North shore at Sunnyside Street
Magnuson Park: Sand Point
Marymoor Park: Sammamish River
40th St. Launch: Bellevue 425-452-4444
Seattle Parks Ramps: 206-684-7249
Seward Park: Andrews Bay
Shilshole Bay Marina: Ballard 206-787-3006
Sixty Acres: Sammamish River
Stan Sayres Park: West shore Lake Washington

REPAIRS / SERVICE
Canal Boatyard 206-784-8408
Coastal Marine Engine 800-223-5284
Gallery Marine: North Lake Union 206-547-2477
North Lake Marina 425-482-9465
Platypus Marine Inc. Port Angeles . . 360-417-0709
Shilshole Bay Marina: Ballard 206-787-3006
Yarrow Bay Marina 425-822-6066
Yachtfish Marine 206-623-3233

SCUBA SITES
Lincoln Park
Seacrest Park

SEWAGE DISPOSALS
Bell Harbor: Pier 66, Pump 206-787-3952
Boat Street Marina 206-634-2050
Carillon Point: Kirkland. Pump 425-822-1700
Elliott Bay Marina 206-285-4817
Fairview Marinas . . . 206-786-1753 Harbor Island Marina
  206-787-3006
Harbour Village Marina: Kenmore. Pump 425-485-7557
Morrison's North Star: Pump 206-284-6600
Parkshore: Rainier Beach. Pump 206-725-3330
Pumpout Guy: Mobile Pumpout . . . 206-437-6764
Salmon Bay Marina. Pump 206-787-3395
Shilshole Bay Fuel Dock: Pump, Dump . . 206-783-7555
Yarrow Bay Marine: Pump 425-822-6066

TAXI
Eastside 425-453-0919
Farwest 206-622-1717
STITA 206-246-9999
Yellow Cab 206-622-6500

TRAILER REPAIR (MOBILE)
Trailer Techs 206-889-0286

TOWING
Dunato's Towing & Salvage 206-730-7227
Fremont Tug 206-632-0151
TowBoat U.S. -
  Lake Union & Lake Washington 206-793-7375
  Seattle (Puget Sound Area) 206-300-0486

VISITOR INFORMATION
Bellevue 425-450-3777
Kirkland 425-822-7066
Seattle 1-866-732-2695

WEATHER
NOAA Recorded Message . . . 206-526-6087 VHF: WX1

"Sailgating" in Union Bay   Photo © John Terry

Visit us at boattravel.com

Chapter 4:
Hood Canal, Admiralty Inlet Northern Olympic Peninsula

Hood Canal to Strait of Juan de Fuca. Port Ludlow, Port Townsend, Port Angeles, Discovery, Sequim & Neah Bays, Marrowstone & Indian Islands.

Port Angeles - photo © Roger Hunsperger

Symbols

[ ]: Numbers between [ ] are chart numbers.
{ }: Numbers & letters between { } are waypoints.

★ Recommended destinations, facilities, and services
⚓: Park, 🚤: Boat Launch, ▲: Campgrounds, 🥾: Hiking Trails, ⊞: Picnic Area, 🚲: Biking
🤿: Scuba

★ See "Important Notices" between Chapters 7 and 8 for specific information on boating related topics such as boating safety, weather, U.S. & Canadian marine radio use, Vessel Traffic Service, security zones, Canadian & U.S. Customs, etc. Due to changing regulations, call ahead to verify latest customs information.

Chart List

NOAA Charts:
18423, 18441, 18445, 18448, 18458, 18460, 18464, 18465, 18468, 18471, 18476-77, 18484-85

Marine Atlas Vol 1 (2018): Pages 13-19

Evergreen Cruising Atlas: Pages 137, 138, 141, 142, 143, 146, 148, 150, 176, 177

Hood Canal
[18441, 18445, 18448, 18458, 18476, 18477]

★ **Hood Canal:** This picturesque fjord indents into the mainland 44 miles, curving at the Great Bend and extending another 11 miles. It ends in tide flats at Lynch Cove. Interestingly, only a few land miles separate Lynch Cove from the head of Case Inlet in South Sound, making one ponder what it would have been like had the waterways met and made the Kitsap Peninsula into a huge island. Hood Canal could be the destination for either an extended vacation or a short get-away cruise. Highlighted by a stop at the marine resort facility in Pleasant Harbor, there are also several marine state parks, Department of Natural Resources shellfish harvesting beaches, and beautiful bays to visit. To add history and variety to the cruise, visit the communities of Port Gamble, Quilcene, Seabeck, Hoodsport, Union and Bangor, home port to naval nuclear submarines.

The shores here are high and wooded and, except for the heads of bays and river mouths, the water is deep. U.S. Highway 101 rims much of the west shore. For many years Hood Canal has been a prime vacation area with summer cabins and permanent residences lining the shores. Photographers have often captured the canal's rich views of the Kitsap Peninsula to the east

Salsbury Point with the Hood Canal Floating Bridge in the background   Photo © WSDOT

Chapter 4 HOOD CANAL & NORTHERN OLYMPIC PENINSULA

The Walker-Ames House in Port Gamble Photo © Jasperdo

and the foothills of the Olympic Mountains to the west. This lush, relatively undeveloped playground is close to the metropolitan cities of Puget Sound. Hood Canal attractions include fishing, camping, beachcombing, swimming, shrimping, clam, mussel and oyster harvesting, dining, wildlife viewing, and just lazy gunkholing. For more information about the things to see and do in Hood Canal visit www.explorehoodcanal.com.

Tidal currents seldom exceed more than two knots. There can be heavy, dangerous rips north of and around Foulweather Bluff when the ebb current of Puget Sound meets the ebb from Hood Canal. Winds in various parts of the canal affect water conditions greatly. In the case of Foulweather Bluff, the rips become even more dangerous during an opposing strong north or northwesterly wind. Further into the canal, in Dabob Bay, rips can occur if a wind blowing from the north meets an opposing southwest wind within the canal. The Great Bend vicinity is also open to conflicting wind patterns. In these cases, smoother waters are found closer to shore.

The Hood Canal Bridge, a fixed pontoon bridge, crosses the canal between Termination and Salsbury Points.

Finally, nuclear submarines from Bangor transit this waterway on a frequent basis. Each submarine is escorted by a fleet of patrol craft. Boaters are required to stay well clear of transiting submarines and avoid any high speeds or maneuvers that might appear to be aggressive. Be aware of the designated restricted areas shown on NOAA chart 18476. During shrimp harvesting season (generally on Saturdays in May), be watchful of shrimp pot markers, which can foul propellers. Before harvesting shellfish, call the Red Tide Hotline at 800-562-5632. Special regulations are enforced in this area, visit http://wdfw.wa.gov/fishing for information or call 360-902-2700.

Foulweather Bluff (1): See current tables for Admiralty Inlet. Like so many other places where large amounts of water move rapidly, this vicinity can be either glassy smooth or rough and very uncomfortable, depending upon wind and tide. Off the point, the ebb current from Puget Sound meets the up to two-and-one-half knot current from Hood Canal. When a north or northwest wind blows during these ebb flows, the rips may be uncomfortable or even dangerous to small vessels. Then it is indeed Foulweather Bluff. During these wind conditions travel during flood tide or close to slack water if possible.

Twin Spits (2): Temporary anchorage in 40 to 50-foot depths, is found south of the spits. This is often a good spot to wait for a tide change or the wind to lay down outside.

★⚓ **Shine Tidelands State Park and Wolfe Property (3):** Bywater Bay lies behind Hood Head, about three miles south of the entrance to Hood Canal. Very shallow, the bay nearly dries at lowest tides, making it suitable only for beachable boats. There are miles of sandy beaches, a lagoon, and nature trails in the 130-acres of undeveloped state park property known as Wolfe Property Park. Wolfe Property Park has a Cascadia Marine Trail campsite and composting toilet. Shine Tidelands State Park, developed from a portion of Wolfe Property, sits between the spit and the bridge. Day use only, no camping, no fresh water, 5,000 feet of tideland, picnic tables, and a primitive hand-carried boat launch. Another launch ramp is found further south near the bridge site. From Bywater Bay to this launch site, tidelands are open for shellfish harvesting. Crabbing, clamming and fishing are popular. Beachcombing, kayaking, and windsurfing are other fun activities at this park.

Squamish Harbor: When heading south into the canal, this harbor is to starboard. Limited, exposed anchorage is possible on a mud bottom off the north shore and near the head of the harbor. Case Shoal is an extensive, marked, shoal on the southeast side that fills a great part of the bay and dries at a minus tide. Deeper water is along the north shore. The launch ramp at W.R. Hicks County Park is not recommended for large boats or for use during tides lower than plus five feet or so.

★⚓ **Salsbury Point County Park (4):** A day use park outside of Port Gamble, at the western end of Teekalet Bluff. There is a good beach (clamming possible at low tides), seasonal restrooms, boat launch, picnic and play areas, and seasonal dock April-Oct. 360-337-5350.

★ **Port Gamble (5):** This is a favored anchorage. Strong currents occur in the entry channel and shoals extend off both sides. The lights on the east side are on shoal and do not mark the exact boundary of the channel. Line up to the range markers for guidance through mid-channel. Beware of the covered shoal about 500 yards northeast from the north end of the lumber mill wharf. Do not tie up to the wharf as it is private. There is good anchorage inside the entrance, on the port side opposite the mill and in the southern portion. Anchor in 25 to 40 foot depths, mud bottom.

Nearby, historic Port Gamble is a restored 1850's company mill town founded by the owners of the Pope and Talbot Lumber Company. The mill closed in 1995, after 142 years of operation. A walking tour through town features many interesting structures including St. Paul's Episcopal Church and the Walker-Ames Home. The elm trees along Main Street came from Maine by way of Cape Horn in 1872.

The historic museum chronicles Port Gamble's development through exhibits of memorabilia owned by generations of mill families. There is a general store, cafe with gifts, ice cream, wine, post office, lodging, restaurant, kayak rental, and shops that sell antiques, art, books, chocolates, and coffee.

★ **Hood Canal Floating Bridge:** [18476] The Hood Canal Bridge is a 1.5-mile floating bridge that connects the Kitsap and Olympic peninsulas. Most smaller boats can pass under the trusses at either end of the bridge depending on the tides. The trusses have a vertical clearance of 31.4 feet at the west end and 50.7 feet at the east end calculated at a MHHW of 7.0. From May 22 until September 30 the bridge will not open for recreational vessels from 3pm to 6:15pm. During all other times, if the bridge must be opened for your vessel, call 360-779-3233 or on VHF CH #13 at least one hour before the intended opening.

Shoals exist around the bridge and strong currents are often present. Because of the shoals, the eastern span is the usual recommended passage. The vicinity of Sisters Rocks, south of the bridge and off the west shore, is extremely hazardous. Shown on the chart, these two rocks are dry at half tide. A large lighted beacon is on the southernmost rock, however, its neighbor is unmarked. If traveling south along the west side of the canal, turn east immediately after passing under the bridge and hug the bridge until mid-span before turning south again. If traveling north, aim for mid-span until very close to the bridge, turn west and hug the bridge until turning north to go under the span.

Concrete launching ramps, usable at all tides are located north of the western end of the bridge. Because of anchor cables extending up to 2000' outboard from the bridge, do not anchor your vessel in the vicinity of the Hood Canal Bridge.

★⚓ **Kitsap Memorial State Park (6):** This 62 acre park, three miles south of the bridge on the eastern shore of the canal, contains cabins, campsites, one mooring buoy, 1.5 miles of hiking trails, swimming beach, showers, picnic facilities, log hall and pavilion. Diving, fishing, kiteflying, volleyball & horseshoes are possible. Reserve cabins/campsites, 1-888-226-7688. General information or to reserve picnic facility, log hall, 360-779-3205.

Thorndike Bay: This bay is too open and shallow for anchorage.

Visit us at boattravel.com

HOOD CANAL & NORTHERN OLYMPIC PENINSULA   Chapter 4   Page 53

Looking out to Hood Canal from the Pleasant Harbor Marina. Photo © Pleasant Harbor Marina

Bangor (7): [18476] {47°33'00"N 122°38'30"W}. Site of the Naval Base Kitsap. Chart 18476 shows an outer restricted area marked by 5 yellow, lighted buoys. The buoys are marked from north to south (A, B, C, D and E). Buoy's "A" and "E" flash yellow every 2.5 seconds and the three in the center ("B", "C" and "D") flash yellow every 6 seconds. A restricted naval operating area extends nearly four miles, north and south of the pier. Avoid this patrolled stretch by staying on the western shore of the canal. If a submarine is in the area, boaters must give it a berth of more than 1,000 yards.

★ **Fisherman Harbor (8):** [18476] When approaching Fisherman Harbor, aim north, traveling opposite the spit. The immediate vicinity is shallow, especially directly opposite the entry. Passage into the harbor must be made near high tide because the entrance dries. There is a natural entry channel. After entering, turn hard to port and follow the spit, then turn to starboard. Depths range from 4' to 17'. The oyster beds are private. On the east entrance to the harbor is the small, close-knit settlement of Coyle. No services are available in Coyle, but a community center hosts year round "Concerts in the Woods", www.coyleconcerts.com. Toandos State Park Recreational Tidelands are outside the harbor, west of the harbor entrance and extending around Tskutsko Point at the west side of Oak Head. Adjacent tidelands are private. Ask prior to taking any shellfish in the vicinity. If permission is granted cover all holes.

★ **Dabob Bay (9):** In season, commercial shrimp pots, with floating buoys attached, are hazards in the bay. Broad Spit, on the western shore, provides some shelter from winds.

Naval operations use much of the bay. There are warning lights on Bolton Point, Whitney Point, Pulali Point, Sylopash Point, and Zelatched Point. Due to testing of torpedoes, submarines, and other underwater vehicles by the Navy, the following restrictions apply to ALL boat operators when in the Dabob Bay Range operating area: Craft should not approach within 100 yds of range vessels and maintain minimum speed within 500 yards AT ALL TIMES.

The Range Control Center at Zelatched Point can be contacted on marine channel 12 or 16, call sign, DABOB RANGE CONTROL, or land line at 360-396-4179 or 4108. RANGE CONTROL may also issue "SECURITE" calls over marine channel 16 to notify craft of ongoing operations. Additionally, small patrol craft may make contact with individual boaters to ensure safety while in the area.

When range warning lights are active, no matter which color, contact Range Control for information and guidance; FLASHING AMBER - operations are in progress but interference issues are minimal. After communicating with Range Control proceed with caution and check frequently for lights to change to flashing red.

FLASHING RED - any of the following situations may exist: TEST VEHICLE about to be launched; SUBMARINE IS SUBMERGED on range: MINIMUM NOISE tests are in progress; GENERALLY HAZARDOUS to boaters.

A DNR beach at the end of Bolton Peninsula is open to shellfish harvesting, as is another state managed beach on the east shore of Jackson Cove, below Pulali Point. These are marked by white and black posts. Anchorage can be found in Jackson Cove. Red Tide: 800-562-5632.

★ **Quilcene Bay (10):** On the west side of Quilcene Bay there is a breakwater-surrounded boat basin, launch ramp and an adjacent park with picnic facilities. The bay dries at the head and both the ramp and the entry to the harbor should be avoided at low tide. The bay is open to southerly winds.

Herb Beck Marina: {47° 48.06' N, 122° 51.92' W} Limited transient moorage, 20 amp power, water, restrooms, launch ramp, pump-out. 360-765-3131.

Walk-around: Quilcene, a pleasant mile and a quarter walk from moorage, is known for its restaurants which feature oysters and other seafoods. Throughout the summer the Linger Longer Stage (next to the Quilcene Historical Museum, 151 Columbia St), hosts shows and events. In September don't miss the *Quilcene Fair, Parade, & Classic Car Show*. Visit www.emeraldtowns.com for other things to see and do in the area. 360-765-4999.

★ **Whitney Point (11):** Site offers picnic table with fire ring, restrooms, and a launch ramp (4-wheel drive definitely recommended). A sand spit encloses a lagoon used for aquaculture. Swimming, beachcombing, and shellfish harvesting in season are possible on the Dabob Bay side of the spit. A restricted Naval operations area is off the point.

Pulali Point: A DNR beach is on the western side of Pulali Point in Jackson Cove. Shellfish harvesting is accessible only by boat. Scuba divers often explore the rocks and steep cliffs off the point. The area from Point Whitney south to Dosewallips Flats is noted for above average salmon fishing. Two miles north of Brinnon near the river flats, Seal Rock Campground, is a good place for clam and oyster harvesting. Campground Info: 360-765-2200.

★ **Dosewallips State Park (12):** Located just south of the town of Brinnon, this 1,064-acre park is accessible mostly by car. There are 5,500 feet of shoreline on Hood Canal and 5,400 feet of freshwater frontage on both sides of the Dosewallips River. Picnic and play areas, 3.5 miles of hiking trails, restrooms, showers, drinking water, tent & RV sites, cabins. Reservations, 888-226-7688. Both fresh and salt water fishing are popular. The part of the beach open for shellfish harvest is marked with orange posts. Hard shell clams, geoducks, and oysters are found. Groceries, gifts, hardware, restaurants, gas, lodging and other services are found within two miles in Brinnon. They also host fun community events like *Shrimpfest* on Memorial Day weekend featuring craft and food booths, belt sander races, exhibits, and live music.

★ **Pleasant Harbor (13):** [18476] This attractive and protected harbor on the west side of Hood Canal is 18 miles south of the bridge. When entering the harbor, stay in mid-channel (at zero tide there is 8' in the middle.) Anchorage is good to depths of 20 to 40 feet on a mud bottom. A boat launch is located on Black Point Road, first left.

2024 Northwest Boat Travel

★ **Pleasant Harbor Marina:** {47° 39.705' N, 122° 55.079' W} Open all year. Guest and permanent moorage, power, water, restaurant, espresso, store, propane, showers/restrooms, laundry, heated pool (May-September), hot tub, gas, diesel, pump-out, on site security. Galley & Pub with outdoor seating upstairs with store and office. See our advertisement on the inside back cover and on page 55. Website: www.pleasantharbormarina.com. Email: reservations@phmresort.com. Telephone: 360-796-4611 / VHF 9 & 16.

Home Port Marina: {47° 39' 52" N, 122° 54' 49 0" W} Annual lease moorage, no liveaboards. 30amp/125 volt power, water, showers, laundry, wifi, security. 360-680-3051.

★ **Pleasant Harbor Marine State Park:** Tucked in behind the sand and gravel spit to the right of the harbor entrance is a small dock. No power. Nightly moorage fees, first-come, first-served. There is a pit toilet. Pump-out and dump site provided. No camping permitted. 360-902-8844.

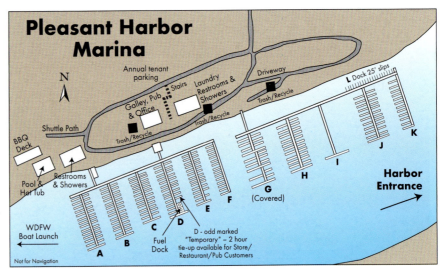

★ **Seabeck Bay (14):** Anchorage, with protection from west and south winds, is possible inside Misery Point. It is open to the north. Shoals extend from the head of the bay. An artificial reef is located off Misery Point, and an excellent launch site is located south of the Point. It is also quick to access from the Salisbury Point Boat Launch near the Hood Canal Bridge, which has a good dock for larger boats to launch. As early as 1853, Seabeck was an active timber town and busy seaport. Today it is a residential community with a general store, restaurant, post office, and excellent fishing, shrimping and crabbing grounds. A private marina is located in the Bay.

Olympic View Marina: Permanent moorage with yearly lease. No utilities or services. Continuing to expand in 2024. 206-941-5932.

★ **Scenic Beach State Park (15):** This park lies one mile southwest of the town of Seabeck. Site of the historic Emel House, originally a homestead and later a resort. To reserve house for event, 360-830-5079. The park has tables and stoves, a kitchen shelter, playground, volley ball, horseshoe pit, campsites, restrooms, showers. Activities include swimming, fishing, hiking, and scuba diving. A WDFW surfaced boat ramp is 1/2 mile east of park. There is above average salmon fishing off Misery Point, Scenic Beach, and in Stavis Bay to the south. 888-226-7688, 360-902-8844.

Hood Canal from Scenic Beach south to Hoodsport: There are several small resort facilities along the western shore of the canal. Most of the harbors are actually estuaries where the rivers empty into the canal.

★ **Triton Cove State Park:** There is anchorage with some protection from south winds. Located about midway between Brinnon and Eldon, this 29-acre day use park has a parking lot, launch ramp, 100' dock, picnic area, and restroom.

Eagle Creek: About 3 miles from Lilliwaup, there are tidelands excellent for harvesting oysters on the south side of Eagle Creek. The north side of the creek is private. A tavern is across the road from the beach.

Lilliwaup: This small town on Highway 101 sits at the mouth of Lilliwaup Creek. There is a store and motel. The bay is very shallow and there is a launching ramp. Lilliwaup State Park has no water or other facilities, but a set of stairs leads from the parking lot to the beach. Scuba diving and swimming are popular in this area. Though rocky and difficult to dig, clams and oysters are harvested here. On the eastern shore, between Tekiu Point and Anderson Cove, and opposite Ayock Point, there are good clam and oyster harvesting spots. At least six beaches have tidelands managed by the DNR. They are bordered by black and white marker posts. Caution advised regarding trespassing on adjacent private property. Directly opposite Lilliwaup is Dewatto Bay. Good clam and oyster beaches are on the north and south shores of this bay. Within walking distance of the bay is a campground managed by the Port of Dewatto.

Mike's Beach Resort: Dock (boats to 20'), mooring buoys, launch (boats to 20'), glamping, cabins, wifi, cinema, play area, small boat rentals, scuba air, shellfish farms. 9 miles north of Lilliwaup. 360-877-5324.

★ **Hoodsport (16):** Originally named Slalatlatltulhu, this is an interesting little town with friendly people. A public waterfront park and beach is located next to the Port of Hoodsport Marina. Public restrooms are located across the street. Nearby is a State Fish Hatchery where tours can be arranged, 360-877-6408. (Mid-Aug to Nov are the best months to view the salmon). Several restaurants, a coffee shop, a real estate office, a bank, post office, library with free Wifi, and gas station, as well as a variety of stores including liquor, hardware, grocery, jewelry and gift shops are available within walking distance of the dock. Should the need arise, there is also a nurse practitioner and a dentist. The Hardware Distillery offers tastings daily in the summer and tours by arrangement, 206-300-0877. The Hoodsport Trail Park, 3 miles up on SR 119 offers lovely walks on forested trails. About one mile south of town on Hwy 101 the Hoodsport Winery, open daily, offers tours (with reservations), tastings and gift shop. 360-877-9894. A boat launch, managed by the Skokomish Tribe, is located about 2 miles away in Potlatch at Saltwater Park across from Tacoma City Light's Cushman No. 2 Plant. A fee applies (free for guests of the Waterfront Resort, 360-877-9422).

Port of Hoodsport Dock: {47° 24' 26.4" N, 123° 8' 24.6" W} Day/overnight moorage, 25' & under. Six 16' slips available. Overnight moorage is $20.00 per night, 1st come/1st served, 24hour limit. Envelopes at Kiosk. No security. Restaurants, grocery store/Ace Hardware & restroom across the street, no power/water. 360-877-9350.

Sunrise Motel & Dive Resort: Lodging, RV sites, scuba air. 360-877-5301.

★ **Potlatch Marine State Park (17):** Located 3 miles south of Hoodsport, at a site where local tribes once held their potlatch ceremony, this 57 acre park has many facilities. Mooring buoys, well offshore in Annas Bay, mark the site. There are tables, stoves, restrooms, hot showers, and campsites, some with hookups. Activities include swimming, fishing, scuba diving, and windsurfing. Canoes or kayaks can be used to explore the estuary of the Skokomish River. Wildlife is plentiful in the vicinity. Park info, 360-877-5361. Reserve campsites, 888-226-7688.

★ **Union (18):** See current tables for Seattle. This tiny town located at the Great Bend of Hood Canal was once named one of America's 20 prettiest towns by *Forbes Traveler*. It is the site of the Hood Canal Marina, Alderbrook Resort, Spa & Golf Course, and a boat launch (on Hwy 106 two miles west of the resort. No fee to launch, plus 5 tide suggested). The historic 1922 Dalby Waterwheel, the region's first hydroelectric plant, is a short walk from the resort. Bring your camera for a great photo op! Other shops and services within a mile include the Cameo Boutique & Wine Shop offering weekend wine tastings, a restaurant & pub, rental cottages, a post office, credit union and café. The marina, two miles from the resort, houses an eclectic market that sells beer, wine, wholesome food, and local art. Visit the new outdoor eatery, Hook and Fork which is open on the weekends. Both the resort and marina participate in Boat U.S. and offer member discounts. The marina is also a home port for a TowBoatUS boat. 2 Margaritas Mexican restaurant is near the marina entrance and the Union Country Store (think fresh baked goods) is across the street. Union Food Mart/Skipper's, on McCreavy & Dalby just over a mile from both the marina and the resort has groceries, gas, diesel, propane, deli items, bait and fishing licenses. Hunter Farms General Store, three miles out on SR 106, has a large nursery, fresh produce, ice cream, some groceries, and hosts a Visitor Information Center. The Lucky Dog Casino is located at the junction of highways 106 and 101. Golfing, hiking and biking trails, in addition to numerous water activities make this hidden secret a perfect paradise. For additional information, www.explorehoodcanal.com.

Alderbrook Resort & Spa: {47° 20' 58 N, 123° 04 46" W} Guest moorage, 30/50amp power, water, free wifi, restrooms, showers, pump-out, seaplane dock, lodging, restaurant/bar, pool/spa, golf, kayak/SUP rentals. Resort & Spa: 360-898-2200. Moorage: 360-898-2252.

Hood Canal Marina: {47° 21' 28 N, 123° 5' 58" W} Permanent and seasonal moorage, limited guest moorage. Non-ethanol gas, diesel, water, power, pump-out, onsite market, off-site dry boat/trailer storage. Market: 360-898-3500. Marina: 360-898-2252.

Pleasant Harbor
Marina & Recreation Community

CALL NOW
360-796-4611

More Than Just A Marina...

YEAR ROUND MOORAGE

- 312 Slip Protected Marina
- 30 & 50 Amp Power
- Non-Ethanol Gas & Diesel
- Vacuum Pump Out
- Heated Pool & Hot Tub
- Permanent/Guest Moorage
- Groceries/Gift Shop

GALLEY & PUB

- Delicious Food
- Local Beers on Tap
- Local Wine Selection
- Roof Top Patio
- 3 Big Screen TVs

ACTIVITIES & ADVENTURES

For up-to-date activities and special events visit our website at pleasantharbormarina.com/marina

Play, Relax, Enjoy
www.pleasantharbormarina.com

Page 56 Chapter 4 HOOD CANAL & NORTHERN OLYMPIC PENINSULA

Tahuya: Located across from Union on the north shore, this small settlement has a post office and resort. The resort rents kayaks, paddle boats, and 4-seater Aquacycles. In the mood for do-it-yourself seafood? They also rent crab & shrimp pots. *Tahuya Day*, the first Saturday in July, features a parade, food, vendor booths, and live music.

Summertide Resort & Marina: {47° 22' 18" N, 123° 04' 16" W} Seasonal docks (May-Sept.). Annual moorage, overnight moorage on docks or buoys for resort guests. 100' of transient dock space, first come, first serve basis for $1.50/foot per night. No sleep aboards. Rental cottages, showers, groceries, beer, wine, ice, RV park, launch ramp (24' max length, launch up to a zero tide), $15.00 for round trip launch. 360-275-9313.

★ **Twanoh Marine State Park (19):** This 188 acre park boasts one of the warmest saltwater beaches in the state. Marine facilities include a pump-out, launch ramp, a dock with float at approximately {47° 22' 48" N, 122° 58' 3" W} and mooring buoys (reported minimum depth at mean low tide is 3 feet). It also has tent and RV sites, restrooms, shower, two kitchens with electricity, and picnic tables. Look for the rustic stone and rock restrooms constructed in 1936 by the Civilian Conservation Corps. Families enjoy badminton, horseshoes, swimming beach and wading pool. Hiking, fishing, waterskiing, shellfish harvesting and crabbing are possible. Park info: 360-275-2222.

Walk-around: Walk Twanoh Park's trails upland along Twanoh Creek and the rain forest-like growth of moss, thick trees, and sprawling ferns. Observe second-growth cedar, fir, and hemlock.

★ **Belfair State Park (20):** This park lies on the north shore, near the extreme end of Hood Canal. It has campsites (including a Cascadia Marine Trail Campsite), RV sites, some hookups, stoves, tables, showers and restrooms. Lynch Cove, bordering the park, is a drying mud flat. Anchorage must be well off shore. An unusual, man-made beach and gravel lined pool has been created for swimming. Trails, horseshoe pits, and volleyball fields. New cabins for rent on first come basis. Campsite reservations: 1-888-226-7688. Park Info: 360-275-0668.

Port of Allyn North Shore Dock: {47° 25' 15.02" N, 122° 54' 7.7" W} Moorage, guest dock 350', 30 amp power, water, portapotty, pump-out to 50', boat launch. Moor here to visit Belfair State Park, located two miles away on North Shore Road. 360-275-2430.

Northern Puget Sound

★ **Kingston:** See Chapter 5

Admiralty Inlet
[18441, 18464, 18473, 18477]

★ **Port Ludlow (21):** Port Ludlow, a two-mile indention, is the site of the Port Ludlow Resort & Marina, as well as anchorage. Shoals extend to the north. When entering or leaving, give at least a 200-yard clearance of Ala Point. Speed restrictions of five mph are in force south of a line extending east of the marina to the east shore of Ludlow Bay. Anchorage in 4 to 8 fathoms is possible in several locations in the outer harbor. The most popular anchorage, however, is a beautiful, usually serene spot in the extreme southwest sector behind the Twin Islands. Enter between the Twin Islands and watch for the rock that is just south of the smaller island. Anchorage is excellent in 4 to 16 feet on a mud bottom. In the mid-1800's, the budding community of Port Ludlow grew up around its earliest industries, boat building and lumber milling. A sawmill, operated by Pope and Talbot helped to make it one of the first logging communities on Puget Sound. While these industries declined years ago, Port Ludlow emerged with a new focus—as a master planned community. The commercial center at the corner of Oak Bay Road and Paradise Bay Road, offers casual dining, a grocery store, gas station, post office and a gift shop. To explore the area from Poulsbo to Port Townsend, take a #7 Jefferson Transit bus that runs on Oak Bay Road near the marina (no service on Sundays). For schedules, 800-371-0497.

★ **Port Ludlow Marina:** {47° 55.30' N, 122° 41.10' W} Come and experience beautiful Port Ludlow! The Port Ludlow Marina offers 300-slips for both permanent and guest moorage and accommodates vessels up to 200'. Marina guests enjoy access to WiFi, a shuttle to the Resort's 18-Hole Championship Golf Course, showers, fresh water, shore power of 30-amp and 50-amp, a Party Barge, covered pavilion and a BBQ pit with gazebo. The convenient Marina Store has gifts, groceries, beer and wine, a full-service fuel dock, gasoline, diesel and pump-out services. The Resort also features fine, waterfront dining at the Fireside Restaurant and guest accommodations at the beautifully appointed Port Ludlow Inn. Yacht Clubs and Rendezvous are welcome. See our advertisement on this page. Marina reservations at 360-437-0513 or 877-344-6725. www.portludlowresort.com. VHF 68.

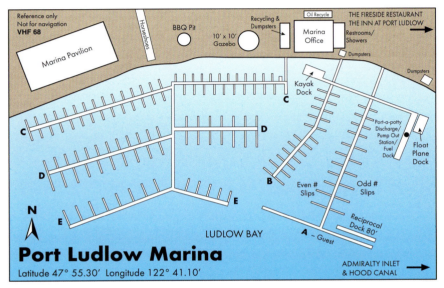

Visit us at boattravel.com

HOOD CANAL & NORTHERN OLYMPIC PENINSULA Chapter 4 Page 57

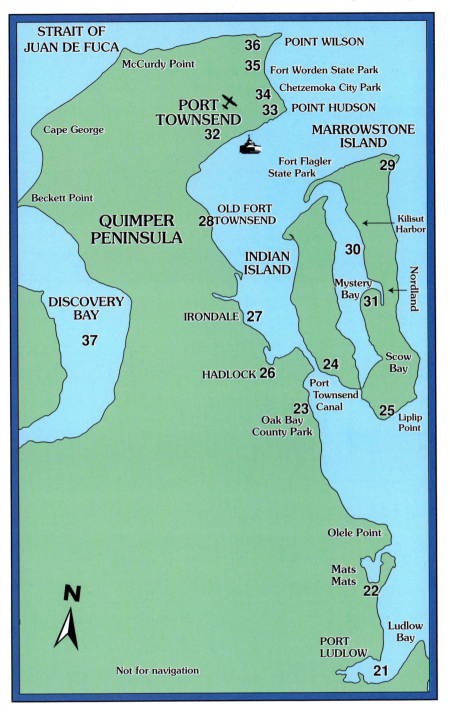

★ **Mats Mats (22):** [18441, 18473] Beware of Snake Rock, Colvos Rocks, and Klas Rock when traveling the 2.5 miles north from Port Ludlow to Mats Mats. Klas Rock is marked-approximate position {47-57-44.8N 122-39-19.2W} with a white flashing light. Mats Mats is a very tiny, well-sheltered bay entered through a tricky 100-yard-wide, well marked, dredged channel from Admiralty Inlet. A day and night range marks center channel. Minimum depths are five feet in the channel. A red nun Coast Guard buoy "8" marks the sandbar on the western shore at the northern entrance to the bay. Depths in the bay range from 3 to 13 feet with the best anchorage in the center. A launch ramp with a floating pier is best used at higher tides. Colvos Rock, Klas Rock and the Mats Mats Quarry are popular dive sites.

★⚓ **Oak Bay County Park (23):** Anchorage is possible in Oak Bay or smaller boats can be beached on the sand and gravel beach. Site of a rock jetty. Campsites, water, picnic tables, toilets, playground, swimming, and fishing. 360-385-9129.

★ **Port Townsend Canal (24):** [18441, 18473] This canal connects Port Townsend with Oak Bay to the south. Separating Quimper Peninsula on the mainland from Indian and Marrowstone Islands, it is a short-cut for boaters and is particularly helpful when seas in Admiralty Inlet are rough and uninviting. The dredged canal is marked by a light at the north entrance, and a light and a day beacon at the south entrance. The passage is about 75 feet wide with a controlling depth of 13 feet. Currents run to three knots, and are strongest on the south end at ebb tide. A fixed bridge with a vertical clearance of about 58 feet crosses the canal. The shoreline surrounding both north and south entrances to the canal offers excellent clam and crab harvesting. Much of this land is county park and open to the public.

★⚓ **Indian Island County Park (25):** Small boats can be beached at this park located across the Port Townsend Canal from Oak Bay County Park. Good clamming, crabbing, scuba diving, picnic shelter with grill, toilets, trails.

★ **Port Hadlock (26):** In 1870, Samuel Hadlock established a sawmill on South Port Townsend Bay. Over the years other industries followed, such as boat building, a clam cannery, and a wood pulp alcohol plant. A hotel & restaurant called the Old Alcohol Plant and Spirits Bar & Grill are located in the old plant. The Port Hadlock Marina, privately owned and operated, is immediately adjacent to the Old Alcohol Plant. It is about a mile from the Port Hadlock commercial district with a large grocery store, hardware store and other shops. The minimum depth at mean low tide at the marina has been reported to be 15'. A voluntary No Anchor Zone, extending from the northeastern point of Skunk Island to the public launch ramp in lower Port Hadlock, is indicated by four marker buoys. Area mooring buoys are private. The Northwest School of Wooden Boat Building campus is just to the north. Just south of the commercial district there is a sandy beach and a launch ramp best suited to small boats. The beach on the spit is private property, no trespassing.

Port Hadlock Marina: {48° 01' 487" N, 122° 44' 69" W} Permanent moorage (to 70'), 30/50 amp power, restrooms, showers, laundry, pump-out, wifi, security, volleyball, fire pit, picnic tables, bbq's. 360-385-6368.

★ **Irondale (27):** There is an underwater recreation area at a wreck off Irondale. Bottle collecting, spear fishing, and shellfish gathering are popular. At the turn-of-the 20th-century, Homer H. Swaney came from Pennsylvania to create a rail and steel manufacturing center, believing the venture would be the largest in the west. By 1900, Irondale was a thriving community. Today only a small dock marks the spot where large sailing vessels once moored and the community is largely residential.

★⚓ **Fort Townsend State Park (28):** {48° 4' 35.76" N, 122° 47' 7" W} The 413-acre park lies south of Port Townsend between Glen Cove and Kala Point. Old pilings, once the fort's wharf, extend into the bay. Mooring buoys are one mile south of Glenn Cove on the west side of Port Townsend Bay. Parklands include tent campsites, picnic shelters and tables. View campsites are on top of a bluff. Camping reservations, 1-888-226-7688. There are also two restrooms, a shower, ball fields and play areas. Activities include swimming, scuba diving, fishing, and hiking on over six miles of trails. Take self-guided history or nature walking tours. Fort Townsend was built in 1856 by the US Army to protect Port Townsend. 360-385-3595.

Indian & Marrowstone Islands

[18441, 18464]

Indian Island: Because of naval installations, give Indian Island a wide berth. The only part of this island open to the public is Indian Island County Park. A man-made causeway connects Indian and Marrowstone Islands and forms the head of Kilisut Harbor. The US Navy has an ordinance handling and storage mission at Naval Magazine Indian Island. No private vessel of any size is allowed within 1,000 yards of the ammunition pier, 100 yards of the island's shore (except when transiting Portage Canal), or 100 yards from any naval vessel in Port Townsend Bay.

2024 Northwest Boat Travel

Page 58 Chapter 4 HOOD CANAL & NORTHERN OLYMPIC PENINSULA

★⚓ **Fort Flagler Marine State Park (29):** Enter Kilisut Harbor in the S-curved channel that is protected by Scow Bay Spit. Boaters will find two boat ramps, 7 mooring buoys, a seasonal mooring dock (removed 9/15-3/25), and fishing pier at the park. Nightly moorage fees. There are groceries, food concessions, fishing supplies available in season. Hot showers, tent and RV campsites, restrooms, kitchen shelter, picnic tables, interpretive displays, and museum. For guided tours and museum, 360-385-3701. The Cascadia Marine Trail has one campsite northeast of the campground. Fishing, hiking, biking, swimming, and scuba diving are popular. An old pier extends into Admiralty Inlet and is the location of an underwater park for divers. Together with the heavy batteries of Fort Worden and Fort Casey, this turn-of-the century Army post guarded the entrance to Puget Sound. Named for Brigadier General Daniel Webster Flagler, construction began in 1897. The facility closed in 1953 and in 1955, became a state park. To reserve one of the historic on-site homes or for campsite reservations, call 1-888-226-7688. Park Info, 360-385-1259.

★ **Kilisut Harbor (30):** [18423, 18464] This long, narrow bay indents four miles between Indian Island and Marrowstone Island. Depths in the entry channel average 11 feet. When following the S-curved entrance between the buoys and markers, refer to charts. Scow Bay Spit is approximately three quarters of a mile in length and is partially submerged at high water. Fort Flagler State Park is to port when entering. There is a mud bottom for anchorage.

★⚓ **Mystery Bay & Mystery Bay Marine State Park (31):** {48° 3' 27" N, 122° 41' 47.77" W} Mystery Bay is on the east side of Kilisut Harbor, about two miles from the entrance. It is protected in most winds and has anchorage in depths of 5 to 25 feet. The marine park is located on the northeastern portion of the bay. A dock/fishing pier, has a long moorage float parallel to shore with 683 feet of moorage (the pier is closed until further notice) and a boat pump-out station. There are also 7 moorage buoys. It has been reported the minimum depth at mean low tide is 4'. This day-use park has a boat launch ramp, vault toilets, 3 fire circles, and picnic tables. Activities include clamming, crabbing, swimming, and scuba diving. The Bay's name harkens back to Prohibition days when alcohol smugglers used Kilisut Harbor to hide from the Coast Guard. Overhanging trees at the north end provided the perfect cover for shallow draft boats. Coast Guard reports indicated the disappearances as "mysterious," hence the name Mystery Bay. 360-385-1259.

Walk-around: From the park head north to Flagler Rd. Turn right at Flagler Rd and it is a 3/4 mile walk to Nordland General Store. Left takes you two miles to the gate of Fort Flagler. Continue until a Y is reached. The right fork will go to the lighthouse. Go straight ahead to the park's main office and to several trails. The left fork ends at the beach.

Nordland General Store: Temporarily closed due to a fire.

Port Townsend
[18441, 18464]

U.S. Customs & Border Protection Clearance: Every boater arriving from foreign who has not otherwise already been granted clearance by CBP through ROAM and plans to continue deeper into the lower Puget Sound region must then clear by the time they reach Port Townsend.

Vessels clearing at Port Townsend can either use the ROAM app (preferred) or they can schedule an appointment for a face-to-face inspection as far in advance as practicable (suggested minimum of 8 hours) by calling the Port Angeles office at 360-457-4311. If the boater does not wish to utilize ROAM they should recognize that failure to schedule an advance apppointment may cause the boater unnecessary delays while they wait for an officer to arrive. NOTE: The advance notice is not required, but it will help facilitate a prompt CBP response time.

Port Angeles is open seven days a week from 8am-6pm. There will be an officer on call till 10pm. Boaters arriving after 10pm should call 360-460-4809.

★ **Port Townsend (32):** Port Townsend Bay is a large body of water that separates the Quimper Peninsula from Indian and Marrowstone Islands. See current tables for Admiralty Inlet.

★ **City of Port Townsend:** This city rims the waterfront on the northwest shore of Port Townsend Bay. Pleasure craft moorage is available at the Port of Port Townsend Boat Haven and at Point Hudson Resort and Marina. Enter the Port of Port Townsend Basin on the northeast side of the breakwater. In summer months, anchorage is possible in the bay, with protection from the prevailing west to southwest winds.

Victorian-era buildings dot the hillside and downtown area of this inviting National Historic Landmark District city and Gateway to the Olympic Peninsula. Overnight accommodations available in Port Townsend include historic homes that are now B & B Inns. In the historic district along Water Street, merchants have paid particular attention to detail and historical accuracy in restoring the old buildings. Union Wharf, located at Water and Taylor Streets, originally constructed in 1867, and then rebuilt in 1932 is seeing new life again. In addition to the wharf and moorage float, there are a variety of restaurants, shops, art galleries, antiques, clothing, and gift shops along the colorful waterfront. Chetzemoka Park and John Pope Marine Park, both located on the waterfront, have playgrounds, picnic and BBQ facilities. Kah Tai Lagoon Nature Park features several species of wildlife and birds, trails, picnic and play areas and restrooms. At the north end of Water Street, next to Point Hudson Marina's southern entrance, is a 290' private dock that often hosts tall ships like Lady Washington and Hawaiian Chieftan as well as local historical schooners like the Adventuress. The dock is part of the two-acre Northwest Maritime Center. 360-385-3628. The NWMC campus is home to the Wooden Boat Foundation, the Wooden Boat Chandlery, Velocity coffee shop, and the H.W. McCurdy Library, all within walking distance from Point Hudson Marina. Waterfront meeting rooms are also available to rent for events. The second week in September NWMC hosts the annual *Wooden Boat Festival*. A block away, the historic City Hall - home of the Jefferson Museum of Art & History features nautical, Native American, Pioneer, and Victorian artifacts as well as a creepy jail gallery in the basement. A plaza across the street has playground equipment and a beautiful bronze sculpture called the Salish Sea Circle. Points-of-interest include the Victorian houses in the Uptown District, Rothschild House and Rose Garden, Haller Fountain, Jefferson County Courthouse, Customs House/US Post Office and Bell Tower. Popular events include the *Rhododendron Festival, Old Fashioned Fourth of July Celebration, Fiddler Tunes Fest, Writers Conference, Mariner's Regatta, Jazz Port Townsend, Salmon Derby, Bike Tour, Wooden Boat Festival, Port Townsend Film Festival,* and *Kinetic Sculpture Race.* For additional events and visitor information, www.enjoypt.com.

First sighted by explorer Captain Vancouver in 1792, Port Townsend was named for the Marquis de Townshend. The city was founded in 1851, six months before Seattle. During the next several decades it developed into one of the leading northwestern seaports at that time. Now it is one of only three Victoria Seaports in the U.S. With the discovery of copper and iron nearby and the development of lumbering and trade, the harbor of Port Townsend became host to many foreign ships.

Visit us at boattravel.com

Boat Haven Marina

A Boatyard. A Shipyard. Three Marinas. Four Haulouts. World's Best Marine Trades. Northwest's Coolest Town.

- **Boat Haven Marina:** With four Travelifts for vessels up to 330 tons, 450 skilled trades nearby and acres of upland work space, this is the working marina. Hundreds of locals and transient slips make it the center of the boating community. Chandlery, fuel, laundy, showers, power, water.

- **Pt. Hudson Marina:** The white-washed buildings of an old Coast Guard station surround this marina with its newly built breakwater. A visitor favorite, it's home of the Wooden Boat Festival and steps from downtown. Laundry, showers, power, water. Also an RV park. Reserve moorage or RV at www.Portofpt.com. 'Point Hudson.'

- **Quilcene Marina:** This intimate marina is on the often warm waters of Quilcene Bay and is perfect for Hood Canal explorations.

Point Hudson Marina

Port of Port Townsend

Boatyard: 360-385-6211   boatyard@portofpt.com

Boat Haven: 360-385-2355   boathaven@portofpt.com

Pt. Hudson: 360-385-2828   pointhudson@portofpt.com

Serving all of Jefferson County
www.PortofPT.com

Quilcene Marina

Chapter 4 HOOD CANAL & NORTHERN OLYMPIC PENINSULA

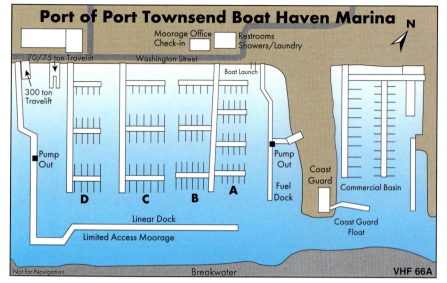

By the 1880's this city was larger than Seattle. Life amid the wealthy merchants and seamen fashioned a style of architecture still present in the city today. With a current population of approximately 9,500, the city's economy is centered around paper making, tourism, seafood packing, lumbering, fishing, and marine-oriented businesses such as boat repair and boat building.

Jefferson Transit offers excellent bus service within the city and through connecting routes to other communities. By bus it is possible to explore Fort Worden and Old Fort Townsend State Parks, Port Hadlock, Port Ludlow, Sequim, and Port Angeles. Port Townsend also has an airport, about a 15-minute drive from downtown.

Walk-around: Charming Port Townsend intrigues visitors and lures them into sightseeing and touring. Be sure to visit Rothschild House Museum at the corner of Franklin and Taylor Streets. Built in 1868, it exemplifies the decor and architecture of the period, and includes original furnishings, carpets, and wallpaper. The residence and its ghosts are on the National Register of Historic Places. Also on Taylor Street, the restored 1907 Rose Theatre now shows contemporary movies.

★ **Port of Port Townsend Boat Haven:** {48° 07'N, 122° 54' W} Permanent and guest moorage is available at this large marina protected by breakwaters. Operated by the Port of Port Townsend, its upland zone is home to a wide variety of marine trades employing 450 who work on all types of boats and boat systems. Although the Port is best-known for work on wooden vessels, companies also specialize in metal and fiberglass boats, along with all systems - mechanical, electric, plumbing, etc. The Port's Boat Yard also welcomes DIY projects. Moorage includes water, restrooms & showers, laundry, 20 & 30 amp power. Two fixed pumpout stations are now joined by a pumpout boat that visits moored vessels. There are four hoists to lift vessels up to 330 tons. There are two wash downs and room for 200 boats ashore. The Harbormaster monitors VHF 66A. An adjacent fuel dock offers gas, diesel and fishing supplies. There are dual boat launch ramps. The Boat Haven is home to a chandlery, restaurants, coffee shops, brewery, with a large grocery store, hardware store and retail boating store nearby. Downtown Port Townsend is a walkable half-mile east. To the west is a seaside walkway and bike trail. See our advertisement on page 59. Mailing address: P.O. Box 1180, Port Townsend, Washington 98368. Website: www.portofpt.com. E-mail: boathaven@portofpt.com. Telephone: 360-385-6211.

Port Townsend Fuel Dock ("Fishin' Hole"): On entering the Boat Haven breakwater, starboard side just past the spit occupied by the U.S. Coast Guard. Gas, diesel, motor oil, pump-out, tackle, fishing licenses, bait, ice. 360-385-7031. VHF 66A.

★ **Union Wharf:** Located at the foot of Taylor, the main cross street in Port Townsend, this restored wharf is the pride of downtown. Its 7,000 square feet extend 200 feet into the bay. Temporary moorage (110 feet) is found on floats adjacent to the wharf. Floats are removed for the winter. To reserve dock for moorage, 360-385-2828. Built in 1867, the old wharf was once the home for steamships and cargo laden vessels. Left in disrepair for many years, it closed in 1981 after a semi truck loaded with dogfish fell through the decayed planking. Today, visitors stroll the pier and gather at the end in the covered, open-sided pavilion to view the city and Port Townsend Bay. Scuba divers will find a short sandy cobblestone beach between Union Wharf and the abandoned ferry pier.

★ **Point Hudson Marina & RV Park:** This intimate harbor is a favorite of Northwest boaters, and each September hosts the Wooden Boat Festival. It will be closed to replace the breakwater until March 2024. The Harbormaster's office is starboard as you enter and monitors VHF 9. It features three restaurants, laundry, restrooms, showers, a pumpout station, power & water. A prime tenant is Sea Marine with its haulout and several marine services. There are also artisan boatbuilders. Point Hudson is adjacent to Northwest Maritime Center and is an easy walk to downtown Port Townsend with its shops, theaters and restaurants. Point Hudson marks the beginning of a beach walk north to Chetzemoka Park and further to Fort Worden State Park and Point Wilson. For boats, 45 slips are open to transients up to 70' LOA, plus linear dock for larger vessels. See the Port of Port Townsend ad on page 59. Address: 103 Hudson St., Port Townsend, Washington 98368. Moorage and RV customers at Point Hudson can make their own reservations through the Port's website: www.portofpt.com. Email: pointhudson@portofpt.com. Telephone: 360-385-2828.

Sea Marine: {48° 111" N, 122° 75.3" W} Full service boatyard, 30 ton haul-outs to 50' long and 15' wide, repairs, indoor paint shop, bottom paint, canvas shop, outboard service, dry storage, brokerage, propane, free WiFi. 360-385-4000.

★ **Chetzemoka City Park (34):** Named for a Klallam chief who befriended early white settlers, this park provides spectacular views of Admiralty Inlet across to Whidbey Island. A popular setting for weddings and family gatherings, the park offers picnic tables, a kitchen shelter, restrooms, water, a playground, rose garden, and bandstand/gazebo. Shakespeare in the Park takes place here in August.

★ **Fort Worden State Park (35):** A 400-foot long, L-shaped pier extends from shore and offers some protection. A moorage float with 120 lineal feet of moorage is attached to the pier. Floats are removed in November and replaced in April. Six mooring buoys are available. The boat launch is closed indefinitely for safety reasons. Temporary anchorage is possible in the buoy area, however winds can pick up and the bottom does not hold well. This 432 acre park is the gem of the park system, attracting over a million visitors each year. There are overnight accommodations, picnic tables and fire boxes, restrooms, tennis courts, athletic fields, RV sites, hot showers, laundromat, heritage sites, Coast Artillery Museum, marine interpretive displays, and learning center. On-site snack bar, grocery, bike, kayak and sports equipment rentals are available seasonally. Swimming, fishing, and scuba diving are popular activities. Fort Worden has landscaped grounds, old barracks, and renovated officer's quarters available for vacation housing. This site is headquarters for the Centrum Foundation. Each summer there is a series of workshops and symposiums featuring famous musicians, dancers, and writers. The Marine Science Center, located on the Fort Worden Pier, offers a Natural History Exhibit that includes a fully articulated Orca skeleton.

Fort Worden was one of the three primary forts built in the early 1900's to guard against

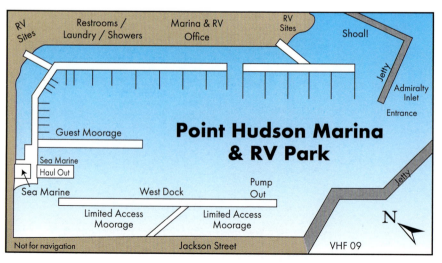

Visit us at boattravel.com

enemy infiltration into Puget Sound. The armaments are a study in naval strategy of the time. During World War II the fort was the headquarters of the Harbor Defense of Puget Sound. Underwater sonar, sensing devices, and radar were used at the site. To reserve dorms/homes/accommodations: 360-344-4400. Camping/Beach Shelters: 1-888-226-7688, Ranger Office: 360-344-4412.

Point Wilson (36): See current tables for Admiralty Inlet. A wind-swept lighthouse is a landmark to boaters traversing the Strait of Juan de Fuca and Admiralty Inlet. It is at this point that the Strait turns and aims southeasterly to become Admiralty Inlet, leading into Puget Sound. There are strong tide rips off the point. When ocean swells and adverse wind conditions exist, seas are uncomfortable and can be hazardous. When the wind is coming from the west and there is an ebb current, tide rips are especially heavy north of the shoals marked by the buoy northwest of Point Wilson light. Avoid this rip by crossing the area near slack water, or by staying close to Whidbey Island until the Point is passed. Some captains suggest passing close to Point Wilson itself, with careful attention to the depth sounder and to charted rocks off the Point. The Point Wilson Lighthouse, commissioned in 1879, has an intriguing history of sightings of a woman's ghost searching for her daughter who was lost when a steamship sank in Puget Sound. Since the 1970's, the lighthouse has been automated and closed to the public.

Northern Olympic Peninsula

[18460, 18465, 18468, 18471, 18484, 18485]

★ **Discovery Bay (37):** Captain Vancouver found this anchorage when re-fitting his ships during his 1792 expedition. Today it remains relatively undiscovered. Unlike its neighbor Sequim Bay which hosts a large marina, many private waterfront homes and a state park, Discovery Bay, with its steep, tree-covered hillsides, has only a few homes and a timeshare development with a private dock. Protection Island, near the bay's entrance cuts off the prevailing west wind and can offer calm waters when winds in the Strait of Juan de Fuca kick up. The island, a National Wildlife Refuge, is closed to the public. A 200-yard offshore buffer is enforced to protect nesting seabirds and harbor seals. Private boat tours around the island are available from nearby marinas. Anchorage can be found in several places in Discovery Bay, but avoid shoaling areas as well as the extreme head where remnants of a sawmill are found. Launching takes place at Gardiner, on the west shore. Within walking distance on Old Gardiner Road you might catch a glimpse of turreted buildings, trolls, or ogres at Troll Haven, a 200 acre private estate with unique rental properties and event venues.

★ **Sequim Bay (38):** With its overlapping spits, which leave only a zig-zag entrance into the bay from the Strait of Juan de Fuca, this is a quiet refuge. The narrow entry passage is between the buoy off Gibson Spit to starboard and Travis Spit to port. The well-marked channel curves around Kiapot Point. Depths average nine feet, but shoals extend from both shores. Keep the "N" buoys to starboard and the "C" buoys to port. Formed in the shape of a vial, the bay is four miles in length. Once inside, good anchorage on a mud bottom can be found in about 35-50 feet of water. An 1800' breakwater along the access channel protects the boat moorage at John Wayne Marina, just three miles from the community of Sequim. In addition to the marina and state park, a boat ramp (18 ft. or less) is also found at Port Williams (Marlyn Nelson County Park.)

★ **Sequim:** Sequim is located about three miles from Sequim Bay. Pronounced S'kwim, the name roughly translates "the place to go to hunt" in the language of the S'Klallam tribe. This friendly town is the northern gateway to the Olympic National Forest and features restaurants, groceries, unique shops, art galleries and tourist attractions. For prehistoric history, visit the Museum and Arts Center on North Sequim Avenue where a locally found specimen suggests that man hunted the mastodon in North America 12,000-14,000 years ago. Land surrounding Sequim has so many irrigation ditches and lines (more than 300 miles) to water the valley's farmlands, that an *Irrigation Festival* is held the first two full weekends in May. It is the oldest continuous festival in the state and includes the biggest parade on the Olympic Peninsula. Also known as the "Lavender Capital of North America," Sequim hosts the annual *Sequim Lavender Weekend* the largest lavender event in North America the third weekend in July. Just west of Sequim on the Dungeness River is Railroad Bridge Park with hiking trails, picnic areas, and a restored railroad trestle that is part of the Olympic Discovery Trail. The Dungeness River Nature Center, offering exhibits, programs and events is located at the park. Still looking for something to do? Go horseback riding or drop a hook in the river to try your luck. The Olympic Game Farm, home to many endangered species and animal veterans of the silver screen, provides opportunities to get face to face with the animals. Other nearby attractions include an award winning winery, the Seven Cedars Casino/Hotel & Golf Course, and the Dungeness Hatchery (open daily, for hours call 360-683-4255). For more information about Sequim stop by the Visitor Center at 1192 E Washington St. (open Mon-Sat), 1-800-737-8462, www.visitsunnysequim.com.

Ride-around: Visit Sequim. Transportation from John Wayne Marina or Sequim Bay State Park is available by taxi, rental car, or bus. On weekdays, Bus Route 52 has service three times daily. Bus service on Saturday is available with 24hr advance notice through Clallam Transit dial-a-ride, 360-452-4511. No bus service on Sunday.

John Wayne Marina: {48° 03.95' N, 123° 02.31' W} Permanent and guest moorage, power, water gas, diesel, oils, restrooms, pump-out, waste dump, showers, laundry, free WiFi, and restaurant. 360-417-3440.

Schooners such as this Thomas Gillmer Blue Moon can be found at the 2024 Port Townsend Wooden Boat Festival occuring September 8-10. Photo © Catherine MacMillan

★ **Sequim Bay Marine State Park:** {48° 2' 26.98" N, 123° 1' 30.01" W} [18471] Encompassing 92 acres, this park is located north of Schoolhouse Point. Tables, stoves, reservable kitchens (888-226-7688), restrooms, showers, campsites, RV sites, trailer dump, one lane launching ramp with side float (available year round), and mooring buoys (in deeper water) are available. The moorage dock is permanently closed due to safety concerns related to age and structural deterioration. Fishing from the pier, tennis, swimming, hiking, ball games, and scuba diving are possible. An interpretive kiosk details information about shellfish harvesting. Park info: 360-683-4235.

★ **Dungeness Bay (39):** [18465] Dungeness Spit, Graveyard Spit, and portions of Dungeness Bay and Harbor are part of the Dungeness National Wildlife Refuge. The Refuge (boundary is marked by pilings in Dungeness Bay) is open to boaters from May 15 to Sept. 30. Refuge waters are a no wake zone and in order to reduce wildlife disturbance boaters are required to stay 100 yards from shore. Boaters may land only at the designated landing spot located due south of the picuresque lighthouse on the bay side of the spit, marked by 2 yellow posts from 9am to 5pm and must have a reservation (call the Refuge Office, 360-457-8451). Public boat ramps are found at Cline Spit County Park (17' and under) and Dungeness Boat Ramp at Oyster House Road (small craft only). Dungeness Spit, five miles in length, is one of the longest natural spits in the world. While the spit is long, it is narrow, measur-

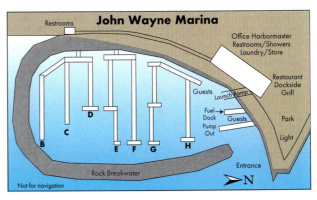

Chapter 4 HOOD CANAL & NORTHERN OLYMPIC PENINSULA

Port Angeles sunrise Photo © Dee

Port Angeles
[18465, 18468]

U.S. Customs & Border Protection Designated Port-of-Entry: Port Angeles is open seven days a week from 8am-6pm. There will be an officer on call till 10pm. For in-person inspection by CBP officer call 360-457-4311. Call ahead for latest customs information. For emergencies or after hours, 360-460-4809.

★ **Port Angeles (40):** Port Angeles is the last major fueling and supply station for those heading for the west coast, across the ocean, or around Vancouver Island. It is also the site of the Black Ball Ferry to Victoria, Canada. Fairchild International Airport, just 3 miles west of town, accommodates small commercial jets, charters, and private aircraft. With the Olympic Mountains looming over Port Angeles in the background, the city's harbor is protected from wind and sea by Ediz Hook, a narrow, three-mile-long natural sand spit that nearly encircles Port Angeles Bay. The U.S. Coast Guard maintains their sector headquarters and air station at the end of Ediz Hook. Much of the harbor is used for light marine industry, major export shipping, and recreation. Moorage is available at the Port Angeles Boat Haven, located behind a breakwater in the southwest portion of the harbor. Anchorage is prohibited in the eastern end and off the north side of Ediz Hook. This city is the commercial center for the Olympic Peninsula, and the gateway headquarters for the Olympic National Park. Restaurants, stores, lodging, and numerous services are found in town. After shopping, take a break near the city fountain downtown and view the murals at nearby 1st and Laurel Streets. Up one block, on 2nd Street, James Park features scenic views of the Strait. Visit the Recreation Corridor off Race Street and enjoy watching the Lefties, a summer collegiate team which is part of the West Coast Baseball League at Civic Field. Right across the street is Erickson Playfield which is home to an amazing playground called the Dream Playground, a world class skate park, newly buildt Pump Track, a Calisthenics Park and Tennis Courts. Walk, bike, or jog the Olympic Discovery Trail (ODT) as it follows the harbor shoreline, providing access to businesses, beaches, and points of interest. The ODT is a planned 130-mile multi-use trail that, once completed, will span from the town of La Push on the west coast, through Port Angeles, to Port Townsend on the east. So far, nearly 75 miles of the ODT have been completed. For further exploration, tour vans and Clallam Transit buses provide access to the entire peninsula from the downtown transit center. Every summer, the City Pier is the site of free, outdoor, live music and performances. These "Concerts on the Pier" occur each Wednesday from 6pm-8pm. The City Pier is also the site of the annual event, the *Dungeness Crab & Seafood Festival*, one of Western Washington's only seafood festivals, held in early October. Another popular event, *The Juan de Fuca Festival*, is held Memorial Day weekend and showcases international dance, music and theater and also features a street fair. The Port Angeles Fine Arts Center features art exhibits and a 5-acre, outdoor, art park that is free to the public. The Waterfront Promenade west of the town's center is an attractive commercial/industrial buffer, including an environmental showcase and interpretive center, with a flag pavilion, historical markers and information. For additional info, contact the Port Angeles Visitor Center: 360-452-2363, or www.portangeles.org.

ing only 50 feet wide at points during high tides and sometimes breaches occur. A shoal, marked by a buoy, extends northeast from the spit. The twisted spit forms a bay and an inner lagoon suitable for shallow draft anchorage. The best anchorage is in five to nine fathoms about one mile southwest of the tip. Avoid the marked cable area. The bay is sheltered from west winds, but exposed to east and north winds. The shallow lagoon at the head may be entered by very small boats.

Walk-around: It is a 5 mile walk from the parking lot to the Lighthouse where volunteers give free tours of the tower 9am to 5pm daily. Built in 1857, the New Dungeness Lighthouse was the first lighthouse north of the Columbia River and has operated continuously ever since. The light station has restrooms, picnic tables and an artesian well for drinking water. Donations to the Lighthouse gratefully accepted.

Dungeness Recreation Area: This Clallam County park is on a bluff with panoramic views. There is no direct water access, but the spit and adjacent tidelands may be explored by entering through the Federal Wildlife Refuge trail. A daily fee of $3 is charged (group of 4 adults, kids under 16 free). Picnic facilities, RV pump-out, trails, playground, restrooms, and fresh water are available. 360-683-5847

Visit us at boattravel.com

★ **Platypus Marine, Inc.:** Platypus Marine is one of the Pacific Northwest's largest indoor/outdoor, full-service shipyards specializing in marine refit, repair and new construction. With our long standing, proven record of excellence, we provide services to government, commercial, fishing and private vessels. Conveniently located off the Strait of Juan de Fuca, our ten-acre facility in Port Angeles, Washington offers 25-foot deep-water, heavy lift haul-out capability. With over 70,000 square feet of enclosed space, our facility is comprised of multiple buildings that include dedicated spaces for our paint shop, metal fabrication shop, fiberglass shop, mechanic shop, carpentry shop, and electrical shop. Platypus Marine's professional, multi-talented tradespeople excel in working with all types of vessels. In addition to our own tradespeople, Platypus Marine utilizes approved contractors that are skilled in specialty trades. Experienced with fiberglass, steel, aluminum and wood, Platypus Marine provides skilled service and repair of propulsion, mechanical, electrical and auxiliary systems. Our experienced and dedicated management team maintains project timelines while ensuring quality and controlling project costs. See our advertisement on pages 46 and 62. Website: www.platypusmarine.com. Address: 518 Marine Dr., Port Angeles, WA 98362. Telephone: 360-417-0709. Fax: 360-417-0729.

Port Angeles Boat Haven: {48° 07.7' N, 123° 27' W} Guest moorage, gas, diesel, power, fresh water, boat hoist, launching ramp, laundry, restrooms, showers, waste pump-out, free WiFi. 360-457-4505.

★ **City Pier and Hollywood Beach:** A 50' tall viewing tower marks this waterfront park and pier. The park has beach and waterfront trail access, restrooms, and picnic tables. Seasonal floats for transient moorage are located at the end of City Pier (moorage limit is 10 consecutive days). A payment box is at the ramp entrance. Boats over 30' moor on the north side of the permanent City Pier dock. The Pier is the site of a popular, annual Summer Concert series. The Feiro Marine Life Center, another pier highlight, is open daily. For hours, 360-775-5182. The Visitor Center is within walking distance and offers maps, brochures, and walking tour information. For a bit more exercise, the Port Angeles segment of the Olympic Discovery Trail leads about 7 miles from the City Pier to the Elwha River.

Port Angeles City Pier Photo © Ramesh Lalwani

Ediz Hook (41): This 3.5 mile-long spit has two small parks with benches and beach access. A lumber mill is at the shore end with adjacent log storage. Currents can be strong in this area. The Coast Guard Air Rescue Station, a small marina, and a large, four lane launch ramp operated by the city are located on the spit. $20 fee is charged for launch ramp, 360-417-4550. The 110' cutter, *Cuttyhunk* is stationed here. The original lighthouse was established by President Lincoln in 1862. A second lighthouse, built in 1908 was deactivated in 1946. Its beacon is now at the tower of the Coast Guard Air Station. A waterfront trail leads from the spit and wraps around the waterfront connecting with the Olympic Discovery Trail.

Freshwater Bay: Located about four miles east of Crescent Bay, this broad open bight, affords anchorage in six to ten fathoms. Scuba diving is popular here.

Crescent Bay: This is a small semi-circular bight approximately one mile in diameter. The east part is shoal. Remains of a wharf on the west shore are to be avoided. This bay only provides shelter in southerly winds.

★ **Salt Creek Recreation Area County Park:** This park in Crescent Bay is accessible by beachable boat and has limited anchorage. Watch for hazards at the entrance to the bay. There are campsites, picnic shelters, water, showers, playgrounds, an RV pump-out and hiking trails. Explore remnants of WWII-era Camp Hayden. Tongue Point, the site of a marine life sanctuary, is one of Washington's most beautiful scuba dive sites. Park info: 360-928-3441.

Pillar Point: Good anchorage can be found with shelter from westerlies. However, it is open to east and northeast winds. A county park onshore has vault toilets and concrete launch ramp for small boats.

★ **Clallam Bay (42):** [18460] Clallam Bay is located about 15 miles southeast of Neah Bay. Clallam Bay is a broad bay about two miles long and one mile wide. Give Slip Point a wide berth of at least one quarter mile to avoid the reef west of it. The reef is marked by a bell buoy. There is often good fishing for salmon and halibut in this area. There is anchorage east of Van Riper's Rocks and off the rocky point, near the middle of the semi-circular beach on the southern shore of the bay. Anchorage is in 20-40 feet of water over a sand bottom and is protected from all but east winds. In addition to fishing, there are great opportunities for hiking and birdwatching. Clallam Bay Spit Park near the mouth of the Clallam River is a good place to do both. The park also has a picnic area and restroom. The small towns of Clallam Bay and Sekiu are on the shore of Clallam Bay. Clallam Bay has a Visitor Center and library with free wifi, a marine supply and repair shop, medical clinic, laundromat, post office, grocery, gift and liquor stores, restaurants and lodging. For more information, www.clallambay.com.

Ediz Hook with the Olympic Mountains in the backdrop Photo © Port Angeles Regional Chamber of Commerce

★ **Sekiu (43):** This interesting town wakes up early during the fishing season. Restaurants, hardware, groceries, and lodging can be found. The waterfront resorts cater to boats less than 22 feet, whose owners have fishing in mind. Moorage may be available for larger craft. Most facilities operate April-October on a first-come-first-serve basis. The Sekiu-Neah Bay area has become a destination for scuba divers, as well.

Cains Auto & Marine Service: Inboard/outboard repairs, parts and accessories, trailers, fishing tackle. 360-963-2894.

Mason's Olson Resort: {48° 15' 51.53" N, 124° 17' 58" W} Moorage to 30', gas & diesel (at fuel dock and gas station), propane, water, showers, laundry, groceries, fishing tackle, launch, lodging, RV & camping sites. 360-963-2311.

Straitside Resort: {48° 15' 4.4" N, 124° 18' W} Moorage available in summer. Lodging, pets allowed with pet fee. 360-963-2173.

Van Riper's Resort: {48° 15' 47"N, 124° 54' W} Moorage, no power, fish cleaning station, boat ramp, groceries, ice, bait, tackle, fishing licenses, boat rentals, lodging, RV/camping sites. 360-963-2334.

★ **Hoko River State Park:** This undeveloped park, located three miles west of Sekiu, contains 3,000 feet of shoreline on the Strait of Juan de Fuca and over 18,000 feet of freshwater shoreline along the Hoko and Little Hoko Rivers. An archaeological site at the mouth of the Hoko River has remains from a 2500 year old Makah Native village.

Snow Creek Resort: {N.48.35.33, W. 124.54.650} This resort is closed. It may be possible to hand-launch smaller, hand-carried boats from shore. Day use only. Vehicle Use Permit or Discover Pass required for parking.

★ **Neah Bay (44):** [18484, 18485] {48° 23' N, 124° 36' W} Located about five miles east of Cape Flattery, Neah Bay has good but limited anchorage, a moorage facility and fuel dock. Enter between Waadah Island and Baadah Point. Favor the south side. The community has a resort with moorage, a general store, a museum, restaurant, espresso stand, and wood fire bakery that serves pizza and has a small hotel above it. Other local lodging options include Hobuck Beach Resort, Cape Resort and campgrounds. Many resorts in this area, known for its great sportfishing, operate April to October. This is the Makah Indian Reservation, home of the Makah Indian Tribe. The Makahs have used sea-going dugout canoes for whale hunting for thousands of years. At the museum, there are preserved fish hooks, seal clubs, harpoons, nets, paddles, boxes, and baskets that were unearthed at the Ozette Archaeological site where they had been covered by a mud slide, perhaps 500 years ago. Replicas depict whaling canoes and salmon drying on overhead racks in the longhouse. A typical Makah conversation is replicated. The museum is open daily, 10am-5pm. 360-645-2711. Each August, *Makah Days* is celebrated with traditional dancing, singing, and canoe races.

★ **Makah Marina:** {48° 22' 5.34" N, 124° 36' 41.76 "W} The final marina before leaving the straits. We offer permanent and overnight moorage for all vessels. For 100' and up vessels, please call ahead as space is limited to accommodate vessels of that size. We offer 30 amp/120 V on docks C-E and 50 amp/125-250 V on docks A & B. Open access to WiFi, shower facilities, on site diver and night watchmen, water and pump-out, fuel (diesel, gas, motor oil) is provided through Makah Mini Mart (360-645-2802). A welcoming community, Washburn's General Store has most of your needs, whether it be food, toiletries, or hardware. Native Grounds Espresso located in Linda's Wood Fire Bakery has your espresso fix and breakfast needs while Linda's covers your lunch and dinner. Warmhouse Restaurant is also another hotspot for meals. Have some extra time on your hands visit the Makah Museum open daily 10am-5pm. The peak season is April-October, with recreational fishing open, we try to accommodate all. See our advertisement on this page. Mailing address: PO Box 137, Neah Bay, WA 98357. Telephone: 360-645-3015. Website: www.makah.com. VHF 16, 66.

Big Salmon Resort: Wet & dry moorage (recreational boats April-Sept.), water, 30/50 amp power, launch ramp, bait/tackle/licenses, deli, charter & rental boats. 1-866-787-1900. Fuel Dock: non-ethanol gas, oils. 360-645-2374. VHF 68.

Makah Mini Mart & Fuel: Diesel & gas (at fuel dock and gas station), motor oil, pizza, snacks, tobacco, ice. 360-645-2802.

Arriving By Sea to La Push: Consult the latest Coast Pilot 7, as well as the most up to date chart prior to transiting the Quillayute River Bar and River. For camera images, evaluations of the bar conditions and restrictions visit, www.wrh.noaa.gov/sew/marine/bars_mover.php. Mariners can contact the Quillayute River Coast Guard Station with questions on Bar Conditions on VHF 16, by phone 360-374-6469, or by AM radio channel WQEL 572.

Arriving by sea, locate the river channel near the southeast shore of James Island. At low tide, James Island is joined to the beach. When winds and waves are from the south, entry into the channel can be dangerous. If there are breakers of any size between the lighted red buoy #2 and the river entrance, contact the Quillayute River Coast Guard before attempting entry. Floodlights to illuminate the entrance channel between James Island and the jetty can be requested - call the Coast Guard Station on VHF 16 and ask them to "Energize the River Lights". The river channel is protected on the southeast side by a jetty. At high water, about 250 feet of the outer end of the jetty is awash. There is shoaling and breakers in that area that should be avoided. A rock dike protects the northwest side of the river channel. Give it wide berth as river currents can easily sweep vessels onto the rocks. During the late summer and fall, watch for fishnets in the channel.

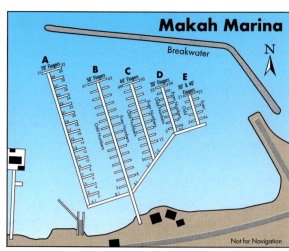

HOOD CANAL & NORTHERN OLYMPIC PENINSULA Chapter 4 Page 65

Inside the entrance, stay on the jetty side of mid-channel. A directional light and seasonal buoys in the channel lead to the small craft basin. The Coast Guard Station is the large white boathouse located at the Eastern most end of the Marina.

Before launching or exiting the marina, consult the diamond shaped "Rough Bar" advisory signs at the boat launch and mounted to the Coast Guard boathouse facing the marina. Two alternating flashing yellow lights on these signs indicate the seas are more than four feet in height and should be considered dangerous for small craft. Weather pennants are also displayed on a flagpole above the Coast Guard boathouse to notify mariners of the forecasted winds. One cone-shaped orange pennant means that a small craft warning is in effect with 25-33 knot winds expected. Two cone-shaped orange pennants means that a Gale warning is in effect with 34-47 knot winds expected. One square flag, with magenta border and black square in the center, means that a Storm warning is in effect with 48-63 knot winds expected. Two square flags means that a Hurricane warning is in effect with 64+ knot winds expected. Be aware that certain conditions including tides of +.5' or less, surf over 20', seas over 30' or winds over 50 knots may limit or prevent Coast Guard response.

★ **La Push (45):** [18480] La Push is located on the Washington Coast about 30 miles south of Cape Flattery. Please read the entry titled "Arriving By Sea to La Push" that follows for more detailed information for boaters. It is an important sportfishing center and the site of a marina at the Quileute village on the Quillayute River's east bank, about 0.4 of a mile above the entrance to the river. Nearby facilities include the Lonesome Creek Grocery, about a half a mile from the marina, with showers, laundry facilities and propane. The River's Edge Restaurant and the Oceanside Resort are also close to the marina. The Resort has lodging, camping sites, RV Park and espresso stand. Access to La Push by car with trailerable boat is by Highway 101, from Port Angeles across northern Olympic Peninsula to just north of Forks and then west on Highway 110 (the La Push turnoff) and proceed on good road 16 miles to La Push. There is a launching ramp at the marina.

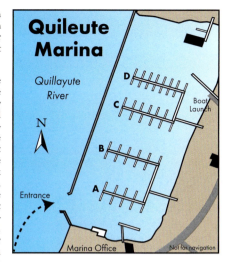

Excellent fishing and annual fishing derbies bring many anglers to this area. Visitors known as "Twilighters" have also been arriving thanks to the wildly popular Twilight books and movies that base much of the action in and around La Push and incorporate Quileute legends. Whale watching, surfing and hiking are among the other activities that bring people to this community.

The Quileute Tribe participates in Native American gatherings promoting traditions of Pacific Northwest canoe voyaging. Handmade cedar canoes from La Push have been paddled to Seattle, to Bella Bella, British Columbia, and to the Commonwealth Games in Victoria. Other traditions are celebrated during *Quileute Days* in mid-July with fireworks, field sports, music entertainment, slow pitch and horseshoe tournaments, Indian dancing, arts and crafts, and the *World Famous Fish Bake* made the Quileute way. For more information about the community and events, call the Quileute Tribal Office: 360-374-6163.

★ **Quileute Harbor Marina:** {47° 54' 39" N, 124° 38' 24"W} The marina can accommodate between 40 to 60 boats up to 50 feet in length. Amenities include 30 amp power, water, porta potty, large launch ramp, waste oil tank. Gas, diesel, hydraulic & two cycle oils are available. Address: 71 Main St., LaPush, WA 98350. Telephone: 360-374-5392. Website: www.quileutenation.org. Channel 16.

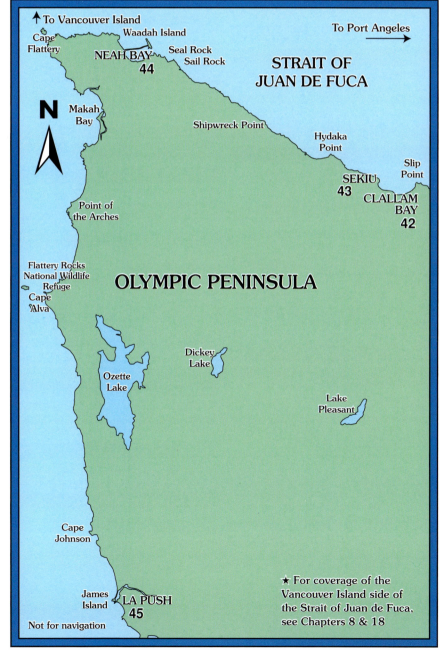

Essential Supplies & Services

AIR TRANSPORTATION
Kenmore Air 1-866-435-9524
NW Seaplanes . . . 425-277-1590, 1-800-690-0086
San Juan Airlines 1-800-874-4434
Seattle Seaplanes 1-800-637-5553

BOOKS / BOOK STORES
Evergreen Pacific Publishing 425-493-1451
The Marine Atlas 253-872-5707

BUS TRANSPORTATION
Clallam Transit: Port Angeles 360-452-4511
Jefferson Transit: Port Townsend 360-385-4777

COAST GUARD
Emergencies . . . . 911, 206-217-6001 VHF 16

– continued on next page –

Essential Supplies & Services — continued

AIR TRANSPORTATION – contd.
Sector Puget Sound (office) 206-217-6200
Vessel Traffic 206-217-6152
Neah Bay . . . . VHF 22A, 360-645-2237
Port Angeles . . . . VHF 22A, 360-417-5990
Quileute . . . . VHF 22A, 360-374-6469

CUSTOMS / BORDER PROTECTION
Due to new security regulations, call ahead for latest customs information.
Port Angeles 360-457-4311
Port Townsend Call Ahead, 8am-4pm . . 360-385-3777
24 hours Pleasure Boat Reporting 1-800-562-5943

FERRY TRANSPORTATION
Pt. Angeles-Victoria 360-457-4491, 250-386-2202
Pt. Townsend-Coupeville 1-800-843-3779

FISHING/SHELLFISHING INFO
Fishing Regulations 360-902-2500
24-Hour Red Tide Hotline 1-800-562-5632
Shellfish Rule Change Hotline 1-866-880-5431

FUELS
Big Salmon Resort 360-645-2374
Herb Beck Marina: Hood Canal 360-765-3131
Hood Canal Marina: Union 360-898-2252
John Wayne: Sequim Bay. Gas, Diesel. . 360-417-3440
Makah Mini Mart & Fuel 360-645-2802
Mason's Olson Resort: Sekiu. Gas, Diesel . 360-963-2311
Pleasant Harbor: Gas, Diesel. 360-796-4611
Port Angeles Boat Haven: Gas, Diesel.
. . . . 360-457-4505
Port Ludlow Marina . . . . . . 360-437-0513 VHF 68
Port of Port Townsend: Gas, Diesel.
. . . . 360-385-7031 VHF 66A
Quileute Marina: Gas, Diesel . . . . 360-374-5392 CH 10

GOLF COURSES
(These courses are accessible from moorage and have rental clubs)
Alderbrook: Hood Canal 360-898-2560
Discovery Bay: Port Townsend 360-385-0704
Cedars at Dungeness: Sequim 360-683-6344
Port Ludlow Resort. 1-888-793-1195
Port Townsend 360-385-4547

HAUL-OUTS
Port Angeles Boat Haven 360-457-4505
Port of Port Townsend 360-385-2355
Sea Marine: Port Townsend 360-385-4000

HOSPITALS
Hoodsport (Mason General) 360-426-1611
Port Angeles (Olympic Medical Ctr) 360-417-7000
Port Townsend (Jefferson Health) 360-385-2200

LODGING
Alderbrook Resort & Spa 360-898-2200
Curley's: Sekiu 360-963-2281
The Resort at Port Ludlow. 1-877-805-0868
Sunrise Motel & Dive Resort 360-877-5301

MARINAS / MOORAGE FLOATS
Big Salmon: Neah Bay . . . . . 1-866-787-1900 VHF 68
Fort Flagler State Park: Marrowstone Island
Fort Worden State Park: Point Wilson
Herb Beck Marina: Hood Canal 360-765-3131
Home Port Marina (Permanent) 360-680-3051
Hood Canal Marina: Union 360-898-2252
Hoodsport Marina 360-877-9350
John Wayne Marina: Sequim Bay 360-417-3440
Jefferson County Parks 360-385-9160
Makah Marina: Neah Bay . . 360-645-3015 VHF 66
Mason's Olson Resort: Sekiu 360-963-2311
Mike's Beach Resort 360-877-5324
Mystery Bay State Park: Marrowstone Isl
Northshore Dock, Port of Allyn 360-275-2430
Pleasant Harbor Marina . 360-796-4611, VHF 16, 9
Pleasant Harbor State Park: Hood Canal
Point Hudson Marina: Port Townsend
. . . . 1-800-228-2803
Port Angeles Boat Haven 360-457-4505
Port Hadlock Marina.(perm) 360-385-6368
Port Ludlow Marina . . .360-437-0513 VHF 16, 68
Port of Port Townsend . . 360-385-2355 VHF 16, 9
Quileute Marina: La Push . . . 360-374-5392 Channel 16
Sequim Bay State Park
Summertide Resort: Tahuya 360-275-9313
Van Riper's: Sekiu. Small boats 360-963-2334

PARKS
Washington State 360-902-8844
Washington Camping Reservations . . .1-888-226-7688

POISON INFO 1-800-222-1222

PROPANE
Mason's Olson Resort: Sekiu 360-963-2311
Pleasant Harbor Marina 360-796-4611
Point Hudson Marina (nearby) . . . 1-800-228-2803
Port Ludlow Marina . . . .360-437-0513 VHF 16, 68
Port of Port Townsend . . 360-385-2355 VHF 16, 9
Sea Marine: Port Townsend 360-385-4000

RV FACILITIES
Belfair State Park: Hood Canal
Dosewallips State Park: Hood Canal
Dungeness County Park: Dungeness Bay
Fort Worden State Park: Point Wilson
Mason's Olson Resort: Sekiu 360-963-2311
Point Hudson Marina & RV Park . 1-800-228-2803
Potlatch State Park: Hood Canal
Rest-a-While: Lilliwaup 360-877-9474
Salt Creek County Park: Crescent Bay
Sequim Bay State Park
Summertide Resort: Tahuya 360-275-9313
Sunrise Motel & Dive Resort 360-877-5301
Twanoh State Park: Hood Canal
Van Ripers, Sekiu 888-462-0803

RAMPS
Big Salmon: Neah Bay . . . . 360-645-2374 VHF 68
Bywater Bay: Hood Canal
Dungeness Bay: Cline Spit County Park and Dungeness Landing
Ediz Hook: Port Angeles 360-417-4550
Gardiner: Discovery Bay
Hadlock Hood Canal Bridge, West End
Herb Beck Marina: Quilcene Bay 360-765-3131
Hoodsport: Hood Canal
Lilliwaup: Hood Canal
John Wayne Marina: Sequim Bay 360-417-3440
Marrowstone Island: Fort Flagler State Park and Mystery Bay State Park
Mats Mats Bay
Mike's Beach Resort 360-877-5324
Mason's Olson Resort: Sekiu 360-963-2311
Misery Point Ramp: Seabeck Bay
Point Hudson Marina & RV Park . 1-800-228-2803
Point Whitney: Hood Canal
Port Angeles Boat Haven 360-457-4505
Port of Allyn Moorage: Hood Canal 360-275-2430
Port of Port Townsend . . 360-385-2355 VHF 16, 9
Port Williams: Marly Nelson County Park
Quileute Marina . . . . 360-374-5392 Channel 16
Salsbury Point County Park: Hood Canal
Sequim Bay State Park 360-683-4235
Summertide Resort: Tahuya 360-275-9313
Triton Cove: Hood Canal
Twanoh State Park: Hood Canal
Van Riper's: Sekiu. Small boats 360-963-2334

REPAIRS
Cains Marine Service 360-963-2894
May Mobile Marine: Hood Canal 360-552-2561
Platypus Marine Inc. Port Angeles. .360-417-0709
Port Angeles Boat Haven 360-457-4505
Port of Port Townsend . . 360-385-2355 VHF 16, 9
Sea Marine: Port Townsend 360-385-4000

SCUBA AIR
Curley's: Sekiu 360-963-2281
Mike's Beach Resort 360-877-5324
Sunrise Resort: Hood Canal 360-877-5301

SCUBA / DIVING SITES
Fort Flagler State Park: Marrowstone Island
Fort Worden State Park: Point Wilson
Lilliwaup: Hood Canal
Mystery Bay State Park: Marrowstone Island
Old Fort Townsend State Park: Irondale
Potlatch State Park: Hood Canal
Pulali Point: Hood Canal
Scenic Beach State Park: Hood Canal
Sequim Bay State Park
South Indian Island County Park

SEWAGE DISPOSALS
Fort Flagler: Marrowstone Island. Dump
Herb Beck Marina: Pump 360-765-3131
John Wayne Marina: Pump, Dump . . . 360-417-3440
Makah Marina: Pump, Dump 360-645-3015
Mystery Bay State Park: Marrowstone Island. Pump. Dump
Pleasant Harbor Marina . 360-796-4611, VHF 16, 9
Pleasant Harbor State Park: Pump, Dump
Point Hudson Marina: Pump, Dump 1-800-228-2803
Port of Allyn Near Belfair: Pump 360-275-2430
Port Angeles Boat Haven: Pump 360-457-4505
Port Hadlock Marina 360-385-6368
Port Ludlow Marina . . . . . . 360-437-0513 VHF 68
Port of Port Townsend: Pump 360-385-2355
Twanoh State Park: Hood Canal. Pump, Dump

TAXI
Port Angeles 360-406-0210
Port Townsend 360-385-1872
Sequim 360-681-4090

TOWING
Tow Boat U.S.- Hood Canal, Port Townsend,
Port Hadlock, ... 360-301-9764

VISITOR INFORMATION
Clallam Bay / Sekiu 360-963-2339
Hoodsport Visitor Information 360-877-2021
North Hood Canal 360-765-4999
Port Angeles 360-452-2363
Port Townsend 360-385-2722
Sequim Dungeness Valley 360-683-6197
Visit Kitsap Peninsula 800-337-0580

WEATHER
NOAA Recorded Message 360-357-6453
VHF WX-1, WX-4

Visit us at boattravel.com

Chapter 5:
North Puget & Possession Sounds & Saratoga Passage

Kingston, Edmonds, Everett, Clinton, Langley, Coupeville, Oak Harbor, Whidbey & Camano Islands.

Oak Harbor Marina - photo © Chris Sublet

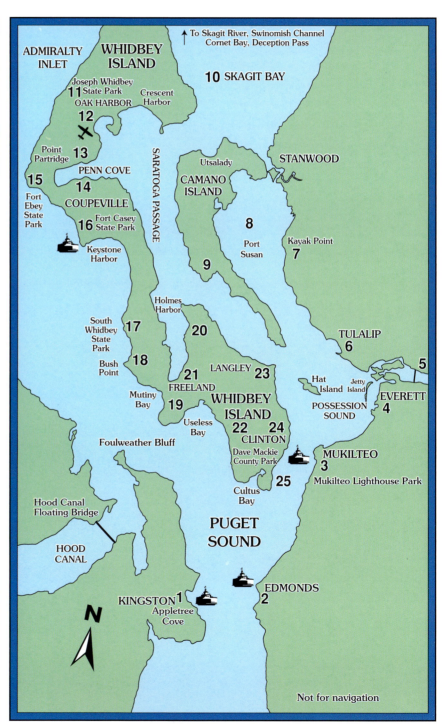

Symbols

[ ]: Numbers between [ ] are chart numbers.

{ }: Numbers & letters between { } are waypoints.

★ Recommended destinations, facilities, and services

⚓: Park, 🚤: Boat Launch, ▲: Campgrounds,

🥾: Hiking Trails, 🎋: Picnic Area, 🚲: Biking

🤿: Scuba

★ See "Important Notices" between Chapters 7 and 8 for specific information on boating related topics such as boating safety, weather, U.S. & Canadian marine radio use, Vessel Traffic Service, security zones, Canadian & U.S. Customs, etc. Due to changing regulations, call ahead to verify latest customs information.

Northern Puget Sound & Admiralty Inlet

[18441, 18445, 18446, 18473]

★ **Port Ludlow:** See Chapter 4

★ **Kingston & Appletree Cove (1):** [18446] Kingston is a North Kitsap town situated on the hillside surrounding the shores of Appletree Cove. The Mosquito Fleet provided early freight and passenger services here until the ferries began running in 1923. Today Kingston is the western terminus of the Edmonds-Kingston auto/passenger ferry, and the Seattle-Kingston passenger ferry, making it the first stop for visitors to the Kitsap and Olympic Peninsulas. For information on Kingston, visit www.KingstonChamber.com or call 360-860-2239.

North of the ferry are four Port of Kingston mooring buoys (boats to 40', no fee, five day maximum stay, requires registration in the port office). Next to the ferry terminal is a port-operated, breakwater-protected marina and double lane

Chart List

NOAA Charts:
18423, 18428, 18441, 18443, 18444, 18445, 18556, 18473, 18477

Marine Atlas Vol 1(2018): Pages 5-6

Evergreen Pacific Cruising Atlas: Pages 129, 133, 137, 142, 144, 145, 147, 154, 160

launch ramp. The visitor's float is parallel to the breakwater. Follow channel markers on approach in and out of the marina, and watch your depths especially during minus tides. Limited anchorage has protection from prevailing winds, however it is exposed to the southeast. When anchoring, please register with the port. Rules for anchoring on state-owned aquatic land do not allow vessels to moor or anchor in the same location for more than 30 consecutive days or in the same area (within a 5-mile radius) for more than a total of 90 days in any 365-day period. Mike Wallace Memorial Park, at the head of the visitor's dock, offers picnic and restroom facilities. From May to mid-October the Kingston Public Market operates at the park on Sundays, 10 am-3pm. 360-728-4471. The park also hosts free *Kingston Concerts on the Cove* put on by the Greater Kingston Community Chamber of Commerce and a Rotary sponsored *Beer Garden* on Saturdays in July and August from 6-8pm. Other events include the *Kingston Wine & Brew Fest* the third Saturday in July, the longest running *4th of July Parade* west of the Mississippi. In December, don't miss *Kingston Cove Christmas* and the *Port's Holiday Light Display* featuring light sculptures containing over ½ million lights! Restaurants, parks, coffee shops, ice cream and gift shops are located near the marina. Banks, post office, as well as hardware and grocery stores are within a half a mile. A community fishing pier where you can also fish for Red Rock Crab is adjacent to the ferry dock.

★ **Port of Kingston:** {47° 47' 45.9024" N, 122° 29' 47.3418" W} The Kingston Marina provides permanent moorage (open and covered), guest moorage to 80', storage for kayaks and canoes, as well as a launch ramp with trailer parking. Seasonal moorage is available from October to May. The onsite fuel dock offers diesel and ethanol free gas, along with motor oil, lubricants, and additives. Marina customers enjoy a full range of amenities including 30/50 amp power, free water, several conveniently located pump-outs, heated restrooms with complimentary showers, a coin-op laundry facility, free WiFi, picnic areas with two covered gazebos, and sturdy tote carts for transporting items. Need to pick up a few supplies in town? Use one of the electric vehicles at no extra charge with paid guest moorage. The marina is located within easy walking distance to the State Ferry Terminal and a variety of shopping and dining options. Reservations recommended. See our advertisement on this page. Website: www.portofkingston.org. Email: info@portofkingston.org. Physical Address: 25864 Washington Blvd., Kingston, WA 98346. Mailing Address: PO Box 559, Kingston, WA 98346. Telephone: 360-297-3545. VHF 65A.

★ **Arness County Park:** Wetlands containing significant wildlife are at the back of the bay, near Arness County Park. Picnic areas and fireplaces are available. With the right tide (a rising tide close to 10-foot high), it is possible to navigate by small craft through a culvert under the road to a lagoon that is popular for swimming. Currents can be strong through the culvert.

Edmonds
[18441, 18445, 18446, 18473]

★ **Edmonds (2):** This picturesque community is the eastern terminus for the Edmonds-Kingston ferry route, with two dozen trips daily to the Kitsap Peninsula. It is also the site of the impressive Port of Edmonds. Visitors may enjoy lovely sunsets over the Olympic Mountains and leisurely strolls along the waterfront where decades ago shingle mills once flourished. Amenities near the marina include restaurants, shopping, lodging, laundry, repairs, and dry storage. The Port is also home to the Edmonds Yacht Club and a unique Weather Center that provides updated weather related data and information. In addition to ferry service, Community Transit bus service and train service by both Amtrak and Sound Transit are options for regional connections. Up from the waterfront, Edmonds' charming streets spoke out from a central fountain and are accented by old-time streetlights draped with colorful hanging baskets. On Saturdays, May to October, this area bustles with a Farmers Market, 9am-3pm. Music lovers can enjoy free, family concerts during July and August at two locations – Sundays 3-4pm at City Park, or Tuesdays noon-1pm and Thursdays 5-6:30pm on the corner of Maple St and 5th Ave. S. Also on 5th Ave. N, the Historical Museum has a room dedicated to marine artifacts open Wed-Sun, 1-4pm. 118 5th Ave. N. Next door the Visitors Center has walking tour brochures, one for historic sites and the other for public art. Art lovers will enjoy visits to the several art galleries in town as well as the Cascade Art Museum with its collection of regional Northwest art. Or perhaps you'd like to take in a live theater or artistic production. For schedule and tickets call the Driftwood Players, 425-774-9600; the Phoenix Theatre, 206-533-2000; or Edmonds Center for the Arts, 425-275-9595. Four parks lie along the waterfront including a 950-foot public fishing pier and a popular 27-acre underwater park for divers. Stop by the Olympic Beach Visitor Station at the base of the Fishing Pier where you'll find a touch tank full of locale marine life (open noon-5pm on weekends, Memorial Day - Labor Day). Birders will enjoy the Edmonds Marsh east of the Marina. Yost Park, one of the 30 diverse parks in this city, has an open-air swimming pool and tennis courts. Community celebrations include the *Edmonds Arts Festival* on Father's Day weekend in June, the *Edmonds Kind of Fourth of July celebration*, a *Sand Sculpting Contest* at Marina Beach in mid-July and *Taste Edmonds* held the following month in August. For more information about Edmonds, www.visitedmonds.com.

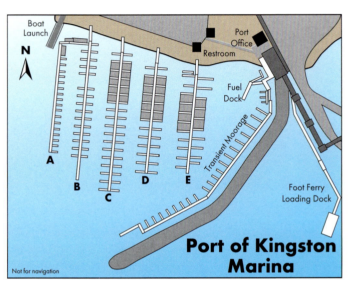

Port of Kingston Marina

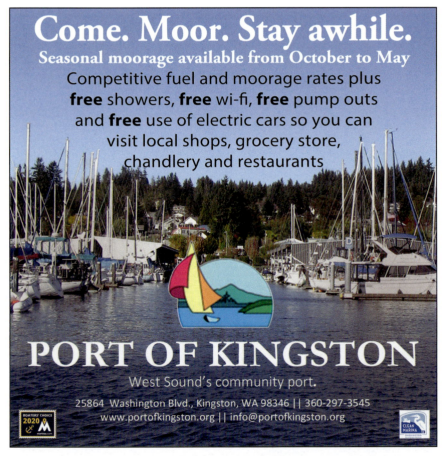

Port of Edmonds: {47° 48.5' N, 122° 23.4' W} This facility offers permanent and guest moorage reservations, water, 30 & 50 amp power available, showers, restrooms, laundry facility, boatyard, dry storage, public sling launch for smaller vessels and 50 ton Travelift for larger vessels by appointment, gas, diesel, and two pump-outs. Ecco Wireless WiFi is available. Waterfront dining and a lovely public plaza are onsite at the marina; the charming shops and restaurants of downtown Edmonds are a short walk away. Public park and dog beach located just south of the marina. Website: www.portofedmonds.org. Address: 458 Admiral Way, Edmonds, WA 98020. Fax: 425-670-0583. For guest moorage reservations: Telephone: Marina Operations: 425-775-4588. VHF 69.

★⚓ **Richmond Beach Saltwater Park:** Over a mile south of Pt. Wells, this City of Shoreline park is used for scuba diving and swimming, has hiking trails, restrooms, playground, and picnic areas. Practical anchorage is limited to a lunch hook.

Port of Edmonds Marina Photo © Joe Mabel

Possession Sound Vicinity
[18423, 18441, 18443, 18445]

★ **Possession Sound:** See current tables for Admiralty Inlet. Possession Sound joins Puget Sound at the southern point of Whidbey Island, extending in a general northerly direction for ten miles to its junction with Saratoga Passage and Port Susan.

Elliott Point (3): Elliott Point is a low spit projecting approximately 200 yards from the high land. Mukilteo Light, 33 feet above the water, is shown from a white octagonal tower on the point. A fog signal is at the station.

★⚓ **Lighthouse Park:** This fourteen acre day-use park near the lighthouse has launching ramps (electronic fee machine onsite), seasonal side floats, trash compactor, tables, covered picnic shelters, a band shell, free standing bbq's, firepits, seasonal beach volleyball court and restrooms. If winds are strong, go to Everett to launch. Parking available, fee applies. No camping. In season, the circa 1905 lighthouse is open for tours 12-5pm weekends and holidays, April through Sept. Scuba diving and fishing are popular in the area. For picnic shelter, band shell, beach volleyball court, wedding circle rentals, call 425-263-8180.

★ **Mukilteo (3):** [18443] Located at Elliott Point, this residential community is the terminus for the Mukilteo-Clinton (Whidbey Island) ferry. An L-shaped fishing pier is near the landing. Beginning in late-spring through early October, the Port of Everett installs seasonal floats on the north side of the ferry landing that are perfect for visiting boaters to tie up at and grab a quick bite to eat upland. The floats accommodate about six boats, 21' and under, 6-hr limit. Construction of a new ferry terminal may affect moorage in 2019 and 2020. Be aware and watch for signed closures. Restaurants, some shops and lodging are within walking distance. Each September the *Lighthouse Festival* features a parade, fireworks, art show, entertainment, and other fun activities.

Everett & Vicinity
[18423, 18443, 18444]

★ **Everett (4):** [18444] Everett is the county seat of Snohomish County, one of the fastest-growing counties in the state. Located 25 miles north of Seattle, Everett is home to Naval Station Everett, the world's most-modern Navy base, as well as the world's largest aircraft manufacturer, the Boeing Company. The Port of Everett links the community to international shipping from around the world and is the largest public marina on the west coast. Everett Station, a model of ingenuity and design, is the city's transportation hub offering local, cross-country and express buses as well as trains, shuttles, taxis and Park-and-Ride facilities.

The Port of Everett Marina is located on the east shore of Port Gardner, about one half mile into the mouth of the Snohomish River. On an ebb tide, currents can be strong. When landing, dock into the current. On approach, you will pass the U.S. Navy Homeport facility. Do not pass within 300-yards of the piers, when approaching the river entrance. Because of the channel buoys which may be confusing, reflections of lights on the water, and debris from up-river, plan to arrive during daylight hours. When entering the channel, keep buoy #3 to port and respect no wake speed. Light #5, located on Jetty Islands' south end helps to mark the entry.

The list of things-to-do and places-to-see in and around Everett is extensive. Just at the port facility itself, one can enjoy hours of attractions and entertainment. Marina Village and Port Gardner Landing compliment the marinas with a pedestrian friendly esplanade, hotel, chandleries and restaurants. The Waterfront Center, at the foot of the North Dock, houses the Port's Administration and Marina offices, as well as restaurants, a distillery, and a number of other businesses including several that offer marine services and repairs.

The 10th Street Marine Park has picnic facilities, a 13-lane boat ramp, and in summer is the site of the Jetty Island Ferry. From June through August there are waterfront concerts at Port Gardner Landing on Thursday and Saturday evenings. The annual *Fresh Paint Arts Festival* occurs each August. Up from the waterfront, a visit to the newly revitalized downtown area will reveal a variety of stores, restaurants, and entertainment venues amid the historic buildings and viewpoints. Funko Headquarters on Wetmore has six-foot pop-culture icons, the Historic Everett Theatre on Colby Avenue features a variety of productions. 425-258-6766. For the younger set, the Imagine Children's Museum on Wall Street offers hands-on fun. 425-258-1006. Angels of the Winds Arena on Hewitt Avenue hosts concerts, rodeos, circuses, and other exciting events. 425-322-2600. The Everett Performing Arts Center features quality, live theatrical productions. 425-257-8600. Taxis, and buses are available to and from the waterfront. Call 425-257-7777 for Everett Transit. Forest Park, the city's oldest and largest park, has a picnic shelter, trails, and water playground. Other local attractions include Future of Flight Aviation Center & Boeing Tours, 425-438-8100 and Everett Aquasox baseball games, 425-258-3673. Golfers can reserve a tee time at the Legion Memorial Golf Course, 2 miles north of the marina. Check out visiteverett.com for additional visitor information.

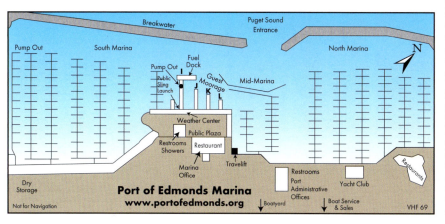

Chapter 5 NORTH PUGET SOUND

★ **Everett Yacht Service:** Everett Yacht Service is under new ownership! We are a sister shop to Pacific Fiberglass in Ballard and operated by Doug Lambeth, Troy Lambeth, and Kyle Messick. We took ownership of Everett Yacht Service in July of 2021. If you are familiar with Pacific FIberglass, you will find the same quality workmanship at Everett Yacht Service with additional mechanical services and a 75-Ton Travelift. We are excited to be up North serving the boating community and building a strong reputation as honest and hard-working boat specialists. See our advertisement on this page. Email: EverettYachtService@outlook.com. Address: 1205 Craftsman Way, Suite 116, Everett, Washington 98201. Telephone: 425-212-9923.

Naval Station Everett: Sailors Choice Marina: Private marina accessible to DoD civilian, reservists, active duty, retired military and disabled veterans only. Any vessel, prior to transmitting to or from the marina, must contact Everett Control on VHF 74. Permanent moorage-no live aboards, water, power, pump-out. 425-304-3449.

Port of Everett: {47° 59' N, 122° 14.1' W} Two lighted markers show the entrance to each of the two marinas. Permanent and guest moorage, 20/30/50 amp power, water, gas, diesel, laundry, restrooms, showers, 75-ton and 50-ton Travelifts, repair yard (DIY or professional), boat storage, waste pump-outs, activity float rentals. Wheelchair/ADA access at East end of South docks. 425-259-6001, 1-800-729-7678.

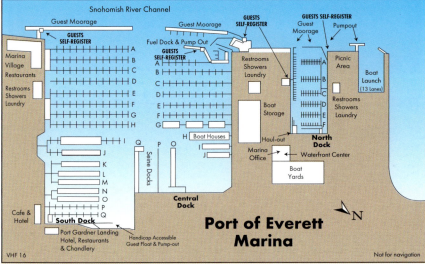

Walk-around: A waterfront public access trail system is a nearly four-mile pathway located between 10th and 18th streets on West Marine View Drive. Along the way, keep an eye out for wildlife and historical markers documenting the rich history of lumber and shingle mills, as well as commercial fishing and boat building industries along the waterfront.

★ **Jetty Island, Jetty Landing and Boat Launch:** Jetty Island, owned by the Port of Everett, is a man-made island composed of river sediment. The original dredged material is more than 100 years old and has been added to over time with each dredging of the Snohomish River Channel. It shelters the Port of Everett Marina from a short distance offshore and is only a five minute boat ride away. A small dock on the east side of the jetty, directly across from the Jetty Landing and Boat Launch (located off 10th Street and West Marine View Drive) provides docking space and limited guest moorage.

Thousands of visitors each year enjoy Jetty Island's sandy beaches, a rarity in the Pacific Northwest. The sand and shallow waters make the water warm enough to swim. Visitors often speak of Jetty Island's untouched natural beauty. With no electricity or plumbing, the island's only structure is the seasonal floating restroom. *Jetty Island Days* occur daily from early July through Labor Day, and features treasure hunts, sandcastle building contests and nature programs. A ferry provides rides to the island from Jetty Landing (adjacent to the 10th St. boat launch). Reservations are required and the cost is $3 a person/2 & under free. For information, call 425-257-8304. Jetty Landing has a number of amenities including picnic/bbq areas, restrooms and fishing opportunities. It is also home to a 13-lane boat launch, rated one of the best in the northwest. The facility is surrounded by miles of waterfront trails connecting various parks and open spaces throughout the marina district.

★ **Snohomish River (5):** The Snohomish is navigable for some distance by canoe, kayak, and shallow draft power boats. About one half mile east of Preston Point is the SR 529 bridge with a vertical clearance of 38 feet above means high water elevation. Moving up-river, Langus Riverfront Park on Smith Island has a boat launch (usable except for extreme minus low tides for boats 20 ft. or smaller), picnic tables, shelter, restrooms, a rowing dock and a 3 mile trail along the Snohomish River. Further inland is the I-5 overpass with a clearance of 66 feet. Explore the main channel for approximately three quarters of a mile past the I-5 overpass where it meets Steamboat Slough and accesses Spencer Island Regional Park with nature trails for bird watching and wetland habitat featuring bald eagles, hawks, ducks, herons and song birds in season.

Dagmars Marina: (On Smith Island) Dry dock boat storage, repairs, ice, bait. 425-259-6124. VHF 77.

Ebey Slough: Caution advised crossing the shallow flats leading to Steamboat and Ebey Sloughs. Pay attention to tide charts. The bar must be crossed at high tide. It is possible to navigate Ebey Slough to the city of Marysville. Use caution. Check channel depths and watch for obstacles. The SR 529 bridge, a fixed span structure crosses over the slough.

Ebey Waterfront Park: Located south of the old Geddes Marina (closed in 2010), this park features a boat launch, restrooms, picnic pavilion, playground, walking paths. For moorage information call 360-363-8400. Observe tide charts closely and allow extra hour to avoid problems loading at low tides. Towne Center Mall is within walking distance.

Located at The Everett Marina Boatyard

Our Services Include But Are Not Limited To:

- ❖ Complete Fiberglass, Paint, and Gelcoat Services
- ❖ Complete Running Gear Services and Repairs
- ❖ Bow and Stern Thruster – New Installation and Repairs
- ❖ Electronics Installation/Repair
- ❖ Mechanical - Marine Engines Including Outboard Motors, Inboard Motors, Diesel, and Gas Engines
- ❖ Bottom Painting and Repairs
- ❖ SEAKEEPER New Installation and Warranty Work

Everett Yacht Service
1205 Craftsman Way Suite 116, Everett, WA 98201
425-212-9923
EverettYachtService@Outlook.com

Visit us at boattravel.com

Gedney Island (Hat Island): This high, wooded island is residential property. The marina is privately owned, no transient moorage. "Pay as you go" guest moorage is allowed for members of yacht clubs with a reciprocal agreement with the Hat Island Yacht and Golf Club, in addition to normal reciprocal privileges. During summer mid-weeks and winter weekends there is usually availability. Call 360-444-6656 to check. Slips for boats to 62', 30/50 amp power, wifi, water, restrooms, showers, no garbage service. The steel breakwater ensures a quiet night. Be aware of shoaling at the entrance of the marina on the North side at low tides. Foul ground extends from the south side of the eastern half of the island. Caution advised. An artificial reef for scuba diving is 3,000 feet south of the island.

★ **Tulalip (6):** Caution advised because of rocks and extensive shoals. Limited anchorage in the shallow bay, located about four miles northwest of Everett. Minimum depths are three feet in most of the bay, however floats near shore may dry. A marina is on the eastern shore. No guest moorage available. South of the marina, the concrete launch ramp with boarding float is for tribal use only. On the hillside, there is an historic Catholic Mission. The surrounding land is part of the Tulalip Indian Reservation. The word Tulalip means "almost landlocked bay".

Tulalip Marina: Private, tribal moorage only. 360-716-4562.

★ **Kayak Point County Park (7):** Tall trees line the extensive gravel beach at Kayak Point. Anchorage is close to shore at the park, or in the bays north and south of the point. There is a launching ramp and a float for loading and unloading. A 300' fishing pier is good for crabbing at high tide. There are campsites, restrooms, picnic shelters, fresh water, and playground.

★ **Port Susan (8):** [18423, 18441] Port Susan is a 12-mile long, 1-mile wide body of water between Camano Island and the mainland. Boaters traveling north from Everett occasionally enter Port Susan by mistake, missing Saratoga Passage. If exploring Port Susan, temporary anchorage is found in the bay on the mainland shore, south of Kayak Point. There is little protection here from southeast winds. A better anchoring spot is Gerde Cove, off Camano Island across from and south of Kayak Point. Although unmarked on charts, it was named in honor of the Gerdes, a seafaring family with many generations fishing the west coast and finally settling on Camano Island. Water depths are 15 to 20 feet with anchorage on a mud bottom. A launching ramp is located at Cavelero Beach County Park on the west shore of Port Susan, south of Triangle Cove. Anchorage is possible. Picnic facilities. Because of the sun-heated tide flats that warm the shallow water in much of the bay, swimming is good. The area in and around Port Susan is known for year round bird watching opportunities. Swans, ducks, raptors, and snow geese are plentiful. The *Port Susan Snow Goose & Birding Festival*, held in February, celebrates these creatures in events, activities, and art. Also in February, the *Great NW Glass Quest* is a unique hunt for hand-blown glass treasures.

Saratoga Passage & Camano Island

[18423, 18441]

★ **Saratoga Passage:** See current table for Admiralty Inlet. Rimming the west side of Camano Island, Saratoga Passage extends approximately 18 miles in a northwesterly direction from its entrance

Port of Everett Marina *Photo © Cindy Shebley*

between Sandy Point and Camano Head. At its north end, this deep waterway connects with Penn Cove and Oak and Crescent Harbors, and leads into Skagit Bay. Winds can funnel through this waterway, and rough water can be encountered when winds meet an opposing tide.

★ **Camano Island:** This island is separated from the mainland shore near the town of Stanwood only by the channels at the mouth of the Stillaguamish River. These river sloughs are navigable only at the highest tides and in shallow draft boats. The beach below 340 foot high Camano Head, at the southern tip of the island, is Tulalip Tribal land and is not open to public use. Camano Island was named after the Spanish explorer Lieutenant Don Jacinto Caamaño. Long before it took this name, the Kikalos and Snohomish Indians knew it as "Kal-lut-chin," translated as "land jutting into a bay" and they came each summer to gather seafood and berries. Today people still come during the warmer months when the island is home to over 16,000 residents. A number of small businesses are found here including grocery stores, lodging, art studios and cafes. There are two wineries and a coffee roasting company that offer tastings and tours (call for appointment), 1-866-833-0209. For fun outdoors, try a round of golf, go ziplining, or hike one of the local trails. Regular bus routes provide service around the island, Mount Vernon and Stanwood, for free, and to Mount Vernon and Everett for a fee. Camano has three boat ramps - Utsalady, Maple Grove, and Cavalero. Fees apply.

Elger Bay: This bay lies on the Saratoga Passage side of the island. There is temporary anchorage with protection from northwesterly winds. The northern extent of the bay is shallow. Favor the Lowell Point side, avoiding some foul ground off the point.

★ **Camano Island State Park (9):** Located at Lowell Point on Saratoga Passage, this 244 acre park has a beach, 77 campsites, 1 Cascadia Marine Trail tent site, 5 cabins, picnic tables, 1 rentable enclosed picnic shelter, water, restrooms, showers, and 1 boat ramp (fees apply). Check bulletin board for interpretive programs. Hiking, biking, swimming, scuba diving, sailboarding, fishing and crabbing are popular in the area. Park Info: 360-387-3031. Cabin Reservations: 1-888-226-7688 or 360-387-1550.

★ **Cama Beach State Park:** Step back in time to a charming historic 1930's fishing resort on the island's southwest shore facing Saratoga Passage. Restored waterfront cabins and bungalows are vacation rentals. No tent camping. The Cama Beach Center has a café and event venue. A satellite facility for The Center for Wooden Boats offers boat building classes, family events and boat rentals. No boat mooring or launching. Reservations/Info: 1-888-226-7688 or 360-387-1550.

Onamac Point: This point is private, do not land onshore. Off the point is an artificial reef for boat dives. There are a variety of bottom fish nearby.

★ **Utsalady:** Utsalady, meaning "land of the berries" was once a summer home settlement and is now a thriving year-round community. A launch ramp is at the small county park on the west side of the bay. Another, the Maple Grove ramp is farther west, around Utsalady Point. Utsalady Bay, formed between Utsalady Point and Brown Point, has depths of 10 to 20 feet. Anchorage is on a mud bottom. The bay is exposed to north and northwest winds and seas from shallow Skagit Bay. Adjoining land is private. More than a century ago, this was a center for lumber milling and ship building. Select timbers, some measuring 125 feet in length and 50 inches in diameter, were shipped as spars to the British and American Navies. One flag staff, made at Utsalady, appeared at the Paris Exposition. In 1857, the enterprising mill owner, Lawrence Gremman, envisioned a canal dug through the middle of Whidbey Island to make a direct shipping lane to the Strait of Juan de Fuca. The mill closed in 1896.

Chapter 5 NORTH PUGET SOUND

Oak Harbor Marina Photo © Chris Sublet

Skagit Bay & Skagit River
[18423, 18427]

★ **Skagit Bay (10):** See current tables for Deception Pass. This bay extends north from Saratoga Passage about 12 miles in a west-northwest direction. The bottom of much of the bay is mud flats that are bare at low water. The mud is intersected by numerous channels caused by the Skagit River outflow. Shoals also extend into the bay from Whidbey Island. A natural channel, marked by buoys and lights, follows the eastern shore of Whidbey Island to the northern point where the channel turns west through Deception Pass. Stay in the marked channel. Approaching from the south, the red nun buoys are to starboard and green cans to port. Velocity and direction of the currents vary throughout the channel. The flood enters through Deception Pass and sets in a generally southern direction. The ebb flows north. This is important to know when west winds are blowing in Juan de Fuca Strait and will clash with an ebb current in the vicinity of Deception Pass.

★ **Skagit River:** The North and South Forks of the Skagit River meet about 1.5 miles south of Mount Vernon, eventually emptying into Skagit Bay, leaving the rich farmlands of triangle-shaped Fir Island between them. The South Fork travels through the flats north of Camano Island. Navigation of the South Fork is not recommended, except by canoeists and kayakers. Launch ramps are at Utsalady.

The North Fork, however, offers an opportunity for owners of small, hand-carried or small-medium sized boats to explore the Skagit River. It is possible to enter the river at most times of the year on a high tide of eight feet or better. The problem spot is the approach channel in Skagit Bay. Entrance to the North Fork is in the channel along the south side of the man-made jetty. Go slow and stay fairly close to the jetty. Once in the river itself, depths are adequate, and unless it is a time of extremely low river height it is even possible to navigate inland by small craft past the city of Mount Vernon. In Skagit Bay, however, the river shallows to wadeable depths at low tide. The Blake family who have owned a resort and marina on the North Fork for many years, share that it is possible to launch a boat (to 30 feet) at their boat ramp, exiting on an 11 or 12 foot tide, go to La Conner to explore, and return at a regular tide. They also recommend fishing for Humpies (pink salmon) in August and September because they are easy to catch, and it is possible to anchor and let the current do all of the work.

The remainder of Skagit Bay, including Swinomish Channel and Similk Bay, are farther north and are described at the beginning of Chapter 6.

Blake's Skagit Resort & Marina: Full RV hookups, daily/weekly/monthly moorage, launch ramp, snacks, showers, laundry, camping, cabins, propane. 360-445-6533.

Whidbey Island
[18423, 18441]

★ **Whidbey Island:** Whidbey Island is described in two chapters in this book. The area along the northern shore, Cornet Bay, and Deception Pass, is outlined in Chapter 6. The area south from Joseph Whidbey State Park and Oak Harbor is described here.

Approximately 55 miles in length, this is the largest salt water island in the contiguous United States. In February 1985, the Supreme Court, in a 9-0 decision, ruled that Long Island, New York is a peninsula rather than an island, leaving the largest island honors to Whidbey. It was named for Joseph Whidbey, a sailing master with Captain George Vancouver in the 1790's. It was Whidbey who discovered Deception Pass between Whidbey and Fidalgo Islands.

Whidbey Island is connected to Fidalgo Island by the Deception Pass Bridge. Ferries provide regular service between Coupeville and Port Townsend, and between Clinton and Mukilteo.

In climate and economy, Whidbey Island's northern half is quite different from the southern half. North Whidbey falls within the lee of the Olympic Rain Shadow, resulting in arid grazing land and an average rainfall of only 17 inches. Even some forms of cacti flourish here. On the island's southern half, the annual rainfall is 35 inches, contributing to the agricultural economic base of this part of the island. Real estate development, logging, and ship building are other south-island industries. The largest employer and economic factor on the island is the Naval Air Station, north of Oak Harbor.

★ **Joseph Whidbey State Park (11):** Located on the Strait of Juan de Fuca, on the west shore of the island, this park is primarily accessible by car. There is a beach for small, beachable boats. Picnic sites and restrooms are available. Day use park only except for one Cascadia Marine Trail campsite. 360-678-4519.

Oak Harbor & Vicinity
[18423, 18428, 18441]

Crescent Harbor (12): [18428] Oak and Crescent Harbors are adjacent to each other. Crescent Harbor, a semicircular bight two miles in diameter, is immediately east of Oak Harbor. Shoal areas are identified on the chart. No marine facilities for civilian pleasure craft, authorized users only. The breakwater, docks, and small craft military vessels support Port Operations. Two launch ramps, authorized users only, are also located here.

★ **Oak Harbor (12):** [18428] Enter Oak Harbor in the marked channel between Blower's Bluff and Forbe's Point. Check depths and stay in the dredged channel between the red and green markers. In order to avoid rocks, do not go between buoy #2 and Maylor Point. Once clear of the last starboard marker, turn sharply to starboard. The city is on the port side and the marina, with abundant visitor moorage, is at the head of the bay. This marina is about 3/4 miles from downtown shops and restaurants. Taxi and bus service are available. The bus is free and runs Monday through Friday, with nearest bus stop just a few blocks away. Destinations of interest include Deception Pass, Ft. Casey and Coupeville. There is a float for small dinghies at the downtown waterfront. Depths are shallow and the float dries at a minus tide.

★ **City of Oak Harbor:** The City of Oak Harbor, thought of fondly as "Paradise of Puget Sound," has many amenities, including restaurants, hotels, gift shops, and grocery stores. Local theaters come in several varieties - live community theater, a multi-screen movie theater and even a drive-in theater featuring go-karts, arcade, and 50's style diner. Northern Oak Harbor is home to Deception Pass State Park and the famous Deception Pass Bridge. Island Transit buses provide free transportation throughout Whidbey Island. The newly renovated Windjammer Park has a splash park, kitchens, a swimming lagoon, playgrounds, exercise course and basketball courts. The grounds are open year-round while the buildings and facilities are open May-October. The city also has a skate park and an indoor swimming pool. A pier, with a float for fishing and landing dinghies, lies along this shore at Flintstone Park. Depths are shallow and the float dries at a minus tide. Annual Oak Harbor Events include the *Whidbey Island Marathon* and *Holland Happening*, a festival celebrating the Dutch heritage) in April. July brings an *Old-Fashioned Fourth of July Parade and Fireworks*. Crabbing in Oak Harbor is always amazing and kicks off with the *Crab Cakes and Cocktails* event. The *Lions Club Car Show*, the *Oak Harbor PigFest* and *Hydro's for Hero's* are held in August. The city welcomes fall with the *Military Appreciation Picnic* (open to all), and the *Oak Harbor Music Festival* in September, and the *Monster Mash/Zombie Crawl* in October. The year wraps up in December with a tree lighting in historic downtown, the *Oak Harbor Yacht Club Lighted Boat Parade*, *Island Ice* (an ice skating adventure) and finally fireworks to ring in the New Year.

The townsite of Oak Harbor, named for the preponderance of Garry Oaks, was first settled in the mid-1800's. By 1891, Oak Harbor's downtown waterfront was booming when steamers made regular freight and passenger runs between the town and Bellingham, Everett, Seattle, and Olympia. In

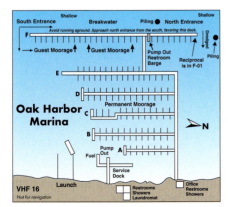

Visit us at boattravel.com

1894, the Dutch arrived from Michigan and the Dakotas, searching for land where they would be free from the age-old fear of floods. The Dutch influence helped to shape the community, as evidenced by the farms, architecture, and gardens.

Oak Harbor Marina: {48° 17.12' N, 122° 38.03' W} Permanent and guest moorage, gas, diesel, pump out, restrooms, showers, laundromat. Shopping and restaurants nearby. 360-279-4575. VHF 16.

Penn Cove & Coupeville

[18423, 18441]

★ Penn Cove (13): Penn Cove is about one mile wide and indents three and a half miles, nearly cutting Whidbey Island in two. Anchorage is possible in several locations in 30-45 feet of water. Most of the bottom is good holding mud. Snakelum Point, at the eastern entrance to Penn Cove, is a narrow spit that extends north for over a half mile. The spit is marked by a buoy. Beware of a wreck in the vicinity. Private homes line this spit. On the north shore, Monroe Landing is home to a launch ramp and picnic area. Also on the northern shore are old wharfs and pilings, reminders of the 1890's when the community of San de Fuca was established on this hillside. At one time San de Fuca had the first schoolhouse on the island, a general store, furniture, and jewelry shops, a tavern, and a fine hotel. The San de Fuca Fire Department building marks the spot today, and the landmark Armstrong House on the hill, has been restored as a residence. On the opposite shore is the historic town of Coupeville.

Farther into Penn Cove, private buoys and aquaculture operations are at the southwest corner. Madrona trees decorate the surrounding hillside approaching Kennedy's Lagoon, at the head of the cove. The Captain Whidby Inn, circa 1907, still operates nearby.

★ Coupeville (14): The wharf provides 400 feet of moorage. Estimate of the minimum depth at mean low tide is approximately 7 feet. There are adequate depths for anchoring nearby.

Several businesses are located on the Wharf, including kayak rentals, a gift shop, a restaurant serving fish and chips, salads, wine and beer & more, coffee shop that serves pastries and locally made products. SUVA, a 1925 schooner moors on the wharf May - September. Information kiosks at the shore-end of the wharf highlight Coupeville's attractions. Stroll Front Street and take in picturesque shops, wine tasting room, deli, bakeries, restaurants, art galleries, museum, historic exhibits, and Victorian era homes. A walking tour guide of the historic homes is available at the Chamber of Commerce. Many of the buildings have been restored as bed and breakfast inns. A small grocery store, post office, and bank are accessible. Lots of fun events are on the calendar each year starting with the *Coupeville Chocolate Walk* in February. The first full weekend in March, thousands of visitors arrive for the *Penn Cove Mussel Festival* featuring mussel bed tours, chowder tasting, and more. The last Saturday in May the Memorial Weekend celebrations include a parade, a musical salute and the town picnic. May is also the month for the *Penn Cove Water Festival*. An *Arts and Crafts Festival* is celebrated in August with arts & craft vendors, wine and beer garden, music and food. In September the town has its annual salmon bake and concert. October is *The Haunting of Coupeville* with haunted Fort Casey, pumpkin patch and pumpkin races. Free public transportation is available. For events and other information, stop at the Visitor Center near the end of the wharf on Alexander Street or visit www.coupevillechamber.com. Coupeville is the county seat for Island County and sits in the heart of the Ebey's Landing National Historical Reserve. The town was founded in the 1850's by Captain Thomas Coupe. At that time about 300 Skagit Natives lived on the lands surrounding Penn Cove. In 1905, the Coupeville wharf was built. It was the only terminal on the island for vessels of any draft. Paddle wheelers and other ships moored to the wharf to off-load farm implements, dry goods and passengers and to load grain and timber from the farms on Whidbey. Commercial boat traffic stopped after the Deception Pass Bridge was built and State Ferries began service to the Island.

Walk-around: A walking tour takes about an hour and includes many restored Victorian homes marked with historical information plaques. Coupeville has the largest collection of territorial buildings (built before statehood) in Washington. Be sure to take in the wonderful Native People-Native Places exhibit and 3 rare dug out canoes at the Island County Museum at the foot of the Coupeville wharf. 360-678-3310.

Port of Coupeville: {48° 13' 22.11" N, 122° 41' 17.56" W} Transient moorage only, gas, diesel, store, showers, restaurant, pumpout station, no power or water. Harbormaster: 360-678-6379. VHF 68.

Captain Coupe Park: A launch ramp with a side float marks the site of this park on the eastern side of town. Parking is provided for cars and boat trailers. There is no wash down hose. The park offers picnic tables, barbecues and a public restroom. Anchorage is limited in the immediate area due to shallow water. 360-678-4461.

Ebey's Landing National Historic Reserve (15): A parking lot, vault toilet, interpretive display, are provided. Hiking, surf fishing, and beachcombing are popular. There are no mooring buoys. A memorial above the beach depicts the life of Colonel Ebey, pioneer commander of an 1855 Militia station who was slain by Haida Indians from the north who sought revenge for the death of their chief.

Fort Ebey State Park: Eagles, bluffs, army bunkers, wild rhododendrons, and sandy beaches can all be found at this 651-acre park on the west side of Whidbey Island. There are over 50 campsites (11 with utility hookups) a restroom, showers, fresh water, and over 25 miles of walking and biking trails. Surfing and paragliding are popular activities. Fort Ebey, built in 1942, joined Fort Casey, Fort Worden and Fort Flagler as the four corners in the defense system of Puget Sound. Gun batteries and bunkers still remain. 360-678-4636. Fort Casey State Park encircles the harbor.

Keystone Harbor (16): Fairly protected by Admiralty Head, Keystone has a small spot for temporary anchorage. The controlling depth at the entrance is 18 feet, with 15 to 18 foot depths in the harbor. Use caution when the tide rips are frothing at the entrance. This small harbor is the Whidbey Island terminus for the Port Townsend-Coupeville ferry. Allow sufficient maneuvering room for the ferry to land.

Fort Casey State Park: There is a boat launch (fee applies), picnic sites, tent and utility campsites, a restroom, and shower. Activities include hiking on the trails, scuba diving at the underwater marine park, visiting the interpretive center in the Admiralty Head Lighthouse, and exploring in the underground rooms. View the concrete bunkers and gun stations from the days of the 1890's when the fort was used in the defense system protecting the entrance to Puget Sound. Gun Battery Tours are conducted June-Aug., call the park at 360-678-4519 for information. Because of the crowded bay, access to the park is primarily by car.

On anchor off Coupeville Wharf

Walk-around: A four-mile walk north along the beach leads to Ebey's Landing. The walk farther north leads to Perrigo's Lagoon and on to Point Partridge.

Walk-around: Crockett Lake (popular for birdwatching), and the beach on Keystone Spit are within walking distance of Fort Casey. In the 1850's, the community of New Chicago was located on the spit. Lots were platted and brought high prices. A wharf and hotel were built, however, a windstorm leveled the hotel, and a proposed railway system never materialized.

★ South Whidbey State Park (17): This 381 acre day use park is near Bush Point. Facilities include picnic tables, a kitchen shelter, restrooms, and pay phone. Campsites closed due to unsafe conditions caused by diseased trees. The beach trail washed out and there is currently no beach access. No mooring buoys. 360-678-4519.

Bush Point (18): This picturesque point is identified by homes rimming the beach and a larger building just south of a boat ramp. The launch ramp is for boats under 22'. Larger boats can be launched but a 1 ton, 4 wheel drive vehicle and extra help is advised. A minimum recommended tide for launching is 0.0'. Boarding floats are available from May to Sept. A restroom is onsite. Trailer/truck parking is available, no overnight parking. Years before the Bush Point Lighthouse was built in 1933, a kerosene lantern hung from a long pole was used on dark nights to warn mariners of the rocks offshore.

Mutiny Bay (19): It is possible to anchor in this indentation between Bush Point and Double Bluff. Dinghy ashore for a picnic on the 300' of public beach extending southward from the launching ramp. Watch for tide rips and shoals that extend 600'.

Greenbank: Located north of Holmes Harbor on the island's east shore, this farming settlement, well known for the cultivation of loganberries and loganberry liqueur, does not have marine facilities for boaters. In the early days of the century, a wharf and a store were established, and the site was a regular steamer stop. By 1908 several Finnish families had settled, and a hotel and school stood near the beach. Today, Greenbank Beach County Park has swimming and picnic sites. Fairly deep water anchorage on a mud bottom, offering some protection in west winds.

★ **Holmes Harbor (20):** Private homes and floats dot the shore of this six mile long inlet. Anchorage is in Honeymoon Bay and off the head, opposite Freeland Park. Open to winds from the north.

★ **Honeymoon Bay:** Anchorage is in a bight on the west shore, south of Dines Point. No floats or docks are available.

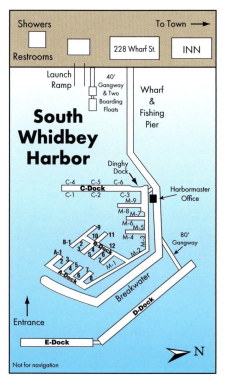

★ **Freeland (21):** The community of Freeland is located at the southern tip of Holmes Harbor. Anchorage can be found at the head, adjacent to the park. It is possible to dinghy ashore and walk to the town center where one will find antique stores and shopping, excellent restaurants, marine supplies, banks, and grocery stores. The Visitor Center is located at 5575 Harbor Avenue, 360-331-1980. Freeland was settled in 1900 when large tracts of land were given to disenchanted Socialists from the Equality colony. Each family grew crops and contributed both money and man power to be used for machinery and construction. A community sawmill was utilized for many years. Today, Freeland is the commercial hub of South Whidbey Island as well as a robust residential community. It is also home to the nationally recognized Nichols Brothers Boat Builders (no marine facilities).

★ **Freeland Park:** Located at the head of Holmes Harbor. Facilities include a launching ramp, picnic sites, playground, and restrooms. The ramp has been extended over 100 feet to permit access at all tides, and floats have been added.

Useless Bay (22): Shallow flats extend from shore and then drop-off abruptly to depths of more than 12 fathoms. This vicinity has been a private summer home haven for many years.

★ **Dave Mackie County Park:** A launching ramp is on the Park's east shore, near Maxwelton. The ramp is closed to trailered boats due to long shore drift, which has covered the ramp with a sand bar. It is difficult to predict when the sand bar will move past the launch and allow normal boat launch operations, but it is not expected anytime soon. Hand launch of smaller boats is possible. Private tidelands are adjacent to the park. The park has picnic tables, restrooms, fresh water, a baseball field and a playground.

Langley
[18423, 18441]

★ **Langley (23):** A breakwater protects the Port of South Whidbey Harbor at Langley moorage basin, where both permanent and guest moorage can be found. There is no fuel service.

Langley sits on a bluff overlooking Saratoga Passage, with Cascades and Mt. Baker views. From March through May, watch for whales from Seawall Park, where picnic tables are available. On summer weekends, free golf shuttle service runs every half hour from the marina into town. Langley received certification last year as a "Washington State Certified Creative District" and we are known for the number of artists and galleries that are located here. There are gift, antique, clothing, jewelry, book and music shops, as well as a grocery store, vintage movie theater, two live theaters, art galleries, a coffee roaster, wine tasting rooms and many good restaurants. Annual events include *Mystery Weekend* the last weekend in February, *Welcome the Whales Day* in April, the free *Island Shakespeare Festival* from mid-July through mid-September, and an old-fashioned *Whidbey Island Fair* in late July. Music lovers won't want to miss the world famous *DjangoFest* celebrating the Gypsy Jazz legacy of Django Reinhart in September. Hiking and biking trails are just outside of town. Rent a kayak at the marina or if you are a diver check out the artificial tire reef just off the breakwater. For information, www.VisitLangley.com.

★ **South Whidbey Harbor at Langley:** {48° 02' N, 122° 24' W} The Harbor boasts deep water moorage on our expanded docks. This breakwater-protected facility offers transient moorage year-round and monthly moorage from October through April. Overnight reservations recommended, day stops upon availability, or call for

★ **South Whidbey Harbor at Langley:** A great little getaway whether close to home or as a stopping place on a longer journey. The Harbor boasts deep water moorage on our expanded docks. This breakwater-protected facility offers transient moorage year-round, and monthly moorage from October through April. Overnight reservations recommended, friendly dockside assistance for arrivals and departures, day stops upon availability, and group reservations up to 1 year in advance. 30, 50 and 100 amp power is available, as well as water, waste pump-out barge, showers and a launch ramp with boarding floats. Laundry facilities in town about 1/4 mile from the Harbor. The charming city of Langley overlooks Saratoga Passage and is a short walk from the waterfront. Visitors will find a full service grocery, wine shops & tasting rooms, several cafes and restaurants, bookstores, clothing stores, gift shops, a classic 1930s movie house, motels, inns, B&Bs, public library, post office and absolutely spectacular views. Annual special events include a Murder Mystery Weekend in February, Whidbey Island Fair in July and Djangofest in September. Check www.visitlangley.com for specific dates. Gray whales are often seen feeding in the shallows just off Seawall Park from March through May. Come enjoy the leisurely pace of Island Time!

www.portofsouthwhidbey.com   Mailing address: Port of South Whidbey, PO Box 872, Freeland WA 98249
Tel: 360-221-1120, VHF 66A, Email: harbormaster@portofsouthwhidbey.com

group reservations. 30, 50 and 100 amp power is available, as well as water, waste pump-out barge, showers, and a launch ramp with boarding floats. See our advertisement on page 74. Website: www.portofsouthwhidbey.com. Email: harbormaster@portofsouthwhidbey.com. Phone: 360-221-1120. VHF 66A.

★⚓ **Seawall Park:** This park runs along the waterfront below the town of Langley, just off First Street. A staircase and steep walkway descend to the beach.

Clinton (24): This is the western terminus for the Clinton-Mukilteo ferry route. A fishing pier and short-stay float for loading is located adjacent to the north side of the ferry wharf. Closed due to storm damage, repairs are underway on the float. A park onshore has restrooms, picnic tables, shelter, and access to Clinton Beach, the pride of local residents. The town with grocery stores, banks, shops, restaurants, and library lies along Highway 525 on the hillside above the ferry terminal.

★⚓ **Possession Beach Waterfront Park:** Located south of Clinton, this park is open dawn to dusk and has a hiking trail, picnic tables, restrooms, and a concrete launch ramp. Boarding floats are available from May-Sept. and end at about a 0.0' tide, so a +3.0' tide is best to use floats. Overnight parking for truck/trailer is available with permit ($10/night). Call 360-579-2451 or visit www.portofsouthwhidbey.com. Red rock and Dungeness crabs are found, along with abundant horse clams.

Possession Point & Cultus Bay (25): [18441, 18445] Possession Point State Park with picnic tables, cascadia marine water trails, campsite and on-site caretaker is located here. Steep trails lead to prominent white bluffs that provide the backdrop for the popular fishing grounds off this point. A bell buoy marks a shoal extending one-half mile from shore, west of Scatchet Head. Another shoal juts 2 1/4 miles offshore from Possession Point. A lighted bell buoy marks the end of this foul ground. An artificial reef with a 240-foot sunken ship is 600 feet west of the buoy. Water depths here are 55 to 100 feet. Anchorage in settled weather can be found fairly close to shore, off the southeast tip of Whidbey, north of Possession Point. Beach homes on shore mark this location. Cultus Bay contains shoals and dries on low tides. A dredged channel on the east side of the bay leads to a private development.

Essential Supplies & Services

AIR TRANSPORTATION
Kenmore Air 1-866-435-9524
NW Seaplanes . . . 425-277-1590, 1-800-690-0086
San Juan Airlines. 1-800-874-4434
Seattle Seaplanes 1-800-637-5553

BOOKS / BOOK STORES
Evergreen Pacific Publishing. 425-493-1451
The Marine Atlas. 253-872-5707

BUS TRANSPORTATION
Everett. 425-257-7777
Greyhound (from U.S.). 1-800-231-2222
Community Transit Snohomish County . 425-353-7433
Island Transit (Camano & Whidbey Islands)
Toll Free 1-800-240-8747

COAST GUARD
Emergencies . . . . 206-217-6001 or VHF 16
Seattle Sector Response. 206-217-6200
Vessel Traffic 206-217-6152

CUSTOMS/BORDER PROTECTION
Small Boat Reporting 1-800-562-5943

FERRY INFORMATION
WA State Ferry 1-888-808-7977

FISHING/SHELLFISHING INFO
https://wdfw.wa.gov/fishing/shellfish
Fishing Regulations 360-902-2500
Red Tide Hotline 1-800-562-5632
Shellfish Rule Change Hotline. 1-866-880-5431

FUELS
Coupeville, Port of: Gas, Diesel. 360-678-6379
Edmonds, Port of: Gas, Diesel.
. . . . 425-775-4588 VHF 69
Everett, Port of: Gas, Diesel. . . . . 425-259-6001 VHF 16
Kingston, Port of: Gas, Diesel 360-297-3545
Oak Harbor: Gas, Diesel . . . . 360-279-4575 VHF 16

GOLF
Gallery Golf Course. 360-257-2178
Holmes Harbor Golf Course:Freeland . . . 360-331-2363
Lan's Links (9 Hole) Oak Harbor. 360-675-3412
Legion Memorial, Everett 425-259-GOLF
Whidbey Golf Club 360-675-5490

HAUL-OUTS
Dagmar's Landing: Smith Island. 425-259-6124 VHF 77

Everett, Port of . . . . 425-259-6001 VHF 16
Mariner's Haven, Oak Harbor 360-675-8828

HOSPITALS
Edmonds (Swedish) 425-640-4000
Everett (Providence) 425-261-2000
Coupeville (WhidbeyHealth) 360-321-5151,
   1-888-903-2345
N Whidbey Community Clinic 360-679-5590

MARINAS / MOORAGE FLOATS
Blake's RV Fishing Resort (Skagit River) 360-445-6533
Coupeville, Port of 360-678-6379
Edmonds, Port of . . . . 425-775-4588 VHF 69
Everett, Port of . . . . 425-259-6001 VHF 16
Kingston, Port of 360-297-3545
Oak Harbor Marina . . . . 360-279-4575 VHF 16
South Whidbey Harbor at Langley. . 360-221-1120

MARINE SUPPLIES
Harbor Marine, Everett 425-259-3285

PARKS
Department of Natural Resources: 360-856-3500
Edmonds City Parks 425-771-0230
Washington State 360-902-8844
Washington State: Central Whidbey 360-678-4519
Washington Camping Reservations . . .1-888-226-7688

PROPANE
Blake's Skagit Resort & Marina 360-445-6533

RAMPS
Blake's RV Fishing Resort (Skagit River)
. . . . 360-445-6533
Bush Point Ramp, Whidbey Island 360-914-1115
Camano Island: Camano Island State Park, Maple
   Grove, Utsalady
Coupeville: Captain Coupe Park
Dave Mackie Park: Maxwelton (CLOSED)
Ebey Waterfront Park Marysville
Edmonds, Port of . . . . 425-775-4588 VHF 69
Everett, Port of . . . . 425-259-6001 VHF 16
Fort Casey State Park: Keystone,
Freeland Park: Whidbey Island
Kingston, Port of 360-297-3545
Langus Waterfront Park: Snohomish River
Lighthouse Park, Mukilteo
Monroe's Landing County Park, Oak Harbor
Oak Harbor Marina . . . . 360-279-4575 VHF 16
Port Susan: Cavelero Beach County Park, Kayak Point
   County Park

Possession Beach Waterfront Park, Whidbey
. . . . 360-579-2451
South Whidbey Harbor at Langley. . 360-221-1120

REPAIRS / SERVICE
Dagmar's Marina: Smith Island . 425-259-6124 VHF 77
Edmonds, Port of . . . . 425-775-4588 VHF 69
Everett Bayside Marine 425-252-3088
Everett, Port of . . . . 425-259-6001 VHF 16
Everett Yacht Service. 425-212-9923
Mariners Haven, Oak Harbor. 360-675-8828

SCUBA / DIVING SITES
Camano Island State Park   Edmonds Underwater Park
Fort Casey State Park   Lighthouse Park
Hat Island   Mukilteo State Park
Richmond Beach Saltwater Park

SEWAGE DISPOSALS
Coupeville, Port of 360-678-6379
Edmonds, Port of: Pump 425-775-4588
Everett, Port of: Pump, Dump. 425-259-6001
Kingston, Port of: Pump, Dump 360-297-3545
Oak Harbor Marina: Pump, Dump 360-279-4575
South Whidbey Harbor at Langley. . 360-221-1120

STORAGE-DRY & STACKED
Dagmar's Marina: Smith Island 425-259-6124
Edmonds, Port of 206-940-1348

TAXI
Everett. 425-259-3333
Oak Harbor Taxi` 360-682-6920
S. Whidbey Island Taxi` 360-678-6666

TOWING
Tow Boat US Dispatch 1-800-367-8222
Tow Boat US - Everett 425-344-3056
N Whidbey Island/Deception Pass 360-675-7900

TRAILER REPAIR (MOBILE)
Trailer Techs. 206-889-0286

VISITOR INFORMATION
Central Whidbey 360-678-5434
Kingston 360-297-3813
Edmonds. 425-776-6711

WEATHER
NOAA Recorded Message. 360-357-6453
VHF WX-1

Chapter 6: Gateway Islands & Mainland

Swinomish Channel to Point Roberts. La Conner, Anacortes, Bellingham, Blaine; North Whidbey, Fidalgo, Guemes, Lummi Islands.

La Conner - photo © La Conner Chamber of Commerce

The La Conner Boardwalk on the Swinomish Channel Photo © Donna Butler

Chart List

NOAA Charts:
   18400, 18421-23, 18424, 18427, 18429-32
Canadian Hydrographic Charts: 3463
Marine Atlas Vol 1 (2018): Pages 6-7, 12
Evergreen Cruising Atlas: Pages 123-125, 128-130, 134-135

Symbols

[   ]: Numbers between [   ] are chart numbers.

{   }: Numbers & letters between {   } are waypoints.

★ Recommended destinations, facilities, and services

⚓: Park, ⛵: Boat Launch, ▲: Campgrounds, ⚐: Hiking Trails, ⊼: Picnic Area, 🚲: Biking, ⚓: Scuba

★ See "Important Notices" between Chapters 7 and 8 for specific information on boating related topics such as boating safety, weather, U.S. & Canadian marine radio use, Vessel Traffic Service, security zones, Canadian & U.S. Customs, etc. Due to changing regulations, call ahead to verify latest customs information.

Skagit Valley
[18400]

★ **Skagit Valley:** The Skagit River descends from the mountains and passes several communities as it meanders through this fertile valley to the Skagit Bay. See Chapter 5. Dairy, bulb, seed, and vegetable farms dominate the landscape. *The La Conner Daffodil Festival* is held in March and *The Skagit Valley Tulip Festival* in April. Skagit Transit offers transportation from moorages in La Conner and Anacortes to nearly all corners of Skagit County, enabling visitors to connect with Mount Vernon, the Bayview Airport, and outlet and shopping malls.

★ **Mount Vernon (1):** See Skagit River information in Chapter 5. Mount Vernon is the county's largest city and the mainland hub for the Skagit Valley. Much of the downtown core lies along the east bank of the Skagit River, and a promenade provides views of the river. Travel on the Skagit River by small boat is possible in the vicinity and also along the North Fork and for some distance into the South Fork to Conway. Some moorage floats for small boats are located along the river bank. Edgewater Park, in West Mount Vernon, south of the bridge, has a launching ramp into the river. Fishermen catch several types of salmon, steelhead, and sometimes sturgeon in the Skagit. ⛵

Swinomish Channel
[18421, 18423, 18427]

Swinomish Channel Updates From The U.S. Army Corps of Engineers:

The Corps dredged in 2018 (finishing at the end of December). The areas dredged included shoals in the southern reach from Skagit Bay to Goat Island, at Hole in the Wall, near Shelter Bay and the Rainbow Bridge and the northern reach from Hwy 20 Bridge to Padilla Bay.

As of the last survey in March 2023, shoaling has occurred in all areas previously dredged. Notable shallow shoals occur immediately south and north of the Hwy 20 Bridge (Twin Bridges). Depths range from 10-12 feet, but shallower areas may occur. Sand waves also occur between Rainbow Bridge and the Hwy 20 bridge, with some sand wave peaks shallower than -12 ft.

The Swinomish Channel is very dynamic. Channel depths and the location of shoals can change rapidly, so boaters should still exercise caution when transiting.

The public can access the latest surveys at the following website: http://navigation.usace.army.mil/Survey/Hydro.

★ **Swinomish Channel (2):** Previously named Swinomish Slough, this natural channel has been dredged for many years.

The Swinomish Channel connects Skagit Bay on the south with Padilla Bay, near Anacortes, on the north. At the northern end, currents flood south and ebb north. The opposite is true at the southern end, resulting in the currents meeting at about the halfway point in the channel. Marked courses for both north and south approaches help boaters avoid the drying tidal flats and rocks that surround the entrances. See entry descriptions that follow. Because of extensive boat traffic, keep the boat's wake as low as possible. If docking at the town of La Conner, located along the channel, it is advisable to head into the current when approaching the dock. If you are unsure as to the direction of the current, a "Land Against Current" arrow is posted at the La Conner Landing fuel dock located midway between the two guest floats.

Entry from the south: Yachtsmen should not turn into the marked channel until the range markers in Dugualla Bay on Whidbey Island are lined up. Before turning east, the boat must be north of the red buoy that marks the southern side of the channel. Next, proceed eastward in the channel, passing to the north of Goat Island. Watch your depths. The channel turns to port at Hole In The Wall. Steep banks are on both sides after the channel curves to port. Shelter Bay, on the port side, is a well established residential community located on Swinomish Tribal lease land. It is home to a 300 slip marina, golf course, many private docks and a yacht club. Guest moorage and reciprocal moorage is available. On the starboard shore there is a shipyard and beyond that is the Rainbow Bridge with a launching ramp at its base. On the other side of the bridge is the town of La Conner. Moorage is available at La Conner Marina and city-owned private floats.

Shelter Bay Marina: {48° 22' 56" N, 122° 30' 41"} Permanent & guest moorage, slips 36'-50', 30 amp power, water, restrooms, showers, private pump-out, oil deposit, boat launch. 360-466-3805.

Entry from the north: From Padilla Bay, keep the red buoys, which line the channel, to starboard, and the cans to port. Do not attempt to cut inside the first (northernmost) red buoy. Keep a watch for commercial crab pot markers. The first bridge is a seldom used railroad bridge. Onshore beyond the railroad bridge, the Swinomish Casino and Lodge is to starboard and Twin Bridges Marina lies to port. A large concrete obstruction, which bares at low tide, lies on the east shore of the channel between the highway bridges and the railroad swing bridge. The Swinomish Channel Boat Launch is at the east approach to the bridge over the channel. Note: the bottom of the ramp is exposed at low tides, wind, currents, and close quarters can make maneuvering from ramp difficult. Navigational range markers for the channel lead to a turn to starboard at the northerly entrance to the town of La Conner. The two Port of Skagit County's La Conner Marina moorage basins are to port after this turn as is the town of La Conner. The Swinomish Reservation is on the west shore.

Twin Bridges Marina: {48° 27' 21.02" N, 122° 30' 37.80" W} North Swinomish Channel. Heated, indoor dry stacked storage, boats to 35' or 22,000 lbs. Inboard/outboard engine repairs onsite, private pump-out. 360-466-1443.

La Conner
[18427]

★ **La Conner (3):** The Rainbow Bridge, built in 1957, is named for its graceful shape. Painted orange (the original primer color that the locals loved), it is a distinctive landmark in this friendly town and historic village on Swinomish Channel. WSDOT data shows the bridge's navigable clearance as 75 feet vertically, 360 feet horizontally. Moorage is available at both basins in the Port of Skagit's La Conner Marina, at city owned floats along the Channel, and at restaurant facilities. The south basin guest docks are only a block from one end of La Conner's shopping district. During summer, there is a golf cart shuttle service from the north basin guest docks. Specialty shops along the waterfront and side streets are open daily, year round. High quality goods, art galleries, three museums and a variety of restaurants attract thousands of visitors from distant places. Don't miss the town's boardwalk for exceptional views of the Swinomish Channel. The Chamber office/Visitor Center open Monday - Friday is located at 210 Morris St. La Conner is the oldest town in Skagit County, dating to the first white settlers in 1864. Thomas Hayes opened a trading post on the site that is now Totem Pole Park. Shortly after, John S. and Louisa A. Conner purchased the post and

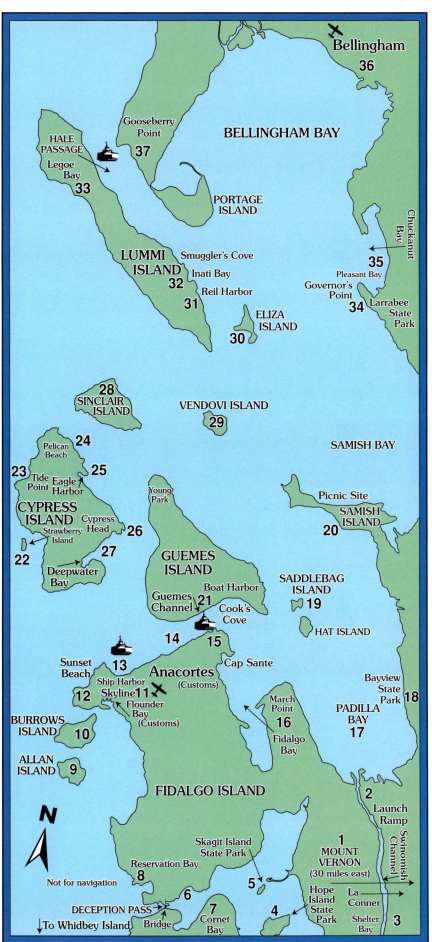

established a post office. The town's original name of Swinomish, was changed to honor Mrs. Conner. From its heritage as a trading post and port-of-call for steamships, the town has retained and restored much of its picturesque New England waterfront flavor. The surrounding farmlands were reclaimed from the river and the sea by diking and draining the land. In spring, extensive bulb fields bloom into a maze of yellow, red, and lavender.

The Skagit County Historical Museum affords beautiful views of these farmlands, looking east to the Skagit Valley. In addition, the museum offers a large selection of interesting and unusual pioneer memorabilia. 360-466-3365. The Gaches Mansion, built in 1891, is home to the Pacific NW Quilt & Fiber Arts Museum, showcasing fiber arts from around the world. 360-466-4288. The Museum of Northwest Art features internationally recognized Pacific Northwest artists and hosts a variety of events. 360-466-4446. On First Street, the Volunteer Fireman Museum houses a circa 1848 fire engine that was used during the 1906 San Francisco earthquake fires.

There are things to do in La Conner nearly every weekend; major events include the *La Conner Daffodil Festival* in March, *Tulip Festival* in April, *Community Celebration* on July 4th, the *La Conner Classic Boat and Car Show* in August, *Beer on the Slough - Beer Fest* in October. *Art's Alive* - an art festival and invitational art show in November, and the *Christmas Lighted Boat Parade & Community Tree Lighting with Santa* in December. For more details, visit www.LoveLaConner.com.

Walk-around: Stroll along La Conner's boardwalk, through historic neighborhoods with carefully restored homes or buy a picnic lunch and walk to Pioneer Park, located at the eastern entrance of the Rainbow Bridge. There are kitchen facilities, picnic tables, fireplaces, restrooms, and an amphitheater. Or walk a little further to Conner Waterfront Park, on the south side of the Rainbow Bridge, to enjoy picnic tables, waterfront access, and one of a kind bridge views.

★ **Port of Skagit's La Conner Marina:** The La Conner Marina, owned and operated by the Port of Skagit, is an easy cruise from the Seattle area to the south and from B.C. ports to the north. Located on the Swinomish Channel at the north end of the Town of La Conner, the marina offers a friendly atmosphere and outstanding customer service for tenants and guests. The marina offers 2,400 feet of transient moorage on F and G docks and nearly 500 permanent moorage slips. See our advertisement on this page. The marina office is located between the two boat basins, just a few blocks from downtown La Conner. Visit www.portofskagit.com. 613 North 2nd St., La Conner, WA, 98257, Mailing Address: PO Box 1120, La Conner, WA, 98257. Telephone: 360-466-3118. VHF 66A.

La Conner Landing: Ethanol free gas, diesel, pump-out, snacks, pop, ice, bait/tackle. 360-466-4478.

La Conner Maritime Service: {48.24.5 N, 122.29.41 W} Complete boatyard services, repairs, haul-out to 110-tons/24' beam. In the north marina basin. 360-466-3629.

⚓ Swinomish Tribal Park Floats: Moorage on west shore of channel for tribal members only.

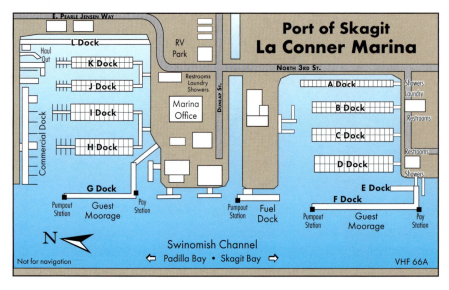

★ **Port of Skagit's La Conner Marina:** Tucked into the east side of the Swinomish Channel, the La Conner Marina is a premier destination for recreational boaters, commercial fishers and marine-related businesses and manufacturers. Located within easy walking distance from the great shopping and dining of downtown La Conner, the marina is a clean, well-maintained facility where we provide outstanding customer service for visitors and tenants alike. Just as important, it's an easy two-hour cruise from the marina into the heart of the beautiful San Juan Islands. The La Conner Marina features two separate moorage basins, together covering about 24 acres.

La Conner Marina has 366 covered moorage slips, 131 open moorage slips and 2,400 lineal feet of guest dock space for overnight moorage.

Boaters' services include: fuel dock, two waste pump-out stations (free), boat service and repairs, yacht sales, haul-out slip with sling hoist, power and water, WiFi, restrooms, showers and laundry, glass, metal and paper recycling and key-fob security.

La Conner Marina
www.portofskagit.com
P.O. Box 1120
613 N. 2nd Street
La Conner, WA 98257
Office: 360-466-3118
VHF Channel 66A

★⚓ **Hope Island Marine State Park (4):** This island park in Skagit Bay has four mooring buoys. Anchoring is also possible. There are primitive campsites, trails, a vault toilet, and a lovely beach. No fresh water, no fires (campfires allowed), no garbage disposal. 360-675-3767. ▲⛺☥

★⚓ **Skagit Island Marine State Park (5):** Two mooring buoys are located on the northwest side of the island. Campsites are primitive and include a Cascadia Marine Trail site. No fresh water, no garbage deposit. A trail encircles the island. Depths between Skagit Island and Kukutali Preserve do not permit passage. According to local legend, Skagit Island was the hideout for turn of the century burglar/smuggler, Henry The Flying Dutchman Ferguson, a member of Butch Cassidy's Hole In The Wall Gang. 360-675-3767. ▲☥

Kiket Island/Kukutali Preserve: In 2010 Kiket Island and Flagstaff Point were formally designated as the Kukutali Preserve. Owned and managed jointly by the Swinomish Indian Tribal Community and Washington State Parks, this preserve is open for public daytime use. Picnic site, portable toilets, 2 miles of walking trails. The waters are fun to explore by kayak or canoe. No motor boats, hunting, fishing, or shellfishing. Flagstaff Island is off limits to protect rare and unique ecosystems. No pets or livestock. The coves near Flagstaff Point are closed to landing kayaks, canoes and dinghies from July through September. 360-675-3767.

★ **Similk Bay (5):** This wide, shallow bay has calm weather anchorage in the outer portion. Often used for log storage, it is open to south winds.

Dewey Beach: This residential area was once a mill townsite. Shoals extend some distance off the beach and drop off suddenly. Anchorage is possible outside the shoals, but the area is open to strong currents and winds.

Deception Pass   Photo © Trish Norberg

Deception Pass Vicinity
[18421, 18423, 18427]

Deception Pass & Canoe Pass (6): The pass narrows to 200 yards at Pass Island. Passage at or near slack water is recommended. Currents run to eight knots and eddies form near the shores. Passage need not be difficult if wind and tide are considered. During strong westerlies, dangerous swells, tide rips, and overfalls may be encountered. Canoe Pass, the narrowest portion, is located on the north side of the main pass. Some boaters prefer it, believing that currents are milder. It has a submerged rock lying on its north side, at the bend. West of the bridge, Lottie Bay, an indentation on Fidalgo Island, offers shelter in an emergency, but nearly dries on a minus tide. If traversing the pass after dark, lights from the bridge and the headlights of passing cars create an eerie sight when looking up from the water.

The passage, first charted by the Spanish in 1791, was named Boca de Flon. In 1792, Captain George Vancouver sighted the indentation, but did not recognize it as a passage separating two land masses. Master Joseph Whidbey made that discovery and Vancouver appropriately named it Deception Pass. He also named the large island to the south in honor of Whidbey. Before the turn-of-the-century, a bridge was envisioned to link Whidbey and Fidalgo Islands. Captain George Morse, credited as the original promoter of the project, was of the opinion that Pass Island was placed there to be a pier for the bridge. A model of the proposed bridge was exhibited at the 1909 Alaskan-Yukon Exposition. However, it was 1934 before the project was funded. A Public Works Project, the bridge was built with workers from the Civilian Conservation Corp and from a penal colony located at a quarry near the site. Shortly after opening in 1935, unofficial tallies showed that 3,000 to 5,000 vehicles crossed the bridge daily. Today, 17,000 vehicles cross this well traveled bridge every day. The bridge was declared a National Monument in 1982.

★⚓ **Deception Pass State Park:** This thickly forested park covers much of northern Whidbey Island and some land on Fidalgo Island. It has campsites, utility spaces, kitchens with shelters, restrooms, showers, a group camp, and learning center. The park provides five saltwater boat ramps, plus 710 feet of saltwater dock. Boating facilities are in Cornet Bay and Bowman's Bay (Sharpe Cove) on Fidalgo Island. ☥▲⛺

★ **Cornet Bay (7):** When entering or exiting Cornet Bay, shoals make the west side of Ben Ure Island unnavigable. Proceed in the channel between the markers. Located at the head of the bay are a marina and repair services. Deception Pass State Park land rims the bay. Several large concrete launch ramps are equipped with side floats. Park floats, dinghy float, restrooms, and waste pump and dump are provided. Moorage fees collected year around. Other state park acreage with saltwater access is on Fidalgo Island. (See Bowman's Bay description.) 360-675-3767, Campsites: 888-226-7688. ☥

Deception Pass Marina: {48° 23' 42" N, 122° 37' 16"} Permanent moorage, transient moorage if space is available, 30 amp power, water, non-ethanol gas, diesel, propane, groceries, beer & wine, ice, bait/tackle. 360-675-5411.

E.Q. Harbor Service & Sales: New/used boats, motors, trailers, and an outboard motor repair/service. 360-679-4783.

Walk-around: It is a pleasant stroll along the road to Hoypus Point to the road-end turn around. Until the completion of the Deception Pass Bridge, a ferry connected Whidbey Island with Blaine Point on Fidalgo Island from this site. A feisty lady named Berte Olson owned and operated the ferry and was the first female captain in the State. Ferry fares were 50 cents per vehicle and 10 cents per passenger. A small gravel beach has views of Mount Baker, Fidalgo, Skagit, and Hope Islands.

Fidalgo Island
[18421, 18423, 18427]

★ **Fidalgo Island:** This island, which some say is shaped like a dog's head, is separated from the mainland on the east by the Swinomish Channel. Bridges cross the channel. Anacortes is the largest city on the Island. To the south, the Deception Pass Bridge connects Fidalgo with Whidbey Island. Fidalgo is named for Lieutenant Salvador Fidalgo of the Spanish ship San Carlos. It is known as "The Heart of the Island Empire".

★⚓ **Bowman Bay (Reservation Bay) (8):** Check your charts and beware of Coffin and Gull Rocks in the entrance. Some of the entrance rocks are covered at higher tides and, near high tide, it is easy to mistake Gull Rocks for Coffin Rocks. It is possible to anchor in the bay, but it is exposed to swells from the strait. Once inside, favor the southeast

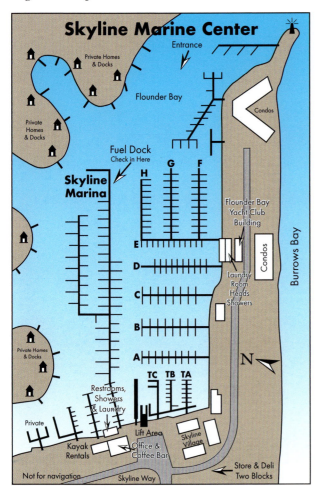

area of the bay in depths of 12-18 feet. There is a dock, campsites (Cascadia Marine Trail sites are south of the pier), launch ramp, and restrooms. Sharpe Cove is located behind some rock out-croppings, in a niche on the northwest side of the bay. Bowman Bay Pier no longer accessible. 360-675-3767. ▲

★ Sharpe Cove (8): A wharf with floats are found in this protected cove. Anchorage is not recommended in this area of Bowman Bay. On shore are cookout shelters, tables, no showers, restrooms. 360-675-3767. 𝄞

Walk-around: A short walk away is Pass Lake, a serene, pastoral lake where fishing is limited to non-powered boats and the use of artificial flies. Another walk is to Rosario Bay to view the statue of The Maiden of Deception Pass.

Rosario Bay: Anchorage is not recommended. There are picnic sites, a kitchen, and mooring buoys that are seasonally available. An underwater park, popular for scuba diving is located south of Rosario Head. Private homes, state park lands, and a college marine facility occupy the shore. There is also a red cedar carving of The Maiden of Deception Pass. It symbolizes Ko-kwal-alwoot, a mythical, self-sacrificing Samish maiden, who gave herself to the gods of the sea, and who safely guides travelers through the passage. Scenes for the movie, The Postman, were filmed here. 𝄞

★ **Burrows Bay:** This long, steep-sided bay on Fidalgo Island's west shore, stretches from Langley Bay, on the south, to Flounder Bay on the north. Avoid Williamson Rocks, a National Wildlife Refuge. Biz Point shelters a community-owned wharf with private mooring float and several private buoys. Beware of reefs in this vicinity. Much of Burrows Bay is open to the southwest and is seldom used as an anchorage. A portion, Alexander Beach, has homes fronting a lovely sandy beach. Temporary anchorage, perhaps as a dinner stop in settled weather to enjoy the sunset, is possible.

Allan Island (9): Named for a naval war hero, this Island was purchased in 1992 by billionaire and Microsoft co-founder Paul Allen. Allen sold the Island in 2013 for $8 million. There are no public facilities.

★ **Burrows Island Marine State Park (10):** Anchorage is found fairly close to shore in Alice Bight, a niche on the northeast side of the island. Tidelands are private. Two Cascade Marine Trail campsites, vault toilet, no fresh water, no hiking trails. The Burrows Island Lighthouse, situated on the southwestern end of the island, warns boaters of the nearby Dennis Shoal and Lawson Reef. The park land around the lighthouse is nearly inaccessible, except for beachable craft landing in tiny Short Bay. Halibut fishing is good off Burrows Point and fishing for chinook is often good off Fidalgo Head. 360-376-2073. ▲

Anacortes
[18423, 18421]

★ **Anacortes:** This friendly, island city is a center for tourist facilities, restaurants, retail stores, and anything boating. Thousands of boats are moored on a permanent basis and hundreds more visit this "boater's paradise." Four full-service marinas, three public boat launches, boat storage, boat building and repair, diving and salvage, marine lumber, marine surveyors, and the list goes on. The weather here is also a plus for visiting boaters. Anacortes averages 26" of rain per year, roughly a foot less than the closest major city. July and August average less than an inch of rain per month, and from April to September the island gets an average 20+ days of sun per month.

Because of its strategic location on the northern and western shores of Fidalgo Island, Anacortes is often frequented by larger vessels and is the terminus for State Ferries to the San Juan Islands and Sidney, British Columbia.

In 1876, when Amos Bowman platted the townsite, he envisioned Anacortes as a different sort of terminus - one for the transcontinental railroad. Bowman established a wharf, a store at what is now the Guemes Island Ferry landing, and a post office that he dedicated as the "Anna Curtis Post Office." The name was later modified and contracted into "Anacortes." By 1890 Anacortes was a bustling community. Fortunes changed with an unsuccessful attempt to move the county seat to Anacortes, and the announcement that Anacortes was not to be the Trans-Pacific port for the northwest. The economy deflated, many people left, and the city was a near ghost town. True to its pioneering spirit residents turned to fishing, fish processing, lumbering, millworking,

Visit us at boattravel.com

and eventually, to ship building. By 1912, the prosperous community had water and electric plants, and paved streets. During World War I ships were built in Anacortes shipyards and on Guemes Island. The next boom came during the 1950's when Texaco and Shell established refineries on nearby March's Point. Today, the refineries and related businesses are still prominent in the economy, as is tourism, fishing, ship building, repair, and other marine services.

US Customs and Border Protection Designated Port of Entry: Boaters entering from Canada may clear customs at Cap Sante Marina. Hours 8am-5pm, Summer 8am-8pm. Telephone: 360-293-2331. If no answer or after hours, call 1-800-562-5943. Stay on your boat. For more customs information see Important Notices between Chapters 7 and 8 in this guide.

An overhead view of Anacortes and Cap Sante Marina

Photo © Chris Teren / TerenPhotography.com

★ **Flounder Bay & Skyline (11) [18421]:** This well sheltered basin is accessed from an entrance on the northern shore of Burrows Bay. There are port and starboard lights at the entrance. Reduce speed before entry so as not to disturb or damage boats moored inside with your wake. The channel and entrance were dredged in 2010, allowing ample depth for boats at low tide. At low tide, deep draft boats should favor the west side of the channel. The inner harbor was dredged in 2016. Skyline is a large residential development of luxury waterfront and hillside homes overlooking Flounder Bay. There is a neighborhood grocery store and shops nearby. A large marina complex includes two full service boatyards, charter companies (including whale watching and fishing), water taxi services, kayak tours, and two yacht clubs with reciprocal privileges. Skyline has condominium boat moorage with slips for sale or lease. Guest moorage is available at Skyline Marine Center. The marina's fuel float is visible once making the turn into the inner bay from the entry channel.

★ **Skyline Marine Center:** Start your San Juan adventure at Skyline. Located on the Northwest side of Fidalgo Island, just minutes from beautiful downtown Anacortes, Skyline puts you closer than anyone else to the San Juan Islands. Offering indoor and outdoor dry storage, moorage, Travelift and monorail boat hoisting, fueling, pump-out services, laundry and shower facilities, and a coffee shop. Skyline Marine Center is everything a boater needs, all in one place. See our advertisement on page 80. Website: skylinemarinecenter.com. Email: info@skylinemarinecenter.com. Address: 2011 Skyline Way, Anacortes, Washington 98221. Telephone: 360-293-5134.

Walk-around: Walk north on Skyline Way to Sunset Avenue. Turn left and walk down the hill to Washington Park and Sunset Beach. See description below.

★ **Washington Park & Sunset Beach (12):** This 220-acre, city-owned park sits on the western shores of Fidalgo Island and offers campsites, boat launching ramp with side boarding floats, sheltered stoves, tables, playground areas, showers and restrooms. A 2.2-mile loop road, as well as an extensive single track trail system, encircles the park. Beaches of small gravel make landing small boats feasible. Scuba diving between Green Point & Fidalgo Head. Campground and boat launch information: 360-293-1927. Other information: 360-293-1918.

Ship Harbor (13): This is the eastern terminus of the ferries to the San Juan Islands and Sidney, British Columbia. Once named Squaw Harbor, whalers beached their boats here to scrape bottoms and make repairs. Later, fish canneries stood on pilings in the harbor.

Guemes Channel (14): Stretching from Shannon Point on the west to Cap Sante on the east, this channel separates Fidalgo and Guemes Islands. Currents exceed five knots at times, flooding east, ebbing west. If winds are strong from the west and you are heading west on a flood tide, heavy rips can be expected where Bellingham Channel (See current tables for Rosario Strait) meets Rosario Strait and Guemes Channel.

★ **Downtown Anacortes (15):** Transient moorage is found at the Port of Anacortes Cap Sante Marina, a sparkling public, park-like facility that boasts a boat launch, fuel dock, large boat slips and pedestrian friendly amenities such as restrooms, benches and tables. Anthony's Restaurant is located next to the marina. Adjacent to downtown Anacortes, this moorage is within easy walking distance of grocery stores, barber and beauty shops, a library with wifi access, hardware stores, marine chandleries, restaurants, pharmacies, post office, wine boutique, banks, furniture and antique dealers, real estate offices, and specialty shops. Many are located on Commercial Avenue, the 40-block-long street which begins at Guemes Channel on the north and stretches southward to the residential hillside.

Nearby, at 7th and R Ave., take a self-guided tour of the W.T. Preston, a historic steam paddlewheeler that for many years served to clear debris that threatened safe navigation in the Skagit River and area bays. The Anacortes Maritime Heritage Center features artifacts and displays illustrating the historical significance of the snagboat and other nautical notables. The nearby Depot Arts & Community Center is housed in a restored Railway Depot and features an art gallery. During the summer, the Anacortes Farmer's Market is held in front of the Depot on Saturdays from 9am-2pm, with community workshops and live music. The Jim Rice Park provides benches and view sites.

Anacortes is sometimes known as "Park Place," because 3,091 acres (almost half of the city's total acreage) are dedicated to community forest lands and parks that are teeming with recreational opportunities including boating, kayaking, fishing, scuba diving, whale and wildlife watching, camping, hiking, and biking. Seafarer's Memorial Park, south of Cap Sante Marina, has showers, restrooms, picnic tables and meeting rooms, as well as a pier and dock to accommodate rowing and sailing dinghies, canoes, and kayaks. In July and August, the Port of Anacortes hosts a Summer Concert Series here. Park landmarks include The Lady of the Sea sculpture, dedicated to those waiting for the return of commercial fishermen, and the Seafarer's Memorial honoring those who have lost their lives while engaged in marine oriented occupations. Other parks include Lower Cap Sante Bluff (Rotary) Park, and Causland Park on 8th Street. The latter, entered on the National Register of Historic Places in 1981 features unique stone mosaics in the walls and other structures, and has long been a popular attraction. The Anacortes Museum, housed in a landmark Carnegie Library, is across the street. Nearby, Anacortes Community Theatre presents spring and fall musicals, as well as comedies and dramas the rest of the year. 360-293-6829.

From performance arts to visual arts, Anacortes takes pride in its reputation as a haven for artists. Many display their works at local shops and at the popular *Anacortes Arts Festival*, held on the first full weekend in August. Evening art walks are held year-round on the First Friday of every month. Bill Mitchell, a local artist, has hand painted more than 100 murals on downtown buildings portraying Anacortes pioneers and historical scenes reproduced from historic photographs. Anacortes' historic past and connection with the sea is also celebrated in fun-filled annual community events including the Anacortes Boat and Yacht Show in mid-May, the *Waterfront Festival* in early June, *Shipwreck Day* in mid-July, and a Crab Pot Christmas Tree as part of the island's *Coastal Christmas* in mid-December. In addition to these events, there are year round events for every interest - quilts, derby fishing, wine, craft beer, antiques, motorcycles, and more. For a list of events or for more community information, visit www.anacortes.org.

Page 82 Chapter 6 GATEWAY ISLANDS & MAINLAND

★ **Cap Sante Marina:** {48° 30.70' N, 122° 36.18' W} By Cap Sante Head, Cap Sante Marina is a modern year round, all weather marina with all the amenities you could need. The 1,000 slip marina located in Anacortes, one of the boating capitals in the Northwest, is centrally located between Vancouver B.C. and Seattle. Cap Sante Marina is also close to Downtown Anacortes' restaurants, shops and any marine service a boater could want. See our advertisement on the inside front cover and on page 83. For more information visit www.portofanacortes.com or call 360-293-0694. Email: marina@portofanacortes.com. Address: 1019 "Q" Avenue, Anacortes, Washington 98221. Fax: 360-299-0998. Harbormaster's Office Telephone: 360-293-0694. VHF 66A U.S.

Anchor Cove Marina: {48° 31' 6" N, 122° 37' 15" W} Condominium ownership marina. Owners rent slips independently short/long term listings at www.anchorcovemarina.com. No transient moorage.

Anacortes Marina: {48° 30' 7" N, 122° 36' 18"W} Annual lease, covered/open moorage, limited liveaboards, power, water. 360-293-4543.

Fidalgo Marina: {48° 29' 49" N, 122° 35' 60" W} Private, condo moorage. Owners may sell their condo slips privately. Laundry, showers, wifi, hot tub/sauna, parking. 360-299-0873.

Guemes Channel Marina formerly Lovric's Sea-Craft Inc.: Located on the Anacortes waterfront on Guemes Channel. 360-293-2042.

Marine Supply and Hardware: Oldest marine supplier operating on the West Coast of the Americas. Rope, blocks, hardware, fasteners, chain, crab pots, brass, decor accessories, galley ware, lamps, rain gear, charts, marine paint. 360-293-3014

North Harbor Diesel: Parts, mechanical/electrical services, repairs, maintenance. Haul-out up to 65'/45 tons, dry storage. 360-293-5551.

Seattle Yachts Service: Full service boatyard, 50-ton travelift beam to 18', boat sales. Fuel dock, retail store, electronics, inflatable boats. 360-293-3145.

March Point (16): Two oil refineries, a waterfront beach area with parking, launching ramp, and RV parking are found on this peninsula.

Padilla Bay To Boundary Bay
[18421, 18423, 18427, 18429, 18430]

Padilla Bay (17): [18427] The entrance to Swinomish Channel is in the southwest part of this shallow bay. Bayview State Park. About a quarter of a mile from the park, the Brezeale Interpretive Center sit on the Padilla Bay National Estuarine Research Reserve (one of 29 National Estuarine Research Reserves in the U.S.).

★ **Bayview State Park (18):** Located on Padilla Bay, west of the city of Burlington, this park is often isolated from navigable water by extensive drying flats and at high water is only accessed by shallow draft boats. The park has tent and utility spaces, six cabins, restrooms, showers, sheltered and unsheltered picnic sites. Activities include fishing, swimming, hiking, and scuba diving. A high-tide only use boat launch, operated by the Dept. of Ecology, is located three blocks south of the park. Park Info: 360-757-0227. Reserve Campsite: 888-226-7688.

Hat Island: Drying flats of Padilla Bay rim the eastern shore of this island. Crabbing is popular. The lack of beaches or coves, and direct exposure

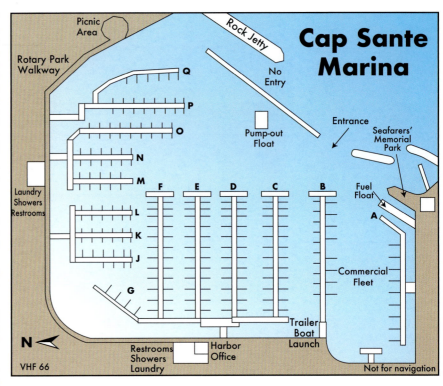

to Guemes Channel winds and currents makes this spot unattractive for anchorage.

★ **Saddlebag Island Marine State Park (19):** This 24-acre marine park (including Dot Island) is east of Guemes Island and north of Anacortes. There is a bay on the north side and another on the south (open to southwest winds). Anchor in either one, depending on wind direction. Onshore are campsites, and a composting toilet, but no fresh water. Marine trail sites are on the south side of the island. Surrounding waters are good crabbing grounds. The Padilla Bay tide flats make the eastern side of the islands unnavigable.

Huckleberry Island: This Island belongs to the Samish Indian Nation. Limited anchoring restricts usage, however there is a small beach for beachable boats. No camping or fires. Contact 360-293-6404 for information.

Samish Island (20): Drying flats prevent anchorage along much of the shore, except at high-tide. On the north, toward shore, there is a picnic spot on a wooded cliff with steps leading down to the beach, first come-first served.

Guemes Island (21): Guemes was named after Senor Don Juan Vicente de Guemes Pacheco y Padilla Orcasites y Aguayo, Conde de Revilla Gigedo, Viceroy of Mexico who funded an expedition of the first Europeans to see the Island in 1792. The Natives who lived here had another name, though. Ken Hansen, chairman of the Samish Tribal Council, said the English translation is Dog Island. Weaving was a specialty of the Samish women and large white Pomeranian type dogs were raised as a source of weaving wool. Guemes Island is still known locally as Dog Island. There are two reefs (west side and north end) both marked by buoys. No facilities for boats, except for boat ramps and private buoys. A ramp and five rental buoys are located at the Guemes Island Resort near the north shore. With buoy rental comes access to the resort's sauna, horseshoe pit, fire pit and guest lounge. A free buoy (upon availabilty) is for boaters who dinghy ashore to shop at the store (ice, beer, snacks) or enjoy a massage. Call ahead to secure a buoy or schedule a massage, 360-

293-6643. In Youngs Park, at North Beach, there are picnic sites, pit toilets, and a swimming beach. On the east side, there is temporary anchorage at Boat Harbor. Often called Square Harbor, this bay is about 400 yards deep and 400 yards wide with six foot depths at a minus tide. Farther south, Long Bay and Cook's Cove provide temporary anchorage on either side of Southeast Point. Open to southeast winds. One drawback to anchorage on the east side of Guemes are the tugs that often run at night between Anacortes and Cherry Point refineries. Their significant wakes, running abeam, can make for a long night. Currents can be strong in Guemes Channel, thus affecting anchorage. Car ferry service connects the south shore of the island with Anacortes. Immediately west of the Guemes Island Ferry dock is a public boat launch. The launch ramp ends at 0 foot tide level which complicates launching and retrieval at minus tides. The concrete surface also is often sanded over and four-wheel drive launch vehicles are essential. There is also a private ramp at Cook's Cove east of the ferry dock. Just up the street from the ferry landing, Guemes Island General Store stocks a range of groceries, beer, wine and snacks, or enjoy an ice cream cone. An onsite restaurant and bar offers live music most Wednesdays, Thursdays and weekends in the summer (all ages welcome). Also enjoy the one acre beer garden on the water located next to the ferry dock. 360-293-4548.

★ **Cone Islands State Park:** Three lovely islets in Bellingham Channel off the east side of Cypress Island are used by owners of small, beachable boats. Good fishing is often found in the vicinity.

★ **Strawberry Island (22):** This is not a recreation site, there are no facilities on shore and no camping is allowed. Visit Pelican Beach or Cypress Island for recreation sites. Anchorage is possible off the Cypress shore, but it is open to south winds. There are strong currents and submerged rocks near shore.

★ **Cypress Island:** This 6,000 acre island is located between Rosario Strait and Bellingham Channel, about six nautical miles northwest of Anacortes. Anchorage or mooring buoys are at Pelican Beach, Eagle Harbor, and Cypress Head. Most of the island

Visit us at boattravel.com

Cap Sante Marina

Leading amenities, unrivaled views, and outstanding customer service make Cap Sante Marina in Anacortes your destination for year-round adventures in the Great Northwest. Centrally located between Victoria, B.C., and Seattle, Washington, Cap Sante offers more than 100 guest slips and accommodates vessels up to 130'. And our beautiful marina is within walking distance of restaurants, boutique shops, and local festivities and amenities in Anacortes' delightful downtown.

Dock | Boat launch | Captain Charlie | West Basin Esplanade | Summer concert Series | Fuel dock

Cap Sante Marina | Anacortes, Washington 98221 | 360-293-0694
VHF 66 US (66a) | portofanacortes.com | marina@portofanacortes.com

is in state ownership, managed by the Department of Natural Resources for Conservation. Cypress Island protects more than 5,100 acres of high quality forest, wetland and grassland plant communities and surrounding state-owned tidelands, and includes the only low-elevation serpentine forest in Washington. There are more than 100 different species of birds living here. There are 21 miles of hiking trail accessed from several locations around the island (pets must be leashed while hiking trails). Locals refer to the waters at the south end of Cypress at Reef Point as the Devil's Hell Hole. The devil appears in the form of waves when strong winds meet opposing tide rips. Salmon fishing is excellent in season along the west side from Tide Point to Towhead Island. Bottom fishing is popular around the island.

Tide Point (23): North of this legendary fishing ground is a curving indentation which provides temporary anchorage. Try fishing along the shore from Tide Point to Eagle Cliff and the north tip of Cypress. An indentation near Eagle Cliff can be used for temporary anchorage.

★ Pelican Beach (24): This Department of Natural Resources recreation site on the NE portion of Cypress Island Natural Resources Conservation Area was named for a Pelican sail boating group which has made this a traditional camping site. Anchorage and mooring buoys (maximum 50' vessel) are open to north winds. Check swinging room to make sure there is adequate clearance from the beach. Small boats can be beached on the gravel beach. There are campsites including five Cascadia Marine Trail sites, picnic sites, fire pits, composting toilets, and access to 21 miles of hiking trails. Keep pets leashed. No fresh water. 360-856-3500. ▲♃⚲

Walk-around: A 1 mile trail leads to Eagle Cliff from a trail junction near Pelican Beach. The Eagle cliff trail is closed February 1 to July 15 to protect nesting raptors. Please keep pets on leash.

★ Eagle Harbor (25): Mooring buoys (maximum 50' vessel) within the harbor provide protection from north winds. Some buoys are located in shallow waters. On low tides, check depths and the swing of the buoys that are near shore. There is a composting toilet and access to 21 miles of hiking trails. Keep pets on leash. No fresh water. 360-856-3500.

★ Cypress Head (26): Cypress Head is a tombolo, a land mass separated from land by a sandspit. It lies within the Cypress Island Natural Resources Conservation Area, and is a Department of Natural Resources recreation site. Mooring buoys (max. 50' vessel) are in the northern bay. Anchorage is best in the northern bight also. The southern bay shallows and has stronger currents. Currents affect anchorage and the swing of the buoys. On low tides, check depths and the swing of the buoys that are near shore. There are campsites (including Cascadia Marine Trail sites), fire pits, two composting toilets, and 21 miles of hiking trails. Keep pets on leash. No fresh water. 360-856-3500. ♃▲⚲

★ Deepwater Bay, Secret Harbor (27): This bay on the eastern side of Cypress provides good, but limited anchorage for small craft. Fish pens are located here and the inner bay is shallow at low tide. This is the site of a private school. No trespassing.

Sinclair Island (28): Caution advised because of extensive shoals off the west and north shores. A small dock, located at Urban, is reported to be in disrepair and unusable. Limited anchorage can be found off the float. The sandy spit on the southwest tip provides some protection from northwesterly winds. In the late 1800's the legendary Smuggler Kelly (who traded in opium and illegal Chinese immigrants) had a farm located here.

Vendovi Island (29): Vendovi Island is a nature preserve owned by the San Juan Preservation Trust. It is open to visitors from 10am-6pm, Thurs-Mon, April-Sept. A breakwater protected dock is located on the north end of the Island, first come/first served, no overnight moorage and no anchoring in the bay. Several trails traverse the island and connect with two publicly accessible beaches. The restroom on the island is closed until further notice, so be sure to hit the head before you hit the island. For more information, 360-378-2461.

Eliza Island (30): This is a private island with a resident caretaker and homeowners association. A private dock (load/unload only) is on the west side of the island. Temporary anchorage is good both north and south of the peninsula that extends to the west and near Eliza Rocks. Good crabbing is found off the eastern shoreline, but it is lined with shoals and rocks. Eliza Island was once home to a chicken ranch, then a fish rendering plant, and later was used as a bombing range for military aircraft during World War II.

★ Lummi Island: This long, mountainous island is easy to identify. Anchorages are found in Legoe Bay on the west side, on Hale Passage in a spot north of Lummi Point, and in Inati Bay on the east side. Lummi Island is connected by car ferry to the mainland at Gooseberry Point. For fares and schedules, call 360-778-6200 or visit www.whatcomchief.org. The small, very rural community includes a general store, post office, library, restaurant and a B & B. Local artists host three "Art Tours" annually over Memorial and Labor Day weekends and the first weekend in December.

★⚓ Lummi Recreation Site (31): This Department of Natural Resources recreation area is located in a small, narrow inlet on the southeast shore, about two miles from the southern tip of the island and one mile south of Reil Harbor. Anchorage is limited and exposed to south winds. There are campsites, five Cascadia Marine Trail tent sites, and vault toilets. No drinking water. 360-856-3500.

Reil Harbor: Fair weather anchorage.

★ Inati Bay (32): This bay is located about a third of the way up on the southeast side of the island from Carter Point on the Hale Passage side. A rock in the entrance is barely covered at high-tide. Enter south of the white buoy. The bay is sheltered from all but northern winds and offers good anchorage in 30-40 feet of water. There are pit toilets, trails, and a beach. No garbage facilities. An old story tells of a bootlegger who, while being chased by the Coast Guard, went over the entrance rock in his small, flat-bottomed boat, while the Coast Guard boat, in hot pursuit, was not as lucky.

Smuggler's Cove: Limited anchorage.

Legoe Bay (33): There is anchorage inside Village Point, but it is open to west winds. A private boat launch and three private mooring buoys are located here. Boaters may use them for a fee, call 360-296-4963. ⚓

★⚓ Larrabee State Park (34): Dedicated in 1923, Larrabee was the first state park in Washington. Located seven miles south of Bellingham, this 2,748-acre camping park is accessible primarily by car. There are shelters, picnic tables, showers, tent, utility and primitive campsites, restrooms, and a high tide launching ramp into Wildcat Cove south of Governor's Point at {48° 39' 41.04" N, 122° 28' 42.96" W}. Swimming, scuba diving, hiking and biking are popular activities. 360-676-2093. ♃ ▲⚓⚲🚴

★ Chuckanut Bay & Pleasant Bay (35): While open to the west, this long indentation in the eastern shore of Bellingham Bay offers shelter on both the north and south ends. The northern portion has anchorage behind the peninsula, offering protection from northwest winds. Anchorage is good, mud bottom. It is possible to dinghy to public

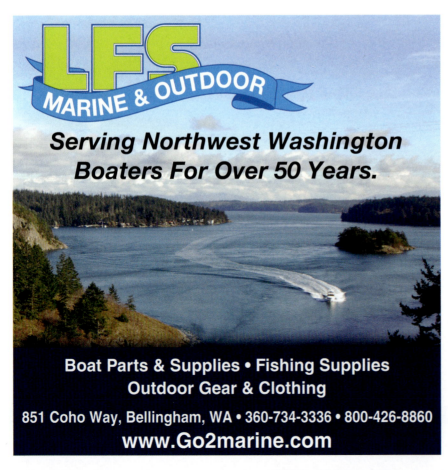

Serving Northwest Washington Boaters For Over 50 Years.

Boat Parts & Supplies • Fishing Supplies
Outdoor Gear & Clothing

851 Coho Way, Bellingham, WA • 360-734-3336 • 800-426-8860

www.Go2marine.com

GATEWAY ISLANDS & MAINLAND   Chapter 6   Page 85

tidelands north of the trestle. Because it dries, enter this lagoon on an incoming tide. A second, tiny anchorage with some protection from the north, is found at the tip of the peninsula, north of Chuckanut Rocks. Chuckanut Rocks, which rim the outer edge of the bay, are hazards as are rocks in the vicinity of Chuckanut Island, farther south. Caution advised. The third anchorage is in Pleasant Bay, inside Governor's Point. It offers good anchorage with protection from south winds. Salmon fishing is often good in the immediate area.

Bellingham

[18421, 18423, 18424]

★ **City of Bellingham (36):** Moorage is available at the Port of Bellingham's Squalicum Harbor and Fairhaven moorage, or for those with reciprocal privileges with the Bellingham Yacht Club. Located on Bellingham Bay, this city is in a strategic location for visiting the San Juan Islands, the Canadian Gulf Islands, and the mainland coast northward to the City of Vancouver and Desolation Sound.

Bellingham is also adjacent to the I-5 freeway, 54 miles south of Vancouver, B.C. and 86 miles north of Seattle. Ground travel options are plentiful - buses, trains, taxis, and rental car services are all available. Several airlines also fly out of Bellingham International Airport. Bellingham is the southern terminus for the Alaska State Ferry System, as well.

The city contains a lively mix of excellent restaurants, art galleries, specialty shops, department stores, motels, hotels, bed and breakfast inns, and colleges. In addition to shopping, other activities include whale watching tours, tennis, swimming, golfing, fishing, sailing races, beachcombing, picnicking, kite flying, sail boarding, rowing, hiking, camping at state parks in the vicinity or enjoying local city parks. A 2-mile promenade rims Squalicum Harbor, providing opportunities for exercise, shopping, and dining. A visit to the Marine Life Center brings you up close and personal with sea creatures in aquariums and touch pools.

Points of interest in downtown Bellingham include the beautifully restored 1927 Mount Baker Theatre, that offers a full season of nationally touring artists. 360-734-6080. The Whatcom Museum has a wonderful collection of fine art, Native American artifacts, and historical items, (many that highlight the city's colorful maritime history). The Museum's campus includes the historic 1892 Old City Hall; the Lightcatcher building housing fine art galleries and the Family Interactive Gallery; and the Syre Education Center, an old firehouse that is home to a photo archive and a collection of taxidermy birds,. 360-778-8930. A few blocks away, the SPARK Museum of Electrical Invention exhibits a world-class collection of early scientific apparatus dating from the 1600's continuing through the 1940's and the Golden Age of Radio. 360-738-3886. Western Washington University's outdoor sculpture collection showcases artworks and sculptures throughout the campus.

★ **LFS Marine & Outdoor:** LFS Marine & Outdoor is located within easy walking distance of the docks at Bellingham's Squalicum Harbor. The well-stocked store carries a large selection of fishing tackle, rods and reels, crab and shrimp gear and other recreational fishing supplies. Safety equipment, rope, anchors, paint, cleaning supplies and marine hardware are available year round. The store also has a great selection of rain gear, outdoor clothing and shoes, including Columbia, Grunden's, Xtratuf, Merrell, Smartwool, Chaco, TEVA, Helly Hansen, Under Armour, Keen, Guy Cotten and Woolrich. Boaters looking for fun will enjoy the many marine-related books, toys and Pacific Northwest souvenirs. See our ad on page 84. Address: 851 Coho Way, Bellingham, Washington 98225. Telephone: 1-800-426-8860 or 360-734-3336. Shop online at www.Go2Marine.com.

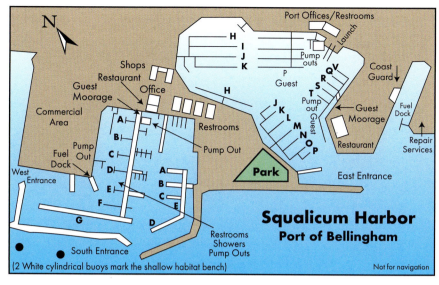

★ **Squalicum Harbor, Port of Bellingham:** {48° 45' N, 122° 30.5' W} Permanent & guest moorage, 110/120 volt, 20/30/50 ampere power, water, gas, diesel, repairs, showers, laundry, provisions. Visitor floats at Gates 3, 9, and 12. Pump-outs at all gates. Community meeting facility on the waterfront. Hotel and restaurants nearby. Additional moorage is found on buoys at the Port's Fairhaven moorage in South Bellingham Bay. Website: www.portofbellingham.com. E-mail: squalicum@portofbellingham.com. Address: 722 Coho Way, Bellingham, Washington 98225. Fax: 360-671-6149. Telephone: 360-676-2542.

Harbor Marine Fuel: (West Entrance Squalicum Harbor) Gas, diesel, oils, fuel additives, absorbent pads, ice. 360-734-1710.

Hilton Harbor Marina: Private dry moorage facility. Gas, hoist, haulouts to 30'/10,000 lbs., not equipped for sailboats. Beer and snack sales. 360-733-1110. Bitterend Boatworks onsite. Mechanical/electrical repairs, mobile services, painting, restoration. 360-676-2407.

Hotel Bellwether: {48° 45' 15.35" N, 122° 29' 52" W} Moorage with power/water for hotel guests (advanced reservation for room and moorage required, fee applies). Complimentary moorage while dining (must call ahead to reserve moorage). Lodging, restaurant, bar, sundries shop. Hotel: 360-392-3100. Restaurant: 360-392-3200.

★⚓ **Boulevard Park:** Located in South Bellingham, this beautiful two level park has viewpoints, bbq's, picnic tables, playground, restroom, interpretive displays, a coffee shop with wifi, and trails. The South Bay Trail fronts the shoreline and meets up with Taylor Dock just beyond the south end of the park. From here, one has access to the Fairhaven neighborhood. Taylor Dock has a pier with floats for temporary moorage (please observe the 2 hour limit). There are no public buoys off the park. Open to winds.

★ **Fairhaven:** Fairhaven is an historic district in Bellingham that is noted for its colorful, 19th century history. Fairhaven once had hopes of being the next Chicago and bustled with hotels, taverns, an opera house, concert garden, restaurants and brothels. Today, many red brick relics of Fairhaven's era survive in the quaint district's six square-blocks and are home to a variety of unique restaurants, pubs, coffee shops, delis, specialty shops, art galleries, antique shops, bookstores, parks and new waterside inns. Sidewalk tombstone markers offer glimpses of Fairhaven's past and what life was like in the late 1890's when more than 35 hotels and boardinghouses were built here to handle the influx of new settlers. This neighborhood also includes the Bellingham Cruise Terminal, home port to companies offering whale watching tours, day and sunset cruises and the southern terminus of the Alaska Marine Highway System. For Alaska Ferry information, 1-800-642-0066. www.dot.alaska.gov/amhs. Nearby Fairhaven Intermodal Station includes the Amtrak and Greyhound terminal.

Fairhaven Moorage: {48° 43' 18" N, 122° 30' 35" W} 600 feet of side-tie linear moorage (3 day limit) and 8 moorage buoys (May - Oct. for vessels to 38'). Water, garbage drop. Kayak/sailboat/SUP rentals. Bellingham Bay Community Boating Center: 360-714-8891.

Gooseberry Point (37): Ferry terminus of mainland-Lummi Island ferry. 360-778-6200.

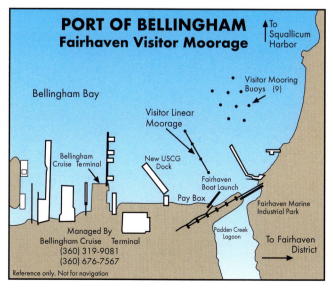

2024 Northwest Boat Travel

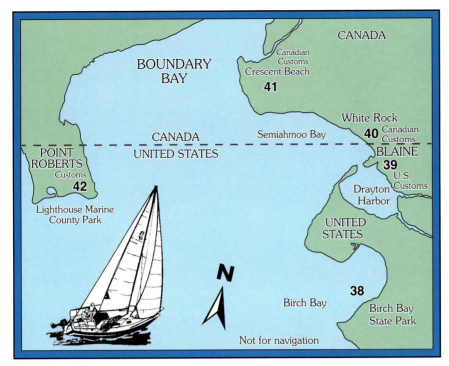

Fisherman's Cove Marina: {48° 43' 49" N, 122° 40' 8" W} Dry moorage only. Gas, hand-carried diesel, propane, boat ramp/parking (fee applies), hoist to 10,000 lbs. Convenience store nearby. 360-758-2450.

Sandy Point: This private residential development is located along the beach and on a system of inland canals that allow homeowners to moor their boats in front of their homes. The community has a small marina, a nine-hole golf course, swimming pool, and club house. The marina is public, but the other amenities are private. Considerable shoaling occurs at the entrance, watch depths and slow to no wake speed.

Sandy Point Marina: Permanent and overnight moorage, slips to 30', 50 amp power, water. Gas available during open hours (call for winter hours). Pumpout, boat launch ($20 includes parking). 360-384-4373.

Birch Bay (38): Birch Bay is very shallow. Summer cabins, sandy beaches, and swimming are popular here. Birch Bay State Park has a boat launch, basketball court, amphitheater, campsites, a kitchen shelter, picnic tables, restrooms, and showers. Park Info: 360-371-2800.

Birch Bay Village Marina: {48° 56' 7" N, 122° 47' 7" W} Private facility, but is a harbor of refuge in an emergency. 360-371-7744.

Semiahmoo Park: At the base of Semiahmoo Spit on the west side of Drayton Harbor, this park, identified by its totem pole, was once the site of a 19th century Indian trading post. There is an interpretive center, 1.5 mile trail, picnic sites, and a good clamming beach. The free Alaska Packer Association Museum is located here. Open Memorial Day through Sept, Fri-Sun, 1-5pm. A restored cannery bunkhouse can be rented as an event venue.

Semiahmoo Marina: {48° 59.30' N, 122° 46'W} Permanent moorage, transient moorage if space is available, gas, diesel, propane, 30 amp power (some 50 amp), water, showers, laundry, pump-out, wifi, marine supplies, provisions, café/coffee shop, dry rack storage. Marine parts delivery available. Semiahmoo Marina Yacht Club reciprocal moorage in fuel dock area. Resort, restaurant, golf nearby. 360-371-0440. VHF 68.

Boundary Bay & Drayton Harbor

[18421, 18423, Canadian Chart: 3463]

★ **Blaine (39):** Blaine, "The Peace Arch City," is a major customs port-of-entry for travelers crossing the border in their cars via the Interstate 5 crossing at International Peace Arch Park. For boaters, Blaine is a stop for those heading north or south along the mainland coast to and from Bellingham, the San Juan Islands, Point Roberts, and Vancouver, British Columbia. Boaters approach Blaine by entering Semiahmoo Bay, passing Semiahmoo Spit, and then proceeding in the channel to moorage at Drayton Harbor. North of Semiahmoo drying mud flats extend for nearly a mile. Use the red and green channel markers to get your bearings. Stay offshore when approaching Drayton Harbor, using a NOAA chart and fathometer for references. The channel's charted depth at mean low water is four fathoms. Semiahmoo, a resort, condominium and marina development is to starboard. To port is Blaine Harbor, a red triangle above the breakwater marks the entrance, beyond is a large moorage basin for small craft. A two lane public boat launch ramp is located at the end of Milhollin Drive and a Seafarer's Memorial is an attraction near the port facility. Marine Park, located across from Blaine Marina, has a nice walking trail, bike route, 4 picnic shelters, amphitheater, two whale sculptures, play area and a public restroom open during the summer. A visitors center is less than 1/2 mile from the park. Walk northeast on Marine Drive and turn right on Peace Portal for 1 block. Pick up a walking tour brochure that highlights many of the city's historic buildings, some dating back 100 years. Three blocks further on Peace Portal the Blaine Produce Market is held Saturdays, May to October. Restaurants, banks, shops, and a library are found in this vicinity.

A courtesy shuttle bus runs seasonally from the harbor to downtown and other area shopping. Check with the harbor office for the schedule. During the summer on weekends, a bicycle and foot passenger ferry links Semiahmoo Spit with Blaine Harbor, allowing boaters to explore the resort, park, and beaches on the west side of Drayton Harbor, and the town of Blaine on the east. The ferry is the historic boat Plover, a classic, 30 foot cedar-planked boat built during World War II. Blaine is also connected to area communities, including Bellingham, by daily bus service. Blaine's annual festivals include *Wings over Water Birding Festival* in mid-March, *Semiahmoo Regatta* in April, the *Old Fashioned Fourth* and the *Blaine Harbor Music Festival* in July, and the *Drayton Harbor Days Maritime Festival* in August. Nearby Peace Arch State Park features the International Peace Arch dedicated in 1921, beautiful gardens, picnic tables, and a rentable kitchen shelter. A calendar of annual events include concerts and sculpture exhibits. Park Info: 360-332-8221.

★ **Blaine Harbor:** {48° 59.30' N, 122° 46' W} Operated by the Port of Bellingham, this facility has moorage, laundry, showers, repairs, waste pump-out and dump. Gas & diesel is available at Semiahmoo Marina. Short walk to downtown Blaine. Easy access to freeway and Peace Arch Border Crossing to Canada. Please use caution when mooring in Drayton Harbor. Drayton Harbor is an environmentally sensitive shellfish harvesting area. Please do not discharge sewage or any other pollutants when anchored in this area. Holding tank pump-outs are available at Blaine Harbor and Semiahmoo Marina. During summer, a passenger ferry connects with Semiahmoo. See our advertisement on page 87. Internet site: www.portofbellingham.com. E-mail: blaineharbor@portofbellingham.com. Mailing address: 235 Marine Drive, Blaine, Washington 98231. Fax: 360-332-1043. Telephone: 360-647-6176. VHF 16/68.

On-Board Marine Services: Full service boatyard, 30-ton Travelift (beam to 15'). 360-332-5051.

★ **White Rock, British Columbia (40):** [18421, Canadian 3463] This seaside city of 21,000, located just north of the U.S. border, is home to Canada's longest pier at 1,542 feet (470 metres) and boasts an oceanfront promenade where you can stroll along the waterfront, take in the view, and visit the many shops and restaurants featuring local fare.

A restored 1913 BNR Station located near the foot of the pier has been converted into the White Rock Museum & Archives which features local history including the legends of the local Semiahmoo people and the iconic rock that sits on White Rock's shores. Known by the Semiahmoo as "P'Quals", the rock is a glacial deposit that is featured in Semiahmoo oral histories as the people who were survivors of the great flood.

White Rock lies along Semiahmoo and Boundary Bay. Nearby moorage is available at Crescent Beach Marina, a 10-minute drive away. (A small government dock for customs use only is located at the end of the Pier. This is not a public/commercial dock

Offering a wide variety of activities and attractions, such as water sports, bird watching, walking nature trails and public art, White Rock hosts many annual events such as the *Polar Bear Swim* (Jan. 1), Sunday Farmers Market (May-Oct.), *Canada Day by the Bay* (July 1), *TD Concerts at the Pier* series (July), *Sea Festival & Semiahmoo Days* (Aug. long weekend), *White Rock Arts Festival* (Oct.) and *Bright Walk in White Rock* (Dec.). For more information visit whiterockcity.ca/events.

GATEWAY ISLANDS & MAINLAND Chapter 6 Page 87

★ **Boundary Bay and Crescent Beach (41):** [Canadian 3463] Boundary Bay lies between the white cliffs at the eastern extremity of Point Roberts and Kwomais Point, 6.6 miles east-northeast. Much of the bay is filled with mud and sand flats. Boundary Bay Regional Park is on the western side of the bay. This region is rich in wildlife and has good fishing grounds. Marshlands are home to herons, ducks, eagles, and geese. Salmon, steelhead and cutthroat trout are abundant in the rivers that empty into Boundary Bay. Commercial crabbing may be present, watch for floats in the water.

In the northeast part of Boundary Bay, the Nicomekl and Serpentine River channels flow through Mud Bay. Crescent Channel light, 0.4 miles southwest of Blackie's Spit is shown from a dolphin with a starboard hand daymark. A marked channel leads up the Nicomekl, past Blackie's Spit (a nature park and bird sanctuary with walking trails), alongside the South Surrey BC neighborhood of Crescent, and onto the Crescent Beach Marina. Navigation is not difficult. Crescent Beach light, a flashing red light in the outer approach to Mud Bay, is shown from a dolphin with a starboard hand daymark. The channel is marked by port and starboard hand daymarks on piles or dolphins. Keep the red triangles to starboard when entering, and the green squares to port. (Red right returning.) Favor the port side because some of the red markers are on drying sand/mud. If possible, traverse the channel at half tide or better and on an incoming tide. A speed limit of four knots is posted in the Nicomekl River. After rounding Blackie's Spit and entering the Nicomekl River, Burlington Northern Railroad Bridge #69 comes into view. This is a swing bridge and when closed, the swing span has a clearance of nine feet at high water. The trestle has a vertical clearance of 12 feet at high water. Clearances are approximate and change with wind and tides. A height clearance gauge is located on the northwest end of the bridge. The swing span shows a red light when closed, and a green light when open. To request an opening, signal three long blasts on the horn or call VHF 66A or by phone 604-538-3233. The bridge is manned seven days a week from 0645 to 2215. Pass on the east side of the bridge both coming and going. Crescent Beach Marina is on the south shore, just past the bridge. The Surrey Public Wharf with a 40' side float, extends from shore at the site of Crescent Beach. Day anchorage can be found on the east side of the wharf. Depths are approximately nine feet. This residential and resort area has stores and restaurants near the wharf. The beach is good for swimming and a large municipal park is on shore. Historic Stewart Farms, located on the banks of this river, has been restored and takes visitors back to the turn of the century. Call Surrey Museum for more information. 604-592-6956.

Blaine Harbor Breakwater   Photo © Ruth Launam

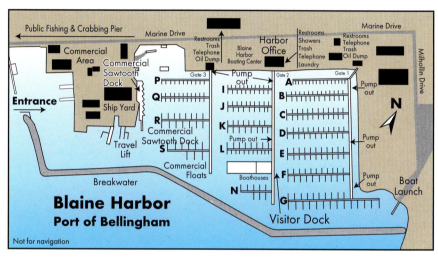

★ **Blaine Harbor:** Cruisers in the northern San Juan and Canadian Gulf Islands enjoy visiting our friendly 630 slip marina on Blaine's historic waterfront. Located right on the international border with Canada, views from the harbor include memorable sunsets over the Straits of Georgia and the iconic Peace Arch monument. Waterfront trails connect the full service marina to the quaint downtown where visitors will find friendly pubs, restaurants and cafes offering something for everyone including local oysters and ice cream. A new seaside playground at the marina has become a popular destination to play and watch the sunset. The harbor features modern concrete docks well protected by a heavy rock breakwater. The entrance to Blaine Harbor is marked by a red triangle to starboard when entering the breakwater

from Drayton Harbor. Visitors can follow signs on the breakwater to the 860 foot guest dock at Gate 2. Harbor amenities include holding tank pump-outs, NEW dock boxes, 30/50 amp 110v power, year-round potable water, clean restrooms, showers, laundry, and WIFI hotspot. Vessel haul-outs and repairs are available. The harbor has a public boat launch and parking. Fuel is available at nearby Semiahmoo Marina.
Internet: www.portofbellingham.com & www.portofbellingham.com/blaine.html & www.boattravel.com/blaineharbormarina.
E-mail: blaineharbor@portofbellingham.com. Address: 235 Marine Drive, Blaine, Washington 98230. Telephone: 360-647-6176. Fax: 360-332-1043. Monitor VHF 16.

★ **Crescent Beach Marina:** {49° 03' 23" N, 122° 52' 12" W} Located in historic Crescent Beach, this marina is the Customs port-of-entry. Moorage from 20' - 50' (year round), boathouses available to 75', transient moorage, 15 & 30 amp power, water, fuel- diesel, premium & mid-grade, full chandlery store, washrooms, laundromat, showers, repairs, parts, haul-outs, dry storage compound, launch ramp and a pump-out station. Close to shopping, fine dining, golfing. Thirty minutes to Vancouver. Please see our advertisement and marina map on page 158. Address: 12555 Crescent Rd, Surrey, B.C. V4A 2V4. Website: www.crescentbeachmarina.com. Telephone: 604-538-9666. Fax: 604-538-7724. VHF 66A.

★ **Point Roberts (42):** [18421, 3463] Point Roberts is a 4.9 square mile peninsula located on the western shore of Boundary Bay. While the peninsula connects to Canada, Point Roberts is part of the United States-the result of the establishment of the 49th parallel as the boundary between the two countries. Access to Point Roberts is possible by a 23 mile highway trip from Blaine, by air to the private airstrip, or by boat. By land it is necessary to cross the US-Canada border at Blaine, drive west to Tsawwassen, BC, and then re-cross the border into the U.S. at Point Roberts.

A large marina and a repair facility are located here. Restaurants, grocery and liquor store, mobile home and RV parks, a campground, bike rentals, post office, library, and banks are available. A newly renovated 18 hole golf course opened in 2018. The Blue Heron gallery featuring local artists is an interesting stop. Be sure to also visit the newly opened Point Roberts History Center located at 1437 Gulf Rd. Nearby Lighthouse Marine Park offers a stretch of beach on the tip of the peninsula, making it ideal for walking, beachcombing, picnicking, and enjoying panoramic views of Mount Baker, the Cascade Mountains, San Juan Islands, and Vancouver Island. Maple Beach Park on the northeast corner of Boundary Bay, has a mile of sandy beach and tidelands perfect for swimming and sunbathing. For wildlife enthusiasts, the Point Roberts area is rich in wildlife including orca whales, deer, eagles, heron and raccoons. Community events during the summer include the bi-annual *Point Roberts Garden Tour* and the *4th of July Parade*. For more information, www.pointrobertsnow.com. ▲⚓

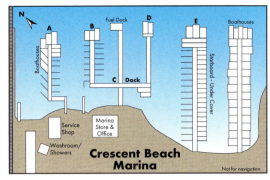

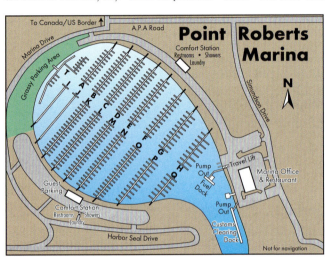

Point Roberts is a U.S. Customs & Border Protection Designated port-of-entry. The customs dock is the first dock to the right. Tie up and walk to the shack. The red phone dials automatically. Summer hours 8am-8pm, the rest of the year 8am-5pm. Info: 360-945-5211.

★ **Point Roberts Marina Resort:** {48° 58' 36" N, 123° 3' 51" W} Point Roberts Marina is superbly located for cruising to and from the San Juan Islands, Active Pass and the Gulf Islands and offers convenient on-site U.S. Customs Clearance. Check out the competitive moorage rates for overnight, monthly and yearly moorage slips with 30/50/100 amp power and water. Other marina amenities include showers, laundry, wifi, and free pump-out facility (slip-side pump-out arranged with advance notice, $5). Gas, diesel, and propane are available at the Fuel Dock where boaters can also purchase ice, bait, fishing licenses, beer/wine and convenience items. Westwind Marine provides mobile repair & service, rigging & mastwork. 360-637-2800. Full service restaurant on site, call Breakwaters at 360-945-2628. See our advertisement on this page. Website: www.pointrobertsmarina.com. Email: prmarina@pointrobertsmarina.com. Mailing address: 713 Simundson Dr., Point Roberts, WA 98281. Fax: 360-945-0927. Phone: 360-945-2255. VHF 66A.

Westwind Marine: Mobile service & repair (Point Roberts, Blaine, Birch Bay, Semiahmoo), rigging & mastwork. 360-637-2800.

★⚓ **Lighthouse Marine County Park:** Lighthouse Park lies at the southwest tip of Point Roberts. There are picnic shelters, barbeques, gravel beach, boardwalk, restrooms, potable water, playground and campgrounds with fire pits. Campsites and kitchen shelter can be reserved online at https://secure.itinio.com/whatcom/lighthouse with 48 hour notice. Park Info: 360-945-4911 or lighthouse@co.whatcom.wa.us. ▲⚓

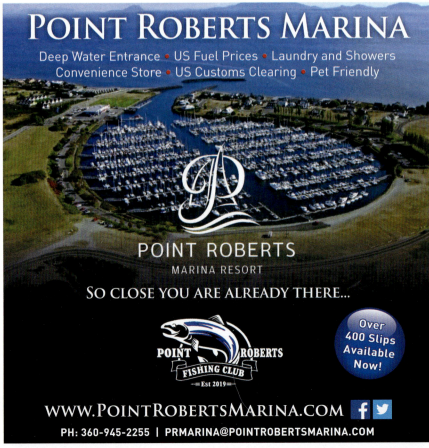

Crystal Water Beach — Photo © Jane Bordignon

Visit us at boattravel.com

Essential Supplies & Services

AIR TRANSPORTATION
Kenmore Air 1-866-435-9524
NW Seaplanes . . . 425-277-1590, 1-800-690-0086
San Juan Airlines. 1-800-874-4434
Seattle Seaplanes 1-800-637-5553

BOOKS / BOOK STORES
Evergreen Pacific Publishing 425-493-1451
The Marine Atlas. 253-872-5707

BUS TRANSPORTATION
Greyhound 1-800-231-2222
Greyhound, Bellingham. 360-733-5251
Skagit Transit 360-757-4433
Whatcom County 360-676-7433

COAST GUARD
Emergencies . . . . 911, 206-217-6001, VHF 16
Sector Puget Sound (office) 206-217-6200
Vessel Traffic 206-217-6152
Bellingham 360-734-1692

CUSTOMS/BORDER PROTECTION
Anacortes 360-293-2331
Canada Border Services Telephone Reporting Centre.
. . . . 1-888-226-7277
Point Roberts 360-945-5211
U.S. Customs Telephone Reporting. . . . 1-800-562-5943

FERRY INFORMATION
www.state.ak.us/ferry 1-800-642-0066
Guemes Island 360-293-6433
Lummi Island 360-778-6200
Washington State 1-800-843-3779

FISHING/SHELLFISHING INFO
Fishing Regulations 360-902-2500
24-hour Red Tide Hotline 1-800-562-5632
Shellfish Rule Change Hotline. 1-866-880-5431

FUELS
Cap Sante Marina 360-293-0694
Crescent Beach Marina . . 604-538-9666 VHF 66A
Deception Pass: Gas, Diesel . . . . 360-675-5411 VHF 16
Fisherman's Cove: Gooseberry Pt. Gas
. . . . 360-758-2450
Harbor Marine Fuels Bellingham. 360-734-1710
Hilton Harbor: Bellingham. Gas 360-733-1110
La Conner Landing: Gas, Diesel 360-466-4478
Point Roberts Marina: Gas, Diesel . .360-945-2255
Sandy Point Marina 360-384-4373
Skyline Marine Center, Anacortes . .360-293-5134
Semiahmoo Marina: Gas, Diesel. 360-371-0440 VHF 68

GOLF
Bald Eagle Golf Club, Point Roberts . . .1-866-460-0368
Semiahmoo Golf. 1-800-231-4425

HAUL-OUTS
Crescent Beach Marina . . 604-538-9666 VHF 66A
Hilton Harbor: Bellingham. 360-733-1110
La Conner Marina . . . . . . 360-466-3118 VHF 66A
La Conner Maritime Services 360-466-3629
North Harbor Diesel 360-293-5551
Seattle Yachts Service, Anacortes. 360-293-3145
Seaview North: Bellingham. 360-676-8282
Walsh Marine 360-332-5051

HOSPITALS
Anacortes Island Hospital. 360-299-1300
Bellingham 360-734-5400
Mount Vernon. 360-424-4111

MARINAS / MOORAGE FLOATS
Blaine Harbor . . . . 360-647-6176 VHF 16
Cap Sante Marina: Anacortes
. . . . 360-293-0694 VHF 66
Crescent Beach Marina . . 604-538-9666 VHF 66A
Deception Pass Marina. . . . . 360-675-5411 VHF 16
Deception Pass State Park: Sharp Cove
Fairhaven Visitor Moorage 360-714-8891
Guemes Channel Marina. 360-293-2042
La Conner Marina . . . . . . 360-466-3118 VHF 66A
Point Roberts Marina . . . . 360-945-2255 VHF 66A
Sandy Point Marina 360-384-4373
Semiahmoo Marina. . . . . 360-371-0440 VHF 68
Skyline Marine Center 360-293-5134
Squalicum Harbor . . . . 360-676-2542 VHF 16

MARINE SUPPLY STORES
Crescent Beach Marina . . 604-538-9666 VHF 66A
LFS Marine & Outdoor: Bellingham. .360-734-3336
Marine Supply & Hardware: Anacortes. . 360-293-3014
Seattle Yachts Service, Anacortes. 360-293-3145
West Marine: Anacortes 360-293-4262

PARKS
Department of Natural Resources. 360-856-3500
Washington State Park Info 360-902-8844
Washington Camping Reservations . . .1-888-226-7688
Whatcom County Parks 360-778-5850

PROPANE
Cap Sante Marina 360-293-0694
Deception Pass Marina. 360-675-5411
Fisherman's Cove: Gooseberry Pt. 360-758-2450
La Conner Marina . . . . . . 360-466-3118 VHF 66
Point Roberts Marina 360-945-2255
Semiahmoo Marina. . . . . 360-371-0440 VHF 68
Skyline Marine Center 360-293-5134

RAMPS
Bayview State Park: Padilla Bay
Blaine Harbor . . . . 360-647-6176 VHF 16
Blaine: Milhollin Road
Cap Sante Marina 360-293-0694
Crescent Beach Marina . . 604-538-9666 VHF 66A
Deception Pass State Park: Bowman Bay, Cornet Bay
Fisherman's Cove: Gooseberry Pt. 360-758-2450
La Conner: Sherman St. Boat Ramp
Larrabee State Park: Bellingham
Lighthouse Marine Park: Point Roberts
Point Roberts Marina . . . 360-945-2255, VHF 66A
Sandy Point Marina 360-384-4373
SR 20 Berentson Bridge: Swinomish Channel
Squalicum Harbor . . . . 360-676-2542 VHF 16
Washington Park: Anacortes

REPAIRS & SERVICE
Bitterend Boatworks: Bellingham 360-676-2407
Blaine Marine Services 360-332-3324
Crescent Beach Marina . . 604-538-9666 VHF 66A
E.Q. Harbor Service 360-679-4783
La Conner Maritime Services 360-466-3629
North Harbor Diesel: Anacortes 360-293-5551
Seattle Yachts Service, Anacortes. 360-293-3145
Seaview North: Bellingham. 360-676-8282

Squalicum Harbor   Photo © Robert James

Skyline Marine Center 360-293-5134
Walsh Marine 360-332-5051
Westwind Marine 360-637-2800

SCUBA DIVING SITES
Rosario Bay
Washington Park & Sunset Beach
Bayview State Park
Cypress Island
Larrabee State Park

SEWAGE DISPOSALS
Blaine Harbor: Pump, Dump. 360-647-6176
Cap Sante Marina: Pump, Dump. . . .360-293-0694
Crescent Beach Marina: Pump
. . . . .604-538-9666 VHF 66A
Deception Pass State Park: Cornet Bay . . Pump, Dump
La Conner Landing 360-466-4478
La Conner Marina: Pump. 360-466-3118
Point Roberts Marina:
  Pump, Dump. 360-945-2255
Semiahmoo Marina: Pump, Dump 360-371-0440
Seattle Yachts Service, Anacortes. 360-293-3145
Skyline Marine Center 360-293-5134
Squalicum Harbor: Pump, Dump. . . .360-676-2542
Twin Bridges Marina. 360-466-1443

TAXIS
Anacortes 360-708-6358
Bellingham 360-220-4990, 360-734-8294
Blaine 360-332-1960

TOWING
TowBoat U.S.- Anacortes 360-675-7900
TowBoat U.S. - Blaine, Bellingham 360-378-1111

VISITOR INFORMATION
Anacortes 360-293-3832
Bellingham . . . . .1-800-487-2032 or 360-671-3990
Blaine Visitors Bureau
. . . . 1-800-624-3555, 360-332-4544
La Conner 360-466-4778, 1-888-642-9284

WEATHER VHF
NOAA Recorded Message. 206-526-6087
Seattle: WX-1, WX-4

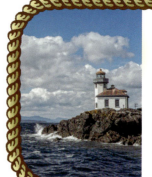

Chapter 7:
San Juan Islands

Blakeley, Decatur, Lopez, Shaw, Orcas, San Juan, Stuart, Waldron, Patos, Sucia, Matia, Barnes, & Clark Islands.

Lime Kiln Lighthouse on San Juan Island - photo © Chris Teren

Mount Baker appears behind Sucia Island — Photo © Chris Teren / TerenPhotography.com

★ See "Important Notices" between Chapters 7 and 8 for specific information on boating related topics such as boating safety, weather, U.S. & Canadian marine radio use, Vessel Traffic Service, security zones, Canadian & U.S. Customs, etc. Due to changing regulations, call ahead to verify latest customs information.

National Wildlife Refuges: Areas designated on charts by the initials NWR are National Wildlife Refuge lands. The San Juan Islands NWR has 83 islands, 81 are closed to the public to protect breeding colonies of seabirds, shorebirds, native plants and marine mammals. Boaters are requested to stay at least 200 yards away from these rocks and islands. Matia and Turn are the only Islands open to the public (moorage and camping through Washington State Parks.) To reduce disturbance to wildlife and habitats, visitors must stay on trail and no pets are allowed. For information, map, and regulations visit www.fws.gov and search for San Juan Islands.

San Juan Islands
[18421, 18423, 18429, 18430, 18431, 18432, 18433, 18434, Canadian 3462]

★ **The San Juan Islands:** First surveyed into townships in 1874, as many as 750 reefs, islets, and rocks can be seen at a minus tide, giving ample reason for more than a casual look at the charts. The commonly accepted number of islands is 457, with approximately 175 being of sufficient size to have been named. The San Juan Archipelago is a prized destination, not only for the residents, but also for boaters and other visitors. Sometimes called the *Magic Islands,* the San Juan Islands do seem to have mystical powers, luring thousands of visitors each year from all over the world. This is a vacationer's paradise and boater's dream come true. In truth, these islands have everything a water lover could want. There are quiet bays with splendid and dependable anchorages, marine parks with docks and facilities, picturesque towns with friendly people and shops, almost inexhaustible beds of shellfish, favored salmon fishing holes, a number of resorts, and an abundance of restaurants and inns. Major communities are found at Eastsound on Orcas Island, and on San Juan Island at Friday Harbor, the county seat of San Juan County. There is ferry service to the four major islands.

The waters of the San Juan Islands lie in the Central Salish Sea, embracing the passages and bays north of the east end of the Strait of Juan de Fuca, and are bounded on the west by Haro Strait and on the north by Boundary Pass. The International Boundary line, which separates Canada from the United States, runs through Boundary Pass and Haro Strait. Tidal currents set north in Haro Strait and Boundary Pass, and ebb to the south with a velocity of one to two knots.

These waterways are used extensively by pleasure craft, ferries, fishing boats, as well as commercial ocean going vessels. Recreational boats abound in June, July, August, and September, but are not totally missing in any month of the year. Ferries run regular trips from Anacortes through Thatcher Pass, Harney Channel, Wasp Passage, San Juan Channel, Spieden Channel, and across Haro Strait to Sidney, British Columbia. Ferry landings are at Upright Head on Lopez Island, at the east entrance to Shaw Island's Blind Bay, at Orcas, on the southern shore of Orcas Island, and at Friday Harbor on San Juan Island.

Oceangoing vessels normally use Haro and Rosario Straits and do not traverse the channels and passes through the islands. Sailing crafts without motors should not attempt the passages against the current, unless the wind is fresh. A reliable auxiliary engine for sailboats is a necessity in. During fishing season, purse seiners and gillnetters may be found, especially in the vicinity of the Salmon Banks, south of San Juan Island. There are several marina facilities and hundreds of anchorages. When anchoring, boaters are cautioned to watch for signs posted on shore, and notations on charts indicating the placement of underwater cables.

For bird-watchers, the San Juan Islands National Wildlife Refuge is a delight, where black oystercatchers, double-crested cormorants, glaucous winged gulls, and other bird species can be counted. Wildlife, including harbor and elephant seals are also common sights.

★⚓ **James Island Marine State Park (1):** This 113 acre hourglass-shaped island has back-to-back bays

Symbols

[ ]: Numbers between [ ] are chart numbers.

{ }: Numbers & letters between { } are waypoints.

★ Recommended destinations, facilities, and services

⚐: Park, ⛵: Boat Launch, ▲: Campgrounds,

⚑: Hiking Trails, ⛱: Picnic Area, 🚲: Biking

🤿: Scuba

Chart List

NOAA Charts:
  18400, 18421, 18423, 18429-34

Canadian Hydrographic Charts: 3462

Marine Atlas Vol 1 (2018): Pages 7-9, 12

Evergreen Cruising Atlas: Pages 101, 107, 109, 123, 125-126, 130-132

Visit us at boattravel.com

on the southwest and northeast sides. The western bay faces Decatur Head and is the most popular. There is one mooring buoy and a seasonal dock large enough for four medium-sized boats (fees apply). The bottom is rock and gravel making anchoring difficult. Strong currents often swirl through the narrow passage between the island and Decatur. Three Cascadia Water Trail campsites and pit toilet are on the hill at the south end of the west cove. Ten other campsites, a composting toilet, pay stations, picnic shelter and two picnic sites are also found on the Island. No potable water or garbage service. On the opposite side of the island, there are 4 offshore mooring buoys in the East Cove. Open to the north and northeast, it is less shelter from winds and gets wave action from the wakes of passing boats in Rosario Strait. Gravel beaches on both sides of the island make it possible to beach small boats. If the dock and buoys are full, overnight anchorage is possible opposite James Island, along the Decatur Island shore's curving beach adjacent to Decatur Head. Good fishing can be found along the Decatur Island shore in Thatcher Pass and near James Island. ▲⛺🚶

Walk-around: 1.5 miles of loop trails around the central and southwest portions of the island offer views from the 200-foot-high hills. Vine maples regally arch the trail. Trails on the northern part of the island are closed to the public.

Decatur Island
[18421, 18423, 18429, Canadian 3462]

★ **Sylvan Cove (2):** When heading west in Thatcher Pass and approaching this bay, caution advised regarding a reef known as Lawson Rock. Marked by a day beacon, this reef off the Decatur Island shore is longer than might be obvious. Sylvan Cove was once known as San Elmo. Boaters visited in the 40's-50's to enjoy chicken dinners at the farmhouse at the head. Today, the site and dock are both private. The view from this bay is a changing scene of passing vessels and a background of radiant sunsets. Open to the northwest, but good protection from southeasterly winds. Depths in most of the bay are about 20 feet. Limited anchorage is possible.

★ **Brigantine Bay (3):** There is good anchorage with protection from northern winds. Anchor close to the beach in about 15 feet of water. This is an attractive half-moon shaped indentation with a private, gravel beach on the southwest shore of Decatur, opposite Trump Island. Shrimping is possible southwest of Trump Island near the Lopez shore in 20 fathoms.

★ **Center Island & Reads Bay (4):** Anchorage, offshore from this private island, is possible in the northern part of Reads Bay, south of Center Island and north of Ram Island, in the passage between Decatur and Center Islands. Note charted hazards.

Blakely Island
[18421, 18430, Canadian 3462]

★ **Behind Armitage Island (5):** Off Thatcher Pass, the waters between Armitage Island and the southeastern tip of Blakely offer shelter. Limited anchorage is possible. Cruise around the bay while checking the depth sounder for suitable depths. There are several private buoys and shallow areas. Both Armitage and Blakely Islands are private. No shore access.

★ **Thatcher Bay (6):** In the spring, a visible waterfall from Spencer Lake marks this wide bay on the west side of Blakely Island. Temporary anchorage is recommended because it is exposed to boat wakes and both southwest and westerly winds. The 12-15 foot depths are fairly consistent. Watch for submerged pilings along the north shore.

★ **Blakely Harbor (7):** This harbor is located off the west end of Peavine Pass. The entrance channel is narrow and sometimes busy with local traffic. Tidal currents can affect maneuvering.

Blakely Island Marina: {48° 35' 5" N, 122° 48' 43" W} Guest moorage, 30 amp power, water, gas, diesel, showers, laundry, wifi, garbage/recycle, general store & deli (seasonal), picnic shelter. 360-375-6121.

Lopez Island
[18421, 18423, 18429, Canadian 3462]

★ **Hunter Bay (8):** Fairly even depths, a mud bottom, protection from all but north winds, and plenty of room to swing, make this an excellent anchorage. The beach is posted and there is no shore access. A day-use county dock and launching ramp are near the tip of the peninsula that separates Hunter Bay from Mud Bay.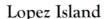

★ **Mud Bay (8):** Mud Bay has drying flats, however anchorage is possible in the northern portion. Open to winds. Note a rock off the eastern shore, well into the bay. Mud Bay Park, with state owned beach and tidelands, is on the southeastern shore. Uplands are private. A launching ramp is on the northeast shore. In 1893, there was a store and post office at Mud Bay.

Lopez Pass (9): See tables for Rosario Strait. This pass connects Lopez Sound with Rosario Strait. A flashing light is on Decatur at the Rosario Strait side of the pass. Lopez Pass is deep with no charted hazards. A tombolo of land extending from Decatur and three islets, Ram, Cayou, and Rim, border the pass opposite Lopez Island. Passage is between Decatur and Rim or between Lopez and Ram. When rounding Ram, give plenty of berth to the charted, kelp-marked rock.

★ **Watmough Bay (10):** A steep-sided bay, this is protected on the south by Watmough Head and gives good shelter in westerly winds. The bottom shoals quickly before the gravel beach at the head. Tricky, overnight anchorage is possible on a rock bottom in about 15 feet of water. Three mooring buoys in the bay are free to use. The buoys are for boats to 45' depending on weight and weather, 72 hour limit. Boaters are encouraged to use the buoys and row in to shore, as anchoring and motors disturbs the sea floor vegetation, impacting the juvenile salmon and other marine life. The beach is a good spot for an afternoon picnic. A few walking trails allow for exploration.

★ **Southern Lopez Island:** Rainfall is less on this wind-swept shore, because it is in the lee of the Olympic Rain Shadow. Cactus grow in profusion. Protected anchorage (exposed to southerlies) is possible in several bays, including McArdle Bay, Hughes Bay, Aleck Bay, and MacKaye Harbor.

Watmough Bay, Lopez Island   Photo © Chris Teren / TerenPhotography.com

★ **McArdle Bay (11):** When approaching from Point Colville, a picturesque, cliff-lined passage between Castle Island and Lopez Island leads to this bay. Private homes look down from the hills to the basin. Open to the Strait of Juan de Fuca and to southwest winds. There is a charted rock, and marsh areas are at both ends of the bay. The bottom is good holding mud. Anchoring depths are 25-35 feet.

Hughes Bay (12): Open to southerly winds, an islet to port upon entry has some protection. Anchor far into the bay.

★ **Aleck Bay (13):** The hills which separate Aleck Bay and Barlow Bay are low and do not offer much protection from west winds. The bay is completely open to the east. The bottom is good holding mud. Favored anchorage is off the southern shore.

Outer Bay: Outer Bay lies between Iceberg Point and Johns Point. Stay clear of foul rock and reefs off Iceberg Point. There are rocks in the bay, but in season, kelp marks many of them. Temporary anchoring on a rock bottom is possible in the south end of the bay, but only in settled weather. Agate Beach Park, in the east end of the bay is a small, day-use park with a beautiful beach, pit toilets, picnic facilities, and sensational views of the cormorants and puffins nesting on offshore rocks. Scuba diving is possible. Private property borders the park.

★ **Iceberg Island State Park:** This undeveloped island in Outer Bay is for day use only. Anchorage possible. No fires or overnight camping.

Davis Bay: This wide bay offers temporary anchorage only, with protection from north winds. Open to Cattle Pass currents and conditions on the Strait of Juan de Fuca. Avoid the rocky areas north of Buck Island and off the western shore. The indentations on the eastern shore are drying flats. Stay in the center in approximately 25' of water. Hard bottom, make sure anchor is hooked.

★ **MacKaye Harbor (14):** [18429] Richardson, located near Charles Island at the western entrance to the harbor, was the site of a landmark general store that stood for 100 years until it was destroyed by fire in 1990. In the early 1900's Richardson was one of the San Juan Islands' busiest ports for steamships. Good anchorage is found in the bays next to the old store site. Avoid rocks near the entrance to Jones Bay. The harbor is large with good anchorage in several spots, especially at the eastern end. Barlow Bay, the southern portion, is shallow and has private docks, as well as a county

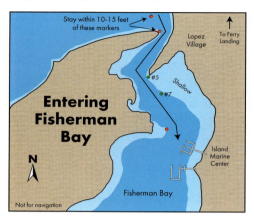

Entering Fisherman Bay

Not for navigation

boat ramp and a grounding float (day use, 2hr limit).

Walk-around: Anchor at the eastern end and row ashore. Walk up to MacKaye Harbor Road and walk south toward Outer Bay and Agate Beach Park to enjoy some lovely views.

★ **Fisherman Bay (15):** [18434] Visitors will find moorage, anchorage, repairs, and restaurants in this long indentation into the western shore of Lopez Island. If approaching from the north, along the Lopez Island shore, give the shore a wide berth to avoid rocks. Most hazardous is a drying rock about three quarters of a mile north of the entrance to the bay. If approaching from the west, give the sand spit a wide berth. Entry into the bay is not difficult. Stay in the narrow, marked channel. If there is any question about adequate depths due to an extreme low tide, enter on an incoming tide. There is only 3 feet of water in the channel at minus one tide. Entry is on a line which divides the approach bay in half and heads toward the channel and past the end of the spit guarding the entrance. Entry channel markers are on concrete pillars and continue after passing the spit. Sandbars and shallows lie outside these markers. The first marker to starboard is red and white checkerboard. Stay close to all markers, keeping in a straight line between them down the center of the channel (red right returning). Keep green (1,5,7) to port. Currents may be strong in this corridor. While transiting this channel, look to port to see the village of Lopez. Winds from the southwest can enter. If anchored, allow adequate room to swing. A low wake maximum speed of six knots is enforced in Fisherman Bay. From moorage, the Village of Lopez is within walking distance. Don't care to walk? Bike and kayak rentals are found nearby, call 360-468-2847. Several B & B's and a golf course are in the vicinity. The Washington State Ferry landing at Upright Head is only 4.5 miles from Fisherman Bay. Daily floatplane flights connect with other islands and major cities. A small airport is also located on the island.

★ **Islands Marine Center:** {48° 31.5' N, 122° 55.2' W} Founded in 1972 by Ron and Jennifer Meng. Complete repair facility with permanent, daily, and temporary moorage. Water, showers, ice, pump-out. Marine parts store, chandlery, and NAPA auto parts store. Haul-outs to 25 tons, dry storage. Authorized boat dealer for Ocean Sport Boats and Pursuit, and authorized sales and service for Yamaha, Volvo Penta, and MerCruiser. See our advertisement on this page. Website: www.islandsmarinecenter.com. Email: imc@rockisland.com and imcservice@rockisland.com. Address: 2793 Fisherman Bay Road, Post Office Box 88, Lopez, Washington 98261. Telephone: 360-468-3377. VHF 69.

Lopez Islander Resort & Marina: {48° 31.5' N, 122° 55.2' W} Guest moorage, 30/50 amp power, water, gas, diesel, restrooms, showers, laundry, marine store, lodging, coffee bar, restaurant/lounge, BBQ, picnic area, swimming pool, hot tub, RV/camping sites. Free guest shuttle from ferry landing or Lopez airport. 360-468-2233. VHF 78A.

Walk-around: Walks are possible along the main road which skirts the bay. One walk leads south to two restaurants, each with a lounge. The other walk to the north, leads to the Village of Lopez. The road meanders through pasture land, passing the library and a picturesque church.

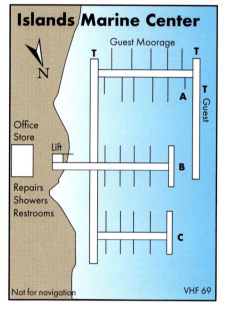

Islands Marine Center

Not for navigation VHF 69

★ **Islands Marine Center:** Islands Marine Center (IMC) is the first marina on the left as you cruise into Fisherman Bay on Lopez Island. Regarded as one of the finest marinas and repair facilities in the San Juan Islands, IMC offers permanent, daily and temporary moorage on modern floats with water, 30 amp power, and a pump-out. Consider Islands Marine Center for your next yacht club rendezvous - we offer a scenic lawn and barbecue pit with tents available with advance arrangement. Or watch the sun set over the marina from our on-site rental apartment with full kitchen and bath at a modest rate. Just across the street from moorage, you will find a marine chandlery and service shop, bathrooms with coin-operated showers, limited garbage disposal and recycling. The fully-stocked chandlery contains hardware, paint, fishing tackle, bait, ice, rain gear, charts, electronics, gifts, and a complete NAPA auto parts store. We are an authorized boat dealer for Ocean Sport Boats and Pursuit and authorized sales and service for Yamaha, Volvo Penta, Yanmar, and Mercruiser. Our factory-trained technicians handle all variety of repairs, rigging, electronic installations, bottom painting, and detailing. Haul-outs to 25 tons and a 13' beam, may depend on the tides. At times, tides, strong currents, and wind can also affect docking. Islands Marine Center offers short or long term dry storage. Lopez Village is a short walk from the marina and offers many shops, grocery stores and restaurants. Don't miss the village's Farmer's Market on summer Saturdays! Other restaurants, bike and kayak rentals, and a fuel dock are located nearby. Just 4.5 miles from the Washington State ferry dock and directly next door to the Kenmore Air float plane dock, Islands Marine Center is ready for your visit!

Website: www.islandsmarinecenter.com. **Email:** imc@rockisland.com and imcservice@rockisland.com.
Address: 2793 Fisherman Bay Road, Post Office Box 88, Lopez, Washington 98261. **Telephone:** 360-468-3377. **VHF:** 69.

Rosario Resort on Orcas Island

★ **Lopez Village:** No floats give direct access to town. However, it is an interesting and easy walk from moorages at Islands Marine Center or Lopez Islander Resort in Fisherman Bay. The Village's first store was opened by early settler H.E. Hutchinson. Today, there are several specialty shops, two espresso bars, restaurants, two food trucks, bakery, tap room, galleries, bookstore, thrift shop, bike shop, pharmacy, natural foods store, grocery, bank, visitors center, library and museum. The museum is open May-Sept, Wed-Sun, noon-4pm or by appointment. 360-468-2049. A community center hosts various performances and events, as well as a farmers market from May to September each Saturday from 10am-2pm. Lopez Island Brewery and Lopez Island Vineyards offer bottles of their libations at the Lopez Village Market. If you visit Lopez in the off-season, keep in mind that retail and restaurant hours are often reduced in winter. Contact the Visitor Center/Chamber of Commerce for year round visitor information at 360-468-4664 or visit www.lopezisland.com.

★ **Upright Channel Day Use Site:** This 20 acre DNR managed day use site is located on the north side of Flat Point. It includes picnic tables, vault toilet, trails and beach access. No water. Garbage must be packed out. Moorage by anchoring only.

★ **Odlin Park (16):** This popular 80 acre park is located about 3 miles from the village on the west side of Lopez, between Flat Point and Upright Head. There are 5 mooring buoys, a small day use dock and a free boat and kayak launch. Anchorage off the park is possible. A sand and mud beach extends into tide flats off shore. Campsites, picnic tables, potable water, vault toilets (no showers), walking trails, a play area and ballfield are found in the park. There are 3 scuba dive sites-the bay, the northern rocky shoreline and the southern shoreline. 360-378-8420.

★ **Shoal Bay (17):** Located between Upright Head and Humphrey Head, shoals extend off the bay. Anchorage is possible in depths of 10-25 feet. Open to north winds. A small private marina and aquaculture operations are located near the lowland which adjoins Humphrey Head. Tidelands are private. No transient boat facilities.

Spencer's Landing Marina: (Adjacent to the Ferry Terminal) Permanent moorage only (no transient moorage), boats 40'-110'. 30/40/100 amp power, bathrooms. 360-468-2077.

★ **Swift's Bay (18):** Although wide and open to ferry wakes and north winds, this bay does offer anchorage. Enter at a lower tide to identify rocks. Leo Reef and Flower Island are opposite the head. Rocky patches, barely covered at high tide, are off Flower Island on a line to the reef. Anchorage is possible in 12-20 foot depths. The shore shoals for some distance. Private homes overlook the bay. A lagoon at Swift's Bay was once the site of Port Stanley, a thriving town until the depression of 1893.

★ **Spencer Spit Marine State Park (19):** This park encompasses a large sand and gravel spit and a lagoon on the eastern side of Lopez Island. Sufficient depths permit passage between Frost Island and the spit at any tide. Stay close to Frost Island. Mooring buoys border both sides of the spit. Because of the park's popularity, it is best to arrive early in the day. Buoys are often empty between 10:30am and noon, after the previous night's boats have departed. Anchorage is excellent on both sides of the spit. Often, wind direction is the deciding factor. No dock. There are tent campsites onshore (including hiker/biker and Cascadia Marine Trail tent sites) as well as trails, fire rings, water, restrooms, and picnic shelters. A log cabin, vintage 1913, serves as one of the picnic shelter. Bike, SUP and kayak rentals are available on the beach mid-May through September, 425-883-9039. Swimming in the shallow, sun-warmed waters along the spit is a popular activity. Excellent scuba diving is also found in the area. Migratory waterfowl, including great blue herons, Canada geese and kingfishers, inhabit the lagoon in season. Rabbits, deer, and raccoons are also frequently seen in the park. Park Info: 360-468-2251.

Orcas Island
[18421, 18423, 18430, 18434, Canadian 3462]

★ **Orcas Island:** This 59 square mile, saddle-bag-shaped island is the largest in the San Juan Archipelago. It is one square mile larger than San Juan Island. Four main communities are spread out over this island. These are Deer Harbor, Orcas Village, Eastsound, and Olga. A public shuttle runs Fri-Sun between the first three communities from mid-June through Labor Day. 360-378-8887. For the boater, many inviting bays indent into the island, and several marine facilities. The island was named by the explorer Francisco de Eliza for the Viceroy of Mexico whose nine-name surname included Horcasitas (orcas).

Point Lawrence (20): This point was named for James Lawrence, whose dying words were "Don't Give Up The Ship." The rugged, steep hillside is a landmark for fishermen who frequent this area.

Peapod Rocks: These rocks found off shore southwest of Doe Bay can be very tricky for boaters. Consult charts and tide books before sailing in this area. This is an Underwater Recreation Park. Shore access prohibited. Diving is popular here and in Doe Bay.

★ **Doe Bay:** Although exposed to the east and Rosario Strait, Doe Bay provides anchorage in 2 to 8 fathoms. Doe Bay is a private resort. There is no public dock, but two private buoys may be available for rent. Call Doe Bay Resort at 360-376-2291 for information. On shore, the resort has cabins, campsites, a yoga studio, the much acclaimed Doe Bay Café and a store with gifts, groceries, beer, wine and supplies. The clothing optional soaking tubs and sauna are available by reservation only and offered exclusively to guests staying at the resort. Boaters who have rented the mooring buoys, or have reservations in the Doe Bay Café, re welcome to come onto the property from the beach. It is highly recommended to call before coming. To make reservations in the Doe Bay Café please call 360-376-8059. ▲

Page 94 Chapter 7 SAN JUAN ISLANDS

★⛺ **Doe Island Marine State Park (21):** Seven-acre Doe Island is a relatively secluded park on the southeast side of Orcas Island. At this time, no public mooring facilities are available. Mooring buoys in the area are private. Two pocket coves in the park are suitable for beachable boats. The park also has one vault toilet, five campsites each with a table and stove, and a .3 mile loop trail. No fresh water, no garbage deposit. Scuba diving offshore is popular. 360-376-2073. ▲🚻🏃‍♂️🤿

★ **Obstruction Pass & Peavine Pass (22):** See current tables for Rosario Strait. These two passes separate Obstruction Island from Orcas and Blakely Islands. When approaching from the west, the view over Obstruction Island toward distant Mount Baker is a photographer's delight. Of the two waterways, Peavine Pass, while narrower, is the easiest to navigate. It is shorter and free of hazards. Rocks south of the eastern entrance are marked. Currents run to four knots at springs. Obstruction Pass, to the north of Obstruction Island, curves and has rocks off the Orcas shore. A launching ramp is on the Orcas shore near the Volunteer Fire Department building. Fishing is popular in and near both passes.

★⛺ **Obstruction Pass State Park:** This park is in a tiny nook on Orcas Island, at the northwest end of Obstruction Pass. The park sign is on a bluff. Good gravel bottom for anchoring. Anchor as close to the shore as depths will permit. Three mooring buoys are available. This park has nine tent spaces, one Cascadia Marine Trail campsite, composting toilets. No potable water, pack out garbage. 360-376-2326, 360-902-8844. ▲🚻

Lieber Haven Rentals: Seasonal summer moorage, ice cream, snacks, wifi, kayak, motor boat and rowboat rentals, sailing school. Open all year. 360-376-2472, 360-228-5405.

★ **Olga (23):** Named after the mother of the village's first postmaster, Olga exudes the pastoral charm of another era. The community dock has about 90 feet of moorage. Fresh water may be available at the head of the dock. Anchorage is possible along the shore south of the dock. Buck Bay is a drying lagoon. The Olga Post Office is across the road from the dock. A little further on, Olga Pottery displays pottery, paintings and other art. A restored historic strawberry barreling plant houses Orcas Island Artworks and the James Hardman Gallery. The Buck Bay Shellfish Farm operates a bistro serving seafood, fish and chips, etc. (open seasonally, usually May - October).

★ **East Sound (24):** [18430] East Sound is a steep sided, forested indentation extending over six miles into the island. Excellent for sailing, the topography of East Sound is such that winds are often present even though surrounding waters are calm. The town of Eastsound lies at the head.

★ **Rosario Resort & Spa:** {48° 38.8' N, 122° 52.2' W} Listed on the National Historic Register, Rosario is a must stop for all boating in the San Juan Islands. Featuring two restaurants, lounge, entertainment, historical museum, fuel (including non-ethanol premium), showers, water, trash disposal, laundromat, indoor pool, two outdoor pools, and a full-service spa featuring whirlpool, sauna and fitness center. See our advertisement on this page. Internet: www.rosarioresort.com. Email: harbormaster@rosarioresort.com. Mailing address: 1400 Rosario Road, Eastsound, WA 98245. Telephone: 360-376-2222, 800 562-8820 ext. 700. VHF 78A.

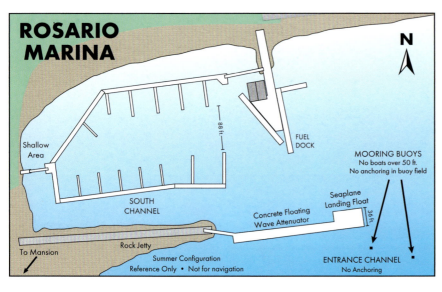

It's About Time

It's your weekend, it's your vacation, it's your valuable free time. We invite you to step back in time at historic Rosario Resort & Spa on beautiful Orcas Island. Slow down to island time with our relaxing spa services, enjoy family time in our waterfront accommodations or marina moorage, taste our locally sourced dishes during meal time, and energize your play time with our many island activities.

www.rosarioresort.com
800.562.8820

Listed on the National Register of Historic Places

ROSARIO Resort & Spa

Visit us at boattravel.com

★ **San Juan Airlines:** Commuter travel to and from the San Juan Islands is within easy reach for business or pleasure. We offer daily flights between the San Juan Islands and Bellingham, Anacortes and Everett. We also offer hundreds of charter options for the ultimate in convenience and flexibility - whether it's a leisurely day trip, family vacation, business commute, or romantic weekend away - you choose the time and location and we'll get you there. Enjoy an unforgettable experience with a bird's-eye view of the San Juan Islands, Mt. Baker, the Skagit tulip fields and more! Avoid the hassle of traffic and spend time being there, instead of getting there. See our advertisement on this page. Visit sanjuanairlines.com or call 1-800-874-4434 for more information or to book your travel.

★ **Cascade Bay:** Cascade Bay, formed by Rosario Point, extends from the eastern shore of East Sound. Anchorage and Rosario Resort buoys are found in the bay. A seaplane dock is located at the end of the rock jetty.

★ **Moran State Park:** Two mountains and five lakes are included in this park. It contains campsites, trout-stocked lakes and the famous lookout tower at Mount Constitution, as well as two ramps for non-motorized boats, picnic tables, and two kitchen shelters with electricity. To reserve shelter, call 888-226-7688. A trail leads up the hill to the dam and the tennis courts near Rosario Lagoon. The trail continues around the north end of Cascade Lake to a swimming beach. At the Y one may veer to the right, cross the Cascade Lake Bridge, and hike around Rosario Lagoon to the main path. Park info: 360-376-2326. ▲⛺🚶

★ **Eastsound (25):** The day-use County dock on the eastern shore gives boaters access to this intriguing community. Small boats can be beached. Ship Bay has anchorage off Madrona Point in 20-35 feet. Fishing Bay has anchorage near Indian Island. Both anchorages are exposed to south winds so check before anchoring. Another niche, Judd Cove, has some anchorage for a few boats. Eastsound is home to a great variety of stores, restaurants, spa and fitness center, bike and kayak rentals, post office, banks, library with internet access, movie theater, and Community Theater. Each year in August, world class musicians perform at the *Orcas Island Chamber Music Festival.* The Orcas Historical Museum, housed in century old homesteader cabins has over 6,000 objects. Call 360-376-4849 for hours. Just north of the museum, a Saturday Farmers Market featuring local arts and crafts, flowers, produce and products is held May through September, 10am-3pm. Not far from town on Mt. Baker Road, Buck Park has a world-class skate park, tennis and basketball courts, pickleball, and baseball field. Visit the Orcas Island Chamber of Commerce's website, www.orcasislandchamber.com for current activities listed in the newsletter or on the calendar.

Walk-around: Dinghy to the County dock from Ship Bay Anchorage. Walk about 5-minutes to downtown Eastsound's shops, large grocery store, and liquor store. (The floating dock in Eastsound is removed during the winter months November 1st to April 1st, so there is no access to the dock during that time).

Guthrie Bay: Some anchorage is in the area marked four fathoms on the chart, but is open to the southeast and to wakes from passing boats. There are rocks on the port side and shallows at the head of the bay.

★ **Twin Rocks:** Located opposite Olga, off the west shore of East Sound, is a day-use park with 800 feet of shoreline. Anchorage is possible, with caution advised regarding shoals off the islands. No fires or camping.

Sunset over Orcas Island   Photo © VPLLC

★ **Grindstone Harbor (26):** [18434, 18430] Two reefs, covered at high tide, appear to block the entrance to this bay, but safe passage is possible on either side of the entry by staying close to the Orcas shore. A drying flat extends from the northeastern side of the bay. The bay is open to winds from the southeast. Grindstone was named because a gentleman named Paul Hubbs operated a trading post with a much valued grindstone at the site in the 1860's. The harbor received prominence again when a wayward Washington State Ferry tried, but failed, to pass safely between the reefs at the entrance.

★ **Orcas Landing (27):** Site of the Orcas Ferry Landing. Adjacent to the Ferry Landing is a day use, short stay county dock. A private marina is east of the Ferry. A grocery store is nearby and on the hillside above the moorage are specialty shops, a hotel, and food concessions.

Bay Head Marina: {48° 35' 52" N, 122° 56' 10" W} Permanent moorage. 855-948-6413.

SAN JUAN ISLANDS Chapter 7 Page 97

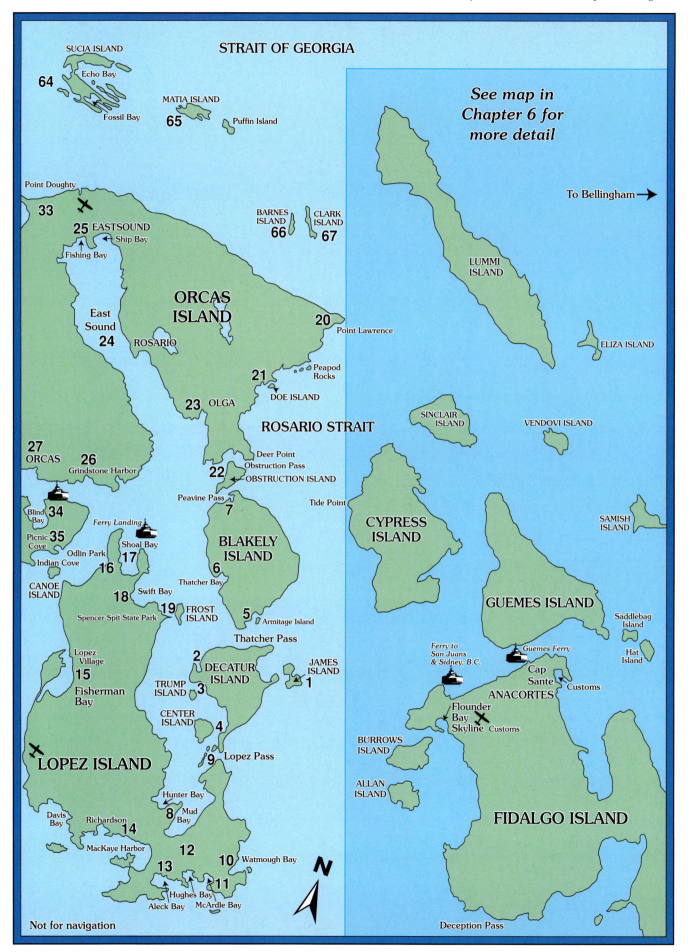

★ **West Sound (28):** Framed by an irregular, winding coastline, this three mile indentation into Orcas Island is especially appealing to those who enjoy exploring nooks and crannies without going ashore. Prevailing north and south winds funnel into the sound, creating ideal sailing conditions. This is the site of the historic Kingfish at West Sound, a restaurant, several B & B's, yacht club, and marina. There is a dock with moorage float for shore access. West Sound Marina is on the east shore, behind Picnic Island.

Massacre Bay, Skull Island and Victim Islands are named for a bloody battle between raiding Haidas from the north and Lummi tribesmen. Skull and Victim Islands are undeveloped park lands (read their descriptions to follow). The west shore of West Sound has several small bights for anchorage, but watch carefully to avoid charted rocks and shoals.

★ **West Sound Marina:** {48° 37' N, 122° 57' W} Located in the lee of Picnic Island. Stay wide, and to the west of Picnic. Approach close to the south float for guest moorage. Family owned and operated full service marina with moorage, gas, diesel, ice, chandlery, haul-outs, pump-out, and complete repair service. Open all year. See our advertisement on this page. Website: under construction. Email: info@westsoundmarina.com. Mailing Address: Post Office Box 119, Orcas, Washington 98280. Telephone: 360-376-2314. Fax: 360-376-4634.

★ **Double Island:** Located near the western mouth of West Sound, there is good anchorage in about 40 feet of water in a small bay on the northwest side. Anchorage is also possible along the Orcas shore, opposite the north tip of Double Island and south of the dock with boathouses. Passage between Orcas and Double Island, even at high tide, is not recommended. Double Island, and Alegria Island to the south, are private.

★⚓ **Victim Island State Park:** Located off the western shore of West Sound, this undeveloped day use park offers good anchorage and beach for landing small boats. Day use only, no fires or camping.

★⚓ **Skull Island State Park:** Located in Massacre Bay near the head of West Sound, anchorage is easily found at this undeveloped park. Give a wide berth to the rock at the entrance to Massacre Bay. Day use only, no fires or overnight camping.

★ **Pole Pass (29):** This passage separates Crane Island from Orcas Island. A low-wake and maximum speed of six knots is enforced in Pole Pass. Few dangers are found on the eastern approach, however rocks are off the Orcas shore at the western entrance and a shoal extends north off Crane Island just west of the indentation that houses a private float. When heading west into Deer Harbor, avoid this shoal and the kelp beds off Orcas Island by maintaining a course about halfway between Crane Island and Orcas Island until clear of the passage about 75 yards before aiming to port toward Reef Island or into Deer Harbor. Strong currents occur on spring tides, however they are navigable at the reduced speed of six knots. It was here that local tribes would tie nets made of cedar bark and kelp between poles across the passage to catch passing ducks - thus the name "Pole Pass".

★ **Deer Harbor (30):** [18434] {48° 37' N, 123° 00' W} Deer Harbor indents into the western side of Orcas Island. Enter the harbor from Pole Pass to the southeast or from North Pass to the west. Fawn Island can be passed on either side, but avoid shoaling off the Island's south side. Continuing on, Deer Harbor Marina, resort, and repair facilities are found on the eastern shore. Watch for seasonal crab and shrimp pots in the vicinity. Further in toward the head of the bay, on the western shore is a private marina. While anchoring is possible, the bay is open to winds from the south. The historic Deer Harbor Inn, built in 1915, serves Island Style Barbecue. Birdwatchers might enjoy a walk to the Frank Richardson Wildlife Reserve viewpoint off Channel Road. Cormorant Bay, a scenic shallow area near the head of the harbor, can be explored by dinghy. If you are lucky, maybe you'll spot one of the deer for which the harbor is named!

★ **West Sound Marina:** Located on the northeast side of West Sound, in the lee of Picnic Island. Enter from the west. Look for the high bay building, gray with green trim, and the landmark weather vane. Guest moorage is found at a 250' float on the south side of the marina, closest to Picnic Island. You may tie on both sides of the float. Thirty amp power, drinking water, and showers are available to moorage patrons. Call on VHF 16. Check in at the marina office on arrival. The fuel dock is adjacent to the guest moorage and dispenses gas and diesel. Waste pump-out is also available at the fuel dock. Expanded in 1999, West Sound Marina is the largest moorage facility on Orcas Island with 180 permanent moorage slips. Some summer sublets are available. West Sound Marina is also the largest repair facility in the San Juans. In addition to the 30 ton hoist, which can handle boats to 18' beam, the yard is an authorized repair facility for Volvo, Yanmar, Ford, and Johnson/Evinrude engines and products. Boats to 60' in length can be repaired under cover in the high bay building on the wharf. The marina store has an extensive inventory as well as a complete stock of engine parts. Ice, propane, charts, and snacks are sold. The Orcas Island Yacht Club and Kingfish at West Sound are only a short walk. Kenmore Air provides scheduled service. Open all year. Hours: Monday-Friday 8:00 a.m.-4:45 p.m. Saturday 10:00 a.m.-3:00 p.m. Sunday (July and August) 10:00 a.m.-3:00 p.m. Closed Sunday in off season. Emergency services can be provided. **Website: under construction. Email: info@westsoundmarina.com. Mailing address: Post Office Box 119, Orcas, Washington 98280. FAX: 360-376-4634, Telephone: 360-376-2314.**

Visit us at boattravel.com

★ **Deer Harbor Marina:** {48° 37'N, 123° 00 W} Open year round, the marina has permanent & guest moorage available, with power, water, gas & diesel, pump-out, restrooms, showers, laundry, groceries & deli store, free WiFi. A restaurant/pub is open in a newly acquired building across the street from the marina. Hotels and restaurants nearby. See our advertisement on this page. Website: www.deerharbormarina.com. Email: mbroman@deerharbormarina.com. Mailing address: P.O. Box 344, Deer Harbor, WA 98243. Telephone: 360-376-3037.

Cayou Quay Marina: {48° 37' 11" N, 123° 0' 22" W} Permanent moorage only, 30 amp power, water, restroom, garbage/recycle, WiFi, no fee launch ramp but parking is for tenants only. 360-376-4560.

Deer Harbor Boatworks: Haulout to 40', mechanical repairs, service calls, small marine store, dry storage, launch ramp (call ahead for availability, fee). Wooden boats are specialty. 360-376-4056.

★ **President Channel (31):** [18432] This five-mile-long waterway separates Orcas and Waldron Islands. Currents run two to five knots. In the early 1900's, this coast was mined for limestone, and ruins of the quarries are visible.

West Beach Resort: Dock/buoy moorage for guests, moorage fee for non-guests. Gas, showers, laundry, pump-out, WiFi, RV/camping sites, cottages, store, cafe, rentals (SUP, kayak, canoe, motor boat), fishing tackle, hot tub, boat launch (dry storage fee for trailers). 360-376-2240.

Freeman Island (32): It is possible to anchor and explore this federally owned park land. Anchor between the island and the Orcas shore. No fires or overnight camping.

★⛺ **Point Doughty Natural Area Preserve: (33):** Located on the northwestern tip of Orcas Island, the DNR managed Point Doughty Preserve includes a small four-acre recreation site. The rest of the area is not available for public use. Boundaries are posted. The site is accessible by water only; there is no overland access. Because of very rocky approaches, the site is primarily used by small boats and kayaks. Anchorage is difficult because of strong currents and hard bottom. Onshore is a Cascadia Marine Trail camping area with 3 campsites and fire rings. No water. Recreation includes beachcombing, scuba diving, and fishing. There is above average salmon fishing off the point. Super-sized ling cod often bite the hook here. 360-856-3500.

★ **North Beach:** East of Pt. Doughty, this area along the north shore of Orcas Island has amazing sunset views, several B & B's and rental cottages, and a small public access beach at the end of North Beach Road. A marina and condominium resort complex are located adjacent to the Eastsound Airport. Entrance to the marina is in a channel at the end of the jetty. The approach depth in the channel between the two steel pilings is 3' at 0 tide. Adjust your approach times accordingly if your draft exceeds the water available for approach. From the marina it is a 20 minute walk into the community of Eastsound. For lodging at the resort call 1-800-488-2097.

Brandt's Landing: {48°42'48.6"N 122°54'30.5"W} Long term moorage, some 20/30 amp power, water. 120' transient moorage, call ahead to reserve. Trailer/boat dry storage, boat launch, porta-potty. Marina: 360-376-4477.

Shaw Island

[18421, 18423, 18434, Canadian 3462]

★ **Shaw Island:** This is the smallest of the four islands served by Washington State Ferries. It is home to about 240 full time residents, strictly residential, except for a general store open seasonally at the ferry terminal. There is a county park at Indian Cove.

Shaw General Store: Limited, short term moorage (25' limit, call ahead). Groceries, ice cream, organic & local produce, fresh pizza & sandwiches, espresso bar, hardware items, gifts, post office. 360-468-2288.

★ **Blind Bay (34):** Blind Bay, adjacent to the Shaw Island ferry landing and about one half mile in width, has good anchorage. Depths in the anchoring basin are approximately 12 to 18 feet, except for a deeper spot south of Blind Island. Being mindful of overnight depths, and the charted rock and shoal area, anchor about 150-200 feet off shore. Another charted drying rock is located south of Blind Island, not far from the state park buoys. Along the south shore is a very small, state-owned island. It is an Oyster Catcher rookery, no trespassing. A hazardous wreck five feet awash at low tide with approximate position {48°34-42.870N 122°56-06.450W} was reported in 2010.

There are hazards to consider before entering the bay. Drying rocks nearly fill the entry to the west between Blind Island and Shaw Island, and passage is not recommended. The safest entry is east of Blind Island, however there is a drying rock (marked by a pole with white day beacon and the words "Danger Rock") located approximately mid-channel. Pass to the west of this rock (between the rock and Blind Island).

★⛺ **Blind Island Marine State Park:** Blind Island is designated a Cascadia Marine Trail site. No fresh water. Mooring buoys are tucked in south of Blind Island in Blind Bay. These offer some protection from north winds and some views of passing traffic in Harney Channel. In the early 1900's, a squatter settled on the two acre island,

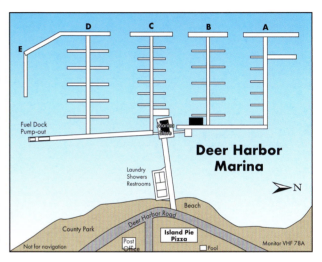

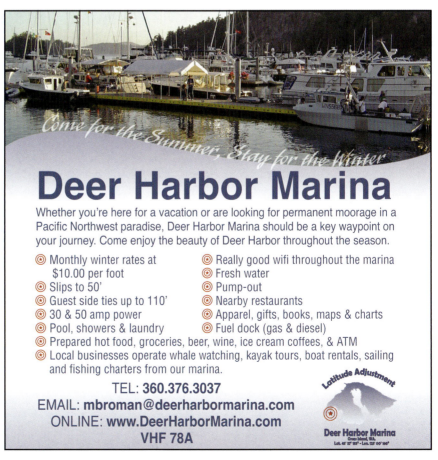

Deer Harbor Marina

Whether you're here for a vacation or are looking for permanent moorage in a Pacific Northwest paradise, Deer Harbor Marina should be a key waypoint on your journey. Come enjoy the beauty of Deer Harbor throughout the season.

- Monthly winter rates at $10.00 per foot
- Slips to 50'
- Guest side ties up to 110'
- 30 & 50 amp power
- Pool, showers & laundry
- Prepared hot food, groceries, beer, wine, ice cream coffees, & ATM
- Local businesses operate whale watching, kayak tours, boat rentals, sailing and fishing charters from our marina.
- Really good wifi throughout the marina
- Fresh water
- Pump-out
- Nearby restaurants
- Apparel, gifts, books, maps & charts
- Fuel dock (gas & diesel)

TEL: **360.376.3037**
EMAIL: **mbroman@deerharbormarina.com**
ONLINE: **www.DeerHarborMarina.com**
VHF 78A

Friday Harbor
Photo © Chris Teren / TerenPhotography.com

supporting his hermit lifestyle by fishing and tilling a small garden spot. Holes that he dug into the rock to be used as cisterns and a concrete retainer that he built around a small spring are still visible. Water from the spring is not safe for human use. 360-378-2044. ▲

★ **Picnic Cove:** Picnic Cove, north of Indian Cove, has depths of six to ten feet at most low tides. There are shoals, especially near the entrance. Anchorage is possible.

★ **Indian Cove (35):** This cove, known locally as South Beach, lies on the southeast side of Shaw Island. Reasonably good anchorage may be obtained in the cove, but it is open to south winds. This is the site of Shaw Island County Park. When entering from the north, favor the Canoe Island side of the channel to avoid a shallow spot in mid-channel. When entering from the south, note the shoal that extends southeast for some distance off Canoe Island and also a rock marked by kelp south of Canoe Island. Canoe Island is private.

★ **Shaw Island County Park:** The park has a picnic area, boat launching ramp, eight campsites, fresh water, and a white-sand beach. The cove waters are warmed by the sun especially in the shallow shoal areas, making it perfect for swimming. Squaw Bay is not a good anchorage.

Hicks Bay (36): Frequently used as a haven by fishermen, this small bay has temporary anchorage with protection from westerlies. It is open to southeasterlies. Rocks to starboard near the entrance are covered at high tide. Tide rips form in the area.

★ **Parks Bay (37):** This is an excellent overnight anchorage. It is sheltered on the southwest by Point George. The bottom is good holding mud. The bay is spacious with anchorage for many boats. Check the chart for the location of old pilings. The western exposure often results in spellbinding sunsets. Deer, eagles, and wild mink inhabit the area. There are no facilities and the land surrounding the bay and the island near the entrance is a "no trespassing" biological reserve.

★ **Jones Island Marine State Park (38):** Located outside North Pass at the southwestern end of Orcas Island, moorage is possible in bays on the south and north sides. A valley between the two hills connects North and South Coves, and walking trails crisscross the area. Mooring buoys are in the southern bay, and anchorage is good on a sand and mud bottom. Picnic sites on the grassy meadow above the bay have good views of the Wasp Islands. The anchorage is open to southerly winds and to the wakes of boats. In the northern bay are three mooring buoys and a dock. Floats are removed in winter. When entering, avoid the marked drying rock about 150 yards off the island's northeast point. The bottom of this northern bay is rock, making anchoring difficult. The favored procedure is to try to secure the hook behind a rock on the bottom and complete a tie to shore to keep the boat from swinging. Tidal action in the bay can add to the problems of anchoring. Campsites (including two Cascadia Marine Trail sites at the west side of the southern bay), fresh water (May to Sept), composting toilets, and fire rings are available. Scuba diving is popular. Because this is a wildlife refuge (deer are especially plentiful) pets must be on a leash on shore. The island is named for Jacob Jones, captain of the 1812 warship Wasp. The remains of a homestead that was built in the 1860's and a few fruit trees found on the south side. 360-378-2044.

Wasp Islands (39): [18434] Also called, *The Rock Pile*, this vicinity has been more profanely named by those who have hit upon one of the many rocks in the area. Even some Washington State Ferries have not escaped the area uninjured. There are many covered and some uncharted rocks and shoals. For example, at or near high tide, rocks lie just under the surface of the water and extend for some distance to the northeast of Bird Rock. Reduced speed, careful attention to chart and sounder, and a visual watch are the only prudent procedures for venturing into this rock pile. Crane Island is the largest and most developed of the Wasps. McConnell, Cliff, Yellow, Reef, Coon, and Bell are the others. There are isolated, one-boat anchorages in the bights around these islands. All, except Yellow Island, are privately owned. There is some unidentified, day use, state parks land on islands northwest of McConnell Island.

McConnell Island: Good anchorage is found in the wide bay on the northeast side of McConnell. The shore is private property.

Yellow Island: Yellow Buttercups that grow profusely each spring inspired the name "Yellow Island." The Island is a Nature Conservancy Preserve with beautiful meadows of wildflowers and birds. It is open to limited public exploration keeping strictly on the trails. A caretaker is on the premises and should be contacted when you come ashore. No camping, no food, and no pets are allowed. Anchor in the southern bay and row ashore.

San Juan Island
[18421, 18423, 18434, Canadian 3462]

★ **San Juan Island:** Second largest in the San Juan group, this island boasts an average of 55 more sunny days per year than Seattle to the south. Most of the population lives around Friday Harbor, the county seat, only incorporated city, and center of commerce for the San Juan Islands. Friday Harbor is reached by boat, ferry, and airplane. Agriculture, real estate, and tourism are the major industries.

About seven miles wide and 15 miles in length, the island has 70 miles of waterfront. The topography varies, with heavily forested hills and shoreline in the northern area, rolling, rich farmlands along the San Juan Valley in the center of the island, and barren wind-swept bluffs and treeless pastures along the southernmost shoreline.

Rocky Bay (40): O'Neal Island lies in the middle of this large indentation into the north shore of San Juan Island. Although there are rocks near shore, anchorage is possible in small coves. Reuben Tarte Memorial Park, with its gravel beach is on shore (day use only, no fires).

★ **Friday Harbor (41):** [18434] This harbor sheltered on the east by Brown Island, is sometimes known as "Friday Island". The passage on the northwest side of Brown Island into Friday Harbor is also used for ferry traffic. The Friday Harbor Laboratories, University of Washington and Cantilever Pier are to starboard. On the southeast side of Brown Island, the passage into the harbor is narrow and restricted by shoals off the Brown Island side. Shallow ground and rocks are marked. Favor the San Juan Island side when traversing this waterway. The southeastern portion of Friday Harbor, known as Shipyard Cove, houses shipyards and repair facilities.

Anchorage is possible in several locations, however space is limited. Avoid anchoring near the breakwater cables at the port facility, and in the traffic lanes of the ferry. Caution is advised because the ferry sometimes backs out toward the south to turn around. Favored anchorage is in the southernmost portion of the harbor, or in the niche between the Marine Laboratories and the port marina. A cable which supplies power, telephone, and water to Brown Island, from Friday Harbor is shown on charts. It is also marked with lighted signs on shore. The Brown Island Owner's Association installed four small marker buoys marked "Do not anchor-cable area" to help boaters avoid the hazard.

Customs check-in: Upon arrival in Friday Harbor, call the Port on 66A or the customs office at 360-378-2080 for tie up instructions. The customs office is open daily, 8am-8pm during summer months. Hours change mid-September. For information, call 1-800-562-5943 or see the Important Notices section between Chapters 7 and 8.

★ **Town of Friday Harbor:** This is one of the northwest's most popular tourist destinations. Shopping, dining, kayaking and whale/wildlife watching top the list of reasons given for visiting, but other popular activities include exploring a local museum such as the Whale Museum, the San Juan Historical Museum or the San Juan Island Museum of Art, playing golf at the San Juan Golf and Country Club, shopping, taking in a movie in the vintage theater or attending a live theatrical or musical production at the San Juan Community Theatre, watching ferries arrive and depart, or just enjoying the leisurely pace of the town. K-9 crew members are welcome and may enjoy a romp in the "Eddy and Friends" dog park on Mullis Ave. Annual events in the community include the *San Juan Marathon*, an *Old fashioned 4th of July Celebration* with a lively parade, 5K foot race, music and fireworks; followed by the *San Juan County Fair* in mid August; *Savor The San Juans*- a month long medley of food, art and culture begins in late October and includes the *Friday Harbor Film Festival*; *Friday Harbor Winterfest* with events throughout the month of December kicks off with the *Island Lights Festival*. Stop by the San Juan Island Chamber of Commerce Visitor Information Center at 165 First Street South for maps and additional island information. A number of small cruise ships include this port-of-call on their itineraries, linking Port Townsend, Seattle and Bellingham. The island is also served by Washington State Ferries from Anacortes on the east. An inter-island ferry connects Friday Harbor with Orcas, Shaw and Lopez Islands. Float planes are active in the vicinity of the harbor. An airport, located less than a mile from town, has scheduled and charter services to other islands and northwest metropolitan cities.

Walk-around: Beginning at the Port of Friday Harbor moorage, walk through Fairweather Park at the head of the ramp. Popeye, a one-eyed resident harbor seal has been immortalized in a sculpture by Matthew Palmer. The granite version of this local celebrity is near the entry to the park. 'Portals of Welcome', carved by Native artist Susan Point, are also located in the park. These Coast Salish houseposts, overlooking the moorage provide a perfect photo op. From July through mid-September, enjoy live entertainment in the park on Saturdays. Stroll along Front Street to Spring Street. On the harborside, a memorial honors San Juan Islands U.S. Army and Navy servicemen who fought in World War I. Nine names are on the plaque - a devastating loss for families in this small, tight knit community. From this vantage point at the foot of Spring Street, look up the hill to get an overall picture of the buildings along the main street. Continue up Spring Street and at First Street a left turn leads to shops and galleries. Walking back to the corner of Spring and First, you will be standing in front of the historic San Juan County Bank building. Cross the street and proceed up the North First Street hillside to The Whale Museum featuring carvings, lithographs, scale models, and video displays. (For hours call 360-378-4710.) Nearby are the vintage San Juan County Courthouse and the Community Theatre. Returning down the hill to Spring Street, a right turn will take you past a variety of shops and provisioning stores.

Warm glow on the town of Friday Harbor

Photo © Chris Teren / TerenPhotography.com

★ **Chris Teren Photography**—A Unique Perspective on Island Life. Inspired by over two decades of island life, Chris Teren's appreciation for the natural wonders of the San Juan Islands is evident in his diverse collection of work. A certified SCUBA diver, pilot, and commercial drone operator, he captures a truly unique perspective—from the wild and wondrous octopi-filled depths of the Salish Sea and breaching orcas at the surface, to soaring heights, beyond the bald eagles, and into the mysterious beauty of the Aurora Borealis. Chris's work has appeared in online, print and local news media, and in area publications and local businesses. Prints and customized photography. See our advertisement on this page. Website: www.terenphotography.com. Phone 360-472-0879.

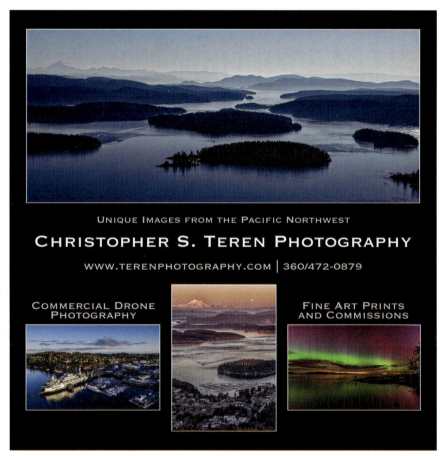

Page 102 Chapter 7 SAN JUAN ISLANDS

★ **Friday Harbor, Port of:** {48° 32.12' N, 123° 01' W} This world renowned marina provides year round shelter for recreational, fishing and permanent customers in the center of the most beautiful cruising waters of the West Coast. This modern full service, amenity-laden marina is open 7 days a week, year round. They offer a Frequent Floater Punch Card Program along with various Moorage Promotions throughout the year (details are available on their website). With the Town of Friday Harbor just blocks away, boaters have easy access to an array of goods, services and attractions including supplies, groceries, restaurants, hardware stores, chandleries, lodging, art galleries, museums, theaters and more. Make daily connections from Bellingham, Port Townsend, and Seattle via passenger vessels or flights. Come start your weekend Where Friday Begins! See our advertisement on this page. Email: contactus@portfridayharbor.org. Website: www.portfridayharbor.org. Address: 204 Front Street, Post Office Box 889, Friday Harbor, Washington 98250. Fax: 360-378-6114. Telephone: 360-378-2688. VHF 66A.

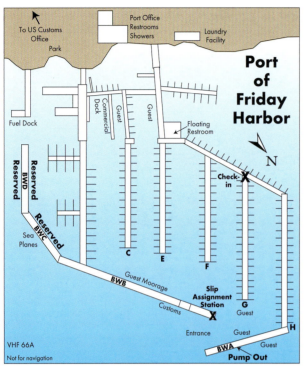

★ **Friday Harbor Seaplanes:** Skip the ferry and fly to San Juan Island in 50 minutes! Scheduled and Charter Flights from Seattle to the San Juan Islands. Daily service to and from Friday Harbor and Roche Harbor, from May through mid October. Located just 15 minutes from the Seattle Airport and downtown Seattle. Shuttle Service to and from SeaTac Airport. Free parking at Renton location. See our advertisement on page 103. Website: www.fridayharborseaplanes.com. Address: 860 W Perimeter Road, Renton, Washington 98057. Telephone: 425-277-1590 for reservations and information.

Port of Friday Harbor Fuel Dock: Gas (with/without ethanol), diesel, lubricants, propane, water, ice. 360-378-3114.

Shipyard Cove Marina: Permanent moorage only. Live-aboards allowed, free parking, restrooms/showers, laundry, boat ramp, dry storage and lockers. 360-378-2688.

★ **University of Washington Friday Harbor Laboratory (42):** Established in 1902, this renowned marine laboratory is about 1-mile from town. Facilities are for educational and research purposes only. Field trips and conferences are scheduled from September through March.

★ **Turn Island Marine Park (43):** Located east of Friday Harbor at Turn Point, this popular park has 2 buoys, campsites, and composting toilets. No fresh water, no fires. Turn Island is a wildlife refuge, no pets allowed. Mooring buoys on the northwest side are somewhat protected, however tidal currents sweep through this area. There is anchorage in the bay south of Turn Island, buoys here are private. Watch for shallow spots, especially off the southern point. The north and west bay beaches are fine gravel and good for beaching small boats. A tide flat on the southwest side of the island has clams. A looped walking trail encircles the island. In 1841, the Wilkes Expedition originally mapped this area as a point of land on San Juan Island and named it Point Salsbury. When it was found to be an island, it was renamed Turn because it was at the turn in the channel. 360-378-2044. ▲ ⛺ 🚶

★ **Griffin Bay (44):** [18434] Anchorage is possible in several niches, such as the bight inside Pear Point, the indentation near the quarry on the north shore, Merrifield Cove along the western shore, and along the Fish Creek shoreline near Cattle Point. Caution is advised near Dinner Island, a pretty islet to see, but watch for hazardous

Photo by Matt Pranger

Stay, play and enjoy the whole day.
Gather with friends so the fun never ends...

Where Friday Begins

PORT OF FRIDAY HARBOR

360-378-2688 * VHF 66A
www.portfridayharbor.org

Visit us at boattravel.com

rocks. North Bay has some protection in westerlies. Little Island, connected by a spit of land to the mainland, once the site of cannery operations, is now home to Jackson Beach Park. Directly behind the spit is the Argyle Lagoon Biological Reserve. Land surrounding Griffin Bay has historical significance. The British fleet trained here with its guns aimed at American Camp. San Juan Town, which burned in 1890, and the settlement of Argyle, were once established communities along the shoreline.

★ **Jackson Beach Park:** A log-strewn beach, free, two sided paved launch ramp, picnic tables, sites with fire rings, restroom, beach volleyball court.

★ **Griffin Bay Campground: (45):** This DNR managed site, located on the western shore is accessible by boat only and may be difficult to spot until one is close enough to shore to see the entry sign. There is no overland access. It is about 1/2 mile north of American Camp, in from Halftide Rocks. There is a charted foul area with pilings. Surrounding lands and the Fish Creek property nearby, are private. The 19 acre recreation site has five campsites (three of those are Cascadia Marine Trail sites), picnic areas, fire rings, and vault toilets. No potable water. Anchorage is possible, subject to submerged hazards. 360-856-3500.

Anchoring off San Juan Island   *Photo © Russ Veenema*

★ **San Juan Island National Historical Park:** This park is composed of two units, English Camp at Garrison Bay (52) and American Camp (46) along the southern shore of Griffin Bay to Cattle Point. These camps were part of the Pig War of 1859, the border-setting confrontation between the United States and Great Britain. This dispute began when an American settler shot a pig belonging to the British-owned Hudson's Bay Company. Except for the ill-fated pig, no other shots were fired and there were no human casualties during the crisis and 12-year joint military occupation of the island. Facilities were constructed to house the troops at both island locations. Kaiser Wilhelm I of Germany was finally accepted by both sides as the arbitrator. In 1872, he ruled in favor of the United States, setting the boundary in Haro Strait and placing the San Juan Islands in the United States. Literature about the Pig War is available at the park. 360-378-2240.

★ **American Camp (46):** This part of the park is primarily accessed by land. There are picnic facilities, a sweeping prairie and beaches. Three original wooden structures remain in and adjacent to the fenced parade ground. A redoubt (or earthwork) constructed during the Pig War crisis is perfectly preserved on a rise overlooking the Strait of Juan de Fuca and Griffin Bay. Fresh water is available except during mid-winter months. Anchorage is possible along the park's shoreline on Griffin Bay. There are no dock facilities, no camping allowed. The park is open daily. Visit the American Camp Visitor Center which has exhibits, park film, a bookstore and rangers on hand to answer questions. Ranger programs are available during June - September.

Walk-around: A historical trail at American Camp includes 10 marked points of interest, including photographs, descriptions, and exhibits.

Cattle Point Natural Resources Conservation Area (NRCA) (47): Situated atop a large sand dune, picturesque Cattle Point Lighthouse, marks the entrance to Cattle Pass. Located north of the lighthouse on the bluff above the Cattle Pass shore, the larger Cattle Point day use area includes an interpretive center, parking, beach access, a picnic area with shelter and restroom, and hiking trails with viewpoints offering outstanding views of the Olympic and Cascade Mountains and surrounding islands. Wildlife is abundant and includes eagles and other birds of prey. No fresh water. Small boats may be beached. Currents are often strong in the pass. Anchoring is not recommended. Cattle Pass is said to have received its name when a boat loaded with cattle wrecked and the cattle had to swim ashore. 360-856-3500.

False Bay (48): This curving bay well deserves its name. Boaters who enter the shallows often find themselves high-and-dry. Nearly all of the bay dries. The land is owned by the University of Washington and is used for marine biological study.

Kanaka Bay: On the chart Kanaka Bay shows as the third indentation north of False Bay. Temporary anchorage only, with some protection from northwest winds. Use Charts 18433 and 18434. This bay is named for the Kanakas, sheepherders who were indigenous natives of Hawaii. The were brought to this island from Hawaii by the Hudson's Bay Company and their main settlement was near Kanaka Bay.

Johns Pass runs between Stuart & Johns Islands Photo © Chris Teren / TerenPhotography.com

Deadman Bay: Temporary anchorage is possible, settled weather only. Avoid shoal areas along north shore. Extensive kelp beds with submerged rock formations are intriguing to scuba divers.

★ **Lime Kiln Point State Park:** This park is named for the kilns once built for the production of local limestone. Accessed by land, this whale-watching park is the first of its kind in the U.S. An interpretive center provides displays and exhibits about the kinds of whales which frequent the area. There are picnic sites, restrooms, and trails. A lighthouse, built around 1919, is on the point. Lighthouse tours and guided walks are offered during summer months. No marine facilities are provided. Diving is possible, but this is considered a very difficult shore dive and strong currents can be dangerous. 360-378-2044.

★ **San Juan County Park & Small Pox Bay (49):** [18433] This park has a launching ramp, campsites, fireplaces, park office, picnic facilities, and restrooms. Temporary anchorage in the bay is possible close to shore, however it is open to winds and wakes from Haro Strait. Scuba diving and snorkeling are popular because of the colorful and sheer mass of marine animals. There are panoramic views of Saanich Peninsula and the lights of Victoria. The bay was named when an epidemic swept through the Indian tribe which inhabited the area. Story tells that in a fever-fighting attempt, the Indians sought relief by diving into the bay, only to contact pneumonia as a result.

Smuggler's Cove: This tiny niche has limited usage for the boater, however it has been witness to the smuggling in of Chinese laborers, opium and diamonds, and during the Prohibition years, liquor from Puerto Rico, Scotland, and Canada.

★ **Mitchell Bay (50):** Located on the west side of San Juan Island, this bay is near the southern entrance to Mosquito Pass. A channel leads through rocky patches to the inner bay. Although the entry may appear tricky, there is no problem if the boater stays mid-channel and to the east of the rocks entering the bay. The center of the bay has a minimum depth of six feet at an extreme low tide.

Snug Harbor Resort & Marina: {48° 34' 15.8" N, 123° 10' 2.4" W} Permanent moorage to 60', transient moorage to 35' (call ahead to reserve), 30 amp power, water, showers, coffee shop, store, gifts, ice, snacks, cabins, suites. 360-378-4762.

★ **Mosquito Pass (51):** [18433] This narrow, shallow waterway stretches over a mile from Hanbury Point on the south to Bazalgette Point on the north. There are both charted and uncharted rocks in the pass. Although hazards are marked, caution is advised. In summer, kelp marks most rocky patches. At times of maximum tidal flow, strong currents are present. Flood tide sets north, ebb south. A county ordinance specifing a low-wake and maximum speed of six knots is enforced in Mosquito Pass.

★ **Garrison Bay (52):** [18433] Garrison Bay and Westcott Bay indent into the San Juan Island shore about midway through Mosquito Pass. Garrison Bay is shallow, however anchorage is good if attention is paid to overnight depths. Check the chart for submerged rocks on the starboard side of the bay. Anchorage is possible in the center near the entrance or to port in the vicinity of Guss Island.

★ **English Camp Unit, San Juan Island National Historical Park:** British Royal Marines landed here in 1860 to share the island with their U.S. Army counterparts already at American Camp, 13 miles south. Several original buildings have been restored, including a blockhouse, commissary, hospital, and a barracks that now has an information center with book and gift shop and audiovisual presentation. In the summer, living history and other programs are presented each Saturday. A formal garden replicates the original planted by the Royal Marines in 1867. There are several giant bigleaf maples, including a 350 year-old specimen. Deer and small animals are plentiful. No hunting permitted, dogs must be leashed. A 115' pier and dinghy dock extend into Garrison Bay providing access. No fresh water or overnight camping.

Walk-around: Begin in the English Camp parking lot, cross West Valley Road, and continue on the trail to The Royal Marine Cemetery found in the clearing near the base of Young Hill. For spectacular island views, hike to the summit of 650-foot Young Hill. Twelve wayside exhibits with photographs, paintings and text are located throughout the parade ground and officers' hill. The dinghy dock gives onto the Bell Point trail. Go left at the top of the steps and follow the relatively flat trail for one mile to the parade ground.

★ **Westcott Bay (53):** This bay is larger than Garrison and somewhat deeper in the center. Grass marks shallow spots. Use a depth sounder or lead line to check the depth within the scope of the overnight anchor rode. Much of the shoreline is private. There is public access and good clamming on the south shore near Bell Point. A trail connects Bell Point with English Camp. Further along the shore, the Westcott Bay Shellfish Company dock offers bow-tie only dinghy access for boaters who visit the retail store. Please note that the dock is private and use is prohibited when the farm is closed. (Open Memorial Day-Labor Day, 11am-5pm). Sit at a communal picnic table onsite to shuck and eat your purchase.

Haro Strait (54): When traversing Haro Strait, note that the ebb sets south and the flood to the north. Currents at springs reach five knots. The deepest water in Haro Strait is off Stuart Island where depths reach 1,356 feet.

★ **Roche Harbor (55):** [18433] The harbor is protected by Pearl Island on the north and Henry Island on the west. Entry from the north is made by passing either side of Pearl Island. On low and minus tides, the western passage is preferred because depths in the eastern pass are shallow to four feet of water. Steer mid-channel in either pass. Entry from the south is made from Mosquito Pass. There is anchorage in the bay in depths of 15-50 feet on a good bottom. Give a wide berth to private docks which extend from shore and from the resort floats.

U.S. Customs & Border Protection Designated Port of Entry: Roche Harbor is no longer a U.S. Point of Entry. There is an unstaffed CBP booth located on Dock G to report arrival via the ROAM app.

Philbrooks Boatyard@Roche Harbor Marine: Haul-outs to 33', marine engine service/repair, parts, chandlery, boat storage. No DIY allowed in boatyard. 360-378-6510.

Roche Harbor: {48° 36.45' N, 123° 09.30' W} Customs-port-of-entry via ROAM app. This marina resort accommodates permanent and guest moorage. Power, water, gas, diesel, propane, launch, showers, laundry, pool, restaurants, lounge and lodging. A paved, lighted airstrip services the resort. Marina: 1-800-586-3590. Resort: 1-800-451-8910. VHF 78A.

Walk-around: Near the entry arches to Roche Harbor is The San Juan Islands Sculpture Park,

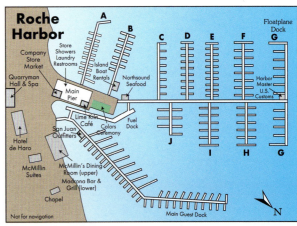

a 20-acre park with trails to stroll and view over 150 outdoor sculptures. $5 donation per adult appreciated. The park is about .5 walk from Roche Harbor Marina.

★⚓ **Posey Island Marine State Park (56):** Named for the profusion of wildflowers that grow here in season, this tiny park has two reservable Cascadia Marine Trail campsites, a composting toilet. No potable water or garbage deposit. Day-use only for motorized boaters. Because the passage between Posey and Pearl Islands is shallow and strewn with rocks, this park is used primarily by canoe and kayak recreationists. ⛺▲

★ **Henry Island (57):** It is possible to imagine that this island is shaped like the letter H. Open Bay and Nelson Bay indent the island's shores. Open Bay is popular for fishing. Beware of the rocks off the southeast tip of the island. They extend some distance from shore, are covered at high tide, and are not well marked. Anchorage with protection from northerly winds is possible near the head of the bay. Nelson Bay has anchorage near its entrance. The inner bay is shallow. A more preferred anchorage in this bay is farther north, past the site of the Seattle Yacht Club out-station at 48° 36.2' N, 123° 10.2' W.

Stuart Island
[18421, 18423, 18432, Canadian 3462]

★⚓ **Stuart Island/Stuart Island State Park (58):** [18423] Home to several families who reside on private land, it is also the site of Stuart Island Marine Park with 20 buoys and 448 feet of dock, as well as a pumpout station. All of these facilities are found in two locations, Prevost Harbor and Reid Harbor. Additionally, there are plenty of good anchorages in Prevost Harbor. Millions of years of natural erosion have left a very irregular and picturesque shoreline on this beautiful island. Douglas fir, madrona, red cedar, juniper, and oak provide a lush forest. Wildflowers are common in spring, and several varieties of mushroom grow in spring and fall. Deer and raccoon, as well as eagles, ravens, and a variety of gulls are commonly seen.

Early settlers on Stuart Island were fishermen and ranchers, as are many of the current residents. An interesting pioneer cemetery includes plots over 100 years old. Other points of interest include a one room school house that served the local population until 2013 and the Stuart Island Treasure Chest (a wooden chest filled with shirts, hats and other items. IOU's and return envelopes are provided for payment by the honor system.) Turn Point Lighthouse overlooking Haro Straight is a local landmark. Currents in this vicinity can run to six knots and dangerous rips form. By water, it is a short three to four miles from Turn Point to the southern Gulf Islands in Canada. Turn Point, a blind point is a Special Operating Area so monitor VHF 11 when in this vicinity to be aware of approaching vessel traffic.

★⚓ **Prevost Harbor at Stuart Island State Park:** Prevost Harbor is located on the north side of Stuart Island, protected by Satellite Island. Enter between Charles Point on Stuart and the northwest end of Satellite. Do not use the rock strewn pass southeast of Satellite Island. There are seven mooring buoys, a dock with moorage floats, and a linear mooring system. Moorage fees are charged all year. There is anchorage in several places. The grassy bottom may foul your patent anchor. Many prefer to anchor in the bight near Satellite's west end. There is a drying rock in the entrance to this bight that is marked by kelp in summer. A pier, used by the Coast Guard and San Juan County, is on the west shore. Campsites, hiking trail, seasonal drinking water (May to September). 360-378-2044. 🚶▲

Turn Point Lighthouse on the northwest tip of Stuart Island

Walk-around: Take the 6-mile round trip trail inside Charles Point that leads to the lighthouse. The correct road is the one straight ahead, not the one to the left past the cemetery. 🚶

★⚓ **Reid Harbor at Stuart Island State Park:** Over 1 mile long, Reid Harbor indents like a crooked finger into Stuart Island. Cemetery and Gossip Islands, near the entrance, are undeveloped marine parks. The bay lies in a northwest to southeast direction. Private homes and State Park lands are on shore. On the north side at the head of the bay, a dock with a mooring float extends from shore. A boat pump out is at the dock. Anchorage is possible in four to five fathoms, mud bottom. There is a linear mooring system, as well as 13 mooring buoys that are spaced strategically throughout the harbor. Park facilities include campsites, fire rings, shelters, picnic tables, composting toilets, fresh water, and a waste pump and dump. Blacktail deer and raccoon are often seen in the park, as are bald eagles, ravens, and seagulls of many varieties. A colony of prickly pear cactus, not a native species, are of special note. 360-378-2044. ⛺▲

Walk-around: A trail at the head diverts foot traffic away from private land between the park and the school house. It winds through woods and marsh and crosses a low, gracefully curved bridge. At the intersection with the public road, hand painted signs, made years ago by the school children, point the way to Turn Point Lighthouse where views stretch to British Columbia.

★ **Johns Pass (59):** This pass separates Stuart Island from Johns Island. Depths are 4 to 11 fathoms. Currents run to five knots on spring tides, ebbing north, flooding south. An extensive reef stretches southeast for over one-half mile from the Stuart Island shore. Foul ground is marked by kelp, but extends farther out than one might expect. Stay in mid-channel to avoid kelp-marked rocky patches. When heading southeast from the pass, aim toward Gull Reef, which has a drying islet. Stay on this heading until well clear of the kelp patches.

★ **Spieden Channel & Spieden Island (60):** The flood current flows east from Haro Strait and west from San Juan Channel often causing heavy rips in Spieden Channel and off Green Point. Green Point on the east tip of Spieden Island shelters a small harbor. There are several homes on this 2 mile long, private island. Spieden is dry and barren on the south side, green and thickly forested on the north. There is no good anchorage. In the early 1970's, the island was stocked with exotic wildlife and birds and renamed "Safari Island" with the intent to promote hunting excursions, but the venture was short lived. Sixteen acre Sentinel Island has been purchased by the Nature Conservancy.

Northern Islands
[18421, 18423, 18431, 18432, Canadian 3462]

★ **Waldron Island (61):** North Bay and Cowlitz Bay offer some anchorage in settled weather. Cowlitz Bay, on the SW corner of the island has a small county dock and private floats. Mail Bay, a tiny niche in the east shore, is rock strewn and has only limited anchorage in the northern section. Minimum depth is six feet. A mooring buoy in approximate position {48-43-09. 7N, 123-01-47.8W} marked "CG" is reserved for government use. This bay was named because mail was delivered here from Orcas. Sandstone bricks were exported from Waldron near the turn of the century. Between Waldron and Patos Islands tide rips and swirls occur off the northern tip of Waldron Island, especially in high winds and ebb currents.

Skipjack Island (62): Named in the 1850's for the skipjack fish caught in the area, this, and neighboring Bare Island, are now wildlife preserves. Boat landing is prohibited. Underwater reefs located here are favorites of divers. 🐟

★⚓ **Patos Island Marine State Park & Active Cove (63):** This park lies a few miles northwest of Sucia Island. Facilities include two mooring buoys in Active Cove, seven campsites, one picnic site, two toilets, and a 1.5 mile loop trail. No potable water, no garbage deposit. Beachcombing, above average cod and salmon fishing, and viewing marine life in the tidal pools among the rocks are popular activities. Entry into Active Cove should only be made off the west end of Little Patos Island at the foot of the wooded hill that bends to the beach. A sandy beach is at the head of the bay. Rocks and ruins of a dock restrict the anchoring area. Mooring buoys are the best choice for overnight stays since the currents can run fairly strong in the cove. Check weather reports before anchoring. Forecasts calling for high pressure systems and westerly winds exceeding 12 knots in southern Georgia Strait can easily cause you to drag anchor and go aground. The word "Patos" means ducks in Spanish. This island is a breeding ground for birds, especially seagulls which enjoy flying bombing missions over peaceful boaters anchored nearby. The automated light at Alden Point is open for tours on some weekends from Memorial Day-Labor Day. 360-376-2073. ▲⛺🚶

Rolfe Cove, Matia Island — Photo © Chris Teren / TerenPhotography.com

★⚓ **Sucia Island Marine State Park (64):** [18431, 18421] This Marine Park includes several islands: Sucia, Little Sucia, Ewing, and the Clusters. North and South Finger Islands and Harnden are private. The island group is located 2½ miles north from Orcas Island. Several bays have anchorage, park buoys, and shore facilities. These include Echo Bay, Snoring Bay, Ewing Cove, Fossil Bay, Fox Cove, and Shallow Bay. In many places, small boats can be beached easily. Sucia has an extensive number of campsites with tables and stoves. Fresh water is available during summer. Primitive roads and hiking trails wind around most of the islands, and fine beaches provide sunbathing and picnic sites.

Fishing is often good for cod, rockfish, and salmon. Irregular coastlines with spectacular rock formations and picturesque bays are a photographer's paradise. Swimming and scuba diving are popular activities. An underwater park marked with a locator buoy in Ewing Cove, is a favorite for divers. Over the years, water has carved hundreds of tide pools into the sandstone. Here, limpets, starfish, snails, sea urchins, sea anemone, and crabs delight old and young marine biologists. Sandstone also played a part in the Island's earlier history when smugglers used the sandstone crevices as hiding places for their hoards of silk, opium, and whiskey. Later, in the early 1900's sandstone bricks from Sucia were used to pave the streets in many Puget Sound towns.

The island's name originated with the Spanish Captain Eliza who labeled it *Isla Sucia* on his map of 1790. In the nautical sense, Sucia means foul. The name was probably chosen because the shore was reef strewn. 360-376-2073, 360-902-8844.

★ **Echo Bay:** [18431] {48° 45' 47.89" N, 122° 54' 37" W} Largest in size, this is a favorite destination for many, although swells often enter from Rosario Strait. Good holding bottom. If anchoring, favor the area behind the Finger Islands. A no anchor zone is in place at the head of the bay. There are 14 buoys and two linear moorage systems in the bay. Potable water available May-Sept. North and South Finger Islands are privately owned. Justice Island, the small island off the tip of South Finger is a state owned wildlife preserve and is closed to the public.

Walk-around: There are over six miles of hiking trails and logging roads. An enjoyable walk is from Echo Bay to Fossil Bay.

★ **Ewing Cove:** {48° 45' 55" N, 122° 53' 9" W} This hideaway cove is found in the north portion of Echo Bay. Caution advised regarding a rock in the entrance from Echo Bay, near the area marked "Fish Haven" on the chart. It is just underwater at low tide. The four buoys here have more protection than those in the wide bay to the south. There are primitive campsites, hiking trail, and a nice beach. This is an underwater park with three sunken vessels for divers.

★ **Snoring Bay:** {48° 4' 55.67" N, 122° 53' 26.99" W} Nearly parallel to Fossil Bay, narrow Snoring Bay is home to 2 buoys, campsites, and hiking trail. It is steep-sided and open to east and southeast winds. Anchoring space is limited, but there is protection during summer months from the prevailing northwest winds.

★ **Fossil Bay:** {48° 45' 0" N, 122° 54' 1.98" W} Perhaps the busiest area is Fossil Bay where there are 16 buoys and two moorage docks. The float behind Harnden Island remains in place all year, the other is removed from late Oct -March. The anchorage basin is a wide area with good bottom. Anchoring depths are adequate, but because this is a relatively shallow bay and winds can enter, especially from the south and southeast, anchorage can be uncomfortable in unsettled conditions. Campsites and picnic areas are on shore. Potable water is available April-Sept. Mud Bay, next to Fossil Bay, is a favorite for those who enjoy exploring by dinghy. It is too shallow for anchorage and dries on low tides.

★ **Fox Cove:** {48° 45' 9.97" N, 122° 54' 47.88" W} Back-to-back with Fossil Bay, anchorage and four buoys are found in this picturesque cove. Little Sucia Island offers some protection. Pay close attention to the chart to avoid extensive reefs off the island.

★ **Shallow Bay:** {48° 45' 43.92" N, 122° 55' 2" W} As its name implies, this popular destination offers anchorage and eight buoys in its one to two fathom depths. The southern portion and much of the bay close to shore is too shallow for overnight anchorage. Located on Sucia Island's west coast, it has the best protection in south and southeast winds. Watch out for strong northwesterlies. Enter between the green and red markers, keeping the green to port. The markers indicate reefs which extend from shore. Camping, hikers hiking the trails and swimming in the warm water are favorite pastimes. As of June 2018, concrete blocks at 48° 45'.842" N, 122° 55' 032 were reported at a depth of 8 feet meaning lower low tide. A scenic marshland at the southern end is popular with photographers, as are China Rock and sunsets framed through the bay's entrance.

★⚓ **Matia Island Marine State Park (65):** This sandstone island is 2.5 miles north of Orcas Island and 1.5 miles east of Sucia Island. Two bights indent the shore near Eagle Point on the island's west side, both are open to winds from the west and northwest. One is quite small. The other, Rolfe Cove, is a deeper indentation that houses a dock and two buoys. Anchorage is difficult because the bottom is rock. Rolfe Cove has six campsites, a sandy beach, one picnic site, a composting toilet, and a loop hiking trail. No fresh water, no open fires, no garbage deposit. Because all but five acres of the park are part of a wildlife refuge, only the Rolfe Cove campsite, the loop trail and the beaches are open for public use.

A small bight on the south side is a beautiful anchorage for a small boat. This bay is sheltered from west and northwest winds. Anchorage for larger boats is in the deeper indentation at the southeast tip of the island. This secluded harbor is unnamed and appears on the chart with a 2.3 fathom mark, and 0 at the head. With the exception of extremely low summer tides, depths are adequate, except at the head of the bay. Check sounder and expected overnight tide depths.

The area between Puffin and Matia is foul with many reefs and kelp beds to mark underwater dangers. If approaching from the direction of Puffin Island, there is a reef with a light on it. There is a passage through the floating kelp between Puffin and a curving bay on Matia's eastern shore. Temporary anchorage is possible in this bight, also marked two fathoms on the chart.

Captain Eliza of the Spanish Expedition of 1792 named the island *Isle de Matia*. The name, pronounced Mah-tee-ah, has many meanings in Spanish, most having to do with lush plant growth. Interestingly, the island was once a fox farm. Puffin Island is a bird sanctuary where cormorants, puffins, and other birds abound. 360-376-2073.

Barnes Island (66): This privately-owned island lies parallel to Clark Island. Water depth is more than adequate for passage in the channel between the two islands. Reefs lie along the Barnes shore.

★⚓ **Clark Island Marine State Park (67):** This lesser known haven for boaters stretches lengthwise in a northwest to south-southeast direction. The island's shape resembles a slender rocket with its exhaust sprinkled out like the cluster of rocks known as The Sisters. When circling the island, avoid the long reef extending from its northwestern tip. While there are no well protected bays on Clark's shoreline, there are indentations which offer some shelter. Gravel and sand beaches are excellent for beaching small boats. Clark Island features nine moorage buoys (no vessels over 45'). Moorage buoys on the west side of the island are subject to strong currents. Mooring buoys on the east side sit in the wide curving bay that is formed by the sweep of beach that extends out from the southeast tip of the island. This mooring is exposed to winds from several directions and to wakes from passing freighters. Sandy beaches on the south have good clamming. Campsites, 1 composting toilet and 2 vault toilets are provided. 360-376-2073.

Essential Supplies & Services

AIR TRANSPORTATION
Friday Harbor Seaplanes
. . . . 425-277-1590, 1-800-690-0086
Kenmore Air 1-866-435-9524
NW Seaplanes . . . 425-277-1590, 1-800-690-0086
San Juan Airlines 1-800-874-4434
Seattle Seaplanes 1-800-637-5553

BOOKS / BOOK STORES
Evergreen Pacific Publishing 425-493-1451
The Marine Atlas 253-872-5707

COAST GUARD
Emergencies . . . . 911, 206-217-6001 or VHF 16
Puget Sound Sector Office 206-217-6200
Vessel Traffic 206-217-6152

CUSTOMS / BORDER PROTECTION
Anacortes 360-293-2331
Canada Border Services Telephone Reporting Centre
. 1-888-226-7277
Friday Harbor/Roche Harbor 360-378-2080
U.S. Customs Telephone Reporting. . . .1-800-562-5943

FERRY INFORMATION
Friday Harbor 360-378-8665
Lopez Island 360-468-4095
Orcas Island 360-376-6253
Washington State 1-888-808-7977

FISHING LICENSES
Roche Harbor 360-378-5562

FISHING/SHELLFISHING INFO
Fishing Regulations 360-902-2500
24 Hour Red Tide Hotline 1-800-562-5632
Shellfish Rule Change Hotline. 1-866-880-5431

FUELS
Blakely Island Marina: Gas, Diesel. 360-375-6121
Deer Harbor Marina: Gas, Diesel.
. . . . 360-376-3037 VHF 78A
Friday Harbor: Gas, Diesel 360-378-3114
Lopez Islander Resort: Gas, Diesel
. . . . 360-468-2233 VHF 78A
Roche Harbor: Gas, Diesel . . 1-800-586-3590 VHF 78A
Rosario Resort. . . . . 360-376-2222 VHF 78A
West Beach Resort: Orcas Island. Gas . . 360-376-2240
West Sound Marina: Gas, Diesel.
. . . . 360-376-2314 VHF 16, 9

GOLF COURSES
(These courses are accessible from moorage and have rental clubs available)
Lopez Island 360-468-2679
Orcas Island 360-376-4400
San Juan Island 360-378-2254

HAUL-OUTS
Deer Harbor Boatworks 360-376-4056
Islands Marine Center
. . . . .360-468-3377 VHF 69, 16
Philbrooks Boatyard@Roche Harbor Marine . . . .
. . . . 360-378-6510
West Sound Marina . . . . 360-376-2314 VHF 16, 9

HOSPITALS/CLINICS
Friday Harbor Medical Center 360-378-2141
Lopez Island Medical Center 360-468-2245
Orcas Island Medical Center 360-376-2561

LIQUOR STORES
East Sound 360-376-2616
Friday Harbor 360-378-4505

LODGING/INNS
Islands Marine Center
. . . . .360-468-3377 VHF 69, 16
Lopez Islander Resort . . . . . . 360-468-2233 VHF 78A
Roche Harbor 1-800-451-8910
Rosario Resort. . . . . 360-376-2222 VHF 78A
Snug Harbor Resort: San Juan Island . . 360-378-4762

MARINAS / MOORAGE FLOATS
Bay Head Marina, Permanent 855-948-6413
Blakely General Store & Marina 360-375-6121
Cayou Quay Marina, Permanent 360-376-4560
Deer Harbor Marina . . . . 360-376-3037 VHF 78A
Friday Harbor, Port of. . . . 360-378-2688 VHF 66A
Islands Marine Center
. . . . .360-468-3377 VHF 69, 16
James Island State Park
Jones Island State Park
Lieber Haven Rentals (summer) 360-376-2472
Lopez Islander Resort . . . . 360-468-2233 VHF 78A
Matia Island State Park
Olga Community Float
Orcas Landing
Prevost Harbor: Stuart Island
Reid Harbor: Stuart Island
Roche Harbor . . . . 1-800-586-3590 VHF 78A
Rosario Resort. . . . . 360-376-2222 VHF 78A
Shipyard Cove Marina, Permanent 360-378-2688
Spencer's Landing Marina, Permanent. . 360-468-2077
Sucia Island State Park
West Beach Resort: Orcas Island 360-376-2240
West Sound Marina . . . . 360-376-2314 VHF 16, 9

MARINE SUPPLY STORES
Islands Marine Center
. . . . .360-468-3377 VHF 69, 16
West Sound Marina . . . . 360-376-2314 VHF 16, 9

PARKS
Department of Natural Resources 360-856-3500
San Juan County Parks 360-378-8420
Washington State 360-902-8844
Washington Camping Reservations . . .1-888-226-7688

PHOTOGRAPHY
Chris Teren Photography
. . . . www.terenphotography.com

PROPANE
Friday Harbor, Port of. 360-378-3114
Roche Harbor . . . . 1-800-586-3590 VHF 78A
Shaw General Store: Shaw Landing 360-468-2288
Sunset Builders, Lopez 360-468-2241
West Sound Marina . . . . 360-376-2314 VHF 16, 9

PROVISIONS
Deer Harbor Marina: . . . . 360-376-3037 VHF 78A
Lopez Village Market 360-468-2266
Roche Harbor . . . . 1-800-586-3590 VHF 78A

RAMPS
Cayou Quay (no parking) 360-376-4560
Deer Harbor Boatworks (call ahead) 360-376-4056
Lopez Island: Hunter Bay; MacKaye Harbor; Odlin Park
Shaw Island: Shaw Island County Park (Indian Cove)
Islands Marine Center . .360-468-3377 VHF 69, 16
Jackson Beach: Griffin Bay
Moran State Park: Orcas Island
Roche Harbor . . . . 1-800-586-3590 VHF 78A
San Juan County Park: Small Pox Bay

REPAIRS/SERVICE
Islands Marine Center . .360-468-3377 VHF 69, 16
Platypus Marine Inc. Port Angeles . . . 360-417-0709
Philbrooks Boatyard @ Roche Harbor Marine
. . . . 360-378-6510
West Sound Marina . . . . 360-376-2314 VHF 16, 9

RESTAURANTS
Deer Harbor Inn 360-376-1040
Downriggers (Friday Harbor) 360-378-2700
Galley Restaurant & Lounge (Lopez) . . . 360-468-2713
Kingfish at West Sound 360-376-4440
Lopez Islander Resort . . . . 360-468-2233 VHF 78A
Roche Harbor 1-800-451-8910
Rosario Resort. . . . . 360-376-2222 VHF 78A

SCUBA SITES
Doe Island Marine State Park   Jones Island
Point Doughty: Orcas Island   San Juan County Park
Sucia Island   Odlin Park
Spencer Spit Marine State Park   Deadman Bay
Ewing Cove

SEWAGE DISPOSAL
Deer Harbor Marina: Pump 360-376-3037
Friday Harbor, Port of: Pump-Out . . . 360-378-2688
Islands Marine: Lopez Isl. Pump
. . . . .360-468-3377 VHF 69, 16
Matia Island State Park: Dump.
Reid Harbor: Stuart Island. Pump, Dump
Roche Harbor: Pump, Dump 1-800-586-3590
West Beach Resort 360-376-2240
West Sound Marina: Pump 360-376-2314

TAXI/SHUTTLE/RENTAL
Orcas Island (Rental) 360-376-7433
Orcas Island (Taxi) 360-376-8294
San Juan Island (Rental) 360-378-5244
San Juan Island (Taxi & Tours)
. . . 360-378-6777, 360-378-3550, or 360-298-6975
San Juan Island Transit 360-378-8887

TOWING
TowBoat U.S. - Friday Harbor 360-378-1111
Anacortes 360-675-7900

TRAILER REPAIR (MOBILE)
Trailer Techs. 206-889-0286

VISITOR INFORMATION
All Islands 360-378-9551, 1-888-468-3701
Lopez 360-468-4664
Orcas 360-376-2273
San Juan 360-378-5240

WEATHER:
CCG Marine Broadcast: Haro Strait 250-363-6880
NOAA Recorded Message 206-526-6087
Port Angeles: WX-4, Seattle: WX-1, Victoria: WX-3

Important Notices

CROSSING THE BORDER

Canada Border Services Agency (or CBSA)

View from the wheelhouse near Bowen Island (page 168) Photo © Russ Veenema

Reporting requirements for private boaters: All private boats entering Canadian waters with fewer than 30 passengers onboard must report their arrival to the Canada Border Services Agency (CBSA) *unless* they meet the following **reporting exemptions:**

You are visiting Canada, you do not land on Canadian soil, do not anchor, moor or make contact with another conveyance while in Canadian waters, and do not embark or disembark people or goods in Canada.

You are returning to Canada, you did not land outside Canada, did not anchor, moor or make contact with another conveyance while outside of Canadian waters, and did not embark or disembark any people or goods while outside Canada.

Making a report: As the operator of the boat, only you are allowed to report to the CBSA. You will need to report:
- the reasons for your trip
- passenger information
- goods to declare

U.S. citizens and other foreign nationals must provide the following:
- full name, date of birth and citizenship
- length and purpose of the stay in Canada
- destination
- visa information (if applicable)
- valid passport, NEXUS of FAST membership card (if applicable), proof of permanent residence i.e. valid driver's license.

Canadian citizens, permanent residents and persons registered under the Indian Act must present the following:
- full name, date of birth and citizenship
- the length of absence from Canada
- one of the following; Canadian passport, Canadian birth certificate, permanent resident card, citizenship card, Secure Certificate of Indian Status card or valid Certificate of Indian Status card.

Reporting Methods: Some vessel reporting stations have a CBSA Officer on duty during the boating season, others utilize a telephone reporting system. Upon arrival in Canada, proceed to a designated station and report to CBSA via telephone. The 24-hour Telephone Reporting Centre (TRC) phone number is 1-888-226-7277. Before calling, gather the following information: Vessel name, length, registration or documentation number, estimated length of stay in Canada and the names, birthdates, citizenship and country of residence of all people aboard the vessel. The CBSA Officer may issue an oral clearance, or may visit the vessel in person if inspection or documentation is required. Only the operator may leave the boat to place the call. Everyone else must remain onboard until the CBSA authorizes entry. No baggage or merchandise may be unloaded until a clearance number has been issued. Once cleared by CBSA, record the date, time and clearance number in your logbook. Follow directions given at CBSA for posting the clearance number on your boat.

CBSA Marine Reporting Sites: Unless otherwise specified, CBSA hours are 24/7. Where, due to weather conditions or other emergencies, the vessel arrives at a place which is not designated for customs reporting, the vessel operator has to report the circumstances to the nearest customs office, the Royal Canadian Mounted Police or by calling the TRC, 1-888-226-7277. NEXUS telephone reporting line, 1-866-99-NEXUS (1-866-996-3987). For a list of CBSA Marine Reporting Sites in B.C., www.cbsa-asfc.gc.ca/do-rb/services/trsm-sdtm-eng.html.

CANPASS Private Boats program members maintain privileges until their memberships expire.

CBSA Marine Reporting Sites arranged by chapters. Please confirm current CBSA Site status by visiting https://www.cbsa-asfc.gc.ca/do-rb/open-poe-temp-pdeouvert/marine-maritime-eng.html

CHAPTER 8
Victoria:
Oak Bay Marina
Raymur Point CBSA Boat Dock
Royal Victoria Yacht Club
Sidney - Tsehum:
Port of Sidney
Sidney RVYC Outstation
Tsehum Harbour
Van Isle Marina
North Saanich: Canoe Cove Marina

CHAPTER 9
Cabbage Island (NEXUS/Marine only)
South Pender Island:
Bedwell Harbour - Friday before Victoria Day until Labour Day, open 8am to 8pm daily. Rest of the year open 9am to 5pm daily.
Mayne Island:
Horton Bay (NEXUS/Marine only)
Miners Bay (NEXUS/Marine only)
North Pender Island:
Port Browning (NEXUS/Marine only)

CHAPTER 10
Galiano Island:
Montague Harbour Marina (NEXUS/Marine only)
Salt Spring Island:
Ganges Harbour (NEXUS/Marine only)
Royal Vancouver Yacht Club Scott Point Outstation (NEXUS/Marine only)
Saltspring Royal Victoria Yacht Club Outstation (NEXUS/Marine only)

CHAPTER 11
Nanaimo:
Nanaimo Boat Basin E Dock
Townsite Marina (NEXUS/Marine only)

CHAPTER 12
Vancouver:
Crescent Beach Marina
False Creek Fisherman's Wharf
Harbour Green Dock
Royal Vancouver Yacht Club Coal Harbour
Royal Vancouver Yacht Club Jericho Dock
Steveston: Steveston Harbour Authority (NEXUS/Marine & commercial vessels only)
Surrey: Crescent Beach Marina
White Rock: White Rock Government Dock

CHAPTER 16
Campbell River Coast Marina
Discovery Harbour Marina

CHAPTER 19
Prince Rupert:
Cow Bay Marina
Fairview Government Dock
Prince Rupert Yacht Club
Rushbrook Government Dock

CBSA Requirements: For detailed information visit www.cbsa.gc.ca or call 1-800-461-9999 (in English) or 1-800-959-2036 (in French). Outside Canada call 204-983-3500 or 506-636-5064.

The following information covers a few of the issues that you might encounter at the Canadian Border:

Proper Identification: Everyone entering Canada must have proof of citizenship. Identification in the form of photo ID and birth certificate, passport, or visa is required. When bringing children into Canada, including your own, you must carry ID for each minor. If the children are not yours or you are not the custodial parent, you must carry a notarized consent letter from the custodial parent authorizing you to take the child into Canada. Proof, such as legal custody documents, is recommended to verify that the person signing the authorization is the custodial parent.

Currency: All currency and monetary instruments of a value equal to or greater than CAN $10,000 must be reported to the CBSA.

Duty Free Entitlements: Fuel that is in the vessel's tanks, clothing, camping and sporting equipment, and a supply of food appropriate to the nature, purpose, and length of stay in Canada may enter duty free. Each adult is permitted the following amount of alcohol and tobacco products: 1.14 litres (40 oz) of liquor, or 1.5 litres (53 oz) of wine, or up to 8.5 litres of beer or ale (24 x 12 oz cans), 50 cigars, 200 cigarettes, 7 oz of manufactured tobacco, and 200 tobacco sticks.

Food, plants, animals or related products: Travelers are required to declare all plant, animal, and food items they bring into Canada. Restrictions on what food items you are allowed to bring into Canada vary, depending on the product. Because pest and disease situations are constantly changing, requirements may be adjusted at any time. Visit www.inspection.gc.ca for helpful information on this topic. Questions? Contact the CBSA BIS line, 1-800-461-9999 in Canada, 204-983-3500 outside Canada.

Pets: Dogs (eight months and older) and cats (three months and older) must have current (within the last three years) rabies vaccinations. Carry a signed, dated certificate from a veterinarian verifying this fact and clearly identifying the animal. For all other animals, refer to www.inspection.gc.ca or call 1-800-442-2342.

Firearms: Declare all firearms in writing to a customs officer at the point of entry to Canada, using the Non-Resident Firearm Declaration form (RCMP 5589). Additional information is available on the Royal Canadian Mounted Police website at www.rcmp-grc.gc.ca, or by calling the Canadian Firearms Program's toll-free information line at 1-800-731-4000.

Prescription Drugs: All prescription drugs should be clearly labeled in the original packaging. If possible, carry copies of the prescription or a letter from your doctor.

CANPASS - Private Boat Program: This program was discontinued in 2018. Current members maintain privileges until their membership expires. Boaters who frequently travel between Canada and the U.S. should consider joining NEXUS.

NEXUS Air/Highway/Marine: This "trusted traveler" program aims to lessen waits at the border. NEXUS card holders arriving via pleasure boat may report by calling 1-800-562-5943. To obtain a NEXUS card by mail, visit www.cbsa-asfc.gc.ca and download form BSF658. The cost is $50 (CAD) and the card is good for 5 years. Applications are also available online at https://ttp.cbp.dhs.gov. An in-person interview will be scheduled and conducted at a NEXUS Processing Center in the U.S. (Blaine) or in British Columbia (Vancouver). Visit www.cbp.gov and click on "Travel" for more information.

Retention of Foreign Pleasure Craft in Canada: Non-residents of Canada who plan to leave their boat for repairs, storage, or any other reason, must document this intent on a Form E29B and keep it available for review upon demand. Generally, foreign pleasure crafts left in Canada more than 12 months for storage and 18 months for repair are subject to duty and tax. Contact the nearest CBSA office to request an extension. For information, visit www.cbsa-asfc.gc.ca.

United States Customs & Border Protection

Customs Information: Clearing U.S. Customs and Border Protection (CBP) is fairly straight forward if you are prepared, so find out about requirements before you travel. Visit www.cbp.gov, go to the travel tab and search "Pleasure Boat & Private Flyers" for helpful information.

Reporting to Customs is the Law: As a general rule of law, the master of every vessel arriving in the U.S. from a foreign place or port must report to U.S. Customs at a designated port-of-entry. Travelers in possession of a NEXUS card or I-68 can still report their arrival by calling 1-800-562-5943 - or use the new CBP One app (refer to the "Reporting Offsite Arrival - Mobile" entry in this section). If travelers arriving by boat have questions about reporting their arrival to CBP, contact the local port of entry or call 1-800-562-5943 (For Puget Sound boat arrivals only). All persons and articles must stay onboard until released by a CBP Officer. Proof of citizenship must be presented (see Proper Identification entry.) Failing to report properly or not following procedures may result in a $5,000 fine, seizure, or criminal penalties.

It will significantly speed your clearance entering the U.S. from Canada if you have a Private Vessel Decal (vessels over 30' in length) or Cruising License, and if you know what items are allowed to cross the border.

The following information covers a few of the issues that you might encounter at the Border:

Proper Identification: When crossing into the U.S. from Canada boaters must present a Passport or Passport Card, a Trusted Traveler Card (NEXUS, SENTRI, Global Entry), or a Washington State EDL. Travelers who are members of the Trusted Traveler Program (Global Entry, NEXUS, SENTRI) should present that information first in lieu of a passport.

Currency: If you or you and your family together are carrying over $10,000 it must be reported to CBP. There is no fee for the importation or exportation of money, however, failure to report more than $10,000 can result in the seizure of all the money and/or an additional penalty.

Duty Free Entitlements: Fuel that is in the vessel's tanks, apparel, sporting equipment, and a two days supply of food can enter duty free.

Each returning U.S. resident is entitled to an $800 exemption once every 30 days provided they are out of the U.S. for at least 48 hours. Adults are allowed one liter of alcoholic beverage, including beer or wine, as well as 100 non-Cuban cigars, 200 cigarettes once every 30 days. If you are out of the U.S. for less than 48 hours or have used your exemption in the last 30 days, you are entitled to import merchandise up to $200 in value. You may include with the $200 exemption your choice of the following: 50 cigarettes and 10 cigars and 150 milliliters (5 fl. oz.) of alcoholic beverages or 150 milliliters (5 fl. oz.) of perfume containing alcohol. Non-residents are allowed a $100 gift exemption every 6 months and adults a liter of alcohol, 50 cigars and not more than 200 cigarettes for personal consumption per trip.

Agricultural Products: As a general guideline, most foods made or grown in Canada or the U.S., and labeled as such are enterable to the U.S. Rules do change from time to time, and the information that follows does not cover every restriction. If in doubt, call a CBP Agricultural Specialist in Blaine at 360-332-1640.

NO lamb or goat, whether fresh, cooked, canned, frozen or as part of another dish (lamb stew for example).

NO pet food made in Canada containing lamb or goat. All pet food must be in the original commercial package.

YES Canadian and U.S. poultry and eggs, swine (pork, ham, bacon), seafood, dairy products, and beef products are all okay. Sausage in lamb casings prohibited. Meats must be identifiable as U.S. or Canadian origin. Meat and other animal products from other than Canada or the U.S. are subject to numerous regulations and restrictions.

NO fresh citrus, regardless of origin. Bananas purchased in Canada are allowed if marked from Western Hemisphere (such as Ecuador or Guatemala).

NO other fresh produce (vegetable or fruit) grown outside the U.S. or Canada, even if purchased in the U.S. or Canada.

Canadian-grown fresh tomatoes, peppers, green onions, leeks or chives are currently not allowed. Canadian grown potatoes are only allowed if in the original commercial package or peeled. Okra and eggplant are prohibited.

YES corn on the cob grown in British Columbia or the Western U.S. is allowed.

NO cherries grown in Ontario, Canada (until fruit fly outbreak contained).

Canned fruits and vegetables are unrestricted.

NO cut flowers or potted plants (they are subject to so many restrictions that it is better to leave them in Canada and avoid the hassle).

NO Firewood is allowed regardless of origin.

Clearing Customs on Foreign Flagged Pleasure Boats: The operator of a foreign flagged pleasure boat must report to CBP immediately upon arriving into the United States. He/she must also make a formal vessel entry on CBP Form 1300 within 48 hours and pay applicable fees. At the time of entry boaters may request a cruising license that provides simplified clearance procedures for visiting boaters (see "Cruising License" entry). Foreign flagged boats without a cruising license are required to have a U.S. Customs Decal (see "U.S. Customs Decal" entry).

Cruising License: Foreign flagged private boats arriving to the U.S. from Canada may apply for cruising licenses from the CBP port director at the first U.S. port of arrival. This license can save time and money. Without it, foreign pleasure boats must obtain CBP clearance and a permit whenever they travel form one place to another within the U.S. Each time they enter the U.S., they must also file a formal entry and clearance, file the appropriate paperwork and pay the applicable fees. Foreign flagged boats traveling without a cruising license must purchase a CBP decal, which is $28.24 for the year.

U.S. Customs Decals: All pleasure boats, 30' or longer, crossing the border into the U.S. must display a Private Vessel Decal. Exemptions include vessels less than 30' and vessels granted a cruising license, under 19 CFR 4.94, during the term of the license. The decal costs $32.62 US. Decals must be purchased in advance online, or by mail or FAX. Visit https://dtops.cbp.dhs.gov. From this screen, either log in with your User ID and password or register for an online account. To mail or fax a form instead, select "Helpful Info", then select "Need a Paper Application?" and print the PDF document. For questions contact the DTOPS help desk at 317-298-1245 (Mon-Fri 8am-4pm EST) or at decals@dhs.gov.

The Canadian Border Boat Landing (I-68) Program: The I-68 program is open to U.S. and Canadian citizens. I-68 holders may report to U.S. Customs by telephone instead of in person.

The information provided has been verified with appropriate agencies and is believed to be correct as of December 2023

IMPORTANT NOTICES

Lady Washington near Stuart Island (page 105) — Photo © Chris Teren / TerenPhotography.com

To obtain an I-68 form, call one of the CBP Designated Port of Entry offices to schedule an in-person interview. Bring proof of citizenship, birth certificate, passport, photo ID and vessel registration number to the interview. The I-68 is valid for one year and costs $16 per person (14 years and older) or $32 per family.

To report your arrival to Customs using the I-68, call the Small Boat Reporting System at 1-800-562-5943 or call a Designated Port of Entry. Everyone on the boat must be an I-68 or NEXUS card holder or you will have to go ashore to report in person.

Reporting Offsite Arrival - Mobile (CBP One): CBP One offers boaters an alternative to reporting arrivals via designated telephone reporting numbers. With the CBP One app, boaters may report their pertinent arrival information by using their personal smart phone or tablet. CBP may opt to continue the interview by way of a video chat or require an in person interview. Download "CBP One" from the Apple App or Google Play stores, then sign in to CBP One via Login.Gov. For more information about CBP One visit, https://www.cbp.gov/travel/pleasure-boats-private-flyers/pleasure-boat-overview#

Small Vessel Reporting System (SVRS): On September 5, 2018 SVRS was discontinued and float plans are no longer accepted. Boaters may report their arrival using the CBP One app in certain areas or report via designated telephone reporting numbers.

U.S. Customs & Border Protection Designated Port-of-Entry: All recreational boaters must report to one of these designated locations identified below upon arrival to the U.S.

- Friday Harbor 360-378-2080
- Roche Harbor 360-378-2080
- Port Angeles 360-457-4311
- Point Roberts 360-945-2314 or 360-945-5211
- Anacortes 360-293-2331
- Ketchikan 907-225-2254

Business hours at these five locations are from 8am to 8pm during the summer boating season and 8am to 5pm from the last week in September through the second week in May. Customs recommends that boaters check-in with the first site upon crossing the border.

U.S. & Washington Notices, Regulations & Resources

Boating Safety Program: "Adventures in Boating," a terrific resource for Washington boaters, contains regulations, safety tips, a pump-out locations map and the course material for the Washington Boater Education Certificate exam. Download a copy at www.boat-ed.com/washington/handbook/book.html or call 360-902-8555.

Boating Website: Washington State's "one-stop" website for boaters, https://boat.wa.gov consolidates and simplifies access to information on a wide variety of boating related topics.

United States Power Squadrons: USPS offers a range of public boating courses and seminars. 1-888-367-8777, www.usps.org.

BoatsUS Boating Safety Courses: Call 1-800-245-2628 or visit www.boatus.org/courses.

Life Jacket Requirement: By law every vessel must carry a life jacket that is USCG-approved and used in accordance with the requirements for every person onboard. On vessels under 19 feet long, children aged 12 and younger must wear life jackets when the vessel is underway unless they are below deck or in a fully enclosed cabin. All boats more than 16 feet long must have a throwable personal flotation device such as a life ring.

Mandatory Boater Safety Education Law: All boaters in Washington are required to obtain a Boater Education Card. The cards cost $10, are good for life, and may reduce boat insurance rates. Boaters born before 1/1/55 are exempt, as are operators of boats with less than 15 horsepower. (Note: Canada and Oregon accept Washington Cards, but do not exempt boaters born before January 1, 1955.) Washington boaters who have a certificate of completion from a Coast Guard Auxiliary or U.S. Power Squadron boating safety class need only to provide a copy of it with an application form and $10 to receive a Boater Ed. Card from WA State Parks. Cards from other states and Canada are recognized, as well. To obtain a card you must pass an approved boating safety education course. For options & price visit http://park.state.wa.us/442/Mandatory-Boater-Education. Information: 360-902-8555.

Charts & Weather

NOAA Chart services: NOAA Office of Coast Survey, 1315 East-West Highway, Silver Spring, MD 20910. 1-888-990-6622. www.nauticalcharts.noaa.gov.

Paper Charts: In early 2016, the U.S. Coast Guard released a policy letter (NVIC 01-16) that provides an option for operators to use official electronic charts in place of paper charts if they choose to do so. NOAA's certified chart agents still provide Print-on-Demand paper charts. https://nauticalcharts.noaa.gov under "Certified Charts & Products".

Raster Navigational Charts: Free downloads of raster charts that are compatible with most navigation software at www.nauticalcharts.noaa.gov under "General Use Charts."

Electronic Navigational Charts: Free downloads of vector charts in the International Hydrographic Organization at www.nauticalcharts.noaa.gov under "Certified Charts & Products."

Print-at-home nautical chart catalogs for regional areas can be accessed at www.charts.noaa.gov/InteractiveCatalog/nrnc.shtml.

Reporting Chart Discrepancies: Boaters who find discrepancies on charts can help by reporting to NOAA, https://nauticalcharts.noaa.gov under "Contact Us Discrepancy Reporting" or 1-888-990-6622.

Distances Between United States Ports, 2012 (12th Edition): Download at https://nauticalcharts.noaa.gov/publications/docs/distances.pdf.

NOAA's National Weather Service. www.weather.gov.

National Weather Service in Seattle: Visit www.weather.gov/sew for current marine observations and forecasts, as well as Satellite and Doppler weather radar images/loops. Call 206-526-6087 or 360-357-6453 for recorded marine forecasts and observations. Call 206-526-6095 ext 0 to talk to a forecaster.

NOAA Weather Radio (NWR): 24 hour, continuous broadcasts to mariners as far south as Olympia and north into Southern British Columbia. Content includes regional and Western Washington's 3-5 day and extended forecasts, marine weather synopsis, warnings, watches, and advisories for conditions. www.nws.noaa.gov/nwr. Among the 16 NWR stations in Washington are:

- Blaine: KAD93, 162.525Mhz
- Forks: KX127, 162.425Mhz
- Neah Bay: KIH36, 162.550Mhz
- Seattle: KHB60, 162.550Mhz
- Puget Sound Marine: WWG24, 162.425Mhz

Live Sea/Weather Conditions by Phone or Internet: Live information, such as wind direction and speed, air temperature and pressure, visibility and more is relayed from specific buoys and Coastal-Marine Automated Network Stations (C-MAN) to the National Data Buoy Center. Mariners can access this helpful information online at www.ndbc.noaa.gov.

To access Dial-A-Buoy, call 1-888-701-8992 (press 1). Then identify the station report you need by its five-digit identifier. Identifiers are found at www.ndbc.noaa.gov or telephone users can press "2" at the beginning of the call to be prompted for a latitude and longitude and receive the closest station locations and identifiers. (Some Washington Buoy/Station Identifiers are listed below.)

Visit us at boattravel.com

IMPORTANT NOTICES   Page 111

WA Buoy/Station Locations and Identification Numbers:
1. Smith Island (Strait of Juan de Fuca, west of Whidbey Island). Enter 74791
2. West Point (West of Discovery Park). Enter 97691
3. New Dungeness, WA (Hein Bank). Enter 46088
4. Neah Bay. Enter 46087
5. Destruction Island (La Push). Enter 33791
6. Cape Elizabeth (45NM northwest of Aberdeen). Enter 46041

U.S. Coast Guard

U.S.C.G. Boating Safety Division: Visit www.uscgboating.org for helpful information about boating safety, recalls, navigation rules, scheduling a courtesy examination and more.

U.S.C.G. Auxiliary: Auxiliary volunteers aid the Coast Guard in a non-law enforcement capacity (vessel safety checks, harbor patrols, search & rescue, safe boating courses, etc.) 1-877-875-6296, www.cgaux.org.

U.S.C.G. Mobile App: Designed as an additional boating safety resource for mobile device users, this app provides the most commonly requested essential services and information to boaters. http://uscgboating.org/mobile/.

U.S. Coast Guard Navigation Information Service: 24-hour navigation information service. 703-313-5900. www.navcen.uscg.gov.

U.S. Coast Guard Local Notice to Mariners (LNM): These weekly notices can be downloaded www.navcen.uscg.gov. There are specific LNMS for each USCG District. The LNM for District 13 covers the waters of Oregon, Washington, Idaho, and Montana. The LNM for District 17 covers Alaskan waters.

Fish and Wildlife, Washington State

Aquatic Invasive Species Prevention Permits: Owners of watercraft registered in another state or country must purchase an Aquatic Invasive Species Prevention Permit before placing or operating the watercraft in any body of water in Washington. The cost is $20 (transaction and dealer fees may apply). For FAQ about the permit and its purchase, visit https://wdfw.wa.gov/ais/.

Vehicle Access Pass (VAP): A VAP, Discover Pass or One Day Discover Pass is required at all WDFW owned recreation sites. Parking in a signed WDFW access site without a pass could result in a fine. A VAP is provided at no cost with the purchase of certain fishing or hunting licenses and is transferable between two vehicles. Remember, the VAP is for use on WDFW lands only, vehicles parked on DNR or State Parks land also need to display a Discover Pass. For information, www.discoverpass.wa.gov.

Sportfishing/Shellfish Information:
  WDFW Fish Program: 360-902-2700 or wdfw.wa.gov/fishing.
  WDFW Fish Hotline (receive regulation updates): 360-902-2500.
  Shellfish Rule Change Hotline: 1-866-880-5431.
  Shellfish Hotline (Dept. of Health Marine Toxins/PSP alerts): 1-800-562-5632.
  Shellfish Harvesting: For a shellfish beach closure map, Paralytic Poisoning (PSP) information, and additional recreational shellfish resources, visit www.doh.wa.gov/CommunityandEnvironment/Shellfish.

Sports Fishing Regulations: Download a copy of the current Washington State Fishing Regulations pamphlet at http://wdfw.wa.gov/fishing, or call 360-902-2700 to request a copy. They are also available where fishing licenses are sold.

Sport Fishing Licenses: Angler Sports Fishers, 15 years or older, must have a fishing license on their person when fishing. All shellfish/seaweed licenses must be displayed on the outside of clothing while harvesting or transporting catch. Licenses are valid from April 1 – March 31.
  For information regarding license types and fees or to purchase a license online: fishhunt.dfw.wa.gov for 600 statewide vendors, call 360-902-2464 or check WDFW website).

Marine Mammal Protection Laws: Laws prohibit the harassment and disturbance of all marine mammals. Violators could incur hefty fines. For marine wildlife guidelines visit www.bewhalewise.org. Remember these guidelines:
- DO NOT APPROACH or position your vessel closer than 200 yards to any killer whale.
- DO NOT APPROACH or get closer than 100 metres/yards to any other marine mammals or nesting birds, whether on the water or on land.
- IF your vessel is not in compliance with the 100 metres/yards approach guideline, place engine in neutral and allow animals to pass.

Killer Whales, in particular, have additional protection in inland waters of Washington State. In 2018, a voluntary 'no-go' zone along Western San Juan Island was established to protect the southern resident killer whales. A map of the area is found at https://wdfw.wa.gov/conservation/orca/.

Fuel Tax

Fuel tax refund: Fuel purchased in Washington is taxed by the state. The majority of this tax is fuel tax, which supports road maintenance and construction. Since boats aren't used on roads, boaters may be eligible to claim a refund. In order to qualify, they must have:
- a current vessel registration
- a valid refund permit with the Department of Washington
- purchased at least 41 gallons of tax-paid fuel within the previous 13 months
- applied for the refund, either electronically or through mail

Boating refunds are subject to the state sales tax and a coastal protection fund fee, which will be deducted from the refund. Depending on the cost of fuel and claim period, the net refund amount ranges from apprx. 25 to 30 cents per gallon. For more information regarding what documentation is required, how to get a fuel tax refund permit and how to file for a refund, visit www.dol.wa.gov/vehicleregistration/ftrefunds.html or call 360-664-1838.

Homeland Security - The Boater's Role

All Boaters Remember to: 1) Keep your distance from all military (at least 100 yards of Navy Vessels or contact vessel at VHF 16), cruise line, ferries, or commercial shipping (see "Security Zones" entry). 2) Avoid commercial port operations. 3) Never stop or anchor beneath bridges or in the channel. 4) Stay vigilant, watch for anything unusual. 5) Don't be an easy target for thieves. Keep an eye on your boat or boat/trailer. When storing your boat, make sure it is secure and the engine disabled. Always take the keys with you.

America's Waterway Watch Program: Report any suspicious activity to 1-877-24WATCH. If there is immediate danger, call 911 or the Coast Guard on VHF 16. www.cgaux.org/aww.php.

Power driven vessels 20 meters/65ft or longer: In Puget Sound, the San Juan Islands and the Strait of Juan de Fuca, during times of increased Maritime Security levels, captains of power driven vessels of 20 meters or more in length may be requested to make radio contact with "Seattle Traffic". Use VHF-FM channel 14 when south of Bush Point in Admiralty Inlet and Possession Point in Possession Sound, and VHF-FM channel 05A when north of these points. Check the latest Local Notice to Mariners or listen for the Broadcast Notice to Mariners for the current status of this requirement, or call Seattle Traffic at 206-217-6050.

Security Zones in Washington State: Security Zones affecting both commercial and pleasure craft have been designated in Puget Sound and the Strait of Juan de Fuca. Security zones apply whether the ship is underway, anchored, or moored. Within these zones, do not pass within 100 yards of any U.S. Military ship, any tanker ship or any passenger vessels (ferries, passenger boats over 100' in length, cruise ships, etc.). If you must pass within 100 yards, contact the vessel or the Coast Guard escort vessel in advance on VHF 13 or 16.
  Always operate at minimum, safe operating speed within 500 yards of any affected vessel. Violators may be charged with criminal penalties and substantial fines.
  If unsure as to whether a particular vessel falls under these requirements, assume that it does and operate accordingly. If no VHF radio is available, slow to a minimum speed, maintain a safe course, and do not turn toward the applicable vessel. For information: 206-217-6215.

Maritime Radiation Detection: In response to the potential for a small vessel being used to attack or deliver materials for an attack in the Puget Sound, technologies and methods for detection of illicit nuclear materials on small vessels are in place. Agency officials may wear radiation detection sensors during routine boat boardings and inspections. Be aware that some medical procedures (such as seed implants, chemotherapy, some stress tests) can cause the detector to react. In this case, a letter from your physician would be a good thing to keep onboard.

Insurance - U.S. Policy Coverage in Canada

Geographic Limits: U.S. boat insurance policy holders who plan extended cruising in Canadian waters should check their policy's geographical limits. Navigation limits vary with each company, but many commonly designate 51 degrees North latitude as the northernmost geographical limit. Requests for alternative geographical limits may result in additional charges. Call your insurance company or broker for specifics.

Marine Trails

Washington Water Trails Association: WWTA (founded 1990) is working to advocate for the right of public access to and from waterways and to steward those waterways and adjoining shore lands. Visit www.wwta.org or call 206-545-9161.

The information provided has been verified with appropriate agencies and is believed to be correct as of December 2023

Parks - Washington State

Washington State Parks Reservations: Reserve a campsite, yurt, cabin, platform tent, group camp or day use facility in more than 60 Washington State Parks. For a list of facilities and locations, trip planning assistance, questions, visit http://parks.state.wa.us or call 360-902-8844 between 8am–5pm, Mon.-Fri. Before making a reservation, have pertinent information ready (credit card number, park sites, arrival/departure dates, alternate choices, etc.). Make reservations (up to nine months in advance) online at washington.goingtocamp.com or by phone, 1-888-226-7688.

Discover Pass: A Discover Pass is required for vehicles on State recreation lands (campgrounds, parks, wildlife/natural/wilderness areas, trails, and water access points). The Pass costs $30 a year (transferable between two vehicles) or $10 for a day-use pass for one vehicle. Transaction and dealer fees extra. A $99 fine applies for not displaying the Pass (reduced to $59 if you provide proof of pass within 15 days). Some exemptions apply. For instance, boaters with annual Natural Investment Permits can launch at State Parks without a Discover Pass (but one is needed at DNR or WDFW sites.) www.discoverpass.wa.gov, 1-866-320-9933.

Marine Parks Information: There are more than 40 marine parks in Washington, all offering different facilities and amenities. To locate a park by name, area, or features, visit http://parks.state.wa.us. Click on "Boating" for specific moorage sites.

Marine Park Moorage Fees: Mooring fees are charged at docks, floats or buoys at WA State Marine Parks between 1pm and 8am. Boaters may pay an annual or daily fee. Annual Permit fees are $5.00 per foot, with a minimum of $60 and are valid from Jan. 1 – Dec. 31. Annual permits may be purchased online at http://parks.state.wa.us, from State Parks Olympia Headquarters, the regional office in Burlington, or on site at State Marine Parks. The daily fee is 70 cents per foot, with a minimum of $15. Moorage buoys cost $15 per night (no boats over 45'). Moorage is first come, first served and is limited to three consecutive nights at a facility. 360-902-8844.

Marine Parks Launch Ramp Fees: Launching a boat at a state park requires one of the following:
- An annual launch permit (Natural Investment Permit). Purchase for $80 online at http://parks.state.wa.us/470/Natural-Investment-Permit, in person at State Parks Headquarters in Olympia, at regional offices or in parks if staff is available. Information: 360-902-8844.
- A $30 annual Discover Pass and a $7 daily launch permit.
- A $10 one-day Discover Pass and a $7 daily launch permit.

For additional information, 360-902-8844 or http://parks.state.wa.us/165/Boating-Fees.

Marine Pump-outs: For pump-out locations, helpful tips and information about using pump-outs visit http://parks.state.wa.us/657/Pumpout.

Moorage and Boat Launch Maps: Washington Water Cruiser is a free online interactive map and smart phone app that shows all state-owned public boat launches and moorage sites, along with amenities for boaters at each site. Visit, www.rco.wa.gov/maps.

Seattle Notices

Seattle Boat Ramp Fees: A permit (Annual or Single Day) is required to use a motorized boat launch ramp. Download an application for an Annual Permit ($150 with up to 4 overnight stay permitted) at www.seattle.gov/parks/reserve/boat-launch-fees or call 206-684-7249. $12 Single Day Launch Permits are purchased on site from gray fee machines or kiosks. For extended stays, overnight permits costing an additional $12 a night for up to 4 nights, can also be purchased.

Seattle Bridges: For descriptions, openings, hours, and contact information, see Chapter 3.

Seattle Parks and Recreation: For general information or to request a Park Guide call 206-684-4075 or visit www.seattle.gov/parks. Visit www.seattle.gov/parks/Boating-and-Sailing for an overview of the City's Boating Program, including topics such as classes and programs, moorage and rental, regulations, fees, fishing piers, etc.

Seattle Police Harbor Patrol: Covers 200 miles of city shoreline using the latest technology in water emergency, dive response, and fire suppression. Boating Regulations brochures, as well as Personal Watercraft Operation Laws are available online or can be picked up from the Harbor Patrol Office at 1717 N. Northlake Place, Seattle. Info: 206-684-4071. In times of distress, 911 or VHF 16. www.seattle.gov/police/about-us/about-policing/harbor-patrol.

Vessels in Washington

Boats Visiting Washington Waters: If you are visiting for less than 60 days and your boat is registered in another state or has current U.S.C.G. documentation paper, no permit is required. For stays longer than 60 days, you must apply for a Non-resident Vessel Permit before the end of the 60th day. For details visit www.dol.wa.gov/vehicleregistration/boatvisit.html or call 360-902-3770.

Hull Identification Number (HIN) Requirements: All state titled vessels must have two identical 12-character hull identification numbers at least ¼ inch high permanently displayed on each boat hull. www.dol.wa.gov/forms/420739.pdf.

Vessel Title and Registration: Most vessels in Washington must be titled and registered. Vessels 10 horsepower or less and under 16 feet are generally exempt. For information regarding other exemptions, to register your boat, renew a registration, report the sale of a boat, or file for a vessel title contact the Dept. of Licensing, www.dol.wa.gov/vehicleregistration/boats.html or 360-902-3770.

Title, Registration and Tax Responsibilities of Boat Owners: This is the title of a very helpful Washington State Department of Revenue publication that provides information on a variety of topics for boaters (both resident and non-resident) https://dor.wa.gov/sites/default/files/legacy/Docs/Pubs/WatercraftVesselTax/BoatBroc.pdf.

VHF Marine Radio-United States Vessels

New VHF Channels Coming: Two digit channels ending with the letter "A" (including 05A, 22A, 66A, and 78A) currently recognized in the US are being phased out. Four digit internationally recognized VHF Channels, beginning with the digits "10" will eventually take their place. That is, US channel 05A will be known as 1005, channel 22A will be 1022, channel 66A will be 1066, and 78A will be 1078. The change will happen as these new channel numbers begin to be displayed on the new models of VHF marine radios. For additional information, https://www.navcen.uscg.gov and click on "Maritime Telecommunications". From here, click on "U.S. VHF Channels & Frequencies."

Restricted Radio Telephone Operators Permit: If you travel to a foreign port and dock there, or communicate with a foreign station, you must have both a Restricted Radio Telephone Operator's Permit and a Ship Radio Station License. (See FCC Forms & Filing).

Ship Station License: U.S. recreational vessels under 20 meters in length, traveling only in U.S. waters, and not transmitting radio communications to a foreign station, are not required to obtain a Ship Radio Station License to operate VHF, EPIRB and marine radar. License or not, you must follow FCC rules for calling other stations, relaying distress messages and the other operating procedures. Boaters can identify themselves over the air by using the FCC issued call sign, the state registration number, the official vessel number, or the vessel name.

U.S. recreational vessels which travel to Canada or any foreign port, or transmit communications to a Canadian station, must have a Ship Radio Station License. Operation of Satellite, SSB, or telegraphy transmitters require a license from the FCC. (See FCC Forms & Filing).

Cellular/Satellite Telephones: Cell phone coverage is good near metropolitan areas and in most open straits, but can be unreliable north of Desolation Sound. Satellite Phones, while more expensive to use, provide reliable coverage.

Cellular phones can't replace a VHF-FM marine radio's ability to communicate marine safety information with multiple marine users at one time.

Marine Operator Radio Telephone Service and Stations: In the U.S., all VHF Public Radio Telephone Service stations closed in 2000. As of March 2010, all Canadian stations shut down and Telus Marine Operator service was cancelled.

VHF Marine Radio Digital Selective Calling (DSC) Capability: If you have a marine radio with DSC capability, you must obtain a nine-digit maritime mobile service identity (MMSI) number and have it programmed into the unit before you transmit. If your vessel requires licensing by the FCC you will obtain an MMSI number during the application/licensing process when you file FCC Forms 159 and 605 with the FCC. If your boat does not require a ship station license, you can apply for an MMSI from BoatsUs and US Power Squadrons.

FCC Forms & Filings

To Obtain FCC Forms: Visit www.fcc.gov/forms or call 1-888-CALL-FCC for additional assistance completing a form.

FCC Form 160-(CORES Registration Form): Submit this form to obtain an FCC Registration Number RFN. FCC Registration Numbers are assigned by CORES and are required for anyone doing business with the FCC.

FCC Form 605 Quick- Form: Application for Authorization in the Ship, Aircraft, Amateur, Restricted and Commercial Operator, and General Mobile Radio Services: This form covers both Ship Station License and Restricted Radiotelephone

IMPORTANT NOTICES   Page 113

Operators Permit filings with the FCC. This includes new applications, modifications or renewals.

FCC Form 159 Remittance Advice: This form must be submitted along with any kind of payment made to the FCC.

Vessel Traffic Service

The Vessel Traffic Service Puget Sound (VTS), or "Seattle Traffic", is a marine traffic service operated by the U.S. Coast Guard Sector Puget Sound. VTS provides navigational assistance to the maritime community by use of:
    1. Radar and Automatic Information Systems.
    2. Vessel movement reporting -VHF-FM radio channels 5A, and 14. Use Channel 5A when located east of Whidbey Island north of Possession Point, or when west of Whidbey Island north of Bush Point and throughout the Strait of Juan de Fuca. Use Channel 14 when south of these areas.
    3. Traffic separation scheme (TSS) -buoys, and charted traffic lanes that direct the flow of traffic.

Recreational Boater Responsibilities: Unless over 20 meters (approximately 66 feet) in length, recreational boats are exempt from participation with the VTS, however all waterborne craft are subject to:
    1. Navigation Rules (See entry for Traffic Separation Scheme that follows).
    2. All direction given by the VTS.
    3. All other practices of safe navigation and prudent seamanship.
    Further participation is voluntary, unless directed by the VTS.

Radio communications: Passive listening of the VTS frequency for your area is highly encouraged! Tune in for free, timely traffic information.

Safe Navigation and Prudent Seamanship: Know and follow the "Rules of the Road." Be aware that specific rules apply when near large ships operating in narrow channels and traffic separation schemes. They have limited ability to see you or maneuver and cannot easily take evasive action. The size and speed of large ships and their wakes can be deceiving, so take early positive action to avoid close quarters situations. Avoid crossing ahead of, or operating close to a deep draft ship. Never cross between a tug and their tow, be wary of submerged apparatus trailing barges.
    Develop a situational awareness of all the vessels in your vicinity. Maintain a proper lookout. Autopilots don't relieve you of the responsibility of keeping a good lookout. Take early and substantial action to indicate your intent to change course and speed. Show a side. Use navigation lights between sunset and sunrise, and in restricted visibility.

Traffic Separation Scheme or TSS: International "Rules of the Road" apply everywhere in the Puget Sound, including Lake Washington, and dictate vessel conduct when meeting, overtaking, or crossing another vessel. They also specify vessel conduct near a TSS. If you are not familiar with the charted traffic lanes in the Puget Sound, obtain nautical charts of the areas you enjoy and familiarize yourself with them. All traffic separation schemes, with separation zones marked in magenta, are printed on nautical charts. The traffic lane network in the Puget Sound begins at buoy J -"Juliet" northwest of Cape Flattery and continues all the way to Tacoma's buoy TC -"Tango Charlie" with Rosario Strait, and Haro Strait bound branches stemming from buoy SA -"Sierra Alpha" near Port Townsend.
    You don't need VTS permission to use these charted lanes! Simply abide by TSS rules: Proceed in the direction of traffic. If joining or leaving the lanes, do so at a TSS buoy by passing the buoy on your port side. When not near a buoy, join or leave a lane with the direction of traffic. Avoid the separation zone as much as possible. If you must cross the lanes (and separation zone), do so at right angles to minimize the time crossing. When not using the lanes, you are responsible for knowing the location of the TSS and avoiding the other vessels using it. Above all, do not impede traffic. Each year, numerous incidents involve boaters impeding a vessel following a traffic lane, or, proceeding the wrong way in a traffic lane.

Canadian Notices, Regulations Resources

Boat Licensing & Registration

Boat Licensing: All Canadian pleasure craft powered by an engine 10 horsepower (7.5 kw) or more must be licensed, unless they are registered. There is a $250 fine for operating a vessel without a license. For information on how to apply for a Pleasure Craft License, visit https://tc.gc.ca. Press Marine and click on Vessels. The license is free and you may choose to submit your request electronically or by post.
    A copy of your Pleasure Craft License must be onboard at all times and the pleasure craft license number must be displayed on the bow of your boat above the waterline on both sides in block characters that are at least 7.5 centimetres (3 inches) high; and in a colour that contrasts with the colour of the bow.

Boat Registration: Boaters who register a pleasure craft are not required to license the vessel. Registration is a title system for ownership of vessels that establishes, among other things, name approval, and mortgage registration. A Certificate of Registry is provided for a fee by Transport Canada and is good for as long as you own your vessel. Visit www.tc.gc.ca/eng/marinesafety/oep-vesselreg-registration-menu-2311.htm. Carry registration documents as well as any other ownership documents on board the vessel at all times to avoid delays or fines when clearing Canada-U.S. Customs.

Boating Safety

Transport Canada Office of Boating Safety: For boating safety information, or for questions regarding regulations for Canadian and foreign recreational boaters in British Columbia waters, contact the Office of Boating Safety at 700-800 Burrard St., Vancouver B.C., Canada V6Z 2J8. 604-666-2681 or visit www.tc.gc.ca/boatingsafety. Click on "Visitor Information" for most everything a visiting boater needs to know, or click "Safe Boating Guide" to download a copy of the guide.

Mandatory Licensing & Education: All operators of power driven pleasure craft must carry proof of competency, proof of residency, and proof of age on board at all times. Non-Residents who stay more than 45 days or who operate a pleasure craft that is licensed or registered in Canada (including rented or chartered boats), must have an operator card, a completed boat rental safety checklist, or proof of competency from their resident state. Your passport is proof of entry and the number of days spent in Canada. For information contact 604-666-2681 or www.tc.gc.ca/boatingsafety or get the Discover Boating app for your smartphone.

Safety Equipment: All boats are required to carry safety equipment. What exactly must be carried depends on the type and size of boat. Download the "Safe Boating Guide" for the requirements for pleasure craft www.tc.gc.ca/boating safety.

Canadian National Defence

Area Whiskey Golf ("WG"): Area "WG" Constitutes a "Defence Establishment" to which the Defence Controlled Access Area Regulations apply. Vessels which do not comply with direction from either Winchelsea control or Range Patrol Vessels may be charged with trespassing.

Canadian Forces Maritime Experimental and Test Ranges – Nanoose Bay, BC:
    The Canadian Forces Maritime Experimental and Test Ranges (CFMETR) tests ship and aircraft systems and torpedoes launched by surface vessels, submarines, or aircraft. No explosives are used, however, a hazard exists due to the possibility of a torpedo homing on vessels and then striking them as it surfaces.
    Testing is usually carried out during daylight hours Monday to Saturday. During testing, area "WG" is "Active". Any vessel within the area is required to clear or stop on demand from the "Winchelsea Island Control" or any of the range vessels or range helicopter. The positions of these coordinates are clearly marked on the diagram found in Chapter 15 of this book.
    A transit area 1,000 yards north of Winchelsea Island and 1,000 yards east of South Ballenas Island is recommended to enable mariners to transit safely around the active area. It also facilitates unimpeded access to marina facilities in Schooner Cove and Nanoose Bay. The active range area is clearly depicted on CHS charts 3512, 3456 and 3459 by means of pecked lines.
    Additional information on active range hours or for safe transit through the area may be obtained from:
    a. Winchelsea Island Control at 1-888-221-1011 (next day's activity only);
    b. CFMETR Range Officer at 250-468-5002 (long range planning);
    c. Winchelsea Island Control VHF CH 10 or 16 (for safe transit area information when approaching Area "WG"); or
    d. VHF 21B or Weather 3 (listen only, for active times).
    Range vessels exhibit a flashing red light in addition to the prescribed lights and shapes. These vessels may operate outside of scheduled hours and should not be approached within 3,000 yards because they may be in a three-point moor with mooring lines extending to buoys 1,500 yards away. Additionally, lighted and unlighted mooring buoys are randomly located within the area. Mariners are advised to use caution when transiting this area during non-active range periods to avoid mooring buoys and lines.

Charts & Weather Service

Official Charts & Nautical Publications: The Canadian Hydrographic Service (CHS) produces and sells navigational products which help to protect lives, property, and the marine environment. Canadian paper and digital charts, Tide and Current Tables and Sailing Directions are sold through over 700 authorized CHS chart dealers worldwide. For an official CHS Chart Dealer near you and other information, www.charts.gc.ca, or contact: CHS, 200 Kent St., Station 12W090, Ottawa, ON K1A 0E6. Tel: 613-998-4931 or 1-866-546-3613. For General Information: chsinfo@dfo-mpo.gc.ca. For marine weather forecasts visit http://weather.gc.ca for marine forecasts, sea surface temperatures and more. Tides, Currents and Water Levels visit http://tides.gc.ca.

The information provided has been verified with appropriate agencies and is believed to be correct as of December 2023

Page 114 IMPORTANT NOTICES

Marine Weather Guide

 Environment Canada Environnement Canada

PACIFIC COAST

MARINE WEATHER GUIDE

Environment Canada's Marine Weather Services for the Pacific Coast

FORECAST PRODUCTS

The **Regular Forecast** includes detailed forecast wind speed and direction, weather and visibility, and any wind and freezing spray warnings in effect for the current and following day. (Days 1 and 2)

The **Extended Forecast** includes a general description of expected wind conditions for the period from the end of the Regular Forecast to the end of the fifth day of the forecast period. (Days 3 to 5)

The **Technical Marine Synopsis** gives a general picture of the position and motion of the main weather features (lows, highs, fronts).

The **Marine Weather Statement** informs of potentially hazardous conditions and/or significant weather features.

The **Wave Height Forecast** describes the expected significant wave height rather than the maximum wave height. Significant wave height is defined as the average of the highest one-third of all waves. Wave heights are described in metres and are measured from trough to crest. Maximum wave heights may be twice as high as the significant wave height.

The **NAVTEX Forecast** is a shortened version of the marine forecast products. It is transmitted by the Canadian Coast Guard and primarily intended for international users in Canadian waters.

MARINE OBSERVATIONS

Environment Canada and its partner organizations provide weather observations and buoy reports along the coast. See maps for observing site locations.

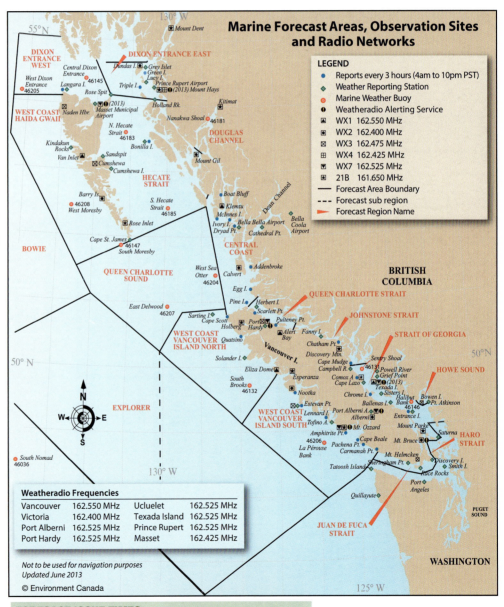

Not to be used for navigation purposes
Updated June 2013
© Environment Canada

Weatheradio Frequencies

Vancouver	162.550 MHz	Ucluelet	162.525 MHz
Victoria	162.400 MHz	Texada Island	162.525 MHz
Port Alberni	162.525 MHz	Prince Rupert	162.525 MHz
Port Hardy	162.525 MHz	Masset	162.425 MHz

FORECAST ISSUE TIMES

All issue times are Pacific Standard or Daylight Saving Time (PST/PDT). Updated forecasts are issued as required.

Regular Forecast and Technical Marine Synopsis:	4 am; 10:30 am 4 pm; 9:30 pm
Extended Forecast:	4 am; 4 pm
Wave Height Forecast:	4 am; 4 pm

Visit us at boattravel.com

IMPORTANT NOTICES Page 115

Marine Weather Guide

 Environment Canada   Environnement Canada

PACIFIC COAST

MARINE WEATHER GUIDE

Environment Canada's Marine Weather Services for the Pacific Coast

FORECAST PRODUCTS

The **Regular Forecast** includes detailed forecast wind speed and direction, weather and visibility, and any wind and freezing spray warnings in effect for the current and following day. (Days 1 and 2)

The **Extended Forecast** includes a general description of expected wind conditions for the period from the end of the Regular Forecast to the end of the fifth day of the forecast period. (Days 3 to 5)

The **Technical Marine Synopsis** gives a general picture of the position and motion of the main weather features (lows, highs, fronts).

The **Marine Weather Statement** informs of potentially hazardous conditions and/or significant weather features.

The **Wave Height Forecast** describes the expected significant wave height rather than the maximum wave height. Significant wave height is defined as the average of the highest one-third of all waves. Wave heights are described in metres and are measured from trough to crest. Maximum wave heights may be twice as high as the significant wave height.

The **NAVTEX Forecast** is a shortened version of the marine forecast products. It is transmitted by the Canadian Coast Guard and primarily intended for international users in Canadian waters.

MARINE OBSERVATIONS

Environment Canada and its partner organizations provide weather observations and buoy reports along the coast. See maps for observing site locations.

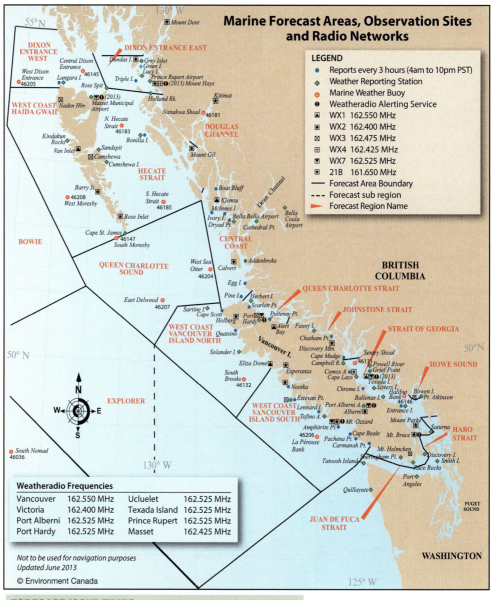

Marine Forecast Areas, Observation Sites and Radio Networks

LEGEND
- • Reports every 3 hours (4am to 10pm PST)
- ◇ Weather Reporting Station
- ○ Marine Weather Buoy
- ⓘ Weatheradio Alerting Service
- ▲ WX1 162.550 MHz
- ■ WX2 162.400 MHz
- ⊠ WX3 162.475 MHz
- ⊞ WX4 162.425 MHz
- ⊟ WX7 162.525 MHz
- ▽ 21B   161.650 MHz
- — Forecast Area Boundary
- --- Forecast sub region
- ▶ Forecast Region Name

Weatheradio Frequencies

Vancouver	162.550 MHz	Ucluelet	162.525 MHz
Victoria	162.400 MHz	Texada Island	162.525 MHz
Port Alberni	162.525 MHz	Prince Rupert	162.525 MHz
Port Hardy	162.525 MHz	Masset	162.425 MHz

Not to be used for navigation purposes
Updated June 2013
© Environment Canada

FORECAST ISSUE TIMES

All issue times are Pacific Standard or Daylight Saving Time (PST/PDT). Updated forecasts are issued as required.

Regular Forecast and Technical Marine Synopsis:	4 am; 10:30 am 4 pm; 9:30 pm
Extended Forecast:	4 am; 4 pm
Wave Height Forecast:	4 am; 4 pm

The information provided has been verified with appropriate agencies and is believed to be correct as of December 2023

Page 116 IMPORTANT NOTICES

Canada Coast Guard

Website: www.ccg-gcc.gc.ca.

Coast Guard Marine Communications & Traffic Services (MCTS): Website: www.ccg-gcc.gc.ca/Marine-Communications/Home. Address: MCTS Regional Office, Canadian Coast Guard - Western Region, Victoria Coast Guard Base 25 Huron Street, Victoria BC V8V 4V9. Phone: 250-363-8904.

The Marine Communications and Traffic Services centre (MCTS) provides marine safety communications co-ordination with the Joint Rescue Co-ordination Centre in Victoria. MCTS centres provide vessel traffic services and waterway management, broadcast weather and safety information; sail plan services in addition to support for other government and marine agencies.

Call the applicable MCTS centre to speak with the shift supervisor:
MCTS   Prince Rupert   250-627-3070
MCTS   Victoria   250-363-6333

Canadian Notices to Mariners: www.notmar.gc.ca.

Coast Guard Notices To Shipping: Visit www.ccg-gcc.gc.ca/eng/CCG/Notship to link to these notices concerning Navigational Aid changes or defects, fishing zones, military exercises, dredging, or other marine hazards.

Coast Guard Search & Rescue: For general information during regular office hours, contact the Victoria Joint Rescue Co-ordination Centre (JRCC) at 250-413-8927.

For emergencies call 1-800-567-5111 (within British Columbia) or 250-413-8933 or via cellular phone #727 (Note: not all cell phone companies provide this service).

The MCTS may also be contacted on VHF channel 16 in case of emergencies. MCTS will relay distress traffic to JRCC and other mariners. Via cellular phone dial *16 (Note: not all cell phone companies provide this service and calls may not be routed to the closest MCTS Centre.) Communication with MCTS via VHF radio is generally a better choice.

Environment Canada

Report A Spill: Marine polluting or oil spills call 1-800-889-8852 24 hours a day.

Pleasure Craft Sewage Discharge: Subdivision 4 of the Regulations for the "Prevention of Pollution from Ships and for Dangerous Chemicals Act" sets out requirements for pleasure craft sewage discharge. Untreated sewage may be discharged not less than three nautical miles from shore. Treated sewage may be discharged not less than one nautical mile from shore. Discharge of untreated sewage is prohibited in inland waters.

Schedule 2 of the regulations sets out designated sewage areas where the discharge of raw sewage is prohibited. The complete text of the regulations can be found at http://laws-lois.justice.gc.ca/eng/regulations/SOR%2D2012%2D69.

Pleasure Craft Sewage Equipment: The "Prevention of Pollution from Ships and for Dangerous Chemicals Act" requires that boats fitted with toilets be equipped with sewage management equipment such as the following:
• Holding Tank - Empty collected sewage at approved pump-out stations on dry land only. Follow all pumping instructions and avoid environmentally harmful disinfectants.

Princess Louisa Inlet (page 179)   Photo © Michael Russell

• Marine Sanitation Devices – Be sure the device you chose meets regulation standards. Only approved devices may be used to receive, treat and discharge in inland waters.
• Temporary Storage – To use temporary storage (such as a porta potti) your vessel must be under 15GT, carry no more that 15 persons, and does not operate on inland waters.

For further sewage discharge information, contact the Office of Boating Safety at 604-666-2681, 1-855-859-3123 or www.tc.gc.ca/boatingsafety.

Fishing & Shellfishing

Sport Fishing: Visit www.pac.dfo-mpo.gc.ca and choose BC Sportfishing, then choose your fishing location for specific information on limits, openings, and closures. Or download a current copy of *B.C. Tidal Waters Sport Fishing Guide* and find helpful information on topics such as how to package your fish properly for transport.

Get The Right Sport Fishing Licenses: Tidal (Salt) Water Sport Fishing Licenses are issued by the DFO and can be purchased online at www.bcsportfishguide.ca. Non-Tidal (Fresh) Water Fishing Licenses for salmon in British Columbia are provided by the Province. Visit www.fishing.gov.bc.ca. For fresh water species other than salmon visit www.env.gov.bc.ca/fw/fish/regulations for additonal information.

Sport Fishing/Shellfishing Phone Contacts:
24 hr. Recorded Notifications, 1-866-431-FISH (Pacific region only) or 604-666-2828. Observe, Record, & Report Line (fisheries violations), 1-800-465-4336 (Pacific region only); or 604-607-4186 in Greater Vancouver. For Recreational Licensing: 1-877-535-7307.

Canadian Salmon Trip Notification: Anglers who plan to fish for salmon in Canadian marine waters and return in their boats with their catch to Washington are required to notify WDFW **before** leaving state waters. The form is available online, http://wdfw.wa.gov/licensing/canadian_catch.php. Anglers will receive an email confirmation that their trip information has been received.

HAM Radio Net

The British Columbia Boaters Net (BCBN) is an Amateur Radio radio net for HAM Radio Operators cruising the Salish Sea (Rosario Strait, Haro Strait, Strait of Georgia), Johnstone Strait and Queen Charlotte Strait as far as the north end of Vancouver Island and the west coast near Tofino. The Net generally begins with call for announcements, then a roll call for vessels that have checked in recently and then a call for new participants. From June to September the net is conducted daily on the 2-meter band at 1700 hr. (5:00 pm) PDT (dates and time subject to change) using the Island Trunk System. Go to www.islandtrunksystem.org for a download of system details. The BCBN operate in an informal way and they enjoy hearing about your day. Traveling north from the San Juan Islands, your first contact would likely be on the repeater near Chemainus: Frequency 146.680 Mhz., offset –600Khz, 141.3hz tone. Call Sign VE7RNA, Elevation 4000'.

A database of participants allows the Net Controller to access basic information about you and your boat. Visit www.bcbn.ca for details about the voluntary registration and other BCBN information.

Harbour Authorities / Fisheries & Oceans

Public Fishing Harbours: Fisheries & Oceans Canada's Small Craft Harbours (SCH) facilities in the Pacific Region are widely distributed and vary greatly in size, scope and make-up, but each reflects local harbour users and communities. Call 604-666-4875 or visit www.dfo-mpo.gc.ca and search "Small Craft Harbours". For additional information on Harbour Authority managed sites, www.haa.bc.ca.

Marine Trails

B.C. Marine Trail Network: A registered non-profit association supporting the establishment of a network of marine trails along the B.C. coastline for the users of small beachable watercraft. For a trail map with campsite, stopovers and launch sites visit www.bcmarinetrails.org.

Visit us at boattravel.com

Parks and Recreation Sites - British Columbia

B.C. Parks Website: www.env.gov.bc.ca/bcparks.

Campsite Reservations: Campsites fill up rapidly so secure your site, visit www.discovercamping.ca or call 1-800-689-9025. Reservations can be placed up to 4 months in advance for Frontcounty campsites or 12 months for group campsites.

Marine Park Fees: Fees are collected for moorage at designated park floats and buoys. The fees are: Floats-$2 per meter (3.28 feet) per night. Moorage buoy fees-$14 per vessel per night. Moorage is offered at a number of Provincial Coastal Marine Parks.

Gulf Islands National Park Reserve: This unique park is a patchwork of protected lands found on 15 Southern Gulf Islands including areas on the Pender Islands, Mayne Island, Prevost Island, Saturna Island, Cabbage Island, Tumbo Island, Russell Island, Princess Margaret (Portland Island), Isle-de-Lis, Sidney Spit, D'Arcy Island, and land near Sidney. Fees are collected for moorage at docks and buoys, and for camping. Dock (Sidney Spit): $2.90 per metre per night. Mooring buoys (Cabbage, Beaumont and Sidney Spit): $14.00 (CAN) per vessel per night. www.pc.gc.ca. 1-866-944-1744 or 250-654-4000.

B.C. Marine Parks Forever Society: This non-profit Society, established by the Council of BC Yacht Clubs and individual boating groups, is dedicated to creating new or improving marine parks for future generations.

Recreation Sites and Trails, B.C.: For an extensive inventory and interactive map of B.C. recreation sites and trails visit, http://www.sitesandtrailsbc.ca.

Canadian Marine Police Units

RCMP Coastal Watch: Boaters are asked to assist the RCMP in the identification of persons, and vessels that may be involved in illegal activities such as drug importation, terrorism, the smuggling of weapons, cigarettes and alcohol; theft of logs/shake blocks and illegal log salvage, persons illegally entering the country; illegal waste discharge, etc. by reporting suspicious activity. Call 1-800-665-6663.

RCMP Patrol Vessels: Most Coastal Detachments and RCMP Border Integrity Units along the West Coast of B.C. operate small coastal watercraft under 8 meters in length. Your boat may be boarded by members of either one. An RCMP boarding is similar to the U.S. Coast Guard boarding checks, checking fire extinguishers, PFD's, and other required equipment. They may also include Criminal Code, Customs, Immigration, and Drug related investigations. If boarded, the RCMP will request identification papers, ships documents, border related clearances and associated receipts or numbers. All RCMP patrol vessels monitor VHF Channel 16.

The Vancouver Police Marine Unit patrols the waters of Vancouver including the Fraser River. They enforce speed limits, check for Proof of Pleasure Craft Operators Proficiency, investigate criminal activity on the waterfront and regularly conduct safe boating seminars. 604-717-3744, VHF Channels 12 or 16.

Center Island (page 91) Photo © Chelsea Frost

VHF Marine Radio Canadian Vessels

Ship radio station license: Canadian recreational vessels operating in U.S. waters must treat this as international travel and are required to have a Station License from Innovation, Science and Economic Development Canada (IC). U.S. recreational vessels operating in Canadian waters must have a Station License from the Federal Communications Commission (FCC).

A ship radio station license is not required if you meet the following criteria:

(1): The vessel is not operated in the sovereign waters of a country other than Canada.

(2): The radio equipment on board the vessel is only capable of operating on frequencies that are allocated for maritime mobile communications or marine radio navigation. To verify whether the frequencies you use are in the maritime mobile band, refer to Regulation by Reference RBR-2. Website: www.ic.gc.ca.

Restricted Operator's Certificate (Maritime): In Canada ALL operators of a VHF Marine Band Radio must have a Restricted Operator's Certificate (Maritime), also known as ROC(M). Canadian Power and Sail Squadrons can administer the exams for the ROC(M), which includes the DSC endorsement. www.cps-ecp.ca. 1-888-277-2628 in Canada, or 416-293-2438 outside of Canada.

Canadian vessels operators may obtain their MMSI from any Innovation, Science and Economic Development Canada (IC) office at no cost. In BC, offices are located in Vancouver (Surrey) and Victoria. Applicants must provide basic information for the Search and Rescue database in order to obtain a MMSI. Website: www.ic.gc.ca, search "MMSI".

VHF Marine Radio Calls: For the correct procedure, channels, and calling etiquette, see the "Marine VHF Radio" pages in the Appendix of this book. When calling marinas in Canada, your VHF radio should not be on international mode.

Vessel Traffic Service

Cooperative Vessel Traffic System (CVTS): The Canadian and U.S. Coast Guards have established the CVTS, managed by Seattle Traffic, Victoria Traffic, and Prince Rupert Traffic.

Seattle Traffic (VHF 5A) provides VTS for both the Canadian and U.S. waters of Juan de Fuca Strait.

Victoria Traffic (VHF 11/12/71/74) provides VTS for CVTS waters encompassing the northeastern portion of Juan de Fuca Strait, both Canadian and U.S. waters of Haro Strait, Boundary Passage, and southern Strait of Georgia. VTS for the Inside Passage to Cape Caution as well as the Strait of Georgia north of a line between Merry Island and Ballenas Island is provided on VHF 71. VTS is provided for the Gulf Islands, Strait of Georgia northward via the inside passage to Cape Caution, and the main arm of the Fraser River up to New Westminster is on VHF 74. Additionally VTS for Howe Sound, English Bay, approaches to the Fraser River (North Arm), Burrard Inlet, and Indian Arm is on VHF 12.

Prince Rupert Traffic (VHF 11/71/74) provides VTS from Cape Caution northward through the Inside Passage, Hecate Straits, and Haida Gwaii Islands on VHF 11. On the west coast of Vancouver Island, Prince Rupert provides VTS on VHF 74 for waters encompassing the western approaches to Juan de Fuca Strait and along Washington State's coastline from 48 degrees north, and from Juan de Fuca Strait northward to Triangle Island. VTS for Dixon Entrance to the Canadian/Alaskan boundary, Chatham Sound, and Prince Rupert harbour are available on VHF 71.

For additional VTS information, visit www.ccg-gcc.gc.ca. Search for "RAMN 2018 Part 3".

The information provided has been verified with appropriate agencies and is believed to be correct as of December 2023

Basic Boat Maneuvering

Moon over Port Ludlow Marina (page 56) — Photo © Port Ludlow Marina

Basic principles: Piloting a boat is not at all like driving a car. With a car, the front end moves right or left as one steers, and the back end usually follows obediently. Not so with a boat. Instead, the stern does the moving, to port or starboard, as one turns the wheel. Thus, the stern must be kept free of obstacles on either side.

As if this is not problem enough, the water under a boat is not a stable substance like a highway. Water moves about with the current, helping or hindering efforts to control the boat. Add to these variables the unpredictable local winds inside small harbors and the close quarters that are frequently encountered, and it's no wonder that many yacht captains have Excedrin headaches.

Not that captains are alone in getting headaches from maneuvering. Most first-mates, given two martinis and an opportunity to speak, can relate at least one instance when their marriage, if not their very life, was called into question by the captain shouting, "What did you do to make the boat do that?" The frustration of such instances sometimes pushes even the most patient first-mate to the verge of a nervous breakdown.

Speed: A frequent mistake novice boat handlers make is using too much speed. A boat speeding about in tight quarters is just asking for trouble. A captain proceeding slowly and cautiously can usually recover from a mistake with little more than embarrassment by simply pushing off the object into which the boat has been carried. There are times, of course, when wind and current require modest amounts of speed in order to maintain headway or sternway. Extreme caution is required at such time.

Observations: Take note of the direction and strength of the wind by observing flags located ashore and on boats. A boat with a relatively flat bottom will be more affected by wind than current. Boats with a deep V-hull, however, are affected more by the current. Which way the current is going to flow can sometimes be determined by knowing whether the tide is flooding or ebbing. Sometimes the current is actually visible in the water, or an object such as a piece of drift wood can be observed moving with the flow. Watch how the current is affecting other boats that are maneuvering in the same area. Make a trial run and note the effect of the current on your boat. The important thing is to take time to decide the best approach, given the present wind and current conditions. Strong preference should be given to heading into the wind or current versus having it at the stern. When landing, it is also preferable for the wind and current to push the boat in toward the dock, rather than away from it.

Backing away from trouble: Many boaters get in trouble because once they decide what they're going to do they keep on doing it, even if things start going wrong. It is best to abort a maneuver that is obviously getting the boat into trouble. Reverse engines, back out into more open waters, and make a change in plans or a better approach.

Docking to portside: Single-screw Yachtsmans usually favor bringing the boat into the dock on the side to which the rotation of the propeller brings the stern of the boat in toward the dock when the engine is in reverse. With right-hand (clockwise rotation) propellers, this is the port side. The reason for this is that when the boat has headway and the engine is in reverse the stern will be driven to port regardless of the rudder's position.

The down-wind or down-current landing: When this landing is a must, have a stern line ready to throw ashore as soon as possible. With the stern secured, the bow will swing into the dock from the pressure of the wind or current. Securing the bow first risks being turned end-for-end. If the wind or current is from the stern, turn the propeller slowly in reverse to hold against them, with rudder only slightly to port. The stern will come in first, so an afterquarter spring line should be secured first.

Leeward-side landing: Occasionally, because of strong winds and seas, it is unadvisable (if not impossible) to land the boat on to the dock. This is a difficult maneuver and there is a risk of damaging the boat. The correct way is to approach the dock bow first, with enough headway to hold into the wind. As the bow line is thrown ashore, engines are reversed to stop headway. Secure the bow-spring line. Turn the rudder to starboard, with engines in forward, just enough to move against the wind. As soon as possible, throw a stern line ashore.

Getting away from a float: If wind or current pushes the boat off the dock, simply loose the lines and let these forces carry the boat away from the dock. If the wind or current is holding the boat into the dock, an after-bow spring line is used. The boat goes ahead on the spring with the rudder set toward the dock. This swings the stern clear allowing the boat to back into the wind.

The same technique works if the wind or current is from the boat's stern. When the stern is out 45-90 degrees from the dock, with the engines in neutral, cast off the bow line. If onshore help is unavailable, double the after-bow spring line so that it comes free and can be hauled aboard when one end is let loose aboard. When the wind or current is from the bow of the boat, a forward-quarter spring is used in the same manner to hold the stern in and let the bow swing out away from the dock.

Using twin screws: By putting one engine in forward and the other in neutral or reverse, a twin-screw boat may be turned around in her own length with the rudder amid-ships. Mastering this technique of steering with the throttles allows the twin-screw captain better maneuverability than with a single-screw.

Inboard-outboard/outboard: The inboard-outboard and outboard maneuver in the same manner as the single-screw inboard, except that the skipper has more control over the boat, because the rudder and propeller are both turned by the wheel.

Well-meaning dock helpers: There are times, such as when the boat is blown off the dock during landing, or onto the dock during the get away, when onshore help is much needed. It is the captain's responsibility to provide correct instructions to these helpers, who may be more well-meaning than knowledgeable. When anticipating a get-away problem, before leaving the dock, it is wise to enlist help and plan a strategy together so that the captain, first mate, and dockhand all have a clear understanding of who does what and when. Difficult approaches are more on a catch-as-catch can basis. It is especially important for the captain and first mate to have an agreed upon procedure, as the first mate may be the only person close enough to a dock hand to yell instructions.

When conditions are calm or after the captain and mate have mastered the art of landing and departing, a well-meaning dock hand may be a detriment. Many a skipper has planned and executed an approach impeccably, only to have a "dockhand" yank on a line, throwing the yacht into an unexpected trajectory. Pull a bow line and the stern leaves the dock. Pull a stern line and the bow will be out of control.

What do you tell a kind person who runs down the dock to help? It helps if the mate understands the captain's plans and can interpret them to helpers. When landing in good conditions, the mate should hand the line to the helper, telling them to hold it, but not to secure or pull on it until requested to do so by the captain.

Visit us at boattravel.com

Basic Boat Anchoring

Although most pleasure boat anchors are patented, sophisticated devices designed to have holding power far beyond their weight, they are neither fool proof, nor immune to the mistakes of the un-enlightened boater! Anchoring is a simple, but precise, skill. It can lead to a satisfying experience and good night sleep, or to hair-raising, ill-fated adventure. The following tips should help the average boater avoid trouble.

Know the bottom. A shale or soft mud bottom will not hold an anchor satisfactorily. Also, extensive grass on the bottom may prevent the anchor fluke from penetrating to the bottom. A rocky bottom requires a special anchoring technique. If the bottom has good holding material, almost anyone can anchor if they avoid "fouling" the anchor. Most of the good-holding bottoms in the Pacific Northwest are found at the head of bays and are a composite of sand and mud or mud and clay.

Use the proper sized anchor. In good bottom, patent anchors like Bruce and Danforth can hold up to 400 times their weight. No single anchor design is best in all conditions, so you may want two anchors aboard (in case one is lost, for use in a different condition, or for stern and bow anchoring in tight anchorages.

Anchor rode: We recommend, as a minimum, enough rode to reach the bottom and allow for sufficient scope in 10 to 15 fathoms. Of the more than 125 anchorages described in chapter 19, Northern British Columbia Coast, over 50% are in the 10 to 15 fathom range. If Chapman's seven times depth rule were strictly followed, some 600 feet of anchor rode would be required. As a practical compromise, we use an oversized Bruce anchor with 100-feet of 5/8" galvanized chain and 200-feet of line. With this tackle, we have anchored successfully in depths up to 20-fathoms in calm weather. In bad weather, we can get a scope of three times depth in 15-fathoms, five times depth in ten fathoms, or seven times depth in seven fathoms.

Watch out for the other guy's anchor. Before anchoring, visualize where the other boats' anchors are set and make a plan to anchor well clear of them. Remember that these boats have prior claim to the territory. If unsure of how much scope or in what direction another boat's anchor lies, ask them.

Never throw an anchor overboard. Always lower the anchor slowly from the boat, observing carefully that it is free from the following chain.

Set your anchor properly with enough scope. Use a depth sounder or lead line to determine the depth where you are anchoring. Then, make a turn or two around the area in which yours will swing. Pay special attention to any rocks or shallow points that may be trouble during a lower tide.

Lower the anchor slowly to the bottom. In the same direction as the wind is expected to blow, gradually back the boat away from the anchor by taking the boat in and out of reverse gear. While backing away from the anchor, gradually let out enough scope to equal approximately three to four times the depth. Grip the anchor line in your hands to cushion the force of the boat when the line becomes taut, or on larger boats, take a turn around the bow cleat. When the line is taut, give it two or three tugs to set the hook. Continue paying out line until your planned scope is reached. In a crowded anchorage on a calm night, you might reduce scope or use a stern anchor.

With the gearshift now in neutral position, tie the line off on the boat. If an extra high tide is expected overnight, pay out additional line to leave plenty of scope. If an extreme low tide is expected, take in some line to keep the boat from swinging too far away from the anchor.

Putting out a stern anchor is possible using a dinghy. Take the dinghy to the desired anchoring spot, lower the anchor slowly, paying the line out slowly, hand-over-hand.

Anchoring with an all-chain rode. A favored way of anchoring with a chain rode is to let all or most of the chain out, letting the boat gently pull against the anchor to set it. Some of the chain may then be winched back to reduce the scope of the swing. Always avoid having the chain pull full force on the anchor. A taut chain may pull the anchor out or, if the anchor is hooked on a rock, the anchor blades may actually bend.

In a wind, the holding power of good-sized chain (3/8-inch or 5/8-inch) is effective because its weight keeps a sag in the line and reduces the pull on the anchor. Again, the chain will not have these qualities if pulled taut, thus chain of sufficient size and length is essential.

Weighing anchor. Should the anchor not come up easily, it may be necessary to dislodge it. Tie off the line on the bow and push forward against it with the boat. If the anchor is pushed in the reverse of the direction in which it was secured, it usually will come loose easily.

On anchor in Kah Shakes Cove (page 261) Photo © Carolin Van Calcar

Laura Cove (page 187) Photo © Bruce Johnson

The information provided has been verified with appropriate agencies and is believed to be correct as of December 2023

Chapter 8:
Southeast Vancouver Island

Portland Island Marine Park - photo © Mary Gasser, courtesy Marine Parks Forever Society

Strait of Juan de Fuca to Saanich Inlet. Victoria, Oak Bay, Sidney, Brentwood Bay, Saanich Peninsula, Tsehum Harbour, Canoe Cove; Discovery, D'Arcy, Sidney, Gooch, Coal, Piers, Moresby, & Portland Islands.

Symbols

[ ]: Numbers between [ ] are chart numbers.

{ }: Numbers & letters between { } are waypoints.

★ Recommended destinations, facilities, and services

⚓: Park, 🚤: Boat Launch, ▲: Campgrounds,

🚶: Hiking Trails, ⛱: Picnic Area, 🚲: Biking

🤿: Scuba

★ See "Important Notices" between Chapters 7 and 8 for specific information on boating related topics such as boating safety, weather, U.S. & Canadian marine radio use, Vessel Traffic Service, security zones, Canadian & U.S. Customs, etc. Due to changing regulations, call ahead to verify latest customs information.

★ **No Dump Zone:** Victoria Harbour

Southeast Vancouver Island

[3313, 3410, 3411, 3412, 3419, 3424, 3440, 3441, 3461, 3462, 3479, 3606, 3647]

★ **Introduction:** By sail or by motor, cruising the inland waterways of British Columbia between Vancouver Island and the mainland is a unique and superlative experience. The ports and places to visit on Vancouver Island, and in the neighboring Gulf Islands, are closely related in climate, topography, culture, and pleasurable experiences. There are numerous marinas and anchorages. These destinations are intimately connected by the attractive inland waterways that lead to them like highways. Boating is a way of life for many people who live or visit here. Harvesting shellfish, fishing, observing marine and bird life, visiting historic sites, exploring anchorages, visiting marinas, walking through Provincial Parks or towns, golfing, hiking, canoeing, kayaking, scuba diving, touring museums, dining in excellent restaurants, staying in fine hotels and inns, and visiting Victoria, Butchart Gardens, Oak Bay, Brentwood Bay, and Sidney are only a few of the possible vacation highlights of this area.

Chart List

Canadian Hydrographic Charts:
3313, 3410, 3411, 3412, 3419, 3424 3440, 3441, 3461, 3462, 3479, 3606, 3647

NOAA Charts:
18400, 18414-18416, 18420, 18421

Marine Atlas Vol 1 (2018): Pages 9, 14, 15

Evergreen Cruising Atlas: Pages 101, 106-107, 121-122

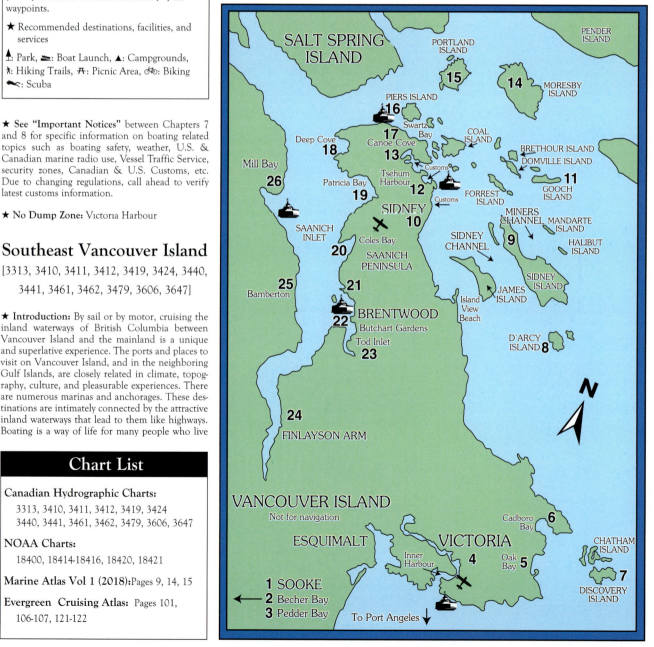

Visit us at boattravel.com

★ **Sooke (1):** [3410, 3411] No customs clearance available. Depending upon your perspective, Sooke's location is either at the gateway to the west coast of Vancouver Island, or the gateway to the east coast of Vancouver Island. See Chapter 18 for description of the harbor and local marinas.

★ **Becher Bay (2):** This bay is located about ten miles from Victoria. At spring tides, currents can run to seven knots at the entrance. In Campbell Cove, anchorage can be found in Murder Bay on the north side, but note on the chart a rock that dries five feet in this cove. The east side of Becher Bay is often used for log booming.

Becher Bay Marina: {48° 19' 44" N, 123° 37' 59" W} Open Arpil 15 - October 15, limited guest moorage, campsites, guest house. 250-642-3816.

Cheanuh Marina: {48° 20' 13"N, 123° 36' 11" W} Permanent moorage, transient moorage if space is available, gas, water, restroom, launch ramp ($10.00), tackle, snacks. 250-478-4880. VHF 16, 68.

★ **Walk-around:** East Sooke Park, located west of Becher Bay, is the largest Capital Regional District Park and contains 31 miles of wilderness hiking trails. Bird watchers visit late September for the peak of the hawk migration. The park is a stop over for the birds as they head south.

Sooke Basin from Roche Cove Bridge — Photo © Michal Klajban

★ **Pedder Bay (3):** Pedder Bay indents nearly two miles, ending in mud flats. While the bay is exposed to southeast winds, anchorage is good but limited near the head. Watch for water and sewer lines. A marina is located at Ash Point. The private dock east of Ash Point belongs to the college there. Orange and white buoys mark the restricted area around Williams Head Institution (minimum security facility).

Pedder Bay Marina: {48° 20' 58.9" N, 123° 34' 43.2" W} Moorage to 56' (call ahead for guest moorage), 30/50 amp power, gas, water, showers, laundry, launch ramp, coffee shop, boat/kayak rentals, tackle/bait, small convenience store, wifi, RV Resort. 250-478-1771. VHF 66A.

Esquimalt: [3419] This natural harbor is home to Canada's Pacific Fleet. The British Royal Navy Establishment at Esquimalt was created in 1865 as an alternate base. In time it grew increasingly more strategic as a support base for the Royal Navy in the Pacific. The name Esquimalt derives from "Es-whoy-malth," an anglicized version of the First Nation word for "the place of gradually shoaling water." Canadian Forces Base Esquimalt Naval & Military Museum, located on the base in Naden, is a great place to visit to learn more about the area's history. No charge, donations suggested. Call 250-363-4312 for hours or visit the museum's Facebook page @NavalAnd Military Museum. All vessels entering or departing Esquimalt Harbour are requested to contact the King's Harbour Master (KHM) Operations on VHF channel 10 or by phone at 250-363-2160.

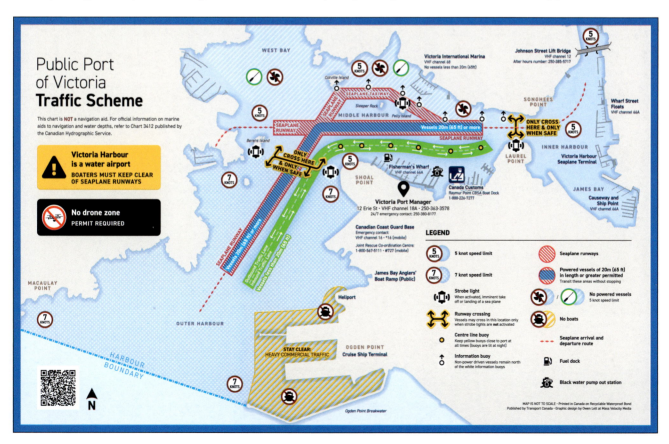

Page 122   Chapter 8   SOUTHEAST VANCOUVER ISLAND

Vancouver's Inner Harbour and the Empress Hotel   Photo © David Leverton

Vessels are at all times to remain 100 metres away from stationary vessels and 200 metres away from vessels underway. Unauthorized intrusions could lead to Federal prosecution. This is primarily a military and industrial area. The closest small craft moorage facility is found in the West Bay off Head Street, but space here is limited. Larger, luxury moorage is available at the Victoria International Marina in Victoria's Middle Harbour. Pleasure craft intending to anchor are to provide KHM with information on their vessel. This information is found at https://www.canada.ca/en/navy/corporate/esquimalt-harbour.html under "Pleasure craft reporting requirements when entering Esquimalt Harbour". Pleasure vessels may only anchor north of a line drawn between the south end of Richards Island and the north end of Smart Island. Every pleasure vessel anchored in Esquimalt Harbour shall be moored with two anchors and in the manner directed by a harbour official. Rafting of pleasure vessels, at anchor, is not permitted. A harbour official must first approve anchoring in any other area of the harbour. This information is found at www.esquimaltharbour.ca under "Practices and Procedures". In addition to the military base, the township of Esquimalt offers dining and lodging options, a golf course, rec-centre and pool, parks, and trails. For township information, visit www.esquimalt.ca.

Sailors Cove Marina: {48° 25.66' N, 123° 23.8' W} Permanent moorage, liveaboards, 20 amp power, water, shower, laundry, private pumpout. 250-385-1831.

Westbay Marine Village: {48° 25' 37"N, 123° 23' 53"W} Permanent moorage, 30/50 amp power, water, showers, laundry, private pump-out. 250-385-1831.

Fleming Bay: East of the Gillingham Islands, this indentation is protected by a rock breakwater. Private floats, a park with picnic area. A whistle buoy painted with a sea life mural is near the launch ramp. The launch fee is $20 or $100 for the year. Free hand rock climbers are often spotted on nearby rock walls.

Victoria Harbour
[3412]

★ **Victoria Harbour Traffic Scheme "Partnership In Safety":** A traffic control system applies to all vessels and seaplanes. Reference Chart #3412. For the purpose of this traffic scheme, Victoria Harbour may be considered in four parts:

• The Outer Harbour extending from the breakwater to Shoal Point
• The Middle Harbour extending from Shoal Point to Laurel Point
• The Inner Harbour extending from Laurel Point to the Johnson Street Bridge
• The Upper Harbour extending north of the Johnson Street Bridge

Two unmarked Seaplane Take-off/Landing areas are located in the middle of the Middle Harbour and extend out into the Outer Harbour. Located parallel to these, (on the southern portion of the Middle Harbour and extending out into the Outer Harbour) are two Inbound/Outbound Traffic Lanes for vessels to 65 feet. The southernmost lane is for inbound vessels. Five lighted yellow cautionary buoys flashing every four seconds are used at the eastern portion (prior to Laurel Point) to divide the inbound/outbound lanes.

All vessels entering or exiting the Inbound/Outbound Traffic Lanes should merge gradually into the appropriate traffic lane, avoiding crossing traffic lanes. If crossing a traffic lane is unavoidable, cross at right angles to the traffic lane.

Cautions: The vertical clearance under the Johnson Street Bridge at high water is 5.9m (19 ft) and the width of the channel between pilings is 37m (122 ft).

White strobe lights located at Shoal Point, Laurel Point, and on Pelly Island alert mariners of imminent seaplane take offs and landings. When lights are activated, use extreme caution.

Three short blasts of a large ferry's whistle (the Coho) means it is in astern propulsion. Stay well clear. Never cross in front of a ferry or in its wake.

Rules and Regulations:
1. Speed Limit is five knots in the Victoria Harbour inside a line from Shoal Point to Berens Island, and seven knots outside the line.
2. Minimize wake to prevent damage.
3. No sailing allowed in Middle, Inner and Upper Harbour. Lower all sails, even when under power.
4. Anchoring is prohibited without the Harbour Master's permission.
5. A Blackwater Discharge prohibition is in effect for all Port of Victoria waters north of Ogden Point as far as the Selkirk Trestle Bridge.

★ **Victoria Harbour & James Bay (4):** Boats arriving from the U.S. that are up to 160' (49m) can clear customs at Raymur Point. Boats over 160' or 40 m should contact CBSA at 1-888-226-7277 to make alternate arrangements. See the entry for the Raymur Point CBSA Boat Dock in this chapter.

Enter Victoria Harbour between Macaulay and Ogden Points. Currents run to two knots in this entrance. Fisherman's Wharf, the first basin on the starboard side when entering the middle harbour, has the only fuel dock in Victoria Harbour. There is no transient moorage available here. The Wharf has a distinct and eclectic flavor, mixing liveaboard boaters, working fishing vessels and colorful float homes on its docks. Nearby waterfront businesses offer ice cream, fish and chips, BBQ, fresh fish, Mexican food, whale watching, kayak tours and more.

Across the middle harbour on the port side is Victoria International Marina. The marina is located just west of downtown Victoria, in the "VicWest" neighborhood, steps away from Lime Bay Park as well as the Songhees Walkway that skirts the shoreline. Boom + Batten, a casual fine dining restaurant with lounge and cafe, is located at the marina. Both offer spectacular views of the City and the bustling harbour traffic.

Continuing on into the Inner Harbour, there are two moorage facilities, the Causeway and Ship Point. Both offer transient moorage. Causeway Docks, located downtown in front of the Fairmont Empress Hotel, hosts prominent events such as Swiftsure, Victoria Harbour Floating Boat Show and the Classic Boat Show. The Causeway docks also provide a front row view of local artists and street performers, as well as the magnificent 3,333 LED light display on the Parliament Buildings. A short walk away on Wharf Street, the Tourism Victoria Visitor Centre can assist with many services such as reservations for accommodations, sightseeing, adventure tours and transportation. (Open daily, except Christmas Day. Extended summer hours.) Ship Point moorage is located on the north side of the Inner Harbour, and from late June through mid-September the Ship Point Night Market features artists, musicians and performers on Friday and Saturday, 6-10:30pm. Each August, the Dragon Boat Festival at Ship Point entertains with two days of unique culture and sport. Keep up with the various harbour area events at www.gvha.ca.

The Victoria Classic Boat Festival occurs August 31 through September 2, 2024 Photo © David Leverton

Just north of Ship Point, the Wharf Street floats offer transient moorage and are convenient to shops, restaurants, and Chinatown. Further up the harbour, is the new Johnson Street Bridge, Canada's largest single-leaf bascule bridge. Just before the bridge are the Johnston Street floats with monthly moorage. Beyond the bridge, the Upper Harbour is surrounded by industrial complexes. A small public float for passenger drop-off only is located at Banfield Park on the Victoria West shore of Selkirk Waterway. The Gorge waterway leads further inland to Portage Inlet. Because of currents and restrictions, passage into the Gorge (even by dinghy) is not recommended.

★ **City of Victoria:** Victoria, the *City of Gardens*, is the capital of British Columbia and one of the northwest's most beautiful cities. In addition, Victoria also boasts more attractions catering to the interests of all ages than cities twice its size. One can explore the B.C. Parliament Buildings or have afternoon tea at the landmark Fairmont Empress Hotel and still find plenty of other places to visit. These include noted specialty shops, Victoria Public Market, art galleries, Miniature World, Thunderbird Park totem poles, Chinatown, Beacon Hill Park & Children's Farm, theaters, rose gardens, heritage homes, and even a Bug Zoo! Take a walk along the Ogden Point Breakwater where Canada's largest mural adorns the inner wall. Let the Royal BC Museum's unique exhibits take you to a turn of the last century British Columbia town, aboard Captain Vancouver's ship *HMS Discovery*, or into the house of First Nations Chief Kwakwabalasami. You can also experience the subtropical surroundings that existed in this region 80 million years ago or feel the chill of the Ice Age at the Green House - Ice Gallery. Want to bring out your inner "foodie"? Victoria has amazing choices to explore from the finest dining establishments to unique food trucks. A burgeoning adult beverage scene includes an array of local craft breweries, cider houses, wineries, and distilleries, some with tours and tastings. Still looking for something to do? Festivals abound here year round, including the *Downtown Victoria Buskers Festival*, *Great Canadian Beer Festival*, *Rifflandia Music Festival*, and *Victoria's Indigenous Cultural Festival*. For events, things to see and do, and visitor information, www.tourismvictoria.com. Many of these attractions, events, and amenities such as a large grocery store, are within walking distance of moorage. Taxis, double-decker buses, horse drawn buggies, harbour cruises, and sight-seeing tours are available. Car ferries connect Victoria with Port Angeles and Vancouver year around. All year, float planes and passenger-only ferries link Victoria with Seattle and Vancouver. Victoria is a center for scheduled bus service to all island communities, and buses board the ferries, taking passengers to Seattle and Vancouver.

★ **Raymur Point CBSA Boat Dock:** {48° 25'23.5" N, 123° 22' 49.8" W} Boats arriving from the U.S. that are up to 160' (49m) in length are to proceed to the Raymur Point Canada Customs Dock (marked by yellow capped pilings and a large red and white Customs sign), just east of Fisherman's Wharf and before reaching the Coast Harbourside Marina. There is a direct line telephone on the dock (reference "Raymur Point CBSA Boat Dock" as the reporting site). If your vessel is over 160' or 49m, contact CBSA at 1-888-226-7277 to make alternate arrangements.

Causeway Marina: {48° 25' 18.4" N, 123° 22' 09.9" W} (Located in Downtown Victoria in front of the Fairmont Empress Hotel and the Lower Causeway). Transient moorage available throughout the summer, with limited availability from Oct-May, and low season moorage Oct-May, vessels to 60'. 30-amp power, water, garbage, compost, and recycling disposal, complimentary WiFi, showers, restrooms and laundry. Marina gate locked 24/7. Mandatory rafting during events and long weekends. The check-in kiosk is open daily mid-June to mid-Sept. Reservations highly recommended. 250-383-8326 ext 235. VHF 66A.

Humpbacks off Mandarte near Sidney — Photo © Chris Teren / www.terenphotography.com

Coast Victoria Harbourside Hotel & Marina: {48° 24' 59" N, 123° 22' 4" W} Daily, monthly, liveaboard moorage. Please call ahead for availability. 20/30, 50, 100 amp power (depending on slip assignment), water, pool, hot tub, sauna, lodging, restaurant. 250-360-1211.

Fisherman's Wharf: {48° 25'21" N, 123° 23' 2" W} (East of Shoal Point). No transient moorage. Float homes, long-term pleasure craft, long-term/short-term commercial fishing vessels. 30/50 amp power, water, fuel dock, showers, restrooms, laundry, garbage, compost and recycling disposal. Pump out on finger B. 250-383-8326 ext. 235.

Fuel Dock at Fisherman's Wharf Marina: Gas, diesel, oil, lubes, waste oil disposal, water, ice, snacks, fishing tackle. 250-381-5221.

Ship Point: {48° 25'21.1" N, 123° 22' 12.3" W} (Located west of Causeway Marina). Transient moorage available throughout the summer, with limited availability from Oct-May, and low season moorage Oct-May, vessels to 280'. 100-amp (single phase) and two, 100-amp (240 v and 408 v) power, water, garbage, compost, and recycling disposal, complimentary WiFi, showers, restrooms, laundry. Marina gate locked 24/7. Mandatory rafting during events and long weekends. Reservations highly recommended. 250-383-8326 ext. 235. VHF 66A.

Victoria International Marina: Twenty-eight slips located in the middle harbour of Victoria. Moorage for yachts between 65 and 175 feet. On-site security, wi-fi, 24/7 concierge services; private captain/crew lounge; restaurant. 778-432-0477. VHF 68.

Wharf Street Marina: {48° 25'31.1" N, 123° 22' 16.6'" W} (In the Inner Harbour north of the Harbour Air Seaplane Terminal). Transient moorage available throughout the summer, with limited availability from Oct-May, monthly and low season moorage Oct-May, vessels up to 150'. 30/50/100 (single phase) amp power, water, garbage, compost, and recycling disposal, complimentary WiFi, showers restrooms, laundry. Marina gate locked 24/7. Mandatory rafting during events and long weekends. Reservations highly recommended. 250-383-8326 ext. 235. VHF 66A.

Oak Bay Area

★ Oak Bay (5): [3424] Entrance is between Turkey Head and the breakwater projecting south from Mary Tod Island. A buoy marks the outer end of a reef extending west from Mary Tod Island. Do not pass between Tod Rock and Fiddle Reef because of shoals. The harbor has a speed limit of four knots. The Oak Bay Marina is located here. Anchorage is usually difficult to find amid the many boats and sunken vessels can pose anchoring hazards. In the early 1900's Hudson's Bay Company personnel established summer homes in the Oak Bay area. Many were designed by architect Sam Maclure in an English Tudor style, but featured timbers on half the house built atop native stone foundations. A contemporary architect, Francis Rattenbury, who designed the Empress and the Parliament Buildings, also had a Tudor style residence here. Others who arrived from England brought their style of life, culture and heritage and that influence continues today. Oak Bay is an inviting place to take a stroll just to admire the fine buildings, or to stop in at a local shop, restaurant, coffee shop, bakery or art gallery. Bus and taxi service is available to and from downtown Victoria. The private Victoria Golf Club (members and reciprocal) is within walking distance of the marina.

Oak Bay Marina: {48° 25'33" N, 123° 18' 11" W} Annual moorage. Short term moorage if space is available, phone ahead. Gas, diesel, 15/30 amp power, water, launch, showers, laundry, chandlery, gifts, restaurant, Customs Dock, kayak tours. Marine repairs onsite (call 250-598-3378). Haulouts to 30', no sailboats. Marina: 250-598-3369. VHF 66A.

Cadbora Bay Beach — Photo © Michal Klajban

★ **Cadboro Bay (6):** Approach to the bay is not difficult with the recommended route being from the north, through Baines Channel, or from the east passing south of Jemmy Jones Island. If coming in from the south, past Oak Bay, there are several well marked islets however use of an updated Canadian marine chart is recommended. Anchorage is very good (mud bottom) near the head of the bay. Several commercial mooring buoys are located in the bay. Dungeness crab fishing is spectacular and standup paddle boarding is popular due to the usually calm summer water conditions. Cadboro Bay is home to the Royal Victoria Yacht Club, host of the world renowned Swiftsure International Yacht Race. On the beach, Gyro Park has a play area with a zipline. The beach consists of pristine white sand and swimming is some of the best in the area. A short walk away, a small community shopping centre has boutique gift shops, grocery store, Starbucks, wine/beer store and other local shops. Public launching ramps are located south of Cadboro Bay at Cattle Point. The Cadborosaurus, a large sea serpent type creature that some say lives in Pacific Northwest waters, was named in part after this Bay. Despite sightings over the years, "Caddy" remains the stuff of legend.

Cadboro Bay and the Royal Victoria Yacht Club   Photo © Lotus Johnson

Royal Victoria Yacht Club: {48° 27.2' N, 123° 17.7' W} Members/Reciprocal visitors only. Canadian Customs point of entry. Moorage, power, water, washroom, showers, laundry, maintenance facility, launch ramp, restaurant, gift shop. 250-592-2441. VHF 09A.

Baynes Channel: Winds are unpredictable and currents can run to six knots at the north entrance, to three knots at the south. Rips are present when wind is against the tide.

Haro Strait: See current tables for Admiralty Inlet. This strait lies between the Strait of Juan de Fuca and Boundary Bay and separates the San Juan Islands from Vancouver Island. The International Boundary between Canada and the United States lies in the center of this busy waterway. Ferries regularly cross the strait en route to Sidney or the San Juan Islands. It is a main shipping route and traffic separation lanes are designated for large vessels. Be cautious and aware of vessel traffic. The maximum velocity of tidal streams reaches four knots on the flood stream, and the strait can kick up significantly when winds are present. A local magnetic anomaly, as much as four degrees from the normal variation, has been observed in the vicinity of Bellevue Point on the east side of Haro Strait.

★ **Discovery Island Marine Park (7):** [3441, 3462] This park is located two miles east of Oak Bay, where Haro Strait meets the Strait of Juan de Fuca. Enter from Plumper Passage or Hecate Passage to the west or into Rudlin Bay from the south. Rudlin Bay access has numerous rocks and reefs so use caution. Because of the location and exposure to winds, there are no sheltered overnight anchorages. Temporary anchorage can be found in a niche on Chatham Island on a good bottom. Kayakers are a common sight in these waters. Many beaches invite picnicking. No fires or pets are permitted. Except for hiking paths, the park is undeveloped. There is a lighthouse on Seabird Point. Tide rips can be dangerous off this point as can the foul ground off Commodore Point. The southern half of the island was donated to the province by Captain E.G. Beaumont. The remainder and nearby islands are First Nations Reserve lands.

Finnerty Cove and Arbutus Cove: These coves are spots for temporary anchorage or gunkholing.

★ **Cordova Bay:** Stretching nearly four and one half miles from Gordon Head on the south to Cowichan Head on the north, this wide bay has shoal areas and some rocky patches. Kelp lines much of the shoreline. It is a popular swimming area. Anchorage in the niche west of Cormorant Point has good holding bottom. While open to north winds, it provides some protection from westerlies.

★ **D'Arcy Island Marine Park (8):** [3440, 3441] This undeveloped park is surrounded by numerous shoals and reefs. Enter from the west to the south of the lighthouse. There are no sheltered anchorages. Boaters may access two newly installed mooring buoys located at the north end of the island. No fires are permitted. Picnic tables, wilderness campsites, pit toilets, and walking paths. No water. From 1891 until 1924 this island served as a Chinese leper colony. Basic supplies were delivered by ship four times a year, but no medical attention was provided. A commemorative plaque remembers the lepers and their story. An orchard and some ruins of buildings may be found amid the brush and undergrowth. Little D'Arcy Island is privately owned.

★ **Island View Beach Regional Park:** This Park has a launch ramp, toilets, RV & tent camping, and over four miles of sandy beach located between Cowichan Head and Cordova Spit. Walk along the loop trail through salt marsh and beach dunes.

★ **Saanichton Bay:** Located between Cordova Spit and Turgoose Point, this bay has good holding anchorage. Mooring buoys are private. A public wharf with a small float is found just south of Turgoose Point (no services, day use only).

★ **James Island:** A good, all weather anchorage is located at The Gunkhole behind James Spit. The entrance is shallow, limiting sailboat access to higher tides. A conspicuous white cliff extends nearly across the south end of this thickly wooded island. Beautiful sand beaches are prevalent, but they, like the entire island are private. Once the site of the third largest explosives plant in the world, today this exclusive island retreat features a 18-hole Jack Nicklaus Signature golf course, docks, airstrip, 5,000 sq. ft house, guest cottages and more. A few years ago, the island was for sale for $75 million. In early 2018, the Tsawout First Nation filed a lawsuit contending that James Island was historically occupied by their people and should be returned to the Nation.

★ **Sidney Spit Marine Park (9):** This picturesque park with its long sandy beach is located on the northwest tip of Sidney Island. Shoaling has made changes in charted depths. Enter from Haro Strait via Miner's Channel or by Sidney Channel. Mooring buoys, and a pier with a dock are available for shore access and overnight stays. Fees charged. Docks removed from Oct. 1-May 14. A covered picnic shelter, camping sites, picnic areas, pit toilets, and drinking water (rather salty!) are available. The white sand beach is irresistible and the perfect place to play or suntan. Several trails traverse the park—one to the lighthouse and one to the site where the Sidney Brick and Tile Company operated on the island in the early 1900's. Another trail leads to the lagoon, a popular spot for watching sunsets or for wildlife viewing. Look for Fallow Deer, introduced in the

Page 126 Chapter 8 SOUTHEAST VANCOUVER ISLAND

The Van Isle Marina Photo © Van Isle Marina

1960's, and Great Blue Herons. A passenger ferry connects the park with Sidney from Memorial Day through Labor Day, call 250-656-7599. For Park Info: 250-654-4000, 1-866-944-1744. ▲⊼⅄

Saanich Peninsula
[3441, 3462]

★ **Saanich Peninsula:** There are hundreds of things to do and see on this strip of land that stretches from Victoria north to Swartz Bay. Although Saanich Peninsula is home to the Victoria International Airport, the Washington State Ferry Terminal at Sidney, and the communities of Brentwood Bay and Sidney, there is a quiet, pastoral quality to the region. The word Saanich means fertile soil and there are many acres devoted to crops and dairy farms.

Visitors reach the peninsula by car ferry from Port Angeles to Victoria and Tsawwassen to Swartz Bay, by passenger-only ferries from Seattle and Vancouver, floatplanes, and by landplane via the Victoria International Airport. The airport, located near Sidney about 20 miles north of Victoria, serves cities around the world. Arrival by pleasure boat is to moorages in Victoria's Inner Harbour, Oak Bay, Sidney, Tsehum Harbour, Canoe Cove, and Saanich Inlet. Marinas at these locations include Port Sidney, Van Isle Marina, Canoe Cove Marina and Angler's Anchorage Marina. These are popular destinations and several are courtesy telephone customs check-in sites. Launching ramps are located at Van Isle, Canoe Cove, and Angler's Anchorage Marinas, Island View Beach, Bazan Bay, Roberts Bay and Shoal Harbour.

Saanich Inlet, which borders the peninsula's western shore, is known for great fishing, but if you aren't interested in fishing, don't worry, there's still plenty to see and do. Other activities include touring beautiful Butchart Gardens, viewing the model engineer and model shipbuilding exhibits at the Saanich Historical Artifacts Society property near the Butchart Gardens, playing golf, tennis and curling. Victoria Butterfly Gardens, located in Brentwood Bay, is a unique tropical haven of gardens, birds, fish and 3,000 butterflies. Located near the Victoria International Airport, the British Columbia Aviation Museum features a collection of vintage airplanes. The University of Victoria in Saanich, offers theatrical and musical performances Oct.-March. Local artists open their studios free to the public for the annual *Spring and Fall Studio Tours*. Major shopping localities are downtown Victoria, Royal Oak, Brentwood Bay, Saanichton, and Sidney. While you're in Sidney, don't miss visiting the Shaw Centre for the Salish Sea.

Sidney
[3441, 3462, 3479]

★ **Downtown Sidney (10):** "Sidney By The Sea," is a lovely waterfront community with nearly 12,000 residents. It is identified by the Bevan Fishing Pier, Beacon Wharf, and Port Sidney Marina.

The entrance to Port Sidney Marina (a Customs Check-in reporting site) is via the southeast end of the breakwater where the two arms overlap. Avoid the reef extending from the north shore. Other floats, located at the foot of Beacon Avenue in downtown Sidney, are not available for visiting boaters nor is customs clearance possible at these sites. Van Isle Marina, just north of the downtown centre in Tsehum Harbour also offers moorage and custom clearance. The Tsehum Harbour vicinity is marine oriented with marinas, restaurants, and other attractions. See "Tsehum Harbour" entry which follows.

Sidney has the feel of a boating destination resort community. The Town of Sidney, and the surrounding Municipality of North Saanich, are agricultural and light industrial based, but a sizable portion is residential. Sidney's shopping options

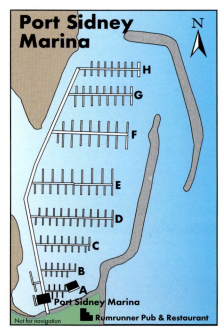

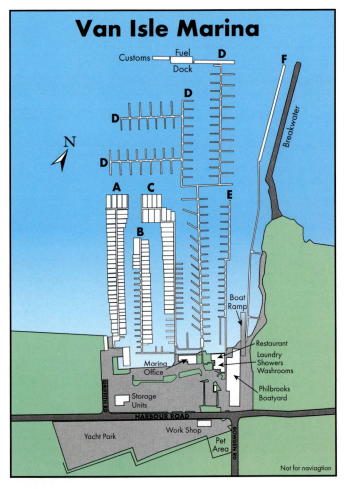

Visit us at boattravel.com

include various small specialty and gift shops, as well as shopping centers, bookstores of every ilk, art galleries, grocery stores, liquor stores, hardware stores, marine supplies, beauty and barber shops, pharmacies, post office, laundry, dry cleaners, and an array of cafes, restaurants and pubs. Medical services include walk-in medical clinics, doctors, dentists, opticians and the nearby Saanich Peninsula Hospital.

The downtown centre is very walkable and there are several attractions like the spectacular Shaw Centre for the Salish Sea featuring the Gallery of the Salish Sea exhibit that makes you feel like the ocean surrounds you. 250-665-7511. The Sidney Museum and Archives at 2423 Beacon Avenue, offers exhibitions, programs, and a permanent collection of over 7,000 items. 250-655-6355. The Mary Winspear Centre, a few blocks away, is home to the Charlie White Theatre featuring stage shows, concerts, dance and lectures. 250-656-0275. At the foot of Bevan Avenue, the Bevan Pier is famous for fishing and crabbing. Offshore, a unique, artificial reef created by 270 hollow concrete spheres attracts different marine life. For more information about Sidney and local attractions, stop by the Visitor Information Centre at 2281 Beacon Avenue. 250-665-7362.

There are also dozens of parks in the Town! Tulista Park has a boat launch ramp, as well as beach access, a Waterfront Walkway, an art gallery, skateboard park, and park trails. Cyclists especially enjoy Lochside Trail, a 20-mile path to Victoria that follows an old rail line.

By land, sea, or air, transportation options here are varied. Taxis and rental cars are available, and BC Transit routes connect with Victoria and other Saanich Peninsula communities. Sidney is connected by ferry to the Gulf Islands and Vancouver from the Swartz Bay Ferry Terminal, approximately 10 minutes north of town by car. The Victoria International Airport is approximately a 10 minute drive southwest of downtown Sidney.

Port Sidney Marina: {48° 39' N, 123° 24' W} Canadian Customs Port of Entry. Hourly, nightly, monthly or annual moorage (reservations recommended), 30/50/100 amp power, potable water, pump out, washrooms, showers, laundry, TV lounge with wifi, pet area, garbage/recycling, security, parking. Complimentary maps/brochures in Marina Office. 250-655-3711. VHF 66A.

Roberts Bay: This bay, with extensive shoaling at the head, lies one mile north of Sidney. Limited anchorage. Keep the day beacon on Graham Rock to port when entering.

★ Isle-De-Lis Marine Park (11): Rum Island, named for rum runners who once frequented this area, is six miles east of the Saanich Peninsula. Three campsites, pit toilets, picnic tables, no drinking water. A trail around the island offers views of Haro Strait. Anchor temporarily in a niche on the north shore in about 30' of water, between the kelp patches, and tie to shore. Currents between Rum and Gooch Islands can affect boat swings. About 150 yards north of Gooch Island {48° 40.094' N, 123° 17.170' W}, a destroyer escort vessel is sunk 100' down. Divers should note that visibility is generally about 25 feet and the currents can be strong in the vicinity.

Tsehum Harbour

[3441, 3462, 3479]

★ Tsehum Harbour (12): [3479] The harbour is easy to enter, but there are rocks along the north shore and in the approach. In season, kelp marks most of the hazards. A courtesy Customs Check-in telephone is at the end of the fuel dock at Van Isle Marina, to port when entering, and also at the Royal Victoria Yacht Club. Marinas, public floats, yacht club outstations, launch ramp, charter agencies, restaurants, marine supplies and repairs, and boatyards are found here. Bus, taxi and rental cars available. Named for the First Nations word for clay, this is an extensive, attractive harbour located only one and one-quarter miles north of Sidney.

★ Van Isle Marina: {48° 40'31" N, 123° 24' 30" W} Owned and operated by the Dickinson family since 1955, this full-service marina has moorage for boats 20' - 200'. Nightly, monthly and annual moorage in 500 berths. 90 spaces for dry-land storage and maintenance. Customs clearance. Fuel dock with mid-grade gasoline, diesel, Chevron oils, ice as well as a sewage pump-out station. Haul-outs and full repair facilities. New & pre-owned yacht sales. Free WiFi. Washrooms, showers, laundry. Complimentary bicycles. Garbage & recycling. 15, 30, 50 & 100 amp electricity. New gas fire table & patio. Good and helpful chandleries. New self-serve Dog Wash Station. Open all year. See our advertisement on this page. Email: info@vanislemarina.com Websites: www.vanislemarina.com & www.boattravel.com/vanislemarina. Address: 2320 Harbour Rd, Sidney, British Columbia, V8L 2P6. Telephone: 250-656-1138. Fax: 250-656-0182. VHF 66A.

All Bay Marine: Fully stocked marine chandlery, splicing, wire crimping. 250-656-0153.

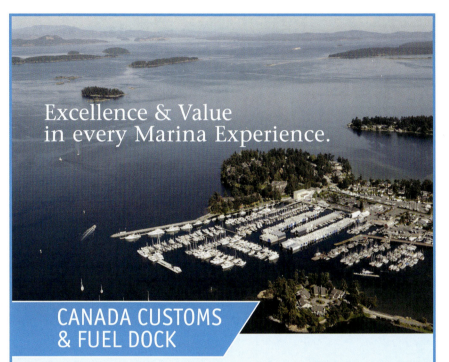

Excellence & Value in every Marina Experience.

CANADA CUSTOMS & FUEL DOCK

- 500 berths for annual, monthly or nightly moorage
- Service for boats 20' to 200'
- Fuel dock & marine store
- Canada Customs Port of Entry
- Haul outs & full repair facilities
- Yacht Park - 90 spaces for dry land storage and maintenance
- 15/30/50/100 amp shore power
- Casual Dining at Sea Glass Grill
- Business centre
- Laundry, showers & washrooms
- *NEW* Dog wash station
- Yacht brokerage & sales
- Free WiFi
- *NEW* Gas fire table & patio

Situated in beautiful Tsehum Harbour by Sidney, British Columbia, Van Isle Marina is just 5 minutes from ferries, Victoria International Airport and shopping.

VAN ISLE MARINA
family owned & operated since 1955

Tsehum Harbour, Sidney, BC | 250 656 1138 | info@vanislemarina.com

vanislemarina.com

Portland Island, Princess Margaret Marine Park   Photo © Mary Gasser, courtesy Marine Parks Forever Society

North Saanich Marina: {48° 40'35" N, 123° 24' 56" W} Privately owned covered moorage, open annual moorage, limited guest moorage if space is available. Gas, diesel, water, ice, snacks, bait, fishing tackle, restrooms. 250-656-5558.

Philbrooks Boatyard (at Van Isle Marina): Full service yard. Haulouts to 120'/150 tons, mechanical, electrical, woodwork, paint, detailing, composite repairs, metal fabrication, canvas. 250-656-1157.

Tsehum Harbour Authority: {48° 40' 14" N, 123° 24' 13" W} Primarily commercial fishing moorage. Very limited transient moorage in summer months, rafting mandatory. 20/30 amp power, water, pump-out, garbage, restroom, showers, security camera. 250-655-4496.

Vector Yacht Services & The Boatyard: 40 & 60 ton Travelifts, vessels to 18 1/2' beam. Haulout with trailer, engine/head services, prop/shaft repairs, inflatable repairs, outboards/outdrives service. 250-655-3222.

Westbay Marina: {48° 40' 10"N, 123° 24' 47"W} Yearly and monthly, liveaboards. Water, 30/50 amp power, private pump-out, laundry, shower. 250-385-1831.

Westport Marina: {48° 40'50" N, 123° 24' 41" W} Permanent moorage, guest moorage if space is available, 30 amp power, water, showers, chandlery, boatyard - full service or DIY, 50 ton TraveLift for vessels to 70' length & 19' beam. 250-656-2832.

Canoe Cove
[3441, 3462, 3479]

★ **Canoe Cove (13):** Iroquois Passage can be used to reach Canoe Cove from either the north or the south. If approaching from the north, keep Goudge Island on the port and Musclow Islet on the starboard. After rounding Musclow Islet turn into the harbour. When arriving from the south, pass between Fernie Island and Goudge. After rounding Rose Rock, a passage leads into the bay.

Canoe Cove Marina & Boatyard: {48° 41' N, 123° 24' W} Canada Customs Check-in (call for information), permanent moorage, guest moorage if space is available, 30/50 amp power, water, laundry, showers, garbage/recycling, chandlery, cafe, pub, dry storage. Service providers onsite for repairs, marine parts, haul-outs to 83 tons. 250-656-5566.

★ **Moresby Island (14):** Anchorage can be found on opposite ends of this thickly wooded island in unnamed bays inside Point Fairfax and south of Reynard Point. The first gives some protection in southwest winds and the latter shelters from northeast blows. Note charts for two rocks that are hazards in this area.

★⚓ **Portland Island, Princess Margaret Marine Park (15):** The principal anchorage is in Princess Bay, a fairly well protected niche at the southern end. Enter north of Tortoise Islets. Favor the islet's shore. An Information Float is found in the bay during the summer. Black Oyster Catchers, with their red beaks and legs, feed and nest nearby. Royal Cove, behind Chads Island, also offers a small semi-sheltered anchorage. For shore access, a dinghy dock is located at the end of the cove (removed from Oct 1 - May 14). A fresh water hand pump is found ten minutes from Royal Cove by trail in the middle of an old farming field. Look for fruit trees and garden plants among the native vegetation—the legacy of Hawaiian immigrants who settled here in the 1880's. Camping is permitted at Princess Bay, Shell Beach, and Arbutus Point. Composting toilets are available, no drinking water, no fires. Reefs and shoals fringe much of the island shore. One notable reef {48° 43.323' N, 123° 21.339' W} is an artificial reef created by the sinking of the M/V Church, a 175 foot freighter. The park's name recalls that in 1958, Portland Island was given to Princess Margaret when she visited British Columbia. She later returned it for use as a park. Today it is part of the Gulf Islands National Park Reserve. No public access is permitted onto the Brackman Island Ecological Reserve. There is temporary anchorage between Brackman Island and Portland Island.

★ **Piers Island (16):** Located northwest of Wilhelm Point, a flashing white light marks three, 70 foot public floats shaped into a triangle. Depths alongside shallow to four feet. The moorage is used primarily by the island's 300 residents. A private ferry for residents and their guests also sails from the government dock.

Swartz Bay (17): Located on the south side of Colburne Pass, this busy site is a major terminal for BC Ferries serving the Gulf Islands and Tsawwassen, on the mainland south of Vancouver. A small public float to the left of the ferry docks primarily serves daily commuters from nearby islands. Minimum depths alongside the float are about two feet. Rock ledges and sand shallows are in the approach and ferry right-of-way are considerations in this vicinity. The ferry terminal has a restaurant and restrooms.

Swartz Bay Public Wharf: The outer float's yellow area is reserved for emergency use, as well as a 15-minute loading/off-loading area. Boat operators must stay with the vessel and move for any emergency vessel. Limited moorage on the rest of the dock, rafting mandatory, maximum stay is 3 days. Payment information is at the head of the ramp. Wharfinger call 250-655-3256.

Saanich Inlet
[3441, 3462]

★ **Saanich Inlet:** This lovely and popular inlet has a reputation for good fishing and a selection of attractions, such as Butchart Gardens, Heritage Acres, Tod Inlet, Finlayson Arm, parks, restaurants, marinas, and the town of Brentwood Bay. Bluebacks are best during March and April. Chinooks and Coho are good almost anytime, with September and October the best as they migrate from the Pacific to spawn in the Goldstream River. Launching can be made at Mill Bay and Tsartlip Reserve in Brentwood Bay.

★ **Deep Cove (18):** Entered between Moses Point and Coal Point, pass on either side of Wain Rock. If time, try a little fishing as you drift by. According to locals, prawning and crabbing are great just off of Wain rock (prawns at 225' and Dungeness crab at 80' deep) The Canadian Hydrographic Service reports an uncharted rock, with a drying height of 0.7 meters. A high-end restaurant, the Deep Cove Chalet, can be accessed by dinghy beached on the NW side of the cove. Keep an eye out for celebrities who are known to frequent the Chalet. Ruins of a government wharf are in the south part. A sunken barge, about 100 yards off the old wharf, is a popular diving site. East of the wharf is a private marina. Caution advised regarding drying rocks, marked by a day beacon and a buoy, in this area. Private buoys are often found in the bay, but limited anchorage may be possible.

Deep Cove Marina: {48° 40'53" N, 123° 28' 41" W} Permanent moorage, 6mos/1yr lease. 250-415-2126.

Patricia Bay (19): Site of the Institute of Ocean Sciences (IOS) and the Victoria International Airport. Department of National Defense vessels operate in the Bay and use orange and white mooring buoys southwest of Warrior Point. University

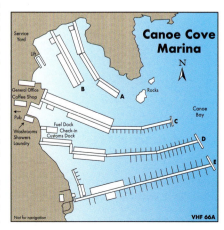

of Victoria's VENUS, or Victoria Experimental Network Under the Sea, is located here and consists of an array of oceanographic instruments connected by cables to the Institute that are marked by a lighted float on the surface. The jetty and small boat basin in the SE corner are for IOS vessels only. Small vessels sometimes anchor in the Bay but it is exposed to the west and care must be taken to avoid charted cables. Victoria International Airport, which is also a seaplane base, is behind the Bay.

★ **Coles Bay and Coles Bay Regional Park (20):** Anchorage, open to south winds, can be found near the head. Avoid shoals extending south of Yarrow Point. The park has a nice beach, picnic area, restrooms, and nature trail.

Thomson Cove (21): Limited anchorage with protection from some winds.

Brentwood Bay
[3313, 3441, 3462]

★ **Brentwood Bay (22):** On approach, a day beacon marks a drying reef about halfway between Brentwood Bay and Daphne Island. This is the heart of the beautiful Saanich Inlet-Brentwood Bay region. Condos, marinas, launch ramp, a government wharf with moorage floats, and the Brentwood Bay-Mill Bay ferry landing are located here. Anchorage is found in Gowlland Tod Provincial Park off Brentwood Bay in Tod Inlet. The Brentwood Bay community covers the hillside and waterfront. A shopping center is located up the hill in the village. Bus service connects with Sidney and Victoria. The Victoria Butterfly Gardens, a Trip Advisor Certificate of Excellence Award winner, is under 10 minutes away by car. 250-652-3822. Once known for salmon fishing, prawning is now the most popular fishery. Each September, the *Wooden Open Boat Festival* has races, demonstrations, tours, and BBQ.

Anglers Anchorage Marina: {48° 34'18" N, 123° 27' 43" W} Annual moorage, transient moorage in summer if space is available, 30/50 amp power, water, showers, laundry, public pump-out by donation, wifi, restaurant. 250-652-3531. VHF 66A.

Brentwood Bay Resort & Spa: {48° 34'39" N, 123° 27' 58" W} Enter keeping red buoy U22 on starboard side. Guest moorage, 15/30/50 amp power, water, cable, laundry, showers. Fitness room, spa, hot tub & pool, restaurant/pub, kayak/SUP rentals. Resort, 250-544-2079. Marina, 250-652-3151. VHF 66A.

★ **Tod Inlet (23):** This lovely inlet has a very narrow entrance. The first bay to the port is the boaters' entrance to Butchart Gardens with a large float for dinghies or float planes only with no overnight moorage permitted. Five buoys (one for boats less than 18', and others for less than 40') are available for Butchart Gardens' visitors on a first come-first served basis for one night only/24 hrs **maximum - no exceptions**, stern ties are mandatory. You must check in with the dock attendant within one hour of mooring. Markers provide anchoring guidelines. Do not anchor near the buoys as the bottom is foul and floatplane access to the docks must be maintained. Please be aware the west side of Butchart Cove can be very shallow at low tide. For anchorage on a mud bottom (3 fathoms deep at low water), proceed farther into Tod Inlet. A buoy to port, just past the entrance, marks a rock near the surface at low tide. The surrounding hillsides cradle the small basin. Check tide tables and take soundings before anchoring. It is possible to stern tie on the shores. Avoid any anchoring in the narrow and relatively shallow entrance fairway to Tod Inlet. According to Butchart Gardens information, "It is not unusual for afternoon warming to create local gusting winds that funnel down the fairway causing vessels to drag anchor and swing around on their stern lines." To visit Butchart Gardens, from Tod Inlet, dinghy over to their wharf in Butchart Cove or go to the BC Parks wharf in Tod Inlet and walk about 15 minutes up to The Gardens Admission Gate located up the hill on Benvenuto Avenue past the vehicle exit. The Gardens are open year round. 250-652-4422.

★ **Finlayson Arm (24):** This beautiful fjord joins Saanich Inlet with the Goldstream River. Depths can reach 600 feet. Famous for fishing and scuba diving waters.

★ **Goldstream Park:** This park has 173 campsites with water and a shower facility, as well as picnic grounds, miles of trails, a scenic waterfall, Visitor Centre and a Nature House. The park is located 2 kilometers from the marina, access by taxi or rental car.

Butchart Cove Dinghy Dock, Tod Inlet
Photo © The Butchart Gardens Ltd, Victoria BC

Goldstream Boathouse Marina: {48° 30' N, 123° 33" W} Permanent and transient moorage, gas, diesel, water, 30/50 amp power, repairs, haul-out to 50', tackle, bait, snacks, boat supplies, launch ramp. 250-478-4407. VHF 66A.

Bamberton Provincial Park (25): This park has 53 campsites, with wood, water, swimming, cold water shower, and picnic areas. When approaching by water, caution advised because a shelf extends about 100 feet out from shore before it makes a sharp drop-off.

Mill Bay
[3441, 3462]

★ **Mill Bay (26):** Site of the Mill Bay Marina, a boat launch and boardwalk just adjacent to the Marina, and the Mill Bay-Brentwood Ferry Landing at McPhail Point south of the marina. This ferry is used by those whose destination is the Saanich Peninsula but they want to avoid traveling the Malahat and around to Victoria. The Mill Bay Visitors Information Booth, located in the Mill Bay Centre at 2720 Mill Bay Road, is open weekdays. Mill Bay has three malls offering groceries, restaurants, liquor stores, hardware stores, banks, pharmacies, medical clinics, coffee shops, fuel, and a library. The South Cowichan Valley also offers wineries, a cidery, golf, hiking trails, picnic sites, swimming, Arts & Music Festivals, renowned private schools and a variety of Bed & Breakfasts. For more information, www.tourismcowichan.com.

Mill Bay Marina: {48° 38'59" N, 123° 33' 10" W} Long term moorage (boats to 88') short term moorage (boats to 300'), gas, diesel, 30/50 amp power, potable water, wifi, washrooms, showers, laundry, sani-pump, Bistro. Shuttle/car rental arranged with advanced notice. Ask about group moorage discounts. Bistro: 778-356-3568. Marina: 250-743-4303. VHF 66A.

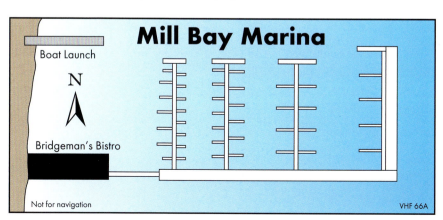

2024 Northwest Boat Travel

Essential Supplies & Services

AIR TRANSPORTATION

To & from Washington
Kenmore Air **1-866-435-9524**
NW Seaplanes . . . **425-277-1590, 1-800-690-0086**
San Juan Airlines **1-800-874-4434**
Seattle Seaplanes **1-800-637-5553**
To & from Islands/Vancouver
Air Canada 1-888-247-2262
Harbour Air 250-384-2215, 1-800-665-0212
Helijet BC 1-800-665-4354
Pacific Coastal Air 250-655-6411, 1-800-663-2872

BOOKS / BOOK STORES

Evergreen Pacific Publishing **425-493-1451**
The Marine Atlas 253-872-5707

BUS TRANSPORTATION

B C Transit, Victoria 250-382-6161
Greyhound 1-800-661-8747
Greyhound, Victoria station: 778-265-1520

CNG CYLINDERS

All Bay Marine Ltd: Sidney 250-656-0153

COAST GUARD

Victoria Coast Guard Radio . . . . VHF 16, 83a
. . . . 1-800-661-9202 (In BC) or 250-363-6611
Victoria Marine Traffic 250-363-6333
Marine Distress, Search & Rescue
 . . . . 1-800-567-5111 (in Canada) or 250-413-8933
Cell Phone (limited to select providers) . . . *16 or #727

CUSTOMS

24 Hour Reporting Centre 1-888-226-7277
CBSA Reporting Sites:
Victoria: Oak Bay Marina, Raymur Point CBSA Boat
  Dock, RVYC Cadboro Bay
Sidney-Tsehum: Port of Sidney, Van Isle Marina
North Saanich: Canoe Cove Marina
For more information, see Important Notices between
  Chapters 7 & 8

FERRY INFORMATION

B C Ferries 1-888-223-3779
Washington State Ferries 1-888-808-7977
Swartz Bay 250-656-5571
Victoria Clipper (passenger only) 1-800-888-2535,
Blackball Ferry (Victoria-Port Angeles)
. . . . 250-386-2202, 360-457-4491

FISHING / SHELLFISHING INFO

24 hr Recorded Notifications (Pacific region only) . . . .
  1-866-431-3474 or 604-666-2828
Recreational Licensing 1-877-535-7307
Observe, Record, & Report Line (fisheries violations) . .
  800-465-4336 or 604-607-4186 (Pacific region only)

FUELS

Canoe Cove: Gas, Diesel 250-656-5566
Cheanuh Marina: Becher Bay. Gas.
 . . . . 250-478-4880 VHF 16, 68
Fuel Dock at Fisherman's Wharf: Gas, Diesel
 250-381-5221
Goldstream Boathouse Marina:
  Saanich Inlet. Gas, Diesel . . . . 250-478-4407 VHF 66A
Mill Bay Marina 250-743-4303
North Saanich Marina: Tsehum Harbour. Gas, Diesel.
 250-656-5558
Oak Bay Marina: Gas, Diesel
 . . . . 250-598-3369 VHF 66A
Pedder Bay Marina: Gas . . . . . . 250-478-1771 VHF 68
Van Isle Marina: Gas, Diesel
 . . . . **250-656-1138 VHF 66A**

GOLF COURSES

These courses are accessible from moorage and have rental clubs available)
Arbutus Ridge, Cobble Hill 250-743-5000
Ardmore, North Saanich 250-656-4621
Glen Meadows, Sidney 250-656-3921
Gorge Vale, Victoria 250-386-3401
Victoria Golf Club (Private) 250-598-4321

HAUL-OUTS

Canoe Cove Marina 250-656-5566
Gartside Marine: Oak Bay 250-598-3378
Goldstream Boathouse Marina: Saanich Inlet . . . .
 250-478-4407
Philbrooks Boatyard: Tsehum Harbour . . 250-656-1157
Van Isle Marina . . . . **250-656-1138 VHF 66A**
Vector Yacht Service: Tsehum Harbour . 250-655-3222
Westport Marina 250-656-2832

HOSPITALS

Healthlink BC (Nurse Helpline) 811
Saanich Peninsula Hospital 250-544-7676
Victoria General Hospital 250-727-4212

LIQUOR STORES

Brentwood Bay
Mill Bay
Sidney
Victoria

MARINAS / MOORAGE FLOATS

Anglers Anchorage: Brentwood Bay (Annual Only)
 . . . . 250-217-7494 VHF 66A
Becher Bay Marina Seasonal 250-642-3816
Brentwood Bay Resort . . . . . . 250-652-3151 VHF 66A
Canoe Cove Marina 250-656-5566
Causeway Floats: . . . . 250-383-8326 Ext. 235 VHF 66A
Cheanuh Marina: Becher Bay 250-478-4880 VHF 16, 68
Coast Victoria Harbourside Hotel & Marina:
Victoria 250-360-1211
Fisherman's Wharf
Floats . . . . 250-383-8326 Ext 235 VHF 66A
Goldstream Boathouse Marina: Saanich Inlet . . . .
 250-478-4407
Greater Victoria Harbour Authority
 . . . . 250-383-8326 Ext 235 VHF 66A
Mill Bay Marina 250-743-4303
Oak Bay Marina . . . . 250-598-3369 VHF 66A
Pedder Bay Marina . . . . 250-478-1771 VHF 66A
Piers Island
Port Sidney Marina . . . . 250-655-3711, VHF 66A
Ship Point . . . . 250-383-8326 Ext 235 VHF 66A
Sidney Spit Marine Park
Tsehum Harbour Authority 250-655-4496
Van Isle Marina . . . . **250-656-1138 VHF 66A**
Victoria International Marina 778-432-0477
Westbay Marina: Victoria 250-385-1831
Wharf Street Marina . 250-383-8326 Ext 235 VHF 66A

RAMPS

Bazan Bay
Boatyard, The: Tsehum Harbour 250-655-1511
Oak Bays Cattle Point
Cheanuh Marina: Becher Bay
 . . . . 250-478-4880 VHF 16, 68
Fleming Bay: Esquimalt
Goldstream Boathouse Marina: Saanich Inlet . . . .
 250-478-4407
Island View Beach
Mill Bay
Oak Bay Marina . . . . 250-598-3369 VHF 66A
Pedder Bay Marina . . . . 250-478-1771 VHF 66A
Roberts Bay
Shoal Harbour
Sidney Tulista Park

REPAIRS/SERVICE

Boatyard, The: Tsehum Harbour 250-655-3222
Boatyard, The: Canoe Cove 250-655-1511
Gartside Marine Engines: Oak Bay . . . 250-598-3378
Goldstream Boathouse Marina: Saanich Inlet . . . .
 250-478-4407
Philbrooks Boatyard: Tsehum Harbour . . 250-656-1157
Sea Power Marine Centre: Sidney 250-656-4341
Vector Yacht Service: Tsehum Harbour . 250-655-3222
Westport Marina: Tsehum Harbour 250-656-2832

RESTAURANTS

Bridgemans Bistro/Mill Bay Marina . . . 778-356-3568
Blue Crab Seafood House Victoria 250-480-1999
Canoe Cove Joe's 250-656-5557
Rumrunner Pub & Restaurant Sidney . . 250-656-5643
Sea Glass Waterfront Grill/Van Isle Marina
 . . . . **778-351-3663**

SCUBA SITES

Finlayson Arms
Ile-De-Lis Marine Park

SEWAGE DISPOSAL

Anglers Anchorage Marina 250-652-3531
Coast Victoria Harbourside Hotel & Marina: Victoria
 250-360-1211
Fisherman's Wharf: Pump . . . . 250-383-8326 Ext 235
Mill Bay Marina 250-743-4303
Port Sidney Marina: Pump 250-655-3711
Tsehum Harbour Authority: Pump 250-655-4496
Van Isle Marina: Pump . . . **250-656-1138 VHF 66A**

TAXI

Esquimalt/Saanich 250-386-7766
Sidney 250-656-6666
Sidney, Greater Victoria 250-656-1111
Victoria 250-381-2222

TOWING

C-TOW 1-888-419-CTOW
Fast Response 250-222-0076
Vessel Assist/TowBoat U.S. 250-883-7865

VISITOR INFORMATION

B.C. Ocean Boating Tourism . . . . **ahoybc.com**
Cowichan Tourism 250-746-4636
Saanich Peninsula Info Centre 778-426-0522
Sidney 250-665-7362
Victoria 250-953-2033

WEATHER:

VHF WX-1, Discovery Island, Esquimalt, Victoria WX-3
Environment Canada Weather Line 250-339-9861
Canadian Coast Guard (recorded) 250-363-6492

Visit us at boattravel.com

Chapter 9:
Southeast Gulf Islands

North & South Pender, Saturna, Cabbage, Tumbo, Samuel, and Mayne Islands.

Horton Bay, Mayne Island - photo © MonicaWorks.com

Symbols

[ ]: Numbers between [ ] are chart numbers.

{ }: Numbers & letters between { } are waypoints.

★ Recommended destinations, facilities, and services

⚓: Park, 🚤: Boat Launch, ▲: Campgrounds,

🥾: Hiking Trails, ⛱: Picnic Area, 🚴: Biking

🤿: Scuba

★ See "Important Notices" between Chapters 7 and 8 for specific information on boating related topics such as boating safety, weather, U.S. & Canadian marine radio use, Vessel Traffic Service, security zones, Canadian & U.S. Customs, etc. Due to changing regulations, call ahead to verify latest customs information.

Gulf Islands
[3313, 3441, 3442, 3462, 3473, 3477]

Chart List

Canadian Hydrographic Charts:
3313, 3441-42, 3462-63, 3473, 3477

NOAA Charts: 18400, 18421, 18432

Marine Atlas Vol 1 (2018): Page 11, 12

Evergreen Cruising Atlas: Pages 106, 108, 109, 117, 120

★ **Introduction:** Boating is a way of life for many who live and visit here. The marinas, anchorages, and other destinations are intimately connected by the attractive waterways that lead to them like highways. The area is bordered on the south by the international boundary, on the north and east by Georgia Strait, and on the west by Vancouver Island, which provides shelter from the Pacific Ocean. Boating visitors return again and again to these islands, discovering hide-aways and communities to explore with each visit. Chapter 9 covers the southern-most islands. Chapters 10 and 11 describe the other islands and the communities located opposite them along the east coast of Vancouver Island.

Salt Spring Island has the greatest population, with the Penders, Galiano, and Mayne following in that order. The main center of commerce is Ganges, on Salt Spring Island. Often, small communities such as Fulford Harbour, Village Bay, Sturdies Bay, and Saturna are located near a ferry landing. Ferry routes link the islands with Vancouver and Swartz Bay.

Fishing, wildlife viewing, visiting petroglyph sites, exploring anchorages, visiting marinas, walking through parks or towns, dining out, touring local wineries, golfing, hiking, canoeing, kayaking, and scuba diving are only a few of the possible vacation highlights of this area.

The Southeast Gulf Islands are also home to a thriving art community comprised of artists and craftspeople of every kind. Art studio tours and cultural events are hosted throughout the year.

The climate is mild with an annual rainfall of less than 30 inches, most which falls between November and March. Summer water temperatures range from 59-63° Fahrenheit, but can be higher in coves where the water is shallow. Normal summer air temperatures range from 54-74° Fahrenheit. In some locales, hot summer days of 84-90° are not uncommon. The sun shines about 60 percent of the time during summer months. The summer fair weather winds are from the northwest. When these northwest winds prevail, they have a predictable pattern to them. Generally, they rise in mid-morning and go down in the late afternoon. As the Coast Salish observed long before the government weather services, if these winds do not go down in the afternoon, it will likely blow for three days. These prevailing winds are modified by local on-shore winds during the afternoons and off-shore winds during the evening. These winds are caused by the heating and cooling of the land masses. When the wind blows from the southeast, it generally indicates a change in the weather or an approaching storm front. The strength of southeast storm winds is difficult to predict and they can result in uncomfortable or even dangerous sea conditions. It is wise to spend such times off the open waters of the straits in one of the well-sheltered marinas or in a very protected anchorage.

During summer months, higher-high tides tend to occur at night while lower-low tides occur during daylight hours. These are the tides that shellfish collectors treasure. Boaters, however, can be surprised by exposed rocks and shelves that can be dangerous to navigation or anchorage. Tidal fluctuations during spring tides, when the moon is full or new, tend to be relatively large, ranging from nine feet at Victoria to seventeen feet at Comox. Tidal runs at springs are usually one to two knots, however maximums of ten knots occur in certain passes. Generally, it is best to head south during an ebbing tide or north during a flood tide since traveling with the current increases speed and saves fuel.

The land in most of this area is composed of layers of sedimentary rock. Centuries of decomposition and erosion have created ridges and valleys which generally run northwest/southeast. Where the valleys slope down to the water, there are often sheltered bays with good holding ground which has been deposited by run-off waters from the valleys.

Otter Bay Marina Photo © Otter Bay Marina

North and South Pender Islands

[3441, 3342, 3462-63, 3477]

★ **Bedwell Harbour (1):** {48° 45' N, 123° 14' W} Named for Captain Edward Bedwell, the master of an 1860 survey ship, this harbour is visited each year by thousands of boaters who come to clear customs and stay to enjoy the area's attractions. Along with a customs dock, a resort with a marina is also found here. Kayaks and bikes (both rented locally) are great for exploring the area. Salmon and crab fishing are popular saltwater catches, while freshwater trout are found in Magic Lake. Not far from the lake, a 27 hole disc golf course challenges frisbee fans. Hiking trails around the harbour afford opportunities to view wildlife. Bird watchers can see eagles, osprey and great blue heron at Medicine Beach Marsh, at the inlet's northend. The beach's unusual name recalls early First Nations people who gathered plants here to be used medicinally. To the southeast, just outside of the harbour, scuba divers can view anemones covering the walls of the Tilly Point Caves.

Customs: May 1 through September 30, boaters arriving from the U.S. who have not cleared by NEXUS Marine, must tie to the customs floats upon arrival. DO NOT tie to the resort dock and walk around to Customs. The customs staff have a boat and are often out and about. Phones on the dock connect directly to the Customs Reporting Centre. 1-888-226-7277.

Poets Cove Resort and Spa: {48° 44'56" N, 123° 13'33" W} Year round moorage, 15/30 amp power, gas, diesel, water, laundromat, showers, garbage/recycle, free WiFi, luxury lodging, onsite dining, liquor, full service spa, pool, hot tub, tennis courts, bike/kayak rentals nearby. Marina amenities vary by season. Onsite Canada Customs dock for guests arriving from U.S. waters. Moorage reservations highly recommended. Resort: 1-888-870-8889. Marina: 250-629-2111. VHF 66A.

★ **Peter Cove:** Private buoys, limited anchorage. Open to wakes. Located to port, when entering Bedwell Harbour from the south.

★ **Egeria Bay:** This bay, starboard upon entering Bedwell Harbour from the south, is the site of a customs port-of-entry and Poets Cove Marina Resort. The graffiti on the cliff by the marina dates to 1905, the work of the crew of the Royal Navy vessel *HMS Egeria*.

★ **Beaumont Marine Park:** Part of the Gulf Island National Park Reserve, this park is nestled against the steep hillside just northwest of Egeria Bay. Mooring buoys, as well as anchorages are found east of Skull Inlet. A beach, picnic areas, campsites, pit toilets, information kiosks, and hiking trails are available. ▲ ⛱ 🚶

Walk Around: Walking trails lead to 890 foot high Mount Norman featuring scenic views of the Gulf Islands and beyond.

★ **Pender Canal (2):** Passage through this narrow, attractive gorge is possible at almost any tide, except for sailboats with masts that won't clear the bridge's minimum 26 feet. When leaving Bedwell Harbour via this canal, pass between the red and the green spar buoys located at the south end of the canal. The red buoy is on a four foot drying rock. Minimum depth in the canal is seven feet. Minimum width is 40 feet at the bridge. Maximum current at springs is four knots. The flood current sets north, ebbs south. Tidal range is 11 feet. Over the years erosion of the banks has become a problem, slow to 5 knots before entering the canal from either side. This man-made waterway was built in 1903 to connect Shark Cove and the head of Bedwell Harbour. The bridge was built in 1955. Shell middens of the Coast Salish, who lived in this area more than 7,000 years ago, are still in evidence. This vicinity is designated as a provincial heritage site.

★ **Shark Cove (3):** There is temporary anchorage in this niche northwest of the bridge over Pender Canal. Two submerged rocks are visible in the cove's emerald green water. To deal with wakes from passing boats, try tying a stern line to shore, keeping the bow facing the wakes. Opposite the cove, Mortimer Spit's extensive gravel beach is popular for picnics and swimming.

★ **Port Browning (4):** Port Browning is a NEXUS Marine only customs check-in site. Enter south of Razor Point, on the west side of Plumper Sound. Anchorage in the harbor is exposed to the east, but protected from prevailing westerlies. One anchoring basin is to port adjacent to Aldridge Point. Water depths are 30-40 feet at high tide on a fairly even bottom. Anchoring off nearby Hamilton Beach, with its white sand and gravel, is possible. To starboard on the north side of the bay is a small public wharf (do not expect overnight moorage, space is filled year round with local rate payers) and a tidal grid. Port Browning Marina Resort is at the head of the bay on the south side, beside the visible stretch of sandy beach. During the summer boaters are sometimes greeted at the marina with the strains of the pipes and drums courtesy of the Pender Highlanders Pipe Band. There are no marine fuel facilities here, but there is a gas station a five minute walk from moorage at the Driftwood Centre. The gas station has gas and diesel as well as marine supplies, parts and accessories, fishing tackle, bait, and a marine mechanic. The Visitor Information Centre and an Information Kiosk are also located at the Driftwood Centre along with a bakery, liquor store, post office, clothing store, hair salon, spa services, flower & pet store, self serve dog wash station, fitness centre, pharmacy, bank, and a restaurant. Tru Value Foods offers groceries, produce, fresh meat and a deli (inquire about a ride back to moorage if purchase is too much to carry). The Centre also offers free Shaw internet. The health clinic, located on Canal Road, provides medical and dental services to visitors on an emergency basis only. Scuba diving lessons and charters, as well as kayak and paddle boat rentals are available locally. Not far away, campers will find tent/vehicle sites at Prior Centennial Provincial Park. If you like wine, Sea Star Estate Vineyards has tours and tastings. ▲

Port Browning Marina Resort: {48° 46' N, 123° 16' W} Transient and long term moorage, 30/50 amp power, showers, laundry, garbage/recycling,

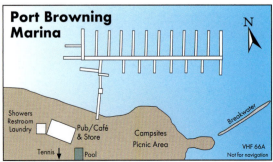

and free wifi for moorage customers. Pub, Bistro, outdoor pool, seasonal convenience store, reserveable tent/RV/glamping sites, 10 minute walk to grocery store. Shuttle service available. 250-629-3493. VHF 66A.

Port Browning Capital Regional District Dock: Located on the north side of the harbour, across the bay from Port Browning Marina. Only 14 spaces are available and these are booked long term by local rate payers. For boaters anchored in the bay, courtesy short term dinghy tie up (2hr limit) may be available on the middle of the two fingers.

★ Hope Bay (5): Navy Channel currents run to three knots, flooding to the east and ebbing to the west. Tucked in behind Fane Island, this bay has a public wharf and 3 floats. Space is limited, with guest moorage most likely found on the seaward side of the main float. Depths are shallow on the inner side of the floats at low tides. Good temporary anchorage is found a short way off in the adjacent bay. Five mooring buoys are in the area. Three are "private" mooring buoys – the one located South of the dock and the other two to the North. Two buoys located in the middle, just east of the dock provide temporary day use moorage for patrons of the landmark Hope Bay Store. A waterfront restaurant, chocolate shop, goldsmith, veterinarian, nature conservancy, art gallery, community studio, Dockside Realty, hair salon, registered massage therapist and other services are found at the store site. The public library, with internet access, is within walking distance. Next to the library, Nu To Yu Thrift store is a local institution that for 40 years has returned its profits to the community. Up the road, the Pender Community Hall hosts the annual *Pender Islands Fall Fair* in August featuring exhibits and demonstrations such as sheep shearing. On Saturday mornings, from May until November, the hall becomes the site of Pender Island's Public Market. Extremely popular, arrival before the 9:30am opening is suggested. Less than a half hour walk along Port Washington Road, there is a store offering organic produce, health foods, and coffee shop. Nearby is a well-stocked hardware store.

Hope Bay Public Moorage: {48° 48.2" N, 123° 16.5' W} Over 300' of moorage space, limited transient moorage, 1st come-1st served. No power, water, or garbage deposit. Washrooms available at the Hope Bay Store during business hours. Wharfinger: 250-813-3321.

Welcome Cove & Colston Cove: These coves afford temporary anchorage, however, they are open to currents.

★ Port Washington, Grimmer Bay (6): Grimmer Bay is divided in half by a shoal which extends to Boat Islet. Some anchorage is possible, however, the niche is open to the west and wakes of large ferries. Mooring floats extend east and west from the dock. When approaching this public dock, note that a rock with a depth of less than six feet lies about 150 feet south of the southeast end of the dock. Local boats have regular moorage here, but visitors may raft up or use available space. No power or water on docks. Do not moor on the reserved space on the most westerly float. This is for emergency vessels, service providers and seaplanes. To reach the Wharfinger, call 250-629-6111. The Southridge Country Store (with cafe, organic produce and food items) and Home Hardware are about a 35 minute walk along Port Washington Road.

★ Otter Bay (7): [3442] Located in the outer portion of the bay is a ferry landing with service to Swartz Bay, Tsawwassen and other Southern Gulf Islands. There is anchorage on a mud bottom in Hyashi Cove, inland from the ferry landing. It is exposed to west winds and some ferry wash. Approaching the marina, keep the green spar buoy located off the corner of the docks to port. Do not pass between the docks and the buoy. The cove is a boating destination with docks, store, bistro, scooter rentals and nearby golf course. A timeshare cottage development, that is not part of the marina, is also onshore. From the dock it is a 1.5 mile walk to the Farmers Market, open Saturdays from May long weekend to Labour Day long weekend. Roesland, which forms part of the National Park, is an interesting place to visit. It was once a pioneer farm belonging to the Roe family. From 1917 to 1991 it was run as a "farm resort." Some of the original cabins still stand, as does the original farmhouse, now restored and re-purposed as the Pender Islands Museum (open weekends from Easter through Thanksgiving). This park also offers a picnic table, walking trails, restrooms, dinghy dock and lovely views off the end of Roe Islet. From the marina, it is a 5 minute dinghy ride across the bay to the Park.

★ Otter Bay Marina: {48° 48.98' N & 123° 18.58' W} In the heart of the Gulf Islands, just five miles from the U.S. Border, is this North Pender Island marina boating destination. Docks accommodate boats of all sizes for both long-term and transient moorage. Amenities include 15/30/50 amp power, potable water (when available on docks), WiFi on docks, showers, café, and store for food items, books and gifts. Relax by the pool or get active! Boat & kayak launch, lawn games, BBQ's available for guest use, fire pit, play area, electric bike rentals, shuttle to golf course, and covered gazebo rental for parties. See our advertisement on this page. Telephone: 250-629-3579. Website: www.otterbay-marina.ca. Email: info@otterbay-marina.ca. VHF 66A.

Thieves Bay (8): Hidden behind a breakwater, this shallow bay is nearly filled with a private marina. A rock, marked by kelp, lies to starboard near the entrance. A launching ramp (high tide only) is near the head. A small park features picnic table, benches, swings and toilet.

Shingle Bay (9): Entirely open to west winds, this bay affords only limited anchorage. The cove north of Mouat Point has adequate depths. The remaining pilings of an old fish reduction plant are hazards. A public beach and campground are onshore.

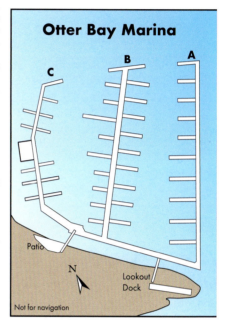

OTTER BAY
MARINA
PENDER ISLAND, BC

Otter Bay Marina is located in the heart of the Gulf Islands, 5 miles from the US border on the west side of North Pender Island, just east of the Ferry Terminal.

- 2 heated swimming pools
- Boat & kayak launch
- 15, 30 & 50 amp power
- Potable water when available on docks
- WiFi on docks
- Store with food items, books and gifts
- Café serving coffee, baked goods & sandwiches
- Local wine, beer & cider
- Firepits and beautiful ocean-front deck seating
- Electric bike rentals
- BBQ's available for guest use
- Dog friendly facility
- Shuttle service available for golf & disc golf at nearby course

www.otterbay-marina.ca   Call (250) 629-3579 or VHF 66A

Tumbo & Cabbage Islands   Photo © Josef Hanus

Tumbo and Cabbage Islands
[3441]

★ **Tumbo & Cabbage Islands (10):** {3313, 3441} Charts are essential. These small islands lie off the southeast tip of Saturna. The area just outside of the reef line, stretching west-northwest from Tumbo and Cabbage, is a favored fishing zone. Do not attempt passage into Reef Harbour between the southeast side of Cabbage and the northeastern shore of Tumbo. A drying reef and mud flats extend between the islands at this location. No approach to Reef Harbour is without hazard. The safest approach is to locate the end of the reef that extends northwestward on a line through Tumbo and Cabbage Islands and Pine Islet. This reef is about one mile long from Cabbage Island. By avoiding the reef, it is possible to head directly toward Saturna. A turn to port is made when the vessel is on a line with Reef Harbour. Proceeding east-by-southeast on a course of about 105 degrees, it is possible to enter between the reef extending west-northwest from Cabbage and the reef extending west-northwest from the western finger of Tumbo. In season, kelp marks some areas to be avoided, but other times of the year it is difficult to navigate this entry. In Reef Harbour one must consult the boat's depth sounder, the chart, and tide predictions for satisfactory overnight anchorage depths. Avoid the drying mud flats to the east-southeast of Cabbage Island. Although this anchorage is exposed to northwest and southeast winds and is difficult to enter, Tumbo Island at least gives protection from seas in southeast winds. Reef Harbour, between Tumbo and Cabbage, has mooring buoys, a sandy beach on Cabbage, and good crabbing along the north shore of Tumbo near the buoys. Anchorage is possible. Tumbo Island has picnic tables, outhouses, and a few short walking trails. No water or camping. Cabbage and Tumbo Islands are part of the Gulf Islands National Park Reserve. Both are managed by Parks Canada. ⚓ 🚶

Cabbage Island is a NEXUS Marine only customs check-in site.

★⚓ **Cabbage Island Marine Park:** Ten mooring buoys are located in Reef Harbour between Cabbage Island and the eastern tip of Tumbo. Camping is permitted on Cabbage only in designated areas (GPS Coordinates: 48.797806, -123.087791). Fees are charged for campsites and mooring buoys from May 15 through Sept. 30. Composting toilet and an information shelter are available. No potable water and fires are not permitted. Keep dogs on leashes at all times. Walking, swimming, fishing, scuba diving and bird watching are popular activities. Bald Eagles and Black Oystercatchers nest here. 🤿

Saturna Island
[3441, 3462, 3477]

★ **Saturna Island:** Although one of the largest of the Gulf Islands, Saturna is relatively undeveloped as nearly two thirds of the island is part of the Gulf Island National Park Reserve. Saturna is accessible by chartered and scheduled float plane, private boat, water taxi, and B.C. ferries (the terminal is located on the point of the peninsula that separates Boot Cove and Lyall Harbour.) A government wharf and marine fuel are found in Lyall Harbour next to the ferry landing. The island is home to a permanent population of 350 residents. Local businesses include several B & B's, convenience and general stores, art studios and galleries, post office, pub, cafe, and coffee shop. The Saturday Summer Market, held from 10am-1pm in the General Store parking lot, highlights the creations of the islands' many talented artisans. Special events include two annual Pig Roasts (May and November) and a Lamb Barbecue on Canada Day (July 1). During the summer, marine experts present "SeaTalks" on topics from plankton to orcas at the Community Hall just up from the ferry landing. Good swimming beaches are found in Veruna Bay, Russell Reef, Thomson Park, East Point Regional Park and Lyall Harbour Beach. There is a public campground at Narvaez Bay and private campgrounds at Breezy Bay and Lyall Harbour. The island has several good hiking trails and roads for biking. Kayak and bike rentals are available in Lyall Harbour. The island was named in 1791 after the schooner Saturnina. For additional information, www.saturnatourism.com.

East Point: An 1888 lighthouse situated here is the reference point for gathering weather conditions for the southern Georgia Strait. The historic light station is part of East Point Regional Park and sits above picturesque sandstone bluffs. The park is known for views east to Mt. Baker and frequent whale sightings. A swimming beach, trails, and toilet are available. There is good fishing in this area. Beware of tidal currents running up to 5 knots around Boiling Reef, off the tip of East Point. 🚶

Narvaez Bay (11): Much of the steep sided land surrounding this long bay is part of the Gulf Island National Park Reserve. There is temporary anchorage near the head and another behind an anvil shaped peninsula off the southern shore. The bay is open to swells of passing ferries and southeast winds. Winds from the west may also funnel into the bay. Unstable bottom, watch for anchor dragging. In areas, the gravel shore allows for beaching dinghies. Hiking is possible on unmaintained trails or along old island roads. A short, but steep uphill hike leads to a meadow. Pit toilet and picnic tables available. ⚓🚶

Saturna Beach (12): A dock is available for shore access. This beach is good for swimming and adjoins Thompson Park, the bluffs and a winery. It is a 15-minute walk up the hill, through the vineyards to the winery. Mount Warburton Pike towers over 1,600 feet above Saturna Beach. Hardy souls can hike a narrow, gravel road leading to the summit and sweeping views. Follow Harris Road to Staples Road. 🚶

Whale watching off Saturna Island   Photo © Miles Ritter

Breezy Bay: Breezy Bay is shallow with depths less than eight feet. True to its name, it is not the best anchorage in rising winds. A dock and orange mooring buoys are part of the Saturna Island Family Estate Winery. The winery is currently not in operation.

★ **Boot Cove (13):** Winds can enter this bay. This steep-sided cove has a narrow, but easily navigated entrance into a basin with suitable depths for anchoring. The bottom is good holding mud. Space is limited by private docks and buoys, and aquaculture. A lodge and restaurant are located near the end of the cove.

★ **Lyall Harbour (14):** There is plentiful and good anchorage here unless a west or northwest wind is expected. It is best to go as far into the bay as overnight depths will permit. The Saturna Island ferry landing is near the harbour entrance. A public wharf with 300 feet of float space is adjacent to the ferry dock. Hand-carried fuel is available nearby. This is the main commercial area on Saturna and stores and services are within a short walk from moorage. A convenience store with ice, snacks, drinks and supplies is located above the The Lighthouse Pub (offering breakfast, lunch and dinner and entertainment on weekends). The General Store, about a fifteen minute walk uphill from moorage, carries groceries, produce, meat, baked goods, liquor, and some hardware. A library with internet is also located in the area (open 10:30am-3pm, Wed. & Sat.). A nearby recreation center with exercise equipment and gym is open to visitors. A "drop in" fee is charged. Kayaks and bicycles can be rented locally. Tent sites, as well as public coin operated showers are available nearby at the Arbutus Point Campground.

Lyall Harbour Government Wharf: Adjacent to the ferry dock. Daily, overnight, monthly moorage. New expanded dock space. First 2 hours free, no power or water, rafting mandatory. 250-889-6318.

Saturna General Store: Groceries, bakery, beer, wine & spirits. 250-539-2936.

Saturna Lighthouse Pub: Hand-carried gas, diesel, WiFi, pub. 250-539-5725.

★⚓ **Winter Cove & Winter Cove Marine Park (15):** This marine park is the site of the Canada Day Lamb Barbecue. There are fire pits, a baseball diamond, picnic areas, pit toilets, walking trails, water, and information kiosks. No camping allowed. There is an unpaved launching ramp, for use at half tide or higher. There are several anchorages in Winter Cove. The bottom is shallow and uneven, but holding is good. This can be a windy area, watch for anchor dragging. When approaching from Plumper Sound, get even with the entrance to Irish Bay, then aim toward Samuel Island until close to the shore. Avoid Minx Reef before turning to starboard and proceeding into Winter Cove. An underwater power cable crosses the west entrance. Areas close to shore are foul. The most favored anchorages are about 100 feet off shore, just southwest of the cable line, between the cables and the ruins of a concrete-supported ramp, north and east of the cable line.

Boat Passage (16): This narrow pass at Winter Point separates Samuel and Saturna Islands. Passage at or near high water slack is recommended. The charted location of the rock in the passage varies with the chart being used. At times the currents tend to carry boats across the rock. Maximum currents run to seven knots at springs. The favored course when going east is along the Saturna Island shore for about 150 yards on the Georgia Strait side. Then turn to port and pass through the break in the kelp beds.

Samuel Island
[3441, 3462, 3477]

★ **Irish Bay (17):** [3477, 3442, 3477] This large, scenic bay has good anchorage on a mud bottom but is open to winds from the southwest and west. Samuel Island is a private estate and a caretaker monitors the beaches, uplands, and private dock year round. Fires are not permitted on the beaches due to the flammable growth on the island and the lack of water and facilities for fire fighting.

Mayne Island
[3441, 3442, 3462, 3477]

★ **Mayne Island:** Public floats are found at Horton and Miners Bays. These sites are also NEXUS Marine locations. Boat launching is possible at David Cove, Village Bay, and Potato (Spud) Point. Regular ferry service connects the island with both Swartz Bay (to Victoria) and Tsawwassen (to Vancouver) at Village Bay. A community bus, with stops including Miners Bay, can meet incoming ferries. Visit https://www.mayneislandchamber.ca/transportation.html. If you are on foot and comfortable with hitching a ride, "car stops" are found at various locations (take lifts at your own risk). Float planes to and from Mayne Island leave from Miners Bay. Kayak and bike rentals are available locally. Mayne Island offers several lodging and dining establishments. Two main commercial hubs are found on the Island, Miners Bay and Fernhill Centre. Miners Bay is considered "towne centre" with a number of stores and services, while Fernhill Centre has an art gallery, bookstore, clothing store, restaurant and hair/nail salon. Tranquil farms and orchards set a leisurely pace for island residents, many of which are artisans who also find inspiration in its beauty. There are a number of historic sites to visit, including the Mayne Museum, St. Mary Magdalene Anglican Church, and Georgina Point Heritage Park and Lighthouse. The lighthouse was originally built in 1885. The museum occupies what was the jail in 1896, and traces the history of Mayne Island from past to present. It is located off Fernhill Road, opposite the Agricultural Hall. The Japanese Memorial Gardens at Dinner Bay Park are also of interest. Prior to World War II and their eviction from the west coast, Japanese farmers established a thriving tomato growing business on the island. These gardens honor their contributions. In addition to the gardens, the park has a putting green, disc golf course, picnic and playground areas, and ballfield. Mt. Parke, located mid-Island off Montrose and Kim Roads, has a variety of trails suited to hikers of all abilities. Visit the Sunny Mayne Bakery for an ice cream and/or snacks. Still looking for something to do? Stop at the Mayne Island Brewery (www.mayneislandbrewingco.com) and have a taster. Annual events include a *May Day Celebration* on May long weekend, *St. Mary Magdalene Annual Church Fair* the second Saturday in July, *Mayne Island Fall Fair* on the third Saturday in August, the famous *Lions Club BBQ* at Dinner Bay Park on Labor Day Sunday and the Made in Mayne Studio tours in both the spring and November. The historic Agricultural Hall (circa 1900) hosts a Farmers Market each Saturday from 10am-1pm, May long weekend through October long weekend. Visit www.mayneisland.com or www.mayneislandchamber.ca for more information.

Horton Bay Community Dock   Photo © MonicaWorks

★ **Georgeson Passage (18):** When entering Georgeson Passage from Plumper Sound, proceed toward Irish Bay. Turn to port and continue north along the Samuel Island shore, keeping Lizard Island to port. Strong currents may be encountered in the Georgeson Passage - Bennett Bay vicinity. Currents reach four knots and maneuvering room is limited. There are reefs in the vicinity of Lizard Island. When approaching Horton Bay from the south, pass south of Curlew Island through Robson Channel. A rock, marked by kelp in season, is kept to port. A rocky ledge off Curlew Island extends to starboard. Minimum depth in this passage is seven feet. Entry to Horton Bay may also be made by proceeding farther north to the end of Georgeson Passage and rounding the north tip of Curlew Island. Avoid the rocks that extend off this tip, proceeding in the direction of Bennett Bay before turning to port and entering the passage between Curlew and Mayne Islands. A private float off Curlew extends into this passage.

★ **Horton Bay (18):** Horton Bay is a NEXUS Marine only customs check-in site. Good anchorage is available in Horton Bay. A submerged rock, well marked on charts, is in the prime moorage area near the head. Check swing room depths on sounder before anchoring. A government dock on the south shore is primarily used by resident boaters, very limited transient moorage, no power or water, rafting required.

★ **Bennett Bay (19):** Entry from the Strait of Georgia is through the narrow passage between Campbell Point and Georgeson Island. Favor the Georgeson Island side. A shoal extends off Campbell Point. Anchorage is possible inside Campbell Point, but tide flats and shallow water extend to the outer end of the long wharf. Two buoys belonging to the Resort are in the bay. Watch for kayakers and keep your wake low as a courtesy. The Mayne Island Resort & Spa and two restaurants are onshore. There is a good swimming beach with a launch site for kayak/SUP rentals, call 250-539-0864. A trail leads to a scenic viewpoint at the end of Campbell Point. The Point and Georgeson Island are part of the Gulf Island National Park Reserve.

★ **Campbell Bay (20):** This bay is protected from northwest winds, but exposed to southeast winds. There are rocks in line with the Belle Chain and extending southward from Campbell Point to beyond Georgeson Island. Anchor near the head on a mud bottom. There is a popular swimming beach onshore.

★ **David Cove (21):** Anchorage in this small niche with minimum depth of seven feet. Exposed to the north. Launching ramp.

Walk-around: At low tide, a shore walk can be made from this cove to the Active Pass Light Station, but the walk is rocky and slippery.

Piggott Bay: There is a good swimming beach here, but reefs and southeast winds are hazards.

★ **Miners Bay (22):** [3473] {48° 51' 7" N, 123° 18' 7" W} Limited moorage. Miners Bay is a NEXUS Marine only check-in site from Oct. 1 to April 30. Open to all boaters the rest of the year. Active Pass has currents to seven knots on spring tides. See Active Pass description in Chapter 10. The northward movement of the flood tide affects the bay. On strong flood tides, with any northerly wind, rips occur from south of Mary Ann Point to Laura Point. Miners Bay is deep, so anchorage must be close to shore. Currents circle around inside the bay. Public dock moorage is open to the wake from BC Ferries, especially at low tide and in a north wind. There is a sunken cable west of the public floats. Float spaces marked in yellow are reserved, not for general moorage. Within walking distance of the floats are an auto & marine store, the museum, farmers market, library with internet access, two grocery stores, consignment shop, a health food store, a liquor outlet, art supply store, art gallery, bakery/deli, pub, and a restaurant.

Active Pass Auto & Marine Ltd.: (1 block from moorage) Hand carried gas, diesel. Propane, postal services, bait/tackle, snacks. 250-539-5411.

Mayne Island TruValue Foods: Groceries, whole/organic foods, frozen products, bulk items. 250-539-2548.

★ **Village Bay (23):** Terminus for the Gulf Islands-Swartz Bay and Tsawwassen ferries. Good mud bottom in 24-40 feet, but ferry wash, northwest winds, and private buoys affect anchorage. Public telephone at terminal. Launching ramp and beach access in bay. Avoid Enterprise Reef. Do not pass between the reef light and the green buoy.

Essential Supplies & Services

AIR TRANSPORTATION
To & from Washington
Kenmore Air 1-866-435-9524
NW Seaplanes . . . 425-277-1590, 1-800-690-0086
San Juan Airlines. 1-800-874-4434
Seattle Seaplanes 1-800-637-5553
To & from Islands/Vancouver
SeaAir Seaplanes . . . 604-273-8900 or 1-800-44SEAIR

BOOKS / BOOK STORES
Evergreen Pacific Publishing 425-493-1451
The Marine Atlas. 253-872-5707

BUS
Mayne Island Community Bus 250-539-0851
Pender Island Community Bus . . . . PenderBus.org

COAST GUARD
Victoria Coast Guard Radio. . . . . VHF 16, 83a
 . . . . 1-800-661-9202 (In BC) or 250-363-6611
Victoria Marine Traffic 250-363-6333
Marine Distress, Search & Rescue
 . . . . 1-800-567-5111 (in Canada) or 250-413-8933
Cell Phone (limited to select providers) . . . *16 or #727

CUSTOMS
Bedwell Harbour
Cabbage Island NEXUS Marine Only
Horton Bay NEXUS Marine Only
Miners Bay NEXUS Marine Only
Port Browning NEXUS Marine Only
For updated information, please visit https://www.cbsa-asfc.gc.ca/do-rb/openpoe-temp-pdeouvert/marine-maritime-eng.html
See Important Notices between Chapters 7 & 8

FERRY INFORMATION
B.C. Ferries. 1-888-223-3779

FISHING / SHELLFISHING INFO
24 hr Recorded Notifications (Pacific region only)
 . . . . .1-866-431-3474 or 604-666-2828
Recreational Licensing 1-877-535-7307
Observe, Record & Report Line (fisheries violations)
1-800-465-4336 or 604-607-4186 (Pacific region only)

FUELS
Active Pass Auto & Marine Ltd
Hand carried Gas, Diesel 250-539-5411
Poets Cove Resort & Spa . . . 250-629-2100, VHF 66A
Saturna Lighthouse Pub: Hand Carried Gas, Diesel
 250-539-5725

GOLF COURSES
(Course accessible from moorage and have rental clubs available)
Pender Island G&CC: North Pender 250-629-6659

GROCERY STORES
Mayne Island Tru Value Foods 250-539-2548
Otter Bay Marina . . . . 250-629-3579, VHF 66A
Pender Island Tru Value Foods. 250-629-8322
Saturna General Store. 250-539-2936

HAULOUTS
Canoe Cove Marina. 250-656-5566
Harbours End Marine (Ganges) .250-537-4202, VHF 16
Maple Bay Marina 250-746-8482

HOSPITALS/CLINICS
Healthlink BC (Nurse Helpline) 811
Mayne Island Health Centre 250-539-2312
Pender Harbour Medical Clinic 250-629-3233
Saturna Island Medical Clinic 250-539-5435

LIQUOR STORES
Mayne Island: Miners Bay
Pender Island: Bedwell Harbour
Saturna Island: Lyall Harbour

LODGING
Poets Cove Resort & Spa . 1-888-870-8889, VHF 66A

MARINAS/MOORAGE FLOATS
Otter Bay Marina . . . . 250-629-3579, VHF 66A
Poets Cove Resort & Spa . . . 250-629-2111, VHF 66A
Port Browning Marina. . . . . 250-629-3493, VHF 66A
Capitol Regional District Small Craft Harbours:
Mayne Island - Horton Bay, Miners Bay
North Pender Island - Hope Bay, Port Browning, Port Washington
Saturna Island - Lyall Harbour

PROPANE
Active Pass Auto & Marine Ltd. 250-539-5411

RAMPS
David Cove
Lyall Harbour: Saturna Island
Otter Bay Marina . . . . 250-629-3579 VHF 66A
Piggot Bay
Port Browning Marina. . . . . .250-629-3493 VHF 66A
Potato Point:
Thieves Bay
Village Bay
Winter Cove Marine Park

REPAIRS
Boatyard, The: Tsehum Harbour. 250-655-1511
Vector Yacht Services (Canoe Cove). . . . 250-656-5515
Harbours End Marine (Ganges)
 . . . . .250-537-4202, VHF 16
Maple Bay Marina 250-746-8482
Philbrooks Boatyard: Tsehum Harbour. . 250-656-1157

RESTAURANTS/PUB
Poets Cove Resort & Spa . 1-888-870-8889, VHF 66A
Port Browning Marina. 250-629-3493
Saturna Island Pub 250-539-5725

SCUBA SITES
Bedwell Harbour
Cabbage Island Marine Park
Port Browning

TAXI
Pender Island 250-629-2222

TOWING
C-TOW 1-888-419-CTOW
Fast Response 250-222-0076
Harbours End Marine 250-537-4202
Vessel Assist/TowBoatUS 250-883-7865

VISITOR INFORMATION
Mayne Island . . . . www.mayneislandchamber.ca
Pender Island . . . . www.penderislandchamber.com
Saturna Island. . . . . www.saturnatourism.com

WEATHER
Environment Canada Weather Line. 250-339-9861
Canadian Coast Guard (recorded). 250-363-6492
Vancouver: WX-1, WX-3

Visit us at boattravel.com

CENTRAL GULF ISLANDS & E. VANCOUVER IS. COAST   Chapter 10   Page 137

Ganges Harbour - photo © Hastings House Country House Hotel

Chapter 10:
Central Gulf Islands & East Vancouver Island Coast

Cowichan Bay to Yellow Point. Ganges, Maple Bay, Crofton, Chemainus, Ladysmith; Salt Spring, Prevost, Galiano, Penelakut, & Thetis Islands.

Symbols

[ ]: Numbers between [ ] are chart numbers.
{ }: Numbers & letters between { } are waypoints.
★ Recommended destinations, facilities, and services
⚓:Park, 🚤: Boat Launch, ▲: Campgrounds,
🚶: Hiking Trails, ⊞: Picnic Area, 🚲: Biking
🤿: Scuba

Chart List

Canadian Hydrographic Charts:
3313, 3441-3443, 3463, 3473, 3475, 3477, 3478
NOAA Charts: 18400, 18412-18415
Marine Atlas Vol 1(2018) Pages 10, 11
Evergreen Cruising Atlas: Pages 101, 104, 105, 106, 111, 113-116, 118, 119

★ See "Important Notices" between Chapters 7 and 8 for specific information on boating related topics such as boating safety, weather, U.S. & Canadian marine radio use, Vessel Traffic Service, security zones, Canadian & U.S. Customs, etc. Due to changing regulations, call ahead to verify latest customs information.

★ **No Dump Zones:** Montague Harbour. Dump gray water only (shower and dish water). Must have approved holding tank on board to enter No Dump Zone.

2024 Northwest Boat Travel

Fulford Harbour   Photo © ShortCreative

★ **Introduction to the Gulf Islands:** See the beginning of Chapter 9.

Salt Spring Island East
[3313, 3441, 3442, 3462, 3463, 3473, 3475, 3477, 3478]

★ **Salt Spring Island East:** This Island is 18 miles in length, with widths varying from two to ten miles. Its largest community, Ganges, is the main centre of commerce for the Gulf Islands. Smaller ports are at Vesuvius and Fulford Harbour. There are several good bays for anchorage. The island, first settled in the 1850's was named for the brine pools at the north end of the island. "Salt Spring" is sometimes spelled as one word and other times as two, even on the same sign! Regardless of its spelling, Salt Spring has become synonymous with the arts. Galleries and studios are everywhere in this enclave of artists and crafts people. Every medium imaginable-paintings, pottery, weaving, stained glass, woodwork, jewelry and quilts are well represented.

Salt Spring is also a treasure trove of wildlife. Deer are prevalent, eagles soar overhead, swans drift out in Fulford Harbour, and geese and ducks parade in Ganges Harbour. Seals are also frequent visitors, especially when the herring run. But, as more people come to the Island to live or visit, the habitat area of these creatures is progressively fragmented. On the Island's north side, McFadden Creek Heronry, once one of the largest heron colonies in British Columbia is now gone. Many residents actively participate in preserving the natural environment and while they welcome visitors, they ask them to be respectful of the wildlife habitat. Local organizations advocating for wildlife include the Water Bird Watch Collective and the Island Wildlife Natural Care Centre. The later, located north of St. Mary Lake, is devoted to the care of Island's sick, injured or orphaned wild animals. Domesticated farm animals are abundant on the island too, and are often seen grazing on the rolling farmlands. In the spring, a visit during lambing season is a lasting memory.

⚓ **Ruckle Provincial Park, Beaver Point (1):** Beaver Point is named for the Hudson's Bay Company ship "Beaver" that ran aground on the point. Several small coves indent the shoreline providing temporary anchorage at this, the largest park in the Gulf Islands. A mooring buoy is often tucked in the first niche north of Beaver Point. In this bay, steamships sailing between Victoria and Nanaimo, docked at the wharf from 1914 to 1951. This is also the terminus of Beaver Point Road, well traveled by visitors making the 10km/7mi trek to the ferry terminal. The park offers picnic sites, fire rings (firewood sold onsite), pit toilets, campsites and water (mid-March through Oct). Popular recreational activities include hiking, sea kayaking, cycling and scuba diving. King's Cove, an indentation farther north, offers temporary anchorage. In 1894, gold was mined north of this cove.

The park is unique in that the Ruckle family still farms near the middle of the park acreage. Henry Ruckle immigrated to Salt Spring from Ireland in 1872 and began a prosperous farm. One hundred years later, most of it was donated to the province, however the Ruckles retained a lifetime tenancy on their farm, making this the oldest continuously run family farm in B.C. The old homestead is located near the park's entrance, as are several historic farm buildings. Park guests and are asked to respect the family's privacy. Public trails are clearly marked by red metal markers. Dogs are only allowed in designated parts of the park and must be leashed. ⛺▲🚶‍♂️

★ **Russell Island:** Located at the entrance to Fulford Harbour, this lovely island is part of the Gulf Islands National Park Reserve. To avoid wakes from passing vessels, anchor between the island and Salt Spring Island. Overnight anchorage is possible in calm weather. Dinghy dock, pit toilets available, no drinking water. A good swimming beach is on the west end. Trails lead to an old homestead. Kanakas (Hawaiians) settled here in the 1880's. Their ancestors had once worked for the Hudson's Bay Company. During the summer, descendants share family stories about life on Russell Island with visitors.

★ **Fulford Harbour (2):** Site of the Swartz Bay-Fulford Harbour ferry landing. Two public floats operated by the Harbour Authority of Salt Spring Island, are located in the harbour. The first, Fulford Outer Harbour is small and exposed, but offers transient moorage with access to Fulford Village, the ferry terminal, and bus service. The second, Fulford Inner Harbour has good protection, but is for long term moorage. Anchorage can be found in 30-40 feet of water on a mud bottom in the center of the bay near the head. A good spot is in the small bight where the creek flows from Stowel Lake. Just northwest of the Inner Harbour Public float is Fulford Landing Marina and Fulford Harbour Marina (the later is no longer operational). Fulford has a grocery store, lodging, a bakery/café and shops. Nearby Drummond Park with playground, picnic tables, and toilets is the site of Fulford Day each year in mid-August featuring food, races and music. A public tennis court is found behind the fire hall. Stowel Lake, off Beaver Point Road, less than a mile from Fulford offers trout fishing and swimming. Two wineries, easily accessed via public transit, offer tastings, sales, and dock delivery for case orders. Call ahead for hours: Garry Oaks Winery. 250-653-4687 and Salt Spring Vineyards. 250-653-9463. Garry Oaks Winery, also offers private tours and tastings by appointment, fee applies. Visit Salt Spring Vineyards website for information on their music and special events for the summer. Picnic items and wine available for purchase from the Vineyard. If craft beer is more to your liking, Salt Spring Island Ales' tasting room makes a fun stop. They also have a picnic area that allows outside food. 778-354-1121. A visit to Ganges is also possible by way of public transit with scheduled stops at the ferry landing.

Fulford Harbour Marina: Closed.

Fulford Landing Marina: Permanent moorage, one transient slip, power, water. 250-930-4996.

Fulford Inner Harbour Public Float: {48° 46' 8" N, 123° 27' 10"W} Long term moorage, transient moorage if space is available, 30 amp power (twist lock plug), water, security cameras, pay phone. 250-537-5711.

Fulford Outer Harbour Public Float: {48° 46' 3" N, 123° 27' 3"W} Transient moorage, security cameras. Derrick crane, emergency 15 amp electrical service available through Harbour Office. 250-537-5711.

Isabella Light: Located near the western entrance of Fulford Harbour, some fair weather anchorage can be found in the bay behind this light. There are rocks from the islet to shore. Approach from the south, aiming toward the pasture and a building. Anchor tucked in behind the islet. The lee of Russell Island might serve as a temporary anchorage.

Walter Bay: This shallow bay in South Ganges Harbour and the encircling spit are part of a wildlife sanctuary. Do not anchor in the area. Observe the 5 knot/10 km per hour speed limit.

Ganges
[3442, 3462, 3478]

★ **Ganges (3):** Ganges (Breakwater Float) is a customs (NEXUS only) check-in location. Upon arrival to Ganges you will be greeted with the picturesque view of boats and float planes tied to moorage floats and boats swinging at anchor in the bay. Boaters should slow to five knots (10 km per hour) when entering Ganges Harbour and then slow to no wake speed.

Transient moorage is available in several locations. The Salt Spring Harbour Authority operates public floats in both the inner and outer harbours. The Government (Centennial Wharf) Boat Basin is located behind the breakwater south of Grace Peninsula. The Outer Harbour public float, Kanaka Visitor's Wharf, is protected by a large breakwater float that extends into Ganges Harbour. There are spaces for float plane passenger pickup, commercial vessels, visitors, and the Coast Guard. It is also the site of a waste pumpout. Ganges Marina and Salt Spring Marina are located at the head of the harbour. If moorages are full, anchorage is plentiful in the harbour in depths of 24-35 feet. For shore access, a dinghy only dock is found alongside the Rotary Marine Park on the water side of Thrifty Foods.

A scenic harbour setting, park-like surroundings, and mountainous backdrop make Ganges an inviting destination. The village continues to expand facilities and attractions while retaining a warm and cozy seaside vibe. Radiating out from Ganges Harbour, over 100 businesses offer an array of services and products, all within easy walking distance.

Ganges Village has been a commercial centre since the turn-of-the-century when Mouat's Brothers Store was established in 1907. Over 110 years later, this store is still operating. A good way to learn about Ganges history is to wander through Mouat's Mall and view exhibits of early photographs, tools and paraphernalia. From these early days, the village now boasts one of the best boutique shopping experiences on the west coast, offering everything from locally made crafts and clothing, fair-trade goods from around the world, specialty food stores featuring local products, liquor stores and specialty services for every need. There are no "chain" stores and almost all stores are unique to the island. Dining options are vast and include upscale fine dining, seaside patios, cafes, bistros and food trucks. There is also a Fish Market open daily featuring local seafood, fish and fresh cooked seafood dishes.

Once one of the largest apple producers in Western Canada, Salt Spring Island boasts 450 varieties of apples today, and continues to produce rich harvests of fruits, vegetables, fresh herbs, hydroponic lettuce, eggs, flowers and meats. Salt Spring lamb is such an honored product that it was served to Queen Elizabeth II at the 1995 Commonwealth Games. Salt Spring Cheese Co. not only produces goat cheese, but in summer is only one of two companies in the province to produce sheep cheese. Fruit and nut trees, some which grow in heritage orchards, bear varieties of apples, pears, plums, walnuts, and hazelnuts. An olive grove planted on the island in 2000 produced the first batch of Canadian olive oil in 2016.

Grapes grow well here and three local wineries produce award-winning vintages. Island grown organic hops are brewed locally by Salt Spring Island Ales. Salt Spring Wild Cider honours the apple growing culture on the island and they will soon be joined by Salt Spring Apple Co. Cider. Salt Spring Shine is a new distillery featuring vodka and gin.

Fresh, local products are on display at several seasonal Farmers Markets. The Salt Spring Saturday Market, boasts over 100 "bake-it, make-it or grow-it" vendors held at Centennial Park from April to October 9am-3pm. The Tuesday Farmers Market highlights local island farmers and food producers and is held from June-October, 1:30-5:30 pm. In addition to hosting these markets, Centennial Park also has a playground, picnic tables, a band stand for concerts and dances, and a war memorial dedicated to island residents who died in service to Canada.

Other island attractions include the 1884 Bittancourt Heritage House Museum, at 351 Rainbow Road in the community owned Farmers Institute. The Museum showcases the history of the island's pioneer families through artifacts, antique equipment and displays. Free Admission. Hours: 11am-3pm. The Farmers Institute also hosts the annual *Fall Fair*, one of the oldest of its kind in B.C. Another Rainbow Road notable is historic Mahon Hall, home of ArtCraft which

Sunrise over Ganges Harbour   Photo © ShortCreative

showcases the work of over 100 Gulf Island's artisans; open daily 10am to 5pm, June-Sept. They also host *WinterCraft* during the holiday season for that special "made-on-Salt Spring-Island" gift.

ArtSpring, a performing and visual art centre, offers world caliber live theater, music, and art exhibits throughout the year featuring local and international talent. There are also dozens of galleries and studios to tour featuring West Coast and First Nations artists, as well as local artists and home-spun talent.

Within a mile radius of Ganges Village are parks, medical and dental centers, a hospital, library with WiFi, the RCMP office, and several churches. If you like to walk, Mouat Provincial Park, located west of the downtown core, has a nice trail, along with disc golf, picnic areas and beautiful towering cedars. Another lovely walk from town takes you along Upper Ganges Road to Churchill Road to scenic Churchill Beach for a stroll on sand made from oyster shells. A more strenuous hike is the three to four hour trek to Mount Erskine or the Channel Ridge Trails.

Land transportation is available to all parts of Salt Spring Island. A free shuttle stops at the marinas in Ganges with service to Upper Ganges where additional shopping and services can be found. A public bus with scheduled stops at the ferry terminals, Fernwood Dock, and Ruckle Provincial Park, runs daily. Also choose from taxi service, scooter and car rentals, or charter sight-seeing tours. Take a side trip to Beddis Beach, about 3.5 miles from Ganges at the end of Beddis Road, a perfect spot for swimming, launching kayaks and enjoying views of passing ferries. Or visit St. Mary Lake, about five miles north of Ganges, to enjoy sunbathing, swimming, and fishing. On Lower Ganges Road toward St. Mary Lake, Salt Spring Cinema ("The Fritz") shows first run films in a 102-year old heritage building.

Keeping active is easy and enjoyable around Ganges. Golf is a great option and the beautiful Salt Spring Golf & Country Club has 9 holes, driving range and practice green. Nearby is outdoor and indoor tennis, a squash court and a jogging track. Bikes, kayaks and SUP's can be rented locally. An indoor swimming pool, a fitness centre and wellness centre, with a full range of services including yoga and fitness classes, are also found in Ganges.

Several annual events and festivals are full of family fun including: the *Blossom Festival*, *Easter Art Festival*, *Canada Day Fireworks*, *The Fall Fair*, the *Harvest Food and Drink Festival* including the *Annual Apple Festival* and *Sip & Savour Salt Spring*. The month of December is a wonderful time to visit for Christmas on Salt Spring. The Visitor Info Centre, located in the heart of Ganges, has free information on the latest events, concerts and activities happening on Salt Spring, the surrounding Gulf Islands, and Vancouver Island. Open daily. Summer: 9am-5pm; spring and fall: 10am-4pm; winter: 11am-3pm. 250-537-5252, 1-866-216-2936 or www.saltspringtourism.com.

Ganges Harbour   Photo © Hastings House Country House Hotel

★ **Salt Spring Marina:** {48° 51' N, 123° 28' W} Located at the head of Ganges Harbour by Moby's Pub and below Hastings House Country Hotel/Spa/Dining. The marina has been recently updated from the seabed up and can accommodate vessels up to 370 ft. Long-term and daily moorage with 30 and 50 amp power, free Wi-Fi, washrooms and laundry (cleaned daily), water, garbage and recycle dropoff, bagged ice. Enjoy the view from Moby's patio with beer, wine, entertainment, great food, take-out, and off-sales. Salt Spring Car & Scooter Rentals is on-site. Salt Spring Adventure Co. offers canoe & Kayak tours. Walk 10 minutes to the village shops and galleries, or BCTransit from all three ferries to the marina. Manager Celeste Cavaliere welcomes yacht clubs, pets on leash, kids and well-mannered parents. See our advertisement on this page. Mind the RED channel markers on the East side–stay between them and the marina. Reservations recommended through Swift Harbour app or our website: www.saltspringmarina.com. For questions or special requests: Telephone: 1-800-334-6629, 250-537-5810. VHF 66A.

Breakwater Float: Transient moorage, 30 amp power, water, wifi, pump-out (fee applies), restricted/reserved areas are painted yellow. Call to verify that showers/restroom are available at Centennial Wharf. 250-537-5711. VHF 09.

Ganges Centennial Wharf: {48° 51.2' N, 123° 29.8" W} Long term moorage, transient moorage (call office to coordinate space), 30 amp power (twist lock plug), water, showers, washrooms, wifi, launch ramp, garbage & waste oil disposal. Call to verify that showers/restroom are available. 250-537-5711. VHF 09.

Ganges Marina: {48° 51.321' N, 123° 29.998' W} Permanent & guest moorage, vessels to 300'. Reservations recommended. 15/30/50 amp power, gas, diesel, lubes, water (restricted usage when Island reservoirs are low), showers, laundry, wifi, garbage drop for moorage customers (fee applies). 250-537-5242. VHF 66A.

Harbours End Marine & Equipment Ltd.: Marine repair & parts, power boat haul-outs to 32', shipwright services, vessel towing, marine chandlery. 250-537-4202.

Hastings House Country Hotel, Relais & Chateaux: The hotel offers 18 luxurious suites on 22 acres overlooking Ganges Harbour next to Salt Spring Marina and exquisite Farm-to-Table dining with extensive wine list from BC and around the globe. Dress casual or come as dressy as you like. Spacious indoor and outdoor dining rooms and terraces. Wellspring Spa offers massages and facials by appointment. We invite you to come early to enjoy the gardens, outdoor sculptures, or perhaps a cozy fire in cooler weather. info@hastingshouse.com; www.hastingshouse.com. 1-800-661-9255 or 250-537-2362.

Kanaka Visitor's Wharf: (Outer Harbour): {48° 51' 25" N, 123° 29.95" W} Transient moorage, long-term moorage from Oct-April, 30 amp twist lock plug power, WiFi, potable water. Rafting required except on header float. Call to verify that showers/restroom are available at Centennial Wharf. 250-537-5711. VHF 09.

Moby's Pub: Located within Salt Spring Marina at the end of Ganges Harbour, has great food and entertainment, with seating indoors and out. Takeout menu and off-sales. www.mobyspub.ca. 250-537-5559.

★ **Long Harbour (4):** This lovely inlet indents into the southeast corner of Salt Spring Island for over two nautical miles. Long Harbour is open to southeast winds, but due to its long, narrow shape, is quite protected, especially further in. The Harbour is the terminus of the Gulf Islands - Tsawwassen Ferry and has many private facilities along its shores. One such facility is the Royal Victoria Yacht Club outstation, located 0.8 nautical miles past the ferry terminal on the west side, {N 48° 51.582", W 123° 27' 832"} Anchorage on a mud bottom is possible in several locations. A favored spot is behind the islets just inside Nose Point. Do not attempt passage on the south side of these islets especially at high tide as there are several submerged rocks just out-west of the main islets. Instead, proceed around the red marker buoy, and then inward between the islets and the Salt Spring shore. Anchoring is also pleasant at the head of the bay in 10 to 15 feet of water where summer sea temperatures can reach the high 70's making the area some of the warmest throughout the Gulf Islands. A beautiful drying lagoon extends from the head waters and is accessible via a short kayak or dinghy sail.

★ **Walker Hook (5):** [3442, 3463] Good anchorage is off a beautiful beach on the east side. The inlet dries. Temporary anchorage on a high tide with some protection from westerlies can be found inside Atkins Reef.

Atkins Reef: Extends northwestward and southeastward from the concrete marker. There are rocks southeast at Walker Hook extending toward the marker.

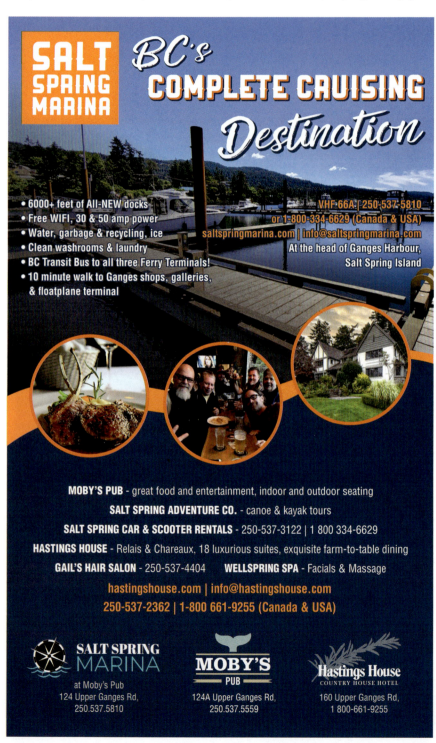

Visit us at boattravel.com

★ **Fernwood (6):** A long public pier juts into Trincomali Channel near Fernwood Point. The mooring float at the end of the dock accommodates only two to three boats. 24-hr limit, no services at dock, no moorage fee, exposed to waves in channel. There is good crabbing off the dock. The Fernwood Road Cafe, across the street from the dock, serves breakfast and lunch. A public bus stops near the cafe with service into Ganges. A one mile walk leads to St. Mary Lake for swimming and fishing. North of the dock off North Beach Road is a boat launch ramp over tidal sand flats.

Southey Point: Site of an Indian midden, the northernmost tip of Salt Spring has a white shell beach, a drying ledge marked by a light, and an adjacent bay. Southey Bay is open to the north. It is nearly filled with private buoys, thus limiting anchorage.

★ **Stonecutter's Bay:** Private homes surround this small bay. Good anchorage. Open to the northwest.

Idol Island: Reports indicate that this is to be part of a park development.

Salt Spring Marina Docks Photo © Salt Spring Marina

Salt Spring Island West
[3442, 3462, 3478]

★ **Vesuvius (7):** Very limited anchorage is possible south of the ferry landing, however private buoys are hazards. A small public float is located adjacent to the landing. A nearby food store sells fresh baked goods and coffee. The Seaside Restaurant serves lunch and dinner and has a dock located just south of the ferry dock that boaters can tie up to while dining. For take out, call 250-537-2249. Several artists studios are within walking distance. Duck Creek Park, about 20 minutes away by foot, has a nice looped walking trail. The closest beaches are found at Quarry Drive Park and Vesuvius Bay Beach. Locals consider the latter to be one of the warmest for swimming. There is public bus service from Vesuvius to Ganges, which is about 4km/2miles away. Good anchorage and views of sunsets can be found in Duck Cove between Dock Point and Parminter Point.

Vesuvius Bay Public Float: {48° 52.9' N, 123° 34.4' W} No facilities, rates are posted, use honor box for payment. Emergency electrical service available through Harbour Office. 250-537-5711.

★ **Booth Bay (8):** There is anchorage, open to westerlies. Tide flats at the head of the bay. It is possible to enter Booth Inlet at high tide in an inflatable, canoe, kayak, or dinghy. Once through the shallow entrance, there is enough water for an outboard. Onshore, the construction of driftwood forts is a popular pastime. A trail just north of the beach connects to Quarry Drive Park.

★ **Burgoyne Bay & Burgoyne Bay Provincial Park (9):** Although open to southeast winds and northwest seas, this bay has anchorage and a 65' public float operated by the Salt Spring Island Harbour Authority {48° 47.6' N, 123° 31.3' W}. Half of the float is reserved, and the other half is for transient use (48 hr max). No services provided. When the drying sand at the head of the bay covers with water on summer days, it is a popular swimming area. Burgoyne Bay was formerly used as a log sorting area, caution advised. The day use Provincial Park has trails and scenic views, no camping or fires are permitted and dogs must be on-leash. A road leads to Burgoyne Valley and Mount Maxwell Provincial Park where Baynes Peak, the Island's highest point, is located. ⚓

Sansum Narrows (10): Currents run to three knots. Erratic winds funnel through the narrows. Sport fishermen frequent this spot. Fishing for Springs is good June through August, while Cohos are best from August through October. To avoid in-season closures, call 1-866-431-3474.

★ **Musgrave Landing (11):** {48° 45" N, 123° 33' 0" W} The public wharf for transient use is seldom empty. No services. Logging roads and trails offer good hiking. Temporary anchorage is possible north of the wharf, but it is unprotected in a south wind.

Prevost Island
[3442, 3462-63, 3478]

★ **Prevost Island (12):** This beautiful island has fingers of land spreading outward in a northwest-southeast direction to form six distinctly different harbours. An Irishman of noble lineage, Digby Hussey deBurge, owned the entire island in the 1920's and tended goats, sheep, and cattle. Today, the deBurge's and a few other families own most of the property, while national park reserve lands are located on the north and south shores of the Island. With its tall trees, red-barked madronas, and moss covered rocks, Prevost Island displays its own special charm. Anchorage can be found in Ellen Bay, Diver Bay, Glenthorne Passage, Annette Inlet, Selby Cove, and James Bay.

★ **Ellen Bay:** Ellen Bay and Diver Bay on Swanson Channel often boast beautiful moonlight vistas on summer evenings. Anchorage on this side of Prevost Island is uncomfortable at times from the ferry wash. Ellen Bay offers good holding anchorage near the head on a mud bottom.

★ **Diver Bay:** Diver Bay, open to the southeast, offers temporary anchorage in 30-40 foot depths. Ferry wakes enter.

★ **Glenthorne Passage:** This harbour is protected by Secret Island and Glenthorne Point. The passage seems to have a south seas flavor that encourages gunkholing by dinghy. The shoreline is private. Enter between Secret Island and the outermost island or from the west along Prevost Island. Depths average 15-25 feet.

★ **Annette Inlet:** Reflections of lingering sunsets often ripple across the water in this long indentation into Prevost Island. When entering, avoid a large kelp patch and rock directly in front of the entrance. Pass either side, then favor center channel because shoals extend from both sides. Anchorage is possible in both the inner and outer bays. In the outer bay, favor the center of the bay. There is a shallow area on the port side and shoals in the cove to starboard. A sand and grass spit extends from the port shore at the opening of the inner bay which tends to separate the inner and outer bays. In the inner bay there is extensive anchorage in the center and on the starboard side. Minimum depths average seven feet. The port side is the shallowest. Bottom is excellent holding, sticky mud. The head of the bay is a large, drying

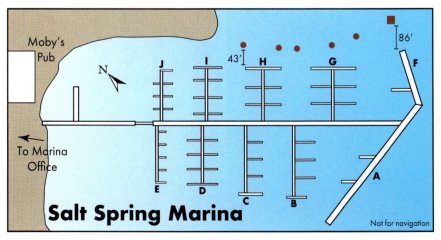

flat. A farm is located here and the shoreline is private. Entertainment is provided by large cormorants which perch in the trees along this shore. After capturing small fish they return to the stark branches to preen their feathers, spreading their wings to dry them.

★ **Selby Cove:** It is possible to go quite far into this bay and anchor over sand and mud near the head. The cove becomes shallow quickly. Anchorage far out in the center is more difficult and anchor dragging has occurred.

James Bay: Most, but not all, of the shoreline and Peile Point Peninsula is part of the Gulf Islands National Park Reserve and remains undeveloped. Early settlers planted orchards, the remains of which can still be found. This bay is exposed to north and northwesterly winds. Temporary anchorage is possible near the head. A ledge, with sunken rocks, is off the southern shore. Walk a sheep trail from the head of the bay to Peile Point.

Active Pass (13): Active Pass separates Galiano and Mayne Islands and is the shipping channel for ferries traveling between Vancouver Island and the mainland. They navigate on a pre-determined course through the passage and have the right-of-way. Currents at springs run up to eight knots. On strong flood tides, when strong north winds are present, there are violent rips in an area that extends from mid-channel south of Mary Anne Point to Laura Point. No dangerous rips occur on ebb tides in the pass. Many fishermen recommend fishing Helen Point on the ebb and Georgina Point on the flood. Also, fish on the north sides of the reefs. This very active passage was not named for the water conditions or boat usage, but was named for the *USS Active, a naval steamer* which did survey work in the area in 1855.

Galiano Island
[3442, 3462, 3463, 3473, 3478]

★ **Galiano Island:** Stretching northwest by southeast along the Strait of Georgia, this long and narrow island enjoys the least rainfall in the Gulf Islands. Many of the island's permanent residents live in the southern portion between Montague Harbour and Sturdies Bay. An atmosphere of relaxation and recreation prevails throughout the island, with it's long and publicly accessible SW facing shoreline.

Bluffs Park, Montague Harbour Provincial Marine Park, Dionisio Point Provincial Park, and other Island parks provide wonderful opportunities for outdoor fun, including camping, cycling, golfing, kayaking, fishing, and hiking. A sixty minute hike to the summit of Mt. Galiano reveals breathtaking, panoramic views all the way south to the San Juan Islands and the Olympic Mountains in Washington. Many talented artists and artisans live on Galiano and display their works at shops and galleries throughout the island. Dining out "Gali Style" is always a treat. From waterfront dining at the marina, to creative farm-to-table cuisine, to Thai or the fantastic food truck fare - the local eateries offer a delicious array of dining experiences. If you need to get around on the island, a new Community Bus service runs Fridays and Saturdays and a charter service is available. Scooters can also be rented at Montague Harbour Marina. On summer afternoons and evenings, Tommy Transit and the Hummingbird Pub Bus runs between the Pub, Montague Harbour Marina and the Provincial Park. Call 250-539-5472. For more information about the island, visit www.galianoisland.com.

★ **Sturdies Bay (14):** Toward the eastern end of Active Pass, Sturdies Bay is the site of the community of South Galiano. The Gulf Islands-Tsawwassen and Sturdies Bay-Swartz Bay Ferry Landing is found here. A small public float, with space for two or three 20 foot boats, is tucked in behind the protection of the pilings, but it is open to northern and easterly winds as well as ferry wake. No services at the dock, payment information at head of the gangway. The small village at Sturdies Bay has a variety of businesses including a couple of restaurants (with internet access), a bakery, a laundromat, a business offering internet access, a bookstore, arts & craft stores (one houses the post office), a propane dealer, and a grocery store/gas station (hand carry gas) that also has an ATM and liquor store on-site. Pick up a map and

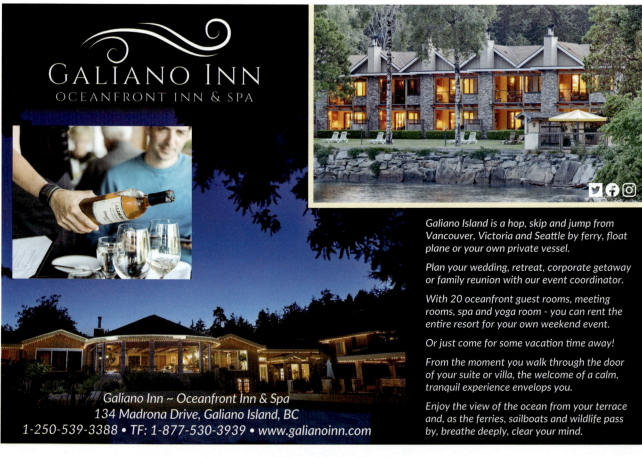

Galiano Inn ~ Oceanfront Inn & Spa
134 Madrona Drive, Galiano Island, BC
1-250-539-3388 • TF: 1-877-530-3939 • www.galianoinn.com

Galiano Island is a hop, skip and jump from Vancouver, Victoria and Seattle by ferry, float plane or your own private vessel.

Plan your wedding, retreat, corporate getaway or family reunion with our event coordinator.

With 20 oceanfront guest rooms, meeting rooms, spa and yoga room - you can rent the entire resort for your own weekend event.

Or just come for some vacation time away!

From the moment you walk through the door of your suite or villa, the welcome of a calm, tranquil experience envelops you.

Enjoy the view of the ocean from your terrace and, as the ferries, sailboats and wildlife pass by, breathe deeply, clear your mind.

art guide at the Tourist Booth in the village and walk to local art galleries and studios. The unique Kunamokst Mural is on display at the Galiano Inn & Spa, a five minute walk from the ferry.

★ **Galiano Oceanfront Inn & Spa**: Set at the water's edge amid beautiful gardens and walking distance to Sturdies Bay Village, this boutique hotel resort offers an award-winning dining room, a casual wood-fired pizza terrace, licensed lounge and luxury spa. A dock is available for boaters while they dine or visit the spa (call ahead for reservations). Smart cars are available for all guests. Boaters staying at Montague Marina can call the resort for transportation options including a summer shuttle. See our advertisement on page 142. Website: www.galianoinn.com. Email: info@galianoinn.com. Address: 134 Madrona Drive, Galiano Island, BC, V0N 1P0. Telephone: 877-530-3939 or 250-539-3388. For Spa: 250-539-3388. Fax: 250-539-3338.

Walk-around: It is a pleasant walk from Sturdies Bay to picnic grounds at Bellhouse Park on Burrill Point. Or walk to Lions Park, on Burrill Road, about 20 minutes from the ferry. In May through October there is a lovely Saturday market at the South End Lions Fiesta Grounds, featuring food, art, music and produce from 10 am-2pm. Another fun idea is to take a picnic lunch and head to Bluffs Park with its old growth forest and panoramic views of the western entrance to Active Pass. From Sturdies Bay, just beyond the Village, turn left on Burrill Road. In about 1.5km/.9mi, this road turns into Bluff Road. Proceed on Bluffs until reaching the park and the path that leads to the edge of the bluff. If you are lucky, you may spot J Pod, a resident Orca pod often viewed from Bluffs Park, as well as Bellhouse Park and Mathews Point Beach. Locals Ralph and Rocky Moyle share this knowledge, "J Pod's feeding cycle is approximately 2 days. They can be seen as they move through Active Pass, head over toward Tsawwassen, veer south to the San Juan Islands and then head north again through Plumper Sound and Navy Channel in search of salmon. They eat approximately 300 Chinook salmon daily."

★ **Whaler Bay (15)**: Guarded from the ravages of the Strait of Georgia by shoals and Gossip Island, this bay was once used to harbour small whaling vessels and still offers anchorage today. Enter between Galiano and Gossip Islands. Favor the west shore south of Twiss Point. A public wharf with four floats is on the port side, well into the bay. Approach with caution as it is shallow. The tidal range in this bay is as much as 16 feet. For a nice walk, head up Whaler Bay Road from the dock to Cain Road. Turn right and continue on until you reach Sturdies Bay Road. To the left, toward Sturdies Bay are restaurants, a liquor store, and bakery. A 3 mile walk in the opposite direction along Sturdies Bay Road leads to other stores, including a hardware store.

Whaler Bay Harbour Authority Float: {48° 53' 0" N, 123° 19' 32" W} Permanent moorage. Transient moorage if space is available, must call ahead), 20/30 amp power, rafting mandatory, no water or garbage disposal. Tidal grid and crane on-site, help with both is available with prior notice. 250-539-2264.

Porlier Pass (16): See current tables for Active Pass. Porlier Pass separates Galiano Island from Valdes Island. The pass lies in a north-south direction. Currents to nine knots at springs flood northwest and ebb southeast. The ebb sets right over Romulus Rock from the direction of Virago Point. Dangerous conditions exist when the tide meets an opposing wind. Traverse the pass near slack water if possible. Blueback fishing is good in the area in April, as is Coho fishing in July. The indentations into Galiano which border Porlier Pass are protected from direct southerlies but are very susceptible to most other winds.

★⛺ **Dionisio Point Provincial Park**: Dionisio Bay offers temporary anchorage, the mooring buoy is for parks staff only. The sandy beach at the head invites sun bathers while the waters invite fishing, kayaking, and scuba diving. Because of the strong currents in the area, divers should be experienced. There are 30 walk-in backcountry camping sites. In Coon Bay there is a picnic area, a hand pump for water (boil before use), pit toilets and information shelter with hiking trail maps. Also of note are archaeological sites in the park that indicate previous use by the Penelakut First Nation as long as 3000 years ago. ▲⛺🚶

★ **Lighthouse Bay**: Anchorage is found in this bay, which lies between Race Point and Virago Point. Avoid the submarine power cable near the entrance.

★ **Reid Island (17)**: Fairweather anchorage is found at the southeast tip where the depth is marked "3" fathoms on the chart. Shoals, which dry five feet and three feet, and an islet enclose the basin at low tide. Since the reefs are covered at high water, the site is exposed to tidal action from Porlier Pass and southerly winds. Some anchorage may be found in an unnamed bight along the southwest shore. The Rose Islets Ecological Reserve is located off the north tip of Reid Island in Trincomali Channel. Established to protect nesting seabirds, this reserve is closed to the public.

★ **North Galiano (Spanish Hills) (18)**: A small public wharf with one float offers loading and unloading only. All other spaces are reserved. This is about one-half mile south of Alcala Point. An unnamed indentation farther south provides limited anchorage. Ruined pilings are in the bay and the northern portion is foul.

★ **Spotlight Cove**: This tiny bight was once used for log storage. Enter with caution and consult charts. Shelter can be found by anchoring and tying to shore.

★ **Retreat Cove (19)**: When entering, favor the south side. The northern part of the bay is shallow and has a few reefs to avoid (unmarked rocks abound.) There is land drying behind Retreat Island. There is barely enough room at the small public float for five or six boats and often locals fill the spots of this favorite moorage. Rafting is mandatory. Two or three boats can usually find space to anchor. This bay offers a small, but helpful, retreat in all but westerly winds. South of the float along the shore is a marine cave carved out of the sandstone. Once inside the mouth, the cave entrance makes a perfect frame for a photograph. A road from the public wharf connects with Porlier Pass Road. A number of artist studios are found off of Porlier Pass Road, south of Retreat Cove. North of the cove approximately 7-9 kms/4-5 miles, Bodega Ridge offers hiking opportunities (easy to moderate difficulty). The reward is worth the effort as the ridge offers spectacular views to Wallace Island and beyond to Salt Spring and Vancouver Islands. Bodega Ridge is also the location of Stone World, a free outdoor art display of huge stone carvings and mini-Stonehenge like arrangements created by eccentric Hungarian forester, Steve Ocsko. You can easily spend an hour or two walking through the fields admiring his unexpected and amazing work.

Walk-around: It is possible to walk across to Pebble Beach, overlooking the Strait of Georgia. Walk on Retreat Cove Road up to Polier Pass Road (Galiano's main road) and turn right. Immediately turn left onto McCoskrie Road, go up over the hill

Cruising Maple Bay   Photo © Carol Messier

and look for the Pebble Beach sign. From here it is a 10 minute hike down the trail to the beach. The trail actually accesses two beaches. First is Cable Bay Beach and around the corner you'll find Pebble Beach - a great place for picnics or for kids to play. The waters on this side of the island are said to be warmer than those of the west side, so swimmers also enjoy this beach.

★ **Montague Harbour (20)**: This beautiful, protected harbour is the site of Montague Harbour Marine Park with dock facilities, mooring buoys, and anchorage. The government dock (one of the most heavily used ports in the South Gulf Islands) and Montague Harbour Marina, just to the southeast, also offer moorage. The government dock, while usually full with local boats, may have transient moorage available. Reserved areas are marked in yellow. Tie dinghies to the dinghy dock only. A payment box is at the head of the gangway. Adjacent to the dock is the Montague Harbour Marina where you'll find scooter and boat rentals (call 250-889-4764), kayak rentals (call 250-539-2442), and local arts and crafts at a small gift shop on-site. Anchorage is good in several areas of the harbour. One such spot is on the shore opposite the park where Winstanley Point forms a sheltered corner. Another possibility is found in Payne Bay on a sand and mud bottom. Private floats extend into this bay and anchorage can be a bit lumpy because of the numerous craft which travel en route to the park. If anchored in Montague Harbour you can dingy over to the dock in the Marine Park, tie up and visit Shell Beach. This is a great spot for a swim (a gradual slope) or an evening walk along the beach and around Grays Peninsula to stretch your legs and enjoy a memorable sunset.

Montague Harbour is also known as the site of an unusual underwater archaeological dig. Researchers in the 1990's explored approximately 250 feet offshore in depths of about 20 feet. A harpoon and floral organic matter found under about three feet of sediment showed through carbon dating that they could be as much as 6,700 years old.

Montague Harbour is a "No Dump Zone," Approved holding tank required.

Montague Harbour is a Customs, Nexus only check-in location.

Montague Harbour — Photo © Dale Simonson

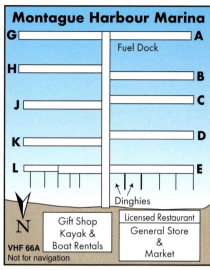

★ **Montague Harbour Marina**: {48° 53' 30" N, 123° 24'W} Located on the sunny south facing shoreline of the harbour, the Marina and licensed restaurant are built on pilings right over the water. The Marina offers a fuel station with gasoline and diesel , WiFi and garbage/recycling drop-off included with overnight moorage, 15 and 30 amp power, a well-stocked market and general store/ice cream parlour. In addition, they are dog friendly, have 5 dining options, a gift shop, moped/boat rentals, and kayak outfitter. Friendly staff and management are always on the docks to assist boats upon arrival and help out anyway they can. There are hiking and walking trails nearby, as well as excellent crabbing and fishing. Large dinghy dock available for any boaters on anchor or mooring buoys who want to enjoy the marina's shopping and dining. Open May - September. Reservations are highly recommended. See our advertisement on page 145 and the outside back cover. www.montagueharbour.com. Phone: 250-539-5733. VHF 66A.

★ **Montague Harbour Marine Park**: {48° 54' 0" N, 123° 24' 15" W} Established in 1959, this beautiful park was the first marine park in B.C. If approaching from the western entrance, be aware of rocks, submerged at high tide, extending off Gray Peninsula. Picnic sites, campsites, sandy beaches, hiking trails, a landing dock for dinghies, boat launch, and 35 mooring buoys (fee applies) are located here. Water is available. Swimming, fishing, kayaking and canoeing are popular aquatic activities.

Parker, Wallace, and Secretary Islands

[3441, 3442, 3463]

★ **Parker Island (21)**: The anvil-shaped piece of land that extends off Parker Island toward Gray Peninsula offers two unnamed bays back-to-back. These bays have anchoring possibilities. The northern bay has a fairly even bottom throughout, becoming shallow only at the head. This provides adequate anchorage, except when northwest winds are expected. The southern bay contains some ruins, dolphins, pilings, and a sometimes-present barge, that need to be considered when finding a spot to drop the hook. When proceeding north from Parker Island it is possible to use the passage between Charles and Wise Islands. Avoid the Ballingall Islets which stretch northwestward for some distance.

★ **Wallace Island Provincial Marine Park (22)**: {48° 56' 32" N, 123° 33' 5" W} This island is near mid-channel at the base of the Secretary Group in Trincomali Channel. All of the island, except two parcels on Princess Bay, is provincial park land. Caution advised off Wallace Island, when entering either Princess Bay or Conover Cove because foul ground, consisting of rocky islets and shoals, extends about 1½ miles in a southeast to northwest direction, framing the west side of the island. Trailer boats access the island by launching at Fernwood on Salt Spring Island. Sheltered anchorage and stern tie rings are available in Conover Cove and Princess Bay. There is also a small dock at Conover Cove, (for vessels less than 36') and a dinghy dock at Princess Bay. Campsites are located at Conover Cove, Cabin Bay, and Chivers Point. No fresh water is available. No fires. Fees charged for dock moorage, rings, and camping. Other park facilities include pit toilets, picnic tables, an information shelter and various walking trails. Sailors find the prevailing winds, which funnel between this island grouping and the steep cliffs of Galiano, excellent for a brisk afternoon sail.

★ **Princess Bay**: An anvil-shaped peninsula separates Princess Bay and Conover Cove. This bay provides overnight anchorage as close to the head of the bay as overnight depths will permit. Stern tie rings on shore. The bottom is even until the shallow shelf at the head. Beautiful madronas surround the cove. Two parcels on shore are private property, and not park land. No trespassing. A trail connects Princess Bay with Conover Cove.

★ **Conover Cove**: Entrance to this well protected nook is very narrow and shallow left of center when going in at low tide. Anchoring space is limited. A float that can accommodate approximately four 30' boats offers moorage. Shallow spots in the cove make it desirable to check overnight depths in the tide book and take soundings to find an appropriate position. Northwest of the float a few pings have been driven into the rocks for shore ties. Pilings near the dock can be used for stern ties. Picnic site and pit toilet on shore.

★ **Secretary Islands (23)**: The two Secretary Islands are connected by a drying sand and gravel ledge. A small bight is formed north of the ledge. Anchorage is possible. Approach from Trincomali Channel, not Houston Passage.

Tent, Penelakut, and Thetis Islands

[3442, 3443, 3463, 3477]

Tent Island (24): This is First Nations reservation land. There is no public access. Anchorage is possible.

Penelakut Island & Lamalchi Bay (25): North of Tent Island, separated by a shoal which is covered at high tide, is Penelakut Island. Previously known as Kuper Island, this island is the home of the Penelakut Band and is a First Nations Reserve. If the bay at Tent Island is too crowded, Lamalchi Bay provides temporary anchorage and a good swimming hole. The bay is shallow, making soundings and reference to tide charts advisable.

★ **Clam Bay (26)**: This large bay is located at the eastern end of the channel separating Penelakut and Thetis Islands. Rocket Shoal and Centre Reef, located in the center of the bay, are well defined by kelp and a red buoy on Centre Reef. Anchorage in 20-30 feet on a mud bottom is found south of Rocket Shoal in the southeast part of Clam Bay, bordering Penelakut Island. When fresh northwesterlies are roaring on Georgia Strait, this anchorage gets rollers and is uncomfortable. Another anchorage, more protected from northwesterlies, is on the northwest shore, avoiding the rocks and shoals to the east.

Boat Passage: [3477] This channel has been dredged since 1905, but silting is continual. Known locally as "the cut," it separates Thetis and Penelakut Islands and, at high tide, serves as a convenient short cut between Telegraph Harbour and Trincomali Channel. This narrow, almost a one-way only passage dries, so it may be used only at or near high water. To check the channel's water depths before entering, read the scale shown on pilings at either end of the channel. On the west end of the channel the marker is kept to port upon entering and starboard when leaving. On the east end, passage is between the two pilings at the entrance. Approach slowly because it is important to minimize wash and to stay in the center as much as possible. There is a sharp curve

near the Telegraph Harbour entrance. Use Fulford Harbour tide chart adjusted for Preedy Harbour. When you have 3 feet at Fulford Harbour, the cut is dry. To determine safe water to transit the cut, add your draft and your safety factor to the 3 feet. If your boat draws 4 feet, you need a minimum of 7 feet at Fulford to clear the cut; the number of feet you add to that is your safety factor. Current floods east, ebbs west.

Thetis Island: Home to about 350 permanent residents, this unspoiled and relatively undeveloped island locale offers a pleasing climate of warm, dry summers and mild winters, and a chance to boat, swim, walk or just relax and enjoy the scenic beauty. A number of businesses, services, and annual summer camps operate here, and a well-trained Fire Department and First Responders are available for emergencies. The *Thetis Island Regatta*, an all-day race around both Thetis and Penelakut Islands is held each May. Visit www.thetisisland.net for a downloadable Visitors' Guide, map, and other helpful information about Thetis Island.

★ **North Cove (27):** Completely exposed to the north, temporary anchorage is possible in the southeast corner and near the entrance to Cufra Inlet. Cufra Inlet cuts into Thetis for about one mile and, although beautiful, is useless to the boater except by dinghy.

★ **Preedy Harbour (28):** Site of the Thetis Island-Chemainus ferry landing. Adjacent to the ferry wharf is a small community float used primarily for emergencies or load/unloading. No overnight moorage allowed. Shoal areas are marked. Anchorage on a mud bottom can be found on the north side of the harbour, north of the sunken cable.

Telegraph Harbour

[3442, 3463, 3477]

★ **Telegraph Harbour (29):** Tucked between Penelakut and Thetis Islands, this attractive harbour has two marinas and limited anchorage with good holding in sand and mud with protection from most winds. Navigation markers delineate the channel in and out of the inner harbour. Watch depths carefully when traversing the channel. Be aware that the channel can be a busy place with boats and seaplane traffic, and remember that there is limited maneuvering room at low water. Private mooring buoys take up much of the inner harbour, so the usual anchorage is south of Thetis Island Marina on the western side. Provisions are available at the marinas and The Howling Wolf Farm Market. A summertime Saturday Market is held 10am-2pm at the latter featuring homemade specialties, baked goods, local artwork and crafts. Be sure to stop and meet Dora Wilson who knits Cowichan Sweaters, which are sold at the market and visit with SolarBud, an artist who creates images using the sun's rays and a magnifying glass. Visitors are welcome to try their hand at the craft during the Fair or daily (provided the sun is out). Other local attractions include what is reported to be the largest Arbutus (Madrona) tree in B.C., and Jollity Farm where organic in-season produce can be purchased on Saturday mornings. A community centre often hosts movies or concerts. On North Cove Road, The Thetis Island Nature Conservancy's Nature House offers beach and forest walks, nature art and crafts, displays, hands on activities and more, three days a week in July and August.

Howling Wolf Farm Market: Where East Meets West! Produce, poultry, meat, eggs, seafood, homemade specialties, award-winning pies. Open year round. For special requests call 250-246-2650.

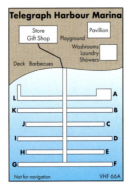

Telegraph Harbour Marina: {48° 58' N, 123° 40' W} Located in the very back of the bay in Telegraph Harbour. Guest moorage, monthly winter moorage, 30 amp power, water, laundry, showers, BBQ/picnic area, covered pavilion, free wifi, store with groceries, produce, deli, esspresso, gifts. 250-246-9511. VHF 66A.

Thetis Island Marina: {48° 65' N, 123° 40' W} Moorage, 15/30 amp power, water, gas, diesel, propane, showers, laundry, free WiFi for guests, lodging, BBQ/picnic area, store, post office, restaurant, pub, liquor store. Marina: 250-246-3464. VHF 66A.

Walk-around: From Telegraph Harbour it is possible to walk to the ferry landing in Preedy Harbour and ferry to Chemainus. Check with Telegraph Harbour Marina for the ferry schedule.

Vancouver Island Central East Coast

[3313, 3441, 3442, 3443, 3462, 3463, 3475, 3478]

★ **Evening Cove (30):** Located between Sharpe Point and Coffin Point, this bay has anchorage near the head in 10-20 feet of water. It is exposed to southeast winds. Private buoys are in the inner bay.

★ **Sibell Bay (31):** Homes overlook a long crescent-shaped beach. A Seattle Yacht Club outstation is located on Ovens Island, the most easterly of the Dunsmuir Islands, which frames the southwest side of Sibell Bay. Anchor in Sibell Bay itself or go around the Dunsmuir Islands and anchor off Bute Island. Log booms are prevalent here and in nearby Burleigh Arm. Commercial oyster beds are also in the vicinity.

Ladysmith

[3443, 3463, 3475]

★ **Ladysmith (32):** Several moorage options, including Fisherman's Wharf, Oyster Bay Marina, and the Ladysmith Marina line the Ladysmith waterfront. All are within walking distance of town. By car, Nanaimo's airport is a 10-minute drive and two BC Ferry terminals connecting to Vancouver, along with the new Hullo Ferry, are only 20 minutes from moorage. On shore is a large concrete, no-fee launching ramp. A tidal grid, for emergency repairs, is by the wharf. Raven Point Inn & Marina is directly across the harbour from the Ladysmith Marina (Oak Bay Marine Group). The Ladysmith Yacht Club is located with Ladysmith Marina (Oak Bay Marine Group). As of June 2018, a wreck with a known depth of 5.1 metres reported in the harbour at 49° 00' 11.6"N, 123° 48' 50.0" W.

Set on a hillside, this delightful, friendly town has many attractions and special events. Hop on the Public Transit Bus to Nanaimo, Chemainus or Duncan and beyond, or call Go Taxi, 250-324-8294/Ladysmith Taxi, 250-210-1027, or walk up the hill from the waterfront to the heritage downtown. Founded in 1904 by James Dunsmuir, the town's name commemorates the British victory ending the siege of Ladysmith in the South African Boer War. Many streets are named for British Generals who served in the Boer War. The community's history of coal and forest industries are highlighted along the Ladysmith Heritage Walking Route. For more historic perspective, check out the museum at 721 First Ave, www.ladysmithhistoricalsoiety.ca/museum, or call 250-245-0423 for hours.

For your shopping needs, Ladysmith has a variety of stores that include grocery, pharmacy, candy, flowers, gifts, an art gallery, housewares, jewelry, hardware, variety, liquor, fashions, a butcher and a bakery. Services include banks, laundry, hair salons, dental, chiropractic, veterinary, auto repair and supply. There are also a number of wonderful restaurants, cafés, pubs and Micro Brewery! For those who enjoy a swim or sauna, the Community Centre pool & fitness centre is on 6th Ave. On the waterfront, Transfer Beach Park has an excellent swimming beach, children's splash park, playground, kayak and SUP rentals/lessons, heritage display boards, and picnic areas. There are Food Trucks at the beach from the May long weekend until Labour Day, daily from 11-7. Along Davis Road, golfers will find a par 3 course. To enjoy the area's natural beauty, walk the 5.8 km Holland Creek Trail loop that winds along both banks and past a waterfall. The Ladysmith Chamber of Commerce/Visitor Information Centre at 33 Roberts Street provides maps of local parks and trails, a self-guided walking tour brochure of heritage buildings and artifacts, and other information about activities and points-of-interest at this, the 49th Parallel Town and the surrounding area.

Summer events include the *Brits on the Beach Car Show* at Transfer Beach, popular *Arts on the Avenue & Light up the Night*, the *Show & Shine* (vintage & antique automobiles), and Sunday evening Concerts in the Park at the waterfront amphitheatre. *Ladysmith Days*, held the first weekend in August, includes a pancake breakfast, downtown parade, fireworks, live music, vendors and activities. Boaters usually anchor off Transfer Beach to watch the fireworks. *Loggers Sports* is typically held at the Transfer Beach Amphitheatre on the Sunday of the Labor Day weekend. For other fun activities and events, www.tourismladysmith.ca.

Ladysmith Fisherman's Wharf: {40° 0' 00" N, 123° 35' 56" W} Permanent and transient moorage, fishing vessels take priority. 30/50 amp power, water, showers (available when Harbourmaster is onsite), washrooms, garbage disposal, two tidal grids (to 50'), launch ramp, derrick. 250-245-7511.

Ladysmith Marina: {49° 0' 15"N, 123° 50' 15" W} Permanent and guest moorage (vessels to 100'), water, 30/50 amp power, showers, wifi available, security. Ladysmith Yacht Club is the floating building. 250-245-4521. VHF 66A.

Oyster Bay Marina: {48° 59' 8.2" N, 123° 48.769 W} Moorage, water, 30 amp power, pumpout, showers, restaurant and laundry. 250-245-1146.

Raven Point Landing Ltd: {49° 00.615 N, 123° 49.389 W} Permanent and transient moorage, 30 amp power, water, laundry, washrooms, free showers, wifi, lodging, restaurant. 250-245-2312 VHF 66A.

Chemainus
[3443, 3463, 3475]

Kin Beach Provincial Park Photo © Chemainus + District Chamber of Commerce

★ **Chemainus (33):** This quaint seaside town has long been on itineraries of many boating families. Limited moorage can be found at the Municipal Marina. Adjacent to the Municipal Marina at the foot of Oak Street in Old Town Chemainus is the Chemainus-Thetis Island-Penelakut Island ferry landing.

Facilities and services include a large variety of specialty and gift shops, restaurants, B & B's, live theatre, park and picnic areas, art galleries, and a laundromat and two well-stocked grocery stores within easy distance to moorage.

Attractions appeal to the entire family. Chemainus boasts Canada's largest outdoor gallery of giant murals, drawn from actual historical photographs and events. At present there are 47 murals in the original Historical Series, 5 murals in the Emily Carr Series and 9 murals in the Community Series as well as 50 sculptures. For a self guided mural tour, follow the footprints painted on the sidewalks or purchase the official Mural Tour Guide Map from the Visitor Centre. All proceeds go to the Festival of Murals Society to refurbish the older murals and paint new ones in the future! Enjoy the horse drawn carriage (seasonally, by appointment) and learn about the history of the town and Cowichan Valley. Lovers of the Arts will also want to visit the landmark Chemainus Lunch/Dinner Theatre with matinée and evening performances, or catch a live, outdoor musical performance during the summer at the Bandshell at Waterwheel Park. A playground, as well as The Chemainus Valley Museum are also located at this park. For Museum hours, 250-246-2445. If you visit at the end of June, don't miss *Summer Fest* featuring musical entertainment, a parade, pancake breakfast and children's activities. The *Giant Street Market Day* on the second Saturday in July (the 13th in 2024) is another fun family event. A weekly market (make it, bake it or grow it) runs every Wednesday, 10am-3pm May to September. Pack a picnic, don your swimsuit and head to Kin Beach Park or Fuller Lake. Both have a playground, boat ramp, and swimming beach. Nearby, Mt. Brenton Golf Course has something for every level of golfer and Fuller Lake Arena offers ice skating fun. Scuba diving is possible just off Chemainus at the Xihwu Boeing 737 artificial reef {48° 56.142N, 123° 43.130W}.

The Chemainus Valley is one of the oldest European settlements on Vancouver Island, dating to the 1850's. A small water-powered sawmill began operations in 1862, and became known for having the longest continuous period of lumber production (over 125 years) in western Canada. Chemainus' Horseshoe Bay became a center for lumber shipments as well as the oldest deep seaport on Canada's west coast. In 1980, anticipating the closing of the mill in this one industry town, residents established a Downtown Revitalization Project with Provincial assistance. From the belief that their history was too important to be forgotten, came the idea of bringing the community's heritage to life on the walls of the village buildings and Chemainus became known as "The Little Town That Did." For more information about Chemainus, visit the Chemainus Visitor Centre in Waterwheel Square or call 250-737-3368.

Chemainus Municipal Marina: {48° 55' 29" N, 123° 42' 54" W} 685' of transient moorage (reservations recommended), water, 30/50 amp power, wifi, showers, restrooms, security gates. Limited space for day use on outside float only, two hour limit, must vacate by 3:00 pm. Limited space for dinghies. Garbage drop for marina guests only. 250-246-4655 or 250-715-8186. VHF 66A.

★ **Crofton (34) [3475, 3442]:** The community of Crofton is located on the hillside behind Osborn Bay. A BC ferry terminal, with ferries connecting hourly with Vesuvius on Salt Spring Island, is found here. Crofton Public Floats are tucked in behind a breakwater, adjacent to the ferry terminal. Expect the public docks to be very full during the commercial prawn season, usually early May-June. A boat launch gives quick access to good fishing grounds. Pubs offer food and weekend entertainment. Two well-stocked grocery stores, some small shops, and restaurants are nearby. Lodging is accessible. The Old Schoolhouse Museum on the waterfront makes an interesting stop. Play and picnic at Osborne Bay Park or Crofton Beach. Marine gas and diesel are available at the Shell station, not on the wharf. Four area parks have good mountain bike and hiking trails. Crofton was founded by Henry Croft in the early 1900's. Croft, a lumber and mining magnate, developed the prosperous Lenora mine at nearby Mount Sicker. He bought the land, named the townsite after himself, and constructed an Opera House, as well as a copper smelter. When copper prices plummeted in 1908, the smelter closed. In 1956, BC Forest Products developed a modern pulp and paper mill north of town that produced for 53 years.

Crofton Public Floats: {48° 51' 55.381" N, 123° 38' 20.4966" W} Permanent & transient moorage, 30 amp power, water, restrooms, showers (key available at ferry toll booth), pay phone, security gates. Laundry one block away. 250-246-4655.

Osborne Bay Resort: {48° 51' 46.88" N, 123° 38' 21.245" W} Moorage for resort guests only, boats to 18', at your own risk. RV/camping sites, cottages, restroom, laundry, play area. 250-246-4787.

★ **Duncan:** While not located on the waterfront, there is easy access to Duncan from Maple Bay Marina by way of shuttles for marina guests (fee applies) or taxi service, rental cars, and nearby bus service. Duncan has a great variety of unique shops, restaurants, grocery stores, and liquor outlets. Located in the heart of a wine producing, culinary, dairy farming and market garden region, Duncan is a commercial and cultural hub approximately midway between Victoria and Nanaimo. The area is home to artisan cheesemakers, bakers, and ice cream makers. It is also a key winery, cidery, brewery and distillery destination, with opportunities for tasting and guided tours. Ask the team at the Cowichan Regional Visitor Centre or Maple Bay Marina for more information. Outdoor activities abound, including hiking and cycling. About 20 minutes south of Duncan is the magnificent Kinsol Trestle, one of the world's largest free standing wooden structures and one of the highest hiking trestles in North America. There are 4 golf courses within 30 minutes of the marina.

Duncan has the distinction of being the world's only dedicated totem city. Approximately 40 unique, original First Nations works adorn the Old Town in Duncan. Cedar Man Holding Talking Stick, the world's widest totem was carved from a tree estimated to be 775 years old. The BC Forest Discovery Centre displays the history of coastal forests and the lumber industry. Take a train ride around the 100 acre site. Throughout the year special event days offer reduced rates, fun activities, crafts, and entertainment. 250-715-1113. At Canada Avenue and Station Street, the Cowichan Valley Museum and Archives, housed inside a 1912 train station, offers free totem tours from mid-June through mid-Sept. 250-746-6612. You can also pick up totem tour maps at

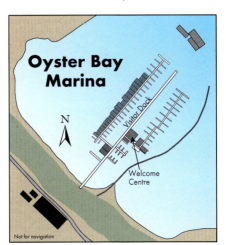

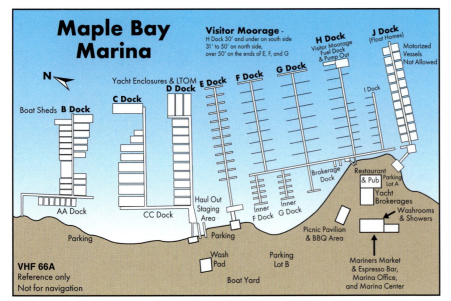

the Cowichan Regional Visitor Centre and take a self-guided totem tour. A year round Saturday Farmers Market, rated one of the best in BC, is held in City Square 10am-2pm. Visit the Hand of Man Natural History Museum, open 365 days a year, 6759 Considine Ave, Maple Bay, 1-888-826-1011 (about a 10 minute drive from Maple Bay Marina). A short drive from town, visitors encounter amazing birds of prey at The Raptors. For open hours and daily scheduled flying demonstrations, call 250-746-0372. The Cowichan Regional Visitor Centre at 2896 Drinkwater Road has maps and information on attractions, events, hiking trails and parks. 250-746-4636 - call to have a visitor package mailed.

Maple Bay
[3442, 3462, 3478]

★ **Maple Bay (35):** [3462, 3478] Entry from the south into this lovely bay is made by rounding landmark Paddy Mile Stone. The bay itself may seem reminiscent of a Swiss lake. The public float, directly west after entering the bay, is open to winds and to wash from boats entering and leaving Bird's Eye Cove. It has 300' of dock space and water is available at the bottom of the ramp. Local facilities and services include marinas, fueling station, a market with provisions and internet, restaurants, repair facilities, float plane service, kayak rentals, and Maple Bay Yacht Club. Downtown Duncan is 11km/6mi from Maple Bay Marina. A shuttle for marina customers is available (fee applies), as are taxis. If you like to hike, there are miles of trails on Mt. Tzouhalem. Stop by Maple Bay Marina for a hiking brochure. Tidal flats and a park reserve at the head of Birds Eye Cove can be explored by dinghy. Afternoon breezes of 10-20 knots in the north part of the bay are normal in summer months, providing good sailing and windsurfing conditions. Scuba diving is popular in the area. Diving and racing markers may be present.

★ **Maple Bay Marina:** {N 48° 47.742', W 123° 35.942'} Famous for breathtaking views and stunning natural beauty, Maple Bay Marina is the largest marina facility north of Sidney and Victoria - superbly sheltered in the Cowichan region on Vancouver Island. The marina features 300 slips (visitor, long term, and covered moorage), fuel dock, pump-out, propane, water, laundromat, showers, a full service boatyard with a 50 ton Travelift, marine supplies, yacht sales office, The Shipyard Restaurant and Pub, Mariners Market & Espresso Bar, as well as a float home community. In addition, regular seaplane service by Harbour Air Seaplanes is available to Downtown Vancouver and the Vancouver International Airport's south terminal. Internet: www.maplebaymarina.com. Address: 6145 Genoa Bay Road, Duncan, British Columbia V9L 5T7. Telephone: Toll Free 1-866-746-8482, 250-746-8482. VHF 66A.

Bird's Eye Cove Marina: {48° 47' 58" N, 123° 36' 7" W} Permanent moorage. 15/30 amp power, water. 250-746-5686.

Sansum Narrows: This passageway has noticeable wave action from the currents. Good fishing. Aquaculture operations are in the vicinity.

★ **Genoa Bay (36):** This bay opens off the northern shore of Cowichan Bay. Keep the red day-beacon on the starboard side and watch the green spar buoy, about 500 yards south of the charted position. There is good anchorage on a mud bottom. Exposure to southeast winds can be a problem, in which case the western shore offers the best protection. A marina, restaurant, and an eclectic mix of floathouses are located here. Exploring the bay by small craft, crabbing, and wildlife watching are popular activities. Hiking is also a possibility, a trail leads from the marina to a scenic viewpoint on Mount Tzouhalem, a 45 minute, moderately difficult hike. Genoa Bay is connected to Duncan and Cowichan Bay by road and taxis are available.

Genoa Bay Marina: {48° 45' 33" N, 123° 35' 55" W} Permanent and transient moorage, 15/30/50 amp power, water, showers, laundry, restroom, launch, store, café, wifi, EBike rentals. 250-746-7621, 1-800-572-6481. VHF 66A.

Cowichan Bay
[3441, 3462, 3478]

★ **Cowichan Bay (37):** Cowichan Bay is a small village, yet reflects the history of being a deep sea port. A rip-rap rock breakwater in the bay has a floating breakwater that accommodates vessels to 100 ft. No power at present. Enter Cowichan Bay with the breakwater to your port side and turn into the harbour. Cowichan Bay is home to the First Nation Cowichan Tribes. In the Hul'qumi'num language, spoken by the Cowichan Tribes, the word "Cowichan" means "warm land". Along the waterfront are marinas, repair facilities, shipyards and a well stocked marine supply store.

Cowichan Bay has a wonderful selection of shops offering an array of services and goods (including the famed Cowichan Sweaters). You'll find a bakery, a custom cheese shop, a pub, post office, artisan's studios, market & liquor store, and some wonderful restaurants. Hotel, motel, and B & B's provide lodging. Kayak and paddle board rentals are also available. The warm climate and fertile soil of the region's sloping terrain are perfect for growing grapes. Several local wineries offer tours, tastings and on-site bistros. Of special interest to visiting families is the Cowichan Bay Maritime Centre featuring classes, workshops, events, exhibits, children's boat building booth and museum displays along an 82 metre pier. Admission by donation. 250-746-4955. The Cowichan Bay Estuary Nature Centre has a touch tank, microscopes, telescopes, interactive displays and an interesting gift shop. 250-597-2288.

Walk to Hecate Park for a picnic or to enjoy the beach area. The park also has a boat launch with trailer parking. Take in a game of tennis or golf or take a short bus ride to Duncan. Annual events include First Nations canoe races, *Spot Prawn Festival* in May, *Cowichan Wooden Boat Festival* in July and the *Cowichan Bay Regatta* in August. Fishing at Sansum Narrows is three miles away and Cowichan Bay is known for some of the best Dungeness crabbing in the area.

Bluenose Marina: {48° 44' 26" N, 123° 37' 21" W} Permanent & transient moorage, 30/50 amp power, laundry, showers, restaurant, ice cream, art for sale, kayak rentals/tours. 250-748-2222.

Classic Marine Ltd: Marine supplies, chandlery, gifts, restaurant, motor boat rentals. 250-746-1093. VHF 66A.

Cowichan Bay Harbour Fisherman's Wharf: {48° 44' 28" N, 123° 37' 3" W} All-tide entry channel behind 500' Floating Breakwater. Permanent & transient moorage (no reservations, call ahead for availability), 30 amp power, water, garbage deposit, washrooms, showers, laundry. Short stays free before 2pm. After 2pm overnight moorage fee applies. 250-746-5911. VHF 66A.

Cowichan Wooden Boat Society: Limited monthly & temporary moorage. Marine ways to 10 tons/12' beam and 6' depth, boat yard, workshop. Services/facilities available to members only. (membership fee $45 for single, $60 for family, per year). 250-746-4955.

Masthead Marina & Restaurant: {48° 44' 29"N, 123° 37' 5" W} Permanent moorage, power. Complimentary tie-up while dining for vessels to 22'. 250-748-3714.

Pier 65 (Dungeness Marina): {48° 44' 27" N, 123° 37' 17" W 48°} Permanent and transient moorage, 30 amp power, water, washroom, showers. 250-748-6789.

Pier 66 Marina: {48° 44' 26" N, 123° 37' 15" W} Permanent moorage, 15/30 amp power, laundry, fuel (mid-grade gas & diesel by appointment only), oil, chandlery, grocery/liquor store, two take-out restaurants, bakery. Marina: 250-748-6789. Store: 250-748-8444.

The Oceanfront Suites at Cowichan Bay: {48° 44.4037 N', 123° 37.077' W} Moorage for hotel guests (no onboard sleeping permitted). Boats must draw less than 3 ½', no power, call ahead for availability. 1-800-663-7898, 250-715-1000.

Visit us at boattravel.com

Essential Supplies & Services

AIR TRANSPORTATION

To & from Washington
Kenmore Air 1-866-435-9524
NW Seaplanes . . . 425-277-1590, 1-800-690-0086
San Juan Airlines. 1-800-874-4434
Seattle Seaplanes 1-800-637-5553

To & from Islands/Vancouver
Air Canada 1-888-247-2262
Gulf Island Seaplanes (Thetis Island) . . . 250-247-9992
Harbour Air 1-800-665-0212
Salt Spring Air 1-877-537-9880
Seair 1-800-447-3247

BOOKS / BOOK STORES

Evergreen Pacific Publishing 425-493-1451
The Marine Atlas. 253-872-5707

BUS TRANSPORTATION

Cowichan Regional Transit 250-746-9899
Greyhound/Pacific Coach Lines 250-385-4411
Salt Spring Island Bus 250-537-6758
Or (24 hr recorded info) 250-538-4282

COAST GUARD

Victoria Coast Guard Radio. . . . . VHF 16, 83a
. . . . 1-800-661-9202 (In BC) or 250-363-6611
Marine Distress, Search & Rescue
. . . . 1-800-567-5111 (in Canada) or 250-413-8933
Cell Phone (limited to select providers) . . . *16 or #727

CUSTOMS

Call 1-888-226-7277
Ganges-Breakwater Float Nexus Marine only
Montague Harbour Marina Nexus Marine only

FERRY INFORMATION

B.C. Ferries 1-888-223-3779

FISHING / SHELLFISHING INFO

24 hr Recorded Notifications
. . . . .1-866-431-3474 (Pacific region only),
Or Call 604-666-2828
Recreational Licensing. 1-877-535-7307
Observe, Record, & Report Line (fisheries violations) . .
1-800-465-4336
Pacific region only. 604-607-4186

FUELS

Ganges Marina: Gas, Diesel . . . 250-537-5242 VHF 66A
Maple Bay Marina: Gas, Diesel
. . . . 866-746-8482 VHF 66A
Montague Harbour Marina 250-539-5733 VHF 66A
Pier 66: Cowichan Bay gas diesel by apt 250-748-8444
Thetis Island Marina: Gas, Diesel
. . . . 250-246-3464 VHF 66A

GOLF COURSES

These courses are accessible from moorage and have rental clubs available)
Arbutus Ridge: Cobble Hill 250-743-5000
Cowichan Golf Club: Duncan 250-746-5333
Duncan Meadows 250-746-8993
Mount Brenton: Chemainus 250-246-9322
Galiano Island: From Montague Harbour 250-539-5533
Salt Spring Island: From Ganges 250-537-2121

HAUL-OUTS

Cowichan Wooden Boat Society. 250-746-4955
Harbours End Marine . . . 250-537-4202 VHF 16 or 66A
Lindstrom Marine, Maple Bay. . 250-748-9199 VHF 66A

HOSPITALS

Healthlink BC (Nurse Helpline) 811
Chemainus Healthcare Center. 250-737-2040
Cowichan District Hospital 250-737-2030
Ganges, Salt Spring Island 250-538-4800
Ladysmith Community Health Centre . . . 250-739-5777

LIQUOR / WINE STORES

Chemainus
Crofton
Fulford
Ladysmith
Thetis Island Maring
Cowichan Bay (Pier 66)
Duncan
Ganges, Salt Spring
Sturdies Bay, Galiano Is

LODGING

Galiano Oceanfront Inn & Spa . . . 1-877-530-3939
Hastings House Country House Hotel, Dining Room &
Spa 1-800-661-9255, 250-537-2362
Oceanfront Suites at Cowichan Bay 250-715-1000
Page Point Inn, Ladysmith 250-245-2312

MARINAS / MOORAGE

Bird's Eye Cove: Maple Bay . . 250-746-5686, VHF 66A
Bluenose Marina: Cowichan Bay. 250-748-2222
Chemainus Municipal Marina . . 250-246-4655 VHF 66A
Conover Cove: Wallace Island
Cowichan Bay Harbour . . . . 250-746-5911 VHF 66A
Crofton Public Floats 250-246-4655
Fernwood: Salt Spring Island
Ganges Marina . . . . 250-537-5242 VHF 66A
Genoa Bay Marina. . . . . 250-746-7621 VHF 66A
Ladysmith Marina. . . . . 250-245-4521 VHF 66A
Ladysmith Fisherman's Wharf 250-245-7511
Lyall Harbour: Saturna Island
Maple Bay Marina . . . . . . 866-746-8482 VHF 66A
Maple Bay Public Float 250-246-4655
Montague Harbour Marina 250-539-5733 VHF 66A
Oyster Bay Marina 250-245-1146
Page Point Inn: Ladysmith . . . . 250-245-2312 VHF 66A
Pier 65 (Dungeness Marina). 250-748-6789
Pier 66: Cowichan Bay, permanent. 250-748-6789
Preedy Harbour: Thetis Island
Retreat Cove: Galiano Island
Salt Spring Harbour Authority: 250-537-5711 VHF 9
Burgoyne Bay, Fulford Harbour (Inner and Outer-
Harbour Floats), Ganges (Breakwater, Kanaka,
Centennial), Musgrave Landing, Vesuvius.
Salt Spring Marina, Ganges. 250-537-5810
. . . . 1-800-334-6629 VHF 66A
Sturdies Bay: Galiano Island
Telegraph Harbour Marina . .250-246-9511 VHF 66A
Thetis Island Marina. . . . . 250-246-3464 VHF 66A
Whaler Bay: Galiano Island. 250-539-2264

MARINE SUPPLIES & PARTS

Classic Marine Ltd, Cowichan Bay 250-746-1093
Harbours End Marine & Equipment
. . . . 250-537-4202 VHF 16
Lindstrom Marine, Maple Bay. . 250-748-9199 VHF 66A
Mouat's, Ganges. 1-877-490-5593
Pier 66: Cowichan Bay 250-748-8444

PROPANE

Thetis Island Marina 250-246-3464

RAMPS

Cowichan Bay, Hecate Park . . . 250-746-5911 VHF 66A
Crofton Ferry Landing Ramp . . 250-246-4655 VHF 66A
Genoa Bay Marina: . . . . 250-746-7621 VHF 66A
Ladysmith Fisherman's Wharf 250-245-7511
Montague Harbour Marine Park
Salt Spring Harbour Authority, Centennial Wharf
(Ganges Boat Basin) . . . . 250-537-5711 VHF 9
Salt Spring Marina: Ganges 250-537-5810 VHF 66A

REPAIRS / SERVICE

Harbours End Marine . . . 250-537-4202 VHF 16 or 66A
Ladysmith Fisherman's Wharf
Lindstrom Marine, Maple Bay. 250-748-9199
Salt Spring Marina: Ganges 250-537-5810 VHF 66A

RESTAURANTS

Cow Cafe, Cowichan 250-597-4353
Galiano Oceanfront Inn & Spa . . . 1-877-530-3939
Moby's Pub 250-537-5559
Hastings House. 800-661-9255
Harbour Grill at Montague Harbour Marina
. . . . 250-539-2226
Rendezvous Cafe 250-537-5810
Shipyard Pub & Restaurant: Maple Bay
. . . . 250-746-1026
Woodley's: Ganges 250-537-4700

SCUBA SITES

Dionisio Point Provincial Park
Ruckle Provincial Park-Beaver Point
Chemainus, Maple Bay

SEWAGE DISPOSAL

Salt Spring Harbour Authority (Ganges Breakwater
Float). Pump . . . . 250-537-5711 VHF 9

TAXI / VEHICLE RENTALS

Chowichan Bay, Genoa, Maple Bay, Duncan
. . . . 250-746-4444, 1-888-748-9400
Galiano (scooter rentals) 250-539-5254
Ganges/Salt Spring Island 250-537-3030
Go Taxi (Ladysmith, Chemainus, Croft. . 250-324-8294
Ladysmith Taxi 250-729-6204

TOWING

C-TOW 1-888-419-CTOW
Fast Response 250-222-0076
Eagle Eye Marine . . . . . . 250-883-7865 (Vessel Assist)
Harbours End Marine . . . 250-537-4202 VHF 16 or 66A

VISITOR INFORMATION

Chemainus & District Chamber of Commerce & Visitor
Information Centre 250-737-3368
Duncan/Cowichan/Maple Bay
. . . . .1-888-303-3337 or 250-746-4636
Galiano Island Chamber 250-539-2233
Ladysmith Chamber of Commerce 250-245-2112
Salt Spring Island 250-537-5252, 1-866-216-2936

WEATHER:

Environment Canada Weather Line 250-339-9861
Canadian Coast Guard (recorded). 250-363-6492
Vancouver WX-3, 21-B

Chapter 11:
Gulf Islands North & Adjacent Vancouver Island East Coast

Kulleet Bay to Departure Bay. Nanaimo, Silva Bay, Pylades, Ruxton, De Courcy, Valdes, Gabriola, Mudge, & Newcastle Islands.

Page's Resort & Marina, Silva Bay - photo © Gloria Hatfield

Symbols

[ ]: Numbers between [ ] are chart numbers.
{ }: Numbers & letters between { } are waypoints.
★ Recommended destinations, facilities, and services
⚓ Park, ⛵: Boat Launch, ▲: Campgrounds,
🚶: Hiking Trails, ⛱: Picnic Area, 🚴: Biking,
🤿 Scuba

★ See "Important Notices" between Chapters 7 and 8 for specific information on boating related topics such as boating safety, weather, U.S. & Canadian marine radio use, Vessel Traffic Service, security zones, Canadian & U.S. Customs, etc. Due to changing regulations, call ahead to verify latest customs information.

★ No Dump Zone: Pilot Bay, Gabriola Island.

★ Introduction to the Gulf Islands: See the beginning of Chapter 9.

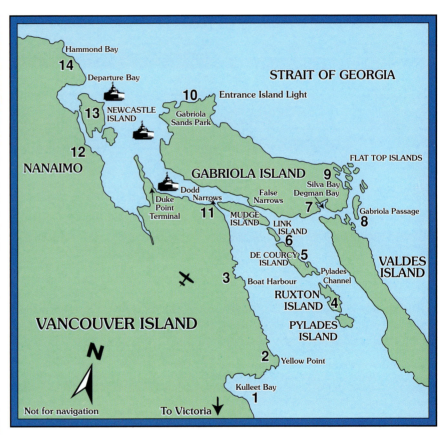

Vancouver Island South Of Nanaimo
[3443, 3463]

★ **Kulleet Bay (1):** This large bay offers anchorage, with protection from northwesterlies. Anchor close in to shore on a sand and shell ledge. Shoal areas are at the extreme head of the bay, and the bottom falls away steeply from the ledges. Open to east winds.

★ **Yellow Point (2):** This is a resort area, located where fish are often biting. Floats are private. North of Yellow Point, a shoal off shore extends southward from the northern shore of the bay and is covered at high tide. The shoal is well marked on charts. Onshore, unique outcroppings of sandstone can be seen.

Chart List

Canadian Hydrographic Charts:
   3313, 3443, 3447, 3458, 3463, 3475
NOAA Charts: 18400, 18402-03
Marine Atlas Vol 1 (2018):   Page 10, 22
Evergreen Cruising Atlas:
   Pages 101, 102, 103, 110, 111, 112, 114

★ **Boat Harbour (3):** Note reefs near the entrance. Anchorage is inside Flewett Point on the south side of the harbour. This harbour is known locally as Kenary Cove. The floats are private. Limited anchorage is possible behind Reynolds Point, farther in the harbour on the northwest side. The harbour is open to easterly winds.

De Courcy Area
[3443, 3463, 3475]

★ **Ruxton Island & Herring Bay (4):** When approaching Herring Bay on the northwest side of Ruxton, keep the day beacon to starboard. The outer limits of the bay are defined by drying reefs. Some kelp marks the reef that forms the eastern side of the entrance channel. Nearly all of the reefs are covered at high tide, making entry at that time more difficult. Entry may also be made from the southwest when the reefs are visible. Depths are 15-30 feet on a good holding sand bottom. Although partially protected by these reefs, this bay is exposed to west and northwest winds and offers little protection in a west wind. If boats shore tie, more space is available for anchorage in this relatively small cove. Seals often bask on the sandstone reefs.

★⚓ **Whaleboat Island Marine Park:** Located off the southeast tip of Ruxton Island, this park has rather unprotected anchorages. One spot is off Pylades Island in Whaleboat Passage. No amenities are onshore and rocky, steep terrain prevents much exploration.

★ **De Courcy Island:** Approximately 30 full time residents call this beautiful island home. Anchorage is found at the north end, in Pirate's Cove, and at the south tip of the island. De Courcy has an interesting history. In the 1920's it was the compound of Edward Arthur Wilson, an English Sea Captain, who, prior to coming to De Courcy, had first settled on Vancouver Island in his Great White Lodge and House of Mystery near Cedar Point. A self-declared prophet, Wilson pronounced that a meteor would destroy everything in the world except this area. His seemingly unbreakable trances through which he shared his visions, swayed many people to believe and become followers. He later moved his operations across to De Courcy and Valdes Islands. He and his companion, Madame Zee, were the highly unorthodox leaders of a cult community on De Courcy. It is said that the pair hoarded over $400,000 in bank notes and gold bricks that may still be hidden somewhere on Valdes Island. If you happen to meet an old-timer who relates these tales, or if you come upon a copy of the book, *Brother Twelve: The Incredible Story of Canada's False Prophet* by John Oliphant, you are in for an interesting story.

South Tip De Courcy Island (5): This bay is back-to-back with Pirate's Cove. The inner bay shallows. Wakes from passing boats can be uncomfortable. Private mooring buoys are in the bay to the west.

★⚓ **Pirate's Cove Marine Park (5):** [3475] When approaching the entrance, aim for the white arrow and range marker. The arrow is painted on the shore next to a set of stairs leading to a summer cabin. Stay well off the shoal to port that extends to the Day Beacon. The reef at the entrance extends well beyond this concrete marker. There is also a shoal on the starboard side, as you enter. It is marked by a red buoy. Pass between the red buoy and the Day Beacon. Anchoring in Pirate's Cove is not as simple as its popularity might indicate. Much of the bottom is soft mud and shale. Because of the crowded conditions, it is difficult to get sufficient scope. Secondly, many a boater has dropped a hook on the shelf that lies along the southern shore of the bay only to find that the anchor will not hold because of the insufficient mud there. Thirdly, a reef extends from the northeastern shore in a westerly direction. This reef dries at low tide. Rings for stern tie-ups are embedded in the rocks. No mooring fees apply. The Parks Department requests that you not tie to trees. Winds entering the cove have a swirling effect so boaters need to watch out for anchor dragging. There are two dinghy docks, one is to port upon entry and another lies to starboard farther into the cove. No overnight tie ups to the docks. The park has campsites, picnic area, drinking water, composting toilets, and hiking trails. No fires allowed. For a beautiful stroll, walk along the park land on the peninsula located on the cove's southeastern shore. Flat rocks, heated in the summer sun, are perfect spots for sun bathers. A path extends south to the cove overlooking Ruxton Passage. ▲🚶⛺

★ **Anchorage between De Courcy and Link Islands (6):** Link Island is connected to the north end of De Courcy Island and the south end of Mudge Island by drying ridges. There is a small niche between De Courcy and Link islands for temporary anchorage. Beware of an uncharted shoal in the center with only three feet of water covering it at low water. When approaching, note that a pesky rock is off the De Courcy shore north-northwest of Pirate's Cove, about 100 yards offshore. Use caution when heading to False Narrows from Link Island or Pirate's Cove. This rock has been coined, *Brother Twelve's Rock*. See history of Brother Twelve above.

Valdes Island: This long island is separated by Gabriola Pass on the northwest side and Porlier Pass on the southeast. Steep cliffs border much of the island. Valdes is a relatively uninhabited island, not linked by ferry service. Unusual rock formations appear to have faces watching you, and a rock house, in the style of Frank Lloyd Wright, is hidden among the ledges. There are attractive beaches near Blackberry, Shingle, and Cardale Points. There is temporary shelter on either side of these points, depending on the wind direction. Much of this land is First Nations Reservation land.

Page's Resort & Marina on Silva Bay — Photo © Gloria Hatfield

On the northern shore, anchorage is found in Wakes Cove near Cordero Point and in a bay formed between the three islets at Kendrick Island and the east shore of Valdes. Known locally as Dogfish Bay, it offers good sheltered anchorage and is often used by tugs awaiting favorable currents in Gabriola Pass.

⚓ **Wakes Cove Marine Park:** Avoid Wakes Cove in a northwest wind. Kelp may affect anchoring. Walking trails, no camping. Bald eagles, minks, otters and harbour seals are commonly spotted here. 🚶

Gabriola Island
[3443, 3458, 3463, 3475]

★ **Gabriola Island:** Gabriola Island has marina facilities in Silva Bay and a public wharf in Degnan Bay (primarily commercial boats). Boat launches are found at El Verano Dr. (False Narrows, watch for tidal currents), Gray Road in Degnan Bay, Silva Bay (fee applies) and Descanso Bay Road (small boats). Descanso Bay, on the island's northend is also the terminal site for the ferry to Nanaimo.

Gabriola has many points-of-interest. These include Drumbeg, Gabriola Sands and Sandwell Provincial Parks, Silva Bay facilities, the Gabriola Museum, the Gabriola Island Golf & Country Club and a working alpaca farm. A community bus known as "Gertie," services the Island, 250-668-6809 and taxi service is also available, 250-247-0049. Recreational activities on Gabriola Island include diving, hiking, biking (rentals available), golfing, kayaking, SUP, fishing, sailing, tennis and swimming. Hours can be spent browsing studios and shopping at Folklife Village and Madrona Marketplace. Annual community events include the *Concert on the Green*, *Cultivate: Theatre+Music+Art* and *Salmon Bar-B-Q* each August and the *Thanksgiving Studio Tour* each October. A seasonal Farmers Market is held each Saturday at the Agi Hall May-October. Some fun competitions each year include The *Brickyard Beast 10K*, *Gabriola 360*, and *The Potato Cannon Contest*. Contact Visitors Information at 1-888-284-9332, www.hellogabriola.ca.

Gabriola Island Cliffs — Photo © David Stanley

Degen Bay (7): Favor Josef Point on entry to avoid the many rocks which surround the island located in the center of the bay. A stone wall at the south end has rings for shore ties. Named after pioneer Thomas Degnen, this bay has limited protected anchorage and a public wharf. There is an unofficial boat launch at the end of Gray Road. Near the head of the bay, on a sandstone rock a few feet above the low tide line, is a petroglyph of a killer whale.

Degnen Bay Government Wharf: {49° 8' 12.6" N, 123° 42' 46.90" W} Limited transient moorage (commercial vessels take priority), 20/30 amp power. Honor box on pier.

Walk-around: A road leads to Silva Bay, about a 40 minute walk. Park is about 1-1/2 miles southeast of Degnen Bay.

★ **Drumbeg Provincial Park:** Located on the north side of Gabriola Pass, east of Josef Point, this day use park is known for its sandstone outcroppings and nice beach. Limited, temporary anchorage for small boats only. Picnicking, fishing, and hiking are popular. Swimming and diving are also available, but be aware of the strong currents that run in Gabriola Passage.

★ **Gabriola Passage (8):** [3475] See current tables for Active Pass. Gabriola Island received its name from the Spanish word gaviota, meaning sea gull. Currents in Gabriola Passage at spring tides reach eight knots maximum, which makes it less than pleasant for the planing hull boats to navigate at maximum runs and difficult, if not impossible, for sail boats and displacement hulls. The average velocity of both flood and ebb currents is four knots. Slack current occurs about 35 minutes before slack water at Active Pass. Flood current sets east, ebbs west. This passage is known as a "world class" dive for experienced divers.

★ **Silva Bay (9):** [3313] Sheltered from seas by Vance, Tugboat, and Sear Island. There are three entrances, each navigable, if you take the hazards into account. The main entrance is between Tugboat and Vance Islands. There is a drying reef which extends northward from Tugboat Island and "Shipyard Rock" lies in mid-channel. The least depth through the channel, north of the reef, is 19 feet. Silva Bay Light (Light List No. 434.3) is exhibited at an elevation of 15 feet from a white circular mast displaying a port hand daymark. Entering the bay, pass this light on the vessel's port side. Continue toward Law Point. Keep the green spar buoy U-39 to port. Do not turn too quickly to aim toward moorage facilities. The facility on Tugboat Island is a private outstation for the Royal Vancouver Yacht Club. The south entrance is between Sear and Gabriola Islands. This channel is about 100 feet wide and has a minimum depth of four feet. Local knowledge suggests staying closer to the Sear Island side where it is deeper and to avoid this entrance, even in shallow draft boats, at extreme low tides. This route may be useful when heavy seas would be encountered while transiting from the south to Commodore Passage in order to reach the main entrance above. The north entrance is between Lily and Vance Islands. Enter at the north end, between Carlos Island and the shoals north of Lily Island. The minimum depth through this channel is 11 feet. An east cardinal buoy, identified as "PA" on charts, marks the drying ledges west of Carlos Island.

Once in Silva Bay, moorage is found at two marinas. Silva Bay is connected by road to Degnen Bay and Descanso Bay, site of the Gabriola-Nanaimo ferry terminal. Gulf Island Seaplanes offers daily air service from Silva Bay to Vancouver.

Walk-around: It is approximately 1.5m/2.4km to Drumbeg Provincial Park on the north side of Gabriola Pass. The extensive sandstone outcroppings and small beach are a favorite spot to sunbathe, wade, and picnic.

★ **Page's Inn on Silva Bay:** (Formerly Silva Bay Inn) New owners Page's Resort Group offer permanent and seasonal moorage, and transient moorage for Inn guests. Farmers' Markets are now held every Sunday through the summer on the lawn at Page's Inn featuring Gabriolan art work, veggies, and baked goods with local musicians entertaining while you wander. The Inn has meeting space accommodating up to 25 people and the suites have kitchens or kitchenettes, wireless high speed internet, propane BBQ, decks looking out over the marina and Silva Bay and a generator back-up. Kayaking, fishing and sailing from the Inn dock. Gift Gallery. The Pier Gallery Artists Collective: A jewel of a gallery, looking right out over Silva Bay, featuring the work of over 25 Gabriola artists. The Fire Truck Grill: A west Coast inspired food truck, featuring flame-grilled meats and seafood, located on the lawn with picnic tables and a dingy dock. See our advertisement on this page. Website: www.pagesresortgroup.com. Email: info@pagesinn.com. Address: 3415 South Rd., Gabriola BC, V0R 1X7. Telephone: 250-247-9351. VHF 66A.

★ **Page's Resort & Marina:** {49° 08.8999 N, 123° 41.807 W} This full-service Resort & Marina on lovely Silva Bay welcomes boaters (and their pets!) to new, expanded moorage with 15/30 amp power, water, showers, laundry, and complimentary wifi. The fuel dock is easy to access and open year round. In addition to marina slips, accommodations include cottages and R/V and tent campsites. The Li'l Market Store is now your corner liquor store for boaters, campers and cottagers at the south end of Gabriola. The Market also continues to offer groceries and over 400 titles of books by Gabriolan authors. Page's spacious, park-like setting includes BBQ and picnic area. A gallery and seasonal Sunday Market are within walking distance. For exploring, rent kayaks and stand up paddle boards on site. A community shuttle also provides service to the golf course and village core. See our advertisement on this page. Website: www.pagesresortgroup.com. Email: info@pagesresort.com. Address: 3350 Coast Road, Gabriola BC, V0R 1X7. Telephone: 250-247-8931. VHF 66A.

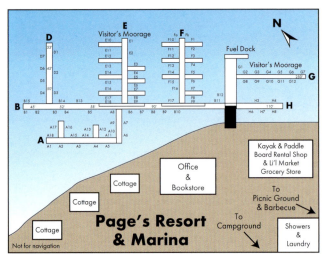

Silva Bay Resort & Marina: {49° 09' 03" N, 123° 41' 55" W} Annual, winter and transient moorage, 30/50 amp power, wifi, garbage disposal, washrooms, showers, and laundry. Marine gas and diesel available at dock. 250-247-8662. VHF 66A.

Area Whiskey Golf: Before crossing Georgia Strait to or from Nanaimo or Silva Bay, read the "Area Whiskey Golf (WG)" from the Canadian Dept of National Defence found in the Important Notices section and in Chapter 15 of this guide.

★⚓ **Gabriola Sands Provincial Park (10):** [3458] Galiano/Malaspina Galleries, a famous erosional sandstone formation, is located south of Malaspina Point. The galleries were noted as early as 1792 when Explorers Galiano and Valdes included drawings of them in their log. This photographer's delight is a sweeping curved roof of sandstone which resembles a giant ocean roller caught upon the point of breaking. The park straddles a narrow neck of land between Pilot and Taylor Bays. Swimming is good at the sandy beaches. An Annual Sand Castle Contest is held here in August. Picnic sites and pit toilets are available; no potable water, no overnight camping. Twin Beaches Shopping Centre is within walking distance. ⛵

Pilot Bay: North end of Gabriola Island. Good anchorage. Protected from SE winds. No dump zone.

Entrance Island Lighthouse: Located off Orlebar Point, this primary weather station reports conditions on the western side of Georgia Strait. The red and white lighthouse, built in 1875, guided coal ships traveling to and from Nanaimo.

Nanaimo Area
[3443, 3447, 3458, 3463, 3475]

Dodd Narrows (11): See current tables for Active Pass. Separating Vancouver Island from Mudge Island, this passage stretches in a southeast-northwest direction. Pleasure craft, tugs, barges, and small log booms pass through the opening at or near slack water. The current sets north on the flood, south on the ebb. Currents reach eight to ten knots at springs. Tide rips occur at the northwestern entrance on the flood and in the vicinity of the overhead cables on the ebb. These overhead cables cross Dodd Narrows about 0.2 miles south of Purvis Point and have a vertical clearance of 37m. There is a harbour speed limit.

False Narrows: Dodd Narrows is the recommended passage between the islands and Nanaimo. False Narrows is a tricky pass to navigate, so always use local charts and B.C. Pilot. The channel is very close to the shores of Gabriola Island and north of a long rocky drying ledge in the middle of the narrows. Tidal streams of four to five knots maximum are referenced at Dodd Narrows. This passage leads from the northwest end of Pylades Channel into Percy Anchorage and is navigable for small craft.

Entrance Island Lighthouse off Orlebar Point   Photo © VPLLC

When approaching from Pylades Channel, favor the Mudge Island shore to avoid a boulder-covered drying area to the north. A beacon range leads from this east end to the five to six feet deep navigable channel. Another set of beacons leads out via the west end. Keep on this west range until close to the Mudge Island shore to avoid a drying spit that extends west from the west range. Thick kelp is a hazard in summer and fall. Temporary anchorage is possible in Percy's Anchorage in 35-50 feet of water on a shell bottom.

Northumberland Channel: Leading northwest from Dodd and False Narrows between Vancouver Island and the southwest coast of Gabriola Island, boaters use this waterway en route to Nanaimo and the Strait of Georgia. Log booms are often rafted against the steep side of Gabriola Island.

Duke Point: Site of the Nanaimo-Tsawwassen Ferry Terminal and the beginning of the freeway north to Courtenay. Located south of the city, near Harmac Pacific mill. When traversing Northumberland Channel to or from Dodd Narrows, or along the northwest shore of Gabriola Island, be watchful for ferry traffic.

★ **Nanaimo (12):** [3443, 3447, 3458] Nanaimo is a customs port-of-entry. The customs office is conveniently located behind the floatplane terminal right along the harbour.

Nanaimo, known as the "Harbour City" is the second largest city on Vancouver Island. This thriving urban centre boasts small city charm, a walk-able waterfront, outstanding parks and trails and a rich cultural heritage. Nanaimo is located on the unceded territory of the Snuneymuxw First Nation. To learn more about the Coast Salish people, take a short foot ferry ride from the downtown harbour and visit Saysutshun (Newcastle Island). On your visit, book a walking tour with a First Nation guide or attend a traditional salmon barbecue to experience the unique culture of the Snuneymuxw people.

Residents and visitors alike delight in the many opportunities Nanaimo offers for outdoor recreation - of the fast and slow variety. Hike beautiful Mount Benson and be rewarded with a stunning view of Nanaimo from the summit. Grab your mountain bike and rip through Nanaimo's world-class trails, or test your skills at the Stevie Smith Bike Park. For a quieter commune with nature, head to Nanaimo River where you can dip your toes in the refreshing pools and float down the river in pure relaxation. If an ocean dip is on your bucket list, head to one of the local beaches like Pipers Lagoon Park and Departure Bay Beach where you can also watch the ferry come in. Nanaimo Harbour offers water sports galore, including stand up paddleboard, kayak rentals, and snorkeling adventures. To stay a bit drier, sign on for a catamaran tour or whale watching expedition.

Closer to the harbour, you can spend the day exploring downtown Nanaimo and the quaint Old City Quarter, with its collection of galleries, restaurants and boutiques. Source locally-made treasures and delight in the city's food culture, which includes three craft breweries, two wineries, a distillery and many varieties of the much-celebrated Nanaimo Bar dessert. A variety of amenities conveniently located near the marina, including retail shops, a grocery store, and marine-oriented businesses. Pioneer Waterfront Plaza provides a viewing platform overlooking Nanaimo's historic waterfront and is home to retail shops and the Nanaimo Farmers' Market open Saturdays from May through October. The Great Canadian Casino Nanaimo, the HBC Bastion, the Nanaimo Museum, the Nanaimo Art Gallery and Port Theatre for the Performing Arts are also notable attractions conveniently accessed by foot from your boat. For further exploration, rental cars and taxis are available, as are tour guides who would happily show you around town.

Nanaimo is a festival filled city, hosting numerous annual celebrations. The popular *Maple Sugar Festival* happens in late February, the *Dragon Boat Festival* and *Silly Boat Regatta* both occur in July. The annual *Marine Festival*, also staged in July, is the reason Nanaimo is known as the "Bathtub Race Capital City of the World." Bathtub racers, start from Swy-a-Lana Lagoon around Entrance Island, head west along Georgia Strait, around Winchelsea Island, and back to Nanaimo for a thrilling finish. In mid-August, *Vancouver Island Exhibition* has crafts, livestock shows, carnival rides and games. Wines from around the world are featured at the *Wine Festival* in October. The unique *Cedar & Yellowpoint Country Christmas Craft Tour* occurs in late November and the *Downtown Art Walk* in early December. November and December play host to several large Christmas craft fairs.

2024 Northwest Boat Travel

Page 154 Chapter 11 NORTHERN GULF ISLANDS

Approaching downtown Nanaimo: The approach to the Port of Nanaimo Boat Basin is either from the northwest through Departure Bay and Newcastle Island Passage or from the east, past the southern tip of Protection Island. When entering Newcastle Passage from the north, keep the buoy near Shaft Point to port and pass in mid-channel between Shaft and Pimbury Points. The enforced speed limit in the channel is five knots. Moorage facilities, repair yards, and fuel docks line the western shore. Oregon Rock is near mid-channel. (Oregon Rock is known locally as "Rowan's Rock" for the late and legendary local mechanic, Johnny Rowan. Prior to the rock being charted and marked by a green can buoy, Johnny made his living salvaging and repairing boats that wandered upon it.) Passage is east of Oregon Rock, between the rock and Newcastle Island. Starboard hand buoy "P14" is on the Newcastle Island side of the Passage. Just north of Oregon Rock is Passage Rock, marked by day beacon with a port hand daymark. Do not pass between these markers. The correct passage is on the east side of the rock off the Newcastle Island shore. To safely transit this area, pass between buoys "P13" and "P14" plus between the day beacon and "P16". Continuing south, the Nanaimo Yacht Club and the Townsite Marina are located here. After passing the floatplane facility, the entrance to the Port of Nanaimo Boat Basin is at the southern end of the floating breakwater close to the fueling dock. The alternative approach to downtown Nanaimo and into Nanaimo Harbour is from the east, in the passage marked by the picturesque lighthouse on the south tip of Protection Island. Keep the red buoy to starboard. Stay to the west of the cardinal buoy marking Satellite Reef. This reef dries at zero tide and should be avoided. Proceed around the 600' cement Visiting Vessel Pier to the inner boat basin tucked in a protected area.

A flashing white strobe light, installed on the windsock on the Central Breakwater, warns of approaching aircraft. Aircraft trigger the strobe light, which flashes for 90 seconds prior to take-off or landing. The Central Breakwater is also the location of the holding tank pump-out station.

Except those with an extended stay permit issued by the Port Authority, recreational boats can anchor in the harbour for a limit of 14 days in a 30 day period.

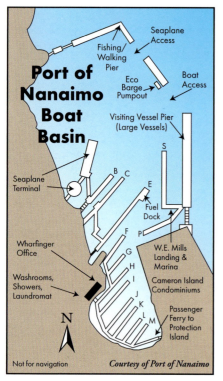

★ **Nanaimo Port Authority Boat Basin:** {49° 10' N, 123° 56' W} The W.E. Mills Landing & Marina, (formerly the Visiting Vessel Pier) off the north tip of Cameron Island, accommodates large pleasure vessels and the adjacent commercial Inlet Basin provides moorage for smaller vessels. Reservations are recommended 48 hours prior to arrival with a $15 cdn reservation fee, although encouraged well before to ensure placement. Full utility services are available including a fuel dock and sewage pump-out. The Wharfinger's office is open extended hours including a secured marina guest washroom with showers and laundry. The Harbourside Walkway extends around the perimeter of the boat basin shoreline and extends for 5 kilometers. Noon cannon firings take place beside the landmark white Hudson's Bay Bastion adjacent to the Pioneer Waterfront Plaza in the summer months only and/or during cruise ship visits. Harbour Air and Sunshine Coast Air offer floatplane passenger service between downtown Nanaimo and Vancouver, to and from Vancouver International Airport and also to the Sunshine Coast. See our advertisement on this page. Mailing address: Post Office Box 131, 100 Port Way, Nanaimo, British Columbia V9R 5K4. Fax: 250-754-4186. Telephone: 250-754-5053. Website: www.npa.ca. Email: marina@npa.ca. VHF 67.

APY Marina: {49° 11' 6.9" N, 123° 56' 46.7304" W} Permanent moorage, 30-amp power, water. 250-591-6966.

Departure Bay Gas N Go: Gas, diesel, oil, fishing tackle, ice and snacks. 250-591-0810. At Stones Marine Centre.

Newcastle Marina & Boatyard: {49° 11' 0.97" N, 123° 56' 42.0" W} Permanent moorage, transient moorage if space is available, call ahead. 15amp/110V power, water, showers, laundry. 60-ton travelift, repairs, maintenance, restoration, services onsite or DIY. 250-753-1431.

Petro Canada Marine (Port of Nanaimo Basin): Gas, diesel, oils, batteries, propane tank exchange, ice, water, bait/tackle, convenience store. 250-754-7828.

Stones Marine Centre Inc.: {49° 11' 17" N, 123° 56' 52" W} Open/covered moorage, visitor moorage by reservation. 30 amp power, water, laundry, showers, restrooms, pub. Boatyard, 83-ton Travelift 85' long x 19.6' beam, onsite repairs or DIY, chandlery, boat storage, yacht charters/brokerage, sailing school & RV park. Marina: 250-753-4232. Boatyard/Marine Store: 250-716-9065.

Townsite Marina: {49° 10' 738" N, 123° 56' 574" W} Permanent moorage only. 30/50 amp power, shower, washroom, laundry. 250-716-8801.

Waterfront Suites & Marina: Annual, monthly, and guest moorage for boats to 90', water, 30/50 amp power, showers, laundry, wifi, security, concierge services for a fee, lodging. 250-753-7111.

Nanaimo Walk-arounds: To orient yourself, remember that the downtown streets are laid out like a wheel - the boat basin is the hub and the streets radiate out like spokes. Self-guided tours are outlined in brochures available at the Visitor Information Centre booth or Wharfingers Office. One tour, "A Walk Through Time," starts at Pioneer Waterfront Park. Steps away from moorage, the Port Place Centre has a Thrifty Foods, London Drugs, Starbucks and clothing & accessory stores. Exit the mall into the southeastern parking lot bordering Terminal Avenue, the location of the Casino Nanaimo and the Italian Fountain. The fountain, built in 1958 is decorated with colorful, inlaid tiles showing fingerlings swimming downstream to the sea. Two, four-ton granite

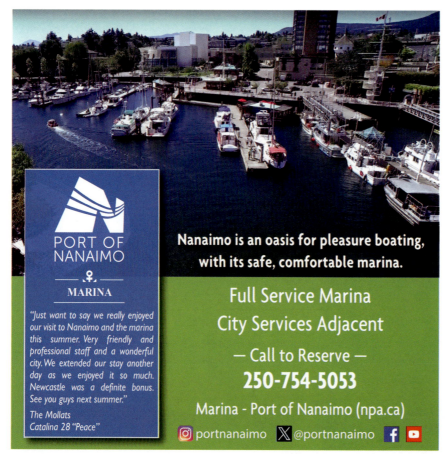

Visit us at boattravel.com

Coho salmon, depict the fight up-river to spawn. Follow Terminal Avenue in a westerly direction to the junction of Terminal and Commercial. Follow Commercial and experience the hustle and bustle of the heart of the downtown shopping district. The Port of Nanaimo Centre houses the Vancouver Island Conference Centre, Shaw auditorium, retail outlets, and museum. Stroll through time in the museum's main galleries - from Nanaimo's earliest settlers, to 19th century mining town, and into the 21st century. To get back to the waterfront, continue on Commercial, turning right on Church Street.

Another tour, "Harbourside Walkway," begins at the Commercial Inlet Boat Basin and ends two and a half miles north. Start on Front Street at the Port Theatre, an 800-seat performing arts theater. Walk up the hill to the Coast Bastion Hotel. Across the street, beside Pioneer Plaza, is The Bastion, a longtime Nanaimo landmark. Originally built as a fort in 1853 by the Hudson Bay Company, it was later used as a jail and is now a part of the Nanaimo museum where visitors take a visual journey through the rich history and culture of Nanaimo's past. From May-September, the Harbourfront Walkway is a summer location for the Tourism Nanaimo Visitor Centre. During these months, visitors can also view an exciting canon firing ceremony accompanied by a bagpiper each day at noon. A nearby flight of stairs leads to Pioneer Plaza where a plaque commemorates the 1854 landing of the Princess Royal Pioneers, a group of skilled coal miners from England who helped to shape the city's coal mining history. Walk in a northwesterly direction along the Princess Elizabeth II Promenade that rims this shore. Go up the stairs to Georgia Park and enjoy fine harbour views. Continue on the promenade to Swy-a-Lana Lagoon and Maffeo-Sutton Park, an extensive green belt along the waterfront that includes Canada's only man made tidal lagoon with the four times a day changes of tide, a swimming beach, playgrounds, landscaped gardens and concession stands. From here a passenger ferry connects with Saysutshun (Newcastle Island Marine Provincial Park. Cross the bridge over the Millstream River or take a side trip under the bridge and follow Mill Street to Barsby Park. Back on the promenade, continue north to the Nanaimo Yacht Club., and further on to Shipyard Point, the Chinese Memorial Gardens, and to stores and restaurants, near the B.C. Ferry Terminal.

Another fun walk is facilitated by the OnThisSpot.ca app, which allows you to experience Nanaimo then and now. This walking tour app engages with you as you walk downtown Nanaimo and shows you historical photos of key landmarks as you stand before them taking in their appearance in present day.

Still want to walk? The City's trail system extends over 170 kilometres. There are paved surfaces for biking and rollerblading, and unpaved surfaces suitable for walking and jogging. For information, pick up a copy of the "Parks & Trails" brochure at one of the City's local recreation centres. Learn more about the things to see and do in Nanaimo at TourismNanaimo.com.

★ **Protection Island:** Nestled in Nanaimo harbour, Protection Island provides a glimpse of simpler, nearly forgotten times. Its eclectic residents enjoy comforts of city utilities but with the feel of rural living. There is a fire station, a small museum (open a few months a year), a community hall and community garden, as well as a small library built by locals. A passenger-only ferry connects residents and tourists to and from downtown Nanaimo. The "must visit" for boaters, though, is The Dinghy Dock Pub and Floating Restaurant, Canada's only registered floating pub. With dock space instead of a parking lot, this unique pub welcomes boaters with a shower, good food and service and wonderful Nanaimo skyline and harbour views. There's even fishing holes for the kids. Call 250-753-2373 for ferry or Pub information. Boaters should not attempt passage between Newcastle and Protection Island. On the south end of the island, there is drying ledge around Gallows Point and nearby Satellite Reef, marked by buoy "PS" dries at zero tide. Stay west of the buoy.

Nanaimo Boardwalk   Photo © GoToVan

Hammond Bay (14): Temporary anchorage in all except northeast winds is available. Enter north of the islets which extend from Lagoon Head. Aim straight in. Avoid foul ground off Neck Point. A submarine pipeline runs down the center of the bay, affecting anchorage position. The Charlaine Boat launch ramp is on shore (tidal dependent).

★⚓ **Saysutshun (Newcastle) Island Provincial Park (13):** [3447] Moorage at public docks ($2 per boat meter) and mooring buoys ($14 per night), campsites, picnic areas, fresh water, showers, restrooms are available at this beautiful park. The Historic CPR Pavilion and Concession is open June to September offering a wide variety of items from burgers and beer to ice cream and camp supplies. Ferry service is also available to downtown Nanaimo from May to October. A park attendant is on duty and monitors the park during low season. Fees are charged for moorage and campsites are booked through BC Parks: www.env.gov.bc.ca/bcparks/reserve. Moorage is limited to 14 days. The use of anchors in Mark Bay is not allowed. Forty-three mooring buoys in the bay are of two types - one for boats to 30' in length, and the other for boats to 40'.

Traditionally known as Saysutshun by the Snuneymuxw people, the Island was renamed after Newcastle-on-Tyne, a famous coal town in England when coal was discovered in 1849.

This family friendly marine provincial park continues to hold a special place in the hearts of Snuneymuxw people or Mustiyuxw, as well as visitors throughout the years. Located within Nanaimo's Harbour, it is a breathtaking place with spectacular panoramic views of the Harbour City and Coast Mountains. On the Island, the restored, 1930-vintage Dance Pavilion is used for weddings, events, and summer entertainment. Wildlife abound, including rabbits, otter, blacktail deer, and raccoons. Trees such as the Douglas Fir, Arbutus, Dogwood and Garry Oaks grow in abundance. Twenty-two kilometers of trail lead around the island's shoreline and to lakes in the heart of the island. Beaches are popular for swimming and sun bathing. Children enjoy the fishing wharf and playground.

A foot passenger ferry runs between Newcastle Island Provincial Park and Nanaimo's Maffeo-Sutton Park. Newcastle Island Info: www.newcastleisland.ca, 1-866-788-6243. ▲⛺🚶

Snake Island: In 1997, the community of Nanaimo, in cooperation with the Nanaimo Dive Association, the Artificial Reef Society of British Columbia, and the Cousteau Society, sank the retired Navy-class destroyer HMCS *Saskatchewan* as an artificial reef just east of Snake Island (49° 12.96' N, 123° 53.070' W). In 2001 the 440 foot Cape Breton was sunk nearby, (49° 12.88' N, 123° 53.067' W). The artificial reef has enhanced fish habitats and recreational diving opportunities. ⚓

Swy-a-Lana Lagoon   Photo © Destination Nanaimo

Essential Supplies & Services

AIR TRANSPORTATION
To & from Washington
Kenmore Air 1-866-435-9524
NW Seaplanes . . . 425-277-1590, 1-800-690-0086
San Juan Airlines 1-800-874-4434
Seattle Seaplanes 1-800-637-5553
To & from Islands/Vancouver
Air Canada 1-888-247-2262
Gulf Island Seaplanes (Silva Bay) 250-247-9992
Harbour Air 250-714-0900, 1-800-665-0212
Sea Air 1-866-692-6440
Sunshine Coast Air . . . 250-591-1810, 1-877-461-5749

BOOKS / BOOK STORES
Evergreen Pacific Publishing 425-493-1451
The Marine Atlas 253-872-5707

BUS TRANSPORTATION
Gabriola Island Bus 250-668-6809
Pacific Coach Line (Greyhound) : 250-385-4411
Regional Transit: 250-390-4531

COAST GUARD
Victoria Coast Guard Radio . . . . VHF 16, 83a
. . . . 1-800-661-9202 (In BC) or 250-363-6611
Victoria Marine Communications & Traffic
. . . . 250-363-6333
Marine Distress, Search & Rescue
. . . . 1-800-567-5111 (in Canada) or 250-413-8933
Cell Phone (limited to select providers) . . . *16 or #727

CUSTOMS
24 Hour Reporting Centre 1-888-226-7277
CBSA Reporting Sites: Nanaimo Boat Basin E Dock
For more information, see Important Notices between Chapters 7 & 8

FERRY INFORMATION
BC Ferries 1-888-223-3779
Newcastle Island: 250-802-0255
Protection Island: 250-753-2373

FISHING INFO/SHELLFISHING INFO
24 hr Recorded Notifications Pacific Region Only
. . . . 1-866-431-3474 Or 604-666-2828
Recreational Licensing 1-877-535-7307
Observe, Record, & Report Line (fisheries violations) . .
. . . . 1-800-465-4336 Or 604-607-4186

FUELS
Departure Bay Gas N Go: Nanaimo 250-591-0810
Nanaimo Port Authority: Gas, Diesel 250-754-7828
Page's Marina: Silva Bay. Gas, Diesel
. . . . 250-247-8931
Silva Bay Resort & Marina, Gas, Diesel . 250-247-9800

GOLF COURSES
(These courses are accessible from moorage and have rental clubs available)
Gabriola Island 250-247-8822
Nanaimo Golf Club 250-758-6332
Pryde Vista (9 Hole), Nanaimo 250-753-6188

HAUL-OUTS
Harbour Homes Marina 250-729-5729
Newcastle Marina: Nanaimo 250-753-1431
Silva Bay Shipyard 250-247-9800
Stones Marine Centre, Inc 250-716-9065

A full day at Page's Resort & Marina Photo © Gloria Hatfield

HOSPITALS
Healthlink BC (Nurse Helpline) 811
Gabriola Medical Clinic 250-247-9222
Nanaimo Regional Hospital 250-755-7691

LIQUOR STORES
Gabriola Island
Nanaimo: Carlos O'Bryans 250-591-3090
Nanaimo: Harbour Park Mall & Terminal Park Plaza

LODGING
Coast Bastion Inn: Nanaimo 250-753-6601
Page's Inn on Silva Bay 250-247-9351
Page's Marina: Silva Bay 250-247-8931

MARINAS / MOORAGE FLOATS
Degnen Bay Government Wharf: Gabriola Island
Harbour Homes Marina 250-729-5729
Nanaimo Port Authority Boat Basin
. . . . 250-754-5053, VHF 67
Newcastle Island Provincial Park 250-754-7893
Pages Marina: Silva Bay 250-247-8931
Silva Bay Resort & Marina 250-247-8662
Stones Marine Centre Inc.: Nanaimo . . . 250-753-4232
Townsite Marina: Nanaimo (Permanent) . . . .
. . . . 250-716-8801

PARKS
BC Parks Reservations 1-800-689-9025
Nanaimo City Parks 250-756-5200
Saysutshun (Newcastle)
Island Marine Park 1-866-788-6243
Cedar: Cedar Ramp (end of Nelson Rd)
Gabriola Island: Degnen Bay, Descanso Bay Rd, El Verano (False Narrows), Silva Bay Marine Resort
Naniamo: Brechin Boat Ramp (1890 Zorkin Rd),
Charlaine Boat Ramp on Hammond Bay Rd

REPAIRS / SERVICE
Newcastle Marina: Nanaimo 250-753-1431
Silva Bay Shipyard 250-247-9800
Stones Marine 250-716-9065

SEWAGE DISPOSAL
Nanaimo Port Authority Boat Basin
. . . . 250-754-5053, VHF 67

SCUBA AIR
Sundown Diving: Nanaimo 250-753-1880

SCUBA SITES
Nanaimo
Silva Bay

TAXI
Gabriola Island 250-247-0049
Nanaimo 250-753-8911, 250-753-1231

TOWING
C-TOW 1-888-419-CTOW
Fast Response 250-222-0076
Harbours End Marine 250-537-4202
Vessel Assist / TowBoatUS - South Gulf Islands,
Nanaimo Harbour 250-883-7865

VISITOR INFORMATION
Nanaimo Tourist Info 250-751-1556
Gabriola Island 250-247-9332, 888-284-9332

WEATHER
Environment Canada Weather Line 250-339-9861
Canadian Coast Guard (recorded) 250-363-6492
Vancouver: VHF WX-1, VHF 21B 604-664-9010

Visit us at boattravel.com

VANCOUVER Chapter 12 Page 157

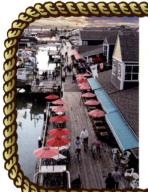

Chapter 12:
Fraser River, Vancouver & Howe Sound

Steveston Boardwalk - photo © Albert Normandin

Tsawwassen, Delta, Richmond, New Westminster, Vancouver, North & West Vancouver, Squamish, False Creek, Burrard Inlet, Indian Arm, Bowen, Gambier, Keats, & Anvil Islands.

★ See "Important Notices" between Chapters 7 and 8 for specific information on boating related topics such as boating safety, weather, U.S. & Canadian marine radio use, Vessel Traffic Service, security zones, Canadian & U.S. Customs, etc. Due to changing regulations, call ahead to verify latest customs information.

Symbols

[ ]: Numbers between [ ] are chart numbers.

{ }: Numbers & letters between { } are waypoints.

★ Recommended destinations, facilities, and services

⊥: Park, 🚤: Boat Launch, ▲: Campgrounds, 🚶: Hiking Trails, ⊼: Picnic Area, 🚲: Biking, 🤿: Scuba

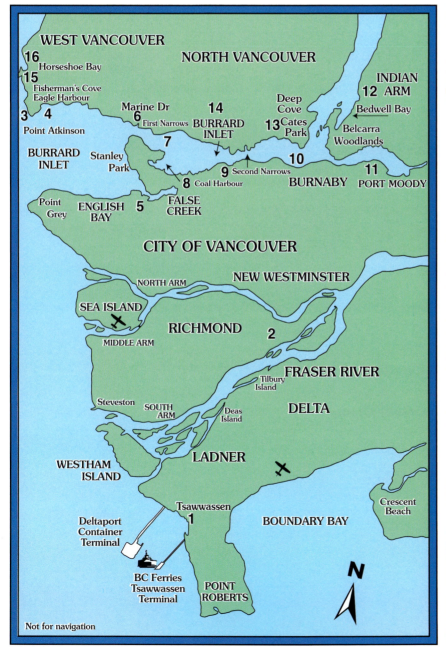

Boundary Bay
[3463]

★ **Point Roberts:** Is a U.S. Customs Port of Entry, for additional information, see Chapter 6. 360-945-5211.

★ **Point Roberts Marina Resort:** {48° 58' 36" N, 123° 3' 51" W} Point Roberts Marina is superbly located for cruising to and from the San Juan Islands, Active Pass and the Gulf Islands and offers convenient on-site U.S. Customs Clearance. Check out the competitive moorage rates for overnight, monthly and yearly moorage slips with 30/50/100 amp power and water. Other marina amenities include showers, laundry, wifi, and free pump-out facility (slip-side pump-out arranged with advance notice, $5). Gas, diesel, and propane are available at the Fuel Dock where boaters can also purchase ice, bait, fishing licenses, beer/wine and convenience items. Westwind Marine provides marine repairs, a boatyard and chandlery, call 360-945-5523. Full service restaurant on site, call Breakwaters at 360-945-2628. See our advertisement on page 88. Website: www.pointrobertsmarina.com. Email: prmarina@pointrobertsmarina.com. Mailing address: 713 Simundson Dr., Point Roberts, WA 98281. Fax: 360-945-0927. Phone: 360-945-2255. VHF 66A.

Chart List

Canadian Hydrographic Charts:
3061, 3062, 3311, 3463, 3481, 3490, 3491, 3492-3495, 3512, 3526, 3534

NOAA Charts:
17517-19, 18400, 18405-09, 18412

Marine Atlas Vol 1 (2018):
Page 12, 20, 21, 25

Evergreen Cruising Atlas: Pages 78-98

2024 Northwest Boat Travel

Crescent Beach & White Rock: For additional information see Chapter 6.

★ **Crescent Beach Marina:** {49° 03' 23.6" N, 122° 52' 12.5" W} Located in historic Crescent Beach, this marina is the Customs port-of-entry. Moorage from 20' - 50' (year round), transient moorage, 15 & 30 amp power, water, fuel- diesel, premium & mid-grade, full chandlery store, washrooms, laundromat, showers, repairs, parts, haul-outs, dry storage compound, launch ramp and a pump-out station. Close to shopping, fine dining, golfing. Thirty minutes to Vancouver. See our advertisement on this page. Address: 12555 Crescent Rd, Surrey, B.C. V4A 2V4. Website: www.crescent-beachmarina.com. Telephone: 604-538-9666. Fax: 604-538-7724. VHF 66A.

Ward's Marina: Permanent moorage. Located on the Nicomekl River in Elgin Heritage Park home of historic Stewart Farm. Picnic area, washroom, trails. ⛱🚶

Tsawwassen (1): [3463, 3492, 3499] Site of a large ferry terminal with service to Swartz Bay, the Gulf Islands, and Nanaimo. The super port has been expanded to include a Container Terminal (Deltaport). Small boats should be aware of increased deep sea and tug movements in this area. For boaters, there is a dredged channel parallel to the south side of the long ferry causeway leading to a mooring basin for temporary anchorage. Temporary anchorage is also possible north of the terminal. Watch depth sounder. There is good fishing between the terminal and the Roberts Bank Superport. A rough ramp for launching at high tide is on the beach along the south side of the causeway going out to the terminal. Great Blue Herons often walk in the shallows between the spit and the coalport. Shallow mudflats extend some distance. ⛵

Fraser River
[3490, 3491, 3492, 3495]

★ **Fraser River:** This waterway is the largest river in British Columbia. Over 2.5 million people live in close proximity to its waters which flow past Vancouver, Richmond, Delta, Ladner, New Westminster, Surrey, Burnaby, Coquitlam, Port Coquitlam, Mission, Steveston, and many other small communities. Two strip charts, #3488 and #3489, cover the Fraser River from Harrison Mills to the Pattulo Bridge. Other charts are #3062 for Pitt Lake and #3061 to Harrison Lake.

Travel on the Fraser requires extra care. Launching can also be tricky. The current is strong, and the water is very murky. Commercial areas are dredged regularly but, further upstream, a guide with local knowledge may be needed to safely navigate between the sandbars. Skippers need to keep a sharp lookout for ever present log handling debris and commercial vessel traffic. Water level is lowest during January, February, and March and is at its highest near the end of June. Currents run to five knots during the summer, with higher rates of flow in narrow places. Waters begin to subside toward

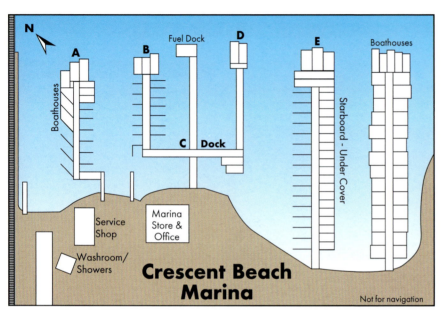

Crescent Beach Marina   604-538-9666

- Port of Entry – Customs
- Launch Ramp & Haul Outs
- Waste Water Treatment System
- Pump Out Station
- Mercury, Volvo & Cummins Certified Technicians
- Fuel Sales – Diesel – Premium – Mid-Grade
- Dry Storage Compound
- Full Chandlery Store
- Fine Dining & Shopping Within 1 Min.
- Golf Course 5 Mins. Away
- Moorage from 20' – 50' (year round) 15 & 30 Amp Power
- Transient Moorage
- 1/2 Hr. to Vancouver

visit: www.crescentbeachmarina.com

VANCOUVER Chapter 12 Page 159

the end of August. September to November are good months for river navigation because the water is still high enough for small vessels to reach Hope, but the current reduces to three or four knots. The river always runs downstream, however, there may be reversal at large flood tides. Turns of the tide are later than those on Georgia Strait. Tide and current tables and detailed charts are a necessity. A northwest wind opposing the flood tide or a southwest wind blowing against the current cause dangerous waves. When entering from the strait, all can buoys to port are green, with odd numbers. Buoys on the starboard are red with even numbers. Lighted buoys to port flash green and those to starboard are red. The river's mouth has several entry channels and arms. Each channel has a boat launching ramp near its mouth.

The Fraser and its tributaries have historically been among the largest natural salmon runs in the world. When they are open to fishing, the mouth of the North Arm and the Main Arm are great spots to catch one of these world famous delicacies.

★ **Fraser River North Arm:** [3491] This arm is used extensively by tugs and barges, as well as pleasure craft. When entering, give the tidal flats at Wreck Beach a wide berth. There is a park on Iona Island with sand dunes and picnic sites. Further inland on the north bank of Sea Island, two launching ramps, picnic tables, restrooms, and a small concessions is found at McDonald Beach. Fraser River Park, at the south end of Angus Dr at 75th Ave in Vancouver, is a fine picnic spot and has a large playfield and a boardwalk through a tidal marsh. Beach area depends on the amount of tide. A marina and boatyard is located just upstream from the park. Also on the North Arm, Fraser Foreshore Park in Burnaby at the south end of Byrne Road has a walkway along the river, picnic and BBQ areas, and fishing.

Milltown Marina & Boatyard: {49°12'16.80"N 123° 8'55.01"W} Permanent moorage, transient moorage if space is available, slips 30' to 80', 30/50 amp power, water, dry stack storage, boat lift (to 30', 10,000 lbs), mechanical/general repair, restaurant/pub. 604-697-9191.

★ **Fraser River Middle Arm:** [3491] Entered south or north of Sea Island, this arm used mainly by pleasure craft. When accessing by the North Arm, keep the North Arm Jetty on your starboard side. At the entrance there will be another jetty on your port side extending from shore. Stay clear of "the flats" when coming up the North Arm. This is extremely shallow water. Once you reach the Arthur Laing Bridge, turn South down the Middle Arm (Moray Channel). Drop your speed to an idle, the Middle Arm is a no wake area. Three bridges span the Middle Arm–the Canada Line Bridge, the Airport Connector Bridge and the Middle Arm Swing Bridge (closed 7am-9am and 4pm-6pm, call 604-270-2845 or VHF 74). Beyond this last bridge, a private marina and a hotel and restaurant are on the right. Sea Island is also the site of Vancouver International Airport. A boat launch is on the southeast side of Sea Island.

Deckside Marina: {49° 11' 24" N, 123° 8' 21" W} Monthly, annual moorage. Transient moorage if space is available. Boats to 100', 30/50 amp power, water, restroom, parking, security. Hotel, restaurant onsite. 604-317-8040.

★ **Fraser River South Arm:** [3490] Avoid approaching when northwest winds oppose a flood tide. This is the main channel of the Fraser. It is entered at Sand Heads. The river is a major transportation link for industry and commerce as well as pleasure craft. Take every effort to avoid hindering the commercial traffic. From July to November, large numbers of gillnetters may be encountered in South Arm, presenting a hazard to navigation.

★ **Steveston:** [3490, 3492] Customs check-in site. This town lies on the north side of the Main Channel at the southwest corner of Lulu Island. Wharves, fueling station, and boatyards line the north side of Cannery Channel. Harbour facilities are found at two main sites, Paramount {49° 7' 7" N, 123° 9' 46" W} and Gulf {49° 7' 29" N, 123° 11' 16" W}. This one time salmon processing center is still home to the west coast's largest fishing fleet and many sell fresh seafood daily from their boats at the newly rebuilt Fisherman's Wharf. Steveston offers over 350 businesses and food services ranging from fish and chips to fine dining. This town is a blend of historic fishing village, quaint tourist destination, and fashionable enterprise. Stores, with rolls of netting, bins

Steveston Boardwalk   Photo © Albert Normandin

of lures, and weights of all sizes, speak of the town's close connection to the fishing industry. There are also unique boutiques and fine gift stores featuring Canadian artisans. Visit the Gulf of Georgia Cannery National Historic Site open year round. For hours and information, 604-664-9009. Steveston Farmers & Artisans Market takes place at 3rd & Moncton, May through September on the first and third Sunday of the month from 10:30am–3:30pm. Other points of interest include Britannia Heritage Shipyard National Historic Site, 604-238-8050 and London Heritage Farm, 604-271-5220. Overlooking the south arm of the Fraser, London Heritage Farm has a restored 1880's farm house, barn, picnic tables, gift shop and tea room. Each July 1st the community celebrates the *Steveston Salmon Festival* features a parade, activities and a BBQ menu that includes 1,200 pounds of wild salmon fillets.

Steveston Chevron Marine: Gas, diesel, lubricants, filters, water, snacks. 604-277-4712.

Steveston Harbour Authority: {49° 7' 3" N, 123° 9' 49" W} Permanent moorage for commercial boats only. Transient moorage if space is available, fishing fleet has priority. Power, water, garbage drop, restrooms, showers, boat launch, 70 ton haul-out, repairs. 604-272-5539.

South of Steveston: There are at least three launch ramp sites on the main arm. Two are on Lulu Island, southeast of Steveston and at the foot of Nelson Road. The third is under the Port Mann Bridge in Coquitlam. Also south of Steveston is Westham Island. Home to the 850-acre George C Reifel Bird Sanctuary, winter home of the Snow Geese and one of Canada's top birdwatching sites. The best times to visit are during the fall and spring migrations. Westham Island is also well known for local produce and berry farms. Canoe Passage, another small arm of the Fraser, separates Westham Island from the mainland. With an up-to-date chart #3492, and a little local knowledge, Canoe Pass is navigable by small craft. The Westham Island Bridge is manned 24/7 from April 1-Dec. 1 and from 6am-10pm the remainder of the year. Call 604-946-0139 or VHF 74 to request a bridge opening (5 mins. average wait time). A launch ramp is on the island, southwest of the bridge.

★ **Ladner:** Ladner is a lively community of about 22,000. Like many communities on the Delta, fishing and agriculture were early economic mainstays and they continue to be strong parts of the spirit of this community. Ladner features a number of independent locally owned shops, cafes and restaurants. many within a 5 to 7 minute walk of the Elliot Street Public Wharf where free moorage is available (3 hr. max). Tie up and enjoy a stroll, do a little shopping or stop for a drink and bite to eat. Be sure to visit the newly completed mural by Delta artist Gary Nay, located at the corner of Elliot Street and 48th Avenue. Ladner Village is host to some major, family-friendly festivities and community celebrations throughout the year. For event information visit www.ladnerbusiness.com. Ladner also has a number of lovely parks including Harbour Park, located about ½ mile east of the boat basin. Trails are plentiful in Ladner and are found in parks and all along the waterfront. For golfers there is a 9-hole course on Admiral Boulevard. There are two public boat launches, one at Wellington Point Park and one at the north end of Ferry Road. **Plan your trip to discover why Ladner Village is the place to live, work and play!**

Ladner Harbour Authority Boat Basin: {49° 5' 31" N, 123° 5' 27"} Permanent and guest moorage (commercial vessels have priority), water, 20/30 power, sewage pump-out. Free 3-hr moorage at Elliot St. Public Wharf. Call Harbourmaster for information. 604-940-6432.

★ **Deas Island Regional Park:** This large park has tree-lined dikes, tidal marshes, and trails. Two historic buildings, a turn-of-the-century residence, and a heritage schoolhouse are open for exploration. Picnicking, canoeing, nature studies, and bar fishing are popular activities.

2024 Northwest Boat Travel

Captain's Cove Marina: {49° 6' 48" N, 123° 4' 41"} Permanent moorage only, 30/50 amp power, water, gas, diesel, wifi, 60-ton travel lift, DIY Boatyard. 604-946-1244.

RiverHouse Marina Restaurant & Pub: {49° 6' 58" N, 123° 3' 48"} On the Deas Slough. Depending on tide, clearance on Hwy 99 Bridge is 11-22'. Permanent moorage, daytime transient moorage, no overnights. 15/30 amp power, water, restaurant, pub. Free moorage while dining, check in with marina. Office: 604-940-4496. Cell: 604-619-8408. Restaurant: 604-946-7545.

★ **Tilbury Island:** Tilbury Island is located in Delta, a suburban area of Vancouver with a population of around 100,000. Most residents live in the residential areas of Ladner, North Delta and Tsawwassen. Tilbury Island, on the other hand, is home to one of the top four business parks in Greater Vancouver with more than 300 businesses representing the aerospace, high-tech, manufacturing, and distribution industries. Right on River Rd, at the west end of the Tilbury district, Bridgeview Marine sells boating supplies, boat parts, new motors, new boat and new trailers and has a full service department for repairs or maintenance. Call 604-946-8566 for information. On the opposite shore is Shelter Island Marina and Boat Yard.

Richmond
[3490]

★ **Richmond (2):** This thriving community, at the mouth of the Fraser River, offers extensive yachting services as well as services and activities for travelers. There are marinas, charter agencies, boat repairs and services, as well as fueling facilities. Day moorage at Imperial Landing at Britannia Shipyards National Historic Site is available. Monthly moorage, as well as some transient space is also available at Steveston Harbour Authority and Shelter Island. Once on land, visitors can explore the city's stores, restaurants and various lodging options, ranging from B&B's to 26 brand name hotels. The Golden Village, in the heart of Richmond, is an Asian Mecca with unique imports, authentic eateries, and many cultural events. Nearly 50 miles of trails offer hours of walking or biking opportunities. A Cultural Art Centre features an art gallery and museum. Several wineries offer tours and tastings. The nearby Historic Fishing Village of Steveston makes a wonderful day trip where sites of interest include the Gulf of Georgia Cannery, London Heritage Farm and the Britannia Heritage Shipyard. Summer events include the *Richmond Maritime Festival*, *Ships to Shore Steveston* and *Steveston Salmon Festival*, all popular events. For current event information, visit www.visitrichmondbc.com or call the Visitor Centre at 1-877-247-0777.

★ **Shelter Island Marina & Boatyard:** {49° 09' 49.9" N, 122° 59' 23.4" W} Come to this Marina, not only for Moorage with power and water, but also to visit Tugboat Annie's Pub & Grille, Tugboat Annie's Liquor Store, as well as Shelter Island's Hardware Store. Haul-out and Storage available. 400 lineal feet of moorage has been added, short and long term available. Two of the largest Travelifts (75 & 220 ton) on the coast, with over 20 acres of boatyard. Connected by bus to downtown Vancouver and surrounding areas. A+ rating with Better Business Bureau. See our advertisement on this page. Website: www.shelterislandmarina.com. Email: infodesk@shelterislandmarina.com. Address: 6911 Graybar Road, Richmond, British Columbia V6W 1H3. Fax: 604-273-6282. Telephone: 604-270-6272.

Imperial Landing Dock: (West of Britannia Shipyards National Historic Site) Transient moorage, 3-day max stay. $1.50 per foot per 24 hours.

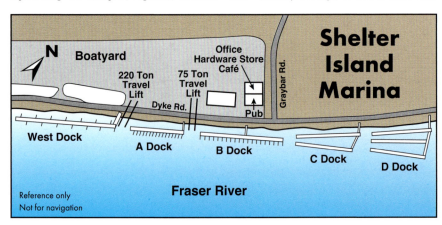

★ **Shelter Island Marina & Boatyard:** Located in South East Richmond on the South Arm of the Fraser River (see Chart 3490/3491), Shelter Island is a full service Marina and Boatyard. Starting with the Yard, Shelter Island is home to the largest Boatyard in B.C. and possesses two of the largest Travelifts along the West Coast (75 and 220 Ton). With over 29 Acres of Boatyard and Marina, Shelter Island offers both short and long term storage to customers with vessels ranging from 20-145 feet in length. What makes Shelter Island unique is that it is an open Boatyard, meaning customers can work on their boats themselves or hire one of the many trades onsite to do the job. In the Marina, Shelter Island has over 9 Acres of Dock space and offers guest Moorage on both short and long term basis; Marina customers are provided with access to cable, water, and power up to 50 amps. Through continuous improvement Shelter Island has expanded its services to offer more to its customers such as: Tugboat Annie's Pub & Grille, Tugboat Annie's Liquor Store, and Jimbo's Café with free Wi-Fi, a 40-50 seat banquet room, and finally a marine hardware store fully stocked with parts, paints, charts, expertise, and so much more. Website: www.shelterislandmarina.com Address: 6911 Graybar Road, Richmond British Columbia V6W 1H3. Fax: 604-273-6282. Telephone 604-270-6272 or toll free 1-877-270-6272. (Shed and Storage space now available)

Visit us at boattravel.com

Pay at parking meter on the pier. Moorage on channel side of dock only, average draft 12.3' on the outside of dock. 15/30/50 amp power, no water, no dumping of black or gray water. 604-238-8038.

Richmond Chevron Marine: Gas, diesel, lubricants, water, snacks. 604-278-2181.

Skyline Marina: {49° 11' 7" N, 123° 8' 13" W} Permanent moorage, 30/50 amp power, water, laundry, showers, washrooms, DIY boatyard, 30-ton Travelift (boats to 42'). 604-273-3977.

Vancouver Marina: {49° 11' 20" N, 123° 8' 11" W} Permanent & transient moorage (call ahead), 15/30/50 amp power, water, WiFi, garbage, fuel dock, restaurant, repairs onsite. 604-278-9787. VHF 66A. Fuel dock: Gas, diesel, public pumpout, ice, bait, snacks, marine charts/supplies. 604-278-3300. Galleon Marine: Mechanical services, parts, boat/motor sales. 604-273-7544. Restaurant: 604-273-7014.

New Westminster's SkyBridge spans the Fraser River   Photo © Dennis Sylvester Hurd

★ **New Westminster:** Located 12 miles east of Vancouver, is the oldest incorporated city in the province. From 1866 to 1868 New Westminster served as the capital of British Columbia. Because it was named by Queen Victoria, it is known as The Royal City. Many fine Victorian and Edwardian buildings are found here. The River Market at Westminster Quay features fresh foods, shops, restaurants and hosts special events during the year. Quayside Park with its maritime play features is a fun stop for kids. Nearby, the last steam-powered sternwheeler to operate in Canada, the 1937 *Samson V*, has been preserved as a museum. One block north, the Skytrain station offers 25 minute connections to downtown Vancouver. For information call 604-953-3333.

Royal City Marina: {49° 10' 45" N, 122°56' 49" W} Permanent moorage, 30 amp power, water. Boat sales. 604-515-1980.

★ **New Westminster to Pitt River:** It is possible, and can be enjoyable, to cruise up the Fraser River beyond New Westminster. Strip charts #3488 and #3489 describe the river from Pattullo Bridge to Harrison River. Because of changing sandbars and deadheads, as well as considerable commercial and recreational vessel activity, it is advisable to have someone with local knowledge on board or to hire a tug or towing captain as a guide. An unmarked channel is maintained with channel depths of 11.8 feet below low-low water line (LLWL) to Whonnock, and 8.2 feet below LLWL from Whonnock to Hope. To starboard are the Fraser Surrey Docks. The Skytrain Bridge connects Westminster and Surrey. Approaching the Pattullo Bridge, keep the red buoys to starboard. Further upstream is the Port Mann Bridge. Douglas Island marks the gateway to Pitt River and Lake.

★ **Pitt River:** [3062] This navigable, 14 mile-long river connects with the Fraser River. It is possible to transit the river and explore expansive Pitt Lake. Port Coquitlam City is on the river's west bank. Several uncharted sloughs empty into the river. There are tidal flats, usually marked by grass. There is a marina at the mouth of the Alouette River, where it joins the Pitt. Two miles north of here on the opposite bank is the DeBouville Slough, site of the Pitt River Boat Club. Look for their sign in the river. Pay attention to depth in the Slough, it can be quite shallow depending on tides/time of year. Several bridges cross the river. Log rafts are frequently stored along the river. Transit Grant Narrows and Grant Channel through a buoy-marked channel, through the flats at the southern part of Pitt Lake. There is a public boat launch at Pitt Polder near the mouth of Pitt Lake. Much of this area is best explored by canoe. It is possible to paddle behind Siwash Island and up Widgeon Creek. This is a wildlife Preserve. It takes 90 minutes by canoe to reach Widgeon Creek Park, with picnic area, campsites, and Forest Service trails.

Pitt Meadows Marina: {49° 15' 5" N, 123° 42' 7" W} Permanent moorage to 28', temporary moorage if space is available, gas, water, 30 amp power, launch (fee applies), convenience store. 604-465-7713.

Pitt River Boat Club: Waitlist for annual moorage/boat launch packages. Gas, water, ice, oil, snacks, restrooms. 604-942-7371.

★ **Pitt Lake:** A voyage to Pitt Lake, one of the world's largest freshwater tidal lakes, is an interesting day trip. Considered by many to be a beautiful, relatively untouched gem of a boating destination, Pitt Lake is deep and adorned with picturesque islands. Due to the topography, wind funnels through in unpredictable patterns. The lake may be choppy at times, even though nearby waters are calm. There are anchorage possibilities off the islands. The Burke-Pinecone Provincial Park, on the west shore, is largely a wilderness area with no facilities. Backcountry camping and hiking are popular here.

★ **Pitt River to Fort Langley and Mission:** Abreast of Douglas Island, heading east, keep to the port side of the Fraser, staying about one third of the breadth of the river from its northern boundaries. The channel is not adequately marked, but the above course is the best choice for reducing the risk of grounding. Barnston Island is peaceful agricultural land suitable for bicycling or walking. No usable beaches. A ferry runs on demand between Surrey to the island from 6:15am-11:55pm daily. Derby Reach Regional Park is on the site of the first Fort Langley, built in 1827. The marshy ground was not easily defended, so the fort was later moved. The park has campsites, picnic areas, and trails, but fishing is the main attraction, especially in fall when the salmon are running. Park Info: 604-530-4983.

Upstream, past Derby Reach, is McMillan Island, a First Nations Reserve. There is also access from the bottom of McMillan Island up Bedford Channel that has better water depth and more dock access since the mill is no longer there. Go past McMillan Island and then turn west into Bedford Channel to visit Fort Langley. The Fort Langley Marina Park and boat launch is to port. Just past the park is a small dock. It may have one or two spots to tie up. There is no other public float. Antique and craft shops, two museums, washrooms, and the restored Hudson's Bay Company Fort, circa 1858, are in the vicinity.

When coming abreast of Crescent Island, keep to the port side of the island. The Stave River flows into the Fraser. Do not pass under the railroad bridge. Keep a third of the way out from the north bank of the Fraser. Pass Benson and Matsqui Islands and have the Mission Bridge in your sights. This bridge connects Mission with Abbotsford and Clearbrook. Immediately up-river from the traffic bridge is the railway bridge. If more than 12 to 15 feet clearance is required, contact the bridge tender on VHF Channel 69 or call 604-826-3117 and request opening the bridge. Just past the Railway Bridge, on the port side, is the Mission dock.

★ **Mission:** Visitor moorage is on the outside of the community dock. The pump-out station is near the bottom of the gangway on the outer breakwater float. Among the local attractions are restaurants, shops, a golf course, performing arts theatre, and a drag racing park. Bus service is available, call 604-854-3232.

Mission Harbour Authority: {49° 7' 42" N, 122° 18' 8" W} Limited moorage (call ahead), 20/30/50 amp power, water, pump-out, garbage, laundry (call ahead), meeting room rental, security gate, water taxi. River pilots can be arranged to travel to Harrison Lake. 24-hr message center. 604-826-4414.

Catherwood Towing: Gas, diesel, assistance with bridge opening, water taxi and river pilot information. 604-826-9221. Fuel: 604-826-9257. VHF 69.

★ **Mission to Harrison River and Lake:** [3061] The ever changing channels of the upper Fraser make it a necessity to hire a guide or pilot for this trip. The natural beauty and abundant wildlife make traveling here highly recommended. The journey on the Fraser ends at Billy Smith Rock

Panoramic perspective of False Creek   Photo © Joe Mabel

where the Harrison and Fraser Rivers come together in a spectacular, powerful array of swirling, frothing multi-colored waters. Further on, waits may be necessary at the CPR Railway Bridge and the Harrison Mills Bridge. After passing the Harrison Rapids, there is a First Nations Reserve to port.

★ **Harrison Hot Springs and Harrison Lake:** [3061] After entering the clear waters of Harrison Lake, pilots will keep a safe distance from the village's shores to starboard. There is a public dock for boats and float planes. A free pump-out station is available adjacent to the public boat launch (fee applies for launch, as well as parking and trailer storage). Another boat launch, no fee, is located on the east side of Harrison Lake at Green Point; part of Sasquatch Provincial Park. Also on the east side of the lake, south of the breakwater, is a red government dock for emergency-only mooring. Beautiful sites in the area include Rainbow Falls on the east side of Cascade Bay. If the angle of the sun is just right, a myriad of rainbows surround the cascading waters of the falls as they tumble into the waters below. Harrison Hot Springs is a lively resort village bustling with activities. There is a post office, mall, art gallery, shops, cafes, a range of lodging options and a public pool filled with natural hot spring mineral waters. A Sasquatch Museum has recently opened in the Visitor Information Centre at 499 Hot Springs Road. Daily tours are available to cruise the lake, the river, or in the fall to view eagles. The Harrison Hot Springs Resort has a spa, a golf course and a dock where several companies offer canoe, kayak, pedal boat, SUP, jet ski, and powerboat rentals. During the summer, there is a large water park in front of the resort. Swimming, fishing, windsurfing, and hiking the local trails are other popular activities. Harrison Hot Springs hopes to celebrate its variety of annual events including the Agassiz Farms Cycle Tour, Harrison Beer Festival Uncorked Wine Festival, and The Harrison Festival of the Arts (an 8-day artisanal festival held each July featuring a variety of performers and artists. For more information about the area visit www.tourismharrison.com.

Harrison Hot Spring Marina: (Adjacent to Marine fueling station). Annual moorage to 60', very limited overnight moorage, some slips with 30 amp power. 604-796-8623.

Killer's Cove Marina: {49° 18' 21" N, 121° 46' 26" W} Daily, weekly, 2 mo., and annual moorage. 30 amp power, gas, snacks. Cell: 604-793-3750. Fuel Dock: 604-796-3856. VHF 68.

Vancouver
[3481, 3493, 3494, 3495]

★ **Vancouver:** Moorage is available at marinas in False Creek and Burrard Inlet. This beautiful city, the third largest in the country, is *Canada's Gateway to the Pacific*. To the east and north, the majestic Coast Mountains overlook this metropolis. To the south, are the lush, green farmlands of the Fraser Valley. To the west, the waters of Burrard Inlet, Vancouver Harbour, False Creek, English Bay, and the Strait of Georgia all embrace the City's shores. Much of Vancouver's economy and recreation are intimately involved with the sea. Blessed with a mild climate, the port is ice free all year. Even fair weather boaters can enjoy a long boating season, from March to well into October. The miles of commercial wharves that line the eastern part of the city's shores are used for shipping coal, potash, sulfur, mineral concentrates, wheat, forest and petroleum products, and general cargo. Storage warehouses and grain elevators are conspicuous along the waterfront.

Vancouver, with its unique cultural and ethnic history, offers hundreds of shopping opportunities. Known for its British influence and treasures, there is an abundance of typical motherland wares, teas, and foods, such as fish and chips served with the typical dash of vinegar. But each neighborhood holds its own special surprises. Gastown is perfect for strolling, shopping, dining, and has re-emerged as one of the hippest neighbourhoods in town. Yaletown-a former warehouse district-is now a friendly shopping and dining district that is home to many of the city's top restaurants. Upscale clothing and jewelry boutiques, as well as well-known national and international retailers are scattered on Robson, Alberni, Granville and Burrard Streets. For an alternative shopping experience, there are a number of public markets, including Granville Island Market, Lonsdale Quay and Westminster Quay. All have waterfront access, fresh local produce, crafts fashioned by local artisans and fresh local seafood. Visitors to the Steveston docks in Richmond can purchase fresh seafood straight off the fishing boats. First Nations arts and crafts are among the top Vancouver souvenirs including carved cedar masks, jewelry, whalebone scrimshaw, and sweaters.

There is always something going on in Vancouver. For cultural enthusiasts there is the summertime *Bard on the Beach Shakespeare Festival*. The *Vancouver International Jazz Festival* is also a summer event and usually begins in June. July's festivities include *Canada Day Celebrations* and the *Vancouver Folk Music Festival*. In English Bay, the *Celebration of Light* fireworks competition events are spectacular. Anchor in the harbour for "front row seats". Early arrival is recommended.

For more information about Vancouver area attractions and events, visit www.destinationvancouver.com. You can also call the Visitor Centre at 604-683-2000 or drop by 200 Burrard Street.

Vancouver Fraser Port Authority: The Vancouver Fraser Port Authority has navigational jurisdiction over a water area that includes the Metro Vancouver region, (Burrard Inlet, Indian Arm, Port Moody, Roberts Bank, and the Fraser River). Download a copy of the Port Information guide containing local rules, procedures and restriction for safe and efficient navigation at www.portvancouver.com/marine-operations.

Burrard Inlet
[3481, 3493]

Point Atkinson: Site of a landmark lighthouse.

Caulfeild Cove: This is a small indentation east of Point Atkinson. It offers a spot for a lunch hook. A small, often crowded, public float extends from the starboard shore. A green meadow provides a blanket for shoreside picnics.

Burrard Inlet (3): The four mile opening of the inlet extends from Point Atkinson on the north to Point Grey on the south. This extensive inlet penetrates eastward over 12 miles where it divides into Indian Arm and Port Moody.

English Bay (4): This bay stretches three miles between Spanish Bank and Stanley Park. Often

VANCOUVER Chapter 12 Page 163

large freighters lie at anchorage in the bay. English Bay Beach, or First Beach, located just below Stanley Park is the site of a striking stone Inukshuk Sculpture, the Inuit symbol for friendship. Shallow, shifting ledges of sand gradually moving into the southern part of English bay have extended beyond the existing markers. False Creek is entered from English Bay.

False Creek
[3311, 3481, 3493]

★ **False Creek (5):** Please note that the speed limit is 10km or 5 knots. No sailing is permitted once you enter False Creek. Tidal streams run to three knots here. Anchoring is allowed in False Creek, stay clear of the navigable channel (refer to "Anchoring in False Creek" entry that follows).

Vanier Park, home to the Maritime Museum and the Pacific Space Centre are to starboard as you enter False Creek from English Bay. A breakwater just inside Elsje Point shelters historic ships in the Museum's Heritage Harbour. Beyond the park, Kitsilano Coast Guard Base is situated on a jetty with floats extending out to the east. One of Vanier Park's public boat ramps is located next to the Base.

Continuing on, pass under the Burrard Street Bridge, clearance 90'. Fishermen's Wharf Terminal is starboard. A courtesy customs telephone check-in site is found at False Creek Fishermen's Wharf, float "F". Further on, under the Granville Bridge is Granville Island where you will find marine businesses, boat brokerages, repair yards, and charter agencies. There is free moorage (3 hr max.) at the Public Market floats on Granville Island.

The next bridge to span False Creek is the Cambie Bridge. Vertical clearance is 46 feet above the high tide line. A condominium marina is at the northwest end of Cambie Street Bridge. Within walking distance of the eastern edge of the grounds is an authentic classical Chinese garden, Sun Yat Sen Classical Chinese Garden. On Carroll Street, in Chinatown, three acres are designed in the tradition of the Ming Dynasty of 2,500 years ago. It is of special interest because the artisans used old techniques and tools to create the garden.

The Plaza of Nations, is on the north shore. This entertainment district includes pubs, eateries, shopping, a casino, and B.C. Place Stadium and Rogers Arena where sports, cultural programs and exhibitions are featured.

False Creek Anchoring Boundary: The area lying east of a line drawn from Kits Point 45 degrees northeast across the mouth of the creek. Visiting boaters wishing to anchor in this area require an anchoring permit. The area to the west falls under the jurisdiction of Transport Canada.

Anchoring in False Creek: Permits to anchor are required if you anchor more than eight hours during the day (9am-11pm) or you anchor anytime between 11pm-9am. Maximum stay 14 days out of 30 from April 1-Sept. 30, and 21 days out of 40 from Oct 1-March 31. Permits are free and available from Heather Civic Marina, 604-874-2814 or online at https://app.vancouver.ca/falsecreek-permit_net.

★ **False Creek Harbour Authority - Fishermen's Wharf:** {49° 16' 21" N, 123° 8' 20" W} This is British Columbia's original 5-Anchor Clean Marine rated facility, open 24 hours a day, all year round. It is located on the south shore of False Creek, west of Granville Island. Please contact the harbour office for docking instructions prior to arrival. Customs clearance is available at the outer end of the fish sales dock. Other services include 20a and 30a power hookups on all docks with some 50a and 100a available, water, washrooms, showers, laundry, ice, pumpout, recycling, waste oil disposal, 24 hour security and free wireless internet. The ramps to shore are 75 feet long and 5 feet wide and fitted with transition plates at each end to make them fully CDPA compliant. Go Fish Seafood Shack's fish & chips are not to be missed and a public fish sales dock is just east of the main docks where you may purchase a variety of seafood directly from the fishermen who caught it. See our advertisement on this page. Website: www.falsecreek.com. Email: Info@falsecreek.com. Address: 1505 West 1st Ave. Vancouver, BC. V6J 1E8. Telephone: (604)-733-3625. VHF 66A.

Burrard Civic Marina: {49° 16' 5" N, 123° 8' 3" W} Permanent moorage, limited transient moorage, 15 amp power, pump-out, launch ramp, garbage deposit. 604-733-5833.

False Creek Fuels: Gas, low sulfur diesel, lubricants, filters, drinks, snacks, ice, marine supplies, fishing licenses, bait & tackle. 604-638-0209. VHF 66A.

False Creek Yacht Club: {49° 16' 21" N, 123° 7' 55" W} Temporary and/or reciprocal moorage (call ahead), 30 amp power, washrooms, showers, laundry, pump-out. Wharfinger: 604-648-2628. VHF 66A.

Heather Civic Marina: {49° 16' 23" N, 123° 7' 20" W} Permanent, monthly, transient moorage, and liveaboard. Water, 15/30/50 amp power, showers, laundry, pump-out. 604-874-2814.

Pacific Boulevard Marina at the Plaza of Nations: {49° 16' 28" N, 123° 6' 29" W} Permanent moorage, call for information on transient, & temporary moorage, 30/50 amp power, water, WiFi, cable. 604-683-7035.

Quayside Marina: {49° 16' 23" N, 123° 7' 12" W} Slips for sale or lease. Limited temporary moorage for boats up to 120', call ahead. 30/50/100 amp power, water, laundry, showers, ice, sewage pumps, garbage, recycling. 604-681-9115. VHF 66A.

★ **Granville Island:** Transient moorage can be found at Pelican Bay Marina and may be available at Fisherman's Terminal when the fishing fleet is out. A free public dock behind the Public Market allows three-hour moorage, first come first

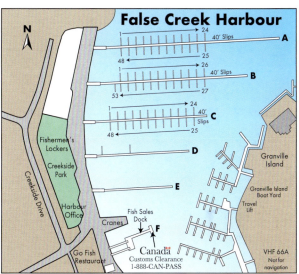

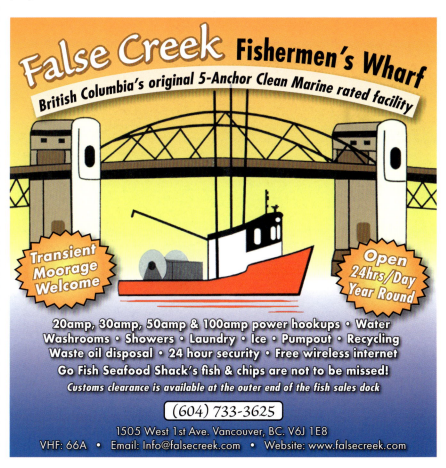

2024 Northwest Boat Travel

Page 164 Chapter 12 VANCOUVER

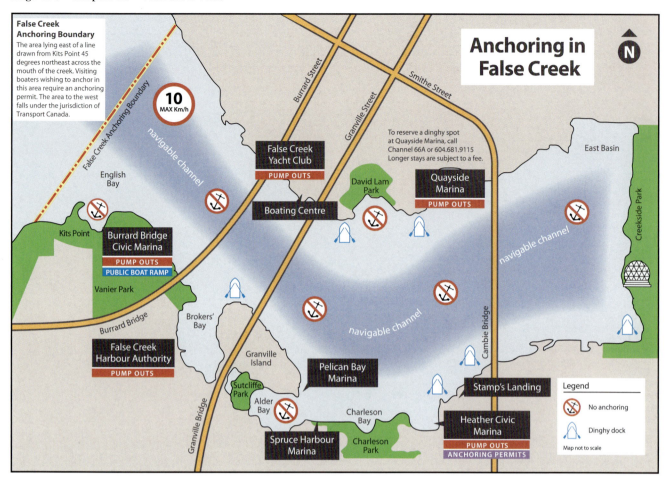

served. Formerly an industrial area, the buildings of Granville Island have been converted to house marine-oriented businesses (including boatyard & repair), restaurants, book and gift shops, a hotel, theaters with live performances, galleries, the Granville Island Brewery, a large public seafood and produce market, and a waterpark for children. Passenger service by False Creek Ferries, 604-684-7781 and the Aquabus, 604-689-5858 make downtown, Yaletown, Chinatown, sports venues, and theaters very accessible. Park lands with picnic facilities and trails are plentiful. Kayak and small boat rentals are available, as are scenic cruises.

Maritime Market and Marina: Annual moorage, power, water, garbage, security. 604-408-0100. Onsite boatyard, travel lift capacity to 70' LOA x 19'8" beam, power/sail services, repairs. 604-685-6924.

Pelican Bay Marina: {49° 16' 7" N, 123° 7' 5" W} Permanent & limited transient moorage, 30/50 amp power, water, washrooms, ice, WiFi. 604-729-1442.

Spruce Harbour Marina: {49° 16' 5.8" N, 123° 7' 42.2" W} Co-op liveaboards. Conventional permanent moorage with 15 amp power, water, parking. 604-733-3512.

First Narrows to Coal Harbour

[3481, 3493]

First Narrows (6): Freighters, tugs, barges, ferries, and small craft traverse the channel between English Bay and Vancouver Harbour. First Narrows, which offers a boat's-eye-view of Stanley Park and the Lions Gate Bridge, is the first of three narrows in Burrard Inlet. Incoming traffic must stay close to Stanley Park. Fishing, cross traffic, sailing or proceeding without mechanical power is prohibited in First Narrows. Listen to VHF 12 for commercial traffic information. Currents in the narrows run to six knots. When a strong northwest wind meets a large ebbing tide, the turbulence can be dangerous in the narrows. Caution advised in regard to strong currents near Prospect Point at the mouth of the Capilano River.

★ **Vancouver Harbour (7):** Vancouver Harbour is the portion of Burrard Inlet east of First Narrows. The north shore rims the City of North Vancouver where the SeaBus ferry terminal at Lonsdale Quay is located. Passenger ferries connect to downtown Vancouver. The west portion of Vancouver Harbour contains Coal Harbour and the shoreline of downtown Vancouver. No sailing is permitted within the Inner Harbour. No scuba diving, water-skiing, or personal watercraft allowed between First and Second Narrows. Vancouver Harbour is a security zone.

Coal Harbour

[3481, 3493]

★⚓ **Stanley Park:** Although there is no direct boater access, beautiful Stanley Park, a 1,000 acre peninsula, borders Coal Harbour. A seawall, with walking path, lines the shore. Activities and facilities include cycle paths, cricket playing, a miniature railway, children's farmyard, pitch and putt course, tennis, concessions, swimming, dancing, rose gardens, and BC's most visited tourist attraction - the collection of nine Kwakwaka'wakw and Haida totems at Brockton Point. The Vancouver Aquarium is also located at the Park and features over 50,000 animals from across the world. Open 365 days a year, call 604-659-FISH.

★ **Coal Harbour (8):** After traversing First Narrows and rounding Stanley Park's Brockton Point, one enters Coal Harbour, where a five knot speed limit is enforced. Anchorage is not permitted, but moorage is available at marinas. Be watchful for seaplane traffic. This area is a seaplane aerodome and hundreds of floatplanes land daily. Royal Vancouver Yacht Club and the Vancouver Rowing Club are headquartered here. The Canadian Customs dock at the foot of Bute Street at the Harbour Green Dock is temporarily closed. Onshore, Harbour

False Creek's Aquabus   Photo © Granville Island Media

Visit us at boattravel.com

False Creek and downtown Vancouver Photo © Ruth Hartnup

Green Park has a water spray feature for kids. FlyOver Canada, a 4-D flight simulation ride is located at Canada Place in Coal Harbour.

Bayshore West Marina: {49° 17' 37" N, 123° 7' 55" W} Permanent moorage, transient moorage if space is available. 30/50 amp power, water, pump-out, garbage/recycling, restrooms, parking. 604-689-5331.

Coal Harbour Chevron: Gas, diesel, lubricants, some filters, water, washrooms, bait, snacks, waste oil disposal. 604-681-7725.

Coal Harbour Marina: {N°49 17.500' W°123 07.600'} Annual and temporary moorage, 30/50/100 amp power, water, laundry, showers, WiFi. 604-681-2628. VHF 66A (24 hrs).

Harbour Green Public Dock: The dock and floating walkway are open. The repairs made have restored the dock as a walkway and space for short-term recreational moorage.

Second Narrows (9): See current tables for Burrard Inlet. This site, where the Seymour River flows into Burrard Inlet, is 4 miles from First Narrows. Conditions are similar to those at First Narrows. No sailing is permitted through the narrows. No anchoring allowed. The Second Narrows Highway Bridge, renamed the Ironworkers Memorial Bridge to honor the 19 workers who lost their lives during its construction, is a local landmark. The vertical clearance at center span is 44 metres or about 144 ft. Approaching the Bridge, the Port Metro Lynnterm Terminal and the Lynnwood Marina & Boatyard are on the North Vancouver shore. Beyond the bridge is a railroad bridge with a minimum height of 35 feet. Taller vessels request lifts on VHF Channel 12 calling "Second Narrows."

Burnaby & Port Moody
[3494, 3495]

★ **Barnet Marine Park (10):** This Burnaby park is the site of the old Kapoor sawmill. Swimming beach, fishing pier, picnic sites, waterside trail, and seasonal off-leash dog area. Anchor east of the pier or in the small niche.

★ **Port Moody (11):** The Port Moody Arm of Burrard Inlet is headed by extensive shallow mudflats designated as Tidal Park. A Designated Anchorage Area, within the boundaries of four buoys based on the coordinates {49° 17'18.06"N, -122° 51' 14.47W}, is the only anchorage allowed for visiting boaters. A permit is required to anchor overnight, dates must be reserved, stays are limited to 21 days within a 40 day period. For details, portmoody.ca/daa or 604-469-4552. A narrow dredged channel, marked with day beacons, leads to Rocky Point Park. Rocky Point Park is home to a wide fee-for-service boat launching ramp, floats for small boats to tie up to, a long lighted pier with benches, a covered pavilion and performance stage, and connections to biking and hiking trails. Park facilities include concessions, swimming pool and spray park, playground, picnic tables, and restrooms. The park also boasts a waterfront restaurant called The Boathouse, Sunday Summer Concerts and Artists in the Park. The Port Moody Station Museum, housed in a 1908 railway station is located nearby. The museum, as well as the annual *Golden Spike Days celebration*, recall the city's early days as the western terminus of the Canadian Pacific Railway. Within short walking distance of the park, the old town city center features shops, liquor store, galleries and restaurants. Port Moody's adopted slogan "City of the Arts" is reflected in the galleries, studios, the Port Moody Arts Centre, the Inlet Theatre, the *Port Moody Canadian Film Festival* in March, the *Golden Spike Days Festival* in July, and the *Summer Sunday Concert Series* is July & August. Visit portmoody.ca/tourism to find out more about local activities, recreation, food/drink, shopping, services, and arts and culture.

Reed Point Marina: {49° 17' 30" N, 122° 52' 49' W} Permanent moorage, 20/30 amp power, water, washrooms, showers, private pump-out, restaurant. Fuel barge with gas, diesel, oil, snacks & beverages (May-Sept), ice. Boatyard onsite, marine services, repairs, parts, 50-ton Travelift. Marina: 604-937-1600. Fuel Barge: 604-937-1606. Boatyard: 604-936-4602.

Indian Arm
[3495]

★ **Indian Arm (12):** This three-mile-wide, ten-mile-long fjord offers a convenient, easily navigated day cruise. Occasionally thermal drafts create down-slope winds and choppy waters, but the waters are generally calm. The arm's deep green waters, home to ling cod and rockfish, lie at the base of peaks which rise to heights of 5,000 feet. Waterfalls plunge down the cliffs in spring and early summer, making the surface water nearly fresh. Speed limits of five knots are in effect in the channel between Twin Island and the mainland, in Belcarra Bay near the floats, in the south end of Bedwell Bay, and between Jug Island and peninsula at the entrance. Much of the shoreline is undeveloped. Three yacht clubs have outstations and there is anchorage near the head of the arm. Caution advised regarding snags in the area. Boats can be beached on the river estuary's sand flats. Wilderness camping is available at Bishop Creek and Granite Falls, near the head of Indian Arm.

★ **Say Nuth Khaw Yum Provincial Park aka (Indian Arm Park):** Located adjacent to Mount Seymour Provincial Park in North Vancouver, the park is situated on the east and west sides of Indian Arm Park and is primarily accessed by water. Park designation protects the shores, old-growth forests, several alpine lakes, a waterfall, numerous creeks, and the Indian River estuary (a vital habitat for five species of salmon, as well as prawns, crabs, waterfowl, and harbour seals). Park beaches are popular

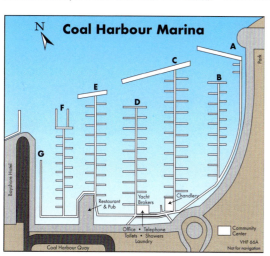

Chapter 12 VANCOUVER

Deep Cove   Photo © Brian H. Wilson

with boaters, kayakers and scuba divers. The park is a wilderness area, no facilities are provided. Please practice the "no trace" policy. Dinghies, kayaks, and canoes may enter the river at the head, however shoaling makes this difficult. A small beach, east of the river, can be used for shore access.

★ **Belcarra Dock in təmtəmíxʷtən/Belcarra Regional Park:** Located near Roche Point, these public L-shaped floats with wheelchair access are often used by commercial boats loading and unloading passengers. Recreational boaters may tie to the dock. No overnight moorage. Depth at floats is 2.4 meters. Picnic shelters, toilets, playground and trails are onshore. Anchorage is possible south of the long wharf or in Belcarra Bay. Drying flats extend from shore. Park info: 604-520-6442.

Deep Cove: This is primarily a residential area of North Vancouver. There is a marina and public float. Moorage for loading and unloading only at the public float. No waterskiing. A five knot speed limit is enforced. The village of Deep Cove has a variety of businesses, including B & B's, gas stations, art galleries, kayak rentals, grocery and gift shops. The Deep Cove Cultural Centre houses an art gallery and gift shop, and the Deep Cove Heritage Society featuring historical photos, maps and documents (call for hours). 604-929-5744. The Centre is also home to a 130-seat air-conditioned studio theatre shared by two theatre companies. For tickets to a production, call 604-929-3200 or 604-929-9456. Two waterfront parks, Deep Cove and Panorama, have swimming, picnic and play areas, as well as boat launches and walking trails. Panorama Park hosts a summer concerts series.

Deep Cove North Shore Marina: {49° 19' 59.88" N, 122° 57' 0" W} Permanent moorage, transient moorage if space is available (call ahead). 15/30 amp power, water, gas, diesel, lubricants, showers, laundry, ice, snacks, boat rentals. 604-929-1251.

★ **Bedwell Bay:** Located at the southeast end of the arm. Good, well-sheltered anchorage. There is an access road to Vancouver.

Woodlands: No marine services. A municipal float has a 24 hour limit. A rock, southwest of the float, is covered five feet at high water.

★ **Raccoon and Twin Islands/Indian Arm Provincial Park:** Temporary anchorage is found near the northwest side of Raccoon. Two rocks which dry are approximately 200' off shore. Other shoals extend off the islands. The waters around these islands are deep. A small public pier for vessels under 30 feet is on the east side of Twin Islands. A limited trail system is provided. Good scuba diving. Limited wilderness camping is permitted only on North Twin Islands. Visitors are asked to observe the "no trace" policy.

Granite Falls: The 165' high falls are the largest in Indian Arm. A BC Parks dock is on the north side of the falls.

★ **Cates Park (13):** One mile northwest of Roche Point, Cates Park offers picnic sites, playground, tennis court, a swimming beach, trails, and seasonal concessions. Each summer, free outdoor concerts are held here. Also of interest is the First Nation canoe on display. For kayak rentals or weekend canoe/kayak tours. 604-985-2925. Scuba diving enthusiasts can explore an artificial reef offshore. Temporary anchorage is possible and there is a launching ramp with a dock for small boats at Roche Point (see Belcarra Dock entry).

North Vancouver
[3481, 3493, 3494]

★ **North Vancouver (14):** Connected to Vancouver by the Lions Gate Bridge and the Ironworkers Memorial Bridge, North Vancouver is home to marinas, waterfront restaurants, repair yards, and chandleries. There are marine businesses along Vancouver Harbour from First Narrows through and beyond Second Narrows. North Vancouver also offers an array of tourist attractions for every interest. Families will enjoy a visit to the animals at Maplewood Farm or attending one of the high quality productions at The Presentation House Theatre. MONOVA (Museum of North Vancouver) newly opened at the end of 2021 in the Shipyards District has lots to offer through stories of North Vancouver through high-quality exhibitions in the Permanent and Feature Galleries. The Polygon Gallery, just one of North Vancouver's art galleries, is located in the revitalized Lower Lonsdale waterfront and is a must see for photography buffs. Also on the waterfront, the Lonsdale Quay Market offers shops, restaurants, boutiques, fresh produce, seafood and other local delights. Check out The Shipyards located adjacent to Lonsdale Quay Market which features 84,000 sq. ft. of mixed use commerical and amenity space. This waterfront destination includes Seaside Boutique Hotel, Capilano University, restaurants, an outdoor covered skating rink (Dec-Mar), water park (late May-early Sept) and other shops and services. From the Market, you can take a 12-minute ride on Sea Bus to downtown Vancouver. Stroll or bike the North Shore Spirit Trail and take in the beautiful views of Vancouver's city skyline. The Squamish Nation Waterfront Greenway, part of the Spirit Trail, links Mosquito Creek Marina & Boatyard with the City's Kings Mill Walk and Waterfront Park. A bit further afoot, Lynn Canyon Park (five miles from moorages) is a great place to picnic and hike amid natural rainforests and old growth cedar trees. The Park is also home to a cafe, suspension bridge, and the Lynn Canyon Ecology Centre featuring a Natural History Museum and interactive exhibits. Capilano Suspension Bridge Park is another must see. Park attractions include the Capilano Suspension Bridge stretching 450'/137m across the Capilano River, Cliffwalk (a cantilevered walkway along the cliffs above the canyon) and Tree Top Adventures (viewing platforms and suspension bridges built right up in the trees). A few minutes drive from Capilano Suspension Bridge is Grouse Mountain offering year round fun for all ages including a Skyride, Ziplines, Grizzly Bear Habitat and much more. For additional information on activities, events, attractions, local shops, sightseeing tours and accommodations stop by the North Vancouver Visitor Centre located in the Lonsdale Quay Market (ground floor, north end), just a few steps away from the SeaBus terminal, or call 604-656-6491. www.nvtourism.ca, www.vancouversnorthshore.com.

Fraser Fibreglass Ltd: Complete yacht service facilities located at Lynnwood Marina. Specializing in yacht/boat painting, shipwrighting, woodworking, boat repair, design & alterations, as well as fibreglass related problems. 604-985-1098.

Lions Gate Marine Centre: {49° 18' 6" N, 123° 06' 8" W} No moorage. Sea-lift (60'/45-ton), haul outs, boatyard services onsite, or DIY, dry storage, launch ramp, pump-out, 604-985-5468.

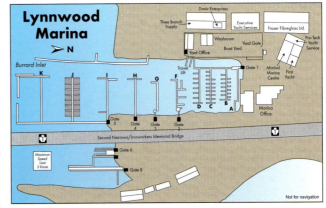

Visit us at boattravel.com

VANCOUVER Chapter 12 Page 167

Lynnwood Marina & Boatyard: {49° 18' 2.63" N, 123° 1' 41.9" W} Haul-outs to 75 tons, indoor and outdoor facilities for repairs, daily yard storage. On-site marine repair and service providers. Open moorage up to 80 feet, boat shed moorage available for annual rental, no transient moorage 604-985-1533.

Mosquito Creek Marina & Boatyard: {49° 18' 38.5" N, 123° 5' 28.2" W} Permanent and guest moorage; power, water, and pump-out services. Showers, laundry, and 24-hour security. Haul-outs to 75 feet, repairs, and dry storage. Easy access to City, restaurants and amenities. 604-987-4113.

West Vancouver
[3481, 3493, 3526]

Point Atkinson: [3481] The first lighthouse on this point was built in 1874. The present building, constructed in 1912, is now automated and is a national historic site. Lighthouse Park, (road access only), has a lighthouse viewpoint, trails, washrooms and parking. For tide here, refer to Atkinson Point, Burrard Inlet.

★ **Eagle Harbour (15):** Eagle Harbour is located 1.5 nautical miles north of Point Atkinson. Look for the highway cut into the hillside above the cove. The entrance to Eagle Harbour is south of Eagle Island, with the Eagle Harbour Yacht Club located behind the barge breakwater. Club reciprocals are available, but anchorage is not possible. Watch for crab buoys, swimmers and small water craft in the area.

Fisherman's Cove: The main entrance to this Cove is located north of both Eagle Harbour and Eagle Island. It is possible, at high tide, to enter the cove from the south side of Eagle Island, using caution over a gravel reef midway. There is a fuel dock at the north entrance. Repairs, haul-outs, mechanics and chandler services are available in the Cove. West Vancouver Yacht Club (reciprocal moorage) is also located in the cove. A marina offers limited transient moorage, advance booking recommended.

Fisherman's Cove Marine Fuels: (at Yacht Club entrance) Gas, diesel, oils, snacks, drinks, ice. 604-921-7333.

Thunderbird Marina: {49° 21' 21" N, 123° 16' 9" W} Permanent moorage, limited guest moorage, power, water, haul-outs (25-ton/50'), services onsite or DIY, chandlery, showers, washrooms. 604-921-7434.

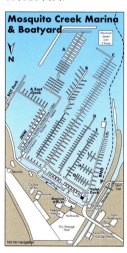

Bachelor Cove: Enter between Bird Islet and Whyte Islet. There is anchorage, open to winds from the south, at the head.

Whyte Cove: Whytecliff Park is onshore. Possible activities include swimming, tennis, picnicking, scuba diving in the underwater marine sanctuary, and low tide walks to scenic Whyte Islet.

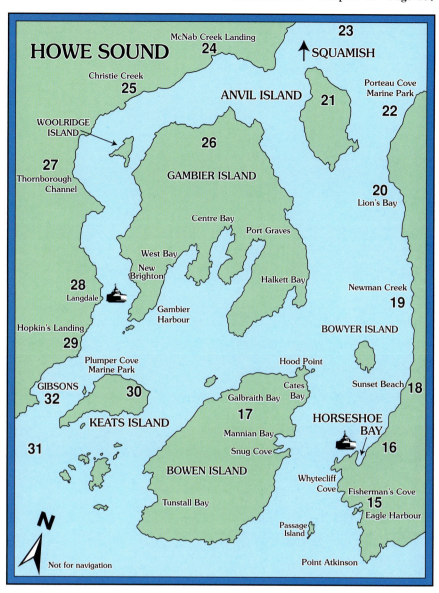

Howe Sound
[3526, 3524]

★ **Howe Sound:** This extensive body of water northwest of Vancouver is entered through one of the four main channels. The steep-sided shores are mountainous and heavily forested. Ferries from Horseshoe Bay cross to Bowen Island, Langdale on the mainland, and Nanaimo on Vancouver Island. Howe Sound is surprisingly undeveloped. Anchorage here is limited because of deep waters. Log tie-ups are often necessary. There are marina facilities in Horseshoe Bay, Snug Cove, Lion's Bay, Sunset Beach, and Gibsons. Porteau Cove and Plumper Cove are marine parks.

Horseshoe Bay
[3481, 3526, 3534]

★ **Horseshoe Bay (16):** A breakwater extends from east to west across the bay, providing protection for the municipal pier and the public float (3 hour limit, no overnight moorage unless in the case of an emergency). The pier is home to the Royal Canadian Marine Search and Rescue vessel and is used by water taxis for pick up/drop off only. A marina in the bay offers limited guest moorage. Provisions, repairs, restaurants, and a park are in the area. Frequent bus service connects to downtown Vancouver. This is the busy arrival-departure center for ferry traffic linking Vancouver Island, Bowen Island and the Sunshine Coast.

Sewell's Marina: {49° 22' 34" N, 123° 16' 26" W} Permanent moorage, some water & power. Guest moorage limited, call ahead. Mid-grade gas, diesel, oil, launch, ice, bait/tackle, sundries, seasonal coffee shop, boat rentals/charters, tours. 604-921-3474.

Bowen Island
[3512, 3526, 3534]

★ **Bowen Island (17):** This beautiful island lies about eight nautical miles northwest of Vancouver. The island is about 20 square miles in size, with a ragged 23 mile coastline. It is connected to Horseshoe Bay by year-round daily scheduled ferry service. Many of the 3,800 residents who live here attend school or work off island and commonly make the 20 minute commute by ferry. In its early history, the island and surrounding waters were

2024 Northwest Boat Travel

Page 168 Chapter 12 VANCOUVER

rich hunting and fishing grounds for the Coast Salish peoples. Bowen Island's ancestral name is Nex̱wlélex̱wm, and is part of the unceded traditional territory of the Skwx̱wú7mesh Nation. In the 1800's settlers worked in the logging mills and camps harvesting local timber. During the steamship era, from 1900 – to late 1950s, Bowen Island was a very popular resort with a hotel, over 200 vacation cottages, six picnic grounds, an outdoor stage and a dance hall that could accommodate 800 couples. Other Island industries have included fishing, a dynamite factory located in Tunstall Bay, and a brickyard that produced bricks from the clay at Deep Bay. Today tourism is the mainstay of the island economy. Moorage facilities are found in Snug Cove. Bowen Island's one public launch ramp is in Tunstall Bay.

★ **Snug Cove:** Site of the Bowen Island-Horseshoe Bay ferry landing, marinas, one public float and a launch ramp at Union SteamShip Marina. Island-wide transportation is provided by Translink community shuttles. There are two shopping areas on Bowen Island, Snug Cove and Artisan Square that feature a variety of restaurants, shops, and galleries that are fun to browse. Pamper yourself with a massage or join a yoga class at one of the island's studios. B&B's offer accommodations. Groceries and liquor are available. A seasonal weekend market offers local products, as well. A community heritage museums is open daily during the summer. Located near the Snug Cove dock is the restored Union Steamship General Store that houses the library. Behind the library, the picturesque heritage cottage is home to the Visitor Centre and The Hearth Gallery, next door, showcases local artists and artisans in the gift store. A short walk from here is the entrance to Crippen Regional Park and the trails to Bridal Veil Falls, the meadow, fish hatchery and Killarney Lake, one of the island's most popular destinations. Bowen Island is well known for wonderful walking and hiking trails, but other outdoor pursuits include biking, swimming, fishing, scuba diving, bird watching, and kayaking (kayak rentals available April-Sept in Snug Cove). There is also a 9-hole golf course with great views of Howe Sound. 604-947-4653 for tee time. For more Bowen Island information, visit www.tourismbowenisland.com.

★ **Union SteamShip Co. Marina:** {49° 23' N, 123° 19' W} Excellent moorage, with power, water, pump-out, wifi, and fishing supplies is found on large, stable floats at this first-class, year around facility. Located adjacent to Snug Cove's parks, village, boutiques, and quality restaurants. Marina office is located in the floating building along with the washroom, shower and laundry facilities. See our advertisement on page 1 and this page. Website: www.ussc.ca. E-mail: marina@ussc.ca. Mailing Address: P.O. Box 250, Snug Cove, Bowen Island, BC V0N 1G0. Fax: 604-947-0708. Telephone: 604-947-0707. Please check in on VHF 66A for berth assignment.

Bowen Island Marina: {49° 22' 48" N, 123° 19' 48" W} The marina and pier have recently sold. Visit www.bowen-island.com for information.

Snug Cove (South) Public Wharf: {49° 22' 44" N, 123° 17' 48" W} Transient moorage for 4 hrs or overnight. Monthly moorage Sept. 16-June 15. Fee info at kiosk at top of the dock. 604-947-4255.

Galbraith Bay: This bay, east of Hutt Island, is the site of the Mount Gardner Dock. No transient space available. 15 minute loading/unloading area only. Monthly moorage (wait list is several years out, 604-947-4255.) A road connects to Snug Cove.

Hood Point: The beaches near Hood Point and Finisterre Island have attracted summer vacationers for many years. Homes and summer cabins line the timbered shore. Anchorage is possible in Smuggler's Cove, Encanta, Columbine, or Cates Bays. Avoid the drying rock in the center of Encanta Bay.

Mannion Bay: Mannion Bay lies directly opposite Horseshoe Bay. Southeast swells enter. There is temporary settled weather anchorage off the head favoring the southwest side. The water tends to be warm in this bay. Charted hazards are sunken and drying rocks. Mannion Bay is managed by the Bowen Island Municipality with a Provincial License of Occupation. Call to verify f moorage is permitted. 604-947-4255.

Seymour Landing: Tthe southwest corner of Seymour Bay, offer some anchorage, but it is open to Horseshoe Bay Ferry wakes. Onshore is a golf course and residential development.

Apodaca Cove: This is a little haven in westerlies. Apodaca Provincial Park, a nature reserve, borders the north side.

East Howe Sound
[3526]

Sunset Beach (18): Site of a marina.

Sunset Marina Ltd.: Wet/dry permanent moorage, limited guest moorage if space is available to 30', gas, water, washrooms, snacks, ice, bait/tackle, boat/engine repairs, marine ways to 24', launch ramp. 604-921-7476.

UNION STEAMSHIP COMPANY MARINA & RESORT
SNUG COVE, BOWEN ISLAND, B.C.
A first-class marina & resort just eight nautical miles from Vancouver.
Guest moorage to 210', Doc Morgan's Restaurant, Chandlery & Gift Shop.
www.ussc.ca 604.947.0707 VHF 66A marina@ussc.ca

Visit us at boattravel.com

VANCOUVER Chapter 12 Page 169

Union SteamShip Co. Marina visited by Navy Yacht Club Everett   Photo © Union SteamShip Co. Marina

Newman Creek (19): Housing development; no marine facilities.

Lions Bay (20): Lions Bay is a small village of 541 homes nestled along the eastern part of Howe Sound on the Sea-to-Sky Highway. There is moorage, fuel, launching ramp and a small provisions store at the marina in the bay. The Village Centre is accessible from the marina by foot; the winding walk takes about 30 minutes up the hill. The Village Centre has a General Store, Post Office, and Café. The Village of Lions Bay has an extensive trail network; details and a map of the trails is online at www.lionsbay.ca, search "trail map".

Lions Bay Marina: Transient moorage, dry stack moorage, water, gas, diesel, propane, haul-out to 30', repairs (no DIY), marine supplies, launch ramp. 604-921-7510.

Alberta Bay: Brunswick Beach, Alberta Bay, is one mile north of Lion's Bay. There is temporary anchorage and a swimming beach.

Anvil Island (21): It isn't hard to imagine how Captain Vancouver chose this island's name in 1792. The 2,500 foot peak on Anvil Island resembles the horn of an anvil pointed upward. A peninsula, also shaped like an anvil, juts into Montague Channel on the east side of the island. The beach along the northern side of this peninsula is a popular picnic and barbecue site. Unpredictable Squamish winds can roar down the inlet in the Anvil vicinity.

★ **Porteau Cove Park (22):** There is one mooring buoy and a floating dock in the park (fees apply). Near the floating dock are two low tide markers. These mark very shallow water and are not mooring buoys. Anchoring is prohibited within the park boundary. Tent and RV campsites and cabins are available. Other amenities include two concrete double width boat launches (avoid low tide launches), boat trailer parking, picnic area, water, showers, toilets, sani-station, fish cleaning station and a change house for divers. There are sunken ships and man made reefs in the vicinity. Walking trails overlook the cove.

Britannia Beach (22): Home of the Britannia Mine Museum with underground train tours, gold panning and more. 1-800-896-4044. Two sunken vessels (a Coast Guard Search & Rescue cutter and a fishing boat) just offshore attract divers to Britannia Beach. Just south of Britannia Beach, golfers won't want to miss playing a round at the Furry Creek Golf and Country Club. 604-896-2224.

★ **Squamish (23) [3526]:** Squamish is located at the North end of Howe Sound. The approach from the north end of Howe Sound is Mamquam Blind Channel located on the east side of the sound. About 1/4 mile up the channel on the starboard side is the Stawamus River. Considerable shoaling across the river's mouth of and into the channel has occurred. Stay mid channel until just before the end of the log booms on the Starboard side. Do not use the range markers beyond this point. Ease over to port and pass closely to the piling that is painted white on top. **Use caution and your depth sounder.** Continue up the channel, keeping the wood pilings close to port. As you enter the harbour there is a minimum depth of 12'. The Squamish Harbour Authority floats are directly to port. Within three blocks of the floats you'll find a park, a hotel, a pub, banks, a post office, and various stores including a grocery store, liquor store, and bookstore. Boat rentals and car rentals, are both available in town. The West Coast Railway Heritage Park, home of the Royal Hudson 2860 Steam Locomotive, has the largest collection of vintage railway rolling stock, locomotives, and artifacts in Western Canada. Open year-round, look for special events, a gift shop, and a miniature railway on site. 604-898-9336. *Squamish Days Loggers Sports* are held the first week in August. Logging and forestry, plus a rapidly expanding tourist industry, are the backbones of the economy. Billed as the "Outdoor Recreation Capital of Canada" Squamish offers year round activities. Rock climbing, hiking and mountain biking are all possible. There are also four local rivers with steelhead, salmon, and giant sturgeon

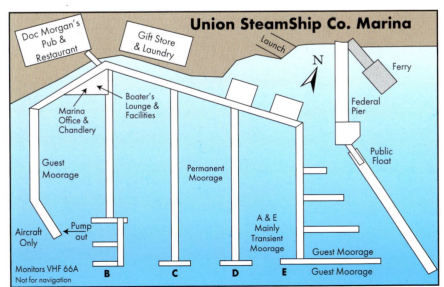

2024 Northwest Boat Travel

West Howe Sound with Union SteamShip Co. Marina in foreground
Photo © Union SteamShip Co. Marina

to tempt the angler. The "spit" in Squamish where Howe Sound and the Squamish River meet is a popular windsurfing and kiteboarding destination. The Squamish River is the winter home of the Bald Eagle and from mid-November through February, record numbers congregate in the area. For panoramic views of the spit and Howe Sound, ride the Sea To Sky Gondola. 604-892-2550. For Squamish Visitor Info. 604-815-5084 or 1-877-815-5084.

Squamish Harbour Authority: {49° 41' 31" N, 123° 9' 17" W} Moorage, 20 amp power, water, metered showers, pump-out. Call ahead to ensure there is a berth available. Office: 604-892-3725.

West Howe Sound

[3526]

There are seven public wharfs in West Howe Sound; one on the mainland at the end of Hopkins Road, four located on Gambier Island and two located on Keats Island. These are all small facilities, most with no services, and used primarily by locals. For information. 604-885-6800.

Zorro Bay: This niche is marked by a small peninsula of land that extends out to form a headland. Avoid the charted rock to the south. Anchorage is possible, but it is open to the north.

McNab Creek Landing (24): A dredged basin is on the east side of the creek mouth. Anchorage is possible off the flats. Potlatch Creek, farther into the sound, has anchorage off the delta.

Christie Creek (25): This tiny bight is south of Stolterfoht Creek. Anchor off south shore with stern tie. Do not block entrance.

Gambier Island

[3526]

★ **Gambier Island (26):** Gambier Island is the largest island in Howe Sound. Water taxis are available to nearby communities. Call 604-921-7451. New Brighton, Gambier Harbour, and West Bay are connected by gravel road. A BC foot passenger-ferry runs between New Brighton and Langdale. Four bays indent the island from the south. These are West Bay, Centre Bay, Port Graves, and Halkett Bay. These bays are deep and afford little anchorage. There are currently no businesses on the island.

Gambier Harbour: There is temporary anchorage here when winds are not from the south or east quadrants. There is a small public dock used mainly by locals, no services, 24 hour limit.

Brigade Bay: Anchorage in calm weather in this bight on the east side of Gambier Island.

★ **New Brighton:** At the head of Thornbrough Bay, New Brighton has a public wharf with mooring floats attached. Of interest in this area is Mariner's Rest, once known as Steamboat Rock, the only official marker for the committal of ashes at sea in British Columbia waters.

★ **West Bay:** A public float is on the west shore. Favor this shore to avoid drying rocks a short distance within the entrance. Anchorage is difficult because of the depths and sunken logs on the bottom. Summer homes dot the western shore.

★ **Centre Bay:** There is protection between the peninsula that juts out from the western shore of Gambier Island. Two yacht clubs maintain outstations here, one on Alexandra Island and one in a niche on the eastern side of the bay.

★ **Port Graves:** Inside Potts Point is the largest anchorage in Howe Sound. A spit of foul ground extends 300 feet off the point. Log booms are often tied near the head of the bay. There is a public wharf with a five-ton crane and a float. Minimum depths at the float are seven feet. No garbage deposit. The land above the wharf and the floats to the east of the wharf are private.

★⚓ **Halkett Bay/Halkett Bay Marine Park:** On the shoreline at the end of Fircom Bay Road, before you enter Halkett Bay, is a small public dock used predominately by locals, no services. Halkett Bay Marine Park offers one mooring buoy and dingy only float. Good anchorage is available without stern ties. The bay is open to the south. The favoured approach is to the steep eastern shoreline. As you enter, a large, square, yellow mooring buoy is on the port side. Be aware that a number of rocks protrude above the water in the middle of the bay. The buoy is before those rocks on the left side. Other marine hazards to note include a series of unmarked drying rocks and reefs in the bay's northwest corner, and an unmarked rock at a depth of less than 6' in mid-fairway near the head. Log booms are common, but tying to them is not recommended as they are frequently towed. No water, no campfires. Wilderness campsites, picnic tables, pit toilet. The HMCS Annapolis, sunk in 2015, provides a habitat for marine life as well as diving opportunities.

Walk-around: A trail leads to Mt. Artaban, a 10 km round trip hike for experienced hikers. At the top are spectacular views and the remains of an old forest service look-out.

Port Mellon (27): This is the site of a pulp mill.

Langdale (28): This is the site of the British Columbia Ferries landing with connections to Horseshoe Bay.

★ **Hopkins Landing (29):** There is a 60' public float at the end of the wharf. Look for the landmark row of oil tanks one mile to the north when locating the site. Note: the Hopkins Landing wharf has been closed until required structural repairs to restore the site to a level considered safe for public use is completed.

Keats Island

[3526]

★ **Keats Island (30):** This island, named to honor Captain Richard Keats, a British naval officer, is a popular recreation island for Vancouverites. It is the site of Plumper Cove Marine Park and a number of summer camps. While the population swells seasonally, full-time residents number less than 100.

Eastbourne: Eastbourne, one-half mile from Cotton Point, has a wharf and float. The mooring buoys are private.

Keats Island Settlement: Many summer homes are in this area. There is a public float, primarily used by residents.

★⚓ **Plumper Cove Marine Park:** Anchorage, eight mooring buoys, and six dock mooring slips can be found in the basin behind the Shelter Islets. There

Squamish Marina Photo © Kyle Pearce

Visit us at boattravel.com

is exposure to winds from the south or southwest. Enter north of the islets. These islets are joined by a drying ledge. According to BC Parks, "A rocky patch at a depth of about 0.5 metres below chart datum is situated about 25 metres off the end of the central mooring float." A display board at the head of the wharf shows the trail routes and campsites. Picnic areas, water and pit toilets available. The beaches are small gravel, so portable boats can be beached. A park ranger is on duty during the summer. ▲ ⊼ ☆

Walk-around : A 1 km trail encircles the park. Observatory Point offers memorable views of Shoal Channel. A 3km trail leads to the Keats Landing Foot Ferry Terminal.

Shoal Channel (31): [3534] This channel separates Keats Island from the mainland. A sand and rock bar extends across mid-channel. Minimum depth is five feet. A rock lies ¼ mile southwest of Steep Bluff. Fishing can be good in this area. Seas break when the wind and tide clash.

★ **Gibsons (32):** This is the southern gateway to the Sunshine Coast. See Chapter 13.

View of Vancouver Island (R) and Keats Island (L) from Gambier Island Photo © Xicotencatl

Essential Supplies & Services

AIR TRANSPORTATION
To & from Washington
NW Seaplanes . . . 425-277-1590, 1-800-690-0086
San Juan Airlines. 1-800-874-4434
Seattle Seaplanes 1-800-637-5553
To & from Islands/Vancouver
Air Canada 1-888-247-2262
Gulf Island Seaplanes 250-247-9992
Harbour Air. 1-800-665-0212
Pacific Coastal . . . . .604-273-8666 or 1-800-663-2872
Sea Air 1-866-692-6440

BOOKS / BOOK STORES
Evergreen Pacific Publishing 425-493-1451
The Marine Atlas. 253-872-5707

BUS TRANSPORTATION
BC Transit. 604-854-3232
Bus Info (Translink) 604-953-3333
Greyhound 800-661-8747

CNG CYLINDERS
Eco Fuel, Langley- Refill certified tanks, no exchange
. . . . 604-888-8384

COAST GUARD:
Victoria Coast Guard Radio. . . . . VHF 16, 83a
. . . . 1-800-661-9202 (In BC) or 250-363-6611
Victoria Marine Traffic 250-363-6333
Marine Distress, Search & Rescue
. . . . 1-800-567-5111 (in Canada) or 250-413-8933
Cell Phone (limited to select providers) . . . *16 or #727

CUSTOMS: See Notices between Chapters 7 & 8
24 Hour Reporting Centre. 1-888-226-7277
CBSA Reporting Sites:
Vancouver: False Creek Fishermen's Wharf, Harbour Green Dock (temporarily closed at time of publication), Royal Vancouver Yacht Club (Coal Harbour & Jericho Dock/English Bay)
Steveston: Steveston Harbour Authority
Surrey: Crescent Beach Marina
White Rock: White Rock Government Dock
US Customs & Border Reporting Sites:
Point Roberts 360-945-5211

FERRY INFORMATION
B. C. 1-888-223-3779
False Creek Ferries 604-684-7781
Sea Bus (Translink) 604-953-3333
Vancouver Aquabus 604-689-5858

FISHING / SHELLFISHING INFO
24 hr Recorded Notifications (Pacific region only)
. . . . .1-866-431-3474 or 604-666-2828
Recreational Licensing 1-877-535-7307
Observe, Record & Report Line (fisheries violations)
Greater Vancouver 604-607-4186
Or Call. 1-800-465-4336

FUELS
Captain's Cove Marina: Ladner. Gas, Diesel.
. . . . 604-946-1244
Catherwood Towing: Mission. Gas, Diesel.
. . . . 604-826-9257. VHF 69
Coal Harbour Chevron: Gas, Diesel. 604-681-7725
Crescent Beach Marina: Gas, Diesel.
. . . . 604-538-9666 VHF 66A

— Continued on next page —

Steveston Village — Photo © Ian Kobylanski

Essential Supplies & Services — continued

FUELS — continued

Deep Cove North Shore Marina: Deep Cove. Gas, Diesel.
. . . . 604-929-1251
False Creek Fuels . . . . 604-638-0209 VHF 66A
Fisherman's Cove Fuels 604-921-7333
Lion's Bay Marina: Howe Sound. Gas. . . 604-921-7510
Pitt Meadows Marina: Mid-Grade Gas . . 604-465-7713
Pitt River Boat Club: Gas 604-465-7713
Point Roberts Marina 360-945-2255 66A
Reed Point Marina: Port Moody. Gas, Diesel.
. . . . 604-937-1606
Richmond Chevron: Diesel 604-278-2181
Sewell's Marina: Horseshoe Bay. Gas, Diesel.
. . . . 604-921-3474 VHF 72
Steveston Chevron: Gas, Diesel 604-277-4712
Sunset Marina: Howe Sound. Gas 604-921-7476
Vancouver Marina: Richmond. Gas, Diesel
. . . . 604-278-3300

GOLF COURSES

Bowen Island (9 holes). 604-947-4653
Links at Hampton Cove (Delta) 9 holes . 604-946-1839
Furry Creek Golf & CC 604-896-2224
Glen Eagles Golf Course (W. Vancouver)
. . . . 604-921-7353

HAUL-OUTS

Captain's Cove Marina: Ladner 604-946-1244
Granville Island Boatyard 604-685-6924
Inlet Marine: Port Moody 604-936-4602
Lion's Bay Marina: Howe Sound 604-921-7510
Lions Gate Marine Centre: N Vancouver
. . . . 604-985-5468
Lynnwood Marina & Boatyard 604-985-1533
Mosquito Creek Marina & Boatyard: . 604-987-4113
helter Island: Richmond 604-270-6272
Skyline Marina: Richmond 604-273-3977
Steveston Harbour Authority 604-272-5539
Sunset Marina: Howe Sound 604-921-7476
Thunderbird Marina: W. Vancouver 604-921-7434

HOSPITALS

Healthlink B C (Nurse Helpline). 811
Lions Gate Hospital: N Vancouver 604-988-3131
Vancouver General 604-875-4111

LIQUOR

Shelter Island Marina: Richmond.
. . . . 604-270-6272 VHF 66A

LODGING

Union SteamShip: Bowen Island.
. . . . 604-947-0707 VHF 66A

MARINAS / MOORAGE

Bayshore West Marina (Coal Harbour) . . 604-689-5331
Bowen Island Marina 604-947-9710
Bowen Island Municipality (Snug Cove)
. . . . 604-947-4255
Burrard Civic Marina. 604-733-5833
Captain's Cove: Ladner, permanent 604-946-1244
Caulfeild Cove: W. Vancouver
Coal Harbour Marina. . . . . 604-681-2628 VHF 66A
Crescent Beach Marina . . 604-538-9666 VHF 66A
False Creek Harbour Authority Fishermen's Wharf
. . . . 604-733-3625 VHF 66A
False Creek Yacht Club . . . . . . 604-648-2628 VHF 66A
Heather Civic Marina. 604-874-2814
Imperial Landing Dock: Richmond . . . .
. . . . 604-238-8038
Ladner Harbour Authority. 604-940-6432
Lion's Bay: Howe Sound. 604-921-7510
Lynnwood Marina & Boatyard: North Vancouver
. . . . 604-985-1533
Mission Harbour Authority 604-826-4414
Mosquito Creek Marina & Boatyard: Vancouver
. . . . 604-987-4113
Pacific Boulevard Marina 604-683-7035
Pelican Bay Marina: False Creek 604-729-1442
Plumper Cove Marine Park: Keats Island
Point Roberts Marina 360-945-2255 66A
Quayside Marina. . . . . 604-681-9115, VHF 66A
Sewell's: Horseshoe Bay. 604-921-3474
Shelter Island Marina: Richmond.
. . . . 604-270-6272 VHF 66A
Skyline Marina: Richmond (permanent) . 604-273-3977
Sunshine Coast Regional District 604-885-6893
  SCRD is reponsible for West Howe Sound docks:
  Gambier Island (Gambier Harbour, Halkett Bay, Port
  Graves, West Bay). Keats Island (Eastbourne, Keats
  Landing). Mainland (Hopkins Landing)
Squamish Harbour Authority:
. . . . .604-892-3725, 604-898-5477
Steveston Harbour Authority 604-272-5539
Sunset Marina: Howe Sound 604-921-7476
Thunderbird Marina: W. Vancouver 604-921-7434
Union SteamShip Marina: Bowen Island.
. . . . 604-947-0707 VHF 66A
Vancouver Marina: Richmond. 604-278-9787

MARINE SUPPLY STORES

Bridgeview Marine 604-946-8566
Crescent Beach Marina 604-538-9666
Shelter Island: Richmond 604-270-6272
Wright Mariner Coal Harbour 604-682-3788

PROPANE

Lion's Bay Marina: Howe Sound. 604-921-7510

RAMPS

Burrard Civic Marina. 604-733-5833
Cates Park: Burrard Inlet
Crescent Beach Marina 604-538-9666
Fort Langley: Fraser River
Kitsilano Beach: English Bay
Ladner: Ferry Road Ramp, Wellington Park Ramp
Lion's Bay Marina: Howe Sound. 604-921-7510
Lions Gate Marine Centre 604-985-5468
Lulu Island: Main Arm Fraser River
Mission Harbour Authority 604-826-4414
McDonald Beach: N. Arm Fraser River
Pitt Meadows Marina 604-465-7713
Pitt Polder: Pitt Lake
Port Mann Bridge: Port Coquitlam
Porteau Cove Provincial Park
Rocky Point Park: Port Moody
Sea Island: Middle Arm Fraser River
Sewell's Marina: Horseshoe Bay. 604-921-3474
Shelter Island: Richmond . 604-270-6272 VHF 66A
Squamish River
Steveston Harbour Authority 604-272-5539
Sunset Marina: Howe Sound 604-921-7476
Tsawwassen
Vanier Park, Vancouver. 604-733-5833
Westham Island: Fraser River

REPAIRS / SERVICE

Bridgeview Marine 604-946-8566
Crescent Beach Marina 604-538-9666
Fraser Fibreglass: North Vancouver . . . 604-985-1098
Galleon Marine, Vancouver Marina. . . . 604-273-7544
Granville Island Boat Yard 604-685-6924
Inlet Marine (Port Moody) 604-936-4602
Lions Gate Marine Centre: N Vancouver. 604-985-5468
Lynnwood Marina & Boatyard: North Vancouver
. . . . 604-985-1533
Milltown Marina Boatyard. 604-697-9191
Mosquito Creek Marina & Boatyard: Vancouver
. . . . 604-987-4113
Shelter Island Marina: Richmond . . 604-270-6272
Sunset Marina. 604-921-7476
Wright Marine: Coal Harbour. 604-682-3788

RESTAURANTS

Go Fish Seafood Shack 604-733-3625
Pier Restaurant & Grill 360-945-7437
Riverhouse Marina Restaurant & Pub. . . 604-946-7545
Tugboat Annie's Pub & Grille 604-270-0364

SCUBA SITES

Halkitt Bay Marine Park, Indian Arm Marine Park,
Whyte Cove, Snug Cove, Porteau Cove Park

SEWAGE DISPOSAL

Burrard Bridge Civic Marina: Pump. 604-733-5833
Coal Harbour Marina. . . . . 604-681-2628 VHF 66A
Crescent Beach Marina: Pump. 604-538-9666
Falsh Creek Mobile Pumpout 778-683-7867
False Creek Yacht Club 604-648-2628
Heather Civic Marina: Pump. 604-874-2814
Lions Gate Marine Centre: N Vancouver. 604-985-5468
Mission Harbour Authority 604-826-4414
Mosquito Creek Marina & Boatyard: Vancouver
. . . . 604-987-4113
Point Roberts Marina 360-945-2255 66A
Quayside Marina. 604-681-9115
Shelter Island Marina: Pump 604-270-6272
Squamish Harbour Authority 604-892-3725
Steveston Harbour Authority 604-272-5539
Union SteamShip: Pump 604-947-0707
Vancouver Marina: Richmond. 604-278-3300

TAXI

Bowen Island 604-250-8294
Squamish 604-898-8888
Vancouver. 604-871-1111

TOWING

C-TOW .1-888-419-CTOW
Catherwood Towing: Pitt River 604-462-9221
Mercury Transport 604-921-7451

VISITOR INFORMATION

Bowen Island Visitor Centre 604-200-2399
North Vancouver Visitor Centre 604-656-6491
Tourism Delta 604-946-4232
Tourism Richmond. 1-877-247-0777
Tourism Squamish 1-877-815-5084
Tourism Vancouver. 604-683-2000
Tourism B.C. 1-800-663-6000

WEATHER

Environment Canada Weather Line 250-339-9861
Bowen Island, Straits of Georgia: . . . . VHF WX-3
Victoria MCTS VHF 21, WX-2 604-666-3655

Visit us at boattravel.com

SUNSHINE COAST Chapter 13 Page 173

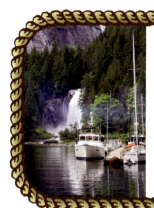

Chapter 13:
Sunshine Coast

Chatterbox Falls - photo © Ryan Van Veen

Gibsons to Lund. Sechelt, Secret Cove, Pender Harbour, Westview / Powell River. Sechelt, Jervis, & Princess Louisa Inlets; Nelson, Hardy, Harmony, Harwood, & Savary Islands.

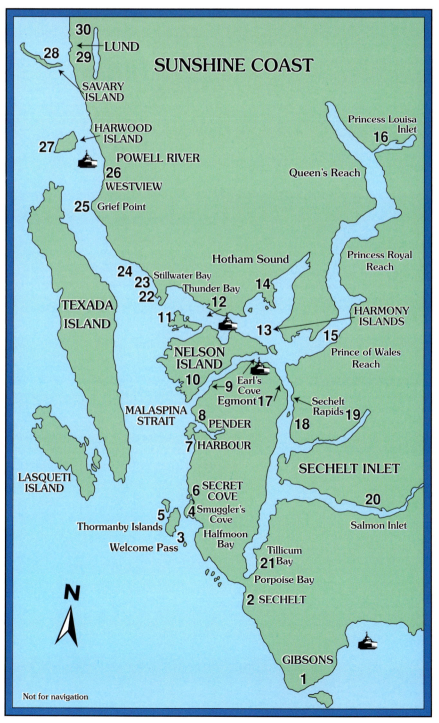

Symbols

[   ]: Numbers between [ ] are chart numbers.

{   }: Numbers & letters between { } are waypoints.

★ Recommended destinations, facilities, and services

⚐: Park, ⛵: Boat Launch, ▲: Campgrounds, ⚹: Hiking Trails, ⊼: Picnic Area, 🚲: Biking
🐟: Scuba

★ See "Important Notices" between Chapters 7 and 8 for specific information on boating related topics such as boating safety, weather, U.S. & Canadian marine radio use, Vessel Traffic Service, security zones, Canadian & U.S. Customs, etc. Due to changing regulations, call ahead to verify latest customs information.

Introduction

★ **The Sunshine Coast:** Well named because of the amount of annual sunshine that warms this area, residents along the Sunshine Coast report that the sun shines 300 days each year. No wonder this stretch of mainland is a popular playground for boaters! They come from near and far, plying the waters to and from Desolation Sound, Discovery Passage, and destinations farther northwest. The coast provides delightful miles of scenic views, inviting coves, sandy beaches, and picturesque fjord-like inlets offering outdoor exploration, fishing, kayaking, swimming, dining, diving, and destination resort comfort. Boaters who have made the cruise through the reaches of Jervis Inlet and traversed Malibu Rapids will never forget the spectacular beauty of the Yosemite Valley-like Princess Louisa Inlet, with its breath-taking Chatterbox Falls. Gibsons, Sechelt, Secret Cove, Pender Harbour, Egmont, and Powell River each offer their own unique variety of scenic wonderland, vacation attractions, facilities, and activities. The entire coast seems rather isolated, yet it is within easy reach of Vancouver by boat, automobile, bus, or air. If traveling by car or RV, two rather short ferry rides add variety to the scenic roadway

Chart List

Canadian Hydrographic Charts:
3311, 3312, 3512, 3514, 3534, 3535

Marine Atlas Vol 1 (2018): Page 22, 26-30

Evergreen Cruising Atlas: Pages 49-51, 62-76

Gibsons Landing
Photo © Sunshine Coast Tourism, Kelly Funk Photography

that permits exploration of the entire length of the coast, ending at Lund. The first ferry is a 40 minute ride and departs from West Vancouver at Horseshoe Bay, taking you to Langdale on the other side of Howe Sound. At Earls Cove, near Egmont, the next ferry is a 50 minute ride, landing at Saltery Bay, on the northwest side of Jervis Inlet. For ferry information call 1-888-223-3779.

Gibsons to Welcome Pass
[3311, 3512, 3526, 3534]

★ **Gibsons (1):** [3534] Situated at the southern end of the Sunshine Coast, just north of Vancouver, Gibsons (population: 5,000) is a quaint town of artists and fishing boats. If approaching from the Strait of Georgia, pass Gower Point and enter Shoal Channel, otherwise known as The Gap. Gibsons is perched on a hillside, overlooking the harbour and nearby islands of Átl'ḵa7tsem/Howe Sound. The town offers excellent breakwater protected moorage and plenty of onshore activities. This area is the traditional, ancestral and unceded territories of the skwxwú7mesh (Squamish) and shíshálh (Sechelt) Nations who have lived here since time immemorial. When colonization occurred, both Nations suffered greatly as the government introduced the Indian Act and residential school system to assimilate and extinguish First Nations cultures. Despite these efforts, both the skwxwú7mesh and shíshálh Nations continue to thrive in their traditional lands today.

The waterfront Landing area's collection of charming shops includes clothing and antique stores, art galleries and studios, and professional services. Walk from the marina to the Sunshine Coast Museum & Archives and the Gibsons Public Art Gallery - their exhibits include ancient Squamish Nation stone tools, Maritime history, and settler history along with a small exhibit with props from the beloved Beachcombers TV Show. Each Autumn, the signature event of the season is The Sunshine Coast Art Crawl. During this three-day event, 100+ galleries, studios and more between Langdale and Earls Cove open their doors to art lovers. For galleries open year-round you'll find the Purple Banner Tour; look for purple banners hung outside studios, a welcome signal for drop-in visitors.

Gibson's thriving culinary scene is a delightful mix- bakeries, cafes, ethnic eateries, west coast cuisine and food trucks serve up locally sourced creations. Three award-winning craft breweries in the area have well-appointed tasting rooms that welcome visitors to experience B.C.'s dynamic craft beer culture.

Located in the heart of Gibsons Landing is the Gibsons Public Market. Home to artists and artisans alike, this community hub features local merchants, an in-house bistro, community kitchen and amenities. It is also home to the Nicholas Sonntag Marine Education Centre featuring a "catch and release" model with 30 + interactive displays showcasing the underwater world of Howe Sound. Farmers Markets run from May - October at the Gibsons Public Market on Fridays, and in Holland Park on Sundays. Annual community events include the Gibsons Jazz Festival, the Sea Cavalcade Festival, the Sunshine Coast Craft Beer Festival and Music in the Landing - a popular series of free weekend concerts.

Uphill from the downtown area are two shopping malls, which include grocery stores and a pharmacy. Nearby parks include Winegarden Waterfront Park overlooking the harbour, and Dougall Park with tennis courts. For more outdoor fun, rent a kayak, SUP or canoe and explore the waters off Gibsons Harbour, or venture over to Keats and Gambier Islands. Beachcomb, swim, or relax on one of the quiet, sheltered beaches: Armours, Georgia, Hopkins Landing, Soames, Granthams Landing, or Secret Beach. Stop by the Visitor Information Centre at 494 S Fletcher Rd, Ste 101 for help with all Sunshine Coast inquiries, including accommodations and things to see and do.

Gibsons Landing Harbour Authority: {49° 23' 58" N, 123° 30' 19" W} Permanent and guest moorage, 4 hr. moorage for minimal fee, 15/30/50/100 amp power, water, laundry, showers, pump-out, garbage deposit, crane, pay phone, airplane float. Fresh fish sales, art gallery, and restaurant onsite. 604-886-8017. VHF 66A.

Gibsons Marina: {49° 23.87' N, 123° 30.42' W} Permanent and guest moorage, 15/30 amp power, water, washrooms, showers, laundry, wifi, launch ramp, chandlery, fishing gear, marine supplies. 604-886-8686. VHF 66A.

Hyak Marine Ltd: (located at Gibson's Marina) Gas, diesel, oil, lubes, batteries, tackle, snacks, ice cream, ice, drinks, water, bathrooms. 604-886-9011.

Roberts Creek: Residential area, beaches, parks, restaurants, shops, art studios, lodging, golf course and launching ramp.

Sechelt (2): Sechelt is unusual in that the community stretches across land which fronts on both the Strait of Georgia and the inland fjord of Sechelt Inlet. On the south shore of Trail Bay, a rip-rap breakwater at Selma Park encloses the Shishalh Nation harbour and shelter is found in the lee of the breakwater. There is a day float at the pier for small craft and one mooring buoy in the bay. Sechelt is a thriving town with all conveniences including a hospital, two malls, as well as various small shops, galleries offering local crafts and carvings, liquor stores, motels, B & B's, marinas (on the Sechelt Inlet shore), and restaurants. Each August the *Festival of the Written Arts* is held in Sechelt. The Shishalh Nation Tems Swiya Museum, located in a building created around the theme of the salmon people, is a popular attraction. Next door, the Ravens Cry movie theater featuring movies nightly, as well as occasional concerts or theatrical productions. Tourist activities include kayaking, paddleboarding, skimboarding, hiking, sailing, fishing, diving, golfing, beachcombing, and mountain biking. You'll also want to visit Chapman Creek Hatchery, as well as the dozens of area artist's studios and galleries. A pedestrian pier is located in Trail Bay, off of Wharf Street in downtown Sechelt. In Sechelt Inlet, also known as The Inland Sea, moorage is available at the Lighthouse Marina at the head of Sechelt Inlet/Porpoise Bay. There is also a lovely, sandy beach at Porpoise Bay Provincial Park. See Sechelt Inlet in this chapter.

★ **Sargeant Bay & Sargeant Bay Provincial Park:** Located west of Sechelt, this bay is open to the south. Anchor in settled weather only as strong northwest winds enter the bay. Anchor off the beach or behind the rock at the north end of the bay. Caution advised regarding a drying rock some distance southwest of the large rock. The day use park includes picnic area (no camping) and trails. Colvin Creek Trail is about 1km long. Sargeants Bay trail leads along the beach to a fish ladder. Windsurfing and kayaking are possible on the bay.

Walk-around: Hike from Sargeant Bay to Trout Lake, where as the name implies, there is good fishing.

Trail Islands: Limited shelter suitable for temporary anchorage.

Welcome Pass to Secret Cove

[3311, 3535]

★ **Welcome Pass (3):** Merry Island, marked by a white and red lighthouse, lies in the middle of the southern end of Welcome Pass. This passage is used extensively by boaters traveling between Nanaimo, Silva Bay, Gibsons, or Vancouver and the Sunshine Coast. There are two unmarked rocks in the pass. Frazer Rock, near Lemberg Point, has about seven feet of water covering it at low tide. Egerton Rock lies south of Lemberg Point. Currents in the pass run to three knots at springs, setting north on flood and south on ebb tides. Merry Island Lighthouse has a fog horn of three long blasts per minute. Pirate Rock has a black, white and green day beacon on it.

★ **Halfmoon Bay (3):** This large and attractive bay can be a welcome refuge to travelers headed toward, or coming from the Strait of Georgia. A public wharf at Priestland Cove at the northeast portion of the bay has a small public float adjacent to it. The irregular shoreline invites exploration by dinghy or small boat. A café and a general store with post office and liquor sales are found here as well. Watch depths carefully when traversing to and from the channel between the islets south of the public wharf as a drying reef extends below the surface. About two miles north of Halfmoon Bay the Homesite Creek Trail leads 1.2 miles through the forest to a waterfall and some limestone caves. South of Halfmoon Bay, Coopers Green Regional Park has a large grassy treed area ideal for family picnics. During the summer you can play beach volleyball on the sandy court, and the park includes a barbeque pit, washroom facilities, swimming beach and a public recreational boat launch. It is also a propular location for divers. In July, the annual *Halfmoon Bay Country Fair* is held here. ⚓🚻🛶

★ **Frenchman's Cove:** Note that Frenchman's Cove is actually one arm of a horseshoe-shaped passage. This secluded anchorage is perfect for adventurous boaters who desire a hidden retreat, are willing to go cautiously "gunkholing" to find the entrance, and can accept the risk of making a mistake. Numerous unmarked drying and submerged rocks, some charted and some not charted, lie offshore, between the entrance to the cove and Welcome Pass. The entrance is so well hidden, that even after you have anchored here numerous times, expect a renewed challenge on each return to find the opening. The entrance is an elusive cut in the high-bank northwest shore of Halfmoon Bay. As you near this shore, locate the houses on the bank at the other end of the horseshoe passage. Then, move your binoculars to the left and examine the shoreline for a large rock that guards the entrance. Even now, you cannot see an opening. Head slowly for that large rock. As you near the rock, the hole in the wall will begin to open in front of you. The width of the passage is about 40 feet, although it seems much narrower. Once through the entrance, the cove widens, giving ample room for one boat, or a small raft of boats, to swing at anchor. There is good holding mud in the cove, with minimum depths of about five feet on a zero tide at Atkinson Point, Burrard Inlet (See current tables for Vancouver, British Columbia). Boaters have commonly ridden out many a high wind, snuggled in this little cove. Locate a rocky area and shoals which extend from shore before setting anchor. Entry can also be made through a narrow pass at the other end of the horseshoe-shaped passage leading into a small basin. Private docks are found here, but very limited anchorage might be available. A drying inlet is at the extreme head of the cove. Drying rocks separate this northern vicinity from the preferred anchorage described above. If traversing the entire passage, do so only at high water and with a shallow draft vessel.

Secret Cove   *Photo © Regan Hately*

★⚓ **Smuggler Cove Marine Park (4):** Look for the "Marine Park" posted up on a rock on Isle Capri. This isle is the north side of the entrance to the park. This narrow entrance with reefs on both sides leads into the popular stopover of Smuggler Cove. Low tide is the optimum time to see the reef and rocks to avoid. Favor the port side (Isle Capri). There is extensive anchorage with fair-to-good holding bottom in two main bays. Good protection for weather is provided by surrounding islands. On the south side of the first bay, there is an uncharted rock about 50 feet out from the house on shore. This rock is covered about five feet at high tide. When entering the inner bay, the reef in the passage, marked by a wooden pointer, extends farther into the passage than one might expect. Rings for shore ties have been driven into the rocks on both sides of the inner cove. Fees charged. A courteous tie to shore makes room for additional boats. Sewage discharge is prohibited. Onshore, a resident beaver dam stands as testament to these industrious creatures. It is possible to walk to a lookout into Frenchman's Cove. This park is accessible by car as well as boat. Wilderness camping, pit toilet, no water. Kayaking, scuba diving and fishing are popular in this area. 🚶🛶

★ **Thormanby Islands (5):** North and South Thormanby Islands are noted for sandy beaches, good swimming, and good fishing grounds. A public wharf is at Vaucroft Beach on the northeast end of North Thormanby Island (15 minutes suggested for load/unload, 24 hour moorage limit, no garbage drop).

★ **Buccaneer Bay:** Located between North and South Thormanby, the entrance to the bay is obstructed by a long ridge of rocks on Tottenham Ledge that extend to the buoy some distance off shore. Silting conditions cause depth variations in the bay. Observe private property regulations. Fine, white sand beaches rim much of the bay. On the southern tip of North Thormanby Island, is Buccaneer Bay Provincial Park. Grassy Point and Gill Beach offer temporary, daytime anchorage and good swimming. This vicinity is unprotected from northwest winds, which usually start after dusk. Anchor behind the Surrey Islands for some protection from southeast and northwest winds, or in Water Bay behind the reef in the center of the bay. Seals and sea lions are common sights.

★⚓ **Farm Bay:** Also on South Thormanby Island are two coves, both suitable for anchorage in settled weather. Farm Bay is the site of Simson Provincial Park and a park sign identifies the location. When anchoring, pay close attention to the chart and identify shoal areas. A second anchorage is in a cove adjacent to Farm Bay. It is also open to the south.

Walk-around: Farm Bay is a good place for a shore walk through unusual rock formations and along old logging roads. Begin at the head of the bay and walk to an old orchard.

Secret Cove

[3311, 3535]

★ **Secret Cove (6):** A marker sits atop a rock at the entrance to this cove. Keep this marker to starboard during entry and reduce speed for courtesy and safety. This is the site of marinas with protected moorage and a repair facility. Anchorage is possible, however dragging anchor often occurs in winds. Many sports fishermen headquarter in Secret Cove because of good fishing grounds nearby.

There are three arms that extend east, northeast, and northwest: (1) The northwest arm lies to port and leads to Secret Cove Marina, the major destination moorage in Secret Cove. There is also a 145' long Government Dock. Bus service connects with points north, and Vancouver. Visit www.sunshinecoastconnector.ca for information. The anchoring bottom is tricky in this arm. In a wind, dragging is not uncommon. (2) The middle (northeast arm) lies almost directly ahead. Buccaneer Marina, fuel and repair facilities are in this arm. According to Marina staff, despite the congestion of boats in the entrance, the arm widens near the end, allowing boats up to 70 ft to reach the end of the arm and turn around. (3) The arm to starboard (east arm) has a narrow entrance and all docks in this arm are private. If entering this east arm, keep the channel marker to port and be aware of the rocks to starboard. At the head of the arm is an extensive drying flat.

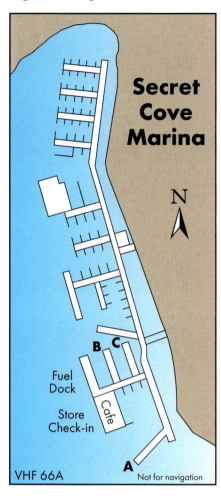

★ **Secret Cove Marina:** {49.534854N, -123.965070 W} Well protected, centrally located, with 20+ dedicated transient slips and lots of amenities, this is a popular moorage for traveling boaters. Gas, diesel, moorage with power, water, store, restaurant (https://www.labettolina.com), internet, liquor, groceries, garbage & recycling, picnic tables, showers, fish cleaning tables. See our advertisement on this page. Internet site: www.secretcovemarina.com. Email: info@secretcovemarina.com. Address: 5411 Secret Cove Rd., Halfmoon Bay, BC. Mailing address: Box 189, Roberts Creek, British Columbia V0N 2W0. Telephone: 1-866-885-3533. VHF 66A.

Buccaneer Marina: {49° 31.9' N, 123° 57.3' W} Permanent moorage, guest moorage if space is available, gas, diesel, water, boat launch, haul-outs to 36', outboard engine sales, repairs, and service, marine accessories, tackle, bait, ice, snacks, water taxi. 604-885-7888, 1-877-885-7888.

Secret Cove Government Dock (Harbour Authority of Pender Harbour): { 49° 32' 03" N, 123° 57' 49" W} 145 ft long dock with transient moorage, if space is available, rafting mandatory, 20 amp power. 604-883-2234.

Secret Cove to Pender Harbour
[3311, 3535]

Wood Bay: Anchorage is possible with some protection from both northwesterly and southeasterly winds. There is aquaculture in the area.

Harness Island: There is anchorage behind the island. Reefs extend between islets. Pass between the tallest islet and Harness Island. A kelp marked rock is a hazard.

★ **Bargain Bay (7):** Access to this anchorage is from Malaspina Strait between Francis Peninsula and Edgecombe Island. The entrance is wide enough to allow easy passage. There are two rocks with less than six feet of water over them, one on each side of the passage. A channel, about 100 yards in width, is between the rocks. Once past the rocks, the head of the bay offers good anchorage in depths of 20-30 feet. Bargain Narrows, known locally as Canoe Pass, connects the head of Bargain Bay with Gerrans Bay. However, the pass is obstructed by a drying bank and is navigable only at high tide and by very small, flat bottomed boats. A bridge with a 13 foot vertical clearance crosses the passage.

Pender Harbour
[3311, 3535]

★ **Pender Harbour (8):** Pender Harbour is a large, deep, protected harbour extending 5km inland. Enter Pender Harbour, {N 49.38 and W 124.02.60}, between Henry Point and Williams Island. Red railings distinguish all three public wharves at Hospital Bay, Welbourn Cove and Gerrans Bay. The inner-harbour seven-knot speed limit is enforced.

Pender Harbour is known for its celebrated "Pender Harbour Spirit," its many communities, friendly residents and its gorgeous, intricately interconnected waterways. With roughly 166 km (103 miles) of scenic shoreline, spectacular islands, tidal pools, coves and bays, visitors find countless recreational opportunities as well as a wide range of world class attractions and amenities to enjoy in and around the hamlets of Garden Bay and Madeira Park.

This one-time steamer stop bustled with commercial fishing, logging, and boat building

---

★ **Secret Cove Marina:** [www.secretcovemarina.com] This resort is a great spot to reprovision on your way to great locations like Princess Louisa Inlet or Desolation Sound. Located close to the beaches of Thormanby Island, this marina has:

- Diesel
- Gas
- Water

The well-stocked store has:

- Groceries
- Liquor
- Clothing
- Tackle
- Marine Supplies

Secret Cove also has an upscale restaurant and over 20 dedicated transient slips with power. Showers, bathrooms, internet, paddleboard and kayak rental are all available. Open daily from mid-May to mid-September, otherwise inquire ahead.

Internet: www.secretcovemarina.com. Email: info@secretcovemarina.com. Address: 5411 Secret Cove Rd, Halfmoon Bay, BC. Mailing address: Box 189, Roberts Creek, British Columbia, V0N 2W0 Telephone: 1-866-885-3533. VHF 66A.

enterprises and served as an important medical waypoint. Today the Pender Harbour area is a year-round destination for recreational boating, fishing, diving, kayaking/canoeing, wildlife viewing, shellfish harvesting, freshwater lake swimming and fishing, golf, horseback riding, hiking and photography. The region also boasts more artists and craft persons per capita than almost any other area in Canada, resulting in a full calendar of cultural activities. Gallery showings, local festivals and live musical offerings, including annual Jazz, Blues, and Chamber Music Festivals, are among the most popular. For a list of artists and events, suncoastarts.com. For music festival information, penderharbourmusic.ca. Summer visitors can tour the harbour and explore local villages via the SloCat Harbour Tours & Shuttle, call 604-741-3796. While there is no public transportation or taxi, most services are within walking distance. Daily bus service to Vancouver is also available. Pender Harbour is also a registered floatplane base.

Sunset on Garden Bay — Photo © Peter Parker

Joe Bay: Joe Bay, at the mouth of Pender Harbour, is the site of historic Irvine's Landing, the area's first non-aboriginal settlement. Once a booming commercial centre, it is now strictly residential. The former government wharf is now privately owned.

Duncan Cove: This cove is to port after Farrington Cove. It is home to the Pender Harbour Resort & Marina. Nearby is Sarah Wray Hall, a renovated historic schoolhouse that serves as a community centre, hosting events, heritage courses and rotating displays of artifacts and photos. Motoko's Fine Art Gallery, a 10-minute walk from the Cove, is open daily in summer, otherwise by appointment, 604-883-9472.

Pender Harbour Resort & Marina: {49° 38' 0.7764" N, 124° 2' 35.8188" W} Permanent & guest moorage (100 slips, vessels to 50'), 30 amp power, water, showers, laundry, free wifi, launch, small store, motel, cabins, heated pool, kayak/motor boat rentals. 604-883-2424.

★ **Hospital Bay:** Continuing into the harbour, to port is Hospital Bay. Hospital Bay was named for the first hospital on the Sunshine Coast, St. Mary's Anglican Mission Hospital. It was built in 1930 when the Columbia Coast Mission "hospital ships" could no longer serve the growing population. When a new hospital opened in Sechelt in 1964, the property was converted into the Historic Seaside Sundowner Inn. The Inn closed a couple of years ago and future plans are uncertain.

Moorage is found at a public float and at John Henry's Marina. There is fuel, a post office, convenience store, liquor store, ATM, and boat launch ramp. A charming footbridge overlooks the marinas and beach, and there are picnic areas near the gazebo.

John Henry's Marina & Resort: {49° 37.9' N, 124° 2.02' W} Permanent, seasonal and guest moorage, 30/50 amp power, water, showers, laundry, garbage/recycling, WiFi, General Store, ice, liquor, propane, café, lodging, kayak/powerboat rentals, float plane service. Fuel Dock with gas, diesel, lube oil, marine batteries, snacks, fishing gear/tackle. 604-883-2336. VHF 66A.

Hospital Bay Government Wharf: (Harbour Authority of Pender Harbour) {49° 37' 55.6" N, 124° 1' 53.1" W} Overnight moorage, 100' of visitor moorage, 15/20/30 amp power, water. 604-883-2234. VHF 66A.

★ **Garden Bay/Village of Garden Bay:** Garden Bay is either a short cruise back to the main channel, easterly to port, or a two-minute walk from Hospital Bay. The Seattle Yacht Club and Royal Vancouver Yacht Club both maintain outstations here, and the Garden Bay Sailing Club holds a mini-regatta every Saturday afternoon.

The village of Garden Bay sits astride two lovely bays, Garden Bay and Hospital Bay. This quintessential seaside village, nestled among rolling coastal hills, is the perfect place to relax and soak up the scenery. Added attractions include nearby freshwater swimming lakes, parks, scenic hikes, historical sites, and art galleries - all within walking distance! Garden Bay is the venue for the *Blues Festival* in June, the *Malaspina Regatta* in July, the *Jazz Festival* in September and the *Art Crawl* in October.

Sunshine Coast Resort Hotel & Marina: {49° 37' 24.84" N, 124° 1' 8.447" W} Long term & overnight moorage to 80', 30 amp power, water, showers, washrooms, laundry, WiFi, hot tub/sauna, lodging. 604-883-9177 or 1-888-883-9177.

★ **Garden Bay Marine Park:** This day-use marine park on the north shore of Pender Harbour, just past Garden Bay features a sheltered anchorage with floating dinghy dock, trail, picnic area, water (boil before consuming) and pit toilets. Activities include swimming, fishing, wildlife viewing, canoeing and kayaking. Steep and rocky access to park upland leads to a small Coast Salish cemetery and a trail to the top of Mt. Daniel - the most spectacular vista in Pender Harbour. From this vantage point, the ancestors of the shíshálh Sechelt First Nation could watch for visitors, friendly or otherwise. A longhouse on the property honours the estimated 5,000 aboriginals who once lived here. The longhouse will host cultural events and displays.

★ **Gunboat Bay:** Enter through the narrow channel at the head of Pender Harbour, outside of Garden Bay. The entry channel is charted to have a drying rock and a minimum depth of four feet. A small part of the upper reaches of Gunboat Bay dry at low tide. The name of the Bay comes from the gunboats HMS Grappler and Forward, stationed here in the 1860's.

Oyster Bay: Gunboat Bay leads to this relatively shallow bay, whose upper reaches dry at low tide. Oysters were introduced here to the West Coast in the 1930s. Uplands are residential.

★ **The Village of Madeira Park/Welbourn Cove:** Located directly across from Garden Bay, Madeira Park was named by an early pioneer after the Island of Madeira in his homeland of Portugal. There is a public wharf and wharfinger office, boat launch, pump-out station and several marinas (some, like Sunshine Coast Resort, Madeira Marina and the Pender Harbour Hotel Marina are found between Gunboat Narrows and Welborne Cove.) Madeira Park is Pender Harbour's commercial centre with a post office, credit union with ATM, pharmacy, grocery stores, liquor store, cafés, veterinarian, law office, spas, barber, hair salons, yoga studio, community hall, reading centre, art gallery, and visitor information booth. The health centre and Rona Building Materials Store are a 20-minute walk from the public docks. Harbour sightseeing and diving tours, as well as fishing charters are offered by local companies. You can also purchase the "catch of the day" directly from fishermen at the floats. Area parks include Seafarer's Millennium Park featuring a gazebo, boardwalk and picnic area. A performance centre overlooking the wharf and park is a venue for several popular annual concerts. Madeira Park is the site of the *April Tools Wooden Boat Challenge*, the *Pender Harbour May Day Celebration* (second-oldest in the country), *Pender Harbour Days* celebrating Pender Harbour's marine heritage with historical boats, land-based heritage displays, sailing competitions, an arts fair, and lots of entertainment, *Pender Harbour Show & Shine* in August, the *Fall Faire*, and the *Attack of Danger Bay*- Canada's largest downhill longboard event.

Madeira Park Government Wharf (Harbour Authority of Pender Harbour): {49° 37' 21.8" N, 124° 1' 30.5" W} Overnight moorage, 500' visitor moorage, 15/30/50 amp plus 3 phase shore power, launch ramp, garbage deposit, recycling, showers, washrooms, pump-out thru appt. Shopping center within 200 yards. 604-883-2234. VHF 66A.

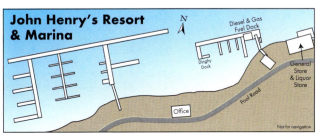

Looking toward Mt. Daniel from Madeira Park Photo © Myrtle Winchester

Coho Marina & RV Resort: {49° 37' 11.78" N, 124° 1' 56.87" W} Annual & transient moorage, 30 amp power, water, launch, clubhouse, laundry, showers, wifi. Walking distance to town. 604-883-2248.

Madeira Marina: Well-stocked marine store, 40-ton marine ways, trailer haul-outs to 30', dry storage. 604-883-2266.

Painted Boat Resort Spa & Marina: {49° 37' 5.41" N, 124° 1' 46.48" W} Moorage available to resort guests who have booked accommodation at the resort and have a confirmed reservation. Moorage should be booked at time of accommodation reservation. Boats to 60', 6' draw or less. 15 amp power and limited 30/50 amp hookups. Water on slips (seasonal). Free day moorage with dining or spa reservations, but moorage must be reserved ahead. 604-883-2456, 1-866-902-3955.

Pender Harbour Diesel: Marine parts, automotive parts, industrial parts, tools, lubes, oils, filters, safety equipment, dock supplies, hardware, rigging and raingear. 604-883-2616.

Pender Harbour Hotel Marina: {49° 37' 29" N, 124° 1' 16" W} Short & long term moorage, 40' to 80' slips, 15/20/30 amp power, water. Hotel, restaurant, pub, liquor store, wifi at hotel & pub. 604-883-9013.

★ **Gerrans Bay (Whiskey Slough):** The entrance to Gerrans Bay is WSW of Madeira Park on the south shore. Enter either side of Mary Islet, but avoid Griffin Ledge between Mary Islet and Welbourn Cove. Once inside Gerrans Bay, look for the channel markers. Onshore is strictly residential. A public wharf, used mainly by local commercial boats, may have overnight spots available. Anchorage is found between Francis Peninsula (Beaver Island) and Dusenbury and Alder Islands, and at the head of the bay.

Gerran's Bay (aka Whiskey Slough) Goverment Wharf (Harbour Authority of Pender Harbour): {49° 36' 55.9" N, 124° 2' 37.1" W} Short term moorage, often room for overnight moorage in summer, rafting offered, 15/20/30 amp power, water. 604-883-2234. VHF 66A.

Agamemnon Channel
[3311, 3312, 3512, 3514]

Agamemnon Channel (9): This is the shortest route when headed for Egmont, Princess Louisa, Sechelt Inlet or Hotham Sound. It also provides a place to run when Malaspina Strait is choppy. If a storm is brewing, the Hotham Sound vicinity can be a nice place to spend time until calmer weather arrives. Agamemnon Channel stretches in a north and northeast direction for about eight miles and is about a half mile wide. Depths range from 20-140 fathoms. There is no place for anchorage except Green Bay. Tidal streams attain rates of one to two knots with the flood tide headed northward and the ebb tide south. Just below Green Bay, on the west side of Agamemnon Channel, a small lagoon with a narrow entrance opens up. This can be entered by shallow draft, small craft. The steep-sided fjord walls of Agamemnon Channel and Jervis Inlet provide superb wall diving on vertical cliffs that plunge several hundred feet straight down. Six foot cloud sponges and enormous fans of gorgonian corals live in the clear waters, where wintertime visibility frequently exceeds 80 feet.

★ **Green Bay:** Green Bay provides well-sheltered anchorage in depths of five to seven fathoms. Rocks near the center and the head of the bay dry at half tide. This bight is often used as a booming ground for logs. The west side forms a nook that offers the most protection. Booming rings that can be used for stern tying are found in the southern side of the nook. On the north side of the bay anchorage is found near the remains of a wharf and cabins.

Agamemnon Bay & Earl's Cove: Site of the Earl's Cove-Saltery Bay ferry which connects the main highway from Vancouver north to the highway's terminus at Lund. Limited anchorage is possible, staying away from the ferry landing. This is the site of a small private marina.

Nelson Island
[3311, 3312, 3512, 3514]

★ **Nelson Island (10):** This Island borders Blind Bay. There are oyster culture beds and popular anchorages nearby. Quarry Bay, Cockburn Bay and Hidden Basin are entered from Malaspina Strait, Ballet Bay from Blind Bay. Vanguard Bay is on the south side of Jervis Inlet.

★ **Quarry Bay:** Use Chart #3512. There is anchorage in the western arm. Watch for a drying rock. There is also good anchorage in the cove in the eastern end, south of the old granite quarry now nearly buried in brush and vegetation. A rock is 200 yards north of the south shore. Watch for drying reefs and rocks. Do not anchor in the northern section of the easternmost arm because of the telephone cable. There is shelter from southeasterlies in the bight to starboard in the entrance. Because of limited swinging room, a shore tie is recommended.

★ **Cockburn Bay:** The narrow entrance to this bay is obstructed by foul ground. Small vessels can enter and leave near high water. Stay mid-channel in the entrance. Favor the north shore for the next 200 feet. Depths inside are around 18 feet at high tide. When anchoring, note the location of the telephone cable.

Billings Bay: An unmaintained public float offers protection from winds.

★ **Hidden Basin:** Entrance to this secluded anchorage is through a narrow entrance in Billings Bay. Pass to starboard of the islet at the entrance. There is about four feet of water in this passage at a ten-foot tide at Atkinson Point, Burrard Inlet. Currents run strong, requiring entry at or near high water slack. Because of the constricted passage, slack water tends to occur about five minutes per foot of change later than the slack outside. There is anchorage in the northeastern portion of this mile-long basin. An uncharted drying rock is in the easternmost end of the cove. Aquaculture operations are along the western shore.

★ **Blind Bay:** Use Charts #3514, #3512 or Chartbook #3312. This bay lies between the northwest side of Nelson Island and the southeast side of Hardy Island. The deep entrance channel is bordered by islets on each side and a sharp lookout for reefs is advised. When winds are kicking up in Malaspina Strait, at the time of an ebb tide in Jervis Inlet, the seas can be rough in the entrance to Blind Bay. Aquaculture operations are prevalent in several areas, and booming grounds are located north of Fox Island and along the south shore of Hardy Island. Anchorage can be found in the indentations along the Hardy Island shore and in Ballet Bay, on the southeast shore of Blind Bay. A popular anchorage is behind Fox Island. Often crowded conditions and a rocky bottom call for shore ties.

★ **Ballet Bay:** Numerous islands shelter this bay, on the southeast shore of Blind Bay. Aquaculture operations are along some of the shoreline. Range markers assist navigation when approaching from the northeast. Recommended entry is from the west. You will be in the correct channel if you see a sign posted on an island to port saying "Clio Island." When approaching from the west, watch for uncharted rocks. There is good anchorage in the outer bay in 30 to 40 feet of water. There is more protected anchorage in the inner bay in 25-30 feet of water at high tide. Much of the bottom near shore is rock. Good holding mud has accumulated in the center of the bay. A path leads from Ballet Bay to Hidden Basin. It is said the bay was named by a ballerina who believed the water flow and motions to be similar to the flowing motions of the dance.

★ **Vanguard Bay:** This is a log booming center. Limited anchorage is north of the islets off the east shore. A rock, which is covered at high tide, lies behind the innermost islet.

★ **Hardy Island (11):** This island is part of the Marine Provincial Park System. Several niches along the Blind Bay shore offer good one or two boat anchorages close in and with a tie to shore. Log booms often provide tie-ups and are breakwaters sheltering some coves. A narrow fjord-like indention into Hardy Island, north of the wider bay, is deep enough for anchorage. For scuba divers, wall dives are made where Ball Point drops vertically to depths of 200 feet.

★⚓ **Hardy Island Marine Park:** This park encompasses Hardy and Musket Islands. Approach from either Malaspina Strait or Jervis Inlet via Telescope Passage. Musket Island is the small island in Blind Bay, just off the south shore of Hardy Island, northwest of Fox Island. Good anchorage. The park has no facilities.

★ **Fox Island Anchorage:** There is a popular anchorage in the bay that is opposite Fox Island. The bottom tends to be rocky. Anchorage is best close in with a tie to shore to secure the hook and to make room for others.

Telescope Passage (12): Picturesque, this narrow channel between the small islands off Hardy and Nelson Islands leads from Blind Bay to Jervis Inlet. A sprawling rock covered by a few feet of water at high tide, lies in this passage. The rock is near mid-channel and spreads out toward the Hardy Island side. Pass close to Nelson Island.

Jervis Inlet
[3311, 3312, 3512, 3514]

★ **Jervis Inlet (13):** High, rugged mountains rim this 46 mile inlet. Currents are weak, however dangerous rips occur at the mouth of the inlet when the wind is against the exiting tide. The summer wind pattern is up inlet winds during the day and light or down inlet winds at night. Winds are strongest during clear weather.

★ **Thunder Bay:** Thunder Bay, and adjacent Maude Bay near the mouth of Jervis Inlet, are two of the few anchorages available in Jervis Inlet. There is anchorage near the sandy beach tucked in behind the point. When entering, stay off the western shore to avoid an unmarked rock. Several summer homes dot the shore.

★⚓ **Saltery Bay & Saltery Bay Park:** Public floats are adjacent to the Saltery Bay-Earls Cove ferry landing. A wheelchair access ramp and a garbage drop are provided. There are camping and picnic sites, water, pit toilets, and a two lane launch ramp. This park is accessible from Highway 101, as well as by water. Underwater, scuba divers search for a nine foot bronze statue of a mermaid. At the turn-of-the century, a Japanese owned and operated fish saltery was near the vicinity of the ferry terminus. ▲⛺🚶‍♂️🚤

Walk-around: A relaxing walk on a well maintained trail around the park's eastern portion ends at Park Creek. Look for salal, hanging moss, 100 year-old stumps in the forest comprised of Douglas Fir and cedar. When you get to the rinse area for divers, take the path east and have a picnic at the tables.

View of One Eye Peak through Princess Louisa Inlet   Photo © Chaz Hitz

St. Vincent Bay: This is a center of commercial oyster culture operations. Fish farms are active here as well. There is very limited anchorage in the bays on both sides of Sykes Island.

Whiskey November (WN): The area between St. Vincent Bay, Captain Island, and the entrance to Hotham Sound is a Department of National Defence military test range. Navy mooring buoys may be present. If the range is active, vessels are requested to remain clear of the area. Interestingly, the deepest "holes" on the Pacific Coast are within this area."

Hotham Sound
[3311, 3312, 3512, 3514]

★ **Hotham Sound (14):** This deep, six mile long sound is surrounded by high mountains. There is temporary anchorage in a niche on the west shore and also in Granville Bay off flats where Lapan Creek enters. Friel Falls, a lovely, tiered waterfall cascades into the sound. The head of the sound has anchorage close to shore in Baker Bay and in the niche to the southeast.

★⚓ **Harmony Islands & Marine Park:** Long a favorite of boaters, please be aware that some of these islands are private and some are included in a provincial park. As with many marine parks, the boundaries between park and private lands are sometimes difficult to discern. According to the B.C. Provincial Park System description, "the park is situated on the east side of Hotham Island, north of Granville Bay and consists of the southernmost island." The two central islands are posted: "Private Island, No trespassing, No stern ties, No kayakers, No fires". Property owners in the vicinity have to struggle to protect their lands from public encroachment. The delicate relationship between the land owners and the thousands of visitors can be enhanced and "harmony" maintained in the Harmony Islands by a little care, thoughtfulness, and respect by all parties.

Anchorage is possible in all areas covered by saltwater, except those areas leased for private buoys, aquaculture, and other purposes. Anchoring may be difficult and takes patience because much of the bottom is rock. Shore ties allowed only to the two Marine Park Islands, not to private lands.

Satisfactory anchorage is possible in the passage between the islands and the mainland shore. Be prepared for mosquitoes when taking a dinghy to the mainland or when anchoring close to shore. Great care needs to be taken to avoid the danger of fires in the area.

Prince of Wales Reach
[3311, 3312, 3514]

★ **Prince of Wales Reach (15):** Prince of Wales, Princess Royal Reach, and Queen's Reach form one long, about 30 mile, waterway leading to Princess Louisa Inlet. Because of great depths, anchorages are few. Behind Patrick Point in Queen's Reach is a nook offering a good place to wait for the tide in Malibu Rapids.

★ **Egmont Village:** Moorage, fuel, and supplies are available. See section on Sechelt Inlet.

Dark Cove: Anchorage in settled weather is close to shore west of Sydney Island. Winds tend to enter the bay and the bottom is not dependable. Goliath Bay to the north is too deep for anchorage.

Killam Bay: There is a small sand beach and limited anchorage.

Vancouver Bay: The shoreline shoals and then drops off rapidly, thus limiting anchorage. Active logging operations in the bay as well.

★ **McMurray Bay:** Limited anchorage is found here, also in the bight just north.

★ **Deserted Bay:** Anchorage is possible in this bay on Princess Royal Reach. A shelf on the southeast corner provides excellent bottom for anchorage. Parts of the shelf are very shallow at low tide. Onshore is First Nations Land.

Chatterbox Falls at the head of Princess Louisa Inlet   Photo © Ryan Van Veen Photography

Princess Louisa Inlet
[3311, 3312, 3512, 3514]

★ **Princess Louisa Inlet (16):** This beautiful inlet with its unique ecological system, is the only true example of fjordland on the Pacific coast. The spectacular marine park at Chatterbox Falls contains mooring buoys, stern pins, a boat dock and a dinghy dock for boaters, as well as an airplane float, a number of campsites, a ranger cabin, picnic shelter and toilets.

★ **Malibu Rapids:** Malibu is 32 miles from Egmont. No fuel is available after Egmont. Currents in the rapids attain rates to nine knots at springs. Because of strong currents and overfalls, the rapids should be entered at or near slack water. High-water slack is preferable because of the added room for navigation in the narrow passage. When waiting for slack, waterfalls located a short distance up the Reach and on the same shoreline, provide diversion. Slack water calculations can be made using standard tide tables. Refer to the time of slack water at Atkinson Point, Burrard Inlet. Slack times vary with the height of the tide. Slack water occurs about 24 minutes after high water and 36 minutes after low water at Atkinson Point. Following a large tidal change the actual slack may be delayed several minutes while pent-up waters move through the rapids. Years of boating experience have proven that while the strip of white water is still visible, looking like a tread across the passage, it is not advisable to go through the rapids. The overfall is caused by the backing-up of water on one side of the narrow, shallow constriction. This results in a different level of water inside and outside the rapids. From the time of the appearance of the overfall until after it disappears, the rapids will be running at full force. Thus, entry is preferable after the slack occurs, as the tidal current actually changes direction, and before the next overfall, rather than just before the slack water. These principles apply during large tidal changes. Following a small change, only a slight current will be encountered a few minutes before and after the current reverses. Because of limited visibility of boats entering at the other end of the rapids, use of VHF 16 to announce your approach is recommended.

The lodge situated at the rapids was originally developed as an exclusive retreat by Thomas F. Hamilton, a pioneer in aviation. Since 1954 the property, known as The Malibu Club, has been a summer camp operated by Young Life. The rest of the year it is available for public bookings. The coordinates are {50° 9' 52.73" N, 123° 51' 4.9" W}. Short tours of the property may be available from 11am-4pm most days June through mid-August. Tour days vary, so check the sign on the deck for availability.

★ **Princess Louisa Marine Provincial Park:** Known to many as the *Eighth Wonder of the World*, this 5mi/8km valley with a boomerang-like curve to port near the head, is breath taking. Picturesque granite walls reach up to 8,000 feet high with seasonal waterfalls cascading to the water below. The most recognizable one, Chatterbox Falls, roars at the head of the inlet. Visitors are asked to respect the calm stillness of this remote location and, in order to prevent wash, there is a speed limit of four knots. The park is staffed from mid-June to mid-September.

In the channel, between the mainland shore and the northeast tip of MacDonald Island, be aware of a rock that is barely covered at high tide. Stern-tie mooring eyes have been placed in the land in a niche to port after entering from Malibu Rapids, on and opposite Macdonald Island. In places where the rock wall shoreline is very steep, two rings or "eyes", one above the other, have been placed to make them reachable at any tide. Check for empty mooring buoys located behind MacDonald Island to port about halfway up the Inlet. Good anchorage is possible, with depths to 60', in the channel near the island, using at least 200 feet of anchor rode. Another two and one-half miles into the inlet, floats provide moorage with a spectacular view of Chatterbox Falls. Vessels must be less than 18m/55ft, 72 hour maximum stay on the floats. Because of popularity, dock space may not be available. One strategy is to moor at MacDonald Island, or anchor in front of the falls and move to the floats when boats depart for the morning slack. There are shore-tie rings on the starboard shore, before reaching the float area. These rings are difficult to use as shore ties for anchorage, because of the depth of the adjacent waters. There are also rings to the left of the falls. Anchorage with stern ties to these rings is possible. Our favorite anchorage is found off the base of the 120 foot-high falls. Set the hook in the silt shallows, very close in, at the foot of the falls (in five to ten feet of water). Put the boat in reverse at low throttle to set the anchor. The ledge drops quickly. Once the anchor catches properly, the current from the falls will keep a constant pull on the anchor and keep the boat facing the falls. A viewing platform with a bronze plaque and the ashes of "Mac" MacDonald, Father of the Inlet, are in a granite wall near the falls. Wildlife is abundant. Mountain goats maneuvering on the high cliffs opposite the floats are a sight to see. Trails, pit toilets, and a picnic shelter at the falls are available. Floats and facilities are provided and maintained by The Princess Louisa International Society through memberships and donations.

Major fund raising efforts are underway to secure monies to purchase some, if not all, of the lands surrounding the inlet. If you'd like more information about how you can help, contact the Princess Louisa International Foundation. Website: www.princesslouisa.bc.ca.

Walk-around: A fairly easy, 1km/.6mi loop trail makes a pleasant walk through the forest to a view of the inlet. Access the trail from the dinghy dock past the campsites. Experienced climbers may want to venture outside the Park and tackle the two hour, steep and difficult climb to the Trapper's Cabin for memorable views of Princess Louisa Inlet, the upper reaches of Jervis Inlet, and of Mount Albert.

Sechelt Inlet

[3311, 3312, 3512]

★ **Sechelt Inlet (17):** Sometimes called an Inland Sea, this large, lovely inlet is actually an arm of Jervis Inlet where the Skookumchuck Narrows are found. Skookumchuck, the Chinook word for "strong waters," aptly describes the turbulent whirlpools and rapid tidal currents, often reaching 14 knots, that occur at change of tide at the Sechelt Rapids. The Skookumchuck Narrows, followed by the Sechelt Rapids form the first three miles of the inlet. Beyond this, the indentation stretches 16 miles and ends in Porpoise Bay. Narrows Inlet and Salmon Inlet branch toward the interior. Together these three inlets, Sechelt, Salmon and Narrows Inlets make up Sechelt Inlets Marine Provincial Park. Beginning in early morning, winds blow up Salmon and Narrows Inlets. Down inlet winds often come at night. Maximum tidal range within the inlet is ten feet. Moorage and supplies are found at Egmont, and Porpoise Bay. Gas and diesel are available at Back Eddy Marina and at Bathgate General Store in Egmont Village. There is a launching ramp at Four Mile Point and at Porpoise Bay. Undeveloped park lands and anchorages are available at Halfway Islet, Skaiakos Point, Tuwanek Point, Nine Mile Point, and Piper Point. Logging operations are prevalent and tugs are a frequent sight. A cottage community called Tuwanek is located in the Sechelt Inlet between 9 mile point and Porpoise Bay. For guests staying overnight, Tranquility Bay Waterfront Inn (the top rated Inn on the coast) offers use of their dock (25' maximum) as a tender and a mooring bouy for larger vessels. No day visits. 604-989-9578. Approximate location is {49° 32' 39.3318" N, 123° 45' 41.403 W}.

★ **Egmont Village (17):** To reach Egmont from Agamemnon Channel or Jervis Inlet cruise along the east coast of the Sechelt Peninsula toward the Sechelt Inlet. Just past the Sutton Islets, Backeddy Resort & Marina offers moorage, fuel, dining and accommodations. Approaching the marina, note the red day beacon and keep it on your port side. Be aware that strong currents can be present in the marina area, keep your bow into the current. Within walking distance of the Backeddy Marina, boaters are welcome to dine, enjoy a spa treatment or book an adventure package at West Coast Wilderness Lodge, 778-280-8610. Continuing down the Narrows is Secret Bay and the village of Egmont. Secret Bay has a well-marked reef and navigating into moorage is not difficult. Just keep the red day marker well to starboard and do not go between the beacons (refer to the Bathgate Marina map for entry & exit route). Moorage is available at Bathgate Resort & Marina (where you will also find fuel, a well-stocked general store, liquor and beer, a marine ways, and lodging). The government dock also has limited moorage. The Village has a small post office and a downtown park with a sports field, tennis court, and playground. There are a number of hiking trails, including one to Skookumchuck Narrows Provincial Park. Near the trailhead, the Skookumchuck Bakery & Cafe is the perfect place to pick up a treat to keep you moving. Once at the park, Roland Point or North Point offer the best views of the spectacle of the powerful tidal surge at the Skookumchuck Rapids. The Egmont Heritage Centre, located across from this Park, is a must see for history buffs. Here, the story of First Nations and early European settlers is told in photos and artifacts. There are also wonderful collections of Vivian and Easthope engines, antique bottles, and Depression era glass. An onsite gift shop features local books, arts and crafts. For hours call 604-883-9994. From Egmont Village, it is a 6 km drive to Earl's Cove and the BC Ferry Terminal. Water taxi and guided kayak, boat and float plane tours are available locally.

★ **Bathgate General Store, Resort & Marina:** {49° 48' N, 123° 56' W} Located on the waterfront in the Sunshine Coast village of Egmont, Bathgate Resort offers beautiful, ocean view accommodations. Campsites for tents, campers and RV's also enjoy scenic water views. Showers, laundry facilities, and water are all available. The fuel dock sells marine fuel, gas and diesel, as well as propane, kerosene, stove oil. Auto gas is also available onsite. Visit the well-stocked general store for groceries, ice, charts, fishing tackle, hardware and marine supplies, along with liquor, beer and wine. The marina is annual moorage only and has a long waitlist. Guest moorage is found nearby at the government docks. See our advertisement on this page. Address: 6781 Bathgate Rd, Egmont, British Columbia, V0N 1N0. Email: info@bathgate.com. Website: http://bathgate.com. Telephone: 604-883-2222. VHF 66A.

Backeddy Resort & Marina: {49° 48' N, 123° 56' W} Permanent & transient moorage, 15/30 amp power, gas and diesel, water, shower and laundry facilities, WiFi, launch ramp, ice, pub. 604-883-2298.

Egmont Public Floats: Annual & transient moorage, 20/30 amp power, water and payment box at top of the dock.

Walk-around: The viewpoint at Skookumchuck Narrows Provincial Park is a 4km/2.5mi hike from Egmont. The path, a quarter mile from the public floats, is marked by a sign. Along the trail there

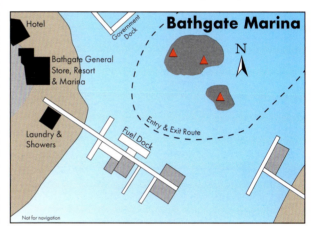

Porpoise Bay Photo © Peter M. Graham

are information signs and restrooms are located at both ends of the trail. Visitors viewing from shore, can best see the incoming current from Rowland Point and the flow of the outgoing current can be spectacular when viewed from North Point. Surf kayakers riding the waves can often be seen. A unique variety of creatures have adapted to life in the raging water flow. Tapestries of dahlia anemones, giant barnacles, encrusting sponges, blue mussels and plumose anemones cling tightly to the rocks and can be seen by scuba divers during the short intervals between the incoming and outgoing currents.

Sechelt Rapids (18): [3514, 3512] Use Volume 5 of the Canadian Tide and Current Tables. Under the heading of Sechelt Rapids are the turns, maximum times, and knots. Because there is no problem going through these narrows at slack water, plan to go through at time of turn. Proper planning is essential to avoid dangerous runs. At spring tides these rapids attain a rate of 15 knots. The preferred route is west of Boom Islet and Sechelt Isle Light. Give Roland Point a wide berth, especially on a flood tide. There can be a spectacular over fall of eight to ten feet. If mooring at Egmont Village and walking in to view the rapids, plan to do so at a maximum time and knots. - means ebb, + means flood.

★ **Narrows Inlet & Tzoozie Narrows (19):** On the south side of the entrance to Narrows Inlet is Cawley Point. Storm Bay offers good anchorage inside the islets east of Cawley Point or behind the point that extends into the middle of the bay. Narrows Inlet is home to Tzoozie Narrows, a marine park, a recreation preserve, coves for anchorage, the fishing grounds of the Tzoonie, and logging operations. Currents run to four knots in Tzoonie Narrows, located about 3.4mi/5.4km up Narrows Inlet. Park land is on both sides and there is a nice beach. Remains of an old homestead are on the north side of the park, and pieces of old logging equipment can also be found in the brush. The recreation reserve is another mile into the inlet.

★ **Salmon Inlet (20):** Power plants and logging operations are at the head. Avoid low hanging power lines. North of Kunechin Point, there is anchorage and park land. Anchor off the northeastern shore near a log float. No fires are allowed at Kunechin Park. A premiere diving site is found off Kunechin Point. The sunken naval vessel *HMCS Chaudiere*, a 365 foot destroyer given over to the diversity of sea life and divers who explore the artificial reef. Its coordinates are 49° 37.694' N, 123° 48.699' W. An artificial reef, created by the sinking of the Canadian destroyer, Chaudiere, attracts marine life (and scuba divers, as well!). An undeveloped park is at Thornhill Creek. North of Thornhill Point is scenic Misery Creek Falls. There is anchorage at the west end of Misery Bay.

Tillicum Bay: Traveling toward the head of Sechelt Inlet past Tuwanek and Lamb Bay is Tillicum bay, site of a marina.

Tillicum Bay Marina: Permanent moorage. Guest moorage if space is available, call ahead. 15 amp power, water, porta-potty. 604-885-2100.

★ **Porpoise Bay (21):** See Sechelt description near the beginning of this chapter. Close to the town of Sechelt, this bay has several floats for moorage and float plane service, a tidal grid, a launching ramp, and marine fuel. There is limited anchorage west of Porpoise Island and off the wharf. A pub and restaurant with free wifi onsite and a well stocked marine supply store are located on the southern shore. Kayak/SUP rentals are available. 604-885-2948. The Provincial Park is found on the northeast shore.

Lighthouse Pub and Marina: {49° 28' 53.1438" N, 123° 45' 28.1478" W} Monthly moorage, limited overnight moorage (call ahead), free 2 hr moorage while dining. 30 amp power, gas, diesel, water, laundry, showers, restaurant/pub, chandlery. 604-885-9494. Chandlery: 778-458-3625.

MacKenzie Sea Services: {49° 29' 11' N, 123° 45' 11" W} Permanent moorage, guest moorage if space is available, haul-out to 45', towing/salvage. 604-885-7851 or cell: 604-740-2495. VHF 08.

Poise Cove Marina: {49° 29' 26" N, 123° 45' 0" W} Permanent annual moorage, guest moorage if space is available up to 26'. Limited power, water. 604-885-5494.

Porpoise Bay Government Wharf: {49° 28.987' N, 123° 45.483' W} Daily & monthly moorage, 30/50 amp power, water, pump-out, electric winch, launch ramp. 604-885-1986, after hours 604-740-6588.

The Spot At Porpose Bay: {49° 29' 8" N, 123° 45' 18" W} Permanent moorage. Overnight moorage for motel guests only if space is available (boats to 25', call ahead). 604-885-7844.

★ **Porpoise Bay Provincial Park** has a one-half mile sandy beach with campsites, showers, toilets, picnic areas, playground, trails. For reservations go to www.discovercamping.ca. Activities include swimming, biking, and kayaking. Walk along Angus Creek into the woodlands and forest. In the fall, spawning salmon can be seen in the creek.

Malaspina Strait
[3311, 3512, 3513]

McRae Cove (22): Although open to south winds, this cove is sheltered from the prevailing westerlies of the Malaspina Strait. Rocks and drying shoals are in the entrance. The head is a drying flat and the bottom is uneven with shallow spots. The Scotch Fir Point vicinity can be dangerous when strong westerly or southerly winds meet an opposing outgoing tide from Jervis Inlet.

Stillwater Bay (23): There is temporary protection from southeasterlies in this bay which lies about 2½ miles northwest of Scotch Fir Point. Booming operations occur frequently. The bay is open to the west. A conspicuous water tower can be used as a landmark.

Lang Bay (24): White sandy beaches line this open, shallow bay at the delta of the Lois River. There is a rock breakwater and often there are log booms. The old public wharf is used by large ships as a fueling station. Good swimming and a visit to the public park are fair weather recreations here.

Powell River
[3311, 3536]

Grief Point (25): {49° 48.3' N, 124° 31.5' W} This point lies two miles south of Powell River. It is marked by a light and beachfront homes. A large rip rap breakwater, housing a marina, is south of the point. When there are wind warnings for this area, rough seas may be encountered off the point.

Beach Gardens Resort & Marina: {49° 48.3' N, 124° 31.5' W} Transient moorage, 15/30 amp power, fresh water and ice, fuel (in season), showers, laundry, garbage disposal, restauarant. 1-800-663-7070, 604-485-6267.

★ **Westview & Powell River (26):** Powell River, for which the community is named, is only about one quarter mile in length, running from Powell Lake to the strait. The boat basins at Westview are located about 3 miles south of Powell River's Historic Townsite and are surrounded by a large rock breakwater which forms two basins, the North Harbour and the South Harbour. The North Harbour has permanent moorage (sublease contracts occasionally available) for vessels from 20' to 60'. A boat launch is located here. The Harbour office is found between the north and south basins. The entrance to the south harbour is located south of the ferry terminal. Follow the breakwater south to the entrance. The South Basin has two moorage facilities, Westview Harbour and South Harbour. Both offer transient moorage for visiting vessels to 150' (max. draft of 20') and are first-come first-served, rafting facilities. Call ahead on 66A for berthing assignment. The fuel dock is located between Float 6 in the Westview Harbour and Float 7 in the South Harbour. A seawalk connects South Harbour and Westview Harbour, making this waterfront a major attraction. Within walking distance of the public wharf are pubs, marine supplies, restaurants, liquor store, hardware stores, and other retail stores. Two shopping malls are a taxi ride away. During July and August a courtesy bus makes daily scheduled runs to the Town Centre Mall and the Town Centre Hotel.

Powell River has a good city bus line. Its stops include malls, the museum, pottery shops, art galleries and the historic townsite where you'll find the Patricia Theatre, the longest continuously running movie theatre in Canada. Centrally located Willingdon Beach Park has RV and tent camping, a playground, and historic walking trail. Across the street, the qathet Historical Museum and Archives' displays include Billy Goat Smith's cabin, the development of the pulp mill, ship and train replicas, and a First Nations display. Open year round. 604-485-2222.

There are an estimated 2,400 hours of annual sunshine in the Powell River area of the "Sunshine Coast." That's plenty of time to enjoy the array of outdoor activities and annual events, such as the Townsite Jazz Festival in April, the July 1 *Canada Day Celebration*, Powell River Logger Sports, and the biennial Kathaumixw choral festival (both also in July), the *B.C. Day Celebration* the first weekend in August, the *Blackberry Festival* in late August, and the *Sunshine Music Fest* over Labour Day weekend. The Farmers Market each Saturday and Sunday as well as Thursday Night Markets each Thursday evening all summer is a weekly treat. Kayaking, canoeing, hiking, mini-golf, ice skating and swimming at the recreation convention center, and golf at Myrtle Point Golf Course are all popular activities. The Mill Lookout is a popular stop. Visitors can peruse historic photos and information displays and enjoy scenic views of the Catalyst tisk^wat Mill, an important part of Powell River history since it first produced paper here in 1912.

The Powell River vicinity is known as a year round hot spot for scuba diving, with 19 dives in the immediate vicinity including the reefs of Vivian Island and Rebecca Rock. The area is also the gateway to Desolation Sound Marine Provincial Park, a boaters paradise.

By car, the town of Powell River is five hours from Vancouver. This entails two ferry trips and a one and one half hour drive between the ferries. Daily bus and air service also connect Powell River with Vancouver. For additional information: Powell River Visitor Info Centre, 4760 Joyce Avenue, 604-485-4701 or gopowellriver.ca.

Westview Fuel Dock: Gas, diesel, lube oils, snacks, water, ice. 604-485-2867. VHF 66A.

Westview Harbour Authority: {49° 50' 9" N, 124° 31' 42" W} Permanent & transient moorage, 30/50 amp power, water, showers, laundry, sewer pump-out, garbage & oil deposit, boat launch. Marine mechanic nearby. 604-485-5244. VHF 66A.

★ **Ahgykson Island/Harwood Island (27):** This is a private island, owned by the Tla'amin Nation. While rock and shoals rim the shores, a small cove at the south end provides anchorage. Beautiful sandy beaches are noteworthy and you are welcome to walk and picnic on the beach, but please take your garbage with you when you leave. Due to archaeological fish traps, canoe skids, and fish weirs on the beach are proteted under the Heritage Conservation Act, please do not move rocks on the beach or do any hunting for artifacts, beads, etc. You must have a Sport Fishing License for any beachharvesting. Also, be aware that hunting is not permitted. Absolutely no campfires during the provincial fire season or Tla'amin Nation fire ban. Permission is required for any access above the high tide. Call 604-483-9646, ext. 154. Members of the Tla'amin Nation use the island frequently.

★ **Savary Island & Keefer Bay (28):** Known for beautiful beaches and Sand Golf, this island is thought to resemble islands in the South Seas. There are private homes, a small public float, B&Bs, and restaurant.

Lund Harbour Photo © Powell River Tourism

There is no power on the island and cell phone service is patchy. Tuesdays in July and August, a Farmers Market with produce, crafts, BBQ and beer is held from 11am-1pm. (Walk about four blocks up hill from the float.) There is limited anchorage in Keefer Bay, inside Mace Point. This is a tricky anchorage because of drying sand beaches, which drop off quickly, poor holding sand bottom, and winds that enter through Manson Passage. Overnight anchorage is not recommended.

Lund
[3311, 3538]

★ **Lund (29):** Entry to the public boat basin is around the north end of the breakwaters. For moorage at the Harbour Authority docks, call upon approach on VHF 73 for slip assignment. Onshore, near the end of the breakwater is a water taxi, as well as additional moorage and a fuel dock at the Lund Resort at Kla ah men.

Long before the arrival of Europeans, the Tla'amin Nation, part of the Coast Salish, had a village here, named Kla ah men. Along with the 100% First Nations acquisition of the former Historic Lund Hotel and treaty settlement lands, a totem pole at the end of the wooden boardwalk in the harbour honors this history. In 1889, the Thulin brothers arrived and began to build a settlement that they named "Lund" after a city in Sweden. Today, Lund lies at Mile "0" of Hwy 101, the northernmost end of the Pacific Coastal Route. Whether you arrive by land or water, you'll find a lovely little village with moorage, marine fuel, marine repairs and boat yard (Finn Bay), a new, larger general store with deli also new public washrooms and public coin-operated showers (private garbage disposal is also available here), liquor sales, post office, artisan galleries and shops, restaurants, an RV park with cabins, waterfront airbnb accommodations, and The Lund Resort at Klah ah men. No trip to Lund is complete without a walk on the boardwalk to the old waterwheel. On the starboard side of the harbour, stop at the Boardwalk Restaurant for the "best fish & chips on the Sunshine Coast" or at Nancy's Bakery for fresh baked blackberry cinnamon buns. Above the Bakery, Terracentric Coastal Adventures has marine charts, tide tables, maps, field guides and guidebooks and offers guided hiking, kayaking, zodiac boat tours, kayak rentals and marine transport/water taxi. Since Lund is considered the "Gateway to Desolation Sound," many other local businesses offer chartered boat tours and kayak rentals for exploring those waters. Water taxis also provide service to Savary and other islands. Public transit between Lund and Powell River is available 4 days/week in the summer months. For more information about Lund visit www.LundBC.ca or www.SunshineCoastCanada.com.

The Lund Resort at Klah ah men: Lodging, marina with fuel dock at approximately {49 °58' 54.2" N, 124° 45'47.8" W}. Limited overnight moorage, strictly first come-first served, with free moorage for hotel guests when available. Garbage/recycling, and access to hotel amenities available with moorage. The fuel dock, open daily year-round carries gas, diesel, and lubricants. Hotel, Marina and Fuel 604-414-0474, 1-877-569-3999. Pub 604-414-0478. Store 604-414-0471.

Lund Harbour Authority: {49° 58' 42" N, 124° 45' 45" W} Permanent and transient moorage, 20/30/50 amp power, water, pump-out, launch ramp, showers, washrooms. No reservations, rafting mandatory. 604-483-4711. VHF 73.

★ **Finn Bay (30):** Just north of Lund, a public float, not connected to shore, is in the bay at approximately {49° 59' 6" N, 124° 46' 9" W}. There is no anchoring due to the water and sewer lines that run to Sevilla Island and other property in the area. A boatyard is located here.

Jack's Boat Yard: Haul-out to 50 tons, dry storage to 20 tons, DIY boatyard, on-site supply store. 604-483-3566.

Thulin Passage: This narrow waterway separates the mainland and Copeland Islands. The courteous skipper will lower his speed and watch his wake for safety and to avoid causing havoc with other vessels.

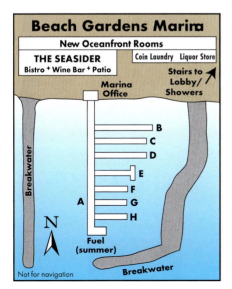

Essential Supplies & Services

AIR TRANSPORTATION
To & from Washington
Kenmore Air 1-866-435-9524
NW Seaplanes . . . 425-277-1590, 1-800-690-0086
San Juan Airlines. 1-800-874-4434
Seattle Seaplanes 1-800-637-5553
To & from Islands/Vancouver
Air Canada .1-888-247-2262
Harbour Air. 1-800-665-0212
Pacific Coastal, Powell 604-485-7216, 1-800-663-2872
Sunshine Coast Air, Sechelt/Gibsons . . . 604-740-8889

BOOKS / BOOK STORES
Evergreen Pacific Publishing 425-493-1451
The Marine Atlas. 253-872-5707

BUS TRANSPORTATION
Greyhound 1-800-661-8747
Powell River, BC Transit. 604-485-4287
Sunshine Coast Transit 604-885-6899
Sunshine Coast Connector 1-844-613-8222

COAST GUARD
Victoria Coast Guard Radio. . . . . VHF 16, 83a
. . . . 1-800-661-9202 (In BC) or 250-363-6333
Marine Distress, Search & Rescue
. . . . 1-800-567-5111 (in Canada) or 250-413-8933
By Cell Phone (limited to select providers) *16 . . .#727

FUELS
Backeddy Resort & Marina: Gas, Diesel.
. . . . .604-883-2298 VHF 66A
Bathgate General Store: Gas, Diesel.
. . . . 604-883-2222 VHF 66A
Beach Gardens Resort & Marina: Gas, Diesel.
. . . . 604-485-7734
Buccaneer Marina: Secret Cove. Gas, Diesel.
. . . . 604-885-7888
Hyak Marine: Gibsons. Gas, Diesel. 604-886-9011
John Henry's Gas, Diesel, 50:1 604-883-2336
Lighthouse Pub & Marina. 604-885-9494
Secret Cove Marina: . . . . 604-885-3533 VHF 66A
The Lund Resort at Klah ah men: Gas, Diesel
. . . . 604-414-0474
Westview: Gas, Diesel. 604-485-2867

GOLF COURSES
(These courses are accessible from moorage and have rental clubs available)
Blue Ocean Golf Club, Sechelt 604-885-2700
Sunshine Coast Golf, Gibson 604-885-9212
Pender Harbour 604-883-9541
Myrtle Point, Powell River 604-487-4653

GROCERY STORES
Bathgate General Store . . 604-883-2222 VHF 66A
Gibsons IGA 604-886-3487
Madeira Park IGA 604-883-9100
Sechelt IGA. 604-885-6331
The Lund Resort at Klah ah men 604-414-0471

HOSPITALS/CLINICS
Healthline BC (Nurse Helpline) 811
Gibsons Medical Clinic 604-886-2868
Pender Harbour Health Centre 604-883-2764
Powell River General Hospital. 604-485-3211
Sechelt St Mary's Hospital 604-885-2224

HAUL-OUTS
Buccaneer Marina: Secret Cove 604-885-7888
Jack's Boat Yard: Finn Bay. 604-483-3566
Mackenzie Sea Services 604-885-7851
Madeira Marina. 604-883-2266

LIQUOR STORES
Backeddy Resort & Marina
. . . . .800-626-0599 VHF 66A
Bathgate General Store Resort & Marina: Egmont.
. . . . 604-883-2222 VHF 66A
Beach Gardens Resort & Marina. 604-485-6267
Gibsons
Halfmoon Bay
John Henry's: 604-883-2253
Madeira Park, Powell River/Westview, Sechelt
The Lund Resort at Klah ah men -Government Liquor
Agency. 604-414-0471

LODGING
Backeddy Resort & Marina
. . . . 800-626-0599, VHF 66A
Bathgate General Store Resort & Marina: Egmont
. . . . 604-883-2222 VHF 66A
Beach Gardens Resort & Marina: Powell River
. . . . 604-485-6267
John Henry's Marina. 604-883-2336
Painted Boat Resort Spa & Marina. . . . 604-883-2456
Pender Harbour Resort. 604-883-2424
Sunshine Coast Resort: Madeira Park . . 604-883-9177
The Lund Resort at Klah ah men 604-414-0474

MARINAS / MOORAGE
Backeddy Resort & Marina
. . . . 604-883-2298 VHF 66A
Bathgate General Store Resort & Marina
(Permanent moorage) . . 604-883-2222 VHF 66A
Beach Gardens Resort & Marina. 604-485-7734
Buccaneer Marina: Secret Cove 604-885-7888
Coho Marina: Pender Harbour 604-883-2248
Egmont Village Public Float
Finn Bay
Gerrans Bay-Whiskey Slough Public Float.
. . . . 604-883-2234
Gibsons Landing Harbour Authority 604-886-8017
Gibsons Marina. . . . . 604-886-8686 VHF 66A
Halfmoon Bay
Hospital Bay Government Wharf. 604-883-2234
John Henry's Marina. . . . . 604-883-2336 VHF 66A
Lund Harbour Authority 604-483-4711
Madeira Park: Harbour Authority of Pender Harbour.
. . . . 604-883-2234 VHF 66A
Pender Harbour Hotel Marina 604-883-9013
Pender Harbour Resort & Marina. 604-883-2424
Porpoise Bay Government Wharf 604-740-7528
Princess Louisa Marine Park
Saltery Bay
Savary Island
Secret Cove Government Dock. 604-883-2234
Secret Cove Marina . . . . . 604-885-3533 VHF 66A
Secret Cove Government Dock. 604-883-2234
Sunshine Coast Resort 604-883-9177
The Lund Resort at Klah ah men Fuel Dock
. . . . 604-414-0474
Westview Harbour Authority. 604-485-5244

MARINE SUPPLY STORES
Pender Harbour Diesel 604-883-2616
Lighthouse Marine 778-458-3625

PROPANE
Bathgate General Store . . 604-883-2222 VHF 66A
John Henry's Marina. . . . . 604-883-2336 VHF 66A
Vanderkemp's: Westview 604-485-9774

RAMPS
Backeddy Resort & Marina
. . . . 604-883-2298, VHF 66A

Buccaneer Marina: Secret Cove 604-885-7888
Coho Marina: Pender Harbour 604-883-2248
Gibsons Marina. 604-886-9011
Halfmoon Bay
John Henry's. 604-883-2336
Lund Harbour Authority 604-483-4711
Madeira Park: Harbour Authority Pender Harbour
Pender Harbour Resort & Marina. 604-883-2424
Porpoise Bay Government Wharf
Sechelt Inlet: Four Mile Pt., Roberts Creek
Saltery Bay
Westview Harbour Authority. 604-485-5244

REPAIRS
Buccaneer Marina: Secret Cove 604-885-7888
Lund Auto & Outboard: Mobile . 604-483-4612 VHF 73
Madeira Marina: Pender Harbour 604-883-2266

RESTAURANTS / PUBS
The Backeddy Marina Pub . . . . 604-883-2298 VHF 66A
Lighthouse Pub & Marina. 604-885-9494
Nancy's Bakery, Lund 604-483-4180
RockWater Secret Cove Resort. 604-885-7038
The Lund Resort at Klah ah men 604-414-0474
The Seasider Bistro + Wine Bar + Patio
. . . . 604-485-0996
Upper Deck Cafe 1-866-885-3533

SCUBA SITES
Halfmoon Bay, Smuggler Cove Marine Park
Pender Harbour, Hardy Island, Saltery Bay-Earl's Cove
Salmon Inlet
Powell River (Vivian Island, Rebecca Rock, Iron Mines)
Skookumchuck Narrows Provincial Park

SEWAGE DISPOSAL
Gibson's Landing Harbour Authority . . . 604-886-8017
Gibson's Marina 604-886-8686
Harbour Authority of Pender Harbour: Madeira Park
. . . . 604-883-2234 VHF 66A
Lund Harbour Authority 604-483-4711
Porpoise Bay Gov't Wharf. 604-740-7528
Westview Harbour Authority. 604-485-5244

SPORTFISHING RESORTS
Beach Gardens Resort & Marina. 604-485-6267
Pender Harbor Resort. 604-883-2424

TAXI SERVICE
Gibsons. 604-886-7337
Longsdale-Secret Cove. 604-989-8294
Sechelt 604-885-3666

TOWING
C-TOW 1-888-419-CTOW
MacKenzie Sea Services 604-885-7851, 604-740-2495

VISITOR INFORMATION
Gibsons. 604-886-2374
Pender Harbour/Egmont. 604-883-2561
Powell River 604-485-4701
Sechelt Visitor Centre 604-885-1036
Sunshine Coast Tourism. 604-740-6170

WEATHER
Environment Canada Weather Line 250-339-9861
Victoria: WX-2. 604-666-3655

Visit us at boattravel.com

Chapter 14: Desolation Sound

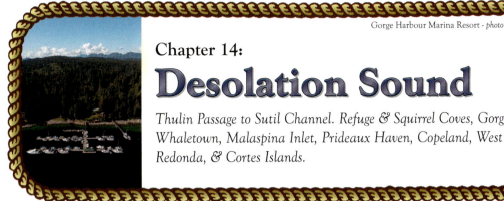

Thulin Passage to Sutil Channel. Refuge & Squirrel Coves, Gorge Harbour, Whaletown, Malaspina Inlet, Prideaux Haven, Copeland, West & East Redonda, & Cortes Islands.

Gorge Harbour Marina Resort - photo © Gorge Harbour Marina Resort

Symbols

[ ]: Numbers between [ ] are chart numbers.

{ }: Numbers & letters between { } are waypoints.

★ Recommended destinations, facilities, and services

⚐: Park, ⛵: Boat Launch, ▲: Campgrounds, 🚶: Hiking Trails, ⊼: Picnic Area, 🚴: Biking : Scuba

★ See "Important Notices" between Chapters 7 and 8 for specific information on boating related topics such as boating safety, weather, U.S. & Canadian marine radio use, Vessel Traffic Service, security zones, Canadian & U.S. Customs, etc. Due to changing regulations, call ahead to verify latest customs information.

★ No Dump Zones: Carrington Bay, Copeland Islands, Cortes Bay, Gorge Harbour, Manson's Landing, Prideaux Haven, Roscoe Bay, Squirrel Cove. Dump gray water only (shower and dish water). Must have approved holding tank on board to enter No Dump Zone.

Thulin Passage
[3311, 3538]

Thulin Passage: This narrow waterway separates the mainland and Copeland Islands. Watch your wake for safety and to avoid causing havoc with other vessels.

★⚐ **Copeland Islands Marine Park (1):** Known locally as the Ragged Islands, a prominent marine park sign welcomes visitors to this collection of small islands. Four larger islands and islets make up the undeveloped marine park. Although there are several indents and bights, protection is limited because of boat wash from Thulin Passage and west side exposure to the Strait of Georgia. A popular anchorage is on the Thulin Passage side about

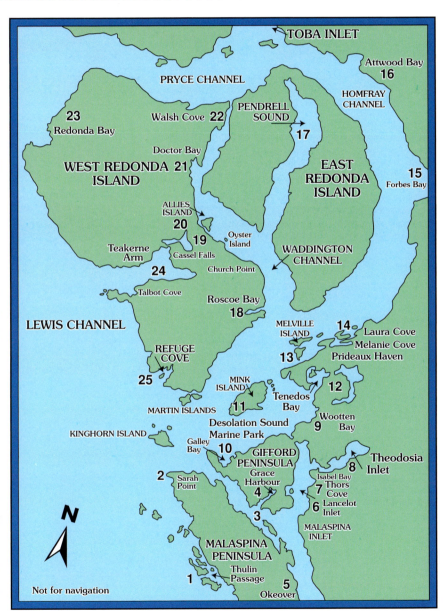

Chart List

Canadian Hydrographic Charts:
3311, 3312, 3538, 3541, 3554, 3559

Marine Atlas Vol 1 (2018): Page 29-32, 34

Evergreen Cruising Atlas:
Pages 49, 52, 53, 59, 63-65, 68, 69, 73

halfway through the passage. Anchorage on the rock bottom is tricky. If the anchor will not hold in the center of the bay, try it close to the shore. Another small bay, with anchoring possibilities, is between two of the northern islets. Another anchorage is in a southerly notch on the west side of the 87 meter island. Excellent destination for kayakers, wildlife viewing, scuba diving, wilderness camping, swimming & fishing.

★ **Bliss Landing:** Situated at the north end of Thulin Passage at the head of Turner Bay is a private gated community of homes and a marina.

Marina at Bliss Landing: Private facility. Transient moorage if space is available, no reservations. 30/50 amp power, washrooms, showers, garbage, wifi, coin laundry, water. Office: 604-414-9417, Cell: 604-483-8098.

Desolation Sound

[3312, 3538, 3541, 3554]

★ **Desolation Sound:** The name alone has intrigued boaters for many years, and once they round Sarah Point and see Mt. Denman in the distance, what Captain George Vancouver described as desolate in 1792, is wide open for interpretation today. Still desolate in terms of development, most boaters experience a feeling of awe when entering this sound. A time period of several days is recommended for exploring the variety of bays and facilities in the Desolation Sound vicinity. Anchorages, fuel, moorages, groceries, liquor, and other provisions are available. During the peak season from July through August, many anchorages and moorage floats become crowded. Reservations at marinas are essential. The lush scenery, warm bays for swimming, tasty shellfish, and bountiful catches of sport salmon, combine to make this a top "bucket list" boating spot for both Canadians and Americans. There is fishing along Mary Point, the shore of Cortes, off Sarah Point past Zephine Head, in Roscoe Bay and in Homfray Channel. Eagles often sit in the trees to watch for fish to eat which may suggest good fishing grounds. The flood streams from north and south meet near Squirrel Cove. Currents from Johnstone Strait meet those from the Strait of Juan de Fuca and Georgia Strait. There is little current, but the area is affected by winds.

★ **Desolation Sound Marine Park:** Desolation Sound falls within the traditional territories of the Tla'amin, Hamalco, and Klahoose First Nations. Current research shows the three Nations have occupied Desolation Sound for over 7,400 years. The First Nations still rely on the abundant sea life in the waters of Desolation Sound to harvest traditional foods. This is one of the largest and most visited parks (the list below is multiple protected areas) in the B.C. Marine Park system. It includes much of Gifford Peninsula, Grace Harbour, Tenedos Bay, Prideaux Haven, Copeland Islands, Teakerne Arm, Walsh Cove, and East Redonda Island Ecological Reserve. However, as with most marine parks, the boundaries between park and private lands are sometimes difficult to discern. Property owners in the vicinity have a struggle to protect their lands from public encroachment. Many private land signs are posted, including the Tla'amin Nation. A little thoughtfulness and respect by all parties concerned are in order. Anchorages (on the water side) are open to the public, since all areas covered by saltwater are public. However, the government has leased certain areas for private buoys, aquaculture, or other purposes. Be aware that there are many archeological sites within Desolation Sound Marine Park, protected under the Heritage Conservation Act, including intertidal features that could be damaged by your anchor. In regard to the shore side, when in doubt, it would be well to attempt to ascertain the proper status to avoid trespassing, and stay on designated BC Park trails and pick up after your pets. If privately owned, obtain permission for tying to shore or coming ashore, and use stern ties within the Park when available. To report a wildfire please call 1-800-663-5555 or *5555 from a cell phone.

Fires are prohibited in Desolation Sound Marine Park, except at Tenedos Bay and Roscoe Bay. Smoking and vaporizers are prohibited on shore in all BC Parks. These parks protect very sensitive ecosystems and cultural values, to help protect these values:

Please stay on designated routes to avoid causing ecological or cultural damage. Designated BC Park Trails are: Grace Harbour to Black Lake, Tenedos Bay to Unwin Lake and Unwin Lake to Melanie Cove, Roscoe Bay to Black Lake, and Teakerne Arm to Cassel Lake. Keep dogs on leash and pick up after your pets. BC Parks Generator hours: 9-11 a.m. and 6-8 p.m. BC Parks 14 Day maximum stay per park per calendar year. Please use stern ties when available. To find locations see: www.marineparksforever.ca/find-marine-parks. Avoid anchoring in less than 20 feet of water to protect intertidal archeological sites such as clam gardens and canoe skids. Federal regulation prohibits the discharge of sewage while at anchor in any waters; it is also prohibited to discharge sewage within 3 nautical miles from shore. Lund Harbour is the closest pump out station.

For more information and to donate to Desolation Sound Marine Provincial Park visit: www.env.gov.bc.ca/bcparks/explore/parkpgs/desolation/.

★ **Sarah Point (2):** This is a popular salmon fishing area. If trolling close in along the shore to Myrmidon Point, avoid Stacey Rock, which is covered at high tide. Sarah Point is the start of the first section of the Sunshine Coast Trail, a hiking trail that ends at the ferry terminal at Saltery Bay in Jervis Inlet.

Malaspina Inlet

[3312, 3538, 3559]

★ **Malaspina Inlet (3):** Several good anchorages, places to explore, and delicious shellfish are found in this lovely and extensive inlet. The entrance channel is not difficult to chart and navigate but tidal streams in the entrance can reach four knots. Although there are rocks and shoal areas, large kelp beds often mark their location during summer months. Most of the inlet waters are a part of Desolation Sound Marine Park, while the Malaspina Peninsula shoreline is designated as a Provincial Park. This inlet is popular with kayakers. There are numerous aquaculture leases in the area which contributes largely to the need for boaters to be ecologically responsible throughout the Malaspina Complex. Many oyster beds are private, so check before you dig.

★ **Parker Harbour:** Two anchorages are in Parker Harbour. One is tucked behind Beulah Island and the other is at the south end behind Thorp Island. Enter north of drying reefs, north of Thorp Island. Give the island a wide berth to avoid shoals. Aquaculture operations are marked by buoys.

★ **Cochrane Islands:** A drying ledge connects these two islands. Watch for rocks. There are anchorages behind the islands. Aquaculture operations are along the shoreline.

★ **Grace Harbour (4):** This large bay is a popular anchorage. The first anchorage is in a bight at Kakaekae Point just before entering Grace Harbour. When passing Jean Island, a Desolation Sound Park sign welcomes boaters. An area behind Jean Island also has anchorage. Shoals are visible. Farther into the entrance, the bay opens into a heart-shaped basin. Anchorage is good both near shore or in the center. Dinghies can be beached at the site of a park information board which illustrates the surroundings. A trail leads to a lake where swimming is possible. The water is quite brown and marshy with several beaver dams. There are many loons in the area.

Treveven Bay: This bay is formed between the Coode Peninsula and Malaspina Peninsula. Aquaculture operations marked by large buoys tend to block the bay. If possible to enter, there is anchorage and shelter in southeasterly winds. Log booms may be in the bay.

★ **Okeover tox^{w}nac^v (Toxw-Nutch) Inlet (5):** Along the western shore are public floats and a provincial park. The eastern shore consists of many aquaculture tenures and the upland is owned by the Tla'amin Nation. Okeover Harbour Authority has a concrete launching ramp next to the public floats. Nearby, visitors can enjoy indoor and outdoor dining at the Laughing Oyster Restaurant, 604-483-9775. North of the wharf is tox^{w}nac^v (Toxw-Nutch, Okeover Arm) Provincial Park. The park has picnic and camping sites, and a hand water pump for water. Absolutely no digging on any of the land. Any shellfish harvesting requires a valid sport fishing license. Anchorage is possible northwest of the Harbour, in Penrose Bay and also to the southeast in Freke Anchorage, near the head of the inlet. The latter offers protection in southeast winds. A water pipeline runs across Freke Anchorage from a local plant. The warm, sheltered waters in this area make this a prolific place for marine life. Scuba divers know the secrets of submarine cave formations found in Okeover tox^{w}nac^v (Toxw-Nutch) Inlet.

Okeover Harbour Authority: {49°59"28.42"N 124°42'40.85'W} Guest moorage, no reservations, first come first served. Outhouse up the hill, pay phone on the wharf head. 604-483-3258. VHF 66A.

★ **Penrose Bay:** This bay is open to the south. There is anchorage at the head of the bay. Onshore at the head of the Bay, Powell River Sea Kayak Ltd is housed in an old log house.

★ **Lancelot Inlet (6):** Anchorage is possible in Isabel Bay, Thors Cove, Wooton Bay, and behind Susan Islets. Enter the inlet between Edith Island and Hillingdon Point. Watch for aquaculture activities.

★ **Isabel Bay:** Isabel Bay is entered from Lancelot Inlet. Pass between Polly Island and Madge Island. A drying rock lies about 100 yards northeast of Polly Island, and drying ledges extend north and northeast from Madge Island. Aquaculture operations are in the bay, but anchorage can be found. West of Madge Island, anchors have fouled on a section of sunken bull dozer track lying at the location marked "4.2m" depth on the large scale chart. The other section of track can be seen high and dry on the nearby rock.

★ **Thors Cove (7):** There is anchorage at the south end of the bay behind the small islet. Enter from the north to avoid hazards. At certain times of the year, the intensity of the green on the surrounding hills and shores of this cove is like something out of a picture book. Aquaculture operations are along some of the shoreline.

★ **Theodosia Inlet (8):** [3559]. The narrow entrance channel has depths of six feet even at low water. Stay in center channel. The head of Theodosia Inlet dries and is used for log storage. Good anchorage is possible in several places on a sticky mud bottom. A favorite spot is behind the islet to port on entering the inlet. Outside the inlet, anchorage is possible near Grail Point behind Susan Islet. An old orchard is a landmark.

★ **Susan Islets Anchorage:** When entering Theodosia Inlet, the Susan Islets will be to port. Good anchorage is found. Locate the rock which dries and a shoal north of the islets before setting the anchor.

★ **Wooten Bay (9):** Located near the head of Lancelot Inlet, anchorage is open to south and southeast winds, but offers some protection from westerlies. Property at nearby Portage Cove is posted as private and is not included in Desolation Sound Marine Park.

★ **Galley Bay (10):** Good anchorage is found, however this harbour is open to the north. Two large drying rocks are shown on charts. The one near the center dries three feet and the one farther in dries 15 feet. Anchorage is possible in the western area and behind the drying shoals and islet in the eastern portion in 30-35 feet of water. Private ramps with floats extend from shore. A stern tie to shore is recommended. Once the site of a commune.

★ **Mink Island (11):** This island is private property, but there is a favorite anchorage on its southeastern side. The outer area of the bay is open to east winds. There is more protected anchorage farther in where the bay turns to the north. Depths are 10-20 feet. A drying lagoon is at the head.

Curme Islands: This cluster of islands stretches along the north-northeast shore of Mink Island. Anchorage, in settled weather, is possible in the passage between the two largest islands in the northernmost group of three islands. The channel is shallow and narrow in spots.

★ **Tenedos Bay (12):** A rock off Bold Head hides its ugly head and has caught many unwary boaters entering or leaving Tenedos Bay. Depths range 200-350 feet in the center. There are coves and niches suitable for anchorage. High, steep cliffs surround the bay. When entering, favor mid channel, aiming straight ahead to the niche that is marked with a 40 on Chart #3312 metric. When adequately past the rock that is to port, turn to port and find anchorage behind the two small, bare islets in the south corner of Tenedos. Farther in on that side is an island that is connected to shore by a drying ledge. Many boaters choose to anchor behind the island in a narrow channel between the island and the mainland. The bottom is mostly rock and quite fickle. A stern line to shore can provide additional room for others, as well as keeping the anchored boat from turning and pulling the anchor out from under the rock where it may be lodged. When a westerly wind arises, it whistles through this area. Unmarked rocks extend from this island in several places. A more popular anchorage is in the area where a stream flows down the bank from nearby Unwin Lake. Anchorage with stern ties to shore is required. Fresh water swims in the lake are popular on hot summer days.

★ **Otter Island (13):** A navigable, very narrow, passage separates Otter Island from the mainland. There is a tiny bight in this passage which provides anchoring room for one or two boats. Sky Pilot Rock, one of the most dangerous hazards in the area, lies north of Otter Island. It waits menacingly out in mid-channel only a few feet under water at high tide. To avoid the rock, favor the Otter Island shore when traveling to and from Prideaux Haven.

★ **Eveleigh Island Anchorage:** [3555] Anchorage is possible in 40 feet on the southeast side of Eveleigh Island.

Prideaux Haven
[3312, 3538, 3554]

★ **Prideaux Haven (14):** No dump zone. The most popular spot in Desolation Sound, Prideaux Haven consists of several sheltered harbours. When approaching, avoid the shelf about 100 yards south of Lucy Point and the three-foot drying rock close to Lucy Point on Eveleigh Island. Approach the narrow entry from the passage between Eveleigh Island and Scobell Island. Kelp may be encountered off the Eveleigh Island shore, but this side, or preferably a mid channel course, is necessary to avoid Oriel Rocks. In the narrow entrance, the white areas that show through the green clear water at some tides are shoals and rocky extensions of the shore. Fires are not permitted on shore. Majestic mountain peaks rise to heights of 4,590 feet. The tidal range is one of the largest in the area. A change of as much as 18 feet on a large tide is not uncommon. Use depth sounder and Chart #3554 or Chart #3312 metric. Once inside Prideaux Haven, anchorage is possible in the south part, in the center, in the larger bay east of William Islands, and in the approach to the indentation that separates Copplestone Island from the mainland.

★ **Melanie Cove:** This is an extremely popular, often crowded anchorage. There may be room for a few boats to swing at anchor in the center, however, most boaters anchor back off toward shore, and tie a shore line. New shore tie pins and chain installed in 2015. The land surrounding Melanie Cove is deeded to the University of British Columbia. A small stream of fresh water empties into the bay near the head of Melanie Cove. On a quiet evening the sound of the bubbling brook may be heard. A hike of about 1/2 mile from the head of Melanie Cove leads to Laura Cove. A trail follows an old logging road and a stream to the old cabin at the head of Laura Cove.

Desolation Sound Photo © Darren Robinson

★ **Laura Cove:** Enter Laura Cove at half tide or better. Do not go west of the charted rock because the passage is blocked from the rock to Copplestone Island. Correct passage is between the rock and Copplestone Point. Shoals also extend from Copplestone Point, making this a narrow entry passage. At peak times during the summer season it is necessary to anchor and tie a stern line to shore to avoid swinging. The land at the head of Laura Cove is an ecological reserve.

★ **Roffey Island:** Drying ledges extend from this island and from the opposite shore on the mainland. A settled weather anchorage can be found behind Roffey Island. The passage behind the island has one particular shoal which stretches nearly across from the island to the mainland. Anchorage is possible both north and south of this shoal. Do not attempt to anchor here unless a detailed chart is used and the captain takes a good cruise around the anchorage with the help of the depth sounder. Two rocks are also hazards.

★ **Homfray Channel:** This channel extends 12 miles from Horace Head on the south end of East Redonda Island to Hepburn Point on the north end of the same island. Unless the clouds are too low and obscuring the mountains, this is some of the best scenery on the south coast of British Columbia. Red snapper fishing is often excellent in Homfray Channel. A lodge is located just behind Foster Point between Attwood Bay and Forbes Bay. For the description of the northern region of Homfray Channel and the extension of Toba Inlet, see chapter 16.

★ **Forbes Bay (15):** This wide bay off Homfray Channel is open to the northwest. Temporary anchorage is possible close in near the head.

Klahoose Wilderness Resort: {50°15'00.0"N, 124°37'48.0"W} Moorage for guests only. All inclusive resort wilderness lodge offering wildlife tours, grizzly bear viewing and cultural packages. Visit www.klahooseresort.com. 250-935-8539.

Attwood Bay (16): Swimming is good in the small bight at the extreme head of this bay. The bay is deep and is too open to southerly winds for good anchorage.

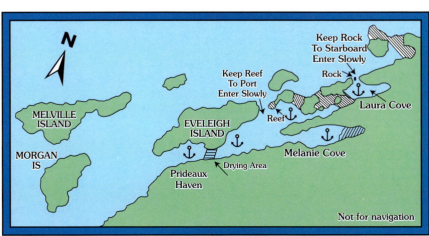

Exiting Gorge Harbour Photo © Gorge Harbour Marina Resort

East Redonda Island

[3312, 3541, 3554]

★ **Pendrell Sound (17):** This six mile indentation into East Redonda Island nearly splits the island in two. High mountains surround the sound. Water temperatures are uncommonly warm, as high as 78 degrees in the summer. Wind patterns vary in different locations. West winds in summer may be strong near the head of the sound. This is one of the largest oyster producing regions in Canada. Posted signs indicate oyster preserves and restrict speeds to four knots to protect oyster spat collecting and propagating equipment. The spat is especially vulnerable to disturbances in July and August. Anchorage is possible near the north end behind the islets, in a niche at the northwest point at the entrance. Another possibility is on the western shore between the island and shore in the bay in front of the lagoon.

West Redonda Island

[3312, 3541, 3554]

Waddington Channel: This waterway separates East and West Redonda Islands and connects Desolation Sound with Pryce Channel. Currents are negligible. Floods north. Anchorage is found in Roscoe Bay, behind the unnamed island north of Church Point (often called Oyster Island), and in Walsh Cove.

★ **Roscoe Bay Marine Park (18):** No dump zone. Use Chart #3312 metric. North of Marylebone Point, Roscoe Bay indents into West Redonda Island. This very protected inlet is the site of a marine park. There is a drying shoal across the entrance, and entry just before or at high water slack is necessary. Plan to stay until the next high tide. Black Lake is within walking distance. For best fishing, carry a lightweight dinghy and fish out in the lake. Swimming is good at the lake, but not recommended in the bay. Water from a small spring drizzles down the rocks, creating a refreshing waterfall sound on a quiet evening. ▲↟

★ **Oyster Island (19):** This small island is unnamed on the charts. Because of the many oysters in the vicinity, it is named Oyster Island by those who frequent the area. Also known as Alfred Island, Elworthy Island, and, most recently, as Cougar Island, this island is north of Church Point. There is good holding ground for anchoring in the passage between the island and West Redonda Island. Enter either side of the island. If approaching from, or exiting to, the north, favor the Oyster Island shore. A rock is in the bay on the north side of the island. There are 20 foot depths in the southern end of the passage and 40 foot depths in the northern end of the passage. Aquaculture operations affect anchoring sites.

★ **Allies Island (20):** Only a short distance north of Oyster Island is Allies Island. There is limited anchorage on the south side in a small indentation. This is open to winds from the southeast. A far better harbour is on the northwest side. Aquaculture operations may be along the shore. There are rocks to port. Maintain a mid-channel course when entering. The bay is deep in the center (110 feet). Anchorage may be obtained close to the Allies Island side by snuggling near the steep rock shore. Venturing north a mile or so from Allies, one will find good anchorage in the shelter of an appendix of land extending from West Redonda Island. A tie ashore is a must.

★ **Doctor Bay (21):** Salmon aquaculture occupies nearly all of the bay. The inlet is open to winds from the southwest but the massive hills provide protection from winds from the northwest. Some foul ground is near the island on the port side when entering. No anchorage available.

★↟ **Walsh Cove Provincial Park (22):** This cove is about one mile from the junction of Waddington and Pryce Channels. Enter from the south and not through False Passage between West Redonda and the Gorges Islands. Look for seven pictographs of red ocher in the granite cliff. This Salish ancient burial site is a marine park. There are several nooks and crannies along the West Redonda shore on the port side when entering. There is good anchorage in the center of the bay if prepared to anchor in 15 fathoms. Anchorage is complicated by the rocky bottom in most of the cove. The first anchorage is an arrowhead-shaped indentation. Five or six boats could tie ashore and raft up with little difficulty. A second bight on the port offers good anchorage. Shoals are easily visible. An uncharted rock has been reported at the entrance to the nook west of Butler Point. The Gorges Islands might well be named the Gorgeous Islands as the rock formations and stately evergreens cast a spell and intrigue the visitor into exploration by dinghy. ↟

★ **Redonda Bay (23):** Settled weather anchorage only because it is exposed to the west and north. The bottom is rock. The old public wharf and float are beyond use. This bay was once a center for logging operations and the site of a busy cannery and a store. Today the bay is deserted, with the possible exception of a small forestry camp. Ruined pilings extend from shore over shoal areas. Rocks in the bay are shown on charts.

★↟ **Teakerne Arm Marine Park (24):** No sewage discharge allowed. Anchoring is difficult in unsettled weather conditions, and is not recommended in this arm because of exposure to northwest winds and the difficulty of securing a proper anchorage. There are often log booms in Teakerne Arm and boom ties may be possible. A lovely waterfall cascades down the bluff from Cassel Lake. There is deep anchorage in the second hollow west of the falls. Look for oysters on the vertical rock faces. A dinghy float is available for shore excursions like a 1 km walk to the lake to swim or fish. While his men fought battles with insects and took showers in the falls, Captain Vancouver became depressed with the excessive rain and named the area Desolation. ↟

★ **Refuge Cove (25):** {50° 07' N, 124° 51' W} On the east side of the cove are public floats with moorage, fuel, potable water, and access to Refuge Cove Store, a café and a gift shop/art gallery. Seaplanes make scheduled stops and this refuge is a popular rendezvous and provisioning location during summer months. An island lies in the center of the cove. A year round aquaculture operation is anchored alongside the island at the northwestern entrance to the cove, and a summer garbage scow is anchored off the innermost point of Center Island. You will find your welcome much more friendly if you slow down well before entering the cove. Wakes from approaching boats can play havoc with boats moored at public floats as well as the private floats around the cove shoreline. If the floats are full, usually during the mid-day period, it is safe to anchor out anywhere in the cove. Before 1930 there were over 200 residents here. At that time, logging, fur farming, and agriculture were the major economic pursuits.

Refuge Cove Store: {50° 07' 22"N, 124° 50' 38"W} Moorage (no reservations), 15 amp power, potable water, gas, diesel, oil, propane, laundry, showers, garbage disposal, wifi, ice, groceries, produce, liquor, marine hardware, fishing tackle, post office, dining. 250-935-6659.

Cortes Island Vicinity

[3312, 3538, 3554]

★ **Squirrel Cove (26):** No dump zone. The First Nations church, government wharf, and Klahoose Multipurpose Centre are landmarks when locating the entrance to Inner Squirrel Cove. The latter is a stunning, award-winning building at entrance. When approaching, avoid the long string of rocks off Boulder Point that are marked by a beacon. This very large anchorage offers excellent protection from bad weather. The harbour also has many fingers that offer good anchorage. Some have mud bottoms, but others are rocky and require care in anchoring and a tie to shore for stability. This prevents swinging and allows room for additional boats. Sunken logs and cables can foul anchors. In the northeast corner, drying rapids lead to a pristine saltwater lagoon. Squirrel Cove is the site of a government dock and at high water there is a private, small day-use dock available in front of the Squirrel Cove Store. The dock is 6' below the local Twin Island tide charts. Larger boats should anchor out and dinghy to the float. Onshore there is a general store, a Shellfish Interpretive Centre and the Cortes Craft Co-Op where locally crafted items are sold by the artists.

Squirrel Cove Government Dock: {50° 07'6" N, 124° 54' 42" W} Rebuilt dock (including floats & wharfhead) reservations required, 20/30 amp power, porta-potty, winch, no water. Supplies available at the store located next door. 250-935-0263.

Squirrel Cove Store: High water dock & boat launch, potable water, gas, diesel, propane, fresh produce, meat & dairy, marine/fishing supplies (quick turnaround on boat parts), liquor, post office, ice, computer use & pay-per usage wifi, tent sites. 250-935-6327.

Walk-arounds: After anchoring in the inner bays of Squirrel Cove, dinghy to the logging skids near the cove entrance. A logging road here joins with the main island road. Turn left and walk about 1.5 km to the store. Another hike that connects Squirrel Cove with Von Donop Inlet begins on a trail found on the beach farther in from the cove entrance. Dinghy to the first indentation that shows a wreck on chart #3538. The hike on the trail takes about 20 minutes.

Seaford: No facilities. To the south, a private float is near Mary Point. There is anchorage in the niche on the north side of Mary Point.

★ **Robertson Cove (27):** This unnamed bay lies at the outlet to Robertson Lake just north of Von Donop Inlet. Robertson Lake, about 1/4-mile away, is a good swimming and trout fishing spot. A painted rock marks the start of the trail. The bottom of the bay is not dependable for holding.

★⚓ **Von Donop Inlet & Provincial Marine Park/Hathayim (28):** The inlet and surrounding lands which comprise this park are part of the traditional territory of Klahoose First Nation who knew it as Hathayim. Some private land remains at the south end and north of the lagoon. There is good anchorage and protection from winds in this three-mile-long, narrow inlet. A large rock marked by kelp at low water is in the center of the narrows. Pass either side, but the starboard (west) side upon entry is recommended. The first anchorage is to port in a bight near the outlet of a lagoon. Rocks restrict the lagoon entrance and currents are encountered from the water flowing to or from this lagoon. At low water, there is as much as a six foot overfall. Farther into the inlet two indentations in the western shore are anchorage possibilities. The most popular overnight anchorages are near the head. A favorite is behind the point which is to port as one turns into the final nook. There is excellent holding bottom of thick, sticky mud in this bay. Depths are 25-30 feet at high water. A rock, which dries at nine feet, is off the eastern shore, almost on a line across the entrance to the bay, opposite the point. Two picnic areas are located on the adjoining peninsula. Another anchorage is in the wide area near the head of the bay.

Walk-around: A trailhead is on the southeast side of the bay. Look for an outhouse that marks the trail to Squirrel Cove. In season, you can enjoy the huckleberries on the way. Robertson and Wiley Lakes, which may be reached by rough trail, are popular for swimming and fishing.

★ **Quartz Bay (29):** Excellent anchorage is in 30-40' of water in the inner harbour. Aquaculture operations and private homes are present.

★⚓ **Carrington Bay/Carrington Bay Park (30):** No dump zone. The lagoon at the head may be visited at high tide by portaging a dinghy over the entrance. Consider the currents caused by the force of the water entering and draining from the lagoon when anchoring. Bottom is rock. Several boats were observed dragging anchor in westerly winds. Hiking and biking trails, fire pit, informal camping, wildlife viewing onshore in the park.

★ **Coulter Bay (31):** Good anchorage is possible with fair protection from westerlies. Tuck in close to Coulter Island. Before anchoring, watch for signs indicating a private water line.

★ **Subtle Islands (32):** These two are connected by a sand and gravel ledge. The northern larger island has a bay for anchorage. The bottom shoals gradually from 60 feet in the middle to 25 feet and then to a shallow ledge fringing the rocky shore. Huge bleached tree stumps are on the beach. There is protection from the south. It is exposed to northwest winds. A sandy, small gravel beach on the Plunger Passage shore has anchorage off the beach in 20-30 feet of water.

★ **Whaletown (33):** This one-time whaling station is now the terminus of the Cortes-Quadra Island ferry. When entering, keep the green-banded white towers on the rocks to port and the red spar Q-10 buoy to starboard. The buoy is on a rock. Shoals extend from shore near the float. A public dock has moorage for fifteen 25'-35' boats (rafting encouraged, commercial boats have priority) as well as a reserved seaplane float. No fuel or provisions are available. The old general store has found new life as the Sunset Suite Vacation Rental. A post office and small library (open 2-3:30pm on Fridays) are also located here.

Whaletown Government Dock: Moorage (reservations required), 20/30 amp power, porta-potty, pay-per usage wifi, winch, kayak launch, no water. 250-935-0263.

★ **Uganda Passage (34):** This well-marked passage between Marina Island and Cortes is not difficult to navigate. Consult tide chart and sounder. When west bound, keep green Q-11 and Q-13 markers to port at the tip of the spit. Green markers are small and may be difficult to see. The red buoy and light are to starboard. Stay inside the channel marked by buoys. The markers are on rocky areas. Temporary anchorage is possible inside Shark Spit. Currents in the passage run two to three knots, flooding north, ebbing south.

★ **Marina Island & Shark Spit (35):** A dangerous reef, studded with boulders, extends a mile from the south end of the island. A red buoy marks the end of the reef. Shark Spit has a good beach and anchorage. Contrary to the name, there are no marinas on this island. The island was named for Marina, Hernando Cortes' mistress and interpreter and mother of his son Martín.

★ **Gorge Harbour (36):** No dump zone. The gorge that forms the entrance to the harbour is less than half a mile long and about 200 yards wide. Currents at springs run to four knots in the passage. Least depth is 36 feet. Passage between the two small islands inside the entrance is blocked by a shoal. Squalls occur because of the harbour's enclosed topography. In strong winds, try the bay on the extreme northwest corner. A rock is in the bay. Good anchorages are found in other areas of the harbour. Moorage is possible at a public dock and Gorge Harbour Marina Resort (hail them on 66A upon entering the Gorge). Over the long weekend in May, the Resort hosts *SeafoodFest* featuring vendors, entertainment and lots of delicious local seafood. A Farmers Market is also held in Gorge Harbour on Saturdays from 10am-1pm. If you like to walk, the Whaletown Commons, a 70-acre green space, offers several short loop forested hikes. The Salish Natives, who once inhabited this harbour, used the caverns on the east side of the entrance for burial caves. They protected their harbour by rolling rocks from atop the gorge onto the canoes of raiding enemies.

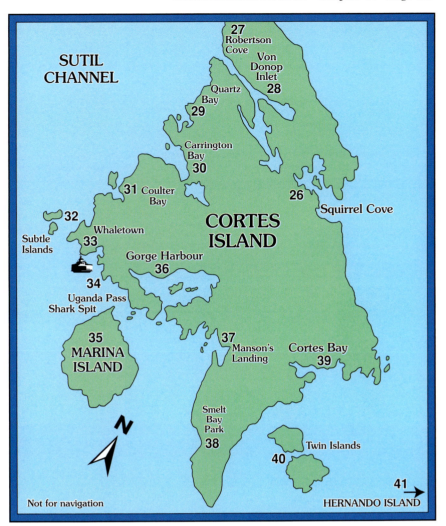

★ **Gorge Harbour Marina Resort:** {50° 06' N, 125° 01' 40" W} Full service marina with moorage, 30/50 amp power, water, gas, diesel, propane, washroom, laundry, WiFi, seaplane dock, general store, liquor store, pool/hot tub, kayak/sup rentals, NEW food & beverage coming 2024 and re-opening in 2024: lodging, RV/camping, and live music during the summer. Open year-round on Cortes Island, BC. See our advertisement on this page. Website: www.thegorgeharbour.com. Telephone: 250-935-6433. VHF 66A.

★ **Walk-around:** Gorge Harbour Park, on the northwest side of the harbour near the resort, has trails and picnic tables. A good hiking road is a half-hour walk to Whaletown, one of three settlements on the island.

★ **Manson's Landing (37):** No dump zone. This is the site of a Provincial Marine Park. Fronting both Hague Lake and Manson Bay, this day use 100 hectares park offers swimming, marine wildlife viewing, pit toilet, day use picnic sites, fresh/saltwater fishing, and trails. No fresh water available. Exposed anchorage is possible in the bay, northwest of the wharf. Avoid the drying bank that extends from the lagoon entrance. There is some protection from southwesterlies between Cat and Sheep Islet and behind Cat Islet. About 1/2 mile up the road from the public float is the Cortes Museum, (call for hours), admission by donation. 250-935-6340. A grocery store, natural foods co-op with in store cafe and bakery, a post office, bookstore, and a B & B are found in Manson's Landing. WiFi available at grocery store and bakery. For java lovers, Becca's Beans, a local coffee roasterie sells organic, fair trade coffee at the co-op and other island stores. A Farmers Market is held at Manson's Hall on Friday noon-3pm all year.

Manson's Landing Public Floats: {50° 4 17" N, 124° 59' 1.1" W} Moorage (reservations required), 20/30 amp power, winch, porta-potty onshore (2 minute walk), pay-per usage wifi, seaplane float. No water. 250-935-0263.

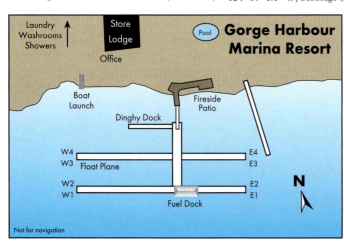

Walk-around: It is a short walk to a lagoon above the landing. In 1887, John Manson established a trading post on the sand spit which separates the bay from the lagoon. In 1973, this entire 117 acres was designated as a marine park. There is a substantial stretch of sandy beach, suitable for picnicking or beachcombing. To reach Hague Lake (noted for excellent swimming and sunbathing beaches), walk south for about 3/4 mile on the paved road, then left about 1/3 mile on another paved road.

★ **Smelt Bay Park (38):** This bay is named for the smelt (capelin fish) that spawn on the sandy beach each Fall. This 20 hectare park about half way between Manson's Landing and Sutil Point may be used by small craft. Approach straight in and anchor close to the beach. A high tide gravel boat launch is located at the northwest corner of the park. There are campsites, pit toilets, picnic areas, and an RV sewage pump-out is located nearby. The park is the site of *Cortes Day* festivities each July with parade, games, food, crafts, and the popular *Nail-Sail-Bail* run. *Sandcastle Day* is another fun event held mid-August. Camping Reservations: 1-800-689-9025.

Sutil Point: For many, rounding this point seems as if it takes forever. The Sutil Point light and bell buoy is almost a mile offshore near the southwest extremity of the rocks and shoals which extend off Cortes Island.

★ **Cortes Bay (39):** No dump zone. Many boaters have found themselves aground if not careful in the vicinity of the Three Islets. Pass south of Three Islets for the safest approach to Cortes Bay. The bay's picturesque entrance has a rock with a flashing beacon that marks a reef. Keep this marker to starboard when entering and to port when leaving. Three moorage facilities, one public and two private, are found in the Bay. In the middle is the Cortes Government Dock, on the south shore is the Seattle Yacht Club outstation, and the Vancouver Yacht Club outstation is on the north shore. The Blind Creek Boat Launch is nearby. The bay is uniformly 20 to 40 feet deep with a

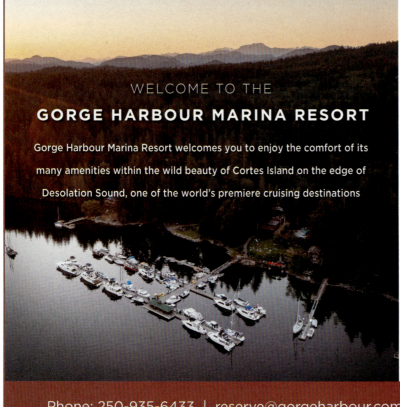

very soft mud bottom that may require additional anchor rode. Coast Guard Rescue Boat 509 is stationed in Cortes Bay. A hiking trail that begins near the yacht club outstation leads to the top of the bluff. Wolf Bluff Castle on Manzanita Road is a notable structure with turrets, courtyard, and dungeon. Originally built as a B & B, "The Castle" is no longer open to the public.

Cortes Bay Public Floats: {50° 3' 46" N, 124° 55' 59" W} Moorage (reservations required), 20/30 amp power, no water, porta-potty, pay-per usage wifi, seaplane float. 250-935-0263.

★ **Walk-around:** The main road from Cortes Bay has good walking opportunities which lead past picturesque fields and farms.

★ **Twin Islands (40):** These islands are actually two humps of a single island connected by a drying ledge. A resident caretaker lives on the premises. Anchorage with protection from westerly winds is possible in Echo Bay. The bay is exposed to the south. A recommended anchorage is on the northwest shore of the northernmost island between the islet and the shore. Depths are 15-20 feet. Central Rock, a hazard off the northwest corner of Twin Islands, dries at low tide.

★ **Hernando Island (41):** Named after Hernando Cortez, Spanish conqueror of Mexico in the early 1500's, this island has many shoal areas containing uncharted rocks. Manson Passage, between Hernando and Savary Islands is not recommended. There is protection from southeasterlies along the beach by Spilsbury Point and in Stag Bay. There is a long, private wharf in the bay.

Good times at Gorge Harbour Marina Resort Photo © Gorge Harbour Marina Resort

Essential Supplies & Services

AIR TRANSPORTATION
To & from Washington
Kenmore Air 1-866-435-9524
NW Seaplanes . . . 425-277-1590, 1-800-690-0086
San Juan Airlines 1-800-874-4434
Seattle Seaplanes 1-800-637-5553
To & from Islands/Vancouver
Air Canada 1-888-247-2262
Corilair 1-888-287-8366, 250-287-8371
Harbour Air 1-800-665-0212

BOOKS / BOOK STORES
Evergreen Pacific Publishing 425-493-1451
The Marine Atlas 253-872-5707

BUS/SHUTTLE TRANSPORTATION
Greyhound 1-800-661-8747
Powell River BC Transit 604-485-4287

COAST GUARD:
Victoria Coast Guard Radio . . . . VHF 16, 83a
. . . . 1-800-661-9202 (In BC) or 250-363-6333
Marine Distress, Search & Rescue
. . . . 1-800-567-5111 (in Canada) or 250-413-8933
Cell Phone (limited to select providers) . . . *16 or #727

FISHING/SHELLFISHING INFO
24 hr Recorded Notifications (Pacific region only)
. . . . 1-866-431-3474 or 604-666-2828
Recreational Licensing 1-877-535-7307
Observe, Record & Report Line (fisheries violations)
Greater Vancouver 604-607-4186
Or Call 1-800-465-4336

FUELS
Gorge Harbour Marina: Gas, Diesel
. . . . 250-935-6433 VHF 66A
Refuge Cove Store: hand carried Gas, Diesel
. . . . 250-935-6659

GROCERY STORES
Cortes Market 250-935-6626

Gorge Harbour Marina Resort 250-935-6433
Refuge Cove Store 250-935-6659
Squirrel Cove 250-935-6327

HAUL-OUTS
Ocean Pacific Marine Supply: Campbell River.
. . . . 250-286-1011

HOSPITALS
Heathlink BC (Nurse Helpline) 811
Campbell River . . . . . . 250-286-7100 or 250-850-2141
Powell River 604-485-3211

LIQUOR STORES
Gorge Harbour Marina 250-935-6433
Squirrel Cove Store 250-935-6327

LODGING
Gorge Harbour Marina Resort 250-935-6433
Homfrey Lodge 250-674-3286
Klahoose Wilderness Resort 250-935-8539

MARINAS / MOORAGE
Cortes Bay Public Floats 250-935-0263
Gorge Harbour Marina . . . 250-935-6433 VHF 66A
Manson's Landing Public Floats 250-935-0263
Okeover Arm Public Floats . . . . 604-483-3258, VHF 66A
Refuge Cove Store 250-935-6659
Squirrel Cove Public Floats 250-935-0263
Whaletown Government Dock 250-935-0263

MARINE SUPPLY STORES
Carmac Diesel: Campbell River 250-287-2171
Ocean Pacific Marine Supply: Campbell River
. . . . 250-286-1011

PROPANE
Gorge Harbour Marina Resort
. . . . 250-935-6433 VHF 66A
Squirrel Cove 250-935-6327

RAMPS
Blind Creek-Cortes Bay
Gorge Harbour Public Dock
Ocean Pacific Marine Supply: Campbell River
. . . . 250-286-1011
Okeover Arm Public Floats
Smelt Bay Park
Squirrel Cove (high tide) 250-935-6327

REPAIRS
Altech Diesel: Campbell River 250-286-0055
Lund Auto & Outboard, Mobile . . 604-483-4612 VHF 66A
Ocean Pacific Marine: Campbell River
. . . . 250-286-1011

RESTAURANTS
Laughing Oyster: Okeover Inlet 604-483-9775
The Floathouse Restaurant (Gorge Harbour)
. . . . 950-935-6433

RV SITES
Gorge Harbour Resort & Marina 250-935-6433

SCUBA SITES:
Okeover Inlet

TAXI
Water Taxi 250-287-7577
Quadra Taxi 250-205-0505

TOWING
C-TOW 1-888-419-CTOW

VISITOR INFORMATION
Campbell River . . 250-830-0411 ext 1, 1-877-286-5705
Cortes Island . . . . info@cibata.ca
Powell River 604-485-4701

WEATHER
Environment Canada Weather Line 250-339-9861
Comox: . . . . WX-21B, 250-339-0748 (recorded)
NOAA Weather Radio WX-1, 162.55

Chapter 15: Northwest Georgia Strait

Nanoose Harbour to Oyster River. Schooner Cove, French Creek, Comox, Courtenay, Ballenas, Hornby, Denman, Lasqueti, & Texada Islands.

Helliwell Provincial Park - photo © Jake Berman

Symbols

[ ]: Numbers between [ ] are chart numbers.
{ }: Numbers & letters between { } are waypoints.
★ Recommended destinations, facilities, and services
⚓: Park, ⛵: Boat Launch, ▲: Campgrounds,
🚶: Hiking Trails, ⊞: Picnic Area, 🚴: Biking
🤿: Scuba

Chart List

Canadian Hydrographic Charts:
3458, 3459, 3512-13, 3527, 3536, PAC 201

Marine Atlas Vol 1 (2018):
Page 23-24, 27, 29

Evergreen Cruising Atlas:
49, 52, 53, 59, 63-65, 68, 69, 73

★ See "Important Notices" between Chapters 7 and 8 for specific information on boating related topics such as boating safety, weather, U.S. & Canadian marine radio use, Vessel Traffic Service, security zones, Canadian & U.S. Customs, etc. Due to changing regulations, call ahead to verify latest customs information.

★ **Area Whiskey Golf:** Mariners in the Strait of Georgia should be aware of Canadian Forces Experimental and Test Ranges near Nanaimo. When active, this area poses a life-threatening danger to vessels and crew. An official notice issued by the Canadian Department of Defence concerning the activities and dangers in this area, can be found in the Important Notices Section.

Vancouver Island Side

[3459, 3512, 3513, 3527]

★ **Nanoose Harbour (1):** {49°15.600 N, 124°09.000 W} This bay can be an important refuge during a blow on the strait. While open to the public, this harbour is administered by the Department of National Defence and considered a Controlled Access Zone. All pleasure vessels are required to register their arrival, intended duration of stay, and departure from the harbour by contacting a Harbour Official, 250-363-2165 or 250-363-7584. Pleasure craft may only anchor south of a line drawn west of Datum Rock and in the vicinity of Fleet Point. By Fleet Point, a marked entrance leads behind a sandspit and breakwater extending from the southern shore. Pilings sit on a mud flat, some of which are hazards because they are covered at high tide. Onshore the Snaw-Naw-As Campground has RV and tent sites, call 250-933-2505. Arbutus Grove Provincial Park is also on the south shore. The Artubus is the only native broadleaf evergreen tree in Canada. The park has no facilities, but there are hiking trails. On the north side of the harbour, the two summits of Nanoose Hill rise above Ranch Point, an Armed Forces Base. Mooring buoys belong to the Canadian Department of National Defence. Inland logging roads and trails are great for exploring. The trail to the top of Notch Hill is the steepest, but rewards climbers with panoramic views. Surrounding waters are good for exploring as well and scuba divers will find a good site at Nanoose Bay. 🚶🤿

Winchelsea Island: Canadian Armed Forces station. Trespassing is not permitted. Winchelsea Control is in charge of Whiskey Golf operations and all vessels traversing the area. See Canadian Department of Defence Notice in our Important Notices Section. Winchelsea Control monitors VHF 10, 16.

★ **Schooner Cove (2):** A large rip rap breakwater protects this marina basin. Enter north of the lighted breakwater and south of Nankivell Point. Inside the breakwater is a rock marked with a red buoy. Keep buoy to starboard. Fairwinds Marina at Schooner Cove is located in the cove. A change in ownership in 2015 has prompted upcoming renovations, so watch for changes in the next few years. Nanoose Head, once known as "Powder Point," was the site of a explosives factory until 1918 when an accidental explosion destroyed the plant. 🚶

Fairwinds Marina at Schooner Cove: Permanent & guest moorage, 15/30/50 amp power, water, gas, diesel, showers, washrooms, laundry, pump-out, boat ramp. Free golf club rentals and shuttle to Fairwinds Golf Club and restaurant with overnight moorage. 250-468-5364. VHF 66A.

NOTICE OF HAZARDOUS AREA
DEPARTMENT OF NATIONAL DEFENCE — **TORPEDO TEST RANGE**

NOTES & INSTRUCTIONS
1. Area WG is a torpedo test range. It is hazardous to vessels when active.
2. For range status information:
   - Call "Winchelsea Control" on VHF 10 or 16
   - Call 250-468-5080 or 1-888-221-1011 (toll free)
   - Monitor VHF 21B or WX3
3. Do not enter "Active Area" unless specifically authorized by "Winchelsea Control".
4. Buoys and moorings may be laid anywhere within WG. Use extreme caution when transiting.
5. See notice to mariners annual edition.

A. 49° 21.35'N 124° 07.70'W
B. 49° 21.00'N 123° 48.40'W
C. 49° 14.38'N 123° 48.40'W
D. 49° 16.75'N 124° 00.90'W
E. 49° 19.35'N 124° 07.70'W

REFERENCE CHARTS: CHS 3512, 3456 & 3459

ISSUED BY COMMANDING OFFICER
CANADIAN FORCES MARITIME EXPERIMENTAL AND TEST RANGES

Visit us at boattravel.com

Walk-around: Trail maps are available at Fairwinds Marina at Schooner Cove or in the Presentation Centre (3455 Fairwinds Drive). Walk or bike through the oceanfront community. Keep an eye out and you might spot a deer, eagles or beavers. Turn left out of the marina parking lot on to Dolphin Drive and in a few minutes you will reach Brickyard Bay, a popular swimming spot. Pieces of brick from a once thriving brickyard lay scattered about the five acre waterfront park.

For a more challenging outing, hike up the scenic, one kilometer trail to the top of Notch Hill. From here it is about half a kilometer down to the Link Place trail head. The Notch Hill trail starts off of Fairwinds Drive, one kilometer down from the Fairwinds Centre on the opposite side of the road (towards Powder Point Road).

Ballenas Islands (3): [3512] Limited shelter is possible in the bay that indents the southernmost island. Navigating the narrow channel between the two islands is tricky. Enter at high water, avoiding rocks in center channel. Anchorage is prohibited due to cables on the bottom of the bay. The north shore has a sand beach. The northern island is the site of an old and picturesque lighthouse and weather reporting station.

★ **Northwest Bay (4):** Pass between the green and red buoys. Avoid the rocky area marked by a red spar buoy. There is anchorage, exposed to northwest winds, near the head of the bay. A breakwater on the eastern shore shelters a marina.

Beachcomber Marina: {49° 18' 9" N, 124° 12' 7" W} Annual moorage only, 30 amp power, water, showers, private boat launch. 250-468-7222. VHF 66A.

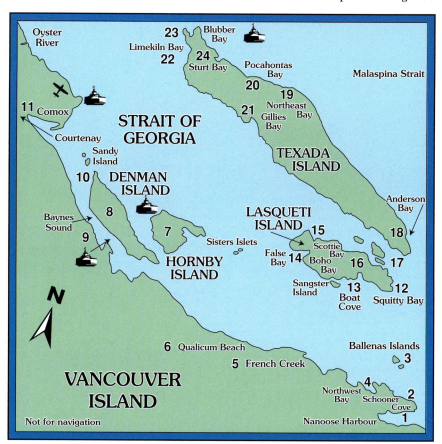

Parksville: A sand beach extends a quarter mile from shore. Anchor offshore in settled weather only. Sandcastle architects claim this beach is one of the best for building such structures, many which are entered in the sand sculpture competition each August during the *Parksville Beach Festival*. The community park on the shore has sport fields, volleyball and tennis courts, skateboard park, play areas, water spray park, and concessions. Accessible shorelines and good weather entice windsurfers and kayakers. Local outfitters offer everything, including lessons. A five minute drive from town, Craig Heritage Park and Museum, is open from May to September. Here you can glimpse the early days of this town named for pioneer and postmaster, Nelson Parks.

★ **Rathtrevor Beach Park:** A gem of the provincial parks. Rathtrevor has 225 campsites, sani-station for RV's, showers, picnic areas, and a lovely sand beach. No marine facilities.

★ **French Creek (5):** [3512] A channel leads to a public wharf and floats that are sheltered by a sturdy breakwater, a hint that conditions get breezy here on occasion, most notably in winter months when winds blow from the southeast. Fuel, groceries, fresh seafood, marine supplies, and a restaurant are available. The Lasqueti Island Passenger Ferry terminal is located adjacent to the boat launching ramp. Additional shops and services are about 10 minutes away by taxi.

French Creek Harbour Authority: {49° 20' 57" N, 124° 21' 27" W} Overnight moorage at docks C, D, E, or 2, 3. 20/30 amp power, water, restrooms, showers, waste oil & garbage deposit, security cameras. 250-248-5051. VHF 66A.

French Creek Seafoods: Gas, diesel, salt ice, seafood store, fresh water with fuel purchase. 250-248-7100.

French Creek-Lasqueti Island Foot Passenger Ferry: Summer sailings daily except Tuesdays. No reservations. 250-927-0431.

Qualicum Beach (6): Miles of beautiful sand beaches with gentle surf and sparkling clear waters comprise the Qualicum Beach shoreline. There are no marine facilities or sheltered coves. Anchor in settled weather only. Onshore art galleries feature local works. Trails for hiking are abundant in the area. An aquatic center offers pool, sauna and steam room. The local museum, open during the summer, is known for its extensive fossil collection.

Qualicum Bay: Eight miles north of Qualicum Beach, this wide bay has good holding bottom for anchoring and offers a limited amount of protection in northwesterly winds. The Qualicum wind blows offshore and results in local choppy waters.

★ **Hornby Island (7):** Hornby offers anchorages, provincial parks, and a public harbour at Ford Cove (fee applies), there are no showers, gas or garbage pick-up at the marina. The nearest gas sales are at Deep Bay or Comox. Anchorage is possible in Tribune Bay with its Hawaiian-like white sand beaches, if the wind isn't blowing from the south. Nash Bank, outside the bay, is a popular fishing spot. This area is designated a marine reserve, so no dumping. Anchorage is also possible north of Shingle Spit in Lambert Channel, however, northwest winds funnel through the channel. A ferry connects Hornby with Denman Island at Shingle Spit. A rock breakwater shelters the landing from southeasterly winds. A launching ramp is located at Shingle Spit, no fee. A funky summer bus runs between Ford Cove and Shingle Spit, giving access to a lot of the Island's highlights. There is a summer cross-Denman connector bus, too. Hitchhiking is also a possibility to get around the island. Of the nearly 1,000 residents living on the Island, many are artists or craftsmen who have working studios open to the public. In May, the *Hornby Island Blues Workshop* features some of Canada's finest instructors. *The Hornby Festival* in August showcases the performing arts - music, dance and more. B & B's, vacation rentals, restaurants and pub, grocery store, gas station, liquor store, and library with WiFi are found on Island. The new restaurant at the Ford Cove marina is open year round. The Pub located next to the

French Creek Harbour Photo © Samantha McLean

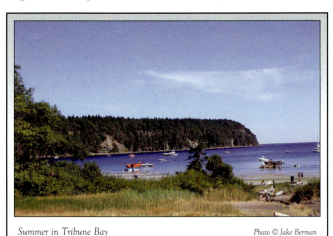
Summer in Tribune Bay Photo © Jake Berman

Ford Cove Harbour Authority: {49° 29' 52" N, 124° 40' 38" W} Call ahead for moorage or register upon arrival. Reservations recommended from June-Sept. Transient moorage on float A, commercial and private moorage on float B. 20/30 amp power, restroom, garbage/recycling, crane, no water, no fuel. Unloading zone, parking. 250-335-0003. VHF 66A.

Walk-around: Hike the path along the shore from Ford Cove to Shingle Spit where there is a pub restaurant.

Shingle Spit ferry terminal allows day use of their dock space during the summer season There is an ATM at the Pub and one at the Co-Op Store, a short walk from Tribune Bay. For fun, stop by the Wednesday and Saturday Farmers Market or visit the 6 tasting/retail rooms at the 2 local wineries, meadery, cidery, micro brewery and distillery. Bike and kayak rentals are available, as are fishing, diving and sightseeing charters. Hornby and Denman Islands are known for scuba diving opportunities. For more information, visit www.hornbyisland.com.

★ **Tribune Bay:** Good anchorage on a sand bottom in depths of about 40 feet is available, with shelter from north and west winds. While the bay is protected from northwesterlies, southeasterlies cause havoc.

★ **Tribune Bay Provincial Park** has white sandy beaches for swimming, trails to hike, tennis court and picnic facilities. No dogs allowed on the beach. Its outdoor education centre provides outdoor education and experiences for youth groups. An RV campground is adjacent to the park. Easy walk to Helliwell Provincial Park at St. John Point or to shops in town.

★ **Helliwell Provincial Park:** Located by road from Tribune Bay anchorage, this relatively undeveloped park also includes the channel south of Hornby Island and up into Lambert Channel where there is an underwater cave and a shipwreck for diving. Also, six gill sharks, normally a deep sea shark rarely found in shallow waters in Canada, are found off Flora Islet and are attractions for divers.

★ **Ford Cove:** The Ford Cove harbour is located near the beginning of Central Road, at Ford Cove, on the southwest side of Hornby Island. The facility is protected by a quarried rock breakwater and a floating breakwater that is fully decked and available for moorage (fees apply). Entry to Ford Cove is between the green spar buoy and the breakwater. The basin is dredged to minimum eight foot depths. Moorage is available at the Harbour Authority docks. There is a timber approach and wharfhead. Dinghy dock is located by the ramp. Anchorage is possible only outside of the harbour authority's water lot. Kayaks can be rented locally. Within walking distance from Ford Cove Harbour is Ford's Cove Marina Ltd., 250-335-2169. They don't have moorage, but do have cottages, tent/RV camping sites and a general store with groceries, fishing licenses/gear, free wifi, and take out pizza. Restaurant is open every day on high season and year round on limited days.

★ **Denman Island & Henry Bay (8):** Temporary anchorage, open to the west, is found in Henry Bay inside Longbeak Point. Anchor well off the oyster beds. On Baynes Sound, about half way down the island is the site of the Denman-Vancouver Island (Buckley Bay) Cable Ferry. A red light shows from both sides when a ferry is underway and the cable is near the surface. Vessels should not transit when the red light is on. A community dock with an upland green/parking area is adjacent to the ferry landing. A boat launch is located between the community dock and the cable ferry landing. Other boat launches on the island include the Bill Mee Boat Launch (about 1 km south of the Hornby Island Ferry landing) and another on the island's northeast side at Gravelly Bay. The latter is in rough shape. A 15 minute walk up the hill from the dock in "Downtown Denman", there is a Post Office and stores that stock books, food and liquor, as well as realty offices, bistros, and a craft store that features the work of local artists. Hardware supplies available at the Denman Island Hardware Empourium, where you'll also find a cafe with WiFi. The General Store, which dates back to the 19th century, carries a variety of local vegetables and meats, as well as island maps and tourist information. The island is also home to many B & B's. The museum in the Activity Centre contains fossils, shells, butterflies, and items used by the original European settlers. The Denman Island Arts Centre & the Community Hall host a variety of cultural activities throughout the year such as art shows, concerts and the annual *Readers & Writers Festival*. The Island's Chocolate Factory welcomes "chocophilic pilgrims" and offers tours by reservation at www.denmanislandchocolate.com. In the summer a Saturday morning farmers' market is held at the Old School Centre. Piercy Farm and Two Roads Farm, close to the Village, also offer local produce. Chrome Island Lighthouse, off the southern tip of Denman Island dates to 1891. Just below the lighthouse, the steamer Alpha sunk in 1900 and today is a popular site for divers. An island Pottery Tour and Art Studio Tour are offered annually, with a bi-annual Home & Garden Tour. For more information about Denman Island, www.visitdenmanisland.ca.

Denman Island Community Dock: Visitor moorage, first 6 hrs. free then fee applies. $1 per ft per day, 5 day max stay. Payment box at the top of the ramp. No garbage drop.

★ **Fillongley Provincial Park:** Ten campsites, picnic facilities, lovely beach, and trails are attractions. Water from hand pump must be boiled. Accessible by car ferry from Buckley Bay.

Baynes Sound

[3513, 3527]

★ **Baynes Sound (9):** This is one of the largest oyster producing regions on the coast. Tidelands are leased. Public harvesting is prohibited. Baynes Sound stretches about 12 miles along the shore of Vancouver Island, and ranges in width between one and two miles. Currents can run to three knots in the southern entrance. This waterway is convenient for those visiting Comox and Courtenay.

Deep Bay: Near the southern entrance to Baynes Sound this bay is the site of a public float complex, as well as a private marina and a tidal marine fuel float. A sandy shoal extends outward from Mapleguard Point. The point was named for the maple trees that once flourished here. Anchoring in the area between the floating breakwater and the Deep Bay Marina is prohibited. There is also anchorage NE of the Deep Bay Marina, but swing room is limited.

Dinghys may be docked at both the Harbour Authority (2 hour limit, contact Harbour Manager) and Deep Bay Marina. The village of Bowser is an hour walk from Deep Bay. Groceries, hardware, postal services, liquor sales, diesel and propane are available in Bowser. Each morning, Tues-Sat., a bus to the Woodgrove Mall in Nanaimo leaves from the marina entrance in the morning and returns late afternoon. Call 250-390-4531 for Route 99.

Deep Bay Harbour Authority: {49° 27' 55.16" N, 124° 43' 44.79" W} Permanent moorage (waitlist), limited guest moorage (call ahead), rafting required. 20/30 amp/120 volt power, water, washrooms, showers, garbage & oil disposal, crane, pump-out. 250-757-9331.

Deep Bay Marina: Permanent moorage, guest moorage if space is available. 15/20/30/50 amp power, water, shower, restroom. 250-586-5560.

Ship and Shore Restaurant & Campground: {49° 27' 51.65" N, 124° 43' 33.72" W} Restaurant/lounge, gas & diesel at tidal fuel float, boat ramp (no launching under a 3' tide). 250-757-8399.

Fanny Bay: A designated federal fishing harbour, Fanny Bay floats are full with local vessels (usually rafting) with no transient moorage available. No fuel or garbage disposal, water dependant on local closures and temperature, port a potty. The drive down unloading dock is for shellfish growers who produce renowned Fanny Bay Oysters. Very limited anchorage near the float, however it is tricky because of the shoals. Onshore, the landmark 1930 Fanny Bay Inn, or "FBI" to the locals, is now a charming pub. Area waterfront B & B's offer stunning Sound views.

Buckley Bay: Denman Island ferry landing site.

Union Bay: Site of a once active coal loading wharf that closed in 1959. Ruins of pilings are hazards. There is anchorage close to shore and a launching ramp to the north, near a rock breakwater. B & B, bank, art studio, dive shop, Union Bay Gaolhouse Museum, and heritage buildings including a restored 1913 post office are found in Union Bay.

Comox Vicinity

[3513, 3527]

★ **Jáji7em and Kw'ulh Marine Park (Sandy Island Marine Park) (10):** Accessible from the water only, this marine park lies northwest of Denman Island and includes Sandy Island (called Tree Island by the locals) and the Seal Islets. Both are part of White Spit extending out from Denman Island. Use caution as many areas are too shallow to navigate. Anchorage is on the south side of the island, in 30-50 feet of water and in nearby Henry Bay. Sandy beaches for sunbathing and swimming, walking trail, and pit toilet onshore.

★ **Comox Harbour (11):** When crossing the Comox Bar from the north, keep the three red buoys to starboard and line up with the range markers on the mainland. The day markers of the range are white with a red stripe. After passing the last red buoy, continue on a bit before turning to starboard. To port, a green can buoy marks the end of the shallows off Gartley Point. Proceed into the harbour with the green can well to port. Anchor avoiding mud flats near Royston, one mile west of Gartley Point. Just south of Gartley Point, two yellow private buoys about 600 metres off shore mark the end of a submarine pipeline intake.

The Courtenay River empties into the harbour. Eddies are caused by the freshwater currents flowing in different directions from the salt water underneath. The north side of the harbour has drying flats nearly to the head of the pier. Anchorage is considered good. It is possible for skiffs or boats with a shallow draft to travel up the river at high tide to Courtenay, but vessels wishing to access the Courtenay Slough need to make arrangements with the Comox Valley Harbour Authority - Fisherman's Wharf (see the entry for Courtenay).

Departing Comox to head north in the Strait of Georgia, it is first necessary to cross the Comox Bar. From the light on Goose Spit, at the entrance to the harbour, head for Sandy Island. Proceed about two miles on that course until you see the three red buoys that should be lined up to indicate the proper course, as shown on Chart #3527. The range markers shown on this chart are lights only, so they are of no benefit during daylight hours. Keeping the red buoys to port, the smoke from the Powell River Pulp Mill across the Strait of Georgia, should be almost dead ahead. The chart shows a least depth of over two meters, so even on a low tide, most boats should have plenty of water. Continuing on this course about two more miles, you must first round East Cardinal Buoy "PJ" (black with a yellow band) to clear the shoals around Cape Lazo. It is about 22 miles from Cape Lazo to the lighthouse on Cape Mudge.

★ **Comox:** The town of Comox has four marinas sheltered by a rock breakwater. A promenade with pier, garbage drop, used oil dump, and public telephone are accessible. A shopping center, golf course, restaurants and pubs are within a short walk. Marina Park, adjacent to the Municipal Marina has restrooms, play area and boat launch. The first weekend in August it is the site of the annual *Comox Nautical Days* featuring dragonboat races, salmon tossing, a parade, dance, live entertainment, fireworks and more.

The name Comox originally came from the native word "kw'umalha," meaning plenty or abundance. Considering that Comox is situated amid the rich agricultural lands of the Comox Valley, the name makes perfect sense. Comox's first wharf was built in 1876, the same year the navy established a base at Goose Spit. The Canadian Armed Forces still operates a base at the spit. Here HMCS Quadra Training Centre hosts over 1,000 Sea Cadets every summer. Visitors are welcome to picnic on the public part of the Spit. Another military presence, 19 Wing Comox is home to the 407 Long Range Patrol Squadron and the 442 Transport and Rescue Squadron. About 14,000 people live in Comox and the city boasts an array of services and facilities, including a large hospital. History, as well as art buffs, will enjoy a visit to 1729 Comox Avenue where the Comox

Comox Harbour Photo © James Wheeler

Museum and the Pearl Ellis Art Gallery are located. 250-339-2885. For golfers a 9-hole golf course is within walking distance of the harbour and a 18-hole course is 10 minutes away by car. Another interesting stop is the Comox Air Force Museum, gift shop and library, open Tues-Sun, 10am-4pm. 250-339-8162. Nearby Heritage Air Park features a collection of RCAF aircraft and vehicles. The first weekend in August the Filberg Heritage Lodge and Park hosts the *Filberg Festival*, an annual arts & crafts and music festival. For Park and Lodge tour info: 250-339-2715. Comox is accessible by land, sea, or air. Daily ferries from Powell River land a bit north, at Little River. Harbour Air provides float plane service from Comox harbour to downtown Vancouver two times daily April-Oct. The Comox Valley Airport, north of Cape Lazo, also features daily flights to Vancouver. Highway 19 connects Comox with communities from Victoria to Port Hardy. For additional information about Comox, visit www.comox.ca.

Comox Marine Gas & Go: Permanent moorage, transient moorage when available, 15 amp power, water, mid-grade gas, diesel, oils, fishing tackle, ice, snacks, wifi. 250-339-4664. VHF 66A.

Comox Municipal Marina: {49° 40' 14.35" N, 124° 55' 41.02" W} Permanent moorage, (currently full). 15/20 amp power, potable water, restrooms, garbage, waste oil disposal, launch ramp, boat trailer parking. Grids available "in person" booking required at Town Hall, 1809 Beaufort Ave. 250-339-2202. Marina: 250-339-3141.

Comox Valley Fisherman's Wharf (Harbour Authority): {49° 41' 9" N, 124° 55' 52" W} Permanent moorage, guest moorage on D, F & G docks. Docks BW1 & BW2 for larger vessels only (up to 160'). No reservations. 20/30/50 amp power (120/250 volts), water, restroom, showers, laundry, pump-out, garbage & waste oil disposal, wifi, winch, ice, pay phone. 250-339-6041. VHF 66A.

Comox Valley Marina: {49° 40.209 N 124° 55.826 W} Permanent and guest moorage, 15/30/50 amp power, water, showers, laundry, garbage deposit, wifi, float plane service. Desolation Sound Yacht Charter has onsite shop for repairs/mechanic. 250-339-7222. Marina: 250-339-2930. VHF 66A.

Courtenay: [3527] The Courtenay River is navigable by very shallow draft boats at high tide but the river has not been dredged in years and sediment has accumulated. Vessels wishing to access the Courtenay Slough need to make arrangements with the Comox Valley Harbour Authority at Fisherman's Wharf. While the channel seldom completely dries, always check local water level conditions before navigating the river. Stay in the marked channel on line with the range lights. Least depth is usually about five feet up to the 17th Street Bridge. Vessels with rigging will not clear this span. 250-339-6041. The Courtenay Slough dock does not allow transient moorage during the summer, but skiffs can tie up for a day trip. Courtenay is a trading center for the mid-Vancouver Island area and features shops, lodging, restaurants, and services. Visit the Comox Valley Farmer's Market for fresh local produce, baked goods, meats, fish, poultry, flowers, plants and more. For locations and information, www.cvfm.ca. Take a walk through Kitty Coleman Woodland Gardens featuring over 3,000 rhododendrons. 250-338-6901. The Courtenay & District Museum highlights Valley history and offers fossil tours. 250-334-0686. The *Comox Valley Exhibition Fall Fair*, held in August, attracts over 15,000 visitors annually. Visitors can also enjoy a variety of live performances at the Sid Williams Theatre. 250-338-2430.

Cape Lazo: See current tables for Seymour Narrows, British Columbia. Interestingly shaped, Cape Lazo has a flat summit and headland with yellow cliffs. It appears to be an island. Hazards extend to the east and southeast. Buoys mark the rock hazard from the cliffs of the cape and from Kye Bay. The lighthouse is a landmark. This is Lighthouse Country with lights on Hornby, Denman, Lasqueti, Chrome, and Sisters Islands.

Little River & Kuhushan Point: This stretch of shoreline north of Cape Lazo has settlements and resorts near the river deltas. Little River is identified by the ferry landing. It is the western terminus of the Vancouver Island-Westview/Powell River ferry. In nor'westers, there is shelter for small boats south of the ferry landing. A launching ramp is next to the resort at the ferry landing.

★ **Kitty Coleman Provincial Park:** This park located about 6km/4mi northwest of Courtenay has two paved boat launches, campsites, picnic area, water and pit toilets. Park Info: 250-338-1332.

Oyster River: An inland boat basin, resort and marina is located just south of the Oyster River. The dredged channel is narrow and has a slight curve in it. At zero tide there is a minimum depth of zero feet of water in the channel. A tide of minimum 7' is needed for a boat with a 4.5' draft. Reference tide table for Mitlenatch Island. Line up and enter between the two entrance pilings from

Chapter 15 NORTHWEST GEORGIA STRAIT

Texada Boat Club in Sturt Bay Photo © Texada Arts, Culture & Tourism Society

at least 200 feet out, follow the navigation markers into the basin. Avoid passage during strong southeast winds or rough seas. Favorite activities for visitors include hiking the nearby trails, birding, fishing for steelhead, sea run cutthroat and trout, and golfing at the 9-hole par 3 course located within walking distance of moorage. Also convenient to moorage is a full grocery store, liquor store, pizza outlet and medical clinic.

Pacific Playgrounds Resort & Marina: {49° 52' 4" N, 125° 7' 5" W} Moorage slips 16' to 40', 15 amp power, water, showers, laundry, Wifi, boat launch, store, RV sites, cabins, pool, playground, playfields. 250-337-5600.

Kuhushan Point: North of Kuhushan Point is another dredged small boat basin. The entrance channel is straight, shallow, and narrow. Orange buoys are range markers. Incoming boats have the right-of-way. Onshore, the Oyster River Nature Walk trail leads about 8km/5mi to the Oyster River Nature Park.

Salmon Point Resort: {49° 53' 44" N, 125° 7' 50" W} Permanent moorage, day use moorage for boats to 32', no overnight sleep aboards. Gas, propane, boat launch, RV park, lodging, ice, wifi, restaurant is under construction with possible opening in 2024. To access marina, channel has a 2' plug which needs to be added to vessel draft for required depth needed. 250-923-6605.

Sunshine Coast Side
[3312, 3512, 3536]

Sisters Islets: These two islets are the site of a light tower, fog signal, and weather reporting station.

Sangster Island: Anchor only in settled weather. The anchorage is northwest of the light. Avoid a drying rock in the entrance to this bight.

★ **Lasqueti Island:** [3512, 3513, 3536] Lasqueti Island is a quiet hideaway for relaxation with fishing and gunkholing spots. The island is about 22km/13.5mi long and the irregular shoreline invites exploration. Logging and fishing were once active pursuits here, but today there is very little industry. False Bay is the center of community activity and home to a public float and the Lasqueti pub, restaurant, and bakery. A gas pump at the pub is open irregular hours. There are a number of B & B's on the island, as well as farms that sell fresh produce. Produce is also available at a Saturday Farmers Market held from 10am-1pm during the summer. It is located a short walk up from the ferry dock. Co-located with the market is an Art Centre that has exhibitions and weekly movie nights. A passenger only ferry runs from False Bay on Lasqueti to French Creek on Vancouver Island. There are no paved roads, no public transportation and no public camp grounds. Island homes are not serviced by an electric company and self sufficient residents often employ solar or micro-hydro sources of power, or they have chosen to live without electricity.

★ **Squitty Bay Provincial Park (12):** This marine park has a public float with moorage for three to four 20' boats. Maneuvering room is limited. There is no space for anchorage. Several rocks obstruct the entrance. The safest passage is along the south shore. The bay is dredged to depths of eight feet. No potable water, no campfires or camping. Picnic tables, pit toilets available. The waters nearby are great for scuba diving and canoeing.

Walk-around: A road from the public float leads to other settlements on the island. Walk up the dirt road and up the hillside for spectacular views. If you have a bike it is 18 km/11 mi to False Bay on the opposite end of the island.

★ **Boat Cove (13):** This niche in the southwestern shore offers anchorage on a good bottom and protection from west winds, but is open to southeast winds. Avoid rocks in the southeast entrance.

★ **Old House Bay:** There is anchorage with protection from northwest winds off the head. Watch for shoals when locating a spot.

★ **Richardson Cove:** Anchorage at the head.

★ **False Bay (14):** [3536] The settlement of Lasqueti is on the east side of Mud Bay. There is a public float with no services, do not moor in areas marked for ferries or seaplane use only. At times evening westerlies and Qualicum winds enter, and moorage at the float is bumpy. Anchorage is on the north side of the bay in three niches in the shoreline. Try east of Higgins Island. There is a good holding bottom. Beware of a drying rock when crossing from the public float. A lagoon has protected mooring, however the entrance, east of Prowse Point, dries in the middle at about half tide. Enter at high water, near slack. A three to four knot current occurs in the channel. Favor the north side, but watch for rock ledges extending from shore and a drying rock located mid-channel.

Lasqueti Island Hotel: Hand carry gas & diesel, call for hours. Lodging, seasonal restaurant, pub, pay showers, water vending machine, store across the street. 250-333-8503.

★ **Spring Bay:** This wide bay has anchorage off the head. Good protection in southerly winds.

★ **Scottie Bay (15):** This small lovely bay provides excellent protection from winds. Enter south of Lindbergh Island. Keep hard to port to avoid a reef off Lindberg Island. There is a private wharf here and a few homes. A road runs about a mile and one half across the island to False Bay.

★ **Tucker Bay:** Anchorage for small craft is possible south of Larson Islet adjacent to Potter Point. Allow at least a 300 foot clearance off the west point of Larson Islet when approaching. Charted Tuck Rock is a hazard in the bay. Much of the bay is open to northwest and north winds.

Jervis Island: There is anchorage between Bunny and Jervis Islands.

★ **Boho Bay (16):** There is anchorage in the harbour between the southern shore of Boho Island and Lasqueti. It is the site of an undeveloped marine park. At times, there are strong currents here.

★ **Skerry Bay:** This bay on the north side of Lasqueti offers good protection in all but northwest winds. Rocks, one of which dries five feet, are in the north entrance. Aquaculture is in the north portion.

★ **Jedediah Island Marine Park & Deep Bay (17):** This beautiful island park has anchorage in several places. Bull Passage, between Lasqueti and Jedediah has several rocky patches, but provides shelter. Jedediah Bay, a small indentation shaped like a dock cleat, offers limited anchorage. An unnamed bay on the southeast end has anchorage and some protection from Rabbit Island. An extremely steep bluff is a landmark.

Deep Bay, a long and narrow bay on the northwest side across from Paul Island, has anchorage. Winds, which tend to swirl around the bay, and the deep bottom, affect anchoring. A tie to shore is advised once the anchor is set. Rings, somewhat difficult to reach at lower tides, are installed on both the south and north shores. Anchorage is also found in the passage between Paul Island and Jedediah. Beaches, grazing land, and old growth Douglas Fir are on the island. Pit toilet, trails to Home Bay, Long Bay, and to the top of Mount Gibraltar, as well as wilderness camping are available onshore.

★ **Texada Island:** This 31 mile-long and 6 mile-wide, mountainous, forested island stretches from Point Upwood on the south to Grilse Point on the north and forms the western boundary of the Malaspina Strait. Texada's continued wealth of limestone was first quarried here in 1897 and is mined today from two major quarry companies at a rate of several million tons per year. The marble, gold, iron and copper mines have all played a part in the economy and leave the island with a rich history. Forestry, tourism and retirees are also the life blood of the current economy. Most of Texada's population of about 1,200 is split between two villages, Van Anda on the northeast at Sturt Bay and Gillies Bay on the southwest side of the island. Sabine Channel, on the southwest end of the island is frequented by towing tugs, so be aware and watchful. Be sure to visit www.texada.org for more information, community events and festivals, and maps.

★ **Anderson Bay (18):** Many boaters have sought shelter in westerlies in this narrow bay located on South Texada Island's eastern shore near the southeast point. Anchorage is possible near the head in 10-20 feet of water. When entering north of the island at the entrance, stay south of the rocks that are in the center and are covered at high water.

★ **Northeast Bay (19):** Although constricted with an island in the center, there is sufficient room for anchorage when seeking shelter from west and southeast winds.

★ **Pocahontas Bay (20):** Although only a small bight, there is shelter here from southeasterlies.

★ **Gillies Bay Village (21):** This bay has some protection in north winds. An extensive drying flat is at the head. Its sandy beaches invite exploration by small boat. Gillies Bay Village has a general store, liquor license, a police station, post office, medical clinic, library with internet, airport with 3,000 ft. paved runway, tennis court, community hall and ballfield that hosts a Sunday Summer Farmers Market featuring local produce and crafts.

Each summer during the lowest tide, *Sand Castle Weekend* is held at Shelter Point Park.

★ **Shelter Point Park (21):** A nationally recognized First Nations Village Archeological Site. View the Artifacts Display that showcases items found onsite of historical and cultural significance. Anchorage, 2 launching ramps, campsites, picnic tables, showers, toilets, seasonal concession, hiking trails, and fresh water.

Limekiln Bay (22): There is temporary anchorage in this shallow bight along the northwest shore. There is a white sandy beach.

Blubber Bay (23): This wide indentation on the north shore between Blubber Point and Grilse Point was once the site of whale rendering operations. On the west side is a landing for ferries from the Westview Terminal connecting to the mainland in Powell River. A float owned by Blubber Bay Quarry offers temporary moorage for sightseers who care to walk up the hill to the Visitor Centre, gift shops and museum. Anchorage on sand and mud is possible, but space is limited and the bay is open to the north and northwest winds. Favored salmon fishing waters are from Grilse Point south to Hodgson Point and Eagle Cove.

★ **Van Anda at Sturt Bay (24):** Good sheltered moorage is available at the Texada Boating Club on dock 4 and the west side of dock 3. Because of the harbour depth and rock bottom, there are no pilings to hold the docks, only concrete weights and chains, therefore no rafting is allowed and vessels over 40 feet must be strategically placed by the wharfinger. Limited anchorage is also possible. Village amenities include a store & liquor outlet, post office, hotel/pub/restaurant, gas station, RV park with laundromat, credit union, community church, Texada Legion, museum, arts and culture centre and local accommodations. A government wharf with tie-up float at Van Anda Bay allows for quick stop shopping.

Texada Boat Club: {49° 45' 35" N, 124° 33' 50" W} Visitor moorage, water, 15 amp power, porta potty. Showers and garbage deposit available for a fee. Wharfinger, Paul Nelson. 604-223-1122. VHF 66A.

Essential Supplies & Services

AIR TRANSPORTATION
To & from Washington
NW Seaplanes . . . 425-277-1590, 1-800-690-0036
San Juan Airlines. 1-800-874-4434
Seattle Seaplanes 1-800-637-5553
To & from Islands/Vancouver
Air Canada .1-888-247-2262
Harbour Air, Comox . . 250-339-5729, 1-800-665-0212
KD Air. 1-800-665-4244
Pacific Coastal, Comox 250-890-0699,1-800-663-2872

BOOKS / BOOK STORES
Evergreen Pacific Publishing 425-493-1451
The Marine Atlas. 253-872-5707

BUS TRANSPORTATION
BC Transit. 250-339-5453
Hornby Island Bus . . . . .www.hornbybus.com
Islandlink Bus Service. . . . . www.islandlinkbus.com
Tofino Bus (Courtenay). 250-334-2475
Greyhound Pacific Coach 1-800-661-8747

COAST GUARD
Victoria Coast Guard Radio. . . . . VHF 16, 83a
. . . . 1-800-661-9202 (In BC) or 250-363-6611
Victoria Marine Traffic 250-363-6333
Marine Distress, Search & Rescue
. . . . 1-800-567-5111 (in Canada) or 250-413-8933
Cell Phone (limited to select providers) . . . *16 or #727

FERRY INFORMATION
B.C.. 1-888-223-3779
Fr. Creek-Lasqueti. 250-927-0431

24 hr Recorded Notifications (Pacific region only)
. . . . .1-866-431-3474 or 604-666-2828
Recreational Licensing 1-877-535-7307
Observe, Record & Report Line (fisheries violations)
Greater Vancouver 604-607-4186
Or Call. 1-800-465-4336

FUELS
Comox Gas & Go Marine: Gas, diesel
. . . . .250-339-4664 VHF 66A
Fairwinds Marina at Schooner Cove: Gas, Diesel
. . . . 250-468-5364 VHF 66A
French Creek Seafoods: Gas, Diesel 250-248-7100
Lasqueti Island: Gas, diesel (hand carry, call for hours)
. . . . 250-333-8503
Salmon Point: Gas 250-923-6605
Ship & Shore Restaurant, Deep Bay: Gas, diesel (tidal float) 250-757-8399

GOLF COURSES
(These courses are accessible from moorage and have rental clubs available)
Comox Golf Club (9 hole). 250-339-4444
Fairwinds Golf Club. 250-468-7666
Glacier Greens (Comox) 250-339-6515
Saratoga Beach (Oyster River, 9-hole).. . 250-337-2208

HAUL-OUTS
Ocean Pacific Marine Supply . . . 1-800-663-2294

HOSPITALS
Healthlink BC (Nurse Helpline) 811
North Island Hospital: Comox. 250-331-5900
Powell River General Hospital. 604-485-3211
Texada Health Centre 604-486-7525

LIQUOR STORES
Comox   Courtenay
Denman Island   Gillies Bay Store
Qualicum Beach   Van Anda

MARINAS / MOORAGE FLOATS
Comox Gas & Go Marina . . . . .250-339-4664 VHF 66A
Comox Municipal Marina, permanent. . . 250-339-3141
Comox Valley Harbour Authority
. . . . 250-339-6041, VHF 66A
Comox Valley Marina . . . . 250-339-2930, VHF 66A
Deep Bay Harbour Authority. 250-757-9331
Deep Bay Marina 250-586-5560
Denman Island Community Dock
False Bay: Lasqueti Island Public Float
Ford Cove Harbour Authority: Hornby Island . . . .
. . . . 250-335-0003
French Creek. . . . . 250-248-5051, VHF 66A
Pacific Playgrounds:Resort & Marina . . . 250-337-5600
Fairwinds Marina at Schooner Cove 250-468-5364
Squitty Bay Provincial Park: Lasqueti Island
Van Anda/Sturt Bay: Texada Island Public Float
Texada Boat Club 604-223-1122
Gillies Bay Store: Texada Island
Salmon Point Resort. 250-923-6605

RAMPS
Comox Municipal Marina 250-339-3141
Deep Bay: Ship & Shore Restaurant . . . 250-757-8399
Denman Island: Bill Mee Boat Launch, Denman Village, Gravelly Bay
Fairwinds Marina at Schooner Cove 250-468-5364
Hornby Island: Shingle Spit
Kitty Coleman Provincial Park
Little River: Salmon Point Resort 250-923-6605
Oyster River: Pacific Playgrounds 250-337-5600
Texada Island: Shelter Point Park
Union Bay

REPAIRS
A & E Marine, Comox 250-339-4422
CV Marine, Courtenay. 250-334-3536
Desolation Sound Yacht Charters/Shop . 250-339-7222

SCUBA SITES
Nanoose Bay   Mardrona Point
Hornby Island   Denman Island

SEWAGE DISPOSAL
Comox Valley Harbour Authority: Pump. 250-339-6041
Deep Bay Harbour Authority: Pump 250-757-9331
Fairwinds Marina at Schooner Cove: Pump. . . . .
. . . . 250-468-5364

TOWING
C-TOW 1-888-419-CTOW
I Charter and Tow 250-228-3585
Vessel Assist -Georgia Strait 250-247-8934

VISITOR INFORMATION
Courtenay-Comox. 250-400-2882, 1-855-400-2882

WEATHER
Environment Canada Weather Line 250-339-9861
Discovery Mt.: VHF WX-4
Texada Island: WX-1, 162.525MHz

Chapter 16: Discovery Passage

Cape Mudge to Dent Rapids. Campbell River, April Point, Quathiaski Cove, Big Bay, Seymour Narrows, Toba & Bute Inlets, Yuculta & Gillard Rapids; Quadra, Reed, Maurelle, Sonora, Octopus, Rendezvous, & Stuart Islands.

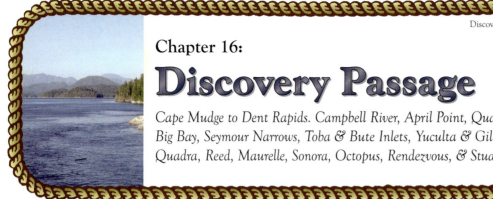

Discovery Passage - photo © David Stanley

Symbols

[ ]: Numbers between [ ] are chart numbers.
{ }: Numbers & letters between { } are waypoints.
★ Recommended destinations, facilities, and services
⚓: Park, ⛵: Boat Launch, ▲: Campgrounds, ⚑: Hiking Trails, ⊼: Picnic Area, 🚲: Biking
🤿: Scuba

Chart List

Canadian Hydrographic Charts:
3312, 3513, 3537-3543

NOAA: 17503

Marine Atlas Vol 1 (2018): Pages 30, 32-35

Evergreen Cruising Atlas:
Pages 42, 43, 44, 54, 55

★ See "Important Notices" between Chapters 7 and 8 for specific information on boating related topics such as boating safety, weather, U.S. & Canadian marine radio use, Vessel Traffic Service, security zones, Canadian & U.S. Customs, etc. Due to changing regulations, call ahead to verify latest customs information.

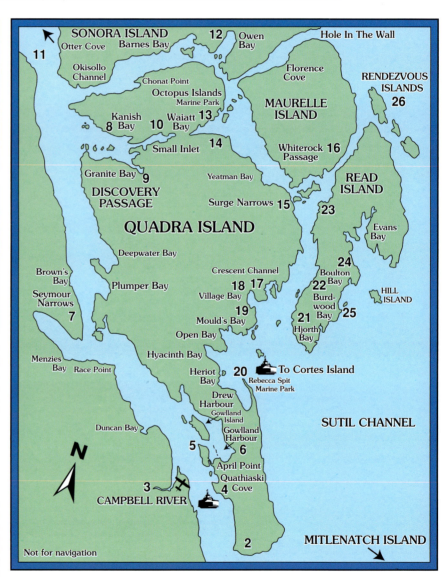

Discovery Passage

[3312, 3513, 3538, 3539, 3540]

Discovery Passage: Named for Captain Vancouver's ship, this passage separates Quadra and Sonora Islands from Vancouver Island. It is the main shipping channel leading northwest from the north end of the Strait of Georgia and is used by tugs, freighters, cruise ships, and fishing boats as well as by pleasure craft. A ferry also crosses the passage from downtown Campbell River to Quathiaski Cove on Quadra Island. Discovery Passage is a designated Vessel Traffic Service Zone. Boaters are advised to monitor traffic on Channel 71. Entry on the south is at Cape Mudge and it is exited on the north at Chatham Point. The flood stream sets south and ebbs north, attaining velocities of five to seven knots on big tides. When the current is strong in mid-channel, try closer to shore where back currents can be helpful to move you against the flood. (See Seymour Narrows, British Columbia current tables). Dangerous rips can form at Cape Mudge where tidal streams can run 7-9 knots. Avoid this area if a southeast wind is blowing on a flood tide. The vicinity of Menzies Bay also gets bad rips. Seymour Narrows, where tidal currents attain speeds of 15 knots, should be transited at or near slack water.

★ **Mitlenatch Island (1):** The Island is home to the Mitlenatch Island Nature Provincial Park where the areas largest seabird colony is found. Park access is through Northwest Bay and Camp Bay, but most of the island is closed to visitors. There is temporary shelter on this rocky, windswept island. Northwest Bay has a fair anchorage that would be treacherous overnight. Beware of two charted, but unmarked rocks located 3/10ths of a mile northeast of this bay. Camp Bay, on the southeast, is small and is exposed in southeast winds. A Coast Salish legend tells that this island is a tribal princess turned to stone and placed there to remind their people to be less boastful. The island was once used by the Manson family of Cortes Island as a sheep farm. Wild flowers and cactus grow profusely, as do many species of birds. Please stay on trails, no pets onshore. One pit toilet available.

Visit us at boattravel.com

Cape Mudge (2): Located on southwest Quadra Island, a cluster of sparkling white, red-roofed, lighthouse buildings are local landmarks. The cape is also famous for salmon fishing. Chinooks to 30 pounds are caught from early June through mid-September. Coho run from mid-June to mid-October. See current tables for Seymour Narrows, British Columbia. The tidal streams in the area run five to seven knots. The flood current flows south, down Discovery Passage, and the ebb flows north. Don't be surprised to see boats going backwards at strong tides. A back eddy close in to Quadra Island makes for easier going when heading up Discovery Passage against the current. In a flood tide and southeast winds, dangerous rips occur off Cape Mudge. When rounding the cape be sure to clear the black can and red spar buoys that mark the end of the Wilby Shoals.

Cape Mudge Village (Yaculta): The Village of Cape Mudge, part of the We Wai Kai First Nation, is set upon the majestic backdrop of Discovery Passage. There is a public wharf, but due to the passing commercial and cruise ship traffic, overnight moorage is not advised. The Village boasts a Band office, playground, historic church, and a cultural centre which houses the Sacred Potlatch Collection along with eight totem poles. Across the street, the Nuyumbalees Native Garden features traditional plants and four beautifully crafted totem poles.

From the south end of the Village, take a half hour walk along the heritage trail to the historic lighthouse. The trail is passable, but rough in spots, so watch your step. The trail leads past an RV Park and Campsite to the lighthouse. The lighthouse keepers cottage, outside (south of) the fenced compound is available as a vacation rental. Contact Tsa Kwa Luten Lodge for rental information. As you stroll along the shoreline watch for dozens of ancient petroglyphs scattered amongst the rocks and only exposed during low tide.

Wildlife viewing, hiking, biking, fishing, diving and kayaking are among the many things to do on Quadra Island. Throughout the season, weekly markets are held beside the Visitors Centre – a fabulous spot to find that perfect hand-crafted treasure.

★ **Campbell River (3):** As you approach, identify the three breakwater-protected moorage basins. Riprap breakwaters extend from shore at each site.

The southernmost basin is the Campbell River Fishermans Wharf. These public floats offer secure berthage in the vicinity of marine repair shops, freight companies, retail stores and other services. The landmark Discovery Fishing Pier, the Maritime Heritage Centre and the Discovery Passage Aquarium are also located beside the wharf. The Maritime Heritage Centre has exhibits and activities and also houses the BCP45 seine boat that once adorned the back of the Canadian five dollar bill. The adjacent Discovery Passage Aquarium showcases local marine species and habitats. This basin is within walking distance to downtown.

To the north, a breakwater protects the Coast Marina, located in the heart of downtown. The marina is situated next to the BC Ferries Terminal to Quadra Island and Tyee Plaza Shopping Centre. The Plaza is home to the Campbell River Visitor Centre and also offers a variety of shops, restaurants, a laundromat and a pharmacy in the immediate area. A grocery store is found just three blocks away.

The northernmost basin encircles the full service Discovery Harbour Marina and the Discovery Harbour Marine Fuel Sales located on the North Floats. Onshore, with close to 40 various shops, restaurants and services, the Discovery Harbour Shopping Centre is the largest shopping centre on Vancouver Island north of Nanaimo. Be sure

Campbell River Government Wharf   Photo © Tourism Campbell River

to stop by the Wei Wai Kum House of Treasures. Designed as a contemporary interpretation of a First Nations Big House, the store carries original, First Nation artwork. Ocean Pacific Marine Supply and Boatyard is also conveniently located here, providing complete marine outfitting and repair services.

Campbell River is one of the most boater friendly boating destinations on British Columbia's coast with ample berth space and most every boat service readily available. The city is centrally located 175 miles from both Victoria to the south and from Cape Scott on the northern end of Vancouver Island, making it the perfect refueling and provisioning stop for travelers in both directions. It is also an ideal base for exploring the Discovery Islands and the Broughton Archipelago.

While you are exploring, take the time to look around this hospitable city. Visitors looking for diversions will find parks, golf courses, an indoor climbing gym, wonderful paved sea walks, great restaurants and shopping, as well as water adventures including grizzly bear viewing and ocean rapids tours. Sequoia Park located just up from downtown, takes its name from a large Sequoia tree overlooking the Discovery Passage. The park is home to a First Nations memorial totem pole and a Ceremonial Torii Gate that honors Campbell River's Sister City, Ishikari, Japan.

Across the street, the Museum at Campbell River has wonderful exhibits highlighting First Nations, Pioneer Life, the Salmon Industry and more.

Campbell River hosts year round events for everyone to enjoy. The "must see" Pier Street Farmers Market is held every Sunday from 10am to 2:30 pm from May through September. Summer activities include *Transformations on the Shore* (an annual wood carving competition), a fun, family oriented *Canada Day Celebration*, and in August is the *Salmon Festival, featuring Logger's Sports and Highland Games*. For more events and information, contact the Destination Campbell River Visitor Centre, open all year. 250-286-6901, 1-877-286-5705.

Cape Mudge Lighthouse   Photo © Patricia Robertson

DISCOVERY PASSAGE Chapter 16 Page 201

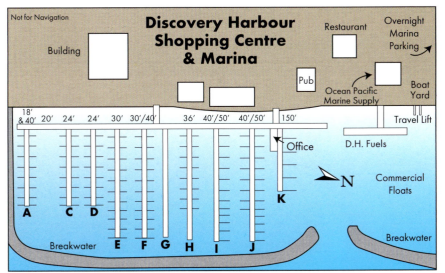

★ **Discovery Harbour Fuel Sales:** Marine Fuels and More! Make us your one-stop marine shop. Gas, diesel, oil and filters, engine and marine maintenance items to keep your vessel moving. A nice selection of tackle, lures, bait, prawn and crab pots for that big catch. Nautical charts, ice, snacks, beverages, and other handy items available, as well as an ATM machine onsite. Located in Discovery Harbour Marina with easy access to the stores and services at the Discovery Harbour Shopping Mall. See our advertisement on page 200. Website: www.discoveryharbourfuel.com. Email: dhfs@telus.net. Address: 1374 Island Hwy, Campbell River, British Columbia V9W 8C9 Canada. Fax: 250-287-3442. Phone: 250-287-3456. VHF 66A.

★ **Discovery HARBOUR Marina:** {50° 02.15' N, 125° 14.40' W} Look for the large riprap breakwater and the Discovery Harbour Fuel Dock sign north of the ferry landing. Moorage, gas, diesel, oils, stove oil, ice, showers, and oil changing are available. See our advertisement on page 200. Website: www.discoveryharbourmarina.com. E-mail: info@discoveryharbourmarina.com. Address: 218-1434 Ironwood St., Campbell River, British Columbia V9W 5T5. Fax: 250-287-8939. Telephone: 250-287-2614. VHF 66A.

★ **Ocean Pacific Marine Supply & Boatyard:** {50° 02.09' N, 125° 14.47' W} North Island's Largest Marine Store and Boatyard. Our fully stocked marine store has a complete inventory of marine parts including Hardware, Sailing Gear, Electronics, Plumbing and Pumps, Fibreglass Supplies & Paint, Cleaning Supplies, Books and Giftware. Visit our website at www.oceanpacificmarine.com. The full service boatyard features a 110 ton Travelift, ABYC Certified Marine Technicians and Electricians, Qualified Fibreglassers, and CWB Welders. Cummins Marine Dealer. Emergency services available. See our advertisement on this page. Website: www.oceanpacificmarine.com. Email: info@oceanpacificmarine.com. Conveniently located in the Discovery Harbour Marina & Shopping Centre. Site: 102-1370 Island Highway. Telephone: 250-286-1011, 1-800-663-2294. Open every day in the summer.

Campbell River Fishermans Wharf: {50° 1.19' N, 125° 14.17' W}: Daily, weekly, monthly moorage. Transient berthage in South Basin finger 5. Drive down loading dock. Rafting optional. 20/30/50/100 amp power, water, pump-out, garbage/recycling deposit, restrooms, showers, wifi, cranes, grid (emergency use). 250-287-7931. VHF 66A.

Coast Marina: {50° 01.81' N, 125° 14.20' W} Permanent and transient moorage to 200', 30/50/100 amp power, water, showers, WiFi, garbage disposal, security & boat monitoring, bar/restaurant, water taxi, fishing & wildlife charters. Ask about free shuttle service & loaner car for moorage customers. 250-204-3900. VHF 66A.

Freshwater Marina on Campbell River: {50° 02.34' N, 125° 16.2' 16"W} Covered monthly moorage, 15/30 amp power, water, porta-potty, boat launch (high tide, fee applies), 50-ton travelift (beam to 20'), DIY boatyard. Travelift: 250-203-2635. Marina: 250-286-0701.

LOCATED IN DISCOVERY HARBOUR MARINA, CAMPBELL RIVER

www.oceanpacificmarine.com

Our Full-Service Boatyard Offers:
- 110 Ton Travelift
- ABYC Certified Marine Technicians & Electricians
- CWB Certified Welders
- NMEA Certified Marine Electronics Technicians
- Fiberglassers, Painting & Detailing
- Convenient Downtown Location

Toll Free:
1-800-663-2294
Local Phone:
250-286-1011

102-1370 Island Highway, Campbell River

FULLY STOCKED MARINE STORE WITH EVERYTHING YOU NEED FOR YOUR VESSEL
FRIENDLY KNOWLEDGEABLE STAFF

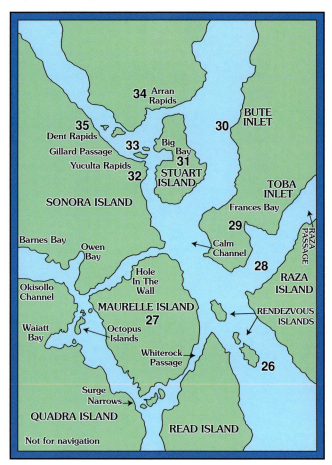

Brown's Bay Resort Photo © Esther Hollink

Quadra Island
[3312, 3539, 3540, 3543]

★ **Quadra Island:** Quadra Island, on the east side of Discovery Passage, is the largest island in the Discovery Passage group. Its name honors the Spanish explorer Don Juan Francisco de a Bodega y Quadra. Several days could be spent circumnavigating and exploring this island, visiting numerous anchorages, parks, and the shore facilities at Quathiaski Cove, Heriot Bay, and April Point. Of five parks on Quadra Island, the Main Lakes Chain is of special significance. For a different experience, launch a hand carried craft into this lake chain and enjoy peaceful, lily studded waterways that meander through the countryside. A portage also leads back out from the lakes to Yeatman Bay, allowing a circuit that is ideal by kayak. This route requires a return through Surge Narrows, so keep an eye on the tidal current tables. About 2,700 people live on the island year round. Many local artists participate each June in the *Quadra Island Studio Tour*. A self-guided tour is available year round. The island is full of recreational opportunities including mountain biking, hiking, camping and kayaking.

★ **Quathiaski Cove (4):** Known as Q Cove, this harbour is located opposite Campbell River on the eastern side of Discovery Passage. Enter north or south of Grouse Island. A natural harbour, Q Cove has a maximum tidal change of 4.6 m and is the site of a marina, public floats, launch ramp, and the terminus of the Quadra Island-Campbell River ferry. This is the commercial centre of the Island. Groceries, accommodations, liquor, a post office, gas, propane, a pharmacy, banking, office & art supplies, art galleries, marine and auto mechanics, cafés, restaurants, hair stylists, a hardware store and a pub are found here. A tourist information booth is open here seasonally, as is a Saturday Farmers Market. The Community Centre at 970 West Road has a climbing wall, skate park, tennis courts, walking trails and also hosts activities and events. 250-285-3243.

Quadra Island Harbour Authority: {50° 02'35.7" N, 125° 12' 59.8"W} Moorage (commercial vessels have priority, rafting is mandatory), power, water, washroom, showers, garbage, WiFi, 1.5 ton winch, boat launch, pay parking. 250-285-3622.

Sea Scape Waterfront Resort & Marina: Under new management.

★ **April Point & April Point Cove (5):** This point of Quadra Island forms a protective windbreak for an appendix-shaped cove which lies south-southwest of Gowlland Island. Here is a beautiful, quiet moorage with wharfage available at April Point Marina or good anchorage on a mud bottom. As you enter the harbour, you will pass the Resort where you will see a red spar bouy. Keep buoy close to your starboard side. Beyond the buoy about 500 metres farther into the cove is the Marina.

April Point Marina, Resort & Spa: {50° 03.52' N, 125° 14' 8"W} Permanent & guest moorage, vessels to 200'. 15/30/50/100 amp power, water, garbage disposal, showers, laundry, picnic areas, ice, wifi, lodging, restaurant, spa. Call ahead for dock assignment or reservations May-Sept. 250-285-3830. VHF 66A.

★ **Gowlland Harbour (6):** There is peaceful and secure anchorage in several places within this large harbour. It is recommended that larger boats enter from the North entrance of Gowlland Harbour. Currents here can reach five knots outside the entrance, but no noticeable current is felt inside. Avoid Entrance Rock to port upon entering. Entry through the narrow passage from April Point at or near the head is not recommended as the passage is rock strewn. Anchorage is good east of Crow Islet, south of Stag Island and Doe Islet, and in the large basin at the head. Tie-ups are not recommended because the area is actively used as a booming ground. Several private floats extend from shore. Gowlland Harbour Resort has complimentary moorage for boats to 24' with advanced dinner reservations. 250-285-3572.

Seymour Narrows (7): Use the *Seymour Narrows, British Columbia* current tables. Powerful currents run to 16 knots at springs, causing overfalls. Travel is advised within a half hour of slack water. The narrows is about two miles long and has high, rugged shorelines on each side. Watch for drift in the waterway. Flood current sets south, while the ebb current sets north. When either stream is running at strength, the eddies and swirls are extremely heavy, and if opposed by a wind, can create very dangerous conditions for mariners. The duration of absolute slack water can range from 12 to 15 minutes, but when there is a large range of tide, the interval of change is less. If weather conditions are extreme, they affect the change also. Race Point, to the south, has strong back eddies on a flood tide. This causes rips, especially if there is wind. Passage at these times is best closer to Quadra Island. When approaching from the south, there is temporary anchorage between Maud Island and the Quadra Island shore. Menzies Bay is also used for anchorage, behind Defender Shoal, marked with an anchor on the charts. When approaching from the north, Deepwater Bay, while open to north-westerlies, does provide temporary shelter. There is a charted rock near Separation Point. Ripple Rock, the cause of several tragic accidents, was located only about a fathom below the surface and near mid-channel until its destruction by explosives in 1958. The three million dollar explosion was the largest non-nuclear explosion to that time.

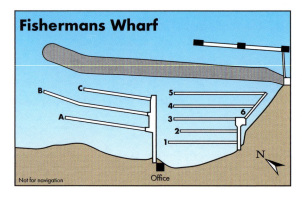

Visit us at boattravel.com

★ **Brown's Bay Resort:** {50° 9' 43.1" N, 125° 22' 26.4" W} Enter the harbour on the north side of the big distinctive breakwater for temporary shelter from the Seymour Narrows. The marina offers slips for vessels up to 100', with 15/30/50 amp power and water; a shower and laundry facility is located right next to the seasonal Floating Restaurant. The marina office located at the head of the marina has a large selection of fishing tackle, ice, bait, and snacks. Fuel up with gas/diesel/water; get the latest on the fishing information or currents for the Narrows. There are two boat ramps with overnight parking availability. Stay for a while and explore all Brown's Bay Resort has to offer including floating rental suites, oceanfront Cabins, "Glamping" tents and a full service RV Park with hot tub, fitness room, playground, clubhouse for weddings and gatherings all with spectacular views of the Inside Passage. See our advertisement on this page. Website: www.brownsbayresort.com. Address: 15021 Brown's Bay Rd., Campbell River, British Columbia, V9H 1N9. Marina Telephone: 250-286-3135. Marina Email: marina@brownsbayresort.com Accommodations Telephone: 250-287-7108. Accommodations email: ripplerockrv@brownsbayresort.com. VHF 66A.

★ **Maud Island:** Temporary anchorage is found in the channel between the island and the Quadra shore. The 366' long *HMCS Columbia* was sunk in 1996 for use as an artificial reef. {50 08.031 N, 125 20.152 W}.

★ **Kanish Bay (8):** This bay indents about two miles into Quadra Island. The Chained Islands, which lie along the southern border of the bay, provide protection and anchorage between the islands and shore. There are rocks and a drying shelf.

★ **Granite Bay (9):** This bay extends southeast off Kanish Bay. The entrance is narrow. A rock is to port near the entrance. Depths within the bay average 30 feet, mud bottom. There is a dock and although there are no shops or other amenities this can be useful when looking for a safe, sheltered harbour while traveling up Discovery Passage. This was once the site of a community of some 500 residents who were engaged in logging, farming, and mining at the Lucky Jim Gold and Copper Mine. Today, there are few residents. A tiny bay between Granite Bay and Small Inlet has some protection from west winds. A road leads to Heriot Bay, Quathiaski Cove, and April Point.

★ **Small Inlet & Small Inlet Marine Provincial Park (10) [3538]:** Small Inlet has, at least, two good anchorages. After negotiating the narrow entrance, the inlet opens up to reveal high mountains and an abundance of greenery. Enter in mid-channel to avoid kelp patches off both shores. Entrance depths at half tide average 18 feet. There is good anchorage far into the bay. The park has no facilities. A rough, 1.5km/1mi trail leads to Newton Lake from the trailhead at the southeast corner of the Inlet.

★ **Otter Cove (11):** Shelter is found from westerlies, and this is also a spot for awaiting favorable current conditions at Seymour Narrows. Enter north of Limestone Island and go close in to the head. Kelp marks dangers near the small island. The southern approach is blocked by extensive kelp and foul ground. The bottom is rock. This cove is part of Rock Bay Marine Park.

Chatham Point: White buildings with red roofs mark the lighthouse at this weather reporting station. Dangerous conditions can exist from tide rips caused when a strong west wind meets an ebbing tide. See current tables for Seymour Narrows, British Columbia.

Rock Bay/Rock Bay Marine Provincial Park: Ruins of a wharf are on the west side. To trailer a boat, an old logging road connects with Hwy 19 and is passable during the dry months. A boat launch is in the park. The park land is strictly along the shore, other area is privately owned. Activities include scuba diving, fishing, paddling, and wildlife viewing.

Okisollo Channel
[3312, 3537, 3539]

★ **Okisollo Channel:** This picturesque 12 mile channel runs along the north shore of Quadra Island. There may be fresh water on the Sonora Island shore, opposite Metcalf Island. A spring, appearing as an especially green spot on the bank, usually cascades down the cliff behind the trees to the water below. It is possible to edge up to the bank to fill containers. In settled weather, there is anchorage behind Metcalf Island. It is possible to avoid much of the current at Lower Rapids and Gypsy Shoal by passing north of the Okis Islands toward Barnes Bay. Gypsy Shoal, with depths of less than six feet, nearly blocks Lower Rapids. Passage is made south of the shoal at slack water only. Heavy overfalls occur on an ebb tide at Upper Rapids, off Cooper Point. Passage in this area is recommended at or near slack. Slack occurs

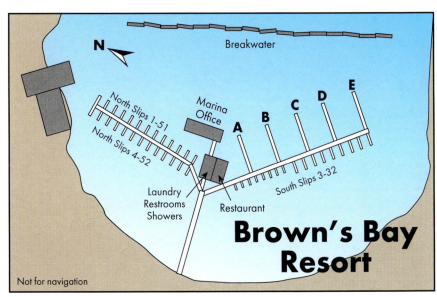

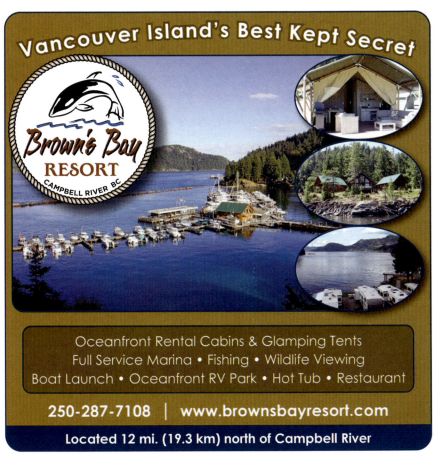

Discovery Passage Photo © David Stanley

at Lower Rapids, Upper Rapids, and Hole-In-The-Wall close to the same time, about 55 minutes before slack water at Seymour Narrows. Use the Seymour Narrows current tables or see the current tables for Seymour Narrows, British Columbia. Hazards are Bentley Rock off Quadra Island, and a reef off Cooper Point. Okisollo Channel continues in a southeasterly direction past the Octopus Islands and Yeatman Bay to Surge Narrows.

★ **Chonat Bay:** Chonat Bay is used primarily for log storage, but anchorage is possible.

Walk-around: A trail leading from the head of the bay crosses over a concrete dam and leads to Chonat Lake. Another small road to starboard, before the bay shallows, leads to Ashlar Lake.

Barnes Bay: Often there are extensive logging operations in this Bay. Anchorage is tricky because the bottom is rock.

★ **Owen Bay (12):** This bay has good anchorage. Enter north of Grant Island. Rocks extend off Walters Point. Another approach can be made south of Grant Island. Rocks and narrow channels make this entrance less inviting. Strong currents are frequent. There is a public float. A lagoon, south of the floats, can be explored by dinghy.

★ **Hole In The Wall:** See current tables for Seymour Narrows, British Columbia. The western end of this channel has rapids which run up to 12 knots at springs. Floods northeast, ebbs southwest. Florence Cove, about halfway through the passage, may provide limited anchorage, but winds funnel into the cove. The eastern end of the passageway is a popular fishing hole.

★⚓ **Octopus Islands Provincial Park (13):** This marine park, west of Hole In The Wall, is part of the BC Marine Trail Association network and is a popular anchorage. Small islets protect larger anchoring basins. One favored entry is from Bodega Anchorage through the narrow northern cut between Quadra and the Octopus Islands. Depths of 15-20 feet are in mid-channel. At the western end of the channel, rocks sitting just below the surface show bright green through the clear water. Anchorage is possible in the first bay to starboard. Avoid a large, sprawling rock to port on entering. Several boats can be accommodated with ties to shore. A second bay, also to starboard, provides more anchorage. The west end is a drying flat. The two largest islands are private. Hiking, swimming, scuba diving, fishing & wilderness camping are possible recreational pastimes.

★ **Waiatt Bay (14):** The safest entry to this bay is the same as the entry to Octopus Islands Marine Park as described above. It is possible to enter from the south, but caution is advised as the fairway is strewn with rocks and kelp. The bottom of Waiatt Bay has depths of 25-40 feet. There is good anchorage near the head of the bay in 15-25 feet of water. Because this bay is protected from prevailing summer westerlies, this anchorage is often mirror smooth. Reflecting in the still water along the shoreline are rock formations called floating totems. Aquaculture operations are on the southeast side. This bay is commonly used by paddlers to portage canoes and kayaks. A portage route to Small Inlet Provincial Park on the west side of Quadra Island can be accessed from this Bay.

Walk-around: A small beach at the head of Waiatt Bay is the site of a path which leads up the hill and offers a vista of Small Inlet, the narrow bay which indents Quadra from Kanish Bay on the other side of the island.

Yeatman Bay: Anchorage is found while awaiting slack at Surge Narrows. An unmaintained trail leads from the bay for about one mile into Main Lake.

★ **Surge Narrows (15):** See current tables for Beazley Passage, British Columbia. This maze of islands and islets is best traversed within a few minutes of slack water. Duration of slack is about 11 minutes. Beazley Pass, between Sturt and Peck Islands, is the navigable passage. Tidal currents run as high as 12 knots at spring floods and 10 knots at spring ebbs. Floods southeast, ebbs northwest. Charted Tusko Rock, just west of Sturt Island, lies very close to mid channel and dries at very low water. It is a frequent cause of collision and groundings. Favor the west side of the pass. Surge Narrows on Read Island has a public float, and a floating Post Office, (open Monday, Wednesday and Friday afternoons, cash only, coffee and treats sometimes available). The small dock on Quadra, in Hoskyn Channel just south of the narrows, is a commuter dock for local, small boats only and gives access to the Quadra road system. This dock is not for recreational use or overnight moorage. No boat launching permitted.

★ **Whiterock Passage (16):** Whiterock Passage is a shortcut from Hoskyn Channel to Calm Channel. It lacks the strong currents found at nearby Surge Narrows. This dredged passage has a least depth of six feet and currents of only two knots. There are rocky patches at the southern entrance. These are easily identified in the clear water. Two sets of range markers mark the passage. Foul ground and shoals are easily avoided if the boat is lined up correctly to match the targets. Passage at half tide or a bit more is recommended. If traversed before actual high water, the shoals are easier to identify.

East Quadra Island
[3312, 3538, 3539]

★ **Crescent Channel (17):** Enter from Hoskyn Channel keeping Bold Island to starboard. There are rocks lying along the Bold Island shoreline. The land in this harbour is private. Anchorage is recommended about halfway into the southwestern channel in five fathoms.

★ **Village Bay (18):** In settled weather, there is fair anchorage near shore, straight in or to the right of the islet near the head.

Walk-around: A trail leads to Village Bay Lake. This lake connects with both Main Lake and Upper Main Lake, making it the longest freshwater passage in the Gulf or Discovery Islands. Good canoeing and bird watching.

★ **Mould's Bay (19):** This bay is tucked in at the northwestern end of the Breton Islands. Anchorage is fair in 25-35 feet of water on a rocky bottom. It is open to southerly winds. Old timers know the bay as once home to a lady who put great store in the readings from her crystal ball.

★ **Heriot Bay (20):** Heriot Bay is a natural harbour where the maximum tidal change is 4.6 m. On the shore to port when entering, lies the historic Heriot Bay Inn and Marina. This bay is the terminus for the Quadra Island-Cortes Island ferry. Southwest of the ferry terminal is the public wharf and concrete loading dock. Anchorage is found out from the public float in the harbour and in nearby Drew Harbour behind the shelter of Rebecca Spit. Taku Resort & Marina is also in Drew Harbour. Kayaks and bikes, both rented locally, are a fun way to explore the area. Groceries are available at Heriot Bay Tru-Value (free delivery to docks). 250-285-2436. A coffee shop, liquor store, post office, and gift shop are located in the same building.

Heriot Bay Inn & Marina: {50° 6' 10" N, 125° 12' 40" W} Moorage, reservations suggested. 15/30 amp power in some slips, gas, diesel, propane, water, showers, laundry, limited wifi (no cellphone reception), RV/tent sites, cabins, rooms, gift shop, restaurant/pub. 1-888-605-4545, 250-285-3322. VHF 66A.

Quadra Island Harbour Authority: Moorage (commercial vessels have priority, rafting is mandatory), 30 amp power, water, showers, garbage disposal, portable toilet, 1.5 ton winch, boat launch, pay parking. 250-285-2855.

★⚓ **Drew Harbour & Rebecca Spit Marine Park (20):** This beautiful area, on the eastern side of Quadra Island, contains many attractions. Drew Harbour and Rebecca Spit Marine Park are southeast of Heriot Bay. Anchorage is good in the bight near the tip of the spit, as close to shore as depths will permit. Anchorage is also possible near the head of the bay in 25-35 feet of water on a mud bottom. Buoys and facilities at the head of the bay

Visit us at boattravel.com

are private. Many artists have found this spit with its white sand and picturesque trees the perfect subject for paintings and photographs. Park acreage is the strand that stretches from the tip of the spit to its base. A sandy beach invites sunbathers and beachcombers. There is also a road for walking, a launching ramp, picnic sites, and pit toilets. No fresh water. Canada Day celebrations are held on the spit each July 1st with a fireworks display in the sky above Drew Harbour.

Taku Resort & Marina: {50° 6' 06" N , 125° 12' 26" W} Moorage, 30/50 amp power, water, laundry, showers, ice, garbage, wifi, lodging, RV/tent sites. Onsite SUP/kayak rentals. 250-285-3031, 1-877-285-8258. VHF 66A.

Read Island
[3312, 3537, 3538, 3539, 3541]

★ **Read Island:** Anchorages are in Hjorth Bay, behind the King Islets, Boulton Bay, Evans Bay and Burdwood Bay. The sites of Surge Narrows and Evans Bay have small public floats. Read Island Provincial Park is located on the southern tip of Read Island. No potable water, wilderness camping allowed. A rustic trail leads to Rosen Lake for fresh water swimming. The park is excellent for wildlife viewing. Bald eagles often nest in the tall trees.

Lake Bay: This bay is deep and offers only limited anchorage with some shelter from northwesterlies.

★ **Hjorth Bay (21):** This picturesque bight and islet, on the west side of Read Island, has anchorage in five fathoms near the head. It is open to west winds, but provides protection in a southerly.

★ **Boulton Bay (22):** This narrow indentation adjacent to Sheer Point has lovely, but limited anchorage near the head. A steep bluff to port cuts off westerly winds, however, the spot is open to the south.

Surge Narrows (23) (15): [3537] This is the site of a public float, post office, and a few homes. Local boats tend to fill the public float so expect limited transient moorage. The post office is open Monday, Wednesday and Friday. In summer, small, informal community farmers markets are sometimes held on Wednesdays on the dock.

★ **Evans Bay (24):** Several indents form anchorages. North winds hit the southern portion of the bay, near the public float. The float has about 100 feet of moorage. When approaching the float, keep the spar buoy to port. The buoy sits on a shoal. South and east winds enter the central portion of the bay. Bird Cove has some anchorage. Many of the nooks have shallow, drying flats at the heads. The niche farther into Evans Bay has anchorage behind the islets. The unnamed arm of Evans Bay that extends farthest north is the preferred anchorage although it is open to southerly winds. Anchor in the center opposite an old wharf in 30-40 feet of water, or near the steep bluffs in 50 feet of water. The old wharf is private and belongs to a kayak lodge. This second anchorage provides a haven of early shade when hot summer sun bakes the bay. This bay is shallow. Swimming is recommended as the water is clear and warm. Shellfish farms extend from all of the beaches except the mud beach in the center. To prevent fecal contamination of the shellfish, please do not walk your dogs on the beach, and use your holding tanks. There is a road access north of the kayak lodge and connects through to Surge Narrows on the west side of Read Island.

★ **Burdwood Bay (25):** Protection in northwesterlies is possible here. Prior to 1900, in the days of the pioneer logging families, Burdwood Bay was the site of Wylie's Hotel and a murder. Anchor in small basin behind chain of islands in southern part of the bay.

Hill Island: Private. Closed to the public.

North of Read Island
[3312, 3539, 3541, 3542]

★ **Rendezvous Islands (26):** Temporary anchorage is possible in a small bight on the southernmost island, behind a small islet and in an unnamed bay on the west side of the middle island. The latter niche has a private float and dolphins extending from shore, restricting space. Lodge on NE Rendezvous Island.

★ **Maurelle Island (27):** Anchorages are not obvious along much of the shore as the hillsides are steep and rocks hide the tiny bights. The vicinity west of Antonio Point is recreational reserve land and includes two small anchorages. Florence Cove, about halfway up Hole In The Wall also offers anchorage.

★ **Surge Narrows Provincial Park** is located on the south end of Maurelle Island. Its name is a reminder of the resulting tidal rapids when the two flood tides converge. High tidal runs make a tide book a "must have" in these waters. No facilities are found at the park. Fishing and wilderness camping are possible. Kayakers should be experienced and exercise extreme caution.

★ **Toba Inlet (28):** This 20 mile inlet is very deep and the mountains rise 8,000 feet above the turquoise blue glacier-fed waters. The Inlet makes an abrupt turn east at Brem Bay. Logging operations are found in the northwest part of the bay. Some sheltered anchorage is found in the northeast corner. Near Brem River, Cutthroat fishing is reported to be excellent during May, June, and July, and the Coho runs are September to October. The fjord ends at the estuary of the Toba River. There are numerous waterfalls in the Inlet during the spring and early summer. Water is available from a spring that empties into the inlet about two and one half miles south of Brem Bay. There is a resort on the mainland at the mouth of the inlet, north of Double Island.

Toba Wilderness Marina: {50°19'.08"50"N 124°47'43.12"W} Overnight moorage only (by reservation), 30/50 amp power, water, restroom, showers, ice, garbage drop (one bag/day), trails & wifi included in rate. Services/amenities are for overnight guests only. Secure boat watch available in the summer. Inquiries@TobaWildernessMarina.com. Call on VHF 66A when approaching.

Snow Bay: Known locally as Blue Ice Bay, this spot provides glacial ice for summer boaters. This bay is in a niche marked 13 fathoms on the chart, on the south side of the inlet. Some anchorage is possible at the head of the bay in the northwest corner; not much protection from winds. Large horse flies may be pests.

Bute Inlet Lodge   Photo © Greg Gage / greggagephotography.com

★ **Frances Bay (29):** Lying off Raza Passage, this bay, also known as Fanny Bay is very exposed to east winds coming down Toba Inlet. Anchorage is not recommended due to logging cable and refuse that foul the bottom. The view of Pryce Channel to Toba Inlet is memorable. Two miles southwest of Frances Bay is Church House. Its landmark church is no longer standing.

★ **Bute Inlet (30):** [3542] Milky, glacier fed waters flow in this inlet. The green water is caused by the mineral content of the glacier run-off. Winds are unpredictable in the inlet and may rise suddenly. The prevailing summer wind pattern is an inflow during the afternoon and an outflow at night and early morning. The inlet is deep, but the bottom often shoals rapidly near shore. Homathko Estuary Provincial Park is at the head of the Inlet. Use caution when approaching as mud flats created by the Homathko River extend far out into the Inlet. The water is very silt laden and visibility is almost nil. The park has no facilities and moorage near the park may be difficult due to extensive mud flats and shallow water. There are drying flats at the mouths of the Inlet's other rivers as well. Lines ashore may be helpful when anchoring. It may be possible to tie to log booms. Temporary anchorages are found close to the drying flats in Waddington Harbour, Orford Bay, and the bights below Purcell Point and Fawn Bluff. Leask Cove, the little bay beneath Fawn Bluff, is the site of the Founders Lodge at Fawn Bluff, a private 340-acre complex complete with concrete dock, lodge, guest house, and lake cottage that is currently for sale. The niche below Leask Lake has a 14 fathom reef near the entrance of a stream that empties from the Lake. Locals boast about the cod fishing over this reef. There is also world class fly fishing found on the Homathko and Southgate rivers. These rivers may rise suddenly and are very difficult to access safely and caution is advised. A lodge is located at the mouth of the Bear River about 10 miles from the head of the Inlet. Mt. Waddington, British Columbia's highest peak is found 31 miles inland from the head of Bute Inlet.

Bute Inlet Lodge: {50° 49' 55" N 124° 57' 18" W} Moorage with lodging only. 250-850-1500.

View from the Dent Island Lodge Photo © Dent Island Lodge

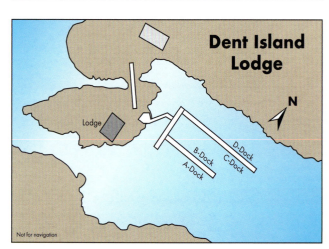

Stuart Island
[3312, 3541, 3543]

Yuculta Rapids (32): [3543] See current tables for Seymour Narrows, B.C. These rapids are in the narrows north of Kellsey Point. The currents are strong and quick to rise. Floods south, ebbs north. The best time to traverse is within one-half hour of slack at Gillard Passage. If planning to continue on west through the passage, arrive before high water slack in order to coordinate times with slack waters at Gillard and Dent Rapids. The *British Columbia Sailing Directions* recommends that low powered small craft headed northwest should approach Yuculta Rapids about one hour before turning to ebb in order to take advantage of a back eddy along the Stuart Island shore until off Kellsey Point. Then cross to the Sonora Island side where there is a prevailing northerly current. This should allow time to transit Gillard and Dent Rapids before the ebb current reaches full force.

Gillard Passage (33): Recommended passage is south of Jimmy Judd Island, between Jimmy Judd and Gillard Islands. Flood currents reach eight knots; ebb ten knots, at springs.

★ **Stuart Island & Big Bay (31):** This attractive island hosts hundreds of fishing vacationers each season. It is home to a number of large, private facilities and docks, as well as one public dock and an airplane float that are situated behind the pile and plank breakwater. Moorage reservations for the public dock are recommended either by phone or email (250-202-3625, stuartisland1964@outlook.com). When entering the bay, head to the public float with signage and a white shade. Surges and tidal currents in the bay amplify boat wakes. A courteous throttle-down upon entry is advisable. Dogs are welcome but must be kept on a leash. Big Bay has a post office, liquor store, gift shop, and a small general store. For anglers, fishing gear and licenses can be purchased or fishing guides arranged at the store. Signs from the store lead to a great hiking trail into Eagle Lake where there is a large population of cutthroat trout. Two floats at the lake are perfect for a summer swim. The annual *Salmon Enhancement Dinner and Auction*, featuring live music, is always a popular event with boaters, please call 250-202-3625 for information on date/time. The other settlement on Stuart Island is at the southwest tip of the island, next to Harbott Point Light. The floats there are privately owned. ⚓

Stuart Island Community Dock: {50° 22' 31" N, 125° 08' 38" W} Moorage for boats to 150' (reservations recommended), water, showers, laundry, wifi, picnic tables, BBQ, ice. Access to walking trails. No power on docks. Profits support salmon enhancement and community programs. 250-202-3625. VHF 66A.

DENT ISLAND LODGE
"The Place To Be"

This hidden treasure is nestled on the islets between Dent Island and the mainland, just a few minutes west of Big Bay. Be sure to make your reservation at this premier resort when cruising north of Desolation Sound this season. Dent Island, well known for outstanding service and friendly staff, upscale marina and facilities. Come and see what all the talk is about!

Amenities available to moorage guests include:

- Breakfast, lunch and dinner service with full bar and a selection of local BC and international wines
- Concrete docks
- 30, 50 & 100 Amp power
- Abundant supply of fresh water
- 24 hour hot tub, sauna, laundry, and showers
- Fitness room featuring Techno Gym equipment
- Experienced local fishing guides and vacuum packing facility
- Ice and garbage disposal
- Wireless Internet throughout property and marina
- Scheduled Sea Plane and Water Taxi Services
- All inclusive cabin packages are available

250.203.2553
www.dentisland.com | info@dentisland.com | VHF 66 A

Visit us at boattravel.com

DISCOVERY PASSAGE Chapter 16 Page 207

Arran Rapids (34): These occur where Cordero Channel joins Bute Inlet. See current tables for Seymour Narrows, B.C. Floods east, ebbs west. Both flood and ebb tides can reach nine knots.

Fishermans Landing and Lodge: {50° 24.411' N, 125° 10.592' W} Moorage, new concrete docks, 30/50/100/200 amp power, filtered water, wifi, laundry, showers, lodging, ice, fishing charters. Permitting underway for fuel and restaurant. Call ahead in 2024 to check on availability. 250-202-0187. VHF 66A.

Dent Rapids (35): [3543] The flood current flows east (095°) and ebbs west (290°). The time of slack water at Dent is identical with that at Arran Rapids. A whirlpool called the Devil's Hole is created at peak flow south of the south point of Little Dent Island. Maximum flood is nine knots, ebb is eight.

★ **Dent Island Lodge:** {50° 24' 48" N 125° 11' 07" W} A superb British Columbia salmon fishing lodge and wilderness vacation resort. Dent Island Lodge is also a preferred BC boating destination with marina and amenities including exercise gym, hot tub, sauna, wireless internet, restaurant and lounge. Come into the area slowly, and after landing you can register at the main office. Site maps and information handouts are available at check-in. See our advertisement on page 206. Open June through September. Internet: www.dentisland.com. E-mail: info@dentisland.com. Mailing address: P.O. Box 8, Stuart Island, British Columbia V0P 1V0. Telephone: 250-203-2553. VHF 66A.

Essential Supplies & Services

AIR TRANSPORTATION
To & from Washington
Kenmore Air 1-866-435-9524
NW Seaplanes . . . 425-277-1590, 1-800-690-0086
San Juan Airlines. 1-800-874-4434
Seattle Seaplanes 1-800-637-5553
To & from Islands/Vancouver
Air Canada 1-888-247-2262
Corilair 250-287-8371, 1-888-287-8366
Pacific Coastal 250-926-6690, 1-800-663-2872
Vancouver Island Air. 250-287-2433

BOOKS / BOOK STORES
Evergreen Pacific Publishing 425-493-1451
The Marine Atlas. 253-872-5707

BUS TRANSPORTATION
Campbell River Transit 250-287-7433
Greyhound Campbell River. 1-800-661-8747
Islandlink Bus . . . . www.islandlinkbus.com

COAST GUARD
Victoria Coast Guard Radio. . . . . VHF 16, 83a
. . . . 1-800-661-9202 (In BC) or 250-363-6611
Victoria Marine Traffic 250-363-6333
Marine Distress, Search & Rescue
. . . . 1-800-567-5111 (in Canada) or 250-413-8933
Cell Phone (limited to select providers) . . . *16 or #727

FERRY INFORMATION
B.C. Ferries: . . . . 1-888-223-3779 (B.C.)

FISHING /SHELLFISHING INFO
24 hr Recorded Notifications (Pacific region only)
. . . . .1-866-431-3474 or 604-666-2828
Recreational Licensing 1-877-535-7307
Observe, Record & Report Line (fisheries violations)
1-800-465-4336 or 604-607-4186 (Pacific region only)

FUELS
Brown's Bay Resort: Gas, Diesel
. . . . 250-286-3135 VHF 66A
Discovery Harbour Fuel Dock: Gas, Diesel
. . . . 250-287-3456 VHF 66A
Heriot Bay Inn: Gas, Diesel, Propane
. . . . 250-285-3322 VHF 66A

GOLF COURSES
(These courses are accessible from moorage and have rental clubs available)
Quadra Island Golf (9-hole) 250-285-2811
Campbell River Golf & Country Club. . . . 250-287-4970
Storey Creek: Campbell River 250-923-FORE

GROCERY STORES
Heriot Bay Tru-Value Foods 250-285-2436
Real Canadian Superstore Campbell River
. . . . 250-830-2700
Stuart Island Community Dock. 250-202-3625

HAUL-OUTS
Ocean Pacific Marine Supply: Campbell River
. . . . 1-800-663-2294
Travelift Campbell River 250-203-2635

HOSPITALS
Healthlink BC (Nurse Helpline) 811
Campbell River 250-850-2141
Qudra Island Medical Clinic 250-285-3540

LIQUOR STORES
Campbell River
Heriot Bay Tru-Value Foods 250-285-2436
Quathiaski Cove

LODGING
April Point Resort & Marina. . . . 250-286-1102 VHF 66A
Brown's Bay Resort 250-287-7108
Dent Island Lodge: Dent Island 250-203-2553
Heriot Bay Inn: Quadra Island. 250-285-3322
Taku Resort & Marina. 250-285-3031

MARINAS / MOORAGE
April Point Marina . . . . 250-286-1102, VHF 66A
Brown's Bay Resort . . . . 250-286-3135 VHF 66A
Campbell River Harbour Authority 250-287-7931
Coast Marina. . . . . 250-204-3900 VHF 66A
Dent Island Lodge 250-203-2553
Discovery Harbour Marina . 250-287-2614 VHF 66A
Evans Bay: Read Island
Fishermans Landing & Lodge. 250-202-0187
Freshwater Marina (Monthly) 250-286-0701
Heriot Bay Inn: Quadra Island. . 250-285-3322 VHF 66A
Heriot Bay: Government Dock. 250-285-2855
Owen Bay: Sonora Island
Quathiaski Cove Harbour 250-285-3622
Stuart Island Community Dock 250-202-3625 VHF 66A
Surge Narrows Public Float
Taku Resort & Marina. 1-877-285-8258
Toba Wilderness Marina. . . . . inquiries@
. . . . TobaWildernessMarina.com VHF 66A

MARINE SUPPLY
Ocean Pacific Marine Supply: Campbell River
. . . . 1-800-663-2294

RAMPS
Brown's Bay Resort 250-286-3135
Freshwater Marina, Campbell River 250-286-0701

Ocean Pacific Marine Supply . . . 1-800-663-2294
Quadra Island: Quathiaski Cove, Heriot Bay, Rebecca Spit

REPAIRS
Altech Diesel, Campbell River. 250-286-0055
Bill Howich RV & Marine 250-287-9514
Carmac Diesel: Campbell River. 250-287-2171
Ocean Pacific Marine: Campbell River
. . . . 250-286-1011

RESTAURANTS
April Point Resort 250-286-1102
Narrows Floating Restaurant/Brown's Bay Resort
. . . . 250-287-3521
Dent Island Lodge 250-203-2553
Heriot Bay Inn: Quadra Island. 250-285-3322

RV SITES / TRAILER PARKING
Brown's Bay Resort 250-287-7108
Heriot Bay Inn: Quadra Island. 250-285-3322
Taku Resort & Marina. 250-285-3031

SCUBA SITES
Rock Bay Marine Park, Maud Island
Octopus Island Provencial Park

SEWAGE DISPOSAL
Campbell River Harbour Authority: Pump
. . . . 250-287-7931, VHF 66A

SPORT FISHING
Dent Island Lodge 250-203-2553

TAXI
287 Taxi (Campbell River) 250-287-8294
Quadra Island 250-205-0505

TOWING
C-TOW .1-888-419-CTOW

VISITOR INFORMATION
Campbell River 250-286-6901
. . . . www.campbellriver.travel
Discovery Island Online Guide
. . . . www.discoveryislands.ca/guide
Quadra Island . . . . www.quadraisland.ca

WEATHER
NOAA Weather Radio WX-1, 162.55
Environment Canada Weather Line. 250-339-9861
VHF WX-1, 21-B

Chapter 17: Johnstone & Queen Charlotte Straits & Adjacent Islands

Chatham Point to Hope Island. Loughborough, Knight, Kingcome, & Drury Inlets; Thurlow, Minstrel, Cracroft, Gilford, Malcolm, Broughton Islands; Port McNeill, Port Hardy.

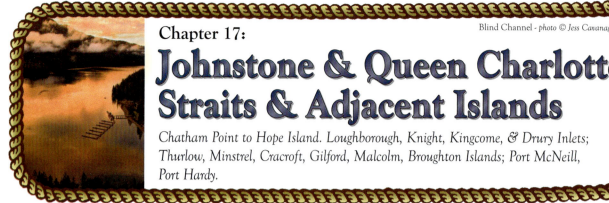

Blind Channel - photo © Jess Cavanagh

Symbols

[   ]: Numbers between [ ] are chart numbers.

{   }: Numbers & letters between { } are waypoints.

★ Recommended destinations, facilities, and services.

⛰: Park, ⛵: Boat Launch, ▲: Campgrounds, 🚶: Hiking Trails, ⌇: Picnic Area, 🚲: Biking, 🤿: Scuba

★ See "Important Notices" between Chapters 7 and 8 for specific information on boating related topics such as boating safety, weather, U.S. & Canadian marine radio use, Vessel Traffic Service, security zones, Canadian & U.S. Customs, etc. Due to changing regulations, call ahead to verify latest customs information.

Seasonal Changes: Many resorts in this area are seasonal or have seasonal hours. May to September is high season. During the off season it is wise to call ahead to check on availability of fuel, provisions, and other services.

Introduction

★ North to Johnstone and Queen Charlotte Straits: Adjacent to the Johnstone and Queen Charlotte Straits are some of the most beautiful and secluded anchorages south of Alaska, and some of the best salmon, cod, halibut, snapper, and prawn fishing anywhere. These are the waters of adventure and exploration. Each year more boaters are lured northwestward, beyond Desolation Sound and Discovery Passage, to the Johnstone Strait and adjacent waters. Here, it is still possible to experience the solitude of having the only boat anchored in one of the hundreds of bays. People who enjoy a leisurely pace-of-life and who are pleased to share a story about the islands, past and present, await. It is impossible to spend much time here without coming away with memories of beautiful scenery and with a respect for the spirit and perseverance of those who live here and those who provide facilities and services for visiting boaters.

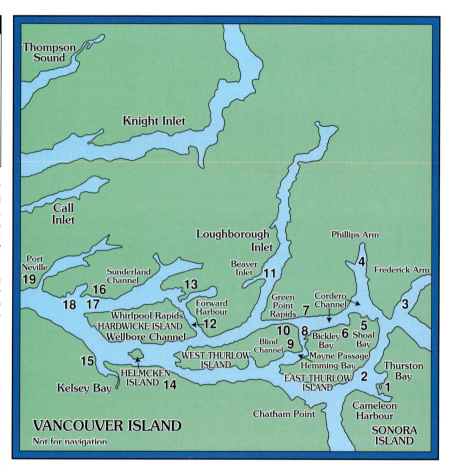

Chart List

Canadian Hydrographic Charts:
  3312, 3515, 3543-3548, 3549, 3564

Marine Atlas Vol 1 (2018):
  Pages 33, 35-41

Evergreen Cruising Atlas: Pages 7-18, 21-29, 31, 34, 35, 42, 43

★ **Facilities:** Each year more facilities are adding power and conveniences. For these out-of-the-way marinas and resorts, bringing in and holding provisions, especially cold items, is an expensive and troublesome task. Power is generated at a much higher cost than power purchased in more populated areas. The season is extremely short. Whenever you pay for overnight moorage at a privately owned float, buy groceries or fuel from these remote provisioners, or dine on a memorable meal prepared by skillful and dedicated chefs, you are supporting the continuance of these "trading-post" style operations.

Weather Patterns: The most common climate from Minstrel Island northward is low clouds and fog in the morning, with clearing in the afternoon. The climate is often refreshingly cooler than the extreme heat of Desolation Sound. The weather is a bit more uncertain than it is to the south. There are more overcast and rainy days. Fog often wraps itself in angel-hair-like chains and patches around the islands and into the fjords. Radar is a significant advantage.

Currents, Winds, & Larger Tidal Changes: A number of the waters in this section are in, or near, passages where current and turbulence can be strong. There is no reason to fear these passages, provided they are traversed with a knowledge of the currents and a respect for the force of the waters. Passage at, or near, slack water is prudent. Tide and current tables list the rate and direction of flow, as well as the slack water times for most navigable passages in the region. Some of the more notable rapids and maximum runs are: Yuculta Rapids, six-seven knots; Dent Rapids, eight-nine knots; Green Point Rapids, seven knots; and Whirlpool

Visit us at boattravel.com

Rapids, seven knots. If adequate planning is done, overfalls and whirlpools can be avoided completely. When in the vicinity of a whirlpool, pass on the side which is moving in the same direction as the boat. This will usually push the boat away from the pool, rather than into it. Even with a faster boat, the speed of the water itself is not the problem, but the overfalls and whirlpools caused by that speed.

Both currents and winds must be considered. The ebbing tide flows northwest; the flooding tide southeast. However, when there is wind, the current that opposes the wind will greatly increase the seas. Since the ebb currents are stronger than the floods (because of residual water), the seas will be the worst with a northwest wind opposing an ebbing tide. For an example of strategic planning, see Wellbore Channel (12). Because of tidal ranges of up to 20 feet at springs, additional allowances for overnight or low tide depths must be made.

Insurance Coverage: Many U.S. boat policies designate 51° (Hope Island) as the northernmost geographical limit. Contact your insurance company or broker regarding an endorsement for extended cruising. Also note that policies commonly restrict cruising dates. May-Sept 15th are often guidelines.

Johnstone Strait
[3543, 3544, 3545, 3546, 3564]

Shoal Bay   *Photo © David Stanley*

★ **Johnstone Strait:** This 54 mile long body of water stretches from Chatham Point to Blinkhorn Peninsula. Eric Borgfjord, manager of the Port of Kelsey Bay and avid boater shares the following: "In the summer months, Johnstone Strait develops a persistent WNW wind, (just like the Juan de Fuca Strait does). The average wind speed for these westerly's is 15 to 25 Knots. The closest automated weather station is Fanny Island (5 Nautical miles from Kelsey Bay) and it reports hourly on WX 1 or WX 8. The reports are also online at http://weather.gc.ca/marine. Click on Pacific-South Coast, then choose 'Johnstone Strait.

The tide heights range from 0 feet to 17 feet with the mean tide about 9 feet. The largest changes occur near the solstices. The average tidal current is 5 knots for both the flood and ebb tides with currents exceeding 8 knots near the solstices. The currents do not change when the tide is at its highest or lowest point, the currents change direction approximately two hours later.

Local Tip: Use the Canadian Tide & Current Tables Volume 6 and divide the current speed for Seymour Narrows in half for a close approximate of the current speed in the area. Also when BC is on Daylight Savings Time the time of the current change is within 15 – 20 minutes.

When the currents are opposing the westerly wind the area does develop large tidal rips where the wave & swell height can exceed 5 meters (15 feet). The cause of the large tide rip is a reef on the Hardwicke Island side combined with several underwater humps in the middle of the strait and the outflow of the Salmon River.

Local Tip: if you are NW bound in Chancellor Channel and there is about a 2 foot wave height (or higher), the wave height in the main strait is usually three times higher.

For shipping lane information, see the Canadian Hydrographic publication, Sailing Directions, PAC 203, and VHF 71.

Lower Johnstone Strait: This is the narrowest portion of Johnstone Strait. Uncomfortable conditions can occur when westerly winds are against even a minimal tide. The old timers' adage is, "Never go to Kelsey Bay on any westerly wind." Perhaps even better would be to avoid the Chatham Point to Kelsey Bay route entirely and stay in the more protected waters of inside channels whenever possible. If traversing Johnstone Strait, after Ripple Point, the waterway narrows to a width of one mile for the next nine miles. Emergency anchorage can be found at Turn Island, between Turn and the East Thurlow Island shore. Currents and winds can enter, but it provides shelter and an indication of conditions on the strait. Another emergency anchorage is in the Walkem Island group, in about four fathoms of water, in the bight on the south side of the larger island and between the two islands. Avoid the bare rock. Little Bear Bay, on the Vancouver Island shore opposite the Walkems, ends in a drying flat with limited protection in southeast winds. Past the Walkem Islands, Mayne Passage joins Johnstone Strait and provides a route to the more protected waters. Continuing northwest in Johnstone, Knox Bay on West Thurlow Island has some protection as a temporary anchorage. Logging operations may be present in the area. On the Vancouver Island shore, limited protection can be found behind the islet in Bear Bight in Humpback Bay and in Palmer Bay, the narrow indentation west of Humpback Bay. Don't be surprised to find logs filling Bear Bight. A drying flat extends from the mouth of the creek in Humpback Bay. Currents become stronger near Camp Point and can reach six knots with heavy tide-rips. Check the Tide and Current tables for Race Passage and Current Passage. See current tables for Seymour Narrows, B.C. Tidal streams run strongly through these passages, attaining five knots on the ebb and flood in Current Passage and six knots on the ebb and flood in Race Passage. Eddies and swirls are numerous. Do not traverse this vicinity when an ebb (westerly flowing) current meets a west wind. Steep-sided Vere Cove, on the west end of West Thurlow is wide open to the west, however shelter is found in a southeast wind. Anchorage is deep (60' plus), but it is also out of the current.

A Vessel Traffic Separation Scheme is in effect. Using Ripple Shoal and Helmcken Island as natural obstacles to divide eastbound from westbound traffic, it is recommended that eastbound traffic use Race Passage and westbound traffic use Current Passage. Boats finding it necessary to do otherwise are asked to notify others in the area by using VHF 71. Caution advised in the area of Ripple Shoal, east of Helmcken Island. Pass north of the shoal. For more on the Helmcken Island vicinity, see chapter 14.

Nodales Channel
[3312, 3539, 3543]

Nodales Channel (1): This waterway runs north and south, connecting Discovery Passage to Cordero Channel. The flood flows north. Rips can form off Johns Point at the north end where flood streams meet. Aquaculture operations are on the west shore. Good anchorages are found in bays on both sides of the channel.

★ **Cameleon Harbour:** Although open to northwest winds, anchorage is possible in this harbour. Marshy land extends from the port side at the head. Anchor favoring the starboard side near the head.

★ **Handfield Bay:** This picturesque, small bay in the northern part of Cameleon Harbour offers good protection and anchorage in depths of 15-25 feet. There is a drying shoal to port in the entrance and a small islet to starboard. The bay shallows quickly. The head is a drying flat. Handfield Bay is part of Thurston Bay Provincial Marine Park.

Walk-around: Ashore, the old orchard can be explored. A path, west of the creek, leads to Anchorage Cove at the south end of Thurston Bay.

★ **Thurston Bay Provincial Marine Park:** Avoid the rocks near the entrance. This undeveloped marine park includes land at the north and south ends of Thurston Bay. Anchorage Cove, at the south end of the bay, is a lovely, lagoon-like spot, with trees down to the water's edge. Depths are adequate for overnight. At the head, there is a marshland, with a drying flat. Other anchorage spots are in the northern portion of Thurston Bay, behind Block Island.

Walk-around: It is possible to walk to the site of the old B.C. Forest Service station and to follow trails and old roads in the vicinity. An unmaintained trail leads about 2.4km/1.5 mi inland to Florence Lake, where there is great trout fishing.

★ **Hemming Bay (2):** This bay is across Nodales Channel from Cameleon Harbour. Entry is made between a point on the south and the Lee Islands.

Page 210 Chapter 17 JOHNSTONE & QUEEN CHARLOTTE STRAITS

Shoal Bay Public Dock — Photo © Viktor Davare

Cordero Channel
[3312, 3543]

Cordero Channel: Beginning in the vicinity of Gillard Pass, this waterway extends in a westerly direction approximately 20 miles until it meets Chancellor Channel.

★ **Frederick Arm (3):** Gomer Island lies at the southeast entrance to Frederick Arm. About three quarters of the way up the inlet, past Egerton Creek is a floathouse and there are logging operations at the head. Good anchorage in ten fathoms is found at the northwest corner of the head of this arm. Open to south winds. It is possible to enter scenic, four mile long Estero Basin in a dinghy. Because of the rapid tidal flows in and out of this uncharted basin, do so at or near high slack tide. The entrance is blocked at low tide. Locate Estero Peak, over 5,000' in height, and let your imagination work to see what it resembles.

Favor the Pinhorn Islet side to avoid Menace Rock that lies in the center of the outer bay. The indentation continues inland, past shoals and islets to port. Anchorage is possible in an area tucked behind the islets, but the bottom is rocky and holding is insecure. The extreme inner bay, which includes a saltwater lagoon, may be explored by dinghy. Much of the land around the lagoon is private property, as is that at the head of the bay where a cabin is found.

★ **Phillips Arm (4):** Anchorage is possible in Fanny Bay or in ten fathoms near the head. The arm shoals quickly and the bottom is covered with weeds and is hard to see. Fanny Bay is a center for logging operations and booms are present. A log boom tie up may be possible.

Visit us at boattravel.com

★ **Shoal Bay (5):** Shoal Bay will be offering transient moorage in 2023. There is a pay box with instructions at the base of the ramp for all boaters to place the moorage. The grounds at Shoal Bay will be available to all overnight moored vessels. In our efforts to reduce environmental impact and heal the land, there is no land access for occupants on anchored boats. Anchored boats are invited to access the beach only. When docking at Shoal Bay please place your boat so as to leave as much room as possible for future boats. Give a helping hand to your fellow boaters. Rafting is allowed and mandatory when necessary. Mark and Cynthia, residents here for more than 20 years have invested much time and resources in revitalizing the creek and local forest and they invite all moored boaters to access the grounds and experience the off-grid lifestyle. Power at Shoal Bay is all generated by a combination of solar and micro-hydro. There are laundry facilities, showers, wifi, a public deck with chairs with a deservedly famous view up Philips Arm to the Coastal Mountains. A you-pick and you-weed vegetable/flower garden, multiple trails, and beautiful hand made ceramics are all on offer. There will be wood-fired pizza and bread experiences this summer and 4pm happy hours at the community deck for moored boaters and our cottage guests. Fresh baked baguettes will be offered on special days.

The Cottages at Shoal Bay: {50° 27' 28" N, 125° 22' 1" W} Moorage is at the public dock. No general food service, catering is available with advance notice-yacht club orders welcome! Cabins, laundry, showers, wifi, organic garden. 250-287-6818.

Walk-around: Hike up the mountainside to a scenic lookout point and an old mine site about an hour away from the bay. The trailhead, (not accessible during high tide), starts at the beach along the creek near the Shoal Bay Lodge & Pub. Volunteers are clearing old trails, expanding the possibilities to explore the area.

★ **Bickley Bay (6):** This bay is on the north shore of East Thurlow Island. There is anchorage on a mud bottom in 20-35 feet of water near the head. Peel Rocks are charted. Favor the port side when entering. The bay is open to northwest winds and currents invade the area. Anchor dragging has been noted.

Cordero Lodge: {50° 26' 49" N, 125° 27' 11" W} Located just east of Greene Point Rapids, tucked in behind Lorte Island. Closed in 2017. At press time, it is unclear if services will be offered in 2024.

Walk-around: A good trail leads to an old logging road, and eventually to a lake.

Tallac Bay (7): Three rocks lie to starboard near the entrance. Pass either side of the rocks and then favor the western portion of this small niche. Set the hook as the boat is aimed toward the logging road on the hillside and then reverse. Tie to shore for overnight stability.

★ **Cordero Islands Anchorage (8):** There is anchorage behind this picturesque group of islets. Good holding in mud bottom and protection from all but strong northwest winds. Avoid big clumps of kelp lining the cove.

Crawford Anchorage (8): The bottom of this anchorage is rock and anchoring is difficult. Rocks lie southeast of Mink Island and in the passage off Erasmus Island. In the niche on Erasmus Island, marked by a "2" on the chart, there is fair anchorage on the west side. A taut tie to shore may add to the security of the ground tackle. There are shoals in the bay. It is possible to walk along the logging road.

Blind Channel Waterfront View Photo © Jess Cavanagh

West Thurlow Island
[3312, 3543]

★ **Mayne Passage (9):** Floods north, ebbs south with currents to five knots at springs. See current tables for Seymour Narrows, B.C. Mayne Passage connects Johnstone Strait with Cordero Channel.

★ **Blind Channel Resort:** {50° 24.50' N, 125° 30.03' W} Blind channel Resort is a full service marina offering accommodations, marine gas and diesel, a well-stocked general store, public laundry and shower facilities. There are seven 80' finger slips accommodating boats in excess of 100'. Enjoy lunch on the seaside patio or a fabulous dinner in the Cedar Post Restaurant. Forest trails lead from the resort offering a chance to see some of the monumental old growth trees that once dominated the coast. Friendly and professional dock staff will assist you to bring your boat into the marina. Scheduled flights from Seattle, Vancouver, and Campbell River, as well as on-site water taxi service and tours. See our advertisement on this page. Email: info@blindchannel.com. Internet: www.blindchannel.com. Address: Blind Channel Resort, Blind Channel, BC V0P 1B0. Telephone: 250-949-1420, 1-888-329-0475. VHF 66A.

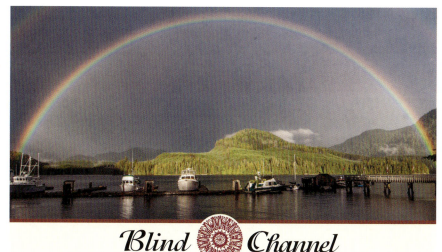

Blind Channel RESORT

TIE UP A favourite destination for boaters for generations. Stay on your boat, or in deluxe rental accommodations overlooking the harbour. Full service marina with 15, 30, and 50 amp power, marine gas, diesel, and propane, filtered spring water, and Wi-Fi. General store offering groceries, gifts, liquor, fishing tackle, ice, a post office and much more. Laundry and shower facilities.

DINE OUT A memorable dining experience, showcasing the owners' German heritage and creative use of fresh, local ingredients. Stunning views from all seats.

EXPLORE Tranquil hiking trails. Guided fishing, wildlife and marine adventure tours. Water taxi service.

info@blindchannel.com   VHF Channel 66A   1-888-329-0475
www.blindchannel.com

Chapter 17 JOHNSTONE & QUEEN CHARLOTTE STRAITS

Celebrating Canada Day at Blind Channel Resort Photo © Jess Cavanagh

Walk-around: The Big Cedar Trail rises to an elevation of 200 feet in less than 1/2 mile. The round trip walk takes about 45 minutes. The Forest Management Trail extends almost a mile from the Big Cedar Trail and intersects a logging road, making extended cross island hikes possible. The Viewpoint Trail is shorter and easily walked in a 30 minute round trip. Maps available at the store.

Knox Bay: This indent into West Thurlow has given shelter from northwesterlies to many boaters. Favor the port side near the head. Although much of the shore is foul, the ledge drops quickly and there is good holding bottom in 45-50 feet of water.

Greene Point Rapids (10): See current tables for Seymour Narrows, B.C. These rapids run to seven knots at springs. Slack water is predicted to occur about one hour and 30 minutes before slack water at Seymour Narrows. Slower boats will want to plan passage within about one-half hour before or after slack. When east bound on a strong flood current, avoid heading toward Erasmus Island.

★ **Loughborough Inlet (11):** [3543, 3555] This inlet stretches inland for 18 miles. A stream cascades down the bank making fresh water accessible near the entrance to the inlet about one-half mile in from Styles Point. Depths are too great for anchorage in most of the inlet. There are no public floats. There are anchorages in Beaver Inlet and Sidney Bay. Log boom tie-ups may be possible in Heydon Bay.

★ **Beaver Inlet:** This inlet lies to port, a short distance in from the entrance to Loughborough Inlet. It is open to northwesterlies because the wind funnels through the draw at the head. There is anchorage at the head, southwest of Dickson Point. Large tidal changes occur in this vicinity. Beware of sunken logs that can foul your anchor when going too far toward the head of the inlet.

★ **Sidney Bay:** Adjacent to Beaver Inlet, Sidney Bay has anchorage at the head in 30-40 feet of water.

Shorter Point: A tiny bight into West Thurlow Island, on the east side of the point, opposite the entrance to Wellbore Channel, has some shelter when there are winds and rips on Chancellor Channel. Anchor close in to the head. The bottom drops quickly to 50 feet.

Wellbore Channel (12): This is the inside passage to the northwestern end of Hardwicke Island. The advantage of using this and Sunderland Channel is that it avoids both Race and Current Passages in Johnstone Strait, where an ebbing tide and northwest wind can cause heavy chop near Helmcken Island and Earl Ledge. If you pass through Greene Point Rapids near high slack when traveling north, you will have the aid of the northbound ebbing tide behind you for several hours all of the way through Wellbore Channel and Whirlpool Rapids. If winds are from the west, however, the wind will be against the ebbing tide and produce heavy rips, especially in Chancellor Channel. For Greene Point Rapids, see current tables for Seymour Narrows, B.C.

Whirlpool Rapids: Currents do not exceed seven knots. The whirlpools form south of Carterer Point on flooding tides and north of this point on ebbing tides. Heading south, if you pass Whirlpool at low water slack, you can cruise 30 miles to Stuart Island with the flood tide pushing you. You will probably have to wait at Dent Rapids until one half hour before high water before starting through. For Whirlpool Rapids, see current tables for Seymour Narrows, B.C.

★ **Forward Harbour & Douglas Bay (13):** [3544] A narrow entrance off Wellbore Channel leads to a long, wide indentation with high mountains and a snowy peak as a backdrop. A small bight to port in the entry, near a grassy knoll, is large enough for one or two boats. Douglas Bay, within Forward Harbour, is the popular anchorage. The crescent-shaped beach encircles an anchorage area that can accommodate 10-15 boats. Rocky shelves extend from shore. Depths average 30-40 feet before a quick drop to 50-60 foot depths. Holding bottom is only fair close in and anchor dragging is not uncommon. The one boat to one anchor rule is prudent here. The holding bottom appears to be better farther out, in the deeper water. Bears are often seen walking the beach. A portion of the land between Douglas Bay and Bessborough Bay is a BC Parks Conservancy.

Walk-around: Hike across to Bessborough Bay's beautiful white sand beach. Tied-on plastic bottles mark the trail. It might be prudent to bring along a cowbell or pan and large spoon to use as a noisemaker to ward off the bears.

Sunderland Channel: Eight miles in length, this passageway leads west-southwest to join Johnstone Strait. When rounding Althorp Point at the head of Wellbore Channel, it is possible to judge sea conditions on Johnstone Strait. If conditions are choppy entering Sunderland Channel, the chop on Johnstone can be expected to be heavier. Bessborough Bay, at the east end, has anchorage and a lovely white sand beach, however, this is open to the west. Jackson Bay on the north side of Topaze Harbour has anchorage and is the site of a logging camp. A bay, east of Gunner Point, has temporary shelter in strong westerlies.

Yorke Island: If passing on the south side, look up the hillside to see remnants of two large gun batteries built in 1939 to guard against any enemy ship that might transit Johnstone Strait. Most of the Island is surrounded by barbed wire, except for two spots. The first is a bight off the channel on the southeast side between Hardwicke and Yorke Islands. Once the site of a World War II dock, today only pilings remain. Because of the continual current and openness to southeasterly winds, make sure your anchor is firmly set and continually monitor the weather to avoid rough conditions in the Strait. Courtenay Bay also offers shore access. Some trail work has been done, but most areas are overgrown or off limits. National Defence conducted a search for live explosives, but the potential is still there. The Island is also home to unique plants and animals, including an endangered species of snail, so be respectful of where you walk.

Helmcken Island (14): This island divides the waters of Johnstone Strait. Current Passage and Race Passage border the island. Billygoat Bay offers an anchorage with protection at {50' 23.92 N; 125 ' 51.99W}. Billygoat Bay North, {50' 24.23 N; 125 ' 52.55W}, is another possibility but it is not safe in ESE winds.

Race and Current Passages: Currents near Earl Ledge run three to six knots in Race Passage and three to five knots in Current Passage. See current tables for Seymour Narrows, B.C. When there is a west, northwest, or southwest wind in Current Passage, tide rips can be amplified and become dangerous. Be alert for commercial vessels that frequent these passages. Race Passage and Current Passage are confined spaces for large vessels. All vessels should monitor the CCG Designated Vessel Traffic channel VHF 71 in addition to VHF 16.

Kelsey Bay (15): Heavy rips form off Kelsey Bay in the vicinity of Earl Ledge in north westerly winds. East of Kelsey Bay, a small bight behind Peterson Islet provides some shelter in westerlies. Another possibility is Nichols Bay on Hardwicke Island, {50' 26.18 N; 125 ' 58.05W} (this bay is not safe to ESE winds). When entering Kelsey Bay from the ESE (Race Passage or Current Passage), keep the sunken freighter breakwater and the log booming grounds on your port side. The entrance to the DFO Small Craft Harbour is behind the wave-reduction breakwater. The entrance to the Sayward Futures Dock is approximately 100 metres (300 ft.) north, behind the cargo pier.

Kelsey Bay Harbours: {50° 23′ 27″ N, 125° 57′ 28″ W} The Kelsey Bay area consists of two unrelated moorage areas. One harbour is the only government dock between Campbell River and Port McNeill in Johnstone Strait. The other harbour site is the Port of Kelsey Bay Wharf which is privately owned and operated by Sayward Futures Society, a non-profit society. A store with snacks and gifts

Visit us at boattravel.com

JOHNSTONE & QUEEN CHARLOTTE STRAITS Chapter 17 Page 213

is located here. No fuel is available in Kelsey Bay (Lagoon Cove or Blind Channel Resort are the nearest places for fuel). Visit the Info Centre for maps to the many hiking trails – from a short walk through the Estuary, to a 23 km on Bill's Trail up to Mt. H'Kusam. Whale watching tour companies claim this area is the number one spot in the world for Orca sightings so keep an eye out and you may spot a passing pod. Do not anchor near the harbours, booming grounds or Salmon River Estuary. There are swift currents and uncharted debris from booming activities. Two boat launches are in the vicinity of the harbours, as is an RV campground with showers, for a fee. A waterfront cafe that serves "Ocean Wise" sustainable seafood has a dock for boating patrons.

Government Small Craft Harbour: Moorage for vessels to 65', 20/30 amp power, water, restroom, showers for a fee, garbage bins. First come-first served, no reservations, rafting mandatory. Tie up and Harbour Manager will collect fees. 250-282-0178.

Sayward Futures Dock: No recreational boat moorage available, the finger float is closed until further notice. The cargo pier is for cargo vessels only (water depth is 30' at low tide). Convenience store with art gallery, Tourist Info Centre (both close in winter). 250-282-0018.

Sayward: The Village of Sayward is about a 15 minute walk from Kelsey Bay Harbours. There is no taxi, but you may be able to hitch a ride with a friendly local. Sayward has a post office, police station, ambulance, fire department, health clinic, school, and library. There is an outdoor tennis court and a recreational centre with gymnasium, exercise/weight room, pool, and hot tub. A small park in town offers RV parking, campsites and pathways amid a picturesque pond setting. Hwy 19 is approximately 11 km/7 mi inland from the Harbours. Adjacent to the highway is the Junction store, a scheduled bus service link to Campbell River or Port Hardy, a restaurant and pub, an art museum and ice cream parlour. There are several B & B's, RV sites, and motels in the surrounding area. Time your visit for the *Canada Day Parade & Events* on July 1st or *Oscar Daze* on the August long weekend featuring a ball tournament, beer gardens, food, a dance and lots of fun (proceeds benefit the Sayward Health Centre). Mid June is the famous *Kusam Klimb Endurance Event*, a timed race up the mountain – not for the out of shape or the faint-hearted!

Central Johnstone Strait
[3544, 3545, 3564]

McLeod Bay (16): This bay provides temporary anchorage when escape from a west wind is desired. Head in toward the logging road and equipment storage.

Tuna Point (17): A small bay tucked in behind Mary Island provides temporary protection during westerlies. Logs may be stored here.

Blenkinsop Bay (18): Blenkinsop Bay has a shallow flat at the head, preventing moorage close enough to shore to find protection from winds.

★ **Port Neville (19):** This seven mile long inlet is used when westerlies invade Johnstone Strait. Anchorage with good holding ground is possible along the west shore opposite the public float, however, strong tidal currents swirl through this area. The public wharf at approximately {50° 29' 35" N, 126° 5' 13" W}, has a float with some moorage. No businesses or services are available. A post office established here in 1895 was the oldest continually operated post office in BC until closing in 2010. Caretaker is on site in summer. Farther into the inlet, Robber's Nob is the site of First Nations petroglyphs. Look on the northwest side. Anchorage is possible southwest of the point. Logging operations may be present in the area. Baresides Bay is recommended for temporary anchorage, but move off shore a little to avoid logs and debris. Clamming and crabbing are possible in the inlet.

Broken Islands (20): These islands lie at the entrance to Havannah Channel. See current tables for Seymour Narrows, B.C. Many boaters know of the Broken Islands because, after rounding them, heading northwest, the waters are more sheltered from sea and winds on the Johnstone Strait. Not to be confused with the Broken Islands of Barkley Sound, on the west coast of Vancouver Island.

Forward Bay & Boat Bay: These indentations, between the Broken Islands and Growler Cove, across from Robson Bight, have some protection in west winds. In Forward Bay, anchor north of the Bush Islets. If attempting to enter Boat Bay, watch for the foul area near the entrance. You can listen to Captains of whale watching cruises talking to each other on VHF 77.

Havannah Channel Vicinity
[3312, 3545, 3564]

★ **Port Harvey (21):** Port Harvey, off Johnstone Strait offers several anchorages, as well as Port Harvey Marine Resort found behind Range Island at the head of the inlet. Barges supporting commercial operations may be anchored offshore opposite the resort. Avoid anchoring in that area. It is possible to anchor north-northwest of the Mist Islets and near the head, north of Range Island. The bottom is mud. Depths range from 15-35 feet. This harbour has some protection from southerly winds and northwesterly winds near Tidepole Islet. Good "gunkholing" by dinghy to site of a meadow. On the western shore there is a private float and house located here supporting logging activities. A drying gorge with large rocks separates Port Harvey from Cracroft Inlet. Do not try to navigate this area.

The Port Harvey Marine Resort, established in 2009, was operated by owners George and Gail Cambridge. Despite setbacks (including having to rebuild and restore services after a barge that held the restaurant, store, restrooms and laundry sank in 2015) they continued to extend a warm welcome to boaters to their resort in the "middle of somewhere". Boaters returned year after year to enjoy the Cambridge's hospitality, the fun events (including the big Canada Day Party) and, of course, to taste the famous, fresh baked cini buns. In 2018 George passed away doing what he loved at Port Harvey. He is missed, not only by his family and friends, but by the boating community. The Resort was sold and is currently closed.

Boughey Bay (22): Anchorage, open to north winds, in 30-40' of water on a mud bottom. Strong southeast winds also tend to funnel into the bay.

★ **Matilpi (23):** Anchor in about 30 feet behind the Indian Islands, off the white shell beach, which marks the site of a midden and an abandoned First Nations village. Approach from the north, around Indian Islands. Outside, in Chatham Channel, lies Tom Islet, nicknamed *Irishman's Hat* for its fluffy green underbrush and feather-like cedar trees.

★ **Burial Cove (24):** This cove was once used as a First Nations burial ground. Anchorage in this bay on the east side of East Cracroft Island is open to winds from the south. Round Island offers some protection. Anchor near the center in 25-40' depths. The head of the bay is a drying flat. Watch for aquaculture operations in the area.

★ **Call Inlet (25):** Steep-sided and deep, Call Inlet extends ten miles into the mainland. A 50' float is reported to be near the head on the north side. Winds tend to funnel down the inlet. The Warren Islands, near the entrance, are reminiscent of the lovely Harmony Islands in Hotham Sound. Anchorage in settled weather is possible in small bights and in the channel, with a tie to shore, in depths of 25-40 feet of water. Streams enter the channel separating the islands at two green grass beach sites. George Cambridge, in the past, shared that the head of Call Inlet can get to 76° F in the summer, which makes for nice swimming. Across the inlet at Squire Point, there is an anchorage in 35-50 feet of water. This bay is open to south winds.

Chatham Channel (26): [3545, 3564]. This five mile long waterway is easier to navigate than the charts indicate. Line up with the range markers. Targets are lighted at night. See current tide table for Sitka, Alaska and current tables for Seymour Narrows, B.C. Kelp extends from both shores. If traversing at a low tide, the kelp will branch out to mid channel and it will be necessary to go through some of it. This should not restrict passage. Strongest current is at Root Point. Flood currents flow to the southeast and ebb to the northwest. Currents do not exceed 5 knots at springs. High water slack is 45 minutes before high water slack at Seymour Narrows. Low water slack is one hour and 25 minutes before slack at Seymour. Watch for No Wake Signs.

★ **Cutter Cove (27):** This long, shallow cove is a popular anchorage, but open to winds. Favor the north shore in westerly winds and the south during easterly winds. The bottom is fair holding mud, but watch for dragging if winds blow up. The head of the cove is a drying flat. At high tide it is possible to explore a series of swamp-like channels which indent inland.

The Blow Hole (28): Separating Minstrel Island from East Cracroft Island, this passage is named for the wind which sometimes funnels through it. Rocks are marked by kelp in summer months. Favor mid-channel, slightly on the Minstrel Island side.

★ **Minstrel Island (29):** There is moorage at a float on the eastern side of Minstrel Island at the northwest end of Chatham Channel just south of Knight Inlet. The property onshore is private. When the Union Steamships made regular stops, Minstrel Island was the region's entertainment center. Minstrel Island and nearby Sambo Point and Bones Bay were said to have received their names because of the traveling minstrel shows that once played here ("Sambo" and "Mr. Bones", played by white actors in Blackface were frequent characters in these shows during the 1800's). At one time, the Minstrel Island Resort and it's pub, now closed and deteriorating, sold more take out beer than any other pub in B.C. Known for being prime grizzly bear country, this area is also rich in other species of wildlife.

Chatham Channel Cabins: {50° 35' 29.08" N, 126° 15' 32.4" W} (2 miles from Knight Inlet & 1 mile from Minstrel Island). Limited shallow water moorage for lodging customers only, water available at dock but no other services. Cabins, tent camping, post office, kayakers welcome. 778-222-2444.

★ **Cracroft Inlet (30):** This inlet contains anchorages, floathomes, lagoon, and a drying gorge that leads to Port Harvey. Passage through the gorge

Chapter 17 JOHNSTONE & QUEEN CHARLOTTE STRAITS

is not possible as a log jam blocks the way and at low tide a good portion of Cracroft Inlet is dry or extremely shallow with rocks. Lagoon Cove Marina is located on the north end of E. Cracroft Island, just south of Minstrel Island. To reach the marina from Chatham Channel, enter through the Blow Hole at the south end of Minstrel Island. From Clio Channel, enter between Perley Island and Farquhason Island. Anchorages are in Lagoon Cove (south of the marina) and behind Dorman and Farquharson Islands in the channel that separates West Cracroft Island from these islands. Be watchful of logging cables fouling both the east and west sides of the inlet. Note the covered rocks on the chart. The inner cove may be explored by dinghy. A nominally priced Shore Pass is available for boaters who anchor in the cove, allowing them to dingy ashore and access the Marina's amenities.

Lagoon Cove Marina: {50° 35.90" N, 126° 18.80" W} Moorage, 15/30 & 2x30 amp power (with your own splitter connection), water, gas, diesel, showers, fishing supplies, gifts, WiFi, open all year. 778-819-6962. VHF 66A US Mode.

Knight Inlet
[3515, 3545]

★ **Knight Inlet (31):** Over 70 miles in length, this narrow, steep-sided fjord is one of the longest indentations into mainland British Columbia. The waters are deep and anchorages are few and far between. Winds are frequently strong, funneling down or up the inlet. It can be difficult to find a nearby place to hide. There is no lack of beautiful scenery, waterfalls, good fishing and prawning, and abundant wildlife, including bear and moose. There are anchorages near the mouths of many streams. Stern ties to shore are necessary to maintain position if anchored on a rocky bottom or if anchored in a narrow niche where swinging is not desired. The bottom is difficult to see in the milky water. A great amount of fresh water from the Klinaklini and Franklin Rivers at the head flows well into the inlet. Much of the surface water is fresh. South and west winds blow up the inlet and, if strong, the rate of the current may also be affected as much as two knots. There are logging camps in the inlet. Generally speaking, the camp operations do not welcome visitors, except in an emergency.

★ **Port Elizabeth:** Anchorages in Maple and Duck Coves provide shelter. The head of Duck Cove is a drying flat. There is another anchorage next to an islet north of Duck Cove. Avoid rocks which extend from shore. They show as a single rock on the chart, but are really a chain of rocks. Log storage and aquaculture operations occupies much of the anchorage.

Tsakonu Cove: Anchorage is fair with some protection from west winds. Hills behind the head are low. Since the bottom is hard and rocky, some dragging is possible.

★ **Sargeaunt Passage:** High hills border each side of this narrow channel. There is anchorage on both sides of the narrows. Favor the east side when anchoring. Fishing boats often use this passage.

Hoeya Sound: Anchorage at the head is possible, but questionable.

★ **Siwash Bay:** Anchorage is along the east shore.

★ **Glendale Cove:** This cove has anchorage near the head and is home to one of the largest concentration of grizzly bears in B.C. Knight Inlet Lodge is located here. See current table for Sitka, Alaska.

Ahnuhati Point: A niche has anchorage and views of waterfalls. There is limited anchorage near the valley, next to the point.

Wahshihlas Bay: Logging operations are located here. Limited anchorage. One possibility is the mouth of the Sim River.

Clio Channel Vicinity
[3545, 3546]

Clio Channel: Clio Channel runs from Minstrel Island to Nicholas Point on Turnour Island where it splits into Beware Passage and Baronet Passage. Possible anchorage.

★ **Bones Bay:** This large bay is the site of an abandoned cannery. The ruins are dangerous, trespassing is not permitted. Anchorage is found near islets on the south shore.

★ **Bend Island:** This island is connected to West Cracroft Island by a drying ledge. There is anchorage behind the island on either side of the ledge. The northern basin is deeper and has protection in westerlies.

★ **Potts Lagoon (32):** This inlet offers anchorage on a mud bottom. The inner bay is somewhat shallow. Large tidal changes must be considered for overnight depths. A lagoon and meadow may be visited by dinghy at high tide. A cove on the east side near the entrance to Potts Lagoon is a bit deeper and also has good anchorage. A grassy patch at the head identifies this anchorage. When proceeding to the inner harbour, the channel is to starboard of the island that is connected to shore by a drying ledge. In the inner harbour, the anchorage basin is opposite the picturesque ruins of a pier in 25-30 feet of water at high tide. Onshore there is an old logging camp and logging road. The island gives some protection in winds. Strong winds can enter this area.

Baronet Passage: Baronet Passage is often used to and from Blackfish Sound and Alert Bay. Tidal currents flood to the west and reach three knots. The vicinity of Walden Island should be navigated cautiously. Preferred passage is the West Cracroft Island side, keeping an eye out for the kelp-marked rock located off the island's southwest tip. Zigzag to pass west and around the kelp. Bell Rocks and strong currents are hazards at the west end, however, the passage is not difficult.

Beware Passage: [3545] Beware Passage is what its name implies. It separates Turnour and Harbledown Islands. Good visibility is necessary to navigate this passage. Do not attempt in fog. There are rocky patches and shoals extend from some of the islets. If traversed at slack on a low tide, with a rising tide, it is not difficult to see the hazards. Approach very slowly. Use depth finder. Tide floods east, ebbs west attaining two-three knots.

Karlukwees: A ruined pier remains at this abandoned First Nations village. There is a steep shell midden and a nice beach. No-see-ums are prevalent, and bears may be a hazard.

Caution Cove: There is anchorage on Turnour Island. Caution Rock dries four feet and marks the entrance. Two other rocks are farther in off the head. The cove is open to northwest winds and logging operations are often present.

★ **Beware Cove:** Also off Beware Passage, Beware Cove, open to southeast winds, has more protection in northwest winds. Anchorage off the northeast end of Cook Island is possible over a mud bottom in 13 to 19 feet.

Canoe Passage: This drying passage separates Village Island from Turnour Island. Winds will funnel through the narrow pass.

★ **Native Anchorage:** There is anchorage that is open to westerlies at the west end of Canoe Passage. East winds can also funnel into the bay. It is a large, attractive basin with anchorage depths of 25-50 feet of water. One anchorage is in the northwest corner. Note shoaling at the head.

★ **Village Island, Mimkwamlis (33):** Charts and maps often call the abandoned village on this island "Mamlilaculla", but that is not an accurate designation or spelling. The actual name is Mimkwamlis, meaning "village with rocks and island out front." Village Island is protected under the Heritage Conservation Act and belongs to the Mamalilikulla First Nation who continue to work on their management plan, including building associated infrastructure for visitors. Currently, there are no services, or public facilities. For permission to go ashore, please contact the Band Office at 250-287-2955. There is a fee of $20 per person to visit the Island. No camping, no fires and please stay out of the buildings. Chief Sumner requested that we let boaters know that the Mamalilikulla First Nation assumes no responsibility for damage or injury to person or property while visiting 'Mimkwamlis and will not be held liable. There is anchorage in the bay, behind the rock islets, in about 25 feet of water. The village's empty structures are decaying, including a fallen totem pole, and the area is greatly overgrown.

★ **Compton Island:** This is First Nations Reserve land. For permission to go ashore, contact the band office at 250-287-2955.

★ **Crease Island:** Anchorage, with protection from west winds, can be found in the bay between the southeast corner of Crease Island and Goat Island. Use chart #3546. Enter north of Goat Island.

★ **Farewell Harbour, Berry Island:** Good anchorage is found in six fathoms on a soft bottom. Farewell Harbour Lodge {50° 36' 3.6" N, 126° 40' 12" W} is a private facility. In favorable weather, anchorage is also possible in the channel between Berry Island and Sarah Islet.

★ **Harbledown Island/New Vancouver:** This Island is home to New Vancouver, a Da'naxda'xw First Nation Village also known as Tsatsisnukomi, located at Dead Point. There is a dock for moorage. Anchorage (and aquaculture operations) can be found between Harbledown and Mound Islands and in the niche behind Dead Point. Parson Bay is wide and open to west winds. Temporary anchorage near the head in settled weather only. The village's small store sells convenience items, local artwork, and take-out hot dogs and burgers. Other local services include tent campsites, some lodging, laundry, and showers. On your visit, explore one of the nearby trails or take a tour of the traditional Big House. With advanced notice, a food sampling can be added to the tour.

Blackfish Sound & Blackney Passage (34): Blackfish Sound, famous for good fishing grounds, connects the southeast portion of Queen Charlotte Strait with Blackney Passage and Johnstone Strait. Currents run to five knots, flooding east, ebbing west. The flood flows north and south of Hanson Island and meets near the south end of Blackney Passage causing a strong tidal race in mid-channel. Strong rips occur near Egeria Shoal and Cracroft Point. Fishing is good off Bold Head and Cracroft Point. Blackney Passage is a very busy shipping channel, with large tows and cruise ships. Traffic on VHF 71.

Visit us at boattravel.com

★ **Hanson Island (35):** This island is on the north side of the western extremity of Johnstone Strait. There are anchorages in Double Bay, as well as a resort with moorage and fuel. Enter on the west side of the bay to avoid the rock and reef at the entrance. Anchorage is also found in six fathoms in the adjacent bay, inside Sprout Islet. These bays offer protection in summer westerlies and south winds.

★ **Growler Cove:** Fishing boats flock to this haven on the western tip of West Cracroft Island. It is known as Pig Ranch Cove by the fishermen. Limited shelter for pleasure craft. The head dries, and rocks are off both shores. Depths are 30-45 feet.

Queen Charlotte Strait
[3547, 3548]

Queen Charlotte Strait: This strait connects Johnstone and Broughton Straits with Queen Charlotte Sound. It is about 15 miles wide, if traveling from Wells Passage to Port McNeill. Although Johnstone and Queen Charlotte Straits have similar weather conditions most of the time, that is not always the case. There may be small craft warnings on one, while the other strait is calm. Flood tides set east-southeast and ebb west-northwest. See current tables for Seymour Narrows, B.C. The prevailing summer wind pattern on a clear morning, is a rising breeze from the northwest, rising in the afternoon and calming just before dark. When checking Alert Bay, WX 1 for the wind reports, note the Alert Bay, Pulteney Point, Scarlett Point and Pine Island readings.

Retreat Passage
[3515, 3546, 3547]

Retreat Passage: Retreat Passage separates Bonwick from Gilford Islands. There is an unusual magnetic disturbance near Meade Bay which can throw off a compass as much as 18 degrees.

⚓ **Broughton Archipelago Marine Park:** This park is a rich, scenic wilderness area with more than 300 islands and abundant marine and bird life. Totaling more than 11,750 hectares, this is B.C.'s largest marine park. The park stretches from Fife Sound on the north to Indian Channel on the south, and from Blackfish Sound on the west to Baker Island/Bonwick Island on the east. The uneven boundary lines dodge in and around some islands, while excluding others. Included are many small islands which have nooks and crannies perfect for secluded anchorages, making it a haven for canoeists and kayakers. There are no moorage buoys and fresh water is difficult to find. Two ancient pictographs, one on Berry Island's northend and one in Village Channel, are reminders of the ancestors of the Kwakiutl First Nation who inhabited this area thousands of years ago.

★ **Bonwick Island (36):** There are several anchorages in indentations off Retreat Passage. The first, Carrie Bay, has anchorage in 25-35 feet of water. Grebe Cove, farther north, shoals gradually to a depth of about 20 feet near the head. This is good anchorage, however the head is rather low and winds can enter. Dusky Cove and Betty Cove have tricky anchorages in settled weather only.

★ **Waddington Bay:** This bay offers outstanding anchorage with views of wildlife. Approach through the northern channel that passes through the Fox Group. The bottom is thick mud and depths are 30-40 feet. Anchorage is good in the bay to starboard upon entry. An uncharted rock is reported in this bay - watch for kelp. There is good anchorage along the southeast shore east of the island that is connected by a drying ledge. This bay is especially good for exploration by dinghy.

★ **False Cove:** There is anchorage at the extreme head of the cove where water flows in from a mountain lake. Open to west winds.

★ **Health Bay:** This bay on Gilford Island has small islets in the entrance and a brilliant green backdrop. There is good protection from southerly winds, but not from westerlies. The best anchorage is at the five fathom mark on the chart, in toward the head. Health Lagoon dries, except for an entrance channel. The brightly painted houses, about 1/2 mile northwest of the bay, are part of a First Nations village.

★ **Crib Island & Sunday Harbour (37):** The small bay on the north side has anchorage with protection in most winds. Sunday Harbour, bordering the southern shore, has been described beautifully in M. Wylie Blanchet's book, *The Curve Of Time*. Sunday Anchorage is a shallow, wide harbour that is open to winds. Anchor in settled weather only. The thick kelp on the bottom makes anchoring questionable, if at all. An indentation into the north shore of Crib Island is more protected.

Tracey Island & Monday Anchorage (37): Monday Anchorage separates Tracey and Mars Islands. It is a large bay with anchorage in several locations. Since it is open to the west, both west and southeast winds will affect anchorage. Anchor in 35-45 feet of water off the northern or southern shores, depending on wind conditions.

Fife Sound
[3515, 3547]

★ **Blackfish Archipelago:** Some refer to this area as Blackfish Archipelago, although no official charts show such a designation at present. We have used the official chart names throughout the area.

★ **Eden Island & Joe Cove (38):** There is anchorage in several unnamed bays behind Fly Island. The larger, thumb-shaped bay is the best. It is protected from winds and, although shallow, can accommodate several boats. Depths are 15-30 feet on a sticky mud, seaweed covered bottom. Adjacent to this bay is another cove that offers anchorage. The head is a drying shelf and large drying rocks restrict too deep an entry into the bay. Joe Cove, on the southeast side of Eden Island, nearly back-to-back with the other bays, has anchorage in about 30-50 feet over mud. Another anchorage, with protection in westerlies, is in an unnamed bay on the south side of Eden Island. Avoid rocks which extend off the port shore at the entrance. The head is a drying flat. The best anchorage is off those flats, but is open to the east.

★ **Cullen Harbour (39):** The most protected anchorage is northeast of Olden Island, in six fathoms. Anchorage in a second cove, on the east side, is open to swells from Queen Charlotte Strait.

★ **Booker Lagoon (39):** Enter through Cullen Harbour and round the tip of Long Island. Avoid the reef off the northeast side of Long Island. The channel narrows and minimum depths are 21 feet in mid channel. Because of strong currents which run in excess of four knots, entry is recommended near slack water. Strong flood current with back eddies along shore create conditions where boats swing a lot at anchor. There is good sheltered anchorage on mud in each of the four arms.

★ **Fife Sound (40):** Fife Sound opens into Queen Charlotte Strait and is frequently used when traveling to and from Port McNeill, Sointula, and Alert Bay. Hazards are few in this deep waterway. There is deep anchorage, with fair protection from west winds, behind Wicklow Point. Farther in, a bight behind Pemberton Point can be used for anchorage.

Indian Passage (40): This narrow, deep passage is nearly parallel to Fife Sound. It is often used as a short cut from Echo Bay and outer islands. Current floods east, ebbs west. There are anchorages in a small bight on the southeast shore of John Island and in the narrow indentation into Davies Island. Old Passage, separating Insect and Baker Islands, is passable and scenic. At times the currents are stronger in this passage than in alternative waterways.

★ **Deep Harbour (40):** Pass either side of Jumper Island when entering this long harbour. Aquaculture pens obstruct the central part of the bay. The extreme head, which looks on the chart to have anchorage, is, unfortunately, blocked by a string of logs attached to shore by cables. An old

Cullen Harbour Photo © Patricia Robertson

Echo Bay Marina and Lodge aka K'wa<u>x</u>walawadi Photo © Patricia Robertson

log skid marks the site of the blockage. Therefore, anchorage is limited. There is a niche on the south shore east of a rock shown on the chart. Check depth and overnight tide when anchoring.

Baker Island: When cruising in the Ragged Island vicinity off northern Baker Island, be on the lookout for Pym Rocks. They are barely under the surface and are hazardous.

★ **Shoal Harbour (41):** There is anchorage on a good holding mud bottom to the right or left of the entry passage. Depths are about 50 feet. To starboard, there is anchorage behind the small islet at the location shown by a three fathom designation on the chart, or temporary anchorage in the inner bay marked by one fathom on the chart. This inner bay is too shallow to be a recommended overnight anchorage. In addition, the entrance to this inner cove is restricted by a drying shoal at a 5.6' tide at Alert Bay. Swamp water often colors the water a dark brown.

Bill Proctor's Museum: Between Shoal Bay and Echo Bay. Excellent to visit. Admission by donation. Hours are 10am-5pm.

★ **Echo Bay (42):** This attractive bay is on the northwest side of Gilford Island off Cramer Passage. Anchorage is not recommended, because the holding bottom is fickle. On the west side of the bay is Echo Bay Marina and Lodge that can be reached using the call sign "Echo Bay Marina". Amenities include a post office, grocery store & fuel dock.

★ **Echo Bay Marina and Lodge aka K'wa<u>x</u>walawadi (formerly Pierre's at Echo Bay):** {50° 45'04.7 N, 126° 29'49.2 W} The resort is open year-round, moorage, 15/30 amp power, gas, diesel, propane, showers, laundry, lodging, post office, gift shop, store, Wifi. 604-973-1802. VHF 66A.

Walk-around: A walk to Scenic View is a great way to spend the afternoon. Plan on at least 3 to 4 hours for the round trip. Start at the old school yard. Walk up the hill, following the water lines to a dam. Continuing past the dam, cross the bridge. From this point the trail veers to the right. Watch for fluorescent markers that lead to a stone wall. Climb over the stone wall onto the logging road and turn left. The lookout is about 4-5km from here, much of it an uphill climb. Your effort will be rewarded with fantastic views from Cramer Pass to the Burdwood Group, including Fife Sound and Penphase Pass.

★ **Echo Bay Marine Park:** The wharf at Echo Bay is unsafe and is closed until further notice. The park is home to a Great Blue Heron rookery. It is also popular with kayakers. Day use picnic area, pit toilet, no water, wilderness camping.

★ **Scott Cove:** [3515] Site of a logging camp and floathouse operation. When entering, check the chart and avoid Powell Rock off Powell Point.

★ **Viner Sound (43):** There is anchorage, open to west winds, in indentations on either side near the head.

★ **Laura Bay (44):** When approaching this cove, avoid the long shoal which extends from Hayle Point. Tucked behind Trivett Island, this bay has adequate anchorage for three to four boats. There is a small islet with a shoal out from it. Enter to port of the islet. An anchorage is north of the islet in 30 feet of water on a zero tide at Alert Bay. This bay is protected from north winds. An uncharted rock lies near the passage that separates Trivett Island.

Burdwood Group (45): This large group of islands lies near the western entrance to Tribune Channel. Anchorage is a matter of gunkholing and is not recommended, except in very settled weather. Salmon farm has been removed.

Tribune Channel (46): Tribune Channel extends along the entire northern and eastern border of Gilford Island to join Knight Inlet. It is used by those who wish to take the inland route from Minstrel Island to Fife Sound.

★ **Watson Cove:** This bay lies off Tribune Channel. A rock lies to starboard at the entrance. Favor the steep hillside to port. Inside, the cove is well protected, except in strong westerlies. Anchoring depths are 40-50 feet at high tide. The shallower anchorage might have room for one or two boats. Anchorage depths vary widely near the head.

★ **Wahkana Bay:** High hills overshadow the entrance channel. The bay is narrow and winds in toward a cut at the head. Anchorage is possible along the shore at the spot marked "5" on the chart. The indentation to port at the head has shoals for some distance off the creek and then a quick drop. The cove to starboard at the head has anchorage in depths of 60-70 feet of water on a 13 foot tide at Alert Bay. It is difficult to get close to shore because of shoaling. It is possble to hike upstream from the creek to a small lake.

★ **Kwatsi Bay:** [3515] When a westerly is affecting Watson Cove, this bay has protected moorage with waterfalls and a stream providing background music. Because of the depths, it is necessary to anchor close to shore in the corners of the bay. A shore tie might be advised. On the east end of the bay, old slide debris extends underwater for 100 feet or so off the shore. Onshore a trail leads to the waterfall.

Kwatsi Bay Marina: {50° 52' N, 126° 15' W} Marina is closed.

Kingcome Inlet & Vicinity
[3515, 3547]

★ **Simoom Sound (47):** Named after her Majesty's Ship *Simoom*, this inlet, entered between Deep Sea Bluff and Pollard Point, has several anchorages in McIntosh and O'Brien Bays. Deep Sea Bluff is noted as a good fishing ground. Buoys marking commercial prawn fisherman traps may be hazards in the vicinity of Louisa Islet. Aquaculture operations may be present to port, after rounding Esther Point.

★ **McIntosh Bay:** After passing Hannant Point, good anchorage and scenic views of Bald Mountain are found in McIntosh Bay. Caution advised regarding shoals and drying rocks which, at low tide, offer platforms for those swimming in the warm water. Anchorage is also found in other indentations into the shoreline.

★ **O'Brien Bay:** Located at the head of Simoom Sound, well protected anchorage with plenty of room to swing is found. The bay's northwest corner offers anchorage at about 50 feet on mud bottom.

★ **Shawl Bay (48):** This popular bay is on Wishart Peninsula, west of Simoom Sound. It is the site of some float houses, and a marina, currently being renovated.

Shawl Bay Marina: {50° 50.90' N, 126° 33.60' W} Sold, under new management. No services currently. Call for 2024 updates. 250-483-4022. VHF 66A.

★ **Moore Bay (49):** A shallow, narrow, but navigable passage separates outer Shawl Bay from

Moore Bay. Two rocky areas off Gregory Island dictate favoring the mainland side of the passage. Minimum depth is zero at a three foot tide at Port Hardy. The Moore Bay Recreation Site includes a ramp and small dock (no vessels over 14' in length), walking trails, picnic tables, several benches, an outhouse, and a fire-wood lean-to. The improvements have been crafted from the huge trees felled during storms. The bay in the southeast corner behind the small island offers protected anchorage in eight fathoms of water, soft bottom. 🚶⛺

★ **Gregory Island:** Views looking up Kingcome Inlet and across Thief Island to the 2,500 foot high Mount Plumridge are spectacular. Coves on the north side have good views and provide anchorage. Milky green waters make it difficult to see the shoaling near shore. Favor the center of either bay in 30-40 feet of water at a five foot tide at Port Hardy. These bights are open to north-northeast winds.

★ **Kingcome Inlet (50):** Long and deep, this inlet stretches 17 miles to the Kingcome River delta. Most of the inlet is too deep for anchorage. Anchorage Cove on the southeast shore, and a small bight to port and inside the entrance to Belle Isle Sound, offer anchorage. If the wind is blowing down Belle Isle Sound from the west, the small bight behind the point, one half mile south of the entrance offers protected anchorage in ten fathoms on a soft bottom. Another anchorage is in an unnamed bay adjacent to Reid Bay. This bay has a rocky bottom with depths of 20-30 feet. A ridge at the head cuts off northwest winds, but the bay is open to the southeast. There are some uncharted rocky patches off the Magin Islets, near the entrance to this bay. Wakeman Sound is a center for logging operations in the region. There is no satisfactory anchorage in Wakeman Sound. There is a small float on the north side of Kingcome Inlet, one half mile past Petley Point. This serves Ukwanalis Village and the logging camp at Petley Point. It is available for temporary moorage. It is possible to dinghy up the river to Ukwanalis Village, described in the book, *I Heard The Owl Call My Name*, by Margaret Craven.

Sir Edmund Bay: A drying rock is a hazard off Hayes Point. Preferred entrance is the channel east of Nicholls Island. Anchorage is possible off a grassy flat in the western corner and behind drying rocks in the southeast corner. Aquaculture operations may be present.

★ **Cypress Harbour (51):** This is one of the prettiest spots on Broughton Island. It is located near the popular fishing areas of Sutlej Channel. Approach with caution, because of Fox Rock and the drying shoal which extends to mid-channel from Woods Point. Enter favoring port. Miller Bay on the east shore has been the site of a fish farm, so the best shelters are in Berry Cove and in the niche between Harbour Point and Blount Point. Bottom fishing is good off the tip of Fox Rock. Farther into the bay, after Roffey Point, there is anchorage in the center. Watch for a rock south of this point marked on chart #3547. BC Forest Service Recreation Site Cypress Harbour is located on Cawston Point. There are campsites with picnic tables, firepits, and a pit toilet. Old logging roads provide a chance to get in some walking. 🚶⛺▲

Greenway Sound

[3547]

★ **Greenway Sound (52):** This boot-shaped sound between North Broughton and Broughton Islands has a number of anchorages. The first anchorages are in the vicinity of Cecil Island. Pass either side of Cecil. The innermost site is behind a small islet with a shoal. A basin with depths of 50 feet is between the islet and the grassy head. There are two rocks near the head. One is covered with yellow seaweed in season. Anchor in the center giving berth to the shoal off the eastern shore. This anchorage is shown by a "5" on the charts. Several boats can be accommodated with shore ties. An outlet from Broughton Lagoon empties into the bay. Another anchorage is close to Cecil Island where a wider passage enters the lagoon. Currents are noticeable making more than temporary anchorage a questionable course of action.

A dinghy trip into the lagoon can be fun and is possible in a substantial dinghy. The North entrance is a reversing rapids that allows about 20-30 minutes inside the lagoon to explore. The trick is to go in about an hour and fifteen minutes after high tide at Alert Bay. At full high tide, the lagoon fills very rapidly, but as the tide lowers, the rapids slow down. Typically, the rapids reverse and the lagoon flows out about an hour and a half after high tide. Your time inside is usually from 1:15 after high tide to 1:45 after high tide. As soon as you enter, note the location of the passage for your return exit passage. It is hard to find from inside the lagoon. The North passage is quite deep. Do not try to go through the South passage as it dries. Continuing into the Sound around the next point, is a large bay. From 1985-2010 the port side of the bay was home to Greenway Sound Marine Resort, a labor of love for Tom and Ann Taylor. Anchoring is possible opposite the port shore, in a bight marked by an "8" fathoms mark on charts.

If traveling farther into the sound, refer to chart #3547 to locate the rock near the center of the waterway, just northwest of Greenway Point. It dries one foot and kelp may not be present to mark it. Watch for shrimp pots in this area. On the west shore at the bend, there is anchorage in the niche marked on the chart as "2" fathoms. Turning the corner of Broughton Point into Carter Passage leads to another anchorage behind the lovely islet at the entrance. There are two other anchorages within this eastern section of Carter Passage. When entering Carter Passage proceed in the narrow, but deep, channel to port of the islet. Continuing into the sound, there is anchorage to starboard prior to reaching Simpson Island. It is marked as seven fathoms. Pass to port of Simpson Island. There is anchorage in a bay straight ahead on the southeast shore, or go around the islet, and continue to the head of the sound. There is good anchorage in 40-50 feet, tucked behind the little peninsula at the head, opposite an old logging road. The extreme head is an active logging operation, unsuitable for anchorage.

Kwakwaka'wakw First Nations cliff art by member Marianne Nicolson in Kingcome Inlet
Photo © Carolyn Van Calcar

Walk-around: On the northern shore of Broughton Island, a dinghy float nearby provides access to the Greenway Sound Rec site onshore. There are two walking trails, one leading to Broughton Lake and the other to Silver King Lake and a lookout over the Broughtons.

Sutlej Channel & Sullivan Bay

[3547]

★ **Cartwright Bay (53):** This indent into North Broughton Island provides good anchorage. Depths are 15-30 feet. A small swampy beach is near the head. There is shelter from both south and west winds, however, it is open to easterlies.

Boyer Point: Good fishing grounds.

★ **Sullivan Bay (54):** Site of Sullivan Bay Resort.

Sullivan Bay Marine Resort: {50° 53' 5" N, 126° 49' 44" W} Moorage, 15/30/50/100 amp power, gas, diesel, propane, showers, laundry, wifi with moorage, store, restaurant, liquor, air service, mail drop, "boat sitting" services. 604-484-9193. VHF 66A (US Mode).

★ **Hopetown Point (55):** Anchorage in 35-45 feet of water over a mud bottom is found in Hoy Bay, east of Hopetown Point. Hopetown Passage may be traversed by shallow draft small craft at high water slack only.

★ **Burley Bay:** Good anchorage, mud bottom.

Jennis Bay Marina   Photo © Patricia Robertson

Mackenzie Sound
[3547]

Watson Point: Seals often frolic in kelp beds off abandoned sawmill site on Watson Point.

★ **Turnbull Cove (56):** This large bay is located off Kenneth Passage. The muddy bottom is very flat with depths of about 30 feet at a 14 foot tide at Alert Bay. Anchorage is possible almost anywhere. The bottom has excellent holding power. There is room here for a large number of boats without any feeling of overcrowding. Forest Ministry has a dinghy dock. Strong southeast winds have been known to swirl around the bay. It is possible to walk to Huaskin Lake. There are often commercial prawn traps near the entry.

Roaringhole Rapids & Nepah Lagoon (57): [3547] The truly adventurous may run the Roaringhole Rapids at high slack water in a shallow draft boat and enter Nepah Lagoon (3-ft draft at low water). Since slack lasts five minutes, tight entrance is dangerous and the visit may have to be short. Depths in the bay discourage or prohibit anchoring. High water slack occurs two hours after high water at Alert Bay. Currents run to eight knots. See current tide table for Sitka, Alaska.

Kenneth Passage: [3547] This passage links Grappler Sound with Mackenzie Sound. First Nations petroglyphs can be seen on the steep cliffs in the area. Pass clear of Kenneth Point and proceed around the islet. Passage is made between the unnamed island in the center and Jessie Point. There is a rock marked by kelp off Jessie Point. Currents swirl through the area causing whirlpools at times. Passage is not restricted and may be made at any tide. It is easiest to go in and out with the tide.

★ **Steamboat Bay:** There is anchorage on a mud bottom. A bright green grassy beach and swampy area are in the background. A shallow area is in mid-bay and a drying rock is to port near the head.

★ **Mackenzie Sound (59):** This is a lovely and isolated area. Heavy moss hangs from the trees along the shoreline. Anchorage is possible. Burly Bay, near the entry to the sound, has anchorage spots near its head and inside Blair Island. Proceeding into the sound, there is a small rock about 100 yards northwest of Turner Island. This rock is especially dangerous because it is covered at high tide. Nimmo Bay and Little Nimmo Bay lie about five miles into the sound. Another anchorage area is at the extreme head of Mackenzie Sound in six to seven fathoms. It is protected from all but west winds. Carvings in the solid rock at the head are believed to be Spanish. The geometric designs, cut with great precision, are of a different nature from those of First Nations origin.

Nimmo Bay & Little Nimmo Bay: Nimmo Bay is shallow with a drying head. A Wilderness Adventure Lodge is located here. The drying rocks in the entry make it appear uninviting. Little Nimmo's entrance has depths sufficient for passage. If you are entering keep to the Port side of centre as you enter straight in perpendicular to the cabins. Near the entrance is a grass and gravel spit. The spit extends about half way across the passage, and is completely covered at high water. The remainder of the bay is open for anchorage.

Grappler Sound
[3547]

★ **Grappler Sound (60):** Many anchorages are found in this vicinity. Embley Lagoon and Overflow Basin, in the north part of the Sound, may be explored by dinghy.

Embley Lagoon: The lagoon is fed by Embley Creek. The water is shallow and there are several rocks to avoid. It is possible to go ashore by dinghy to explore the fish ladder. Land at high water on the west side near the ruins. Logs are tied together at the trail head. Beware of bears. Take a ten minute hike to the left, past a shack, uphill. Check to see if the rotting bridge is still safe to cross. Once across the bridge, uphill and to the right, the fish ladder is in sight. This can be spectacular when the pink salmon are climbing the ladder. The lagoon seems to boil with the jumping salmon during runs. The confined, shallow entry to the lagoon prohibits overnight anchorage.

★ **Woods Bay:** Anchor off the south shore in 30-40 feet of water.

★ **Claydon Bay:** One of the most popular anchorages in the area, shelter is found in either the northern or southern section depending on wind direction. Drying patches in the entrance are clearly marked on charts. Favor the south shore when entering. An islet has reefs extending from it. A sharp rock sits atop the westerly reef. Pass west of this rock when entering the northern basin. Anchorage is possible.

★ **Carriden Bay:** Large, with a curving shoreline and fairly even bottom, this bay offers excellent holding on hard mud. The shore is skirted with drying flats. Anchor near the center in 25-35 feet of water. Adequate protection for south and west winds is possible.

Stuart Narrows (61): This passageway extends from Morris Islet to Leche Islet. Since currents run to seven knots, flooding west, ebbing east, plan to enter or exit at slack water. Depths are adequate for low water entry. High and low water slack are 10 and 15 minutes respectively after high and low water slack at Alert Bay. Welde Rock, a large drying, nearly flat rock is a hazard in the center of the narrows. Covered at high water, it dries eight feet and has kelp to help identify it. Pass either side.

★ **Drury Inlet (61):** There are some excellent anchorages in this scenic inlet surrounded by low, rolling hills. It is the lesser traveled part of the Broughtons and finding a private anchorage is still possible. This is logging country and debris covers the bottom of most of the anchorages. To avoid fouling, an anchor buoy is recommended.

Richmond Bay: Turning into the bay, pass to the north of Leche Islet, and give a wide berth to rocks in the center of the bay. One anchorage site, on the east shore, is marked with "4" fathoms on the chart. It is open to westerlies. The other, with more protection, is at the extreme southern head, marked by a "3" fathoms on the chart.

Tancred Bay: Open to northwesterly winds.

Davis Bay: There is anchorage on the north side, marked "2" fathoms on the chart. Beware of sunken pilings.

Jennis Bay: First visited by Captain Vancouver and his crew in the early 1790's, Jennis Bay was a well-known logging camp starting in about 1890. Today, a quaint marina and resort is located 15 km west of Sullivan Bay, 10 km through Stuart Narrows on your right. The beautiful and well protected bay and its fascinating surroundings offers many opportunities for adventure and exploration. There is excellent fishing and kayaking in Drury Inlet and the many nearby lakes. Jennis Bay itself affords miles of logging roads for mountain biking and hiking, as well as access to magnificent Huaskin Lake. There is excellent anchorage in the lagoon to the northwest, opposite the peninsula.

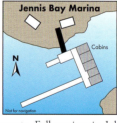

Jennis Bay Marina: {50° 54.866' N, 127° 01.632' W} Moorage for approximately 20 boats. Showers, wifi access, cell phone boosters, gift shop, rental cabins, covered party deck, organized get-togethers for guests. Full services in July & August. 250-954-8112. VHF 66A.

★ **Sutherland Bay:** This bay is large and shallow. There is good anchorage, with protection from most winds.

Actress Passage, leading to Actaeon Sound: This pass is rock strewn and hazardous. Passage at slack water is recommended. Pass west of Dove Island. Avoid Skene Point by favoring the Bond Peninsula shore.

Walk-around: Take a walk from the west side of Actress Passage to the southwest tip of Bond Lagoon by way of a logging road. Halfway between Charlotte Point and Charters Point there is a small peninsula. The road begins on the north side of this peninsula and runs inland toward the northeast. The lagoon overlook is about a half mile walk, but the road continues on into the timber.

★ **Skeene Bay:** Good sheltered anchorage, though easterly winds can kick up waves. When entering stay toward the southern shore. Shallows extend from the islet on the north end. Good holding in sand about halfway to the head of the bay.

★ **Bond Lagoon:** Good anchorage, however, the entrance dries three feet, leaving you land-locked at lower tides. Enter at high-water slack and stay directly in the center of the channel. There are shoals off the south shore and rocks along the north shore. Anchorage can also be found in Hand and Creasy Bays and behind the islet in the niche formed by England Point.

Creasy Bay: Anchorage is possible in the northwest corner of the bay in about 36 feet. The bottom is silty and holding is poor. The western shore is the site of logging operations and various pieces of machinery, both old and new can be seen. Nice views of the bay are possible from the top of a steep logging road. A creek empties into the bay from Creasy Lake. This pretty little lake is accessed by a trail on the east side of the creek. Once you get past the steep entry with all of the undergrowth the trail is fairly good. It veers off from the creek to a marshy area and then opens onto the lake.

England Point Cove: Entry is east of the islet. Stay to the south shore of Actaeon Sound. When you are beyond the east entrance turn to the northwest as a reef extends off the islets's southeast shore. Good holding in mud bottom.

Tsibass Lagoon: Located at the end of Actaeon Sound, the entrance to the lagoon is marked by strong currents and tidal rapids. Water rushes out of the lagoon with surprising force, churning up a white foam that can be seen floating in the basin to the south. The narrow entrance has least depths of two feet and should be explored only by dinghy at high water slack which occurs 2 hours and 20 minutes after high water slack at Alert Bay. Beyond the rapids the lagoon's islets, one about midway in and a couple at the head, are fun to explore.

Wells Passage Vicinity

[3547]

★ **Tracey Harbour (62):** Tracey Harbour was once a major center for logging operations. Remnants of booms may still be in Napier Bay. Trailers, trucks, and a few boats remain active at the camp site. Anchorage is excellent in six fathoms mud bottom, at Napier Bay opposite the camp. In addition, a pleasant anchorage is in the inlet next to Carter Point. The bottom is rock until near the head, however, good anchorage is found in 30 feet of water at a 16 foot tide at Alert Bay. A shoal extends from shore.

★ **Carter Passage (62):** Since this passage is blocked by a boulder-covered drying shelf two and a half miles from its western entrance, it may be better to describe the passage as two inlets, separated by the drying obstruction. Anchorage is found at both ends of the passage. When approaching the western entry, pass either side of the cluster of rocks and islets just outside the entrance. Currents in the narrow pass run to seven knots, ebbing west, flooding east. Plan to enter or leave at high water slack. There is 17 feet of water on a 12 foot tide at Alert Bay. The starboard shore on entering has kelp covered rocks. Favor the left center of the fairway. Inside are three unnamed anchoring sites. The two to port are sheltered from the north with anchorage in 30-40 feet of water. The bay to starboard, while open to northwest winds, is smaller, with anchorage in 35-45 feet on a good mud bottom. A shoal, covered at high water, is to port near the entrance to this bay. The head of this bay is a drying flat. The eastern portion of Carter Passage is reached from Greenway Sound. Keep to port when passing the islet off Broughton Point. Adequate depths for passage are found in this narrow channel. Anchorage can be found in the bay to starboard, behind the islet and in niches on both sides farther into the waterway. Survey the area to check out small reefs protruding from shore.

Wells Passage: This well traversed waterway opens from and to Queen Charlotte Strait. It is a primary passage for those heading to or from Port Hardy or Port McNeill to the islands and for those heading to or from Northern British Columbia and Alaska. Numas Islands are offshore, providing a landmark when locating the entrance. When approaching Wells Passage from the southeast, the opening is wide. Polkinhorne Islands, Vincent, and Percy Islands dot the starboard side but provide little shelter. Any anchorages in the Polkinhornes are open to the northwest, thus open to prevailing winds. When approaching from the west, avoid Lewis Rocks which extend southeastward far off the peninsula that borders Lewis Cove. It is possible to pass between the rocks and the peninsula, then to give a wide berth when rounding Boyles Point. Once in the pass, the waterway narrows and Ommaney Islet is to starboard. Pass to port between the islet and the famous fishing grounds off James Point. The nearest anchorages adjacent to Wells Passage are adjacent to Popplewell Point (temporary anchorage), in the bay on the northeast side of Dickson Island, Carter Passage, and Tracey Harbour.

★ **Dickson Island:** Good anchorage is found in the bay on the northeast side. Kelp patches mark a rock and shoals off the small island. The extreme head is shallow, however anchorage can be found. Depths in the main anchoring basin are 40-55 feet. The low hills do not block strong westerlies.

Vancouver Island Side

[3545, 3546, 3548, 3549]

Robson Bight/Michael Biggs Ecological Reserve (63): This reserve is at the mouth of the Tsitika River, directly opposite the West Cracroft light. The area is a major gathering site for pods of killer whales who like to rub barnacles off their stomachs on the shallow beaches. The reserve was established in 1982 to protect the whales and to continue the research of biologist Michael Biggs. Two boundary makers on the shore mark the east and west end of the areas that are closed to the public. Offshore eastern boundary is {50° 29.65'N 126° 30.23'W}. Offshore western boundary is {50° 30.33'N and 126° 37.47'W}. The "no enter" zone extends a half nautical mile into the strait. By way of interest, a pod consists of five to 20 whales. Nineteen of about 30 pods that travel between Washington State and British Columbia are found in the Johnstone Strait area. Killer whales travel between six-eight knots. By law boaters must give the whales a wide berth, never coming closer than 200 metres or yards.

★ **Bauza Cove (64):** Entry is made either side of Bauza Islet. This picturesque, deep cove provides anchorage and protection in westerlies.

★ **Telegraph Cove (65) [3546]:** In the sheltered niche just southwest of Ella Point at the entrance to Beaver Cove, is the picturesque harbour of Telegraph Cove. Boaters can moor at one of two marinas in the cove. The community also has RV and tent camping sites, launch ramps, a gallery, restaurant, pub, coffee shops and general store. A Whale Interpretive Center near the cove's entrance has a complete fin whale skeleton among its collection. Many of the old buildings, connected by boardwalks, sit on stilts above the water - a testament to the days when the village was the site of a 1911 telegraph station, a 1920's fish packing operation, the Telegraph Cove Sawmill (which operated for 60 years), and a stop for Union Steamship Company vessels. A visit to today's Telegraph Cove is like experiencing the past and viewing the future simultaneously. Historic restorations stand with the modern conveniences that provide a thoroughly enjoyable cruising destination. Motorists can also reach Telegraph Cove via a paved road off Highway 19.

Telegraph Cove Marina: {50° 32.956'N and 126° 49.742'W} Moorage to 70', potable water, 15/30/50 amp power, fish cleaning stations, handicap-accessible washrooms, showers, laundry, Wifi, extra wide launch and wash down station. Annual moorage available. 250-928-3163. VHF 66A.

Telegraph Cove Resort: {50° 32' 43'"N and 126° 49' 59"W} Moorage (boats to 25'). No power or water on docks. Gas, showers, laundry, general store, restaurant/pub, coffee shops, boat ramp, RV/tent campsites, lodging. 250-928-3131, 1-800-200-4665.

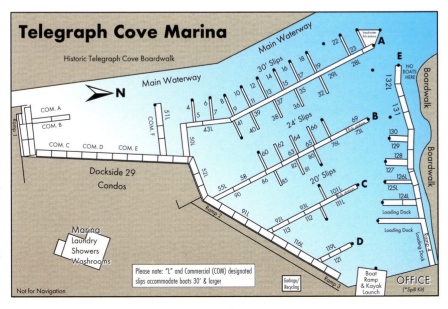

Turnbull Cove   Photo © Patricia Robertson

Beaver Cove (65): Enter between Ella and Lewis Points. There is deep, temporary anchorage in the cove that offers protection in westerlies. This is the site of an old ferry landing, sawmill, and log storage so beware of sunken logs that may foul the anchor line. An area called Englewood is in the extreme head of Beaver Cove. Log booms often provide tie-ups.

Broughton Strait Area
[3546]

★⚓ **Cormorant Channel Provincial Park:** This park encompasses the Pearse and Plumper Island groups, including Stubbs Island, a well-known diving destination. The 740 hectare, mostly water park, offers opportunities to view killer whales, sea lions, otters, porpoises, and other marine life. The park does not have protected anchorages. Strong tidal currents occur in the area, fog is common, and even in the summer the wind can whip up rough seas.

Broughton Strait: This channel lies between Johnstone Strait and Queen Charlotte Strait, separating the Pearse Islands, Cormorant Island, Haddington Island, and Malcolm Island from Vancouver Island. A rock, which dries six feet, is located one half mile west-northwest of Pearse Reefs. If crossing between eastern Malcolm Island and eastern Cormorant Island, set a course to miss this rock. The reference point for weather conditions is Pulteney Point. Currents can reach four knots. While currents do not greatly affect Port McNeill, moorings in Sointula and Alert Bay may be affected.

★ **Alert Bay (66):** The Alert Bay Boat Harbour is sheltered by a rock breakwater. At the base of the breakwater, the B.C. Ferry Terminal has daily scheduled service to Port McNeill and Sointula. Southwest of the breakwater, good anchorage can be found on the sandy bottom at depths of 40-50 feet. In the center of the bay, a Government Wharf offers temporary moorage for six to eight boats with water, but no power, and no breakwater at this location. Alert Bay has two boat launch ramps located about a half mile apart. One is on Front Street, and the other is on Fir Street by the Government Wharf.

Alert Bay is located on Cormorant Island. Both names recall British ships that surveyed the area in the mid-1800's - the H.M.S. Alert and the H.M.S. Cormorant. Together, the Village of Alert Bay, 'Namgis First Nation, Whe-la-la-u Area Council and the Regional District of Mount Waddington have approximately 1,200 to 1,500 residents. Known as the *Home of the Killer Whale*, the historic fishing village of Alert Bay features a number of interesting sites like the century old Anglican Church. A must see, the U'mista Cultural Centre, houses various exhibits including the repatriated Potlatch Collection featuring treasured masks and ceremonial objects. For open hours and information. 250-974-5403, www.umista.ca. In July and through the third week in August the T'sasala Cultural Group perform traditional dances in the Big House, on Saturday at 1:15 pm. Special group performances (25 or more) call Andrea Cranmer, 250-974-8097. Throughout the community of Alert Bay you will see a number of Totem Poles, including the world's tallest Totem Pole. Memorial Poles and other Totem Poles adorn the 'Namgis First Nation burial grounds (please view from the road only). Other local attractions include the Ecological Park and the 'Namgis Big House. For a unique, hands-on cultural experience like cedar weaving, preparing a traditional salmon bbq, or Nusa story telling with Ada, call Culture Shock, 250-974-2484 (advanced reservations required). Some fun events celebrated annually include *June Sports* featuring a First Nations Soccer Tournament, a parade, Crowning of Salmon Prince & Princess, kids races and more. You'll also want to mark the calendar for the *Alert Bay 360* on the BC long weekend when kayaks race around Cormorant Island for cash and prizes, www.alertbay360.com. Check closer to Event times to confirm. During the summer visitors can also take a whale tour or walk or bike on the nearby network of Island trails. Taxi service is also available 40K Taxi & Charters, 250-974-5525.

From the harbour you can walk to downtown Alert Bay where there are grocery, hardware, liquor, beer and wine stores, as well as gift shops and galleries. Services available include a Post Office, hospital, pharmacy, gas station, restaurants, accommodations, and library-museum. The Alert Bay Library-Museum offers free internet access (1/2 hour, donations accepted). For open hours call 250-974-5721. For community information, contact the Alert Bay Visitor Centre: info@alertbay.ca, www.alertbay.ca.

Alert Bay Boat Harbour: {50° 35' 24" N, 126° 65' 25" W} Moorage, 20/30 amp/110 volt power, water, waste pump-out, garbage drop, wifi, washrooms, showers, laundry, credit cards accepted. 250-974-5727. Cell 250-974-8365. VHF 66A.

★ **Sointula (67):** Malcolm Island has breakwater protected moorage in Rough Bay, one mile north of the town of Sointula. The boat launch located here is best used at high tide. Sointula is also reached by car and passenger ferry from Port McNeill and Alert Bay. Sointula, meaning "place of harmony," was settled by Finnish immigrants in 1901 as a utopian colony. Descendants of the original settlers still live here and the ties to the old country are strong. The museum houses displays reflecting the Finnish heritage of the Island. In summer, the museum is open daily, noon-4pm. Historically, fishing was the main source of livelihood, and while the industry isn't what it once was, this is still a working commercial fishing harbour. An historic anchor and "Lost at Sea" Memorial at the harbour honor this legacy. Today tourism and the community based cooperative and non-profit organizations are central to the economy. Many of the 700 island residents also work within the tri-port region (Port McNeill, Alert Bay and Port Hardy). The Co-op, founded in 1909, is the oldest and largest on the west coast. It has groceries, dry goods, marine hardware, liquor (closed Sun. & Mon.), ATM and gas station. The town has a post office, medical center, library, bakery, campgrounds, B & B's, and a hotel with a pub and ATM. Several art studio shops offer open hours to the public, while other home studios are open by appointment only. A truck delivers fuel to the docks on Tuesdays and Thursdays. To arrange a delivery call 250-973-6717. Haul-out and mechanical services are also available. Bikes that are free to borrow and are specifically for use by boaters are found at the harbour. Free green bikes for general public use are found at the Sointula Resource Centre located opposite the ferry terminal. Hiking trails and whale watching and fishing charters provide wonderful opportunities to explore the area. Bere Point Regional Park (6km/3.7 miles from town) has campsites, 2 picnic areas, outhouse, and beach with views of Queen Charlotte Strait. No potable water. For more community information, www.sointulainfo.ca.

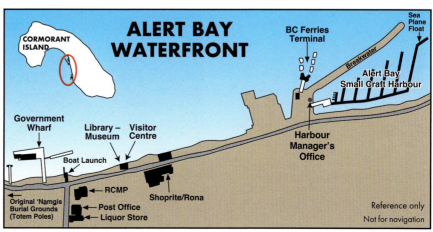

Visit us at boattravel.com

JOHNSTONE & QUEEN CHARLOTTE STRAITS Chapter 17 Page 221

Port McNeil & North Island Marina Photo © Steve Jackman

Malcolm Island Lions Harbour Authority: {50° 37' 37" N, 127° 1' 10" W} Moorage (no reservations), 15/20/30 amp power, water, showers, laundry, garbage drop, pump-out, wifi, summer boat minding service, winter boat storage. 250-973-6544. VHF 66A (summer only).

Tarkanen Marine Ways: Haul-out to 70' long/20' wide. Repairs, maintenance, welding, fibreglass. 250-973-6710.

Mitchell Bay: Located near Donegal Head, there is a public wharf and anchorage in the bay. Fishing, whale watching and scuba diving are popular in the area. Call ahead to Dunroven Farm to see if they have fresh eggs for sale, 250-973-6030. To walk to the farm from the float, turn right and walk to Lands End Road. Go up the hill and on to the right to 20 Lands End Road. Look for the farm's sign. Lodging is available on the farm at the "Sea Cottage" (you must book through Airbnb).

Pulteney Point: See current tables for Seymour Narrows, B.C. Site of lighthouse, fog signal, and weather reporting station. Avoid a kelp patch 1 1/2 miles northwest of the point. This is one of the few remaining manned lighthouses in B.C.

Port McNeill

[3546, 3548]

★ **Port McNeill (68):** Located next to the ferry landing, the Port McNeill Harbour offers guest moorage for boats of all sizes at both the North Island Marina, as well as the Port McNeil Harbour Authority facility. Anchorage is also possible. Housed with the harbour office, the Information Centre offers information for local and the North Island region, as well as high speed wifi. Boaters will find that this coastal community is not only a convenient supply center, but that it offers modern facilities and amenities, as well as abundant recreational activities all in an amazingly scenic setting. Most services are found within easy access of the waterfront. Port McNeill has health and dental facilities, banking services, marine and automotive repair and supply, post office, library with Internet access, laundromat and other service-oriented businesses. Retail options are varied and include a liquor store, sporting goods and clothing shops, galleries, gift shops, and a grocery store. The local pubs and theatre offer up excellent entertainment. Restaurants range from fast food to five star dining to please every palate and pocketbook. Burn off those calories with a visit to the outdoor seasonal swimming pool, ball field, or nearby golf courses. Tours of every kind including whale watching, kayaking, hiking and more are also available. The harbour seaside walk is perfect for a stroll. The Port McNeill & District Museum, housed in a beautiful log cabin structure, shares the area's pioneer and logging history with visitors. For hours, call 250-956-3881. Near the museum, a huge, record breaking natural wood burl tips the scales at nearly 30 tons. If you visit in August don't miss *Orca Fest* featuring fun activities including a salmon barbecue and picnic, children's activities, Outdoor Market, and huge Invitational Baseball Tournament. Travel to and from Port McNeill is possible via several means. By car, the Island Highway 19 extends into the North Island region. Chartered float planes and helicopters are available. Two regional airports, Port Hardy and Comox, provide scheduled air service within and to the North Island. The BC Tri-Island Ferry also runs daily to Alert Bay and Sointula from the Port McNeill terminus. Mount Waddington Regional Transit bus system offers regularly scheduled service for a minimal fee.

North Island Marina: {50° 35' 29" N, 127° 5' 25" W} Moorage (vessels to 285'), reservations available, 30/50/100 amp power, water, garbage, recycling. Marine diesel & gas, jet fuel, avgas, propane, marine parts/service, chandlery, laundromat, free WiFi, courtesy vehicle, dockside delivery provisioning services, BBQ & patio area, gated marina, long stay boat watch programs. Marina: 250-956-4044. Winter Office: 250-956-3336. VHF 66A.

Port McNeill Harbour Authority: {50° 35' 29" N, 127° 5' 20" W} Moorage, call upon approaching breakwater. 20/30/50/100 amp power (208 volts), boat launch ramp, garbage & oil disposal, water, showers, washrooms, cardboard recycling. 2 hour courtesy loading dock with pump-out. 250-956-3881. VHF 66A.

Port McNeill IGA: Complete grocery experience. 250-956-4404.

★ **Beaver Harbour [3548]:** There are three entrances to this harbour. One is through Daedalus Passage to the north on the west side of Peel Island. The second is to the south of Peel Island, watching out for Twin Rocks on the south side of the passage. The third entrance is to the south between Deer Island and Thomas Point. One anchorage is on a soft bottom on the west side of the southernmost tip of the Cattle Islands in five to seven fathoms of water. Shell Islands, to the south of the Beaver Harbour anchorage, have several large First Nations middens on them.

★ **Patrician Cove:** Lying in the northwest corner of Beaver Harbour, there is anchorage in seven fathoms, on a soft bottom. On shore at Fort Rupert, former site of a Hudson's Bay Company Fort (1839), there is a gift shop where resident native artists' work is on display.

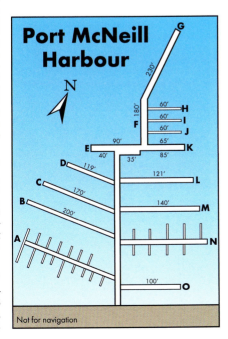

Quarterdeck Marina, Port Hardy   Photo © District of Port Hardy

Port Hardy
[3548]

★ **Hardy Bay (69):** Hardy Bay is a long indentation culminating in the drying flats of the Quatse and Glen Lyon Rivers. Shoals extend from shore in several places. Use charts and keep the red markers well to starboard when entering Hardy Bay.

Bear Cove: This cove, located in Hardy Bay, is the site of the Bear Cove Recreational Site which offers a picnic area, free boat launch, parking, free day-use moorage and weekly moorage by reservation (30' max length). Water is available on the docks. Open seasonally from June 1-Sept 1. Call 250-902-7145. A marine fuel dock, a ferry landing with service to Prince Rupert and the mid-coast, and rental cabins are also located in the cove. Cabin info: 1-877-949-7939.

Coastal Mountain Fuel: Gas, diesel, propane, lubricants, filters, convenience store, ice, bait, waste oil disposal & water. 250-949-9988.

★ **Port Hardy:** This community is to starboard when entering Hardy Bay. Fishing, logging, and tourism are local industries. The Coast Guard station is located near the Government Dock. Stop by the Visitor Centre on Market Street to browse their gift shop or to pick up a map and information showing all the city amenities including a hospital, library, museum, galleries, hotels, shopping centers, restaurants, coffee shops, bakeries, laundromat, clothing, hardware, and liquor stores.

Visitor attractions include local artisan & First Nation art galleries, cultural tours and aboriginal experiences (cedar weaving & drum making), as well as scenic wildlife boat tours. Port Hardy also has full gym and facilities, an indoor swimming pool, ice arena, tennis courts, bowling alley, kayaking, a nearby golf course and shallow and wreck diving sites (diving charter/rentals are available, but limited). Storey's Beach, with swimming and beachcombing opportunities has a covered pavilion and the Commuter trail. Take a guided day trip to the West Coast of Northern Vancouver Island to explore beaches in Cape Scott Provincial Park. The Quatse Salmon Stewardship Centre & hatchery offering guided interpretive tours, a salmon fry tank, mini cinema & gift shop makes an interesting stop. The museum on Market Street features exhibits depicting the early days of First Nation and white settlements on Vancouver Island North. The gift shop includes the works of local First Nation artists. Points of interest in the area include Fort Rupert, the museum at Coal Harbour and the Harbour Front Estuary trail. In the fall watch for salmon spawning up the Quatse River. You may even sight a bear doing some fishing. The Alice Loop features geographic interests such as the Eternal Fountain, and the Devil's Bath - both are half day trips from Port Hardy. Nearby Marble River Provincial Park has a 4.2km hike into Bear Falls and the Emerald Pools.

Special community events include *Filomi Days* held the third weekend in July. Festivities include a parade, First Nations dancing, street hockey, soap-box races, local art vendors, food, entertainment and fishing derby. *Oceans Day* in early June opens with First Nations dancing and features shore walks with a marine biologist, touch tanks, interactive activities and arts & crafts.

Local transit bus service linking Port Hardy Storeys Beach, Coal Harbour and other neighboring North Island communities is available Monday through Saturday. Contact Tofino Bus for travel to and from all points south, including Nanaimo, Victoria and Vancouver. Chartered float plane, scenic overflights and helicopter tours are also available in Port Hardy. The Port Hardy Airport, about 12km/7.5mi from town, has daily scheduled flights to and from Vancouver. For more information about exploring Port Hardy, www.visitporthardy.com.

Port Hardy Berthage: The inner basin is a NO Anchor Zone. A no wake zone commences at the navigation markers. Watch for float plane traffic indicated by a flashing white light. Port Hardy has four moorage facilities. Three are public and are managed by Port Hardy Harbour Authority - Seagate Pier (the most northernly moorage at 8500 Granville St.), the Seine Docks (further south at 8500 Glenview Rd), and Fisherman's Wharf (located inside the breakwater). Also inside the breakwater, the Quarterdeck Inn and Marina, is a privately owned marina. Laundry, restaurants, and marine supply stores are easily accessed from moorages.

Fisherman's Wharf: {50° 42' 49.2258" N, 127° 29' 29.5254" W} Moorage, 20/30 amp power, fresh water, garbage/recycling, sewage pump-out, boat ramp, tidal grid (for changing zincs), winch/derrick, payphones, wifi available by office. Rafting required. 250-949-6332, cell (after hours/emergency) 250-949-0336. VHF 66A.

Quarterdeck Inn & Marina: {50° 42' 44" N, 127° 28' 59" W} Moorage for vessels to 165', 15/30/50 amp power, water, gas, diesel, lubes, outboard oil, propane, laundry, showers, wifi (with paid moorage), convenience store, lodging, restaurant. Inn: 250-902-0455. Restaurant/Pub: 250-949-6922. Marina: 250-949-6551. VHF 66A.

Seagate Pier: Summer T-floats available June-Sept, 30 amp power, fresh water. No rafting. For Main Pier moorage, call ahead to confirm availability. 250-949-6332, cell (after hours/emergency) 250-949-0336. VHF 66A.

The Seine Docks: A floating structure, commercial vessels only. 20/30/50 amp power, potable water, waste oil/bilge water/antifreeze disposal. 250-949-6332, cell (after hours/emergency) 250-949-0336. VHF 66A.

Walk-around: A sidewalk leads to downtown from the moorage basin. Visit the waterfront at the north end of Market Street for walks along the seawall and views of Hardy Bay. The seawalk passes famous "Carrot Park" and ends at Gwa'Sala-'Nakwax'xw Park and Playground.

★ **Bell Island (70):** [3549] There are good protected anchorages on the south side of Bell Island and between Bell Island and Heard Island. These islands lie between Goletas Channel and Gordon Channel, about four miles north of Duval Point or seven miles north of Port Hardy moorages. Depths vary from seven to 11 fathoms. There is limited anchorage in the passage between Bell and the two islands directly south. Be aware of the hazards on both sides. These are marked with kelp in season. There is a large First Nations midden on the south side of Bell Island in this passage.

★⚓ **God's Pocket Marine Park:** On the north side of Goletas Channel at the entrance to Queen Charlotte Strait, this 2,036-hectare park includes Hurst, Bell, Boyle and Crane Islands. It is known as a world-class cold water diving destination.

★ **Hurst Island (71):** On the west side of the island, God's Pocket offers boaters welcome relief from foul weather conditions in the strait.

God's Pocket Resort: {50°50.398 N, 127°35.535 W} Limited moorage, cabin rentals, family style meals provided, diving air, kayak & diving charters. 250-949-1755. VHF 16 (call for Hurst Isle).

★**Nigei Island (72):** Anchorage is found where rocks and islets form a line at the entrance to an unnamed bay across from Cardigan Rocks off Browning Passage. Entry is possible between the southeastern end of the chain of islets. Anchor in the middle of the main channel, not in the lower basin. Port Alexander, a steep-sided, wide, long bay is open to the southeast. Pass Fraser Island and anchor near the head. Anchor in settled or northwest wind weather only. Loquililla Cove, on Goletas Channel, has anchorage and protection from west winds. Avoid kelp covered rocks at the southern entrance.

★ **Hope Island & Bull Harbour (73):** [3549] For area description and complete local moorage information refer to "Bull Harbour" in Chapter 18.

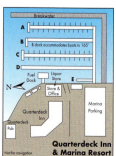

Essential Supplies & Services

AIR TRANSPORTATION

To & from Washington
Kenmore Air 1-866-435-9524
NW Seaplanes
. . . . 425-277-1590, 1-800-690-0086
San Juan Airlines. 1-800-874-4434
Seattle Seaplanes 1-800-637-5553
To & from Islands/Vancouver
Air Canada 1-888-247-2262
Pacific Coastal Air. . . . 250-949-6353, 1-800-343-5963
Vancouver Island Air. 250-287-2433

BOOKS / BOOK STORES

Evergreen Pacific Publishing 425-493-1451
The Marine Atlas. 253-872-5707

BUS TRANSPORTATION

Waivin Flags Transportation 250-230-8294
Mt. Waddington Transit 250-956-3151
Tofino Bus 1-866-986-3466

COAST GUARD

Victoria Coast Guard Radio. . . . . VHF 16, 83a
. . . . 1-800-661-9202 (In BC) or 250-363-6611
Victoria Marine Traffic 250-363-6333
Marine Distress, Search & Rescue:
. . . . 1-800-567-5111 (in Canada) or 250-413-8933
Cell Phone (limited to select providers), *16 . . . . . #727

DIVER'S AIR

God's Pocket Resort. 250-949-1755

FERRY INFORMATION

Port Hardy Terminal . . . . 1-877-223-8778 Ext 3
Port McNeill-Alert Bay
. . . . 250-956-4533, 1-888-223-3779

FISHING/SHELLFISHING INFO

24 hr Recorded Notifications (Pacific region only)
. . . . 1-866-431-3474 or 604-666-2828
Recreational Licensing 1-877-535-7307
Observe, Record & Report Line (fisheries violations)
. . . . 1-800-465-4336

FUELS

Blind Channel Resort: . . . 250-949-1420 VHF 66A
Coastal Mountain Fuel: Port Hardy 250-949-9988
Echo Bay Marina & Lodge: . . . . 604-973-1802 VHF 66A
Sointula Gas Bar, Gas, Diesel (Tues/Thurs Deliveries,
    Pre-arranged orders only) 250-973-6717
Lagoon Cove Marina: Gas, Diesel 778-819-6962
North Island Marina. Gas, Diesel
    . . . . 250-956-4044, 250-956-3336 VHF 66A
Quarterdeck Marina: Gas, Diesel. 250-949-6551
Sullivan Bay Resort: Gas, Diesel.
    . . . . 604-484-9193 VHF 66A
Telegraph Cove Resort: Gas 250-928-3131

GOLF COURSES

Cedar Park Golf: Port McNeil (9-hole) . . 250-956-2270
Seven Hills: Port Hardy. 250-949-9818

GROCERY STORES

Alert Bay Shoprite. 250-974-2777
Echo Bay Marina & Resort . . . . 604-973-1802 VHF 66A
Port McNeill IGA. 250-956-4404
Save On Foods, Port Hardy. 250-949-6455
Telegraph Cove Resort 250-928-3131

HAUL-OUTS

Tarkanen Marine Ways: Sointula. 250-973-6710

HOSPITALS & MEDICAL CENTERS

Healthlink BC (Nurse Helpline) 811
Alert Bay Health Centre. 250-974-5585
Port Hardy Hospital 250-902-6021
Port McNeill Hospital 250-956-4461

LIQUOR STORES

Alert Bay 250-974-5450
Blind Channel Resort . . . . 778-785-1161 VHF 66A
Port Hardy 250-949-6636
Port McNeill 250-956-4142
Sointula. 250-973-6912
Sullivan Bay Marine Resort. 604-484-9193
Telegraph Cove Resort 250-928-3131

LODGING

Blind Channel Resort . . . . 250-949-1420 VHF 66A
Chatham Channel Cabins 778-222-2444
Dockside 29 Suites at Telegraph Cove
    . . . . 250-928-3163 VHF 66A
Echo Bay Marina & Lodge . . . . 604-973-1802 VHF 66A
Jennis Bay Marina . . . . 250-954-8112, VHF 66A
Quarterdeck Inn 250-902-0455
Telegraph Cove Marina. 250-928-3163
Telegraph Cove Resort 250-928-3131

MARINAS / MOORAGE

Alert Bay Boat Harbour: . . . . . 250-974-5727, VHF 66A
Blind Channel Resort . . . . 250-949-1420 VHF 66A
Bull Harbour
Echo Bay Marina & Lodge . . . . 604-973-1802 VHF 66A
Jennis Bay Marina . . . . 250-954-8112, VHF 66A
Kelsey Bay Government Dock. 250-282-0178
Lagoon Cove Marina: . . . . 778-819-6962 VHF 66A
Malcolm Island Lyons Harbour Authority
    250-973-6544
Mitchell Bay: Malcolm Island
North Island Marina. Gas, Diesel:
    . . . . 250-956-4044, 250-956-3336 VHF 66A
Port Hardy Public Harbour . . . . 250-949-6332 VHF 66A
Port McNeill Boat Harbour 250-956-3881
Quarterdeck Inn & Marina: Port Hardy
    . . . . 250-949-6551 VHF 66A
Shoal Bay Public Wharf
Sullivan Bay Marine Resort. . . . 604-484-9193 VHF 66A
Telegraph Cove Marina. . . . . . 250-928-3163 VHF 66A
Telegraph Cove Resort 250-928-3131

MARINE SUPPLIES

North Island Marina
    . . . . 250-956-4044, 250-956-3336 VHF 66A
Sointula Hardware 250-973-6986
Port Hardy Marine Hardware 250-949-6461

PROPANE

Alert Bay Propane-Shoprite 250-974-2777
Blind Channel Resort
    . . . . 250-949-1420 VHF 66A
Coastal Mountain Fuel: Port Hardy 250-949-9988
Echo Bay Marina & Resort: . . . . 604-973-1802 VHF 66A
Sullivan Bay Marine Resort. . . . 604-484-9193 VHF 66A
North Island Marina. Gas, Diesel.
    . . . . 250-956-4044, 250-956-3336 VHF 66A
Quarterdeck Inn & Marina: . . . . 250-949-6551 VHF 66A
Sointula Gas Bar. 250-973-6717

RAMPS

Alert Bay Shipyards, Bear Cove, Beaver Harbour Park,
    More Bay, Port Hardy, Port McNeill.
Kelsey Bay Harbour
Port Hardy Public Harbour 250-949-6332
Port McNeill Boat Harbour 250-956-3881
Telegraph Cove Marina. 250-928-3163

REPAIRS

Progressive Diesel: Port McNeill. 250-956-2700
Stryker Electronics: Port Hardy. 250-949-8022
Tarkanen Marine Ways: Sointula. 250-973-6710

RESTAURANTS

Blind Channel 250-949-1420
Quarterdeck Restaurant & Pub: 250-949-6922
Seahorse Cafe, Telegraph Cove Marina:
    . . . . www.seahorsecafe.org

RV PARKS

Telegraph Cove RV Park 250-928-3163
Telegraph Cove Resort 250-928-3131

SCUBA SITES

God's Pocket. Mitchell Bay, Port Hardy

SEWAGE DISPOSAL

Alert Bay Boat Harbour. . . . . . . 250-974-5727 VHF 66A
Port Hardy Fisherman's Wharf: Pump.
    . . . . 250-949-6332 VHF 66A
Port McNeill Boat Harbour: Pump 250-956-3881
Sointula Boat Harbour 250-973-6544

TAXI

Alert Bay. 250-974-5525
Port Hardy/Port McNeill 250-230-7655
Port Hardy Town Taxi. 250-949-7877

TOWING

C-TOW 1-888-419-CTOW

VISITOR INFORMATION

Alert Bay. 250-974-5024
Port Hardy 250-949-7622
Port McNeill 250-956-3881
Sointula. 250-973-2001

WEATHER

Environment Canada Weather Line. 250-339-9861
Alert Bay: 250-974-5305 (recorded)
Discovery: WX-4, 21-B
Fanny Island: WX-1, WX-8

Chapter 18: West Coast Vancouver Island

Sooke to Cape Scott. Bamfield, Ucluelet, Tofino, Gold River, Tahasis, Zeballos, Port Alice, Coal & Winter Harbours; Barkley, Clayoquot, Nootka, Kyuquot, Quatsino Sounds.

God's Pocket - photo © Jennie Takata

Symbols

[   ]: Numbers between [ ] are chart numbers.
{   }: Numbers & letters between { } are waypoints.
★ Recommended destinations, facilities, and services.
⛰: Park, ⛵: Boat Launch, ▲: Campgrounds,
⚑: Hiking Trails, ㍻: Picnic Area, ⚙: Biking
⚓: Scuba

Chart List

Canadian Hydrographic Charts:
3411, 3461, 3549, 3602-06, 3623-24, 3646-47, 3651, 3668, 3670-71, 3673-75, 3677, 3679-81, 3683, 3685-86

NOAA Charts:
17541-46, 17548-50, 17489, 17491, 17495, 18400, 18460, 18465, 18480, 18484-85

Marine Atlas Vol 1 (2018 ed.):
Pages 13-14

Marine Atlas Vol 2 (2020 ed.):
Pages 1-12

West Coast of Vancouver Island Evergreen Cruising Atlas: 4, 5, 18, 138, 139

★ See "Important Notices" between Chapters 7 and 8 for specific information on boating related topics such as boating safety, weather, U.S. & Canadian marine radio use, Vessel Traffic Service, security zones, Canadian & U.S. Customs, etc. Due to changing regulations, call ahead to verify latest customs information.

Vancouver Island

★ **Vancouver Island:** This heavily forested island is the largest pacific island of North America, extending half the length of the B.C. coast and about half the distance from Washington to Alaska. It is 282 miles long, about 70 miles across at its widest point. About 90 percent of the population lives along a narrow coastal strip, between Sooke and Victoria, on the south, and Campbell River, on the north. About half of this population lives in the greater Victoria area. The remainder of the island, including about 75 percent of the coastline, is very sparsely settled. Several chapters in this guide cover the waterways along the island's eastern shoreline from Victoria to Port Hardy. This chapter deals only with the outer coast.

★ **Circumnavigating Vancouver Island:** A cruise around Vancouver Island, a complete circumnavigation, is a challenge that lures many Northwest mariners, both sail and power. It is a shorter trip than the Inside Passage to Skagway or Glacier Bay, but is in several ways more difficult and more dangerous. The western Vancouver Island Coast is remote and beautiful, with many inviting sounds and inlets. The winds and water conditions along this coast can be extremely dangerous, and have been responsible for more than their share of shipwrecks, both large and small. There are enough villages to provide fuel, water, supplies, and ice, if proper travel plans are made. For this trip, the boat needs to be better equipped and the captain more experienced than for cruises in the more sheltered waters of the Inside Passage.

★ **A cruise of Vancouver Island's west coast:** This is most often done as a circumnavigation of the whole island. Otherwise, unless continuing on from the north, one would be retracing his steps—which is not all bad because there is much to see and do on that beautiful coast! This direction of the circumnavigation is typically in a counter clockwise direction. That is because most of the population and repair facilities are found on the inside of the island where they're more likely to be required during the first part of the voyage. This route is also preferred because of the protection afforded on the inside of the island. One of the biggest advantages for the counter clockwise route is the prevailing wind. The typical summer afternoon westerlies are much easier to run with, than against. Once on the outside of the island, the typical northwest wind of late summer, along with the big ocean waves, would all be going in the direction of travel. Unfortunately however, this is not always the case. Winds on the west coast can shift to southerly, bringing rough seas. It is during these rough seas that our vessels are challenged most and when boat equipment or structural failures are most likely to occur. Sailing this long stretch, though, can be one of the highlights of a circumnavigation.

The only community of any size on the west coast is Port Alberni, at the end of a 40 mile inlet from the Pacific Ocean, and 15 miles overland from the Georgia Strait. The only others are a dozen or so small fishing and logging villages, some with no land access at all. Paved roads cross the island to Ucluelet, Tofino, Port Renfrew, Gold River in Nootka Sound, Coal Harbour, and Port Alice. Gravel logging roads, most of which are open at all times to the public, lead to Bamfield, Tahsis, Zeballos, Fair Harbour, Holberg, and Winter Harbour. Traveling these logging roads can be hazardous and it is imperative to inquire locally about access before using them. The longest stretches of open water are the two approaches at the north and south ends of the island. One can avoid these by trailering to Port Alberni, Ucluelet, or Tofino and then cruising Barkley and Clayoquot Sounds or even Nootka Sound. In the north, one can trailer to Coal Harbour and cruise Quatsino and adjoining sounds. There are good ramps, serviced by paved roads. If it is preferable not to trailer or if the boat is large, there are commercial haulers available.

Fog: From June to October, the surface of the ocean is frequently warmer offshore than immediately along the west coast of Vancouver Island. This is the primary cause of sea-fog, when the wind is blowing onshore. These fogs may come and go several times a day, or last for many days. They do not necessarily follow the typical pattern one would expect with this type of fog, where morning fog dissipates by afternoon. In fact, the afternoon westerlies can even blow in more fog. This can cause some real problems when trying to locate an entrance to one of the inlets. Radar is recommended equipment for this voyage. Even with radar, approaching a narrow entrance in fog can be hazardous. Because electronic equipment can fail, basic navigation is still essential. In these waters, the use of dead reckoning, using time, distance and speed to determine boat position, can be important to fall back upon. The problem is not so much in the fog itself, but the rocks. Hitting a rock in the protected waters of the San Juan Islands, for instance, is one thing, but coming down a big Pacific Ocean wave onto one is quite another. Even for an experienced boater, it's surprising how fast an object can burst out of the murky surroundings. On the other hand, fog is so common on this coast that it's hard to avoid and with some experience, it's not such a problem. Radar is not as important as a good depth sounder, compass and loran or GPS. A radar reflector and horn are also musts. Most important, however, is to slow the boat down in fog, listen, at least through an open window, and watch carefully in all directions. With these basics, most of the open inlets along this coast can be safely approached in fog.

Storms: While traversing the coastline, the mariner is fully exposed to any adverse weather on the Pacific Ocean. Large swells are often encountered in the outer waters of some inlets, even during calm wind conditions. Although there are numerous sounds and inlets offering protection, the mariner must be especially alert to weather forecasts and able to interpret storm signs in time to run for cover. The numbers of large ships that have been lost along this coast confirm that it is no playground for the unwary.

"Roughness" of the sea, however, is not usually the problem one would think here. Even on the open ocean, there's usually hardly enough wind for a sailboat to sail effectively. In fact, the distances between ports often makes such leisurely sailing impractical. On the other hand, storms with gale-force winds are common along this coast. During

WEST COAST VANCOUVER ISLAND Chapter 18 Page 225

one recent summer, there were two storms with winds of actual hurricane force. Plan some extra time for such a voyage because of the likelihood of being holed up for an extra day or two.

Rain too varies greatly, even between early and late summer. During one recent June in Tofino, right in the middle of this coast, there was rain every single day and in Uchucklesit Inlet the average annual rainfall is 300 inches. For this reason, the best time to plan for such a trip is mid to late summer. The drawback to this time of year is that statistically, parts of this coast have roughly twice the number of foggy days in July as June and twice again as many in August.

Rocky coast: Not only is the coastline itself rocky, but there are many offshore rocks, making careful navigation important. Many of the sounds and inlets also have numerous underwater rocks present. A good fathometer and a complete set of charts are absolute necessities. Nothing can substitute for an alert and knowledgeable navigator aboard.

Points: The points of land along this coast can be particularly rough. This can be a problem for both power and sailboats. The repeated heavy seas can loosen debris in fuel tanks, clog filters, stop a motor, or break a traveler or mast step on a sailboat. With such breakdowns, a great deal of time may be required to make repairs.

Winds: Calm mornings are often the rule. Prevailing summer wind is from the southwest and west, with winds rising in late afternoon.

Anchoring: Knowing, and adhering to, correct principals of anchoring is more important along the West Coast than in more protected inland waters. First, because there are so few docks, a mariner is forced to anchor most of the time. Secondly, this area is more exposed and subject to storms. Winds can funnel into the inlets, as well as down mountains. The primary anchor should be heavy, and an even heavier auxiliary anchor should be available in case the primary is lost or doesn't hold. It's best that the auxiliary anchor be of a different type than the primary one, so that, if one doesn't hold on the particular bottom, the other may. Both anchors should have at least 30' of chain and 200' of line. Using, two or three times the depth for the anchor scope may work for protected areas, but much more rode is sure to be needed on this trip. The main thing to do is to back away from the anchor, after it is set, using plenty of power, although beginning slowly so as not to dislodge the anchor when the line is made abruptly taut. Once anchored, watching the shore off the side of the vessel, a range between a near tree and far hilltop beyond it, should not change. Using a stern anchor or a stern line to shore may not work here, because such a tie does not allow the boat to swing freely with the wind, and may hold the boat broadside to wind and/or waves. Two anchors, both set from the bow, can help. Prior to anchoring it is wise to not only circle the perimeter of probable swing during the night, but the adjacent area as well.

Important Items For This Trip
1. A reliable and seaworthy boat
2. All Canadian Hydrographic charts for the area
3. An accurate, compensated compass
4. A fathometer
5. A marine VHF two-way radio, with weather and emergency channels
6. A radar
7. RDF or GPS
8. Sailing Directions British Columbia Coast, PAC 202 (Vancouver Island, West Coast and Coastal Inlets)
9. A captain experienced in boat handling and navigation
10. Ample time for the cruise to allow for weather changes
11. Inflatable dinghy

This last item can be invaluable for a voyage on the West Coast. A quality inflatable, with an outboard powerful enough to plane, vastly expands the exploring possibilities. A dinghy is the best way to get around in many of these coastal towns, some of which are built right along the water or are divided by bodies of water. Dinghies often provide the most direct route, avoiding a long distance trek. Planing at two or three times the speed of a main boat, inflatables can quickly get to and into tight little spots that are otherwise inaccessible to a larger boat, even via "gunkholing". For scouting shorelines, even in open waters, an inflatable can be safer than the main boat, because it can bounce off rocks and ride big seas. These inflatables also work well in the open ocean.

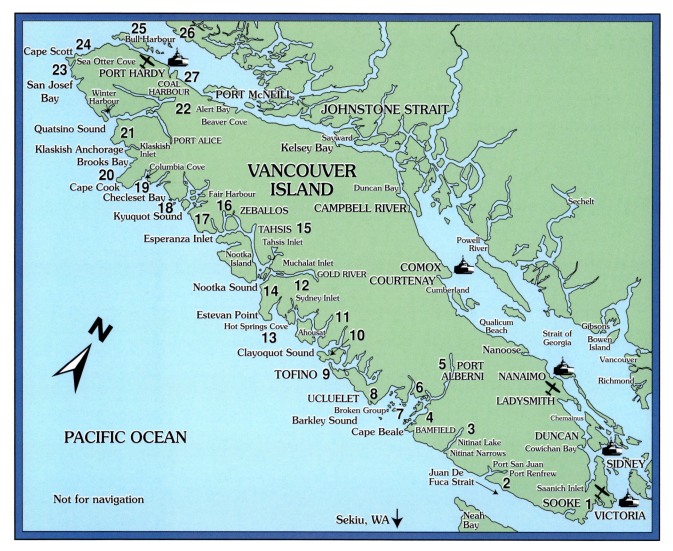

2024 Northwest Boat Travel

Strait Of Juan de Fuca To Barkley Sound

[3461, 3602, 3606]

★ **Sekiu, Washington:** See information near the end of Chapter 4. Sekiu is located in the northwest corner of Clallam Bay. It is 39 nautical miles west of Port Angeles, the closest Customs Port of Entry. The small craft basin has a curved, stone breakwater on the west shore of Clallam Bay. There is a marina with moorage, water, ice, and a good launching ramp. Grocery, motels, and restaurants are 1/8 mile from the marina. Anchorage is open to the north.

★ **Neah Bay, Washington:** Located 14 nautical miles from Sekiu. The well protected harbor houses marinas with diesel, gas, water, ice and ramps. See Chapter 4.

Crossing Juan de Fuca Strait: It is 40 nautical miles across the mouth of Juan de Fuca Strait to Cape Beale.

Traveling from the Puget Sound to Barkley Sound, Juan de Fuca Strait must sooner or later be crossed. Crossing early and following the Canadian coastline is more scenic and less populated. After Port San Juan, there are no communities or safe harbours over this 37 mile distance to Barkley Sound. The only people seen here are those hiking the West Coast Trail, established in 1909 after 126 survivors from the shipwrecked Valentia were unable to make it out by foot. Miles of this shoreline are composed of multicolored, tilted sandstone with caves, arches, blow holes and waterfalls. One waterfall is 80 feet high.

The best time of day to traverse this long section is morning. This avoids much of the typical afternoon westerlies, but means leaving very early in the morning. The summer westerlies are created by the daily heating of the mainland, and often result in strong winds funneling down the strait. Compounding that, the stronger ebb currents, flowing against the wind, can cause severely choppy seas, which not only require hours longer to travel, but can be a danger, even capsizing a smaller boat caught abeam steep breaking waves. These conditions must be anticipated and avoided because, once in them, it's too late to simply speed up and run the long distances for cover.

Traveling in the other direction, from Barkley Sound eastward, can be quite a contrast and reason enough, if circumnavigating the island, to do so in a counter clockwise direction. Traveling eastward, with the combination of the westerly wind and a flood current, a boat can double its normal ground speed for many miles. For the sailor, this can also provide one of the best and longest sails of a circumnavigation.

Fog is common in the strait and it can last all day. An advantage of traveling this coastline when fog is present is that there are no obstacles within one mile of land. This distance can be maintained, with a depth sounder and chart, by following between a 15 and 30 fathom curve. Although land may never be seen, this way the distance from it will always be known.

Current: Juan de Fuca Strait funnels a lot of water, like the neck of an hourglass between the ocean and two inland seas—Puget Sound and the Strait of Georgia. This causes significant currents. Also, the "mixed tides" in this area result in a great variation between every other high and low tide. That's because, especially in early summers when the moon is high in the Northwest, it exerts a direct gravitational pull on the water, causing an extreme high and low tide along with their correspondingly strong currents. Then, by the time the next high and low tides come, the earth has rotated to another position, such that these are much less and the corresponding currents are less too.

The places this current is most dramatic on the routes to Barkley Sound are at the points of land. The primary such points are Point Wilson, near Port Townsend, Discovery Island, near Victoria and Race Rocks, near Sooke. Where different currents meet each other, especially at places like this, they result in tide rips. While tide rips can be only areas of swirling water in places like the San Juan Islands, in the above three areas, they can be hazardous and even flip a smaller boat. Such severe tide rips can be avoided by carefully studying the following: the *U.S. Pilot*, the *British Columbia Coast Sailing Directions*, the *Pacific Coast Current Tables*, the *Canadian Tide and Current Tables*, and the fine print on the large-scale charts. The main precaution is to either try to wait out the times of these worst rips or skirt them widely. As an example of how currents can vary widely within a general area, at two specific places near Point Wilson only five miles apart, the difference in the times of the same slack current is 3 1/2 hours and the difference in strength is ten times.

Traveling from Juan de Fuca Strait, the current usually does not present a problem. In fact, contrary to the inside of Vancouver Island, where the transits of many waterways may have to be timed around the slack current, there are no such problems on the entire West Coast of Vancouver Island, with the possible exception of Quatsino Narrows, near Coal Harbour.

Race Rocks: Now automated, this 89 foot tall lighthouse is made of granite blocks which were shipped around The Horn from Scotland in 1860. Other landmarks are the keepers white house with its red roof and grass lawn. The light transmits in Morse Code. The fog signal is three blasts every 60 seconds. When this station was manned, the keeper on duty climbed the 114 steps each day to check the light.

Sooke

[3411, 3461, 3606, 3647]

★ **Sooke (1):** Sooke is at the gateway to the west coast of Vancouver Island. There is a government float moorage and fuel is found at the end of Sooke Basin at Sunny Shores. Sooke is a major fishing center and much of the harbour is used by commercial and sport fishermen. When entering, line up the outer range markers before crossing the bar. The bar extends from Parsons to Simpson Points and has a least depth of 14 feet of water. When approaching the tip of Whiffin Spit, favor the Simpson Point side. Foul ground, marked by kelp, extends for some distance from the western shore to port. Currents run to four knots and the streams set toward that shore. When rounding Whiffin Spit, stay about 100 feet offshore and keep Grant Rocks to starboard. Grant Rocks consist of three rocks–one that dries and two that are covered. Strong currents tend to push toward the rocks. The harbour has shallow areas, usually marked by kelp in summer. When proceeding to the marine businesses, public floats, and the community of Sooke, give Woodward Point a wide berth and follow the channel marked by red spar buoys and cardinal buoys. Keep these to starboard. If the range light is your marker, the white sector shows the preferred channel.

A government wharf, with finger floats, is located on the western shore. The municipal boat ramp is located in front of the nearby Prestige Hotel. Hardware, liquor, grocery, laundromat, pharmacy, post office outlet, and other stores are within walking distance of the government wharf. Hosting a population of over 12,000, this is among the oldest settlements on the coast. Exhibits at the outstanding Sooke Region Museum reconstruct the history of the southwest coast of Vancouver Island. These consist of logging, fishing, and Coast Salish artifacts, as well as the Historic Triangle Island Lighthouse and Moss Cottage (built in 1870), one of the oldest standing buildings west of Victoria. For lighthouse & Moss Cottage tours, call the Museum at 250-642-6351, or 866-888-4748. The Visitor Centre, co-located with the Museum has maps and information about things to see and do in the region. The *Sooke Fall Fair*, held every September at Sooke Community Hall is a perennial favorite with both locals and visitors. Also widely known, the *Sooke Fine Arts Show* is held each summer (July/Aug). Each Thursday from 5-8pm, June-August, the museum hosts a Night Market featuring food, crafts, produce, and entertainment. For the latest happenings, check the Calendar of Events at www.sookeregionmuseum.ca. Regularly scheduled buses run throughout Sooke and to Victoria. The Galloping Goose Trail, skirting the Sooke Basin, is a favorite place to walk or cycle. Thrill seekers can ride zip lines through the tree tops east of Sooke. 250-642-1933. ⚓🏨⛽

Sooke Harbour Authority: {48° 21' 57" N, 123° 43' 36"W} Moorage, 20/30 amp power, potable water, garbage disposal, security gate/cameras. 250-642-4431.

Sooke Harbour Resort & Marina: {48° 21' 57.5172" N, 123° 43' 41.1096" W} Permanent & guest moorage to 50', 30/50 amp power, water, showers, launch, garbage/recycling, fish cleaning stations, accommodations, WiFi, bike/kayak rentals. 250-642-3236.

Sunny Shores Resort & Marina: Moorage, 15 amp power & water at some slips, gas, diesel, launch, haul-out, showers, lodging, campground, playground, mini golf. 250-642-5731. CB 13, VHF 16.

Sheringham Point: Eight nautical miles from entrance to Sooke Inlet, a lighthouse and fog signal are located here.

Port San Juan (2): [3647] Port San Juan can be identified by a huge gap between two mountain ranges. A light and fog signal are on San Juan Point. The fog signal is one blast every 30 seconds. The entrance is 49 nautical miles from Victoria, 35 miles from Sooke. The inlet extends three and one-half miles inland. It is exposed to southwest winds and a gale from that direction may produce large swells in the inlet. Some anchorage can be found in six fathoms about one mile from the head, in a small niche on the south side, off the west shore north of Quartertide Rocks, offshore from the mouth of Hobbs Creek, or behind the breakwater near the fuel dock at Port Renfrew.

★ **Port Renfrew:** In summer, the best anchorage is in the San Juan Bay. A community dock in Snuggery Cove provides shore access and is within walking distance of most amenities. Seasonal wharfs provide some transient moorage from late-May to mid-September. A bit further east of Snuggery Cove along the southern shoreline is the Pacific Gateway Marina, which offers better protection during winter. There are also several moorages on the Gordon River, including Butch's Moorage, Pacheedaht Shores and Port Renfrew Marina. It is necessary to go up the river to get to these marinas. Because of shallow water, this is not recommended for sailboats. Power boats, with over three-four foot draft, should cross the entrance only at high tide. Monitor VHF 9. Port Renfrew has seen quite a bit of growth recently that has contributed to the reinvention of the community from a former fishing and logging community. A cottage development offering waterfront rentals and older establishments like the Port Renfrew

WEST COAST VANCOUVER ISLAND   Chapter 18   Page 227

Hotel & Pub and the West Coast Lodge have been redeveloped. Other businesses and services in Port Renfrew include accommodations, dining, fishing charters, post office, rec-centre, a general store with groceries, liquor, and gifts, gas station on Parkinson Rd. Port Renfrew is connected to Victoria by Highway 14 (Pacific Marine Circle Route). It is the southern entrance to the famous West Coast Trail and the northern terminus of the Juan de Fuca Marine Trail. It is also home to the world famous Botanical Beach and Botany Bay, as well as Avatar Grove, home of the world's gnarliest tree. There are also a number of local hiking trails in the area. Every year in June, the *Tall Tree Festival* is held on a nearby hillside. Attendees, 19 and older, enjoy three days of music and camping. For more information about Port Renfrew visit www.portrenfrew.com.

Butch's Marina: Seasonal moorage, late April-late Sept. No reservations, no power, water (provide your own hose or bucket), cleaning station.

Pacheedaht Campground: Check in at campground office 9am-9pm. showers, RV/tent sites, snacks & drinks. Open year round. 250-647-0090.

Pacific Gateway Marina: {48° 33' 20" N, 124° 24' 53" W} Daily, monthly, seasonal moorage, vessels to 80', reservations recommended. Gas, diesel, limited power and fresh water on the main dock. Full service restaurant, fishing charters, bait, ice, boat launch, vehicle/boat trailer parking. 250-412-5509. VHF 66A

Port Renfrew Marina & RV Park: Moorage to 30'. Gas, diesel, ice, tackle/bait, pay phone, ATM, launch ramp, camping/RV sites. Opposite Port Renfrew at entrance to Gordon River. Watch tides, 3' depth required for easy passage. Open May 1 - Oct. 15. 250-483-1878. VHF 06.

Bonilla Point: Reefs extend south and west of the point.

Carmanah Point: Light and fog signal. This is the northwest entrance point to Juan de Fuca Strait. A Canadian troller fisherman passed on the tip that there are often reverse currents close to the Vancouver Island shore during strong tides. Ebb tides are the strongest.

Nitinat Narrows and Nitinat Lake (3): [3647] Very hazardous during adverse weather conditions. Under these circumstances no vessel should attempt to enter. Even with good weather, an ebb tide meeting incoming swells on the entrance bar will make for very hazardous conditions. There are no marine facilities. This is the site of an abandoned First Nations village.

Cape Beale: [3671] This is 86 nautical miles from Victoria. A light and fog signal are located here at the entrance to Barkley Sound. The temptation, once Barkley Sound is in sight, is to cut right in toward it. Resist this desire, because Cape Beale is the worst obstacle encountered so far along this route. Rocks surround it for about one-third of a mile in all directions. Give it plenty of leeway.

Barkley Sound looking toward Port Alberni   Photo © David Abercrombie

Barkley Sound
[3602, 3604, 3646, 3670, 3671]

★ **Barkley Sound:** There are three main entrance channels, Trevor, Imperial Eagle, and Loudoun Channels. The sound is 15 miles wide and indents about 25 miles into the island. This body of water, with all of its small and large islands and numerous channels, has great attraction for both the sailor and the power boater. Once behind the outer islands, the waters are relatively protected, as witnessed by the number of kayaks and canoes seen in Pacific Rim National Park. However, the sound is exposed to the full sweep of the Pacific Ocean, resulting in heavy swells during stormy conditions. Even during calm weather, swells may be present. Thus, quiet and safe anchorages can be found only in the inner protected areas. In recent years, primarily due to a successful salmon enhancement program, Barkley Sound has become well known for its excellent chinook salmon fishing. There are also many cohos and sockeye in these waters. Fishing peaks about Labor Day. Barkley Sound, with all of its rocks and reefs, also offers some great bottom fishing.

Entering Barkley Sound by way of the first channel, Trevor Channel, the ocean waves usually quickly subside; however, don't be lulled. Barkley Sound is a sea of rocks and many are pyramid shaped. Because of the shape of these rocks, a depth sounder doesn't help much, because the top of the rocks emerge too fast. Charts must be carefully followed.

★ **Deer Group:** This small group of islands has anchorage in Dodger Channel. The scenery quickly improves upon entry to Trevor Channel. The Deer Group of islands to the west are thickly forested and to the east are several long sand beaches separated by rugged headlands. There are sculptured rock towers crested with tortuous Sitka spruce. Anchorage is possible in some of these bays, but watch for rocks and kelp. Ocean waves can swing in, so anchor securely. Much of this area is First Nation Reserve land and permission to go ashore should first be obtained. The beaches are nice for walking and most of the headland can be scaled.

Another way to these beaches is by a trail at the head of Bamfield Inlet, but the wharf there is only usable at higher tides. A second trail in the Bamfield vicinity leads four miles to the Cape Beale lighthouse, however this trail is unmaintained and in poor condition.

★ **Bamfield (4):** [3646] Bamfield straddles Bamfield and Grappler Inlets. There are four public floats - Port Desire, the Eastside Huu-ay-aht dock, and two on the Westside. Anchorage is also possible near Burlo Island and in Grappler Inlet. Mean depths are 50', good holding bottom. Please note there are water lines and telephone cables that run under the inlet. Entering the harbour, the Canadian Coast Guard Station is on your starboard side. Immediately following is the West Public Wharf. A general store with liquor agency is located next to the West Public Wharf. A public use composting toilet is a short walk from the store. A post office is also found on the west side. Lodging is available at several locations, as well (reservations are a must in the summer). Many lodges have their own floats for easy access. Midway down the harbour is the Bamfield Harbour Authority public float. Look for the red triangle marker just off the southeast corner of the dock. Prominent on your port side is the Bamfield Marine Station. The East Side Huu-ay-aht Wharf provides access to a hospital, motel and additional lodging options, a pub, general store with liquor agency, restaurant, and an ATM machine (there are no banks in Bamfield). Marine repairs are available at Breaker's Marine, 250-278-3281 located 1/8 mile from the dock on Grappler Road. A tourist information booth and small museum are also found on Grappler Road at Bamfield Centennial Park near Port Desire at the head of Grappler Inlet. The museum is open July 1 until Labour Day, donations gratefully accepted. The annual *Music By the Sea Festival*, held at the Rix Centre for Ocean Discoveries, offers a wide variety of musical genres with musicians from around the world. For information and dates call 250-728-3887, or www.musicbythesea.ca.

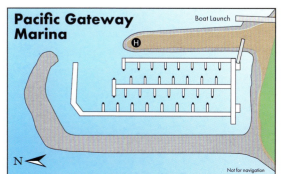

Chapter 18 WEST COAST VANCOUVER ISLAND

Bamfield is connected to Port Alberni by an industrial logging road, as well as year-long steamer, water taxi, and float plane service. Bamfield is also the northern end of the West Coast Life Saving Trail, now known as The West Coast Trail. The 45m/75km trail was originally cleared in 1907 to help those stranded by coast wrecks. Now rebuilt, the trail attracts thousands of hikers each year, reservations/permits required. Brady's Beach, about a 30 minute hike to the west side, has spectacular views and is a favorite spot to picnic and swim. Keeha and Pachena Beaches on the east side are equally spectacular and worth a visit. From May through September, the West Coast Trail Express operates bus service from Victoria and Nanaimo to Bamfield. 250 477-8700, 1-888-999-2288.

Bamfield, lying 92 nautical miles from Victoria, was the eastern terminus of the Trans-Pacific Cable from 1902 to 1959. The 4,000 mile cable connected to Fanning Island near the Equator. A newer cable has since been laid from Port Alberni to Hawaii and the old Cable Station on the hillside is now the home of the West Canadian Universities Marine Biological Station. For more information about the community, visit www.bamfieldchamber.com.

Bamfield Harbour Authority Dock: {48° 46' 49" N, 125° 8' 15" W} Moorage (reservations recommended June through end of September), 20/30 amp power, water, no garbage deposit, fish cleaning station. Located in West Bamfield. On right side when entering Bamfield Inlet, midway down the harbour. Contact Dock Manager at 250-720-7548.

McKay Bay Lodge: {48° 49' 52" N, 125° 08' 47" W} Gas, diesel, fill-up water for a small fee. Lodging/meals/moorage pkgs. Flash freezing, tackle. Boaters may dine here, reserve 1 day in advance for dinner. 250-728-3323.

Mills Landing: Adjacent to Harbour Authority Dock. BYO Boat moorage available with reservations 5/15-9/15. Cottages, bait, tackle, saltwater ice, fish cleaning station, freezer space, charters. 250-728-2300.

Pacific Gateway Wilderness Lodge: {48° 50' 16.5114" N, 125° 8' 20.7744" W} Located at the mouth of the harbour. Limited transient moorage if space is available. Lodging. Boaters may dine with reservations made 24 hours in advance, if space available. 250-728-3646.

★⛺ **Pacific Rim National Park Reserve:** The park contains three units: Long Beach, the Broken Group Islands, and the West Coast Trail, an iconic 75km/47mi backpacking trail. For the seasoned hiker, this is an adventure to be savoured. Winding between Port Renfrew and Bamfield (with a mid-point entrance at Nitinaht Village offering a half trail option), hikers will find themselves wading through rivers, climbing ladders, pulling cable cars across river crossings and negotiating steep slopes and muddy terrain. The West Coast Trail is open May 1-Sept 30. Park Entry and Backcountry permits are required. Reservations for 2024 will open mid January. Spaces fill quickly, so consider setting up an account prior to January 12, 2024. Please call 1-877-737-3783 the beginning of January for specific date reserations open.

★ **Grappler Inlet:** This inlet is entered from the east side of Bamfield Inlet about one-quarter mile from the entrance. Port Desire, one-half mile inside Grappler Inlet, has a small public float and launching ramp. Two campgrounds are within walking distance of the public float. Anchorage is possible, but the depth is shallow.

★ **Poett Nook:** Good, protected anchorage, in three fathoms of water. A logging road connects with Port Alberni (65 km) and Bamfield.

Poett Nook Marina: {48° 52'.52" N 125° 02' 55.37" W} Open year round. Moorage to 35' (larger boats by prior arrangement), marine gas, showers, water, ice, campground, fish freezer, fishing gear, some groceries. 250-720-9572.

★ **San Mateo Bay:** Anchorage is found in Ritherdon Bay at the entrance to San Mateo Bay. A public float is moored on the south side of Bernard Point. Aquaculture operations are in the vicinity.

★ **Port Alberni (5):** [3668] Port Alberni is located at the head of Alberni Inlet, 30 nautical miles from Cape Beale. Supplies, equipment, parts, marine ways, fuel floats with diesel, gasoline and water. Marinas are located in the harbour, on the Somass River, and at China Creek (30km/19mi up the Alberni Inlet). The latter two have multiple lane, concrete launching ramps. The Port Alberni Yacht Club has facilities located at the north end of Fleming Island in Robbers Pass. In 1891 the first paper mill in British Columbia was established here. Today, Port Alberni is a shipping center for lumber products and has a population of about 18,000. Commercial fishing is also a big industry. Activities for visitors include swimming, roller skating, golfing, racquet ball, wind surfing, paddleboarding, soaring, tubing down the river, horseback riding, and hiking. Camping is also popular and numerous sites are found throughout the Alberni Valley. The Alberni Harbour Quay is the site of a view tower, shops and The Spirit Square Farmers Market on Saturdays, 9am-12pm year round and The Market on Margaret, Wed. evenings June 13-Aug 29th. The Maritime Discovery Centre, a unique hands-on maritime museum, housed in the heritage lighthouse is also found here. Call 250-723-6164 for open hours. The museum at Port Alberni's Echo Centre, 250-720-2863 features Alberni Valley and West Coast history, artifacts of the First Nations culture & historical collection of research & photos. Tours available. Annual events such as *Fall Fair* and the *Port Alberni Salmon Festival* are enjoyed by residents and visitors alike.

China Creek Campground & Marina: {49° 9' 14" N, 124° 47' 48" W} Breakwater protected moorage, gas and diesel, boat launch, open moorage to 35', 20/30 amp power, water, showers, laundry, garbage, fish cleaning tables and 250 site campsite. 250-723-9812.

Clutesi Haven Marina: {49° 15' 28" N, 124° 48' 53" W} Open and covered moorage to 32', 15/20 amp power, water, washrooms, picnic areas, launching ramp, fish cleaning station. Located at the mouth of the Somass River. 250-724-6837. VHF 69.

Harbour Quay Marina: {49° 13' 56" N, 124° 48' 50" W} Breakwater protected moorage to 50', side ties for larger vessels, 20/30/50 amp power, showers, washrooms, laundry, garbage, wifi, fish cleaning tables. 250-723-1413.

Petro Canada, Port Alberni: Across the street from Clutesi Marina. Gas, diesel, marine fuel, propane, oils (are to be hand carried to boat), ice, convenience store items, restrooms. 250-724-2626.

Port Alberni Fisherman's Harbour: {49° 14' 11" N, 124° 48' 51" W} Moorage (primarily commercial vessels, but pleasure boats welcome), 15/20/30/ and select 50 amp power, water, washroom, shower, wifi, garbage, sani-pump-out, (hydraulic) electric winch. 250-723-2533.

Port Alberni Marine Fuels & Services Ltd: (Located adjacent to Fisherman's Wharf at Tyee Landing). Gas, diesel, oil, convenience and sundry items, bait/tackle, ice (cubes & fish ice). 250-730-3835. VHF 06.

Tyee Landing: {49° 14' 15" N, 124° 48' 58" W} Moorage up to 60', 20/30 amp and select 50 amp power, water, garbage and fish cleaning station. Same float as Alberni Fuels. Shower at Fishermen's Harbour next door. 250-723-2533.

★ **Trailering to Port Alberni:** It is possible to trailer a boat to Port Alberni, avoiding the exposed waters of Juan de Fuca Strait. This can be accomplished from French Creek or Nanaimo. The ramp at Nanaimo, located at the north end of the channel, between Vancouver Island and Newcastle Island, makes an excellent loading spot. The distance from Nanaimo is only 54 miles. The road is good, but there are steep hills, even though the actual summit is relatively low. For boaters who do not have a trailer or prefer not to use a trailer, several commercial haulers are available at reasonable prices. Most are equipped to haul large boats, both sail and power, up to 40 feet.

★ **Nahmint Bay:** Temporary anchorage is found close to shore, near ruins of a former wharf. A 100 foot float for the emergency use of small craft is moored in a bay 7/10 of a mile northeast of Nahmint Bay. Depth is about seven feet.

★ **Limestone Bay:** Sheltered anchorage is available in four to five fathoms of water.

★ **Uchucklesit Inlet (6):** From 1903 to 1960 the Kildonan Cannery operated here. Although it was demolished in 1962, some of the old pilings remain. Kildonan is a small community and has no commercial centre, but a point of interest is the post office - one of the last floating post offices in Canada. The historic M/V Frances Barkley makes regular stops here bringing mail, supplies and passengers. Anchorages can be found in the inlet. Green Cove, just inside the entrance, has anchorage in five to ten fathoms with a rock and sand bottom. Snug Basin, at the head of the inlet, has completely protected anchorage in eight to ten fathoms of water, mud bottom.

Green Cove Store: Temporarily closed for upgrades. Call ahead in 2024 for available services. When complete, the store will offer overnight moorage, gas, marine gear, bait & tackle, groceries, homemade goodies, snacks, ice. Tribal Office: 250-724-1832. VHF 06.

★ **Sproat Bay:** This anchorage off Tzartus Island has fair protection in the southern portion of the bay in two to three fathoms of water.

★ **Roquefoil Bay:** Fairly sheltered anchorage is available in eight to ten fathoms.

★**Robbers Passage:** Use Charts #366 and #3671. This Passage between Tzartus and Fleming Islands is shallow and narrow. Caution should be used. A day beacon is on a drying rock in the eastern entrance. The preferred channel is to the right. A yacht club is located on Fleming Island. Hiking trails and beaches are onshore.

Port Alberni Yacht Club: {48° 53' 33" N, 125° 7' 5" W} Moorage for members. 1st come-1st served visitor moorage. Water, showers, picnic tables, pit toilets, fish cleaning station. PO Box 37, Port Alberni, BC V9Y 7M6.

Satellite Passage: Anchoring is prohibited because of submarine cables.

Imperial Eagle Channel: During south or south-

WEST COAST VANCOUVER ISLAND   Chapter 18   Page 229

west gales there is a very heavy sea in this channel. Use Charts #3670 and #3671.

Ecoole: Ecoole is in Junction Passage, which connects Trevor and Imperial Eagle Channels. It is located in a small bay on the southeast side of Seddall Island.

★ **Useless Inlet:** The entrance to Useless Inlet is rocky but attainable by small craft. Fatty Basin, near the head of Useless Bay, is best explored by dinghy.

Vernon Bay: Entrance is between Palmer and Allen Points. The shore is high and rugged. Depths prohibit anchorage. Jane Island, at the head of the bay, is in the entrance to a deep, sheltered basin, Jane Bay.

Jane Bay: Entrance is about 100 yards wide. A resort is situated on the west side of the bay, while a fish farm operates on the eastern shore. Stretch your legs and walk the beach or explore local hiking trails. ⚹

Eagle Nook Resort: {49° 0" N, 125° 09"} Nestled between Jane Bay and Vernon Bay in a deep, sheltered basin. Moorage, power, water, ice, wifi, accommodations, dining/lounge, kayaking, SUP & hiking. 604-357-3361. VHF 73.

★ **Alma Russell Islands:** Sheltered anchorage for small craft is found in Julia Passage. The periphery of Barkley Sound along with some of these inlets are partially inhabited with houseboats.

★ **Julia Passage:** This passage can be entered at its north end, but it's tight and the trees on either side must be watched.

★ **Pinkerton Group:** Continuing counter clockwise around Barkley Sound, the small, low Pinkerton Group of islands are particularly scenic. Rocks, however, are numerous here and very slow boat speed is recommended.

★ **Pipestem Inlet:** Located on the northwest side of Barkley Sound, Pipestem Inlet is a four and one-half-mile-long fjord. It is steep sided, fairly easy to navigate, and worth the side trip. Anchorages are at the entrance, east of Refuge Island, and east and southeast of Bazett Island. The latter has mud bottom, abundant oysters, and room for several boats. Check the Shellfish Hotline. 250-720-4440. Travel to the end of Pipestem Inlet at ebb tide to gather larger oysters. Use your dinghy because depths at the head are too deep for anchorage. Temporary anchorage can be found in 20 metres on the northwest end. See description of Lucky Creek below.

Lucky Creek: This is located at the west end of Pipestem Inlet, north of Bazett Island. With a flat bottom dinghy, go to three tiered Lucky Creek Falls at any time. Watch the depth finder closely and have someone on the bow watching for rocks. The channels run on the outside of the curves. With a deeper draft dinghy, go about an hour before flood and leave about an hour after flood. Tie up to a tree on the east side, close to the wall. Climb the trail leading to the left of the first level of falls. A beautiful secluded place to sun, picnic, swim (cold). Especially good for children. Oysters are abundant in Lucky Creek Bay.

Stopper Islands: Just beyond Pipestem Inlet, this group of two primary islands offers only provisional anchorage because it is open to Loudoun Channel. Anchor in 18 metres between Larken Island and South Stopper Island. Enter from the north.

★ **Broken Group Islands (7):** [3670] This archipelago of islands, about 100 in all, are part of the Pacific Rim National Park. The group consists of islands, islets and rocks, lying between Imperial Eagle and Loudoun Channels. There are several passages through the group, but only two, Sechart and Coaster Channels, are marked by lights. All other channels are hazardous, and unless in possession of local knowledge, should be approached cautiously. Parks Canada has a float and primitive office on the north side of Gibraltar Island. Primitive camping areas are on Hand, Turret, Gibraltar, Willis, Dodd, Clarke and Gilbert Islands. There is no potable water available on the islands. There are few good smaller craft anchorages in the Broken Group. Approaching from Coaster Channel, Effingham Bay or between Cooper and Batley Island are possibilities. Island Harbour, approached from Imperial Eagle Channel by way of Harbour Entrance is another. A sheltered anchorage is also made by Walsh, Turtle, Dodd, and Willis Islands. In addition to camping, kayaking is extremely popular. Five thousand kayakers explore the islands each year. Three First Nations reserves on the islands are not open to the public.

★ **Effingham Island & Effingham Bay:** The bay is on the northwest side of the island. Good anchorage, on a mud bottom, and room for a number of boats. Many kayakers and canoeists are in the area and the designated campsites are only for their use. From the head of Effingham Bay's southwest bight, a short trail leads across the island to one of about 100 First Nation village sites where a total of about ten thousand natives once lived. Just up from the shore is a 300' terrace which is actually a 30' deep midden, where for centuries, natives ate shellfish beside their fires. On close examination, some of the logs in this zone are seen to be squared rather than rounded, identifying them as round house beams.

★ **Walk-around:** Walking the beach toward the ocean, the seascape is rugged but the scenery and caves make the walk worthwhile. One cave is 100' deep and can be entered at lower tides. When exploring such caves great caution is required to avoid being trapped inside by a rising tide. Likewise, caution is also needed when beach walking along the West Coast because the dense underbrush along the shoreline can be impenetrable and one can be trapped by an incoming tide.

Jaques Island: While Jaques Island lagoon is intriguing for gunkholing, it is very rocky and shallow and for most boats is only accessible at higher tides.

Eagle Nook Resort & Spa   Photo © Eagle Nook Resort & Spa

Wouwer Island: This is one of the best examples of a rugged out-island on the coast. This close to the ocean, anchoring is precarious; however, in reasonable weather, there is provisional anchorage on the inside of the island. Entering this area from the west, the seas breaking all around on the nearby rocks can be intimidating. Entering from the east, there is an unlikely approach which is smoother but the extreme of gunkholing. Although this is not recommended, on higher tides and in mild weather, the tiny slit between Batley and Wouwer Islands is barely passable for most boats. Once inside, there are tight anchorages in the next two bays of Wouwer Island. Another way here is by dinghy from a more protected inland anchorage.

After taking the dinghy ashore, there's a short trail from the deepest bay to the other side of the island, directly facing the ocean. The beach here is jam-packed with drift logs. Walking the beach, over logs, around teeming tide pools and climbing

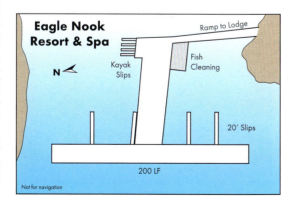

2024 Northwest Boat Travel

Chapter 18 WEST COAST VANCOUVER ISLAND

Tofino Harbour Photo © VPLLC

around headland here can be a highlight of the trip. There are thick carpets of mussels, dozens of roaring sea lions and eagles clinging to shreds of storm-torn trees. For any such walk, it's important to allow plenty of time because the walking is slow. Also take a flashlight because some of the trails like this are actually tunnels of dense salal and after dark they're absolutely black.

★ **Loudoun Channel:** Most of this channel is too open for good anchoring, but there are some locations at the north end. The southeast corner of Mayne Bay, off David Channel, is one. Another anchorage is in Pipestem Inlet, behind Bazett Island. The latter is more sheltered, but caution should be used because of rocks on both sides of the entrance. During fair weather, Toquart Bay offers sufficient shelter for anchoring in several small bays and coves. There is access to Toquart Bay by logging roads. Camping and launching facilities are very primitive.

★ **Ucluelet (8):** [3646] This picturesque fishing village is perched on the Ucluth Peninsula, located at the west entrance to Barkley Sound, 22 miles from Bamfield and is on the traditional territory of the Yuucluth-aht Yuułuʔiłʔatḥ people. Ucluelet, is pronounced you-clue-let, which means 'people of the safe harbour' in Nuu-chah-nulth. Yuułuʔiłʔatḥ (Government) is a modern treaty government, located in the village hitacu (on the starboard side of the inlet upon entering about .4km south of Port Albion). There are several public floats in the inlet, including the Eagle Marine fuel float with diesel, gas, and water. There is no longer a Canada Border Services Agency reporting site in the Ucluelet Harbour. The Otter Street Harbour, also known as "52 Steps", for the stairs that lead to the floats, is the deepest public moorage in Ucluelet and is the choice for large, commercial vessels. Space for recreational vessels may be available on the inside of the dock closest to shore. Ucluelet West, also known as Small Craft Harbour, is the most likely moorage for recreational boaters. This is the west coast's most comprehensive marine facility and is a classic example of a true working harbour. The facility has 20-amp service, fresh water, a maximum draft of 12 feet and is within walking distance of the village center. A launching ramp is just west of the Harbour. Various amenities can be found on Peninsula Road and Main Street including banks, a post office, grocery stores, pharmacies, and a laundromat. Accommodation options abound including motels, B & B's, lodges, and luxury accommodations. Throughout town there are shops and galleries, delis, bakeries, breakfast spots, food trucks, a vegan cafe and award-winning restaurants. You will also find fair trade, locally roasted artisan coffee, hand-blended teas, a microbrewery, and an award-winning distillery. Marine and electronic repair facilities are accessible at Pioneer Boatworks or Eric Larsen Diesel. Ucluelet is connected to Port Alberni by Hwy 4. Ucluelet is a growing tourist destination offering coastal beauty and recreation. Don't miss The Wild Pacific Trail (rated one of the top trails in BC), a great walking trail along the ocean and through the rainforest as well as the seasonal Ucluelet Aquarium (open March-November). This catch-and-release aquarium showcases intertidal life, including touch tanks and displays. Other activities include surfing, fishing, whale watching, kayaking, camping, hiking, and biking. Go to www.discoverucluelet.com to plan your trip.

Eagle Marine: Gas, diesel, oils, lubes, filters, batteries, water, marine supplies, rain gear, ice, bait/tackle. 250-726-4262.

Island West Resort: {48° 56' 47" N, 125° 32' 56" W} Moorage, 15 amp power, water, showers, laundry, sani-dump (for guests only), motel, launch ramp, RV sites, ice, store with snacks, restaurant/pub. 250-726-7515.

Ucluelet Otter St.: {48° 56' 28" N, 125° 32' 26" W} Moorage, water, garbage deposit, pay phone, 250-726-4241.

Ucluelet West Small Craft Harbour: {48° 56' 47" N, 125° 33' 9" W} Located west of the north tip of Lyche Island. Moorage, 30/50 amp power, pump-out, WiFi, water, washroom, laundry & shower, pay phone. 250-726-4241.

Barkley Sound To Clayoquot Sound

[3603, 3646, 3671, 3673, 3674, 3685]

★ **Carolina Channel:** Carolina Channel is the most direct route between Barkley and Clayoquot Sounds. Because of this and because it's also the most direct route to the fishing grounds, this fairly narrow channel is often crowded with fishing boats. Ordinarily none of this is a problem except in fog, which is often thick here. Between all the boats and reefs surrounding the channel, navigation is critical.

Long Beach: Accessible by land only with no moorage or shore access, this is a popular part of Pacific Rim National Park. Miles of sand and surf, numerous picnic areas and campsites are located near motels and restaurants. From late June to September, park service naturalists present programs. A large airport, established during the war, is still in use today.

★ **Tofino (9):** [3685] When approaching, watch for shoal areas in the harbour. A number of floats, both public and private line its waterfront. Among the public floats are the First Street Government Dock (no public moorage, loading/unloading only), Wingen Lane Dock, The 4th Street Dock, Lyons Gate (commercial vessels only) and the Crab Dock. The Harbour Office, located at the 4th Street Dock is open daily, May-Sept., 8am-5pm. No reservations, first come first served for Wingen Lane, 4th Street & the Crab docks.

Tofino is a small community in Clayoquot Sound. Since the Sound is made up of many inlets & fjords surrounded by old growth forests, boat exploration is ideal. Tofino's population is approximately 1,800 residents. Local facilities include a hospital, liquor store, bakery, bank, library, pharmacies and post office. Explore the local history at the Tofino Clayoquot Heritage Museum and schedule a walking tour. Accommodation options include resorts, hotels, motels, B & B's and vacation rentals. Shopping options include gift shops, art galleries and boutiques. Tofino offers a variety of restaurants from casual to fine-dining, a chocolate shop sure to satisfy any sweet tooth, as well as a coffee roaster, and a brewery that offers tastings. Also offered are a variety of activities and sightseeing opportunities. These include miles of sandy beaches, the Tonquin Trail and the Tofino Botanical Gardens with 12 acres of garden & forest trails leading down to the shoreline where bird watching is ideal. Tofino's seaplane companies offer scenic flights around picturesque Clayoquot Sound. Flights to the Hot Springs Cove can also be arranged. Tofino has a 9-hole golf course, kayak, bike and surf rentals, and charter companies offering fishing and guided tours including kayak, dug-out canoe, bird, whale, hot springs and bear watching, and skydiving. Tofino hosts many festivals throughout the year celebrating *Whales, Shorebird, Feast, Food & Wine, Carving Film and Oyster Festivals*. From May to September there is a public market every Saturday in the Village Green. In July, former NHL player Brendan Morrison hosts the *Tofino Saltwater Classic Fishing Derby* and in October the *Queen of the Peak* surf competition is held. A paved road connects Tofino and Ucluelet, with access to trails and majestic beaches found within Pacific Rim National Park Reserve. Tofino Bus operates all year round. 866-986-3466.

Tofino Harbour Authority: Crab Dock (Armitage Point): Transient moorage, 35' & under (rafting mandatory), 20/30 amp power, water. Services at 4th St Dock. Call in when you approach to confirm there is space. 250-725-4441. VHF 66A

Tofino Harbour Authority, 4th St. Dock: {49° 9' 17" N, 125° 54' 18" W} Transient moorage, 42' & under, (rafting mandatory), 20/30 amp power, water, laundry, washrooms, showers, wifi, boat launch & pump-out. Call in when you approach to confirm there is space. 250-725-4441. VHF 66A.

Visit us at boattravel.com

Tofino Harbour Authority, Wingen Lane {49° 9' 17" N, 125° 54' 18" W} No transient moorage. Dries at low tide. 250-725-4441. VHF 66A.

Tofino Resort + Marina: {49° 09.081 N, 125° 53.716 W} Annual and transient moorage, vessels to 130', reservations recommended. Gas (volume discount), 15/30/100 amp power, water, shower, laundry, security, wifi, gym, lodging, restaurant, pub, guided adventure tours. 844-680-4184. VHF 66A.

Method Marine Supply: Fuel, lube oil, propane, marine hardware & electronics, fishing/scuba gear. 250-725-3251. VHF 09.

Stubbs Island: Private wildlife reserve. No services for boaters. A fur trading post was established here in 1875.

★ **Yarksis:** Anchorage in the bay is possible in nine to 15 feet of water. Ruins of a former Native village are situated on Father Charles Channel on the southeast side of Vargas Island.

★ **Tofino Inlet:** Entering Tofino Inlet from Tofino, is more of a challenge than indicated from a glance at the chart. Traveling east from the main part of town, the channel becomes narrower. At the last dock, the Crab Dock, there's not enough room to easily turn a boat around between the dock and a sand bar to the north. Furthermore, the flood current is strong enough to sweep a boat into a reef just beyond the dock. Instead, a sharp left turn is required between two tight buoys. Also there's an uncharted rock right off the Tofino Resort and Marina dock. To avoid all this, especially on a flood tide, it is safest to use one of two more preferred but more indirect routes. One is through Heynen Channel and west of Morpheus Island and the other is through Duffin Passage and between Strawberry and Riley Islands. Because of these problems in the vicinity of the Crab Dock, the preferred dock, which is accessible unless full with fishing boats.

Tofino Inlet is a dead end. Because of this, fewer boats are found, yet the area contains some of the best and most secluded anchorages in Clayoquot Sound. If you dinghy to shore for a walk, be sure to tie the dinghy high and dry, or with the tidal range in this area, you could return to find the anchor under water. Much of the Inlet has been logged and may not be as scenic, but there are miles of logging roads to walk, some with spectacular views. Many roads appear to be close to the water, but reaching them may be nearly impossible due to an impenetrable maze of slash. Berry bushes are abundant along the roadsides, so be aware of bears and make plenty of noise. Wolves are often heard howling at night, even on a beach.

Grice Bay: There is a good paved ramp, parking, and a small campground here, but no floats. The bay is very shallow. This is a favorite spot for park naturalists who lead canoe and kayaking groups through this area.

★ **Island Cove:** At entrance to Tofino Inlet, there is protected anchorage in eight to nine fathoms of water. Use the passage north of the island in the entrance.

★ **Gunner Inlet:** Just north of Island Cove, this inlet has several protected anchorages.

★ **Kennedy Cove:** Found at the entrance to Kennedy River. Anchorage is possible in two to four fathoms of water in either the north or south side of the cove.

★ **Meares Island (10):** Mosquito Bay, in the northeast corner of Meares Island, has good anchorage in two to six fathoms of water. The passage west of Kirshaw and Wood Islets has the fewest obstructions. Also, Ritchie Bay, in the northwest corner, has good anchorage in four to five fathoms of water.

Clayoquot Sound to Nootka Sound

[3603, 3624, 3673, 3674, 3675]

★ **Hecate Bay and Cypress Bay:** These are opposite the northwest corner of Meares Island. Several very good anchorages are available. A unique floating complex, known as Freedom Cove, painted bright turquoise and pink is found in Cypress Bay. This combination art installation/dwelling is the self sustaining creation of artists Catherine King and Wayne Adams.

★ **Matilda Inlet:** This niche is in the southeast corner of Flores Island and has several attractions. Anchorage in the inlet is difficult and not recommended. One suggested spot is about 0.6 miles south of Matilda Inlet light, in 27m on a mud bottom. Ahousat, a settlement on the west side of the inlet, has a private float and a general store that, among other items, also carries local artwork. There is also a seasonal restaurant and a motel. Another restaurant, open all year, is located a short walk from the "old Hydro" deck. On the east side of Matilda Inlet is the Ahousaht First Nations village of Marktosis (known as Maaqtusiis in the Nuu-chah-nulth language). Local knowledge is advised when approaching Marktosis as the harbour approach can be hazardous. It is best visited with a skiff in good weather, approach the village on its east side. The Aa-uuk-nuk Lodge is located here and for hikers, there is an 11 km rustic trail known as the "Walk on the Wild Side". From a boardwalk in the forest to long stretches of beach (and occasional muddy spots), the trail leads from Ahousat to Cow Bay. Before hiking the trail visit the trail office in the village, info@wildsidetrail.com, or call 250-725-2169. There is a trail use fee of $25.00 per person ($15.00 for trail use and an additional $10.00 for camping). ⚐

Ahousat General Store: {49° 16' 55" N, 126° 4' 16" W} Gas, diesel, stove oil, water, groceries, marine railway for DIY haul-out, very limited moorage, post office. 250-670-9575. VHF 68.

★⚓ **Gibson Marine Park (11):** This BC Provincial Marine Park is located on the north shore of Whitesand Cove. Enter from Russell Channel. Ahousat Hot Springs are found in the park on Matilda Inlet. No marine facilities. A primitive hiking trail goes from Ahousat through the park to the broad, sandy beaches of White Sand Cove. ⛺⚐

★ **Cow Bay:** This is the local name for the bay just north of Russell Channel, into which Cow Creek flows. This is the most likely place to see gray whales. The beach at cow bay is the last beach on the "Walk on the Wild Side Trail." From here, the trail follows Cow Creek inland to the peak of Mt. Flores.

★ **Whitepine Cove:** Although this cove is open and exposed, just to its west is a portion of the cove which is fully protected. It is entered through the channel west of the charted 310 foot island and continuing south of the 240 foot island. At this point, the water is very shallow, however even at a fairly low tide, traveling slowly, the rocks can be seen and avoided. Inside, there's a wide area for anchorage.

Bawden Bay: The inner side of Bawden Bay has several little nooks to explore, however the whole bay is exposed to the north and the nooks are too small for proper anchoring.

★ **Ross Passage:** On the south side of Ross Passage there is presently a fish farm, but the north side is uninhabited and scenic. Inside the charted 200 foot island, there is anchorage and the channel there is passable.

★ **Gibson Cove:** This cove, on the east side of Herbert Inlet, offers good anchorage in six fathoms of water in the southeast corner.

★ **Sulphur Passage, East of Obstruction Island:** The bay in the southwest corner of the passage offers anchorage in seven to nine fathoms of water. The north end of this passage has many rocks and is not recommended.

★ **Riley Cove (12):** Located at the junction of Shelter Inlet and Sydney Inlet, this area has good shelter for anchoring. There is a mud bank in the harbour that should be located while looking for an anchoring location. A tie to shore might be a good idea.

★ **Sydney Inlet:** [3674] Sydney Inlet is a classic example of a fjord, spectacular to see, but too deep for good anchorage. It is an extensive, inviting waterway, enclosed with tall cones. The dense foliage is "trimmed" by the salt water, precisely to the high-water line, forming a horizontal line as far as the eye can see. A branching fjord, Stewardson Inlet, is also good for exploring.

★ **Young Bay:** This bay, located in Sydney Inlet, two miles north of Starling Point, offers secure anchorage in six to nine fathoms. A short walk to freshwater Cecelia Lake rewards the explorer with clean water and swimming. The trail has become nearly obliterated in places and is not an easy walk. The ruins, at the north side of the entrance, is that of a pilchard plant. Bays like this one offer about as much beauty as one could desire.

★ **Holmes Inlet:** This eastern branch of Sydney Inlet, offers some especially good gunkholing and unusual anchorages. The first unnamed bay entering Holmes Inlet on the east is called "Still Cove" because of its quiet serenity. It is entered through a bottleneck entrance with two narrow but passable constrictions. Inside the bay there's ample room for a good choice of anchorages.

Continuing north and east of a charted 225 foot island is another anchorage adjacent to the remains of an abandoned oyster farm. North of that, through a very narrow passage, is a tiny bay to the east with more remnants of the oyster farm. This bay is just large enough for one boat to anchor, with minimal scope in what feels like a mountain lake. From here there are two of the most narrow passages possible for gunkholing. The one leading west and north of the 225 foot island, has underwater rock shelves extending out from its sides. The other passage, to the north, is hardly discernible through the trees and at higher tide. It is barely negotiable, staying between the trees in mid-channel.

Pretty Girl Cove: The name alone makes this bay irresistible to see. The bay is scenic and the tidal grass at its head looks like an immense lawn. The anchorage, however, is not good because the bay is wide open. Also, as is typical of the heads of some of these bays that have streams entering them, the deltas formed by the streams end suddenly and drops like a cliff, here to 80 feet.

Exiting Sydney Inlet, toward the ocean, there are some tempting little bays along the western shore. These can be entered, but with the swells and the typical rocks, close navigation is necessary. The largest of these bays is behind a charted 190 foot island, where there is reasonably secure anchorage. This island is an example of places with forests of original growth.

★⚓ **Hot Springs Cove/Maquinna Provincial Park (13):** Part of the Maquinna Provincial Park, this cove is located at the northern entrance to Clayoquot Sound. To the east of the harbour entrance on Sharp Point is a light and a fog signal. On the west side is the Mate Island light. Favor a mid-channel course when entering the harbour. Approaching Hot Springs Cove from the north, there's a contrast between the way things look on a chart and how they actually are on the water. The narrow entrance is barely discernible until one is almost there, when finally, the two points forming its entrance separate. About two-thirds of the way into the bay on the north side is a First Nations Village. There is good anchorage available here, as well as public floats, mooring buoys, fuel, and as the name suggests, hot springs. The public wharf with an information shelter, toilet, and picnic area located at its head charges $2 per metre/night fee for moorage, no rafting. A boardwalk trail (2km/1mi long) leads from here to the hot springs. Anchoring near the springs to avoid the walk is not recommended and would be extremely difficult due to the surf. The Native word for the site is Mok-seh-kla-chuck, meaning smoking water, and during the peak months of July and August it draws up to 300 visitors daily. There is a $3.00 user fee (per person, per day). At the hot springs, water streams over a falls, through pools cut into the black rock, and into the ocean surf. This is a good place to sit among the rocks and watch the ocean sparkling below. If you like hot baths, try the higher pools. Bubbling out of the earth at about 117 degrees Fahrenheit, the water continues to cool gradually as it cascades to the pools below. The natural beauty of this area is spectacular. For an interesting side trip take a dinghy into the slit inside inner Mate Island. This requires about a mid-tide and you will need to secure the dinghy to the Vancouver Island side to protect it from the ocean. The beach that stretches to the northwest is some of the most rugged and scenic of the coast. Please note the Openit Peninsula portion of the park is a day use area and has some special restrictions. For restrictions information and park notices visit https://bcparks.ca or call 250-725-2169. ⚓🚶

★ **Nootka Sound (14):** [3675] It is about 28 nautical miles from Hot Springs Cove to Friendly Cove, allowing for plenty of clearance for Estevan Point and Perez Rocks on the Hesquiat Peninsula. With reasonable weather and good visibility, most of the first part of this coastline between Mate Island and Hesquiat Point can be taken close enough to see the large caves. It is possible, in good weather to land on some of these beaches and even in the entrances to the caves; however there are some important precautions. Because many of these caves were native burial sites, first obtain permission from Hesquiat band members to explore. Also, remember that when landing a dinghy on beaches exposed to the ocean you must be prepared for an unexpected swamping. Protect your valuables from the water and try to land the dinghy straight in, jumping quickly ashore with the painter. It is also possible that the waves breaking on the beach may not allow for an exit and the steep sides of caves may not allow for an escape. In such cases, there is a real advantage in taking a portable VHF radio when exploring.

A light and fog signal are on Estevan Point. Shoals extend a great distance. It would be possible to enter Hesquiat Harbour about seven nautical miles from the entrance to Hot Springs Cove. There are several good anchorages, but the Hesquiat Bar stretches across the entrance to this bay. There are rocks with kelp and shoals. Do not cross in rough weather. The most protected anchorage is Roe Basin at the head of the bay. When entering Hesquiat Harbour, the bar shallows to eighteen feet and is covered with kelp. Once inside, the remaining waves still make for a rolling anchorage, especially in the outer portions of the harbour. Extensive beaches, covered with clam shells, line most of the harbour. In the vicinity of Hisnet Lake there are some smaller caves which, with a little rock climbing, can be explored. In addition to caving, surfing off Nootka Island is gaining popularity, as is scuba diving in the Sound where the six gill sharks have been spotted. Nootka Sound has historical importance because it was the first place where Europeans entered the coast of British Columbia. ⚓

⚓ **Hesquiat Peninsula Provincial Park:** Situated between Nootka Sound and Hesquiat Harbour on the Hesquiat Peninsula. No developed trails, but a coastal route from Escalante Point to Boat Basin is traversed by experienced hikers. Fishing and windsurfing, as well as kayaking in Hesquiat Harbour are possible. Also of note is "Cougar Annie's" homestead and garden heritage site near Boat Basin.

★ **Friendly Cove:** There is a public pier and float available during the summer. No services at the docks. A village member is on hand to collect a landing fee and a small moorage fee (cash only). Considered the ancestral home of the Mowachaht/Muchalaht tribes, archaeological evidence indicates their presence in Yuquot for over 4,300 years. This spot, on the southeast corner of Nootka Island, just north of the San Rafael Island light, was also where Captain James Cook landed in 1778. Natives came to meet him and trade for goods. Four years earlier the natives had traded with Captain Juan Perez of Spain, but Perez did not actually come ashore. This fact eventually led to British sovereignty, but not before years of tension and near war between the two countries. A church onshore is adorned with native carvings and stained glass windows commemorating the meeting of Captain Vancouver and Commander Quadra which lead to a treaty in 1792 returning the cove to Britain. The Church is currently being renovated. The village of Yuquot in Friendly Cove was once lined with long houses, but today only one family lives here. The lighthouse overlooking the cove is probably the most accessible on this coast to visit. The lighthouse keeper is happy to show visitors the tower. Area campsites and cabins may be reserved. Call 250-283-2015 for information. Experienced hikers, for a $50 fee, can traverse the Nootka Trail. Every summer the *Yuquot Summerfest* features a traditional salmon BBQ. Many celebrants arrive by canoe. 🚶

★ **Santa Gertrudis Cove:** Nicknamed Dolly's Cove, this secluded, small bay about one half mile from Friendly Cove, offers protected anchorage. The very narrow entrance has rocks in the center and northern side. Even shallow draft boats should use extreme caution and enter only at high tide.

★ **Nootka:** About one and one half miles north of Friendly Cove, protected anchorage is available, but use caution as there are many underwater objects such as broken piles. This was once the town site of Nootka and the location of a thriving cannery. By 1982 the cannery was closed and in disrepair. Today, the cannery has new life as a fishing lodge.

Nootka Island Fishing Lodge: BYO boat moorage package includes room and meals. May-Sept, 604-909-4155. Oct-April, 604-960-0461.

★ **McKay Passage:** Between Saavedra Islands and Nootka Island.

★⚓ **Plumper Harbour:** Good sheltered anchorage can be found on the west side of Kendrick Inlet.

★ **Bligh Island, Bligh Island Provincial Marine Park:** [3664] Bligh Island fills the center of Nootka Sound. It is here where Captain Cook, accompanied by the infamous Captain Bligh, cut spars from the tall trees for their ships, Resolute and Discovery. At the extreme end and western bight of Ewin Inlet of Bligh Island is one of the most secluded anchorages anywhere. The park includes the south part of Bligh Island, Villaverde Islands, Pantoja Islands, Verdia Island, Vernaci Island and Spouter Island. ⚓

Tuta Marina: {49° 40' 32" N, 126° 28' 12" W} Located in Hanna Channel. Moorage, no power or water at dock, showers, freezers, ice, bait, launch ramp (tide dependent), RV & tent sites. 250-283-7550. ⚓▲

Gold River: [3675] This one time logging port at the head of Muchalat Inlet now hosts marine and seaplane access to smaller communities in the area. There is a municipal dock and a float plane dock. Nearby is a rough paved ramp (fee applies in summer). The town itself is eight miles inland, and is connected by paved highway to Campbell River. ⚓

Gold River Municipal Wharf: Very limited moorage, no amenities. 250-283-2202.

★ **Tlupana Inlet:** North of Bligh Island, this inlet has several anchorages in its bays and coves. As you travel into the Inlet, Galiano Bay, on the starboard shore is home to Nootka Sound Resort. Further up the inlet, near its head is a box canyon which wings into the end of Tlupana Inlet to the west and Nesook Bay to the east. Perpendicular Bluff at this junction is well named. It is so steep that a boat passing alongside would bump the inlet's sides before touching bottom, making anchoring in the vicinity difficult.

Nootka Sound Resort: {49° 42.391' N, 126° 28.251' W} BYO All-inclusive floating resort. Guided fishing, rental boats, BYO packages. Seasonal accommodations (June through August) bait, ice, gift shop. 1-877-337-5464.

★ **Hisnit Inlet:** This Inlet, branching west from lower Tlupana Inlet, has fair anchorage near its head and better anchorage in Valdez Bay. Near the head of Hisnit Inlet, at the mouth of the Conuma River in Moutcha Bay is the site of Moutcha Bay Resort Marina. Watching closely along the western shore near the head of the inlet, some weathered piles of gigantic marble slabs are visible. Small marble samples are easy pickings here and many other places along the coast. Oysters are plentiful, too, but always call the shellfish hotline, 604-666-2828 or visit www.pac.dfo-mpo.gc.ca for PSP (Red Tide) closures before harvesting. The Inlet is in Area 25-4. Valdez has a permanent year round sanitary closure.

Moutcha Bay Resort & Marina: {49° 47.280' N, 126° 27.67' W} Gas, diesel, propane, moorage, boat launch all offered year round. Seasonal services May to Sept: Full service marina, guided fishing, rental boats, snacks & beverages, bait/tackle, restaurant/pub, lodging, luxury yurts, RV/campsites, govt. inspected fish processing. 1-877-337-5464. ⚓

Critter Cove: Approximately one mile south of Argonaut Point, this unnamed cove is now known as Critter Cove after the marina located here. Charts show two rocks, one that dries 1.5m, located in the narrow channel leading to the inner basin behind Critter Cove. Small craft may find anchorage, but private float homes make it very tight.

Critter Cove Marina: {49° 42' 39" N, 126° 30' 22" W} Moorage, marine gas, lodging, restaurant, showers, ice, bait, tackle. Mid June to early Sept. 250-283-7364. Sat Phone: 250-412-6029. VHF 7.

★ **Tahsis Inlet:** [3604, 3624, 3675] The wind commonly funnels up or down this long fjord, providing sailors with one of the best spinnaker runs of the whole voyage. Gunkholing through Princesa Channel and behind Bodega Island, some protected anchorage is attainable. Mozino Point in the Tahsis Narrows has a coral grove that attracts scuba divers.

★ **Tahsis (15):** Located at the head of Tahsis Inlet this was once the winter village of Maquinna, the Nootka Chief who hosted Vancouver and Quadra here in 1792. In later years it was a sawmill town and port for overseas shipments of forest products. Today, tourism is the main industry. The village has public floats, marinas, fuels, repairs, water, ramp, showers, liquor, post office, library, groceries, hardware store, marine supplies, medical clinic, RV park with laundry facilities, restaurants, bed & breakfasts, and a modern recreation center with pool and exercise facilities that can be used for a small drop-in fee. 40 miles of good road connects the town to Gold River. Visitors can enjoy a multitude of activities including world-class fishing, wildlife viewing, hiking trails, windsurfing, kayaking, scuba diving, and spelunking. The InfoCentre and local Historical Museum are open during summer months. The Centre has a number of brochures available including an Historical Walking Tour Guide. Each July, *Tahsis Days* is celebrated with a parade, food, races, and lots of other fun activities. For more information on Tahsis visit www.villageoftahsis.com.

Tahsis Harbour Facility: {49° 54' 35.26" N, 126° 39' 44.29" W} Small craft harbor, deep at low tide, temporary moorage (2-hr limit, small fee applies) tide dependent launch ramp, parking for fee. 250-934-6344.

Westview Marina & Lodge: Permanent and transient moorage, gas, diesel, 15/30/50 amp power, water, showers, lodging, provisions, ice, laundry, restrooms, restaurant, floating patio/pub, live music Fri. nights June-Sept., fishing supplies, WiFi, mechanic on site. Great place for crew switch out (2.2 hr drive from Campbell River). 250-943-7672, 250-287-1394 (cell) or 1-800-992-3252. VHF 06.

★ **Esperanza:** [3624] There is a settlement on the north side of Hecate Channel with a small community dock and a DIY boat ways. Gasoline, diesel and tackle available year round. For service call on VHF 06 or ring the horn at the top of the dock. In addition to moorage they provide free wifi, access to laundry facilities and access to their greenhouse. Outgoing mail can be dropped off at the community post office. Each August the community operates as a summer camp for coastal youth. (During this time, no moorage, showers or laundry services are available to visiting boaters.)

Esperanza Marine Service: Gas, diesel, water, moorage, laundry & showers by donation, pop, snacks, ice & fish tackle. Free ice cream with purchase of gas or diesel. 250-483-4125. VHF 06.

★ **Ceepeecee:** This old cannery site is one mile northeast of Esperanza. The floats are private.

★ **Zeballos (16):** Zeballos is a quiet little village where visitors are welcomed. It's the kind of place where the locals will offer to phone the museum curator to give you a private tour or a chance meeting on the street might provide inside tips about the best local fishing spots. In 2017, Zeballos' water (which comes from a well) was named the "Best Tap Water in B.C.". Businesses and services

Zeballos — Photo © Lyn Hawley

here include a variety of lodging options, two general stores, liquor agent, ATM, Fuel dock (marine & road fuel) museum, library, campsite, RV site, secure parking, public washroom with shower, post office, medical clinic, ambulance station, float plane dock and concrete boat launch. As you walk along the main streets, historical interpretive signs provide a glimpse into the gold rush past of Zeballos that began with the discovery of gold in the 1920's. Hiking, fishing, camping, kayaking, caving, bird, whale and wildlife observing are popular recreational activities. A stretch of 42km/25 mi of active logging road connects the town to the paved Island Highway. Residents say that depending on the time of year, the ride almost always includes spotting bear, deer, elk or eagles, waterfalls, and gigantic boulders in the river sporting full grown trees. At Canyon Hill, a 5 inch wide vein of what may be quartz goes almost straight up about 40 feet. Village Office: 250-761-4229. www.zeballos.com.

Zeballos Fuel Dock & Marina: Transient & permanent moorage, water, marine gas & diesel, road gas & diesel, oil products, propane, hardware, sea ice, fishing tackle. 250-761-4201.

Zeballos Harbour Facilities: {49° 58' 45.1914" N, 126° 50' 37.2402" W} Small craft harbour. Draft is 10' deep at low tide. Moorage, 30 amp power, water, garbage/waste oil deposit, wifi, pay phone. 250-761-4333.

Espinosa Inlet: The Otter Islands mark the mouth of Espinosa Inlet. Once inside the inlet Newton Cove is to port and is the site of a fishing resort.

Newton Cove Resort: {49° 52' 26.5" N, 126° 56' 35.8" W} Luxury all-inclusive floating resort. Fully-guided and BYO boat packages with advanced reservations. Gas & diesel available for guests from July to Sept., bait, ice, gift shop. 1-877-337-5464.

★ **Queen Cove:** In Port Eliza, this cove has good anchorage in six fathoms on a mud bottom. Excellent for a relaxing stop over. Very protected. The entrance to the channel is narrow. Further into the inlet, past Eliza Island at about {49.88.510 N, 127.01.594 W} is the Port Eliza Lodge offering BYO Boat packages. For availability, call 949-456-3791.

★ **Nuchatlitz Inlet:** Although this inlet is somewhat out of the way for boats traveling in or out of Esperanza Inlet, with an extra day or two, its remoteness and beauty are worth the side trip. Its entrance is particularly rocky and right off the ocean like this, careful navigation is required. Once inside the rocks, there are several secluded anchorages. The most protected is Mary Basin, near the end of Nuchatlitz Inlet and behind Lord Island. This basin is large with a choice of anchorage sites.

★ **Inner Basin:** Beyond Mary Basin is the almost irresistible three mile Inner Basin. Its entrance is extremely narrow and rocky. It also has strong currents that are not listed in the tables, so the only safe way to enter is by waiting for a near slack current and, because of the shallow rocky entrance, this should preferably be the slack high water. This means you either make a quick trip, exiting again with the same slack current, or spend the night in the basin and return with the next day's high slack. Anchorage in the basin is possible along some of the shorelines, perhaps with a stern line ashore.

Nuchatlitz and Nuchatlitz Provincial Park: [3675, 3676] This First Nations village is in another part of the bay, not so far out of the way from Esperanza Inlet. The village itself is nearly abandoned now and the entrance is tricky and more easily accomplished by anchoring farther out and going by dinghy. The Park encompasses the northwest tip of Nootka Island along with some of the nearby small islets including Rosa Island. When ashore be aware that black bear are common to the islands.

★ **Esperanza Inlet (17):** [3624] This is the northern access to the inlets of Nootka Sound. Gillam Channel is the preferred approach because it is marked by navigational aids. Catala Island Marine Park is located in Esperanza Inlet.

★ **Catala Island Provincial Marine Park:** [3624] This island is accessible from anchorage in Queen Cove. An unusual beach on the southeast side is composed of mid-sized rocks so that they roll downhill with the beach walker. On the northeast side of the island, accessible at lower tides, is a series of interconnected caves. Rough trails lead to a lake and marshy area at the Island's center. Saltwater fishing, wildlife viewing, scuba diving and sea kayaking are among the recreational options. One pit toilet, no potable water, and wilderness camping available.

Rolling Roadstead: There is anchorage here in calm weather. Traveling to or from the northwest, Rolling Roadstead is a shortcut from the preferred Gillam Channel route. This shortcut not only saves a few miles but also avoids the usually rough ocean here. The portion of this route between Obstruction Reef and High Rocks, however, is reasonably close to some rocks which break heavily.

Nootka Sound to Kyuquot Sound

[3603, 3623, 3624, 3651, 3675, 3677]

★ **Clear Passage:** Traveling north, this passage is another shortcut which is easier to negotiate than Rolling Roadstead. Immediately before McQuarrie Islets, there is a break in the inner reef, through which a nearly direct inward turn can be made. Then stay in the middle of Clear Passage and turn back out just after Grogan Rock, a jagged 23 foot spire.

★ **Kyuquot Sound (18):** The distance from the outer marker in Gillam Channel to the outer marker for Kyuquot Channel is 13 nautical miles. Kyuquot Sound is the smallest of the five large sounds on the West Coast of Vancouver Island. Surrounded by fairly high mountains, Kyuquot Sound has two main inlets, Kashutl and Tahsis, and many islands and islets.

Dixie Cove: This cove on Hohoae Island is small, but has protected anchorage with no swells. A second anchorage, adjacent to Dixie Cove, is entered through the narrow channel. There is 20 feet of water here, even on a minus tide.

★ **Rugged Point Marine Provincial Park:** [3682] Accessible only by boat this park is home to one of the most beautiful shorelines on the west coast and offers spectacular views of the open Pacific Ocean and Kyuquot Sound. Safe places to anchor at Rugged Point make this park a popular destination. In bad weather, more sheltered anchorages can be found in nearby Dixie Cove, 5 miles to the east. Walk-in wilderness camping, small day-use/picnic area with a pit toilet, bear-proof food cache and open-walled cooking/picnic shelter near the beach. Kapoose Creek runs through the park to empty into the Pacific, providing a supply of fresh water for boaters and campers.

★ **Kyuquot & Walters Cove:** Walters Cove is a village located on the north side of Walters Island. The entrance to Kyuquot requires intricate and precise navigation because this entire area is a garden of rocks. Boaters and other visitors are advised to check in at the Ka:'yu:'k't'h'/Chek'tles7et'h' First Nations office, 250-332-5259, VHF 14. A public dock with two floats provides moorage with water and electricity found at {50° 1' 34" N, 127° 22' 30" W}. A general store that houses the post office is near the top of the ramp and is stocked with ice, fishing gear, bait, groceries, hardware, and produce, (generally open Mon., Wed., Fri. afternoons, 250-332-5211). Lodging and a seasonal restaurant are found here, as well. The Kyuquot Health Centre has a resident nurse who can be reached at 250-332-5289 or 250-332-5259 ext 205. Help is also available on VHF 6. Rose bushes line some very pretty lanes and the walkway resembles that of an English country village. Plans for a new Bighouse that will serve as a cultural and community centre are under-

way. Across the bay from the village, on Treaty Settlement Lands, there is another general store with ice cream, snacks, canned & dry goods, frozen meat and bread, open 7 days a week. The owner, Leo Jack, also runs Voyager Water Taxi email, vwt@gmx.com. Leo tells us that Jane Watson, a marine biologist who comes to Kyuquot to count sea otters every year in August says there are 200 otters in the raft inside of Spring Island and 2500 otters in Kyuquot alone. Valued for their pelt, B.C. sea otters were almost driven to extinction by the late 1920's. Sea otters from Alaska were transplanted to the northwest coast between 1969-1972. The present population on Vancouver Island is estimated at 3,000. In addition to wildlife viewing, kayaking, salmon fishing, camping and hiking are among the things to do here.

★ **Fair Harbour:** Entering through Kyuquot Channel, the first good anchorage is about ten miles in, on the east side. Some anchorage on a mud bottom can be found in either the east or west end. During north gales the wind may funnel into the harbour, but the holding ground is good. Fair Harbour is connected to Zeballos by 20 miles of logging roads. This is the only land access to Kyuquot Sound. A public dock with a float and a launch ramp are found in the harbour. A fuel station is located nearby. Campsites with picnic tables, fire rings, and pit toilets are located about one-half mile from the wharf.

Fair Harbour Marina and Campground: Moorage, gas, diesel, propane, outboard oil, boat launch, fishing tackle, convenience store, showers & laundry facility, camping telephone, wifi. Rental cabins and fishing charters are available. 250-483-3382. VHF 12.

★ **Kashutl Inlet:** Anchorages can be found in Hankin Cove, on the east side of the inlet in 40-60 feet of water. The cove is a booming ground with logging operations. There are no anchorages in Tahsis Inlet. Easy Inlet, on the west side of Kashutl Inlet, is another anchorage with good holding ground. Small craft anchorage is also available in Wood Cove.

★ **Crowther Channel:** Heading north from Kyuquot Sound, the route through this channel is much shorter than the more preferred Kyuquot Channel route. There is a narrow but deep exit between Amos Island and a charted 26 foot rock to the south.

Kyuquot Sound to Quatsino Sound

[3604, 3623, 3624, 3651, 3677, 3679, 3680, 3683, 3686]

Checleset Bay (19): The 56 mile stretch from Kyuquot Sound to Winter Harbour is one of the longer runs on the West Coast. One must cross Checleset Bay and round Cape Cook on Brooks Peninsula. There are three smaller inlets in Checleset Bay that offer shelter (Malksope, Ououkinsh, Nasparti), but the approaches have many hazards, especially during poor weather conditions. The coast along the southeast side of Brooks Peninsula, northeast of Clerke Point is locally known as Shelter Shed and is used by fishermen in northwest winds. Columbia Cove, inside Jackobson Point in Nasparti Inlet has good shelter. Entrance is between Jackobson Point and the unnamed island. A drying rock spit extends from Jackobson Point. Watch depths as silting has been reported. Very large swells can be encountered rounding Cape Cook, even for those traveling a good two miles outside of Solander Island.

Checleset Bay Ecological Reserve: Includes the waters of the Bay, as well as those of the west side of Gay Passage adjacent to Big Bunsby Marine Provincial Park. No motorized vehicles, no hunting, fishing, or camping on the reserve.

★ **Bunsby Islands/Big Bunsby Marine Provincial Park:** Bunsby Islands offer some of the best of gunkholing as well as dinghy exploring. Scow Bay, West Nook and South Cove are some of the better anchorages along both sides of Gay Passage. Getting to the Bunsby Island from Kyuquot, is a protected passage inside the Barrier Islands. Entering this passage at St. Paul's Dome, use careful navigation between the inner and outer set of reefs. Big Bunsby Marine Provincial Park is found here. Fishing, kayaking, canoeing and wildlife viewing are activities that visitors enjoy. The park is located with the traditional territory of the Kyuquot/Checleset First Nation peoples. First Nations reserves located within the Bunsby Islands are not for recreational use. Visitors are encouraged to contact the band office in Kyuquot prior to exploring the Bunsby Islands. 250-332-5259.

Battle Bay: Battle Bay is very rocky, but has some areas offering reasonable anchorage. The Bay is part of the Checleset Bay Ecological Reserve.

★ **Nasparti Inlet:** The Inlet area has several choices of interesting anchorages. Dinghy exploring into lagoons, like Johnson Lagoon, with a narrow entrance, however, holds a risk. Always size up the entrance carefully for currents before approaching. Unless the entire entrance way can be seen, there is the danger of capsizing.

Cape Cook: Exiting the interior of Checleset Bay in any direction, navigation is especially important. The reefs here are probably more extensive and difficult to identify than any along the coast. With the constant ocean swells breaking over their exposed and unexposed rocks, these kinds of reefs are the most dangerous. Rounding Cape Cook from this direction, another hazard is the first prominence of Brooks Peninsula, Clerke Point. Surrounded by kelp one-and-one-half miles out, this broad shallow grounds must be given a wide berth. Cape Cook, along with the entire Brooks Peninsula, juts farther out into the ocean than any other prominence of the coast. Because of this, the wind is accelerated and it is likely to be the roughest part of circumnavigation, hence the moniker "Cape of Storms." On the other hand, surfing with the wind in a sailboat here, can be one of the most thrilling parts of the voyage. There are no adequate anchorages all the way around the end of the peninsula. The route often taken by local fishing boats inside of Solander Island is tricky to navigate, doesn't save much distance and is not recommended. Because the outside of Solander Island is deep, the island can be taken close enough for a good view of the extensive population of sea birds and sea lions on this barren monarch of an island. This general area of Vancouver Island is particularly desolate and other mariners are less frequent. Yet in these waters, the boat often parts tens of thousands of common murrs, rhinoceros auklets, sooty shearwaters and tufted puffins.

★ **Brooks Bay (20):** [3624, 3651, 3680] This is the most remote major bay along the coast. Even during the peak of the summer, a mariner is likely to be the only one here.

★ **Klaskish Inlet & Klaskino Inlet:** These inlets indent into Vancouver Island north of Brooks Peninsula. Klaskish Inlet is deep. The basin at the head has protected anchorage from the seas, however, strong winds can blow down from the mountains. There are public mooring buoys in the basin. Klaskino Inlet, farther north, is entered north of Heater Point. There is an anchorage southeast of

Anchorage Island and a few public mooring buoys are east of the island. A fresh water stream exits the delta south of there, with a three foot deep pool of water about 100 yards upstream.

★⛺ **Lawn Point and Lawn Point Provincial Park:** [3680] The entire reef surrounded prominence of Lawn and Kwakiutl Point are examples of why it is a good rule to give most of the west coast of Vancouver Island a two mile berth. Kelp beds obscure hazardous rocks especially in waters just south of Lawn Point. The park, popular with kayakers has wilderness camping, no facilities.

★ **Quatsino Sound (21):** [3605, 3624, 3679, 3686] This is one of the largest sounds on the west coast of Vancouver Island. It has several communities in it, all but one connected by road to Port Hardy. There are strong tidal currents in parts of the sound, especially in Quatsino Narrows, where the maximum is usually five knots, but can reach eight at springs. Heavy tide-rips are also encountered at times. Please note that logbooms travel both directions in Quatsino Narrows. They have the right of way & monitors Channel 06.

★ **Winter Harbour:** This interesting fishing community is at the head of Forward Inlet, 15 miles from Holberg and 47 miles from Port Hardy by logging roads. There is sheltered anchorage in eight fathoms of water over mud. About a dozen residents live here year round, but the summer population swells to nearly 300. Commercial and recreational moorage can be found at a public dock, as well as two private marinas. This is a stop on the biennial Van Isle 360 International Yacht Race. The community also has a public telephone, garbage & recycling, launch ramp, B & B's and a general store that is open all year and has satellite internet WiFi. Marine gas and diesel are available. A community center houses a library, post office, and restrooms. Take a stroll along the old wooden waterfront boardwalk, or through towering old growth trees on the Botel Trail leading to the beach.

Qualicum Rivers Winter Harbour Fishing Lodge & Resort: Moorage at Government Wharf. Fishing charters, flaked ice, wifi. 1-800-960-2646. VHF 68.

The Outpost at Winter Harbour: {50° 30' 40" N, 128° 1' 44" W} Moorage, gas, diesel, coin-operated laundry & showers, washroom, store, liquor, ice, fishing supplies, pay per use Satellite Internet wifi hot spot, lodging, camping/RV sites by reservation, fish cleaning tables. 250-969-4333. VHF 19. ▲

Winter Harbour, Harbour Authority: {50° 30' 46.4796" N, 128° 1' 45.051" W} Moorage, 15/20/30 amp power, water, washroom, garbage, recycling, waste oil bin, grid, pay phone. During summer call 1-800-960-2646. VHF 68.

Winter Harbour Marina & RV: Moorage, water, some power, fish cleaning tables. Washroom, launch ramp, RV sites, cabin rentals, fishing charters, ice, fish freezer rentals. 250-969-4325.

★ **North Harbour:** On the west side of Forward Inlet, North Harbour also offers sheltered anchorage in seven fathoms of water. Mooring buoys.

★⛺ **Koprino Harbour & Quatsino Marine Park:** Anchorages are west and north of Schloss Island. The park has campsites and a small dock. A rough, unmaintained trail leads to Koprino Lake, in the center of the park. ▲

★ **Pamphlet Cove:** Land around this cove has been purchased as a recreational reserve. It is on the north side of Drake Island and has sheltered anchorage.

Port Alice Rumble Beach Marina Photo © Darrell McIntosh, North Island Images

★ **Julian Cove:** Southeast of Banter Point in Buchholz Channel is small but has anchorage for small craft.

Quatsino: This small, remote hamlet stretches along 8 km of gravel road. It has a public dock, but no fuel services. Settled as a Norwegian colony in 1895, Quatsino is one of the North Island's earliest European settlements. Find out more about this heritage on historical signage found throughout the community. Points of interest, listed on an information board near the government wharf, include: two small cemeteries, historic St. Olafs' Anglican Church (built in 1896 it is one of the oldest buildings still in use on Northern Vancouver Island), Quatsino Elementary School (built in 1935, closed in 2008 and awaits a required enrollment minimum of just 9 students to reopen.) The Quatsino Museum & Archives with a unique local wildlife display out front, makes an interesting stop. Free internet access is available at here. Open: 1-2pm daily during July and August, and weekends the rest of the year. (Or open by request, quatsino.museum@recn.ca). The community also has a fire department with 911 service, a recycle facility, a full service post office, open 9am-5pm on Monday and Thursday and noon-5pm on Tuesday and Wednesday. The Colony Lake Trail starts across the road from the post office. This new, 1km trail is an excellent walk with lots of nice bridges along the way. It accesses a great place to picnic and swim. An outhouse is available at the trail's end. Quatsino has several sportsfishing and guest lodges, some open year round. Area waters are great for fishing, kayaking and scuba diving.

Kagoagh Resort & Fishing Lodge: {50° 32' 58.1388" N, 127°36' 11.9412" W} Located in Hecate Cove. Overnight moorage if space is available. Moor while dining with advanced reservations. Lodging, laundry, showers, hot tub, fish charters advance reservations required. 250-902-0434.

Quatsino Lodge: Deep water overnight moorage with advance notice. Water, freezer facilities, laundry (available upon request). Moor while dining with advanced reservations. Kayak tours/rentals, guided fishing. 1-866-279-5061.

Jeune Landing, Neroutsos Inlet: A small logging settlement with a public dock and float. Transient moorage if space is available, contact phone numbers are posted at the dock. No services. Located a mile from Port Alice.

★ **Port Alice:** [3679, 3681] Just 30 minutes off of Highway 19, this community of 800 at the end of Neroutsos Inlet is known as the Gateway to the Wild West Coast, providing access to prime fishing and recreation areas such as Side Bay, Gooding Cove and Winter Harbour. Moorage facilities for recreational boaters are offered at the Municipal Float (Rumble Beach Marina). The Port Alice Yacht Club Float {50° 25' 25"N, 127° 29' 6"W}, is a private facility.

Within walking distance from the marina, the Village of Port Alice offers overnight accommodations, RV sites, laundry facilities, a golf course, an ice rink, restaurants, grocery store, gas station, bank, a liquor store, RCMP and a medical clinic. For information on fuel, call Port Alice Petroleum, 250-284-3530.

Local trail systems are fun to explore and the sheltered waters surrounding Port Alice are perfect for kayaking, scuba diving and fishing. For Village information, call the municipal office at 250-284-3391.

Port Alice Municipal Float (Rumble Beach Marina): {50° 25' 25"N, 127° 29' 6"W} Moorage for vessels to 100', no reservations. Potable water, garbage disposal, public washrooms, fish cleaning station. Paved ramp, parking for fee. May-Oct call 250-209-2665.

★ **Coal Harbour (22):** This harbour is 12 miles from Port Hardy by paved road. This is the best access to Quatsino Sound for trailer boaters. There is wharf with marine fuel, as well as a good paved ramp with adequate parking next to the dock area. Mechanical repairs are available. Other amenities in Coal Harbour include fishing charter, water taxi & seaplane. Originally a coal-mining site, Coal Harbour became a seaplane base for Catalinas in the 1930's. The infrastructures that remained were later used for the whaling industry. This village was a whaling station through 1967 where whales were brought ashore for processing. One hanger where whale blubber was rendered still exists and is home to a floatplane company. The rings to which cables were fixed for hauling the whales ashore as well as jaw bones of whales can still be seen adjacent to the boat ramp.

Sunset Fishing by the Quatsino (Kains Island) Lighthouse   Photo © Qualicum Rivers Winter Harbour Lodge & Resort

Quatsino First Nations Dock: {50° 35' 53" N, 127° 34' 44" W} Moorage, 10/20 amp power, water, laundry, shower, restroom, kayak launch. Gas, diesel, oils (call for hours). 250-949-6870.

DH Timber Towing: Operates tugs, water launch, emergency towing in Quatsino Sound. 250-949-6358. VHF 06.

★ **Holberg:** This once thriving logging community is at the head of Holberg Inlet. There is a community dock, launch ramp, general store with gas, post office, restaurant/pub with grocery store. Don't miss the shoe tree which is a large cedar covered in hundreds of shoes.

★ **Varney Bay, Rupert Inlet:** Anchorage in this bay is near the inlet entrance. There is a large drying flat at the head of the bay. From Varney Bay, a dinghy can be taken at higher tides into the box canyon of nearby Marble River, with its overhanging caves. Utah Copper Mines, on the inlet's north side, has an ore loading facility for large ships.

Quatsino Sound to Port Hardy

[3549, 3605, 3624, 3679]

★ **Kains Island:** Leaving Quatsino Sound, fishing boats often take the route inside Kains Island; however, without local knowledge, the route outside the island is the safest.

⚓ **Raft Cove Provincial Park:** This park, located at the mouth of the Macjack River is undeveloped, remote, and open to winds and high waves. Anchorage is possible only in good weather. The park is accessed by land via gravel logging roads out of Holberg. It is a 40 minute walk along a rough, often muddy trail between the parking lot and the long, sandy beach in the bay. Board surfers, in growing numbers are discovering the challenges of the Pacific surf. Scuba diving is possible here as well. River otters are often viewed at the estuary at the mouth of the river. Be aware of black bears. Backcountry camping ($5 PP) & pit toilets, no fresh water.

★ **Sea Otter Cove (23):** Heading north from the entrance to Quatsino Sound, it is 56 nautical miles to the first secure anchorage at Bull Harbour. Sea Otter Cove is a possible stop along the way. Use Chart #3624. The cove, which is well used by small crafts during the summer, lies east of Cape Russell and is marked by a light. Kelp covers most rocks and reefs. The entrance is very shallow and should be approached cautiously. There are mooring buoys in the cove. There is a fresh water stream on the north shore.

★ **Hansen Bay:** Although Hansen Bay is exposed, in reasonably calm weather, provisional anchorage is possible for a brief dinghy trip into Hansen Lagoon. In lagoons like this, however, being caught in a dropping tide can mean a long muddy wait for the next high tide.

Cape Scott Provincial Park: This cape is the northwest corner of Vancouver Island. The weather is often windy and tidal currents of up to three knots can cause heavy tide-rips and overfalls on both sides of Scott Channel, between the Cape and the Scott Islands. When the wind is against the tide these areas can be dangerous. Rounding Cape Scott is probably the highlight of a Vancouver Island voyage. It is the point where the mariner turns the boat clear around, heading back the other way. Cape Scott is connected to the mainland of Vancouver Island by a half mile sand isthmus that can be accessed from either its north side in Experiment Bight, when the weather is from the south or from its south side in Guise Bay, when the weather is from the north. Either of these bays can be used for protection and provisional anchorage in the case of storms. Experiment Bight is open, but Guise Bay takes some navigating to get between a reef in the middle of its entrance and rocks on either side. Once ashore, this extensive and desolate isthmus can be crossed for some beautiful beach walking on both sides. Use caution and watch for signs showing the way. There is an ongoing wolf awareness advisory. Call 1-877-952-7277 to report aggressive wildlife. Backpackers need to come adequately prepared as this is a rugged wilderness area.

Scott Islands: The five Scott Islands extend 25 miles west from Cape Scott. None offer very protected anchorage and they are so exposed, venturing there can be risky - as illustrated by the Triangle Island Lighthouse, destroyed by a storm despite being braced and cabled to the island.

Nahwitti Bar (24): See current tables for Seymour Narrows, BC. This bar stretches across the west entrance to Goletas Channel. It is best crossed at times of slack. Because of shallowing depths as low as six fathoms, waves break over the bar. If traveling from north Vancouver Island around Cape Scott, it is possible to cross Nahwitti Bar at high slack and ride the ebb tide out. With a west wind opposing a falling tide, there can be very heavy breaking and dangerous seas. The alternative is to go around Hope Island.

★ **Bull Harbour & Hope Island (25):** [3549] This harbour, on the south side of Hope Island, is marked by an entrance light. Use caution as finfish aquaculture pens are located near the entrance There is a three knot speed limit in the harbour. Pass to the right of the island in the entrance. Anchorage is possible between the two docks in mid-bay. Do not go too close to the head because it shoals rapidly. The harbour is open to southeast winds. All of Hope Island, including the Village of Bull Harbour, is the property of the Tlatlasikwala First Nation. There are no services, or public facilities available at this time on Hope Island so visitors are asked not to go ashore until the Tlatlasikwala First Nation have completed their management plan and building of associated infrastructure for visitors. Please treat Hope Island as you would private property. Moorage on wharf docks is first come, first served. $25.00 Cdn/night, or $1.00/foot of vessel/night – whichever is greater. Please make payment to: Tlatlasikwala First Nation, P.O. Box 339, Port Hardy, BC, V0N 2P0. Docks and slips may be undergoing repairs. Please do not tie up on the last (northern most) section of floating dock, it is reserved for float planes. For latest information visit www.tlatlasikwala.com. VHF 6, 16.

★ **Goletas Channel:** See current tables for Seymour Narrows, British Columbia. Inside Nahwitti Bar extends east southeast from Godkin Point, the entrance to Bull Harbour, to Duval Point, the northwest entrance to Port Hardy. It is deep and free from obstructions. This is a good place to troll for silvers. Try Buzz Bombs near the surface while traveling at three knots.

★ **Loquillia Cove:** This cove can be used for anchorage in settled weather or in northwest winds. Open to the southeast. Avoid kelp covered rocks at southern entrance.

★ **Shushartie Bay:** Open to the northwest. There is anchorage in five fathoms of water on the east shore near the entry.

★ **Port Alexander:** There is anchorage at the southeast corner of Nigei Island.

★ **God's Pocket (26):** This niche on Christie Passage has been a favorite shelter for fishermen for many years. Anchorage can be found on the west side of Hurst Island. God's Pocket Resort is on shore. See information in Chapter 17. The waters around God's Pocket are among the world's best cold water diving areas.

★ **Port Hardy (27):** This area is described in Chapter 17.

Visit us at boattravel.com

Essential Supplies & Services

AIR TRANSPORTATION
To & from Washington
NW Seaplanes... 425-277-1590, 1-800-690-0086
San Juan Airlines........... 1-800-874-4434
Seattle Seaplanes........... 1-800-637-5553
To & from Islands/Vancouver
Air Canada 1-888-247-2262
Harbour Air..................... 1-800-665-0212
Pacific Coastal Airline . 250-725-1230, 1-800-663-2872
Tofino Air 1-866-486-3247
Vancouver Island Air................. 250-287-2433

BOOKS / BOOK STORES
Evergreen Pacific Publishing 425-493-1451
The Marine Atlas.................... 253-872-5707

BUS TRANSPORTATION
Tofino Bus (The Island Bus) Locations 1-866-986-3466
  Tofino 250-725-2871
  Port Alberni 250-724-1266
  Ucluelet...................... 250-726-4337
Port Alberni Transit................. 250-723-3341
West Coast Trail Bus 250-477-8700

COAST GUARD
Prince Rupert Coast Guard........... 250-627-3082
Marine Distress, Search & Rescue
  .... 1-800-567-5111 (in Canada) or 250-413-8933
Cell Phone (limited to select providers) ... *16 or #727

CUSTOMS 1-888-226-7277

FERRY INFORMATION
Gold River/Nootka/Kuyquot/Tahsis (Passenger, freight only) 250-283-2515
Bamfield / Port Alberni/Ucluelet (Passenger only)
.... 250-723-8313

FISHING/SHELLFISHING INFO
Recorded Notificiation 250-723-0417
Port Alberni DFO..................... 250-720-4440
Tofino DFO........................... 250-725-3500
Nootka Sound Hotline................. 604-666-2828

FUELS
Ahousat General Store: Gas, Diesel
.... 250-670-9575 VHF 68
China Creek: Port Alberni. Gas, Diesel .. 250-723-9812
Coal Harbour QFN.................... 250-949-6870
Critter Cove: Gas............... 250-412-6029 VHF 7
Eagle Marine: Ucluelet............... 250-726-4262
Esperanza: Gas, Diesel .... 250-483-4125 VHF 06
Fair Harbour Marina .... 250-483-3382 VHF 78A
Hot Springs Cove (First Nation Village)
McKay Bay Lodge: Bamfield. Gas, Diesel 250-728-3323
Method Marine Supply: Tofino, Gas, Diesel
.... 250-725-3251 VHF 09
Moutcha Bay: Gas, Diesel.......... 1-877-337-5464
Pacific Gateway Marina: Gas, Diesel.. 250-412-5509
Poett Nook: Gas 250-720-9572
Petro Canada: Port Alberni, Somass River . Gas, Diesel
  (Must Hand Carry to Boat) 250-724-2626
Port Alberni Marine Fuels & Services Ltd: Gas, Diesel..
.... 250-730-3835 VHF 06
Port Alice Petroleum (Call Ahead)...... 250-284-3530
Port Renfrew Marina: Gas, Diesel...... 250-483-1878
Quatsino First Nation Dock, Gas, Diesel . 250-949-6870
Sunny Shores Marina: Sooke. ... 250-642-5731 VHF 6
Tofino Resort & Marina: Gas 1-844-680-4184 VHF 66A
Westview Marina: Tahsis ..... 250-934-7672 VHF 6
Winter Harbour: Gas, Diesel 250-969-4333
Zeballos Fuel Dock. Gas, Diesel 250-761-4201

GOLF
Port Alberni...................... 250-723-5422
Port Alice Golf & Country Club....... 250 284-3213
Tofino 9-hole 250-725-3332

HAUL-OUTS
Ahousat General Store .... 250-670-9595 VHF 68
CME Engineering: Port Alberni....... 250-723-0111
Sunny Shores Resort & Marina .250-642-5731. VHF 16

HOSPITALS
Healthlink BC (Nurse Helpline) . 1-866-215-4700 or 811
Bamfield (Health Center)............. 250-728-3312
Kyuquot .... 250-332-5289 (Nurse) VHF 6
Port Alberni (Hospital) 250-731-1370
Port Alice Health Centre 250-284-3555
Tahsis Health Centre................. 250-934-6404
Tofino General Hospital 250-725-4010
Ucluelet (Dr. office)................... 250-726-4443
Zeballos Health Clinic 250-761-4274

LIQUOR STORES
Bamfield   Tahsis
Gold River   Tofino
Port Alberni   Ucluelet
Port Alice   Winter Harbour
Sooke   Zeballos

LODGING
Eagle Nook Resort 604-357-3361
Island West Resort.................. 250-726-7515
Pacific Gateway Wilderness Lodge..... 250-728-3646

MARINAS / MOORAGE FLOATS
Ahousat
Bamfield Harbour Authority 250-720-7548
China Creek Marina................... 250-723-9812
Clutesi Haven: Port Alberni..... 250-724-6837 VHF 69
Critter Cove.................... 250-412-6029 VHF 7
Eagle Nook Resort 604-357-3361
Esperanza .... 250-483-4125 VHF 6
Esperanza Marine Service...... 250-483-4125 VHF 06
Fisherman's Harbour: Port Alberni 250-723-2533
Gold River Municipal Wharf 250-283-2202
Harbour Quay: Port Alberni............ 250-723-1413
Island West: Ucluelet .... 250-726-7515 VHF 66A
Kyuquot
Maquinna Resort & Tahsis Marina Hotel 250-934-6200
Moutcha Bay Resort.................. 877-337-5464
Pacific Gateway Marina............... 250-412-5509
Poett Nook Marina 250-720-9572
Port Alberni Yacht Club
Port Alice Municpal Float 250-209-2665
Port Renfrew Marina & RV Park.. 250-483-1878 VHF 6
Sooke Harbour Authority 250-642-4431
Sooke Harbour Resort & Marina....... 250-642-3236
Sunny Shores Resort & Marina
.... 250-642-5731. CB 13, VHF 16
Tofino Resort + Marina............. 1-844-680-4184
Tofino Harbour...................... 250-725-4441
Tuta Marina: Gold River 250-283-7550
Tyee Landing 250-723-2533
Ucluelet Small Craft Harbour 250-726-4241
Westview Marina 250-934-7672
Winter Harbour Harbour Authority 800-960-2646
Winter Harbour Marina & RV 250-969-4325
Winter Harbour (The Outpost) 250-969-4333
Zeballos Fuel Dock & Marina 250-761-4201
Zeballos Harbour 250-761-4333

PROPANE
China Creek, Port Alberni 250-723-9812
Fair Harbour Marina & Campground.... 250-483-3382
Method Marine: Tofino .... 250-725-3251 VHF 9
Moutcha Bay Resort & Marina 1-877-337-5464
Petro Canada: Port Alberni 250-724-2626
Zeballos Fuel Dock 250-761-4201

RAMPS
China Creek: Port Alberni 250-723-9812
Clutesi Haven: Port Alberni..... 250-724-6837 VHF 69
Coal Harbour
Esperanza Marine Service...... 250-483-4125 VHF 06
Fair Harbour 250-483-3382
Island West Resort: .... 250-726-7515 VHF 66A
Pacheedaht Campground, Port Renfrew. 250-647-0090
Pacific Gateway Marina............... 250-412-5509
Poett Nook Marina 250-720-9572
Quatsino First Nations Dock 250-949-6870
Sooke Harbour Resort 250-642-3236
Sunny Shores: Sooke .... 250-642-5731 VHF 16
Bamfield, Gold River, Grappler Inlet, Grice Bay, Holberg,
  Port Alberni, Port Alice, Tahsis, Tofino 4th St Dock,
  Ucluelet, Winter Harbour, Zeballos

REPAIRS
Breakers Marine: Bamfield 250-728-3281
CAE Engineering: Port Alberni 250-723-0111
Pioneer Boatworks, Ucluelet........... 250-726-4382
Westview Marina,Tahsis.............. 250-934-7672

RESTAURANTS
Critter Cove Marina.................. 250-283-7364
Eagle Nook Resort 604-357-3361
Eagle's Nest 250-726-7515
Moutcha Bay Resort & Marina 877-337-5464
Pacific Gateway Marina............... 250-412-6121
Westview Marina & Lodge 250-934-7672

SCUBA SITES
Ucluelet, Mazino Point, Tahsis

SEWAGE DISPOSAL
Port Alberni Fisherman's Harbour: Pump
.... 250-723-2533
Tofino: Pump 250-725-4441
Ucluelet: Island West. Dump. 250-726-4241

TAXI
Port Hardy (North Island)............. 250-949-7877
Port Alberni...................... 250-723-2121
Port McNeill 250-230-2655

TOWING
C-TOW 1-888-419-CTOW
DH Timber Towing 250-949-6358

VISITOR INFORMATION
Bamfield (Centennial Park)........... 250-728-3006
Sooke 250-642-6351
Tahsis Village Office 250-934-6344
Tofino/Long Beach 250-725-3153

WEATHER
VHF WX-1, 2, Race Rocks WX-3, Port Alberni WX-7,
  VHF Cape Scott, Quatsino, Holberg, Esperanza,
  Nootka VHF 21B
Environment Canada Weather Line..... 250-339-9861

Chapter 19:
Northern British Columbia

Blunden Harbour to Portland Canal. Bella Bella, Shearwater, Ocean Falls, Bella Coola, Klemtu, Kitimat, & Prince Rupert; Seymour, Smith, Rivers, Fish Egg, Kynock, Roscoe, Mussel, Laredo, Khutze, Lowe, Kumealon, Khutzeymateen, & Observatory Inlets; Banks, Princess Royal, Pitt & Haida Gwaii (Queen Charlotte Islands).

Cow Bay - photo © Lonnie Wishart

Symbols

[ ]: Numbers between [ ] are chart numbers.

{ }: Numbers & letters between { } are waypoints.

★ Recommended destinations, facilities, and services.

⛺: Park, 🚤: Boat Launch, ▲: Campgrounds,
🥾: Hiking Trails, ⛱: Picnic Area, 🚴: Biking
🤿: Scuba

Important Notices

★ See "Important Notices" between Chapters 7 and 8 for specific information on boating related topics such as boating safety, weather, U.S. & Canadian marine radio use, Vessel Traffic Service, security zones, Canadian & U.S. Customs, etc. Due to changing regulations, call ahead to verify latest customs information.

Fuel, Supplies, & Services Availability & Seasonal Changes: Many facilities appearing in this chapter are seasonal or have seasonal hours. May - Sept is high season. Other times of the year it is wise to call ahead to check on availability of fuel, provisions, and other services. We have provided telephone numbers and VHF frequencies when available and known at publication time. See the Essential Supplies & Services page at the end of this chapter.

British Columbia Marine Parks: Several Provincial Marine Parks and protected areas are included in this chapter, including Penrose Island, Green Inlet, Codville Lagoon, Oliver Cove, Jackson Narrows, Union Passage, Lowe Inlet, Kitson Island, and Klewnuggit Inlet, Gilttoyees Inlet, Bishop Bay, Weewaniee Hot Springs, and Sue Channel. These join Hakai Luxvbalis Conservancy, Fiordland Recreation Area, and Sir Alexander Mackenzie Provincial Park in the park system. These are remote wilderness parks and do not have facilities of any kind. Access by boat or float plane only.

Insurance Coverage: Many U.S. boat policies designate latitude 51.0 as the northernmost geographical limit. Verify your policy limits with your insurance broker/company. An endorsement for extended cruising may be required.

Introduction

The Lure of the North Coast: For most boaters, the North Coast of British Columbia starts in the Port Hardy/Wells Passage area, even though it technically does not begin until Cape Caution, some 40 miles farther northwest. There are thousands of miles of island-studded channels stretching northwest into southeast Alaska, waiting to be explored by those who love natural surroundings and quietude. Facilities are more primitive, less amenity laden and farther apart.

Queen Charlotte Sound and Cape Caution comprise the most difficult waters of the entire Inside Passage. While these waters should be treated with caution, a safe and enjoyable passage is possible if one is well prepared and willing to wait for good weather. Good ground tackle, reliable electronic gear, a complete spare parts kit, VHF radio, and if possible, radar, are basic equipment. An extensive collection of charts is advised. CHS Sailing Directions, PAC 205E and PAC 206E are an invaluable resource.

Each summer many trailer boats are launched at Port Hardy, bound for Rivers Inlet for the salmon fishing. Many boaters who venture past Cape Caution are intent on getting to Southeast Alaska as soon as possible and hurry single-mindedly through the waters to Prince Rupert without taking the time to cruise into the various inlets along the North Coast of British Columbia. They are missing the boat (so to speak)! These waters are some of the best on the entire Inside Passage. The scenery in such places as Roscoe Inlet, Kynoch Inlet and Gardner Canal is equal to any in Southeast Alaska. The only thing missing might be a tide water glacier calving icebergs into the salt water. British Columbia's glaciers have retreated up the valleys and mountains, but they are still visible.

Anchoring and Tie-up: Adequate ground tackle and log tie-up equipment are essential when traveling these waters. Recommended, as a minimum, is enough rode to reach the bottom and allow for sufficient scope in 10 to 15 fathoms. Over 50% of the anchorages described in this chapter are in the 10 to 15 fathom range. Please refer to "Basic Boat Anchoring" at the end of the Important Notices section of this guide.

Log tie-up fenders: Tie only to the extreme outside of a log boom. Booms are often unstable and move with the wind and tide. A tie to a side or the inside could result in the boat being trapped against the shore. To protect the boat, cylindrical-shaped fenders with an eye on each end and a few ten pound lead weights tied to the bottom ends of the fenders, are handy. Lower the fenders to the proper depth, keeping them between the log and the boat. Tie them off in the usual manner. Regular fenders will float out of place and fail to give protection from the log.

Fuel Availability: The lack of available fuel between Port Hardy and Prince Rupert can present a problem for gas powered boats. From south to north: Rivers Inlet: Gas and diesel at Dawsons Landing and Duncanby Landing. Shearwater: Gas and diesel. Bella Bella: Gas and diesel. Klemtu: Gas and diesel. Hartley Bay: Gas and diesel. Fuel is also available at Bella Coola and Kitimat, however these are a considerable distance off the beaten track. Since many dispensers depend upon fuel being barged to them, it is wise to call ahead to check availability at any of the above locations. See the telephone numbers listed under "Fuel" at the end of this chapter.

Approaches to Cape Caution

[3547, 3548, 3549, 3550, 3552, 3921]

★ **Blunden Harbour (1):** [3548] This chart is necessary because of hazards in the entrance. Good anchorage can be found on a mud bottom in depths of 40-55 feet of water. Secure anchorage is found over mud in front of the beach. Posted signs prohibit digging in abandoned Nakwoktak Native shell middens and cairns. The anchorage in the outer basin is equidistant between Edgell Island, Brandon Point and Augustine Island. Bradley Lagoon is extensive and may be explored by dinghy. The entrance dries more than ten feet. Tidal currents become strong in the shallow entrance. Kelp may make entry difficult. Rockfish and ling cod are found near kelp patches outside.

Jeanette Island Light: Temporary anchorage is possible east of Robertson Island in seven to eight fathoms. It is somewhat exposed, and currents run through the passage.

★ **God's Pocket (2):** Here is a good jumping off point if going across Queen Charlotte Sound by way of Pine Island. This little cove, on the west side of Hurst Island, is not named on charts, but is much used by fishing boats seeking its shelter. It is off Christie Pass, about 1 1/2 miles southwest of Scarlett Point Light. Several marked trails for

Chart List

Canadian Hydrographic Charts:

3547-3550, 3552, 3721, 3728, 3737, 3741, 3742, 3781, 3789, 3800, 3807-09, 3811, 3825, 3853, 3855, 3859, 3868-69, 3890-3892, 3894-95, 3902, 3908-3912, 3920-21, 3931-3942, 3944-45, 3947, 3948, 3955-58, 3960, 3963, 3964, 3974, 3977, 3985

Marine Atlas Volume 2 (2020 ed.):
Pages 13-28

Evergreen Cruising Atlas: Pages 2-5, 19

Visit us at boattravel.com

NORTHERN BRITISH COLUMBIA COAST Chapter 19 Page 239

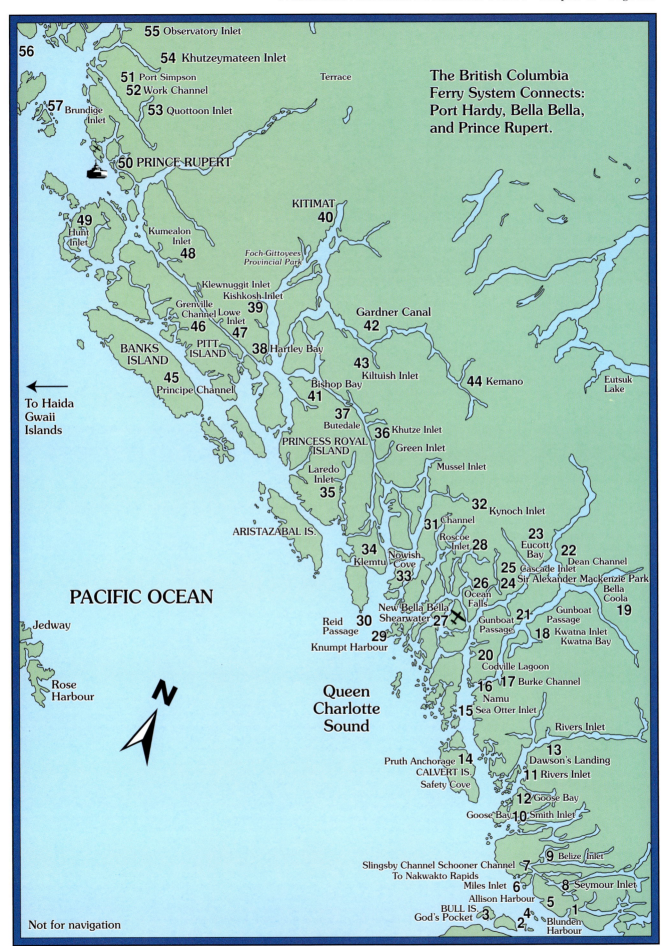

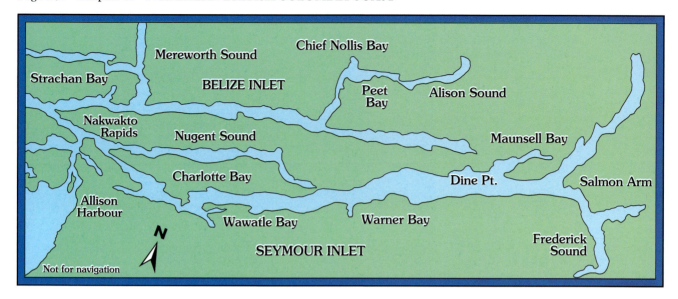

hiking on shore. Area waters are among the best in the world for cold water diving.

God's Pocket Resort: {50°50.398 N, 127°35.535 W} Limited moorage, cabin rentals, family style meals provided, diving air, kayak & diving charters. 250-949-1755. VHF 16 (call for Hurst Isle).

★ **Bull Harbour (3):** This is another useful anchorage if going directly across Queen Charlotte Sound. For local moorage information, see entry for "Bull Harbour" in Chapter 18.

★ **Walker Group (4):** This island group lies approximately 11 miles north of Port Hardy. Anchorage is between Kent Island and Staples Island in three fathoms, soft bottom. Good protection. Access is from the west or east entrances.

Deserters Group: There are no good anchorages in this group of islands. There is good fishing for salmon and bottom fish on both sides of Castle Point and on the south and east side of Echo Islands.

★⚓ **Allison Harbour/Allison Harbour Marine Provincial Park (5):** This protected, short inlet has several small coves and tidal flats at the head. It is known for being the last all-weather anchorage for boaters traveling north around Cape Caution, as well as a good position for an early morning crossing of the sound. There are no facilities here, but at one time the harbour was a centre for commerce and communication north of Port Hardy. Ruins of cannery, store and post office buildings remain. Avoid the reef off the east shore and drying rock farther in on the east side. Depths in the upper harbour are about 28 ft. The bottom is very soft mud and is difficult to hold at times. Allison Harbour Marine Park, with three pocket beaches and two creeks, is located mid-way along the southern shore. A cabin and pit toilet are situated at the Park's southern boundary. The park protects important habitat for resident gray whales during the summer.

★ **Skull Cove:** There is good anchorage here on a good, sticky mud bottom. Very sheltered anchorage is possible in the first basin in 25 foot depths, equidistant from the three nearest points. It is possible to observe sea conditions outside while in the shelter of this anchorage. If going in to the back or northernmost basin, keep to the west side to avoid the two drying rocks shown on the chart.

★ **Miles Inlet (6):** A small, sheltered anchorage is in about three fathoms of water on a mud bottom. The best spot is right in the cross of the "T" shaped inlet. It is possible to take a skiff into the lagoon at the north end, but only at high slack. There are overfalls at both ebb and flood. This is the closest anchorage to Cape Caution. It is hard to see the entrance at first, but McEwan Rock is a good landmark.

Slingsby & Schooner Channels to Nakwakto Rapids (7): [3552] Nakwakto Rapids are included in the Canada Tide & Currents Tables, Volume 6.

★ **Schooner Channel:** [3921] This channel has moderate currents, but is narrow with several hazards. The least width is 200 feet and the least depth about two fathoms. The northern approach, via Slingsby Channel, can have extremely strong tide rips in its western entrance, caused by strong ebb tides meeting the swells that are usually present in Queen Charlotte Sound. The entrance is wide and deep, but should be approached with caution on even a moderate ebb tide. Rocks foul both sides of the channel. Kelp marks some of these trouble spots, but not all of them so be very watchful.

★ **Treadwell Bay:** Sheltered anchorage is in the inside of Slingsby Channel in 45 feet of water, mud bottom.

★ **Nakwakto Rapids:** Tide and current tables are necessities for entering these rapids and are not included in this book. Use Canada Tide and Current Tables, Volume 6. These rapids are among the fastest in the world and should be approached with caution. The maximum currents are 16 knots on the ebb and 14 knots on the flood, caused by the six inlets drawing through this one narrow passage. In the inlets inside the rapids, the average tidal range is just four feet while outside the average range is 12 feet. Fortunately not all tides are large spring tides, and in most months, and certain phases of the moon, the maximum rate will not reach four knots on the smallest tide of the day. It is best to make the transit as close to slack water as possible. Passage is possible on either side of Turret Rock (or Tremble Island as it is sometimes called) but the west passage is the preferred one. The passage is short, straight, relatively wide, and deep, if one avoids the shoal southwest of Turret Rock.

Inside of Nakwakto Rapids are two large inlets, Seymour and Belize, 35 miles and 24 miles in length respectively. There are also four smaller sounds, Nugent, Mereworth, and Alison, each about ten miles in length, and Frederick Sound about six miles in length. Each of these waterways is surrounded by mountains, and offers beautiful scenic attractions. There are several good anchorages in each of these inlets, but there are no facilities of any sort for boaters. The only habitations are an occasional floathouse or logging camp. There is good radio reception, including VHF, so getting weather reports is no problem. On warm, clear days expect some fairly strong afternoon up channel breezes, as in most coastal inlets.

Seymour Inlet
[3552, 3921]

★ **Charlotte Bay (8):** This bay, five miles from the rapids, is the first good, protected anchorage. Anchor in four to five fathoms, mud bottom. Look out for the charted rocks in the northern part of the bay.

★ **Harriet Point:** At Harriet Point, Seymour Inlet narrows and makes a dog leg turn to the north. Anchorage is possible in the small bay directly across from Harriet Point, behind the small 26 meter island on the chart, in two to three fathoms. There is some kelp in this bay.

★ **Wawatle Bay:** Anchorage is found at the head of this bay.

★ **Frederick Bay:** As Seymour Inlet continues to the east it becomes wider, and the shores more mountainous. Anchorage is possible in a small nook at the west end of Frederick Bay in about five fathoms, soft bottom.

Warner Bay: Some anchorage is found here. Beware of the drying rock in the center of the bay.

★ **Dine Point Vicinity:** Proceeding east there are two anchorages about seven miles from Warner Bay. The cove on the north side, about one mile west of Dine Point, is not named on the chart, but is known as, Jesus' Pocket. There is room for only one or two boats, in four fathoms, with protection.

★ **Towry Point Vicinity:** Directly across the inlet, on the south side there is good anchorage on the east side of Towry Point in ten fathoms, mud bottom, with protection from all but east winds.

Maunsell Bay: Located on the north side of Seymour, this bay is large and too deep for anchorage. A cove at the east end does offer sheltered anchorage in 12 fathoms, mud and gravel bottom.

NORTHERN BRITISH COLUMBIA COAST   Chapter 19   Page 241

To the Head of Seymour Inlet: Another three miles to the east of Martin Point is Eclipse Narrows, the entrance to Frederick Sound. Seymour Inlet turns northeast here, and continues for another eight miles to its head where there may be a logging camp on the east side. The only possible anchorage would be at the very head of the inlet. The bottom is steep-to and there is no shelter from prevailing winds blowing in the inlet. Temporary anchorage in ten fathoms of water is possible if one wishes to explore the Seymour River. The river is large and may be explored by dinghy for about two miles where there are some big falls.

Frederick Sound

★ **Frederick Sound:** Currents in Eclipse Narrows, at the entrance to the sound, run four to five knots. Changes are about $1/2$ hour after tide changes at Nakwakto Rapids. This sound is about six miles long. Anchorage is possible in ten fathoms at the head of Frederick Sound, or at about the same depth in the northeast corner of Salmon Arm, which lies on the east side of this sound. The Salmon Arm anchorage is the more scenic of the two anchorages, but don't anchor in less than ten fathoms because there is a drying deadhead farther into the cove.

Nugent Sound

★ **Nugent Sound:** Entered $1\frac{1}{2}$ miles southeast of Nakwakto Rapids, this sound is ten miles long and very attractive. The best anchorage is three miles from the entrance in the bay on the north side, across from Nugent Creek on the south side. Depths are eight fathoms, good holding on a sand bottom. The anchorage is well protected with room for several boats. Anchorage is also possible at the head of the sound in 8-12 fathoms, mud and sand bottom, open to the southwest. The entrance to Schwartzenberg Lagoon is less than three feet deep with currents to five knots and is passable only by dinghy.

Belize Inlet

★ **Belize Inlet (9):** The entrance is at Mignon Point, about two miles northeast of Nakwakto Rapids. There is good, relatively protected anchorage at the very head of Rowley Bay, two miles west of Mignon Point, in ten fathoms, soft bottom. Some exposure to east winds. Better anchorage can be found at the head of Westerman Bay, on the north side of the inlet four miles northwest of Mignon Point in the cove at the north end in three fathoms on mud with good protection. Belize Inlet stretches 24 miles to the east from Mignon Point. It is straight, lined by mountain ranges on both sides. The only possible anchorage appears to be at the very head of the inlet, in the southeast corner in about 15 fathoms, but with no shelter from frequent, up inlet winds. Good anchorages, however, are found in Mereworth Sound and Alison Sound, which branch off to the north of Belize. These sounds are also very scenic.

Mereworth Sound

★ **Mereworth Sound:** Excellent anchorage is found in the cove at the southwest corner of Strachan Bay in seven fathoms, mud bottom. There is plenty of room, and good protection from all directions. Village Cove, about two miles into the sound, has anchorage in seven to eight fathoms on mud. There is good protection if one anchors in the northwest corner of the cove. Another good anchorage is in the cove southwest of Rock Island on the south side of the sound. There is good protection and plenty of room in eight to ten fathoms, mud bottom.

Alison Sound

★ **Alison Sound:** This sound is the most scenic of the six sounds. The entrance is about 18 miles east of Mignon Point. Beware of the three meter shoal on the west side of the entrance. Obstruction Island lies in the narrows about $1\frac{1}{2}$ miles inside the sound. Currents run to five or six knots, and the preferred channel on the west side is about 300 feet wide and 30 feet deep. Current changes seem to follow closely to those at Nakwakto Rapids. The passage offers no problems. The best anchorage in this sound is in Peet Bay about $1\frac{1}{2}$ miles past the narrows in five to six fathoms, soft bottom. The bay is small, but has good protection. Other possible anchorages are in the cove about one mile north of Obstruction Island in 15 fathoms, mud and sand bottom, good protection. Chief Nollis Bay has anchorage in 12-13 fathoms and Summers Bay has anchorage in 13-15 fathoms. The last two have limited protection.

Smith Sound & Smith Inlet
[3931, 3934]

★ **Smith Sound and Egg Island (10):** There are three entrances to Smith Sound. One is Alexandra Passage, just south of Egg Island, between North Iron Rock to the south and Egg Rocks to the north. The clearest passage, and the best one to use, if visibility is minimal, is Loran Passage between Egg Island to the south and Table Island to the north. The last, and northernmost passage, has three possible entries, Radar Passage, Irving Passage, or the innermost, between False Egg Island and Tie Island, often used by commercial fishermen going from Smith Sound to Rivers Inlet. There are no facilities for boaters in Smith Sound or Smith Inlet. Egg Island is the site of a manned lighthouse. When passing Egg Island, you can call "Egg Yolk" to say hello to the caretakers. Fog horn discontinued.

★ **Millbrook Cove:** [3934] Anchorage is available on the north side of the sound, near the entrance. The cove is marked by red spar buoy "E-6", with a radar reflector on it. Best anchorage is at the north end of the cove, behind the island marked 30 meters on chart #3934 and 100 feet on the older charts. It may be passed on either side. If using the wider eastern entrance, give the island plenty of clearance. Anchorage is in four fathoms on mud.

★ **Jones Cove:** Southeast of Macnicol Point is a little cove with fair protection, that provides an emergency anchorage. Avoid the reef 600 feet southwest of Turner Islands. At Jones Cove entry is around the east point with a minimum of 300 foot clearance.

★ **Fly Basin, Takush Harbour:** The entrance to Takush is rock strewn, first to the east, then to the west. But the chart shows the hazards. A huge landlocked basin provides protected anchorage with flat shallow anchorage in four to six fathoms on good holding sticky mud.

★ **McBride Bay:** This bay has anchorage in about 12 fathoms.

★ **Margaret Bay:** This bay is located on the north side of the inlet and has anchorage in eight to 12 fathoms.

★ **Ethel Cove:** Adjacent to Margaret Bay, this cove offers protection in six to eight fathoms with good holding mud and sand bottom. Anchor mid-channel to avoid dumped logs and snags. Watch for grizzlies on shore.

★ **Finis Nook:** This nook is off Boswell Inlet. Protected anchorage in depths of three or four fathoms.

★ **Anchor Cove & Quascilla Bay:** This cove, on the south side of Smith Inlet, is about nine miles east of the entrance to Smith Sound. There is anchorage in ten fathoms.

★ **Smith Inlet:** [3931] This chart made exploration possible for the first time. The inlet is about 18 miles long, from the entrance at Ripon Point to the head in Walkum Bay. The mountain scenery is beautiful, but anchorages are scarce. Anchorage might be possible off the flats in Walkum Bay, but the shoaling is very steep-to, and there is exposure to up-inlet winds. A temporary anchorage is possible off the Nekite River flats, in the cove on the east side of Jap Island.

★ **Boswell Inlet:** This eight mile long inlet is entered north of Denison Island. The ruins of the former settlement of Boswell are on the north shore of the inlet. Security Bay appears to be a good anchorage. The narrows, about one and $1/2$-mile farther east, are wide and deep and present no problems. An excellent, protected anchorage is $1/2$-mile above the narrows in the unnamed cove to the west, in five fathoms, soft bottom. Anchorage is possible at the head of Boswell Inlet in 10 to 13 fathoms. Beware of very rapid shoaling. The head of Boswell is very scenic.

Rivers Inlet
[3921, 3932, 3934, 3994]

★ **Rivers Inlet (11):** This thirty five mile long inlet is known as a prime fishing area. Commercial salmon fishing began here in 1882 and at one time there were as many as 17 operating canneries located in the inlet. Today it is an active fishing resort area and during summer season float planes deliver fishermen looking to hook a trophy salmon. Rivers Inlet boasts some of the largest sport caught Chinook in the world. This inlet is also a good place to spot Orca or Humpback Whales.

Rivers Inlet proper culminates in the big, two mile wide bay ending in the Wannock River flats to the east and Kilbella Bay and its flats to the north. The waters are always discolored, either by mud after a rain, or glacial silt at other times. A small public dock is found north of the Wannock River at the head of the Inlet. It is not suitable for larger boats. Logging operations and a First Nations Village are located on the river flats. Anchorage is possible off the river flats. Old cannery remains can be seen in Kilbella Bay on the western shore. Kibella Bay offers anchorage with good holding. Another anchorage is in the small bight behind McAllister Point in six to eight fathoms, good holding bottom, protected from all but east winds.

★ **Goose Bay (12):** Islets and drying rocks are in the entrance. Pass either east or west. Duncanby Lodge, a private fishing lodge, is on the east side of the entrance to Goose Bay at {51°24'16.63"N 127°38'43.69"W}. While the lodge once provided moorage and fuel, they stopped to focus on the fishing lodge enterprise. No fuel or other services are available to private boaters.

Wadhams: This one-time cannery site is now a private lodge.

★ **Finn Bay:** Sheltered, but deep anchorage can be found here. Private floats are in the bay. Beware of a rock, covered less than six feet, two tenths of a mile inside the entrance on the north shore.

Klaquaek Channel: [3994] This channel leads north from Rivers Inlet between Ripon and Walbran Islands to the east and Penrose Island to the west. There are several possible entrances from the south. The northern entrances are rocky, and the western-most, next to Penrose Island, is probably the best. Darby Channel is at the north end of the channel. There are several good anchorages in 10 to 15 fathoms on either side of Klaquaek Channel. Penrose Island's, Frypan Bay, on the west side of Klaquaek Channel, is a nice, small indentation. Anchorage is possible in seven fathoms, mud bottom.

★ **Penrose Island Marine Park:** [3921] This scenic park has anchorage and a network of narrow channels that are perfect for exploring by kayak or dinghy. There are inviting beaches and good diving sites. The southwestern shore of the island offers sandy, shell strewn beaches, lagoons, and islets. On the east side are two deep inlets which provide excellent anchorages protected by a steep wooded shoreline. Clamming is prohibited.

★ **Schooner Retreat:** [3934] Located on the southwest side of Penrose Island, Schooner Retreat is composed of three anchorages: Frigate Bay to the southeast, Exposed Anchorage to the northwest and Secure Anchorage in between. Anchorages are in 10 to 15 fathoms, much of it on mud, but rather exposed to southeast and southwest winds. The entrances and anchorages have many rocks requiring close attention to the chart.

★ **Fury Island:** There is a bay between Fury Island and Penrose Island that can be entered through the channel north of Heathcoat Island. Although not well protected from winds, anchorage is otherwise excellent and it is possible to note sea conditions on Queen Charlotte Sound.

★ **Dawsons Landing (13):** The very small public wharf with a float is for government fisheries vessels.

★ **Dawsons Landing General Store:** Secure moorage, water, gas and diesel, bait, tackle, showers, laundry facilities, a well stocked general store with frozen foods, fresh vegetables, dairy products, gifts, souvenirs, chandlery, cube & block ice, Post Office and Liquor store. See our advertisement on this page. Website: www.dawsonslanding.ca. Email: dawsonslanding@hotmail.com. Address: Dawsons Landing, British Columbia V0N 1M0. Phone: 604-629-9897. VHF 06.

Darby Channel: [3934] This channel runs from Fitz Hugh Sound to Dawsons Landing, and saves several miles of travel. There are several hazards, but, with caution, passage is easy.

★ **Sandell Bay:** Located about five miles north of Dawsons Landing, Sandell Bay offers relatively protected anchorage in five fathoms, soft bottom, open to the south.

★ **Taylor Bay:** On the east side of Walbran Island, Taylor Bay offers a small, but secure, anchorage in 11 fathoms of water over mud.

★ **Johnston Bay:** Traditionally, there has been good, well protected anchorage in this bay just south of the lodge and at the head of the bay in ten to twelve fathoms, mud bottom. Avoid the reef in the outer bay and other hazards by keeping to the west side all of the way in. Some old abandoned net floats are at the head of the bay. This is a delightful place.

Good Hope Bay: Across from Dawsons Landing near Ida Island, Good Hope Bay is the site of a cannery built in 1894. In 1965, the dilapidated structure was restored and reopened as a private fishing resort. The mouth of the Sandell River is found on the east side of the bay.

★ **Weeolk Passage:** An unnamed cove on the east side of the passage provides good, relatively sheltered anchorage in 50 feet of water over a mud bottom. A rocky ridge on the north side is a hazard. The charted rock in the entrance is best passed on the south side.

Moses Inlet: Moses Inlet runs 14 miles north from McAllister Point to the drying flats at its head. Half way up it has a dog-leg to starboard, and is constricted by Nelson Narrows. The island in the center can be passed on either side. A day beacon marks a shoal to be avoided on the port side. Depths are adequate and currents are negligible. Three to four thousand foot mountains line the sides of the inlet. The only anchoring possibilities are off the steep-to Clyak River flats at the head of the inlet, or in the northeast corner of Inrig Bay, but both are exposed. The head of the Inlet and the river estuary wetlands, known as the Clyak Estuary Conservancy, are home to trumpeter swans and western grebes, as well as grizzly bears and juvenile salmon.

★ **Hardy Inlet:** Six mile Hardy Inlet takes off to the west from Moses Inlet, two miles north of McAllister Point. Mountains range to 2,500 feet on both sides, and again the inlet is deep. Two coves at the very head of the inlet offer the best anchorages. The cove straight ahead is the best, with a soft bottom and anchorage in eight fathoms, protected from all but east winds. The scenery looking back down the inlet is wonderful. If the wind is up the inlet from the east, the bight on the south side affords some protection in about the same depths.

★ **Dawsons Landing General Store:** Serving boaters and fishermen for over 60 years, this store and fueling facility is located on the west shore of Rivers Inlet, opposite the northeast end of Walbran Island. Secure moorage, with fresh water on floats that rim the front of the buildings. Gas and diesel available. New showers and laundry facilities have been added. The well stocked store carries a large selection of canned and frozen goods, fresh vegetables and dairy products, liquor, gifts, souvenirs, chandlery items, block & cube ice, and is the site of the post office. Bait and tackle are sold. Internet service available. Accommodations are available with reservations advised. Located in the heart of the fabulous fishing grounds of Rivers Inlet, Dawsons is headquarters for the sports fisherman, as well as commercial and pleasure craft. Daily scheduled float plane service links with several communities along the coast, both large and small. Lots of humpbacks have been spotted on the Rivers Inlet the past couple of years so come see us in 2024. Proprietors Nola and Robert Bachen. Email: dawsonslanding@hotmail.com. Address: Dawsons Landing, British Columbia V0N 1M0. Phone: 604-629-9897. VHF 06. Internet: www.dawsonslanding.ca.

Draney Inlet
[3931]

★ **Draney Inlet:** [3931] This chart, on a scale of 1:40,000, covers this inlet for the first time. Draney is an 11 mile long inlet, on the east side of Rivers Inlet. It is entered through Draney Narrows. The narrows is shown on an inset to the chart. Currents run to ten knots. The narrows are best entered at or near slack tide. The narrows is known for good Chinook and Coho fishing.

★ **Fishhook Bay:** This bay is one mile past the narrows. Anchorage is in two to four fathoms, with good protection.

★ **Robert Arm:** There is very good anchorage in this arm, in about seven fathoms, mud bottom and good protection from all but east winds.

★ **Allard Bay:** At high tide, there is anchorage in six to nine fathoms in the entrance. There is more room than might be apparent on the chart and the bottom is mud. Several boats could snuggle here, but check overnight tidal depths vs. present depths. The head of Draney Inlet has an excellent, protected anchorage in 15 fathoms, mud bottom.

Fish Egg Inlet
[3921]

★ **Fish Egg Inlet:** These interesting waters are entered to the east of Addenbroke Island, and its lighthouse. They present excellent waters for "gunkholing" and there are numerous good anchorages. Entry is either by Convoy Passage to the south, or Patrol Passage and Fairmile Passage to the north.

★ **Green Island Anchorage:** [3921] This lies at the entrance to Illahie Inlet. Protected anchorage is in seven fathoms, mud bottom off the island that gives the cove its name. The southeast entrance is the safest one. This chart shows Fish Egg Inlet and Allison Harbour, metric, scale 1:20,000.

★ **Illahie Inlet:** Anchorage with good protection on a mud bottom is possible in the cove at the head. When weighing anchor, be ready with hose or bucket water to clean chain.

★ **Joes Bay:** This bay, located at the entrance to Elizabeth Lagoon, has protected anchorage in ten fathoms. The entrance to the lagoon has tidal rapids and many obstructions and is best avoided.

★ **Waterfall Inlet:** This inlet has a nice protected anchorage at its head, in the northeast corner, in ten fathoms, mud bottom. An uncharted rock lies just off the east shore, about 200 yards south of the head of the inlet. It is clearly visible at lower tides.

★ **Mantrap Inlet:** A well protected anchorage is found at the southern end in ten fathoms. Because of the very shallow, rocky entrance, it is better to enter or exit on the top half of the tide. Currents are weak in the entrance.

Gildersleeve Bay: Open to the north. Two anchorages in the southwest corner are not good. The northernmost is too shallow, and the southern one has a rocky bottom.

★ **Eastern Section of Fish Egg Inlet:** East of The Narrows are some nice anchorages. The farthest eastern cove has a good, protected anchorage in 6½ fathoms on a mud bottom. Oyster Bay has a well protected anchorage in four fathoms, mud bottom. Fish Trap Bay has an anchorage in its very small cove.

Addenbroke Island Light Station — Photo © David Stanley

Hakai Pass & Fitz Hugh Sound
[3921, 3934-37]

★ **Hakai Luxvbalis Conservancy** [3937]: Located about 130km north of Port Hardy and 115km southwest of Bella Coola. Hakai Luxvbalis Conservancy is almost 15 times the size of Desolation Sound Marine Park and is the largest marine park on British Columbia's west coast. The park boundaries stretch from Fitz Hugh Channel on the east, the top half of Calvert Island to the south, Goose Island on the west, to the northern half of Hunter Island. Major anchorages include Pruth Bay on Calvert Island, Crab Cove in Sea Otter Inlet, the north end of Triquet Island near Spider Anchorage, Spider Anchorage southeast of Spider Island and Bremner Bay on Hunter Island. No developed facilities. Popular fishing spots are Odlum Point, The Gap, and Nalau Passage. Experienced sea kayakers and scuba divers will find plenty of places to enjoy these activities. Please respect First Nations Cultural Heritage Sites.

★ **Safety Cove (14):** Located just above Calvert Island's southernmost tip, this cove offers good anchorage in 8 to 15 fathoms of water on mud. This is the first anchorage on Calvert Island, after crossing Queen Charlotte Sound.

Addenbroke Island Light Station: Located four miles north of Safety Cove on Calvert Island. At the time of this writing, the principal lightkeepers appreciated receiving VHF calls and mail from old and new friends. They say the coffee is always on! In settled weather, anchoring is possible in 60', sand bottom, near the lighthouse boat launch. New road, derrick pad, hydraulic engines, and lights. Do not anchor in too closely to the old cannery site. Kayakers find good camping for large groups & houses for smaller groups. Call on VHF 09 or 82 to be met. During winter months 82A is used exclusively. Call "Addenbroke Lighthouse" on either channel or, on VHF 82, you can also use "Late for Supper".

★ **Pruth Bay & Kwakshua Inlet:** [3921] This well-protected inlet has good anchorage in 40-50 feet near mid channel, sand and mud bottom. The bottom is hard along the south shore. The bay is home to the Hakai Institute, a teaching, research and conference center offering a variety of programs in cooperation with BC universities and colleges, BC Parks, First Nations, NGOs and local schools community groups. Hakai Institute property is extensive and encompasses the shorelines of Pruth Bay, West Beach and North Beach and the connecting trails. The Institute also has a dock in the bay. When necessary, the marine park ranger vessel uses the dock.

Hakai Institute: Visitors will notice Hakai's scientific buoy as they enter the eastern end of Kwakshua Channel. It's part of a global network of similar devices monitoring ocean acidification (goa-on.org). Visitors may moor dinghies to the wooden floats at the back of the dock. Do not interfere with the outer side of the T, which is used by aircraft. All visitors are encouraged to stop at the Welcome Kiosk at the shore end of the dock to sign the guest book. Then enjoy hiking the trails to the beaches and viewpoints on Hakai Institute property and in the surrounding conservancy. Trails to North Beach and the beach lookout are much more accessible since significant upgrades were made in 2012. www.hakai.org, welcome@hakai.org, VHF 06, call sign 'Hakai Institute'. ★

Hakai Passage: This open passage to the Pacific lies at the north end of Kwakshua Channel and Hecate Island. This is a famous sport salmon fishing area, especially around Odlum Point, but beware of strong swells and currents. Anchorage is possible at the north end of Choked Passage in nine to ten fathoms, between the north end of Calvert Island and Odlum and Starfish Islands. While there is protection from the seas, there is not much protection from strong west and southwest winds.

★ **Goldstream Harbour:** Anchorage can be found here in depths of 40-60 feet on a mud and sand bottom. Evening Rock is located in the center of the bay. It dries four feet and fishermen often mark it. Favor the Hat Island side unless Evening Rock is showing so it can be avoided easily. Kelpie Point, at the northernmost tip of Hecate Island and Hakai Passage are noted for good salmon fishing.

Kwakume Inlet: [3935] On the east side of Fitz Hugh Sound, about six miles north of Addenbroke Island Light, Kwakume Inlet offers protected anchorage in seven to ten fathoms with almost unlimited room. Use caution in the entrance. The small treed island that appears to be in the center of the entrance should be passed on the north side. There is a least depth of 25' in this 250' wide northern channel. There is a rock one tenth of one mile west of the entrance.

Chapter 19 NORTHERN BRITISH COLUMBIA COAST

Bella Coola Harbour   Photo © Lonnie Wishart / www.lonniewishart.com

★ **Koeye Point:** This bay is at the mouth of the Koeye River. An uncharted rock is near the entrance to the narrow boat channel. There is anchorage off the point to starboard after entering. Trout fishing is said to be good in the river. The river may be traversed by dinghy for some distance. The ruins of an old mine wharf and a cabin are about 1/2 mile up the river. There is a white sandy beach. Note the white quartz and the pockets in the marble made by water action. In fishing season this small harbour may be crowded with commercial fishermen.

★ **Lewall Inlet:** [3935] Indenting Sterling Island, this shallow, narrow, L-shaped inlet has good anchorage. Very isolated, pretty, many jellyfish. Avoid shallow spot to starboard, near the end of the entrance passage.

★ **Hunter Island & Sea Otter Inlet (15):** On the west side of Fitz Hugh Sound, Sea Otter Inlet offers anchorage with excellent protection near the head of the south arm in ten fathoms, or in five fathoms in the north arm, called Crab Bay.

Warrior Cove: This is a pretty spot, south of Namu. Anchor in the back of the cove, behind a small peninsula.

Namu (16): [3935, 3936] Beware of Loo Rock. This charted rock is marked with an orange bobber. Namu's first white inhabitants arrived about 1893, but archaeological evidence, including ancient stone tools and a 6,000 year old fish trap points to aboriginal use for nearly 10,000 years. The remains of a B.C. Packers Cannery, now badly deteriorated and collapsing sits on the shoreline. There are no longer any floats or caretakers at Namu. These buildings are unsafe and boaters should keep their distance. Onshore a one mile trail leads to Namu Lake. Anchorage is in Inner Warrior Cove or Rock Inlet. Rock Inlet is good for smaller craft, enter east of Verdant Island, watch for islets and rocks.

Burke Channel
[3938-3940, 3974]

★ **Burke Channel (17):** Burke Channel leads off to the northeast from Fitz Hugh Sound about two miles north of Namu, at Edmund Point. It continues in a northeast direction for 55 miles to the village of Bella Coola, which is connected to the town of Williams Lake in the interior by a 300 mile long road, largely unpaved. This is some of the best scenery on the British Columbia coast, if the weather cooperates. Strong winds often blow up and down this inlet. Caution advised at Mesachie Nose. Known locally as Dancing Waters, dangerous tide rips form at this location.

★ **Fougner Bay:** Anchorage is possible in the outer part of the bay in seven to ten fathoms.

★ **Restoration Bay:** This anchorage was first used by George Vancouver in 1793 to overhaul his ships. It has good holding in 55 feet of water. The Bay is exposed to the southwest. Caution must be used when approaching the head because the bay shoals very rapidly.

★ **Cathedral Point:** Anchorage is possible in the small cove right on the point in 25 feet of water over a mud bottom. There is not much room, but it is satisfactory in settled weather. If an east wind is blowing down Burke Channel, the anchorage will be uncomfortable.

★ **Kwatna Inlet & Kwatna Bay (18):** This scenic inlet lies to the south of Burke Channel. The entrance is between Mapalaklenk Point and Cathedral Point. It extends 12 miles southwest from the latter point and is very scenic and uncrowded. There is excellent anchorage in ten fathoms at the head of the inlet. Be cautious, because there is much shoal water at the head, but there is plenty of room to anchor before reaching the shallows. This is a very nice anchorage, with beaches to explore. Kwatna Bay, on the east side, about four miles south of Cathedral Point, is too deep for anchorage, and the mud flat at the head is steep. There is a logging camp at the head of Kwatna Bay.

★ **South Bentinck Arm:** This 19 mile inlet has some of the most beautiful scenery on the British Columbia coast. Spectacular mountains on either side are covered with glaciers and snow. Anchorages are in Larso Bay in ten fathoms, or at the head of the inlet in the southwest corner in 11 fathoms. About six miles in from the entrance of South Bentinck Arm, hot springs warm a pool created with rocks and man-made structures.

★ **Bella Coola (19):** [3911, 3912, 3974] Public floats are located in a sheltered small boat harbour located about 1 1/2 miles from the center of town. There is an easy access float for boats over 45 feet. Visitor Information is available June-Sept. in the Copper Sun Gallery in downtown Bella Coola. The downtown also has shopping facilities, post office, telephone, liquor store, restaurants, motels, showers, and a hospital. Car rentals are available and there is a Community Bus (call one day in advance and leave a call back number to arrange a ride. 250-799-0079). The Bella Coola area, the only land access to the Great Bear Rainforest, offers numerous recreational options like hiking for all levels, rafting, eco-tourism, and fishing. There is also an opportunity to enjoy a wide array of Nuxalk carvings and paintings and personal contact with this vibrant First Nation. Highway 20 to the BC Interior accesses the fabulous "wild frontier" of the Chilcotin Plateau via one of the steepest roads in North America. Bella Coola is a stop on the B.C. Ferries Discovery Coast Passage route from Port Hardy and scheduled air service to Vancouver is also available.

The Nuxalkmc people have long inhabited the Bella Coola Valley. The first European visitor, Alexander Mackenzie, ended his trip across Canada at this point in 1793 accomplishing the first land crossing of the North American Continent. A monument commemorating this event is on the north shore of Dean Channel, about two miles west of Cascade Inlet at Elcho Point. The Bella Coola Valley was later settled by Norwegian immigrants from Minnesota in 1894. Items they brought with them are displayed in the museum which is located in a school house and a land surveyor's cabin. Open June-September. Local events include the *Bella Coola Rodeo* over Canada weekend, the *Bella Coola Music Festival* in July, and the *Fall Fair* in September. For more information, visit www.bellacoola.ca.

Bella Coola Harbour: {52° 22' 30" N, 126° 47' 30" W} Moorage, 30 amp power, potable water, launch ramp, tidal grid, gas, diesel, laundry facilities (April 15-Oct 31), washrooms, showers, and pay phone. Rafting mandatory. Salt flake ice for sale (if available). Summer office hours 8am-4pm. 250-799-5633. VHF 06.

Tallheo: On the north shore of North Bentinck Arm, 2 miles across from Bella Coola, is the site of a former cannery that has been restored as a B & B. Guided Historic Tours of the Cannery Buildings are available with advanced notice. Call 604-992-1424. There are no longer any facilities here for boaters, except one small float.

Fisher Channel
[3939]

★ **Kisameet Bay:** Passing Burke Channel and Humchit Island in Fitz Hugh Sound, tuck to the northeast behind Kipling Island. Proceed northeast behind Kisameet Island, carefully avoiding charted rocks. Kisameet Bay offers sheltered anchorage in six to ten fathoms on good holding mud bottom. Remains of a cabin are on shore on the small island with a rock shelf baring at very low tide. This "window to Fitz Hugh Sound" at the anchorage site shows rocks which block transit at low tide. On the chart, note Kisameet Lake to the northeast.

★ **Codville Lagoon Marine Park (20):** The entrance to Codville Lagoon is located off Fisher Channel at the head of Lagoon Bay. The narrow, tree-lined entrance off the channel gives protection to this lovely area. There are obstructions, including a rock just north of mid-channel, but they are easily avoided. There is good, all weather anchorage in six to seven fathoms in the cove behind Codville Island. Watch for logs and deadheads on the southeast side of the lagoon. Wildlife is plentiful in this small park. A sign on shore at the north end of the lagoon indicates the trail to Sagar Lake is 1.2km. A wooden boardwalk covers much of the trail, but there are some rough "stairways" of tree roots to maneuver. The 20-minute walk ends at the lake where there is a nice, reddish colored sand beach and swimming possibilities. ⚲

★ **Evans Inlet:** Good anchorage in 12 fathoms is found at the head of this four mile inlet. The head of the inlet shoals rapidly.

Port John: Port John, about 1 1/2 miles north of the entrance to Evans Inlet, has a temporary anchorage in its northeast corner in seven fathoms, soft bottom. Open to the southwest. If traveling from Evans Inlet to Port John via Matthew Passage, beware of Peril Rock in the center of the passage.

★ **Gunboat Passage (21):** [3938, 3940] This narrow, rocky, but well marked passage is the shortest route between Dean Channel/Ocean Falls and Shearwater/Bella Bella. The charts and the Canada Hydrographic Services' PAC 205 *Sailing Directions: Inner Passage, Queen Charlotte Sound to Chatham Sound* should be consulted. Gosse Bay, on the north side of the passage, offers good, protected anchorage in eight fathoms. Anchorage is also possible in the bay lying northwest of Stokes Island, at the east end of Gunboat. Anchor in 15 fathoms next to Stokes Island near the head of the bay. The bottom is hard, but held when tried in settled weather.

Dean Channel

[3781, 3789, 3939, 3944, 3945, 3974]

★ **Dean Channel (22):** This channel is about 53 miles long, extending northeast from Rattenbury Point, where it meets Fisher Channel to its head at the Kimsquit River flats. The scenery is wonderful, especially in the upper sections, past Edward Point, where it meets Labouchere Channel, which connects it to Burke Channel. Mountain peaks reach 6,000 and 7,000 feet on both sides of the channel.

★ **Eucott Bay (23):** Twenty-five miles from Bella Coola by way of North Bentinck Arm and Labouchere Channel, this bay has a hidden surprise at every turn. High stony mountains, several waterfalls that cascade down hundreds of feet, hot springs, marshes on shore, skunk cabbage, and bears, Arctic loons, mallards, and Canada Geese. Anchorage in this bay is good, and well sheltered, though quite shallow. Depths are greatest near the east side of the bay, 2 to 2 1/2 fathoms, and good mud.

★ **Carlson Inlet:** This is a deep anchorage in 20 fathoms at the very head, but well sheltered. The current from the stream will probably keep the boat headed toward it at all times.

Kimsquit Bay: Deep anchorage is possible here, at least 20 fathoms, and there is a private float. Anchorage might be possible in front of the ruins across the channel, just north of Kimsquit Narrows. The head of the inlet is very deep, and the flats steep.

★⚓ **Sir Alexander Mackenzie Park (24):** [3738-40] Located just east of Elcho Point, on the north shore of Dean Channel. A 43' high monument commemorates the first land crossing of the North American continent in 1793 by Sir Alexander Mackenzie. A trail from a small, light gravel nook

Ocean Falls Harbour   *Photo © Janice Plante*

near the monument may be passable. Dinghy to this nook. However, because of the steep bank, it might be easiest to use binoculars to view the chiseled inscription. Look directly below the cairn, high on the rock face, to read: "Alex Mackenzie from Canada by land 22d July 1793". The original writing by Mackenzie was done with red pigmented grease.

★ **Elcho Harbour:** Good, protected anchorage in about 11 fathoms, soft bottom, is available in the northeast corner. In August watch for bears and eagles pursuing salmon heading up the river.

★ **Cascade Inlet (25):** This 13 mile long inlet is well worth exploring because of its numerous waterfalls. Anchorage is possible in the northeast side at the head in ten fathoms, soft bottom, even though the flats are very steep-to.

Nascall Hot Springs: The old hot tubs have been removed. This is a private facility. Anchorage is possible, however it is exposed to southeast winds.

★ **Ocean Falls (26):** [3944, 3945, 3781] This historic former paper mill town, whose heyday was in the 1960's and 1970's, is experiencing new life through tourism. The remote community, located at the head of Cousins Inlet has a winter population of about 60 with over 100 in the summer. There is no road access, but it is accessible by plane, pleasure craft, or ferry as it is a stop on the B.C. Ferries Discovery Coast Passage route from Bella Coola and Port Hardy, or Prince Rupert via Bella Bella.

"The Shack," a floating building on the public dock, is open for visiting boaters to use as a covered lounge. There is limited free WiFi at the dock. Ocean Falls has an unlimited supply of some of the best water in the world to replenish tanks and the cheapest moorage rates on the West Coast.

Once a populated settlement prior to the closure of the pulp mill, many local buildings now serve new purposes. The Ocean Falls Gift Shoppe on a corner of the Marine Ways building offers handmade offerings from local residents, Christmas items, many small keepsakes and ice sales. Norm Brown passed away in January of 2022, but his unofficial museum is still on the top floor of the Marine Ways building and is filled with an eclectic collection of items that were left abandoned in Ocean Falls when the mill closed. Les and Toni are the current owners of the Ways and time permitting, give free tours of the building and Museum (donations collected go to the maintenance of the building). The Ways building is the broadcast location for CBC radio. Central coast marine weather broadcasts every morning at 5:30 am. The former CIBC building, now the Old Bank Inn, is a full-board accommodation that also offers showers, as well as wash and fold laundry service and is open year round. Beside the Old Bank Inn is The Little Licker Store where you can buy hard ice cream cones, coffee, tea, pop, bread and baked goods during the warmer months. You may also buy "To Go" hot breakfast sandwiches between 7 am and 9 am. The "Company House" on the hill has 5 bed and bath suites and is available to rent by the week for families and groups. The former Court House is home to the Post Office and the Town (Improvement District) Office, as well as apartments available on the second floor to rent for 6 month or longer leases.

Most residents live at the end of the one-mile paved road to Martin Valley. Renovation of older homes in the valley is becoming more common and attractive to people looking for a simpler lifestyle. Martin River Lodge (Ken & Shelly) provides accommodation with meals or without and also short-term rental homes. Fishing is a popular pastime in Ocean Falls and fishing charters as well as water taxi services are available. A launch ramp is found in this area which also serves as our plane ramp. The popular Saggo's Saloon should reopen sometime in 2023 with new owners Dustin and Chantale. The pub has limited hours; check for postings in the Shack.

This is a great place for hiking and short walks, but be aware that wildlife may share the trails and townsite. A short walk up from the townsite is the dam that supplies power for Ocean Falls, Shearwater, and Bella Bella. Link Lake is pristine, 17 miles long and offers great canoeing, kayaking and trout fishing activities as well as a small swimming beach and free picnic and tenting area. To the left of the parking area is a marked route to the top of Caro Marion, our tallest mountain and an easier branch trail that ends up at Lost Lake, about a 45 minute hike.

Check the information board in The Shack, by the longhouse or inquire at the Post Office for local information. For historical perspective, read the book *Rain People: The Story of Ocean Falls* by Bruce Ramsey that can be purchased locally. For Ocean Falls events or to inquire about available services, visit the Facebook group "Ocean Falls - Embers amongst the Ashes". ⚓⚲

Ocean Falls Public Dock: {52° 21' 14" N, 127° 41' 45" W} Moorage, potable water, 20/30 power plug-ins, free WiFi, washroom, garbage/recycling. Wharfinger: 250-289-3315. VHF 06, 09.

Jenny Inlet: On the south side of the channel, anchorage is possible at the head in 11 fathoms, mud bottom. This inlet was logged about 25 years ago and a dock for loading/unloading supplies is still here, as are logging roads that provide a good place to stretch your legs.

Bella Bella & Shearwater Area

[3911, 3938, 3939, 3940, 3941, 3945]

★ **Bella Bella & Shearwater Area (27):** These two communities, a few miles apart, provide a good base for exploring some of the most beautiful waters on the west coast. There is scheduled land plane service to each community from Port Hardy, Bella Coola, and Vancouver. BC Ferries also offer routes from Port Hardy, bound for either Ocean Falls and Bella Coola, with stops at McLoughlin Bay/Shearwater. Return southbound voyages leave from Bella Coola.

★ **Waglisia (Bella Bella):** Home of the Heiltsuk Nation is on the East coast of Campbell Island and West shore of Lama Passage. The Village of approximately 1500 people have services such as the Lama Pass Fuel station, which offers marine and auto fuel. The Waglisla Band Store offers groceries and houses the liquor store and Post Office. Also in the community, there is the Bella Bella Hospital (with pharmacy) and Clinic along with the R.C.M.P. facility that services Bella Bella and the Ocean Falls, Shearwater, Klemtu, and Namu areas. The Qatuwalas or "The Gathering Place", is a beautiful place to learn about the Heiltsuk Nation's history, both past and present. It also displays Heiltsuk artists and supports local enterprises. The Heiltsuk Cultural Education Centre makes another interesting stop, it is inside the Bella Bella Community School building. The Cultural Centre highlights Heiltsuk culture and history with an interesting collection of photos, maps, transcribed stories and more. There is also a Community Hall with a fitness center in the basement. All of these facilities are central to the village. On the North end of Bella Bella lays the Airport with services from Pacific Coastal and Wilderness Sea Planes. On the South end of Bella Bella known as McLoughlin Bay (Gelc) which is the location of the Heiltsuk Fisheries Mgmt. Ltd. (the Fish Plant), Salmon Enhancement program and BC Ferry Terminal with services to Port Hardy, Klemtu, Ocean Falls, Bella Coola, and Prince Rupert. In the centre of town is a government wharf for general marine use, including Lama Pass Fuels; and Martins' Cove, a marina for fishers and workboats. Shearwater Resort and Marina is on Denny Island 3.5km east of Bella Bella and is now owned and operated by the Heiltsuk Nation. Shearwater has accommodations and many services such as the Fishermans Bar and Grill, laundromat, grocery store, marine store, gas bar, moorage, shipyard and a BC Ferries Port with services to OceanFalls and Bella Coola.

Lama Pass Fuels: Gas, diesel, stove oil, propane, naptha, oils, lubricants, marine batteries, good water, garbage deposit at head of the ramp. 250-957-2440. VHF 06, 10.

Bella Bella: The British Columbia Packers sold all the facilities at Old Bella Bella on the eastern shore of Lama Passage to the Heiltsuk Nation several years ago. Although there are no facilities, there is some moorage and the fisheries office is here.

★ **Shearwater:** This community is on the west side of Kliktsoatli Harbour on Denny Island, about two miles southeast of New Bella Bella. Both moorage and anchorage are found here. Anchor in 10 to 12 fathoms throughout this large bay. Shearwater is a full-service marine centre offering a full range of services. For transportation, Shearwater is connected to New Bella Bella by water taxi service and B.C. Ferries provide service seasonally from Port Hardy or Bella Coola. There is also scheduled daily air service to and from Vancouver and Port Hardy. Shearwater was originally established as a RCAF base to provide anti-submarine air patrols during World War II. A hanger still stands and is used by the boatyard. A bomb shelter also remains and can be reached by a short hike.

Shearwater Resort Hotel & Marina: {52° 08' 8" N, 128° 05.4' W} Moorage (reservations advised), 15/30/50 amp power, water, gas, diesel, propane, lubricants, laundry, showers, restrooms, repairs, 70 ton Travelift, towing, restaurant, pub, post office, gifts, groceries, liquor, marine hardware, WiFi, ecotours, helicopter tours. 250-957-2666. VHF 66A.

★ **Kakushdish Harbour:** This well protected harbour, 1 1/2 miles east of Shearwater, offers anchorage in seven fathoms, mud bottom. There are shoals in the entrance and on the south side near the head. There is adequate room for anchoring in the channel. A First Nation reservation, with some inhabited cabins, is at the head.

★ **Campbell Island:** This harbour's entrance, about ½ mile north of New Bella Bella, is marked by a green spar buoy. Keep well north of the buoy because of shoals. There are several floats behind the rock breakwater, rafting is often necessary. In addition to the public floats there is a marine repair facility with a marine railway.

★ **Troup Passage & Troup Narrows:** [3938, 3939, 3940] This passage, northeast of Shearwater between Cunningham and Chatfield Islands, has no problems except at Troup Narrows at the northeast end. The Narrows is shallow and rocky, and must be navigated with caution. Tidal information is given in the Tide Tables, Volume 6. A nice, protected anchorage is found in the unnamed bay ½ mile west of the south end of Troup Narrows. Depth is six fathoms, soft bottom. An even more protected anchorage is in the bay to the east on the north end of the narrows, on mud in four to five fathoms. When approaching Troup Narrows from the north, the best course is along the east side of the bay.

★ **Roscoe Inlet (28):** [3940, 3974] This spectacular inlet extends north and east for 21 miles from its entrance, at the junction of Johnson and Return Channels, about ten miles northeast of New Bella Bella. At one point, just southwest of Hansen Point, a sheer cliff 1,200 feet high rises from the water. The inlet is quite narrow and crooked, and if the weather is good, there is some really beautiful scenery. Good anchorages in 10 to 15 fathoms can be found in Clatse Bay, Boukind Bay, and at the head of the inlet. Quartcha Bay is too deep for most boats to anchor.

★ **Kynumpt Harbour (29):** This harbour, located on Campbell Island, on the south shore of Seaforth Channel, offers good, secluded, sheltered anchorage in 45-60 feet of water on a sandy mud bottom. A wild mint patch is on the south shore. Big, white butter clams and little neck steamers are found here. Wild blackberries grow in profusion.

★ **Dundivan Inlet & Lockhard Bay:** Located one mile east of Idol Point, this inlet has several possible anchorages. The best are in Lockhart Bay's two arms in eight to ten fathoms, soft bottom and good protection. The West Arm is especially protected. Idol Point is a favorite salmon fishing area.

St. John Harbour: This is an excellent, well protected anchorage six miles south-southwest of Ivory Island Lighthouse. There is a red spar buoy marking the reefs on the starboard side on the approach. Raby Islet may be passed on either side. Anchorage is in Dyer Cove in ten fathoms of water on a mud bottom.

Reid Passage Mathieson Channel

[3728, 3910, 3911, 3938, 3942]

Reid Passage (30): [3910] This route offers a more sheltered alternative to going out into Milbanke Sound at Ivory Island and then continuing north in Finlayson Channel. The entrance, which lies just east of Ivory Island, and its lighthouse, marked by starboard and port markers, is 13 miles west of Dryad Point Light. Carne Rock, the main hazard in the passage, is now marked by a beacon. There is ample room for safe passage on the east side.

Mathieson Channel (31): [3728, 3910, 3911, 3942] This 35 mile channel extends north from Milbanke Sound to Sheep Passage. It is off the regularly traveled route, and offers beautiful scenery.

Perceval Narrows: [3910] Located at the south end of Mathieson Channel. Currents run to five knots ebbing south and flooding north. Listed in *Canadian Tide and Current Tables* Volume 6. Strong tide rips can be encountered south of the narrows on an ebb tide when there are swells coming in from Milbanke Sound.

★⚓ **Oliver Cove Marine Park:** This is a popular anchorage in Reid Passage about one mile north of the light on Carne Rock. There is a charted rock in the entrance and a ledge on the north side of the entrance. Good protected anchorage in the center of the bay in six fathoms with a soft bottom.

★ **Boat Inlet:** On the west side of Reid Passage, anchorage is possible in two to three fathoms, soft bottoms.

★ **Cockle Bay:** Anchorage in ten to fifteen fathoms, soft bottom, but open to winds from the northeast. Beautiful sand beach.

★ **Tom Bay:** [3728] Well protected anchorage in five fathoms, mud bottom is available. If the hook won't hold, it is probably because of kelp on the bottom. Try ten fathoms in the center of the bay.

★ **Arthur Island:** A well protected anchorage in the eastern most of two coves on Dowager Island is just north of Arthur Island. Ten fathoms, soft bottom.

Salmon Bay: If the wind is not from the west, this is a nice anchorage with a soft bottom, in ten to twelve fathoms. A favored spot for eagle watching.

★ **Rescue Bay:** This is an excellent, large, protected anchorage at the east end of Jackson Passage. Depths of eight to ten fathoms, over a soft bottom. Log rafts may have the prime anchorage site.

Oscar Passage: This is the easiest passage west to Finlayson Channel and Klemtu.

★⚓ **Jackson Passage & Jackson Narrows Marine Park:** [3938, 3941] This picturesque passage narrows at the east end due to rocks and drying reefs. The passage should be navigated only at high slack. On the ebb, current in Jackson Passage flows east. The park is found where the east end of the passage connects with Mathieson Channel. There are no facilities. Two Kitsasoo/Xaixais fish farms are located in Jackson Passage - one in Jackson Pass and one in Lochalsh Bay.

★ **James Bay:** [3942] This bay on the west side of Mathieson Channel offers good anchorage on a soft bottom in eight to ten fathoms, but it is open to winds from the south. Beware of shoaling on west side at head of the bay. Good crabbing.

Fiordland Recreational Area

[3942]

★⚓ **Fiordland Recreational Area:** This large marine park includes Mussel and Kynoch Inlets and Pooley Island. The topography here is reminiscent of the fjords of Norway and New Zealand.

★ **Kynoch Inlet (32):** This 8 1/2 mile inlet is near the north end of Mathieson Channel contains some of B.C.'s most spectacular scenery. A waterfall near the entrance of the inlet cascades from Lessum Creek. You may see goats on the cliffs, grizzly bears fishing in the streams, and dozens of cascading waterfalls. When ashore be watchful for grizzlies. Hiking is not recommended. Anchorage is possible at the head of the inlet, off the drying flat, in about ten fathoms of water. The best anchorages are on the north side, but note that it shoals very rapidly at the head. This can be a rough anchorage when the wind blows up the inlet, but it is worth it. Fishing for trout and salmon is possible in the creek entering the inlet.

★ **Culpepper Lagoon:** Culpepper Lagoon, to the east, should be entered only at or near high slack tide. Tides are said to run to eight knots in the narrows and can develop small rapids. Use Bella Bella tide information. The only anchorage is off the flats at the head of the lagoon, in about 15 fathoms at high tide. When you enter on a high tide, it will not be possible to see the flats when anchoring. The chart does not show the true location of the flats on the north side. They extend very far out, drying at low tide. This anchorage is usually better protected than those at the head of Kynoch Inlet, but strong wind gusts can enter. The lagoon is a lovely setting, providing mountain views when the clouds lift.

★ **Desbrisay Bay:** Deep and exposed, this scenic bay on the north side of Kynoch Inlet has anchorage in the northwest corner in ten fathoms, soft bottom.

Sheep Passage: Sheep Passage connects Mathieson Narrows and Mussel Inlet. South and west, the passage leads to Finlayson Channel and north and east to Poison Cove and Mussel Inlet.

Griffin Passage: Not recommended. There are several tidal rapids in the passage. The narrows at the south entrance and at another spot in the northern part, are dangerous.

Mussel Inlet: There are several waterfalls in this inlet, one from McAlpin Lake, and two which enter Oatswish Bay. Because of the depths, anchoring is difficult.

David Bay: Too deep for good anchorage.

★ **Mussel Bay:** Anchorage is possible in this bay at the head of Mussel Inlet. Anchor in nine fathoms, in front of the river. Beware of rapid shoaling. On shore, watch out for grizzly bears. A Kitasoo Guardian Watchmen is stationed here Aug.-Oct., call on VHF 06 for fishing protocol.

Boat Bluff Lighthouse near Klemtu   *Photo © Carolyn Van Calcar*

Oatswish Bay: Oatswish Bay is deep, but a temporary anchorage is in ten fathoms near its head, on the west side. It may be too exposed to up-inlet winds for overnight. Lizette Creek Falls may be the most beautiful on the British Columbia Coast.

Poison Cove: Named by Captain Vancouver, whose crew members were poisoned by eating shellfish, probably mussels. The cove is too deep to be a good anchorage.

★ **Bolin Bay:** The mountains rise to 3,000' around this little bay making it a spectacular anchorage in 11 fathoms, mud bottom. Protected in all but east winds. Beware of the drying flats at the head of the bay.

★ **Windy Bay:** There is plenty of anchorage here in 10 to 20 fathoms. The best protected anchorage is behind the island at the east side of the entrance.

Finlayson & Tolmie Channels

[3902, 3911, 3938, 3941, 3943, 3945]

★ **Nowish Cove & Nowish Narrows (33):** This lovely cove in Susan Island is protected by Nowish Island. Entry must be made from the west, north of Nowish Island. The deep cove requires anchorage in 70-80 feet of water. Use plenty of scope because an eddy current sweeps the cove. Bottom is coarse sand. Nowish Narrows, south of the cove, has currents to six knots. Charles Narrows is strewn with rocks and should not be used. These narrows lead into Nowish Inlet. Exploration into the inlet by dinghy is possible, however, currents are strong.

★ **Klemtu (34):** Located on Swindle Island, three miles south of the Boat Bluff Lighthouse, Klemtu is home to the Kitasoo/Xai'xais Nation. The lighthouse keeper stands by on Channel 82A. This is the only stop for fuel between Bella Bella and Prince Rupert. Most residents hold jobs in the aquaculture, forestry, or tourism industries, all of which the community is working to enhance. Boaters are often surprised and pleased to find that Klemtu also has cell phone service for most cell phones. Other services here include a grocery store, a restaurant with wifi, a lodge, and a wharf and floats at {52° 35' 25.8576" N, 128° 31' 25.086" W}. There is no charge to tie up at the dock if space is available. Moorage is exposed to the wakes of passing boats. Anchorage is also possible in the bay. Please note the strict No Wake Zone in Klemtu Pass starts just before the Fish Processing Plant/Gas dock on the northern side of the village and the Spirit Bear Lodge dock on the south end. There is a point marked with a cross just before you get close to the No Wake Zone and there are also signs in the pass that state where to slow down. Spirit Bear Lodge offers all inclusive packages from Vancouver, however, accommodation and tours are accessible for boaters subject to availability (best to call in advance). The best way for boaters to inquire is to stop in at Spirit Bear Lodge when they arrive in Klemtu or email explore@spiritbear.com as dock is not open to the public. A Big House Walking Tour may be available by calling 250-839-1096 or the Band Office at 250-839-1255, by email at admin@kxsa.ca or after hours call on VHF 06. Access to the museum is currently limited due to renovation. Klemtu is on the B.C. Ferries route from Port Hardy. In case of an emergency while in Klemtu territory, a Kitasoo Guardian Watchmen patrol vessel may be called on VHF 06 to assist.

First Nations Fuel: Gas, diesel, oils, propane. Hail "First Nations Fuel" on VHF 06.

★ **Alexander Inlet:** This five mile inlet off Meyers Passage, six miles north of Klemtu, is overlooked by many boaters. It is very scenic, especially the first part, and offers an excellent, protected anchorage in the cove at the head in five fathoms, soft mud.

★ **Bottleneck Inlet:** A good, protected anchorage in six fathoms, mud bottom. No problems at the entrance. Beautiful reflections when the water is smooth.

★ **Goat Cove:** Entrance is 1/2 mile east of Goat Bluff. The inner basin, east of the stream at the head, has well protected anchorage with good holding in gravel and sand in 6 1/2 to 10 fathoms.

★ **Cougar Bay:** Cougar Bay is located ten miles north of Klemtu on Tolmie Channel. Anchor in the bight on the east side of the bay. Depths are ten fathoms on the east and south sides.

★ **Work Bay:** Located on the east side of Sarah Island. Good anchorage can be found at the far northeast end of the bay in seven fathoms. Well protected from all but south winds.

Hartley Bay Photo © Lonnie Wishart / www.lonniewishart.com

★ **Carter Bay:** This bay, at the junction of Sheep Passage, offers anchorage in 12-15 fathoms, near the wreck of the Ohio, but it is fully exposed to the south. The steamer Ohio was beached in 1909 after striking a rock (now known as Ohio Rock) in Finlayson Channel, about three miles southeast of where she now lies. At low tide, parts of her bow are still visible.

Hiekish Narrows: These narrows extend 5 miles north northwest from Finlayson Head to Sarah Head at the north end of Sarah Island. The narrows floods to the north at a maximum rate of four knots and ebbs south a maximum rate of 4½ knots. Most days the maximum current run is 2½ to 3½ knots. The best course is on the east side of the buoy on the reef at Hewitt Rock which is marked for passage on either side. Fishing can be excellent on this reef at slack water.

Graham Reach to Fraser Reach

[3944, 3902]

★⚓ **Green Inlet Marine Park:** A tiny, sheltered anchorage is in Horsefly Cove. The cove is just off Graham Reach at the entrance to Green Inlet, 196 kilometers south of Prince Rupert. Anchor in about 13 fathoms of water.

★ **Khutze Inlet (36):** [3944] Just off Graham Reach, Khutze lies near the route that most cruising boats take beyond Klemtu. This four mile, deep inlet ends in a drying mud flat where anchorage is possible. Anchor to starboard of the largest waterfall and stream in 11 fathoms (facing the falls). This clears the mud flats, as well as the wreck at the southwest extremity of the mud flats. Commercial crab traps may limit the anchorage area. Watch for eagles feeding on salmon at the stream southeast of the flats and deer swimming the channel. Salmon, flounder, and small cod are caught. Anchorage is also possible on the east side of the kelp area, marked Green Spit on the chart, in about 15 fathoms. Tide and currents need to be considered. This anchorage can be rough when south winds blow up Graham Reach and bounce off the mountains on the inlet's north side. The valley at the head has deer, Canada geese, and mink. A three mile hike up the river valley leads to an abandoned gold mine.

Aaltanhash Inlet: Anchorage at the head of the inlet is possible, but the bottom is very rocky. There are strong currents from the two rivers, and there is exposure to the wind. Good halibut fishing and beautiful scenery.

Butedale (37): Located on beautiful Princess Royal Island. Anchorage is possible, however it is open to winds. Established in the early 1900's, Butedale was a prosperous fishing, mining, and lumbering community. The cannery closed in the 1950's and workers left. Butedale became a "ghost town" and over the years the buildings deteriorated. New owners are undertaking clean-up and stabilization efforts, but the future of the property remains to be seen. The uplands are considered a constuction site and are closed to visitors. Rudimentary floats are still there (use at your own risk), but there are no services and nothing is open for business. Butedale Falls, a magnificent 1/4 mile cascade of water can be viewed from the channel below.

★ **Klekane Inlet:** This inlet, across from Butedale, offers anchorage with some protection in 12 fathoms of water off Scow Bay. Open to the south. Anchorage is also found at the head of the inlet in the northwest corner in 10 - 14 fathoms.

Douglas Channel & Gardner Canal

[3902, 3908, 3945, 3948, 3977]

★ **Hartley Bay (38):** Four public floats are behind the breakwater at {53° 25' 29.05" N,129° 15' 4.59" W}. Anchorages are found in Stewart Narrows. Hartley Bay is the home community of the Gitga'at Nation and has a year round population of about 180. Limited provisions, fuel, towing, and minor engine repairs are available. Major credit cards accepted. It is a dry (no alcohol) community. In 2018, Hartley Bay assumed the Harbour Authority, and plans are under way for improved services at the docks including bathrooms, and pay per use showers and laundry. A Community Hall/Cultural Centre is used for local gatherings throughout the year and is the site of several beautiful totems. In 2006, the Hall was used as an aid centre for the passengers of the Queen of the North after it sunk. Residents of Hartley Bay were first on the scene to pick up survivors. For their initiative and selflessness, the community received the Governor General's Commendation for Outstanding Service. Scheduled float plane flights and a ferry twice per week connect to Prince Rupert for supplies or passengers. The Band Administration Office is open Monday-Friday. 250-841-2500. CB 14. VHF 6, 60.

Hartley Bay Fuels: Open year round. Diesel, gas, small selection of oils, water at end of ramp. 250-841-2675. VHF 06.

Walk Around: Inquire about visiting the salmon hatchery and walking to a lake.

★ **Curlew Bay:** On the northeast corner of Fin Island, there is anchorage in eight fathoms, soft bottom, protected.

★ **Kiskosh Inlet (39):** On the west side of Douglas Channel, anchorage is less than ideal in this 5.5 mile inlet. Just inside the narrow, shallow entrance lies a mud flat. Crabs, clams, scallops, cod and flounder are common. This inlet is worth exploring for these delights, and the startling luminescence of the water at night.

★⚓ **Foch-Gilttoyees Provincial Park and Protected Area:** Douglas Channel adjoins this terrain stretching from sea level to mountain top. It includes old-growth forests, waterfalls, tidal estuaries, unique tidal narrows, snow-topped mountain peaks, and a receding glaciers cap. Along with Gitnadoiks River Park and Protected Area to the north, Foch-Gilttoyees completes a contiguous protected area corridor between the Douglas Channel, south of Kitimat, and the Skeena River, west of Terrace. Boaters can explore six mile-long Foch Lagoon and seven mile-long Gilttoyees Inlet, both of which have exceptional natural features. Highly productive tidal estuaries are known for good Chinook, Chum, Pink Salmon, Steelhead, and especially Coho salmon. Wildlife includes Grizzly bear, wolverine, hawks, Peregrine Falcon, Trumpeter Swan, Short Eared Owl, and even the Coastal Tailed Frog. Granite walls along Gilttoyees Creek attract rock climbers, but no trails in the park make access difficult. Scuba divers are often seen near the entrance to Foch Lagoon located off the head of Drumlummon Bay. Enter Foch Lagoon at slack tide and use caution due to strong tidal streams in the narrow entrance. The entrance to Gilttoyees inlet is on the north side of Douglas Channel, about 16 miles southwest of Kitimat. The scenery in this narrow inlet is spectacular when the cloud cover does not obscure the tops of the tall mountains. The best anchorage is in the small bay on the east side, 2.5 miles south of the drying flats at the head. Anchorage is in eight fathoms, mud bottom, with excellent protection. No crabs, but plenty of huge starfish. ⚓

★ **Kitimat (40):** [3908, 3977] When traveling up the inlet, the prevailing winds are calm in the mornings with rising inland winds in the afternoon. This town of 9,000 residents is located at the head of Kitimat Arm, an extension of Douglas Channel. Guest moorage is available at MK Bay Marina, about 11 km/7 mi from town. Cab service to town is available. For further travel, Kitimat is connected to the interior by good paved roads and scheduled air service from the Terrace-Kitimat Airport 55 km/34 mi north. There are supermarkets, as well as shops, post office, banks, drug stores, liquor store, hospital, and restaurants. Points of interest include the Hirsch Creek Golf & Winter Club, Sam Lindsey Aquatic Centre, Coghlin Park Viewpoint, Minette Bay West Park, Moore Creek Waterfalls, and the Giant Spruce Tree. The Kitimat Museum & Archives also makes an interesting stop featuring exhibitions highlighting Haisla heritage, early valley pioneer and missionary settlement, and the massive Alcan smelter development in the 1950's. Call 250-632-8950 for hours. If you like to fish, local waters offer great fresh and salt water fishing. Tours of the Kitimat River Fish Hatchery are available June 1-August 31. 250-639-9888. For a little exercise, try a game of racquetball or tennis, or pick up a hiking map at the Kitimat Visitor Centre: 250-632-6294. www.kitimatbound.ca.

Minette Bay Marina: 6/12 mos. leased moorage, 10 amp power, water hose at dock, dry land storage, float plane dock. Medium to high tide arrival or departure only. 250-632-3177.

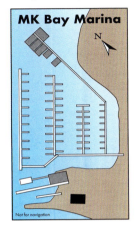

MK Bay Marina: Located at the head of Douglas Channel. Annual, monthly (Oct. 1 - April 30), and daily moorage (no reservations). Power, water, washroom, laundry, free wifi, RV sites, store with boating supplies & fishing gear, snack bar, ice, boat launch and parking. Haul-outs for vessels up to 36'. 250-632-6401. VHF 68.

★ **Bishop Bay (41):** Located off Ursula Channel, Bishop Bay is the site of a well known hot springs and part of the Bishop Bay-Monkey Beach Conservancy. Entry is between Riordan Point and Tomkinson Point. Fair anchorage is in 10 to 15 fathoms around the head of the bay. There are also three mooring buoys and a small dock. Boats over 36' should moor offshore. Slightly south of the dock, reports indicate an uncharted shoal extending into the bay. Walk the boardwalk to three pools (two outdoor and one inside). Tent platform, toilet, and picnic shelter. Salmon fishing is often good in early June. ⚓

★ **Kitsaway Anchorage:** Situated on the east side of Hawkesbury Island, this spot offers excellent protected anchorage in 6 to 13 fathoms on mud. Good crabbing.

★ **Weewanie Hot Springs Provincial Park:** Located in Devastation Channel, about 2½ miles northeast of Dorothy Island Light and about 17 miles south of Kitimat. There is a bath house for soaking, a campsite, picnic area and pit toilet. One mooring buoy is located in this semi-protected bay and anchorage is in eight fathoms or more. {53° 41'49" N; 128° 47'.21" W} ⚓ ▲

Sue Channel: Anchorage is available here in the bight on the north side of Hawkesbury Island, about two miles west of Gaudin Point, in ten fathoms. This site is not well protected from the wind. A bay on the south side of Loretta Island, while better protected, is deep, but does offer potential anchorage.

★ **Gardner Canal (42):** [3948] This is one of the most beautiful spots on the whole coast, and one of the least visited. The canal is 45 miles long, narrow and winding, with snow covered mountains over 6,000 feet high on either side. The entrance is at Staniforth Point, about 26 miles south of Kitimat.

★ **Triumph Bay:** Protected anchorage is in the bight on the east side of the bay, about one mile south of Walkem Point in 70 feet of water, mud bottom.

★ **Kiltuish Inlet (43):** [3948] Anchorage is in 12 fathoms in the bay just west of the entrance to the inlet. The inlet itself is about three miles long after going through the very rocky narrow entrance. Least depth in the entrance is six feet, but because of swift currents, entrance should be near high slack. This passage is hazardous and should be approached very cautiously. The scenery inside is very good, with towering peaks on either side. There is plenty of room to anchor inside with reasonable depths.

★ **Europa Point:** Site of lovely hot springs. It is possible to soak and cast a line into the water at the same time.

★ **Kemano Bay (44):** [3736, 3948] A First Nation graveyard and fishing village is on Kemano Spit. This was the traditional home of the Haisla until, after a 1940's smallpox epidemic, the survivors from the Kitlope and Kemano areas moved to Kitimat and Kitimaat Village. Since 1950, the bay has been utilized by Rio Tinto Alcan to offload people and supplies for the company town of Kemano. Automation eventually reduced the need for workers and by 2000 the town's residents had all left. There still is a docking station in Kemano Bay, it is private and for the express purpose to moor the company's passenger vessel. Protected anchorage is possible in the bay at under 20 fathoms depth, but use caution. The bay shoals suddenly near the tidal flats.

★ **Kemano (44):** In 2000, the town of Kemano, located about ten miles from Kemano Bay, was closed. Today Kemano is a worker campsite for the sole purpose of maintaining Rio Tinto Alcan's powerhouse. There are no services offered to the general public and the private work site is totally off limits.

★ **Chief Mathews Bay:** This bay, about seven miles south of Kemano, is said to be too deep for anchorage, but is worth exploring because of the huge glaciers that can be seen on the mountains at the head of the inlet. Anchorage may be possible off the drying flats at the head.

★**Kitlope Heritage Conservancy/ Huchsduwachsdu Nuyem Jees:** This region, at the head of Gardner Canal, is described as the world's largest undisturbed coastal temperate rain forest. It is also considered one of the loveliest places on the coast with hanging glaciers, waterfalls cascading down 2,000' granite cliffs, and thermal springs, as well as abundant wildlife including black bears, harbour seals, beaver, eagles, mountain goats, caribou, moose, and various waterfowl. This is a haven for the photographer. The land is protected under the supervision of B.C. Parks and the Haisla First Nations. For more information and permission to visit, contact Na na kila Institute in Kitimaat Village. 250-639-9361. A BC Parks/ Kitlope Watchmen Cabin is on the south side of the Kitlope River {53° 12.95' N; 127° 51.78' W}. Interpretive programs may be possible between May and October.

★ **Kitlope Anchorage:** At the head of Garner Canal, Kitlope Anchorage has silted in, use caution and watch for changing depths. While here, dinghy the Kitlope River Estuary and river. As mountains diminish, a wide valley containing sandbars and grassy knolls spreads out. Strong river currents can make travel difficult and the milky-blue water makes depths hard to determine. About a half-mile up river please report in at the Na na kila watchmen's cabin. One-mile up river, look for a cave in a cliff that served to hide Haisla from enemy raiding parties. Another 1.5 mile is an old logging camp now used for the Haisla Rediscovery Program. It is possible to go nearly six miles up the river to Kitlope Lake.

Principe Channel, Banks, Princess Royal, & Pitt Islands

[3721, 3737, 3741, 3742, 3902, 3910, 3911, 3912]

Meyers Passage: [3721, 3910, 3911, 3912] See current table for Wrangell Narrows. This is the southern entry to the west side of Princess Royal Island. The route along the west sides of Princess Royal and Pitt Islands is an alternative for travel from Klemtu to Prince Rupert. The distance is about the same, there are many anchorages and less traffic, but there is more exposure to storms. Passage should be made at or near high tide. The least depth, at zero tide, is only three feet.

The McNaughton Group — Photo © Carolyn Van Calcar

Anger Island Anchorage   Photo © Carolyn Van Calcar

★ **Parsons Anchorage:** Located at the south end of Kitasu Bay on the northwest corner of Swindle Island, this bay has anchorage in six fathoms, soft bottom. Open to northwest winds.

★ **Laredo Inlet (35):** [3737] Eighteen mile Laredo Inlet is the longest of the dozen or so inlets that are encountered between here and Prince Rupert. Laredo Inlet is very scenic, with high mountains on both sides. There are a half dozen good anchorages in the inlet.

★ **Alston Cove:** Anchorage is possible in six fathoms, mud bottom with good protection.

★ **Fifer Cove:** This cove is eight miles farther north on the east side of the inlet. An excellent, beautiful anchorage in ten fathoms, mud bottom, and good protection in front of the large stream at the head of the cove.

Brew Island: Located at the head of Laredo Inlet. The inlet has a temporary anchorage on its northwest corner in ten fathoms, soft bottom. Limited protection from up-inlet winds.

★ **Weld Cove:** Located on the west side of Pocock Island, this cove offers anchorage in 10 to 12 fathoms, mud bottom, with entry on either side of Kohl Island. The entrances are rocky, and caution must be used when entering or departing.

★ **Bay of Plenty:** Good, scenic and well protected anchorage in nine fathoms is on the southwest side at the head of the bay, mud bottom.

★ **Mellis Inlet:** Anchorage in 12 fathoms in the cove at the head, soft bottom. Open to winds from the south. Beautiful scenery with high mountains on both sides.

★ **Trahey Inlet:** [3737] Lying just west of the entrance to Laredo Inlet, there is well protected anchorage at the head of its west arm in six to seven fathoms, mud bottom. Entry is possible on either side of Jessop Island, but because of many hazards, extreme caution is necessary. This chart, scale 1:77,429, is the only chart available, and it isn't very helpful.

Kent, Helmcken, Commando, & Evinrude Inlets: [3719] These inlets indent Princess Royal Island on the east side of Laredo Channel. The chart above is essential for entering any of these waters. Kent and Commando have strong tidal currents and should be entered only at slack water, preferably high slack. Evinrude Inlet has a shoal on the north side of its entrance. Anchoring depths are fairly deep. Helmcken Inlet should be entered south of Smithers Island. Anchorages are also deep in this inlet. The best choice is in the small bight on the east side of Smithers Island, in 11 fathoms, on a soft bottom. There is good protection from winds. The cove on the southwest side of Smithers Island is too exposed to west and southwest winds to be a good anchorage.

★ **Surf Inlet:** [3737] This 11 mile inlet is the most beautiful of all the inlets on the west sides of Princess Royal and Pitt Islands, with steep sides, and a relatively narrow channel. Anchorage is possible at the head of the inlet in eight to ten fathoms, but very little protection from winds up or down the inlet. The mountain scenery is beautiful. Port Belmont was once the site of a gold mining operation. Remains of a dam and abandoned power house are still visible.

★ **Penn Harbour:** This harbour, four miles from the head of Surf Inlet, is by far the best anchorage. Anchorage is in nine to ten fathoms, soft bottom, and excellent protection. Some nice waterfalls are at the head of the bay.

★ **Cameron Cove:** Located in Barnard Harbour on the northwest corner of Princess Royal Island, the head of this cove has well protected anchorage in seven fathoms, soft bottom.

★ **Monckton Inlet:** [3721] Located on the west side of Pitt Island. The first anchorage is near the head of the large cove on the north side of the inlet, about 1/2 mile north of Roy Island in nine fathoms, mud bottom, and good protection. Additional anchorages are in the cove to the northwest of Monckton Point in nine to ten fathoms, and near the head of the inlet in six to ten fathoms. Entrance to Monckton Inlet is easy.

★ **Port Stephen:** Good, well protected anchorage in the first cove to the northeast of Littlejohn Point. Anchorage is in ten fathoms, soft bottom. Another anchorage is in the cove to the north of the west entrance to Stephen Narrows in 11-12 fathoms, soft bottom, fair protection.

★ **Buchan Inlet:** [3721] This inlet, five miles north of Monckton Inlet, is entered north of Tweedsmuir Point. Both the inlet and the point are named for the author, John Buchan, Lord Tweedsmuir, the former Governor General of Canada. The inlet offers sheltered anchorage in nine to ten fathoms just north of Elsfield Point, and for the more adventurous, several anchorages in the inner basin. Don't try this without the above chart. Least depths of six feet are reported in the narrows.

★ **Patterson Inlet:** This inlet is about six miles north of Buchan Inlet. Anchorage is possible in either of the two coves at the head of the inlet, in six fathoms in the north cove and 10 to 12 fathoms in the southern one.

Mink Trap Bay: [3721] The best anchorage is in Moolock Cove, in the basin on the far south end, in ten fathoms with a mud bottom. Good protection from seas, but there is limited shelter from south and west winds. Wind can come in over the low ground around the cove. Because of numerous shoals and rocks, caution must be exercised when entering. Both of the anchorages in Patterson Inlet are more secure and easier to enter.

Petrel Channel: [3984] This channel is entered at Foul Point on Anger Island. It runs 23 miles north and west to Comrie Head, where it meets Ogden Channel. Tidal currents can run to three knots in Petrel Channel. Principe Channel continues northwest from Foul Point. Three excellent anchorages lie off of Petrel Channel.

★ **Hevenor Inlet:** This inlet is five miles long and has a well protected anchorage in six to eight fathoms, soft bottom, at the very head of the inlet.

★ **Newcombe Harbour:** This harbour is four miles north of Hevenor Point. It is a large, scenic, well protected anchorage in nine fathoms, mud bottom, just south of the prominent point on the west side at the head of the bay.

★ **Captain Cove:** The best protected anchorage is near the head of the cove, on the south side, just east of the islets, in 10 to 12 fathoms, mud bottom.

Principe Channel (45): Not many pleasure boaters venture into Principe Channel. Most prefer Grenville Channel, en route to Alaska. If crossing to Haida Gwaii, however, one can use this route.

Larson Harbour: On the northern tip of Banks Island, this protected anchorage is often used by boats waiting to cross Hecate Strait to Haida Gwaii (Queen Charlotte Islands). Two lights mark the entrance. One must sail directly through thick kelp beds to approach it. Inside are six mooring buoys and space to anchor.

Grenville Channel to Prince Rupert

[3946]

Grenville Channel (46): See current table for Wrangell Narrows. This trench-like channel is very narrow, deep and straight, and extends northwest 45 miles from Sainty Point to Gibson Island. From Gibson Island it is another 27 miles to Prince Rupert Harbour. The tidal currents in the channel can reach two knots on springs, flooding from each end, meeting near Evening Point, just south of Klewnuggit Inlet.

★⚓ **Lowe Inlet Provincial Marine Park & Nettle Basin (47):** Anchorage is possible in Nettle Basin in front of beautiful Verney Falls. Anchor in or on either side of the falls depending on the tide and wind. Strong currents can lead to dragging anchor. Our favored anchorage is south of the stream on a sandy mud bottom. Anchorage is in 70-90 foot depths. It is possible to approach the foot of the falls where salmon put on a show while awaiting high tide and the chance to jump the falls leading to the lake above. Bears and seals are also seen here. At the outlet of the falls in Nettle Basin one can still find the remnants of ancient stone fish traps. A short trail to the left of the falls leads to the lake where anglers will find good trout fishing. Much of the shoreline is undeveloped parkland. The falls and the trail to the lake is First Nations Reserve land. On the north side of Nettle Basin, on private land, stand the remnants of an old cannery that operated from 1890 to 1934. Parts of the wharf are still visible.

Dodge Cove on Digby Island Photo © Lonnie Wishart / www.lonniewishart.com

★⚓ **Klewnuggit Inlet Provincial Marine Park:** This undeveloped park consists of East Inlet and the two lakes above. Good anchorage is at the north end of East Inlet in nine fathoms over a good bottom. Crabbing is good here. Brodie Lake is separated from the inlet by a small rock step. There is an unmarked trail from Exposed Inlet to Brodie Lake near its river outlet and a trail on the northwest side of the river between Brodie and Freda Lakes.

Kxngeal Inlet: Anchorage in 10 to 14 fathoms near the inlet's head. Although exposed to south winds, this provides welcome shelter when strong north winds catch you out in Grenville Channel.

★ **Baker Inlet:** Enter north of Griffon Point by way of 200 foot wide Watts Narrows. Be aware of strong currents in Watts Narrows. A light marks the entrance to this four-mile long inlet. The entrance is not as difficult as it looks. There is plenty of water. Use the chart inset and go through near slack water. Slack water is about the same as the turn at Prince Rupert. Drying reefs and shoals are on the south side. Anchorage is found in 11 fathoms at the head of the inlet, south of the small island. It has good holding bottom, and is very well protected. A family of seven wolves was once observed on shore.

★ **Kumealon Inlet (48):** An attractive anchorage in six fathoms is found inside the island near the entrance of this inlet located 28 miles from Lowe Inlet and 37 miles from Prince Rupert. Anchorage is also possible in 15 fathoms, mud bottom, behind the small island at the head of the inlet. Pass to the north side of this island when entering.

★ **Lewis Island Anchorage:** Bloxam Pass lies between Lewis Island and McMicking Island. Enter from Arthur Passage just north of the light on Herbert Reefs. Relatively protected anchorages in five to ten fathoms, soft bottom, are available in several locations in the passages on the northeast side of Porcher Island. The most protected is off the west side of Lewis Island in five to six fathoms, good bottom. Entrance or exit is also possible to the north via Chismore Passage. Kelp Passage, to the south, is not recommended because of obstructing reefs. These anchorages are about 18 miles south of Prince Rupert.

Porcher Island

★ **Porcher Island:** See current tide table for Prince Rupert, BC. Oona River Harbour is located on southeast Porcher Island. The harbour can be approached comfortably for most vessels two hours either side of the high tide. Look for the entrance dolphin that indicates a marked depth in feet. The depths mark the depth at the shallowest part of the route. Using the range marker on the end of the breakwater, find your position and follow that route in to and then around the breakwater. Before you reach the breakwater, you will pass a marker that should be kept to port as the area behind the marker is very rocky. The small community of Oona River (population 22) has moorage, a post office, and accommodations with reservations. There are no retail or other services available. Hiking trails are onshore, as well as a fish hatchery. The fish hatchery can be visited with prior arrangements.

Oona River Harbour Authority: Moorage, 30 amp power, non-potable water, rafting when required, arrange showers and laundry at the post office. Call ahead for moorage, 778-884-1359.

★ **Hunt Inlet (49):** This bay, located on the northwest side of Porcher Island, has shelter in all winds. A dangerous rock ledge is near the entrance. A public float is on the west side at approximately {54° 4' 4.9002" N, 130° 26' 38.6916" W}. There are no services.

Kinahan Islands: Anchorage is in seven fathoms over a mud bottom in the bay between the two islands with exposure to southeast winds.

★ **Port Edward:** Named for King Edward VII this community is located about six miles south of Prince Rupert on the Tsimpsean Peninsula. The Port Edward Harbour Authority is a commercial fishing dock that welcomes recreational vessels. This is a private dock with public access. The facility has two drive down ramps that are used for the maintenance and the loading and off loading of supplies. About three miles from the harbour, the Porpoise Harbour Boat Launch has free temporary moorage for loading/unloading only. It is convenient to Chatham Sound and popular fishing grounds. The North Pacific Cannery National Historic Site, a major tourist attraction is located in Port Edward. Twenty-eight historic buildings, some dating to 1889, house a cafe, bunkhouse hostel, and gift shop. Visitors enjoy tours, performances, exhibits and displays illustrating the historic importance of these canneries and the workers who kept them running.

Port Edward Public Moorage (Porpoise Harbour): {54° 13' 23" N, 130° 18' 3" W} Private dock with public access. Power, potable water on main float, restrooms, showers, laundry, 35-ton Travelift. Harbour Authority: 250-628-9220.

★⚓ **Kitson Island Provincial Marine Park:** Kitson Island and adjacent Kitson Islet at the southern entrance to Prince Rupert Harbour, northeast of Smith Island and south of Ridley Island, comprise this undeveloped park. Enter from Chatham Sound, and be alert for shoals. When the wind blows against the current, expect choppy conditions around the island. Sandy beaches with landing areas for kayaks. No sheltered anchorages.

★ **Digby Island:** Directly west of Kaien Island where Prince Rupert is located, Digby Island is home to the Prince Rupert Airport. A ferry runs between Fairview Harbour in downtown Prince Rupert and Digby Island to transport travelers to the airport. 250-624-6274. The small, residential community of Dodge Cove is located on the eastside of Digby Island. Boat building and commercial fishing fueled the local economy. A welding and woodwork business, Leakey Boats and Lumber, currently operates out of one of the historical boatsheds that remains. There are no other commercial services, paved roads or cars. Water taxi service to and from Prince Rupert is only a few times a week. The Digby Island Art Group along with several independent artist studios have hosted some annual art shows. A moorage float is at {54° 19' 0" N, 130° 19' 0" W} with 30 amp power and internet access. Fee applies, no water.

Prince Rupert
[3955, 3957, 3958]

★ **Prince Rupert (50):** Entry is from the south between Digby and Kaien Islands. All vessels transiting Prince Rupert Harbour, Venn Pass, and Porpoise Harbour should observe the five-knot speed limit and minimize wakes. Exercise extreme caution in the vicinity of the Digby Island Ferry Landing and within 600 yards of the harbour shoreline.

Chapter 19 NORTHERN BRITISH COLUMBIA COAST

Cow Bay Photo © Lonnie Wishart / www.lonniewishart.com

Prince Rupert lies at the heart of the traditional territory of the Coast Tsimshian Indigenous People. More than half the population of Prince Rupert consists of Indigenous people from a number of different communities. Their history, culture, and tradition helped to shape this community and continue to enrich it today.

Modern day Prince Rupert began with the construction of the Grand Trunk Pacific Railway. Prince Rupert grew from a railroad town to a thriving fishing and port community in the early 1900s. Canadian and American troops flooded the community during World War II when Prince Rupert was an American sub-port and staging area for troops and munitions.

Many buildings from Prince Rupert's early days still stand in the historic downtown shopping district. In fact, a statue of the Grand Trunk Pacific Railway's first president, Charles Hays, stands with totem poles beside City Hall on Third Avenue. Visitors will find a variety of grocery and department stores, shops, and art galleries nestled in a scenic setting with fountains, gardens, and totem poles sprinkled among the historic architecture. Views of the stunning harbour and distant islands are prominent from almost all main intersections in downtown Prince Rupert.

Prince Rupert's fishing heritage is recalled in Cow Bay. During the heyday of the canneries, so much fresh halibut was shipped from Prince Rupert that it earned the name "Halibut Capital of the World." Historic buildings, many of them built on pilings, are still found in Cow Bay. This trendy shopping district offers a variety of boutiques, souvenir and gift shops, restaurants and coffee shops, local tour companies, and moorage facilities.

Prince Rupert is a vibrant port city, home to cultures from all over the globe. It has become a centre for commerce and transportation, a meeting point for both British Columbia and Alaska ferries, the terminus of the Haida Gwaii Islands ferry, and the place where the Yellowhead Highway and VIA Rail meet the sea. Visitors come to this cosmopolitan city to experience 10,000 years of living culture, world-class sport fishing, and spectacular wildlife viewing.

Your first glimmer of what you will experience unfolds as you cruise into the harbour. Immense tidal changes create continually changing landscapes, sometimes linking isolated islands with clam-filled sandbars. The rugged coastline hosts a variety of wildlife including bears, moose, wolves, and deer. The sky is often filled with eagles and ravens. Spend a quiet moment along the waterfront and you may a glimpse of a harbour seal or one of many species of seabirds, and on rare occasions, even humpback or killer whale.

Here nature and history are vital to daily life, and Prince Rupert has a variety of shore excursions available that explore both. One tour turns back the clock at the historic North Pacific Cannery, a National Historic Site. Others focus on nature, wildlife, and the outdoors (kayaking, whale watching, nature hikes, sport fishing, floatplane and helicopter tours, and bear watching at the Khutzeymateen Grizzly Bear Sanctuary). Prince Rupert is also home to the world class Museum of Northern British Columbia, at which tours can be booked by calling 250-624-3207. The Lester Centre of the Arts, the Jim Ciccone Recreation Centre, and the Prince Rupert Golf Course also offer visitors alternate activities. For city information and activities, visit www.visitprincerupert.com or call the Visitor Information Centre at 250-624-5637.

Banks, restaurants, hotels, B&Bs, retail centres, grocery and liquor stores, marine supply stores, and marine repair services are all located in the area and easily accessed.

CBSA Customs check-in: 24 hr. Customs service. 1-888-226-7277, or 1-888-CANPASS.

Prince Rupert Berthage: Pleasure craft moorage is available in Cow Bay and Rushbrooke Harbour. Fairview Harbour is primarily for commercial craft, with moorage available when the fleet is out. The public floats are protected by breakwaters. Please note: No hourly or short term moorage is available at the public docks. Once you tie up, the daily rate applies. Stays past midnight, incur a charge for another day. For general port information: Port Edward Harbour Authority. 250-628-9220.

★ **Shutter Shack:** Northwestern BC's premier photography shop since 1975, Shutter Shack is a must-stop during any visit to Prince Rupert. Shutter Shack offers all ID photos, photographic printing, custom framing, and a wide selection of art, locally made souvenirs, and gifts featuring the work of renowned photographer Lonnie Wishart. There's even a camera museum! See our advertisement on this page. 221 Third Avenue West, Prince Rupert. Phone: 250-624-4233.

★ **Cow Bay:** Local lore attests that in 1906 the first dairy herd arrived via ship. With no dock to unload the cargo, the cows were unceremoniously dumped overboard and swam ashore. Today a harbour front walk leads to dining, shopping, and historic buildings. The *Udder Fest Theatre Festival and Cow Bay Regatta* occur in August.

• Lonnie Wishart Gallery • Post Cards • Camera Museum
• Locally Handmade Souvenirs • Custom Framing • Photo Printing

Proud to be Northern British Columbia's Premier Photo Lab

Shutter Shack

est 1975

221- 3RD AVE WEST • PRINCE RUPERT • 250.624.4233
(BESIDE EAST WIND EMPORIUM)

Visit us at boattravel.com

NORTHERN BRITISH COLUMBIA COAST Chapter 19 Page 253

Harbour Authority floats are the closest public floats to town at {54° 19' 10" N, 130° 19' 7" W}. There is a garbage drop, but no power or water. Because of lack of amenities, these are usually used by boaters for come and go stops while visiting the town to shop.

Facilities for transiting pleasure craft are available adjacent to the Cow Bay floats at the Cow Bay Marina and at the Prince Rupert Yacht and Rowing Club.

★ **Cow Bay Marina**: {54° 19' 9.45" N, 130° 19' 14.33" W} Customs Approved, Cow Bay Marina is located in the heart of Prince Rupert's tourist area with great stores and restaurants that are within walking distance. With the capacity to berth 51 vessels, including larger yachts, the marina is an ideal re-supply stop for boats traveling to and from Haida Gwaii and Alaska. Located at the Atlin Terminal in Cow Bay, the new marina offers slips for vessels that are up to 100 feet, with a capacity to moor larger vessels on the dock's breakwater. The breakwater is covered by a walkway and is accessible to Prince Rupert residents, who now have a dedicated space to stroll the harbour. Visiting yachters will have access to a plethora of shops and services all located within a five block radius. Boutique shopping includes gift stores, art galleries and artisan shops. Marine re-fitters and supply stores are within easy walking distance. People can provision easily, with access to several grocery stores and a liquor store. Great restaurants offer a variety of international cuisine. There is a pub and microbrewery all within walking distance. See our advertisement on this page. Website: www.cowbaymarina.ca. Address: 209 Cow Bay Rd, Prince Rupert, BC V8J 1L7. Phone: 250-622-2628. VHF 66A.

Linde Canada: Dry ice. 250-624-4301.

Northwest Fuels-Cow Bay: Gas, diesel, filters, marine batteries, lubricants, fuel additives, marine supplies, oil/garbage disposal, showers, water, snacks, ice, bait & tackle. 250-624-4106. VHF 71.

Prince Rupert Rowing and Yacht Club: {54° 19.245' N, 130° 19.244' W} Customs clearance. Member, reciprocal & public moorage, reservations welcome, 30/50 amp power, showers, laundry, water, phone, garbage/recycling, WiFi. 250-624-4317. VHF 73.

★ **Rushbrooke Harbour:** This basin is a commercial fishing dock that welcomes recreational vessels. Enter through the northern breakwater entrance. When mooring at either the Rushbrooke or the Yacht Club floats, be aware of strong currents which may affect maneuverability. Stop by the Harbour Managers office to pick up literature describing what to do and see in Prince Rupert. It is about a 15 minute walk to town.

Rushbrooke Harbour Floats: {54°18' 30" N, 130° 18' 18" W} Permanent and guest moorage, 20 amp power, water, washroom, showers, telephone, boat launching ramp, garbage deposit. Rafting is common. No reservations. Harbour Manager: 250-624-9400 or 250-628-9220.

Bridgeview Marine: Boating supplies, new/used boat sales, trailers, engines, maintenance and repairs, dry land boat storage. 250-624-5809.

Fairview Harbour: {54° 17' 32" N, 130° 21' 14" W} One breakwater shelters the floats extending east to west. Fairview is a commercial fishing dock that welcomes recreational vessels. Power, washroom, showers, laundry, water in loading areas, with electric derrick, garbage drop. Located at the bottom of Park Ave, 1.5 km (about a 25 min walk) from downtown Prince Rupert. Stop by the Harbour Managers office to pick up literature describing what to do and see in Prince Rupert. Harbour Manager: 250-624-3127 or 250-628-9220.

★ **Venn Passage:** [3955, 3957, 3959, 3985] Both northbound and southbound approaches to Prince Rupert may be shortened by about ten miles by traversing this passage, known locally as Metlakatla Pass. The twisting channel is reef infested, and requires extreme caution. It is well marked with buoys and segmented lights. Currents run to three knots. Coast Guard approved charts and a sounder are musts. The large Tsimshian native village of Metlakatla is on the north side of the passage. Traffic should slow down when passing the floats in front of this village.

Prince Rupert — Photo © Lonnie Wishart / www.lonniewishart.com

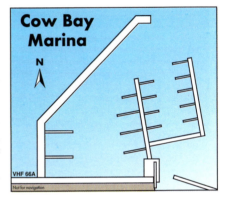

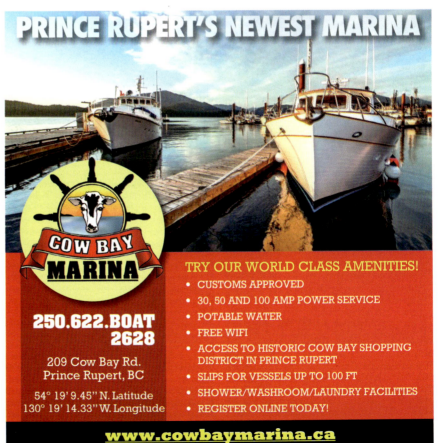

2024 Northwest Boat Travel

Langara Point Lighthouse at the north end of Haida Gwaii
Photo © Lonnie Wishart / www.lonniewishart.com

There is a short cut to the north, about ¾ of a mile west of Metlakatla, that is about three miles shorter than following the old route around Enfield Rock. It goes east of Tugwell Island into Duncan Bay, and then northwest to pass on either side of Hodgson Reefs. Pay close attention to the channel markers to avoid numerous shoals.

★ **Tuck Inlet & Tuck Narrows:** [3964] This inlet is a continuation of Prince Rupert Harbour. It is entered at Tuck Point, five miles north of Rushbrooke Harbour. This is a convenient anchorage, if Prince Rupert moorage is full or you want a quieter place. A rock at approximately {54° 18' 18.9" N, 130° 14' 56.5" W} covers and uncovers with a drying height of 0.09 metres. Anchorage is in the bight 3/8 of a mile west of Tuck Point in 8 to 10 fathoms on a mud bottom with protection from all except down-inlet winds. Another spot is at the head of the inlet in 16 fathoms on a mud bottom. There is protection from all but up-inlet winds. Be aware that the head shoals rapidly, especially to port. Currents at Tuck Narrows run to six knots, but the channel is short, wide and deep. See current tide table for Wrangell Narrows.

Prince Rupert to Alaska Border
[3800, 3933, 3960, 3963]

★ **Port Simpson/Lax Kw'alaams (51):** [3933] Port Simpson may be approached by Cunningham Passage from the south or Inskip Passage from the north. This harbour offers good anchorage. There are no tidal streams and approach is unobstructed. It is sheltered from all but west winds. This is a good jumping off place for crossing Dixon entrance. Lax Kw'alaams is a derivative of a word meaning "Island of the wild roses". An ancient camping spot of the Gispaxlo'ots tribe, in 1834 it became the site of a Hudson Bay Company trading post called Fort Simpson, and later Port Simpson. Today the residents of this Tsimshian community are mainly engaged in the fishing industry. Fuel is available during the fishing season, Monday and Wednesday between 1pm and 4pm, and Friday from 1pm to 3:45pm. Receipts MUST be purchased at the Band Office. Moorage floats are on the east side of Village Island, {54° 33' 39.6288" N, 130° 25' 52.3668" W}. Call the local taxi on CB radio channel 2. Port Simpson has a post office, five stores, two take-out food joints, and a pool with hot tub, sauna, and fitness room. Lodging is available at Knotts Landing B & B. A ferry, water taxi and plane service provide connections to Prince Rupert.

There are several large inlets in British Columbia located north and east of Port Simpson that are passed up by most boaters, but are worth exploring. These waterways are Work Channel, Quottoon, Khutzeymateen, Observatory, and Portland Inlets, and Portland and Pearse Canals. (The latter three are covered in Chapter 20.) Most are surrounded by beautiful, high mountains, some with glaciers, abundant wildlife, and Observatory Inlet even has three ghost towns - Alice Arm, Kisault, and Anyox.

Brundige Inlet
[3909]

★ **Brundige Inlet & Dundas Island (57):** This excellent anchorage is on the north end of Dundas Island, and 35 miles north of Prince Rupert via Venn Passage. It is a good jumping off place for crossing Dixon Entrance. The best anchorage is in the far south end of the inlet, in seven fathoms of water, or in the bay on the port side, in about halfway, in five fathoms of water. Good holding bottoms. To anchor near Fitch Island, to port after entry, pass Fitch Island, then slowly turn in, keeping it to port and use a depth finder to ease between Fitch Island and the baring mound, labeled "18" on the chart. Keep the mound to starboard and go into the head of the cove for secure holding bottom in four fathoms. At low tide, observe the baring mound and record the location for future use. Ketchikan, the first port in Alaska, is about 55 miles from here.

Work Channel
[3963]

★ **Work Channel & Trail Bay (52):** Enter at Maskelyne Point on the north end of Maskelyne Island. Dudevoir Pass, south of this island, has a least depth of three feet, and, though used by some commercial fishermen, is not recommended. Paradise Passage, two miles inside Work Channel on the north side, is not recommended for the same reason. Work Channel is about 28 miles long, is bordered by high mountains, and is very scenic, especially Quottoon Inlet. Anchorages are rare, but there are a few good ones. The first anchorage is in Trail Bay, six miles southeast of Maskelyne Point. Anchor either at the head of Trail Bay in about ten fathoms, sand and gravel bottom, or at a better more protected anchorage in Zumtela Bay, on the west side of Trail Bay, in eight fathoms, sand bottom. Legace Bay, about five miles southeast of Trail Bay could be used as an anchorage, but it is deep, about 15 fathoms, and not too well protected.

★ **Quottoon Inlet & Quottoon Narrows (53):** Also known as the North Arm, this inlet branches off to the north about 19 miles from the entrance of Work Channel. Good, protected anchorage in Quottoon Inlet is in the unnamed cove just north of Quottoon Narrows, in 10 to 11 fathoms, well protected. Quottoon Inlet is surrounded by 3,000' to 4,000' mountains, and is the main reason for exploring Work Channel. Tidal currents are strong in Quottoon Narrows, but it is wide, 450 feet. Favor the east side of the narrows when making the passage. In summer, the three miles remaining to the head of the inlet offer spectacular scenery, with snow capped peaks and beautiful waterfalls. The inlet is too deep and the flats at the head too steep, to offer any anchorages. From Quottoon Point, Work Channel continues another nine miles to its head in Davies Bay.

★ **Davies Bay:** Well protected anchorage is possible in about 8 to 10 fathoms of water on gravel on the east side at the head of Davies Bay. Davies Lagoon dries 9 feet, according to the chart, and may be entered by small craft at or near high water.

★ **Union Inlet:** This inlet is entered at John Point about two miles northeast of Maskelyne Point. Anchorage is possible near the head in 15 to 17 fathoms, on a mud bottom.

Khutzeymateen Inlet
[3909]

★ **Khutzeymateen Inlet (54):** Khutzeymateen Inlet is 13 miles long and is entered between Keemein and Welgeegenk Points. The entrance is 9 miles northeast of Maskelyne Point, up Steamer Passage. Water depths can vary considerably with the tides, especially near the estuary. High winds are also common. The scenery at the head of Khutzeymateen Inlet is very beautiful. There is a very large seal population and Killer Whales sometimes come here to hunt seals. Khutzemateen Inlet has a good sized Grizzly Bear population, and for that reason, the Khutzeymateen Provincial Park (aka Khutzeymateen/K'tzim-a-deen Grizzly Bear Sanctuary) was established as a Class A Park in 1994 - the first area in Canada to be protected specifically for grizzly bears and their habitat. Boaters entering the sanctuary should keep to the centre of the inlet to avoid disturbing bears and must register at the K'tzim-a-deen Ranger Station upon entering the inlet. VHF l8 U.S. The Khytzemateen Guardians will explain regulations and guidelines. Entry into the estuary is restricted to those with permitted guides only (advanced reservations required). No land based access is permitted in the sanctuary. Fishing on the Khutzemateen River is closed. Review the *Tidal Waters Sport Fishing Guide* for fishing regulations within the tidal waters of the sanctuary. Hunting of wildlife is prohibited below 1,000m. Check the latest regulations at the district office.

★ **Sommerville Bay:** This bay, on the north end of Sommerville Island, offers good anchorage in 11 fathoms, sand bottom, with protection from all but northeast winds.

Observatory Inlet
[3920, 3933]

★ **Observatory Inlet & Perry Bay (55):** This inlet begins at Nass Point at the north end of Portland Inlet. Kincolith, or Gingolx is a First Nation village located about one mile southeast of Nass Point. The public boat harbour is protected by a rock breakwater, but it is shallow and very small. When local gillnetters are in, the harbour may be full. An unprotected small float lies just west of the breakwater that could be used temporarily. The public wharf in front of the village can only be reached at high water. It is about a 20 minute walk to town from the harbour. There are grocery stores, but no fuel or water available. There are several walking trails including one with a wonderful lookout of the village.

The first 22 miles up Observatory Inlet are bounded by 4,000 foot mountains. All of these waters are very deep, and anchorages are rare. Salmon Cove, 16½ miles north of Nass Point, has a possible anchorage in 11-12 fathoms, but there is very little protection from winds blowing up or down the inlet. Brooke Point is 22 miles northeast of Nass Point. Continue up Paddy Passage and Liddle Channel for 4 miles to the entrance of Perry Bay, the best anchorage in the area (well protected anchorage in 9 to 10 fathoms, mud bottom). This is a good base from which to explore the surrounding waters. There are black bears around the bay, and good crabbing. Exercise caution at the entrance to Perry Bay as there are shoals on both sides.

★ **Alice Arm:** Extends northeast nine miles from Liddle Island in its entrance. There are no suitable anchorages, but mooring is possible at Alice Arm float located at the head of the inlet. One can walk into the "ghost" town of Alice Arm, a former gold mining community, a distance of about 1/2 mile by road. Largely uninhabited save for a year round caretaker and a number of homeowners that return seasonally. ★

Kitsault: This abandoned molybdenum mining town lies across the arm. This large establishment was built in the 1970's but shut down in 1983 when the world market for this mineral, used as an alloy in steel manufacturing, collapsed from over production. The town was sold in 2005 and is currently owned by Kitsault Resorts Limited. Future plans are to establish an LNG plant, refinery, and export terminal in Kitsault. There is a private gravel road connecting the town to Terrace, B.C. A security staff remains on the premises.

★ **Hastings Arm:** [3920, 3933] This scenic inlet extends 13 miles north from Davies Point, and has high mountains on both sides. The head of the inlet is about 20 miles north of Prince Rupert and about 65 miles southwest of Ketchikan, Alaska. Anchorage might be possible at the head of the inlet. An abandoned cabin and a buoy are on the east side, and the flats are steep-to. There is temporary anchorage 4½ miles south of the head of Hastings Arm off the mouth of the creek in 9 to 10 fathoms on a soft bottom. No protection from winds blowing up or down the inlet.

★ **Granby Bay & Anyox:** The dominant feature in this bay on the west side of Observatory Inlet is the abandoned copper mining town of Anyox and its smelter. The copper smelter was built in 1915, and the town and copper mines precede that date. A fire in 1923 exploded the plant's powder magazines and destroyed the town. No one was hurt, and since much copper remained, the town was soon rebuilt. It continued to operate until low copper prices shut it down in 1935. In 1942 forest fires destroyed the town, leaving the remains of brick buildings and smoke stacks. Granby Bay is very deep, and the best anchorage is in the bay on the west side of Granby Peninsula in about ten fathoms, with good protection. The barren landscape around the town is the result of the fumes once emitted by the smelters.

Haida Gwaii
(Queen Charlotte Islands)
[3800, 3807, 3808, 3809, 3811, 3825, 3853, 3855, 3859, 3868, 3869, 3890,-3895, 3960]

★ **Haida Gwaii (Queen Charlotte Islands) (56):** This is the historic home of the Haida Nation. These islands were first sighted by Europeans in 1774 and named in 1787 after Queen Charlotte, wife of King George III. In 2009, as part of a reconciliation agreement between the Haida Nation and the Province, the Queen Charlotte Islands officially became known as Haida Gwaii, which means "islands of the people" in the Haida language.

In this 190 mile island chain there are some 200 islands and islets, along with numerous narrow and intriguing passages that are isolated from British Columbia's mainland by 60 miles of Hecate Strait. These islands lie roughly in a triangle about 65 miles across the top and tapering to a point at the south end. Graham, Moresby, and Kunghit are the three largest islands. The north end of Graham Island is about 45 miles from Alaska's border. The larger communities are Masset, Daajing Giids (Queen Charlotte) and Skidegate Landing on Graham Island and Sandspit on Moresby Island. The total population of the Haida Gwaiis is about 6,000. Industries include fishing, logging, and tourism. Haida artisans are famous for their work including argillite and silver carvings.

The climate of the Haida Gwaiis is considered to be mild. Summer temperatures are similar to those in northern and central B.C. and winter

Chapter 19 NORTHERN BRITISH COLUMBIA COAST

A sunny day near Sandspit Harbour — Photo © Murray Foubister

temperatures are moderated by the Japanese current. These islands also have a reputation for rain. While the west coast averages 180 inches of annual rainfall, the eastern side is less, as it lies in a rain shadow created by mountains. July is the driest month, October the wettest.

When cruising the islands, boaters are wise to carry extra fuel, water, oil, stove fuel, charts, a spare anchor, and a good dinghy that is capable of carrying serveral people. Most nights are spent anchored or tied to a buoy. There are boat launches at Sandspit, Copper Bay, Daajing Giids (Queen Charlotte) and Masset.

B.C. Ferries run between Prince Rupert and Skidegate Landing, with frequent sailings during June-September. The two largest islands are then connected by a ferry between Alliford Bay and Skidegate. Several charter agencies run tours through the islands. Car rentals are possible in Masset, Daajing Giids (Queen Charlotte) and Sandspit. Logging roads can be explored with 4-wheel vehicles, but check in first with the Visitor Centre. There is daily scheduled airline service to Sandspit and Masset from Vancouver, and from Prince Rupert to Masset. Reservations are recommended between July and late September. For additional visitor information call 250-559-8050 or www.gohaidagwaii.ca.

★ **Masset & Graham Island:** [3892, 3895] Graham Island has miles of sand dunes. Masset, the largest island community is home to about 800 residents. An additional 700 people reside in Gaw Tlagée (Old Massett), as well. The Canadian Forces Station, once a bustling site of 700 has downsized to only about 10 military families. If you visit during the May long weekend, you can join in with the residents to celebrate *Harbour Days*, complete with a parade, concessions, games, bbq's and more. The Haida culture is important in this community and it is proudly displayed in totem poles and in local art galleries that sell arts and crafts made by local artisans. In Gaw Tlagée (Old Massett) there is a carving shed where you might view an artist at work. A gallery/gift shop is also nearby. For the old village sites in the northern area of Graham Island, contact the Gaw Tlagée (Old Massett) Village Council at 250-626-3337. Another interesting stop in Massett is the Dixon Entrance Maritime Museum. If you like to hike, there are a number of trails, including some found in the Naikoon Provincial Park. The Cape Fife Trail (10 km each way) follows an old settler's path. One can hike to the Blow Hole, climb Taaw Tldáaw (Tow Hill), or collect agates, glass balls, driftwood, and shells at Agate Beach. Surfers come from all around to catch the waves at North Beach (for surfing supplies and tips, call 250-626-SURF).Clamming and crabbing are possibilities as well. Local rivers like the Sangan, Chown, Hiellen rivers are good for coho and trout fishing. Golfers will enjoy the 9-hole Dixon Entrance Golf Course. At the Delkatla Wildlife Sanctuary, more than 140 species of water fowl and shore birds have been seen. There are three viewing towers and bird watching walks are available. Local charter companies offer birding and sightseeing tours. Air service is available at the Masset Municipal Airport. Masset is also connected by road to Daajing Giids (Queen Charlotte). Services in Masset include liquor and grocery stores, restaurants, lodgings, RV Park, library, hardware, retail shops, car rentals, and boat launching. The boat basin inside Delkatla Inlet has a public dock and a private marina (longterm leases only). A fuel dock is about .5km from the public floats. For additional community information, call the Masset Visitor Centre at 250-626-3982.

Masset Harbour Dock: {54° 0' 32" N, 132° 8' 25" W} Moorage (10' max draft), 20/30 amp power, water, waste oil/garbage deposit. 250-626-7362.

North Arm Transportation Ltd.: Gas, diesel, lubricants, water. 250-626-3328. VHF 7A.

★ **Daajing Giids (Queen Charlotte):** [3890] This community is found on the south shore of Graham Island on Skidegate Inlet. The public floats are well protected and accessed by a single approach. Rafting is not usually necessary. Daajing Giids (Queen Charlotte) also has restaurants and coffee shops, a credit union, bank machine, many bed and breakfasts, laundry, liquor, clothing, and hardware stores are accessible. Artwork by local artists can be found in many of the shops. If you visit in June, join in the fun during the annual *Hospital Day Celebration* with a parade, games, races, and music and in August you can check out the *Edge of the World* music festival in Tll.aal (Tlell). There are many different trails throughout the island and free maps can be found at the Visitor Centre, located to the right of the dock on Wharf Street. 250-559-8316, www.queencharlottevisitorcentre.com. The Centre also offers free brochures and information about different activities, accommodations, and attractions, and has a computer with internet access, as well as wifi. Fishing charters and land tours are available, as well as boat tours to Gwaii Haanas, the National Park Reserve. There is fishing in the Yakoun River and Yakoun Lake is a scenic spot to explore. A boat launch is located halfway between the town and Skidegate Landing. Ferry service to Prince Rupert as well as Alliford Bay (Sandspit) is provided 3 miles away in Skidegate Landing. The main highway passes through the communities of Daajing Giids (Queen Charlotte), Skidegate, Tll.aal (Tlell), Gamadiis (Port Clements) and Massett.

Queen Charlotte Harbour Authority: {53° 15' 5" N, 132° 4' 31" W} Moorage, 15/30 amp power, water, restroom, shower, garbage, oil disposal, security cameras. 250-559-4650. VHF 06.

Fast Fuel: Gas, diesel, spill supplies. Open June-August from 5-8pm or by appt. Also by appt. the rest of the year. Call ahead for oils/lubes by the case. 250-559-4611.

Tll.aal (Tlell): This tiny community of artisans includes shops, animal clinic, and restaurant. Beaches and sand dunes are lovely along the Tll.aal (Tlell) River. A good hike is to the shipwreck of the barge *Pezuta*. Site of the annual *Edge of the World Music Festival* held the 2nd weekend in August.

★ **Gamadiis (Port Clements):** [3893] The public boat dock and boat launch are centrally located in Stewart Bay. The community has lodging options including a local motel, B & B's, and a hostel. Other amenities include: post office, health clinic, library, pub, grocery store, gas station with cafe, liquor and propane. The Port Clements Historical Society runs an interesting heritage museum north from the docks that also acts as a visitor information centre and has a walking trail on its grounds. Not far from the museum is St. Mark's Church, a restored heritage church which also has a gift shop. Surrounding the Church is Millennium Park where a sapling of the Golden Spruce tree is growing. About two blocks away, the Community Park has a playground, soccer field, gravel running track, baseball field, and picnic tables. Local businesses offer fishing charters, sightseeing, logging and ecotours. The Yakoun River, known for world class fishing, also offers boating and picnicking opportunities. For a hike, try the 6.5km/4 mi Sunset Park Trail that starts near the museum and includes a multi-level bird tower overlooking the Yakoun Estuary, as well as tent and RV campsites. Another trail winds 1km/.6 mi through old growth forest to the Golden Spruce heritage site just beyond the village on the road to Juskatla. Gamadiis (Port Clements) also hosts the *Canada Days* event which includes a parade, a baseball tournament, mud bog car racing, logger sports and a dance. For more Gamadiis (Port Clements), information, visit www.portclements.ca.

Gamadiis (Port Clements) Small Craft Harbour: {53° 41' 23" N, 132° 11' 9" W} Moorage, 20/30/50 amp power, water, boat launch. All vessels must check-in at the Village Office to sign a moorage agreement form in order to moor at harbour. 250-557-4295.

★ **H1Gaagilda (Skidegate):** [3890] The Council of the Haida Nation is asking all visitors to sign the Haida Gwaii Pledge and take the Haida Gwaii Visitor Orientation before preparing to travel to Haida Gwaii. The Pledge can be found at https://haidagwaiipledge.ca. This Haida community of about 800 residents offers lodging, restaurants, groceries, gas, propane, and stores selling souvenirs, clothing, local art and more. It is 1.5k/1mi. from the site of the ferry landing. Rich in Haida tradition, six monumental poles mark the Haida Heritage Centre which houses the Haida Gwaii Museum. Another prominent totem pole by Master carver Bill Reid is found at the Kay Centre. Visitors to the carving shed can view local artists engaged in their craft. The canoe shed holds the famous 50 foot cedar Loo Taas Canoe. To watch Haida canoes race and enjoy lots of other fun activities, come in July for Skidegate Days. Visit the Haida Heritage Centre in August and join in on the Kay Anniversary celebrations starting with a Clan March, vendors, cultural sharing and the biggest event, the Mens and Womens Dance Competitions. Please visit the Heritage Centre or Go Haida Gwaii to confirm dates and times.

NORTHERN BRITISH COLUMBIA COAST Chapter 19 Page 257

Walk-around: The Spirit Lake trail makes a good family hike. A beautiful carved cedar gateway marks the trailhead. ⚲

Skidegate Narrows: This passage is narrow, rocky, shallow, and well marked. If possible, follow a local boat through at high water slack. There is anchorage in Dawson Harbour, in five fathoms, behind the small island on the south side. There is a buoy at the east end of the narrows, on the south side.

★ **Gwaii Haanas:** The southern half of Moresby Island, and adjacent smaller islands, are designated as Gwaii Haanas National Park Reserve/ Haida Heritage Site. All visitors traveling between May 1 - Sept 30 must have a reservation and register before entering the park. 1-877-559-8818. Boaters who plan to stay at Sandspit Harbour on the way to visit Gwaii Haanas National Park and want to take the mandatory orientation session in Sandspit (fee applies), must make those arrangements in advance. Download a trip planner at www.pc.gc.ca/gwaiihaanas for more information.

★ **Sandspit & Moresby Island:** [3890, 3894] The Parks Service has some facilities on South Moresby, including untreated fresh watering stations at Shuttle Island {52° 40.00'N, 131° 43.80'W} and Louscoone Inlet {52° 11.64'N, 131° 15.37'W}. To verify the availability of park services, call 250-559-8818. Tasu, a former mining operation and supply stop on Moresby's west coast, is closed and nothing much remains.

Sandspit is the largest community on the island. The majority of approaches to Sandspit Harbour are from the east crossing Hecate Strait, over Dogfish Banks, into Skidegate Inlet, and direct to Sandspit. Not surprisingly, Sandspit is named for an actual sandspit that stretches out north of the community. Avoid passing too close to the bar as it can be very shallow. While the crossing can be "lumpy" at times, the prudent mariner with an eye on the weather and tides will have no problems with the well-charted and marked channel. Lit ranges and other aids to navigation can help guide you. Monitor weather channel VHF 3 for up-to-date information. Use Charts #3890 and #3894 and the North Coast Sailing Directions. Sandspit Harbour is located about 2 miles/3kms from the town's central hub. Lodging and provisions are available. Laundry facilities and showers are available at the 501 Campground (250-637-5473) just up the road from the Marina. Campground operates generally in July, August, part of September. Groceries and rental cars can be delivered to the marina. Activities here include camping, swimming, beachcombing at Gray Bay, or exploring the numerous walking and hiking trails. The Dover Trail starts by the Harbour, wandering through old growth cedars, spruce groves and along a scenic creek. It takes about two hours to hike the loop, sturdy shoes required. Wildlife viewing opportunities are spectacular - birds, deer, bear, whales, sea lions and more are common sights on the islands. Fishing is also popular, especially mid-May to early September. An annual Coho derby runs for four consecutive weekends starting the weekend after Labour Day. Each July, Logger's Sports Day features a variety of logging skill contests and ends with a community hall dance. The Sandspit Airport has daily flights to and from Vancouver via Air Canada Jazz. There is an Airport Shuttle operating during Air Canada flight times only between the airport and Alliford Bay ferry terminal. Pre-booking is required (250-559-4461). Non-airport travelers can use the service but only during the scheduled airport runs. Helicopter tours are available. Bikes can be rented at the Sandspit Visitor Centre, located in the airport terminal. The Centre is open year round. 250-637-5362. Daajing Giids (Queen Charlotte) Visitor Centre closes down in the winter. 250-559-8316, www.daajinggiidsvisitorcentre.com. If you plan to visit Gwaii Haanas National Park, National Marine Conservation Area Reserve, and Haida Heritage Site, please refer to the "Gwaii Haanas" entry in this chapter. A ferry landing with a shelter and pay phone is located out of town. The ferry crosses to Graham Island where the Village of Daajing Giids (Queen Charlotte), Skidegate, the Haida Heritage Centre, and Masset are located.

★ **Sandspit Harbour:** {58° 14.3' N, 131° 51.8' W} Located just east of Haans Creek on Moresby Island. Moorage, gas, diesel, 15, 30, 50 ampere power, fresh water, showers, launch ramp. Fishing and tour charters. Recreational activities nearby. See our advertisement on this page. Internet: www.sandspitharbour.com. E-mail: sandspitharbour2@outlook.com. Address: Post Office Box 477, Sandspit, British Columbia V0T IT0. Harbour Phone: 250-637-5700. Fax: 250-637-5701.

Bridgeview Marine: Boating supplies, new/used boat sales, trailers, engines, maintenance and repairs, dry land boat storage. 250-637-5432.

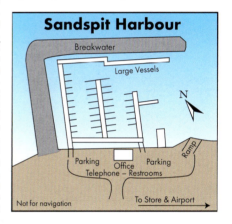

★ **Sandspit Harbour:** [3890, 3894] The gateway marina to the Gwaii Haanas National Park Reserve / Haida Heritage Site is a state-of-the-art facility. (53 14.3 N, 131 51.8 W , NAD 27) Situated in the heart of the picturesque Queen Charlotte Islands-Haida Gwaii, Sandspit Harbour is ideally located for exploring the islands and Gwaii Haanas. Visitors take away fond memories of the natural beauty of the area and the breathtaking island sunsets reflecting off the water around the harbour. Eighty-four slips are available for permanent and transient moorage, accommodating vessels up to 114' in length. Fuel: regular, premium gas & diesel are dispensed at the fuel dock; potable water, dockside electricity (15, 30, 50 ampere), storage yard, seaplane float, restrooms, showers, garbage bins, public phone and launching ramp are all located in this quiet, well-protected harbour. Spacious fairways allow for safe and easy maneuverability. Recreational activities such as deep sea and fresh water fishing, kayaking, canoeing, photography, scuba diving, hiking, mountain biking, sightseeing, whale or bird watching, golfing, beachcombing, helicopter tours, and many others are available right in Sandspit. Groceries, restaurants, pub, post office, liquor store, hair salon, cappuccino bar, propane, fishing supplies and licenses, marine supplies, airport, and lodging accommodations are located within two miles. When travelling the north coast of British Columbia, a stay at this modern, well equipped harbour is a must. Reservations for the busy summer season are strongly recommended **Call ahead on VHF 73 to contact the Wharfinger.** Internet: www.sandspitharbour.com. E-mail: sandspitharbour2@outlook.com or Address: Post Office Box 477, Sandspit, British Columbia V0T 1T0. Harbour Phone: 250-637-5700. Fax: 250-637-5701.

Essential Supplies & Services

AIR TRANSPORTATION

To & from Washington
NW Seaplanes 425-277-1590, 800-690-0086
San Juan Airlines. 1-800-874-4434
Seattle Seaplanes 1-800-637-5553
To & from Islands/Vancouver
Air Canada 1-888-247-2262
Helijet Haida Gwaii 1-877-569-4354
Inland Air 250-624-2577, 1-888-624-2577
Pacific Coastal . . . . .250-957-2285 or 1-800-663-2872

BOOKS / BOOK STORES

Evergreen Pacific Publishing 425-493-1451
The Marine Atlas. 253-872-5707

BUS TRANSPORTATION

Eagle Transit (Queen Charlotte) 250-559-4461
BC Transit: (Prince Rupert/P. Edward) . . 250-624-3343
BC Transit: (Kitimat) 250-632-4449
Greyhound (Prince Rupert). 250-624-5090

COAST GUARD

Marine Distress, Search & Rescue
. . . . 1-800-567-5111 (in Canada) or 250-413-8933
Prince Rupert Coast Guard, Radio VHF 16
or 250-627-3081
Prince Rupert Vessel Traffic . . . .250-627-3074, VHF 71
Cell Phone (limited to select providers) . . . *16 or #727

CUSTOMS

Ketchikan 907-225-2254
B.C. 1-888-226-7277

FERRY INFORMATION

Alaska Ferries 800-642-0066
B.C. Ferries . . . . .1-888-223-3779 (B.C.)
B.C. Ferries 1-877-223-8778
(ext. 1 for Prince Rupert, ext. 2 for Skidegate)

FISHING/SHELLFISHING INFO

Recorded Notifications 1-866-431-3474
Recreational Licensing 1-877-535-7307

FUELS

Bella Coola: Gas, Diesel 250-799-5633
Cow Bay Petro: P.R. Gas, Diesel. 250-624-4106 VHF 71
Dawsons Landing: Gas, Diesel
. . . . .604-629-9897. VHF 6
Hartley Bay: Gas, Diesel . . . . . . 250-841-2675 VHF 06
Klemtu: Gas, Diesel. . . . . VHF 06
Lama Pass Fuels: (New Bella Bella) Gas, Diesel
. . . . 250-957-2440 VHF 10
M K Bay Marina: Kitimat. . . . .250-632-6401 VHF 68
Masset: Gas, Diesel . . . . 250-626-3328 VHF 7A
Queen Charlotte: Gas/Diesel 250-559-4611
Sandspit Harbour, Moresby Island: Gas, Diesel.
. 250-637-5700
Shearwater Resort & Marina: Gas. Diesel
. . . . 250-957-2305 VHF 66A

GOLF COURSES

Dixon Entrance Golf: Massett (9 hole) . . 250-626-3735
Hirsch Creek: Kitimat 250-632-GOLF
Prince Rupert Gold Club: 250-624-2000

HAUL-OUTS

M K Bay Marina: Kitimat. 250-632-6401
Port Edward 250-268-9220
Shearwater Resort 250-957-2305

HOSPITALS

Healthlink BC (Nurse Helpline) 811
Bella Coola 250-799-5311
Kitimat 250-632-2121
Masset 250-626-4700
Prince Rupert 250-624-2171
Queen Charlotte 250-559-4900

LIQUOR STORES

Bella Coola
Dawsons Landing. 604-629-9897
Kitimat
Masset
New Bella Bella
Prince Rupert
Queen Charlotte
Shearwater Marina . . . . 250-957-2305 VHF 66A

LODGING

Dawsons Landing . . . . 604-629-9897 VHF 6

MARINAS / MOORAGE FLOATS

Bella Coola Public Dock . . . . 250-799-5633 VHF 16
Cow Bay Marina. 250-622-2628
Cow Bay: P.R. 250-628-9220
Dawsons Landing . . . . 604-629-9897 VHF 6
Digby Island
Fairview Harbour: P.R.
. . . . 250-624-3127 or 250-628-9220
Hartley Bay 250-841-2500
Hunt Inlet
Kincolith
Klemtu . . . . VHF 6
M K Bay Marina: Kitimat. . . .250-632-6401 VHF 68A
Masset Public Dock 250-626-7362
Minette Bay Marina (permanent) 250-632-3177
New Bella Bella
Ocean Falls Public Dock 250-289-3315
Gamadiis (Gamadiis (Port Clements)) Small Craft
  Harbour
. . . . 250-557-4295
Port Edward (Porpoise Harbour) 250-628-9220
Port Simpson
Prince Rupert Yacht Club . . . . . 250-624-4317 VHF 73
Queen Charlotte . . . . 250-559-4650 VHF 06
Rushbrooke: P.R. . . . . . 250-624-9400 or 250-628-9220
Sandspit Harbour: Moresby Island
. 250-637-5700
Shearwater Marina . . . . 250-957-2305 VHF 66A
Skidegate: Moresby Island Alliford Bay

PHOTOGRAPHY

Shutter Shack . . . . www.LonnieWishart.com

PROPANE

Lama Pass Fuels: (New Bella Bella) Gas, Diesel
. . . . 250-957-2440 VHF 10
Sandspit Harbour, Moresby Island
. 250-637-5700
Shearwater Resort
. . . . 250-957-2305 VHF 06, 66A

RAMPS

Bella Coola Harbour 250-799-5633
Moresby Island: Copper Bay, Moresby Camp in
  Cumshewa Inlet
Hartley Bay
M K Bay Marina: Kitimat. 250-632-6401
Masset
Ocean Falls
Port Edward (Porpoise Harbour) 250-268-9220
Gamadiis (Port Clements). 250-557-4295
Rushbrooke: P.R. 250-624-9400
Sandspit Harbour. 250-627-5700
Shearwater Marina. . . . . 250-957-2305 VHF 6, 66A

REPAIRS

Bridgeview Marine: Prince Rupert . . . 250-624-5809
Bridgeview Marine: Sandspit 250-637-5432
Command Marine: Kitimat. . . . . 250-632-6676 VHF 74
DC Marine: Electronics, PR. 250-624-4178
MK Marina Kitimat . . . . .250-632-6401 VHF 68A
R G's Marine: Kitimat 250-632-7722
Rocky's Equipment Sales: Queen Charlotte City
. . . . 250-559-8311
Sea Sport Outboard Marina: PR. 250-624-5337
Shearwater Marine Ltd. . . . . . . 250-957-2305 VHF 66A

SCUBA SITES

Shearwater Harbour
Gilttoyoes Inlet
Rennell Sount

SEWAGE DISPOSAL

Bella Coola Harbour 250-799-5633
Sandspit Harbour, Moresby Island . .250-637-5700

TAXI/CAR RENTAL

Bella Coola Car Rental 250-982-2146
Kitimat: Haisla Taxi 250-632-2100
Prince Rupert Skeena Taxi . . . . . . 250-624-2185 VHF 8
Sandspit Car Rental 250-637-5688

TOWING

C-TOW 1-888-419-CTOW
Shearwater Marine Ltd . . . . . 250-957-2305 VHF 6, 66A

VISITOR INFORMATION

Gwaii Haanas 877-559-8818
Kitimat 800-664-6554
Masset 250-626-3982
Gamadiis (Port Clements). 250-557-4576
Prince Rupert 250-624-5637, 800-667-1994
Queen Charlotte 250-559-8316
Sandspit 250-637-5362

WEATHER

Klemtu, Swindle Island, Van Inlet: VHF WX-1
Barry Island, Calvert Island, Dundas Island, Langara
  Island, Mt. Gil: VHF WX-2
Sandspit, Morsby Island, Port Hardy: WX-3
Masset: WX-4
Prince Rupert: VHF 21B, WX-7
Continuous Marine Broadcast (North) . . 250-624-9099

Visit us at boattravel.com

Chapter 20: Southeast Alaska

Portland Canal to Lynn Canal. Ketchikan, Wrangell, Petersburg, Juneau, Haines, Skagway, Sitka, Craig, Misty Fjords, Ford's Terror, Glacier Bay, Prince of Wales, Kupreanof, Admiralty, & Baranof Islands.

Symbols

[ ]: Numbers between [ ] are chart numbers.

{ }: Numbers & letters between { } are waypoints.

★ Recommended destinations, facilities, and services.

⛰: Park, ⛵: Boat Launch, ▲: Campgrounds, 🚶: Hiking Trails, ⊼: Picnic Area, 🚴: Biking, 🤿: Scuba

Important Notices

★ See "Important Notices" between Chapters 7 and 8 for specific information on boating related topics such as boating safety, weather, U.S. & Canadian marine radio use, Vessel Traffic Service, security zones, Canadian & U.S. Customs, etc. Due to changing regulations, call ahead to verify latest customs information.

Airline Connections: There is passenger and cargo plane service by jet to six airports in SE Alaska: Ketchikan, Wrangell, Petersburg, Sitka, Juneau, & Gustavus/Glacier Bay.

Alaska State Parks: 907-269-8400 or SE Alaska-907-465-4563. For a map of Marine Parks in SE Alaska visit http://dnr.alaska.gov/parks and choose "Regions". From the drop down menu, click on "Southeast."

Charts and publications: In addition to the charts for the waters in which one will cruise, three NOAA publications are absolute necessities. (1) the latest edition of the *United States Coast Pilot 8*; (2) *Tidal Tables, West Coast of North and South America*; and (3) *Tidal Current Tables, Pacific Coast of North America and Asia*.

Crossing the border: The border between British Columbia and Alaska is about two miles north of the north end of Dundas Island in Dixon Entrance. The exposure to the Pacific Ocean continues until one is behind Duke Island, a distance of about 20 miles. The U.S. Coast Pilot 8 gives the mileage from Seattle to the border as 615 miles. Alaska has its own time zone and it is one hour behind British Columbia and the rest of the west coast that are on Pacific Time.

Customs & Border Protection: The (CBP) Port-of-Entry is Ketchikan. 907-225-2254. All vessels arriving at Ketchikan from a foreign port or place must report immediately, regardless of the time of arrival. Travelors holding a Trusted Traveler document (Global Entry, NEXUS and SENTRI) should present this information first, in lieu of the passport. Have passports, passport card, enhanced drivers license, or NEXUS card ready for identification. Private boats may obtain pre-approval for overnight anchor at Foggy Bay by calling the CBP Ketchikan POE prior to crossing the border. When calling, be prepared with vessel and traveler information (legal names, dates of birth, travel document type, and document numbers for all aboard). CBP Trusted Travelers, including Global Entry and Nexus, will be processed expeditiously (i.e. telephonic clearance at CBP discretion upon arrival) but are still required to make initial arrival into a manned CBP Port of Entry. Boaters who have downloaded the Reporting Offsite Arrival - Mobile, or CBP One app may report their pertinent arrival information by using their personal smart phone or tablet. CBP may opt to continue the interview by way of a video chat or require an in person interview. For information regarding CBP One, please visit https://www.cbp.gov and search CBP One Overview.

Glacier Bay National Park & Preserve: 1 Park Rd, PO Box 140, Gustavus, AK 99826. 907-697-2230. For boating and camping permit information call 907-697-2627. VHF 12 or 16 KWM20 Bartlett Cove. Visit www.nps.gov/glba for information, reservations, and to download park brochures, maps and visitors guides.

Sportfishing/Shellfishing in Alaska: Alaska Dept. of Fish & Game. Headquarters: 907-465-4180. Call to be connected with the various SE Alaska offices. Website: www.adfg.alaska.gov.

Fishing licenses: Everyone, 16 and older (18 for residents) who fish in Alaska must purchase a license. Non-resident licenses are good for 1, 3, 7, or 14 days. Annual licenses are also available. Fees are from $15-$100. Fishing for King salmon requires a King Salmon Stamp. Non-resident fees range from $15/one day to $100/annual stamp.

Paralytic Shellfish Poisoning Information: The Dept. of Environmental Conservation (DEC) warns that the risk of Paralytic Shellfish Poisoning (PSP) is real. PSP occurs widely in Alaska and strikes people nearly every year. People should NOT harvest or consume shellfish from recreational beaches because the DEC does not routinely monitor these shellfish for PSP. Commercially harvested shellfish are routinely tested and are considered safe. Information: Shellfish Permit Coordinator. 907-269-7636. http://dec.alaska.gov/eh/fss/shellfish/paralytic-shellfish-poisoning.

Chart List

Canadian Hydrographic Charts: 3935

NOAA Charts:

17300, 17301-17303, 17314-17318, 17320-17324, 17331, 17333, 17336-17339, 17360, 17362, 17363, 17367, 17375, 17378, 17384, 17385, 17387, 17400, 17403-17405, 17407, 17408, 17420, 17422-17424, 17426, 17428, 17430-17438

Marine Atlas Vol 2 (2020 ed.):

Pages 29-66

Cruising Thorne Bay — Photo © WayneBenner

Thorne Bay - photo © Wayne Benner

Page 260 Chapter 20 SOUTHEAST ALASKA

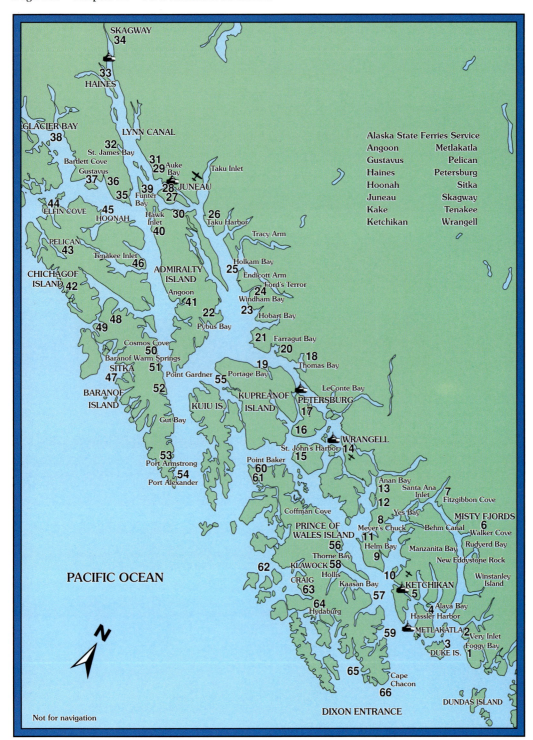

Alaska State Ferries Service
- Angoon
- Gustavus
- Haines
- Hoonah
- Juneau
- Kake
- Ketchikan
- Metlakatla
- Pelican
- Petersburg
- Sitka
- Skagway
- Tenakee
- Wrangell

U.S. Forest Service Cabins: Tongass National Forest has about 150 public recreational cabins available for a reasonable fee per night. Permits to use the cabins must be reserved in advance. www.recreation.gov. or calling 1-877-444-6777.

Introduction

★ **Southeast Alaskan Panhandle:** [17300, 17320, 17360, 17400, 17420] Hundreds of islands and inlets are found among the more than 11,000 miles of coastline contained in southeast Alaska. The entire territory is over 400 miles long and about 125 miles wide. The majority of channels are wide and deep. Hundreds of freighters, ferries, cruise ships, tugs and barges, fishing boats, and pleasure craft ply this marine highway each year. Sixty percent of the region consists of hundreds of islands covered with dense deep-green forests of spruce, hemlock and cedar. Above the timberline on the mainland are snow-capped peaks and glaciers moving slowly down the valleys to the sea. Southeastern Alaska lies at the same latitude as Scotland, Denmark, and southern Sweden. Warmed by ocean currents, this region experiences relatively mild, warm summers with July temperatures averaging about 60 degrees. An occasional heat wave may go into the 80's. Winters are cool but not severely cold, sub-zero temperatures being uncommon. The region experiences considerable rainfall, averaging more than 160 inches annually with the heaviest in late fall and a lighter average in summer. Almost all of Southeast Alaska lies within the Tongass National Forest which, at nearly 17 million acres in size, is the largest National Forest in the U.S. These forests once provided Southeastern's major industry, timber harvesting. Today, government, fishing/fish processing, and tourism are the three major contributors to the economy, while timber constitutes a small part. Seventy five percent of the population lives in the five major communities of Juneau, Ketchikan, Petersburg, Sitka and Wrangell. The Forget-Me-Not is the state flower and the Sitka Spruce is the state tree. By way of interest, the Sitka Spruce can grow to 49 feet in circumference and 213 feet in height. The state flag, a deep blue with stars in the pattern of the Big Dipper was designed by a 13 year old boy. The Big Dipper, part of the constellation Ursa Major or the "Big Bear" connotes strength and the North Star represents the most northern state and its bright future. Alaska was purchased from Russia in 1867 for only $7.2 million (a bargain at two cents an acre!). Sitka was the first capital city. Juneau is the capital today.

Portland Inlet, Canal, & Pearse Canal
[17420, 17425, 17427]

Portland Inlet & Portland Canal: This inlet begins five miles north of Port Simpson and continues for 90 miles north to the Ports of Stewart, British Columbia and Hyder, Alaska. The scenery at the head of Portland Canal is beautiful, with mountain peaks over 7,000 feet, covered by glaciers and large snow fields. When boating to the head of the canal be aware that the wind that often blows up or down the waterway with considerable force. When blowing against the tide it can create very uncomfortable conditions. Good anchorages are rare in Portland Canal. The international boundary more or less follows the center of the canal. If planning to fish both sides of Portland Canal you'll need fishing licenses from both countries.

★ **Halibut Bay (Alaska):** This is the best anchorage in Portland Canal. It is 47 miles north of Port Simpson and 46 miles south of Stewart. Anchorage is possible in seven fathoms, good holding bottom, on the bay's west side. However, if the wind is blowing up the canal, as it often does, seas will come right into the anchorage.

Visit us at boattravel.com

★ **Whiskey Bay (British Columbia):** This little cove at the north end of Pearse Island offers anchorage in five to seven fathoms, soft bottom. When the wind is blowing in Pearse and Portland Canals there is protection here from all but north winds. In that case, go down Pearse Canal, with the seas behind you, to Winter Inlet, also on Pearse Island.

Pearse Canal: Lies between Pearse Island, British Columbia, and the Alaska mainland. The international boundary runs down the canal. These waters are more protected than those of Portland Canal and Inlet.

Hidden Inlet (Alaska): Ruins of a former cannery are on the north shore of the canal west of Hidden Inlet. This is also the site of a fishing resort. The currents in and out of Hidden Inlet are very strong.

★ **Winter Inlet (British Columbia):** This inlet at the west end of Pearse Island offers good, protected anchorage in seven fathoms, on mud bottom.

★ **Wales Island (British Columbia):** Anchorage can be found in Wales Harbour and near Swaine Point.

★ **Wales Harbor (British Columbia):** On the north side of Wales Island. Good anchorage in eleven fathoms, on mud, at the head of the harbor.

★ **Swaine Point (British Columbia):** Anchorage in seven fathoms of water with fair shelter is possible in the small bight immediately west of this point on the east side of Wales Island. Good salmon fishing may be found at Swaine Point.

★ **Regina Cove (Alaska):** Offers protected anchorage in ten fathoms, on the north side of Pearse Canal.

Fillmore Inlet Notice: The chart of Fillmore Inlet on Chart #17437, 9th edition has been reported to have significant offset (as much as 500 yards) and shoreline irregularities. Mariners navigating in Fillmore Inlet using chart #17437, 9th Edition or electronic charts derived from this chart should use extreme caution.

★ **Nakat Harbor (Alaska):** Finding the entrance to the harbor can be tricky. This bay, on the east side of Nakat Bay, has anchorage in 12 fathoms, mud bottom, at the head of the north arm. It has some protection, but not from south or southwest winds. Well protected anchorage with a good holding bottom is also possible in the southwest arm, between the mainland and the island to the west in ten fathoms just short of the rock that bares four feet.

★ **Hyder, Alaska:** At the head of Portland Canal, this town once bustled with the business of mining. By the mid-1950's most of the major mines had closed. Today, tourism is the mainstay of this community known as the "Friendliest Ghost Town in Alaska." Recreational fishing and hunting, heliskiing, snowmobiling, camping, and hiking are among the possible activities. By paved road, Fish Creek is 4 miles away. During July and August you can see bears fishing for salmon in the creek. Hyder has a post office, library, museum, motel, bars and restaurants. The fish & chips at "The Bus", a summertime seafood restaurant, were even recommended in *Travel and Leisure* magazine. Moorage is available at a dock located at {55° 54.364' N, 130° 00.687' W}, no water or power. The harbor needs to be dredged and boats will likey run aground at low tide. A launch ramp is nearby. Due to tidal flats, do not launch below a one foot tide. It is less than a mile walk into town from the dock. While there is no ferry service, float plane service to Ketchikan is available.

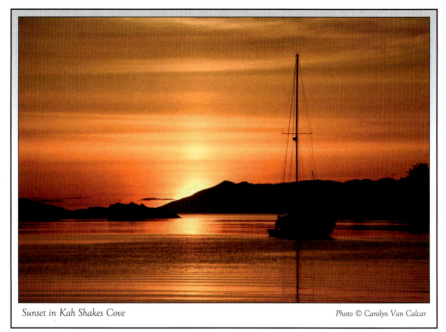
Sunset in Kah Shakes Cove — Photo © Carolyn Van Calcar

★ **Stewart, British Columbia:** This is a place of natural beauty and friendly people. Moorage, boat launch (somewhat steep, 4-wheel drive recommended), a seaplane base, lodging, restaurants, groceries, post office, library, a health centre, and cell phone service are all available here. This community is connected to the rest of B.C. by paved road. To reach Stewart, drivers take Highway 37A from Meziaden Junction. Highway 37 to Cassiar goes near the Grand Canyon of Stikine, regarded as one of the province's most spectacular land formations. Dease Lake or Iskut are day trips. Another picnic site is Bear Glacier, which laps into a turquoise blue lake between Stewart and Meziadin Lake. It is a 60-minute drive to Salmon Glacier, the 5th largest glacier in the world that is accessible by road. To reach the glacier, travelers pass through Hyder, Alaska and then re-enter Canada, so be sure to bring your passport. The films *Bear Island*, *The Thing From Planet X*, and *Insomnia* were filmed here.

Port of Stewart Dock: {55° 55' 20" N, 130° 0' 20" W} Moorage, 20 amp power and a few 50 amp. Water and fuel available by advance request. For info: Gody or Maya Appenzeller, 250-636-2626, 250-636-2802 (home) or 250-845-4352 (cell).

Dixon Entrance To Wrangell

[17420, 17434]

★ **Foggy Bay, Very Inlet (1):** [17434] Use U.S. Coast Pilot 8 when entering Foggy Bay. Hundreds of gillnetters fish the Tree Point area. Stretched nets are a hazard. The bay, a mile south of Very Inlet, has a tiny, narrow, but deep entrance. Anchorage is possible in 30-40 feet on a sticky mud bottom. Favored anchorage is behind an islet on the east side. The north entrance is the deepest. The south entrance bares at half-tide and should not be attempted. There is good protection from seas in Revillagigedo Channel. A Fish and Game Warden is stationed here most of the summer. It is possible to explore Very Inlet. Boaters who have entered the US from Canada and wish to weigh anchor in Foggy Bay should call ahead to Customs at 907-225-2254 to receive a clearance to do so.

★ **Kah Shakes Cove (2):** [17434] This anchorage, named for a Tlingit Chief, is about 30 miles south of Ketchikan. Several rocky islets extend in a westerly direction off the north side of the cove. The entrance is narrow, but the chart is an adequate guide. Favored anchorage is east of the two inner points. Some swells from the south may come in the area farther westward and closer to the entrance. Excellent clamming beds near the entrance uncover at a plus five foot tide. Anchorage depths are 35-45 feet on a sandy mud bottom. Good holding in winds. Loons, eagles, minks, and seals frequent this area. A smokehouse is available for use, if you provide your own alder.

★ **Boca de Quadra:** This is off the beaten path. The 25 mile long inlet, and its five smaller inlets, provide intriguing cruising waters and several good anchorages. Entrance is between Slate Island Light on the north side and White Reef on the south side. An alternate, if coming from the south, is to pass to the east side of Black Rock Light and White Reef. There are no facilities for boaters in Boca de Quadra. A sport fishing camp is located at the entrance to Mink Bay.

★ **Vixen Bay:** The anchorage is toward the head between Raven Island and Gosling Island, on the east side of the bay in 12 fathoms, soft bottom, good protection.

★ **Mink Bay:** Anchorages are in the cove on the west side at the entrance, just south of Cygnet Island in eight fathoms, mud bottom, good protection, and at the head of Mink Bay in 10 to 15 fathoms. This anchorage is just south of the tidal flat that extends almost across the inlet. Caution must be observed when passing the flats.

Boca de Quadra and Marten Arm: These two inlets extending 15 and 5 miles respectively from Bactrian Point, are very scenic, but too deep for anchorage.

★ **Weasel Cove:** Good protected anchorage in 16 fathoms, soft bottom with plenty of room.

Ray Anchorage, Duke Island (3): [17434] This anchorage is sheltered from south winds, but open to the northeast. Anchorage is on a hard bottom in 10 to 20 fathoms of water.

Creek Street in Ketchikan   Photo © Bernard Spragg

Ketchikan
[17420, 17428, 17430]

★ **Customs Check-in at Ketchikan:** When leaving British Columbia and entering the United States, the captain is required, regardless of the time of arrival, to notify U.S. Customs immediately to make notice of arrival. Captains with the CBP One app can use their smart phone or tablet for notification, others should call 907-225-2254. Have the pertinent information readily available for this phone call and for the in-person inspection to follow once you arrive in Ketchikan. This information includes boat registration or documentation number, Canadian customs clearance number, pet vaccination records, passports, passport card, enhanced drivers license, or NEXUS card, and current U.S. Customs decal number (to avoid delays, purchase customs decals prior to visiting Alaska, http://dtops.cbp.dhs.gov). A duty officer is available 24 hours-a-day. If you reach a recording, contact information will be provided.

★ **Morse Cove:** This cove to the west is protected and has a mud bottom. The entrance is narrow and rock strewn. It is wise to consult the U.S. Coast Pilot 8 and Chart #17434 before considering anchorage in Morse Cove. Foggy Bay, across Revillagigedo Channel, is a better choice of anchorage.

★ **Moth Bay:** This is good anchorage at the entrance to Thorne Arm, about 13 miles south of Ketchikan. Relatively protected anchorage in ten fathoms, mud bottom.

★ **Thorne Arm:** [17428] This ten mile long inlet is entered between Moth Point and Cone Point, about 11.5 miles southeast of Ketchikan. The head of the arm is broad with relatively low shores. Several anchorages are possible at the head of the arm. The most protected is on the west side of the northernmost of the Minx Islands in eight to ten fathoms, soft bottom. There are two Forest Service buoys, and a Forest Service cabin on the east side of the arm.

★ **Carroll Inlet:** [17428] Twenty miles in length, this inlet is the most scenic of the three inlets on the southwest side of Revillagigedo Island, with high mountains on both sides at its head. Anchorage with good protection is possible in Gnat Cove, six miles up the inlet on the east side in seven to eight fathoms. Two more anchorages are two and a half miles farther north. One is in the area just north of Osten Island, protected by an unnamed island to the east and reefs to the west. Anchorage is in six to ten fathoms, soft bottom. The second is 1/2 mile northwest on the Revillagigedo Island shore between two small islands, in three to four fathoms. Anchorage would also be possible off the flats at the head of the inlet, subject to winds up or down the inlet. A Forest Service Buoy is at the entrance to Shoal Cove (white with blue tape in 30-80' of water).

★ **George Inlet & Coon Cove:** [17428] This 12 mile long inlet lies north of Mountain Point, four miles southeast of Ketchikan. Private homes, summer cabins, logging operations and log booms can be seen along the shores of this inlet. A road connects from Ketchikan to Beaver Falls Creek, about a quarter of the way into the inlet on the port side. Before you get to the falls is George Inlet Lodge. This restored cannery bunkhouse (circa 1940) was towed from Hidden Inlet in the 1970's and now hosts experiences for tourists. The Lodge's dock space is private. The best anchorage in George Inlet is in the cove north of Bat Point, at the head of the inlet, in ten fathoms, mud bottom, and excellent protection. Anchorage is also possible in Coon Cove on the east side of the inlet in 10 to 13 fathoms, with good protection.

Annette Island & Hassler Harbor (4): [17434]. Located between Pow Island and Annette Island, Hassler Harbor offers shelter from southeast winds, with a good holding bottom in ten fathoms. Metlakatla, also on Annette Island, is the site of a fuel facility. See description of Metlakatla later in this chapter.

★ **Ketchikan (5):** See customs and berthage information below. Ketchikan, "Alaska's First City," is located on Revillagigedo Island and is a customs port. Ketchikan Creek, running through the heart of town, was originally the site of a fish camp used by Tlingit Natives. During the 1880's the settlement grew as fishing and later logging became lucrative industries. Today, Ketchikan is the state's seventh largest community and is known for its scenic beauty, spectacular sports fishing, rich native culture, and ample "liquid sunshine"-over 150 inches annually! That rainfall helps maintain the lush, green vegetation of the surrounding Tongass National Forest. The community of Ketchikan is built along the waterfront (often on pilings) and up the hillsides that overlook the channel. There are many things to see and do within the city limits and most are accessible on foot. Downtown Ketchikan offers a number of shops and services including restaurants, cafes, bars, a movie theater, and banks. There is a public bus, taxi services, and rental cars. Looking for another way to travel? Bicycles, electric carts, kayaks and skiffs can all be rented locally. From May through September artistically decorated "Salmon Run" free shuttle buses run every 20 minutes between the tour ship docks and points of interest including SE Discovery Center, Creek Street, Totem Heritage Center and the Tongass Historical Museum. Visitors will enjoy the museum, featuring artifacts and exhibits illustrating local history, art, and native culture. 907-225-5600. The natural and cultural history of the area is also highlighted through exhibits, films and presentations at the SE Alaska Discovery Center. The Center is also a great resource for visitor information on recreation, wildlife and Native Culture. 907-228-6220. Other downtown attractions include the Great Alaskan Lumberjack Show where log-rolling contestants often take a dip and Dolly's House Museum which offers a glimpse into the days when Creek Street was the town's red light district. From Creek Street, a funicular provides panoramic views on its way up to Cape Fox Lodge and Restaurant. Within walking distance of downtown is City Park and the Totem Heritage Center featuring historic poles. 907-225-5900. Charters, tours, flight seeing, sightseeing; every activity from A (amphibious tours) to Z (zip line adventures) can be arranged. For brochures, maps and information

The Rock tells the story of how Ketchikan became Alaska's "first city."   Photo © Carolyn Van Calcar

SOUTHEAST ALASKA   Chapter 20   Page 263

about Ketchikan, stop by the Visitor Information Center on the corner of Front and Mission Streets, or their satellite facility two blocks north, at cruise ship berth #3. 907-225-6166, 1-800-770-3300. www.visit-ketchikan.com. Ketchikan has the largest collection of totem poles in the world and some of the most magnificent examples are found at Saxman Totem Park (2.5 mi. S. Tongass Hwy) and Totem Bight State Historical Park (10 mi. N. Tongass Hwy). Potlatch Park, located next to the latter, is a replicated native village with a resident carver. There is also an antique firearms and antique car museum. Hiking opportunities for all fitness levels abound in the Ketchikan area. Ward Lake trail, located 8 miles north of town, is great for beginners. Not far from downtown, the Deer Mountain Trail, with its series of switchbacks, poses a much bigger challenge. Local events include the month long *Alaska Hummingbird Festival* each April featuring fun educational and recreational activities. In July, the *Fourth of July Celebration* has a parade, food and game booths, contests, fireworks. The *Blueberry Festival* occurs the first Saturday in August and features local arts and crafts. Ketchikan has an international airport and an Alaska State ferry terminal.

The City Float in Ketchikan   Photo © Richard H. Van Cleave

★ **Tongass Trading Company**: Tongass Trading Co. Marine and Outdoor is your local source in SE Alaska for all your commercial marine gear, outdoor clothing and footwear, boating and safety, marine hardware, fishing tackle, camping equipment, guns, ammo and hunting supplies. We also provide commercial and sport licenses and much much more! Plus we do special orders. Get special pricing on non-stocked items. If we don't stock it, we will try to find it for you. See store for details. We accept phone orders. We pride ourselves with the most knowledgeable local sales staff. We are conveniently located in Ketchikan next to Bar Harbor docks, close to grocery stores, banks and gas stations. Our summer store hours are Monday-Saturday, 8am-6pm, Sunday, 8am-5pm. Web store: www.tongasstrading.com. See our advertisement on this page. Address: 2521 Marine Works Way, Ketchikan, Alaska 99901. Telephone: 1-800-235-5102, 907-225-5101. Tongass Trading Co. since 1898 - Quality costs no more.

City of Ketchikan Port & Harbors Berthage: Transient moorage is available at Thomas Basin, Ketchikan Yacht Club, Casey Moran Harbor (City Float), Hole-In-The-Wall, Knudson Cove, Bar Harbor South, and Bar Harbor North. All transient moorage (except at the Ketchikan Yacht Club) is parallel to the dock unless the Harbormaster assigns a finger slip. The Harbormaster is located in Bar Harbor, north of downtown. Call 907-228-5632 or VHF 16, 73.

Bar Harbor Facilities: {55° 20.979' N, 131° 41.082' W} One mile north of Casey Moran Harbor. Moorage to 110', potable water, 30/50/100 amp 208 V power, garbage drop, pump-out, launch ramp. Drive down loading dock with crane and tidal grid requires reservation. Close to post office, supermarket, motels, laundromat, showers, restaurants and repairs. 907-228-5632. VHF 16, 73.

Casey Moran Harbor (City Float): {55° 20.597' N, 131° 39.119' W} North of Thomas Basin, behind the floating cruise ship berth. Transient moorage (first come, first served, no moorage where you see paint), 30/50 amp power, potable water, garbage drop, pump-out. 907-228-5632. VHF 16, 73.

Doyon's Landing: {55° 19.747' N, 131° 37.212' W} Private yacht moorage. 50/100 amp power, water, garbage, wifi, yacht fueling, Customs/Immigrations services. 1-877-228-4656, 907-225-5155.

Hole-In-The-Wall Floats: {55° 19.117' N, 131° 31.215' W} Very limited transient moorage to 26'. No power. Seasonal potable water. Located seven miles south of the city center. 907-228-5632. VHF 16, 73.

Ketchikan Moorage: {55° 20.736' N, 131° 39.644' W} Private yacht moorage, vessels to 170', 30/50/100 amp, single & 3 phase power, water, wifi, customs services, gated ramp. 907-220-6384.

Ketchikan Petro Marine Service: (located south of downtown by USCG Base) Gas, diesel, propane, oils, lubricants, solvents, filters, batteries, water, ice, bait. 907-225-2106. VHF 16.

Ketchikan Yacht Club: {55°20.5' N, 131°38.7' W} In Thomas Basin. Limited visitor's moorage on Float 2, fourth float inside the breakwater, 46' or less. First come first served. Call posted number for assignment. Moorage includes use of showers, galley stoves/refrigerators, clubhouse tables, picnic table. Power, internet additional cost. 907-225-3262.

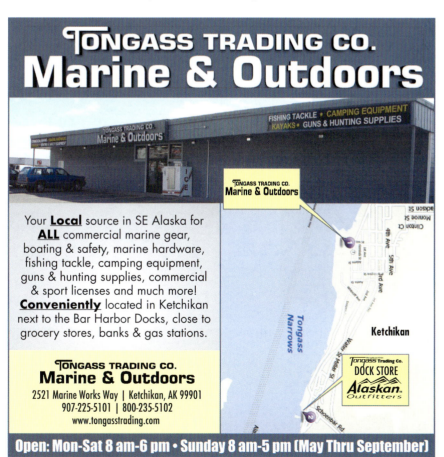

2024 Northwest Boat Travel

Misty Fjords National Monument   Photo © Jeremy Keith

Refuge Cove Marina: Private marina with transient moorage for small boats and boats up to 110'. Power, water, garbage. Telephone: 907-225-1958, Cell Phone: 907-617-2829.

Thomas Basin: {55° 20.306' N, 131° 38.584' W} Permanent moorage, transient moorage on south side of Float 4. 30/50 amp power, potable water, garbage drop, pump-out. Tidal grid, 2 ton hoist, reservations required. Located in historic downtown area. Restaurants and welding shop within walking distance. 907-228-5632. VHF 16, 73.

Tongass Narrows: [17428, 17420] Resembling the letter "Y" Tongass Narrows stretches 13 nautical miles from Nichols Passage to Guard Island. It is only about a quarter of a mile wide at its narrowest point. Well marked shoals extend from both shores. On the eastern shore are the cities of Saxman and Ketchikan. Tongass Avenue, the main thoroughfare parallels the channel. This is a busy waterway with an enforced speed limit of seven knots. When possible, travel perpendicular to, or parallel with, the main channel. Be aware of the constant stream of floatplanes landing and taking off. Use caution and watch your wake near kayakers. Traveling north up the Narrows is Ward Cove. The pulp mill in Ward Cove, once a major contributor to the economy of Ketchikan closed in 1997. There are no facilities for pleasure craft here, but a marina is located in Refuge Cove, the next bay to the north.

Air Marine Harbor: Located in Refuge Cove. Limited moorage, call ahead. No power or water at docks. Repairs, DIY Boatyard, 50 ton Travelift, dry storage for airplanes and boats. 907-225-2282.

★ **Misty Fjords National Monument (6):** [17422, 17424, 17434] This is one of 18 National Monuments in Alaska. This area east of Ketchikan includes eastern Behm Canal, Rudyerd Bay and Walker Cove. It is beautiful, off the beaten path, and worth taking time to explore. There are glaciers, mountain peaks which rise to 3,000 feet, three main rivers and many small streams, and an amazing assortment of wildlife. A continuation around the north end of Revillagigedo Island and down western Behm Canal circumnavigates the island, ending in Clarence Strait, just north of Ketchikan. Stops can be made along the way at the many anchorages. Mooring buoys can be found at Alava Bay, Anchor Pass, Bailey Bay, Blind Pass, Ella Bay, Princess Bay, Winstanley Island, and Burroughs Bay. Check the fishing regulations before fishing for salmon in the eastern portion of Behm Canal as some areas may be closed. The western part of Behm Canal is a popular area to fish for coho, sockeye, pink, king, and chum salmon. The SE Alaska Discovery Center sells a Forest/Wilderness map of Misty Fjords National Monument. 907-228-6220.

★ **Alava Bay:** The bay offers a sheltered anchorage in a southeast wind. A Forest Service cabin is onshore and a large white can buoy in the bay.

★ **Sykes Cove:** On the east side of the entrance to the east arm of Behm Canal, this anchorage is in seven fathoms with protection from all but northeast winds.

★ **Winstanley Island:** Anchorage is possible in Shoalwater Pass between the island and the mainland. The best choice is the northern anchorage where the shoal at the entrance has a least depth of nine feet. Anchorage is on the west side of the passage in seven fathoms, mud bottom, and good protection. A Forest Service cabin and a mooring buoy are located here.

New Eddystone Rock: At 237' high, this prominent feature in Behm Canal was named in 1793 by Captain George Vancouver. The rock's unusual shape reminded him of Eddystone Lighthouse off Plymouth, England. There are shoals extending off the rock's base.

★ **Rudyerd Bay:** Spectacular cliffs and waterfalls are found here, especially in Punch Bowl Cove. A private mooring buoy is in Punch Bowl Cove.

★ **Manzanita Bay:** Located on the west shore of Behm Canal, anchorage is possible in 15 fathoms in the cove in the southeast corner. Exposure to northeast winds, soft bottom. A Forest Service shelter is on the north shore.

★ **Walker Cove:** Farther along Behm Canal, this is another scenic inlet. Summer anchorage is possible in the entrance to the cove, in six and one-half to twenty fathoms of water. There is usually good bottom fishing to be had on the shoal at the entrance. There is a private buoy in a bight on the south side of the cove.

★ **Fitzgibbon Cove (7):** [17424] At the north end of eastern Behm Canal there is an excellent and beautiful anchorage in 11 to 13 fathoms of water, with a mud bottom. Note the warnings in the U.S. Coast Pilot 8 before entering.

★ **Anchor Pass:** Anchorage is possible in three fathoms, soft bottom, in the little cove on the west side, just south of the restricted north entrance to Anchor Pass. The least depth in this pass is only one and one half feet. A mooring buoy is in the bay. A Forest Service cabin is onshore.

Bell Island: The former resort located on this island is now private, not open to the public.

★ **Bailey Bay:** This deep bay off Bell Arm has a lovely waterfall at the head. A Forest Service buoy is in the bay. The Shelokum Lake Trail onshore leads about 2 miles to the Lake Shelokum shelter and hotsprings.

★ **Short Bay:** East of Bailey Bay, this bay has good anchorage in 17 to 20 fathoms of water near its head. A privately maintained mooring buoy is near the flat.

★ **Yes Bay (8):** [17422] This bay has anchorage in the cove south of the first narrow spot. Depths are about eight fathoms on a mud bottom. Newcomers should navigate the bay at low tide, when the rocks are visible. Enter in mid channel and then favor the north shore. Pass 40 yards south-southwest of the resort and favor the north shore until the basin opens up.

Yes Bay Lodge: Restaurant (advanced reservations only), lodging, gift shop, internet, fishing tours. The dock is private, moorage is available for dinghies of guests booked for dining or lodging. Pick-up service is available from anchored vessels for booked dining guests. 907-302-5490. Marine 10.

★ **Hassler Pass:** The unnamed bay on the east side of this pass has anchorage in 11 fathoms, well protected, and soft bottom. Beware of shoals on all sides of the head of the cove.

★ **Spacious Bay:** Anchorage is possible in eight to ten fathoms between Square Island and the mainland. Exposed to north and southeast, but satisfactory in settled weather, soft bottom.

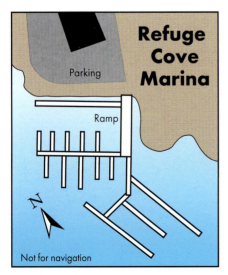

Visit us at boattravel.com

★ **Helm Bay Float (9):** [17422] {55° 37.887' N, 131° 58.668' W} A 10' x 100' state float, located in Helm Bay, 20 miles from Ketchikan, no facilities and no shore access. It is used as a haven in a storm for lay-over purposes. Sometimes this float is crowded on weekends. At low tide, the shore side of the float is in shallow moorage depth. A forest service cabin is located on the west end of the bay. Just south of Helm Bay is a Forest Service buoy for the Smugglers Cove Day use area.

★ **Naha Bay & Loring:** At the turn of the century, Loring bustled with canning operations. Today it is a popular salmon fishing, hiking, and kayaking area. The public floats in Loring at approximately {55° 35.982' N, 131° 38' W} are exposed to high seas during southwesterly winds and depths may be shallow. No power or water. A short walk from the float, the Art Cache has artwork and organic coffee (beans and take out). Nearby, the Loring Gardens are open daily for self-guided tours. Ready to get a work-out? Climb the stairway and visit the historic Cannery House Museum featuring cannery era photos and artifacts. The museum is housed in the historic Heckman home. Built around the turn of the century, it is believed to be the oldest existing home in Loring. The museum is open May to September. In addition to moorage at the float, anchorage is possible between Dogfish Island and Revillagigedo Island in fifteen fathoms, good protection, or at the head of Naha Bay, where there is also a small Forest Service float. Nearby, Roosevelt Lagoon can be entered at high tide, slack water. A trail from the float goes around the lagoon and leads to Heckman Lake. ★

★ **Moser Bay:** Anchorage is possible in the bight on the west side of the entrance to this bay in seven fathoms, soft bottom, and well protected. The small cove is crowded by some old float houses, and there are several houses onshore. A small art gallery features local artwork. Walking trails lead through the forest around the bay.

★ **Clover Pass Vicinity (10):** [17422] Fishing resorts and anchorages are located here. Knudson Cove Marina and Clover Pass Resort are connected by highway to Ketchikan.

Clover Pass Resort: {55' 28.443" N, 131' 48.884" W} Boat/skiff rentals, lodging and fish processing for fishing package guests. 907-247-2234, 1-800-410-2234. VHF 16.

★ **Knudson Cove:** Located 15-miles north of Ketchikan, this small bay on the south side of Clover Passage offers good anchorage in four fathoms of water. Day beacons mark the entrance. The city of Ketchikan maintains small craft floats on the east side of Knudson Cove. {55° 28.385' N, 131° 47.929' W} Vessels to 30', no water or power. Floats are usually very crowded. Launch ramps nearby. Harbormaster: 907-228-5632. VHF 73.

Knudson Cove Marina: {55° 28.338' N, 131° 47.855' W} Moorage limited, vessels to 28'. Gas, diesel, propane, water, coffee shop, liquor, bait, ice, snacks, lodging, boat rentals, fishing licenses, charter fishing. 907-247-8500. VHF 16.

Wrangell from Mt. Dewey Trail   Photo © Hans-Jürgen Hübner

Clarence Strait
[17420, 17423]

Clarence Strait: This strait can be dangerous in some winds. Check the weather forecasts from Ketchikan before starting the 21 mile trip from Camano Point to Lemesurier Point, at the entrance to Ernest Sound. Plan ahead for places to hide, if need be, along both sides of the strait. The strait itself is over 100 miles long and about 15 miles wide at the south end, and five to six miles wide in the northwest reaches. Flood is from the south, ebb from the northwest. Currents can reach four knots. When wind and strong tidal currents oppose each other, extremely rough conditions can result.

★ **Meyers Chuck (11):** [17423] Meyers Chuck is a small harbor 40 miles northwest of Ketchikan, on the east side of Clarence Strait. Its shelter can be a welcome relief if high wind and seas are kicking up in the strait. The narrow entry can be seen by lining up north-northwest of the tall flashing tower (visible from some distance) and north of Meyers Island. Do not enter via shoals south of Meyers Island. Keep "#3" green triangle to port and "#4" red to starboard, turning south just after clearing "#4" red. Anchorage is possible in the arm. A state operated float at {55° 44.4' N, 132° 15.5' W} has fresh water and tidal grid. There is also a seaplane float and helicopter pad. By foot, visitors can walk to a unique art gallery that features a wide variety of work from local artisans including homemade crafts, cedar bark baskets, beaded art, wood turned art and more. Dinghy over to the Post Office (open Weds., 8am-4pm or whenever the flag is flying). In addition to postal services, you can purchase a fishing license here.

★ **McHenry Anchorage:** Indenting Etolin Island, McHenry is 7.5 miles north of Ernst Point. It offers shelter except from west winds. Anchor in five to seven fathoms of water in the southeast portion, about 250 yards west of the wooded island. Avon Island, on the north side of the entry, is small and close to shore. Give a wide berth of 250 yards. A reef extends approximately 400 yards southeasterly from the southeast side of Avon Island. Caution advised regarding a rock 1/2 mile west-southwest of Avon Island.

★ **Kindergarten Bay:** [17360, 17382] This deep cove on Etolin Island, two miles north of Pt. Harrington, is one of the best anchorages in the area. It affords protection in most winds, except when strong winds blow down from the hills. Enter mid-channel, south of the wooded islet. Anchor in five to seven fathoms of water, soft bottom. Avoid a large rock southwest of the largest islet, near the head of the bay. It is covered four to six feet at high tide.

Wrangell Area
[17360, 17385]

★ **Wrangell Area:** [17360, 17385] After passing Lemesurier Point, just north of Meyer's Chuck, it is about 52 miles to Wrangell, following the ferry route through Clarence and Stikine Straits. Two alternate routes to the east offer more protection and some inspiring scenery. These are Zimovia Strait between Etolin Island and Wrangell Island, and Blake Channel and Eastern Passage, between Wrangell Island and the mainland. Zimovia is two miles shorter than the Stikine Strait route, and Eastern Passage is about eight miles longer. The chart will help you through either Zimovia Strait or Eastern Passage. Both passages are marked by buoys, day beacons, and lights. Tides run to 1.7 knots in the former, and 2.2 to 3 knots in the latter. The tides meet from north and south at the narrows in both passages. In making a transit of Zimovia Strait, strict attention must be paid to the channel markers. The course is very crooked and there are shallows on either side.

★ **Vixen Harbor:** A snug little anchorage just southeast of Union Point, about five miles east of Lemesurier Point. It is a very restricted entrance, but not difficult if one is cautious. Look out for the submerged ledges if you are not going in at low tide. Well protected anchorage is in five fathoms.

★ **Santa Anna Inlet (12):** [17385] This inlet is about midway between Ketchikan and Wrangell. There is excellent anchorage in ten fathoms near the head. Avoid a shoal which extends 200 yards off the southwest shore, one-half mile from the entrance. A river empties from Lake Helen. There is good fishing here for Rainbow trout.

Chapter 20 SOUTHEAST ALASKA

Petroglyph Beach in Wrangell — Photo © Carolyn Van Calcar

★ **Anan Bay (13):** [17385] Anchorage is fair near the Forest Service cabin. The bottom of the bay is sticky mud. The 25' float in front is for use by occupants of the cabin only. Day users of the site should use the Anan Trailhead landing designated by a red and white diamond marker located about 1/4 mile south of the Forest Service cabin. An observatory deck, where it is possible to watch brown and black bears fishing for salmon in Anan Creek, is about 1/2 mile from the trailhead. From July 5 through August 25, a $10 pass is required to visit the observatory. Only 60 passes per day are available, so plan ahead. Permits are reservable starting Feb 1st at www.recreation.gov. Search for "Anan Wildlife Observatory Permits." For additional information on permits or to rent a cabin call 907-874-2323 or 1-877-444-6777.

★ **Fool's Inlet:** This inlet is located five miles northeast of Found Island and is acceptable fair weather anchorage when Anan Bay is crowded. Anchor in 11 fathoms to starboard of the north islet at the head. Mud flats extend .9 miles from the head, nearly to the two small islets.

★ **Bradfield Canal:** Bradfield Canal extends 12 miles to the east from Anan Bay with mountains on both sides creating spectacular scenery. Caution must be used in front of Harding River where a shoal extends much farther across the inlet than one might expect. The inlet's waters are full of silt, making it impossible to see to any depth. Anchorage is possible at the head of the canal in eight to ten fathoms. The bottom shoals very rapidly and there is no protection from up or down channel winds. The flats are a good place to see both brown and black bears as well as numerous eagles. Anchorage is said to be possible in the cove in the inside of Duck Point, but on inspection it does not look very desirable.

★ **Zimovia Strait, Thom's Place:** On the east side of the strait this bay has protected anchorage in seven to eight fathoms.

★ **Zimovia Strait, Anita Bay:** [17382, 17382] On the west side of the strait this bay affords good anchorage in ten fathoms on a mud bottom at the head of the bay. This is one of the most beautiful anchorages in Alaska. With its snow covered mountaintops it feels like being anchored on a mountain lake.

★ **Blake Channel-Eastern Passage:** This is the most beautiful route to Wrangell and the navigation is easier than Zimovia Strait. There are two good anchorages, one on each side of the narrows where the flood tides meet.

★ **Berg Bay:** A well protected anchorage in front of the Forest Service cabin and float. Depths in the bay are from 5-11 fathoms.

★ **Madan Bay:** Good protective anchorage in seven to eight fathoms north of the projecting point on the west side near the head of the bay, soft bottom.

★ **Wrangell (14):** [17360, 17384] Wrangell is 750 miles from Seattle. Three harbor basins provide moorage - Etolin Harbor in downtown Wrangell and Heritage Harbor and Shoemaker Bay Harbor, both located south of town. The city is also home to two fuel docks, a boat repair/storage yard with 150 and 300 ton travelifts, three seafood processing companies and other local businesses related to the fishing and tourism industries. Wrangell's airport offers twice daily scheduled jet service and the city is also served by Alaska State ferries. Named after an 1831 governor of Russian America, Baron Von Wrangell, it is the only Alaskan city to have been under three flags - Imperial Russian, British, and United States. In the years between 1860 and 1898, gold strikes brought a bustle of activity to Wrangell. The museum, housed in the Nolan Center, reflects Wrangell's colorful past. For hours, 907-874-3770. For more ancient history, Native rock carvings at Petroglyph Beach State Historic Park are thought to be as much as 8,000 years old. Wrangell is a good place to walk or hike (read suggested "walkabouts" that follow below). For an entirely different experience, take a charter boat day trip up the wild and scenic Stikine River, or go fishing for salmon or halibut. In July and August visiting the Anan Bear and Wildlife Observatory is a once in a lifetime experience. (See Anan Bay) Other fun activities include a visit to Garnet Ledge, the historic site of an 1880's mine or golfing at the USGA rated 9 hole Muskeg Meadows Golf Course. During the summer, weekend tournaments are open to the public. Other summer events include the annual *King Salmon Derby* from June 14-June 22, the great hometown 3 day *4th of July Celebration*, and *Alaska Bearfest* the end of July, with research symposium, workshops, music, salmon feed and other activities. For Wrangell Visitor Information, call 1-800-367-9745.

Walk-around: Volunteer Park Trails, near the elementary school on Bennett Street, are flat and easy loops through muskeg or forested areas. The trailhead is located between the ballfields.

Walk-around: To tour downtown, walk along Front Street through the business district. Cross the plank bridge in Wrangell Harbor to Shakes Island, the site of the Chief Shakes Community House and collection of totems. This is an entertaining place to look around, however, visiting hours for inside the Tribal House are very restricted. The James & Elsie Nolan Center at 296 Campbell Drive in downtown Wrangell houses the Visitor Center, movie theater and meeting rooms, and Museum. For a great vista of Zimovia Straits and town overlook, hike Mt. Dewey trail, beginning at the steps on the corner of Reid Street and Mckinnon St. a short trail but with steps.

Walk-around: Walk to Petroglyph Beach State Historic Park, located about 3/4 miles from the ferry dock. Time your walk to arrive at low tide. Walk north on Evergreen Avenue, follow the signs to the accessible boardwalk and interpretive platform. Take the steps to the beach, turn right, and walk toward the large outcropping of rocks in the tidal area where the most visible petroglyphs are found. The Killer Whale, the most unique petroglyph is located along the grass line.

Visit us at boattravel.com

Walk-around: The Rainbow Falls Trail, across the road from the boat basin at Shoemaker Bay, is a one mile hike on steps and boardwalk to the falls. Two additional trails split off near the Falls. Institute Trail leads to an overnight shelter and an overlook of Zimovia Straits. The High Country Trail, with two overnight shelters, travels a ridge line back toward town. Both trails are steep in areas and hiking boots are a must. ↟

Wrangell Port & Harbors operates three full service recreational and commercial harbor basins which can accommodate everything from 18' skiffs to 200+' yachts, tenders and tugboats. A Marine Service Center offers up to 330 ton lift capacity and repair service vendors, in a convenient downtown location. The Harbor Office is located in the Downtown Harbor right above Reliance Float, N56° 27.98' W132° 22.80'. 907- 874-3736. VHF 16.

Heritage Harbor: Deep draft harbor. Permanent & transient moorage. 30/50/100 amp power, water, waste oil & garbage collection, restroom, all tides boat launch, and a sewage pump-out station located one half mile from downtown. 907-874-3736. VHF 16.

Inner Harbor Float: Located in Downtown Harbor, east side of Chief Shakes Island. Permanent moorage for vessels under 40'. Power, water, waste oil & garbage collection. 907-874-3736. VHF 16.

Reliance Harbor Float: Located in Downtown Harbor. Transient moorage. Power, water, waste oil & garbage collection, tidal grid for vessels under 40', hydraulic hoists, high tide boat launch, and a sewage pump-out station. 907-874-3736. VHF 16.

Shoemaker Bay Harbor: Permanent moorage. Transient moorage here is only by advanced arrangements with the Harbormaster. Power, water, waste oil & garbage collection. Tidal grids, hydraulic hoist, all tides boat launch available. 907-874-3736. VHF 16.

Wrangell Petro Marine Services: (Reliance Harbor area) Gas, diesel, water, lubricants, oils, batteries, filters, restroom. 907-874-3276.

Petersburg Area
[17360, 17375, 17382]

Approaching Petersburg: If you didn't visit Wrangell, you are headed for Petersburg, continuing north through Clarence Strait, around Zarembo Island to the south end of Wrangell Narrows. If coming from Wrangell, you will approach Wrangell Narrows through Sumner Strait.

★ **St. John Harbor (15):** [17382] Located at the northwest corner of Zarembo Island, St. John Harbor offers good anchorage in 10 fathoms of water on a mud bottom. The harbor is protected from all directions but north. Although it is best to approach the harbor from the north, it is possible to approach from south of Southerly Island. This is a good place to wait for the tide in Wrangell Narrows.

★ **Wrangell Narrows (16):** [17375] Tidal currents enter from both ends and meet just south of Green Point. Transiting either north or south, it is best to start on the end of a rising tide, arriving at Green Point around high slack, therefore having a following tidal current all of the way. Currents can

The LeConte Glacier calving   Photo © John Yeager

run from five to seven knots on large tides. There are 63 numbered navigational aids in the 21 mile length of the narrows, as well as some unnumbered range markers. Two public floats, 100 and 62 feet in length respectively, are located at Papkes Landing, 13 miles south of Petersburg. These are open for public moorage, no water or power. A second public float extends into Wrangell Narrows at West Petersburg.

★ **Petersburg (17):** [17375] Small town charm, unique cultural heritage, great salmon, halibut and crab fishing, beautiful scenery, and abundant wildlife that includes humpback whales, sea lions, otters and more and are all part and parcel of this wonderful little city. LeConte Glacier is nearby making it possible for you to see the southernmost tidewater glacier in the northern hemisphere known for its "shooter" icebergs that calve off underwater and shoot up. Because they cannot negotiate Wrangell Narrows, the large cruise ships don't stop here, which makes Petersburg a haven from the hustle and bustle of thousands of visitors hitting town at the same time. While large cruise ships don't moor here, plenty of commercial and recreational boats fill the three modern harbors. Petersburg Harbor is home to one of the top fishing fleets in the world, so it is no surprise that many local businesses serve the needs of boaters including marine parts supplies and services, shipwrights, haul-out, trailer lift, and fuel. Grocery stores, liquor store, gift shops, galleries, banks, laundromat, hardware stores, a drug store, cafes and restaurants, a movie theatre, lodging and other businesses are also available, many within walking distance of moorage.

The borough of Petersburg is home to about 3,150 residents. It was founded by Peter Buschmann of Tacoma and settled by Norwegians in 1897. Still known as Little Norway, Norwegian rosemal storefront paintings and Velkommen signs are common and entice visitors into a festive mood. Other styles of art are also found in the downtown shopping area. There are brass sidewalk inlays designed by Tacoma artist Henry Balazs. Two totem poles, the Raven and the Eagle are beautiful examples of Tlingit art and culture. Three large outdoor murals include "Our Town," which is a composite of Petersburg, while "Flowers" and "Sealife" feature local flora and fauna. On the third weekend in May, a *Norwegian Constitution Day* celebration is held. Another celebration takes place on the 4th of July. The camera buff will enjoy views of the Sons of Norway Hall, Clausen Memorial Museum, the viking ship Valhalla, Sing Lee Alley, Eagle's Roost Park, the canneries, the Fiske Fountain, and the homes along Hammer Slough. About 17 miles south of Petersburg is Crystal Lake Hatchery, one of the oldest currently operating hatcheries in SE Alaska. It is open daily during the summer, no formal tours but someone is always on hand to answer questions. Alaska Airlines flies daily scheduled jet service to Seattle and Juneau. Petersburg is also served by the Alaska Ferry System.

Walk-around: The Clausen Memorial Museum has a *Heritage of the Sea* wing, as well as antiques and the world record 126 lb King salmon. Walk the picturesque street where the Sons of Norway building sits on pilings over Hammer Slough. Several outdoor fishing and picnic spots (handicapped accessible) are available. The Visitor Information Center is at First and Fram Streets. 907-772-4636. ⚓ ↟

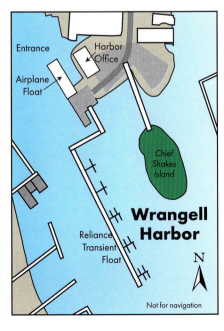

Page 268 Chapter 20 SOUTHEAST ALASKA

★ **Petersburg Harbor** {56° 48.713' N, 132° 57.867' W} Moorage, 30/50/60/100 3 phase amp power, water, showers, waste oil disposal, boat launch, crane, tidal gridirons. Call our 24-Hour Harbormaster 30 minutes prior to arrival for moorage assignment. See our advertisement on this page. Email: gwollen@petersburgak.gov. Website: www.ci.petersburg.ak.us. Telephone: 907-772-4688. VHF 16, CB-9.

Petersburg Petro Marine Services: Gas, diesel, water, batteries, filters, oils, lubricants. Free popcorn & coffee. 907-772-4251. VHF 16.

City of Kupreanof (West Petersburg): Kupreanof is located across the Wrangell Narrows from Petersburg. Remnants of the past are still visible and attest to the various ventures, including sawmills, mink farms, and a clam cannery that were once found on the site. Today most of the land is owned by the City and the Forest Service, however, the beach front homes are privately owned. Kupreanof does not have any stores and is a roadless community. Many residents make a living as fishermen, while others commute by boat to jobs in Petersburg. The public float at {56° 48.844' N, 132° 58.728' W} does not have any power or water and the float is dry at a -3 low tide. Be sure to pay attention to the tide table because there is a -4 to a 22 foot tide difference at various times of the year. There is a public shelter just to the north of the Kupreanof Dock. Locals take pride in their lovely boardwalk hiking trails and welcome visitors to enjoy a "Walk Into the Wilderness" with the following requests - follow the signs, stay on the trails and not on the vegetation, and do not trespass on private property. Three hiking trails begin at the Kupreanof Dock. The Petersburg Creek Trail and the Kupreanof Loop Trail are both easy 45 minute hikes and the Petersburg Mountain Trail is a difficult hike that takes about 6 hours to complete. For more information about Kupreanof, www.cityofkupreanof.org. Click on the "Trails Guide" tab at the top right of the website for an interpretive brochure about the history of Kupreanof and trail maps and videos. ⚲

★ **Thomas Bay & Spray Island (18):** [17360, 17367] There is good anchoring in this bay with its milky-gray glacial silt water. Baird and Patterson Glaciers are at the ends of the arms. Excellent holding bottom with depths of 60 to 70 feet can be found southeast of Spray Island. There is good shrimping here. Another anchorage is in Scenery Cove. It is possible to dinghy to the flats and explore the area of the face of the glacier. Another anchorage is in a bight on the south end of Ruth Island in seven fathoms of water.

★ **Portage Bay (19):** [17367] There is protected anchorage in this bay on the south side of Frederick Sound. The entrance is 150 yards in width. Use directions in U.S. Coast Pilot 8 recommends entry at high slack. Anchor in mid-channel in five fathoms of water. Shoals extend from the head and 40-60 feet out from the sides.

★ **Farragut Bay (20):** [17367] This bay is across Frederick Sound from Portage Bay. Best anchorage is in Francis Anchorage, in a small bight on the point on the south side of the anchorage. There is a good holding bottom in 14 fathoms of water. Avoid the mud flats on the east side.

Frederick Sound & Stephens Passage
[17360, 17365]

★ **Nearby Waters:** [17360] At this point some comments may be helpful regarding the waters to the north and west. A glance at Chart #17360 will tell you that Frederick Sound and Stephens Passage have some wide stretches of water. Strong winds can kick up some very rough seas so pay attention to the weather reports and forecasts. It is also possible to encounter ice floes from LeConte Glacier to the south and the three glaciers in Holkam Bay to the north.

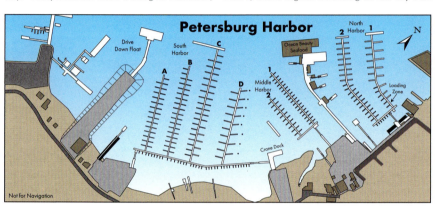

24-Hour Harbor Master on Duty for the Three City Operated Boat Harbors
150-ton Tidal Grid • 30-50 Private Travel Trailer • Reservations Suggested for Boats Over 100 feet
Close Proximity to: Banks • Markets • Laundromat • Restaurants • Drug Store • Liquor Stores

Harbor Master Office: 223 Harbor Way, Petersburg, AK 99833
Mailing address: PO Box 329, Petersburg, AK 99833

907-772-4688
VHF 16, CB-9

www.ci.petersburg.ak.us
Email: gwollen@petersburgak.gov

Visit us at boattravel.com

★ **Cleveland Passage (21):** [17365] Cleveland Passage is located just north of Cape Fanshaw between Whitney Island and the mainland. U.S Coast Pilot 8 recommends entering from the north. Anchorages can be found in Cleveland Passage in four to eight fathoms of water near the southeast end behind Whitney Island. Rollers enter Steamboat Bay near Foot Island, however anchorage is possible. The Five Finger Light Station, automated in 1984, was both the first and last manned light station in Alaska.

Admiralty Island East Side

[17360, 17336, 17362, 17363]

★ **Chapin Bay:** Located on Admiralty Island, this bay has rocks at the entrance. Entry at low tide is recommended to insure locating the channel. The steep-sided indentation has anchorage in the inner bay where a stream enters from the head.

★ **Pybus Bay:** Three channels provide entrance into Pybus Bay. One is through the San Juan Islands. The largest is between the southern San Juan and Elliot Island, and the third is south of Elliot Island. Anchorage can be found in the most northerly entrance, in the small bight in the middle of the south San Juan Islands. Dangers are exposed at low tide making the anchoring basin easier to identify. Kelp marks a shallow patch and foul ground off Pybus Point. Cannery Cove, the site of a cannery from 1918-19 3, affords the most sheltered anchorage. Anchor left of the head in 45 to 50 feet of water.

★ **Gambier Bay (22):** [17362] Several anchorages are found here. A convenient one is in a small cove east of Good Island, between the island and the peninsula to the east in 10 to 15 fathoms, mud bottom. The Inner Bay or Gambier Bay proper has several excellent protected anchorages. Entry is to the west of Gambier Island with a light at Point Gambier at its south end then northwest three miles to the entrance light, northeast of Gain Island. Pass fairly close to it in order to avoid the reef to the south. Then head north around the unnamed island north of Gain Island, entering the inner bay. Snug Cove in the southwest corner of the bay offers good anchorage in ten fathoms, mud bottom. There are several other good possibilities for anchoring. First on the reef southeast of the Gambier Bay entrance light, and then on the reef north of the unnamed island three miles north where you enter the inner bay. Halibut fishing is said to be quite good in these waters.

★ **Hobart Bay (23):** [17363] Found between Port Houghton and Windham Bay, this bay offers protected anchorage when weather kicks up in Stephens Passage. Entrance Island has a small niche on the east side with a state refuge float at Lat 58-11.745N, Long 136-20.836W with no amenities, suitable for six boats. Look for the buildings to port on shore when rounding the south tip of the island. Turn into the bay immediately following this site. The float is on the port side of this niche. The outsides of the floats have water depths of seven feet at a minus two tide at Juneau.

★ **Windham Bay (24):** [17363] This old town site was once a gold mining town. Chum salmon fishing is often excellent here. Some anchorage is possible far into the bay, on the north shore near the town site. The bay is deep, with a sticky mud bottom. Shoal areas are near the head. Another anchorage, on a hard bottom, is found in the small cove inside the entrance on the south side.

Petersburg   *Photo © Kim*

★ **Holkham Bay (25):** [17360] Holkham Bay, with its two big arms containing tide water glaciers, plus Ford's Terror, is one of the most spectacular places in all of Southeast Alaska. It is well worth spending several days exploring. Holkham Bay is at the base of Tracy and Endicott Arms. The best anchorage is near the entrance to Tracy Arm, see paragraph on Tracy Arm. In south winds, there is anchorage at Wood Spit in the second niche away from the spit. Anchor in 35 to 50 feet of water at a 13-foot tide at Juneau. The sandy bottom rises quickly to shore. Limit scope accordingly. Boats also anchor in the niche formed by Point Ashley. Harbor Island, in the middle of Holkham Bay, has range markers. In a north wind there is anchorage in a small cove on the south shore of Harbor Island in front of an abandoned fur farm. Anchor just outside the points and about equidistant from them in 25 feet of water, 100- foot rode at 16-foot tide at Juneau. Hard bottom, but good holding. Currents affect the amount of swing. This was once the home of the Sumdum tribe of the Tlingit Natives who guided John Muir on his exploration in 1897. The word "Sumdum" comes from the Native interpretation of the roar of the fjord's calving icebergs. Views across Holkham Bay to Sumdum Glacier are gorgeous in the late afternoon sun.

★ **Endicott Arm:** Spectacular views and some of the largest icebergs are seen in this fjord that stretches southeast from Holkham Bay. Ford's Terror, opening to port, about 13 miles from Holkham Bay, is a "must see" for adventuresome boaters. Sumdum anchorage is in Sanford Cove. A suitable anchorage is difficult to find and it is safer not to recommend anchoring here. Some anchorage has been found near the west shore on line from the unnamed point to Rock Point in about 50 feet of water on a hard bottom. The beach shoals and then drops rapidly, not allowing room for sufficient rode. Sanford Cove is also subject to entry of icebergs and winds. At the turn-of-the-century, the Sumdum Chief Mine was located here. It produced nearly a half million dollars in gold and silver. Dawes Glacier, at the head of the arm, extends into the water and calves off large amounts of ice that are always present. If going in close to the glaciers expect slow going because the arms become choked with ice floes. Do not approach the faces of the glaciers too closely because large chunks of ice fall into the water creating swells as high as 25 feet. The swells are easy to ride if the boat does not get caught between icebergs and is kept heading into the oncoming swells.

★ **Fords Terror:** [17360] This is one of the most beautiful and isolated fjords in the northwest. If warm days have caused rapid calving off of Dawes Glacier, entry through Endicott Arm may require slow and careful maneuvering through tightly-packed icebergs. Allow three to four hours from Wood Spit to the narrows in Fords Terror, making eight knots when not in congested ice floes. Plan to traverse the narrows on high tide slack with sufficient daylight before and after for navigation. Entry at low slack is not recommended because of a one-quarter fathom controlling depth at zero tide at Juneau. The narrows in Fords Terror are about 1.3 miles inside the inlet. Lay off the largest waterfall, opposite the narrows. Perhaps 10 to 25 minutes after high tide at Juneau, the turn in the narrows can be observed by the gradual slowing of the movement of ice and debris. This time will vary depending upon the amount of tidal change for the day. This is the time to enter. While currents in the narrows can run to 15 knots at springs with a seven-foot over fall, high slack passage is easy, with minimum depths of 17 1/2 feet at a 16-foot tide at Juneau, with only slight current and whirlpools.

Once through the narrows, a deep-walled fjord stretches ahead with camera-ready spectacular waterfalls and scenery. At the head of the fjord, the northeast finger is worth viewing, but doesn't have the best anchorage. It is also windy when the west finger is dead calm. A drying bar stretches across the northeast finger where the grassy shore to port on entry juts into the waterway. Minimum depth observed was eight feet at a 15-foot tide at Juneau. The best anchorage is in the west arm, near the waterfall in the northwest corner. Drying flats extend out from the falls and the starboard shore on approach. A quick-rising bottom affords good holding mud off these flats. Anchor in about 55 feet of water at a 14' foot tide at Juneau. Unless there is wind, the force of the current from the falls will keep the boat facing the falls on all tides. Several other falls are visible across the fjord on the south side. There are black bears, seals, plentiful fresh water, and blackberries in season. Plan to spend more than one night in this scenic spot. This is a more isolated location than most boaters have experienced. There is no VHF radio contact and it is entirely possible to spend several days here without seeing or hearing from another boat. In the event of an unforeseen circumstance like engine trouble, it is wise to have enough food, water, and cooking fuel onboard to survive for a week. It would also be prudent to notify someone of your plans and expected time of return. Exit

Waterfall in Tracy Arm Photo © Carolyn Van Calcar

through the Narrows at 10 to 25 minutes after high water at Juneau. Fords Terror received its name from navy man H.R. Ford who, in 1889, entered the narrows in a rowboat. After exploring the fjord, the unsuspecting sailor returned to the narrows at a full run and was so frightened by his white water ride that his officers named the fjord accordingly.

★ **Temporary anchorage in the small bight outside Fords Terror narrows:** If necessary to wait until high slack, temporary anchorage is possible in a bight opposite the entry to the narrows, just north of the falls. Shoals and rocks in the west half of this bight are marked by kelp and/or icebergs at most tides. Anchor in 45 to 50 feet of water at a plus 16-foot tide at Juneau. Fending-off icebergs may be required during the last three hours of flood tide and the first three hours of ebb tide. Overnight anchorage in this bight is not recommended because of danger from icebergs.

★ **Tracy Arm:** [17300] Enter by keeping the stern on the Harbor Island Range, the bow on the RW beacon on the east side of Holkham Bay. Markers are about three miles apart, one on the north tip of Harbor Island, the other on a line of about ten degrees magnetic to the mainland shore. The best base-station anchorage for exploring this area is in the unnamed bay about two and one-half miles from Harbor Island on the western shore of the Arm. Turn for entry when depths show that the bar has been cleared. Avoid a rock off the southeast tip of the small island which forms the northeastern shore of the bay. Enter in the center of the bay between the island and the mainland shore. Anchor at the head in 35 feet at a 16-foot tide at Juneau. Hard, rocky bottom. Shoaling near shore. Tracy Arm indents 26 miles and has North and South Sawyer glaciers at the head. Both are calving glaciers. Icebergs abound, and a sightseeing excursion from Juneau is often taken by pleasure boaters. The scenery in Tracy Arm provided by the steep rocky walls on both sides of the arm, as well as the two glaciers at its head, is unsurpassed.

★ **Taku Harbor (26):** [17300, 17314] Anchorage is found in the south end of the bay in seven fathoms of water on a soft mud bottom. There is also a 400' small craft, state float on the east side of the harbor. Submerged pilings are hazards near the old cannery wharf. This harbor was once the home of both Father Hubbard, The Glacier Priest, and a hermit, Tiger Olson.

Taku Inlet: [17300, 17315] No secure anchorage. This inlet has many shoals and tends to be quite windy. As the Taku Glacier moves, small lakes open up providing resting grounds for geese.

Juneau Area
[17300, 17315]

★ **Douglas (27):** When traversing Gastineau Channel, note that the current floods northwest up Gastineau Channel toward Juneau and ebbs to the southeast. Clearance under the Douglas Bridge is 60' at MLLW in the center of the navigation channel. A basin for small craft, operated by the City of Juneau, is located at Douglas, behind Mayflower Island, three miles south of the bridge. Water depth in the moorage basins is at least 12'. The Harbormaster can provide more information. The Douglas basin has a lighted, 250' floating concrete breakwater that protects the entrance to the facility. The floats are well maintained and protected. Douglas Island is connected to downtown Juneau by 2 miles of road and taxi service is available. No groceries are available in Douglas, but restaurants are within walking distance. Douglas was the site of the Treadwell Gold Mine, once the world's largest mining operation. Before it flooded and caved in, it gave up $70 million in gold. The Treadwell Mine Historic Walking Trail is located in Savikko Park at Sandy Beach which is near moorage. The trailhead is just south of the second covered picnic shelter in the park.

Douglas Boat Harbor: {58° 16' 35.74" N, 134° 23' 17.79" W} To port side coming into Juneau. The Juneau Harbormaster may direct you here for transient moorage on inside of C-float. 30/50 amp power, water, pump-out, launch ramp. 907-586-5255. VHF 73.

Juneau/Douglas Petro Marine Services: Gas, diesel, oils, batteries, water, ice, bait. Free coffee and popcorn. Located directly across channel from Harris Harbor. 907-586-4400.

★ **Juneau (28):** See berthage information that follows. The nominal height of the Juneau-Douglas Bridge is 66.4' on a 0.0 tide. A gauge on the bridge measures the current height. When approaching Juneau, Alaska's capital city, look to starboard and spot the landmark ruins of the Alaska Juneau Mine. When leaving Juneau, retrace your path and exit down Gastineau Channel. The shallow channel to Auke Bay dries at 10' on Juneau tides.

Aurora Harbor: {58° 18' 15.18" N, 134° 25' 58.47" W} Located next to Harris Harbor. No transient moorage allowed without specific assignment. 30/50/100 amp power, water, garbage/oil deposit, cranes. 907-586-5255. VHF 73.

Harri Commercial Marine: (downtown Juneau) Boatyard, 35-ton travelift, welding, fiberglass repairs, some engine work. 907-321-0389, 907-723-1456.

Harris Harbor: {58° 18' 01.75" N, 134° 25' 44.35" W} First harbor to starboard after the Douglas Bridge. The Juneau Harbormaster may direct you here for transient moorage. Near downtown. 30/50 amp power, water, garbage, porta potty, pump-out, boat launch, tidal grid to 85'. 907-586-5255. VHF 73.

Intermediate Vessel Float: {58° 17' 40.19" N, 134° 23' 57.55" W} Located downtown. Assigned moorage only, vessels to 200'. Water depth is over 20'. 30/50/100 amp power, potable water, garbage. Moorage reservations are only available from May 1-Oct 1. 907-586-5720. VHF 73

Petro Marine Services: (south of downtown) Diesel, oils, lubes, fuel additives, absorbents, water in the summer, free cup of coffee. 907-586-4400.

Seadrome Marina: (downtown Juneau) Private, full-service facility, reservations required. Guest moorage, vessels to 200', 30/50/100 amp power, water, pump-out, garbage disposal, dockside fueling, (#2 diesel, larger vessels only). Marina: 907-463-8811. Fuel: 907-586-4400.

★ **Exploring Juneau:** Be sure to pick up a free copy of the *Southeast Alaska Traveler* in the Harbormaster's Office or stop by a visitor information center and pick up a downtown map illustrating points of interest such as museums, historic buildings, public art and facilities.

This busy Alaska capital city and popular cruising destination sits amid the scenic backdrop of Mount Juneau and Mount Roberts. Juneau serves as the center of commerce for outlying communities. The economy centers largely around government and tourism; transportation, medical and education services; and as the hub for a growing mining industry that includes the Kensington Mine just north of Juneau and the Greens Creek Mine located on nearby Admiralty Island.

When exploring the heart of downtown Juneau, a car is not necessary except to transport provisions back to moorages. Local taxi companies can readily meet this need. Public bus service also connects downtown Juneau to adjacent Douglas Island and to the Mendenhall Valley, where the airport and Mendenhall Glacier are located about nine miles north. To explore Juneau and the surrounding area, and to avoid walking up the steep hillsides, car transportation should be considered. Rental car agencies, located at or near the airport, are plentiful.

The downtown area, which includes a seven block historic district, has many attractions and notable buildings such as the St. Nicholas Russian Orthodox Church. Built in 1894, it is the oldest original and continuously used Church in southeast Alaska. The Capitol Building, open for guided tours is a few blocks away. The Juneau Douglas City Museum, across from the Capitol, offers historic walking tours (May-Sept, call 907-586-3572 for details). The Governor's House, with pillared terrace, is easy to locate on the hillside. A few blocks away is the House of Wickersham. Built in 1898 this Victorian-style home housed some of Juneau's most prominent early residents.

Visit us at boattravel.com

907-586-9001 for hours of operation. Down hill, closer to the water on Whittier Street, is where the newly renovated Alaska State Museum is located. The nearby Arts & Culture Center houses the Juneau Arts & Humanities Council, an art gallery and hosts events year round. There is also a health food store and several bakeries found in the downtown neighborhood. Street vendors dot the narrow streets selling Cajun, Thai, Vietnamese, Mexican, and Italian specialties in addition to American fare.

Along downtown Juneau's waterfront colorful decorative banners and an abundance of flowers set a pretty stage. There are viewing platforms and wide walkways with benches, a marine park, an information kiosk, concessions, picnic sites, public art and memorials, restaurants, a visitor information center, and the lower terminal of the Mt. Roberts Tramway.

Want to wander a little further? One excursion possibility is to the beautiful Mendenhall Glacier. The impressive Mendenhall Glacier Visitor Center has exhibits, powerful telescopes and staff to explain the fascinating qualities of the glacier, as well as a bookstore and gift shop. Easily accessible trails lead to waterfalls, salmon rearing streams, and great photo opportunities. On the west side of Mendenhall Lake, tour operators can arrange raft trips down the Mendenhall River. Beyond the glacier other attractions await, including the charming Chapel-by-the-Lake overlooking placid Auke Lake. Twenty-three miles out the Glacier Highway is the serenely beautiful Shrine of St. Therese, and just beyond that is the Jensen-Olson Arboretum.

Indoor and outdoor tennis, hiking on well-maintained trails, rock and ice climbing, biking and paragliding are popular local activities. For a game of golf, play the nine-hole Mendenhall Golf Course, located near the airport. Rental clubs available. Cash only. 907-789-1221. Flightseeing by helicopter and small planes is also available. If you are visiting Juneau during the 4th of July holiday, take in the local parade and enjoy the nation's earliest 4th of July fireworks show, held at midnight on July 3.

★ **Auke Bay (29):** Statter Harbor moorage facility is located 14 miles north of Downtown Juneau in Auke Bay. This deep draft harbor has the capability of handling large vessels. There are two private marinas nearby, but they do not have transient moorage. A convenience store that sells some groceries and two restaurants are within walking distance of the harbor. The University of Alaska Southeast Campus is across the street. Bus service is available to downtown and shopping. Juneau has taxi and rental cars as well. There are large shopping centers along the Auke Bay-Juneau Road about four miles from moorage.

Auke Bay Commercial Loading Facility: Cranes, loading ramp, drive down float, by reservation only. 907-789-0819. VHF 16, 74.

Karl's Auto & Marine Repair: Honda and Suzuki outboard servicing, boat hauling, boat storage, boat and marine repair. 907-789-3883

Petro Marine Services: Gas, diesel, water, oils, lubes, bait, free popcorn. 907-790-3030.

Statter Harbor/Auke Bay: {58° 22' 57.52" N, 134° 39' 16.71" W} Transient moorage for boats to 250', first come/first served, reservations available for vessels greater that 65'. Breakwater moorage reservable (no electricity). 20/30/50 amp power, first come/first served, water, showers, pump-out. 907-789-0819 or VHF 74.

★ **Admiralty Cove (30):** Just west of Point Young on the north side of Admiralty Island, this cove offers anchorage to mariners traversing Saginaw Channel. Shoals extend from shore. In summer, blooming fireweed gives an impression of velvet cloth on a cushion of green. Anchorage is found southwest of the island on the southwest side of Admiralty Cove in five fathoms of water. It is open to the west and somewhat to the north.

Lynn Canal

[17300, 17316, 17317]

Lynn Canal: This body of water, which extends about 85 miles from Icy Strait to Skagway, is often ignored by boaters. This is regretful because it offers some truly beautiful scenery, with high mountains and glaciers on both sides. None of the glaciers reach the salt water, so ice is not a concern. At the north end you will find Skagway, the end of the Inside Passage. This city was once considered the main port for the gold miners in the Klondike Gold Rush of 1898. The only commercial facilities are in Skagway or Haines, about 15 miles south of Skagway. There is a separate VHF weather and wind forecast for Lynn Canal.

★ **Tee Harbor (31):** Tee Harbor is situated on the east side of Favorite Channel, two miles north of Point Lena. There is a private marina in the harbor. A road connects the harbor to Auke Bay and Juneau. Anchorage is possible in the center of the harbor in 12 to 15 fathoms. The north arm has shallower anchorage in five to ten fathoms and better protection from north winds.

Donohue's Marina: Private marina. Fuel dock is for marina customers with appointment. 907-789-7851.

★ **Saint James Bay (32):** Located on the west side of Lynn Canal, Saint James Bay offers anchorage in 40-foot depths. The bottom is sticky mud. This bay is open to winds from the north and southeast. There are shoal areas near the head.

★ **Bridget Cove and Mab Island:** The best anchorage is in the small cove opposite the north end of Mab Island in five fathoms of water. Don't get in too far, because this little cove has large drying flats. Anchorage is also possible in the passage between Mab Island and the mainland. This area is often used by commercial fishermen, especially gillnetters.

★ **Echo Cove:** Anchorage is possible in ten fathoms near the head of the cove. Enter the cove along the northeast shoreline. Watch charts closely. The entrance is narrow and shallow until past the bar which extends from the southwest shore. Good holding, soft bottom with good protection. Many commercial crab pots affect anchorage. The City of Juneau issues permits for the use of the public boat launch. A small public camp area with seven campsites is available on a first come-first serve basis. Private property adjoins the campsites and is posted.

★ **Haines (33):** [17317] This town, 92 miles northwest of Juneau, has the largest concentration of American Bald Eagles during the fall and winter months in the world. Called Dei-shu, meaning end of the trail, Haines has a population of about 1,900, spectacular mountain scenery, and less rainfall than Ketchikan, Sitka, or Juneau. Restaurants and overnight accommodations are available. There are well-stocked provision stores, in town laundromat and showers. Many local art galleries and shops display works of local artists. Specialties include woodcarving, silver carving, fine art, photography, Native artwork and items from Interior Natives. The Haines Sheldon Museum and Cultural Center, located across from the small boat harbor, features other examples of Tlingit art, as well as historic pioneer and military pieces illustrating early life in the Chilkat Valley. 907-766-2366. The world's first Hammer Museum is found across from the Sheldon Museum. Over two thousand hammers dating from Roman times to the present are on display. Another interesting stop is the American Bald Eagle Foundation featuring an aviary and live bird presentation. Each May the annual *Great Alaska Craftbeer & Homebrew Festival* highlights local microbrews. A July 4th *Independence Day Celebration* offers a parade, races, and activities throughout the community. The *Southeast Alaska State Fair* is held in July. Car rental gives access by highway to Whitehorse, Haines Junction, and the Alaska Interior. Just 1.5 miles from downtown is the Valley of the Eagles Golf Links and Driving Range, with pro shop, rental clubs, and lessons. 907-766-2002. Chilkoot Lake State Recreation Site, about 10 miles from town is a well-known bear viewing area. Another very exciting side trip is a scenic flight from the Haines, or Skagway airports over Glacier Bay National Park and Haines' Chilkat Valley. Muir Glacier, in Glacier Bay, is on the other side of the mountains, only about 30 miles from the Haines airport. For the adventurous in spirit, rafting, kayaking, 4x4 and jet boat excursions can be arranged. For more information about Haines, or to pick up maps, guides, fishing regulations, tide books and brochures stop by the Visitor Center, 122 Second Ave. The Visitor Center is open daily in the summer. From the Boat Harbor, walk two blocks up Main, take a left at the stop sign, two blocks down on the left. 907-766-6418.

Walk-around: Lookout Park, near the harbor on the waterfront, has a picnic area and viewing platform and is near Tlingit Park which has a historic cemetery and a native longhouse. Tlingit Park has a historic cemetery. Visit expansive Chilkat State Park. There are hiking trails and glacier views. It is possible to moor at Haines and walk to Fort William H. Seward, the first military outpost in Alaska. Interpretive signs are provided along the way.

Haines Propane: Propane, new tanks. 907-766-3191.

Haines Small Boat Harbor: Permanent and transient moorage, 30/50 amp power, water in the summer, pumpout, recycling/waste disposal, launch ramp, tidal grid, fuel dock with gas, diesel, and access to a crane. 907-766-6450. Harbor Cell: 907-314-0173. VHF 12, 16.

★ **Letnikof Cove:** Located five miles from Haines, seasonal floats (April-Sept.) for transient moorage will not be available in 2024. A boat launch ramp operated by the Haines Borough and pit toilets are available. 907-766-6450. VHF 12, 16.

★ **Taiasanka Harbor:** [17317] This well protected harbor, located about five miles from Haines, has anchorage in five fathoms of water on a soft bottom. Use the United States Coast Pilot 8.

★ **Skagway (34):** [17317] Situated in Southeast Alaska in a lush valley at the edge of a deep-water fjord called the Lynn Canal, Shgagwéi was its first name meaning "bunched up or roughed up water" in traditional Tlingit language. This charming Borough's Boat Basin has moorage that is convenient to fuel, groceries, restaurants, supplies and laundry. The Harbor office is a "hot spot" for WiFi for a fee and free internet is available at the Skagway Public Library, Shoreline Park and City Hall. A well-stocked hardware store, located less than a mile from moorage has a motto that never fails to get a laugh, "If we don't have it, you don't need it." Some 1.3 million visitors, arriving

Page 272 Chapter 20 SOUTHEAST ALASKA

Haines Small Boat Harbor   Photo © Lauri Stepansky

by cruise ships, ferries, boats, highway, railroad and air, come to Skagway each year. Activities and attractions include riding old street cars, panning for gold, walking in gardens, enjoying live vaudeville shows, visiting museums, the Gold Rush buildings, gift shops, arts & crafts exhibits and galleries. Tours of every kind - zip line, dog mushing, glass blowing, ocean rafting, hiking, and more are available. Call 907-983-3900 for details. Dining out is also an experience. In addition to over 25 restaurants, food carts and coffee joints, Skagway also has two micro breweries and a distillery. Menus for all the restaurants in town, as well as free town maps, trail maps and historic walking guides are offered by the Visitors Center. For additional information, maps, activities and events contact the Skagway Visitors Bureau. 907-983-2854, www.skagway.com. The center is housed in the Arctic Brotherhood Hall, featuring a unique facade composed of thousands of driftwood pieces. The Klondike Gold Rush National Park is a great place to start your visit. They offer free films, lectures and guided ranger tours. Outdoor recreation includes basketball, softball, and hiking trails. While much of the town is walkable, the SMART Shuttle is another option. It operates year-round on call, and on a regular schedule during the cruise season for $3 one way or $5 for an all day pass. They have a stop just south of the Small Boat Harbor for a shuttle into town. Please visit https://www.skagway.com/listing/skagway-municipal-and-regional-transit-smart-bus/126/ for more information. The South Klondike Highway connects Skagway with Whitehorse, Yukon Territory, Interior Alaska, and the rest of North America. Since the Gold Rush, the 4th of July has been a big holiday. Contests, a barbecue, and a parade are featured.

Walk-arounds and side trips: In 1898, Skagway had 30,000 residents. By 1900, the Gold Rush was over and Skagway was nearly a ghost town. Allow plenty of time to learn about the heritage and enjoy the attractions of this historic site. Stroll the wooden boardwalks of Broadway or hike one of the trails found close to town. Rent a car and drive to the ruins of Dyea, at the foot of the Chilkoot Trail, and walk to historic Slide Cemetery. Or take a ride in a vintage parlor car of the White Pass and Yukon Route narrow gauge railroad. A three hour round trip includes the summit of White Pass. 1-800-343-7373. Another option is to continue by bus to Whitehorse. Flightseeing tours of Glacier Bay, Gold Rush sites, or the Juneau Ice Cap are also available.

Skagway Boat Basin: {59° 26.938' N, 135° 19.317' W} Moorage to 150', 30/50-amp, 110-volt power. Water, seasonal restrooms and showers, pump-out, garbage, waste oil deposit, haul-outs to 20-tons or 40-feet, 74' grid, launch ramp. 907-983-2628. VHF 16.

Skagway Petro Marine Services: Gas, diesel, batteries, water, oils, lubricants. 907-983-2259.

Icy Strait
[17300, 17316]

Couverden Island (35): There is a state float situated in Swanson Harbor near the spit of land connecting the tumbolo off Couverden Island, opposite Ansley Island. No facilities. Designed primarily as protected moorage for refuge in bad weather on Icy Strait. Use extreme caution when navigating the dredged channel and only navigate during the daylight.

★ **Excursion Inlet (36):** [17316] There is a small settlement on the east side of the inlet with the same name. A cannery was built here in 1908 that later served as a prisoner of war camp during World War II, and today is home to a small store and museum. A seafood processing plant, owned by Ocean Beauty Seafoods is also located in the Inlet and is generally operational from June 1 to September 1. While there are services like fuel, water and some supplies available in an emergency (call VHF 11), this is a commercial operation and not a boater's destination. No tours given. When the cannery is not in operation, a caretaker is present. A small craft float is about one-quarter mile north of the cannery dock. The currents can be very strong at the float. This is a unique little community in a beautiful setting. Fish traps, now outlawed, are beached at the head of the inlet.

★ **Gustavus (37):** [17302] This community on the north side of Icy Strait has a dock, floats offering temporary tie-ups, and fuel services at the dock during the summer from 5-9am, Mon-Sat. There are cafes, inns and lodges, a grocery store, gift shops, art galleries, taxi service and rental cars, and a building supply store. The grocery is 2.5 miles from the dock. The community's location, adjacent to Icy Straits, places it near some of the best whale watching waters in Alaska. Excursion and charter fishing boats are available for halibut and salmon charters. Visitors hike on miles of beaches or bike to Glacier Bay Park. The annual 4th of July celebration is a highlight with locals and visitors alike. The airport at Gustavus handles jet traffic from Juneau. There are also several small air carriers that service the area. Flights from Gustavus serve the regional hub of Juneau for easy access to this and other southeast communities. Flight seeing tours of Glacier Bay can be arranged with local charter operators. A paved road connects Gustavus and the airport with park headquarters at Bartlett Cove. Ferry service through Juneau and Hoonah is offered twice a week during the summer. For local events and information, www.gustavusak.com.

★ **Glacier Bay National Park & Bartlett Cove (38):** [17300, 17302, 17318] This large national park is accessible only by boat or plane. There is a dock (no overnight moorage), seasonal fuel dock, and a lodge with accommodations in Bartlett Cove. Boaters must hail KWM20 Bartlett Cove before entering or exiting Glacier Bay. Entry by private vessel into the park or Bartlett Cove, between June 1 and August 31, is by permit only. For reservation instructions and the boater application, see www.nps.gov/glba/planyourvisit/cruising.htm. There is no fee for the permit, but the number of permits issued are limited, so plan ahead. When approaching, be aware that rips can occur in lower Glacier Bay and there are often swells off the strait. Prevailing winds off Cross Sound are from the southwest. Tidal range is 25 feet. There are speed and route regulations within the park and some areas are closed to vessel traffic. Please contact the park for specific information prior to your arrival. Hail KWM20 Barlett Cove on VHF 12 or 16, or call 907-697-2627 within 48 hours of your scheduled permit time to confirm your reservation. Failure to confirm prior to 10am on the day of your schedule visit will result in a cancellation.

Upon arrival in Glacier Bay, permit holders must go ashore at Bartlett Cove and check in at the Visitor's Information Station for a Boaters' Orientation. The T-shaped head pier is for the National Park Service and the *Daily Tour Boat* and, if space permits, for a three hour visit ashore for larger vessels. Check the dock bulletin board for location of three hour maximum moorage for smaller vessels. A "no anchor zone" extends for 300' off the head of the pier.

Pets are not permitted on shore, except on a leash within 100-feet of roadways in the Bartlett Cove area. While firearms aboard your vessel are permitted, you may not discharge them in the national park.

A 5 minute walk from the Visitor Information Station is the Huna Tribal Clan House where Huna Tlingit history, culture, and life ways are shared with visitors through programs that are scheduled almost daily throughout the summer months. Guided tours of the park are also available, for tour reservations call 1-888-229-8687. Glaciers, whales, fish, scenic fjords, and over 200 species of birds and assorted flora and fauna can be seen. Most glaciers within the park are currently receding, but continue to calve into the sea.

Walk-around: At Bartlett Cove, well maintained trails near the lodge offer hiking options. There is a one mile forest trail, and the five mile round trip Bartlett River Trail. For a full day of hiking, Bartlett Lake is a perfect destination. Rangers also lead daily walks originating in the lodge lobby. Wildlife and water birds are subjects for the camera fan with a telephoto lens.

Bartlett Cove Dock: No overnight moorage, 3-hr max stay if space is available. Seasonal fuel dock (call for open hours), waste pump-out. Call ahead to the lodge on VHF channel 16 for service. VHF 12 or 16, KWM20 Barlett Cove or 907-697-2627.

Glacier Bay Lodge: Operates late May-early September. Restaurant/lounge open to non-guests. Showers, laundry for fee (ask for a key at the front desk). 907-697-4000, 1-888-229-8687.

Popular Glacier Bay anchorages and inlets:

★ **North Sandy Cove:** Icebergs are rarely found in this cove which offers good protection in any winds. Watch for bears on the beach. Anchor in four to six fathoms with good holding ground between the mainland and two islands about 1.2 miles east of Sturgess Island.

★ **South Sandy Cove:** Located immediately south of North Sandy Cove, this cove offers excellent anchorage. Try the bight to the southeast of the head in five to eight fathoms on a mud and sand bottom. It is open to southwest winds and the water is more stagnant here. To enter, pass south of the rock 250 yards south of the small islet on the north side entry. Avoid the boulders fringing the southeast shore. Two rocks are .5 miles west of the south entry point. The south rock uncovers 12 feet and the north rock uncovers two feet. Do not try to go between the rocks and the point. Nearby South Marble Islands are closed to hiking to protect nesting bird colonies and sea lions.

★ **Sebree Cove:** There is good holding ground here, although it is exposed to south winds. Ice seldom floats in here. There is an islet at the entry about .5 miles south of Tlingit Point. Small boats may anchor between Tlingit Point and south Sebree Island.

★ **Wachusett Inlet:** Carefully avoid the reef which uncovers at nine feet one mile from the entry and 500 yards from the south shore. Favor the north shore. Anchorage is possible in shallow water in a cove two miles west of Rowley Point. The mountains on the south side of this inlet are beautiful and, after the inlet turns northwest seven miles from its entrance, there are also views of Carroll Glacier.

Muir Glacier Face: From the Junction entry it is about 24 miles to Muir Glacier Face. The rapid retreat in the last few decades has exposed a spectrum of glaciated land. Muir Glacier is grounded out and no longer calves.

Berg Bay: This bay is located ten miles above the Glacier Bay entry. To enter pass midway between 3/4 fathoms and the low-water line on the north side of the channel. Be careful until you are past the shoals on the south shore. It is advisable to go in at or near high water. This entry is between the northwest Lars Island and the southeast side of Netland Island. Passage north of Netland Island is not recommended as rocks constrict Glacier Bay end and low water on the Berg Bay end of the channel. Strong outflow winds may pour out under some conditions.

★ **Shag Cove:** This two mile long cove is one mile within the entry to Geikie Inlet on the south shore. The inlet extends eight miles southwest from the south shore of Glacier Bay. Protected anchorage is in 5 to 20 fathoms at the cove head on a soft bottom. Rocks extend 300 yards offshore from the entry point and from a small island at the southwest cove entry. The foul area extends toward a large island .2 miles to the north northeast. Strong outflow winds may pour down Geikie Inlet.

★ **Tyndall Cove:** This is two miles southwest of Shag Cove. Anchor in 10 to 20 fathoms at the head, on a soft bottom. Note the comment above that in some summer conditions, strong outflow winds may be expected.

★ **Blue Mouse Cove:** This popular anchorage offers two possibilities - either in the far west corner in five to seven fathoms or on the east side in eight to ten fathoms. Good holding bottom and protection from all but north winds. The cove on the west side one-half mile inside the entrance provides even more shelter. A national park float cabin is moored here.

★ **Reid Inlet:** This anchorage is an excellent base for exploring the huge glaciers in Tarr and Johns Hopkins Inlets, if ice accumulations allow you entry. Anchorage is south of the spits on the east and west sides of the inlet at the entrance. Depths are 5 to 7 fathoms on the west side and 10 to 12 fathoms on the east side. Less ice was experienced on the east side, although this may vary from time to time. Use this anchorage only in good weather. Down-inlet winds off Reid Glacier can be severe. Grand Pacific and Margerie Glaciers at the head of Tarr Inlet, and Johns Hopkins Glacier at the head of the inlet with the same name, are truly spectacular and worth visiting. Go no closer than one-quarter to one-half nautical mile from the face of any glacier.

Tarr Inlet   *Photo © David Baron*

Admiralty Island West Side

[17300, 17312, 17339]

★ **Funter Bay (39):** Two state floats are located here. Funter Bay Refuge Float {56° 14.635' N, 134° 53.030' W} is not connected to the shore and lacks protection from north and west winds and seas entering the bay. It has 300 ft of moorage in depths of about 38 ft. Funter Bay Harbor Float {58° 15.299' N, 134° 53.750' W} is connected to shore and has more protection, but in unsettled weather, wind and swells can enter the bay making it very uncomfortable. Good anchorage is also found in Coot Cove and Crab Cove. Funter Bay has a seaplane float and water is available. There are white sandy beaches and about 30 summer cabins on the shores. Funter Bay was a gold mining area from 1877-1920 and also the site of an old fish cannery that was used as an internment camp for Aleuts during World War II. In summer, Bare Island is covered with beautiful fireweed wild flowers. Eagles are often seen catching fish from the bay and devouring their treasures on rocky ledges onshore.

★ **Hawk Inlet (40):** [17300, 17312] Give wide berth to foul areas when approaching from the south. Keep the green day beacon #3 to port to avoid the extensive shoal area. Continue East NE and keep Hawk Inlet Light 5 to port. This light marks the end of the shoal. Then continue North and keep Hawk Inlet Light 6 & 8 to starboard. The old cannery location is now the site of Green's Creek Mine operations. Anchorage is possible here. Continue mid-channel up the inlet. The entry to the basin at the head has shoals. Depths are about ten feet in the channel, which opens to a shoal-surrounded basin. The large basin has extensive shallow areas and care must be taken to locate an anchorage with sufficient depth within swinging room. There is good VHF radio reception to and from Juneau. Seaplane traffic is extensive overhead and a seaplane, if needed, could land easily in this large basin.

West side of Admiralty Island Photo © Carolyn Van Calcar

★ **Angoon (41):** [17339] Access the boat harbor through the Kootznoowoo Inlet with a maximum tidal flow of approximately 7 knots on outgoing tides. Slack water is the best time to approach. During big tide changes of 18 feet or more boats can enter the inlet safely on incoming slack or low tides. Boaters should run right of Rose Rock as opposed to motoring through Stillwater when making the approach to the boat harbor. This Tlingit village of 350 residents is located on the west side of Admiralty Island. It has the distinction of being the only community with the status of a National Monument. Guided by the wisdom of the elders and with a lot of hard work, Angoon petitioned for and was granted this status thus protecting the old growth forest for generations to come. Today they are a part of the Admiralty Island National Monument, a 1,493 sq. mile preserve. As stewards of the land, they are watchful of making responsible progress while still preserving the past. Several cultural Tlingit Totem poles stand in the downtown area. Part of the Angoon's history includes the 1882 Angoon Bombardment, when the USS Corwin destroyed the village. This attack resulted when a Tlingit shaman was accidentally killed by a whaling vessel's misfire. As was customary, the Village demanded 200 blankets as payment for the dead man's family. Taken as a threat, the bombardment was the response. In 1973, the Federal Government agreed to an out-of-court settlement for the bombardment.

The Angoon Trading Company is about a mile from the harbor and sells a wide variety of goods including groceries, supplies, hardware, electronics, and marine batteries. 907-788-3111. If you plan to stock up with more than you can carry, ask about a ride to and from the harbor. It is the only place to purchase supplies before exploring the Mitchell Bay Water Complex and Chatham Strait. Lodging is available at the Kootznahoo Inlet Lodge and the Favorite Bay Lodge (1-866-788-3344). The Favorite Bay Lodge, located just west of the harbor above the float plane dock, and Whalers Cove Lodge, a nearby seasonal fishing lodge on Killisnoo, both offer breakfast, lunch and dinner on a space available basis with 24 hour advance reservations (1-800-423-3123). This facility can prove to be a safe harbor during rough weather. Angoon is serviced by regularly scheduled air and ferry stops.

Angoon Boat Harbor: {57° 29.65' N, 134° 33.907' W} Located in the inner harbor by Favorite Bay. Moorage (call to see if improvements are done). 907-788-3653.

Angoon Oil: Gas, diesel. Located adjacent to city boat harbor. Call ahead for open hours. 907-788-3436.

Point Gardner: This point at the southwest corner of Admiralty Island, where Frederick Sound and Chatham Strait meet, can be unpleasantly rough at times. When ebbing tides from the north and east meet winds and/or swells from the south, heavy tide rips form in a large area around Point Gardner. Try to round this point at slack water. Murder Cove, adjacent to the point, has been the site of a whaling station, coal mine, and salmon cannery. Anchorage in settled weather only.

Chichagof Island
[17300, 17320, 17321, 17322]

★ **Chichagof Island:** This large island lies south of Glacier Bay, across Icy Strait and Cross Sound. If coming from, or going to Sitka to the south, passage can be on either the east side of the island, through Peril Strait and Chatham Strait, or via Lisianski Inlet down the west side. The course on the west side offers very interesting and beautiful waters with exposure only at the north and south ends of the trip. If you take the "inside passage" behind the islands use the charts.

★ **West Side Chichagof Island (42):** [17303, 17321, 17322, 17323] Beginning from the south, good starting points are two inlets on the north end of Kruzof Island. Sukoi Inlet offers well protected anchorage in 8 to 15 fathoms of water on a mud bottom. Kalinin Bay offers well protected anchorage in four to five fathoms of water on a soft bottom, but is more difficult to enter because of rocks in the entrance. A bit of shelter may be found by going inside of Kolkachef Island. Keep well off shore because this is a very rocky coast. A short-cut into Slocum Arm through the islands and rocks northwest of Khaz Head is not worth the risk. The safer route is by way of Khaz Bay, which has a marker in its rocky entrance.

★ **Slocum Arm:** Anchorages are in Waterfall Cove, two miles southeast of Falcon Arm. The west bight, in seven fathoms of water with a good bottom, is best. The east bight dries far out. The head of Falcon Arm has good, protected anchorage on mud in five fathoms of water. Elf Cove in Ford Arm has good anchorage in nine fathoms of water with a soft bottom. Island Cove, four and one-half miles southeast of Falcon Arm, is the location of the abandoned mining town of Cobol. Some buildings remain. Anchorage is in the southeast end of the cove, in 16 fathoms of water. Bears, otter, seals and eagles may be seen in Slocum, with mountains on two sides.

★ **Klag Bay:** [17322] Klag Bay, at the end of Kahz Bay, has a narrow rocky entrance best entered at slack tide and preferably low slack when hazards are visible. The entrance, called The Gate, is well marked and leads into Elbow Passage. The abandoned mining town of Chichagof is at the head of Klag Bay. Several ruins remain. When at its peak of activity in 1938, there were 200 residents. Anchorage is possible at the head of the bay in front of town, but beware of the hazards shown on the chart and especially the unmarked shoals in front of the ruins. There is good halibut fishing off the south end of Borata Island.

★ **Ogden Passage:** Continuing north along the east side of Herbert Graves Island through this passage will bring you into Portlock Harbor.

★ **Kimshan Cove:** [17321] On the east side of Surveyor Passage this cove offers excellent anchorage in seven to ten fathoms, mud bottom, anywhere in the cove. The ruins of the Hirst Mine operation are on the south shore of the cove. In 1938, the town had 100 residents. Gold, silver, minor lead and copper deposits were the objects of production in this area lasting from 1905 to 1940.

★ **Didrickson Bay:** On the east side of Portlock Harbor, there is good anchorage at the head of the bay in 11 fathoms of water, on soft mud. Keep to the west side of the bay, because it shoals very rapidly in front of the waterfalls. Entrance to, or exit from Portlock Harbor is best made through Imperial Passage. There is a light on Hill Island on the north side of the passage. It is nine miles from Imperial Passage to the bell buoy off the entrance to Lisianski Strait. Keep well off the shore because there are many rocks. Turning at the bell buoy into Lisianski Strait, a second marker is on the starboard side, entering the strait. The scenery in both Lisianski Strait and Lisianski Inlet is beautiful, with snow-covered peaks all around.

★ **Pelican (43):** [17303] This supply center for Cross Sound fishermen received its name from a fish packer, The Pelican. The buildings are on stilts, surrounded by boardwalks. The harbor has room for about 98 vessels. Transient moorage is along B dock, the dock with the sea plane float. Temporarily unoccupied berths may also be available. Moorage is arranged with the Harbormaster. Please pay upon arrival. Pelican has a bar and grill, a restaurant, lodging (B & B, inns, cabins and rooms for rent), marine supply store, gift shop, liquor store, public library with internet access, friendly people, good moorage, limited repairs, fuel, four tidal grids (up to 50 feet), and a post office. Showers and laundry are located not far from the harbor. The only vehicles in town are fire, garbage, oil trucks, and a few ATV's and golf carts. A stroll along "Salmon Way" is a pleasant walk. In September the large stream at the end of the boardwalk is full of spawning salmon. There is emergency 911 service and a health clinic open Mon-Fri. The Alaska Ferry, from Juneau, stops once a month. Scheduled daily air service is available. Fishing, sightseeing, and kayak charters, as well

Visit us at boattravel.com

as boat/skiff/kayak rentals are available. Annual community events include the *King Salmon Derby* in June and a downhome *4th of July Celebration*. www.pelican.net.

Pelican Harbor: {57° 57.51' N, 136° 13.727' W} Moorage, water, power, restroom, tidal grids to 50'. 907-735-2201. VHF 16, 09.

Pelican Fuel Dock: Gas, diesel, propane, heating fuel, oils, filters & lubes. 907-735-2211. VHF 16.

★ **Elfin Cove (44):** [17302] Moorage can be found on floats in two locations, the outer harbor at {58° 11.745' N, 136° 20.836' W} and inner harbor at {58° 11.558' N, 136° 20.679' W}. Outer harbor moorage has spectacular views, but is susceptible to swells during north winds. In 2023, a controlling depth of 10 feet was dredged in the channel to the Inner Harbor. Deep draft boats must be aware of low tide entrances and be prepared to be patient and wait for a higher tide to leave the inner harbor. Following the navigation channel is important, the remainder of the waterway is quite shallow. There is no current harbormaster and docks are 1st come-1st served. Moorage for approximately 46 boats is open on a space available basis which, during the summer is limited so rafting is encouraged. Water is accessible at the fuel dock located in Elfin Cove. The drinking water, tested monthly, comes from spring boxes high upon the mountain above Elfin Cove. Please do not use to wash boats due to limited supply.

Named after a boat owned by a pioneer resident, Elfin Cove is one of the nicest places in all Southeast Alaska. The community is located on a peninsula just behind the outer floats. A boardwalk crosses over the neck of the peninsula to the inner harbor and continues around the outer perimeter of the peninsula, until it reaches the starting point. Along the boardwalk are a fishing lodge (one of several), the post office, a souvenir gift shop, several homes, a restaurant, a laundry with shower and coin-op washers and dryers, and a general store. Near the post office there is a museum of local history. Next door, in the community shop, there is a public telephone (long distance accessed with a phone card). Cell service inside Elfin Cove can be limited and is more reliable outside the cove. There is a store that offers fresh produce and a variety of food and fishing supplies in the summer. Elfin Cove has no solid waste facilities: please take your garbage with you when you depart. For a fun side trip, visit Granite Cove about .25 mi away by boat. Anchor and dinghy ashore to explore. A maintained trail leads to a WWII era cannon and beautiful views of Cross Sound. The hike is 2 mi round trip. Bring hot dogs and marshmallows to roast on the beach. For additional information about Elfin Cove, visit https://www.facebook.com/ElfinCove.

Elfin Cove Fuel Dock: Gas, diesel (#1 & #2), propane, oils, batteries, filters, water. Open year round. Call for open hours. Off-hours fueling on call, $50 charge. 907-239-2208. VHF 72.

★ **Hoonah (45):** [17302] Enter inside of Pitt Island. A white buoy with a white light flashes every 2 seconds in Port Frederick in position {58° 06'51" N, 135°27'30"W} to alert mariners to the local no wake zone. Hoonah has two moorage facilities, Hoonah City Float and Hoonah Harbor. Hoonah City Float is the wooden float located at the city center, a few blocks away from Hoonah Harbor. This moorage is open to strong southwest winds. Hoonah Harbor is located behind the breakwater, past the Hoonah Cold Storage. This protected inner harbor has concrete floats. The transient float, attached to a wharf, is the first float to port when entering the basin.

This community of nearly 970 residents offers a laundromat, lodging, restaurants, coffee shop, and hotel. Local stores sell groceries, hardware, tackle and marine supplies, as well as gifts. The Hoonah Trading Company is a 15 minute walk from the harbor. Just go up the ramp and take a left at the road. A 35-ton hydraulic boat lift and repairs are available, as is upland fenced storage with security cameras. A 220-ton Travelift with wash down is located by the ferry terminal. There is ferry service two times a week and a small airport and float plane dock accommodates regularly scheduled air flights.

The name Hoonah means "village by the cliff" in Tlingit. This is the principal ancestral village of the Huna people from the Tlingit tribe. Residents have always relied on the sea for their livelihood, whether it be commercial or subsistence fishing. Tourism is currently the up and coming industry. A new cruise ship berthing facility offshore accommodates the cruise ships that are making Hoonah a regular stop. About a mile from town, a renovated cannery has shops and a cultural center. Shore and wildlife excursions can be arranged here, on a space available basis after cruise ship bookings are made. In the center of town, two Tlingit totems stand beside the community center. The local school and City Hall also have a totem pole on display. A totem carving project is ongoing during the summer months and boaters can talk to local carvers as they work on new totems. The Forest Service office, less than a mile from downtown on Garteeni Hwy, has brochures and a road guide for hiking and biking adventures. www.visitHoonah.com is also a helpful resource. ⚓

Hoonah City Float: {58° 06.66' N, 135° 26.955' W} The floats have wifi and security cameras. Potable water available in the loading zone, no shore power. 907-945-3670. VHF 16.

Hoonah Harbor: {58° 06.400' N, 135° 26.881' W} Permanent moorage stalls have power and water. Transient dock has potable water, no power. Harbor has laundry, showers, wifi, security cameras, tidal grid, and launch ramp. 907-945-3670. VHF 16. Working Channels 9, 14.

Hoonah Trading Co.: Hardware, groceries, produce, clothing, sporting goods, gifts. Gas, marine fuel and propane at fuel dock and service station. Tie up to float at the end of the dock while shopping. 907-945-3211.

Huna Propane: Propane. 907-945-9697.

Pavlof Harbor: This is on the south shore of Freshwater Bay. A lake is within walking distance.

Freshwater Bay — Photo © Cynthia Meyer

★ **Tenakee Inlet (46):** [17300, 17302] This long inlet is the site of Tenakee Springs and several bays which permit anchorage. This is a busy place when fishing season is open. Crab Bay, Saltery Bay, Lang Bay, and Seal Bay have anchorage. There is little, if any, radio reception from this area.

★ **Tenakee Springs:** A boat basin, capacity 56, provides moorage one-half mile east of center of town at {57° 46.686' N, 135° 09.587' W}. Power on floats, non-potable water. 16' X 51' grid available. Additional moorage is found on the inside of the floating breakwater with a dinghy ride ashore. Check-in at the floats with the harbormaster upon arrival as there are specific transient moorage spaces. City personnel monitor VHF Channel 16 to assist visiting boaters. In an emergency, a speedy 26 foot Munson Landing Craft serves as the Rescue Boat. Tenakee Springs is home to about 100 residents. A fuel wharf with gas and diesel, non-potable water, shops, meals, and groceries can be found. A museum that showcases Tenakee's unique history opened in 2017. The Community Center hosts events and classes. The entire community seems to center around the hot springs bath at Dock and Main Streets. Separate bath hours are designated for men and women. Take your own soap to pre-wash. Because of sulfur in the water, remove all jewelry. The oil truck and fire engine are the only vehicles in town. Fishing for halibut, Dolly Varden, cod, salmon, and crab may prove fruitful near the moorage basin. The ferry makes scheduled stops to Tenakee Springs.

Tenakee Fuel Facility: Gas, diesel, marine batteries, oils, lubricants, gas additives, fuel filters. Open year round, call for hours. 907-736-2288. VHF 16.

Tenakee Springs City Hall: Moorage. 907-736-2207. VHF 16.

Page 276 Chapter 20 SOUTHEAST ALASKA

Tenakee Springs Market: Groceries, organic & gluten free, liquor. Phone for days/hours open. 907-736-2205.

★ **Crab Bay:** Good anchorage on the south side of Tenakee Inlet. Anchor in five to 25 fathoms, avoiding mud flats on the south side and at the head.

★ **Saltery Bay:** The narrow entrance opens to a wider basin. Flats extend 1.2 miles from the head. Anchorage is soft mud and gravel bottom. A four fathom shoal is on the north side of the entry.

Seal Bay: This bay is ten miles west northwest of Tenakee Springs on the south side of the inlet. Shoals are at entry at $6^{1}/_{4}$ fathoms and $1^{1}/_{2}$ fathoms. See Coast Pilot for specifics regarding latitude and longitude. The flat is .8 of a mile from the head, plus a rock near the middle, $1^{1}/_{2}$ miles inside the entry, is covered at high water. Between this rock and the flat, depths are 19 to 29 fathoms on a soft bottom.

★ **Long Bay:** This bay is located 12.5 miles from town on the southwest inlet side. See U.S. Coast Pilot 8 for Pacific Coast Alaska. From the northwest entry point, a reef, covered at half tide, extends east .5 miles. Depths are 5 to 15 fathoms, secure mud bottom anchorage. From the head, a mud flat extends .6 miles. On the north shore of upper Tenakee Inlet is a portage 300 yards to Point Frederick in Icy Strait.

★ **Basket Bay:** The cave at the head will be of interest to explore. Anchor in about seven fathoms off the flats at the head. Open to southeasterly winds. The tides in Chatham Strait meet near the vicinity of Basket Bay, except during spring tides when the meeting place is farther south.

★ **Sitkoh Bay:** [17320, 17338] Fair anchorage is found off the flats at the head, past the old Chatham Cannery site. A rough, 3.5 mile trail starts near the cannery, following along Sitkoh Creek to Sitkoh Lake where a Forest Service cabin is located. Bring a pole and fish for Cutthroat or Dolly Varden. ⚓

Baranof Island
[17320, 17324, 17326, 17327, 17331, 17336, 17337, 17338]

★ **Baranof Island:** Named after Alexander Andreievich Baranov, the first governor of the Russian-American colonies, this mountainous island was the first place in Southeast Alaska settled by the Russians (a fact confirmed by the predominance of Russian place names).

★ **Goddard Hot Springs Bay & Kliuchevoi Bay:** [17326] Located on the east shore of Baranof Island, is the scene of nice hot springs. Kliuchevoi Bay is a good anchorage, but be careful in the entrance. Use the east one. Going in, there is a rock sticking up in the entrance. Keep to the right of the rock as you turn around it, but stay close to it because the shore to the right is foul. Another submerged rock is just beyond the first one. Go between the two rocks. Once inside, there is no problem. According to the City of Sitka, GPS navigation charts do not correctly locate the rocks at the Kliuchevoi Bay entrance. Several boats have hit the rock using GPS data. Printed navigation charts are correct. The buoys, float and property in the inner part of Kliuchevoi Bay are private. The hot springs are to the south, just outside Kliuchevoi Bay. You should see a clearing up from the shore. There are two bath houses with hot tubs, a boardwalk, and outhouse. The bay immediately in front of the springs is foul. A recreational cabin rented

Baranof Warm Springs Dock Photo © Carolyn Van Calcar

through the City of Sitka is located northwest of Goodard on Yán Ayawa Glaakw Island (formerly Kolash Island). A white buoy with blue tape is available for cabin guests.

★ **Aleutkina Bay:** The inner bay is very protected with good holding. Keep well over to the left shore and watch the depth sounder on the way in. Gravel bars extend farther than you might expect, or that is shown on the chart.

★ **Silver Bay:** There is a shallower spot for anchoring at the extreme south end behind the island. Good holding. A Forest Service buoy in the southwest end of the Bay is near a trailhead that accesses Salmon Lake. Other trails in the area lead into the mountains. One takes off slightly towards a power plant, just beyond some old abandoned buildings. It has been marked with surveyor's tape. There are old mines in the area.

★ **Sitka (47):** [17324] This is the oldest Russian established city in southeast Alaska and was in fact the colonial capital of Russian America from 1804 until the transfer to the United States in 1867. Many believe it also claims the title of being most beautiful. During the summer you can see performances of the Naa Kahidi Native Tlingit Dancers or the New Archangel Dancers (Russian dances in authentic costumes). Other attractions include the Sitka Historical Museum, Sitka National Historical Park, Sheldon Jackson Museum and St. Michael's Russian Orthodox Cathedral. The first cathedral was completed in 1848. It was destroyed by fire in 1966, but artwork, icons and other treasures were salvaged and are in a rebuilt replica of the original structure. The Cathedral is a working Church and open for regular services. During the summer tour hours vary, check posted hours on the church door. On Sundays and in the winter, tours by appointment only. For information, hours, and appointments: 907-747-8120. Another attraction is the Russian Bishop's House. Built in 1842 it is the oldest intact Russian building. Take a free guided tour of the restored second floor living quarters and chapel. Call Sitka National Historic Park for information, 907-747-0110. For those interested in the Native culture, the Sheldon Jackson Museum features one of Alaska's oldest collections, or visit the Sitka National Historical Park to view the site of a Tlingit Fort and the battlegrounds of 1804. A fine collection of Haida and Tlingit totem poles were moved to this park from the 1904 Louisiana Exposition in St. Louis. Also within walking distance of the downtown area, the Alaska Raptor Center (open year round) offers views of recovering eagles and other wild raptors, as well as special shows scheduled May - Sept. 907-747-8662. The *Sitka Summer Music Festival*, Alaska's premier chamber music festival, takes place in June. For information. 907-747-6774. The Sitka Sound Science Center features an aquarium with touch tanks, killer whale skeleton, and hatchery. 907-747-8878. About five miles from town, the Fortress of the Bear is an education and rescue center for orphaned brown bear cubs. Enjoy tours, viewing area, and gift shop. 907-747-3550. A Visitor Information Center located at the downtown Lincoln St. stoplight is open year-round M-F 10am-4pm. Seasonal Visitor Information Kiosks at Harrigan Centennial Hall or O'Connell Bridge Dock are open on large cruise ship port days mid-May through mid-September.

Sitka's name is said to have come from the Tlingit name Sheet'Ka, meaning "on the outside of Baranof Island." The Natives developed a culture, exemplified by the totem poles which depicted family history and legends, and the creation of baskets, tools, artworks, and clan houses. Russian fur traders first sighted Sitka in 1741 and returned to settle under the leadership of Alexander Baranov in 1799. The Tlingit defeated and expelled the Russians in 1802, but the Russians returned in 1804 and won a multi-day battle for control. By 1848, Sitka, dubbed "Paris of the Pacific", was said to have been the busiest port on the Pacific Coast. Furs from the sea otter and fur seal were the valuable attraction. On October 18, 1867, at the Baranof Castle Hill site, the transfer of Alaska from Russia to the United States was made for the price of $7,200,000. Sitka was the capital of Alaska until 1906 when it moved to Juneau. For more information contact Visit Sitka. 907-747-8604. www.sitka.org.

Berthage: Upon entering the Sitka Channel, contact the Harbormaster on VHF 16 7:30am-11:30pm to register and to be assigned a slip. The inner harbor is a no wake zone, slow to 3 mph. Crescent Harbor and Sealing Cove Harbor are strictly permanent moorage harbors. Eliason, ANB and Thomsen Harbors offer the only moorage for transient recreational vessels. There is a reserved moorage policy for slips ranging from 100' to 150' and for the 180' private bridge facility. For large vessel reservations call 907-747-3439 or www.cityofsitka.com. Choose departments, then harbors for further information.

SOUTHEAST ALASKA Chapter 20 Page 277

Eliason Harbor: {57° 03.344' N, 135° 21.065' W} Located about .5 mi from downtown. Transient moorage for vessels 32' to 150'. Some 30/50 amp power, water, restrooms, showers, fish cleaning stations, waste oil/garbage drop. Laundry facilities, groceries, supplies, sporting goods, marine hardware are nearby. 907-747-3439. VHF 16.

Sitka Petro Marine Services (North Plant): Gas, diesel, propane, heating fuel, oils, filters, water, waste oil disposal, free popcorn. 907-747-3414. VHF 16.

Sitka Petro Marine Services (South Plant, located by the bridge): Gas, diesel, water, batteries, filters, oils, free popcorn. 907-747-3414. VHF 16.

Delta Western: (at Halibut Point) Gas, diesel, propane, oil, lubes, filters, ice. 907-747-4999, VHF 16. Halibut Point Marine is onsite and has an 88-ton Travelift, call 907-747-1089.

★ **Neva Strait and Olga Strait:** These straits are well marked with navigational aids. Watch closely for hazards like submerged rocks and floating logs. Currents run to about 1.5 knots. Neva Strait floods to the south, and Olga Strait to the northwest. The ideal situation is to reach Krestof Sound, situated between the two Straits, at high slack. State Ferries routinely use these Straits and give about ten minutes warning on VHF Channel 16 of their approach. There are several spots where one might not want to meet them.

★ **Sergius Narrows:** The channel is 24 feet deep and 450 feet wide. Flood currents set northeast, ebb southwest. Currents can run to 5.9 knots on the flood and 5.5 on the ebb. Use the current tables and transit at or near times of slack water.

★ **Appleton Cove (48):** [17338] This cove is located on the south side of Rodman Bay, which is on the south side of Peril Strait. Good, well-protected anchorage is available on the east side of the cove in eight fathoms of water on a soft bottom. Some anchor fouling has been reported. A good anchorage is at the south end of the cove northeast of Andersen Island. Salmon fishing is recommended between Point Benham and the buoy in the mouth of Rodman Bay.

★ **Magoun Islands:** Located in Krestof Sound, the bay formed by these islands is very pretty and well sheltered. Enter through the north passage. There are no obstructions in the entrance, and the holding bottom is good. Keep an eye out for a small wreck on the south shore.

★ **St. John the Baptist Bay (49):** [17323] Located at the north end of Neva Strait, this bay has anchorage in 11 fathoms of water on a soft bottom, near the head of the bay. Anchorage is also possible in the bight behind the island off the south side near the entrance, in seven fathoms of water on a soft bottom. However, there is not much room at this second location.

Trader's Islands: This group is located at the eastern end of Peril Strait. The shoreline of Catharine Island is foul. Favor the Traders Islands and anchor in one of the several small bights along the southern shore. This is a good anchorage only in settled weather.

Point Lull: This is open to the southeast, however there is anchorage in six fathoms of water with protection from north winds.

★ **Cosmos Cove (50):** [17337] This is a popular anchorage during the fishing season. Flats extend from the head of the cove.

Red Bluff Bay Photo © Carolyn Van Calcar

★ **L Cove:** This is a lovely little nook, adjacent to Takatz Bay. The small indentation, in the shape of a reversed L, is unnamed and barely shown on charts. This is an excellent anchorage in about seven fathoms on a rocky bottom.

★ **Baranof Warm Springs (51):** [17337] Located in Warm Springs Bay, on the east side of Baranof Island, is a 200' small craft float with moorage on both sides. A moorage payment box is onsite. Water is usually available on the floats. Water is from the river and not treated so it should be filtered prior to drinking. Because of currents caused by the falls at the head of the bay, landing may be easier on the inside of the floats and heading into the current. Watch out for the rock directly beyond the float that sits at 9' below LMW. Anchorage is possible in the two coves on the south side of the bay. The westernmost cove is preferable as it shows shallower water, 12 to 15 fathoms. At the head of the bay is a boardwalk that is lined with about a dozen private cabins and ends near the spectacular waterfalls. The Alaska Whale Foundation (AWF) field station is on the boardwalk, as is a picnic shelter and three public, semi-enclosed bathtubs with lovely views of the falls. Bath use is by donation, proceeds help to maintain the tubs. The Baranof Wilderness Lodge, a private seasonal lodge, is located nearby. It is possible to visit the hot springs pools. Walk up the dock onto the wooden boardwalk and continue all the way past the turn off to the falls and the AWF field station. The trail winds through the forest for about a quarter of a mile. There are stretches in the boardwalk interspersed with a mud path veined with tree roots. A sign points off to the left down to the hot pools, again by of a mud path again veined with tree roots. It is not difficult, just muddy. The lowest pool, in the series of three, is cold. The path continues past the hot pools turnoff to Baranof Lake.

★ **Red Bluff Bay (52):** [17336] Named for the red rock cliffs on the north side, this bay has waterfalls and a river flat at the head. Anchor at the head.

★ **Gut Bay:** Anchor near the head.

★ **Port Armstrong (53):** Use [17333] The one time site of a whaling plant, a herring oil plant, and now a research fish hatchery, operates here. Good anchorage can be found in the niche near the plant site.

★ **Port Alexander (54):** [17331] This is a small, quiet fishing community of about 60 residents. There are two floats with first come first served transient moorage. During the busy summer months boats sometimes raft four deep. The first harbor when rounding the red navigation nun buoy is the main harbor. {56° 14.799' N, 134° 38.911' W}. It is the site of a Seaplane Float and 450' float. There is no harbormaster. Moorage payments can be made at the top of the dock in the drop box. No power. Fresh water is at both ends of the main float and pay phone is onshore. There is room enough to anchor here, but stay to the sides to avoid floatplane traffic. The northernmost float, known as the back dock, is harder to get to and requires local knowledge. There is a nearby 18 X 48 grid. Groceries are accessible, fuel may be available during the summer-ask a local. Bear Hall, the city building, has a small library. There is also a small museum and cafe close to the dock. Main St. General Store, open seasonally, sells gifts and locally made crafts. Laughing Raven Lodge offers guided fishing, lodging and meals with advance notice. 907-568-2266. Each 4th of July the community celebrates with a parade, kids games and barbecue. In mid-August the annual *Troll Closure Open* is held. It is the longest running golf tournament in SE Alaska, and second in Alaska.

Keku Strait: This strait separates Kuiu Island from Kupreanof Island. Navigational aids have been replaced by the Coast Guard and an updated chart is available. However, the passage is narrow and currents can cause problems in some places. Recommended for passage only by skippers with considerable cruising experience. In case of trouble, it could be days before anyone ventures by to offer help.

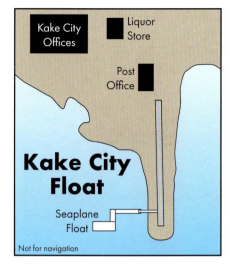
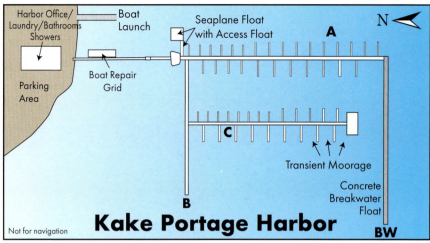

★ **Kake (55):** [17368] The City of Kake Harbor Department operates and maintains one boat harbor and one dock and seaplane float. At the Kake Portage Harbor {56° 56.780' N, 133° 53.826'}, there is moorage for transient and commercial vessels. The transient moorage rate is $.50 per foot. Harbor amenities include 30/50 amp power, potable water, restroom, laundry, shower, a tidal grid, boat launch and floating ramp, and a garbage receptacle at bottom of ramp. During the summer, the city's harbors host all kinds of vessels – commercial fishing, recreation and sport fishing, and an ever more increasing number of large transient yachts. At the Kake dock and seaplane float, small boat daily moorage is offered. Just up from the ramp is the center of downtown Kake where the post office and liquor store are located. From here, the grocery store, clinic, lodges, and one of the world's largest totem poles at 132 feet are all within walking distance. See our advertisement on this page. City of Kake: Telephone: 907-785-3804. Fax" 907-785-4815. Email: cityclerk@cityofkake.org.

Prince of Wales Island

[17360, 17423, 17426, 17432, 17433, 17436]

★ **Prince of Wales Island:** This island, with 1,000 miles of coastline, is the third largest island in the entire United States. It is 135 miles long and 45 miles across. Eleven islands and several small islets surround Prince of Wales Island. There are many bays, coves, and inlets around this island. Winds flow mainly from the northeast or southwest in the summer. Direction varies with local topography. This area has historically been populated by Tlingit and Haida Natives. Recently, this has become the home of miners, loggers, and commercial fishermen. The communities of Craig, Klawock, Hydaburg, Coffman Cove, Hollis, and Thorne Bay are connected by road. Prince of Wales Island has a road network of over 1,000 miles, the largest in southeast Alaska. Vehicles can arrive by ferry from Ketchikan to Hollis, or cars can be rented. A picnic site with an outstanding view of Clarence Strait is located at Sandy Beach, six miles north of Thorne Bay. There are tables, fire rings, and toilets. No fresh water. Exchange Cove, 15 minutes by car from the community of Whale Pass, has three campsites. Lake #3, 30 minutes by car from Thorne Bay, has fishing, hiking, canoeing, and two campsites. No developed water supply. All water in these wilderness areas must be boiled at least five minutes before using. Black bears are found on Prince of Wales Island. Make plenty of noise while hiking to warn bears that you are around. A startled bear is a dangerous bear.

East Side Prince of Wales Island

[17360, 17382, 17401, 17420, 17423]

★ **Clarence Strait:** This strait extends about 110 miles along the entire east side of Prince of Wales Island from Dixon Entrance on the south, to Sumner Strait at the north. Currents run to four knots. The strait is broken by several large sounds and bays in the southern half. Snow Passage, at the north end of Clarence Strait, has strong currents and can be very uncomfortable when wind is added.

★ **Exchange Cove:** Located on the east side of Prince of Wales Island, about two miles northwest of Kashevarof Passage. Heed the channel marker west of West Island and avoid numerous shoal and rocky areas, when approaching from either north or south. Exchange Cove is the largest well protected anchorage in this area and has room for several boats. The entry depth is ten fathoms, with gradual shoaling toward the head. Avoid the drying mudflat. Anchor in ten fathoms, excellent holding soft bottom. This cove is a popular spot with locals for beach camping. ▲

★ **Coffman Cove:** {56° 0' 39" N, 132° 49' 55" W} This one-time logging camp has become a destination for visitors who seek an unspoiled landscape, thriving wildlife, and outdoor adventure (which of course includes boating!). The dock has moorage space for over 100 slips. Transient boats usually moor on the outside. There is water at the dock,

Visit us at boattravel.com

shore power and a launch ramp is nearby. The cove is sheltered with good anchorage. In addition to boating, there are many other activities to enjoy such as hiking, kayaking, and fishing. The bird and wildlife viewing opportunities are amazing - bears, deer, whales, herons, and sea lions are commonly seen. Come to Coffman Cove for some exciting events: "By The Sea" Arts & Seafood Festival held in August, Silver Salmon Tournament July 3rd and King Salmon Derby May 1st - August 31st. The city's amenities and services are sure to make your stay more comfortable. There is a library with wireless internet, a gas station, fully furnished lodges, B & B's, and rental cabins. There is a hamburger and sandwich joint, and for groceries and a little bit of everything there is the Riggin Shack. Local transportation options include the float plane service Island Air Express out of Klawock, IFA Ferry out of Hollis and Breakaway Adventures Water Taxi out of Wrangell. Coffman Cove is the only community on the north end of Prince of Wales Island that is accessible by paved roads. Rent a car and see the caves or explore the other island communities. Visit www.ccalaska.com for links to local businesses, transportation information and more. City of Coffman Cove: Telephone: 907-329-2233. Harbormaster: 907-329-2233. VHF 16.

Walk-around: Stroll to Rhody Park within walking distance from moorage, and enjoy a water view from the lookout area or explore other nearby trails.

Ratz Harbor: Fair anchorage, but open to wakes.

★ **Snug Anchorage:** Favor the west shore when entering. Anchor north of the islet.

★ **Thorne Bay (56):** [17423] This large bay is the site of the City of Thorne Bay, with guest dock space and slips, several seasonal and year round lodges, a couple of B & B's and numerous anchorages. The narrow entrance channel is marked by navigation aids and easily accessed by small tour boats and tugs pulling barges. Docks, located at city center, have power and water. A boat launch and boat grid are located nearby. This is a friendly, walkable town to visit. The residents actively participate in the community events and businesses. Shopping includes clothing, gifts, groceries, hardware, tackle, liquor, marine supplies, and car and boat rentals. The community also has a post office and library with internet. The City's emergency medical volunteers are available 24/7. A city map with directions to local services is available at the harbor, city hall or at businesses in town.

Thorne Bay, built by the timber industry, is an entry point to the over 1,500 miles of road on Prince of Wales Island. Scheduled float plane and weekly barge service to and from Ketchikan bring supplies to the entire island. By car, Thorne Bay is reached via the Inter-Island Ferry to Hollis. For information, 1-866-308-4848. Both salt and freshwater fishing can be excellent. Thorne Bay was once the largest logging camp in the United States and became a city in 1982. The four major employers are the City of Thorne Bay, the U.S. Forestry Service, Southeast Island School District, and Thorne Bay Market.

For current information regarding local services or for additional City information, visit www.thornebay-ak.gov.

★ **City of Thorne Bay:** {55° 41.01.88'N, 132° 31.21.71'W} Year round moorage, propane & diesel, fresh water, power (check in with Harbormaster or City Hall before plugging into power), restroom, shower, boat grid, boat launch, float plane dock, Thorne Bay Market & liquor store within easy walking distance. Harbormaster or City Hall available year round Monday-Friday 8am to 4pm, and on call weekends. Please call City Hall at 907-828-3380 or Harbormaster cell at 907-204-0815 or either one on VHF Channel 16. Website: www.thornebay-ak.gov.

The Tackle Shack at Thorne Bay: Located near the main dock. Sporting goods, hunting and fishing licenses, bait, propane, gifts, hull cleaning, zinc inspection and replacement. 907-828-8212.

The Port at Thorne Bay: Located one-half mile from the main dock. Fuel and float plane docks. Gas, diesel, oils, post office, convenience store, gifts, and snacks or light fare. 907-828-3995.

The Thorne Bay Market: Located a short walk from the harbor. Groceries, produce, deli, ice and bait, ATM. Courtesy ride to the dock for heavy purchases. 907-828-3306.

Riptide Liquor Store: Just up the hill from the harbor. Wine, beer, liquor, ice. 907-828-8233.

McFarlands Floatel: {55° 41' 7.8" N, 132° 31' 55"W} Located two miles by water from Thorne Bay. Lodging, gifts, sporting & boating supplies. 541-571-8304. VHF 16.

★ **Lyman Anchorage:** A small, well protected anchorage. The entrance is narrow, and depths may be minimal at very low tides. Good holding bottom in eight fathoms. This anchorage is on the west side of Clarence Strait, about 22 miles north of Ketchikan.

★ **Kasaan Bay (57):** [17426] This 25 mile long bay is interesting, but the shoreline is relatively flat in comparison to the west side of Prince of Wales Island. Kasaan is a native Haida village with breakwater, floats, and sea plane float {55° 32.217' N, 132° 23.910' W}. There is a library, post office, and health clinic in town. Kasaan has a totem park and Whale Clan House. From the early to mid-1900's this was the site of a busy cannery.

★ **Kina Cove:** Is on the south side of Kasaan Bay, about 15 miles from the entrance. Sheltered anchorage in seven fathoms is at the head of the cove.

★ **Hollis (58):** [17426] Hollis is the site of a 150' moorage float at {55° 28.918' N, 132° 38.767' W} with a separate float for seaplanes. No water, power, garbage or waste oil disposal. The float approach is quite shallow and restricted, and the float is often full. Anchorage in front of the launching ramp is possible. Next to the docks, Hollis Adventure Rentals rents boats, kayaks, canoes, camp gear, cars and trucks. This small residential community also has a school and library. About 4 miles from the dock, a nice trail runs along the Harris River where there is excellent fishing and a covered picnic shelter. Plans are to extend this trail into Twelve Mile Arm, a waterway that continues after Hollis for another 7 miles. In nearby Clark Bay there is a float plane dock and the Inter Island Ferry Terminal with daily trips to Ketchikan. There is no public moorage in this bay. In the early 1950's Hollis was the main logging camp on Prince of Wales until 1962 when the center of activity shifted to Thorne Bay. In the 1980's, the State of Alaska made private land available here and Hollis began the transition to a permanent community.

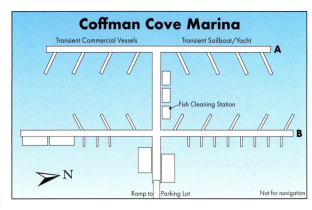

★ **Skowl Arm:** [17426, 17436] Anchorage is possible in seven fathoms on mud bottom in Saltery Cove. In some places the bottom is rocky. There is a large sport fishing lodge and several private residences.

★ **McKenzie Inlet:** This is entered at Khayyam Point and extends south for about five miles. McKenzie Rock should be given a wide berth. Anchorage is possible in the cove to the east of Thumb Point, .5 mi south of McKenzie Rock, in nine to ten fathoms, soft bottom, and protected from all but north winds. There is also good anchorage near the head of the inlet in seven to ten fathoms, soft bottom on the west side of Peacock Island. The entrance to Polk Inlet, at the west end of Skowl Arm, is foul and entering may not be worth the risks involved.

★ **Cholmondeley Sound:** [17436] Pronounced Chomly, this sound is entered between Chasina Point and Skin Island. This sound extends about 16 miles to the end of its West Arm.

★ **Lancaster Cove:** The first anchorage after entering the sound is in Lancaster Cove, about one mile southeast of Hump Island, and behind the island in the center of the cove. The north cove is the best choice.

Kitkum Bay: This bay lies to the southwest of Lancaster Cove, but because of all the hazards in its entrance, may not be worth exploring.

★ **Dora Bay:** Three miles long, this bay lies off the south side of the sound. The best anchorage is in the tight little cove at the far south end, just before the flats, in eight to ten fathoms, soft bottom. When weather permits there are beautiful views of Mount Eudora.

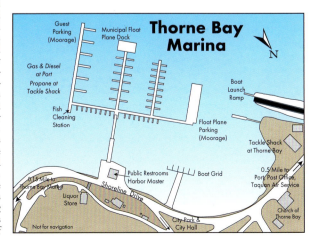

★ **Cholmondeley Sound South Arm:** Seven miles long, the South Arm lies just west of Dora Bay. There are two coves at the head, the one on the east side is probably best, being shallower, and less subject to strong winds coming through from Klakas Inlet on the west side of Prince of Wales Island. Anchorage in the east cove is in seven to eight fathoms, soft bottom, with plenty of room. When the mountains are visible, this is a beautiful place.

★ **Cholmondeley Sound West Arm:** Three possible anchorages are found in its six mile length. First is the little cove 1.5 miles into the arm on the south side, just past the remains of old pilings and a building or two. They mark the site of an old settlement called Chomley. The second anchorage may be the best and is farther west just past the first group of seven or eight islets, in front of the creek that flows into the sound. Anchorage is in eight to ten fathoms, well protected, and a soft bottom. The third possibility is at the head of the arm in 12-15 fathoms, but it may be subject to winds funneling through from Hetta Inlet. Another anchorage is in Sunny Cove, on the north side of the sound, about five miles west of Hump Island. Protected anchorage in 12-15 fathoms is available.

★ **Port Johnson:** [17432] Entrance is between Wedge Island and Adams Point. Beware of the reef shown off Inner Point, it extends quite far off shore. Port Johnson is three and one half miles long. The cove at the west end is a very nice, protected anchorage in 10 to 12 fathoms, soft bottom, just to the south of the small island shown on the chart.

Dolomi Bay: This is a small, narrow inlet, about one and one quarter miles in from the entrance to the inlet, and would be a nice anchorage in eight to ten fathoms at the head. A logging camp and log booms may be present. The abandoned gold mining town of Dolomi is located here.

★ **Moira Sound:** [17432] This sound has beautiful scenery and good anchorages in its seven or more arms. Four mile long North Arm is entered at Point Halliday, three miles west of Moira Rock. This is in the entrance to Moira Sound.

★ **Clarno Cove:** The best anchorages are both in Clarno Cove. The first is at the head of Clarno in eight fathoms, soft bottom, and the second is in the entrance to Aiken Cove in eight to nine fathoms, soft bottom. There is an excellent view of 3,500 foot Mount Eudora. Additional anchorages are in the unnamed cove on the south side of Clarno Cove, with a least depth of one fathom in its entrance, and in Nowiskay Cove and Cannery Cove.

★ **Niblack Anchorage:** Entry is at Safety Rock, three and one half miles west-southwest of Moira Rock. Anchorage is in six to eight fathoms, mud bottom, and good protection in the cove at the head of this inlet. The buildings onshore are those of a mining company doing exploration work in the area. They are on the site of the former copper mining town of Niblack, founded around 1900 and abandoned in 1909.

★ **Kegan Cove:** This small scenic cove lies off the north side of Moira Sound. When entering or departing, do so on the top half of a tide, as the chart shows a depth of only five feet at zero tide. Favor the west side when entering. Anchorage in the inner cove is in six to seven fathoms, mud bottom, plenty of room, and well protected. A Forest Service cabin is on shore and a buoy is in the cove (no boats over 26'). A trail leads from the cabin about a half mile to Kegan Lake, where another Forest Service cabin is located.

★ **Dickman Bay:** This is an inlet in the West Arm of Moira Sound. Dickman Bay extends four miles northwest from its entrance and is clear of dangers except for the narrow passage just prior to entering the cove at the head of the bay. The chart shows seven foot depths in the narrows at zero tide. A fair current flows through the anchorage, but not enough to create a problem. Anchorage is in six fathoms in the far west cove, soft bottom, and good protection. The cove to the south shows a rocky bottom. This is a beautiful anchorage. There are two more anchorages in Dickman Bay, the eastern most has anchorage in 15-17 fathoms, and the western in five to eight fathoms, both with mud bottoms, and good protection.

★ **Frederick Cove:** This inlet extends two and one half miles further west from the west end of Moira Sound. Anchorage near the head is in six to eight fathoms, soft bottom, well protected.

★ **South Arm of Moira Sound:** Anchorage is found at the head of this four mile inlet in seven fathoms, over soft bottom, with protection from all but northeast winds up the inlet. Except for rocky 2,500 foot Bokan Mountain on the east side, the shoreline is low. Beware of the rocks, not visible at high tide, in the center of the inlet about one and one half miles south of the entrance. The best course is along the eastern shore until you are certain that you are past the rocks.

★ **Johnson Cove:** [17432] Johnson Cove lies just east of the South Arm. Is is 2.5 miles long, and has a large, well protected anchorage at its head with depths of ten fathoms, soft bottom. Passage from the South Arm to Johnson Cove is possible in the narrow channel south of the largest island on the west side of the entrance to Johnson Cove.

Menefee Anchorage: Located on the south side of the entrance to Moira Sound, this has depths of 25 fathoms, but shallower anchorages can be found around the edges.

★ **Ingraham Bay:** [17432] This bay is located about four miles south of Rip Point on the south side of the entrance to Moira Sound. The best anchorage is in the one mile long north arm in seven to eight fathoms, mud bottom, good protection, and nice scenery. There are at least six fathoms of water in the entrance to the north arm. The two mile long south arm is so rock infested that entry is not worth the risks involved.

★ **Kendrick Bay:** [17433] Located about six miles south of the entrance to Ingraham Bay, Kendrick Bay can be entered on either the north or south side of the Kendrick Islands. The south side is the easiest. Stay well offshore to avoid the numerous rocks, which afford excellent bottom fishing for large rockfish and ling cod. There is a mooring buoy in the bay.

South Arm: This has an anchorage in seven to eight fathoms, bottom may be hard. May be best used as a temporary anchorage.

West Arm: Extreme caution is necessary in entering this arm because of numerous charted and uncharted hazards. The first uncharted rock is in the main part of Kendrick Bay, a short distance to the east of the two islets in the center of the bay. From these islets, or rocks, the course to the West Arm is south of the two small islands in water shown on the chart as 15 fathoms. Just past the second of these islands three underwater rocks are shown extending out into the channel. Two reefs are shown to the west, with above water rocks. They should be passed to the north, giving them plenty of clearance, as there are some uncharted rocks to the north which are only visible at low tide. The Coast Pilot's excellent advice is to traverse this passage near low tide. The best anchorage is found in the bight on the south side in nine to ten fathoms, soft bottom. The large float in the bay is private and used by UCore Rare Metals for support of their Bokan Mountain mining operations.

★ **Gardner Bay:** Gardner Bay is entered on the south side of the island in its entrance. There is a good anchorage in 13 fathoms over mud in the basin at the head of the bay. This is a beautiful spot, surrounded by big mountains. Anchorage is also possible in the small bight on the south side, showing six and one half fathoms. This spot is more protected than the head of the bay. The head is subject to "willawaw" winds.

★ **McLean Arm:** McLean Point is about four miles north of Cape Chacon, and McLean Arm is entered north of the light on the point. This four mile inlet is straight and unencumbered by hazards. Anchorage is possible at the head of either the north or west arms, but they can be subject to "willawaw" winds. The small bight on the south side, just west of the point showing 3 fathoms has a more protected anchorage in 12 fathoms, soft bottom.

West Side Prince of Wales Island
[17378, 17387, 17400, 17403-17408, 17431-17433]

★ **West Side Prince of Wales Island:** This stretch of water covers about 150 miles from Point Baker on the northwest corner of the island to Cape Chacon, its southern tip in Dixon Entrance. It offers some of the most scenic and protected waters in southeast Alaska with many narrow passages and untold numbers of anchorages. Good salmon fishing is to be found in several locations, especially along the outer islands.

★ **Point Baker (60):** Located at the north end of Prince of Wales Island, this lovely, sheltered harbor is the site of a float, sea plane float, Lodges & B & B's. The float accommodates about 27 vessels and has power and seasonal water. There is a grid nearby. Sport fishing is good in the immediate vicinity, as are opportunities for eagle, whale, and dolphin watching. Visit the World Class caves discovered at nearby El Capitan Mountain. The Caves are open May - Sept. For open hours, age restrictions, and other information, call weekdays to 907-828-3304.

★ **Port Protection (61):** [17378] This small settlement is in Wooden Wheel Cove on the east side of Port Protection. There is 250-foot, state float and seaplane float, some houses and private floats, and a general store. A grid is located near the private floats. Anchorage is found farther into the bay on the east side, south of Wooden Wheel Cove, behind the small islands, in ten fathoms of water on a mud bottom. George Vancouver named this site when he sought refuge from a storm in Sumner Strait. Stretch your legs on a walk around the boardwalk. If you visit in June, bring a dish to share and enjoy food, music, art and fun at the annual Solstice Festival. ⚓

Wooden Wheel Cove Trading Post: Gas, diesel, lubes, potable water, showers, laundry, hardware, groceries, liquor, mail drop, bait, tackle, fishing licenses. 907-489-2222. VHF 16.

★ **Shakan Strait:** [17387] Shakan Bay and Shakan Strait lead to the north entrance to El Capitan Passage, between Prince of Wales Island and Koscuisko Island.

Bay at Marble Creek: This bay is being used by commercial boats involved in the mining operations at Maple Creek. If there is room, anchorage is in six fathoms of water on mud.

Calder Bay: This bay has anchorage, on the east side in five fathoms of water on a soft bottom, however, it is open to prevailing winds and can be uncomfortable.

★ **El Capitan Passage:** This is the most spectacular part of this trip. The first three and one-half miles from Shakan Strait to Aneskett Point have been dredged through several shoals. Controlling depth in Dry Pass is seven feet for a width of 70 feet. Currents in Dry Pass run to 1.8 knots to the east on the flood, and 0.9 knots to the west on the ebb. High and low water in this area occur at about the same time as Sitka. El Capitan Passage continues south for 18 miles to Sea Otter Sound.

★ **Sarheen Cove:** This little cove on the east side of El Capitan Passage offers well protected anchorage in seven to eight fathoms, soft bottom.

Tokeen: A marble quarry and fish processing facility were formerly located here on the west side of El Capitan Island, at the south end of El Capitan Passage. Some floats and a store, where gas may be available, have been at the site.

★ **Sarkar Cove:** This cove is located on the east side of El Capitan Passage, about 18 miles south of Shakan Strait. Anchorage is in seven fathoms of water over a mud bottom. The ruins of the abandoned mining town of Deweyville are on the north side of the cove. Continuing south, you must decide which side of Tuxekan Island to traverse. To the west, the route continues in El Capitan Passage and Sea Otter Sound and Karheen Passage. To the east are Tuxekan Narrows and Tuxekan Passage. Both are marked with navigational aids. The two routes join at the south end of Tuxekan Island at Kauda Point. The route continues south through Tonowek Bay and San Cristoval Channel into San Alberto Bay and Klawock Inlet. There are two villages in Klawock Inlet.

★ **Sea Otter Sound:** [17403] Good salmon fishing around Surf Point at the entrance to the sound.

★ **Port Alice:** Anchorage possible near the head in 8 to 15 fathoms.

★ **Edna Bay:** When entering the harbor use caution and watch for the shoals marked by buoys. There is a State float in East Edna Bay that connects to the shore, {55° 56.99' N, 133° 39.60' W}. No water, power, garbage or waste oil dump facilities. Grid is available. Use honor box to pay for moorage. Edna Bay timber was used to build Howard Hughes' "Spruce Goose."

★ **Heceta Island:** [17360, 17404] A cove on the northeast corner of the island about 1¼ miles southwest at the light on Peep Rock offers well protected anchorage in eight fathoms, mud bottom.

★ **Nossuck Anchorage:** This anchorage, about one mile southwest of Tonowek Narrows, has good anchorage in nine fathoms, on a mud bottom.

Harmony Islands: If the seas are rough in Tonowek Bay, it is possible to avoid some of them by passing to the east of these islands, located about three miles southwest of Tonowek Narrows. At the south end you can come out either between Culebra and St. Philip Islands, or continue east of St. Philip.

★ **Gulf of Esquibel:** Good salmon fishing, coho, at the San Lorenzo Islands on the west side of the sound. The fish were in shallow water along the southeast shore of the eastern most of the two islands.

Prince of Wales Island — Photo © Andrea Izzotti

★ **Steamboat Bay:** Located on Noyes Island about 20-25 miles from Craig, there are some facilities here for commercial fisherman. Anchorage is possible near the head of the bay in 12-18 fathoms, soft bottom. There is exposure to the north and swells may enter the bay.

★ **Klawock (62):** [17405] This Tlingit village of 800 is the site of the first salmon cannery in Alaska, built in 1878. Locals are proud of their Totem Park situated just above the harbor where 22 outstanding poles have been relocated from Tuxecan, on the north end of POW Island. Totem restoration is an ongoing process, and new poles are always raised amid great ceremony. In 2018, a totem pole to honor Alaska Veterans was raised in a three day celebration. It stands in Veterans Memorial Park, up the hill from Totem Park. Another place of interest is Klawock's fish hatchery, the second oldest hatchery in Alaska. A public float and grid are near the town center. Contact the Harbormaster at 907-755-2260. Water is available (use your own hose), no power for transient moorage. A boat launch ramp is north of the cannery. A fuel stop with gas and diesel, a supermarket, restaurant, bank, and a Liquor/Tobacco store are all found about 1.5 miles away on the main highway. Groceries are delivered to the dock at no charge, call 907-755-2722. An airstrip lies a few miles northeast of Klawock.

★ **Craig (63):** [17405] This bustling town of 1,200 residents, was named after turn-of-the-century salmon salter Craig Millar. The use of his first name illustrates the casualness and friendliness of the town. Craig is home to the Healing Heart Totem, carved by Tsimpsian master Stan Marsden. Raised by the community in 1995, this magnificent pole stands in a totem park about one half mile east of the harbors. Craig has a supermarket one block east of the harbors that delivers to the docks, spend $50 to get free delivery. Call 907-826-3394. The town has a full range of services including several restaurants, a garage, hardware stores, public swimming pool, library, post office, hotels, medical and dental clinic, banks, rental cars, engine and marine repairs, laundromat, gift shops and internet access. An ice house for commercial and public flake ice is located about one quarter mile north of Craig on False Island right next to Petro Marine Fuels. There is also a 3.6-ton crane, a public sport fishing dock for cleaning fish (no moorage), and a boat launch at this location. The harbor department operates a haulout that accommodates vessels up to 52' and up to 50-tons. Boat harbor floats are located in the north and south coves, as well as City Float in the old downtown area. The entrance channel to South Cove has been dredged to minus eleven feet. Be cautious maneuvering in and approaching the harbor. Check your chart carefully. The Harbormaster suggests, "When approaching Craig from the north, pass on the east side (fuel dock side) of green buoy #7 and watch the chart carefully." The North Cove transient float is just inside the floating breakwater and is T-shaped. South Cove has a dog-leg shaped transient float just as you enter the harbor. Heading southwest from Craig, the route is through Ulloa Channel, after rounding Cape Flores. For additional community or harbor information, www.craigak.com.

Craig City Dock: {55° 28.667' N, 132° 09.105' W} Moorage, water, grid, 3,800lbs/1.9-ton hoist. 907-826-3404. VHF 16.

Craig Petro Marine Services: Gas, diesel, oils, propane, marine batteries, water. 907-826-3296. VHF 16.

North Cove Harbor: {55° 28.685' N, 133° 08.650' W} Moorage, 30/50 amp power, water, oil waste deposit, grid, launch ramp. 907-826-3404. VHF 16.

South Cove Harbor: {55° 28.505' N, 133° 08.589' W} Moorage, 30/50 amp power, water, grid, Harbormaster's Office, restroom, coin-op showers. 907-826-3404. VHF 16.

Early morning crossing of the Dixon Entrance Photo © Carolyn Van Calcar

Port Estrella: About seven miles south of Craig, and just east of Cape Flores, this bay offers anchorage in seven fathoms, mud bottom. It is exposed to west winds, however, and may be uncomfortable under some circumstances.

★ **Port Refugio:** Port Refugio is about three miles south of Cape Flores, down Ulloa Channel. This bay offers good, well protected anchorage in six to seven fathoms on mud, at the head of the bay, on the south side of the small island. Waterfall Resort, is found across from Point Bocas on Ulloa Channel. The resort, once the site of a busy cannery, is now a private fishing lodge.

Port Real Marina: [17406] This passage between Lulu Island and Baker Island leads to Siketi Sound and the Pacific Ocean. Good salmon fishing reported around south end of Cone Island in Siketi Sound. At the east end the bight between Santa Rita Island and St. Ignace Island offers the best anchorage in the area in ten fathoms, soft bottom.

★ **North Bay:** [17407] About 2½ miles south of Tlevak Narrows, this anchorage on the east side of Dall Island offers well protected anchorage in 10 to 12 fathoms, mud bottom.

★ **Hydaburg (64):** [17407] This hospitable Haida Native village of 500 has a large harbor with a dock and approach located about 1.5 miles north of town. The facility primarily serves the local resident fishing fleet, but transient moorage is possible if space is available. The city's Search & Rescue vessel and active EMS team can be reached by calling "The Haida Watchman" on VHF channel 16 or 65 should you need assistance. Gas and diesel can be purchased at a landbased station. There is a grocery store at the south end of town near the cold storage. The cold storage, which is no longer in operation, still affords a good place to tie up for a short time. A new Seafood Specialty Plant processes value added seafood and includes a retail shop stocked with a line of local products like teas and berries. Tie up to the newly renovated dock adjacent to the plant while you shop. Hydaburg's Totem Park is a big attraction and includes 21 replicated totems. There is also often open where visitors can view Haida carvers at work. The Haida longhouse holds cultural events. The community holds a Culture Camp each year during the last full week in July and welcomes attendees from around the state and country. Hydaburg is about 40 miles from Craig by road. After leaving Hydaburg, the course is to Cape Chacon on the southeast tip of Prince of Wales, through Sukkwan Straight and Cordova Bay.

Hydaburg City Dock: {55° 12.667' N, 132° 49.833' W} Moorage, 30 amp power, water, oil deposit, boat launch, grid. Harbormaster: 907-401-1742. City: 907-285-3761.

★ **Hetta Inlet (65):** [17431] This 12 mile long inlet starts at Eek Point, about 12 miles southeast of Hydaburg. Around the turn of the century it was the site of several copper mines, and at least one smelter, long ago abandoned. There are two good anchorages. Eek Inlet has well protected anchorage in nine fathoms on mud, and Deer Bay, about 6 miles farther north offers protected anchorage in seven fathoms, good holding.

★ **Kaasa Inlet:** There is good, protected anchorage at the head of the north arm in nine fathoms, soft bottom.

★ **Mabel Bay:** This is an excellent anchorage behind Mabel Island, which is two miles southeast of Mellen Rock light. The anchorage is at the east end of the bay in 12 fathoms of water over a mud bottom. It is attractive as well as being well protected. The final decision in getting to Cape Chacon is whether to go by Round Island light and the outside, or through Eureka Channel in the Barrier Islands. The latter is well marked and offers more protection.

★ **Jackson Island:** [17431] This island in Cordova Bay off the southeast end of Sukkwan Island is a good spot for chinook and coho salmon fishing along its southeast shore. The unnamed bay on Sukkwan Island one mile north of Jackson Island has anchorage in ten fathoms, soft bottom, but open to the southeast. A good temporary anchorage.

★ **Long Island:** [17431] Elbow Bay on the northeast shore of Long Island has an anchorage at the head of its southeast arm in ten fathoms. Soft bottom, good protection. Enter Elbow Bay to the south of the two small islands in the entrance then avoid the shoals on the east side and the center of the bay. Long Island has been heavily logged so the scenery is not the best.

★ **Cape Chacon (66):** [17433] See current table for Wrangell Narrows. The charts have warnings of tide rips in two locations, and they are undoubtedly present under the right conditions when swells, wind, and/or tidal currents oppose each other. When approaching the cape, weather information for Dixon Entrance should be available from both Annette Island (Ketchikan) and Prince Rupert. There are more decisions to be made at Cape Chacon, (1) Prince Rupert is 72 nautical miles to the southeast, (2) Brundige Inlet on the north end of Dundas Island is about 40 miles. Both lie across Dixon Entrance. There are some charted, but unmarked, rocks and shoals to avoid. The third, more protected route is northwest to the end of Annette Island, then along the north side of Duke Island to Danger Passage and into Revillagigedo Channel, where one turns south to Dundas Island and Prince Rupert. A fourth possibility is northeast to Ketchikan, about 45 miles, through Nichols Passage.

Annette Island

★ **Metlakatla (67):** [17434, 17435] In 1887, lay missionary William Duncan and 826 of his followers settled this community of Tsimshian people. Located on Port Chester, which is on the east side of Nichols Passage, Metlakatla is now home to 1,400 permanent residents. Two protected harbors are within the village, both offering electrical hookups and water access. The marine ways is covered and capable of handling boats to 60'. Local retail shops are convenient to the harbors. Groceries are available at AC Company Market and the Mini Mart. The Mini Mart also features fresh baked goods, fast food and videos. Metco is a small hardware/variety store. The Metlakatla Hotel and Laughing Berry Inn offer public lodging. Tourism is a new enterprise for Metlakatla. Duncan Cottage Museum and community totem poles are among the local sights to visit. During the summer cruise ship season, Metlakatla Tours offers performances of Tsimshian Dancers in full regalia at the Tribal Longhouse and a visit to the Artist's Village. Here stores, including the Laughing Berry Gift Shop, House of the Wolf, Raven Dancer Creations and others carry hand crafted local jewelry, carvings and baskets, as well as t-shirts and other souvenirs. For visitor information, contact Metlakatla Tourism at 907-886-TOUR, May through October. Silver Bay Seafoods operates a cold storage year round for the community-owned fishing fleet, which harvests seafood such as salmon, halibut, and sea cucumbers. Metlakatla is accessible from Ketchikan by boat and floatplane. Pacific Air offers the 10-minute plane ride on daily schedules. Metlakatla is homeport to M/V Lituya, a 180' Alaska State ferry that makes two scheduled round trips between Metlakatla and Ketchikan on Thursdays through Sundays. There is no ferry service on Tuesdays or Wednesdays.

Annette Island Gas Services: Delivers gas, diesel and oils to the Port dock. Propane also available. 907-886-7851.

Metlakatla Harbor: {55° 07.856' N, 131° 35.098' W} Moorage, no power at transient float, water at port dock, haul-out (60' long, 17' wide). Harbormaster: 907-886-4646 or 907-886-4011. VHF 16, 80.

Duke Island

★ **Ryus Bay (68):** On the north side of Duke Island, Ryus Bay offers a sheltered anchorage in seven to ten fathoms of water over a mud bottom.

Essential Supplies & Services

AIR TRANSPORTATION
Alaska Airlines 1-800-252-7522
Alaska Seaplanes 907-789-3331
Pacific Airways Ketchikan 907-225-3500
Seattle Seaplanes 1-800-637-5553
Taquan Air 907-225-8800, 1-800-770-8800
Ward Air, Juneau 907-789-9150

BOOKS / BOOK STORES
Evergreen Pacific Publishing 425-493-1451
The Marine Atlas 253-872-5707
**Tongass Trading Co
.... 1-800-235-5102, 907-225-5101**

COAST GUARD
All areas: VHF 16, HF 2182 mhz
*CG from cell phone (limited providers)
Ketchikan: VHF 13, 16, ... 907-228-0340
Prince Rupert: VHF 16, 83A 250-627-3081
Rescue Coordination: Ketchikan - VHF 22, Petersburg, Sitka - VHF 28

CUSTOMS
Ketchikan 907-225-2254
Canadian 888-226-7277

FERRY INFO
www.state.ak.us/ferry ... 907-465-3941, 800-642-0066
Inter-Island 907-530-4848, 1-866-308-4848

FISHING / SHELLFISHING INFO
Shellfishing (PSP info) 907-269-7630
Sportfishing recorded info
Haines, Skagway 907-766-2625
Juneau 907-465-4116

FUELS
Annette Island: Gas, Diesel 907-886-7851
Angoon: Gas, Diesel 907-788-3436
Auke Bay: Gas, Diesel 907-790-3030
Bartlett Cove: Gas, Diesel .... VHF 16
Clover Pass Resort: Gas, Diesel 907-247-2234
Coffman Cove: Gas, Diesel 907-329-2233
Craig: Gas, Diesel, Propane .... 907-826-3296 VHF 16
Delta Western, Sitka: .... 907-747-4999 VHF 16
Elfin Cove: Gas, Diesel ...... 907-239-2208 VHF 72
Fisherman's: Auke Bay. Gas, Diesel 907-789-7312
Haines Gas, Diesel ...... 907-766-6450 VHF 12,16
Hoonah: Gas, Diesel ...... 907-945-3211 VHF 11
Juneau/Douglas Petro Marine Services: Gas, Diesel. . . . 907-586-4400
Kake 907-465-7730
Ketchikan Petro Marine: Gas, diesel, propane
.... 907-225-2106 VHF 16
Knudson Cove: Gas, Diesel ... 907-247-8500 VHF 16
Metlakatla: Gas, Diesel .... 907-886-7851, VHF 72
Pelican: Gas, Diesel Propane ... 907-735-2211 VHF 10
Petersburg Petro: Gas, Diesel ... 907-772-4251 VHF 16
Petro Marine Services Juneau: Gas, Diesel
.... 907-586-4400
Petro Marine Services: KTN South. Gas, Diesel
.... 907-225-2106
Petro Marine Services: KTN North, Gas, Diesel
.... 907-225-1731
Port Protection: Gas, Diesel .... 907-489-2222 VHF 16
Sitka Petro: (South) Gas, Diesel
.... 907-747-3414 VHF 16
Sitka Petro: (North) Gas, Diesel. 907-747-3414 VHF 16
Skagway Petro: Gas, Diesel 907-983-2259
Tenakee Springs: Gas, Diesel ... 907-736-2288 VHF 16
Thorne Bay: Port at Thorne Bay 907-828-3995
Wrangell: Gas, Diesel 907-874-3276

HAUL-OUT
Air Marine Harbor: Ketchikan 907-225-2282
Craig 907-826-3404
Halibut Point Marine: Sitka 907-747-1089
Harri Commercial Marine: Juneau 907-321-0389
Harri Commercial Marine: Auke Bay.... 907-789-5250
Hoonah Harbor 907-945-3670
Metlakatla 907-886-4646
Skagway Boat Basin .... 907-983-2628 VHF 16
Shoemaker Bay Harbor 907-874-3736
Wrangell 907-874-3736

HOSPITALS / CLINICS
Juneau Hospital 907-586-2611
Kake Health Clinic 907-785-3333
Ketchikan Medical Center 907-225-5171
Metlakatla Clinic 907-886-4741
Petersburg Medical Center 907-772-4291
Sitka Community Hospital 907-747-3241
Skagway Clinic 907-983-2255
Wrangell 907-874-7000

LIQUOR STORES
Craig   Ketchikan   Port Protection
Haines   Meyer's Chuck Sitka
Juneau   Petersburg   Wrangell

Thorne Bay 907-828-8233

MARINAS / MOORAGE
Angoon Boat Harbor 907-788-3653
Clover Pass Resort .... 907-247-2234 VHF 16
Coffman Cove .... 907-329-2233 VHF 16
Couverden Island
Craig .... 907-826-3404 VHF 16
Douglas Harbor 907-586-5255
Doyon's Landing 907-225-5155
Edna Bay, Elfin Cove, Entrance Island, Gustavus
Haines Small Boat Harbor ... 907-766-6450 VHF 12,16
Helm Bay, Hobart Bay, Hollis
Hoonah .... 907-945-3670 VHF 16
Hydaburg City Dock 907-401-1742
Hyder
Juneau .... 907-586-5255 VHF 73
Kake 907-465-7730
Kasaan
Ketchikan Harbors .... 907-228-5632 VHF 16, 73
Ketchikan Moorage 907-220-6384
Ketchikan Yacht Club 907-225-3262
Klawock 907-755-2260
Knudson Cove Marina .... 907-247-8500 VHF 16
Letnikof Cove
Metlakatla .... 907-886-4646 VHF 16
Meyers Chuck
Papkes Landing: Wrangell Narrows
Pelican .... 907-735-2201 VHF 9, 16
Petersburg Harbor ..... 907-772-4688 VHF 9, 16
Port Alexander
Port Protection
Refuge Cove Marina 907-225-1958
Sitka: All moorages .... 907-747-3439 VHF 16
Skagway .... 907-983-2628 VHF 16
Statter Harbor/Auke Bay ..... 907-789-0819 VHF 16
Stewart: British Columbia 250-636-2626
Taku Harbor
Tenakee Springs .... 907-736-2207 VHF 16
Thorne Bay .... 907-828-3380, 907-965-4138 VHF 16
West Petersburg
Wrangell .... 907-874-3736 VHF 16

MARINE SUPPLY STORES
**Tongass Trading Co
.... 1-800-235-5102, 907-225-5101**

RAMPS
Craig, Echo Cove (Juneau), Hollis, Hyder, Kake,
Air Marine Harbor: KTN Refuge Cove ... 907-225-2282
Auke Bay 907-789-4225
Douglas Harbor 907-586-5255
Halibut Point Marine: Sitka ..... 907-747-4999 VHF 16
Haines Small Boat Harbor ... 907-766-6450 VHF 12,16
Heritage Harbor 907-874-3736
Hoonah Harbor 907-945-3670
Juneau .... 907-586-5255 VHF 16
Ketchikan: Bar Harbor, Mountain Point, Knudson Cove
Klawock 907-755-2260
Letnikof Cove 907-766-6450
North Cove Harbor 907-826-3404
Piston & Rudder Services, Petersburg .. 907-772-4500
Reliance Harbor Float .... 907-874-3736 VHF 16
Shoemaker Bay Harbor .... 907-874-3736 VHF 16
Skagway Boat Basin .... 907-983-2628 VHF 16
Thorne Bay .... 907-828-3380, 907-965-4138 VHF 16
Wrangell .... 907-874-3736 VHF 16
Willies Marine: Juneau 907-789-4831

REPAIRS
Air Marine Harbor: Ketchikan 907-225-2282
Canal Marine: Haines 907-766-2437
Harbor Marine: Hoonah 907-945-3722
NC Machinery: Juneau 907-789-0181
Northern Communications: Juneau 907-789-0008
Piston & Rudder Services, Petersburg .. 907-772-4500
Tanner's Service: Douglas (outboards) .. 907-364-2434
Willies Marine: Juneau 907-789-4831

TAXIS
Ketchikan 907-225-5555, 907-225-2133
Ketchikan Rental Company 907-225-5000
Juneau 907-780-6400, 907-790-5555
Petersburg 907-772-2222
Sitka 907-747-5001
Wrangell 907-874-4646

SEWAGE DISPOSAL
Auke Bay: Pump
Aurora Harbor: Juneau: Pump
Douglas Harbor 907-586-5255
Haines Pump .... 907-766-6450 VHF 12,16
Juneau .... 907-586-5255 VHF 16
Ketchikan: Thomas Basis, Casey Moran Harbor & Bar Harbor: Pump
Petersburg Harbor .... 907-772-4688 VHF 9, 16
Skagway Pump .... 907-983-2628 VHF 16
Wrangell: pump .... 907-874-3736 VHF 16

VISITOR INFORMATION
Gustavus 907-500-5143
Haines 907-766-6418, 1-800-458-3579
Juneau 907-586-2201, 1-888-581-2201
Ketchikan 907-225-6166
Pelican 907-735-2202
Petersburg 907-772-4636
Prince of Wales Island 907-755-2626
Sitka 907-747-8604
Skagway 907-983-2854
Thorne Bay 907-828-3380
Wrangell 907-874-2829, 1-800-367-9745

WEATHER
Ketchikan: WX-1, Petersburg: WX-1 Dundas Island, WX-2
Juneau: WX-1 907-586-3997
Sitka 907 747-6011
Wrangell: WX-2 907-874-3232
SE Alaska 1-800-472-0391 (4)

Crossing The Straits & Other Large Bodies Of Water

Gorge Harbour (p. 189-190)   Photo © Gorge Harbour Marina

Preparing for crossings: There are a few general rules that apply to the crossing of any large body of water, or to preparation for any long cruise. First, it is a good idea for the captain to become familiar with the boat, trying it out in local calm and rough waters before tackling unfamiliar seas. The second is to learn to be aware of, and to travel with, the wind and the tide. Waiting for calm weather, not being in a hurry, and timing travels to the encountered weather will make for a more pleasant and safer trip. Before and during crossings, maintain weather watches on VHF weather channels. The vessel should have plenty of fuel, water, and supplies. Furnishings and gear should be secured and stowed before rough seas are encountered.

Strait of Juan de Fuca: This body of water connects Puget Sound and the Pacific Ocean. It is 12-16 miles wide and extends in length about 80 miles from Whidbey Island to Cape Flattery. Since the winds on this strait tend to rise in the afternoon, the best time of day for crossing this strait is usually in the early morning. Wind flow in the central strait is either east or west. Western entrance weather is more like the west coast of Vancouver Island. This is the Strait of Juan de Fuca forecast and conditions that are given on Canadian weather stations. The inland strait has weather more like that in the lower Georgia Strait. These are the weather forecast and conditions given on American weather stations. Sea fog near the west entrance is caused when northwest air is pulled over the cold water. There are more fog banks on the south side of the entrance than on the Victoria side. Tides for this strait are listed in the Canadian Tide and Current Tables, Volume Five. Between Sooke Inlet and Race Rocks the flood stream is strongest near the Canadian shore. When wind and sea collide, choppy, sometimes dangerous seas result in some areas. Especially heavy rips are found off Cape Flattery, Race Rocks, New Dungeness, Point Wilson, between Beechey Head and Esquimalt, and off the Trial Islands.

Strait of Georgia: This body of water, 125 miles long and about 20 miles wide, is not the biggest strait along the Inside Passage, but it is the most traversed by pleasure boaters. While this body of water is certainly deserving of a great deal of respect, the use of knowledge and good judgment is the best assurance of a good crossing. Most boaters take advantage of the protection afforded by Texada Island and use Malaspina Strait, on the east side of Texada, to travel the Sunshine Coast. For this crossing, the problem is getting to the southeast end of Texada Island. Boaters headed north from Vancouver, pass Howe Sound, Gibsons, and Sechelt on their way to Welcome Pass. This does not require crossing the strait, but there is a run of about 16 miles along the northeast shore from Gower Point to Merry Island. Boaters headed north from the Gulf Islands must choose between three routes: (1) Nanaimo to Welcome Pass; (2) Silva Bay to Welcome Pass; and (3) Nanaimo to Ballenas Islands and north about eight and one-half nautical miles to Point Upwood on Texada Island. The first is about five miles shorter than the others. The second has a favorable heading for quartering seas caused by prevailing summer winds out of the northwest. The third avoids military range Whiskey Golf, making it a possible route when Whiskey Golf is active, and it also leads to exploration of the Vancouver Island side of the Strait. Finally, for those travelling between Vancouver and the Gulf Islands, the Burrard-Point Grey to Silva Bay-Gabriola Pass crossing is about 20 miles and the Burrard-Point Grey to Porlier Pass crossing is about 21 miles.

One complicating factor in the Nanaimo-Welcome Pass area is the Canadian Naval area known as Whiskey-Golf. This area is designated on government charts. In the water, the active area is marked by orange can-buoys. The Canadian and American Armed Forces use this range for firing of non-explosive surface or air launched torpedoes. There are uncharted, lighted and unlighted, buoys within the area, as well as range vessels. During operations, this area is extremely dangerous to mariners. For a chart of the area, details, and times of operation, see Canadian National Defense Notice in Chapter 15 of this guide. Also see Important Notices between Chapter 7 and Chapter 8. If necessary, call Winchelsea Control on VHF Channel 10 or 16.

It is possible to avoid area Whisky-Golf by crossing from Silva Bay-Flat Top Islands to Merry Island on a heading of 310 degrees magnetic or by leaving Nanaimo on a course heading for Bowen Island, turning to port after passing area Whiskey-Golf. If the latter course is used, care must be exercised to avoid the natural tendency to change course too early and cross the eastern end of the active area. Another possible route is from Departure Bay, passing north of Winchelsea Island and east of Ballenas Island in a designated non-firing area.

Valuable information may be obtained on your VHF marine radio. Boaters who travel regularly in Canadian waters should install channels 21B (161.65) in addition to WX-1 (162.55), WX-2 (162.40) and WX-3 (162.475). These channels have continuous Canadian weather broadcasts and are received at different locations along the coast. See the Marine Weather Guide in the Important Notices section of this book for more information. Channels 84 and 26 are also useful for obtaining information. You may also call Victoria Radio first on Channel 16 and then switch to Channels 84, 26 or 83A to talk to the operator. It is important to note that sea conditions will often vary widely on the two sides of the strait. Thus, you may begin crossing in what appears to be very flat water only to find yourself half-way across being battered by seas you did not expect. Getting current sea conditions for both sides of the strait is helpful. The wind and sea conditions at Merry Island (on the Welcome Pass side) and Entrance Island (on the Nanaimo side) will provide information about the two sides of the strait. The wind reports taken at Sisters and Ballenas Islands will describe the middle of the strait. For those making the Burrard Inlet to Silva Bay crossing, the wind and sea conditions at Sand Heads will be helpful on the Burrard side, as will the Entrance Island conditions on the Silva Bay side. To enter the Georgia Strait without knowing both present conditions and the forecast is foolhardy indeed.

Wind and sea conditions on the Georgia Strait are quite different from those on the Juan de Fuca Strait or the Queen Charlotte Sound. Developing an adequate plan for crossing requires specific knowledge about the strait. There are a few axioms concerning the Georgia Strait that have served yachtsmen well for some years.

(1) The probability is that the weather tomorrow will be more like the weather today than it will be like any other day.

(2) If the wind comes up in the morning, it will go down in the late afternoon. This illustrates the wisdom of the First Nations, who navigated the waters of this strait long before white men appeared. In the summer, the prevailing wind on the Georgia Strait is from the northwest. This

is a fair-weather wind and must be distinguished from a storm wind which generally flows from the southeast. Many prefer to cross the strait in the afternoon when this fair weather wind goes down. The seas on the Georgia Strait calm down quickly following these warm-weather winds. Once the wind is down in the later afternoon, it is unlikely that it will come up again until after dark. Thus, a boater leaving Nanaimo or Welcome Pass at 5:00 or 6:00 p.m., after having observed that the wind has gone down, is quite likely to have several hours of calm wind to traverse the Strait of Georgia in peace. Some boaters prefer a morning crossing as the water is often as smooth as glass at daybreak. But this crossing can be treacherous because the wind will often begin to rise before the crossing is completed.

(3) Another First Nation axiom holds that if the northwest fair weather wind does not go down in the late afternoon, it will blow for three days. Not only can you assume that you are probably in for a three-day blow, but it is also unlikely that there will be an opportunity to cross the strait comfortably and safely for the next few days. Following such a three-day blow, be alert for the subsiding of the wind in the late afternoon. This is your opportunity to cross, an opportunity that may not come again for another three or four days.

(4) When a southeasterly wind is blowing, there is no preferred crossing time, and it will be best to forget crossing until the storm is over.

(5) If the decks are wet with dew in the evening, it is almost a sure sign that the following day will be bright and clear and that the prevailing fair weather winds will be blowing.

Discovery Passage and Johnstone Strait: Although this strait is only about two to three miles wide, the waters of this 50-mile stretch from Cape Mudge to Blackfish Sound, can be difficult. Tide rips of dangerous proportions may be encountered off Cape Mudge on a flood tide and strong south winds. Seymour Narrows has tides of up to 16 knots at springs. Passage here is recommended near slack waters, using the British Columbia Tide and Current Tables. At Ripple Shoal, Current, and Race Passages, tides can run five to seven knots, with heavy tide rips possible. The main problem in all of these waters is having the tides, which can be strong, and winds opposed to each other, causing very uncomfortable conditions with quite steep seas.

One very popular alternative to Discovery Passage and southeastern Johnstone Strait is to take the more protected eastern route from the Desolation Sound-Discovery Passage area to the Stuart Island area, passing through Yuculta, Gillard and Dent Rapids, Cordero Channel, Green Point Rapids, Chancellor Channel, Wellbore Channel, Whirlpool Rapids, and Sunderland Channel, escaping the lower part of the Johnstone Strait entirely. The rapids are traversed easily at times of slack water, using the Tide and Current Tables. The flood tides come around the north and south ends of Vancouver Island, meeting near Cape Mudge and Stuart Island. Careful planning with the current tables can make it possible to approach either of these points travelling with the flooding tide, crossing the point of the meeting currents near slack water, and proceeding on the other side with the ebbing tide.

Clark Island (p. 106)   Photo © Chris Teren / TerenPhotography.com

From the west end of Hardwicke Island to Broken Islands there is no choice but to tackle the strait for about 12 miles. This area is often windy and tide rips can be encountered. Port Neville offers the best shelter, if escape is needed. The eight miles between Port Neville and the Broken Islands are usually the roughest part of this passage. At the Broken Islands the alternatives are to enter Havanna Channel, and go through Chatham Channel to Clio Channel or Knight Inlet, or to continue on 20 miles west to the end of Johnstone Strait. Weather conditions may make the decision for you.

Queen Charlotte Strait & Queen Charlotte Sound: Queen Charlotte Strait, to the southeast of Queen Charlotte Sound, lies between Queen Charlotte Sound and Johnstone Strait. Weather and wind patterns sometimes resemble Queen Charlotte Sound, and sometimes resemble Johnstone Strait. Weather conditions can be determined by listening to WX-1, Alert Bay weather. Queen Charlotte Strait is adjacent to the beautiful islands rimming the mainland in the Fife Sound and Kingcome Inlet areas.

Queen Charlotte Sound is often the most difficult of the Big Waters to traverse safely. There is about a 40 nautical mile stretch that is open to the Pacific Ocean and sizable swells. The topography of the sound is such that the bottom rises from the continental shelf to a depth as shallow as 17 fathoms. This has an amplifying effect upon swells and waves. During the ebbing tide there are currents coming from the straits, sounds, and inlets to the south, north, and east. These ebbing currents collide with each other and with the incoming swells in the sound. This is a recipe for rough waters, especially if the wind is blowing. Indeed, unusually strong tidal currents and wave heights have occasionally been observed in this area. The British Columbia Sailing Directions reports observations of waves as high as 90 to 100 feet in storm and hurricane force winds. Even after the passage of such storms, the effects on the currents in the area can last three to four days.

Fortunately, gale and storm force winds are rare in summer months, so many crossings are made in quiet waters. Fog can be encountered anytime, but is most frequent from August through October. Many sport fishermen put their boats in the water at Port Hardy and make the 50-mile crossing to Rivers Inlet. Port Hardy makes a good starting point to prepare for the crossing and to study the weather reports and patterns. The most critical point is Egg Island. The lighthouse located there gives local conditions on the Alert Bay Radio weather reports on WX-1. When passing Egg Island, may want to call "Egg Yolk" on VHF 16 to say "Hello" to the caretaker. It is also possible to call Alert Bay Radio on Channel 16, switch to Channel 26, and request the latest sea and weather conditions and forecast for the Queen Charlotte crossing.

Nearby provisioning points include Alert Bay (no fuel), Echo Bay Marina and Lodge, Sullivan Bay Marina Resort, Telegraph Cove Marina, Port Hardy, Port McNeill, and Sointula (fuel by arranged delivery). Starting points include Allison Harbour, Blunden Harbour, Bull Harbour, God's Pocket, Miles Inlet, and Skull Cove. Destination points include Rivers Inlet, Pruth Anchorage, Safety Cove, and Smith Sound.

Milbanke Sound: The exposure here is for a short duration compared to Queen Charlotte Sound and Dixon Entrance. Most of the direct exposure to the Pacific Ocean is during the seven miles from Ivory Island to Vancouver Rock. This sound can be avoided by travelling through Reid Channel, or partially avoided by heading east-north-east toward Mathieson Channel after rounding Ivory Island.

Dixon Entrance: Topographically, this deep trough separates the north end of the Haida Gwaii Islands from Dall and Prince of Wales Islands. Fog plagues these waters from July to October. The crossing is about 20 miles. Nearby starting points are Brundige Inlet or Port Simpson. The closest destination harbor is Foggy Bay in Very Inlet.

Other big southeast Alaska waters: Even though the waters of southeast Alaska are part of the Inside Passage and are "protected" from the Pacific Ocean by one or more islands, there are still some large areas of water where wind and wind against tidal current can cause some very rough seas. Frederick Sound, Chatham Channel, Stephens Passage, Clarence Strait, Lynn Canal, and Icy Strait all deserve respect and careful navigation with an ear and eye to weather and current conditions.

VHF Marine Channels for Pleasure Vessels in Washington & British Columbia

Washington Waters

05A SECTOR PUGET SOUND VESSEL TRAFFIC SERVICE— North of Bush Point and East of Whidbey Island. Vessels not required to participate are highly encouraged to maintain a listening watch. Contact with VTS is encouraged if essential to navigational safety.

06 INTERSHIP SAFETY. Only for ship-to-ship use for safety communications. For Search and Rescue (SAR) liaison with Coast Guard vessels and aircraft.

09 INTERSHIP & SHIP-SHORE ALL VESSELS. Calling & Reply For Pleasure Vessels (optional, U.S. only).

13 Vessel BRIDGE to vessel BRIDGE, large vessels. May also be used to contact locks (in Seattle only) and bridges BUT use sound signals in the Seattle area to avoid dangerous interference to collision avoidance communications between large vessels.

14 SECTOR PUGET SOUND VESSEL TRAFFIC SYSTEM— South of Bush Point and West of Whidbey Island. Vessels not required to participate are highly encouraged to maintain a listening watch. Contact with VTS is encouraged if essential to navigational safety.

16 INTERNATIONAL DISTRESS AND CALLING. Used only for distress and urgency traffic, for Safety calls and contacting other stations. Listen first to make sure no distress traffic is in progress; do not transmit if a SEELONCE MAYDAY is declared. Keep all communications to a minimum. Do not repeat a call to the same station more than once every two minutes. After three attempts wait fifteen minutes before calling the same station.

22A LIAISON AND SAFETY BROADCASTS. A government channel used for Safety and Liaison Communications with the U.S. Coast Guard. Broadcasts announced on channel 16. Canadian Coast Guard does not monitor this channel.

66A PORT OPERATIONS. All marinas in Puget Sound and B.C. are being encouraged to use this common frequency for arranging moorage.

67 INTERSHIP ONLY FOR ALL VESSELS (U.S. only, Puget Sound). Working Channel.

68 INTERSHIP & SHIP-SHORE FOR PLEASURE VESSELS ONLY.

69 INTERSHIP & SHIP-SHORE FOR PLEASURE VESSELS ONLY.

70 DIGITAL SELECTIVE CALLING ONLY (no voice) FOR DISTRESS, SAFETY AND CALLING.

72 INTERSHIP ONLY FOR ALL VESSELS (U.S. only, Puget Sound).

78A INTERSHIP & SHIP-SHORE FOR PLEASURE VESSELS ONLY (In the U.S. only). All marinas in Puget Sound are being encouraged to use this as a secondary working channel.

British Columbia Waters

05A SECTOR PUGET SOUND VESSEL TRAFFIC SERVICE— Juan de Fuca Strait west of Victoria, Rosario Straits, San Juans. Vessels not required to participate are highly encouraged to maintain a listening watch. Contact with VTS is encouraged if essential to navigational safety.

06 INTERSHIP SAFETY. Only for ship-to-ship use for safety communications. For Search and Rescue (SAR) liaison with Coast Guard vessels and aircraft.

09 INTERSHIP & SHIP-SHORE. All Vessels.

11 VESSEL TRAFFIC SERVICE VICTORIA—Strait of Juan de Fuca east of Victoria; Haro Strait; Boundary Passage; Gulf Islands; Strait of Georgia.
VESSEL TRAFFIC SERVICE PRINCE RUPERT—West Coast of Haida Gwaii, Queen Charlotte Sound, Hecate Strait and Inside Passage.

12 VESSEL TRAFFIC SERVICE VICTORIA —Vancouver Harbour, English Bay, and Howe Sound.

16 INTERNATIONAL DISTRESS AND CALLING. Used only for distress and urgency traffic, for Safety calls and contacting other stations. Listen first to make sure no distress traffic is in progress; do not transmit if a SEELONCE MAYDAY is declared. Keep all communications to a minimum. Do not repeat a call to the same station more than once every two minutes. After three attempts wait fifteen minutes before calling the same station.

66A PORT OPERATIONS. All marinas in Puget Sound and B.C. are being encouraged to use this common frequency for arranging moorage.

67 INTERSHIP & SHIP-SHORE. All Vessels. Working Channel.

68 INTERSHIP & SHIP-SHORE. For Pleasure Vessels Only.

69 INTERSHIP & SHIP-SHORE. For Pleasure Vessels Only.

70 DIGITAL SELECTIVE CALLING ONLY (no voice) FOR DISTRESS, SAFETY AND CALLING.

71 VESSEL TRAFFIC SERVICE PRINCE RUPERT—Dixon Entrance to Prince Rupert.

72 INTERSHIP. Pleasure Vessels. Working Channel.

73 INTERSHIP & SHIP-SHORE. Pleasure Vessels. Working Channel.

74 VESSEL TRAFFIC SERVICE VICTORIA—Fraser River. VESSEL TRAFFIC SERVICE PRINCE RUPERT—West Coast of Vancouver Island.

83A COAST GUARD LIAISON. A government channel used for Safety and Liaison Communications with the Coast Guard (B.C. Waters). Also known as Channel 83 in the U.S. mode.

Even though you may use alternate communication means, such as cellular phone, **Monitor VHF 16**. The safety of yourself, your family and your friends is enhanced by a watch on 16 by all vessels.

Radio Emergency Signals

MAYDAY	Vessel threatened by grave and imminent danger and requests immediate assistance.
PAN PAN	Urgent message concerning safety of vessel or person on board or in sight.
SECURITÉ	Message concerning safety of navigation or meteorological warning.
SEELONCE MAYDAY	Mayday in progress, do not transmit normal communications.
SEELONCE FEENE	Resume normal communications.

Visit us at boattravel.com

Marine Distress Communications Form

Complete form now (except for items 5 through 8) and post near your VHF for use in distress.

SPEAK: SLOWLY — CLEARLY — CALMLY

1. Turn VHF on and select Channel 16 (156.8 MHz).
2. Press and hold microphone button and say: **"MAYDAY—MAYDAY—MAYDAY."**
3. Say: **"This is:** _____ _____ _____."
   Your boat name and call sign or registration number repeated three times.
4. Say: **"Mayday** _____."
   Your boat name.
5. **TELL WHERE YOU ARE** (what navigation aids, landmarks or other vessels are near?).
6. **STATE THE NATURE OF YOUR DISTRESS.** (Taking on water, fire aboard, etc.)
7. **GIVE NUMBER OF PERSONS ABOARD AND CONDITIONS OF INJURED.**
8. **ESTIMATE PRESENT SEAWORTHINESS OF YOUR BOAT.**
9. **BRIEFLY DESCRIBE YOUR BOAT:** _____ FEET _____; _____ HULL;
   Length — Type — Color
   _____ TRIM; _____ MASTS:_____
   Color — Number — Anything else you think will help rescuers find you.
10. **SAY "THIS IS** _____, **OVER."**
    Your call sign/boat name.
11. Release microphone button and listen. Someone should answer.

    IF THEY DO NOT, REPEAT CALL, BEGINNING AT ITEM NO. 2 ABOVE.

    If there is still no answer, switch to another channel and begin again.

Consider having every one put on their PFD. If you are drifting without power, putting your anchor out may keep you off the shore. Have your flares or other visual signaling items available for use.

VHF Call Sign or Vessel Name _____

Vessel Registration No. _____

Proper understanding and use of VHF Radio Procedures is essential in order to ensure that VHF remains a useful and reliable safety and communications tool.

VHF Do's and Don'ts

DO	Use Channel 16 only for Distress and Calling.
DO	Call marinas on the working channel (66A or 78A) instead of 16.
DO	Keep all calling to an absolute minimum on Channel 16.
DO	Call coast stations on their working channel and not Channel 16.
DON'T	Try to sneak in short messages on Channel 16.
DO	Listen before transmitting to make sure no distress traffic is in progress.
DO	Stop transmitting when a *SEELONCE MAYDAY* is declared. Resume normal communications when *SEELONCE FEENEE* is declared.
DO	Instruct children on the proper use of the VHF and that it is not a toy.
DO	Call the same station no more than once every two minutes and after three tries wait fifteen minutes.
DO	Use low power at all times. It is required on 13, 14, 5A, and 66A.
DO	Keep all communications to the minimum necessary.
DON'T	Use Channel 16 for radio checks with the Coast Guard. It is not permitted by FCC rules and the Coast Guard doesn't like them on 16. Do your radio checks on a working frequency.
DO	Pick a working channel appropriate to the type of intended communication.
DO	Eliminate idle chit-chat; keep communications to those necessary for the needs of the vessel.
DON'T	Talk on Channel 70–it is reserved for Digital Selective Calling (DSC) for distress, safety and General calling using DSC techniques.
DON'T	Use Channels 1-4 or 60-64 in Puget Sound. They are assigned to land stations only.

For additional information call the FCC Consumer Assistance Branch (888) 225-5322.

DISTANCE TABLES

Place	Page #
Cordero Channel	291
Desolation Sound	291
Discovery Passage	291
East Coast Vancouver Island	289
Georgia Strait	290
Gulf Islands	290
Johnstone Strait	291
Juan de Fuca Strait-South Georgia Strait	288
Northern BC Coast	292
Pender Harbour - Sechelt Inlet	291
Prince Rupert - Haida Gwaii	292
Prince Rupert/Alaska Border	292
Puget Sound	288
Southeast Alaska	292
Sunshine Coast	291
West Coast Vancouver Island	289

Distances in Juan De Fuca Strait, Admiralty Inlet, Puget Sound, and the S.E. part of the Strait of Georgia

Figure at the intersection of columns opposite the places in question is the approximate distance in nautical miles between the two.

Courtesy of the Canadian Hydrographic Service

Port Townsend	Port Ludlow	Port Gamble	Everett	Eagle Harbor	Seattle	Bremerton	Tacoma	Olympia	Anacortes	Bellingham	Blaine	New Westminster	Nanaimo
16													
21	10												
34	25	28											
40	32	34	29										
40	32	34	29	8									
49	41	44	38	13	14								
60	52	55	49	25	25	29							
84	76	79	73	50	50	50	34						
29	42	47	49	66	66	75	86	110					
43	56	61	63	80	80	89	100	124	16				
58	71	76	78	95	95	104	115	139	35	37			
91	104	109	111	128	128	137	148	172	69	70	47		
97	110	115	116	134	134	143	154	178	74	74	53	46	
92	105	110	111	129	129	138	149	173	68	70	47	40	34

Distances in Juan De Fuca Strait, Admiralty Inlet, Puget Sound, and the S.E. part of the Strait of Georgia

Figure at the intersection of columns opposite the places in question is the approximate distance in nautical miles between the two.

Example: Victoria, B.C. is 71 nautical miles from Seattle, Wash.

Courtesy of the Canadian Hydrographic Service

Cape Flattery (Tatoosh Id. Lt. Ho. brg. 150°, 3.5 miles)	Neah Bay	Port Renfrew	Sooke Harbour (Entrance)	Race Rocks Lt. Ho. brg. 000°, 1.5 miles	Port Angeles	Victoria (Ogden Point)	Point Wilson Lt. Ho. brg. 225°, 1 mile	Port Townsend	Port Ludlow	Port Gamble	Everett (See Note 3)	Eagle Harbor	Seattle	Bremerton	Tacoma	Olympia	Anacortes	Bellingham	Blaine	New Westminster	Nanaimo
10																					
16	14																				
43	35	36																			
51	43	44	10																		
61	54	54	21	12																	
61	53	54	20	10	19																
84	76	77	43	33	29	31															
87	79	80	46	36	32	34	3														
100	92	93	59	49	45	47	16	16													
105	97	98	64	54	50	52	21	21	10												
118	110	111	77	67	63	65	34	34	25	28											
124	116	117	83	73	69	71	40	40	32	34	29										
124	116	117	83	73	69	71	40	40	32	34	29	8									
133	125	126	92	82	78	80	49	49	41	44	38	13	14								
144	136	137	103	93	89	91	60	60	52	55	49	25	25	29							
168	160	161	128	117	113	115	84	84	76	79	73	50	50	50	34						
92	84	85	51	41	42	35	26	29	42	47	49	66	66	75	86	110					
106	98	99	65	55	55	49	40	43	56	61	63	80	80	89	100	124	16				
111	103	104	70	60	65	53	55	58	71	76	78	95	95	104	115	139	35	37			
138	130	131	97	87	91	79	88	91	104	109	111	128	128	137	148	172	69	70	47		
143	35	136	102	92	100	85	94	97	110	115	116	134	134	143	154	178	74	74	53	46	
138	130	131	97	87	92	80	89	92	105	110	111	129	129	138	149	173	68	70	47	40	34

Notes:
1. Distances from ports in Juan de Fuca Strait to New Westminster, Nanaimo, and Vancouver are via Boundry Pass. For distances via Active Pass *deduct* 8 miles for Nanaimo, and 7 miles for New Westminster and Vancouver.
2. Distances from ports in Admiralty Inlet and Puget Sound to ports in the S.E. part of the Strait of Georgia are via Rosario Strait and adjacent channels.
3. Distances from Everett, Wash. to Anacortes, Bellingham, and ports in the S.E. part of the Strait of Georgia are by way of Saratoga Passage and Deception Pass. For distances over route west of Whidbey Island and via Rosario Strait *add* 11 miles.

Visit us at boattravel.com

DISTANCE TABLES Page 289

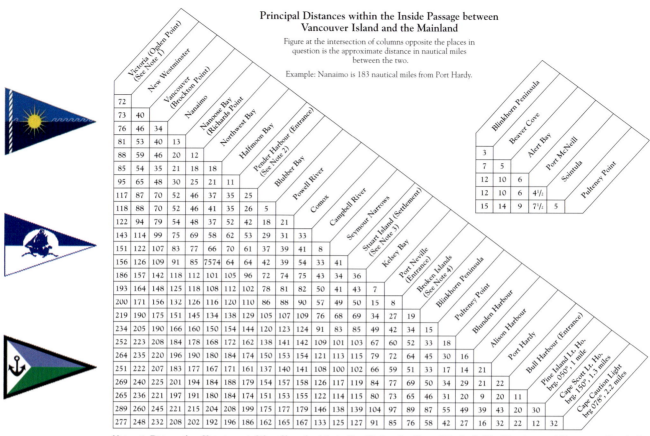

Principal Distances within the Inside Passage between Vancouver Island and the Mainland

Figure at the intersection of columns opposite the places in question is the approximate distance in nautical miles between the two.

Example: Nanaimo is 183 nautical miles from Port Hardy.

Notes:
1. Distances from Victoria are via Sidney Channel and Active Pass. Via Boundary Pass, *add* 7 miles for New Westminster and Vancouver and 8 miles for the remaining places.
2. For the head of Jervis Inlet and Porpoise Bay in Sechelt Inlet, *add* 46 miles and 30 miles respectively.
3. Distances westward from Stuart Island are via Cordero and Chancellor Channels.
4. For Port Harvey, *add* 3 miles.

Courtesy of the Canadian Hydrographic Service

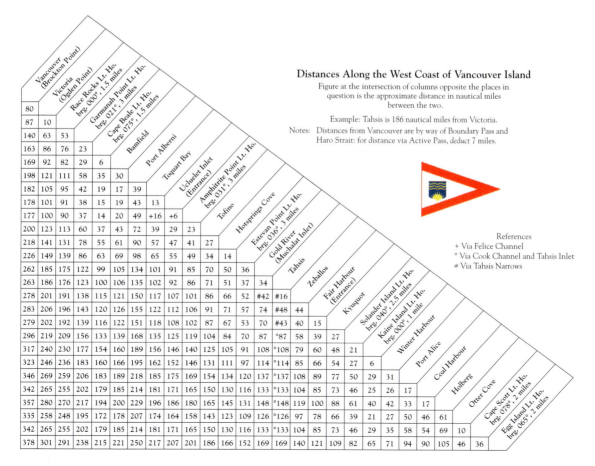

Distances Along the West Coast of Vancouver Island

Figure at the intersection of columns opposite the places in question is the approximate distance in nautical miles between the two.

Example: Tahsis is 186 nautical miles from Victoria.

Notes: Distances from Vancouver are by way of Boundary Pass and Haro Strait: for distance via Active Pass, *deduct* 7 miles.

References
+ Via Felice Channel
° Via Cook Channel and Tahsis Inlet
Via Tahsis Narrows

2024 Northwest Boat Travel

Page 290 DISTANCE TABLES

Distance Table
Distances in the Strait of Georgia

Victoria (Ogden Point)	New Westminster	Vancouver (Brockton Point)	Nanaimo	Nanoose Bay (Richards Point)	Northwest Bay	Halfmoon Bay	Pender Harbour (Entrance)	Blubber Bay	Powell River	Comox	Campbell River	Seymour Narrows
72												
73	40											
76	46	34										
81	53	40	13									
88	59	46	20	12								
85	54	35	21	18	18							
95	65	48	30	25	21	11						
117	87	70	52	46	37	35	25					
118	88	70	52	46	41	35	26	5				
122	94	79	54	48	37	52	42	18	21			
143	114	99	75	69	58	62	53	29	31	33		
151	122	107	83	77	66	70	61	37	39	41	8	

Note: Distances from Victoria are via Sidney Channel and Active Pass. Via Boundary Pass add 7 miles for New Westminster and Vancouver and 8 miles for the remaining places.

Distances in the Gulf Islands and San Juan Archipelago

Figure at the intersection of columns opposite places in question is the approximate distance in nautical miles between the two.

Example: Victoria is 51 miles from Chemainus

Victoria (Ogden Point)	Cadboro Bay (Entrance)	Sidney	Tschum Harbour	Fulford Harbour	Friday Harbor (Wash.)	Roche Harbor (Wash.)	Reid Harbour	Bedwell Harbour	Lyall Harbour	Ganges	Sturdies Bay	Montague Harbour	Cowichan Bay	Maple Bay	Crofton	Chemainus	Telegraph Harbour	Ladysmith	Porlier Pass	Dodd Narrows	Gabriola Passage	Nanaimo	New Westminster	Vancouver (Brockton Point)
8																								
24	15																							
24	17	2																						
32	23	9	9																					
27	25	19	19	24																				
23	15	10	10	17	11																			
23	16	10	10	14	11	3																		
28	20	10	10	10	16	9	8																	
35	27	17	18	14	20	16	14	9																
39	30	16	16	12	28	20	18	14	13															
39	31	16	16	13	28	20	18	14	11	10														
39	31	17	17	13	28	20	19	15	11	7	7													
38	29	15	15	11	30	21	20	18	22	20	21	21												
42	33	19	19	15	34	25	24	22	25	24	25	@18	8											
46	37	22	23	19	38	29	27	26	@29	@20	@15	@15	12	5										
51	42	28	28	24	43	34	33	29	@26	@22	@22	@17	17	11	6									
51	42	28	28	24	43	34	33	29	@25	@21	@21	@16	17	11	7	3								
56	47	33	33	29	48	39	37	35	@31	@27	@27	#21	22	15	11	6	7							
50	41	27	27	#23	39	31	29	25	21	17	#17	11	20	13	9	11	10	14						
#60	#52	#38	#38	#34	#49	#42	#40	#36	32	28	#28	22	30	23	19	14	13	14	13					
#58	#49	#35	#35	#32	#47	#39	#38	#33	30	26	23	20	29	22	18	14	14	14	9	7				
#*65	#*57	#*43	#*43	*39	*54	*47	*45	*41	*37	*33	33	*30	*35	*28	*24	*19	*18	*19	-24	5	-16			
°72	°64	°50	°50	°46	°61	°53	°52	°47	°44	°43	°34	°40	°54	+43	+40	+42	+41	+45	31	+44	35	46		
°73	°64	°50	°50	°46	°61	°53	°52	°47	°44	33	°40	°54	+41	+47	+39	+42	+42	28	36	27	34	40		

References
* Via Dodd Narrows   # Via Trincomali Channel
° Via Active Pass   + Via Porlier Pass
@ Via Houston Passage   - Outside the Gulf Islands

Visit us at boattravel.com

DISTANCE TABLES   Page 291

STRAIT OF GEORGIA
* via Sabine Channel   + via Malaspina Strait

Agamemnon Channel (South Entrance/Entrée Sud)								
50	Campbell River							
6	44	Cape Cockburn						
43	16	37	Cortes Bay					
24	47	26	44	False Bay				
54	16	48	17	52	Heriot Bay			
31	75*	34	70+	29	79*	Nanaimo		
24	31	18	20	29	32	51+	Powell River	
42	89	45	82+	46	93+	28	63	Vancouver (Pt. Atkinson)

Ref. Chart 3312, Courtesy of the Canadian Hydrographic Service

DISTANCES: PENDER HARBOUR TO PURPOISE BAY VIA AGAMEMNON CHANNEL

Pender Harbour Francis Point 1 mile NE							
10.5	Earls Cove						
14.5	4	Egmont					
16	5.5	1.5	Sechelt Rapids				
24	13.5	9.5	8	Kunechin Islets			
25.5	15	11	9.5	1.5	Nine Mile Point		
30.5	20	16	14.5	6.5	5	Four Mile Point	
33	22.5	18.5	17	9	7.5	2.5	Porpoise Bay Anchorage

DESOLATION SOUND

Bliss Landing								
4	Cortes Bay							
13	12	Gorge Harbour						
18	17	8	Heriot Bay					
4	5	15	20	Malaspina Inlet (Entrance/Entrée)				
10	11	21	26	7	Prideaux Haven			
6	6	16	21	4	7	Refuge Cove		
7	7	17	22	6	10	3	Squirrel Cove	
15	13	3	6	16	23	18	19	Whaletown

DISCOVERY PASSAGE - JOHNSTONE STRAIT

Campbell River								
2	Cape Mudge							
38	40	Chancellor Channel (West End/Bout Quest)						
16	14	54	Cortes Bay					
16	15	54	17	Heriot Bay				
28	30	10	44	44	Mayne Passage (West End/Bout Quest)			
22	24	16	38	38	6	Nodales Channel (West End/Bout Quest)		
18	20	20	34	34	10	4	Okisollo Channel (West/Quest)	
9	11	29	25	25	19	13	9	Seymour Narrows

POINT ATKINSON TO LUND AND BULL PASSAGE

Point Atkinson											
16.5	Roberts Creek										
22.5	6	Sechelt									
27.5	11	5.8	Merry Island Light								
32.5	16	10.8	5	Secret Cove							
37.5	21	15.8	10	5.8	Pender Harbour/Francis Cove 1' NE						
37	21	17	11	8.7	Bull Passage						
45	28.3	23	17.5	13	7.5	14	Cape Cockburn				
52	35.5	30.1	24.3	20	14.5	21	7	Still Water			
60.5	44	39	33	28.8	24	*32 / 28	14.5	9	Vananda		
65	49	44	38	33	29	*30	19	14	5	Blubber Bay	
69	53	48	42	37	33	*34	17	11	4.5	4	Westview
81	65	60.5	54.5	49	45.5	46.5	29	23	16	13	12.5	Lund

Reference   * Via Algerine Passage

CORDERO AND / ET NODALES CHANNELS MAYNE PASSAGE

Arran Rapids								
28	Chancellor Channel (West End/Bout Quest)							
3	25	Dent Rapids						
10	24	7	Frederick Arm (Head/au fond)					
2	27	2	9	Gillard Passage				
16	12	13	12	15	Greene Point Rapids			
20	17	17	16	19	5	Mayne Passage (West End/Bout Quest)		
15	28	12	12	14	16	20	Nodales Channel (West/Quest)	
14	22	11	10	13	10	14	14	Phillips Arm (Head/au fond)

DISTANCE TABLES

Inside Passage — Prince Rupert to Cape Caution via Grenville, Princess Royal, and Seaforth Channels, lama Passage, Fitz Hugh Sound.

Note - The distances given in the tables on this and subsequent pages are approximate only. They are based on the most frequently used tracks which may not be suitable for all vessels.

Prince Rupert												
72	Sainty Point											
100	28	Butedale										
121	49	67	Kitimat									
158	58	65	57	Kemano								
135	63	35	102	104	Boat Bluff							
161	89	61	126	128	26	Susan Rock						
180	108	80	147	145	45	20	Bella Bella					
190	118	90	157	155	55	30	10	Pointer Island (E. end Lama Pass)				
210	138	110	167	176	63	50	30	20	Ocean Falls			
255	183	165	213	211	119	86	61	56	54	Bella Coola via Burke Chan.		
203	131	103	181	179	68	42	23	12	33	56	Namu	
222	150	122	189	191	87	61	42	32	51	66	20	Safety Cove
232	160	132	199	201	98	71	52	42	61	86	30	10	Dugout Rocks
245	173	145	212	214	110	84	65	55	74	99	43	23	13	Cape Caution 078°, 2.2 miles

Prince Rupert to East Coast Haida Gwaii Islands

Prince Rupert								
9	Holland Rocks							
28	19	Seal Rocks						
95	86	67	Cumshewa Head					
99	90	71	11	Reef Is.				
122	113	94	38	27	Scudder Point			
128	119	100	44	33	6	Copper Is.		
136	127	108	56	45	18	12	Garcin Rocks	
158	149	130	73	62	35	29	17	Cape St. James

Canadian Hydrographic Service

Figure at the intersection of columns opposite places in question is the approximate distance in nautical miles between the two.

INSIDE PASSAGE DISTANCES
SEATTLE, WASH. TO CAPE SPENCER, ALASKA

Figure at intersection of columns opposite ports in question is the nautical mileage between the two. Example: Ketchikan, Alaska is 220 nautical miles from Juneau, Alaska.

Distances to Sitka are partly outside

Seattle, Wash. 47°36.2'N., 122°20.3'W.																
72	Victoria, Canada 48°25.0'N., 123°23.5'W.															
664	612	Dixon Entrance, Alaska 54°28.0'N., 132°52.0'W.														
690	638	169	Hyder, Alaska 55°54.2'N., 130°00.6'W.													
640	588	34	136	Cape Chacon, Alaska 54°40.6'N., 131°59.7'W.												
660	608	66	148	32	Metlakatla, Alaska 55°07.8'N., 131°34.2'W.											
659	608	79	144	45	16	Ketchikan, Alaska 55°20.5'N., 131°38.7'W.										
716	664	77	212	76	109	121	Craig, Alaska 55°28.7'N., 133°09.2'W.									
749	697	157	234	123	104	89	111	Wrangell, Alaska 56°28.2'N., 132°23.2'W.								
788	737	126	273	125	143	129	49	75	Cape Decision, Alaska 55°59.4'N., 134°08.1'W.							
812	761	150	297	149	167	153	73	99	25	Port Alexander, Alaska 56°14.8'N., 134°38.8'W.						
771	719	180	256	146	126	112	113	40	76	100	Petersburg, Alaska 56°48.8'N., 132°57.8'W.					
883	832	221	368	220	238	224	144	170	95	82	159	Sitka, Alaska 57°03.1'N., 135°20.5'W.				
989	937	332	464	331	334	320	255	248	206	186	207	79	Pelican, Alaska 57°57.6'N., 136°13.8'W.			
879	827	288	364	254	235	220	206	148	157	140	108	162	123	Juneau, Alaska 58°17.9'N., 134°24.7'W.		
950	898	359	435	325	305	291	253	219	204	186	179	176	138	88	Haines, Alaska 59°13.8'N., 135°26.1'W.	
962	910	371	447	337	317	303	264	231	215	198	191	187	148	100	14	Skagway, Alaska 59°26.8'N., 135°19.3'W.
938	886	290	423	289	293	278	213	208	164	147	166	136	45	82	96	108	Gustavus, Alaska 58°23.3'N., 135°43.6'W.
976	924	319	451	318	321	307	242	235	193	173	195	85	18	110	124	136	32	Cape Spencer, Alaska 58°10.0'N., 136°38.3'W.

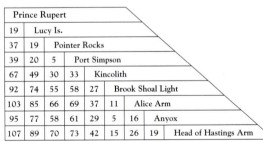

Prince Rupert							
19	Lucy Is.						
37	19	Pointer Rocks					
39	20	5	Port Simpson				
67	49	30	33	Kincolith			
92	74	55	58	27	Brook Shoal Light		
103	85	66	69	37	11	Alice Arm	
95	77	58	61	29	5	16	Anyox
107	89	70	73	42	15	26	19	Head of Hastings Arm

Visit us at boattravel.com

Index of Anchorages, Parks, Ports-of-Call, Marinas, Moorages, Facilities, & Services

15th Street Public Dock ... 16

A

Aaltanhash Inlet ... 248
Aaron's Marine Service ... 18
Actaeon Sound ... 218
Active Cove ... 105
Active Pass ... 142
Active Pass Auto & Marine Ltd ... 136
Actress Passage ... 218
Addenbroke Island Lighthouse ... 243
Admiralty Cove ... 271
Admiralty Inlet ... 56
Admiralty Island, East Side ... 269
Admiralty Island, West Side ... 273
Agamemnon Bay ... 178
Agamemnon Channel ... 178
Agate Passage ... 30
Ahgykson Island ... 183
Ahnuhati Point ... 214
Ahousat General Store ... 231
Ahoy British Columbia ... 123
Air Marine Harbor ... 264
Alava Bay ... 264
Alberta Bay ... 169
Alderbrook Resort and Spa ... 54
Aleck Bay ... 91
Alert Bay ... 220
Alert Bay Boat Harbour ... 220
Aleutkina Bay ... 276
Alexander Inlet ... 247
Alice Arm ... 255
Alison Sound ... 241
Alki Point ... 38
All Bay Marine ... 127
Allan Island ... 80
Allard Bay ... 243
Allies Island ... 188
Allison Harbour ... 240
Allison Harbour Marine Provincial Park ... 240
Allyn ... 22
Allyn Waterfront Park Dock ... 22
Alma Russell Islands ... 229
Alston Cove ... 250
American Camp ... 103
Amsterdam Bay ... 18
Anacortes ... 80
Anacortes Downtown ... 81
Anacortes Marina ... 82
Anan Bay ... 266
Anchor Cove ... 241
Anchor Cove Marina ... 82
Anchor Pass ... 264
Anderson Bay ... 197
Anderson Island ... 18
Andrews Bay ... 49
Anglers Anchorage Marina ... 129
Angoon ... 274
Angoon Boat Harbor ... 274
Angoon Oil ... 274
Anita Bay ... 266
Anna Smith County Park ... 33
Annapolis ... 35
Annette Inlet ... 141
Annette Island ... 262
Annette Island ... 282
Annette Island Gas Services ... 282
Anvil Island ... 169
Anyox ... 255
Apodoca Cove ... 168
Appleton Cove ... 277
Appletree Cove ... 67
April Point ... 202
April Point Cove ... 202
April Point Marina, Resort & Spa ... 202
APY Marina ... 154
Arabella's Landing ... 20
Arbutus Cove ... 125
Area Whiskey Golf ... 153
Area Whiskey Golf ... 192
Armitage Island ... 91
Arness County Park ... 68
Arran Rapids ... 207
Arthur Island ... 246
Atkins Reef ... 140
Atlantic City Boat Ramp ... 49
Attwood Bay ... 187
Auke Bay ... 271
Auke Bay Commercial Loading Facility ... 271
Auke Bay Petro Marine Services ... 271
Aurora Harbor ... 270

B

Bachelor Cove ... 167
Backeddy Resort & Marina ... 181
Bailey Bay ... 264
Bainbridge Island ... 28
Bainbridge Island City Dock ... 29
Baker Inlet ... 251
Baker Island ... 216
Ballard ... 43
Ballard Mill Marina ... 44
Ballard Pier - 24th Avenue Landing ... 43
Ballenas Islands ... 193
Ballet Bay ... 178
Bamberton Provincial Park ... 129
Bamfield ... 227
Bamfield Harbour Authority Dock ... 228
Bangor ... 53
Bar Harbor Facilities ... 263
Baranof Island ... 276
Baranof Warm Springs ... 277
Bargain Bay ... 176
Barkley Sound ... 227
Barkley Sound ... 230
Barnes Bay ... 204
Barnes Island ... 106
Barnet Marine Park ... 165
Baronet Passage ... 214
Bartlett Cove ... 272
Bartlett Cove Dock ... 273
Basic Boat Anchoring ... 119
Basic Boat Maneuvering ... 118
Basket Bay ... 276
Bathgate General Store, Resort & Marina ... 181
Battle Bay ... 234
Bauza Cove ... 219
Bawden Bay ... 231
Bay at Marble Creek ... 281
Bay Head Marina ... 95
Bay of Plenty ... 250
Baynes Channel ... 125
Baynes Sound ... 194
Bayshore West Marina ... 165
Bayview State Park ... 82
BC Ocean Boating Tourism Association ... 123
Beach Gardens Resort & Marina ... 182
Beachcomber Marina ... 193
Bear Cove ... 222
Beaumont Marine Park ... 132
Beaver Cove ... 220
Beaver Harbour ... 221
Beaver Inlet ... 212
Beaver Point ... 138
Becher Bay ... 121
Becher Bay Marina ... 121
Bedwell Bay ... 166
Bedwell Harbour ... 132
Belcarra Dock/Belcarra Regional Park ... 166
Belfair State Park ... 56
Belize Inlet ... 241
Bell Harbor Marina ... 40
Bell Island, AK ... 264
Bell Island, BC ... 222
Bella Bella ... 246
Bella Coola ... 244
Bella Coola Harbour ... 244
Bellevue ... 48
Bellevue Marina at Meydenbauer Bay ... 48
Bellingham City of ... 85
Bend Island ... 214
Bennett Bay ... 136
Berg Bay ... 266, 273
Berry Island ... 214
Beware Cove ... 214
Beware Passage ... 214
Bickley Bay ... 211
Big Bay ... 206
Big Bunsby Marine Provincial Park ... 234
Big Salmon Resort ... 64
Bill Proctor's Museum ... 216
Billings Bay ... 178
Birch Bay ... 86
Birch Bay Village Marina ... 86
Bird's Eye Cove Marina ... 148
Bishop Bay ... 249
Blackfish Archipelago ... 215
Blackfish Sound ... 214
Blackney Passage ... 214
Blaine ... 86
Blaine Harbor ... 86, 87
Blake Channel-Eastern Passage ... 266
Blake Island Marine State Park ... 35
Blake's Skagit Resort & Marina ... 72
Blakely Harbor ... 28, 91
Blakely Island ... 91
Blakely Island Marina ... 91
Blenkinsop Bay ... 213
Bligh Island ... 232
Blind Bay ... 178
Blind Bay ... 99, 178
Blind Channel Resort ... 211
Blind Island Marine State Park ... 99
Bliss Landing ... 185
Blow Hole The ... 213
Blubber Bay ... 197
Blue Mouse Cove ... 273
Bluenose Marina ... 148
Blunden Harbour ... 238
Boat Bay ... 213
Boat Cove ... 196
Boat Inlet ... 246
Boat Passage ... 135, 144
Boat Shed Restaurant ... 33
Boat Street Marina ... 46
Boating Safety, Canada ... 113
Boating Safety, US ... 110
Boca de Quadra ... 261
Boho Bay ... 196
Bolin Bay ... 247
Bond Lagoon ... 219
Bones Bay ... 214
Bonilla Point ... 227
Bonwick Island ... 215
Booker Lagoon ... 215
Boot Cove ... 135
Booth Bay ... 141
Boston Harbor ... 24
Boston Harbor Marina ... 24

Boswell Inlet 241
Bothell Landing 47
Bottleneck Inlet 247
Boughey Bay 213
Boulevard Park 85
Boulton Bay 205
Boundary Bay 87, 156
Bowen Island 167
Bowen Island Marina 168
Bowman Bay 79
Boyer Point 217
Bradfield Canal 266
Brandt's Landing Marina 99
Breakwater Float 140
Breakwater Marina 17
Breezy Bay 135
Bremerton 32
Bremerton Marina 32
Bremerton Waterfront Park 32
Brentwood Bay 129
Brentwood Bay Resort & Spa 129
Brew Island 250
Bridget Cove 271
Bridgeview Marina 33
Bridgeview Marine 253, 257
Brigade Bay 170
Brigantine Bay 91
Britannia Beach 169
Broken Group Islands 229
Broken Islands 213
Brooks Bay 234
Broughton Archipelago Marine Park 215
Broughton Strait 220
Brown's Bay Resort 203
Browns Point Lighthouse Park 14
Brownsville 31
Brownsville Port of 31
Brundige Inlet 254
Buccaneer Bay 175
Buccaneer Marina 176
Buchan Inlet 250
Buckley Bay 194
Budd Inlet 24
Bull Harbour 222, 236, 240
Bunsby Islands 234
Burdwood Bay 205
Burdwood Group 216
Burfoot County Park 24
Burgoyne Bay 141
Burgoyne Bay Provincial Park 141
Burial Cove 213
Burke Channel 244
Burley Bay 217
Burnaby 165
Burrard Civic Marina 163
Burrard Inlet 162
Burrows Bay 80
Burrows Island Marine State Park 80
Bush Point 73
Butch's Marina 227
Bute Inlet 205
Bute Inlet Lodge 205
Butedale 248

C

Cabbage Island 134
Cabbage Island Marine Park 134
Cadboro Bay 125
Cains Marine Service 64
Calder Bay 281
Call Inlet 213
Cama Beach State Park 71
Camano Island 71
Camano Island State Park 71
Cameleon Harbour 209
Cameron Cove 250
Campbell Bay 136
Campbell Island 246
Campbell River 199
Campbell River Fishermans Wharf 201
Canada Border Services Agency (CBSA) 108
Canadian Marine Police Units 117
Canadian National Defence 113
Canoe Cove 128
Canoe Cove Marina & Boatyard 128
Canoe Pass 79
Canoe Passage 214
Cap Sante Marina .... IFC, 82, 83
Cape Beale 227
Cape Chacon 282
Cape Cook 234
Cape Lazo 195
Cape Mudge 199
Cape Mudge Village 199
Cape Scott Provincial Park 236
Captain Coupe Park 73
Captain Cove 250
Captain's Cove Marina 160
Carillon Point Marina 48
Carlson Inlet 245
Carmanah Point 227
Carolina Channel 230
Carr Inlet 21
Carriden Bay 218
Carrington Bay 189
Carrington Bay Park 189
Carroll Inlet 262
Carter Bay 248
Carter Passage 219
Cartwright Bay 217
Cascade Bay 95
Cascade Inlet 245
Case Inlet 22
Casey Moran Harbor 263
Catala Island Provincial Marine Park 233
Cates Park 166
Cathedral Point 244
Catherwood Towing 161
Cattle Point NRCA 103
Caulfeild Cove 162
Causeway Marina, Victoria Harbour 123
Caution Cove 214
Cayou Quay Marina 99
Ceepeecee 233
Center Island 91
Centre Bay 170
Chapin Bay 269
Charlotte Bay 240
Charts - Canadian 113
Charts & Weather, US 110
Chatham Channel 213
Chatham Channel Cabins 213
Chatham Point 203
Chatterbox Falls 180
Cheanuh Marina 121
Checleset Bay 234
Checleset Bay Ecological Reserve 234
Chemainus 147
Chemainus Municipal Marina 147
Chetzemoka City Park 60
Chichagof Island 274
Chichagof Island, West Side 274
Chico 33
Chief Mathews Bay 249
Chief Seattle Park 30
China Creek Campground & Marina 228
Chinook Landing Marina 15
Cholmondeley Sound 279
Cholmondeley Sound South Arm 280
Cholmondeley Sound West Arm 280
Chonat Bay 204
Chris Teren Photography 101
Christie Creek 170
Chuckanut Bay 84
City of Kake 278
City of Thorne Bay 279
Clallam Bay 63
Clam Bay 144
Clarence Strait 265, 278
Clark Island Marine State Park 106
Clarno Cove 280
Classic Marine Ltd 148
Claydon Bay 218
Clayoquot Sound 230
Clear Passage 234
Cleveland Passage 269
Clinton 75
Clio Channel 214
Clover Pass 265
Clover Pass Resort 265
Clutesi Haven Marina 228
Coal Harbour 235
Coal Harbour Chevron 165
Coal Harbour Marina 165
Coal Harbour, Vancouver 164
Coast Guard, Canadian 116
Coast Guard, US 111
Coast Marina 201
Coast Victoria Harbourside Hotel & Marina 124
Coastal Mountain Fuel (Bear Cove BC) 222
Cochrane Islands 186
Cockburn Bay 178
Cockle Bay 246
Codville Lagoon Marine Park 244
Coffman Cove 278
Coffman Cove Marina 278
Coho Marina & RV Resort 178
Coles Bay 129
Coles Bay Regional Park 129
Colston Cove 133
Colvos Passage 11
Commando Inlet 250
Commencement Bay 14
Community Paddlers Dock at Ancich Waterfront Park 19
Comox 195
Comox Harbour 195
Comox Marine Gas & Go 195
Comox Municipal Marina 195
Comox Valley Fisherman's Wharf 195
Comox Valley Marina 195
Compton Island 214
Cone Islands State Park 82
Conover Cove 144
Coon Cove 262
Copeland Islands Marine Park 185
Cordero Channel 210
Cordero Islands Anchorage 211
Cordero Lodge 211
Cordova Bay 125
Cormorant Channel Provincial Park 220
Cornet Bay 79
Cortes Bay 190
Cortes Bay Public Floats 191
Cortes Island 188
Cosmos Cove 277
Cottages at Shoal Bay, The 211
Cougar Bay 247
Coulter Bay 189
Coupeville 73
Coupeville Port of 73
Courtenay 195
Couverden Island 272
Covich-Williams Chevron 44
Cow Bay 231, 252
Cow Bay Marina 253
Cow Bay Northwest Fuels 253
Cowichan Bay 148
Cowichan Bay Harbour Fisherman's Wharf 148
Cowichan Wooden Boat Society 148
Cozy Cove 48
Crab Bay 276
Cracroft Inlet 213
Craig 281
Craig City Dock 281
Craig Petro Marine Services 281
Crawford Anchorage 211
Crease Island 214
Creasy Bay 219
Crescent Bay 63
Crescent Beach 87, 158
Crescent Beach Marina 88, 158
Crescent Channel 204

Visit us at boattravel.com

INDEX Page 295

Crescent Harbor ... 72
Crib Island ... 215
Critter Cove ... 232
Critter Cove Marina ... 233
Crockett Lake ... 73
Crofton ... 147
Crofton Public Floats ... 147
Crossing The Border ... 108
Crowther Channel ... 234
CSR Marine ... 14
Cullen Harbour ... 215
Culpepper Lagoon ... 247
Cultus Bay ... 75
Curlew Bay ... 248
Curme Islands ... 187
Current Passage ... 212
Cutter Cove ... 213
Cutts Island Marine State Park ... 21
Cypress Bay ... 231
Cypress Harbour ... 217
Cypress Head ... 84
Cypress Island ... 82

D

D H Timber Towing ... 236
D'Arcy Island Marine Park ... 125
Daajing Giids (Queen Charlotte) ... 256
Dabob Bay ... 53
Dagmar's Marina ... 70
Dalco Passage ... 13
Darby Channel ... 242
Dark Cove ... 179
Dash Point Park & Pier ... 14
Dash Point State Park ... 14
Dave Mackie County Park ... 74
David Bay ... 247
David Cove ... 136
Davies Bay ... 254
Davis Bay, B.C. ... 218
Davis Bay, WA ... 91
Dawsons Landing ... 242
Dawsons Landing General Store ... 242
Day Island ... 18
Day Island Yacht Harbor ... 18
De Courcy Island ... 150
Deadman Bay ... 104
Deadman Island ... 21
Dean Channel ... 245
Deas Island Regional Park ... 159
Decatur Island ... 91
Deception Pass ... 79
Deception Pass Marina ... 79
Deception Pass State Park ... 79
Deckside Marina ... 159
Deep Bay ... 194, 196
Deep Bay Harbour Authority ... 194
Deep Bay Marina ... 194
Deep Cove ... 128, 166
Deep Cove Marina ... 128
Deep Cove North Shore Marina ... 166
Deep Harbour ... 215
Deepwater Bay ... 82
Deepwater Bay ... 84
Deer Group ... 227
Deer Harbor ... 98
Deer Harbor Boatworks ... 99
Deer Harbor Marina ... 99
Degnen Bay ... 152
Degnen Bay Government Wharf ... 152
Delin Docks Marina ... 15
Delta Western (Halibut Point) ... 277
Denman Island ... 194
Denman Island Community Dock ... 194
Dent Island Lodge ... 206, 207
Dent Rapids ... 207
Departure Bay Gas N Go ... 154
Des Moines ... 13
Des Moines Marina ... 13
Desbrisay Bay ... 247
Deserted Bay ... 179
Deserters Group ... 240
Desolation Sound ... 186
Desolation Sound Marine Park ... 186
Dewey Beach ... 79
Dickman Bay ... 280
Dickman Mill Park ... 16
Dickson Island ... 219
Didrickson Bay ... 274
Digby Island ... 251
Dine Point, Seymour Inlet ... 240
Dionisio Point Provincial Park ... 143
Discovery Bay ... 61
Discovery Harbour Fuel Sales ... 200, 201
Discovery Harbour Marina ... 200, 201
Discovery Island Marine Park ... 125
Discovery Passage ... 198
Diver Bay ... 141
Dixie Cove ... 234
Dixon Entrance ... 261
Dock Street Marina ... 15
Dockton Park ... 12
Doctor Bay ... 188
Dodd Narrows ... 153
Doe Bay ... 93
Doe Island Marine State Park ... 94
Dolomi Bay ... 280
Don Armeni Park ... 38
Donohues Marina ... 271
Dora Bay ... 279
Dosewallips State Park ... 53
Double Island ... 98
Douglas ... 270
Douglas Bay ... 212
Douglas Boat Harbor ... 270
Douglas Channel ... 248
Downtown Seattle Waterfront ... 39
Downtown Sidney ... 126
Doyon's Landing ... 263
Draney Inlet ... 243
Drayton Harbor ... 86
Drew Harbour ... 204
Drumbeg Provincial Park ... 152
Drury Inlet ... 218
Duanto's Marine Services ... 46
Duke Island ... 261
Duke Island ... 282
Duke Point ... 153
Duncan ... 147
Duncan Cove ... 177
Dundas Island ... 254
Dundivan Inlet ... 246
Dungeness Bay ... 61
Dungeness Recreation Area ... 62
Duwamish Waterway ... 38
Dyes Inlet ... 33

E

E Q Harbor Service & Sales ... 79
Eagle Creek ... 54
Eagle Harbor ... 29, 84
Eagle Harbor Marina ... 29
Eagle Harbor Waterfront Park Float ... 29
Eagle Harbour ... 167
Eagle Island Marine State Park ... 18
Eagle Marine ... 230
Eagle Nook Resort & Spa ... 229
Earl's Cove ... 178
East Passage ... 12
East Point ... 134
East Quadra Island ... 204
East Redonda Island ... 188
East Sound ... 94
Eastbourne ... 170
Eastsound ... 95
Ebey Slough ... 70
Ebey Waterfront Park ... 70
Ebey's Landing National Historic Reserve ... 73
Echo Bay Marina & Lodge ... 216
Echo Bay Marine Park ... 216
Echo Bay, BC ... 216
Echo Bay, Washington ... 106
Echo Cove ... 271
Ecoole ... 229
Eden Island ... 215
Ediz Hook ... 63
Edmonds ... 68
Edmonds, Port of ... 69
Edna Bay ... 281
Effingham Bay ... 229
Effingham Island ... 229
Egeria Bay ... 132
Egg Island ... 241
Egmont Public Floats ... 181
Egmont Village ... 179, 181
El Capitan Passage ... 281
Elcho Harbour ... 245
Eld Inlet ... 26
Elfin Cove ... 275
Elfin Cove Fuel Dock ... 275
Elger Bay ... 71
Eliason Harbor ... 277
Eliza Island ... 84
Ellen Bay ... 141
Elliott Bay ... 38
Elliott Bay Marina ... 41
Elliott Point ... 69
Embley Lagoon ... 218
Endicott Arm ... 268
England Point Cove ... 219
English Bay ... 162
English Camp Unit ... 104
Entrance Island Lighthouse ... 153
Environment Canada ... 116
Esperanza ... 233
Esperanza Inlet ... 233
Esperanza Marine Service ... 233
Espinosa Inlet ... 233
Esquimalt ... 121
Ethel Cove ... 241
Eucott Bay ... 245
Europa Point ... 249
Evans Bay ... 205
Evans Inlet ... 245
Eveleigh Island Anchorage ... 187
Evening Cove ... 146
Everett ... 69
Everett Yacht Service ... 70
Everett, Port of ... 70
Evergreen Pacific Publishing ... 7, 8, 9
Evergreen Rotary Park ... 33
Evinrude Inlet ... 250
Ewing Cove ... 106
Ewing Street Moorings ... 44
Exchange Cove ... 278
Excursion Inlet ... 272

F

Fair Harbor Marina ... 22
Fair Harbor, Washington ... 22
Fair Harbour Marina & Campground ... 234
Fair Harbour, BC ... 234
Fairhaven ... 85
Fairhaven Moorage ... 85
Fairview Harbour ... 253
Fairview Marina ... 46
Fairweather Bay ... 48
Fairwinds Marina at Schooner Cove ... 192
False Bay ... 103, 196
False Cove ... 215
False Creek ... 163
False Creek Fuels ... 163
False Creek Harbour-Fishermen's Wharf ... 163
False Creek Yacht Club ... 163
False Narrows ... 153
Fanny Bay ... 194
Farewell Harbour ... 214
Farm Bay ... 175
Farragut Bay ... 268
Fast Fuel ... 256
Fauntleroy ... 13, 49
Fay Bainbridge Park ... 29
FCC Forms & Filings ... 112
Fernwood ... 141

Fidalgo Island 79
Fidalgo Marina 82
Fife Sound 215
Fifer Cove 250
Fillmore Inlet 261
Fillongley Provincial Park 194
Filucy Bay 21
Finis Nook 241
Finlayson Arm 129
Finlayson Channel 247
Finn Bay 183, 242
Finnerty Cove 125
Fiordland Recreational Area 247
First Narrows 164
First Nations Fuel 247
Fish & Shellfishing, Canada 116
Fish & Wildlife, Washington State 111
Fish Egg Inlet 243
Fish Egg Inlet, Eastern Section 243
Fisher Channel 244
Fisheries Supplies 44, 45
Fisherman Bay 92
Fisherman Harbor 53
Fisherman's Cove 167
Fisherman's Cove Marina 86
Fisherman's Cove Marine Fuels 167
Fisherman's Landing & Lodge 207
Fisherman's Wharf Small Craft Harbour 222
Fisherman's Wharf, Victoria 124
Fishermen's Terminal 43
Fishhook Bay 243
Fitz Hugh Sound 243
Fitzgibbon Cove 264
Fleming Bay 122
Fletcher Bay 30
Flounder Bay 81
Fly Basin 241
Foch-Gilttoyees Provincial Park 248
Foggy Bay 261
Fool's Inlet 266
Forbes Bay 187
Ford Cove 194
Ford Cove Harbour Authority 194
Fords Terror 268
Fort Casey State Park 73
Fort Ebey State Park 73
Fort Flagler Marine State Park 58
Fort Langley 161
Fort Townsend State Park 57
Fort Ward Park 35
Fort Worden State Park 60
Forward Bay 213
Forward Harbour 212
Foss Harbor Marina 15
Foss Landing Marina 15
Foss Waterway Seaport 16
Fossil Bay 106
Fougner Bay 244
Foulweather Bluff 52
Fox Cove 106
Fox Island 18
Fox Island Anchorage 179
Frances Bay 205
Fraser Fibreglass Ltd. 166
Fraser Reach 248
Fraser River 158
Fraser River, Middle Arm 159
Fraser River, North Arm 159
Fraser River, South Arm 159
Frederick Arm 210
Frederick Bay 240
Frederick Cove 280
Frederick Sound 241, 268
Freeland 74
Freeland Park 74
Freeman Island 99
French Creek 193
French Creek Harbour Authority 193
French Creek Seafoods 193
French Creek-Lasqueti Island Ferry 193
Frenchman's Cove 175
Freshwater Bay 63
Freshwater Marina on Campbell River 201
Friday Harbor 100
Friday Harbor Port of 102
Friday Harbor Seaplanes 102, 103
Friday Harbor Town of 101
Friendly Cove 232
Fuel Dock at Fisherman's Wharf 124
Fuel Tax 111
Fulford Harbour 138
Fulford Harbour Marina 138
Fulford Inner Harbour Public Float 138
Fulford Landing Marina 138
Fulford Outer Harbour Public Float 138
Funter Bay 273
Fury Island 242

G

Gabriola Island 151
Gabriola Passage 152
Gabriola Sands Provincial Park 153
Galbraith Bay 168
Galiano Island 142
Galiano Oceanfront Inn & Spa 142, 143
Gallery Marine 46
Galley Bay 187
Gamadiis (Port Clements) 256
Gamadiis (Port Clements) Small Craft Harbour 256
Gambier Bay 269
Gambier Harbour 170
Gambier Island 170
Ganges 138
Ganges Centennial Wharf 140
Ganges Marina 140
Garden Bay 177
Garden Bay Marine Park 177
Gardner Bay 280
Gardner Canal 249
Garrison Bay 104
Gedney Island 71
Gene Coulon Memorial Park 49
Genoa Bay 148
Genoa Bay Marina 148
George Inlet 262
Georgeson Passage 135
Gerran's Bay 178
Gerran's Bay Government Wharf 178
Gibson Cove 231
Gibson Marine Park 231
Gibsons 174
Gibsons Landing Harbour Authority 174
Gibsons Marina 174
Gig Harbor 19
Gig Harbor Marina & Boatyard 20
Gildersleeve Bay 243
Gillard Passage 206
Gillies Bay Village 197
Glacier Bay Lodge 273
Glacier Bay National Park 272
Glen Cove 21
Glendale Cove 214
Glenthorne Passage 141
Goat Cove 247
God's Pocket 236, 238
God's Pocket Marine Park 222
God's Pocket Resort 222, 240
Goddard Hot Springs Bay 276
Gold River 232
Gold River Municipal Wharf 232
Golden Gardens Park 41
Goldstream Boathouse Marina 129
Goldstream Harbour 243
Goldstream Park 129
Goletas Channel 236
Good Hope Bay 242
Goose Bay 241
Gooseberry Point 85
Gorge Harbour 189
Gorge Harbour Marina & Resort 190
Gowlland Harbour 202
Grace Harbour 186
Graham Island 256
Graham Reach 248
Granby Bay 255
Granite Bay 203
Granite Falls 166
Granville Island 163
Grapeview 22
Grappler Inlet 228
Grappler Sound 218
Green Bay 178
Green Cove Store 228
Green Inlet Marine Park 248
Green Island Anchorage 243
Greenbank 73
Greene Point Rapids 212
Greenway Sound 217
Gregory Island 217
Grenville Channel 250
Grice Bay 231
Grief Point 182
Griffin Bay 102
Griffin Bay Campground 103
Griffin Passage 247
Grimmer Bay 133
Grindstone Harbor 95
Growler Cove 215
Guemes Channel 81
Guemes Channel Marina 82
Guemes Island 82
Gulf Islands, Introduction 131
Gulf of Esquibel 281
Gunboat Bay 177
Gunboat Passage 245
Gunner Inlet 231
Gustavus 272
Gut Bay 277
Guthrie Bay 95
Gwaii Haanas 257

H

Haida Gwaii (Queen Charlotte Islands) 255
Haines 271
Haines Propane 271
Haines Small Boat Harbor 271
Hakai Institute 243
Hakai Luxvbalis Conservancy 243
Hakai Passage 243
Hale Passage 19
Halfmoon Bay 175
Halibut Bay, Alaska 260
Halkett Bay 170
Halkett Bay Marine Park 170
Hamilton Park 16
Hammersley Inlet 26
Hammond Bay 155
Handfield Bay 209
Hansen Bay 236
Hanson Island 215
Harbledown Island 214
Harbor Island 38
Harbor Island Marina 38
Harbor Marine Fuel, Bellingham 85
Harborview Marina 20
Harbour Authority of Pender Harbour 178
Harbour Green Public Dock 165
Harbour Marina, The 29
Harbour Quay Marina 228
Harbour Village Marina 47
Harbours End Marine & Equipment Ltd. 140
Hardy Bay 222
Hardy Inlet 242
Hardy Island 179
Hardy Island Marine Park 179
Harmony Islands 179
Harmony Islands 281
Harmony Islands Marine Park 179
Harness Island 176
Haro Strait 104, 125
Harper 35
Harri Commercial Marine (Juneau) 270
Harriet Point 240

INDEX

Harris Harbor	270
Harrison Hot Springs	162
Harrison Hot Springs Marina	162
Harrison Lake	162
Harrison River	161
Hartley Bay	248
Hartley Bay Fuels	248
Hartstine Island State Park	22
Harwood Island	183
Hassler Harbor	262
Hassler Pass	264
Hastings Arm	255
Hastings House Country Hotel, Relais & Chateaus	140
Hat Island	82
Havannah Channel	213
Hawk Inlet	273
Health Bay	215
Heather Civic Marina	163
Hecate Bay	231
Heceta Island	281
Helliwell Provincial Park	194
Helm Bay Float	265
Helmcken Inlet	250
Helmcken Island	212
Hemming Bay	209
Henderson Bay	21
Henderson Inlet	24
Henry Bay	194
Henry Island	105
Herb Beck Marina	53
Heriot Bay	204
Heriot Bay Inn & Marina	204
Heritage Harbor	267
Hernando Island	191
Herring Bay	150
Herron Island	22
Hesquiat Peninsula Provincial Park	232
Hetta Inlet	282
Hevenor Inlet	250
Hicks Bay	100
Hidden Basin	178
Hidden Cove	29
Hidden Inlet, Alaska	261
Hiekish Narrows	248
Hill Island	205
Hilton Harbor Marina	85
Hiram M. Chittenden Locks	42
Hisnit Inlet	232
Hjorth Bay	205
HlGaagilda (Skidegate)	256
Hobart Bay	269
Hoeya Sound	214
Hoko River State Park	64
Holberg	236
Hole In The Wall, BC	204
Hole-In-The-Wall Floats, AK	263
Holkham Bay	269
Hollis	279
Holmes Harbor	74
Holmes Inlet	231
Home Port Marina	54
Homeland Security	111
Homfray Channel	187
Honeymoon Bay	74
Hood Canal	51
Hood Canal Floating Bridge	52
Hood Canal Marina	54
Hood Point	168
Hoodsport	54
Hoonah	275
Hoonah City Float	275
Hoonah Harbor	275
Hoonah Trading Co.	275
Hope Bay	133
Hope Bay Public Moorage	133
Hope Island	222, 236
Hope Island Marine State Park	23, 79
Hopetown Point	217
Hopkins Landing	170
Hornby Island	193
Horsehead Bay	21
Horseshoe Bay	167
Horton Bay	135
Hospital Bay	177
Hospital Bay Government Wharf	177
Hot Springs Cove	232
Hotel Bellwether	85
Hotham Sound	179
Howe Sound	167
Howe Sound, East	168
Howe Sound, West	170
Howling Wolf Farm Market	146
Huckleberry Island	82
Hughes Bay	91
Huna Propane	275
Hunt Inlet	251
Hunter Bay	91
Hunter Island	244
Hurst Island	222
Hyak Marine Ltd	174
Hydaburg	282
Hydaburg City Dock	282
Hyder, Alaska	261
Hylebos Marina	15
Hylebos Waterway	14

I

I-68 Canadian Boat Landing Program	109
Iceberg Island State Park	91
Icy Strait	273
Idol Island	141
Ile-De-Lis Marine Park	127
Illahee	31
Illahee Marine State Park	31
Illahie Inlet	243
Imperial Eagle Channel	228
Imperial Landing Floats	160
Important Notices	108
Inati Bay	84
Indian Arm	165
Indian Arm Park	165
Indian Arm Provincial Park	166
Indian Cove	100
Indian Island	57
Indian Island County Park	57
Indian Passage	215
Indianola	29
Ingraham Bay	280
Inner Basin	233
Inner Port Madison	29
Introduction	5
Irish Bay	135
Irondale	57
Isabel Bay	186
Isabella Light	138
Island Cove	231
Island View Beach Regional Park	125
Island West Resort	230
Islands Marine Center	**92**

J

Jack Hyde Park on Commencement Bay	16
Jack's Boat Yard	183
Jackson Beach Park	103
Jackson Island	282
Jackson Narrows Marine Park	246
Jackson Passage	246
James Bay	142
James Bay (Mathieson Channel, B.C.)	247
James Bay, Victoria Inner Harbor	122
James Island Marine State Park	90
James Island, B.C.	125
Jane Bay	229
Jaques Island	229
Jarrell Cove Marine State Park	23
Jarrell's Cove Marina	**23**
Jeanette Island Light	238
Jedediah Island Marine Park	196
Jennis Bay	218
Jennis Bay Marina	218
Jenny Inlet	246
Jerisich Dock	19
Jervis Inlet	179
Jervis Island	196
Jetty Island	70
Jetty Landing	70
Jeune Landing	235
Joe Bay	177
Joe Cove	215
Joemma Beach State Park	22
Joes Bay	243
John Henry's Resort & Marina	177
John Wayne Marina	61
Johnny's Dock Restaurant & Marina	16
Johns Pass	105
Johnson Cove	280
Johnson Point	23
Johnston Bay	242
Johnstone Strait	209
Johnstone Strait, Central	213
Jones Cove	241
Jones Island Marine State Park	100
Joseph Whidbey State Park	72
Juan de Fuca Strait, Crossing	226
Julia Passage	229
Julian Cove	235
Juneau	270
Juneau Petro Marine (Douglas)	270
Juneau, Intermediate Vessel Float	270

K

Kaasa Inlet	282
Kagoagh Resort & Fishing Lodge	235
Kah Shakes Cove	261
Kains Island	236
Kake	**278**
Kakushdish Harbour	246
Kanaka Bay	103
Kanaka Visitor's Wharf	140
Kanish Bay	203
Karl's Auto & Marine Repair	271
Karlukwees	214
Kasaan Bay	279
Kashutl Inlet	234
Kayak Point County Park	71
Keats Island	170
Keats Island Settlement	170
Keefer Bay	183
Kegan Cove	280
Keku Strait	277
Kelsey Bay	212
Kelsey Bay Harbours	212
Kemano	249
Kemano Bay	249
Kendrick Bay	280
Kendrick Bay, South Arm	280
Kendrick Bay, West Arm	280
Kenmore	47
Kenmore Air	**45, 47**
Kennedy Cove	231
Kenneth Passage	218
Kent Inlet	250
Ketchikan	262
Ketchikan Moorage	263
Ketchikan Petro Marine Service	263
Ketchikan Yacht Club	263
Ketron Island	18
Keyport	30
Keyport Naval	29
Keyport Port of	30
Keystone Harbor	73
Khutze Inlet	248
Khutzeymateen Inlet	254
Kiket Island	79
Kilisut Harbor	58
Killam Bay	179
Killer's Cove Marina	162
Kiltuish Inlet	249
Kimshan Cove	274
Kimsquit Bay	245
Kina Cove	279

Kinahan Islands ... 251
Kindergarten Bay ... 265
Kingcome Inlet ... 217
Kingston ... 67
Kingston Port of ... 68
Kirkland ... 48
Kirkland Homeport Marina ... 48
Kirkland Marina at Marina Park ... 48
Kisameet Bay ... 244
Kiskosh Inlet ... 248
Kitimat ... 248
Kitkum Bay ... 279
Kitlope Anchorage ... 249
Kitlope Heritage Conservancy ... 249
Kitsap Marina ... 35
Kitsap Memorial State Park ... 52
Kitsault ... 255
Kitsaway Anchorage ... 249
Kitson Island Provincial Marine Park ... 251
Kitty Coleman Provincial Park ... 195
Klag Bay ... 274
Klahoose Wilderness Lodge ... 187
Klaquaek Channel ... 242
Klaskino Inlet ... 234
Klaskish Inlet ... 234
Klawock ... 281
Klekane Inlet ... 248
Klemtu ... 247
Klewnuggit Inlet Provincial Marine Park ... 251
Kliuchevoi Bay ... 276
Knight Inlet ... 214
Knox Bay ... 212
Knudson Cove ... 265
Koeye Point ... 244
Kopachuck Marine State Park ... 21
Koprino Harbour ... 235
Kuhushan Point ... 195, 196
Kukutali Preserve ... 79
Kulleet Bay ... 150
Kumealon Inlet ... 251
Kundson Cove Marina ... 265
Kupreanof City of ... 268
Kwakshua Inlet ... 243
Kwakume Inlet ... 243
Kwatna Bay ... 244
Kwatna Inlet ... 244
Kwatsi Bay ... 216
Kwatsi Bay Marina ... 216
Kxngeal Inlet ... 251
Kynoch Inlet ... 247
Kynumpt Harbour ... 246
Kyuquot ... 234
Kyuquot Sound ... 234

L

L Cove ... 277
La Conner ... 77
La Conner Landing ... 78
La Conner Marina, Port of Skagit's ... 78
La Conner Maritime Service ... 78
Ladner ... 159
Ladner Harbour Authority ... 159
Ladysmith ... 146
Ladysmith Fisherman's Wharf ... 146
Ladysmith Marina ... 146
Lagoon Cove Marina ... 214
Lake Bay ... 205
Lake Union ... 44
Lake Washington ... 47
Lake Washington Bridges ... 47
Lake Washington Ship Canal ... 43
Lakebay Marina Resort ... 21
Lakes to Locks Water Trail The ... 37
Lakewood Moorage ... 49
Lama Pass Fuels ... 246
Lamalchi Bay ... 144
Lancaster Cove ... 279
Lancelot Inlet ... 186
Lang Bay ... 182
Langdale ... 170
Langley ... 74
Langley Harbor, Port of South Whidbey's ... 74
LaPush ... 65
Laredo Inlet ... 250
Larrabee State Park ... 84
Larson Harbour ... 250
Lasqueti Island ... 196
Lasqueti Island Hotel ... 196
Laura Bay ... 216
Laura Cove ... 187
Lawn Point ... 235
Lawn Point Provincial Park ... 235
Legoe Bay ... 84
Les Davis Fishing Pier ... 16
Leschi ... 49
Leschi Moorage ... 49
Leschi Yacht Basin ... 49
Letnikof Cove ... 271
Lewall Inlet ... 244
Lewis Island Anchorage ... 251
LFS Marine & Outdoor ... 84, 85
Liberty Bay ... 30
Liberty Bay Marina ... 31
Lieber Haven Rentals ... 94
Lighthouse Bay ... 143
Lighthouse Marine County Park ... 88
Lighthouse Marine Gig Harbor LLC ... 20
Lighthouse Park ... 69
Lighthouse Pub & Marina ... 182
Lilliwaup ... 54
Lime Kiln Point State Park ... 104
Limekiln Bay ... 197
Limestone Bay ... 228
Lincoln Park ... 49
Linde Canada ... 253
Link Island ... 151
Lion's Park ... 33
Lions Bay ... 169
Lions Bay Marina ... 169
Lions Gate Marine Centre ... 166
Lisabuela Park ... 12
Little Nimmo Bay ... 218
Little River ... 195
Lockhard Bay ... 246
Long Bay ... 276
Long Beach ... 230
Long Harbour ... 140
Long Island ... 282
Longbranch ... 21
Longbranch Improvement Club Marina ... 21
Longship Marine ... 31
Lopez Island ... 91
Lopez Islander Resort & Marina ... 92
Lopez Pass ... 91
Lopez Village ... 93
Loquillia Cove ... 236
Loring ... 265
Loudoun Channel ... 230
Loughborough Inlet ... 212
Lowe Inlet Provincial Marine Park ... 251
Lower Johnstone Strait ... 209
Lucky Creek ... 229
Lummi Island ... 84
Lummi Recreation Site ... 84
Lund ... 183
Lund Harbour Authority ... 183
Lund Resort at Klah ah Men The ... 183
Luther Burbank Park ... 48
Lyall Harbour ... 135
Lyall Harbour Government Wharf ... 135
Lyman Anchorage ... 279
Lynn Canal ... 271
Lynnwood Marina & Boatyard ... 167

M

M K Bay Marina ... 249
Mab Island ... 271
Mabel Bay ... 282
MacKaye Harbor ... 91
MacKenzie Sea Services ... 182
Mackenzie Sound ... 218
Madan Bay ... 266
Madeira Marina ... 178
Madeira Park Government Wharf ... 177
Madeira Park The Village of ... 177
Magnuson Park ... 47
Magoun Islands ... 277
Makah Marina ... 64
Makah Mini Mart & Fuel ... 64
Malaspina Inlet ... 186
Malaspina Strait ... 182
Malcolm Island Lions Harbour Authority ... 221
Malibu Rapids ... 180
Manchester ... 35
Manchester State Park ... 35
Mannion Bay ... 168
Manson's Landing ... 190
Manson's Landing Public Floats ... 190
Mantrap Inlet ... 243
Manzanita Bay, Alaska ... 264
Manzanita Bay, Washington ... 30
Maple Bay ... 148
Maple Bay Marina ... 148
Maple Hollow ... 21
Maquinna Provincial Park ... 232
March Point ... 82
Margaret Bay ... 241
Marina at Bliss Landing ... 185
Marina at Browns Point ... 15
Marina Island ... 189
Marina Mart ... 46
Marina Park ... 48
Marine Atlas ... 8
Marine Park, Tacoma ... 16
Marine Supply and Hardware ... 82
Marine Trails, BC ... 116
Marine Trails, Washington ... 111
Marine View Drive ... 14
Maritime Market and Marina ... 164
Maritime Pier, Gig Harbor ... 19
Marrowstone Island ... 57
Marten Arm ... 261
Martin Marina ... 25
Marymoor Park ... 48
Mason's Olson Resort ... 64
Masset ... 256
Masset Harbour Dock ... 256
Masthead Marina & Restaurant ... 148
Mathieson Channel ... 246
Matia Island Marine State Park ... 106
Matilda Inlet ... 231
Matilpi ... 213
Mats Mats ... 57
Maud Island ... 203
Maunsell Bay ... 240
Maurelle Island ... 205
Maury Island ... 12
Maury Island Marine Park ... 12
Mayne Island ... 135
Mayne Island Tru Value Foods ... 136
Mayne Passage ... 211
Mayo Cove ... 21
McArdle Bay ... 91
McBride Bay ... 241
McConnell Island ... 100
McFarlands Floatel ... 279
McHenry Anchorage ... 265
McIntosh Bay ... 216
McKay Bay Lodge ... 228
McKay Passage ... 232
McKenzie Inlet ... 279
McLane Cove ... 23
McLean Arm ... 280
McLeod Bay ... 213
McMicken Island Marine State Park ... 22
McMurray Bay ... 179
McNab Creek Landing ... 170
McNeil Island ... 18
McRae Cove ... 182
Meares Island ... 231
Melanie Cove ... 187
Mellis Inlet ... 250
Menefee Anchorage ... 280

Visit us at boattravel.com

INDEX Page 299

Mercer Island	48
Mereworth Sound	241
Method Marine Supply	231
Metlakatla	282
Metlakatla Harbor	282
Meydenbauer Bay	48
Meyers Chuck	265
Meyers Passage	249
Michael Biggs Ecological Reserve	219
Mike's Beach Resort	54
Miles Inlet	240
Mill Bay	129
Mill Bay Marina	129
Millbrook Cove	241
Miller Bay	29
Miller Bay Marine	30
Mills Landing	228
Milltown Marina & Boatyard	159
Miners Bay	136
Minette Bay Marina	249
Mink Bay	261
Mink Island	187
Mink Trap Bay	250
Minstrel Island	213
Mission	161
Mission Harbour Authority	161
Misty Fjords National Monument	264
Mitchell Bay, B.C.	221
Mitchell Bay, WA	104
Mitlenatch Island	198
Mobey's Pub	140
Modutech Marine, Inc	15
Moira Sound	280
Moira Sound South Arm	280
Monckton Inlet	250
Monday Anchorage	215
Montague Harbour	143
Montague Harbour Marina	**OBC, 144, 145**
Montague Harbour Marine Park	144
Moore Bay	216
Moran State Park	95
Moresby Island	257
Moresby Island	128, 257
Morrison's North Star Marine	46
Morse Cove	262
Moser Bay	265
Moses Inlet	242
Mosquito Creek Marina & Boatyard	167
Mosquito Pass	104
Moth Bay	262
Mould's Bay	204
Mount Vernon	76
Moutcha Bay Resort & Marina	232
Mud Bay	91
Muir Glacier Face	273
Mukilteo	69
Murden Cove	29
Murphy's Landing	20
Musgrave Landing	141
Mussel Bay	247
Mussel Inlet	247
Mutiny Bay	73
Mystery Bay	58
Mystery Bay Marine State Park	58

N

Naha Bay	265
Nahmint Bay	228
Nahwitti Bar	236
Nakat Harbor, Alaska	261
Nakwakto Rapids	240
Namu	244
Nanaimo	153
Nanaimo Port Authority Boat Basin	**154**
Nanoose Harbour	192
Narrows Inlet	182
Narrows Marina	18
Narvaez Bay	134
Nascall Hot Springs	245
Nasparti Inlet	234
Native Anchorage	214
Nautical Landing Marina	46
Naval Station Everett	70
Naval Station Everett Marina	70
Neah Bay	64
Neah Bay, Washington	226
Nelson Island	178
Nepah Lagoon	218
Neroutsos Inlet	235
Nettle Basin	251
Neva Strait	277
New Brighton	170
New Eddystone Rock	264
New Vancouver Dock	214
New Westminster	161
Newcastle Island Provincial Park	155
Newcastle Marina & Boatyard	154
Newcombe Harbour	250
Newman Creek	169
Newport Yacht Basin Assn.	48
Newton Cove Resort	233
NEXUS	109
Niblack Anchorage	280
Nigei Island	222
Nimmo Bay	218
Nisqually Delta	23
Nitinat Lake	227
Nitinat Narrows	227
Nodales Channel	209
Nootka	232
Nootka Island Fishing Lodge	232
Nootka Sound	232
Nootka Sound Resort	232
Nordland General Store	58
North Arm Transportation Ltd, Masset	256
North Bay	282
North Beach, Orcas Island	99
North Cove	146
North Cove Harbor, Craig Alaska	281
North Galiano	143
North Harbor Diesel	82
North Harbour	235
North Island Marina	221
North Lake Marina	47
North Pender Island	132
North Saanich Marina	128
North Sandy Cove	273
North Vancouver	166
Northeast Bay	197
Northern Islands	105
Northern Olympic Peninsula	61
Northumberland Channel	153
Northwest Bay	193
Northwest Fuels -Cow Bay	253
Northwest Seaplanes	**49**
Nossuck Anchorage	281
Nowish Cove	247
Nowish Narrows	247
Nuchatlitz	233
Nuchatlitz Inlet	233
Nuchatlitz Provincial Park	233
Nugent Sound	241

O

O'Brien Bay	216
Oak Bay	124
Oak Bay County Park	57
Oak Bay Marina The	124
Oak Harbor	72
Oak Harbor City of	72
Oak Harbor Marina	73
Oakland Bay	26
Oakland Bay Marina	26
Oatswish Bay	247
Observatory Inlet	255
Obstruction Pass	94
Obstruction Pass State Park	94
Ocean Falls	245
Ocean Falls Public Dock	245
Ocean Pacific Marine Supply & Boatyard	**201**
Oceanfront Suites at Cowichan Bay	148
Octopus Islands Provincial Park	204
Odlin Park	93
Ogden Passage	274
Okeover Harbour Authority	186
Okeover Inlet	186
Okisollo Channel	203
Olalla	11
Old House Bay	196
Old Man House Park	30
Old Town Dock	16
Old Town Historic District	16
Olga	94
Olga Strait	277
Oliver Cove Marine Park	246
Olympia	24
Olympic View Marina	54
On-Board Marine Services	86
Onamac Point	71
Oona River Harbour Authority	251
Orcas Island	93
Orcas Landing	95
Oro Bay	18
Osborne Bay Resort	147
Oscar Passage	246
Ostrich Bay	33
Otter Bay	133
Otter Bay Marina	**133**
Otter Cove	203
Otter Island	187
Outer Bay	91
Outpost at Winter Harbour The	235
Owen Bay	204
Oyster Bay	33
Oyster Bay Marina	146
Oyster Bay, BC	177
Oyster Island	188
Oyster River	195

P

Pacheedaht Campground	227
Pacific Boulevard Marina at Plaza of Nations	163
Pacific Gateway Marina	227
Pacific Gateway Wilderness Lodge	228
Pacific Playgrounds Resort & Marina	196
Pacific Rim National Park Reserve	228
Padilla Bay	82
Page's Resort & Marina	**152**
Pages Inn on Silva Bay	**152**
Painted Boat Resort Spa & Marina	178
Pamphlet Cove	235
Parker Harbour	186
Parker Island	144
Parks Bay	100
Parks, British Columbia	117
Parks, Seattle & Washington	112
Parkshore Marina	49
Parksville	193
Parsons Anchorage	250
Passports	109
Patos Island Marine State Park	105
Patricia Bay	128
Patrician Cove	221
Patterson Inlet	250
Pavlof Harbor	275
Peapod Rocks	93
Pearse Canal	261
Peavine Pass	94
Pedder Bay	121
Pedder Bay Marina	121
Pelican	274
Pelican Bay Marina	164
Pelican Beach	84
Pelican Fuel Dock	275
Pelican Harbor	275
Pender Canal	132
Pender Harbour	176
Pender Harbour Diesel	178
Pender Harbour Hotel Marina	178
Pender Harbour Resort & Marina	177
Pender Island	132
Pendrell Sound	188
Penelakut Island	144

Peninsula Yacht Basin 20
Penn Cove 73
Penn Harbour 250
Penrose Bay 186
Penrose Island Marine Park 242
Penrose Point Marine State Park 21
Perceval Narrows 246
Percival Landing Marine Park 26
Perry Bay 255
Peter Cove 132
Petersburg 267, 268
Petersburg Harbor 268
Petersburg Petro Marine Services 268
Petrel Channel 250
Petro Canada Marine-Nanaimo 154
Petro Canada, Port Alberni 228
Petro Marine Serves-Ketchikan 263
Philbrook's Boatyard 128
Philbrooks's Boatyard@Roche Harbor Marine 104
Phillips Arm 210
Phinney Bay 33
Pickering Passage 23
Picnic Cove 100
Pier 65 (Dungeness Marina) 148
Pier 66 Marina 148
Piers Island 128
Piggott Bay 136
Pillar Point 63
Pilot Bay 153
Pinkerton Group 229
Pipestem Inlet 229
Pirate's Cove Marine Park 151
Pitt Lake 161
Pitt Meadows Marina 161
Pitt Passage 21
Pitt River 161
Pitt River Boat Club 161
Platypus Marine 46, 62, 63
Pleasant Bay 84
Pleasant Harbor 53
Pleasant Harbor Marina .... IBC, 54, 55
Pleasant Harbor Marine State Park 54
Pleasurecraft Marina 20
Plumper Cove Marine Park 170
Plumper Harbour 232
Pocahontas Bay 197
Poets Cove Resort and Spa 132
Poett Nook 228
Poett Nook Marina 228
Point Atkinson 162
Point Atkinson 167
Point Baker 280
Point Defiance Marina & Boathouse 17
Point Defiance Park 16
Point Doughty Natural Area Preserve 99
Point Gardner 274
Point Hudson Marina & RV Park 59, 60
Point Lawrence 93
Point Lull 277
Point Monroe 29
Point Roberts 88, 157
Point Roberts Marina Resort 88, 157
Point Robinson Park 12
Point Wilson 61
Poise Cove Marina 182
Poison Cove 247
Pole Pass 98
Porcher Island 251
Porlier Pass 143
Porpoise Bay 182
Porpoise Bay Government Wharf 182
Porpoise Bay Provincial Park 182
Port Alberni 228
Port Alberni Fisherman's Harbour 228
Port Alberni Marine Fuels & Services Ltd 228
Port Alberni Yacht Club 228
Port Alberni: Petro Canada 228
Port Alexander, Alaska 277
Port Alexander, B.C. 236
Port Alice Municipal Float 235
Port Alice, Alaska 281
Port Alice, BC 235
Port Angeles 62
Port Angeles Boat Haven 63
Port Angeles City Pier and Hollywood Beach 63
Port Armstrong 277
Port Browning 132
Port Browning Capital Regional District Dock 133
Port Browning Marina Resort 132
Port Clements 256
Port Clements Small Craft Harbour 256
Port Edward 251
Port Edward Public Moorage 251
Port Elizabeth 214
Port Estrella 282
Port Gamble 52
Port Graves 170
Port Hadlock 57
Port Hadlock Marina 57
Port Hardy 222, 236
Port Hardy Berthage 222
Port Harvey 213
Port John 245
Port Johnson 280
Port Ludlow 56
Port Ludlow Marina 56
Port Madison 29
Port McNeill 221
Port McNeill Harbour Authority 221
Port McNeill IGA 221
Port Mellon 170
Port Moody 165
Port Neville 213
Port of Allyn North Shore Dock 56
Port of Anacortes, Cap Sante Marina .... IFC, 82, 83
Port of Bellingham, Blaine Harbor 86, 87
Port of Bellingham, Squalicum Harbor 85
Port of Bremerton 32
Port of Brownsville 31
Port of Edmonds 69
Port of Everett 70
Port of Friday Harbor 102
Port of Friday Harbor Fuel Dock 102
Port of Hoodsport Dock 54
Port of Keyport 30
Port of Kingston 68
Port of Nanaimo Boat Basin 154
Port of Olympia 25
Port of Port Townsend 59, 60
Port of Poulsbo 31
Port of Seattle 40, 42, 43, 44
Port of Silverdale 33
Port of Skagit's La Conner Marina 78
Port of South Whidbey's Harbor at Langley 74
Port of Stewart Dock 261
Port of Tacoma 14
Port Orchard 34
Port Orchard City of 34
Port Orchard Marina 34
Port Orchard Railway Marina 35
Port Orchard Strait 34
Port Plaza 24
Port Protection 280
Port Real Marina 282
Port Refugio 282
Port Renfrew 226
Port Renfrew Marina & RV Park 227
Port San Juan 226
Port Sidney Marina 127
Port Simpson 254
Port Stephen 250
Port Susan 71
Port Townsend 58
Port Townsend Canal 57
Port Townsend City of 58
Port Townsend Fuel Dock 60
Port Townsend Port of 59, 60
Port Townsend's Boat Haven 59, 60
Port Washington 133
Port Washington Narrows 33
Portage Bay, Alaska 268
Portage Bay, Washington 46
Porteau Cove Park 169
Portland Canal 260
Portland Inlet 260
Portland Island 128
Posey Island Marine State Park 105
Possession Beach Waterfront Park 75
Possession Point 75
Possession Sound 69
Potlatch Marine State Park 54
Potts Lagoon 214
Poulsbo 30
Poulsbo Marina 31
Powell River 182
Preedy Harbour 146
President Channel 99
Pretty Girl Cove 231
Prevost Harbor 105
Prevost Island 141
Prideaux Haven 187
Priest Point Park 24
Prince of Wales Island 278
Prince of Wales Island, East Side 278
Prince of Wales Island, West Side 280
Prince of Wales Reach 179
Prince Rupert 251
Prince Rupert Berthage 252
Prince Rupert Rowing and Yacht Club 253
Princess Bay 144
Princess Louisa Inlet 179
Princess Louisa International Society 180
Princess Louisa Provincial Marine Park 180
Princess Margaret Marine Park 128
Principe Channel 250
Protection Island 155
Pruth Bay 243
Puget Creek Natural Area 16
Puget Marina 23
Puget Park 16
Puget Sound 10
Pulali Point 53
Pulteney Point 221
Pumpout Guy 4
Puyallup River 14
Pybus Bay 269

Q

Quadra Island 202
Quadra Island Harbour Authority 202, 204
Qualicum Bay 193
Qualicum Beach 193
Qualicum Rivers Winter Harbour Fishing Lodge & Resort 235
Quarry Bay 178
Quarterdeck Inn & Marina 222
Quarterdeck Restaurant & Pub 222
Quartermaster Harbor 12
Quartermaster Marina 12
Quartz Bay 189
Quascilla Bay 241
Quathiaski Cove 202
Quatsino 235
Quatsino First Nations Dock 236
Quatsino Lodge 235
Quatsino Marine Park 235
Quatsino Sound 235
Quayside Marina 163
Queen Charlotte 256
Queen Charlotte City Harbour Authority 256
Queen Charlotte Strait 215
Queen Cove 233
Quilcene Bay 53
Quileute Harbor Marina 65
Quottoon Inlet 254
Quottoon Narrows 254

R

Raccoon Island 166
Race Passage 212
Race Rocks 226

Visit us at boattravel.com

INDEX Page 301

Raft Cove Provincial Park ... 236
Raft Island ... 21
Rainier Beach ... 49
Rathtrevor Beach Park ... 193
Ratz Harbor ... 279
Raven Point Landing Ltd. ... 146
Ray Anchorage ... 261
Raymur Point CBSA Boat Dock ... 123
Read Island ... 205
Reads Bay ... 91
Rebecca Spit Marine Park ... 204
Red Bluff Bay ... 277
Redonda Bay ... 188
Redondo ... 14
Reed Point Marina ... 165
Refuge Cove ... 188
Refuge Cove Marina ... 264
Refuge Cove Store ... 188
Regina Cove, Alaska ... 261
Reid Harbor ... 105
Reid Inlet ... 273
Reid Island ... 143
Reid Passage ... 246
Reil Harbor ... 84
Reliance Harbor Float ... 267
Rendezvous Islands ... 205
Renton ... 48
Rescue Bay ... 246
Reservation Bay ... 79
Restoration Bay ... 244
Retreat Cove ... 143
Retreat Passage ... 215
Rich Passage ... 35
Richardson Cove ... 196
Richmond ... 160
Richmond Bay ... 218
Richmond Beach Saltwater Park ... 69
Richmond Chevron Marine ... 161
Riley Cove ... 231
Riptide Liquor Store ... 279
RiverHouse Marina Restaurant & Pub ... 160
Rivers Inlet ... 241
Roaringhole Rapids ... 218
Robbers Passage ... 228
Robert Arm ... 243
Roberts Bay ... 127
Roberts Creek ... 174
Robertson Cove ... 189
Robson Bight ... 219
Roche Harbor ... 104
Roche Harbor Marina & Resort ... 104
Rock Bay ... 203
Rock Bay Marine Provincial Park ... 203
Rocky Bay ... 22, 100
Roffey Island ... 187
Rolling Roadstead ... 234
Roquefoil Bay ... 228
Rosario Bay ... 80
Rosario Resort & Spa ... 94
Roscoe Bay Marine Park ... 188
Roscoe Inlet ... 246
Rosedale ... 21
Ross Passage ... 231
Royal City Marina ... 161
Royal Victoria Yacht Club ... 125
Ruckle Provincial Park ... 138
Rudyerd Bay ... 264
Rugged Point Marine Provincial Park ... 234
Rumble Beach Marina ... 235
Rupert Inlet ... 236
Rushbrooke Harbour ... 253
Rushbrooke Harbour Floats ... 253
Russell Island ... 138
Ruston Way ... 16
Ruxton Island ... 150
Ryus Bay ... 282

S

Saanich Inlet ... 128
Saanich Peninsula ... 126
Saanichton Bay ... 125
Saddlebag Island Marine State Park ... 82
Safety Cove ... 243
Sailors Cove Marina ... 122
Saint Edwards State Park ... 47
Saint James Bay ... 271
Salmon Bay Marina ... 44
Salmon Bay, B.C. ... 246
Salmon Bay, Washington ... 43
Salmon Beach ... 17
Salmon Inlet ... 182
Salmon Point Resort ... 196
Salsbury Point County Park ... 52
Salt Creek Recreation Area County Park ... 63
Salt Spring Island East ... 138
Salt Spring Island West ... 141
Salt Spring Marina ... 140, 141
Saltery Bay Park ... 179
Saltery Bay, Alaska ... 276
Saltery Bay, B.C. ... 179
Saltwater State Park ... 14
Samish Island ... 82
Sammamish River ... 47
Samuel Island ... 135
San Juan Airlines ... 95
San Juan County Park ... 104
San Juan Island ... 100
San Juan Island National Historical Park ... 103
San Juan Islands ... 90
San Mateo Bay ... 228
Sand Point ... 47
Sandell Bay ... 242
Sandspit ... 257
Sandspit Harbour ... 257
Sandy Island Marine Park ... 195
Sandy Point ... 86
Sandy Point Marina ... 86
Sangster Island ... 196
Sansum Narrows ... 141, 148
Santa Anna Inlet ... 265
Santa Gertrudis Cove ... 232
Sarah Point ... 186
Saratoga Passage ... 71
Sargeant Bay ... 174
Sargeant Bay Provincial Park ... 174
Sargeaunt Passage ... 214
Sarheen Cove ... 281
Sarkar Cove ... 281
Satellite Passage ... 228
Saturna Beach ... 134
Saturna General Store ... 135
Saturna Island ... 134
Saturna Lighthouse Pub ... 135
Savary Island ... 183
Say Nuth Khaw Yum Provincial Park (Indian Arm Park) ... 165
Saysutshyun (Newcastle) Island Provincial Park ... 155
Sayward ... 213
Sayward Futures Dock ... 213
Sayward, Government Small Craft Harbour ... 213
Scenic Beach State Park ... 54
Schooner Channel ... 240
Schooner Cove ... 192
Schooner Retreat ... 242
Scott Cove ... 216
Scott Islands ... 236
Scottie Bay ... 196
Sea Marine ... 60
Sea Otter Cove ... 236
Sea Otter Inlet ... 244
Sea Otter Sound ... 281
Sea Scape Waterfront Resort & Marina ... 202
Seabeck Bay ... 54
Seacrest Park ... 38
Seadrome Marina ... 270
Seaford ... 189
Seagate Pier ... 222
Seahurst Park ... 13
Seal Bay ... 276
Seattle ... 37
Seattle Boat Co. ... 48
Seattle Seaplanes ... 44
Seattle Waterfront Map ... 39
Seattle Yacht Services ... 82
Seawall Park ... 75
Sebree Cove ... 273
Sechelt ... 174
Sechelt Inlet ... 181
Sechelt Rapids ... 182
Second Narrows ... 165
Secret Cove ... 175
Secret Cove Government Dock ... 176
Secret Cove Marina ... 176
Secret Harbor ... 84
Secretary Islands ... 144
Seine Docks The ... 222
Sekiu, Washington ... 64. 226
Selby Cove ... 142
Semiahmoo Marina ... 86
Semiahmoo Park ... 86
Sequim ... 61
Sequim Bay ... 61
Sequim Bay Marine State Park ... 61
Sergius Narrows ... 277
Seward Park ... 49
Sewell's Marina ... 167
Seymour Inlet ... 240
Seymour Landing ... 168
Seymour Narrows ... 202
Shag Cove ... 273
Shakan Strait ... 280
Shallow Bay ... 106
Shark Cove ... 132
Shark Spit ... 189
Sharpe Cove ... 80
Shaw General Store ... 99
Shaw Island ... 99
Shaw Island County Park ... 100
Shawl Bay ... 216
Shawl Bay Marina ... 216
Shearwater ... 246
Shearwater Resort, Hotel & Marina ... 246
Sheep Passage ... 247
Shelter Bay Marina ... 77
Shelter Island Marina & Boatyard ... 160
Shelter Point Park ... 197
Shelton ... 26
Shelton Yacht Club ... 26
Sheringham Point ... 226
Shilshole Bay ... 41
Shilshole Bay Fuel Dock ... 42
Shilshole Bay Marina ... 42
Shine Tidelands State Park ... 52
Shingle Bay ... 133
Ship & Shore Restaurant & Campground ... 194
Ship Harbor ... 81
Ship Point ... 124
Ship To Shore Marine Supply ... 20
Shipyard Cove Marina ... 102
Shoal Bay, B.C. ... 211
Shoal Bay, Washington ... 93
Shoal Channel ... 171
Shoal Harbour ... 216
Shoemaker Bay Harbor ... 267
Short Bay ... 264
Shorter Point ... 212
Shushartie Bay ... 236
Shutter Shack ... 252
Sibell Bay ... 146
Sidney ... 126
Sidney Bay ... 212
Sidney Spit Marine Park ... 125
Silva Bay ... 152
Silva Bay Resort & Marina ... 153
Silver Bay ... 276
Silverdale ... 33
Silverdale Waterfront Park ... 33
Similk Bay ... 79
Simoom Sound ... 216
Sinclair Inlet ... 34
Sinclair Inlet Marina ... 35
Sinclair Island ... 84
Sir Alexander Mackenzie Park ... 245

2024 Northwest Boat Travel

INDEX

Sir Edmund Bay ... 217
Sisters Islets ... 196
Sitka ... 276
Sitka Petro Marine Services ... 277
Sitkoh Bay ... 276
Siwash Bay ... 214
Skagit Bay ... 72
Skagit Island Marine State Park ... 79
Skagit River ... 72
Skagit Valley ... 76
Skagway ... 271
Skagway Boat Basin ... 272
Skagway Petro Marine Services ... 272
Skanskie Brothers Park ... 19
Skeene Bay ... 219
Skerry Bay ... 196
Skidegate ... 256
Skidegate Narrows ... 257
Skipjack Island ... 105
Skowl Arm ... 279
Skull Cove ... 240
Skull Island State Park ... 98
Skyline ... 81
Skyline Marina ... 161
Skyline Marine Center ... 80, 81
Slingsby Channel ... 240
Slocum Arm ... 274
Small Inlet ... 203
Small Inlet Marine Provincial Park ... 203
Small Pox Bay ... 104
Smelt Bay Park ... 190
Smith Inlet ... 241
Smith Sound ... 241
Smuggler Cove Marine Park ... 175
Smuggler's Cove ... 84, 104
Snake Island ... 155
Snohomish River ... 70
Snoring Bay ... 106
Snow Bay ... 205
Snow Creek Resort ... 64
Snug Anchorage ... 279
Snug Cove ... 168
Snug Cove Public Wharf ... 168
Snug Harbor Resort & Marina ... 104
Sointula ... 220
Sommerville Bay ... 254
Sooke ... 121, 226
Sooke Harbour Authority ... 226
Sooke Harbour Resort & Marina ... 226
South Bentinck Arm ... 244
South Cove Harbor, Craig AK ... 281
South Pender Island ... 132
South Puget Sound ... 10
South Sandy Cove ... 273
South Whidbey State Park ... 73
South Whidbey's Harbor at Langley, Port of ... 74
Southeast Alaskan Panhandle, Introduction ... 260
Southeast Vancouver Island ... 120
Southern Lopez Island ... 91
Southey Point ... 141
Southworth ... 35
Spacious Bay ... 264
Spanish Hills (N Galiano Island) ... 143
Spencer Spit Marine State Park ... 93
Spencer's Landing Marina ... 93
Spieden Channel ... 105
Spieden Island ... 105
Spotlight Cove ... 143
Spray Island ... 268
Spring Bay ... 196
Sproat Bay ... 228
Spruce Harbour Marina ... 164
Squalicum Harbor ... 85
Squamish ... 169
Squamish Harbor ... 52
Squamish Harbour Authority ... 170
Squaxin Island ... 23
Squaxin Park ... 24
Squirrel Cove ... 188
Squirrel Cove Government Dock ... 188
Squirrel Cove Store ... 188

Squitty Bay Provincial Park ... 196
St. John Harbor ... 267
St. John Harbour ... 246
St. John the Baptist Bay ... 277
St. Vincent Bay ... 179
Stan Sayres Memorial Park ... 49
Stanley Park ... 164
Statter Harbor (Auke Bay) ... 271
Steamboat Bay ... 218
Steamboat Bay ... 281
Steilacoom ... 18
Stephens Passage ... 268
Steveston ... 159
Steveston Chevron Marine ... 159
Steveston Harbour Authority ... 159
Stewart, British Columbia ... 261
Stillwater Bay ... 182
Stone's Marine Center Inc ... 154
Stonecutter's Bay ... 141
Stopper Islands ... 229
Strait of Juan de Fuca ... 226
Straitside Resort ... 64
Strawberry Island ... 82
Stretch Island ... 23
Stretch Point Marine State Park ... 23
Stuart Island Community Dock ... 206
Stuart Island State Park ... 105
Stuart Island, BC ... 206
Stuart Island, Washington ... 105
Stuart Narrows ... 218
Stubbs Island ... 231
Sturdies Bay ... 142
Sturt Bay ... 197
Subtle Islands ... 189
Sucia Island Marine State Park ... 106
Sue Channel ... 249
Sullivan Bay ... 217
Sullivan Bay Marine Resort ... 217
Sulphur Passage ... 231
Summertide Resort and Marina ... 56
Sunday Harbour ... 215
Sunderland Channel ... 212
Sunny Shores Resort & Marina ... 226
Sunrise Motel & Dive Resort ... 54
Sunset Beach ... 168
Sunset Beach, Anacortes ... 81
Sunset Marina Ltd. ... 168
Sunshine Coast Resort Hotel & Marina ... 177
Sunshine Coast The ... 173
Suquamish ... 30
Surf Inlet ... 250
Surge Narrows ... 204, 205
Surge Narrows Provincial Park ... 205
Susan Islets Anchorage ... 186
Sutherland Bay ... 218
Sutil Point ... 190
Sutlej Channel ... 217
Swaine Point, British Columbia ... 261
Swantown Marina and Boatworks ... 25
Swartz Bay ... 128
Swartz Bay Public Wharf ... 128
Swift's Bay ... 93
Swinomish Channel ... 76
Swinomish Tribal Park Floats ... 78
Sydney Inlet ... 231
Sykes Cove ... 264
Sylvan Cove ... 91

T

Tackle Shack at Thorne Bay ... 279
Tacoma ... 14
Tacoma Fuel Dock ... 16
Tacoma Narrows ... 17
Tacoma Port of ... 14
Tacoma Yacht Club ... 17
Tahlequah ... 13
Tahsis ... 233
Tahsis Harbour Facility ... 233
Tahsis Inlet ... 233
Tahuya ... 56
Taiasanka Harbor ... 271

Taku Harbor ... 270
Taku Inlet ... 270
Taku Resort & Marina ... 205
Takush Harbour ... 241
Tallac Bay ... 211
Tallheo ... 244
Tancred Bay ... 218
Tanglewood Island ... 18
Tarkanen Marine Ways ... 221
Taylor Bay, BC ... 242
Taylor Bay, Washington ... 22
Teakerne Arm Marine Park ... 188
Tee Harbor ... 271
Telegraph Cove ... 219
Telegraph Cove Marina ... 219
Telegraph Cove Resort ... 219
Telegraph Harbour ... 146
Telegraph Harbour Marina ... 146
Telescope Passage ... 179
Tenakee Fuel Facility ... 275
Tenakee Inlet ... 275
Tenakee Springs ... 275
Tenakee Springs City Hall ... 275
Tenakee Springs Market ... 276
Tenedos Bay ... 187
Tent Island ... 144
Teren Photography ... 101
Texada Boating Club ... 197
Texada Island ... 196
Thatcher Bay ... 91
The Port at Thorne Bay ... 279
The Spot at Porpoise Bay ... 182
Thea Foss Waterway ... 15
Theodosia Inlet ... 186
Thetis Island ... 146
Thetis Island Marina ... 146
Thieves Bay ... 133
Thom's Place ... 266
Thomas Basin ... 264
Thomas Bay ... 268
Thomson Cove ... 129
Thormanby Islands ... 175
Thorndike Bay ... 52
Thorne Arm ... 262
Thorne Bay ... 279
Thorne Bay City of ... 279
Thorne Bay Harbor ... 279
Thorne Bay Market ... 279
Thors Cove ... 186
Thulin Passage ... 183, 185
Thunder Bay ... 179
Thunderbird Marina ... 167
Thurston Bay Provincial Marine Park ... 209
Tide Point ... 84
Tides Tavern ... 20
Tilbury Island ... 160
Tillicum Bay ... 182
Tillicum Bay Marina ... 182
Titlow Park ... 17
Tlell ... 256
Tll.aal (Tlell) ... 256
Tlupana Inlet ... 232
Toba Inlet ... 205
Toba Wilderness Marina ... 205
Tod Inlet ... 129
Tofino ... 230
Tofino Harbour Authority ... 230, 231
Tofino Inlet ... 231
Tofino Resort + Marina ... 231
Tokeen ... 281
Tolmie Channel ... 247
Tolmie Marine State Park ... 23
Tom Bay ... 246
Tongass Narrows ... 264
Tongass Trading Company ... 263
Totten Inlet ... 26
Townsite Marina ... 154
Towry Point, Seymour Inlet ... 240
Tracey Harbour ... 219
Tracey Island ... 215
Tracy Arm ... 270

Visit us at boattravel.com

Tracy Owen Station 47
Tracyton 33
Trader's Islands 277
Trahey Inlet 250
Trail Bay 254
Trail Islands 174
Trailer Techs 6, 49
Tramp Harbor 12
Treadwell Bay 240
Trevenen Bay 186
Tribune Bay 194
Tribune Bay Provincial Park 194
Tribune Channel 216
Triton Cove State Park 54
Triumph Bay 249
Troup Narrows 246
Troup Passage 246
Tsakonu Cove 214
Tsawwassen 158
Tsehum Harbour 127
Tsehum Harbour Authority 128
Tsibass Lagoon 219
Tuck Inlet 254
Tuck Narrows 254
Tucker Bay 196
Tulalip 71
Tulalip Marina 71
Tumbo Island 134
Tuna Point 213
Turn Island Marine Park 102
Turnbull Cove 218
Tuta Marina 232
Twanoh Marine State Park 56
Twin Bridges Marina 77
Twin Islands 166, 191
Twin Rocks 95
Twin Spits 52
Tyee Landing 228
Tyee Marina 15
Tyndall Cove 273
Tzoozie Narrows 182

U

Uchucklesit Inlet 228
Ucluelet 230
Ucluelet Otter Street 230
Ucluelet West Small Craft Harbour 230
Uganda Passage 189
Union 54
Union Bay, BC 194
Union Bay, Washington 46
Union Inlet 254
Union SteamShip Co. Marina 1, 168, 169
Union Wharf 60
University of Washington Friday Harbor Laboratory 102
Upright Channel 93
US Customs & Border Protection Information 109
US Customs Designated Port-of-Entry 110
Useless Bay 74
Useless Inlet 229
Utsalady 71

V

Valdes Island 151
Van Anda Bay 197
Van Isle Marina 126, 127
Van Riper's Resort 64
Vancouver 162
Vancouver Bay 179
Vancouver Fraser Port Authority 162
Vancouver Harbour 164
Vancouver Island 224
Vancouver Island, Central East Coast 146
Vancouver Island, South of Nanaimo 150
Vancouver Island, Southeast 120
Vancouver Marina 161
Vanguard Bay 179
Varney Bay 236
Vashon Center 10
Vashon Island 10
Vaughn Bay 22
Vector Yacht Services & The Boatyard 128
Vendovi Island 84
Venn Passage 253
Vernon Bay 229
Very Inlet 261
Vessels in Washington 112
Vesuvius 141
Vesuvius Bay Public Float 141
VHF Marine Radio, Canada 117
VHF Marine Radio, US 112
Victim Island State Park 98
Victoria City of 123
Victoria Harbour 122
Victoria Harbour Traffic Scheme 122
Victoria Inner Harbour 122
Victoria International Marina 124
Village Bay, Mayne Island 136
Village Bay, Quadra Island 204
Village Island 214
Viner Sound 216
Vixen Bay 261
Vixen Harbor 265
Von Donop Inlet 189
Von Donop Provincial Marine Park 189
Von Geldern Cove 21

W

Wachusett Inlet 273
Waddington Bay 215
Waddington Channel 188
Wadhams 241
Waglisia (Bella Bella) 246
Wahkana Bay 216
Wahshihlas Bay 214
Waiatt Bay 204
Wakes Cove Marine Park 151
Waldron Island 105
Wales Harbor, British Columbia 261
Wales Island, British Columbia 261
Walker Cove 264
Walker Group 240
Walker Hook 140
Wallace Island Provincial Marine Park 144
Walsh Cove Provincial Park 188
Walter Bay 138
Walters Cove 234
Ward's Marina 158
Warner Bay 240
Warrior Cove 244
Washington Park 81
Washington Sea Grant 4, 46
Wasp Islands 100
Waterfall Inlet 243
Waterfront Suites & Marina 154
Waterman Pier 35
Watmough Bay 91
Watson Cove 216
Watson Point 218
Wawatle Bay 240
Waypoint Marine Group 44
Weasel Cove 261
Weeolk Passage 242
Weewanie Hot Springs Provincial Park 249
Welbourn Cove 177
Welcome Cove 133
Welcome Pass 175
Weld Cove 250
Wellbore Channel 212
Wells Passage 219
West Bay 170
West Bay Marina 26
West Beach Resort 99
West Redonda Island 188
West Seattle 49
West Seattle's Western Shore 49
West Shore Marina 20
West Sound 98
West Sound Marina 98
West Thurlow Island 211
West Vancouver 167
Westbay Marina 128
Westbay Marine Village 122
Westcott Bay 104
Westport Marina 128
Westview 182
Westview Fuel Dock 183
Westview Harbour Authority 183
Westview Marina & Lodge 233
Westwind Marine 88
Whaleboat Island Marine Park 150
Whaler Bay 143
Whaler Bay Harbour Authority Float 143
Whaletown 189
Whaletown Government Dock 189
Wharf Street Marina, Victoria Harbour 124
What is Northwest Boat Travel? 6
Whidbey Island 72
Whirlpool Rapids 212
Whiskey Bay, British Columbia 261
Whiskey November 179
Whiskey Slough Government Wharf 178
White Rock 158
White Rock, BC 86
Whitepine Cove 231
Whiterock Passage 204
Whitney Point 53
Whyte Cove 167
Winchelsea Island 192
Windham Bay 269
Windy Bay 247
Wingehaven Park 12
Winslow 29
Winslow Wharf Marina 29
Winstanley Island 264
Winter Cove 135
Winter Cove Marine Park 135
Winter Harbour 235
Winter Harbour Harbour Authority 235
Winter Harbour Marina & RV 235
Winter Inlet, British Columbia 261
Wolfe Property Park 52
Wollochet Bay 19
Wood Bay 176
Wooden Wheel Cove Trading Post 280
Woodlands 166
Woods Bay 218
Wooten Bay 187
Work Bay 247
Work Channel 254
Wouwer Island 229
Wrangell 266
Wrangell Narrows 267
Wrangell Petro Marine 267
Wrangell Port & Harbors 266, 267
Wrangell, Inner Harbor Float 267

Y

Yachtfish Marine NW 35, 46
Yarksis 231
Yarrow Bay Marina 48
Yeatman Bay 204
Yellow Island 100
Yellow Point 150
Yes Bay 264
Yes Bay Lodge 264
Yorke Island 212
Young Bay 231
Yuculta Rapids 206
Yukon Harbor 35

Z

Zeballos 233
Zeballos Fuel Dock & Marina 233
Zeballos Harbour Facilities 233
Zimovia Strait 266
Zittel's Marina 24
Zorro Bay 170

Index of Advertisers

Arabella's Landing	20
BC Ocean Boating Tourism	123
Bathgate General Store, Resort & Marina	181
Bell Harbor Marina	40
Blaine Harbor, Port of Bellingham	86, 87
Blind Channel Resort	211
Bremerton Marina	32
Brown's Bay Resort	203
Cap Sante Marina	IFC, 82, 83
Christopher S. Teren Photography	101
City of Des Moines Marina	13
City of Kake Ports & Harbor	278
Cow Bay Marina	253
Crescent Beach Marina	88, 158
Dawson's Landing General Store	242
Deer Harbor Marina	99
Dent Island Lodge The	206, 207
Discovery Harbour Fuel Sales	200, 201
Discovery Harbour Marina	200, 201
Dock Street Marina	15
Elliott Bay Marina	41
Everett Yacht Service	70
Evergreen Pacific Publishing	7, 8, 9
False Creek Harbour Authority-Fishermen's Wharf	163
Fisheries Supply	44, 45
Fishermen's Terminal	43
Friday Harbor Seaplanes	102, 103
Galiano Oceanfront Inn & Spa	142, 143
Gorge Harbour Marina Resort	190
Islands Marine Center	92
Jarrell's Cove Marina	23
Kake Ports & Harbor	278
Kenmore Air	45, 47
LFS Marine & Outdoor	84, 85
La Conner Marina, Port of Skagit's	78
Langley Harbor, Port of South Whidbey	74
Lonnie Wishart Photography	252
Makah Marina	64
Maple Bay Marina	148
Montague Harbour Marina	OBC, 144, 145
Nanaimo Port Authority Boat Basin	154
Northwest Seaplanes	49
Ocean Pacific Marine Supply & Boatyard	201
Otter Bay Marina	133
Page's Inn on Silva Bay	152
Page's Resort & Marina	152
Petersburg Harbor	268
Platypus Marine Inc.	46, 62, 63
Pleasant Harbor Marina	IBC, 54, 55
Point Defiance Marina & Boathouse	17
Point Hudson Marina & RV Park	59, 60
Point Roberts Marina Resort	88, 157
Port Ludlow Marina	56
Port of Anacortes, Cap Sante Marina	IFC, 82, 83
Port of Bellingham, Blaine Harbor	86, 87
Port of Bellingham, Squalicum Harbor	85
Port of Bremerton	32
Port of Friday Harbor	102
Port of Kingston	68
Port of Nanaimo Boat Basin	154
Port of Olympia, Swantown Marina & Boatworks	25
Port of Port Townsend Boat Haven	59, 60
Port of Poulsbo	31
Port of Seattle-Harbor Services	40, 42, 43, 44
Port of Skagit's La Conner Marina	78
Port of South Whidbey Harbor at Langley	74
Port Orchard Marina	34
Poulsbo Marina	31
Pumpout Guy	4
Rosario Resort & Spa	94
Salmon Bay Marina	44
Salt Spring Marina	140, 141
San Juan Airlines	95
Sandspit Harbour Society	257
Seattle Seaplanes	44
Secret Cove Marina	176
Shelter Island Marina & Boat Yard	160
Shilshole Bay Marina	42
Shutter Shack	252
Skyline Marine Center	80, 81
Squalicum Harbor, Port of Bellingham	85
Swantown Marina & Boatworks, Port of Olympia	25
Teren Photography	101
Tongass Trading Co.	263
Trailer Techs	6, 49
Union SteamShip Co. Marina	1, 168, 169
Van Isle Marina	126, 127
Washington Sea Grant	4, 46
West Sound Marina	98
Wishart, Lonnie Photography	252

Visit us at boattravel.com